THE
COMPLETE
HANDBOOK
OF
Astrology

WHSMITH

EXCLUSIVE · BOOKS ·

Editor Caroline Bugler
Designer David Ashford
Production Craig Chubb

Produced exclusively for WH Smith Limited by
Marshall Cavendish Books (a division of Marshall Cavendish Partworks Limited), 119 Wardour Street, London W1V 3TD

Printed and bound in Singapore

ISBN 1 85435 462 0

Most of this material was previously published in the Marshall Cavendish partwork ZODIAC

CONTENTS

SUN SIGNS

Popular 'star sign' columns intrigue most people, while for many they represent a jumping off point into a deeper study of the subject. Sun sign astrology simply divides the population up into 12 basic personality types. The people in each group derive their characteristics from the sign the Sun was passing through during the month they were born.

The Sun Signs and You
So why do some people seem to be typical of their sign, while others fail to display a single characteristic associated with it? This is where a proper study of astrology comes in. For the Sun is only one of ten planets in anyone's horoscope or chart. It represents the inner self, and the way we prefer to deal with things. For example, someone with Sun in Aries would typically approach life with energy and impulsiveness, while someone with Sun in Capricorn would probably

7

opt for caution. But if the Aries person had a concentration of planets in Earth signs (Taurus, Virgo and Capricorn) their fundamental urge for action could be considerably slowed down.

Studying the Sun signs is an excellent way to learn the basics, and can be surprisingly accurate. However, astrology teaches that each of us is a complex and subtle blend of traits symbolised by all the planets, and where and how these traits operate is determined by the ascendant, or rising sign.

The word *horoscopos* is Greek for 'I watch that which is rising'. So the word horoscope originally referred simply to the ascendant, that is the point of the zodiac rising over the horizon at the precise moment of birth.

Once you know your rising sign, you may find that the 'Sun sign' descriptions for that sign are, in fact, more meaningful for you. However, nothing is as accurate, or as fascinating, as a proper birth chart.

ASTROLOGY AND PERSONALITY

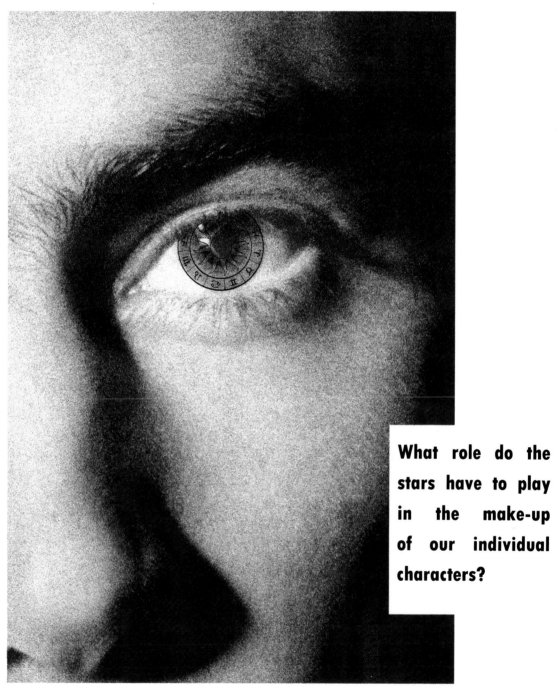

What role do the stars have to play in the make-up of our individual characters?

A very strong link exists between the time of year at which you were born and the type of personality you have. Everyone who was born during a specific astrological period – that is, people who share the same Sun sign – will have the same basic characteristics only of that sign; while further aspects of personality can be ascertained from a more detailed chart prepared for the day, and preferably the hour, when you were born.

The twelve signs of the zodiac form the basic 'clock' relating to the journey of the Sun through the heavens, a cycle which takes a year to complete. This astrological year starts in late March at the time when the Sun enters

Aries. Thereafter, the signs change at monthly intervals. However, the zodiac also breaks down into smaller cycles, each having its effect on the personality.

The main astrological indicators of personality are the Sun, the Moon, the Ascendant and the Mid-Heaven.

The cycle of the Moon takes 28 days to complete; so, while the Sun is journeying through one sign, the Moon will have travelled through all twelve. There is also a daily cycle related to the sign rising over the horizon as the Earth rotates. It is these cycles which provide the subtle colouring to the basic astrological Sun sign personality.

The Four Elements

The twelve signs of the zodiac are divided into four elements. Each elemental personality type interacts with the world in a different way. The Fire signs (Aries, Leo and Sagittarius) are basically out-going, energetic people who function well on the intuitive level. The Water signs (Cancer, Scorpio and Pisces) are inherently inward-looking, emotionally orientated people who feel things very deeply. The Air signs (Gemini, Libra and Aquarius) are communicative and concerned with things of the mind, operating most comfortably in the mental realm. Earth signs (Taurus, Virgo and Capricorn) are cautious and practical people who function through the physical senses, although Virgo is also somewhat mentally inclined.

Extrovert or Introvert?

The Sun signs can also be divided into the outward-looking, active 'extrovert' signs (Aries, Gemini, Leo, Libra, Sagittarius and Aquarius) and the more inward-looking, receptive, 'introvert' signs (Taurus, Cancer, Virgo, Scorpio, Capricorn and Pisces). Generally, those born under an introvert sign are happiest when alone at home or with small groups of people.

The urge to communicate with one's fellow men is believed to be much stronger among the 'extrovert' signs.

They also make good listeners. On the other hand, individuals belonging to an 'extrovert' sign

THE MOON

Closely associated with our fundamental emotional responses, the Moon is also linked with our past, with our roots and with habits laid down in childhood.

Its position on the birth chart can reveal much about your instinctive nature and personality, too. If it was positioned in a Water sign (Cancer, Scorpio and Pisces), for instance, it is likely to have produced a highly sensitive and moody individual. Air Moon personalities may be cool and detached (Gemini, Libra and Aquarius); while Fire Moon people (born with the Moon in Aries, Leo or Sagittarius) are able to express their feelings more easily. Those with Earth Moons, however (born with the Moon in Taurus, Virgo or Capricorn) are likely to find self-expression rather more challenging.

The Moon has long been known to exert influence over the tides (left) and (above) over the individual's personality too.

THE ASCENDANT

The sign which is rising over the horizon at the moment of birth and which can only be calculated from an accurate birth time is known as the Ascendant or rising sign.

Someone born at dawn has the Sun on the Ascendant. But an individual born earlier or later in the day, on the other hand, will have a different Ascendant to the sign in which his or her Sun falls. Each Sun sign has twelve possible Ascendants, and each rising sign will affect rather differently how we see the outside world, as well as how in turn other people see and form their impression of us.

Your Ascendant thus influences the protective colouring which your Sun sign adopts in its approach to the outside world, providing the outward expression of personality.

If the Sun sign Cancer, for example (a moody and emotional sign), has a Virgo Ascendant, it will give the outward impression of an efficient and well organized individual. A Gemini Ascendant would make for a lively communicator; while Sagittarius as a rising sign would project the aura of an adventurous free spirit. Each of these facades would overlie the basically sensitive, home-loving Cancerian nature.

are likely to enjoy the company of others and may feel lonely and unhappy when they have only themselves for company.

The Sun signs can also be divided into three groups having what are known as Cardinal, Fixed or Mutable qualities.

The Cardinal Personality

Aries, Cancer, Libra and Capricorn are Cardinal signs, and as such are concerned with initiating matters. Vigorous and ambitious in their actions, the Cardinal signs are extremely good at beginning projects, but often lack the staying power to see them through – except for Capricorns who have the cautious practicality of their element Earth behind them.

The Fixed Personality

Taurus, Scorpio, Leo and Aquarius – as Fixed signs – are concerned with conserving things, and are very resistant to change. They are thus often steadfast, supportive individuals who can be relied upon to see things through, but who may find it difficult to start things off – with the exception of Aquarians who always seem to be one step ahead of everyone

else but who can still seem set in their ways at times.

The Mutable Personality

Gemini, Sagittarius, Virgo and Pisces are Mutable signs with an adaptable energy and marked versatility. While they are extremely good at picking up an idea and then developing it, they lack the stability to deal with routine for long – except for Virgos, who are stabilized by the element Earth.

THE MID-HEAVEN

A point 'overhead in the sky', shown at the top of the birth chart, the Mid-heaven can only be calculated if the time of birth is known. It represents the way in which an individual will interact with the outside world. Often linked to the career choice which a person makes, the Mid-Heaven may also indicate the specific vocation – such as medicine (Scorpio), nursing (Virgo), or religion (Pisces) – to which a person is particularly suited.

The Mid-Heaven can also indicate qualities which an individual values and seeks to develop as life progresses. Sagittarius on the Mid-Heaven, for example, may show that

knowledge is held in high regard, so that the individual may become the perpetual student who never stops learning. Cancer on the Mid-Heaven, however, may indicate that particular store is set by emotional sensitivity which the individual seeks to express through interaction with children or as a social worker, for instance.

An Islamic astrologer calculates the Mid-heaven, which is often linked with career choice.

Discover what the Sun signs can reveal about character

ARIES	**Enthusiastic, impulsive, independent, pioneering, insensitive, excitable**
TAURUS	**Practical, generous, patient, purposeful, constant, obstinate**
GEMINI	**Inquisitive, versatile, dextrous, articulate, cheering, inconsistent**
CANCER	**Protective, tenacious, changeable, tough, caring, possessive**
LEO	**Extravagant, creative, dignified, domineering, passionate, haughty**
VIRGO	**Meticulous, critical, analytical, methodical, practical, pedantic**
LIBRA	**Diplomatic, amenable, charming, romantic, courteous, narcissistic**
SCORPIO	**Magnetic, intense, secretive, wilful, penetrating, understanding**
SAGITTARIUS	**Optimistic, freedom-loving, idealistic, philosophical, honest, undisciplined**
CAPRICORN	**Dutiful, industrious, loyal, enduring, ambitious, selfish**
AQUARIUS	**Humanitarian, intuitive, sociable, detached, individualistic, cranky**
PISCES	**Sensitive, self-sacrificing, dreamy, compassionate, imaginative, vague**

Sun sign CHARACTERS

March 21 ARIES April 19

THE BRIGHT SIDE   The Aries personality is fiery and warm, passionate and self-expressive with an urge to act – now! This is not a patient sign: everything is done on impulse, and with great urgency.

Enterprise

Aries is a courageous leader, not averse to taking risks, but will often feel that 'I know best'. As Aries has a quick grasp of the essentials of any situation, this may well be so; but Aries rarely hangs around to check out the details. However, give Aries a good cause for which to fight, a problem to solve, or a new idea to pioneer and this enterprising personality comes into its own.

Intolerance

THE DARKER SIDE   Strangely enough for such an active sign, one of its main failings is that of procrastination. Although Aries is extremely impatient and intolerant of delay, the Aries personality is prone to put off what must be done (tax returns, for example) if the matter to be put underway is simply not interesting. Similarly, Aries may resort to lies rather than undergo the inconvenience, or boredom, of being forced into doing something Aries would rather not do. Arians can also be blunt, often causing offence, or employ bullying tactics in a selfish desire to have their own way.

EGOTIST

Aries is the first sign of the zodiac, and 'Me First' is the Arian motto! Active and outgoing, the Arian personality is all set to make its mark on the world – but this can lead to a selfish, egotistical attitude to life. In a vulgar manner, this often proves successful: because the simple fact of the matter is what Arians want, they usually tend to get.

April 20 TAURUS May 20

THE BRIGHT SIDE   Taurus has a patient, steadfast and reliable personality. People generally know where they are with Taurus – unless they make the mistake of goading one too far! The Taurean personality is also warm and sensual, with an appreciation of fine things.

Security

As Taurus is firmly motivated by a need for security, this sign is often excellent at business matters and can be trusted to plan and carry things through carefully with resolute attention to detail. An Earth sign, Taurus also values the environment and will do everything possible to preserve its well-being.

THE DARKER SIDE   Unfortunately, the Taurean personality can be so committed to self-preservation and so cautious in approaching anything new that it may become boring – although many people are prepared to brave the possibility of a tedious evening in view of the excellence of the food served at Taurean dinner parties!

Taureans at their best are typically 'strong, silent types', but all too often they appear ignorant and wilfully obstinate to others.

ENDURER

The typical Taurean personality is earthy, solid and enduring, continuing with dogged persistence long after everyone else has given up. However, Taureans can be particularly resistant to change, unable to adapt to new and innovative ways of thinking.

Explosive

Taureans have two other main difficulties in interacting with people: a very slow-to-rouse but terrible temper, and possessiveness. Sexual jealousy, another Taurean trait, can often lead to explosions of anger.

May 21	**GEMINI**	June 20

June 21	**CANCER**	July 22

THE BRIGHT SIDE   The Gemini personality is bright, witty and adaptable. Very little ever troubles a Gemini, or stops one talking for long — Geminis can argue  their way out of any situation. Having a lively curiosity, Gemini also excels at gathering information, processing it, and expressing it in an accessible way to the waiting world. This personality can do almost anything — so long as it does not cause boredom, anathema to Geminis. With so many talents and an ability to make something out of nothing, Gemini's difficulty lies in deciding where, and how, to concentrate. Geminis are almost always doing at least two things at once, you will usually find.

Volatile

THE DARKER SIDE   The Gemini personality's greatest faults are inconsistency and superficiality. Other people never quite know what to expect; indeed, Gemini cannot be relied upon to do anything. All that chasing about and mind-changing leave little time for them to go within and assess things on a deeper level, and this can lead to mental overload.

Cunning

There is a side of Geminis which can be quite a surprise to admirers of their other qualities, since there can be a deep streak of cunning and also a tongue which can become positively lethal at times, when provoked.

COMMUNICATOR

The self-expressive Gemini personality simply has to communicate, knows everything, forms strong opinions and is always right — except that Geminis can change their minds so quickly that they may end up contradicting themselves. Consequently, Geminis can appear indecisive or hypocritical.

THE BRIGHT SIDE   At their best, Cancerians are sensitive, kind and sympathetic with an urge to nurture and care for people which expresses itself particularly strongly through the home and family. This is the 'soft' side of the Cancer personality. Meanwhile, the 'hard' side is very enterprising, shrewd, and also self-assured.

PROTECTOR

The Cancer personality is extremely protective of a vulnerable underside. There is a hard shell which is outwardly tough and impenetrable; but, inwardly, Cancer is highly sensitive and caring, even if this tendency is well hidden from the rest of the world.

Imaginative

When attuned to the rhythms of their own nature, Cancerians are intuitive, imaginative and resourceful, knowing when to reach out to others and when to withdraw into their inner self for sustenance.

THE DARKER SIDE   Cancerians have great trouble deciding between the tough, ambitious and outgoing side of their nature and the sensitive, emotional, inward-looking part. This can create great conflict and swings of mood which makes it impossible for other people to assess how the somewhat contrary Cancerian will react at any time.

Possessive

Cancer also has a deep inferiority complex, so that any hurt, real or imagined, is brooded upon. Cancer sometimes shows, too, a tendency to look back at,  and hold on to, things of the past and can be a very possessive sign. This highlights an inherently conservative aspect of their nature although, as a Cardinal sign, they will also often initiate changes.

| July 23 | **LEO** | August 22 | | August 23 | **VIRGO** | Sep 22 |

THE BRIGHT SIDE This aspect of Leo is very bright indeed, for this is a personality very much attuned to the vital life-giving qualities of the Sun.

Flamboyant

The typical Leo personality is flamboyant and generous with tremendous charm and magnanimity of spirit which draws people close. The fixed quality of the sign, meanwhile, helps to restrain the Fire element's tendency to over-exuberance. Leos are also loyal, full of self-assurance and hard-working, being excellent organizers (so long as they are the boss). Leo's ability to play hard and the value placed on pleasure makes for an excellent companion.

THE DARKER SIDE This aspect of the Leo personality usually emerges when Leo is being ignored, which may result in sulking, or when inferior mortals challenge the divine right to rule. Leos can be very self-opinionated and consequently bombastic and overbearing. One of Leo's most characteristic traits is pride, and there is a tendency, too, towards pomposity and snobbery.

KING

Leos are warm, sunny and outgoing but just love to be adored and looked up to. Those who fail to recognize a Leo's innate need to be superior may find themselves on the receiving end of a right royal snub, or the victims of typically aristocratic wrath.

Touchy

It can be difficult to spot when Leo is hurt (and this sign is surprisingly touchy): but the sudden drop in temperature as Leo retreats back into regal dignity provides a clue. In long-term disagreements, Leo can also prove to be something of a formidable enemy.

THE BRIGHT SIDE The Virgo personality is marked by a very sharp intellect which is used to analyse the natural order of things. Virgos generally tend to be methodical and precise, being drawn only to  such knowledge as can be applied usefully. They will happily share this with anyone, however, as it confirms their own usefulness in the world, and brings them out of their normally reserved shells, eager as they are to play their part.

Achievement

Caution is another Virgo trait which, if positively used, bestows on those under this Sun sign a fine sense of discrimination between the practical and the fanciful. They will usually develop skills which will enable them to improve themselves and their immediate surroundings, and place great pride in tangible achievements.

Obsessive

THE DARKER SIDE In their urge to categorize the mechanics of life and the forces that hold them together, Virgos can become obsessed with the notion of order. Anything that upsets this harmony and understanding potentially exposes them to fear of the unknown. For Virgos, there is a place for everything and everything has to have its place: and they will do anything to achieve this.

REALIST

Virgos are typically labelled as perfectionists. But their concern with high standards has little bearing on the pursuit of ideals; it is more a reflection of a need to have a tight grip on their environment. Virgos will also tend to immerse themselves in the minutest details of how something works in order to enrich their understanding.

Sep 23	**LIBRA**	Oct 22

Oct 23	**SCORPIO**	Nov 21

THE BRIGHT SIDE The Libran personality is one which is easy-going, charming and pleasant, and for whom relationships are all-important. This sign above all simply cannot do without other people, and so makes an excellent host or hostess.

Peaceful

Libra is also a sign which values peace — often at all costs — and which is very fair-minded, so that other people like being around Librans as they will always seek a compromise if an argument is threatened. (However, those dealing with Librans should remember that things are not always what they seem. Librans can, if so minded, charm the birds out of the trees!)

THE DARKER SIDE The famous indecisiveness of Librans means that they either sit on the fence and wait, or swing wildly from one point-of-view to another. So it is not the most reliable of signs and is often accused of being two-faced. It is perhaps less well known that Libra is also a very self-centred sign which always insists on its own way.

Devious

What Libra wants, Libra gets in the end, and all kinds of devious ploys may be used in the meantime. But a reluctance to dirty their hands gives Librans a streak of laziness which may mean a delay in getting their many plans off the ground.

THE BRIGHT SIDE Although they often get a bad press astrologically, Scorpios have very intense personalities with hidden depths of perspicacity and a compassion which reaches out to troubled people, even though this may not always show on the surface. Being deeply emotional themselves, Scorpios understand and accept the feelings and pain that other signs often find they cannot handle.

Magnetism

Scorpio is not afraid to go into darkness, so this sign makes an ideal therapist, and many doctors and surgeons are Scorpios, using their incisive skills in a constructive way. Scorpios also have incredible personal magnetism and can be very loyal and devoted friends or lovers.

THE DARKER SIDE Scorpios have a hidden and secretive side and are not averse to using their very deep understanding of other people for their own ends — usually directed towards gaining power.

Grudges

Indeed, Scorpio has a fascination with power, how to use it, how to master it, and how to hold it over people. At times, this can extend into extreme cruelty, for Scorpio is a vindictive, brooding sign which never forgets a grudge. Scorpio can also have an inner self-destruct button which is pushed compulsively from time to time.

Nov 22 SAGITTARIUS Dec 21

THE BRIGHT SIDE Sagittarius is an optimistic, out-going and adaptable Fire sign. Sagittarian personalities seek to interact spontaneously with life as they go on their great quest for meaning. Sagittarians also need a great deal of freedom, and are equally willing to offer that freedom to others.

SEEKER

Sagittarius is a great traveller and adventurer, not only physically but in the mind. It is a sign that simply has to know the answers to life's big questions. Although they are as pleasant as could be when these answers are discovered, frustrating their quest could produce sparks.

Understanding

Sagittarians have an open-minded and intellectual curiosity which means that they are willing to learn about other people in an effort to understand them, and to be trusting and open with them in return. Sagittarians say exactly what they mean with devastating frankness.

THE DARKER SIDE Tactlessness, boastfulness and thinking with one's mouth are Sagittarian faults which tend to upset other people. And so, too, does a Sagittarian tendency to moralize and 'preach' what other people should do — without, of course, following the same rules themselves.

Loyalties

One of the great Sagittarian difficulties lies in relationships. They find it extremely easy to be entirely faithful to two people at once. And bored Sagittarians are a danger to themselves and others. Anything goes, is their attitude, so long as it is found to be stimulating. This tendency to over-indulge can lead them to burn the candle at both ends, and health may suffer.

Dec 22 CAPRICORN Jan 19

THE BRIGHT SIDE One of the Capricorn personality's most positive features is its sense of humour. This is something which often sustains Capricorn in its efforts to impose some order on the world, or wisely master its resources. Although the humour is likely to be dry, it does involve contact with other people (something that the self-contained Capricorn does not excel at). What the Capricorn personality *is* very good at is everything that others (except for Earth signs) find a little tedious. Capricorn is endlessly patient, prudent, reliable, persevering and disciplined.

Inhibited

THE DARKER SIDE Capricorns can be extremely rigid and pessimistic in their outlook; and gloomy and depressed (and depressing) in their interaction with other people. They can also be emotionally cold and inhibited. The prudent and cautious side of the Capricorn nature can be taken to extremes, too, sometimes into the unsociable realm of the miser.

CONSERVER

Most Capricorns are in favour of conserving assets and are firm supporters of all things traditional and conventional. Capricorn's basic motivation is security. They can also become fanatical moralists, opposing anything that contradicts their view of the world. But they are also widely known for their generosity of nature.

Authoritarian

The Capricorn's need to be in control can even extend to the outer limits of authoritarianism. They distrust anything spontaneous, if it tends to deflect them from their sense of purpose which is to go all out to change their environment to suit their needs.

| Jan 20 | **AQUARIUS** | Feb 18 |

THE BRIGHT SIDE Aquarians are lively, inventive and original. Anything goes with Aquarius, and being an individual does not worry this sign: in fact, Aquarius is always out of step with the rest of the world and revels in anything that is 'different'.

Humanitarian

The Aquarian personality is one of the most impersonal and detached, yet Aquarius has a deep care and concern for humanity. A progressive reformer, Aquarius is also full of humanitarian ideals, but these can be somewhat vague, giving Aquarians a reputation for keeping their heads in the clouds.

Eccentric

Aquarius is also one of the most happily eccentric of the signs. Although it can be extremely difficult to get close to an Aquarian, this is a Fixed sign and so is loyal and faithful. Ask an Aquarian for help and you will immediately get it, for this sign is a very soft touch and would willingly give some people the shirt off its back if necessary.

Unpredictable

THE DARKER SIDE The Aquarian personality can be chaotic and unpredictable, stubborn and rebellious, cranky and perverse. It is a sign which can be totally dedicated to being unconventional, whilst remaining stuck in a rigid, unrecognized pattern. It is also a sign which can become detached to the point of coldness, making it very difficult for ordinary mortals to relate to them. Aquarians do not care what the world thinks, however, so that social conventions are sometimes thrown out of the window in favour of anarchy. The isolation this can sometimes bring can come as a surprise to them as they find it difficult to see how they might have behaved unreasonably.

| Feb 19 | **PISCES** | March 20 |

THE BRIGHT SIDE Pisces is sympathetic and compassionate, and cannot bear to see another human being in pain. Indeed, Pisceans feel very deeply about other people as they do not have a strong sense of separation and individuality.

Intuition

Pisces is an intuitive sign which can receive great inspiration from beyond. Pisceans are thus the natural mediums and mystics of the zodiac who can communicate their inner vision through either the arts or sciences. Pisces can also be a sign of selfless or self-sacrificing devotion, and is capable of truly unconditional love for others.

Guilt-ridden

THE DARKER SIDE The Pisces personality has a number of sub-personalities who are likely to take over at the drop of a hat. They include the victim, the martyr and the saviour or rescuer; and once Pisces gets locked into these patterns, it can be very difficult to shift. This can be hard on other people involved, too, for Pisceans can inflict, or receive, considerable suffering when they enter into a guilt-ridden phase. The other negative Piscean trait involves the illusion and confusion which surrounds their ability to tell the truth — known as lying by the more pragmatic signs. Pisceans tend to be too imaginative for their own good.

DREAMER

The Piscean personality is the most unworldly one in the zodiac. It is the poet, the dreamer, or the psychic who enjoys being taken away from the mundane reality of everyday life. If Pisceans become trapped by circumstances in any one place, they will seek solace from their own inner world.

ASTROLOGY AND ROMANCE

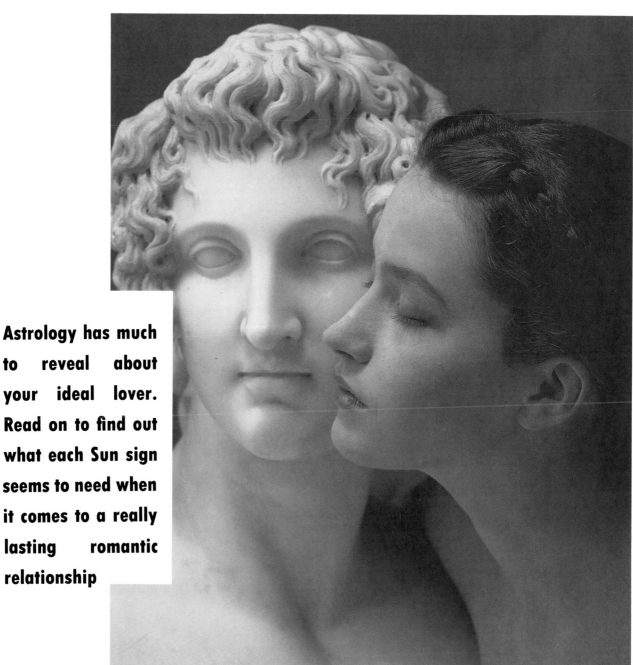

Astrology has much to reveal about your ideal lover. Read on to find out what each Sun sign seems to need when it comes to a really lasting romantic relationship

I t is fate, some say, that works to propel us into love. Be that as it may, there is certainly a lot to be said for a means of coming to understand more precisely your own innate requirements for a loving and enduring relationship.

Astrology offers much in this respect. In turn, too, it can guide you in the attempt to find a suitable life partner.

Perhaps, for instance, you have noticed how often we are attracted to those who seem to have the very qualities we lack. Opposite Sun signs, astrologers have found, often make for rather dynamic or difficult partnerships. Who, then, should you seek as *your* ideal lover?

Do **Opposites Attract?**

In astrology, each Sun sign has what is known as its polar, or opposite, sign.

Although the characteristics of each pair appear to be very different, each sign counteracts the deficiencies in its opposite, often with some very fascinating results.

The Arian's impetuosity is tempered by the Libran's diplomacy; and the ardent Arian will also spark the romantic Libran sexually. Taurean faithfulness comes as a relief to the suspicious and jealous Scorpio. A philosophical Sagittarian will broaden and deepen a Gemini's superficial way of thinking. Although moody and highly strung, the Cancerian can soften the austere Capricorn heart. A not too possessive Leo can learn a lot from an independent and freedom-loving Aquarian. Dreamy Pisceans are brought firmly down to earth by ever-practical Virgos.

Strong magnetic attractions between opposite signs may, however, generate tension unless there is compromise.

OPPOSITE SUN SIGNS

Consult the above chart to find your opposite sign. For example, Libra lies diametrically across the zodiac from Aries. Opposite signs have very different characteristics which in love may cause sparks, unless there is a certain amount of give and take between partners.

PLANET OF LOVE

Venus, also known as the Evening Star, is the brightest planet. Consisting mostly of carbon dioxide, it is the hottest, too.

Traditionally, the planet Venus rules over our relationships, affection and harmony. She took her name from the Roman goddess who presided over beauty, sensuality, the arts, fertility and money.

In astrology, she represents our ability to attract and respond romantically to others. She embodies the highest of our ideals – finding the perfect partner, aesthetic beauty, inner peace and well-being. She also reflects our struggle to achieve these.

The planet Venus, shown above, represents love and harmony, as depicted symbolically, left, in a 15th century manuscript.

Elementary Attraction

Astrologers arrange the twelve signs of the zodiac into four groups, which correspond to the four elements of ancient and medieval philosophy: Fire, Earth, Air and Water. Each of these groups contains three Sun signs, which are influenced by their element in particular ways. Signs which share the same element will also have more insight into and understanding of certain aspects of their personalities than do members of other element groups.

Fire Signs

The Fire signs – Aries, Leo and Sagittarius – are assertive, enthusiastic, energetic and creative. Full of life, warmth and enthusiasm, these individuals have a direct and immediate influence on their surroundings.

It is a very forceful combination when two Fire signs meet, as they usually spur each other on in all sorts of ways, and make the most of any exciting opportunities that arise.

The expansiveness so typical of the Fire signs can also result in extravagance when two of them get together.

Fire signs are on the same emotional wavelength, and love means a great deal to them. They share a need for a warm, loving relationship and are often very passionate.

Earth Signs

The Earth signs – Taurus, Virgo and Capricorn – are practical and materially-minded. Innately cautious, careful and restrained, Earth signs have a great deal in common. They like stability and work hard to improve and consolidate their situation in life. When two of them get together, they find it very reassuring to meet someone who shares their down-to-earth outlook.

F \ M	FIRE	EARTH	AIR	WATER
FIRE	Certainly a fiery relationship, with plenty of emotion and excitement. But there may not be a problem in keeping the fire burning.	A good emotional match, but with plenty of fireworks. The Earth signs may prove too stubborn for their partner.	Will find each other endlessly fascinating, with plenty to talk about, although the Air partner may not share the Fire sign's passion.	A very passionate combination, although the Water sign may prove difficult with tears and tantrums.
EARTH	This could be a tricky relationship as the Fire signs need plenty of room to breathe, even though their enthusiasm is inspiring.	This will prove to be a very secure relationship, although not entirely lacking in passion.	Can be filled with fun, until the Earth sign tries to tie down the light-hearted Air sign, which will frighten the partner off.	You adore the emotional security that you give each other, but try to bring out your imagination more.
AIR	A successful relationship filled with good times. The stronger the emotions, the happier it will be.	Although operating at very different levels, this may still work. The Earth partner provides stability.	A magical combination for the mind although it may be difficult to express emotions.	Needs careful handling so that the romantic dreams of the Water sign are not destroyed.
WATER	Wonderful at first, although problems may arise when the Water sign tries to use emotional blackmail.	These signs need the same things in life – love and security – and this will lead to a very supportive relationship.	The Air sign can be entrancing, although emotional differences may prove to be a stumbling block.	These two signs understand each other perfectly. This can be a wonderfully sensitive partnership.

Use the chart above to find which elemental partner would be ideal for you. Women should read down from the top line, and men across from the left.

Earth signs are marvellously faithful, and will stand by each other. Permanent relationships are very important to them.

Air Signs

The Air signs – Gemini, Libra and Aquarius – are traditionally the least emotional of the four groups. They tend to value mental compatibility in romance more than passion or looks. They love conversation and discussing their thoughts. But shaping new ideas is generally far more exciting to them than carrying them through.

They especially enjoy the company of other Air signs, although they can find it very difficult when it comes to expressing emotions. They also tend to worry about committing themselves to anything or anyone, in case they change their minds later.

Air signs are unhappy in claustrophobic relationships, so they are ideally suited to each other. There will be little danger of them making emotional demands that cannot be satisfied.

Water Signs

The Water signs – Cancer, Scorpio and Pisces – are governed by powerful emotions, making them intense and sensitive. The best person to understand the needs of a Water sign is another Water sign; for others may interpret their traits as an unwillingness to communicate or even moodiness.

In a relationship between two Water signs, emotions are of paramount importance. They can be very protective towards each other, creating a very cosy, caring partnership.

However, these strong emotions can also have the opposite effect, leading to games that can destroy the relationship.

ATTRACTION CHART

LOVE CHART

How compatible are you? Read down for the man and across for the woman to find out.

M ＼ F	ARIES	TAURUS	GEMINI	CANCER	LEO	VIRGO	LIBRA	SCORPIO	SAGITTARIUS	CAPRICORN	AQUARIUS	PISCES
ARIES	Fiery	Very erotic	Light-hearted	Many differences	Hot and cold	Unstoppable	Sensual	**Very ardent**	Adventurous	Lots of passion	Intriguing	Difficult
TAURUS	Passionate	Well suited	Not a success	Caring and sharing	Intense	Hot and cold	Quite magnetic	Very rocky	Sensual	Terrific	Very strong	Traumatic
GEMINI	Promising	A difficult combination	Could be fickle	Steer clear	Good fun	Erratic	**Absolutely wonderful**	Off key	Fun-loving	Don't see eye to eye	Good friends	Charming
CANCER	Poor match	A cosy atmosphere	At odds	**A dreamy affair**	**Extremely loving**	Stimulating company	Heavy going	Sparks fly	Troublesome	A caring couple	Upsetting	Highly charged
LEO	Memorable	Truly emotional	**Full of laughter**	Loving	A battle of wills	A difficult match	Great fun	A clash of egos	Very powerful	Short but sweet	Can be difficult	Sparks fly
VIRGO	Poles apart	Steady and enjoyable	Quite unusual	Problematic	Divided opinions	Can be boring	Hard going	Truly passionate	Different needs	In tune	Troubled waters	**Heavenly**
LIBRA	Opposites attract	Very sensual	Sublime	Hard work	Invigorating	Discordant	Too indecisive	Too flighty	Emotionally rewarding	Not a good bet	**Marvellous match**	**Quite rewarding**
SCORPIO	Long-lasting	Rewarding relationship	Volatile	Paradise	Powerful attraction	Slow start	Heady stuff	Explosive	Can be strained	Entrancing	**Up and down**	**Absolutely superb**
SAGITTARIUS	**Wonderfully romantic**	Some confrontation	Hot and cold	Too distant	Truly passionate	Powerful	Sheer enjoyment	Chalk and cheese	Filled with excitement	Conflicts galore	Rather heated	Can be difficult
CAPRICORN	May argue	Good prospects	Hard work	A great match	Very different	Can be strong	Not a winner	Very strong	Unsuitable	Long lasting	**Tremendous**	**Sensual but erratic**
AQUARIUS	Very lively	Too stubborn	On the cool side	Too hurtful	Most entertaining	Not harmonious	**Superlative**	Many conflicts	Requires effort	Can be tricky	Truly amazing	Can lead to tears
PISCES	Needs dedication	An excellent match	Needs insight	Quite entrancing	A romantic couple	Quite supportive	Fairytale romance	Tantalising and fun	Too many problems	Thoroughly passionate	Take care	**Absolute bliss**

sun signs FOR LOVERS

| March 21 | **ARIES** | April 19 |
| April 20 | **TAURUS** | May 20 |

As the first sign of the zodiac, Arians cannot help putting themselves first, although they are very affectionate and generous towards their loved ones. They have warm and enthusiastic natures and can be very demonstrative.

Gregarious, sociable and extrovert, Arians are great people to  have around as they are usually the life and soul of any party, thanks to their bouncy, enthusiastic natures. Sometimes, however, the Arian face becomes creased with frowns when he or she is crossed in love.

Heartbreak

This usually occurs when they have been let down in love, which is something they take very seriously. Despite their cheery exterior, Arians are very soft-hearted and vulnerable.

They often fall in love at first sight and instantly put their partner on a pedestal. This is when the trouble starts. Unless the couple are able to talk through differences, the Arian will be disappointed on discovering that his or her partner is only human after all.

The idea of being faithful to one person forever appeals to the Arian's strong sense of romance; but if things begin to turn sour, he or she may prefer to stray elsewhere in search of more excitement, attention and love.

ARDENT LOVERS

Arians have a heedless attitude to love and are not content with half measures. They are true optimists, refusing to accept defeat, and frequently rush in without thinking when they believe they have found true love. They are sentimental and impulsive, sometimes to the extent of being foolhardy.

Taureans are extremely faithful, with a strong need for security and a settled routine. Although they have Earth as their element, they can be highly romantic and sensitive when it comes to love.

Security

Security is of paramount importance to Taureans, and emotional contentment and stability come high on their list of priorities.

Although passionate, they are steadfast which may not appeal to those who crave constant excitement. Nevertheless, there are many who fall for that Taurean charm, those film star good looks and that placid, easy-going nature.

Taureans like to take things slowly, and they make no exceptions to this rule when it comes to love. In fact, they like to be extra sure of sweethearts before they commit themselves, so they often spend lots of time getting to know them well.

Reliability is second nature to Taureans, which means that they are faithful lovers. But they can be overpoweringly possessive. They need to learn to let go and give their partners the freedom they need, or they may end up alone. When in a serious relationship, marriage is often a better solution than living together, since it helps boost their much-needed sense of security. They are often traditionalists who prefer not to fly in the face of convention.

FAITHFUL MATE

Although they do not sweep prospective lovers off their feet, Taureans are incurable romantics and shower their loved ones with gifts. Once in love, they are prepared to make a commitment and remain very faithful.

| May 21 | **GEMINI** | June 20 | | June 21 | **CANCER** | July 22 |

Geminis are renowned for their dual personalities and ability to change mood from moment to moment. Although they hate to be tied down, they make lively, entertaining and romantic partners, even if rather fickle at times.

Natural communicators, Geminis do not suffer fools gladly; so once they are attracted to people, they have to ensure that they are not dull or mundane. They will spend ages chatting to them about every subject under the sun, just to find out what makes them tick.

Independence

Variety is the spice of life for Geminis, especially when it comes to love. At the first hint of boredom, they will frantically plot their escape, whether temporary or perhaps permanent.

Faithfulness is difficult for Geminis, and most of them are born flirts. Their curiosity makes them wonder if they are missing out on meeting the great love of their life, even if happily married.

A few of them will take this to extremes and thrive on the excitement of leading a double life. But they are so quick with words that they can usually talk their way out of trouble. Just keeping up with a Gemini can prove a full-time occupation, as they are constantly busy. They have so many different interests that their partners may feel exhausted just watching them.

FLIGHTY SPIRIT

Gemini lovers keep changing their minds. Their flighty spirit means that they do not like to be tied down. Partners may find them unreliable and a constant source of surprise as they are forever dithering, unable to reach a final decision! Most are also incorrigibly flirtatious.

Emotions play a very important role in the lives of Cancerians. Although naturally defensive and afraid of being hurt, they put their hearts and souls into relationships and are faithful, loving and loyal partners.

Sensitivity

Cancerians crave the security of being near the one they love. Soft-hearted and also highly emotional, Cancerian feelings are never far from the surface, particularly when it comes to romance.

DEVOTED LOVER

The Cancerian heart is filled with emotions but they will only expose them very gradually. Faithful and loyal, Cancerians think carefully before committing themselves to anyone, lest their emotional security is threatened and their trust broken.

There are no half measures when Cancerians fall in love; they really do fall hook, line and sinker. Because of their need for permanent partnerships, Cancerians are not at all interested in light-hearted flirtations. Without some love in their lives, Cancerians feel unfulfilled and unhappy.

Fidelity

Cancerians are very faithful indeed, and they expect the same loyalty in return. They lavish much love and affection on their partners, but they can sometimes be so caring that they become overprotective and very possessive. Indeed, their loved ones can sometimes feel as though they are being suffocated, to the extent that they have no life of their own. They often find it very hard to say goodbye at the end of a relationship, and sometimes choose to suffer the consequences of painful meetings rather than let go.

July 23	**LEO**	August 22

August 23	**VIRGO**	Sep 22

Expansive, generous and caring, Leos revel in love affairs and all things romantic. They are passionate and demonstrative, and like nothing better than spoiling their loved ones.

Emotions

Happiness knows no bounds for Leos in love. Their big hearts and warm emotions really come into their own when they fall for someone. Then their true Leonine personalities emerge. Because they value love above all else, Leos are naturally faithful, and very loyal. But they can sometimes almost over-whelm their partners with adoration.

They invest all their emotions in their love affairs; but if things go wrong, they come down to earth with a bump. Once a Leo heart is broken, it takes a long time to mend.

Problems can arise if a Leo forgets that he or she is one half only of a partnership, and begins to act in the role of boss. Although outwardly they seem to be bursting with self-assurance and confidence, and often revel in being the centre of attention, underneath their showy exterior Leos can be very sensitive, but usually they hate to admit it.

FULL OF PASSION

Leos spare no expense when courting a new love. They are very demonstrative and loyal, and are almost continually in the throes of passion, remaining very faithful. They only lose their sparkle when love begins to fade.

Their fiery feelings and expansive emotions have to find an outlet and they yearn to express their inner-most thoughts to their partner. However, they almost always expect an equally heartfelt sentiment to be returned by the loved one.

Although they may seem shy, introverted and self-conscious on the surface, Virgos blossom and relax once love comes their way.

Virgos sometimes find it hard to show their love. They have a thoughtful approach, and always look before they leap, analyzing all the possible consequences of a relationship.

Inhibitions

When looking for a partner to sweep you off your feet with tender words of love and steamy nights of passion, it is wise to think twice before picking a Virgo.

It is often a real effort for them to make the first move in the game of love — they are so sure that they are going to fail. Although they may long to cast caution to the wind, they have to conquer their emotional inhibitions first. But with the help of a loving, patient and understanding partner, love will blossom.

Once they have found a true love, Virgos can be very faithful and will work hard to keep the relationship alive and exciting. However, they can nag, carp or fault-find whenever their partners fail to come up to scratch.

Because they have such high standards, it can be a constant battle for the Virgo's partner who has to struggle to fulfil these expectations. Rows begin when they unintentionally deeply offend their loved one in this way.

COOL CUSTOMER

Dependable and sincere as lovers, Virgos have few illusions about affairs of the heart. Rather than lavishing affection on their partners, they prefer to show their love in small gestures and are cautious in the extreme about making a first move. They are also often far too down-to-earth to be swept away.

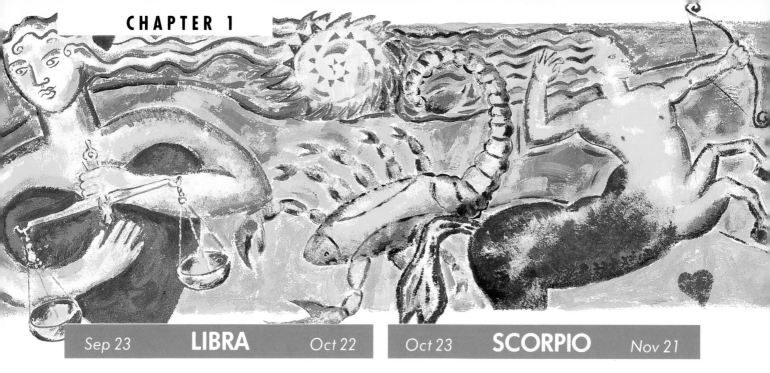

| Sep 23 | **LIBRA** | Oct 22 | Oct 23 | **SCORPIO** | Nov 21 |

Falling in love comes naturally to Librans, whose whole reason for living centres around happy and enduring relationships.

For them, a life without love is not worth contemplating, since they find it hard to  function properly without someone special in their hearts. They long for the emotional security of knowing that they are loved.

Infatuation

As a result, many Librans can fall in love with the idea of love, confusing infatuation with the real thing. There are lots of sad Librans who married in haste at an early age and lived to regret it. They prefer to endure an unhappy relationship rather than leave and live on their own again.

Romance

Romance could have been invented by Librans, who use everything from poetry to expensive dinners when wooing a prospective partner. They are born flirts, but often do not change even when they have met the partner of their dreams. Instead, they want to practise on other people, just to make sure that they have not lost their touch! Librans are one of the most attractive signs, oozing great charm and diplomacy. They enjoy the good things in life and ensure that their partners do, too.

TRUE ROMANTIC

Librans are in love with love. Loving relationships are the centre of their world and they expend a great deal of energy achieving harmony. For them, romantic partnerships are virtually an art form, but problems arise when an innate inability to make a definite and binding decision about a relationship comes to the fore.

The intensity and passion of Scorpios makes them unforgettable partners when it comes to love. They take their love affairs very seriously, which sometimes leads to jealousy. Their innate secrecy can also make it difficult for them to confront problems in a romantic relationship.

Passion

There is no mistaking it when Scorpios really fall for someone because they pull out all the stops. Once they are deeply involved in a relationship, they show just  how passionate they can be. When love comes their way, they are convinced that this is the relationship that they have always been waiting for, and will invest in it all their energies. Scorpios are very suspicious, and can easily work themselves up into a state of jealousy if they imagine that their other half is being untruthful. They will soon gather up the evidence and challenge their loved one. This is when the volcanic Scorpio temper can emerge, often with very frightening results.

POSSESSIVE MATE

They may be cool on the surface, but underneath Scorpios are intensely passionate, both physically and emotionally. When love is sweet, they are very loyal, but when things go wrong they may show a sting in their tail.

Intensity

Renowned for being introverted and intense, Scorpios bury their deepest emotions well under the surface and positively relish their resulting mysterious image. They are very faithful and need the security of permanent relationships. If they are badly let down in a love affair, they may decide to play tit for tat.

Nov 22 SAGITTARIUS Dec 21

Although they often prefer to be footloose and fancy free, once involved in a relationship Sagittarians will make it as much fun and as enjoyable as possible.

Sagittarians are usually very gregarious people, but they gladly find the time for one important loving relationship. They are very warm and caring, although their light-hearted affections may seem a bit too casual for some of the more passionate Sun signs, who prefer more security.

CASUAL ROMANTIC

Sagittarians may plunge into a love affair whole-heartedly, but do not commit themselves too easily. They enjoy the chase of a new romance and often prefer casual relationships to something more permanent which denies them freedom.

The Chase

As the hunters of the zodiac, there is nothing Sagittarians like better than the thrill of the romantic chase. However, some of the them lose interest once they have captured the heart of the person they have been pursuing, and will then set their sights on someone new.

Freedom

Independence is vital to Sagittarians, who can quickly start to feel trapped in a suffocating relationship. Some of them expect their partners to wait around while they pursue their own interests; and their tendency to blow hot and cold can be very confusing. They usually possess suitably warm emotions and also a wonderful zest for life which is often filled with endless absorbing interests. Naturally optimistic, they will always tend to shrug off defeat.

Dec 22 CAPRICORN Jan 19

Once Capricorns conquer their natural reserve and shyness, they make terrific partners: for although they are cautious and introverted, they can be very faithful when in a relationship. They need a partner who will support them emotionally and give them a much-needed boost in confidence.

Confidence

Some Capricorns are so frightened of rejection and the possibility of being hurt that beginning a relationship can be difficult and opportunities are often missed. They may be short of self-confidence and are convinced that no one will ever find them attractive enough to embark on a long-term meaningful relationship.

Rivals

Flirtations do not appeal to most Capricorns, who prefer a permanent relationship that gives them emotional security. The partner of a Capricorn may find that the only serious rival for his or her affections is the Capricorn's career. Although they can often seem a touch too introverted for the first few meetings, once they relax and feel more comfortable with someone, they are able to reveal more of themselves. One of their most appealing traits is a fantastic sense of humour, even when the joke is at their expense. Once trust is established, their confidence blossoms.

CAUTIOUS LOVER

The head rules the heart for Capricorns and they never marry without being totally sure about their partner. They are steady and careful in love rather than being full of surprises, and usually prove to be faithful and trusting lovers. Their ultimate goal in love is to feel secure.

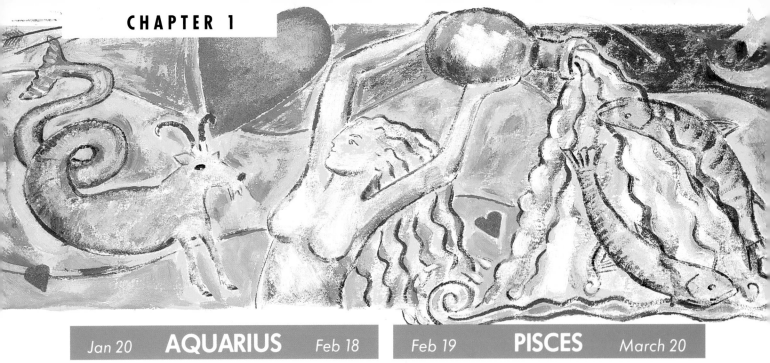

Jan 20   AQUARIUS   Feb 18

Feb 19   PISCES   March 20

Aquarians are strongly independent and cannot bear to be tied down. Their firm views and opinions can quickly change to obstinacy and stubbornness when provoked. Nevertheless, they are faithful and supportive in the right relationship. They may become ensconsed in a committed relationship but need to preserve their privacy and independence.

FREE SPIRIT

Aquarians do not like showing their real feelings. An independent nature also means that they take their time to settle in steady relationships. They find it hard to build up trust but will remain very faithful once a relationship is established.

Honesty

Although they are naturally very straightforward, do not expect Aquarians to be clear-cut because they are often very unpredictable, and will almost certainly keep their loved ones guessing. Not all Aquarians find it easy to show their feelings, and they are often uncomfortable about the more romantic aspects of love.

Extrovert, entertaining, intelligent, and often very idealistic, Aquarians usually have many friends who play an important role in their lives. Although they are very loyal and trustworthy, their partners may often become jealous over the bond between an Aquarian and his or her friends. In some cases, their strong feelings and attitudes can turn into insistence and tremendous arguments if aroused, which can make life difficult for their partners.

Aquarians also often have difficulty in handling their own as well as other people's emotions, which may mean that they sometimes ignore a partner's most intimate feelings and insecurities.

The most idealistic, romantic and highly-strung sign, Pisceans are only too happy to lose themselves in their relationships. Being loved is central to their well-being. They are very caring, and make compassionate partners.

Ideals

Deeply sensitive and soft-hearted, Pisceans revel in highly-charged relationships. Unfortunately, they are so easily hurt that they often emerge battle-scarred from a relationship with their dreams shattered. Many Pisceans also view their loved ones through rose-coloured spectacles, refusing to admit that their idealized lover is only human after all.

As a result, they sometimes turn a blind eye to transgressions that would provoke some of the more down-to-earth signs. Some Pisceans become willing victims in destructive relationships, without realizing it.

However, if Pisceans become involved with those who are too realistic and unable to stimulate a vivid imagination, they may well start to stray to pastures new through sheer boredom.

IDEALISTIC MATE

When in love, Pisceans are filled with aspirations. Often seeking a spiritual life with their partner, they are probably the most romantic sign of the zodiac and can be very caring and sensitive. But the fact that they are dreamers can cause problems since expectations may be too high.

Love affairs are the essence of romance for Pisceans. They like nothing better than to escape from their everyday routine into a dream-world. Probably the only occasion on which they will be unfaithful is in their imaginations, for they may fantasize about dramatic love affairs that in reality do not exist.

HEALTH
AND ASTROLOGY

Are you more likely to become ill in certain ways that relate directly to your Sun sign?

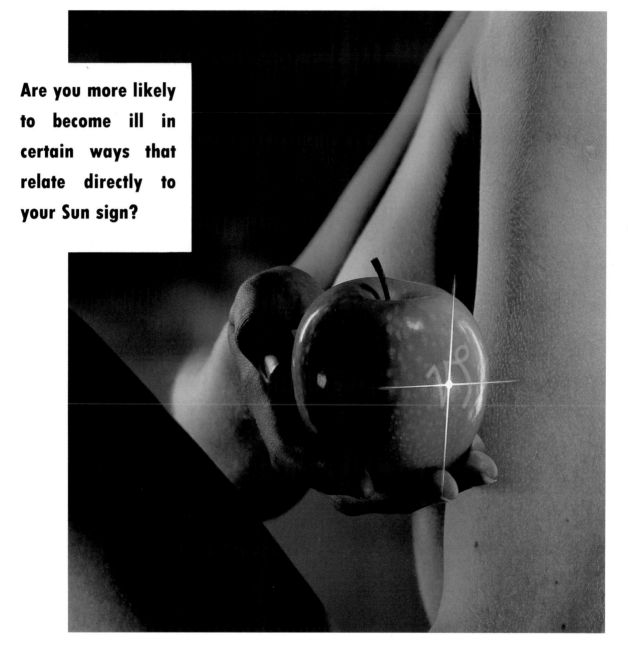

Over thousands of years, certain parts of the anatomy and vital organs have come to be associated with particular signs of the zodiac. Astrologers maintain that this ancient system of correspondences can help you pinpoint potential bodily strengths and weaknesses according to your star sign. A comprehensive picture of your health can thus be obtained from an analysis of your birth chart.

The four astrological elements – Fire, Earth, Air and Water – are also said to have a bearing on our health. Each represents a particular type of energy that flows through the body. The distribution of these four energy currents in a birth chart allows for the anticipation of stressful situations and even physical illness. Although the most complete picture of your health will be gained if you look at your birth chart, you can identify your basic type from the element ruling your Sun sign.

Particular Sun signs are associated with different parts of the body. Aries rules the head and brain; Taurus, the throat area; Gemini, the lungs and nervous system; Cancer, the stomach and breasts; Leo, the heart area; Virgo, the abdomen; Libra, the kidneys and lower back; Scorpio, the sex organs; Sagittarius, the hips and thighs; Capricorn, the skeleton, teeth and skin; Aquarius, the circulatory system; and Pisces, the feet and lymphatic system. This does not necessarily mean that these parts are susceptible; it can give them extra strength.

Fire:
Aries, Leo, Sagittarius

The Fire element relates to the warming, vital function of the circulatory system. Since it exemplifies enthusiasm and self-motivation, it is important for their health that Fire sign people should be allowed to act freely and impulsively. If this element is balanced by the others in a chart, serious disorders will be met head-on and conquered. Vigorous physical exercise stimulates people born under Fire signs, and they usually have good digestion.

Too much emphasis on Fire produces restlessness and excessive self-centredness, however. People with this tendency are often so obsessed with leaving their mark on the world that they literally 'burn out'.

Earth:
Taurus, Virgo, Capricorn

The Earth element represents the physical body of the individual, and the processes necessary to sustain it. Earth signs are finely attuned to the practical

requirements of material survival; and they know that diet and exercise are essential to healthy living.

An over-emphasis on Earth in an individual's chart creates someone who is too preoccupied with material concerns. Sometimes this can show itself in an unhealthy attachment to food, or as an obsession with the body's needs, which can lead to hypochondria.

Those lacking the Earth element find it difficult to accept their limitations, often forgetting even to eat and rest.

Air:
Gemini, Libra, Aquarius

Air is the element associated with the body's life support system. It regulates how people think, breathe and adapt to their environment. When it is well-balanced in a chart, the Air element enables an individual to view his or her emotional and physical needs in a rational manner, and to change poor health habits in an innovative way.

People who have Air as the dominant element are inclined to 'live in their heads'. Although they may be highly intelligent, they can be out of touch with their bodies. They are mentally over-active and prone to pounding their highly-charged nervous systems into a state of exhaustion. Rest, relaxation and frequent changes of scenery are necessary in order to prevent worry and anxiety.

HEALING WITH HERBS

Herbs have been used for centuries for their medicinal properties. Modern herbal medicine uses all parts of the plant which can be taken internally as a medicine or rubbed on to the skin in the form of an ointment. Deciding which herbs are suitable for particular ailments can be achieved using Sun signs.

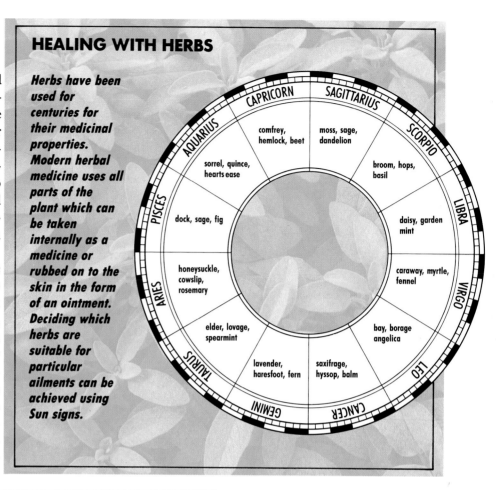

THE TWELVE HOUSES

A birth chart, which shows the position of the planets at the time of birth, is divided into twelve 'houses', each of which represents an aspect of your life. The way that the planets fall within the houses tells us in which area of life their influence is likely to operate. The beginning or 'cusp' of the first house, known as the 'Ascendant', marks the moment of birth. Progress through the houses can be viewed as a journey through life, starting with the development of our basic needs (houses 1-3), moving on to how we grow into our surroundings (houses 4-6), our response to other people (houses 7-9), and our involvement with the wider world (houses 10-12).

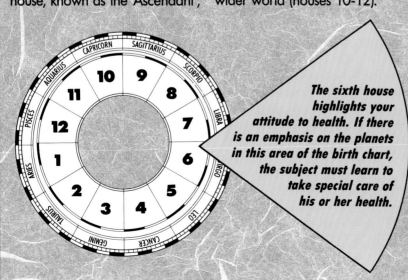

The sixth house highlights your attitude to health. If there is an emphasis on the planets in this area of the birth chart, the subject must learn to take special care of his or her health.

Water:
Cancer, Scorpio, Pisces

The Water element cools, soothes and heals. It is linked to the body processes responsible for filtering out impurities and to emotional states. When Water is balanced by the other elements in a chart, the individual is in touch with his or her feelings and has great sensitivity in handling the emotions of others. Water, incidentally, features prominently in the charts of most natural healers and those working in alternative medicine such as homeopaths reflexologists and natural healers.

When Water predominates, the person will tend to be at the mercy of emotional currents. Physically, it may indicate that the body is constantly eliminating poisons accumulated through an over-sensitivity to life's stresses. There may be a tendency for water retention, puffiness or bloating.

HEALTHCHART

Astrologers have found that certain parts of the body and vital organs, as well as diseases and many chronic physical conditions, relate quite closely to a person's Sun sign. This chart pinpoints the most likely trouble spots or strengths.

Sign	PARTS OF BODY	GLANDS, NERVES AND ARTERIES	POSSIBLE DISORDERS
ARIES	head, brain, eyes, bones of face	pineal gland, arteries to head and brain	headaches, acne, fainting, brain fever, neuralgia
TAURUS	neck, throat, larynx, chin, lower jaw, ears, tongue, vocal cords	jugular vein, tonsils, thyroid	laryngitis, throat inflammation, goitre, tonsillitis
GEMINI	shoulders, arms, hands, fingers, upper ribs	bronchial tubes, trachea, thymus, nervous system	bronchitis, asthma, chest disorders, accidents to arms, shoulders and hands
CANCER	alimentary canal, ribs, sternum, womb, digestive organs	pancreas, breasts	gastric disorders, heartburn, obesity
LEO	heart, upper back, spleen	spinal cord, aorta	back complaints, spinal meningitis, heart diseases
VIRGO	intestines, abdomen	lower dorsal nerves	bowel diseases, indigestion, colic, intestinal infection
LIBRA	kidneys, lumbar region, haunches	adrenal glands, lumbar nerves, blood vessels	kidney and bladder disorders, eczema, lumbago, abscesses
SCORPIO	bladder, sex organs, coccyx, cervix, anus	genito-urinary system, prostate gland	bladder disorders, genito-urinary diseases, prostate or menstrual problems, piles
SAGITTARIUS	hips, thighs, pelvis, sacrum, liver	sciatic nerve, arterial system	injuries and diseases of hips and thighs, liver disorders, sciatica, paralysis of limbs
CAPRICORN	bones, knees	skin	rheumatism, skin complaints, knee injuries, bone diseases
AQUARIUS	ankles, calves, shins	circulatory system	calf and ankle injuries, varicose veins, poor circulation, blood diseases, heart palpitations
PISCES	feet and toes	lymphatic system, pituitary gland	bunions, chilblains, drink and drug problems, lymphatic and glandular disorders

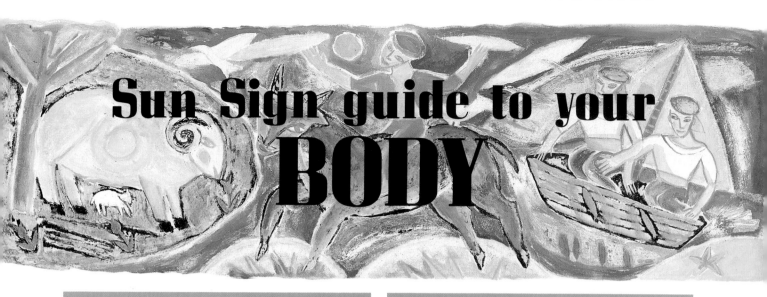

Sun Sign guide to your BODY

March 21	**ARIES**	April 19

This sign has more than its fair share of vigorous health. In fact, always impatient to meet the next challenge, Arians cannot spare the time to be ill. They have remarkably quick powers of recovery; and since Aries rules the head, typical ailments of this fiery sign are raging headaches and fevers which seem to 'burn off' in no time.

Stamina

Headstrong Arians appear to live off adrenalin. This makes them tireless workers when their energy is properly channelled; but when this lacks direction, their stamina tends to suffer. They can be prone to irritability or temper tantrums, too. Resentments add to stress and this tends to affect the blood circulation to their brain and eyes.

Relaxation

Arians need to accept they are not invulnerable, and that relaxation is important. Bracing country walks or a competitive sport should work off excess aggression.

They are also inclined to experience wildly fluctuating energy levels. Diet is important to every sign, but Arians in particular should avoid coffee and white sugar as these can place added stress on the nervous system and adrenal glands.

Few Arians have a problem with weight; they are far too active.

IRRITABILITY

If frustration gets out of hand, Arians may fall victim to their own impetuous behaviour. They always seem to be at war with themselves, and have the cuts and bruises to prove it. They have to learn the Libran art of co-operation since, even if this slows them down, it will be less damaging to their emotional and physical health in the long run.

April 20	**TAURUS**	May 20

By nature, Taureans are slow and persistent. They settle into a comfortable groove and need a great deal of persuading before they will change. But while they generally have sturdy constitutions, their earthy attraction to the good life often leads to over-indulgence. Indeed there is nothing more appealing to the Taurean palate than rich and sweet foods, and nothing more difficult for them to forfeit. But discipline with eating habits is essential to their well-being. Taurus rules the thyroid gland, which regulates the body's metabolism. Unless high-calorie, fatty diets are avoided, weight problems will plague their later years.

Fitness

Exercise is another key to Taurean health. It is not easy to persuade normally passive Taureans to rouse themselves, however, since they tend to accept being overweight as the yoke they must carry. But they do love to dance, and enjoy the more sensual therapies such as body massage and saunas.

Tension

This sign also rules the throat, neck and voice. Overdoing things often results in muscle tension in this area, or laryngitis. Regular, gentle massage should ease stiffness in the neck muscles. Their natural weak spot in the throat may lead to long-lasting colds. If this happens, Taureans should re-think their diet and take up some form of exercise.

SORE THROATS

The throat is traditionally a vulnerable point for Taureans, and problems here represent a refusal to change. Typically, Taureans need to learn to look critically at their habits and understand that they alone can alter their health patterns for the better.

| May 21 | **GEMINI** | June 20 | | June 21 | **CANCER** | July 22 |

Restless Geminis tend to live on their nerves, consuming enough energy for two. Distracted by their inquisitive minds, they even often forget bodily needs as

basic as eating and sleeping. As Gemini rules the nervous system, mental and nervous exhaustion are potential trouble spots.

The Mind

Relaxation techniques will be beneficial; and Geminis need to learn that a quiet, controlled mind is more efficient than constant mental whirring. Geminis are famous for a 'dual' personality, their sociable, effervescent side having a moody, unresponsive counterpart. This is reflected in naturally erratic energy levels, so that regular meals and sleep are vital to reduce the wilder fluctuations in their moods.

Colds and 'Flu

Geminis always seem to suffer more with colds and 'flu than most. In part, this arises from their reluctance to take to their beds, but also because they never seem to recognize the body's plea that 'Enough is enough!'

Gemini also rules the lungs, pointing to a need to guard against chest infection.

The shoulders, arms, hands and fingers fall under Gemini's domain as well. If tension in the shoulder becomes painful, it should be treated with gentle massage before it 'freezes'.

COLDS

For Geminis, colds can be a persistent problem, since congestion in the respiratory organs is a reflection of the Geminian tendency to block the mind with too many thoughts at once. Geminis should learn that correct breathing also helps to decongest the mind: and an orderly mind means a healthier body.

Beneath the tough outer shell of the crab, there is a soft under-belly; and so it is with Cancerians. However cool they appear on the surface, they are highly responsive to emotional upsets. Watery Cancer rules the stomach and alimentary canal, and the Cancerian's sensitive digestive system is the area most likely to register any distress. Those born under this sign tend to bottle things up; and resulting long-term tension may lead to stomach ulcers. While they are very supportive of those around them, they are likely to suffer in silence. They do not communicate easily, which makes it difficult for others to support them.

GASTRIC TROUBLES

Cancerians like to feel secure in their surroundings, but uncertainty may give rise to depression. They tend to churn things over, and are therefore vulnerable to gastric disorders. For Cancerians, the challenge is to try and let go of anxieties by learning to talk through their problems.

Home Cooking

But whatever the pressures, food is very important to Cancerians. They like good home cooking and plenty of it, but they need to take great care over what they eat, and should avoid high-fat diets. Water-retention is another common disorder, so that drinking habits require control as well. Should they neglect themselves, Cancerians will soon discover that theirs is one of the more 'rounded' signs: the waistline can disappear and a moon-shaped tummy may develop as the calories mount up. Any form of water-sport is natural to Cancerians, and swimming is probably the most enjoyable way for them to keep fit. Cancerians are great worriers, which tends to make them over-eat.

| July 23 | **LEO** | August 22 | August 23 | **VIRGO** | Sep 22 |

Radiant and energetic, Leos bring so much light into other people's lives that they can be blind to the needs of their own, especially where health is concerned. Their need to be appreciated drives them on to endless feats of achievement; and because they have so much natural vitality, they refuse to ease up.

Vitality

While some will approach middle life with more energy than those half their age, Leos will have to come to terms with their own mortality sooner or later. If not, the rich foods and wines they find irresistible will be their undoing.

Excesses

Leo rules the back and the heart, and it is these two areas that are most vulnerable to Leonine excesses. Exercise and a careful diet are obvious remedies for an expanding waistline. Leos often go on until they drop, so regular holidays away from it all will re-charge those exhausted batteries.

There is no unhappier sight than an unadmired or unloved Leo. This can cause tremendous depression and may bring on nagging back troubles, as a sign of lack of the emotional support they so greatly need.

Back problems can be added to if the Leo becomes overweight: a daily brisk walk will tone up the whole body, keeping the muscles in the back supple so that they are more able to take the strain.

BACK COMPLAINTS

Leos have an enthusiasm which will lead them to put their back out for anybody, except themselves. They do not like to be reminded that they are made of all-too-brittle bones, and will often moan about a bad back while doing very little about it.

A passion for attention to detail has given Virgoans a reputation for hypochondria. Mind and body are as one to them. Information is like food: it is digested, and only what is useful is absorbed.

Stomach Upsets

If anything threatens this orderly process, then both mind and body are affected. Such a preoccupation with health is the Virgoan's attempt to make sure everything goes perfectly to plan. The trouble is that they can worry too much about getting the balance right, and in the process wear themselves to a frazzle. Virgo rules the abdominal organs, intestines and bowels. Any undue stress and anxiety tends to create nervous indigestion, heartburn or stomach upsets.

Pressure

Virgos also find it difficult to 'switch off'. As pressures build up, they can suffer from insomnia, lose their appetite and become hunched up with nervous tension. Their lesson is to relax and sometimes let life happen spontaneously. As an Earth sign, they are very resourceful, however, and can weather physical setbacks that would daunt other less resilient signs.

Any stress in their lives can be counteracted with a 'relaxing' habit such as meditation or deep breathing.

NERVOUS TENSION

Fastidious Virgoans can be very self-critical, and this can wreak havoc on their sensitive stomachs. These upsets relate to a desire to be in total control and also to fear of letting go. Regular stretching exercises and massage should ease such tension. Virgoans can also take preventative measures by sticking to a healthy diet and relaxing.

LIBRA
Sep 23 — *Oct 22*

SCORPIO
Oct 23 — *Nov 21*

As the sign of the scales, Libra's main concern is to weigh up options and arrive at correct decisions. The sharp Libran mind shows good judgement in the affairs of others. But in their own lives, the spectre of indecision rises to haunt them.

Rather than confront emotional issues honestly, they will sometimes prefer to settle for peace at any price. In so doing, they may lose their way and become angry and frustrated as they suppress their deepest desires. This frustration may lead to illness.

Skin and Kidney Troubles

The difficulty for Librans is that, while they are easily upset by arguments, they can create even greater inner stress by not asserting themselves. Typical Libran stress symptoms are eczema, weak backs and kidney trouble.

Another area Librans must watch is their weight, since they are often easily tempted to seek emotional refuge in a box of chocolates. More often than not, this is a sign of their insecurity.

STRESS

Difficulties in close relationships can cause great stress for Librans, leading to nervous tension, irritability and maybe sexual problems. Exercises that require mental and physical balance — like the graceful martial art of Aikido or the movement meditations of Hatha Yoga or T'ai Chi — will help them achieve the greater self-control they probably need.

Over-eating

Persistent over-eating can denote depression. But with their strong and wiry constitutions, there is no reason why Librans should not occasionally indulge a sweet tooth. Balance is a key word for their health and for their general well-being.

Of all the Sun signs, Scorpios are easily the most misunderstood. They are commonly associated with the rawest human emotions, such as malice and retribution, as well as sexual obsession. Scorpio's rule over the sex organs only seems to bear this out. But while this may be true of some Scorpios, it by no means describes the majority.

Psychosomatic Illnesses

Part of this misrepresentation arises from an intensity of emotions running at a very deep level which manifests itself in strong physical needs. The determination of Scorpios gives them greater powers of self-denial than most; but once in a relationship, they are capable of unbridled passion. It is in this sense that they are highly-sexed; and if such urges are repressed, problems such as anger, lower back pains and premenstrual tension in women may develop. As they prefer to feel bad than to feel nothing at all, Scorpios are also prone to mysterious psychosomatic complaints.

Generally, they are extremely energetic and recuperate very quickly from illness. But they are rarely moderate in their health habits, either eating, drinking and smoking furiously, or totally abstaining. As Scorpio also rules the organs that eliminate toxins from the body, Scorpios should learn to rid themselves with regularity of both physical and emotional excesses in their lives.

SEXUAL TENSIONS

Scorpios tend to be very attuned to their sexual nature: but sometimes such feelings can be so intense that they feel guilty about them. When this happens, they need to cleanse the body of tension built up from frustration with a suitable distraction.

Nov 22 SAGITTARIUS Dec 21

Dec 22 CAPRICORN Jan 19

Sagittarians approach life on a grand scale, whether through their words, deeds or eating habits. They love excitement and adventure; and what they fear most is the prospect of being immobilized by illness. But constant restlessness drives them to use up enormous reserves of energy, endangering the mobility which they value so much.

A tendency to swing from the heights of unbounded enthusiasm to deep depression may also often appear out of proportion to the events that triggered such emotions; but like the other Fire signs, Sagittarians do not take kindly to advice about their health habits.

WEIGHT PROBLEMS

Sagittarians are traditionally known for their energy and love of sport. But they can also be lazy, expecting a naturally fine physique to absorb the excesses of a careless diet. It is not easy to get an out-of-condition Sagittarian back to fitness, although acupuncture might help.

Health Worries
In this respect, they are their own worst enemies. For while they may make light of personal worries and ailments, there is often hidden anxiety about health and the secret fear that one day luck may run out.

Binges
As if to test their fate, Sagittarians will sometimes dull this mental torture in heavy bouts of eating or drinking. If this becomes a habit, those areas most vulnerable in the Sagittarian anatomy — liver, hips and thighs — may well suffer.

The most important thing for them to do is to temper their exuberant nature with some rest and relaxation.

Proceeding through life cautiously and methodically, Capricorns seem to have an instinctive awareness of their abilities, which they apply resourcefully in the pursuit of definite goals. When their heads are down, little will distract them. However, they may have bouts of depression due to the hard tasks they set themselves, and find it difficult to let off steam.

Rigidity
While they are very tenacious in achieving their goals, Capricorns tend also to be rigid in their work patterns. This may be because they do not readily trust others to carry out their long-term plans. But they are also inclined to belittle the value of relaxation unless it serves a useful end — like a round of golf with the boss. Significantly, this rigidity in their character corresponds to those Capricorn ailments which restrict movement, such as rheumatism and arthritis.

Disciplined
Generally, Capricorns approach their health with the same discipline as their careers. They are a naturally active sign, but will only allow themselves the luxury of exercise if it fits into their scheme of things. There must always be a goal for them to set their sights on — a high mountain peak to conquer or a very challenging yoga position to achieve, for instance.

REPRESSION

Serious Capricorns can get bogged down in long periods of work which may gradually erode their health. Instead, it would be wise for them to develop interests involving a complete change of mood, and to realize the healing properties of playing just for play's sake on a regular basis in order to combat stress.

Jan 20 AQUARIUS Feb 18

Idealistic Aquarians are full of suggestions for changing the state of the world, but this often means they overlook their own condition. They are frequently fascinated by health issues, especially in the area of new healing techniques. Yet they can easily neglect themselves. They are simply far too absorbed in their thoughts.

A tremendous zest for life gives them enormous staying power; but, extremely self-willed, they will stubbornly resist any advice to slow down.

VARICOSE VEINS

This traditional Aquarian ailment is said to represent a feeling of being overworked and overburdened. Gregarious Aquarians also often find themselves in emotional situations in which they feel trapped. Quite literally, they feel they cannot circulate freely.

Fatigue

Tiredness can produce loss of concentration and may induce contrary and over-wrought behaviour. Other Aquarian symptoms of stress are muscular tension or spasms. These can build up over a long period of time, eventually leading to circulatory disorders — another Aquarian concern. They are often unpleasantly surprised when their bodies let them down, and they make difficult patients.

Exercise

When taking exercise, Aquarians should tread warily. Unexpressed anger makes them susceptible to accidents. Typically vulnerable areas in the lower limbs are the shins, calves, ankles and also the Achilles tendons, which are often prone to bruising and strain.

Feb 19 PISCES March 20

Piscean sensitivity is so finely tuned that it reacts like blotting paper to atmospheres. When nursing the sick, for instance, Pisceans are apt to reflect a patient's own symptoms themselves. Indeed, Pisceans often have problems defining the boundaries between fact and fiction in general.

Addiction

In difficult circumstances, especially in relationships, this can lead to a tendency to withdraw from reality, with drink or drugs as a possible escape. Apart from the obvious disadvantages to health, such flights might further loosen a weak grasp of self-identity, causing deep depression. With such a tendency to addiction, Pisceans would do well to avoid painkillers and tranquillizers, using natural remedies instead whenever possible.

Indecision

The glyph for this sign shows two fishes swimming in opposite directions. Pisceans can be so whimsical that all their energies are consumed in the plans they dream up; and in the end, they simply cannot say which direction they are facing. Pisces also rules the feet: and indeed Pisceans often need to be grounded, and to feel themselves in their own bodies. Any massage method would be suitable, but a particularly appropriate one is reflexology, which works through the feet.

SENSITIVE FEET

Pisceans' feet and toes cause them the most anxiety. This is perhaps not surprising as, symbolically, it is the feet that keep this fanciful sign earthbound. They might find it therapeutic to 'feel the ground' beneath them by walking barefoot occasionally, or to use massage and reflexology to ease the strain.

ARIES AFFINITIES

MARCH 21 – APRIL 19

W ho works from morn to set of Sun
And never likes to be outdone?
Whose walk is almost like a run?
Who? Aries

The sign of the Pioneer, the Warrior

Symbol: the Ram
Element: Fire
Quality: Cardinal
Planetary ruler: Mars
Colour: red
Gemstone: garnet
Metal: iron

Perfume: Dragon's Blood
Keywords: assertively, energetically, urgently
Rules: the First House (outer personality, appearance, self-image, mode of expression and action).

Mythology: the Ram was a supernatural being sent by Zeus to rescue Phirxus and Helle from their wicked stepmother. Helle fell from the Ram's back and was drowned in the sea, but Phirxus arrived safely and sacrificed the beast to Zeus who placed its form in the heavens. The Ram's fleece turned to gold and was hung in a sacred grove protected by a dragon. This was later found and captured by Jason in the course of his adventures with the Argonauts.

KEY SAYING
"One small step for man, one giant leap for mankind"
– Astronaut Neil Armstrong, 1969

Positive traits: forceful, pioneering, adventurous, enterprising, courageous, direct, energetic, freedom-loving, self-assertive.
Negative traits: Selfish, unsubtle, impulsive, rash, quick-tempered, impatient, quarrelsome, aggressive.

THE ARIAN BODY
Parts of the body ruled: head, eyes, face, muscles, pineal gland.
Acupuncture meridian: kidney meridian.
Arian ailments: accidents, acne, brain disorders, burns, fainting, headaches, head injuries, inflammation, neuralgia, stress, swellings, sunstroke.
Beneficial foods: rhubarb, tomatoes.

ARIAN ASSOCIATIONS
Herbs and Plants: anemone, basil, briony, chillies, coriander, crow's foot, flax-weed, garden cress, garlic, ginger, honeysuckle, mustard, onions, peppers, tobacco, thorny trees.
Objects: cars, fires, knives, machinery, motor cycles, tools, weapons.
Professions and Trades: armed forces, blacksmith, butcher, dentist, explorer, engineer, engine driver, fireman, trade union leader, mechanic, metalworker, professional sportsman/woman, self-employed businessman/woman, steeplejack.
Sports and Hobbies: acting, car maintenance, dancing, hockey, football, hang-gliding, martial arts, metalwork, motor racing, rugby.

ARIES AND THE WORLD
Aries represents the idea of nationhood, national characteristics and self-image.
Countries ruled by Aries: England, Germany.
Cities ruled by Aries: Florence, Marseilles.

The archetypal Arian: Who else but Adam in the Garden of Eden? First in everything, his impetuousness and desire always to go one better eventually proved his undoing.

TAURUS AFFINITIES

APRIL 20 – MAY 20

Who smiles at life except when crossed?
Who knows or thinks he knows, the most?
Who loves good things, boiled or roast?
Oh, Taurus

The sign of the Builder

Symbol: the Bull
Element: Earth
Quality: Fixed
Planetary ruler: Venus
Colours: blue, violet
Gemstone: diamond
Metal: copper

Perfume: storax
Keywords: possessively, permanently, practically
Rules: the Second House (personal and material resources, possessions and attitudes towards them).

Mythology: Zeus disguised himself as a white bull to court and seduce a mortal woman named Europa. He carried her from her home in Tyre to Crete, where he made love to her before changing back to his normal form. Europa bore him three sons. Zeus commemorated the event by placing the form of the bull among the stars.

> *KEY SAYING*
> **"Give me a firm spot on which to stand and I will move the earth"**
> – *Archimedes*

Positive traits: practical, reliable, patient, persistent, solid, determined, industrious, strong-willed, sensuous, affectionate, warm-hearted, trustworthy.
Negative traits: lazy, possessive, self-indulgent, dull, inflexible, unoriginal, unimaginative, greedy, stubborn, resentful, hidebound by routine.

THE TAUREAN BODY

Parts of the body ruled: neck, throat, larynx, chin, lower jaw, ears, tongue, vocal chords jugular vein, tonsils, thyroid gland.
Acupuncture meridian: triple generator.
Taurean ailments: earache, goitres, gout, laryngitis, obesity, tonsillitis, swollen neck glands, throat inflammations, constipation.
Beneficial foods: beans, celery.

TAUREAN ASSOCIATIONS

Herbs and plants: almond, apricot, ash, beans, cloves, colt's foot, cowslip, elder flower, ferns, gooseberry, grape, groundsel, lily, lovage, mint, pecan, primrose, red cherry, sorrel, spearmint, tansy, thyme, violet, wheat.
Objects: antique furniture, china and glass, jewellery, perfume, musical instruments, silverware.
Professions and Trades: accountant, architect, financier, art dealer, banker, builder, civil servant, farmer, horticulturalist, jeweller, model, property dealer, sculptor, singer, surveyor.
Sports and Hobbies: ballroom dancing, cookery, flower arranging, gardening, interior design, music, pottery, singing, sculpture, soft furnishings, woodwork, wrestling.

TAURUS AND THE WORLD

Taurus represents all aspects of production and in the world relates to banks, financial institutions, material resources, security and national heritage.
Countries ruled by Taurus: Iran, Iraq, Ireland.
Cities ruled by Taurus: Lucerne, St Louis.

The archetypal Taurean: Bilbo Baggins, the Hobbit. Never changing, despite his many adventures, he forever longed for the comforts of home.

GEMINI AFFINITIES

MAY 21 – JUNE 20

Who's fond of life, jest and pleasure?
Who vacillates and changes ever?
Who loves attention without measure?
Why? Gemini

The archetypal Gemini: Pinocchio, the naughty puppet whose curiousity gets him into all sorts of scrapes before he at last finds his heart.

The sign of the Storyteller

Symbol: the Twins
Element: Air
Quality: Mutable
Planetary ruler: Mercury
Colour: yellow
Gemstone: agate
Metal: mercury

Perfume: wormwood
Keywords: adaptably, communicatively, variably
Rules: the Third House (short journeys, mental abilities, all communication, perception, peers, siblings, early school).

Mythology: the constellation of Gemini is associated with the twins Castor and Pollux, who were born of the union of Leda and Zeus (who disguised himself as a Swan). After Castor was killed in a fight, Pollux grieved until Zeus restored his dead twin to life. In payment, the pair were obliged by Zeus to live alternate days in Hades and Olympus.

KEY SAYING
"I think therefore I am"
— Rene Descartes

Positive traits: versatile, adaptable, intellectual, witty, charming, logical, energetic, spontaneous, lively, chatty, amusing, youthful, up-to-date.
Negative traits: changeable, restless, cunning, inquisitive, inconstant, fickle, inconsistent, two-faced, fidgety, superficial, gossipy, transparent.

THE GEMINI BODY

Parts of the body ruled: arms, hands, fingers, shoulders, upper ribs, lungs, bronchial tracts, trachea, thymus gland, nervous system.
Acupuncture meridian: liver meridian.
Gemini ailments: asthma, accidents to the upper body especially the collarbone, bronchitis, pneumonia, nervous exhaustion.
Beneficial foods: lettuce, cauliflower.

GEMINI ASSOCIATIONS

Herbs and Plants: carrot, cress, dill, garlic, haresfoot, hogweed, lavender, liquorice, mandrake, mulberry, parsley, pomegranate.
Objects: address book, filofax, computer, magazines, newspapers, radio, telephone, television, word processor.
Professions and Trades: broadcaster, writer, chauffeur, commentator, commercial traveller, journalist, lecturer, light manual worker, linguist, navigator, postman, salesman, secretary, shop assistant, teacher, telephone operator, travel agent.
Sports and Hobbies: conjuring, crosswords, doodling, fencing, gossiping, socializing, telephoning, writing.

GEMINI AND THE WORLD

Gemini represents all forms of communication, trade and the distribution of goods. It also has links with education, the media, and a country's infrastructure and transport system.
Countries ruled by Gemini: Belgium, Wales.
Cities ruled by Gemini: London, Melbourne, Plymouth, San Francisco.

CANCER AFFINITIES

JUNE 21 – JULY 22

W ho changes like a changeful season
Holds fast and lets go without reason?
Who is there can give adhesion
To Cancer?

The sign of the Protector

Symbol: the Crab
Element: Water
Quality: Cardinal
Planetary ruler: Moon
Colours: silver, pale blue
Gems: moonstone, pearl
Metal: silver

Perfume: onycha
Keywords: defensively, tenaciously, sensitively
Rules: the Fourth House (home and domestic life, the supportive parent, hidden motivations, old age).

Mythology: the constellation of Cancer immortalizes the Crab sent by the goddess Hera to combat her old enemy, Hercules. As the hero embarked on the second of his Twelve Labours – the destruction of the nine-headed serpent, Hydra – the Crab nipped at his ankles but was crushed underfoot. Hera raised it to the heavens as a reward.

KEY SAYING
"People who live in glass houses shouldn't throw stones"
– Proverb

Positive traits: kind, sensitive, sympathetic, imaginative, maternal or paternal, solicitous, protective, cautious, patriotic, tenacious, shrewd, thrifty, resourceful, good homemaker.
Negative traits: over-emotional, hypersensitive, moody, devious, changeable, self-pitying, unforgiving, unstable, gullible, untidy.

THE CANCERIAN BODY
Parts of the body ruled: alimentary canal, lower ribs, breasts, breast bone, womb, digestive tract, upper digestive organs, pancreas.
Acupuncture meridian: stomach meridian.
Cancerian ailments: gastric disorders, heartburn, indigestion, obesity, ulcers.
Beneficial foods: watercress, milk.

CANCERIAN ASSOCIATIONS
Herbs and Plants: cabbage, cardamine, chick weed, flax, lettuce, maple, mushroom, olive, pumpkin, saxifrage, turnip, water violet, white rose.
Objects: boats, cooking utensils, gardening tools, home appliances, photographs, potted plants, souvenirs, swimming pools.
Professions and Trades: antique dealer, businessman/woman, caterer, fisherman, food scientist, historian, hotelier, housewife, kindergarten teacher, museum curator, nurse, publican, sailor.
Sports and Hobbies: cooking, DIY, memory quizzes, sailing, sewing, water-skiing.

CANCER AND THE WORLD
Cancer represents the common people, mass ideologies, national sentiment, and opposition to government. It also has ties with a country's agriculture and all produce of the land.
Countries ruled by Cancer: Holland, New Zealand, Scotland.
Cities ruled by Cancer: Amsterdam, Manchester, Milan, New York, Venice.

The archetypal Cancerian: Snow White, the innocent whose trust was betrayed but who found comfort and shelter in the bosom of her tiny family!

LEO AFFINITIES

JULY 23 – AUGUST 22

*Who praises all his kindred do
Expects his friends to praise them too
And cannot see their senseless view?
Ah, Leo*

The archetypal Leo: Mr Toad, whose stubbornness and extravagant, boastful behaviour cost him his beloved home – and nearly his friends, too!

The sign of the Leader, the Ruler

Symbol: the Lion
Element: Fire
Quality: Fixed
Planetary ruler: Sun
Colour: golden yellow
Gems: amber, ruby
Metal: gold

Perfume: olibanum
Keywords: creatively, authoritatively, dramatically
Rules: the Fifth House (self-expression, creativity, children, love, pleasure, speculation, recreation).

Mythology: the constellation of Leo commemorates the Nemean Lion – a ferocious beast sent by the goddess Hera to test her enemy, Hercules, in the first of his Twelve Labours. Arrows proved useless against the animal's thick hide, so Hercules trapped the Lion in its lair and choked it to death with his bare hands despite losing a finger. Afterwards he cloaked himself in the Lion's skin as a protection against all future enemies.

KEY SAYING

"From the sublime to the ridiculous, it only takes one step"
– Napoleon Bonaparte

Positive traits: creative, generous, enthusiastic, good organizer, broad minded, expansive, dramatic.
Negative traits: vain, proud, bullying, pompous, snobbish, intolerant, dogmatic, stubborn, patronizing, egotistical, conceited.

THE LEO BODY

Parts of the body ruled: heart, upper back, spleen, spine, circulation, aorta.
Acupuncture meridian: heart meridian.
Leo ailments: backache, palpitations, fainting, blood disorders, fevers, dizziness, heart problems.
Beneficial foods: oranges, peas.

LEO ASSOCIATIONS

Herbs and Plants: almond, angelica, bay, celandine, chamomile, frankincense, juniper, lemon, marigold, mistletoe, orange, poppyrice, rosemary, saffron.
Objects: cut glass, designer clothes, fireplaces, gold jewellery, limousines, luxuries, perfume, trophies, wood-burning stoves.
Professions and Trades: actor/actress, astrologer, chairman, charity organizer, commissionaire, dancer, farmer, hairdresser, jeweller, managing director, professional sportsman/woman, teacher, youth worker.
Sports and Hobbies: athletics, amateur dramatics, giving parties, interior design, opera, painting, sculpture, showjumping.

LEO AND THE WORLD

Leo represents a nation's creative activities, its art and culture. It has ties with all forms of sport and entertainment, ceremonies, children, the birth rate, the stockmarket and national lotteries.
Countries ruled by Leo: France, Italy, Romania.
Cities ruled by Leo: Bath, Bristol, Chicago, Los Angeles, Philadelphia, Prague, Rome.

VIRGO AFFINITIES

AUGUST 23 – SEPTEMBER 22

Who criticizes all she sees
Yes e'en would analyse a sneeze?
Who hugs and loves her own disease?
Humph, Virgo

The sign of the Critic, the Technician

Symbol: the Virgin
Element: Earth
Quality: Mutable
Planetary ruler: Mercury
Colour: grey, navy blue
Gemstone: sardonyx
Metal: mercury

Perfume: narcissus
Keywords: critically, analytically, dutifully
Rules: the Sixth House (work, service, working relationships, health, diet, the balance between mind and body).

Mythology: the constellation of Virgo immortalizes the goddess Astraea, who was sent by her father, Zeus, to live among mortals and instructed to teach them to obey the laws of nature. For a time, all went well and the world enjoyed the so-called 'Golden Age' when peace reigned and there were harvests in abundance. But eventually, mankind began to fall into increasingly evil ways and Astraea, disgusted, resumed her rightful place among the gods.

> *KEY SAYING*
> **"It is much easier to be critical than it is to be correct"**
> *– George Bernard Shaw*

Positive traits: discriminating, fastidious, analytical, meticulous, modest, precise.
Negative traits: fussy, self-conscious, cynical, hypercritical, finicky, over-conforming.

THE VIRGO BODY

Parts of the body ruled: intestines, abdomen, lower dorsal nerves, bowels, nails, spleen.
Acupuncture meridian: large intestine.
Virgo ailments: anorexia, bowel problems, indigestion, intestinal infections, appendicitis, malnutrition, hernia.
Beneficial foods: lemons, caraway seeds.

VIRGO ASSOCIATIONS

Herbs and Plants: azalea, balm, caraway, fenugreek, endive, fennel, hazel, lily of the valley, marjoram, myrtle, sage, savory, valerian.
Objects: practical clothing, domestic pets, reference books, small objets d'art, miniature paintings, reference books, stamp collections.
Professions and Trades: accountant, craftsman, critic, dentist, doctor, gardener, inspector, nurse, policeman, secretary, statistician, teacher, writer.
Sports and Hobbies: ballet, collecting, evening classes, handicrafts, housework, languages, model making, pastry cooking, reading, writing.

VIRGO AND THE WORLD

Virgo represents the working classes, labour organizations and public institutions – the armed forces, the civil service, the police. It also has links with public health and hygiene.
Countries ruled by Virgo: Greece, Turkey, Switzerland.
Cities ruled by Virgo: Basle, Boston, Cheltenham, Jerusalem, Lyons, Paris, Reading.

The archetypal Virgo: enslaved by her ugly sisters, Cinderella's devotion to duty was finally rewarded when she met Prince Charming.

LIBRA AFFINITIES

SEPTEMBER 23 – OCTOBER 22

*W*ho puts off with promise gay
And keeps you waiting half the day?
Who compromises all the way?
Sweet Libra

The archetypal Libran: Eve, who listened to the Voice of Reason (the Serpent) but could do nothing until she had persuaded her mate (Adam) to join her.

The sign of the Diplomat

Symbol: the Scales
Element: Air
Quality: Cardinal
Planetary ruler: Venus
Colours: pale blue, pink
Gemstone: emerald
Metal: copper

Perfume: galbanum
Keywords: harmoniously, diplomatically, perfectly
Rules: the Seventh House (the 'other half', marriage, all close relationships, open enemies, the legal process).

Mythology: the constellation of the Scales is thought to take its name from the ancient Babylonians, who believed that the god *Zibanitu* – the Scales – sat in judgement weighing the souls of the living and the dead. In Greek mythology it is associated with the goddess Athene, who confounded her high-handed and imperious fellow gods by holding a court of justice among mortals.

KEY SAYING
"To be or not to be: that is the question"
– Shakespeare, Hamlet

Positive traits: charming, easy-going, romantic, diplomatic, idealistic, refined, far-sighted.
Negative traits: indecisive, resentful, frivolous, changeable, flirtatious, easily influenced, highly susceptible to flattery.

THE LIBRAN BODY

Parts of the body ruled: kidneys, lumbar region of the back, adrenal glands, lumbar nerves, blood vessels, skin.
Acupuncture meridian: circulation.
Libran ailments: eczema, skin diseases, kidney and bladder infections, diabetes, abcesses, lumbago, vein disorders.
Beneficial foods: strawberries, plums.

LIBRAN ASSOCIATIONS

Herbs and Plants: apple, artichoke, chestnut, daffodil, daisy, foxglove, groundsel, lily, mint, parsley, pennyroyal, potato, rose, walnuts, yarrow.
Objects: expensive bath oil, paintings, perfume window garden, sculptures, sports coupe.
Professions and Trades: barrister, beautician, designer, diplomat, judge, personnel officer, receptionist, valuer, welfare worker.
Sports and Hobbies: collecting objets d'art, cooking, cricket, dancing, decorating, flower arranging, needlework, shopping, socializing, sunbathing.

LIBRA AND THE WORLD

Libra represents all formal relationships with other countries such as treaties, diplomatic initiatives and wars. It also reveals national characteristics that a country 'projects' on to its enemies.
Countries ruled by Libra: Austria, Burma, Canada, Egypt, Japan, Tibet.
Cities ruled by Libra: Copenhagen, Frankfurt, Lisbon, Vienna.

SCORPIO AFFINITIES

OCTOBER 23 – NOVEMBER 21

Who keeps an arrow in his bow
And if you prod, he lets it go?
A fervent friend, a subtle foe —
That's Scorpio

The sign of the Investigator

Symbol: the Scorpion
Element: Water
Quality: Fixed
Rulers: Pluto, Mars
Colour: deep red
Gemstone: opal
Metal: steel

Perfume: saimeze benzoin
Keywords: intensively, penetratingly, secretively
Rules: the Eighth House (procreation, birth and death, sex, rebirth, mysteries, the occult, hidden meanings).

Mythology: the constellation of Scorpio immortalizes the Scorpion summoned by Hera from the underworld to destroy Orion – a hunter who had previously boasted to the gods that he could kill any creature on earth. Later the Scorpion halted the horses which pulled the gods' Sun-chariot after Phaidon, son of Apollo, had taken it on a joyride. The creature's reward was to be raised to the heavens (where, incidentally, he joined Orion!)

KEY SAYING
"The heart has its reasons which the mind knows nothing of"
– *Blaise Pascal*

Positive traits: powerful feelings and emotions, committed, loyal, imaginative, discerning, subtle, persistent, determined.
Negative traits: jealous, resentful, obstinate, unforgiving, inflexible, secretive, suspicious, vindictive.

THE SCORPIO BODY

Parts of the body ruled: genitals, bladder, cervix, anus, genito-urinary tract, prostate gland.
Acupuncture meridian: bladder meridian.
Scorpio ailments: bladder disorders, cystitis, genito-urinary diseases, venereal diseases, piles, prostate trouble, PMT.
Beneficial foods: prunes, hops.

SCORPIO ASSOCIATIONS

Herbs and Plants: aloes, briar, broom, capers, cactus, furze, garlic, ginger, ginseng, horseradish, leeks, nettles, radish, tobacco, thistle.
Objects: chess set, classic car, crime novel, occult paraphernalia, safe, Tarot cards, unusual ornaments.
Professions and Trades: analyst, butcher, businessman/woman, chemist, detective, farmer, financial consultant, policeman, plumber, psychologist, research scientist, soldier, surgeon, spiritualist healer, tax collector, undertaker.
Sports and Hobbies: food, investigating mysteries, psychology, potholing, scuba diving, seduction, sex, solving puzzles, occult subjects.

SCORPIO AND THE WORLD

Scorpio represents global resources, international finance, multinational corporations and the death/rebirth of nations. It has strong ties with organized crime, undercover organizations and the recycling of waste products.
Countries ruled by Scorpio: Algeria, Morocco, Norway, Syria.
Cities ruled by Scorpio: Liverpool, New Orleans, Washington D.C.

The archetypal Scorpio: the Snow Queen, whose icy beauty and jealous heart lured many an innocent child to her frosty fortress.

SAGITTARIUS AFFINITIES

NOVEMBER 22 – DECEMBER 21

Who loves the dim, religious light?
Who always keeps a star in sight?
An optimist, both gay and bright —
It's Sagittarius

The sign of the Gypsy

Symbol: the Archer
Element: Fire
Quality: Mutable
Planetary ruler: Jupiter
Colours: blue, purple
Gemstone: topaz
Metal: tin

Perfume: lign-aloes
Keywords: extensively, expansively, philosophically
Rules: the Ninth House (the 'higher mind', philosophy, further education, religion, all links with foreign cultures).

Mythology: the constellation of Sagittarius immortalizes the centaur, Chiron – a creature born out of the union of Philyra and the god Cronos. On being discovered *in flagrante*, Cronos turned himself into a horse and galloped away; Philyra, dismayed at her child's appearance, turned herself into a linden tree. Chiron became a healer philosopher and prophet, famed for his wisdom and righteousness. He instructed the gods in music making and taught Achilles to hunt before being raised to the heavens as a reward.

> *KEY SAYING*
> **"Every cloud has a silver lining"**
> *– Proverb*

Positive traits: jovial, optimistic, versatile, open-minded, philosphical, sincere, frank, visionary.
Negative traits: tactless, restless, careless, boisterous, irresponsible, apt to exaggerate, boastful, lazy, wasteful, moralizing.

THE SAGITTARIAN BODY
Parts of the body ruled: hips, thighs, arterial system, pelvis, femur (thighbone).
Acupuncture meridian: spleen meridian.
Sagittarian ailments: injuries to hips and thighs, falls, hip problems, obesity, baldness.
Beneficial foods: asparagus, cucumber.

SAGITTARIAN ASSOCIATIONS
Herbs and Plants: almond, apricot, ash, borage, chervil, cloves, dandelion, mint, myrrh, rhubarb, sage, sugarcane, tomato.
Objects: back-pack, Bible, books, evening wear, riding equipment, souvenirs, travel guides.
Professions and Trades: barrister, bookseller, explorer, horse trainer, interpreter, jockey, lawyer, lecturer, librarian, philosopher, priest, professor, publisher, professional sportsman/woman, teacher, travel agent, vet, writer.
Sports and Hobbies: all sports, gambling, horse racing, motoring, practical jokes, reading, studying, travelling.

SAGITTARIUS AND THE WORLD
Sagittarius represents morality, religion, international law, and all forms of long-distance communication – especially shipping. It has strong connections with higher education, publishing, foreign relations, the media and the law.
Countries rules by Sagittarius: Australia, Hungary, Spain, USA.
Cities ruled by Sagittarius: Budapest, Cologne, Naples.

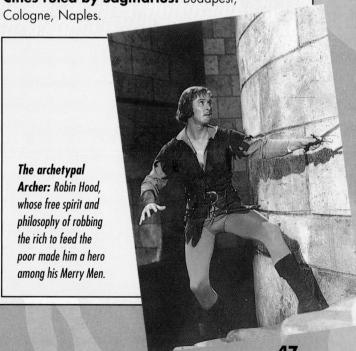

The archetypal Archer: Robin Hood, whose free spirit and philosophy of robbing the rich to feed the poor made him a hero among his Merry Men.

CAPRICORN AFFINITIES

DECEMBER 22 – JANUARY 19

W ho climbs, schemes for wealth and place
And mourns the brother's fall from grace?
But takes what's due in any case –
Safe Capricorn

The sign of the Achiever

Symbol: the Goat
Element: Earth
Quality: Cardinal
Planetary ruler: Saturn
Colours: black, grey
Gemstone: jet
Metal: lead

Perfume: musk
Keywords: rationally, prudently, determinedly
Rules: the Tenth House (ambitions, career, public recognition, status, authority figures, the dominant parent).

Mythology: the constellation of Capricorn takes its name from the fish-tailed Goat, Amaltheia, who suckled the baby Zeus while he was in hiding from his evil father Cronos. Later, when he became Lord of the gods, Zeus took one of the Goat's horns. This was the fabled Cornucopia – the Horn of Plenty, said to overflow with whatever its fortunate owner desired.

Amaltheia was raised to the heavens by Zeus as a reward for her kindness.

KEY SAYING
"When the going gets tough, the tough get going"
– Proverb

Positive traits: reliable, determined, ambitious, careful, prudent, disciplined, patient, hard-working, persevering, far-sighted.
Negative traits: rigid, harsh, ruthless, cold, over-exacting, pessimistic, over-conventional, miserly, licentious, a 'wet blanket'.

THE CAPRICORN BODY
Parts of the body ruled: bones, skin, knees, joints.
Acupuncture meridian: gall bladder.
Capricorn ailments: arthritis, rheumatism, skin complaints, knee injuries, bone diseases, depression, eczema.
Beneficial foods: cabbage, kale.

The archetypal Capricorn: Dick Whittington, the poor youngster who went to London to make his fortune and rose to become Lord Mayor.

CAPRICORN ASSOCIATIONS
Herbs and Plants: barley, beech, beet, burdock, comfrey, cypress, deadly nightshade, elm, hemlock, holly, ivy, onions, spinach, willow, yew.
Objects: antiques, clipboard, clock, classic shoes, designer labels, large ornaments, vintage wine, watch, wellington boots.
Professions and Trades: administrator, antique dealer, architect, builder, civil servant, dentist, engineer, farmer, head teacher, musician, politician, scientist, surveyor.
Sports and Hobbies: collecting, investing, jogging, knitting, gardening, music, rock-climbing.

CAPRICORN AND THE WORLD
Capricorn represents national prestige and the ruling classes – established government, royal families, chiefs, and party leaders. It also has ties with national traditions and heavy industry.
Countries ruled by Capricorn: Afghanistan, Bulgaria, India, Lithuania, Mexico.
Cities ruled by Capricorn: Brussels, Oxford.

AQUARIUS AFFINITIES

JANUARY 20 – FEBRUARY 18

Who gives to all a helping hand
But bows his head to no command
And higher laws doth understand?
Inventor, genius – Aquarius

The sign of the Thinker

Symbol: the Water-bearer
Element: Air
Quality: Fixed
Rulers: Uranus, Saturn
Colour: electric blue
Gemstone: aquamarine
Metal: platinum

Perfume: galbanum
Keywords: independently, detachedly, unconventionally
Rules: the Eleventh House (ideals, group involvements, friends, humanitarianism, hopes and wishes).

Mythology: there are various myths associated with Aquarius, including the Egyptian god Hapi, from whose water jars poured the River Nile. In Greek mythology the sign may be linked with the legend of Prometheus, who stole fire from Zeus so that mortal man might be enlightened. Uranus, the sky god, was slain and castrated by his son Cronos after being imprisoned in the Underworld.

KEY SAYING
"A radical is a man with both feet planted firmly in the air"
– Franklin D. Roosevelt

Positive traits: humanitarian, independent, quirky, friendly, willing, progressive, original, inventive, progressive, loyal, idealistic, rational.
Negative traits: unpredictable, eccentric, rebellious, contrary, tactless, stubborn, perverse, emotionally oblivious.

THE AQUARIAN BODY

Parts of the body ruled: ankles, calves, shins, Achilles tendon, circulatory system, breath, eyesight.
Acupuncture meridian: lung meridian.
Aquarian ailments: injuries to lower legs, varicose veins, poor circulation, blood disorders, nervous disorders.
Beneficial foods: pomegranates.

AQUARIAN ASSOCIATIONS

Herbs and Plants: comfrey, golden-rain, heartsease, hemp, mandrake, moss, pansies, parsnips, pine, quince, rushes, sorrel, spinach.
Objects: art deco, bicycle, car parts, comics, computers, electronic equipment, kitcsh objects.
Professions and Trades: archaeologist, astrologer, astronomer, broadcaster, charity worker, computer programmer, electrical engineer, inventor, pilot, radiographer, scientist, sociologist, writer.
Sports and Hobbies: collecting gadgets, computer games, debating, discussing, flying, inventing, minority sports, ufology.

AQUARIUS AND THE WORLD

Aquarius represents all democratic institutions — parliaments, assemblies, local authorities, and so on. It also has links with humanitarian groups and the revolutionary overthrow of established orders.
Countries ruled by Aquarius: Poland, Sweden, USSR, Zimbabwe.
Cities ruled by Aquarius: Hamburg, Moscow.

*The archetypal **Aquarian:** the Tin Man who, in spite of his rational, friendly nature, had to search long and hard before he found his heart.*

PISCES AFFINITIES

FEBRUARY 19 – MARCH 20

*Who prays, serves and prays some more
And feeds the beggar at the door —
And weeps o'er loves lost long before?
Poor Pisces*

The sign of the Dreamer

Symbol: the Two Fishes
Element: Water
Quality: Mutable
Rulers: Neptune, Jupiter
Colours: sea green, lilac
Gemstone: bloodstone
Metal: zinc

Perfume: ambergris
Keywords: impressionably, nebulously, compassionately
Rules: the Twelfth House (the unconscious, secret enemies, repressed emotions, dreams, surrendering to a higher cause).

Mythology: the constellation of Pisces is said to commemorate the Fishes who rescued the goddess Aphrodite and her son Eros after they hurled themselves into a river to escape the wrath of the giant Typhon. The Fishes were raised to the heavens as a reward, and their tails tied together by the gods so that they should never be separated.

KEY SAYING

"The easiest thing of all is to deceive oneself; for what a man wishes he usually believes to be true"
– Demosthenes

Positive traits: artistic, kind, sympathetic, intuitive, visionary, sensitive, adaptable, receptive.

Negative traits: impractical, vague, careless, spiteful, confused, weak-willed, indecisive, easily led astray, greedy, immoral.

THE PISCEAN BODY

Parts of the body ruled: feet, lymphatic system, glandular system, mucus, gastro-abdominal system.
Acupuncture meridian: small intestine.
Piscean ailments: bunions, chilblains, alcoholism, drug addiction, lymphatic and glandular disorders, forgetfulness, insanity.
Beneficial foods: raisins, dates, cereals.

PISCEAN ASSOCIATIONS

Herbs and Plants: aniseed, balm, birch, chestnut, currants, daisy, dandelion, dock, fig, kelp, lime, marjoram, nutmeg, oak, sage, strawberry, water lily.
Objects: beer glasses, boats, bric-a-brac, fancy dress costumes, objects from work, photographs, shells, watercolours, wigs.
Professions and Trades: actor/actress, artist, chiropodist, fishmonger, hospital worker, photographer, priest, prison worker, sailor, spiritual healer, vet, writer.
Sports and Hobbies: cinema, darts, daydreaming, drinking, painting, photography, poetry, storytelling, swimming.

PISCES AND THE WORLD

Pisces represents all in the world that is spiritual, universal and intangible. It also has ties with all places of seclusion and confinement, secret societies, and the oil industry.
Countries ruled by Pisces: Portugal, Tonga, Tanzania.
Cities ruled by Pisces: Alexandria, Seville.

The archetypal Piscean: Don Quixote, the knight who was ridiculed for tilting at imaginery windmills but who in the end found spiritual fulfilment.

INTERPRETATION

Interpreting a birth chart is a fascinating adventure. All the more so if the chart belongs to you, or someone close to you. And it is an art which develops and changes with you, so you never really stop learning.

As a beginner, you may find it helpful to start with a computer calculated chart. Mathematical accuracy is crucial in astrology; a mistake in calculating the ascendant, for example, may result in the wrong rising sign and will certainly alter the house divisions round the chart. Secondly, interpretation itself has much to teach you about the structure of a chart.

When you come to drawing up one yourself you will, therefore, feel much more at home with the symbols for the planets, signs and aspects.

When interpreting, it is important to adopt a flexible and positive attitude towards your discoveries. Nothing is absolute, which is why many modern astrologers prefer to talk about 'hard' and 'soft' aspects rather than positive or negative ones.

Astrology's Changing World

Centuries ago, astrology dealt with a less sophisticated world. Most people believed in heaven and hell, heroes and heroines rarely revealed

flaws, and villains were one hundred per cent evil. Astrologers considered character traits, naturally, but the birth chart was viewed in a much more fatalistic fashion. Planets were termed 'malefic' (Mars and Saturn, for instance) or 'benefic' (Venus and Jupiter). Those with 'difficult' planetary combinations were left with scant room for compromise, self knowledge, or inner change. With the development of psychology and psychiatry, our ways of viewing things have changed irrevocably. We now accept the presence of a personal inner world, and are certainly inclined to take

unconcious motives into account.

This chapter shows you how to begin your interpretations on three levels. These are the internal level, how this relates to the outside world, and how it suggests external manifestations. The section on Affinities in Chapter One is particularly useful when considering external things such as careers and personal interests.On an inner level, interpretation becomes more delicate and requires a certain amount of objectivity. Every chart like every human being contains some areas of conflict, difficulty or repression. Some you may recognise, some may seem alien or depressing to you. You may assign a power to your chart and the planets within it which neither truly posesses. At such points, remember that you are in control, and can work towards expressing the most positive manifestations of the combined planetary energies.

Approached in the spirit of curiousity and adventure, your birth chart can be a valuable map of your potential and indicate ways you may realise this.

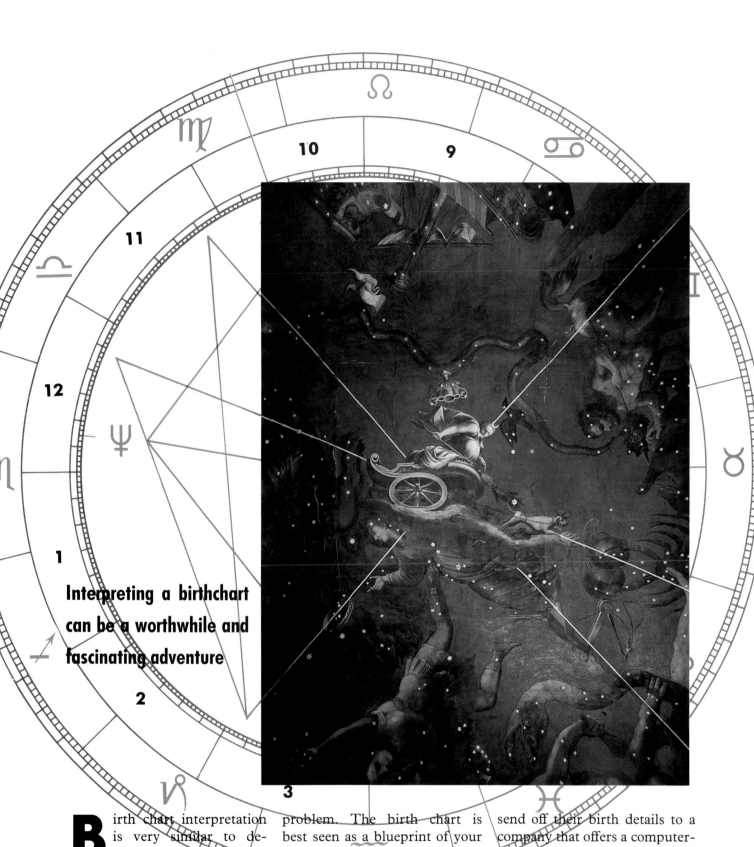

Interpreting a birthchart can be a worthwhile and fascinating adventure

Birth chart interpretation is very similar to detective work. A large number of clues need to be sifted through and analysed before they can be assembled into a pattern of possible trends.

However, unlike the detective, the astrologer cannot hope to come up with a final solution to a problem. The birth chart is best seen as a blueprint of your potential, but it is up to you how that potential is expressed. It is, of course, possible to work out your own birth chart, using tables of planetary positions and various mathematical calculations; but many people find the process laborious, and prefer to send off their birth details to a company that offers a computerized birth chart service. For those who have personal computers, there are a number of software programmes, available through specialist shops and magazines, that will do all the necessary calculations.

Whether you have had your

birth chart cast by a professional astrologer, sent off for a computerized chart, or set it up yourself, it is well worth trying your hand at astrological interpretation. Not only will it help you make sense of your own chart and give you the chance to compare your skills with those of the professionals, but you may well progress on to interpreting those of other people.

Unlike astronomy, which takes the Sun as the centre of our solar system, astrology looks at the skies purely from the point of view of the Earth, tracing the apparent movements of the planets around it.

This does not mean that astrology dismisses the findings of astronomy. It simply asks us to look at the cosmos through a different lens; one through which our thoughts and actions are seen as part of a larger pattern of events.

The Concept of the Zodiac

As seen from Earth, the journey of the Sun across the heavens appears to steer a course through a broad circular band – approximately 18° of latitude wide – which encircles our planet. This

▲ *In this 18th-century map of the constellations, the signs of the zodiac mingle with other symbols.*

◄ *The Sun (yellow) as seen from the Earth (green) appears to move through the zodiac belt.*

imaginary wheel is referred to as the 'zodiac belt', and contains the 12 constellations of stars that give their names to the astrological signs. It is these constellations which form the visible backcloth to the Sun's apparent path through the zodiac.

Astrology divides this path – known as the 'ecliptic' – into 12 equal sections of 30°, which are referred to as the signs of the zodiac. These divisions do not correspond to the size or the positions of the constellations bearing the zodiac names, how-

ever. They are purely symbolic, marking out the seasonal cycles of the Sun.

While the Sun acts as the astrological timekeeper, taking a year to pass through all the signs of the zodiac, the Moon and the eight planets also have their own cycles. They appear to move through the heavens very close to the ecliptic, so that the zodiac is also a reference grid for their positions. Their speeds vary enormously: the Moon takes approximately 28 days to pass through all the signs; while Pluto, the slowest moving planet, takes about 210 years.

Map of the Heavens

The birth chart is a personal map of the heavens as they were at the exact time and place of your birth. It is drawn as a circle divided into 12 segments and shows the precise positions, in degrees, of the Sun, the Moon and the planets in the signs. The areas where the planet-sign combinations fall in the chart – known as Houses – are determined by the Ascendant or rising sign, which is the degree of the ecliptic that was rising on the eastern horizon when you were born. Once this point or angle has been established, all the positions of planets and houses can be entered on the chart.

Principles of Interpretation

There are four fundamental components which make up the basis for chart interpretation.

1 The eight planets, the Sun and the Moon, each of which represents a particular kind of energy which manifests itself in the individual as instinctive drives.

2 The 12 Sun signs, which modify the way a planetary energy expresses itself. For example, Venus in a birth chart signifies the way in which an individual forms close relationships with others. If it is placed

ASTROLOGY SINCE ANCIENT TIMES

While the earliest astrological records are some 5,000 years old, the earliest known horoscope, or astrological chart, is a Babylonian one dating from 409 BC.

But it was not until the 3rd and 2nd centuries BC that the Ancient Greeks developed the idea of the 12 signs of the zodiac that we know today. (Zodiac is Greek for 'circle of animals'). The Greeks of this time noted that there was a relationship between people's personalities and their season of birth. They identified

12 types of character, which they connected to the 12 zodiac signs which took their names from 12 constellations of stars.

The influence of astrology faded in Europe with the decline of the classical world, however. It was attacked by the early Christian Church, which claimed that it went against the will of God. But the Persians kept the science alive. By the 8th and 9th centuries AD, it had been absorbed by the expanding Islamic cultures and was in turn passed on, via Spain, to the rest of Europe. Astrology then enjoyed a revival which lasted from the early Middle Ages to the 16th century.

The scientific discoveries of the 'Age of Reason', during the late 17th century and 18th century, conspired against anything that smacked of mysticism. And astrology's association with the occult arts contributed to its second major

eclipse. Yet by the mid-19th century, serious astrology was once again popular, interest possibly having been sparked off by the discovery of the planets Uranus in 1781 and Neptune in 1848. This revival prepared the ground for today's reawakened interest in astrology.

Stonehenge may have been built as a Neolithic observatory.

in Aries the sign will bring out spontaneous and fiery qualities in friendship and love affairs. But Venus in Taurus will manifest itself in a slower, more sensual manner.

3 The 12 houses, which indicate the main areas of the individual's life where all this activity will find an outlet. As with the signs, not all houses share the same level of importance in a chart. Some are 'empty' with no planets in them, others may be occupied by more than one planet. The Ascendant marks the beginning of the First House and, according to the commonly used 'Equal House' system, the other houses follow on at intervals of 30°. So if, for example, your Ascendant is 25° Libra, your second house will begin at 25° Scorpio, your third house at 25° Sagittarius, and so on through the zodiac.

4 The aspects, which represent the geometrical angles that the planets make to one another as seen from Earth. In the birth chart, they signify dynamic points of contact between two different types of energy, bringing either harmony or challenge to those areas of life connected with the planets concerned.

You can learn to fill in your own birth chart, placing the planets in the signs and houses, and drawing in the Ascendant and Midheaven.

A Picture of the Personality

As the eight planets, and the Sun and the Moon, may be located in any of the 12 signs and houses, the various permutations are considerable, even before the aspects have been taken into account. The skill and fun of interpretation lies in blending together all these various factors to form a complete picture of the personality. It may seem incredibly complicated at first, but proceed slowly and a clear pattern will soon begin to emerge.

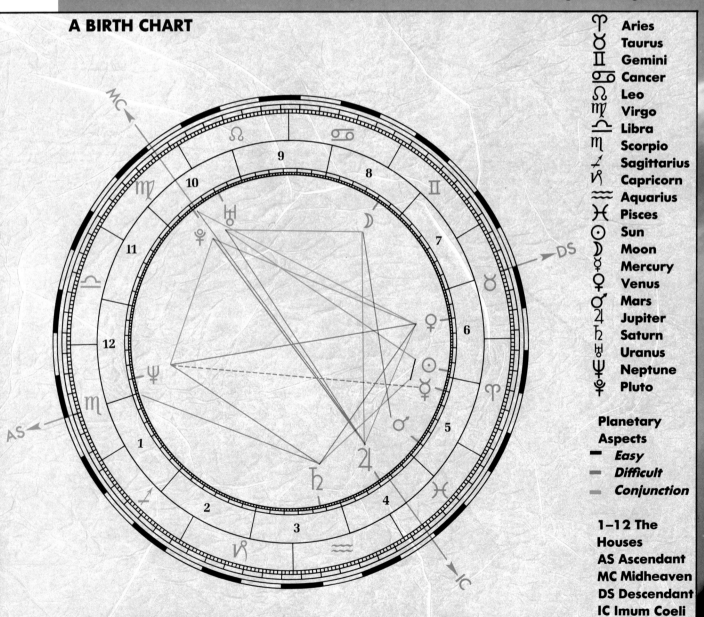

A BIRTH CHART

♈	Aries
♉	Taurus
♊	Gemini
♋	Cancer
♌	Leo
♍	Virgo
♎	Libra
♏	Scorpio
♐	Sagittarius
♑	Capricorn
♒	Aquarius
♓	Pisces
☉	Sun
☽	Moon
☿	Mercury
♀	Venus
♂	Mars
♃	Jupiter
♄	Saturn
♅	Uranus
♆	Neptune
♇	Pluto

Planetary Aspects
— *Easy*
— *Difficult*
— *Conjunction*

1–12 The Houses
AS Ascendant
MC Midheaven
DS Descendant
IC Imum Coeli

Placing the signs, planets and houses on the zodiac wheel

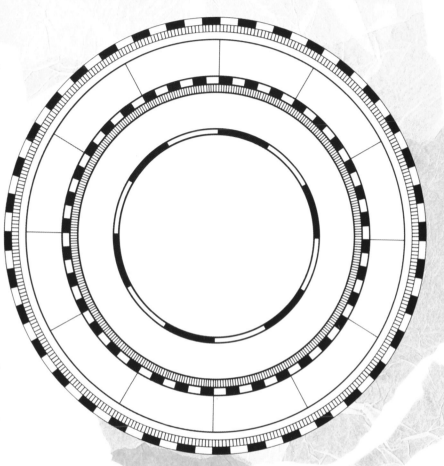

I f you visit an astrologer for a chart reading or write off for a computer analysis, you are unlikely to receive a copy of the zodiac wheel itself. You may be given a list of planet positions on the front page of the computer character analysis, or these may appear as marginal annotations in the text. However, this can be very frustrating if you decide you would like to learn more about your own chart and the workings of astrology in general, for the zodiac wheel provides a very graphic and compact picture of all the information you need.

One solution to the problem is to transfer the information to a birth chart yourself. There are many different ways to present information on a zodiac wheel, but the method described here is probably the simplest for the beginner.

Blank Charts

You can start with blank birth chart sheets, which are easily bought from 'occult' bookshops, and are very cheap. Alternatively, you can make up your own chart by copying the drawing above. You will need a ruler, a compass to draw the various circles, and a 5–6 inch protractor to mark off the degrees of the outer circle – 360 in all, with every fifth one emphasized to

make it easier when working out the positions of the Ascendant, Midheaven and House divisions (cusps). Remember that each

sign takes up exactly 30° of the zodiac wheel, although these cusps are usually marked in the blank birth charts.

Step 1: The Signs

It is simplest to fill in the details of your chart by entering the signs first in the outer section of the wheel. Traditionally, astrologers begin with the Ascendant, or Rising sign – Scorpio, in our example – placing it in the first section below the horizontal line to the left of the zodiac wheel. The other signs are then filled in anti-clockwise in their chronological order, so the second section is Sagittarius, the third Capricorn and so on.

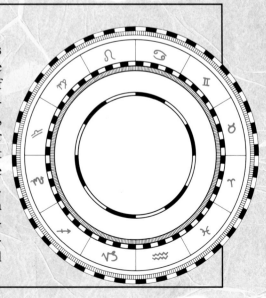

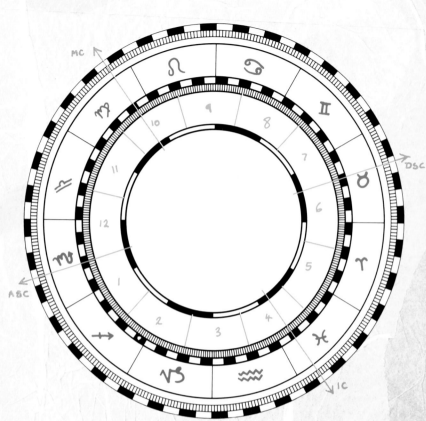

possible and line it up with exactly the same degree in the opposite sign of Taurus. You can check that you are doing this correctly, as the ruler should pass directly across the central point of the wheel.

Start to draw a line between these two points, but leave the space in the centre blank. This process can be repeated for the remaining Houses, and for the sake of clarity, it helps to number the Houses as you go along in the inner ring. As we are using the Equal House System, each House cusp is 30° from the last, so the cusp for the Second House is at 17°50′ Sagittarius, and its opposite – the Eighth – at 17°50′ Gemini. When the Houses have been entered, fill in the Midheaven and its opposite point the IC, in the same way. This axis and the Ascendant-Descendant axis are very important in a birth chart interpretation and most astrologers give them a strong visual emphasis by adding arrow heads to the Ascendant and Midheaven to make them easy to find.

Step 2: The Houses

The next stage is to draw in the Houses. Again, you should start with the Ascendant, which marks the beginning, or cusp, of the First House, and in our chart is at 17 degrees and 50 minutes of Scorpio – written 17°50′. Place your ruler as near to the 17–18 point of this sign as

Step 3: The Planets

In our sample chart, the Sun, for instance, is at 19°33′ Aries and in the Sixth House. You should place this and the other planets in the largest ring of the wheel, so that both the sign and House they fall in can be easily identified. If you find the symbols difficult to draw, practise on a notepad and you will soon master their shapes. It also helps when it comes to plotting the aspects if you mark approximately the position of the planets on the inner ring of the wheel.

Using different-coloured pens – as in the illustration – is helpful when marking signs, glyphs and cusps.

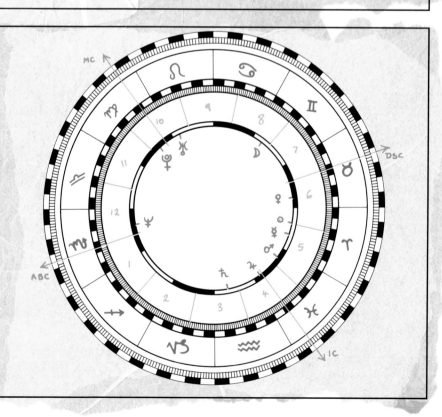

The various aspects between the planets in your chart may pinpoint areas of harmony or conflict

The final stage in preparing your chart is to determine the aspects. These are angular relationships between the planets, which combine their energies to create dynamic patterns of expression. They point to areas of potential harmony or tension in your personality. If the birth time is known to be accurate, aspects to the Ascendant and Midheaven are also important. Not all the planets make aspects to each other – just the ones that are certain distances apart.

Some computerized birth charts give the aspects in a box diagram, while others will list them as marginal annotations. Like the signs and planets, they have their own set of symbols. In the blank birth chart forms that can be bought from specialist bookshops, an aspect grid is provided for the aspect symbols to be filled in against the appropriate planets.

At this stage we will deal only with the category traditionally known as the 'major' aspects. The following descriptions show the symbol, the exact degree and the distance in degrees (known as the 'orb') allowed either side of the exact degree for each aspect. For example, in our sample chart (right) the Sun and Mercury are both in Aries, about 7½° apart. They do not make an exact aspect – they would both have to occupy the same degree and minute of the sign to do that – but they fall within the allowable orb for a 'conjunction'.

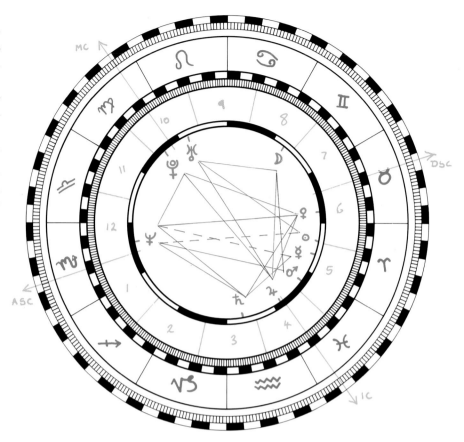

Understanding Aspects

These are the general rules for interpreting the aspects, although the nature of the planets in aspect to each other must also be considered. Any contact between Saturn and Pluto, for example, whether a conjunction, trine or square is regarded by most astrologers as very testing. Yet the 'difficult' aspects (i.e. square, or opposition) between, say, Venus and Jupiter – two planets that harmonise well – are not thought to be too serious.

The aspects can be plotted across the centre of the birth chart using different coloured pens. Planets opposite or square each other are joined by a line in one colour (usually red); the inconjunctions by a broken line in the same colour. For trines and

---

Squares 90° apart, orb 8°: these represent challenge and conflict leading to frustration, but they also provide the drive to overcome difficulties. Change is brought about by developing the positive side of the planets involved.

Oppositions 180° apart, orb 8°: pinpoint the need to balance these opposing energies. Like squares, they can be difficult to handle, but are easier to see and reconcile.

Inconjunctions 150° apart, orb 3°: represent the conflict between personal desires and the demands of others. Their effect is invariably frustrating.

Conjunctions 0° apart, orb 8–10°: combine the functions of two or more planets in a positive or challenging way, according to sign and house position, the planets involved and the type of aspects these planets make to any others, if any.

Trines 120° apart, orb 8°: usually considered to be a helpful combinations, but can also indicate the path of least resistance in people who find it difficult to motivate themselves.

Sextiles 60° apart, orb 8°: like the trines they usually emphasize the constructive qualities of the planets, although they do require some effort.

sextiles you should use a different coloured pen (perhaps blue or green). Conjunctions can be marked by a small black loop joining the planets.

Interpreting the chart

It is important to remember that what you are aiming for in a chart interpretation is an understanding of what makes the person concerned behave the way he or she does. This can be a fascinating and, at times, baffling exercise, for you have to bring together the often contradictory data supplied by the planets in the signs, their house positions, and the aspects between the planets into a recognizable and coherent whole. Like the detective gathering forensic evidence, you are looking for motives.

It is always helpful to look at the general impression a chart creates before breaking it down into its component parts. There are in fact several patterns that emerge at first sight which can tell you a great deal about the basic personality type of the individual under the astrological microscope.

The Chart Shapes

Once you have drawn up a chart, the most immediate impact is the shape that the planets in their signs and houses seem to form. There are seven principal shapes and they offer a general insight into the psychological make-up and expected life experiences of the individual. Most charts fall into these categories.

The Splay Shape (1)

This is the most common and least defined shape, with the planets evenly spread throughout the chart. Often this shape indicates a healthy distribution of abilities and activities, but if the planets do not connect strongly by aspect, especially to the Ascendant and Midheaven, the individual may have difficulty in bringing them out.

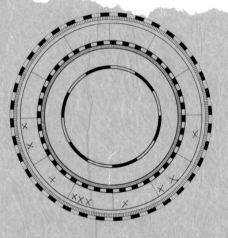

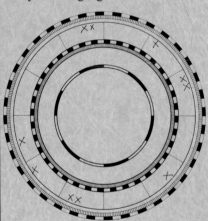

The Bowl Shape (2)

All the planets fall within one half of the chart. If the planets are placed in the top half of the chart – taking the Ascendant-Descendant axis as the dividing line – the focus is on the conscious, external activities of the individual. In the bottom half, the experiences are much more subjective, bringing personal, unconscious issues to the surface.

The left side hemisphere – divided by the Midheaven-IC axis – is concerned with taking direct control of one's destiny, while the right side is associated more with the influence others have on your life.

The Bucket Shape (3)

This is like the Bowl except that one planet, or a conjunction of planets, forms a 'handle'. It is less one-sided than the Bowl, as the handle provides access to the empty half, often creating a funnel of highly concentrated energy. Aspects from the other planets to the handle will show how and where this energy will manifest itself.

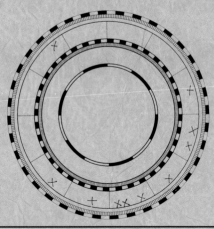

The Locomotive Shape (4)

One third of the chart or the equivalent of four consecutive signs, contains no planets. The empty section indicates the vulnerable part of the personality which may need careful attention.

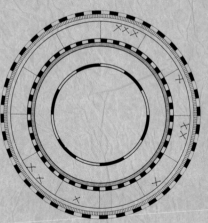

The Bundle Shape (5)

This is the opposite to the Locomotive with all planets contained within one third, or 120°, of the chart, This is a fairly rare combination, but people with this shape tend to have highly

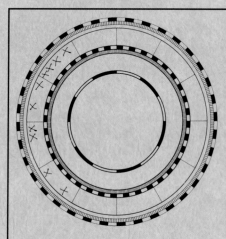

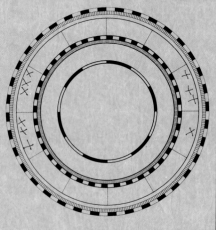

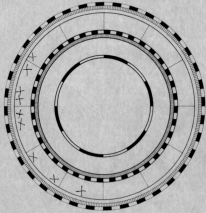

centrated section. The Sling is similar to the Bucket, except that the attention on the separate planet or planets is even more intense. People with this configuration are often driven by a vocational calling.

focused objectives at the expense of any others. It can be the mark of the highly-strung genius, or the obsessive personality!

The Sling Shape (6)
This is the Bundle with a planet, or conjunction, outside the con-

The See Saw Shape (7)
As the name suggests, this shape consists of two planetary groupings opposite each other. Behaviour patterns can fluctuate abruptly from one group to the other, often resulting in contradictory actions.

Positive and Negative
Psychology tests have shown that there is a strong correlation between the positive signs and the extrovert personality types, as well as the negative signs and introverted types. In the birth chart, the planets in the signs, together with the sign positions of the Ascendant and Midheaven, are counted to find out the balance between introversion and extroversion. Fire and Air signs are positive, while the Earth and Water signs are negative.

The planets, the Ascendant and Midheaven are also checked to see how they break down into the elements (also known as Triplicities) and qualities (or Quadruplicities).

The elements – Fire, Earth, Air and Water – describe four basic psychological types and the

signs belonging to the same element all share something in common: the Fire signs are restless, energetic, optimistic and assertive; the Earth signs, practical, sensual, persevering and reserved; the Air signs, objective, sociable, independent and mentally active; the Water signs, emotional, sensitive and intuitive.

The Qualities
Three qualities – Cardinal, Fixed and Mutable – define how we act and react to situations, although this will be coloured by the element to which each sign belongs. Cardinal signs are enterprising, self-motivated and like to initiate and involve themselves in projects. Fixed signs consolidate what the Cardinal signs begin: they are determined, dependable, loyal and often resistant to change. Mut-

able signs, by contrast, are adaptable, flexible, unpredictable and stimulated by new ideas.

Once you have accounted for all the planets by their element and quality you will have a strong overview of the distribution of the basic psychological categories in the birth chart. You can look immediately to see whether there is, for instance, an undue emphasis on planets in Negative, Earth, or Fixed signs. This would suggest a purposeful, reflective and probably stubborn individual who might find it hard to change his or her ways. Similarly, you may find that there are few or no planets belonging to a particular element or quality. Without going into any detailed chart analysis, you can establish early on likely strengths and weaknesses by looking at these patterns.

	FIRE	EARTH	AIR	WATER
CARDINAL	Aries	Capricorn	Libra	Cancer
FIXED	Leo	Taurus	Aquarius	Scorpio
MUTABLE	Sagittarius	Virgo	Gemini	Pisces
	POSITIVE	NEGATIVE	POSITIVE	NEGATIVE

The so-called 'angles' – the Ascendant, the Midheaven and their opposite numbers – are of supreme importance in chart interpretation

Our time and place of birth are vital pieces of data for astrologers. As well as enabling them to plot precisely where the planets and signs fall in our birthchart, they establish the positions of four especially sensitive points – commonly known as the *angles*.

The first two angles are the *Ascendant* – the exact degree of the sign rising over the eastern horizon at the time and place of birth – and the *Descendant* – its opposite on the western horizon. The third is the *Midheaven* (often referred to by its Latin name *meridian coeli* or simply MC), which is the highest point directly above the horizon. The fourth is the MC's opposite number on the lowest point below the horizon, and is called the *IC* (immeum coeli).

Traditionally the Ascendant is held to be the most significant, followed by the Midheaven. But it is also worth considering the other angles, as together they seem to symbolize heightened points of self-awareness.

The Ascendant represents our instinctive sense of self and also the way that we try to express it – the image we have of ourselves and how we present it to others. This applies particularly to the first impressions we create. Generally, the Ascendant governs the most visible aspects of our personality – and according to some astrologers, our physical appearance too.

The Descendant represents our sense of self in relation to others. It shows what we seek – whether consciously or otherwise – from relationships, and determines which side of our personality will be brought out through them. It also governs how we react to relationships, and the environment in which they are likely to take place.

The Midheaven represents our sense of self as we would want to impress it on the outside world. It shows the qualities we admire and strive to develop as we mature;

Taurus rising in Elvis's chart indicates a capacity for hard work.

the direction we wish to take; our need for status, recognition and achievement; our ideal career or vocation.

The IC signifies the exact opposite: our innermost, least consciously acknowledged sense of self, and where we are coming from. In adults it often points to past influences such as home and family background, defining our sense of 'belonging' and deepest motivations.

The four Angles of the birthchart – Ascendant, Descendant, Midheaven and IC. Together, they represent the chart's most sensitive points.

Aries

ASCENDANT/DESCENDANT
Typical traits: decisive, impatient, impulsive, combative, assertive. Needs to find creative outlets for restless energy. Once channelled, actions are fearless and inspired, but lack of purpose can lead to frustration.
Dangers: being too pushy and egocentric. With Libra on the Descendant, the challenge is to accommodate other people's feelings and points of view.

MIDHEAVEN/IC
Looks to take initiative, adopting own methods to achieve aims. Likes to be seen as optimistic and confident, leading from the front. Can come across as arrogant, impulsive and over-hasty. With a Libra IC, the family background may provide the equilibrium for Arian individuality to flower.

Taurus

ASCENDANT/DESCENDANT
Typical traits: cautious, purposeful, practical, reliable, industrious. Needs to create a secure framework within which to achieve aims. Enormously patient and persevering, but can become overly fond of routine.
Dangers: lazy habits and possessiveness. Scorpio on the Descendant calls for outmoded patterns of behaviour to be transformed.

MIDHEAVEN/IC
Seeks dignity, tangible results and often public recognition. Sees patience, hard work and, above all, professional security as virtues. Can be too conservative, inflexible or stubborn. Scorpio IC stresses the need to look inwards – possibly to face childhood issues – to gain emotional security.

Gemini

ASCENDANT/DESCENDANT

Typical traits: inquisitive, sociable, versatile, ingenious, analytical. Needs constant and varied stimuli to occupy the mind. Excellent at communicating and people-handling, but can be too talkative and superficial.

Dangers: diffusing energies by being too easily diverted. Sagittarius on the Descendant teaches the value of breadth and depth of vision.

MIDHEAVEN/IC

Drawn by an urge to explore as many outlets as possible. Likes to be at the centre of activity without being tied to it. Often accused of a butterfly mentality and lack of purpose. Sagittarius IC can supply enough breadth of vision – either through travel or from childhood influences – to fuel big ambitions.

Cancer

ASCENDANT/DESCENDANT

Typical traits: intuitive, tenacious, protective, sympathetic, shrewd. Needs to use acute sensitivity in a nurturing, rather than a defensive way. Supportive when helping others, but may be reluctant to unburden own emotions.

Dangers: excessive irascibility and moodiness. Capricorn Descendant provides the strength to contain wildly fluctuating feelings.

MIDHEAVEN/IC

Tends to develop a tough outer shell to protect sensitivity, and is intensely aware of public reputation. Wants responsibility, but is wary of limelight. Tenacious and supportive, but may cling to outworn values and harbour resentment. Capricorn IC may mean that true vocation is shaped by limitations of one's background.

The Greatest: not surprisingly, Muhammad Ali has Leo rising.

Leo

ASCENDANT/DESCENDANT

Typical traits: authoritative, generous, dramatic, enthusiastic, dignified. Must feel appreciated to make most of creative flair. Lack of recognition of leadership qualities may sap confidence.

Dangers: self-importance and tyranny. Aquarius Descendant brings a wider lens to self-centred views, plus the ability to give without expecting any return.

MIDHEAVEN/IC

Seeks admiration, but can devote enormous energy and organizing abilities to realizing ambitions. Believes in self-promotion and glamour, but others may see it as rampant egotism. Aquarius IC suggests aspects of the home background are unconventional. Eventually, human issues must be included in personal ambitions.

Sean Connery's Scorpio MC makes him a true 007, on or off-screen.

Virgo

ASCENDANT/DESCENDANT

Typical traits: discriminating, reserved, analytical, methodical, conscientious. Needs to acquire practical, detailed knowledge of how things work. Good at learning but often unable to 'let go'.

Dangers: hypercritical, obsessed with correctness. Pisces Descendant invites greater spontaneity and breaks down over-rigid boundaries.

MIDHEAVEN/IC

Strives for an orderly career in which intellectual abilities are employed. Fussy about image, and prefers to be thought efficient. May be seen as aloof and lacking spontaneity. Pisces IC can romanticize home and family environment, weakening one's sense of individuality. Spiritual yearnings may emerge later in life.

Libra

ASCENDANT/DESCENDANT

Typical traits: tactful, charming, perfectionist, idealistic, considerate. Needs to establish balance and harmony in all interactions. Finely tuned sense of co-operation can lead to 'people pleasing' just to keep the peace.

Dangers: indecisiveness and insincerity. Aries Descendant encourages the instinct to stand up and fight for what is sought.

MIDHEAVEN/IC

Cultivates charm, diplomacy and fortunate contacts in pursuit of aims. Indecision often masks the need to gain co-operation of others, especially those offering professional advancement. Seen as unctuously calculating by some. Aries IC may present the challenge to find a sense of purpose free from family ties.

Scorpio

ASCENDANT/DESCENDANT

Typical traits: loyal, secretive, penetrative, passionate, steadfast. Needs to channel intense emotions constructively. Has ability to draw on hidden resources, but does not always know when to pull back.
Dangers: destructive, manipulative and vengeful tendencies. Taurus Descendant can temper more extreme urges.

MIDHEAVEN/IC

Desires the independence to follow own path, and can be fiercely anti-establishment. More interested in the potential for transformation than in establishing a reputation. Often destroys to rebuild, which can be seen as needlessly ruthless. Taurus IC stresses the importance of traditional values in building lasting structures.

Sagittarius

ASCENDANT/DESCENDANT

Typical traits: opportunist, freedom-seeking, frank, utopian, jovial. Needs to feel free to experience life as an adventure. Optimistic when energy and enthusiasm are directed, otherwise may be depressed and restless.
Dangers: taking others for granted, arrogance and self-pity. Gemini Descendant should help to ride less roughshod over others.

MIDHEAVEN/IC

Aims for high standards and fulfilment, rather than material success. Hates routine and may be hopelessly impractical. Views self as natural leader, often with high-minded goals, but can be loud-mouthed and self-inflated. Gemini IC hints at a need to reach a precise understanding of one's deepest motives to realize ideals.

Princess Caroline's Capricorn MC points to lofty worldly ambition.

Capricorn

ASCENDANT/DESCENDANT

Typical traits: resourceful, cautious, disciplined, reserved, cool. Needs to feel self-sufficient and in control. Has tremendous ability to withstand hardship in pursuit of ambition, but can become trapped by conformity.
Dangers: selfish, calculating and unfeeling. Cancer Descendant may soften inflexible emotions and lack of sensitivity to others.

MIDHEAVEN/IC

Sensitive to how others react, but ploughs a solitary, cautious furrow. Driven by worldly ambition and equipped with patience and determination to succeed — eventually. May be seen as self-centred and obsessed with status. Cancer IC stresses the need for a sense of belonging.

Robert Redford's Pisces Ascendant softens his powerful Leo Sun.

Aquarius

ASCENDANT/DESCENDANT

Typical traits: independent, original, humanitarian, sociable, progressive. Needs to experience the human condition as a totality rather than from a personal viewpoint. Thinks in broad concepts which can verge on the dogmatic.
Dangers: naive and dismissive of personal emotions. Leo Descendant calls for warmth and respect of individuals' rights.

MIDHEAVEN/IC

Is fascinated by innovation, and likes to work in unconventional or future-orientated areas. A need to feel part of the 'winds of change' sometimes fails to take account of the virtues of tradition and individuality. Leo IC shows that sense of self can grow without having to reject background.

Pisces

ASCENDANT/DESCENDANT

Typical traits: compassionate, impressionable, imaginative, sensitive, visionary. Needs freedom from inflexibility. Selflessness can result in acts of great service or creativity, though sometimes at the expense of individuality.
Dangers: self-victimization and drowning of sorrows destructively. Virgo Descendant gives power to live within one's own limits.

MIDHEAVEN/IC

May indicate a longing to be revered by the public which, more often than not, results in hard work for little recognition. Ability to be all things to all people, leads to confusion about personal identity and ambition. Virgo IC shows a need to develop a more conscious sense of one's deepest motivations.

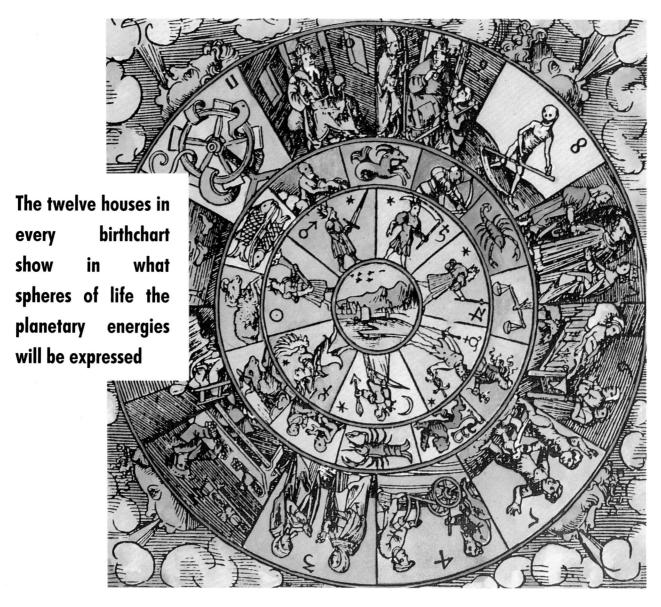

The twelve houses in every birthchart show in what spheres of life the planetary energies will be expressed

I f the planets in a birthchart represent particular energies, or modes of action, and the signs show the way in which these energies are expressed, then the houses describe the areas of life in which all this activity is most likely to occur.

Regardless of which method is used to calculate the houses (and there are several – see House Systems overleaf), there are always twelve in a birthchart. They are counted anti-clockwise, beginning at the Ascendant.

Just as the twelve signs each embrace different human qualities under the same banner, so the twelve houses each encompass several different areas of life experience. Sagittarius, for example, is associated both with a love of freedom and with a desire to explore deeper philosophical concepts. Similarly, the Sagittarius-ruled Ninth House may refer equally to adventure in foreign lands, or to some form of higher education.

Deciding which meanings apply is never easy, as it depends on the complex interrelationship between the planets. Often astrologers must rely on their own intuition; it is here that astrology changes from science to art.

THE TRADITIONAL MEANINGS OF THE HOUSES

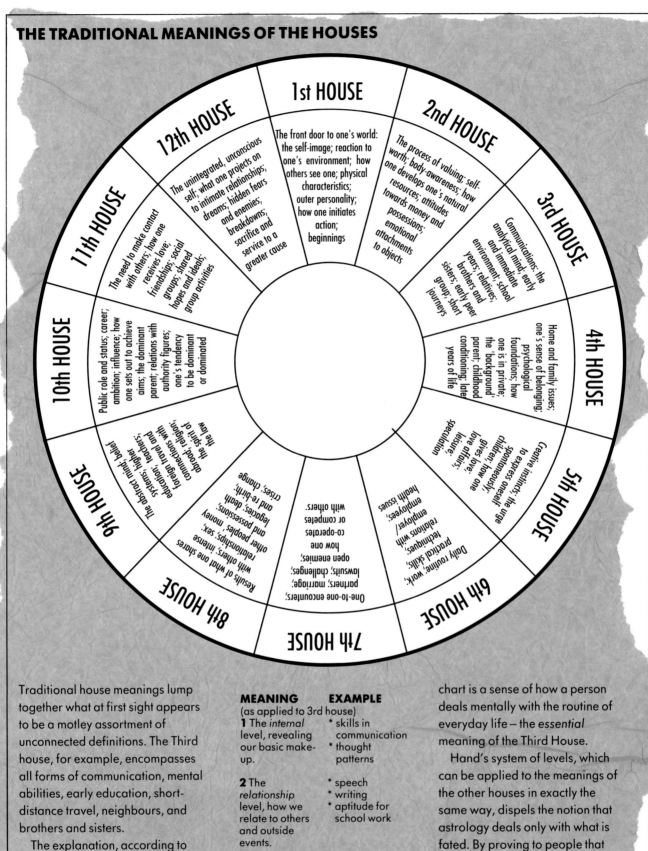

1st HOUSE
The front door to one's world: the self-image; reaction to one's environment; how others see one; physical characteristics; outer personality; how one initiates action; beginnings

2nd HOUSE
The process of valuing: self-worth; body-awareness; how one develops one's natural resources; attitudes towards money and possessions; emotional attachments to objects

3rd HOUSE
Communications: the analytical mind; early environment; school years; relatives; brothers and sisters; early peer group; short journeys

4th HOUSE
Home and family issues; one's sense of belonging; psychological foundations; how one is in private; the 'background' parent; childhood conditioning; later years of life

5th HOUSE
Creative instincts; the urge to express oneself; children; how one gives love; love affairs; leisure; speculation

6th HOUSE
Daily routine; work; practical skills; techniques; relations with employer/employees; health issues.

7th HOUSE
One-to-one encounters; partners; marriage; lawsuits; challenges; open enemies; how one co-operates or competes with others.

8th HOUSE
Results of what one shares with others; intense relationships; sex; other peoples' money and possessions; legacies; death and re-birth; crises; change

9th HOUSE
The abstract mind; belief systems; higher education; foreign travel and connections with abroad; religion; the spirit of the law

10th HOUSE
Public role and status; career; ambition; influence; how one sets out to achieve aims; the dominant parent; relations with authority figures; one's tendency to be dominant or dominated

11th HOUSE
The need to make contact with others; how one receives love; friendships; social groups; shared hopes and ideals; group activities

12th HOUSE
The unintegrated, unconscious self; what one projects on to intimate relationships; dreams; hidden fears and enemies; breakdowns; sacrifice and service to a greater cause

Traditional house meanings lump together what at first sight appears to be a motley assortment of unconnected definitions. The Third house, for example, encompasses all forms of communication, mental abilities, early education, short-distance travel, neighbours, and brothers and sisters.

The explanation, according to American astrologer Robert Hand, is that planetary energies within the houses can operate simultaneously on three levels as demonstrated in the chart for the Third House shown right.

Linking all the meanings in the

MEANING
(as applied to 3rd house)

1 The *internal* level, revealing our basic make-up.

2 The *relationship* level, how we relate to others and outside events.

3 The *external* level, showing how other people and outside events can indirectly affect us.

EXAMPLE

* skills in communication
* thought patterns

* speech
* writing
* aptitude for school work

* school
* short journeys
* neighbours
* brothers and sisters

chart is a sense of how a person deals mentally with the routine of everyday life – the *essential* meaning of the Third House.

Hand's system of levels, which can be applied to the meanings of the other houses in exactly the same way, dispels the notion that astrology deals only with what is fated. By proving to people that their own psychological make-up is inextricably linked with the outside circumstances that can affect them, the system encourages them to take control of their own destiny, rather than simply be led by it.

House Relationships

Just as the various meanings ascribed to individual houses have common links, so the houses themselves are related to one another. They must never be considered purely in isolation.

The most obvious relationship is between opposite houses – the First and the Seventh, the Second and the Eighth, and so on. This becomes especially relevant when a planet in, say, the First opposes a planet in the Seventh.

The issue in this particular case focuses on the contrast between the person's urge to put themselves first and their need for close relationships. Does the person identify with one planet, while at the same time unconsciously causing others to act out the role of the opposing planet? Or does he or she flip erratically from one to the other?

Deciding which levels of meaning apply is largely a matter for the astrologer's own intuition. Questions like these are certainly beyond the scope of a computerized interpretation.

Another way to group the houses is to see them as stages in a person's life. The journey begins at the Ascendant, the moment marking birth; Houses 1–3 then go on to represent the development of basic needs. Houses 4–6 show how the person acclimatizes to their surroundings in preparation for Houses 7–9, which are concerned with their response and adjustment to other people. Last are Houses 10–12, which reveal the nature of the person's involvement in the wider world.

Planets in Houses

There are several ways in which a planet can be seen to work through a house:

1 The planet occupies the house. This is the most obvious way, and is generally agreed by

HOUSE SYSTEMS

There are several systems for dividing up the birthchart into houses. Astrologers still argue about which is the most accurate, and the astronomical arguments for preferring one to another are extremely complicated. The two most commonly used in Britain, are Equal House and Placidus.

The Equal House is the simplest to operate, since it divides the zodiac into houses of exactly 30° each, starting from the degree of the Ascendant. However, it also allows the Midheaven/IC axis to 'float' anywhere between the Eighth-Second and Eleventh-Fifth Houses. Critics point out that given their significance as Angles, the MC and IC should always mark the cusps of the Tenth and Fourth Houses respectively.

The Placidus system answers this criticism, but in doing so raises another problem. Because it works out the house divisions according to the observed movement of the heavens, calculations for latitudes near the Poles cause some houses to grow exceptionally large, while others disappear altogether! And even where it does work, the Placidus system creates houses of unequal size, allowing planets to fall in houses different from those calculated when using the Equal House system.

For the aspiring astrologer, there is no solution to this dilemma. The only answer is to spend some time experimenting with both systems until you find the one which appears to work best for you. Or you may make your own choice according to the individual chart.

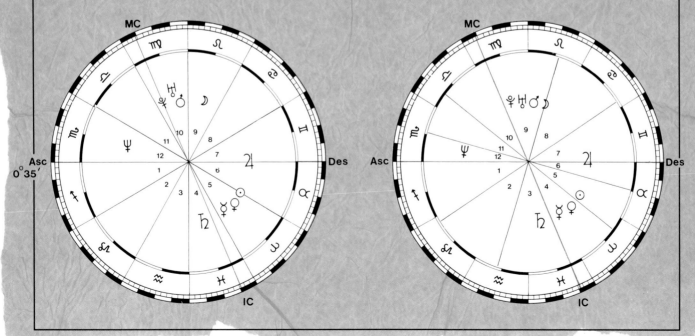

astrologers to be the most powerful.

2 The planet aspects another planet in another house, thereby affecting the other house. This is a development of (1), and is not always accurate. Sometimes such an aspect between two planets bears no apparent relation to the houses in which the planets fall.

3 The planet makes an aspect to the house cusp. This is particularly important when the cusp is one of the Angles (Ascendant, Midheaven, Descendent, IC). Most astrologers agree that planets in these positions have a very strong bearing on the chart, while the other house cusps appear to be less critical.

4 The planet rules the sign on the house cusp, or the sign following it. Unless a person's Ascendant is 0°, each house will embrace the sign on the cusp and part of the sign which follows. So if the Ascendant is 15° Aries, both Mars (ruler of Aries) and Venus (ruler of Taurus, which follows) are involved, and their aspects, signs and house positions will all have a bearing on First House matters. For a full interpretation, this complex procedure must be applied to all the houses.

'Empty' Houses

Houses with no planets in them will naturally have less emphasis in the chart than houses that do. But this does not necessarily mean, for example, that an 'empty' Seventh House rules out the chance of close relationships.

To find out how such a house will be energized, the astrologer looks to the sign on the cusp and the sign following on. He or she then notes the planetary rulers of the two signs and checks their positions in the chart.

The Chart Ruler

Most astrologers agree that of all the planets 'ruling' houses, the one ruling the sign on the First House cusp is the most important because it modifies the way the Ascendant is expressed. For example, Cancer rising calls for the Moon's position by sign and house and aspect to be given special prominence in the interpretation; the chart is said to have a 'lunar' flavour which will colour the whole picture.

THE NATURAL ZODIAC

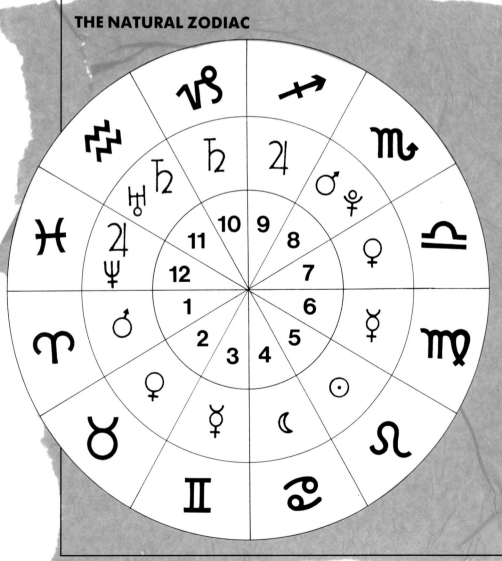

The basic links between the signs, planets and Houses are symbolized by what is called the Natural Zodiac, which takes 0° Aries as its Ascendant, 0° Taurus as the cusp of the Second House, and so on. Both Aries and the First House have an affinity with Mars and are said to be 'ruled' by this planet. The same applies to the other signs, houses, and planets, as shown left.

Some confusion exists as to why Scorpio, Aquarius and Pisces should each have two planetary rulers. The reason is that the links in the Natural Zodiac were established long before the discovery of Uranus, Neptune, Pluto – at a time when there were only seven planets to share between the twelve signs and houses.

Over the years, by popular – though not universal – consent, Pluto was linked with Scorpio, Uranus with Aquarius and Neptune with Pisces. Many astrologers, however, continue to use the traditional sign and house rulers in conjunction with the new.

☉ *the sun*

In the birthchart the Sun, by sign, house position and – above all – the aspects it makes to the Angles and other planets, describes a person's motivating force; what essentially that person is seeking to become. This is reflected in the Sun's glyph – a dot, representing potential, in a circle signifying completeness or maturity.

On other levels the Sun also corresponds to the masculine principle – willpower, courage, creativity, purpose, growth, one's sense of uniqueness, authority, the father, the ruler.

This last image is particularly helpful to an understanding of the Sun's astrological function. In life, the ruler is the figurehead under which the disparate social groups of a nation either unite, or divide. Similarly, the Sun symbolizes the process by which other planetary energies in the birthchart are integrated, or wasted. For a more detailed look at the Sun through the signs, please refer to Chapter One. Overleaf you will find the essential keywords for the sign and house positions.

THE SUN THROUGH THE SIGNS

ARIES Assertive, impulsive, independent, pioneering, enthusiastic, insensitive, direct, aggressive, impatient, self-centred.

TAURUS Calm, determined, patient, even-tempered, deliberate, inflexible, industrious, hedonistic, possessive, grasping.

GEMINI Mentally agile, inquisitive, adaptable, restless, stimulating, fickle, superficial, dishonest, apt to scatter energies.

CANCER Emotional, nurturing, protective, touchy, outwardly tough, shrewd, intuitive, changeable, sentimental, possessive.

LEO Spontaneous, generous, theatrical, creative, dignified, overbearing, passionate, intolerant, snobbish, haughty.

VIRGO Reserved, practical, analytical, methodical, critical, pedantic, conscientious, anxious, lacks self-worth, emotionally repressed.

LIBRA Diplomatic, congenial, co-operative, idealistic, romantic, perfectionist, narcissistic, over-amenable, indecisive, lacking confidence.

SCORPIO Intensely emotional, secretive, wilful, penetrative, transformative, extremely jealous, perceptive, imaginative, suspicious, vindictive.

SAGITTARIUS Freedom-loving, idealistic, deep-thinking, sincere, outspoken, benevolent, moralistic, optimistic, undisciplined, arrogant.

CAPRICORN Persevering, resourceful, industrious, possessed of enormous staying-power, ambitious, prudent, rational, conformist, selfish, unfeeling.

AQUARIUS Individualistic, sociable, detached, humanitarian, intuitive, dogmatic, progressive, rebellious, cranky, erratic.

PISCES Highly sensitive, compassionate, impressionable, receptive, imaginative, submissive, escapist, self-sacrificing, impractical, gullible.

THE SUN THROUGH THE HOUSES

FIRST The urge to leave one's mark; natural qualities of leadership; may radiate infectious enthusiasm or appear overbearing and proud.

SECOND Acquires money and possessions as a mark of individuality; able to manage material resources; the need to develop a unique sense of self-worth.

THIRD Achieving distinction through knowledge; wanting to be respected for one's mental abilities; 'streetwise' skills; intellectual arrogance; the need to develop depth of understanding.

FOURTH Establishing a strong, sometimes tyrannical sense of self through the home; often indicates early struggles against the family background, especially the father figure.

FIFTH A spontaneous need to express oneself through romantic or creative pursuits; a desire to prove one's strengths and abilities; extravagant self-confidence leading to recklessness.

SIXTH Distinguishing oneself through hard work; a need to be of useful service and to be recognized for one's skills; focus on employment issues, or on health and dietary habits.

SEVENTH Enhancing individuality through close partnerships; striking a balance between independence and reliance on others; a danger of inflicting one's will on partners.

EIGHTH Learning to share resources and possessions with partners; intense emotional and sexual bonds; transforming oneself through inner development or the outer accumulation of wealth.

NINTH A need to create one's own set of moral or spiritual values; an intellectual appetite for learning; bigoted views; identity often expanded through contact with foreign lands or cultures.

TENTH A need to be taken seriously professionally, or to be seen as authoritative in some area; dependent on the outward trappings of success; drawn to a prestigious partner; a powerful parent, often an ambitious mother.

ELEVENTH Seeking recognition via group activities, or organizations; needing to cultivate own beliefs as distinct from group ideas; influential friends; selfish exploitation of friendships or groups.

TWELFTH Sacrificing personal identity to collective needs; recognition through service to others; work behind the scenes; yearnings for approval often thwarted; powerful secret enemies; own worst enemy.

☾ the moon

Just as the Moon reflects the Sun's light, so in astrology it signifies a person's instinctive, emotional response to their environment. Where the Sun is connected with action, the Moon's domain is reaction.

These feelings are largely unconscious in childhood, only coming to light as we become aware of our true selves as signified by the Sun. As a result, the Moon by sign, house position and aspects can reveal a great deal about a person's emotional development as a child, and how these patterns are likely to re-emerge in later life.

The Moon also corresponds to the 'feminine' principle – the protective instinct; the home environment; our sense of 'belonging'; natural habits; eating patterns and preferences; attitudes to the past; changing moods and fortunes (reflecting the cycles of the Moon); the imagination; the ability to reach the public; and women, especially the mother.

ARIES Hasty reactions; a short-fused temper which quickly burns out; independent; intolerant of interference; may possibly seek to dominate others emotionally.

TAURUS Instinctively finds emotional stability in material security; stimulated by beauty and the good life; often lazy, acquisitive and habit-bound.

GEMINI An ability to rationalize emotions can lead to losing touch with feelings; restless spirit may seek stimulus through constantly changing surroundings; superficial.

CANCER Great emotional strength and sensitivity; highly responsive to the moods of others, though easily wounded by imaginary slights; brooding; smothering affections.

LEO Proud feelings and dramatic reactions; feels 'at home' in the limelight; powerful instinct to give and receive; loyal in affections; can be stubborn and self-centred.

VIRGO Tendency for the head to govern the heart; difficulty in 'letting go' results in concern for order and correctness; shy; over-anxious; prudish; driven by a need to be useful.

LIBRA Sensitivity to others means that emotional responses may be unduly influenced by partners; hates disharmony; loves beauty and elegance; can be fickle and hypercritical.

SCORPIO Intense emotions, which can range from total self-denial to compulsive indulgence; capable of noble sacrifice or bearing deep grudges; stubborn; brooding and unforgiving.

SAGITTARIUS A strong emotional attachment to childhood moral values; optimism and high ideals give a child-like innocence to responses; lacks objectivity; intuitive; restless.

CAPRICORN Reluctant to express emotions for fear of exposing vulnerability; cautious, reserved and practical; reactions to others tend to be guided by material considerations.

AQUARIUS Detached concern for others resulting from a dread of being restricted by personal involvements; intuitive; difficulty in dealing with emotions; needs freedom at home.

PISCES Hypersensitivity can lead to unconscious absorption of other people's emotions; highly imaginative; easily wounded; has difficulty accepting worldly reality; escapist; addictive.

FIRST The feeling nature is heightened, especially the ability to tune into immediate surroundings; highly subjective; difficulty in distinguishing between own and others' needs.

SECOND Material values endorse emotional security; difficulty in releasing emotional attachments; greedy; strong family ties; liable to experience changeable financial fortunes.

THIRD Thought processes coloured by moods; intuitive about what others think; learning equals security; an ability to influence through writing or speaking.

FOURTH A strong sense of belonging within the family framework; the need to create a home as a sanctuary; childhood patterns or issues may re-emerge in later life.

FIFTH An instinctive need to be creative; natural artistic ability; the possibility of reliving aspects of the 'mother' through love affairs or children; public appeal.

SIXTH The need to be emotionally fulfilled by work; dealing with other people's emotions; working to perfect daily habits, especially how to handle stress; needing to be needed.

SEVENTH Seeking a partner for 'completeness'; nurturing relationships; sometimes looking for 'mother' in the partner; family issues affecting the marriage.

EIGHTH A subtle awareness of how to use other people's resources; responsive to partner's sexuality; emotional crises leading to a renewed sense of worth.

NINTH A fascination with concepts that broaden the mind; travel; foreign connections; an ability to tune into future trends and to gauge public opinion; 'gut' convictions.

TENTH Blending in with the status quo; seeking public approval; sensitivity to public reputation; intuitive feeling for public taste; unresolved issues with parents, especially the mother.

ELEVENTH A sense of belonging through friends or organizations; falling in with the crowd; supporting emotive causes; female friendships; fluctuating goals throughout life.

TWELFTH Susceptibility to others' emotions; the need to withdraw to find a sense of self; hidden or repressed emotions; vivid dreams; deep-rooted phobias; caring for the less fortunate.

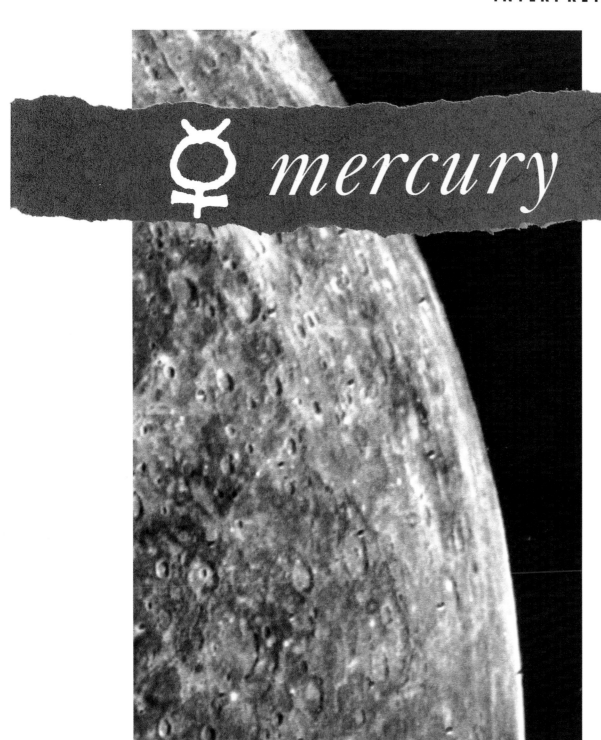

☿ *mercury*

Mercury, in his mythological role as Messenger of the Gods, was responsible for conveying information between mortals and the deities residing on Mount Olympus. In the birthchart, his planetary counterpart fulfils a similar function; Mercury carries the torch of conscious thought to the rest of the chart, offering the opportunity of greater self-awareness along the way.

More specifically, Mercury by sign, house position and aspects to other planets reveals the mental frequency on which we operate – how we think and generally communicate. He also shows our aptitude for learning, and – especially through the contact he makes to other planets – whether our opinions are likely to be based on logic or feelings and habits.

In his highest expression, Mercury symbolizes the power of wisdom and self-knowledge; in his lowest, the mind of the trickster, full of deceit and low cunning. On other levels Mercury corresponds to the workings of the rational, objective mind; early school experiences; reading and writing; languages; debate and discussion; transport; commerce; short-distance travel; and the tools of communication – books, newspapers, telephones, television and computers.

MERCURY THROUGH THE SIGNS

ARIES A quick, decisive mind, capable of producing highly intuitive ideas; impulsive decisions, often ill-thought out; lacking patience and attention to detail; argumentative.

TAURUS Slow, deliberate thought processes; reluctant to change mind; shrewd and practical head for business; strong powers of concentration; commonsensical; opinionated.

GEMINI A logical, versatile mind, capable of processing a lot of information quickly; often articulate and witty; good at problem-solving; easily distracted; fickle opinions.

CANCER Thoughts shaped by emotional responses; retentive memory; imaginative; susceptible to what others think; good business acumen; sentimental.

LEO Strong-minded with a good overview, but poor grasp of details; slow to form and change opinions; thoughts expressed authoritatively, sometimes arrogantly; good at selling ideas.

VIRGO An analytical, rational mind that concerns itself with the practical application of ideas; efficient and attentive to detail; can be over-fussy and obsessed with order.

LIBRA A sharp, active mind capable of weighing all the options and reaching balanced decisions; may try to please others and compromise own opinions; good for business planning.

SCORPIO An intuitive mind which can penetrate the most insoluble problems; communicates only when necessary, hence seen as secretive and scheming; instinctive business sense; may be sharp-tongued.

SAGITTARIUS A philosophical mind, finely tuned to dominant social attitudes; can overlook facts for the sake of an idea; may either have almost visionary insight or bigoted beliefs.

CAPRICORN An organized, practical mind, capable of great concentration; thinking is slow, often sceptical, but thorough; drawn to ideas that are well tested; resourceful in business.

AQUARIUS A free-thinking, inventive mind, always seeking mental stimulation; humanitarian views can be either benevolent or dogmatic; obsession with objective truth may obscure subjective values.

PISCES A highly sensitive mind with a vivid imagination, but prone to being overwhelmed by fluctuating and unconscious emotions; difficulty in communicating deepest thoughts; artistic leanings.

MERCURY THROUGH THE HOUSES

FIRST Restless mental activity, always seeking to communicate; observant, perhaps with a gift for mimicry; may be over-talkative, even argumentative.

SECOND Communication skills can be deployed to earn money; a sharp understanding of the value of things – either objects, such as antiques, or abstract activities, such as economics.

THIRD A need for constant mental stimulation, especially through study, or work which involves travel; the ability to exploit knowledge commercially; strong mental ties with siblings.

FOURTH A background where learning is important; how one develops a rational perspective on one's upbringing and family environment; may indicate frequent changes of home.

FIFTH The urge to identify with one's 'rational' mind; a need to express one's thoughts creatively; independent or narrow-minded thinking; communication with children often emphasized.

SIXTH Developing communication skills in one's work; seeking mentally stimulating work; learning how to synthesize detailed and varied information; an interest in health issues.

SEVENTH Seeking a strong mental affinity in close relationships, especially marriage; how one adjusts to the opinions of others; the ability to sell an idea; possibly a younger partner.

EIGHTH An interest in subjects that penetrate the the mind, such as psychology, mysticism, and sex; handling other people's resources in business; intense mental contact in close relationships.

NINTH An attraction to interests that broaden the mind, such as religion, philosophy, politics and foreign cultures; travel and further education are highlighted; possibly dogmatic opinions.

TENTH May indicate the need for public speaking skills; educational qualifications as a means of furthering one's career; wanting to be taken seriously for one's ability with words.

ELEVENTH Intellectual concern with humanitarian or social issues; thoughts shaped by friends or group organizations; the ability to be a group spokesperson; groups of like-minded people.

TWELFTH A highly active imagination stirred by deeply felt, often unconscious, thought patterns; possible 'psychic' abilities; can indicate mental blocks stemming from early learning difficulties.

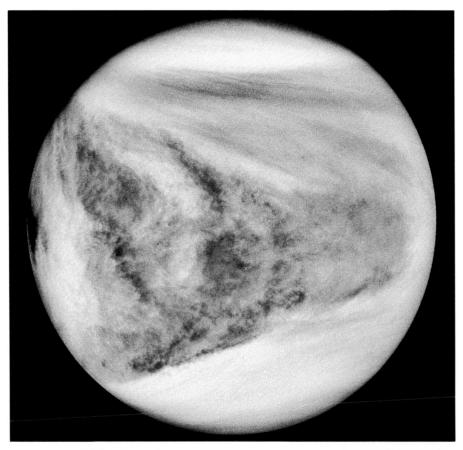

♀ *venus*

Named after the the goddess of love, beauty and sensuality, the planet Venus traditionally refers to our need for relationship, affection and harmony. At a more fundamental level, however, Venus is concerned with what attracts and repels us, and how we respond to these influences.

The process involved is one of weighing up – of trying to decide what is good or bad according to how we perceive our needs. More often than not, this results in sharing or co-operative behaviour, since most people find dealing with others preferable to being lonely and unpopular.

In terms of love, Venus reveals our reaction when we meet it, rather than how we express ourselves emotionally (which is more a function of Mars). Venus rarely gives without expecting something in return, hence our ability to attract harmonious relationships will depend on its sign and house position, and more specifically on the nature of the planets it aspects.

On other levels, matters which fall within Venus' portfolio include the arts; style; taste; physical attraction; close partnerships of all kinds; women and feminine sexuality; physical wellbeing; money and all means of exchange; diplomacy and vanity.

VENUS THROUGH THE SIGNS

ARIES Socially dynamic and openly flirtatious; affectionate, but prone to impulsive attractions; competitive instinct is sharpened by the chase, but can lead to overbearing, self-centred behaviour.

TAURUS Can be passionate and loyal in love, though also possessive if emotional security is uncertain; highly sensual; artistic ability a common feature.

GEMINI Seeks variety in both romantic and social spheres; needs space and a strong mental rapport in a relationship; fear of strong emotional contacts may lead to fickleness and superficiality.

CANCER May be moody and hyper-sensitive in relationships; compassionate and highly protective – if not smothering – regarding partners or children; preoccupied with financial and domestic security.

LEO Delights in courtship and in being the centre of attention; passionate and loyal, but expects due recognition in return; a natural talent for dramatizing feelings; a strong sense of colour.

VIRGO May undervalue self, both socially and romantically, leading to shyness; standards may be too high in relationships; a practical approach to love based on shared work and mental compatibility.

LIBRA Usually romantic, affectionate and companionable; need for beauty may be projected on to partner; desire to accommodate others may lead to over-conformity and suppression of true desires.

SCORPIO Passions run high and sexual desire is at its most intense; capacity for self-sacrifice can lead to great bitterness if loyalty is betrayed; feelings in love are either all or nothing.

SAGITTARIUS Enthusiastic nature needs room to explore fun-loving relationships; many contacts often preferred to deep commitments; may try to mould partner to own outlook; love of high living.

CAPRICORN Emotional stability linked with material status, so love and marriage may be used to advance socially or professionally; reserved but loyal in affections; objects of beauty seen as investments.

AQUARIUS Resistance to being conventionally 'tied down'; detached emotions may confuse friendship with love; need for unorthodox contacts may result in disappointment if experiment does not succeed!

PISCES Must temper compassionate nature with a sense of discrimination; vulnerable to seduction and exploitation; tendency to become emotionally dependent on partner, or to play the martyr.

VENUS THROUGH THE HOUSES

FIRST Refined; needs harmonious surroundings; prone to instant attractions; over-accommodating for the sake of peace; charming, but needs flattering in return; expects things to fall into place.

SECOND Sets a high premium on beauty and material possessions; a strongly marked sensuality; tendency for indulgent and expensive habits; powerful emotions which can lead to possessiveness.

THIRD Sensitive to the immediate environment; a sympathetic listener who can communicate easily; inclined to say what people want to hear; a sparkling love of words; an elusive magnetism.

FOURTH Creates beauty and harmony in the home; clings to ancestral values; emotional stability; tied to parental influences; may romanticize about one parent; a need for dependency in relationships.

FIFTH An urge to be popular and desirable; a passionate need to be 'in love'; liking for style and luxury; creative talents developed for the enjoyment they bring; easy contact with children.

SIXTH Acquiring practical values; refining techniques and skills; learning to accept spontaneous desires; close relationships might develop through, or interfere with work.

SEVENTH An attraction for social gatherings and the 'good life'; finds own sense of worth in a partner; too great a dependency on others; possible disappointments in search for 'ideal' partner.

EIGHTH A need to share at the deepest level, especially through sex; crises in relationships which are destructive or transformative; possible benefits through marriage or inheritance.

NINTH Developing an idealistic set of values; able to inspire others through own enthusiasm; a love of adventure, travel or foreign cultures; one to one relationships may be seen as restricting.

TENTH Natural gifts used to advance career; places status and security above romance; seeks recognition for own style, taste, or beauty; possible loneliness in love by appearing too aloof.

ELEVENTH Brings a spirit of co-operation to friendships or social contacts; many acquaintances; finds love through friendship and mutual interests.

TWELFTH Yearns to submerge self in partner; strong subconscious emotional and sexual urges; falling for the unavailable; finding love at enormous personal sacrifice; often denotes strong artistic leanings.

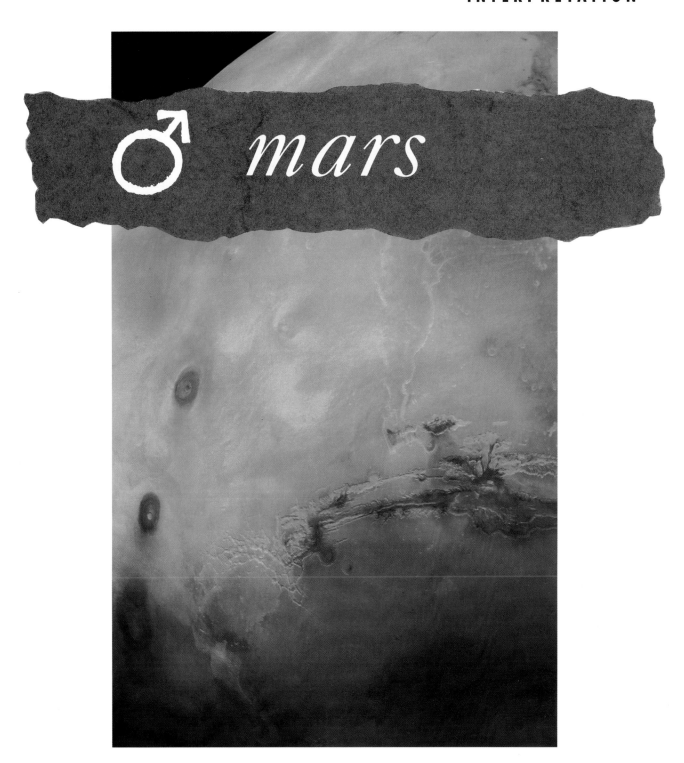

♂ *mars*

At an instinctive level, Mars represents our determination to battle for survival. When threatened, we can either confront a likely aggressor or flee. As we will only fight for what we value, the implications of Mars in our birthchart have to be seen in conjunction with Venus.

While Venus describes what we value, Mars shows how we obtain or preserve it. Conse-quently, Mars symbolizes all those qualities which help us achieve our desires and therefore enhance our self-image, such as initiative, courage, physical strength and stamina.

It is through the impulse Mars gives us to assert ourselves that it has acquired its reputation for conflict. In the birthchart, Mars's sign, house position and aspects show how we arouse ourselves to conscious action and reveals the way we spontaneously express our emotions.

On other levels, Mars is associ-ated with athleticism and sport; war and all military affairs; all forms of coercion; men and male sexuality; selfish desires; anger; passion; panic; frustration; guns, iron and all sharp metal instru-ments; machines and mechanics; technicians; engineers; explo-sives; fire; fever; inflammation and accidents and operations.

MARS THROUGH THE SIGNS

ARIES An urge to take the initiative; courageous; determined to achieve desires; infectious enthusiasm; lack of consideration for others; erratic energy levels; aggressive under pressure.

TAURUS Slow, but purposeful; deep reserves of strength; a capacity for hard work; practical, conservative aims; possessive emotions may lead to acquisitiveness; obstinate, even prejudiced, views.

GEMINI Mentally assertive and competitive, though argumentative if threatened; good at problem-solving; an often biting wit; restlessness leading to a lack of consistency and purpose.

CANCER Actions motivated by deeply felt emotions; lack of self-control in headlong confrontations; indirect approach to aims; moody when thwarted; repressed anger; an aptitude for DIY.

LEO Tirelessly and consistently enterprising; can uplift others through self-confidence; tremendous vitality and passion; impractical schemes; a tendency to be self-publicizing and extremely vain.

VIRGO Cautious and methodical; precise; analytical; often critical of own or others' actions; highly strung; overly controlled emotions; moralistic.

LIBRA Able to act strategically, but may be too dependent on others' support; indecisive; can confuse own aims with those of others; handling others' conflicts; quarrelsome relationships.

SCORPIO Tenacious and sometimes ruthless pursuit of goals; stamina in adversity; secretive methods; overbearing with others emotionally and sexually; destructive; power-conscious; intense grudges.

SAGITTARIUS A crusading spirit; pitching own strengths against others'; extravagant, ill-conceived actions; seeking fulfilment through an unfettered sense of freedom.

CAPRICORN Well orchestrated plans and realistic ambitions; decisive actions calculated to bring tangible results; perservering; exploitative; controlled emotions for fear of seeming vulnerable.

AQUARIUS Needs to act rationally; unorthodox methods; contributing to teamwork or to the betterment of the human condition; stubbornness born of a fierce need to act in one's own way.

PISCES Passive attitude to aims; struggles for acknowledgement; works behind the scenes; self-confidence eroded by hyper-sensitivity; avoids confrontations; escapist; unreliable emotions.

MARS THROUGH THE HOUSES

FIRST Finding outlets for self-expression; taking control of own destiny; competitive situations; impulsive actions; gratifying one's desires; a strong physical presence.

SECOND Learning about the power of money; possessions as a reflection of self; fighting for what is valued; business initiative; rash use of financial resources; strongly expressed sensuality.

THIRD Tuning the mind to perfection; speaking one's mind forcefully or bluntly; a restless mentality which needs relaxing outlets; fighting for survival in early childhood; possible tension with siblings.

FOURTH Emotional issues concerning the family; an urge to dominate in the home; finding ways to let off steam at home; abilities or resentments which slowly surface; conflicts with the father.

FIFTH Expressing vitality through creative pursuits; passionate and spontaneous love affairs; impulsive speculation; a love of sport; an ability to work with the young; egotistical attitudes.

SIXTH Learning skills which enhance pride in work; fighting for recognition of worth; punishing the body through over-exertion; possible conflicts with co-workers; obsessed with details; self-sufficient.

SEVENTH Cultivating contacts in pursuit of aims; a partner who takes the initiative; needing others to confirm one's worth; rashness and disharmony in relationships; defending the downtrodden.

EIGHTH Thriving on close emotional ties and joint enterprises; dealing with deep emotional and sexual instincts; meeting life as a series of crises and transformations; exploiting other's resources.

NINTH A love of contests; grappling with belief systems or cultural issues; challenging higher authorities; invoking moral principles to justify actions; pioneering travel; religious bigotry.

TENTH Wanting to be seen as influential and assertive; choosing a career for personal status; ambitions influenced by parents; clashes with people in authority; ruthless in achieving ends.

ELEVENTH Finding confidence through group activities; competitive and possibly off-hand with friends; championing causes; clear-cut objectives.

TWELFTH Finding a higher sense of purpose; trouble discriminating between own and other people's aims; covert operations; feeling ineffectual; self-destructive; passive resentments; violent dreams.

♃ jupiter

As the largest planet in the solar system, it is perhaps not surprising that Jupiter has long been associated astrologically with growth and expansion.

This can be taken in the physical sense, in that Jupiter corresponds to the growth of the body – in particular, cellular development and digestion. But the main significance of Jupiter in the birthchart is its function as a 'social' planet – a role it shares with Saturn. The Sun, Moon, Mercury, Venus and Mars all deal with strictly personal aspects of our character without any reference to inherited or environmental factors. Jupiter, by contrast, shows how we grow throughout life to fulfil the potential of our birthright.

Growth in this context means how we develop in response to the prevailing beliefs in society, and to what extent we blend in with, or challenge them. In our quest to find a place in the world, Jupiter by sign, house and, above all, aspect, shows our social expectations and ideals, and also how we go about creating opportunities to realize them.

On other levels, Jupiter corresponds to religious faith, wisdom, our understanding of God; the spirit of the law, philosophy and all theoretical thought. It also embraces, politics, higher education, morality, travel, exploration, anything to do with places abroad, spiritual or material prosperity, over-consumption, obesity and wastefulness.

JUPITER THROUGH THE SIGNS

ARIES Learning to take the initiative to earn success; leading by example; inspiring others with one's faith; thoughtless and over-hasty actions; exaggerated optimism; inflated self-importance.

TAURUS A sense of power through financial security; exploring the social uses to which money can be put; realistic expectations; over-indulgent habits; self-gratification; snobbish values; conventional.

GEMINI Seeking breadth of experience; improving one's mental abilities; a need to keep abreast of social issues; many social contacts; wide, though superficial, knowledge; intellectual conceit.

CANCER A strong sense of family; seeking to create a comfortable environment; supporting others in need; powerful emotions which cloud reason; faith based on 'gut' feeling; sentimental about the past.

LEO Driven by a mission to achieve; radiating self-confidence; needing to feel important or popular; inspiring optimism in others; a tendency to sensationalize; reckless gambling; ostentatious.

VIRGO Practical service to a social ideal; a hunger for information; tension from taking on too much responsibility; learning to delegate; technical excellence; sceptical of 'spiritual' values.

LIBRA A wide range of personal contacts; influence through popularity and social prestige; a strong sense of fair play; a philosophical outlook; too dependent on others; companionship at all costs.

SCORPIO Digging for the truth; obsessive or unbending beliefs; acquiring power over others; the drive for wealth and pleasure; an accentuated sexuality; delusions of invincibility.

SAGITTARIUS Spiritual quests; far-sighted aims; expanding horizons through travel and study; slavishy following social trends; moral preaching.

CAPRICORN A preoccupation with social responsibilities; finding a philosophy to justify ambitions; a high regard for reputation; executive skills; concern with correct behaviour.

AQUARIUS Philanthropic ideals; crossing the barriers of class or race; insight into human nature; progressive views on society; detached personal commitments; dissipating energies.

PISCES Powerful spiritual yearnings; looking for a spiritual figurehead; service to humanity; visionary; indiscriminate altruism; enjoyment of solitude and tranquillity; lack of discipline.

JUPITER THROUGH THE HOUSES

FIRST Drawn to social, moral or spiritual issues; actions and gestures on a grand scale; the need for an adventurous environment; a dignified bearing; self-important; an authoritative presence.

SECOND Searching for stability in a material or spiritual creed; the ability to realize one's ideals; money-consciousness; financial luck; complacency; powerful desires; hedonistic.

THIRD Developing one's mental faculties; analytical abilities; understanding prevailing social trends; over-emphasizing the power of the rational mind; intellectual arrogance; many 'streetwise' contacts.

FOURTH Powerful moral or religious issues around one's upbringing; finding one's true home; burdensome family ties; focusing on one's need for inner growth; a spirit of adventure in later life.

FIFTH A pressing need to express one's natural abilities; involvement in large scale ventures; lusty romantic adventures; pushing beliefs on to children; many interests; living life to the full.

SIXTH Perfecting skills which are of practical use; over-dutiful in one's work; excessive or obsessive dietary habits; understanding the relationship between a healthy mind and body; healing abilities.

SEVENTH Striking a balance between independence and security in relationships; issues around infidelity and jealousy; investing a partner with larger-than-life qualities; expectations others have of one.

EIGHTH Deep sexual unions, or an insatiable appetite; reconciling beliefs with instinctive drives; intuitive touch with money; benefits through other people; probing hidden meanings.

NINTH Expanding one's understanding of life through religion, philosophy, travel or higher education; communicating truth to others; inflated belief in one's own mission or importance.

TENTH Seeking high office or prominence in career; wanting a reputation for integrity and hard work; a sense of duty; hypocritical posturing.

ELEVENTH Expanding one's influence through friendships and groups; an active social life; influencing others to support personal goals; foresight into future trends; parasitical friends.

TWELFTH Evolving an inner optimism in life; periods of confinement for self-examination; working in the healing professions; over-supportive of others; escapism through over-indulgent habits.

♄ saturn

In counterbalance to Jupiter's expansive nature, Saturn's astrological function is to restrict. This is often a painful but none the less vital part of our development, for Saturn keeps Jupiter's urge to grow within manageable bounds.

Saturn's position in the birthchart shows where and how we most want to make our mark in society. The aspects it makes to the Angles and the other planets focus on the obstacles we are likely to meet on the way. These may be self-inflicted or brought about by events which appear to be beyond our control.

In both cases, Saturn teaches us – through harsh confrontation with reality and through limiting circumstances – what we must change in ourselves before we can achieve our ambitions. Since few of us accept delays or hardship gracefully, these lessons are seldom learned without pain.

At its most constructive Saturn imparts wisdom born of a true understanding of the virtues of patience, hard work, tradition and self-discipline. But if the Saturnian energy is ignored or becomes too dominant, it may also be repressive – inhibiting our self-confidence and frustrating our aims.

Saturn's rule extends among other things to all rules and regulations, the government and all authority figures, exams and teachers, the physical laws of the universe, economic recession, time, the ageing process, depression, fear and loneliness.

SATURN THROUGH THE SIGNS

ARIES Strong ambitions which require great effort to realize; developing patience and self-discipline in actions; self-reliant; struggling to find motivation; repressive; the path of the loner.

TAURUS Practical, long-term aims which are methodically executed; a dogged sense of purpose; inflexible principles; frugal to the point of self-denial; pre-occupation with what one owns.

GEMINI A well-ordered, sometimes calculating mind; an aptitude for research; good concentration; a distrust of the irrational; precise, or inhibited expression; an intellectual inferiority complex.

CANCER Strong attachments to people or places; sensitive to the demands of others; shrewd business ability; performing to high family expectations; emotional inhibition from a fear of rejection.

LEO A steady, self-assured pursuit of goals; a compulsive need to be in charge, or to have one's own way; easily slighted; resentful of external restrictions; high-handed, possibly autocratic.

VIRGO A laborious concern for detail and order; over-conscientious about duties; a fear of the unknown; prone to excessive worrying.

LIBRA Ambitions realized through teamwork; responsibility through organizing others; putting a great deal of effort into close partnerships to make them work; harsh on the failings of others.

SCORPIO The urge to exploit every resource in pursuit of success; an ability to unravel insoluble problems; a fear of being betrayed; stubborn, even extreme principles; guarded emotions.

SAGITTARIUS A conflict between grand ideas and the need for detail; practical application of concepts; coming to terms with everyday reality; strict moral or ethical views; intellectual arrogance.

CAPRICORN Striving for worldly achievements and public recognition; putting self-reliance above all else; grafting for long-term aims; faith in traditional views of authority; a fear of failure.

AQUARIUS The ability to test new ideas; distrusting change or progressive views; mental self-discipline; placing too much value on the rational mind; insensitive to emotions; highly dogmatic.

PISCES Requiring great self-discipline to be effective in the world; a feeling of being restricted by invisible forces; the need to develop an objective view of oneself.

SATURN THROUGH THE HOUSES

FIRST Reluctant to assert oneself; a serious approach to life; feeling one's early environment to be unsupportive; pessimistic expectations.

SECOND Insecurity about self-worth may lead to proving one's earning power; feeling restricted by material commitments; worry over finance may give rise to meanness; secure long-term investments.

THIRD A fear of being ignorant, or mentally inadequate; early childhood, especially school, as a restrictive experience; a serious attitude to learning or diminishing its value altogether.

FOURTH A deep feeling of being hemmed in by, or a need for, tradition; an absence of family support; a frosty or disciplinarian parent; a sense of alienation from one's background.

FIFTH Spontaneity limited by fear of disapproval; frustration from feelings of blocked creativity; inhibited in love out of a dread of rejection; may find child-rearing a burdensome issue.

SIXTH Dissatisfaction in one's work; suffocating routines; acquiring skills which have a useful social function; health issues which force one to work within one's mental and physical limitations.

SEVENTH Picking holes in partners when relationships turn faulty; lessons in mutual responsibility; a reluctance to become too close or dependent; burdensome or infrequent relationships.

EIGHTH A distrust of letting go emotionally; resisting change; a reluctance to probe beneath the surface; inhibited sexuality; controlling or being burdened with other people's assets or liabilities.

NINTH Learning the value of discipline and self-denial; giving practical meaning to abstract concepts; puritanical beliefs; oppressive moral or religious influences; a frustrated urge to travel.

TENTH The need for social acceptability; making one's mark in society; a slow progress to the top with many delays and obstacles; fulfilling parental expectations; the need to become self-reliant.

ELEVENTH Lasting, or onerous friendships; a preference for older friends; the loner who finds friendship and group activities difficult; administrative abilities; dogmatic beliefs.

TWELFTH Meeting unpleasant aspects of oneself in other people; hidden doubts and fears; feelings of loneliness, or being alienated from society; the need for a clearly defined self-image.

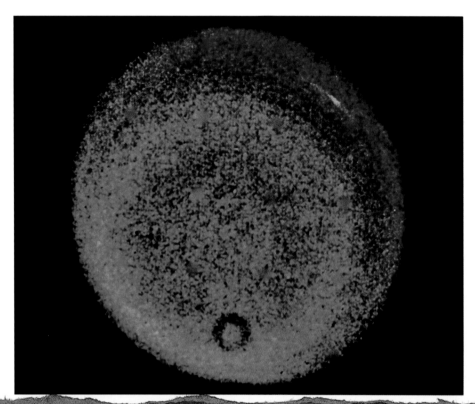

Uranus

Discovered in 1781, at a time of great social unrest and upheaval, Uranus has come to symbolize unexpected and traumatic change. Usually this happens when the Saturnian principles of order and control become too rigid – either in either our personal lives or in society as a whole.

Some people in life display powerful Uranian drives, either by spearheading progressive reforms, or – less constructively – by standing out from the crowd through shocking or anti-social behaviour. Whatever the level of expression, Uranian individuals seem to crackle with a mysterious force that generates excitement, eccentricity or danger.

For most of us, though, the influence of Uranus is not so consistently evident. It tends to take us by surprise when it is activated in our personal lives, for few of us are receptive to the wholesale change it often demands.

As a result Uranus is often felt to work disruptively, breaking down attitudes or situations which have become fossilized. Yet no matter how painful these rude awakenings may be, they offer us the chance to take control of our destinies and live our lives in accordance with our deepest wishes. In this sense, Uranus can be seen as a truly liberating agent.

On other levels it corresponds to electricity; lightning; any sudden illumination or original discovery; eccentricity; all innovative technologies; the abstract sciences; revolutionary ideals; reforms; anarchy; democracy and civil liberties.

URANUS THROUGH THE SIGNS

ARIES Pioneering change and new ideas; a marked spirit of adventure; highly self-willed; an often disruptive impulse to act one's own way; a thoughtless disregard for past values.

TAURUS Dogged persistence, or extreme impatience in working for change; inventive ways of resolving practical issues; breaking free from materialism.

GEMINI Independent thinking; innovative ideas and methods; love of new or unusual social contacts; restlessness leading to uncompleted projects; poor mental self-discipline; unreliable; impractical.

CANCER Emotional independence; highly intuitive, or cutting off from feelings; difficulty in asking for support; erratic mood swings; a need for space; emotionally excitable; sudden rebellious outbursts.

LEO The urge to be seen as different or unconventional; championing radical causes; breaking free from authority; overbearing self-importance; stubborn refusal to take advice.

VIRGO Upheavals through resistance to change; breaking away from inflexible methods; rigid adherence to principles; extreme points of view; outspoken criticism; anti-disciplinarian.

LIBRA Unconventional or exciting relationships; sudden attractions and repulsions; self-reliant or self-centred; resisting mutual responsibility; rebelling against accepted social standards.

SCORPIO Electrically charged emotions; generating or seeking intense sexual excitement; ruthless, decisive action; sudden, violent outbursts which may be wilfully destructive; extreme courage.

SAGITTARIUS Shaking others out of outmoded beliefs; fanatically non-conformist; exposing religious humbug, or hypocrisy in social morals; challenging educational values; radical thinking; scepticism.

CAPRICORN A fear of rapid change; making new ideas work; rebelling against authority and tradition, or resisting progress; cautious reform, or forcing change through.

AQUARIUS A progressive mind; breaking down social barriers; fighting for individual rights and freedoms; lack of thought for emotional issues in pursuit of the truth or a cause; individualistic.

PISCES Heightened receptivity; sudden inspiration; escaping from unpalatable truths or situations, leading to unexpected upheavals; impractical idealism; emotionally erratic; mystical leanings.

URANUS THROUGH THE HOUSES

FIRST An exciting, highly individualistic personality; the need to find a true role in life; sudden or drastic events, especially if personal environment is felt to be stifling.

SECOND Breaking with conventional values; using money as a means to freedom, or renouncing its accepted value; unexpected gains and losses; realizing special talents; an off-beat lifestyle.

THIRD Sudden, intuitive insights; frustration with orthodox schooling; mental acrobatics; restless for constant stimulation; original, inventive mind.

FOURTH Rebelling against one's background, or the need to look at it in a new light; unusual views on family values; an unorthodox parent; sudden changes in residence; radical change in later years.

FIFTH A heightened need to express individuality; dissatisfaction with the fruits of one's labours; explosive or unusual love affairs; looking for constant excitement; erratic with children.

SIXTH Seeking fulfilment in work; avoiding numbing routines; disruptive working relations; sudden illnesses; nervous disorders; innovative ways of addressing the balance between mind and body.

SEVENTH Difficulty in settling into conventional relationships; learning to respect one another's needs; looking for a stimulating or charismatic partner; attracting people who force one to change.

EIGHTH Exposure to deep or murky passions; the need to release oneself from unstable emotions; breaking through sexual taboos; inconsistent sex drive which may lead to experimentation.

NINTH Evolving beliefs from personal experience rather than received wisdom; rebelling against tradition; far-reaching but not always practical aims; the ability to sense future trends.

TENTH An agent for social change; radical views which touch the public; finding one's particular vocation; sudden career changes brought on by unforeseen events; success on one's own terms.

ELEVENTH Sudden friendships that catalyse change; drawn to groups or people sharing the same ideals; the ability to bring fresh ideas into an organization, or too independent to fit in.

TWELFTH Fearful of facing changes necessary for inner growth; a need to free what is buried in the subconscious; experiencing or seeking heightened states of consciousness; predictive dreams.

Ψ neptune

As the planet of unreality – of unlimited possibilities and things we cannot touch or see – Neptune's function is to break down the boundaries that keep us contained within the realities of the physical universe.

Both personally, and in society as a whole, the effect is to undermine the limitations imposed by harsh, practical Saturn. Neptune offers us the promise of other realities, and in so doing, fuels our dreams of transcending the routine and the humdrum.

In its positive expression, Neptune enables us to shift the focus of our lives from purely selfish concerns to a vision of the Greater Whole of which each of us is a part. It can heighten perception, inspire the imagination and deepen our understanding of other people. The ideals it spawns are both universal and spiritual.

The darker side of Neptune emerges when our wishes bear little relation to what we are capable of achieving. If, for whatever reason, we are reluctant to face undesirable qualities in ourselves, then our Neptunian values become distorted. When this happens, Neptune brings confusion, self-deception, greed, deceit, loss, disillusionment and a flight from reality through drugs, alcohol or idle fantasy.

Other correspondences to Neptune include water in all its forms; shipping; oil; chemical gases; leaks; scandal; films; photography; mysticism; altruism; martyrdom; spiritual salvation; artistic inspiration; altered states of consciousness; and illusion or confusion.

NEPTUNE THROUGH THE SIGNS

LEO (1914/16–1928/9) Struggling to find a clear self-image; needing to follow one's own ideals; strong charitable instincts; attracted to the glamorous or the fashionable; false optimism; delusions of grandeur; unattainable standards.

VIRGO (1928/9–1942/3) Mental sensitivity and a powerful imagination which need practical outlets; highly perceptive or intuitive; easily influenced by those with strong beliefs; false judgements; disorganization due to a confused state of mind.

LIBRA (1942/3–1955/7) A need to refine one's emotions, especially in close relationships; idealistic or unrealistic expectations of partnership; an intense desire for peace; lacking self-motivation; artistic inspiration.

SCORPIO (1955/7–1970) A need to suppress intense desires; fluctuating between extremes of self-denial and self-gratification; an awareness of other people's true motives; confused or misled by others; misinterpreted ambitions.

SAGITTARIUS (1970–1984) Looking for spiritual meaning or inspiration in life; grand schemes which come to nothing; a tendency to escape from reality; aimless wandering in pursuit of elusive dreams; unreal values or beliefs; extremely intuitive.

CAPRICORN (1984–1998) Mixing practicality with idealism; shrewd foresight; the need to incorporate spiritual values in one's life; allowing fantasies to over-ride commonsense; dissatisfaction with over-materialistic life-style; dedication to duty.

THE OUTER PLANETS

The three planets beyond Saturn – Uranus (1781), Neptune (1846) and Pluto (1930) – are relatively recent additions to the planetary picture. Because of the length of time they spend in each sign (an average of 7, 14 and 21 years respectively), they are thought to apply more to generations, or to mankind as a whole, than to individuals.

Traditionally, it is their house positions and the aspects they make to the Angles and personal planets which give the outer planets significance in the birthchart; the impact of their energies is most evident when they appear on the Ascendant. Contrary to custom, some of the likely personal meanings of Uranus, Neptune and Pluto through the signs have been included here.

NEPTUNE THROUGH THE HOUSES

FIRST Heightened awareness of surroundings and others; uncertainty about the boundaries between oneself and others resulting in impressionability or self-victimization; a confused self-image.

SECOND Experiencing the illusory nature of money and possessions; learning to value one's natural abilities; intuitive at earning money; confused or fluctuating finances; glamorizing money.

THIRD Difficulties with analytical thought; inspired sense of imagery and story-telling; embroidering the facts; highly receptive to other people's thinking; vague or weak-minded.

FOURTH Sensitivity to atmospheres in the home; a romanticized memory of childhood; an idealized or 'absent' parent; a need to loosen family ties; searching for one's spiritual home.

FIFTH The ability to play roles; susceptible to other people's approval; finding creative outlets that release the imagination; highly idealistic or falling for the unavailable in love.

SIXTH Dissatisfaction with humdrum practicalities; looking for ideal working conditions; confusion or deception with working colleagues; either neglectful of health or else pre-occupied with it.

SEVENTH A yearning for the perfect relationship leading to disappointments; playing the martyr in relationships; understanding the meaning of selfless love; addictive or inspirational partners.

EIGHTH The urge to lose oneself through physical intimacy; vulnerability to other people's values; encouraging others to develop their talents.

NINTH Looking for salvation in a belief system or a spiritual leader; the ability to act as mouthpiece for others; the eternal student or wanderer; spiritually drawn to foreign countries or cultures.

TENTH Catching the public's imagination; either worshipped by the public, or working for little recognition; fantasizing about glamour and fame; sacrificing career for a more fulfilling path.

ELEVENTH Submerging oneself in, or being overwhelmed by the group identity; an indulgent social life; acts of altruism; supportive or deceitful friends; chasing elusive dreams.

TWELFTH Swamped by strong unconscious emotions; an active dream life; feeling ineffective in the outer world; seeking to escape the harshness of reality; letting go through transcendental experiences.

pluto

Most astrologers now agree that tiny, distant Pluto represents in the birthchart the process of fundamental transformation – of death and rebirth. In contrast to Uranus – which disrupts the Saturnian structures we create in both society and our personal lives – and Neptune – which turns them inside out – Pluto breaks them down completely so that a new level of awareness can be brought into being.

Like the other slow-moving planets, the effect of Pluto in any particular sign is to raise issues which are experienced by a generation. In the birthchart, it is Pluto's house position and the contacts it makes to the Angles and personal planets which show in what area of life we are most likely to respond or contribute to these collective pressures.

Pluto's domain in the birthchart is the subconscious mind, where primitive instincts often lie buried because we have been taught they are socially undesirable. If we refuse to recognize them, they can result in negative Plutonian patterns of behaviour such as compulsions and obsessions, or give rise to events beyond our control which threaten our very survival.

Yet if we can bring these instincts to the surface, Pluto will enable us to refine them so that eventually all aspects of our personality can be brought under conscious control. Such a process of change may be extremely testing, since it involves breaking down old self-images before a new and more complete self is able to emerge.

Pluto also governs any aspect of society that is potentially undermining but which we are unwilling to face – the criminal underworld, subversive groups, taboos, urban decay and corruption; earthquakes and volcanic eruptions; self-transforming therapies and healers; charlatans; any form of uncontrolled power; nuclear energy; depth psychology; sexual reproduction; and the orgasm.

PLUTO THROUGH THE SIGNS

CANCER (1912/3–1938/9) Emotional intensity; hiding emotions from view, or trying to suppress them; family upheavals; skeletons in the family cupboard; the need to rebuild one's notion of family or country; understanding the darker side of human nature.

LEO (1938/9–1957/8) Prone to excessive pride; re-evaluating one's understanding of what power means, perhaps leading to misuse; fighting for one's individuality by resisting tyranny or mass ideologies; using arrogance to disguise lack of confidence.

VIRGO (1957/8–1971/2) Intense dissatisfaction with meaningless routines, forcing one to find more fulfilling methods; re-defining the quality of life; the need for increased awareness of one's environment; ideas that transform one's attitude to the relationship between mind and body.

LIBRA (1971/2–1983/4) Emotional disappointments through inharmonious relationships; the need to face the real issues of commitment to another; clinging to outworn relationships out of a deep fear of being unlovable; learning to trust another person's love for what it is; new awareness of the power of appearance.

SCORPIO (1983/4–1995) Intense desire for intimate unions; penetrating the surface of life to find the common thread that unites everything, yet also learning to tolerate individual differences; the exposure of the abuse of power, especially sexual power; breaking down sexual taboos.

PLUTO THROUGH THE HOUSES

FIRST A powerful personality that can reach out to influence many, or turn inwards to create continual crises in personal life; the need to face one's buried instincts; life as a fight for survival.

SECOND The ability to transform something of little worth into something valuable; over-concern about finances for fear of losing everything; financial crises forcing one to change one's material values.

THIRD A laser-like mind, suited to research; a cutting tongue; revolutionary ideas; mental breakdown leading to changes in the way one thinks.

FOURTH Wrestling with one's deepest feelings, bringing inner turmoil, or release from unconscious behaviour-patterns; a family background which is disruptive; domineering in the home.

FIFTH A profound need to express creative instincts spontaneously; the need to overcome creative blocks; impulsive, passionate love affairs; driven by the need to be someone special.

SIXTH The ability to transform one's working conditions; power struggles in the workplace; a tendency to bury oneself in one's work; illnesses that transform one's attitude to life.

SEVENTH Relationships that force drastic personal changes, or that tap buried feelings of vulnerability; projecting one's more primitive nature on to partners; a powerful partner.

EIGHTH Either repressing or learning to master one's instinctive nature; pent-up energy which may be expressed as sexual frustration; emotional crises which bring change; manipulating others.

NINTH Crises of conviction which make one reassess one's beliefs; an overbearing belief in one's own views; an intense search for the meaning of existence, or a denial of spiritual values.

TENTH A desire to be influential, or to hide from public attention; asserting one's will in order to succeed; crises in career which may result in new directions; struggles with authority figures.

ELEVENTH Ideals or groups that have a deep effect on one's thinking; powerful friends that help one achieve objectives; using friends or groups for selfish motives; highly competitive friendships.

TWELFTH A need to confront unpleasant aspects of oneself deeply buried in the unconscious; a fear of being unacceptable; transforming other people's circumstances, for better or worse.

The aspects between planets are one of the most important areas of modern chart interpretation

When astrologers speak of *aspects* in a birthchart, they mean the relationships that are constantly forming and re-forming between the planets.

While astronomy tells us that the planets of the solar system are in perpetual orbit around the Sun (and that the Moon is in orbit around the earth), from earth itself it seems as if all ten of the other bodies follow a circular path through the sky – the 360° of the zodiac. When a birthchart is drawn up for a certain time and place, each of these bodies is at a different point on the circle.

Astrologers came to discover that there were certain distances between the ten 'planets' – expressed as degrees of the zodiac circle – which corresponded to certain patterns of behaviour in people on earth. These distances, which became known as *aspects*, now form a significant part of the foundation of modern birthchart interpretation.

While the planets signify particular kinds of energy and the signs show the way in which those

ASPECTS TO THE ANGLES

Just as planets can form aspects to one another, so they can form aspects to the Angles in the chart – the Ascendant and Midheaven (and by definition, their opposite numbers – the Descendant and IC). In this respect the Angles can be seen as extremely important outlets for the other planetary energies – but only if the exact time of birth is known.

energies will be expressed, it is the aspects which indicate whether the energies will flow easily or with difficulty.

Good or Bad?

Once it was thought that certain aspects between the planets were 'good' and helped to make life easy, while others were 'bad' and hindered progress or brought misfortune. Modern astrologers no longer believe this. Instead, they classify the aspects as 'hard' and 'soft' (or sometimes, 'easy' and 'difficult').

If you imagine planetary energies as flows of traffic, then the aspects are the traffic lights. 'Hard' aspects are the red lights that cause congestion or hold-ups; soft aspects allow the traffic to flow more easily.

Continuing the example, if the traffic were to flow too easily there would be chaos – things would be almost as bad as if the traffic were permanently snarled up. The same happens in the birthchart. A free flow of aggressive Martian energy might be fine for achieving goals, but at what and whose expense? To be easily

moved to tears might seem on the surface to imply weakness, yet it may also denote compassion and depth of feeling.

The fact is that most charts contain both hard and soft aspects, which is just as well. The hard aspects create the tensions in the personality that urge us to get moving and go somewhere; the soft aspects help us to get there, but only if we know where that 'somewhere' is.

As well as the hard and soft aspects there is the conjunction (0°), which is often described as 'neutral'. In other words it can be hard or soft or both, according to the planets involved and depending on the aspects they make to other planets.

There are also the 'subtle' aspects, so-called because their effects show themselves in a much more subtle way. While the conjunction is very important, even for beginners, subtle aspects are generally only used by professional astrologers.

Major and Minor

Traditionally, the various types of aspect were classified as 'major'

and 'minor' according to the importance they were believed to have. But most astrologers now agree that 'minor' aspects which are nearly exact are every bit as (if not more) significant as 'major' aspects which only just fall within their prescribed distance.

Defenders of the old view maintain that 'major' aspects relate to the issues central to a person's life, while the 'minor' ones are only at work below the surface. Generally speaking, though, any aspect which is close to being exact is likely to be important and warrants being looked at carefully.

Lack of Aspects

Many charts appear to have no aspects at all – at least, no major ones – but this does not mean that the subject is a 'non-person'. A closer look will reveal a host of minor aspects, which naturally take on greater significance than they might otherwise have had.

Professional astrologers today use this example to underline their argument that minor aspects are in fact an important part of the birthchart.

ORBS OF ASPECT

Although each aspect has its own prescribed distance – expressed in degrees of the zodiac – this distance does not have to be exact for the aspect to take effect. There is a 'margin for error' of a few degrees either side – commonly known in astrology as the *orb*.

Generally speaking, major aspects have a wider orb than minor ones. It is also customary to add a couple of extra degrees to the orbs of aspects involving the Sun and the Moon, since the influences exerted by these planets are so important.

When two planets are moving towards an aspect with each other

they are said to be 'applying' – in other words, the aspect can only become stronger. After making an exact aspect, the planets then move

apart and are said to be 'separating' – the aspect can only get weaker.

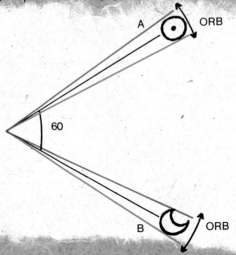

THE MAJOR ASPECTS

CONJUNCTION 0° (Neutral) Orb:8°
When two or more planets are in conjunction there is a union or coming together of the principles represented by those planets. They function as one, and yet each gains the support of its neighbour. They do not lose their individuality but provide a powerful focus of energy in the birthchart.

The natures of the planets involved in the conjunction will determine whether this is likely to be hard and challenging or soft and harmonious.

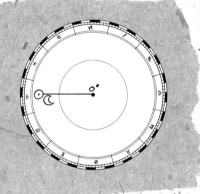

TRINE 120° (Soft) Orb:8°
Everyone has the potential to be creative. The trine shows how easily that creativity is expressed. Sometimes it comes too easily, in which case there is a danger that in-born talents are taken too much for granted and not developed as fully as they might be. It is often helpful to have hard aspects which link up with trines in a chart, as these can often generate the kind of inner tensions which tend to inject the creative instinct with the determination to succeed.

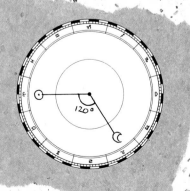

SEXTILE 60° (Soft) Orb:4–5°
Sextiles link planets in signs of different but compatible elements. The flow of energy is similar to that of the trine, but not quite so easy – there is enough difference to create the kind of friction that stimulates effort, and less risk of complacency. For this reason, the talents indicated by a sextile can be more valuable than those of a trine, though there may also be a tendency to live by one's wits.

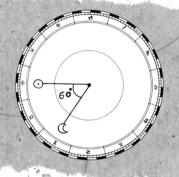

SQUARE 90° (Hard) Orb:8°
There is a sense of being boxed-in with the square, as the planetary energies are operating in mutually antagonistic signs. The tension that builds up as a result can be difficult to handle, bringing uncertainty and apparent obstacles to progress. However, squares are by and large less extreme than oppositions, forcing the kind of action that eventually leads to change – and to a new set of challenges. In fact without this aspect, the urge to push forward and prove oneself is considerably weakened. It is through the square that the individual acquires the determination and self-discipline to rise above their circumstances.

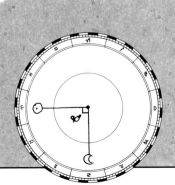

OPPOSITION 180° (Hard) Orb:8°
As its name implies, this aspect gives a tendency to fluctuate from one extreme to another, according to the energies represented by the planets and the signs. In early years, this is likely to be experienced as a feeling of being pulled apart, as if the individual is unable to satisfy themselves or anyone else. It is rather like trying to be in two places at the same time; one side of the opposition will always lose out. Even so, this aspect offers the chance to balance out the opposing factions so that with maturity and increasing self-awareness, what seem like incompatible facets of the personality can be reconciled. A supporting soft aspect can be helpful in creating openings in the conflicting energies and opportunities for personal growth.

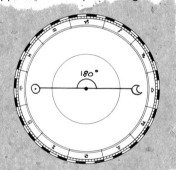

QUINCUNX 150° (Hard) Orb:2–3°
This aspect implies tension which can prove very frustrating, since the planetary energies are working through signs that have little in common with one another. Out of such frustration can spring great achievement – but not without considerable effort.

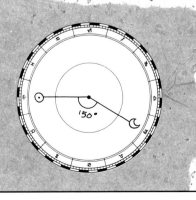

THE MINOR ASPECTS

SEMI-SEXTILE *30° (Neutral) Orb:1–2°*
This aspect could be described as both soft and hard, for it links the two zodiacal signs immediately next to each other. Rather like neighbours, they have to learn to get along – which is not always easy! On its own the semi-sextile is not generally considered very important, but its significance grows when it acts as a 'bridge' between other aspects in a chart that would otherwise be unconnected.

SEMI-SQUARE *45° (Hard) Orb:2–3°*
Similar to the square, the semi-square indicates tension. But the changes it brings are often more sudden and unexpected, possibly because the conflict within the personality – represented by the planets involved in the aspect – are less conscious.

SESQUIQUADRATE: *135° (Hard) Orb; 2–3°*
This aspect is similar to the square and semi-square. The difference is that the changes are usually triggered by external events in a way that enables the tension to be released more easily than is the case with the square.

QUINTILE *72° (Subtle) Orb:1–2°*
BI-QUINTILE *144° (Subtle) Orb:1–2°*
These aspects often reveal potential talents or gifts, although they may not show themselves unless there are some supporting hard aspects giving the individual the discipline and resolve to develop them.

DISASSOCIATION

There is one big difficulty concerning the aspects which those who study and practise astrology have so far only partly managed to resolve.

Hard aspects are usually formed between planets in mutually unsympathetic signs. But if one planet is near the beginning of a sign and the other planet is near the end of another sign as in the example shown, then it is perfectly possible for them to form a hard aspect in mutually sympathetic signs. Exactly the same condition may apply to soft aspects, which usually involve sympathetic signs but can equally embrace unsympathetic ones.

Astrologers disagree as to the significance of these so-called 'disassociate' aspects. For the beginner, the best advice is to think of a disassociate hard aspect as being 'softer' than it might otherwise be, and in the same way, to think of a disassociate soft aspect as being slightly 'harder'.

There is also a body of opinion which holds that any two planets in unsympathetic signs have something of a 'hard' connection between them whether they are in aspect or not, and that similarly, any two planets in sympathetic signs have some kind of 'soft' link. These subtle distinctions, however, are normally beyond the scope of the beginner.

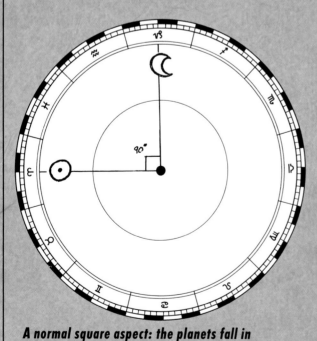

A normal square aspect: the planets fall in 'unsympathetic' Fire and Earth signs.

A disassociate square: the aspect is the same, but both planets fall in signs of the same element.

Discover how aspect patterns can provide valuable clues when assessing someone's basic personality

Every birthchart has its unique combination of aspects, assuming, of course, that the precise time of birth is known. Even if two people are born within minutes of each other in the same place, the Ascendant and Midheaven will have moved, along with the cusps of the other Houses. Over such a short time the aspects between the planets will stay virtually the same. Even so, the shift in the House cusps is often enough to alter the aspects to the all-important Angles, and for other planetary aspects to move into different Houses.

Yet in spite of each chart's uniqueness, people born on the same day, month or even year have certain planetary aspects in common. More often than not, aspects between two planets do not happen in isolation, but link up to other aspected planets to form a network of contacts known as aspect patterns. These patterns are important chiefly because they give astrologers an immediate idea of the way planetary energies are flowing – they are the 'keys' that help to unlock the rest of the chart. However, many aspect patterns also involve the slower-moving planets, giving added insight into how the subject will respond – against a backcloth of family values – to generational issues that affect us all.

Aspect patterns are divided into two categories: major and minor. The major patterns are the most powerful, pointing to complex and often conflicting attitudes within the subject's character. The minor patterns are more subtle, and symbolize less visible personality traits. As a general rule, however, the more planets involved in a pattern, the more intense the effects.

No Aspect Patterns
Strictly speaking no chart is devoid of aspect patterns, since any aspected planets which also make contacts to other planets create a similar flow of energy. It is quite common for none of the major or minor aspect patterns to appear in a chart, but this does not mean that the subject is a weak or insignificant person – simply that for them the focus of planetary energies is different.

THE GRAND CROSS

The Grand Cross, as its name implies, incorporates planets in square and opposition to each other and involves all four signs of a particular Quality – Cardinal, Fixed or Mutable. It is sometimes referred to as the 'Dilemma', in that when it is triggered – especially by a transiting planet – everything seems to happen at once. As a result, people with this tricky combination often seem to lurch from crisis to crisis as if their mettle is constantly being tested. But if and when they finally master their formidable energies, they may be capable of quite exceptional results. People with a Cardinal Grand Cross have tremendous drive and energy, but also meet with a great deal of resistance in achieving their aims. While they may blame others for the frustration they experience, much of it is self-induced, for they seldom plan or think carefully before they act and insist on doing everything their own way. Those with a Fixed Grand Cross tend to do everything within their considerable power to keep things as they are. Valuing reliability and preservation above all else, they will passionately hold out against anything or anyone who tries to upset their sense of order; when change inevitably comes it is usually dramatic and sudden. Mutable Grand Cross types have no difficulty accepting change – in fact, this is their problem. Rather than face a challenge they tend to alter their course in the vain hope that by changing their external circumstances they can avoid unwanted difficulties. The lesson they have to learn is that their conflicts arise from within, as a result of a lack of consistency and a tendency to spread themselves too thinly.

Actor Marlon Brando has a Fiery Grand Trine involving the Sun/ Moon in Aries, Neptune in Leo and Jupiter in Sagittarius, giving him energy and dramatic flair but also a tendency to over-indulge.

THE GRAND TRINE

The Grand Trine consists of a triangle of three or more planets – including sensitive points such as the Ascendant and MC – which all make trine aspects to each other in one of the Elements (Fire, Earth, Air, Water). Traditionally, the Grand Trine was thought to be extremely fortunate, but the modern view is that on its own it may be too fortunate. Since it shows natural talents which usually emerge early on in life, there may be a tendency to take these gifts for granted and a corresponding lack of resolve to develop them.

The effects are much more positive when one or more of the

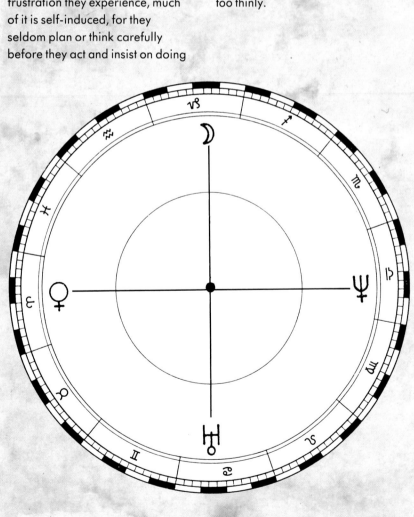

THE STELLIUM

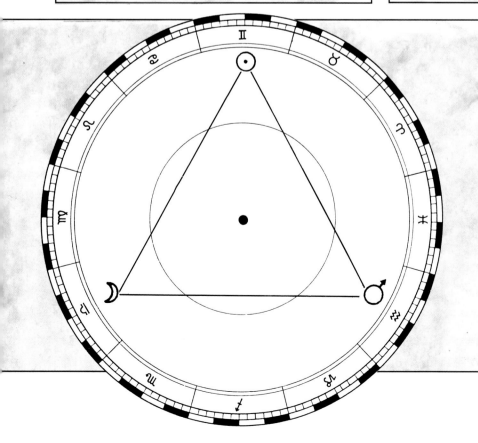

A Stellium (also known as *Satellitium*) is an aspect pattern made up of three or more planets which are either in the same sign or in the same house (although if they are only in the same house and their signs are different, the effect is less intense). The group of planets form a chain of conjunctions, so that while the first and last planets in the chain may not be in aspect to each other, they are joined through their conjunctions to the planets in between. The effect is to exaggerate the qualities of the sign(s) and house(s) in which the stellium falls – although sometimes overpoweringly so, at the expense of any planets which do not happen to aspect this relatively common configuration.

THE T-SQUARE

The T-Square – an opposition with one (or more) planets squaring both ends – is similar to the Grand Cross, except that it has one 'arm' missing. It is held to be easier to handle than the Grand Cross, for the empty arm offers an escape route and creates less of a feeling of being torn four ways. The tensions it sets up can also be released through any planet(s) which makes sextile or trine aspects to one of the planets within it.

The same sort of dilemmas apply to the Cardinal, Fixed and Mutable qualities of the T-Square as to the Grand Cross. However, because the planetary energies are not as prone to being bottled up, people with this combination usually manage to sort out their inner problems more easily.

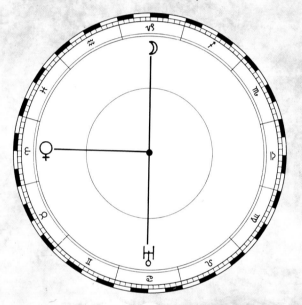

planets in the Grand Trine also makes a hard aspect – such as a square or opposition – to another planet. This stiffens the 'easy come, easy go' attitude, urging the subject to put more effort into channelling their planetary energies purposefully. A more common version of the Grand Trine is the Minor Grand Trine, which occurs when two planets trine each other and at the same time make a sextile aspect to another planet. The effects are similar, but often more dynamic, since the sextiles introduce a sense of perseverance that may otherwise be lacking.

MINOR ASPECT PATTERNING

The Finger of Fate (Yod) is a rare pattern in which two planets in sextile to one another are both quincunx (150°) to a third. The Yod takes its name from the Hebrew meaning 'blessed' and is

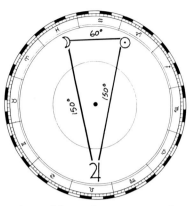

reputed to have a quality of fate about it - in other words, the planets and houses involved point to a certain direction in life. This is not an easy pattern to work with, but if the tensions it shows can be resolved, great achievements are possible.

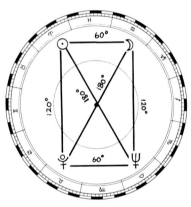

The Mystic Rectangle is a complex pattern consisting of two oppositions, the ends of which form sextiles or trines to each other. Because of its shape, the flow of energy may be limited to the

soft aspects, missing out the hard ones altogether and leaving important issues unresolved, as with the Grand Trine. However, if the oppositions are integrated, the blend of hard and soft aspects can result in the kind of dynamic tension that enables people to develop their natural abilities to the full.

The Kite occurs whenever three planets in a Grand Trine link up to another which opposes one and is sextile to the other two. Its effect is much the same as the Mystic Rectangle in that the many

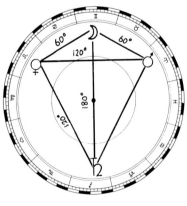

soft aspects can lead to a reluctance to face the difficulties shown by the planets in hard aspect. But again, if the issues shown by the opposition are confronted, the potential rewards are high.

DISSOCIATE PATTERNS

A Dissociate Grand Trine occurs when one planet of the triangle falls in a different Element from the other two. This can only happen when the planets involved are either very near the end or at the beginning of their respective signs. Because one of the planets in this configuration falls in an inharmonious sign, the flow of energy is less stable than the pure Grand Trine. The errant planet introduces a quality of tension – rather like a square – to the aspect pattern, and offers a greater chance of using the planets' collective energies assertively. Dissociate Grand Crosses and T-Squares are also softer versions of their pure forms. At least one planet in the configuration falls in a different Quality to the others, and consequently tones down the overall level of tension. The same principles apply to all dissociate aspect patterns.

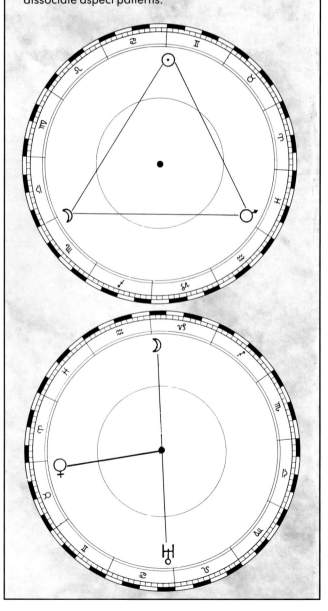

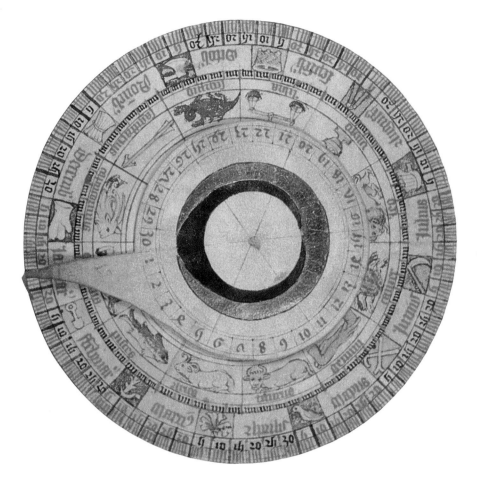

Examining aspects between the planets strengthens and adds depth to interpretation

Although aspects between planets are a key part of chart interpretation, this does not mean that unaspected planets are unimportant. In fact, they may be exceptionally revealing.

If a planet has no aspects, or those present are very weak, then either its energy will be blocked and it will have trouble blending in with other planets, or it will take on a magnified importance.

People with an unaspected Sun, for example, may struggle to find their purpose in life, or be excessively self-centred. An unaspected Moon can point to weak emotional ties in childhood for which the individual tries to compensate in later life. Mercury unaspected suggests trouble with self-expression, although people with this configuration may also be obsessed with developing their mental faculties.

Shyness often dominates those with an unaspected Venus; they may struggle to form close relationships, while at the same time hiding their inhibitions by being overly sociable. A lack of self-motivation commonly afflicts those with an unaspected Mars. It is not that they are short of energy; simply that they do not know what to do with it!

With Jupiter, weak or no aspects can lead to problems in creating opportunities, although much energy may be wasted through misplaced optimism. Those with an unaspected Saturn rarely know their own limitations, and often set themselves impossible tasks.

A solitary Uranus suggests a person who has difficulty developing their individuality, mistaking frankness and anti-social behaviour for the same thing. Neptune on its own describes people who may confuse their own feelings with spiritual inspiration. For those with an unaspected Pluto, there may be a profound resistance to plumbing their own emotional depths, coupled with a compulsion to project their fears on to others instead.

aspects to the sun

SUN-MOON

Conjunction: Strong emotional family ties; a lack of objectivity in close relationships; a reluctance to let go of the past.

Soft: A contented nature; good relations with family and partners; possibly too self-satisfied.

Hard: Argumentative and highly strung; difficulty in changing habits; may see family life as 'unsafe'; striving to overcome family patterns of behaviour.

SUN-MERCURY

Conjunction: Independent-minded; mentally alert and talkative; may be opinionated while seeming rational. (Mercury is never more than 28° away from the Sun so only the conjunction is possible.)

SUN-VENUS

Conjunction: An emphasized need for relationships; learning to love oneself; seeking popularity; refined and artistic; over-compromising; self-indulgent.

(Venus is never more than 48° away from the Sun, so only a conjunction, semi-sextile or semi-square can occur. The semi-square is linked to breakdowns in relationships.)

SUN-MARS

Conjunction: A desire to achieve and be in charge; fiercely competitive and combative; hot-blooded, impulsive and full of energy.

Soft: Enormous vitality; channelling energy constructively; decisive; enterprising; vigorous.

Hard: Fluctuating energy levels; impetuous; argumentative; injury-prone; over-stressed; rash.

SUN-JUPITER

Conjunction: Optimistic; generous; fortunate contacts; visionary; humorous; high aspirations.

Soft: Tolerant; high expectations; benevolent; indulgent; easy-going; high expectations.

Hard: Wasteful; boastful; showy; restless; undisciplined; lazy; misplaced idealism; greedy.

SUN-SATURN

Conjunction: Serious; solitary; ambitious; self-denying; selfish; unsympathetic; undemonstrative.

Soft: Slow but steady progress; well organized; reliable; patient; cautious; dedicated; enduring.

Hard: Feeling inferior; self-conscious; pessimistic; inhibited; austere; unfortunate.

SUN-URANUS

Conjunction: Original; over-powering; stubborn; eccentric; magnetic; unorthodox; independent.

Soft: Progressive; a leader; frank; dramatic; seeking change; zestful; supporting the underdog.

Hard: Anarchic; rebellious; compelled to change things; self-destructive; domineering.

SUN-NEPTUNE

Conjunction: Sensitive; dreamy; impractical; a weak sense of self; gullible; artistic; receptive.

Soft: Inspired ideas; visionary; compassionate; idealistic; strong creative potential.

Hard: Confused identity; highly emotional; self-victimizing; impressionable; open to deception.

SUN-PLUTO

Conjunction: A power complex; many upheavals; extreme ambition; a need for self-knowledge; tyrannical.

Soft: Notable achievements; forceful; crises may prove beneficial; creative potential.

Hard: Obsessed with self; ruthless; dynamic; stressed; fanatical.

JANE FONDA (Sun in Sagittarius)

Jane's birthchart contains a disassociated Grand Trine in Fire and Earth involving the Sun, Moon and Midheaven. This is indicative of her privileged, supportive upbringing and of her capacity to turn creative ideas into reality through the sheer force of her personality. However, her Sun in a Mutable T-Square with Saturn opposite Neptune suggests that in spite of the many favours which have come her way, she has been dogged by feelings of insecurity and a confused identity.

aspects to the moon

MOON-MERCURY

Conjunction: A retentive memory; imaginative; intuitive; full of common sense; perceptive; talkative.
Soft: Expressive; language skills; shrewd; sensible; adaptable; reasonable; humorous.
Hard: Devious; quick-witted; scornful; hypersensitive; highly strung; erratic; gossiping.

MOON-VENUS

Conjunction: Great charm; peaceful; co-operative; fair-minded; a love of beauty; tender.
Soft: Social graces; a strong sense of taste; supportive; popular; diplomatic; pleasure-seeking.
Hard: Struggles to express feelings; misunderstandings with partners; shy; moody; frustrated in love.

MOON-MARS

Conjunction: Fiery emotions; thoughtless courage; direct; strong-willed; a fighting spirit.
Soft: Vigorous health; candid; energetic; independent; fond of daredevil pursuits; warm-hearted.
Hard: Poor health; exaggerated reactions; irritable; intolerant; short-tempered; ambitious; pushy.

MOON-JUPITER

Conjunction: Generous; protective; an urge to travel; emotionally demanding; self-indulgent; selfish.
Soft: Warm-hearted; benevolent; optimistic; generally fortunate; a keen social conscience; a traveller.
Hard: Harshly critical; careless; lazy; faulty judgement; wasteful; greedy.

MOON-SATURN

Conjunction: Powerful concentration; a poor mother image; self-denying; hardworking; dutiful; inhibited; mean.
Soft: Loyal; reliable; industrious; organizing skills; controlled; down-to-earth; traditional; limited.
Hard: Depressive; pessimistic; afraid of failure; looking for 'mother'; a sense of being hard done by; low self-esteem; lonely; worrying.

MOON-URANUS

Conjunction: Original; unorthodox; extremely independent; highly strung; erratic emotional reactions.
Soft: Highly intuitive; capable of making instant decisions; prone to sudden mood changes; progressive; ambitious; offbeat.
Hard: Extremely tense and prone to stress; demanding; difficult to live with; an exaggerated need for space.

MOON-NEPTUNE

Conjunction: Highly romantic; selfless; extremely sensitive to surroundings; secluded; escapist.
Soft: Imaginative; visionary; kind; difficulty in understanding own limitations; idealizing the family.
Hard: Prone to self-deception; impractical; addictive; seducible; confused emotions; misplaced ideals.

MOON-PLUTO

Conjunction: Intense but buried feelings; extreme reactions; a powerful mother; skeletons in the cupboard.
Soft: Resilient; able to express and transform deepest feelings; a vivid unconscious mind; passionate.
Hard: Thwarted needs; bouts of jealousy; impulsive or even violent reactions; obsessive; fated events; emotional blackmail; crises in home life.

TWIGGY (Sun in Virgo)

Twiggy has a shy, retiring Sun in Virgo in the Twelfth House, but counterbalancing this is a powerful Stellium aspect pattern comprising the Moon, Mars and Pluto in Leo in the Eleventh. Such a configuration at least partly explains her public impact as fashion leader for an entire generation.

aspects to mercury

MERCURY-VENUS

Conjunction: An elegant way with words; charming; sociable; vain; amusing; superficial relationships. (Mercury and Venus are never more than 76° apart; so only the conjunction; semi-sextile; semi-square and quintile are possible. Soft aspects mirror the more amiable qualities of the conjunction, while the semi-square emphasizes the lazier (and more conceited side)!

MERCURY-MARS

Conjunction: Mentally alert; needle-tongued; argumentative; a sharp mind; nervous tension; outspoken.
Soft: A skilled speaker; ready wit; common sense; courageous; decisive; determined; a strong nervous system.
Hard: Capable; tends to overwork; irritable; critical; sarcastic; litigious; cheeky; self-important.

MERCURY-JUPITER

Conjunction: A need to expand the mind; travel-hungry; optimistic; a mass of ideas; conceited; popular.
Soft: A fertile mind; eager for information; humorous; articulate; constructive ideas; self-satisfied.
Hard: Over-confident; a lazy mind; arrogant; poor judgement; negligent; original; deceitful; indiscreet.

MERCURY-SATURN

Conjunction: Concentration; patient; methodical; great mental effort; depressed; dull; slow-witted; inhibited expression; deep thoughts.
Soft: Organizational and practical skills; serious; reliable; honest; blunt speech; profound; ambitious.
Hard: Shy; over-concerned with detail; anxious; unconfident; harsh; lonely; inhibited; a rigid mentality.

MERCURY-URANUS

Conjunction: The mind of the genius; great originality; intuitive; highly strung; erratic; misunderstood.
Soft: Forward-looking; inventive; adaptable; dramatic; a good memory; single-minded; self-reliant; astute.
Hard: Nervous tension; wasted energy; eccentric; selfish; inflated belief in own views; tactless.

MERCURY-NEPTUNE

Conjunction: Imaginative; sensitive; creative; self-deluding; vague; poetic; gullible; impractical.
Soft: Highly sympathetic; easily hurt; inspired; an interest in the spiritual; receptive to ideas.
Hard: An extremely rich but troubled imagination; lack of self-belief; worrying; dishonest; deceitful.

MERCURY-PLUTO

Conjunction: A penetrating mind; mental stress; critical of others; persuasive; vigorous.
Soft: Incisive understanding; fast thinking; a restless, intense mind; a black sense of humour; cunning.
Hard: Tense; rushed thinking; over-straining the mind; fits of temper.

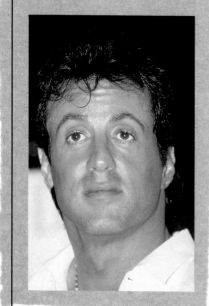

SYLVESTER STALLONE (Sun in Cancer)
'Sly' Stallone has his Sun and Saturn square Jupiter in Libra, indicating the numerous personal problems which he has encountered despite riding the crest of a wave of success in his career.

JOHN TRAVOLTA (Sun in Aquarius)
John has his Moon in conscientious Virgo sextile Saturn in deep, penetrating Scorpio, telling of the hard-working and dedicated way he responds to the challenge of each new screen role.

A tricky problem for any astrologer is how to interpret the likely strengths and weaknesses of two (or more) planets when they are in aspect to each other. The traditional approach is to follow a planetary pecking order, in which the planets furthest from the Sun are given more weight than those which are nearer. For example, when Venus is in aspect to Pluto (the most distant planet), it is Pluto's influence which takes precedence.

But although this is a helpful way to learn how the planets work, most astrologers today keep an open mind on which planet in an aspect plays the dominant role. They resist drawing any firm conclusions until they have considered the chart as a whole.

Returning to our example, Venus may be involved in other strong aspect patterns, or be prominent either through its position or as the chart ruler, in which case it will hold sway over Pluto. Equally, if Scorpio or Pluto are strong in the chart, then Pluto's energies will be to the fore.

Relative Strengths

Another delicate question is how to interpret the relative strengths of aspects. Aspects are strongest when they are exact, give or take one degree of orb. But it is usual for the orbs to be wider – up to eight degrees – in which case the aspect will either be *applying* or *separating*.

When an aspect is applying, it has yet to reach exactitude and its full effects will be felt after birth. The opposite is true of a separating aspect, since it was exact before birth.

Some astrologers believe that applying aspects refer to conditions that will be met in the future, while separating aspects deal with circumstances that the subject is born into and so have an hereditary quality about them.

aspects to venus

VENUS-MARS

Conjunction: Passionate in love; sensual; strong sex drive; sensitive feelings; tactless; lewd; impulsive.
Soft: Warm and affectionate; expressive; appetite for sex may lead to many love affairs; creative.
Hard: Easily offended; stressful sex life; lustful; blowing hot and cold; discontented; insatiable; impatient.

VENUS-JUPITER

Conjunction: Popularity through charm and generosity; a taste for luxury; high expectations of partners.
Soft: Sociable; pleasure-seeking; an eye for quality; graceful; able to handle people; extravagant.
Hard: Over-dramatic; conflicts in love; lazy; vain; many love affairs through high ideals.

VENUS-SATURN

Conjunction: Inhibited; slow to form relationships; sense of duty; cold; lonely or deprived; faithful.
Soft: Responsible; controlled feelings; lack-lustre social life; stable love; lacking spontaneity.
Hard: Love sacrificed to ambition; unhappy loves; poverty; low self-worth; undemonstrative; selfish.

VENUS-URANUS

Conjunction: Emotionally independent; magnetic attractions; erratic feelings; highly strung; eccentric tastes.
Soft: Many friends; charismatic; romantic; free with affections; will not be tied down; creative talents.
Hard: Problems with commitment; troubled loves; nervous tension; sudden changes in finances.

VENUS-NEPTUNE

Conjunction: Highly idealistic and romantic; finding love confusing or disappointing; overly compassionate.
Soft: Imaginative; unworldly; sensitive; artistic flair; image-conscious; a tendency to daydream; highly musical.
Hard: Unrealistic ideals leading to disappointments; indecisive; easily deluded; victimized; escapist.

VENUS-PLUTO

Conjunction: Powerful and deep feelings; obsessive or destructive loves; intense sexuality; demanding.
Soft: Passionate nature; dynamic; financial ability; intensely loyal; dramatic; magnetic; highly creative.
Hard: Strong likes and dislikes; lusting after money or sex; deep unhappiness; upheavals in love.

GOLDIE HAWN (Sun in Scorpio)
One of the most powerful women in films today comes in a deceptively doll-like package. But Goldie's Venus in Scorpio in a difficult square aspect to her Sun-sign ruler, Pluto, reveals a deep need to have total control over her life and work.

RICHARD GERE (Sun in Virgo)
With Mars in sensual Cancer opposing Jupiter in chilly Capricorn, the heart-throb who can safely count himself among Hollywood's biggest earners actually dislikes the trappings of wealth and much prefers the simple life.

aspects to mars

MARS-JUPITER

Conjunction: Driving physical energy; competitive; open and direct; decisive; self-important.

Soft: Positive and enterprising; confidence in own actions; high energy levels; capable; willpower.

Hard: Restless; unfocused energy; a dislike of routine; disruptive; hasty; arrogant; challenging authority.

MARS-SATURN

Conjunction: Accident-prone; physical suffering; hardships; learning to endure delays; hard-working; frugal.

Soft: Disciplined; persevering; strong survival instinct; organizing skills once motivated; practical; possibly unimaginative.

Hard: Poor staying power; negative attitudes; a fear of being cowardly; lack of purpose; injuries; harsh.

MARS-URANUS

Conjunction: Individualistic; sharp reflexes; courageous; wilful; high tension may lead to breakdown.

Soft: Intuitive snap decisions; heightened awareness; aims achieved; a need to channel impulsive urges.

Hard: Tense; temperamental; hasty; undisciplined; argumentative; brash; stubborn; carrying a high risk of accidents.

MARS-NEPTUNE

Conjunction: Impractical daydreams; strong sexual fantasies; compassion; inconsistent energy; escapist.

Soft: Inspired goals which are often achieved; charitable; idealistic; a rich imagination; powerful emotions.

Hard: Longing for the impossible; discontent; escape through drink or drugs; diffused energy; depraved.

MARS-PLUTO

Conjunction: Explosive or destructive energy; ruthlessly determined; cruel; violent emotional outbursts.

Soft: Ambitious; a tireless worker; great courage; remarkable feats against the odds; self-confident.

Hard: Obsessive emotions; obstinate; riding roughshod over others to attain goals; over-reaching aims.

aspects to jupiter

JUPITER-SATURN

Conjunction: Slow progress; need to persevere in the face of opposition; optimism tested; brooding; tenacity.

Soft: Steady but sure advancement; realistic beliefs; highly motivated; conscientious; modest; constructive.

Hard: Easily discouraged; unstable; pessimistic; confused ambitions; a need to work within limitations.

JUPITER-URANUS

Conjunction: Forward-looking; grand-scale ambitions; a pressing need for independence; restless.

Soft: Leadership qualities; radical thinking; unconventional beliefs; unexpected luck; sudden insights.

Hard: Stubborn resistance to change; rebellious; missed chances; wilful; dogmatic; argumentative; outspoken.

JUPITER-NEPTUNE

Conjunction: Idealistic; perceptive; unrealistic dreams; inflated pride; spiritual longings; artistic talent.

Soft: Kind-hearted; championing the underdog; a need for solitude; visionary; effortless gains; sloppy.

Hard: Hypersensitive; confused spiritual ideas; muddled finances; aimless wandering; scandal.

JUPITER-PLUTO

Conjunction: Power complex; extreme self-confidence; unflinching; major accomplishments; leadership.

Soft: Single-minded pursuits; desire to influence; organizing skills; the ability to unearth the truth.

Hard: Fanatical beliefs; wasteful; self-destructive; militant; great gains and losses; scheming or manipulative.

aspects to saturn

SATURN-URANUS

Conjunction: Conflict between radical change and convention; great inner struggles; depression; excitability.

Soft: Mixing initiative with caution; perseverance; sudden major changes late in life; administrative skills.

Hard: Extreme nervous tension; conflicts with authority figures; difficult separations; displays of rebellion.

SATURN-NEPTUNE

Conjunction: A need to discipline the imagination; realizing dreams; fear of letting go; self-obsessed.

Soft: Working hard to realize dreams; a structured imagination; methodical; conservative.

Hard: Emotionally inhibited; strange disorders; disappointed dreams; self-torment; impractical aims.

SATURN-PLUTO

Conjunction: Unpredictable; deeply ingrained obsessions; hard-hearted; severe; suppressing pain.

Soft: Overcoming frustrations; remarkable powers of endurance; great dedication; eventual success.

Hard: Lack of compassion; thwarted ambition; self-centred; destructive; severe losses; physical hardship.

aspects to uranus

URANUS-NEPTUNE

Conjunction: Remarkable talents; unstable events; an original mixture of intuition and imagination.

Soft: Strong humanitarian instinct; visionary; intuitive; idealistic.

Hard: Fear of the unknown; bigoted; a need to make dramatic changes; chaos; emotionally unstable.

URANUS-PLUTO

Conjunction: An urge to transform environment or exploit it mercilessly; huge creative potential.

Soft: Dynamic; a desire for change and self-improvement; self-awareness through facing traumas.

Hard: Suffering through resistance to change; subversive; inner tension which explodes violently; impatient.

aspects to neptune

NEPTUNE-PLUTO

Conjunction: Happens about every 490 years; those born with this aspect during the 1890s were at the centre of the huge upheavals resulting from two World Wars.

Soft: From 1945 to 2036 these two planets remain more or less in sextile to each other, coinciding with adjustments that have to be made in society following the effects of the conjunction.

Hard: Will not happen in the lifetime of the reader! Historically connected with prolonged periods of crisis and extreme reactions.

Learn all about the relative strengths of the ten planets in certain signs and the aspects they form to the Angles

One thing never to forget when interpreting a birthchart is that whatever the aspects the planets make to each other, they are also always profoundly affected by the sign which they occupy. Some planetary energies flow more smoothly in certain signs, while in others their expression is less harmonious.

In principle, planets are at their 'purest' when they occupy the sign they rule and are said to be in **dignity**. However, in traditional astrology every planet also has one sign in which it is believed to function most effectively, known as its sign of **exaltation**.

In these signs, planets seem to acquire an extra dimension which encourages a higher level of expression. For example Saturn is 'exalted' in Libra, and while this may point to difficult or inhibited relationships, it also inspires – through experience – a responsible attitude and sense of duty towards such commitments.

When a planet is in the sign opposite to its dignity, it is in **detriment**. This placement is considered to be weak since the sign is a poor vehicle for the planet's energies. Similarly, planets in the opposite signs to their exaltation are said to be in

their **fall** – a position which restricts their free expression. The planet Mars, for example, 'falls' in Cancer because the direct, assertive nature of this planet is camouflaged by the defensive, non-confrontational quality of the sign.

Occasionally, two planets are found in signs ruled by each other – for instance, Mercury in Aries or Mars in Gemini. In this case they are said to be in **mutual reception** – a combination similar to the conjunction, although not as powerful.

The full list of planetary dignities, exaltations, detriments and falls is shown on the right, though astrologers are not completely in agreement about the relatively newly discovered 'Outer Planets'.

In fact, many modern astrologers tend to disregard these planetary strengths altogether, while others only use them cautiously. Even so, for the beginner, they are a useful way of learning how the planets and signs interact.

PLANETARY STRENGTHS

Planet	Dignity (Sign ruled)	Detriment	Exaltation	Fall
Sun	Leo	Aquarius	Aries	Libra
Moon	Cancer	Capricorn	Taurus	Scorpio
Mercury	Gemini	Sagittarius	Virgo	Pisces
	Virgo	Pisces	(Aquarius)	(Leo)
Venus	Taurus	Scorpio	Pisces	Virgo
	Libra	Aries		
Mars	Aries	Libra	Capricorn	Cancer
	Scorpio	Taurus		
Jupiter	Sagittarius	Gemini	Cancer	Capricorn
	Pisces	Virgo		
Saturn	Capricorn	Cancer	Libra	Aries
	Aquarius	Leo		
Uranus	Aquarius	Leo	Scorpio	Taurus
Neptune	Pisces	Virgo	(Cancer)	(Capricorn)
Pluto	Scorpio	Taurus	(Pisces)	(Virgo)
			(Aquarius)	(Leo)

NB: Astrologers have yet to agree about the Exaltations and Falls given in brackets

planetary aspects to the angles

the sun

the moon

mercury

SUN-ASCENDANT
Conjunction: A radiant personality; self-centred; happy; seeking fame.
Opposition: Looking for fulfilment through relationships and partners.
Soft: Likeable; confident; desire to shine; well-adjusted; recognition.
Hard: Over-confident; unpopular; overcoming obstacles to ambition.

SUN-MIDHEAVEN
Conjunction: Powerful urge to be recognized; single-minded ambition.
Opposition: Need for privacy; self-conscious; resolving family issues.
Soft: Positive outlook; easily motivated; self-aware; successful.
Hard: Arrogant belief in own abilities; setbacks lead to loss of confidence; the hard road to success.

MOON-ASCENDANT
Conjunction: Strong family ties; caring; moody; highly subjective.
Opposition: Strong contacts with women; over-dependent.
Soft: Adaptable; receptive; easygoing; emotional needs satisfied.
Hard: Touchy; over-reacting; emotional discord; changeable.

MOON-MIDHEAVEN
Conjunction: Instinct for what the public wants; women, especially the mother, influence direction in life.
Opposition: Powerful link with family tradition; sense of history.
Soft: Sentimental; well-balanced emotions; flexible; urge to nurture.
Hard: Restlessness leads to many career changes; unsettled home life.

MERCURY-ASCENDANT
Conjunction: Inquisitive; versatile; many contacts; articulate; restless.
Opposition: Looking for lively partners; sensitive nervous system.
Soft: Chatty; charming; business-minded; stimulating company.
Hard: Gossiping; hypercritical; nervous disorders; fickle; rude.

MERCURY-MIDHEAVEN
Conjunction: A passion for learning; seeking recognition for mental abilities; influential contacts.
Opposition: Feeling mentally inferior; lack of self-motivation.
Soft: In tune with public; planning skills; a 'professional' attitude.
Hard: Indecisive; unreliable; aimless; many career changes.

venus

VENUS-ASCENDANT
Conjunction: Personable and usually physically very attractive; a love of luxury; somewhat vain.
Opposition: Motivated by others' needs; high expectations of partner.
Soft: Diplomatic; kind-hearted; sociable; charming; creative.
Hard: Extravagant; self-indulgent; pretentious; inclined towards idle pleasure-seeking.

VENUS-MIDHEAVEN
Conjunction: Drawn to an artistic career; a need for partnership.
Opposition: Conflict between home life and career may dull ambition.
Soft: Easy expression of feelings and talents, though often lazy.
Hard: Feelings of being unloved; rivalry in partnerships; vain.

mars

MARS-ASCENDANT
Conjunction: Strong-bodied; highly energetic; competitive; imposing; a strong physical presence.
Opposition: Argumentative or bossy partners; over-exertion; abrasive.
Soft: Leadership qualities; dynamic; honest; practical; hard-working.
Hard: Stressful; a need to direct powerful emotions purposefully; rash.

MARS-MIDHEAVEN
Conjunction: Determined; fiercely ambitious; a love of challenge.
Opposition: Frustrated goals; struggling to become independent; disruptive influences at home.
Soft: Enterprising; organizational skills; resolute; realistic goals.
Hard: Conflicts with authority; over-worked; many disputes; hasty.

jupiter

JUPITER-ASCENDANT
Conjunction: Hugely optimistic; great flair; self-important; idle.
Opposition: Difficulty reconciling need for freedom with obligations to others; 'lucky' partnerships.
Soft: Easy-going; optimistic outlook, usually vindicated.
Hard: Arrogant; poor judgement; over-generous; hedonistic.

JUPITER-MIDHEAVEN
Conjunction: Career success; a need to influence; confident.
Opposition: Quietly optimistic, or exaggerated expectations of life due to parental influence.
Soft: Expansive; humanitarian interests; generous; achieving goals.
Hard: Inflated self-importance; drawn to get-rich-quick schemes.

Hollywood star Jack Nicholson has Pluto on his Ascendant, Jupiter on the Descendant, and Venus sitting on the Midheaven. As well as ensuring career success, the combination endows him with a fatally attractive quality as far as women are concerned – although relationships may well be undermined by the force of his own compelling personality.

♄ saturn

SATURN-ASCENDANT
Conjunction: Serious; capable; feeling unsupported; ambitious.
Opposition: Difficulty in expressing emotions in relationships; partner's age or outlook may differ markedly.
Soft: Reserved; reticent; a late developer who eventually succeeds.
Hard: Underlying shyness prevents intimate contacts; self-conscious.

SATURN-MIDHEAVEN
Conjunction: Hardworking; a lonely position of authority; setbacks.
Opposition: Inhibited ambition; a desire to become self-sufficient.
Soft: Patient; practical; the slow road to success; conscientious.
Hard: Thwarted ambition; self-doubt; pessimistic; difficult challenges.

♅ uranus

URANUS-ASCENDANT
Conjunction: Erratic; excitable; scattered energies; temperamentally 'different'; independent; magnetic.
Opposition: Unusual partner; sudden change through relationships.
Soft: Ingenious; continually changing; thriving on the unusual.
Hard: Explosive; nervous tension; unpredictable; compulsive.

URANUS-MIDHEAVEN
Conjunction: Sudden twists of fate; eccentric choice of career; original.
Opposition: Unable to settle; cut off from or rebelling against family.
Soft: Fortunate though unexpected events; original methods; dynamic.
Hard: Hasty decisions; many career changes; unreliable; stubborn.

With the Moon in Cancer conjuncting her Ascendant, Aquarian Farah Fawcett has made a name for herself projecting an image of wholesome femininity. Interestingly, her domestic affairs have never been far from the public eye!

With Jupiter conjuncting his IC, it seems likely that Paul McCartney's rise to fame and wealth stemmed from feelings of optimism and expectation acquired as a child. Neptune on the Descendant shows a rather idealized view of relationships.

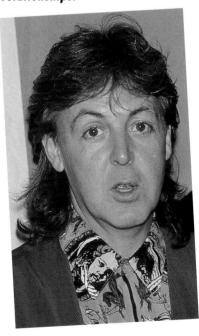

♆ neptune

NEPTUNE-ASCENDANT
Conjunction: Hypersensitive; dreamy; confused; escapist; deluded; gentle.
Opposition: Highly idealistic about relationships leading to sacrifices or disappointments.
Soft: Compassionate; romantic; easily influenced; unrealistic.
Hard: Misled; betrayed; insincere; confused motives; poor sense of self.

NEPTUNE-MIDHEAVEN
Conjunction: Longing for the ideal career; hard work for little reward.
Opposition: Idealized memories of childhood; lack of security/purpose.
Soft: Attracted to the artistic; yearning for the impossible.
Hard: Confused objectives; easily deceived; lacking confidence.

♇ pluto

PLUTO-ASCENDANT
Conjunction: A complex personality; dramatic changes in life; intense; inner strength; domineering.
Opposition: Obsessive quality about relationships; dictatorial partner.
Soft: The ability to heal past wounds and begin anew; influential.
Hard: Drastic upheavals; inner turmoil; deep-rooted obsessions.

PLUTO-MIDHEAVEN
Conjunction: Hungry for fame; career may seem 'fated'.
Opposition: A need to explore one's origins; rebuilding a sense of self.
Soft: Organizing abilities; staying power; visionary; authoritative.
Hard: Unforeseen events which thwart ambition; foolhardy.

CHAPTER 3

FUTURE POTENTIAL

With advanced astrology the patterns you learned to interpret in the birth chart begin to shift and change. Future potentials may be glimpsed, as you work with the patterns of planetary energies and their effects upon the natal map.

The idea of predicting the future is a heady one, and many astrologers have tried it, some with uncanny success. However, that is not really what advanced astrology is all about.

Centuries ago our view of the world, and consequently of astrology, was much simpler. Aspects between certain planets were characterised as either good or bad. and the planets themselves were either 'malefic' such as Saturn and Mars, or 'benefic' such as Jupiter or Venus. A challenging aspect, such as a square, between two 'malefics' was, therefore, occasion for predictions of doom and disaster.

And, sometimes, these proved correct. The Master Astrologer William Lilly, for example, made an astonish-ing prediction in 1651 when he forecast the Great Fire of London in 1666 with such accuracy that he was briefly suspected of starting it. But his name was soon cleared, and reputation permanently enhanced.

A thought-provoking modern example of startlingly accu-rate prediction may be found in THE OUTER PLANETS AND THEIR TRANSITS (1983) by Dr. Liz Greene. Looking at the forthcoming transits for Russia's chart she writes:

'I would understand those

transits in part to mean that there is some kind of severing of the interconnecting countries that make up the Soviet Union, which of course they could only do if the central government were to collapse ... it may be that Pluto takes on the very literal meaning of death, and the Union of Soviet Socialist Republics will no longer be a union.'

An Inner Journey

But prophesying events with such clarity is difficult, for each of the planets symbolise a wide spectrum of meanings. And while such meanings are interconnected, how they express themselves can often prove surprising and unexpected. Monitoring inner changes and developments through astrology is on the whole less glamorous, but ultimately more satisfying. Transits and progressions map the course of an inner journey, filled with challenges and rewards, mirroring the course of life itself. Adopting this attitude towards predictive astrology can be extremely positive, enabling you to understand yourself and others with more compassion and acceptance.

Discover how the transits of the planets through the skies can be used to predict important future events

An astrologer's work does not end with drawing up and interpreting a birthchart. In fact, it has only just begun. The birthchart is like a blueprint of our potential, but on its own it can only hint at how that potential may unfold during the course of a lifetime. This is where transits take over.

The birthchart is like a snapshot of the solar system taken from a specific place at the exact moment of birth. Thereafter, the planets continue on their never-ending journeys, forming aspects to the natal planets and house cusps (the most important being the Angles). These aspects are called *transits*, and their effect is to transform the still photo of the birthchart into a running film.

Looking to the Future

Transits have long been employed as one of the main ways of predicting the future. Traditionally, they were believed to indicate events that happened to us during our lives – some good, some bad, according to the planets and aspects involved. But to astrologers of today, this smacks too much of a blind belief in Fate, and also implies that the planets are somehow 'responsible' for our lives.

The modern approach is to see nothing as inevitable unless we make it so through our actions – or lack of actions. Transits are still used to look at future trends, but from a different perspective; depending on which planets are involved, they are now thought to coincide with phases in our lives when certain issues are more likely to surface than others.

Nothing which happens during these phases is pre-ordained, for the planets do not 'cause' anything; they are merely symbols for our inner energies. Transits simply show how, at specific times in our lives, we can use these energies in response to the issues at hand.

HOW TO INTERPRET TRANSITS

What orb should I allow for transits?

The orbs used for transits to natal planets and Angles are much tighter than those allowed in birthchart interpretation. Most astrologers use an orb of only one degree (1°), although this may be extended when a number of transiting planets gather around a key point in the natal chart.

How long do transits last?

Transits from the inner planets to natal planets or Angles are short-lived, varying from about three hours for the Moon, to a day to several weeks for Venus and Mars. Transits from the outer planets last much longer: despite the tight orb allowance, Jupiter and Saturn can hover over a natal planet for up to one year, while Uranus, Neptune and Pluto may linger for 18 months or more.

Are all transits equally important?

No. Transits from the faster moving planets are too brief to be of any great significance on their own. The only exception is when a cluster of faster moving planets combine on the same day to form a network of aspects which also focus on a natal planet or Angle.

Transits from the slower moving planets are much more important. Although on their own they may not coincide with any noticeably dramatic events, they represent undercurrents of change which may surface when 'triggered' by one (or more) transits from the faster moving planets – notably, the Sun and Mars.

Multiple transits from the slower moving planets to a natal planet or Angle are the most likely indicators of major crises or turning points in the subject's life – especially when they are joined by transits from the planets that move faster.

Can events signified by transits be 'timed'?

Yes, roughly – by looking at when the 'trigger' transits from the faster moving planets hit those made by the slower moving ones. More precise timing in-volves a lot more work and is beyond the scope of the amateur astrologer.

What about retrograde planets?

A transiting planet which turns retrograde over a natal planet or Angle will usually aspect it three times – once as it passes over, once as it goes back, and once as it moves forward again.

This can be a particularly challenging time, especially with the conjunction and opposition. But if any serious difficulties arise, there are also more opportunities to resolve them.

How do transits affect planets in aspect?

Transits between planets which aspect one another in the birthchart are especially important, since they pick up on issues inherent in the subject's personality. As a rule, the natal aspect defines the essential character, while the transit offers a different slant on it.

The only exception is when the transit is the same as the natal aspect – an indication that the

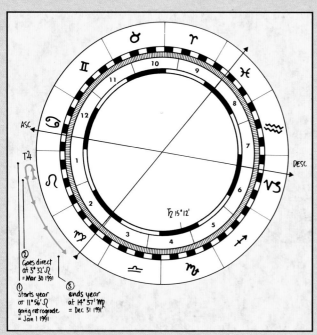

The transit of Jupiter over a period of 12 months as it moves up to affect natal Saturn.

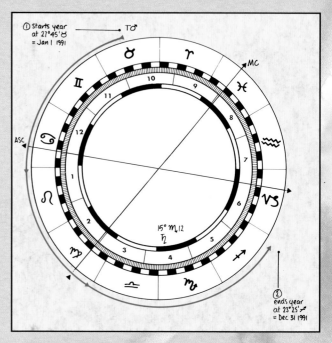

The transit of Mars – a faster moving 'trigger' planet – travels much further during the same period.

transiting planet has 'returned' to its position in the birthchart and is re-activating natal aspects. This is often a time of reappraisal.

Are all transits equally important?

Newcomers to transits are best advised to concentrate on the major aspects – conjunction, opposition, square, sextile and trine. Even so, sudden changes or disruptions which seem to occur independently of any major transit aspects can often be traced back to the so-called 'minor' aspects. As you become more experienced, you can turn to these for more information.

Signs and Houses

A transiting planet acts like a 'trigger' on natal planets, activating their energies according to the signs, house positions and aspects involved. The guidelines for interpreting transits by sign and house are the same as for the birthchart, but the sign of the transiting planet is of only secondary importance. Far more significant is the transiting planet's house position – especially if it is

transiting one of the Angles – since it shows in which area of the subject's life the need for change is likely to arise.

The Scope of Transits

Transits must be interpreted with an understanding of what they can and cannot do. Astrologers have found that even when a complex of astrological factors points to a major 'event' around a certain date, it is extremely risky to predict how that event will manifest itself.

It may, for example, be felt on a psychological level – perhaps as a slow build-up of pressure or a gradual change in awareness. On the other hand it might be experienced through relationships, or as a sudden happening which occurs out of the blue. Usually it is a combination of all three, but for those new to transits, it is much safer to concentrate on the timing of the event and the subject's own response.

It can be helpful to look back at previous transits to see how they manifested in your life. Never forget that transiting planets also carry their natal aspects.

MIDPOINTS

Many astrologers argue that it is a mistake to concentrate solely on transits to the natal planets and Angles. They believe there are other subtle points in the birthchart which can give more information about the nature, timing, and possible outcome of transits. These are known as the *midpoints*.

As the term suggests, a midpoint is the exact degree and minute halfway between two natal planets (or a planet and an Angle). Midpoints exist between all the planets and Angles in a birthchart, thereby linking planetary factors which at first sight may appear to be totally unconnected.

There are two midpoints for every planetary pairing – one on the shorter arc (distance) between the two, and one on the longer arc. Both are thought to be highly sensitive to transits, as they symbolize points where the energies of the two natal planets merge.

Midpoint interpretation is one of the more advanced areas of astrology and is beyond the scope of this book. Even so, it is a must for all serious students; *Horoscope Symbols* by Robert Hand provides a good introduction to the subject.

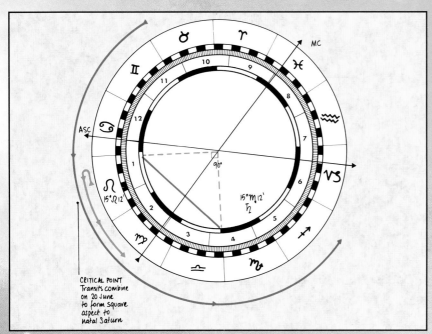

CRITICAL POINT
Transits combine
on 20 June
to form square
aspect to
natal Saturn

When the transits are combined, you can see that transiting Mars conjuncts transiting Jupiter at the same time as both planets square natal Saturn.

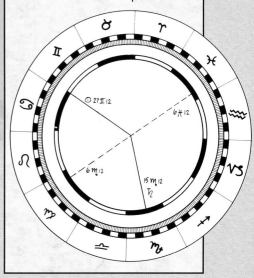

TRANSIT CYCLES

When a transiting planet makes a conjunction to a natal planet, it begins a cycle which will only be completed when it returns to the same point. For example, if transiting Saturn conjuncts natal Mercury, it will make every conceivable aspect to Mercury over the course of its 29-year cycle before it conjuncts it again. During the same period transiting Mercury will make an identical pattern of aspects to natal Saturn – except that it will do so about 29 times!

This creates a permanent and subtle link between the two planets – a link which applies equally to planets not in aspect in the birthchart. Each transit aspect marks a new stage of development in the relationship between the two planetary energies, as follows:

Conjunction The first stirring of a new process – sometimes accompanied by a sudden burst of energy – depending on the nature of the planets involved. The energy represented by the transiting planet often overwhelms the natal planet, so that at this stage of the cycle it is not always clear what is going on.

Separating Sextile What happened at the Conjunction becomes clearer. A helpful time to make adjustments for the next stage.

Separating Square The first real test. Opportunities are limited, and decisions made at the Conjunction are challenged. If this time is dealt with successfully, it should pay dividends at the Opposition; if not, the consequences will have to be faced later on.

Separating Trine A time of relative ease, or for revising plans if the previous Square led to major changes. It may also be a time when things are taken for granted, leading to a false sense of security. This is a good time to pay heed to the writing on the wall!

Opposition If decisions have worked out well, this is time when prizes can be claimed! If previous decisions and actions were inappropriate, this can be a very difficult time. On the other hand, it offers the chance to sweep past errors away to one side and start all over again.

Applying Trine This may mark a 'second harvest' when things appear to go well and changes are easily made, or it may act in a similar way to the Separating Sextile if new activity was begun at the Opposition. Whatever the circumstances involved, there could be a tendency to rest on one's laurels.

Applying Square Often brings a sudden demand to adapt to new situations, even if there were no apparent difficulties before. There is a need to let go or to radically change old structures and attitudes. Resistance to change at this stage can lead to collapse at the next Conjunction, but it can also act like a Separating Square – especially if a new cycle was begun at the Opposition.

Applying Sextile The final preparation which makes way for the next cycle and hopefully a brand-new burst of energy. Alternatively, it may act like the Separating Trine.

Second Conjunction Represents the beginning of a new cycle, but can also mark the same kind of changes as the Opposition, particularly if there is a strong reluctance to face up to change.

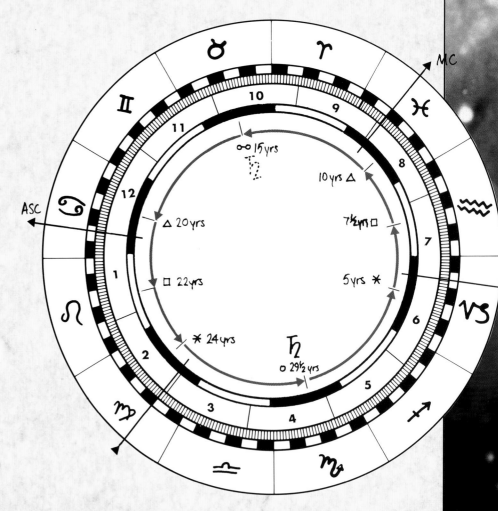

The transits made by Saturn to its natal position during its 29-year cycle. Only the major aspects are shown.

Discover what the transits of the Sun, Mercury, the Moon and Venus may hold in store for you

Transits are aspects between planets on the move and sensitive points in the birthchart which remain fixed. At first sight they may seem complicated, but it is worth remembering that they are derived from exactly the same principles as those governing natal chart interpretation.

As with natal aspects, the old distinction between 'good' and 'bad' transits has largely been dropped, since the way a transit unfolds depends entirely on how the individual copes with the flow of energies symbolized by the particular planets involved.

The first rule of transit interpretation is to decide at the outset if the planets involved are compatible. For example, Mars-Pluto contacts are never easy, whereas Venus and Jupiter hardly ever combine stressfully. You must also decide which transit aspects to work with. Most astrologers concentrate on the harder ones – conjunction, opposition, square, semi-square and sesquiquadrate – as these seem to be much more indicative of change.

Softer aspects represent the kind of circumstances in which a person is not pressurized into changing, and often nothing happens as a result! Even so, it is wise not just to cast them aside without trying them out, and they should always be used when they connect with hard aspects from other transiting planets. Of the inner planet transits described overleaf, those of the Sun are the most important – but only when they are combined with long-term transits from the outer planets.

Of the other three, Venus' transits are perhaps the most interesting, since they can have a major bearing on relationships.

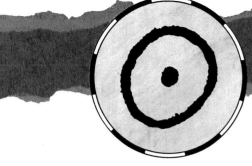

transits of the sun

The transits of the Sun to the natal planets occur at the same time each year. On one level, they show our internal response to the changing seasons, like a personal clock marking individual high and low spots during the course of the year.

For example, the transits of the Sun to natal Saturn – especially the hard aspects – are almost invariably times when vitality is low and a faint air of pessimism creeps in. We do not need an astrologer to tell us that there are certain times of the year we feel more subdued than others.

On their own, the Sun's transits are not thought to be long enough to signify major events or changes. The Sun simply accentuates issues connected with the house and planet it transits.

However, when the Sun joins a lingering transit from one or more outer planets to a natal point, its arrival frequently coincides with a decisive turn of events. In fact, many astrologers have found that without the Sun to act as a trigger, even long-term transits can pass by without any significant events occurring.

The Sun's transits last two to three days at the very most. Like the Moon, the Sun never goes retrograde.

To the Sun: Of the Sun's transits, the most important is its return to its natal position around a person's birthday. Known as the Solar Return, a chart set up for this moment gives a foretaste of what is likely to be in store over the next 12 months.

To the Moon: Highlights personal, domestic and emotional issues, as well as focusing on unconscious habits, or matters connected with the past. Problems arise only if there are negative emotions that need to be dealt with. The conjunction acts like a New Moon, paving the way for changes; the opposition corresponds to the Full Moon – a time of possible inner tension and conflict.

To Mercury: Stimulates an exchange of ideas; good for travel and business arrangements, communications, and paperwork.

To Venus: Sociable occasions and a time to enjoy other people's company; sometimes signifies the beginning of a new love affair; good for financial dealings, although it can also indicate extravagance.

To Mars: Emphasizes initiative and motivation; in the mood to do battle; increased physical energy; maybe a tendency to be too pushy.

To Jupiter: An optimistic, expansive time; good for studying; with hard aspects, opportunities may be wasted due to over-confidence.

To Saturn: Brings one's duties and responsibilities to the fore; good for tidying up any loose ends, or planning new ventures; energy levels tend to be low, so there is a tendency to feel dispirited.

To Uranus: A sudden impulse to do something different and break away from rigid routines; a rebellious spirit which can create friction with people in authority; ideas may not go according to plan with the hard aspects, causing a build-up of frustration.

To Neptune: Increased sensitivity and compassion, but possible confusion and unwillingness to face facts; a bad time to confront.

To Pluto: Powerful external forces may appear to obstruct one's path, but this only reflects a need to look within and make changes where necessary; dealings with others will be intense.

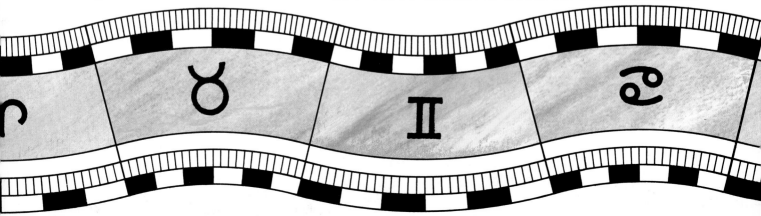

transits of venus

Venus is a 'passive' planet, representing our ability to attract what is desired – mainly love, but also money, power, or simply a good time. Little effort is required to enjoy the fruits of this planet's transits, which are usually associated with agreeable events. Since many of them pass without too much fuss, most astrologers pay no more than passing attention to transiting Venus.

Aspects of Love

All the same, it would be rash to dismiss Venus transits entirely. While it is true that they are too brief to indicate major new love affairs – or even significant changes to existing ones – relationships can nevertheless 'take off' or alter course during a Venus transit. Indeed, some of the hard aspects – notably those to Mars, Saturn and Pluto – sometimes trigger short-lived crises in a relationship which may appear to blow over quickly, but in actual fact reflect unconscious energies deeply buried in the psyche. If the causes are not confronted at the time, they may re-emerge later on with even greater force.

Venus transits last for two to three days, unless Venus turns retrograde over a natal planet, in which case it can stay there for up to three weeks.

To the Sun: A perfect day for partying, looking one's radiant best, and for falling in love, though the latter cannot be guaranteed; not good for work with a challenging routine.

To the Moon: An affectionate, romantic mood prevails, coupled with a general feeling of well-being; all the same, minor conflicts may arise if one is emotionally too demanding.

To Mercury: A light-hearted time, perfect for indulging romantic tastes; good for rubber-stamping business deals, but not for sorting out serious differences of opinion.

To Venus: Possibly a new love affair, but only if other factors support it; good for co-operative ventures; a danger of going on a spending spree; normally a lazy time.

To Mars: Definitely a time when passions are easily aroused; intense sexual feelings; a new attraction is likely to be impulsive, so it is not a good time to embark on a stable relationship; disagreements with lovers; good for artistic endeavours.

To Jupiter: Traditionally, the conjunction is held to be good for weddings; generally speaking, relationships will be harmonious, although the urge to relax coupled with a complete lack of self-discipline may possibly lead to over-indulgence.

To Saturn: Duty takes precedence over pleasure; a good time to tighten one's belt financially; dissatisfaction with others; possible break-ups in love; feelings of loneliness.

To Uranus: Surprise happenings; in the mood to experiment; a new love now would be exciting but unstable; sudden financial gains or losses.

To Neptune: Heightened romantic yearnings can lead to unrealistic expectations; good for work which requires a touch of inspiration; poor for practical matters.

To Pluto: Intense and possibly stressful feelings in love and relationships; hidden resentments are likely to come to the surface; inner compulsion may lead to a new infatuation.

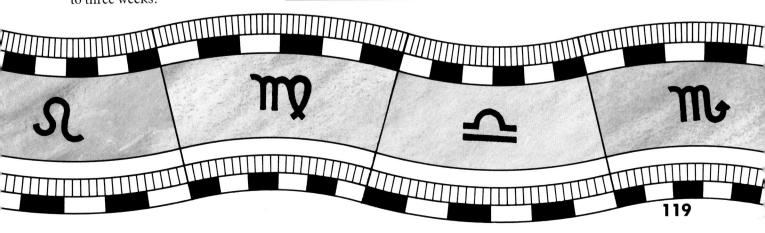

transits of the moon

The Moon's transits are so brief (two to three hours) that they usually amount to little more than a fleeting mood, which as often as not passes by unnoticed. Unless the Moon ties in with other transiting factors, its transits tend not to be taken too seriously by modern astrologers.

The main exception to this is when a New or Full Moon falls on a sensitive natal point, in which case the 'effects' – according to the planets and Houses involved – are quite likely to last for anything up to a month.

To the Sun: A fresh burst of vitality; minor irritations with others; traditionally, the conjunction is an unfavourable time for surgery.

To the Moon: A chart drawn up for the conjunction (Lunar Return) can be used to predict emotional responses over the following month.

To Mercury: Thinking is affected by moods; good for expressing feelings, but not for rational decisions under hard aspect.

To Venus: A day for socializing, entertaining at home, or spending money freely; a temptation to over-indulge in food and drink.

To Mars: May attract quarrels through irritability, or hasty actions; good for bold initiatives, but care is needed to avoid accidents.

To Jupiter: A benevolent, confident mood; tolerant of others; can also trigger exaggerated reactions; a danger of over-confidence.

To Saturn: Feelings of being weighed down by domestic duties; a difficult time to resolve emotional problems; pessimistic attitudes.

To Uranus: Reacting rashly, seemingly out of character; poor concentration; impatient; hidden tensions spring to the surface.

To Neptune: Heightened sensitivity; strange, dreamy moods; easily discouraged; confused feelings may create misunderstandings.

To Pluto: Powerful emotional responses to others which express deeply buried feelings; possible confrontations on the domestic front.

To the Sun: A day for knowing and speaking one's mind; a need to be on the move; possibly a tendency to be self-opinionated.

To the Moon: Responsive to other people's feelings; emotions tend to cloud judgment; possible stress under hard aspect.

To Mercury: Mentally alert; good for studying and putting ideas across; idle chatter; new acquaintances; opinions may be challenged.

To Venus: Stimulates a spirit of compromise; good for clearing the air in relationships; also favourable for business deals.

To Mars: Increased mental stamina makes this a good time for getting plans off the ground; a lack of tact may provoke needless arguments.

To Jupiter: Good for taking a fresh look at old ideas, and preparing an overall plan of action, but not for work needing detailed analysis.

To Saturn: A day for serious, concentrated thinking; negative attitudes may colour outlook; generally uncommunicative.

To Uranus: Mental processes are speeded up; good for sudden insights and original ideas, but trying to rush things may lead to exhaustion.

To Neptune: Assists artistic inspiration, but woolly-mindedness may confuse matters; not an easy time to be direct or honest.

Pluto: Good for research and putting ideas across persuasively; wilfulness or a sharp tongue may spark off conflicts.

transits of mercury

Operating principally in the realm of ideas, Mercury transits stimulate all forms of mental activity. As it breezes through the houses, the aspects it makes to the natal planets focus on routine and day-to-day dealings.

Mercury transits are thought to be lightweight unless they are linked to the more substantial transits of the outer planets; their contribution is usually to clarify the issues at stake. They last about two days, unless Mercury is retrograde, when they may last up to 11 days.

To get the most out of transits, it is important to interpret them in the context of what has already happened in the subject's life. This may appear obvious, but it is often forgotten, and can result in vague – or worse, totally inaccurate – predictions.

A helpful way of establishing what future trends are likely to hold in store is to refer an imminent major transit from an outer planet to previous transits involving the same transiting and natal planet. For example, a conjunction of transiting Saturn to the natal Sun should be interpreted in the light of what happened over the previous 14 or so years – when Saturn opposed, trined and then squared the Sun. By looking at each transit as part of a cycle, you can assess how the subject has dealt with this energy in the past and get a good idea of how he or she is likely to respond to it this time around.

This method is particularly useful for the transits of the outer planets – most notably, Jupiter, Saturn and Uranus, since their cycles seem to correspond closely with the critical stages of our development from childhood through to maturity. The inner planets complete their cycles too quickly to coincide with anything more than subtle or minor issues, while Neptune and Pluto only ever complete part of their cycles during the average lifetime.

transits of mars

Mars brings energy and drive to the houses and planets it transits – sometimes in uncontrollable doses. Still uncharitably referred to as 'the Lesser Malefic', this planet has earned a reputation for being the planetary equivalent of dynamite.

Without doubt, some people experience the transits of Mars as particularly trying periods – usually because they find it hard to deal with the sudden fluctuations in energy levels. If they are not confident in themselves, they may unconsciously seek to prove their strength through aggressive and disruptive behaviour.

But it is not true that Mars transits always end up in explosive conflicts or accidents. Many people take them in their stride, barely noticing the difference apart from a sensation of stepping up a gear or two in vitality and stamina. They can be productive times, when hard work produces positive results.

Another thing to remember about the transits of Mars is that they are short compared with the those of the other outer planets – just four days when Mars is direct; up to several weeks when it goes retrograde. Consequently, on their own they seldom amount to much.

But in common with the Sun, when the transits of Mars join forces with those of the slower moving planets, they seem to act as a kind of 'trigger'. The arrival of Mars on the scene often 'sets off' an event corresponding to the nature of the other planetary transits involved.

To the Sun: A good transit for any activity requiring high levels of physical energy; can be uncompromising towards others, stirring up opposition to plans; frustration may spark off explosive bursts of anger.

To the Moon: Tempers are likely to be on a short fuse, especially in close relationships; intense emotional reactions may cause minor disagreements to be over-dramatized; a good time to air grievances.

To Mercury: Great mental energy provides the enthusiasm to promote ideas; a tendency to react to even the most constructive criticism as a personal affront; a poor time for subtle negotiations.

To Venus: Heightens sensuality and the sex drive; a new love affair under this transit will probably be extremely physical, if short-lived; a good time to find creative ways to express feelings.

To Mars: Surplus energy needs a healthy outlet to avoid hasty actions; a need to prove one's effectiveness may result in unusually forceful or overbearing behaviour; a good time to 'get things done'.

To Jupiter: Good for making 'fortunate' decisions, partly because belief in oneself is high; the energy to cope with almost anything; resistance to any restrictions; rushing headlong into conflicts.

To Saturn: A limiting, restricting time when it is difficult to let off steam; depleted energies; efforts appear to be blocked by circumstances beyond control; temporary feelings of impotence.

To Uranus: Expect the unexpected; a spirit of rebellion may suddenly surface, disrupting normal life or prompting escape from obligations.

To Neptune: Feeling listless and easily depressed; muddle-headed aims may cause self-doubt; a poor time to draw up new plans; try to avoid diffusing energies; good for solitude and inspiration!

To Pluto: Increased self-confidence and physical stamina; good for making constructive changes, but the need to win may be too intense.

To the Ascendant: A time to assert oneself and get ideas off the ground; a spirit of compromise will head off conflicts with others.

To the Descendant: Tension between personal goals and the need for others' support can lead to stormy relationships.

To the MC: A time to be recognized for one's achievements, although any impulse to 'go it alone' is likely to meet with resistance.

To the IC: Pressures of home life may have an effect on work; quarrels are likely if differences are not settled calmly.

transits of jupiter

Benevolent Jupiter, true to his larger than life mythology, has, by tradition, a somewhat inflated reputation in astrology. Known as 'the Greater Benefic' (Venus being the Lesser), this planet was thought to be the direct opposite of Saturn – bringing hope, good fortune and success to anyone lucky enough to be under its generous 'influence'.

Although Jupiter is one of the 'pleasure' planets, its transits are no longer seen to be firm guarantees of prosperity. It is not that Jupiterian energy is inherently difficult – in fact, quite the opposite. It is precisely because everything seems to be going our way during Jupiter's transits that they can turn out to be so disappointing.

Symbolizing the urge to expand and widen our boundaries, Jupiter transits often coincide with genuine opportunities for growth – usually according to the House and planet involved. The down side is that this planet does not always know when to stop.

Unless transiting Saturn is also close at hand, Jupiter's blind optimism can easily over-step the mark, arousing the kind of hopes that have no foundations in reality. Jupiter transits can end in shattered dreams just as much as in golden opportunities. The truth is that some effort is required to cash in on them; Jupiter's gift is to signpost the way generously – not to hand things out on a plate.

Jupiter transits last from about two weeks up to six months if it goes retrograde.

To the Sun: Can bring a ray of sunlight into one's life, especially if it coincides with other difficult transits; traditionally good for health; advisable to avoid sitting back and trusting entirely to luck.

To the Moon: A pervasive mood of emotional well-being; good for property investment or moving home; with the hard aspects, a danger of being too demanding of others; a possible gain in weight.

To Mercury: A wealth of ideas and opportunities which require careful attention if anything is to come of them; good for business deals and settling legal matters; beware of over-confidence and sharp practices.

To Venus: Enhances popularity and the urge to indulge in just about everything pleasurable; favourable for a new romance, though under hard aspect, too carefree an attitude may lead to conflicts.

To Mars: An ebullient time, perfect for improving one's physical condition; the energy to achieve aims, especially in career; a good time to settle disputes; a lack of moderation may upset superiors.

To Jupiter: The conjunction marks the start of a 12-year cycle bringing opportunities for growth which must be seized, not wasted.

To Saturn: The principles of expansion and restriction join forces; either an unsettled time when dissatisfaction urges a break from old commitments, or a time to achieve through patience and hard work.

To Uranus: Sudden benefits or changes in direction; the urge to become more independent; a good time to review one's beliefs.

To Neptune: The possibility of a dream coming true; a bubble of idealism is likely to burst out of misplaced optimism; not a time for practical ventures, so care is needed in finances and relationships.

To Pluto: Good for taking the lead and organizing things one's own way; the urge to change one's circumstances drastically; a danger of squandering potential success by using unscrupulous means.

To the Ascendant: A positive time for enlarging social contacts and position; a liking for self-indulgence may come across as arrogance.

To the Descendant: Increases opportunities through partnerships of all kinds; possible clashes in outlook; favourable for legal actions.

To the MC: Traditionally an auspicious time for advancing one's professional standing; can also lead to nothing through complacency.

To the IC: The focus is on improving the quality of home life; good for building a solid base from which to launch oneself into the world.

transits of saturn

In the astrology of our forebears, Saturn was known as the 'Greater Malefic'. Roughly speaking, this meant that on a scale of one to ten, this planet scored maximum points for its ability to bring misfortune into a subject's life.

Despite the fact that modern astrologers no longer take this old, simplistic view, few of them look forward to Saturn's transits with glee. The reason is that this planet invariably plays the role of examiner in our lives; its transits through the houses – especially the sensitive natal points – frequently coincide with times when our attitudes and actions (as symbolized by the relevant planets and houses) are tested to the core, often with painful results.

The Teacher Within

Even if these tests of strength appear to be forced on us by external events or other people's actions, it is important to remember that Saturn represents 'the teacher within'. Restricting or burdensome circumstances often come about through our reluctance to see that we may have outgrown the people, places and ambitions which seem to mean so much to us. But it is our inability to let go that leads to losses and difficulties – not the transits themselves. Indeed, it is perfectly possible to experience positive results under a Saturn transit – it is just that any success is usually hard-earned.

Saturn's transits can last for about a month, or for the best part of a year if it goes retrograde over a natal point.

To the Sun: Either a time to reap the rewards of past endeavours, or to accept and sort out failures; life will be a struggle even if successful; low vitality; an end to burdensome relationships.

To the Moon: Emotional balance undermined by feelings of loneliness and of not being up to scratch; good for reassessing past deeds and seeing oneself in a more realistic light; emotional separations.

To Mercury: Serious, possibly gloomy thoughts; good for activities requiring mental endurance; a danger of being too single-minded and narrowing one's options; obstacles to ideas; lack of confidence.

To Venus: Inhibitions or a sense of reality may pervade relationships to test them; feeling unloved; seeking emotional stability.

To Mars: Events appear to conspire to test one's strength and ability to endure setbacks; a time to keep one's head down and work steadily and hard; important to find constructive outlets for pent-up energies.

To Jupiter: Patience and caution will be rewarded with opportunities for sustainable progress; a time to adjust expectations to reality; a need to shake free from restrictions and have more time to oneself.

To Saturn: Saturn's transits to its natal position represent periods of self-examination; attitudes and achievements are tested; often a time to (reluctantly) let go of unrewarding parts of one's life.

To Uranus: A desire for change battles against the instinct to hang on, creating inner tension; an urge to break free from rigid routines.

To Neptune: An unnerving time of uncertainty, pessimism and self-questioning moods; dissatisfaction with the drearier realities of life; a good time to decide how to set about realizing one's dreams.

To Pluto: A feeling of being hemmed in by circumstances; a need to live within restricted means; clinging on to old ways, or the end of a chapter and a time to start aiming for more control of one's life.

To the Ascendant: A time to review one's obligations and role in life; relentless demands to get things done; frustrated by others.

To the Descendant: Relationships can become more stable and sober, or so restrictive that they break down; new responsibilites.

To the MC: Great tenacity needed to persevere with aims; new commitments test one's ability to deal with responsibility.

To the IC: Possibly weighed down by domestic and family obligations; a good time to find a secure base and put down roots.

Discover how the transits of Uranus, Neptune and Pluto can affect events far into the future

There are occasions – admittedly few – when major events or turning points in our lives do not appear to be backed up by any significant transits, or when major transits do not seem to reflect what is happening in our lives. There are several reasons why this should be so, the most common being human error. For newcomers to astrology, it is all too easy to overlook some of the less obvious indicators, just as it is tempting to put too much emphasis on the major ones. So remember, when plotting or interpreting transits:

● Those of the slower moving planets – especially Uranus, Neptune and Pluto – can last up to 18 months. During this time, nothing remarkable may happen unless other transiting planets become involved.

● If the transits on a day when something important happened to you do not seem to reflect the event, check that you have not forgotten the minor aspects – especially the semi-square (45°) and the sesquiquadrate (135°) – and double-check the positions of the inner planets.

transits of uranus

There are good grounds for arguing that Uranus is the joker in the astrological pack. The only safe prediction to be made about a transit from this planet is that the outcome will be unpredictable!

Often referred to as the planet of the 'higher mind', Uranus represents the potential within us to break away from our early conditioning and become independent-minded individuals. For most of us, this urge has to contend with our varying needs for stability and predictability. It makes for an uncomfortable arrangement, because while one part of us wants to rebel against set patterns in our lives, another always prefers to settle for the devil it knows.

Need for Change

More often than not, the conformist within us wins out – but by clinging to old habits and views, we may neglect the Uranian side of our personality. If we are resistant to change, a transit from this planet is likely to jolt us out of our sleepy ways and force us to acknowledge that, according to the natal planet and house under transit, we are in danger of becoming living fossils.

Uranian transits – notably the hard aspects – are rarely dull, frequently disruptive and sometimes painful. But it is helpful to remember that they are only made difficult by our reluctance to face the truth about ourselves or our fear of taking risks. Uranus' great gift is to free us from our past so that we can become more truly ourselves.

To the Sun: A sudden impulse to change course and improve one's circumstances; considerable unrest and inner tension; either striving for greater freedom, or unexpected setbacks which restrict liberty.

To the Moon: A time of emotional turmoil, possibly because of unsettling changes on the home front; a need to become more independent – often at the expense of personal or family ties.

To Mercury: Great mental excitability; a time to break free from old ideas and develop an original line of thinking; exhaustion through a tendency to rush things; others may challenge opinions.

To Venus: A conflict between the need for love and greater freedom; a new love affair now is likely to be impulsive, unusual and unstable; existing close relationships may require greater flexibility.

To Mars: Energy levels are extremely high and potentially explosive; a need to find a goal which demands extraordinary effort; a tendency to blast one's way through obstacles; spoiling for a fight.

To Jupiter: A fortunate turn of events, or sudden recognition; missed or wasted opportunities; a good time to broaden horizons through travel or education; one's outlook on life may be severely tested.

To Saturn: Great tension resulting from a conflict between the urge to rebel and the instinct to conform; unexpected upheavals in job or personal relationships; resistance to change may prove restrictive.

To Uranus: The major transits tie in with critical stages of life; the square at 21 (breaking away from adolescence) and the opposition at about 42 (the mid-life crisis) are especially significant.

To Neptune: A time when radical ideas may inspire a vision of a new order or slide into vague idealism; a desire to escape empty routine.

To Pluto: A period of traumatic or rapid changes – possibly through social upheaval which has an indirect effect on one's circumstances.

To the Ascendant: Sudden and often disruptive events which overturn the status quo; an unconscious urge to break away from commitments.

To the Descendant: Personal relationships may become tense or need to be redefined; sudden new contacts; unexpected legal conflicts.

To the MC: An irresistible urge to free oneself from suffocating obligations; fortunate changes for the better, or sudden upsets.

To the IC: Unforeseen changes within the home – including a sudden move of house; events that force a new level of self-awareness.

transits of neptune

For most of us, a transit from Neptune often coincides with a time of considerable confusion. Neptune's trick is to show us that nothing is what it appears to be, so that the issues connected with a natal planet or house under transit no longer unfold in their customary way. Invariably, the source of this confusion lies within ourselves, even though it may seem at times as if other people are conspiring to undermine our position.

A Neptune transit often begins with a creeping dissatisfaction with everyday life, followed by a longing to experience something out of the ordinary. Sometimes this results in a blind rush to escape whatever ties us down and chase a heartfelt dream – although in fact we are merely fleeing from problems of our own making. At other times, we may actually take on new commitments in an unconscious or a misguided attempt to give our lives more meaning.

It is because Neptune operates on such a deep, feeling level that the effects of its transits can only truly be assessed long after they have passed. Even if we fall victim to our own illusions and go off the rails, there is more to Neptune transits than the disappointments that so often seem to accompany them.

On the positive side, Neptune makes us aware that there is more to life than meets the eye. By loosening our grip on mere reality, it helps us become more sensitive to the less tangible influences around us.

To the Sun: Stimulates the imagination; good for creative inspiration, but poor for making intentions clearly known; a risk of becoming involved in unrealistic or dishonest schemes.

To the Moon: Heightens sensitivity to surroundings and the need to help people in trouble; overwhelmed by strange, irrational feelings; exploitable as a result of being too receptive to others' wishes.

To Mercury: Opens the mind to subtle, new influences which can also be confusing; favourable for developing intuition; a temptation to bend the truth stresses the importance of being honest and direct.

To Venus: Intensifies one's sense of beauty and romantic yearnings; a dreamlike infatuation which ends in disappointment; the need to infuse ideals and hopes with a strong measure of practicality.

To Mars: Lack of drive and initiative, or circumstances that seem to conspire against one's best efforts; a crisis of confidence that helps one to accept failure and redirect energies realistically.

To Jupiter: The stirring of unfulfilled dreams; new spiritual insights; a desire to escape from humdrum existence; a danger of living in a cloud of optimism and over-reaching oneself.

To Saturn: Frequent swings of mood, or feelings of dissatisfaction with one's lot; a time to re-assess spiritual and material needs and tailor one's life accordingly; a fear of letting go of the 'old order'.

To Uranus: Changing states of consciousness which affect most people through issues that embrace the whole of society, if not the world!

To Neptune: The square occurs during the 'mid-life crisis', the trine at 55 and the opposition at about 84; they involve facing up to one's deeper desires by letting go of, or chasing, unrealized dreams.

To Pluto: A generational influence, producing a groundswell of profound dissatisfaction with 'establishment' values.

To the Ascendant: Increases sensitivity; obscures one's grasp of 'self'; a danger of becoming a victim of one's circumstances.

To the Descendant: A tendency to lean or be leant on by others; misunderstandings in close relationships; a betrayal of trust.

To the MC: Uncertain about direction in life; devotion to a cause; feeling unfulfilled in career; a deep need for spiritual nourishment.

To the IC: Confusing feelings of inadequacy may affect sense of purpose; a time to withdraw and sort out one's true needs and aims.

transits of pluto

What Mars and Saturn were to the ancients, Pluto has become to modern astrologers – the dark hand of fate. But while this may well be the case in mundane astrology (world events), Pluto's transits in a birthchart are by no means a guaranteed omen of doom and destruction.

Although in the years since its relatively recent discovery, Pluto has come to be associated with drastic upheaval, the other side to this planet is that it only destroys what is decaying or useless to clear the way for positive change and reconstruction. This may sound like cold comfort for anyone anticipating a 'hard' Pluto transit, but Plutonian change **can** happen without the world falling around our shoulders.

Deep Powers

Many astrologers believe it is impossible to know what to expect from a Pluto transit. Part of the problem is that Pluto seems to represent energies buried deep in the psyche – so deep, in fact, that the effects of its transits may not materialize for years.

Far from signifying catastrophic change, a Pluto transit can just as easily mark the beginning of a slow process of psychological growth which only becomes clear much later – perhaps when another planet transits the same part of the birthchart. All the same, there are times when Pluto transits coincide with events that cast us into the depths of despair – a kind of psychological death that enables us to be reborn with renewed strength.

To the Sun: A time of sudden, though not easy, progress; seeking to become more influential and effective; a risk of overestimating one's strengths; a need to face one's less pleasant personality traits.

To the Moon: Powerful emotional outbursts, usually triggered by deep-seated insecurities; obsessive behaviour often connected with childhood; good for bringing subconscious feelings to the surface.

To Mercury: Intensifies powers of observation and the ability to uncover the truth; a danger of being drawn to fanatical views, or opposed for one's own; nervous exhaustion through mental effort.

To Venus: Emphasizes sexual drive and the need for love; a love affair begun under this transit is likely to be compulsive and highly sexual; difficulties point to a need to transform attitudes to love.

To Mars: A period of extraordinary energy; increases the will to overcome through sheer effort; though the urge to win at all costs can lead to ruthless behaviour or create violent opposition.

To Jupiter: Increases the desire to achieve and improve oneself; possible public influence; a rebirth of optimism or spiritual faith; conflicts with authority; inflated self-importance; traumatic losses.

To Saturn: A stressful time because Saturn resists change whereas Pluto makes it inevitable; the end of an old order and the chance to relinquish what is no longer essential to one's self-development.

To Uranus: Stimulates the zeal to change and break away from old conventions; often coincides with a period of upsets, intolerance and fanaticism; trying to achieve aims by disruptive or forceful means.

To Neptune: An inner transformation of beliefs and values which only becomes clear much later. The effects are generational.

To Pluto: Only the sextile and square are possible in a lifetime; may correspond to issues and changes affecting an entire generation.

To the Ascendant: A tendency to be too heavy-handed and wilful in dealings with others; a dramatic change in circumstances.

To the Descndant: Intimate relationships may be subject to great pressures; people who strongly influence one's view of life.

To the MC: Dramatically alters one's direction in life; either a gain in authority and influence, or a calamitous fall from power.

To the IC: A period of inner transformation; breaking with the past; upheavals within the family or on the domestic front.

Although widely used in astrology, transits are only one among a host of predictive techniques that have evolved over the years. Another method which is every bit as popular in natal astrology is a system commonly referred to as *'day-for-year' progressions*.

The principle on which this system works is – as the name implies – that every day after your date of birth is equivalent to one year of your life. So if, for example, you were born at 17.48 GMT on 25th April 1970, the positions of the planets and Angles at exactly the same time the following day (26th April) would correspond to your first birthday – 25th April 1971.

Continuing the conversion, the positions of the planets and Angles on 27th April would correspond to your second birthday, their positions on the 28th April would correspond to your third birthday, and so on.

Charts drawn up using this 'day-for-year' method are known as *progressed* charts, and are said to herald issues or events for the years in question.

In other words, if your birthday is 25th April 1970 and you want to see what your twentieth year is likely to hold in store, you draw up a chart showing the planets' exact positions on 15th March (20 days on from your birthday – corresponding to 25th April 1990), then look at how these positions compare with each other and with those in your own birthchart.

INTERPRETING PROGRESSIONS

How do progressions differ from transits in interpretation?

The traditional view is to see them as indicators of inner psychological growth and change, while transits relate more to external events and conditions we meet in the world around us. A growing number of astrologers refute this, however, arguing that as far as interpretation goes, there is no clear distinction between the two systems. They look at transits **and** progressions before drawing any conclusions, though as always in astrology, there is no substitute for personal experience.

What are the advantages of using progressions?

Progressions are strong where transits are weak – namely, with the inner planets and the Angles. As far as transits are concerned, these move too quickly to have more than a fleeting significance, and the emphasis is always on the slow-moving planets.

With progressions, the focus switches to the inner planets and Angles because on a day-for-year basis the rate at which these move, or 'progress', is much slower – slow enough, in fact, for them to make significant aspects to planets and Angles in the birthchart.

Another advantage of progressions is that you can – preferably with the help of a computer and the appropriate astrological software – progress the entire birthchart, so that from year to year the planets, Angles **and** house cusps inch their way forward (unless, of course, a planet is retrograde).

Astrologers who do this claim that it can provide an extremely detailed map of approaching trends in a subject's life, although this method should never be used on its own, without reference to the birthchart.

THE DAY-FOR-YEAR PRINCIPLE

Whereas transits track the actual movements of the planets as they circle the zodiac, day-for-year progressions correspond to purely symbolic planetary movements. It may seem strange that the Sun or any other planet's position on the twentieth day after your birth has any bearing on conditions surrounding your twentieth year. But quite apart from the fact that the day-for-year method of progressing the birthchart produces highly accurate results, there are good astrological grounds for taking seemingly different timescales – such as a day and a year – and treating them as one.

In the course of a day, the Earth rotates once on its axis, and in so doing completes one full circuit of the zodiac. Over a period of a year, the Sun (as seen from Earth) also circles the zodiac once. Moreover, if you were to plot a chart for each day after you were born, using exactly the same data for your time and place of birth, you would find that after 365 days, your Ascendant, MC and house cusps would have progressed through every degree of the zodiac to end up in exactly the same position as they were in your birthchart.

So while day-for-year progressions work on a symbolic timescale, there is still a clear link – based on the Earth's movement relative to the Sun – between a day and a year. Hence their adoption as the most popular method of progressing a birthchart.

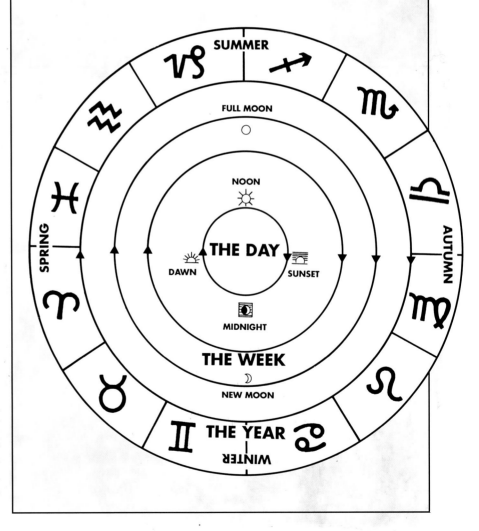

How long do progressions last?

The generally accepted view is that a progression lasts as long as it takes the progressed planet to pass 1° either side of a natal planet or Angle.

However, the energies symbolized by the progressed and natal planets will be at their most intense when the aspect is exact.

With the inner planets, the progressed Sun takes just over two years to move over a natal point, Mercury and Venus an average of about a year, and Mars about three years. Only the Moon, which travels 12–14° over a progressed year, covers any significant ground, and its aspects last a correspondingly shorter time – usually no more than a couple of months.

Are the outer planets used in progressions?

Over a 'progressed' lifespan of, say, 75 years, the outer planets will not move a great deal – after all, this period is equivalent to only 75 'real' days. During this time, Jupiter would need a full head of steam (when it is not 'slowed down' by a bout of retrograde motion), to progress as far as 17°. And from Saturn to Pluto, the planetary momentum never for a moment rises above a snail's pace.

Clearly, there is little point looking at progressions from the slow-moving planets to the natal planets and Angles, as in the vast majority of cases the outer planet will already be aspecting that point in the birthchart. The one exception is when the aspect from the outer planet is applying and is within a close enough orb to become exact during the subject's lifetime. This point is usually marked by some memorable event or a critical stage of development for the subject in keeping with the planetary energies involved.

Progressions were traditionally thought to relate more closely to psychological change while transits referred to specific events in life.

Can events actually be timed by progressions?

Yes, over the period of a year it is possible to predict major events, but generally only if the progressions involve the Angles and the Sun. It also requires experience – beginners are best advised to consider only the general outlook of a progressed year.

How important are the signs and houses in progressions?

Very – just as for transits, except that the sign of a progressed planet or Angle is given more prominence in progressions. This is especially true when a progressed planet or Angle changes sign, as this is believed to represent a new phase of personal experience or growth.

For example, if you have a Cancer Ascendant, the Moon will be your lifetime ruling planet. But when your Ascendant progresses into Leo (the timing of which depends entirely on the degree of your natal Ascendant) the Sun takes on a powerful significance; although it will always be secondary to the Moon, you may start to approach life with a renewed sense of vitality.

The house cusps are also important. Aspects between the progressed planets and the natal cusps, and from the progressed cusps to the natal planets are thought to highlight the affairs of that house, making them more noticeable than normal. However, this is really a matter for a professional astrologer.

PERPETUAL NOON DATE

Name: SAMPLE X

House System: EQUAL

AGE: 20	Day	Month	Year
Noon positions on:	15	5	1970
Correspond to:	28	1	1990

A SAMPLE PROGRESSED CHART

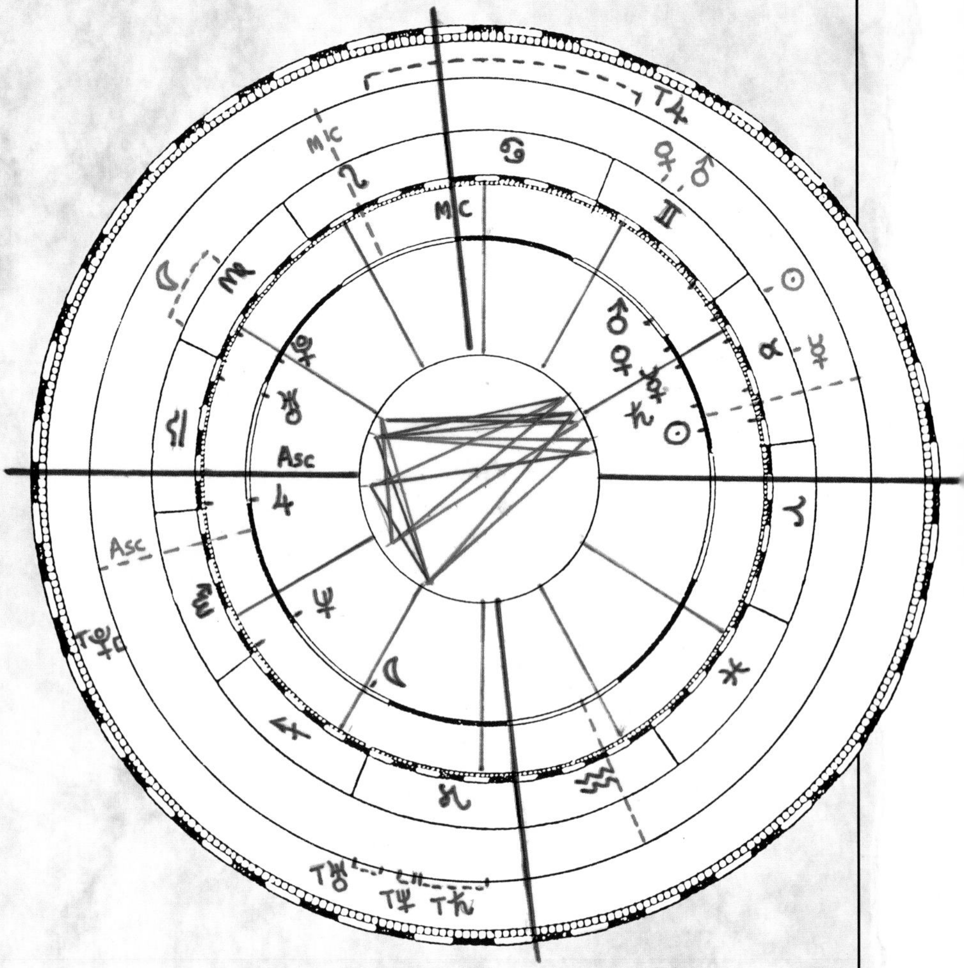

POSITIONS OF PROGRESSED PLANETS

☉: 24 ♉ 14   ♀: 4 ♊ 27

☽: 16 ♍ 48   ♂: 18 ♊ 9

  Asc 7 ♏ 42

☿: 14 ♉ 50 R   MC 19 ♌ 36

THE PROGRESSED MOON OVER ONE YEAR

MONTH	Position	Aspects to Natal Planets/Angles	Aspects to Prog Planets/Angles
28th JAN	♍ 16° 48'		
28th FEB	17° 48'	□ ♂	
28th MAR	18° 49'		
28th APR	19° 49'		
28th MAY	20° 50'	□ ♀	
28th JUN	21° 50'		△ ☿
28th JULY	22° 51'		
28th AUG	23° 52'	△ ☉ ♂ ♇	
28th SEPT	24° 53'	♂ ♇	♂ ♇
28th OCT	25° 54'		♂ ♇
28th NOV	26° 55'		□ ☽ △ ♇
28th DEC	27° 56'		
28th JAN	28° 57'		

PROGRESSIONS OF SUN, MERCURY, VENUS, MARS, ASC & MC

YEAR	Aspects to Natal Planets/Angles	Aspects to Progressed Planets/Angles
1990	☉ △ ♇	☉ △ ♇ ☿ ♂ ♄
1991	☉ △ ♇ ☽ ⚹ ♆ ☽ ⚹ MC ♀ △ Asc ☽ ♂ ♃	☉ △ ♇ ☽ ⚹ ♆ ☿ ♂ ♄ ☽ ♂ ♄
1992	☉ △ ♇ MC □ ☿ ♀ △ Asc ☽ ♂ Asc	☿ ♂ ♄ ☽ ⚹ MC ☽ △ ♀ ♀ □ ♇ ☽ △ ♂
1993	☉ ♂ ♀ ☽ ♂ ☉ ♀ □ ♇ ☽ ♂ Asc ♀ ♂ ☽ MC □ ☿	☿ ♂ ♄ ☽ ♂ ♃ ♀ □ ♇
1994	☉ ♂ ♀ Asc ♂ ♄ ♀ ♂ ☽ MC ⚹ Asc	☿ ♂ ♄

Copying this layout will enable you to keep all your progression information neatly organized.

In the top box, fill in the data for the progressed year in question, including the subject's Perpetual Noon/Midnight Date.

In the box below it, enter the positions of the progressed planets and Angles from your Ephemeris for the appropriate Progressed Date. You do not need to enter the positions of the slower planets.

Next draw up the progressed chart. The natal planets and Angles go on the inner wheel. Outside them go the progressed planets and Angles. The outermost ring can then be used to plot the transits for the year, as shown here.

In the Progressed Moon box, enter the Moon's average monthly motion and the aspects it makes to natal and other progressed points over the year — starting from the Perpetual Noon/Midnight Date.

Repeat for the remaining planets and Angles. As these are slower, you can fill in their progressions over the next five years.

It is all too easy to look at progressions (or transits) for a year and get carried away by a particularly sparkling aspect – for example, a conjunction between the Ascendant and Venus. Equally, there may be a temptation to wallow in despair if progressed Mars on the natal MC also forms a menacing square to natal Pluto. The fact is, though, that aspects involving progressions should never be interpreted on their own, or without first considering the natal condition of the planets involved.

A 'favourable' progressed aspect between the Ascendant and Venus is far less likely to promise a happy time if natal Venus is part of a testing T-square involving Saturn and Pluto. Similarly, a progressed Mars square to Pluto will most probably be softened if natal Mars is well aspected.

Individual Interpretations

But even these guidelines cannot be taken at face value, for just as different people respond to the same things in different ways, so the 'effects' of planetary aspects (whether in progressions, transits or in the birthchart) can never be the same for everyone – not even those born within a few minutes of one another.

When astrologers interpret progressions accurately, it is not because they have some mystical insight into how they work; it is because they observe one of astrology's golden rules – that any 'predictions' must be based not only on what is shown in the birthchart, but on the way each of us goes about handling our planetary energies.

aspects between progressed Angles and planets

SUN – Hard: Loss of position or status; struggling to achieve goals; a need for privacy; conflict between domestic and professional life.
SUN – Soft: Public recognition; growing prestige, sometimes on account of partner's achievements; gain through land or property.

MOON – Hard: Adverse publicity; loss of popularity; dashed hopes; upsetting changes on the home front; lowered vitality.
MOON – Soft: An increased need for security; strong links with women; in a man's chart, marriage (usually if Venus is also active).

MERCURY – Hard: Unhappy changes of residence; domestic squabbles; fraudulent activities; notoriety through slander or libel.
MERCURY – Soft: Increased opportunities to travel; communicating to a wider public; academic achievements; successful commercial ventures.

VENUS – Hard: Misdirected feelings, attracting the 'wrong' sort of lover; loss of creature comforts; financial extravagance.
VENUS – Soft: Greater popularity; new friendships; romance, and in a man's chart, marriage; also divorce if this restores 'harmony'.

MARS – Hard: Accidents resulting from hasty actions; strife at home; loss of or damage to home; setbacks through upsetting others.
MARS – Soft: Successful endeavours; marriage in a woman's chart (if Venus is also active); preparing the ground for future actions.

JUPITER – Hard: Loss of face through poor judgement or taking unsound advice; financial troubles through over-expansion; legal problems.
JUPITER – Soft: Helpful contacts from 'people in high places'; greater prosperity and popularity; an engagement, marriage or birth.

SATURN – Hard: Setbacks from lack of discipline or staying power; illness to, or separation from, loved ones; missed opportunities.
SATURN – Soft: Hard work with slow but steady progress; mettle-testing commitments; greater domestic security or social reputation.

URANUS – Hard: Sudden upsets, including separations or divorce; reacting against change, or rebelling against established patterns.
URANUS – Soft: Setting up new ventures; new contacts; greater independence; a sudden end to troubles; rapid progress; parenthood.

NEPTUNE – Hard: A shattered dream; involved in a scandal, or dishonest practices; failure through vague aims or impracticality.
NEPTUNE – Soft: Realizing a long-cherished dream; catching the popular imagination; willingly making a sacrifice for an ideal.

PLUTO – Hard: A ruthless attitude to others (or vice versa); damage to home; financial upheavals; power struggles; loss of a loved one.
PLUTO – Soft: Determination to succeed pays off; beginning a new direction in life; improved finances; increased influence in public.

In day-for-year progressions, the Midheaven, Ascendant and their opposite points appear to play more or less the same part as the Sun and Mars do in transits; they are the triggers which activate other planetary energies.

As far as interpretation goes, there seems to be no difference in meaning between aspects made by progressed Angles to natal or progressed planets, and those made by progressed planets to natal Angles. In fact, it is quite possible for aspects between both sets of Angles and planets to happen simultaneously – for example, for progressed Mars to oppose the natal MC, while the progressed MC trines natal Mars.

No Difference
Some astrologers also believe that there is little to distinguish between the Angles themselves. So while we may have grown used to thinking of the MC in terms of our position in the world, and the Ascendant more as a mirror of our immediate environment, we should not cling to these distinctions too tightly – at least not when interpreting progressions!

One word of caution: progressing the angles only works if your birth time is accurate. Four minutes can make the difference of one degree, which in the day-for-year timescale is the equivalent of a year. So if the birth time is unknown or uncertain, the progressed Angles can only be of limited value.

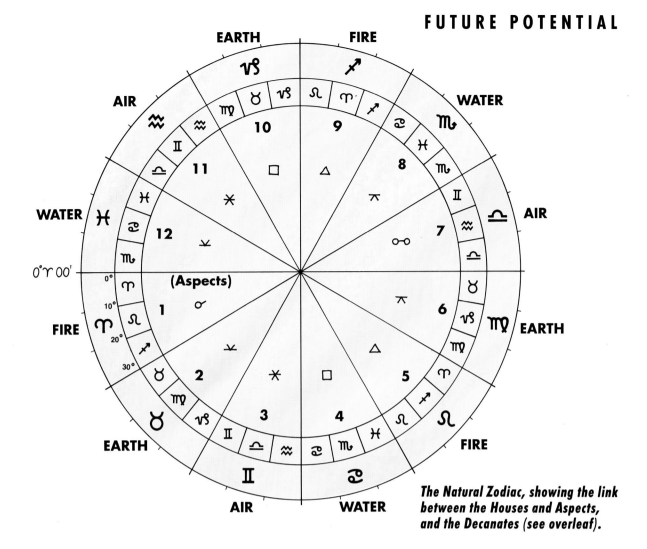

The Natural Zodiac, showing the link between the Houses and Aspects, and the Decanates (see overleaf).

Astrologers cannot agree on how relevant the Signs and Houses are when it comes to interpreting the aspects in progressions. It seems there is no cut and dried answer – indeed, many of the conflicting standpoints each have something to recommend them!

One traditional way of interpreting the aspects is to relate them to the Signs and Houses in the Natural Zodiac. In this system, the degrees of an aspect are measured in both directions from 0° 00' Aries (known as the *First Point of Aries*) to find the corresponding Sign and House, and hence the meaning of the aspect. For example, the square, being a 90° aspect, is 90° away from the First Point of Aries.

It therefore lines up with, and draws its meaning from, Cancer and Capricorn – as well as from the Fourth and Tenth Houses of the Natural Zodiac.

ASPECT CORRESPONDENCES

The Conjunction (0°): Corresponds to the Aries and First House. Signifies a new cycle of experience, which is often unconscious at the outset.

The Semi-sextile (30°): Corresponds to Taurus and Pisces, and to the Second and Twelfth Houses. Signifies the potential to expand/integrate energies, bringing greater stability to the subject's life.

The Sextile (60°): Corresponds to Gemini and Aquarius, and to the Third and Eleventh Houses. Signifies harmony in surroundings and social contacts; a mind at ease with itself.

The Square (90°): Corresponds to Cancer and Capricorn, and to the Fourth and Tenth Houses. Signifies conflict between sudden changes in the subject's professional (conscious) and personal (unconscious) life.

The Trine (120°): Corresponds to Leo and Sagittarius, and to the Fifth and Ninth Houses. Denotes easy opportunities for growth and gain on all levels – sometimes too easy!

The Inconjunction (150°): Corresponds to Virgo and Scorpio, and to the Sixth and Eighth Houses. Signifies a need for the subject to face up to and overhaul areas of life in need of improvement.

The Opposition (180°): Corresponds to Libra and the Seventh House. Signifies conflict or union, depending on how the two opposing energies can be merged.

The Semi-square (45°) and **Sequiquadrate (135°)** correspond respectively to Taurus and Aquarius, and Leo and Scorpio. Although they don't fit neatly into the House system, together they form a Grand Cross at 15° of the Fixed signs – which perhaps explains why they are said to represent sudden and unexpected change.

PROGRESSIONS AND THE DECANATES

Although progressions involving the Angles are important, there are other, more subtle influences connected with the progressed Ascendant and Midheaven which can give clues to developments and changes in the subject's life. One such influence is that of the *Decanates* – a system whereby each sign is divided into three parts of 10° each. Within each sign, the First Decanate is the sign's purest expression, the Second has a flavour of the next sign from the same Element, and the Third has a flavour of the last sign from the same Element.

For example, with the Fire sign Aries, 0°–10° belongs to Aries itself, 10°–20° belongs to Leo, and 20°–30° to Sagittarius; with the next Fire sign, Leo, the First Decanate is ruled by Leo, the Second by Sagittarius and the Third by Aries. And so it goes, through the signs and Elements.

When an Angle progresses from one sign to another, it often coincides with a big change in direction; when it changes Decanates, the shift in emphasis is less marked. All the same, the use of Decanates in progressions can shed considerable light on the quality of experiences we are likely to draw to ourselves.

THE MEANING OF THE DECANATES

Aries (Aries): Plenty of energy and opportunities to make changes, get ahead in life and realize goals.

Aries (Leo): A sense of being rejuvenated, coupled with new experiences that deepen one's feelings.

Aries (Sagittarius): An awakening spirit of exploration may lead to travel or further studies.

Taurus (Taurus): A time to get practical affairs in order; stubbornness may make it hard to change.

Taurus (Virgo): A need to sharpen critical talents and re-evaluate oneself in a more objective light.

Taurus (Capricorn): A time of stirring ambitions; new commitments, and maybe public recognition.

Gemini (Gemini): Increased restlessness and curiosity as the mind speeds up; hunger for knowledge.

Gemini (Libra): Emphasizes the need to see and experience life from as many sides as possible.

Gemini (Aquarius): A period of mental stability, and a chance to focus deeply on one area of life.

Cancer (Cancer): May put the spotlight on domestic issues; opens up a whole new world of feelings.

Cancer (Scorpio): Traditionally thought to denote a time of loss and sorrow; releases buried feelings.

Cancer (Pisces): Increased sensitivity to surroundings needs to be offset by periods alone.

Leo (Leo): Awakens the urge to give emotionally; a time of greater vitality, and *joie de vivre*.

Leo (Sagittarius): Opportunities to expand on all levels; a good time for developing intuition.

Leo (Aries): Stimulates a spirit of enterprise; a risk of being thwarted through being too assertive.

Virgo (Virgo): Not a time for 'making it' in the world; keeping one's head low and working hard.

Virgo (Capricorn): Much better for stirring one's ambitions; honour or gain through perseverance.

Virgo (Taurus): Tempers Virgo's more critical side; opportunities to improve financial position.

Libra (Libra): A strong need for peace and harmony; partner(s) may be especially influential now.

Libra (Aquarius): Learning to be more decisive; contacts who awaken one's humanitarian instincts.

Libra (Gemini): A more active mind seeks travel, a better social life or creative expression.

Scorpio (Scorpio): A greater determination to succeed; new and intense feelings and experiences.

Scorpio (Pisces): A need to guard against the less than honest; seeing the sad side of life.

Scorpio (Cancer): Domestic upheavals; over-sensitive to others; strange romantic attractions.

Sagittarius (Sagittarius): Foreign travel or living abroad; a spiritual quest, or spirit of rebellion.

Sagittarius (Aries): Greater independence of mind; suffering through being over-wilful and impulsive.

Sagittarius (Leo): A phase of falling in love rather too easily; over-dramatizing emotions.

Capricorn (Capricorn): A chance to leave one's mark on society – through merit or mere social climbing.

Capricorn (Taurus): The single-minded pursuit of fixed goals can lead to financial gain.

Capricorn (Virgo): A suitable period to sow for the future; a danger of becoming too self-obsessed.

Aquarius (Aquarius): Either swept off one's feet by new ideas and friends, or sticking to old views.

Aquarius (Gemini): An excitable, erratic mentality; living in one's head; seeking a marriage of minds.

Aquarius (Libra): A more balanced state of mind; a binding commitment; a sharpened sense of justice.

Pisces (Pisces): A need to develop stronger resolve in dealings with others; heightened awareness.

Pisces (Cancer): Learning self-reliance; hyper-sensitivity to surroundings; clinging to the past.

Pisces (Scorpio): A danger of becoming ensnared by negative feelings; a need for self control.

As with transits, it takes time to learn how to use progressions. Part of the problem is that there are so many different shades of meaning attached to each planetary combination that it is very hard to establish on which level to pitch your 'forecast'.

The answer, to begin with at least, is not even to try. The first step is to discover how the subject responds to the energy patterns indicated by the planets and their signs, houses and aspects in the birthchart. With a progression involving the Sun and Saturn, for example, some people may draw experiences that reflect the gloomier or more selfish side of this aspect. Others, however, may find events have a sunnier twist to them – perhaps as they gain some reward or recognition for their efforts.

Whatever the outcome, progressions do not hold the key; they merely point to the nature of the 'event'. Another reason for not relying on progressions (or transits) to 'predict' what will happen is that the full effects of a progressed aspect will not necessarily be obvious straight away. Even though a major event or change of direction is on the cards, it may take months or years for it to materialize.

As a guideline, it is safe to say that progressions involving the Angles and the Sun are more powerful indicators of major events than those of the other planets, the exception being those progressions of the chart ruler.

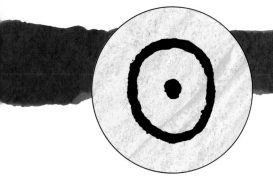

progressions of the sun

To the Sun: These happen at roughly the same age for everyone – the semi-sextile is at 30, the semi-square at 46 and the sextile at 61. It is impossible to say what 'effects' might be expected without detailed reference to the Sun's placement in the birthchart.

To the Moon: Most astrologers only consider progressions of the Sun to the natal Moon, which represent a process of inner change which gradually turns outwards. But also important are the progressed New Moon, which marks a time for change through personal initiative, and the progressed Full Moon, which implies changes through confrontation and breaking with the past.

To Mercury: The conjunction from the progressed Sun to Mercury (or vice versa) is the most significant aspect, as it occurs early in life (early 20s at the latest). It often coincides with changes or events connected with experiences at school or in further education.

To Venus: The conjunction is traditionally linked with marriage, or failing that, with increased popularity and rosier prospects. Of the hard aspects, only the semi-square and square are possible; they may coincide with disappointment in love or friendship, and money worries.

To Mars: All these aspects are associated with turbulent times, since the will to achieve is heightened. A tendency to over-reach oneself may lead to accidents. In a woman's chart there may be marriage. Hard aspects often correspond to domestic break-up – even divorce.

To Jupiter: Traditionally, the conjunction marks public honour and general good fortune, though modern astrologers place the emphasis on striving for success. Possibly marriage in a woman's chart. Even the hard aspects can be helpful, though over-confidence may lead to loss.

To Saturn: A character-forming progression: it invariably brings greater responsibility which either furthers ambitions or is seen as an unwanted burden. The soft aspects are good for investments or career promotion. Hard aspects often coincide with a fall from grace.

To Uranus: Behaviour becomes erratic, old ways of life seem stifling and there is a need to be 'more oneself'. The hard aspects can be especially stressful, representing sudden reversals and separations.

To Neptune: A longing for spiritual enlightenment; dissatisfaction with present circumstances; experiences that point out character faults; a sacrifice made in order to gain one's heart's desire.

To Pluto: A powerful progression linked with events that bring about a major change of direction in life – often accompanied by a feeling of inevitability. Discovering and following one's true vocation. The hard aspects can symbolize organized opposition to one's schemes.

Whether you are looking at progressions, transits, or an ordinary birthchart, never forget that the Sun is the focal point of all the other planetary energies. Astrologically, the Sun mirrors its function in the solar system: it is fundamental to our existence – so much so, in fact, that it is hard to define what its function is!

One way of looking at the Sun is as our essential 'life force', pushing us to discover our true purpose. While it may not tell us specifically about our mission in life (which is for each of us to choose), it can nevertheless show how we set about looking for it – or not, as the case might be!

Core Issues

Along with those of the Angles, the Sun's progressions are thought to be the most important, for they raise issues that affect us to our very core. But how we cope with these issues cannot be gauged simply from the progressed aspects and planets involved; as always, the answer lies in the Sun's placement in the birthchart by sign, house and aspect.

There will be years when neither the progressed nor the natal Sun are involved in any progressions. This does not mean that life will be uneventful – there are always the transits to consider – but it does suggest that changes or developments during these 'fallow' periods might not affect us radically. It is important, too, to check the Sun's progressions into a new sign or house, as these will bring new issues to the surface.

progressions of the moon

As a rule, progressions from the planets to the natal Moon are more important than progressions of the Moon itself, as the Moon progresses so rapidly. But aspects from the progressed Moon to a natal or progressed outer planet are worth watching, since these can last up to six months.

Where the progressed Moon really comes into its own is when it joins progressions from the other progressed planets to the planets or Angles in the birth-chart. Under these conditions the Moon can act very much like a trigger, setting off a chain of events which reflect the nature of the planets involved.

To the Moon: The Moon completes a full cycle every 28 years; the progressions to its natal position depend on its natal aspects.

To Mercury: A lightweight combination; may focus on day-to-day issues at the office or at home; an emphasis on travel; adverse publicity.

To Venus: Denotes the path of least resistance; does not promise much on its own, as there is no drive to succeed; an emotional attraction.

To Mars: Highlights restlessness; an urge to travel; tempers can run high; feelings blown out of proportion may create discord all round.

To Jupiter: New social contacts; a change of residence; sometimes events during this time have an almost fated quality about them.

To Saturn: Brings stability to lunar affairs; attractions to older people; feelings of loneliness brought on by inhibited emotions.

To Uranus: Unusual encounters or experiences may trigger changes; emotional crises; marriage in a man's chart; estrangements.

To Neptune: Heightened emotions; increasingly sympathetic; helping the less fortunate; over-idealizing friendships; escape from reality.

To Pluto: People or events that spark off fundamental changes; an awakening of intense emotions; mass popularity – or unpopularity.

progressions of mercury

To Mercury: More concerned with mental development than outside events, unless the natal aspects of Mercury suggest otherwise.

To Venus: Not a serious planetary combination in progressions; may highlight social life, or financial affairs of friends and partners.

To Mars: Sharpens the mind, bringing an added measure of common sense to all affairs; impatience may lead to ill-considered actions.

To Jupiter: Chances to expand the mind through travel or study; hard aspects may warn of dishonest practices, libel or legal troubles.

To Saturn: Dealing with feelings of not being mentally up to scratch; confidence undermined through a gloomy outlook; ambitious ideas.

To Uranus: An acute state of mental excitement; increasingly outspoken – and probably less popular; strained family relations.

To Neptune: Inspires the imagination; new ideas lead to a broadening of horizons, or mental confusion results in self-deception.

To Pluto: An inquisitive mind; a perfect time to embark on any work involving in-depth research; consumed by self-destructive notions.

Operating as it does in the realm of the mind, the effects of Mercury tend to be less visible than those of other planets. But just because its progressions may not be immediately obvious does not mean they should be ignored. In fact, progressions to or from Mercury often coincide with specific developments – such as travel, a change of residence, or the start of a commercial venture – which affect not only our state of mind, but the way we choose to live our lives in the future.

progressions of venus

To Venus: Without other progressions or transits to point the way, this progression is thought to be more or less insignificant.

To Mars: Emotionally impulsive and prone to 'love at first sight' encounters; a danger that the heart may rule the head; if reason prevails, a more balanced attitude to relationships is on the cards.

To Jupiter: Prosperity, comfort and emotional fulfilment are the 'positive' benefits of this progression, although it is equally possible to fritter away opportunities and end up with nothing.

To Saturn: Often coincides with a strong, permanent relationship – sometimes with someone older; good for investment, but can also indicate financial hardship; leant on by friends and loved ones.

To Uranus: Unexpected financial benefits – or losses; sudden friendships or love affairs; breakdowns in relationships and upheavals on the home front, forcing one to become more independent.

To Neptune: Greater emotional sensitivity to others; idealized feelings of love can lead to romantic infatuation – and possible deception; a risk of falling for 'get-rich-quick' schemes.

To Pluto: An intense, all-consuming affair that is fraught with obstacles; emotional upsets which dramatically alter one's sense of values; learning to love unconditionally; discovering hidden talents.

Although Venus is traditionally the goddess of love, progressions involving this planet do not necessarily mean wedding bells. While it is fair to say that when other progressions or transits bear them out, Venus progressions may well coincide with marriage or a major new love affair, this is because Venus itself embodies the principle of balance and harmony – a condition we most commonly experience when in love.

When this sense of inner well-being is completely absent from a relationship, we might just as easily expect progressions involving Venus to redress the balance – even if initially, this means a painful break-up.

progressions of mars

To Mars: Only the semi-sextile and semi-square are possible in an average lifespan, and their meaning is not clear.

To Jupiter: An increase in drive and initiative can bring gains – especially good for expanding the business; marriage in a woman's chart; losses through lack of restraint; ill-judged risks.

To Saturn: Something of an endurance test – with both hard and soft aspects, progress is slow; issues that demand courage, or which call on one to prove oneself; a time to focus on the bare necessities.

To Uranus: Unexpected opportunities for 'overnight' success; often an exciting, adventurous time highlighting the need to be resourceful in the face of unforeseen circumstances; rash behaviour and accidents.

To Neptune: Favourable for artistic inspiration; the hard aspects often bring out escapist tendencies; attractions to peculiar – even deceptive – people or beliefs.

To Pluto: Total resolve in all actions, which may come across to others as ruthless determination; situations in which negative emotions such as anger or fanaticism have to be confronted.

When Mars becomes active by progression, whichever part of our lives is stirred by its arrival certainly won't be dull – and may never be the same again! Traditionally, Mars was seen as an 'evil' influence, and even the soft aspects were given a luke-warm reception by astrologers. But although the energies symbolized by Mars can easily be disruptive if we fail to channel them constructively, when handled wisely, they can also give us the strength of will to move mountains.

Discover how, by comparing a couple's charts, you can learn a great deal about what makes their relationship tick

Where personal relationships are concerned, the birthchart alone is of limited value. It may show what we seek in the world, and how we set about finding it, but it cannot reveal the flip side of the coin – in other words, what the world seeks in us. Astrology's solution to this dilemma is both simple and effective. By comparing the charts of the people involved in a process called *Synastry*, it becomes possible to build up a picture of the unique qualities of their relationship – for better or for worse.

There are several techniques for comparing the astrology between two (or more) people, one of which – the *composite chart* - involves merging the separate birthcharts into one (ideally, with the aid of a computer). Happily, the most commonly used method of synastry is much less complicated. You simply draw up the two birthcharts in the usual way, then look at the aspects formed between their respective planets and Angles.

In theory, any two charts can be compared – between friends, business partners, parent and child, teacher and pupil, or even boss and company! Not surprisingly, though, the greatest demand for synastry tends to come from would-be lovers, or people in long-term relationships.

How to Use Synastry

Synastry is a symbolic language which shows how people 'talk' to each other on many different levels – some of them conscious, some of them not. It can pinpoint areas of mutual attraction or tension, and suggest ways of resolving problems, but it cannot reveal whether a relationship is 'meant to be', or even how long it will last; that rests on how much the two people involved want the relationship to work!

The theory is that an abundance of hard aspects in synastry may create too many blocks for the relationship to survive, while a proliferation of soft aspects implies harmony and mutual understanding. However, this guideline should not be followed rigidly.

There are many examples of couples with supposedly disastrous, synastry who manage to pull through against all apparent odds. Similarly, a host of gentle aspects is no guarantee of a strong or lasting relationship; it can just as easily suggest a relationship that will disintegrate at the first sign of trouble, or run out of steam as soon as the initial flurry of passion is exhausted.

Bearing these limitations in mind, the best way for a beginner to approach chart comparison is to employ the same step-by-step procedure as that used for interpreting an ordinary birthchart.

STEP 1

Before making any comparisons, start by assessing the main focal points of each chart. In particular, look at the signs, sign rulers and any planets (as well as the aspects to them) that fall in the Seventh and Eighth Houses of each chart. Although neither House can be considered in total isolation, both have a major bearing on what sort of relationships we seek.

STEP 2

Using the blank aspect grid given in Starfile – Drawing Up a Birthchart 4, fill in all the aspects between the two charts. Beginners should concentrate on the major aspects, and use the standard orbs.

In the process make a note of the balance of Elements and Qualities between the charts. These show at a very basic level what each of us tends to look for in another – usually to compensate for what is actually missing in ourselves.

This is especially true when one or both charts shows a relative emphasis/lack of one or more Elements or Qualities.

STEP 3

Next, look at the Angles and see where they fall in each other's charts. It is safe to say that no relationship will get very far without planetary contacts from one person's planets to the other's Angles, and this applies to both the Ascendant-Descendant and the MC-IC axis.

Aspects between the Ascendant rulers are important, as they throw light on the nature of the couple's attraction. Contacts between their Angles – for example, when the Ascendant of one conjuncts the Ascendant or MC of the other – are also significant, as these reflect similarities of outlook on life.

STEP 4

Compare the signs and House positions of the so-called personal planets – the Sun, Moon, Mercury, Venus and Mars. These represent the basic thrust of the relationship, and show how and in what area, the feelings, emotions and mental attitudes of one party affect and influence those of the other.

While Mercury is said to be 'neutral', strong aspects between the 'male' planets (the Sun and Mars) and 'female' planets (the Moon and Venus) are the clearest indicators of sexual attraction. For an affair of the heart to get off the ground, there must be some form of contact between the male and female planets – whether the aspects are hard or soft.

STEP 5

Finally, repeat the same process for the outer planets – Jupiter to Pluto. Aspects between these are not critical unless their position in one or other of the charts is especially powerful (for example, on, or ruling, the Ascendant). Even so, they should not be ignored, since they can throw light on issues which arise as a result of age differences.

Aspects from the outer to the personal planets must always be considered in synastry. They symbolize deep and powerful emotional responses within the relationship which at times may be almost compulsive. In fact, the way these energies are handled will, to a large extent, determine whether the relationship stands or falls by the wayside.

The following pages provide you with a detailed interpretation guide to help you put the theories and techniques of synastry into practice.

Discover the precise meanings of aspects made between the Sun, Moon and Mercury in two charts

As in birthchart interpretation, you have to tread cautiously when following the 'rules' governing synastry – the comparison of two charts. By tradition, for example, the most highly prized sign of compatibility was when a man's Sun aspected a woman's Moon – preferably by conjunction. If the woman's Sun also happened to touch the man's Moon, this was held to be the perfect union.

The danger of following this principle to the letter, though, can be seen by looking at the pairing of a Sun-Leo, Moon-Scorpio man with a Sun-Scorpio, Moon-Leo woman. Even if these planets do not actually form squares to each other natally, or between the two charts, they are still square by sign – and being Fixed signs, they constitute a highly formidable combination.

It might be that the combined energies of the planets blend naturally. But equally, they could signify a high level of competition and emotional tension within the relationship. Beyond the perfectly reasonable observation that this particular mixture is the planetary equivalent of dynamite, there is little more that can be said without referring back to the couple's birthcharts to see what each of them is looking to contribute to the relationship.

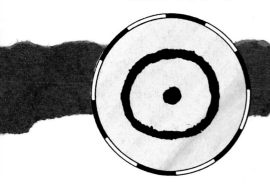

sun contacts

In synastry, the Sun is a vitally important agent in the 'glue' of a relationship. But that does not mean one partner's Sun has to be compatible with the other's for the relationship to hold together. Admittedly it helps if the two Suns make soft aspects to one another, or failing that, fall in mutually sympathetic signs. But if they don't, it is by no means the end of the world.

Just as important are the aspects made between the couple's Suns and their other planets. As the bringer of light, the Sun of one person energizes the planets it aspects in the other's chart, and it is these aspects which give the relationship its sense of purpose. Without strong solar contacts, neither partner is likely to have a lasting effect on the other one, and the two will probably drift apart.

In most cases, a smattering of hard aspects (preferably involving both Suns, to keep the balance even) is just what is needed to give a stimulating, dynamic twist to the relationship. On the other hand, too many will create friction which in time may become intolerable.

By contrast, a relationship with mostly soft solar aspects will have a sense of ease and spontaneity, but may also lack direction. Even though the attraction is likely to be a strong one, there may not be enough tension to make it binding. A healthy spread of hard and soft aspects means that there is incentive to change and grow with each experience – and to do so with confidence.

To the Sun: The conjunction can either bring harmony, or the kind of friction that comes through being too similar. Soft aspects blend most easily, although they may lack the dynamic tension of a square, or the balanced viewpoint of an opposition.

To the Moon: A traditional indicator of a strong physical attraction, as well as friendship – especially with the conjunction. With the hard aspects, the initial pull is likely to fade if the Sun becomes too overbearing, while the Moon may be seen as indecisive and moody.

To Mercury: A stimulating mental rapport with many interests in common. Differences of opinion implied by the hard aspects need not become a problem providing each is prepared to hear the other out.

To Venus: An excellent sign of sexual attraction, especially if the woman's Sun contacts the man's Venus. Of the hard aspects, only the square and inconjunction indicate possible tension in affections.

To Mars: Action-packed and volatile, this is not for the faint-hearted. The hard aspects in particular need outlets to vent anger. Often a strong pull when the man's Sun contacts the woman's Mars.

To Jupiter: All aspects point to opportunities to learn from one another. There is mutual support with the soft aspects, whereas more effort is needed to tolerate differences with the hard aspects.

To Saturn: Sombre Saturn can quickly deflate the Sun's confidence, and both sides may have to swallow some painful truths. With patience the Sun can energize Saturn and learn self-discipline in return.

To Uranus: A sudden, magnetic attraction which is likely to be short-lived if the novelty proves too much. A mixture offering the chance to open up to new ideas on relating; never likely to be dull.

To Neptune: The Sun is beguiled and nurtured by Neptune, the spell breaking only when reality forces both sides to face up to more worldly matters. A risk of falling into saviour-victim roles.

To Pluto: Pluto can either raise the Sun's level of awareness, or indulge in power games. Change on a deep level is probable with this contact, although it is likely to be resisted if the pace is forced.

To the Ascendant-Descendant: A combination that is likely to have a powerful impact. Even though this is one of the traditional signs of compatibility, each can end up blaming the other for joint failures!

To the MC-IC: The Sun often identifies strongly with issues concerning the other person's MC-IC axis, although it might just as easily be tempted to hog the limelight.

moon contacts

The Moon represents our emotional response to (and expectations of) life at a very basic level. Our 'gut' feeling when we first meet someone, or the type of person we instinctively feel drawn to, reveals a great deal about our own lunar energy. But the astrological reasons as to why a particular relationship seems to 'make' people behave the way they do only become clear when we compare the positions and aspects of the Moons in the couple's charts.

Light and Dark

It is worth bearing in mind that psychologically, the Moon in a relationship has both a light and a dark side. And since it also tends to reflect the nature of any planets which it aspects in the other person's chart, there are times when it is hard to know who is triggering which reaction in whom! As a rule, soft aspects from one person's Moon to the other's speak of a strong emotional bond, based on intuitive understanding and an urge to protect and support one another. But soft aspects can also encourage one or both parties to indulge in compulsive habits (usually connected with unconscious behaviour patterns from the past) which may prove hard to break.

Hard aspects point to areas in the relationship where feelings of inhibition or rejection are likely to surface. The intense feelings involved mean that there is no soft option: these issues will eventually have to be faced and resolved one way or another.

To the Moon: Contacts between Moons are like tuning into an emotional frequency. The soft aspects – and also the conjunction – show that the signals between both sides are being received loud and clear; with such mutual sensitivity, it is second nature to adjust to one another's moods. Although there are distinct signs of 'interference' with the opposition, there is usually enough give and take in the relationship to outweigh the differences. The squares are extremely difficult to handle because something is felt to be missing at a deep level and neither side ever feels truly 'at home' with the other.

To Mercury: There is usually an instinctive understanding, plus an ability to air and work out any grievances, with these two planets. The hard aspects denote more tension and less objectivity.

To Venus: All these aspects are extremely positive, bringing a soothing hand to soften any friction elsewhere. With the square, the attraction may be compulsive but feelings will be no less genuine.

To Mars: Highly strung and hot blooded – a relationship where the crockery is likely to fly. Sexual energy is high as well, but it may not be enough to offset the explosive conflicts of the hard aspects.

To Jupiter: These two planets feel good together, offering mutual support and protection. However, this combination also needs space – especially with the hard aspects – to avoid exaggerating differences.

To Saturn: Often an indicator of emotional barriers. Saturn may cause the Moon to close up and feel unwanted, while the Moon may be too intuitive for Saturn. Emotional stability is prized above all else.

To Uranus: An electric, unusual combination which may prove too highly charged after the intitial attraction wears thin. The 'on-off' quality means that nothing is predictable – even the outcome!

To Neptune: Seeking an out-of-the-ordinary relationship, couples with this contact are as likely to lose their way through making unrealistic demands on each other as they are to fulfil their dream!

To Pluto: Symbolizes a journey into unchartered waters which is likely to dredge up deeply buried emotions. This contact offers much but there is also a danger of possessiveness and emotional blackmail.

To the Ascendant-Descendant: Traditionally a sign of strong physical attraction, but the emotional bond is also powerful. Often this contact stirs strong feelings of 'deja vu', even with the square.

To the MC-IC: The Moon is usually tremendously supportive of the MC-IC partner, relating instinctively to (and often blending in with) his or her deepest feelings. The square points to family interference.

mercury contacts

While the other personal planets are traditionally regarded as symbolizing classically 'male' or 'female' energies in synastry, Mercury is often described as a 'neutral' or non-sexual planet. But this is misleading, for the Messenger of the Gods is certainly no eunuch when it comes to romantic or sexual encounters! Often he makes his presence felt from the moment Cupid's arrow strikes its target. He is 'responsible', among other things, for the oily charms of the seducer, and it is he who is absent when we open our mouths only to be lost for words.

Mercury contacts in synastry reveal whether we are likely to have a good mental rapport with our partner, the kind of mutual interests we enjoy, and whether or not we share the same sense of humour – one of the greatest aphrodisiacs of all. Easy contacts may also symbolize an unspoken understanding – almost as if, to quote one astrologer, 'we naturally learn to speak each other's language'.

Even if we are not tuned into each other intuitively, positive Mercury contacts show that a relationship is unlikely to break down due to poor communications! – and as long as couples talk, there is always a chance that problems can be sorted out. Difficult aspects from one Mercury to another often show themselves more clearly once the physical side of the relationship has settled down. It is at this stage that people often discover if there is something to build on.

To Mercury: Soft aspects and the conjunction are particularly important in synastry, as they show mental compatibility and the likelihood of shared interests outside the bedroom! The opposition gives objectivity and an ability to appreciate the different ways in which one another's minds work; the square and inconjunction may indulge in cutting remarks, and can also prove difficult when it comes to everday decisions or listening to each other's viewpoint.

To Venus: This pairing shows a natural urge to express affections and be sensitive to one another's feelings. There may be a tendency to suppress grievances, though less so with the hard aspects.

To Mars: Sparks are likely to fly, as Mercury and Mars both enjoy locking antlers mentally or letting off steam. With the hard aspects, early passionate disagreements may stop a relationship flowering.

To Jupiter: A strong indication of mental compatibility. Even when they don't see eye to eye, they complement one other – Mercury is good with details, Jupiter likes to orchestrate the overall picture.

To Saturn: Saturn can block Mercury's flow, although this may be just what is needed when Mercury goes into overdrive. Better for business than love, as Saturn may strip away any romantic illusions!

To Uranus: Mentally this is a bit like being connected to a live wire. Both planets stimulate each other to question and challenge accepted beliefs. Likely to be exciting, but with the hard aspects there is a habit of taking the opposite view just for the sake of it.

To Neptune: Rational Mercury is easily overwhelmed by Neptune's formless, and often unreachable, world. Communication may be almost telepathic and the exchange of ideas inspired. But just as often there is impracticality, confusion or downright lying.

To Pluto: At their best, Pluto and Mercury combine to unearth what makes a relationship tick. With the hard aspects, old prejudices and patterns of thinking may have to be faced. It is important that both sides learn to accept the other's views in the process.

To the Ascendant-Descendant: This combination stresses the importance of a marriage of minds. Sometimes a couple may think as one, but they may also be drawn to the kind of healthy disagreements that stimulate debate – although with the square, they may easily become too analytical for their own good.

To the MC-IC: An extremely positive combination in business. In love, life is likely to be stimulating – and with the square, maybe even controversial. Other factors will show if the difference in opinions is serious enough to have a major effect on the relationship.

Taking a detailed look at the aspects formed by Venus, Mars and the outer planets

In the excitement of comparing planetary aspects between two charts to see whether or not they are compatible, it is all too easy to overlook other important synastry factors – especially the signs and houses. For example, an enticing trine between a man's Mars in Aries and a woman's Venus in Leo is not just different in substance from the same trine in Taurus and Virgo. There would also be a subtle change of emphasis if the signs were reversed – with his Mars in Leo and her Venus in Aries. Similarly, the balance of sexual and emotional energy would shift if his Venus were in Aries and her Mars in Leo. It may not weaken the attraction, but it would be interesting to speculate as to who wore the trousers in the relationship!

The same careful consideration must be given to precisely where one person's planets fall in the other's chart. For example, Venus in the partner's Second House will not have the same 'effect' as when it falls in the Fifth. The first denotes a shared interest in the good and beautiful things in life; the second will really fire up the couple's sexual chemistry!

On the other hand, if a Venus-Pluto square happens to fall between the partner's Second and Fifth Houses, the affairs of both houses will be brought into play. In this case, the relationship might have to deal with issues of possessiveness on both a material and romantic level.

venus contacts

Venus represents the principle of attraction, and also its opposite – repulsion! Its main function in the birthchart is to sort out our likes from our dislikes at every level – a process we tend to feel most acutely when we are attracted to someone else. But although Venus may show us where our heart's desire lies, it does not produce any tangible results on its own. Being passive by nature, Venus in synastry needs to contact one of the would-be partner's 'active' planets for the attraction to lead anywhere.

Aspects from Venus to the partner's Sun, Mars or Angles were traditionally thought to offer the best odds on an attraction developing into something more substantial than a mere fluttering of hearts. Nowadays, astrologers consider the outer planets to be powerful magnets, too.

Mutual Satisfaction

Soft aspects from Venus to a partner's planets or Angles show that the couple enjoy each other's company, and share similar tastes and values. If Mars is involved in the synastry, there is also a strong probability that the couple will be sexually compatible.

A surfeit of hard aspects to Venus is commonly found in love affairs that have an 'eyes met across the table' quality about them. The attraction is usually compulsive, pushing one (if not both) partners to behave destructively, though on the positive side, relationships as intense as these can in some cases lead to a deeper level of self-awareness.

To Venus: Couples with a conjunction or soft aspects tend to find each other's company soothing. Those with hard aspects may not share the same values, but are still likely to find each other appealing. The differences signified by hard Venus aspects rarely become serious unless other factors also point in this direction.

To Mars: Mars arouses Venus' desires. Contacts here indicate tremendous magnetic attraction and show how a relationship functions physically. With soft aspects, the physical and emotional side of the relationship will be well balanced. With hard aspects, the sexual atmosphere may be steamier – perhaps compulsively so at times.

To Jupiter: All these contacts promise great warmth and affection, although with the conjunction and soft aspects there is a tendency to accept things as they are. The hard aspects put backbone into the relationship in a way that is mutually beneficial.

To Saturn: The classic 'going steady' relationship – cool and reliable. Feelings are genuine but largely inhibited. Hard aspects often hint at 'bad timing'; the attraction is there but somehow the relationship never gets off the ground. This combination can also show great commitment, but not necessarily for the right reasons.

To Uranus: Zappy Uranus can wreak havoc with Venus' sense of values – often in a thrilling way. This planetary pairing brings a spirit of exploration to a relationship, and any attempt to settle into a cosy routine is likely to end in tears. The unexpected ups and downs – particularly with the hard aspects – may be too much for some.

To Neptune: These highly idealistic contacts point to a search for the 'beautiful' partner which as often as not ends in shattered dreams – especially with the hard aspects. A planetary duet which often starts with a romantic fanfare, only to find the harsher truths of the affair disappointing. Can inspire tremendous feelings of love.

To Pluto: There is nothing lightweight these contacts. Venus and Pluto are both adept at playing power games in love, and a relationship with this pairing often has a compulsive love-hate or manipulative side to it. With the hard aspects, the compulsion is often unconscious and only becomes clear after the couple have parted.

To the Ascendant-Descendant: Traditionally one of the best signs of compatibility. Both sides are affectionate and want to give what the other needs. With the square, Venus offers the other half a break from life's toils, though both draw strength from just being together.

To the MC-IC: Often prominent in the charts of people who look good together in public. With Venus on the partner's IC, the emphasis is likely to be more on enjoying each other's company in private.

mars contacts

Mars represents quite the opposite energy to Venus. On a psychological level it shows our need to be our 'own person', whereas Venus symbolizes our desire to link arms with someone else. In synastry the balance between these two forces is critical in deciding whether the relationship is likely to be harmonious or unstable.

Balancing Act

When Mars is prominent in synastry, the chances are that one or both sides will be more concerned with looking after their own interests than supporting the other. On the other hand, few or no aspects to Mars suggests a lack of impetus to become involved at all – even if other synastry contacts indicate a strong attraction!

Soft aspects from Mars to the partner's chart imply that the couple are temperamentally well suited and have compatible sex drives – especially if Venus and Jupiter are in the picture. With the possible exception of aspects to Saturn or Neptune, both sides should gain individually from being together.

Hard aspects – and with Mars, this includes the conjunction – do not mean that the relationship is doomed to failure, but it is vital that the energies of Mars are not suppressed, otherwise the pressures may become intolerable. Often sexual energy is extremely high, providing an outlet for bottled-up feelings. However, there is also a danger that passions may run out of control, or simply be 'out of synch'.

To Mars: The impulsive energies of Mars can prove quite a handful when they combine in synastry. The hard aspects often point to tempestuous emotions and a spirit of confrontation. Sexual energy is high, but there is often a lack of tenderness. With the soft aspects – and to a lesser extent the conjunction – passions continue to be easily stirred, but with more consideration for the other party.

To Jupiter: Releases great physical energy, although there is a meeting of minds as well. Jupiter has faith in Mars' ambitions, while Mars can make Jupiter more dynamic and active, as well as finding outlets for their combined energies. Sexually, this is a compatible blend – particularly with the conjunction and soft aspects.

To Saturn: The direct opposite to Mars-Jupiter, bringing feelings of frustration and a sense that both hot and cold taps are running at the same time! Saturn thinks Mars is too self-centred, while Mars finds Saturn harsh and obstructive. The truth is that with all the aspects, both sides must give each other plenty of room to breathe if there is to be any chance of a lasting relationship.

To Uranus: This combination often occurs between two people seeking (consciously or not) to break away from previous relationship patterns. The attraction is usually immediate, extremely physical and off-beat. A once-in-a-lifetime affair that may not last, but has a lasting effect, opening the door to a new way of relating.

To Neptune: These are difficult energies to work with. Mars gets befogged by Neptune's other-worldliness, while Neptune finds it hard to appreciate Mars 'go out and prove yourself' approach. The combined effect is rather like a hall of mirrors in which the relationship becomes distorted through a total lack of mutual undersatnding.

To Pluto: This combination frequently starts off as an unconscious power struggle in which Pluto seeks to dominate Mars, who in turn tries to get Pluto to show his cards. Both sides have to prove themselves right – though less compulsively with the soft aspects. At times the relationship may resemble a battlefield, in which case the powerful sexual attraction may not be strong enough to sustain it.

To the Ascendant-Descendant: These aspects tend to magnify other factors in the chart. The effect on the relationship depends on whether the couple see themselves primarily as a team or (especially with the square) as individuals. Probably best in a working relationship where disagreements can be kept under tight rein!

To the MC-IC: Mars can help the MC-IC partner make it in the world or be fiercely competitive. Similarly, home may be a stimulating environment, or a cauldron of arguments and accusations! This combination demands a spirit of compromise to be of mutual benefit.

CHAPTER 3

contacts between the slower planets

In synastry, aspects between Jupiter, Saturn and the outer planets are less significant than aspects from these slower moving bodies to the 'personal' planets.

In the case of Uranus, Neptune and Pluto this is not surprising: they travel around the zodiac so slowly that most couples either have them in the same sign, or in the sign next door. Only if there is a big age gap will they make substantially different aspects from those in the birthchart.

Yet although aspects between the slower moving planets may have little to say about how a relationship gets off the ground, they can reveal a great deal about what keeps it together or pulls it apart. Contacts between Jupiter and the partner's outer planets, for example, raise a relationship's expectations. There is an optimistic, fun-loving streak which keeps things on an even keel, although hard aspects can also bring out Jupiter's extravagant side.

Saturn, by contrast, restricts or inhibits any planet it contacts, and can unfortunately kill all the romance and spontaneity. Yet Saturn also has the power to bring a relationship down to earth and teach some important lessons about living together – the kind of lessons that most of us need to learn from time to time!

jupiter contacts

To Jupiter: Even if the aspects are hard, these contacts usually signify that both sides are likely to broaden the other's mind.

To Saturn: Despite symbolizing opposite principles of growth and limitation, these planets combine well and balance each other out.

To Uranus: Hard aspects make Jupiter over-reach himself, though soft aspects and the conjunction often indicate a telepathic link.

To Neptune: Denotes great sensitivity. Good for sharing one another's spiritual goals, but poor for day-to-day practical matters!

To Pluto: Relationships with this pairing often have a deep level of understanding; the hard aspects may point to a lack of co-operation.

To the Angles: Whatever the outcome, these aspects suggest that the relationship offers a valuable opportunity for mutual growth.

saturn contacts

To Saturn: Shows how both parties deal with the other's inhibitions and insecurities, and what kind of ambitions they share.

To Uranus: Usually indicates tension through Uranus being too rebellious and Saturn too restrictive for each other's liking.

To Neptune: Slippery Neptune is too elusive for Saturn, who can be too rigid for Neptune; the conjunction may help dreams become reality.

To Pluto: Although Saturn might feel threatened by Pluto, and Pluto distanced by Saturn, this pair can survive great hardship.

To the Angles: Saturn can either be a restrictive influence or bring a much-needed sense of structure and stability to the partner's life.

Uranus: This planet tends to disrupt any attempt to settle into a conventional relationship; an unstable influence with the square.

Neptune: Can indicate an inspired, spiritual bond, or an affair which loses itself in a web of illusion, false hopes and deception!

Pluto: Deep, fascinating and intense, Pluto usually acts on an unconscious level as an agent of transformation or destruction.

CALCULATIONS

Perhaps you have chosen to start here, or perhaps your curiosity has been aroused and you have decided to get to grips with the fundamentals of astrology.

Drawing up charts by hand may seem a daunting prospect for the novice astrologer. And with computer programmes and charts so easily available you might wonder why you should bother with it at all. But there are good reasons.

Why Bother?

Firstly, learning to cast a chart by hand enables you to verify a machine calculated one. Even machines make mistakes, and without this foundation knowledge you may be unable to spot them.

Secondly, the process facilitates a deeper understanding of the chart as a whole. As it takes shape, you begin grasp the principles of astrology in a practical way. Like a butterfly emerging from a chrysalis, the chart unfolds its secrets step by step. The glyphs and

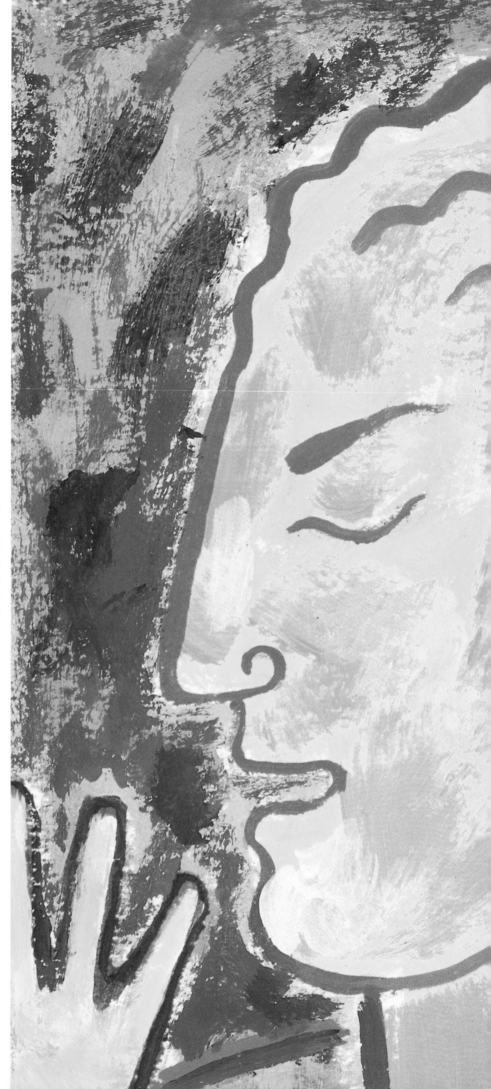

symbols begin to form a meaningful language.

And when you learn how to plot transits, or progress the chart, you can more easily see those patterns as part of a cycle too. You can see where a transit has been in the past, and where it is heading on its journey around the chart. You can see clearly that a progressed chart is a development of the natal map, and not simply a frozen entity on a computer print out.

Indeed, some astrologers regard drawing the chart as a meditation, as the moment when thoughtful interpretation begins. Certainly, a well-drawn chart is a beautiful thing in itself. And even if you eventually opt for a computerised short cut, you will never be at the mercy of a machine. You will have studied a new language, and understood its ancient roots to which you can always return.

A step-by-step calculation guide to your own birthchart, planetary progressions and transits

Sooner or later, anyone with a developing interest in astrology wants to interpret their birthchart – and probably other people's too! But how do you get one drawn up?

Today, there are three options, each of which has its pros and cons. Option 1 involves getting someone else to do it for you, Option 2 is only feasible if you own a computer. Option 3 involves calculating the chart yourself, which is time-consuming but not as difficult as some people think. This chapter shows you how to tackle the mathematical process in easy-to-manage stages.

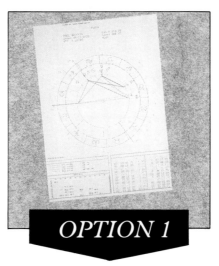

OPTION 1

Nowadays it is possible to have your chart calculated (and usually interpreted, too) by one of the many computer 'read-out' companies. The cost of a basic calculation can be offset against the time taken and books needed to do it yourself.

Computer interpretations are fun, and very accurate as far as they go. The drawback is that computers can only ever give a standard description of what the various planetary combinations in your chart mean.

For a deeper understanding of the way these combinations refer specifically to you and your life, you must either learn to interpret them yourself or visit a professional astrologer.

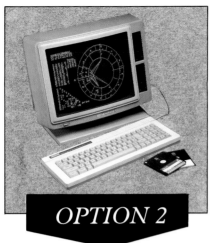

OPTION 2

If you own a personal computer (eg Amstrad PCW, IBM PC, Amstrad 1640) and you want to study astrology seriously, a chart calculation program could prove an excellent investment. Most practising astrologers find them indispensable, since they will draw up and print out all kinds of charts at the touch of a button and save the details on file. Good calculation programs are readily available, and some also have interpretation programs which

you can 'add on' at extra cost. All these programs are widely advertised in the specialist computer or astrology press.

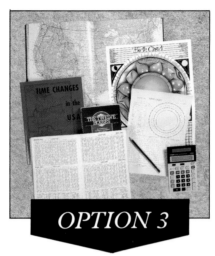

OPTION 3

This is the old method – calculating and drawing up the chart by hand. At first sight it can appear a little daunting, but in fact the maths are not that complicated. The only serious drawback is the number of reference books you need to obtain before you can start drawing up the chart.

The essential books are:
An Ephemeris for the positions of the planets for each day, either at noon or midnight. One is included at the back of this book, plus Tables of Houses for the Northern Latitudes.
A Table of Houses for working out where the Ascendant, Midheaven and House cusps fall.
An Atlas giving the longitude and latitude of major cities and towns around the world.
A Book of Time Changes around the world. There are in fact three – one for the USA, one for Canada and Mexico, and one for the rest of the world. With any luck, you should find some of these books in the second hand section of a reasonable occult bookshop. You also need:
● Some blank charts (these are easily available from occult bookshops; it is very tedious drawing up your own).
● A calculator (ideally one which will work in hours and minutes).

CONSULTING AN ASTROLOGER

Plenty of astrologers advertise in the specialist magazines, but if you know someone who has been before, and whose judgement you trust, personal recommendation is probably the most reliable way to choose one.

The astrologer will need to know your date, time and place of birth. If you do not know your time of birth, it is possible to have a reading based on a chart set up for noon on the day you were born. This will not be as precise as a proper chart, but should still reveal some of your basic personality traits. It may even provide a platform for the astrologer to deduce your birth time by working back through the major events in your life. However, this process – called rectification – is time-consuming, and therefore costly.

Most chart readings take the form of face-to-face interviews. Remember that astrology is not the same as clairvoyance, although all good astrologers are highly intuitive. Your chart is not a record of all your thoughts and deeds, but a coded list of your potential strengths and limitations.

In order to crack the code, an astrologer has to establish which areas of your personality you have developed, and which seem to be as yet untapped. Most astrologers take between 1–1½ hours to give a personal consultation. Prices vary considerably, so do check first.

Face-to-face consultations enable astrologers to blend basic chart data with their own intuition.

Place, Date and Time

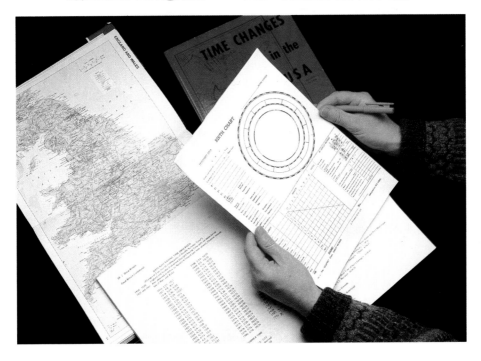

Having decided to calculate a birthchart yourself and assembled the necessary equipment (see part 1 of the course), start by sorting out the data.

The Birth Place. If this is a large city or town, look it up in an atlas and find its *latitude* (expressed as degrees/minutes – °/' – North or South of the Equator) and *longitude* (expressed as degrees/minutes East or West of the Greenwich Meridian).

If you cannot find the exact place, you have no choice but to take the nearest town and then 'guesstimate'.

The Birth Date. Note this down, writing the name of the month out in full to avoid confusion – eg 25th April 1970. Note, when only digits are used, the month may be given before the day – eg in the USA, 4/12/73 means 12th April, not 4th December.

The Birth Time. Write this down using the 24 hour clock to avoid confusion – eg 5.30pm = 17:30 **Now double-check your data.**

STAGE 1

Converting the time

The first stage of birthchart calculation is to convert the time given in the birth data to Greenwich Mean Time (GMT) – the standard on which all world times are based, and the time quoted in all astrological tables.

Step 1: Establish time of birth
If you were born in the UK you are lucky. Britain has worked on GMT since 1880, so all you have to do is make an allowance for *Daylight Saving* (see step 3).

Most other countries work on zone standards based on GMT (see map). Thus, the time in Bangkok is seven hours **ahead** of GMT (+7); the time in New York is five hours **behind** GMT (–5). However, some countries only switched to zone standard time relatively recently. Before that they used *Local Mean Time* (LMT), based on the sun's position relative to their own country (as did the UK before 1880). And in the USA, some states (and even counties) have changed their time zones from year to year.

Because of this confusing situation, the only way to be absolutely sure what time standard is or was in force for places abroad is to consult the various time change books. There is one for the USA, one for Canada and Mexico, and another covering the rest of the world.

Step 2: Convert to GMT
If your birth time is in a zone standard **ahead** of GMT, then all you need do to convert it is

subtract the number of hours quoted for that zone.

Example: Bangkok is 7hr ahead of GMT. A time of 14.34 Bangkok local time thus becomes 07.34 GMT (14.34 – 7hr).

If your birth time is in a zone standard **behind** GMT, then to convert it **add** the number of hours quoted for that zone.

Example: New York is 5hr behind GMT. A time of 14.34 New York local time thus becomes 19.34 GMT (14.34 + 5hr).

If your birth time is quoted as LMT, you can calculate the GMT on the basis that the sun moves 1° of longitude every 4 min.

Example: for a time of 14.34 LMT Moscow on 30th December 1925:
- *Find the longitude for Moscow (= 37° 42'W)*
- *Use the table in your time change book to find out how long the sun takes to travel from Moscow to Greenwich (= 2hr 30min 48sec).*
- *Subtract 2hr 30min 48sec from LMT (14.34.00). This gives a final result of 12.03.12 GMT*

Step 3: Check Daylight Saving.
Daylight Saving (eg 'British Summer Time') has been in force on and off around the world for years. The table given below left shows British Daylight Saving dates. For other countries, check your time change books.

Where the tables say '+1', this means local time was one hour ahead of the zone standard time for the date shown. So if a '+' figure is given, **subtract** it from the adjusted time. In certain cases (eg World War 2) some countries adopted 'Double Summer Time'. **Subtract** 2 hours from the adjusted time.

Example: on 19 June 1955, British Summer Time (+1) was in force. Therefore, for a local time of 05.45, subtract 1 hr = 04.45 GMT.

Note: After performing these calculations, you may find that the GMT time carries the Birth Date back to the day before or forward to the day after. Either way, be sure to use this new *GMT date* for all further calculations – not the given birth date.

DATE PLACE AND TIME

DATE/PLACE

	d	m	y
Birth Date			
Birth Place			
Latitude (N/S)			
Longitude (E/W)			

TIME

	h	m	s
Birth Time as given			
Zone Standard (+E -W LMT)			
Allowance for Daylight Saving			
GMT Time			
(Adjusted GMT Date)			

Use the blank chart above as a guide when converting the time (or photocopy this page). Shown right is a filled-in example for Paris.

DATE/PLACE
	d	m	y
Birth Date		25 April 1970	
Birth Place		Paris, France	
Latitude (N/S)		48° 50' N	
Longitude (E/W)		2° 20' E	

TIME
	h	m	s
Birth Time as given	18	48	
Zone Standard (+E -W LMT)		+1 (subtract)	
Allowance for Daylight Saving		(not used in 1970)	
GMT Time	17	48	
(Adjusted GMT Date)		—	

DAYLIGHT SAVING TIMES

Change at 2 am except * = change at 3 am ** = change at 12 am

1916–1920: Daylight Saving only observed in England and Scotland.

1921–onwards: Daylight Saving also observed by N. Ireland, Channel Islands, Isle of Man and Wales

1916 (+1) 21/5–1/10	1949 (+1) 3/4–30/10
1917 (+1) 8/4–17/9	1950 (+1) 16/4–22/10
1918 (+1) 24/3–30/9	1951 (+1) 15/4–21/10
1919 (+1) 30/3–29/9	1952 (+1) 20/4–26/10
1920 (+1) 28/3–25/10	1953 (+1) 19/4–4/10
1921 (+1) 3/4–3/10	1954 (+1) 11/4–3/10
1922 (+1) 26/3–8/10	1955 (+1) 17/4–2/10
1923 (+1) 22/4–16/9	1956 (+1) 22/4–7/10
1924 (+1) 13/4–21/9	1957 (+1) 14/4–6/10
1925 (+1) 19/4–4/10	1958 (+1) 20/4–5/10
1926 (+1) 18/4–3/10	1959 (+1) 19/4–4/10
1927 (+1) 10/4–2/10	1960 (+1) 10/4–2/10
1928 (+1) 22/4–7/10	1961 (+1) 26/3–29/10
1929 (+1) 25/4–6/10	1962 (+1) 25/3–28/10
1930 (+1) 13/4–5/10	1963 (+1) 31/3–27/10
1931 (+1) 19/4–4/10	1964 (+1) 22/3–25/10
1932 (+1) 17/4–2/10	1965 (+1) 21/3–24/10
1933 (+1) 9/4–8/10	1966 (+1) 20/3–23/10
1934 (+1) 22/4–7/10	1967 (+1) 19/3–29/10
1935 (+1) 14/4–6/10	1968 18/2–1971 31/10 (+1)
1936 (+1) 19/4–4/10	1972 (+1) 19/3–29/10
1937 (+1) 4/4–3/10	1973 (+1) 18/3–28/10
1938 (+1) 10/4–2/10	1974 (+1) 17/3–27/10
1939 (+1) 10/4–19/11	1975 (+1) 16/3–26/10
1940 (+1) 25/2–31/12**	1976 (+1) 21/3–24/10
1941 (+1) 1/1–31/12	1977 (+1) 20/3–23/10
1941 (+2) 4/5–10/8*	1978 (+1) 19/3–29/10
1942 (+1) 1/1–31/12	1979 (+1) 18/3–28/10
1942 (+2) 5/4–9/8*	1980 (+1) 16/3–26/10
1943 (+1) 1/1–31/12	1981 (+1) 29/3–25/10
1943 (+2) 4/4–15/8*	1982 (+1) 28/3–24/10
1944 (+1) 1/1–31/12	1983 (+1) 27/3–23/10
1944 (+2) 2/4–17/9*	1984 (+1) 25/3–28/10
1945 (+1) 1/1–7/10	1985 (+1) 31/3–27/10
1945 (+2) 2/4–15/7*	1986 (+1) 30/3–26/10
1946 (+1) 14/4–6/10	1987 (+1) 29/3–25/10
1947 (+1) 16/3–2/11	1988 (+1) 27/3–23/10
1947 (+2) 13/4–10/8	1989 (+1) 21/3–29/10
1948 (+1) 14/3–31/10	1990 (+1) 25/3–29/10

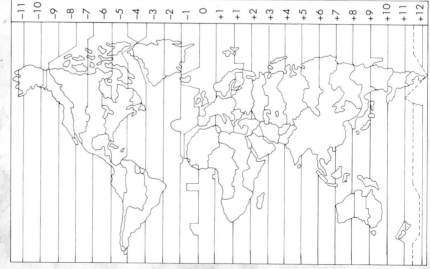

Finding the Ascendant and Midheaven

You find the Ascendant and Midheaven for the birthchart by looking up the Birth Time in a Table of Houses and reading off the relevant degrees. But there is just one snag.

All astrological tables use *Sidereal Time*, which is based on the rotation of the earth relative to the fixed stars and has been used by navigators for centuries. Your adjusted GMT Birth Time is *Tropical Time* ('Clock Time'), which is based on the rotation of the earth relative to the sun.

The difference between a day of Sidereal Time and a day of Tropical Time is 3min 54sec. The two are now so 'out of sync' that they bear no relation to one another, so the next step is to convert the *GMT Time at Birth* to the *Local Sidereal Time at Birth*.

STAGE 2

Convert GMT to Sidereal time

Step 1: Write down the GMT Time at Birth, then below it write the Latitude and Longitude of the Birth Place.

Step 2: Turning to your Ephemeris, look up the Sidereal Time for Midnight (00.00) or Noon (12.00) at Greenwich on the Date of Birth, depending on which one the Ephemeris gives. If you had to adjust the Birth Date, use the adjusted date).

Step 3: Work out the time difference in hours and minutes between the GMT Time at Birth and Midnight (or Noon, if you are using a Noon Ephemeris). This is called the *Interval*.

For a **Midnight** Ephemeris, **add** the Interval to the Sidereal Time you have just looked up.

For a **Noon** Ephemeris, **subtract** the Interval if the GMT Time at Birth is **before** midday; if it is **after** midday, **add** it.

Step 4: To allow for the slight variation between Sidereal and Tropical time during the Interval you have to make one further calculation – astrologers call it the *Acceleration on the Interval*.

Allow 1sec for every 6min of the Interval (ie 10sec per hour). As in Step 3, if you are using a **Midnight** Ephemeris, **add** this to your existing time. If you are using a **Noon** ephemeris, **subtract** it for a time **before** midday; **add** it for a time **after** midday.

Step 5: What you have before you is the *Sidereal Time at Greenwich at Birth*. This figure must now be

157

adjusted to the *Local Sidereal Time at Birth*.

- First work out the distance in degrees Longitude between the Birth Place and Greenwich (0°).
- The sun takes 4min to move through 1° of Longitude. So, if you multiply the distance in degrees and minutes by 4, you get the time difference (in minutes and seconds) between the *Sidereal Time at Greenwich* and the *Local Sidereal Time*. This is called the *Longitude Equivalent in Time* (LET). (Time Change books have tables which get around the need to make this calculation).

Example: To convert 112° 40'E to hours, minutes and seconds east of Greenwich:
112°×4 = 448min = 7hr 28min
40'×4 = 160sec = 2min 40sec
TOTAL = 7hr 30min 40sec

- If the Longitude of the Birth Place is **West** of Greenwich, **subtract** the LET from your Adjusted GMT Time (see part 2); if the Longitude is **East** of Greenwich, **add** it.
- If the figure in front of you is over 24 hours, subtract 24.

You now have the *Local Sidereal Time at Birth*.

SOUTHERN LATITUDES

Tables of Houses are normally only given for Northern latitudes. If the Birth Place is in the Southern Hemisphere, find the Local Sidereal Time at Birth as if it were for the equivalent Northern Latitude, then:

- Add 12 hours. If the total comes to over 24, subtract 24.
- Turn to your Table of Houses and find the column giving the equivalent Northern Latitude.
- Look up the Ascendant and Midheaven, then simply change the signs to their opposites in the zodiac. Thus 3° 4' Gemini becomes 3° 4' Sagittarius; 23° 25' Leo becomes 23° 25' Aquarius.

TIME CALCULATION CHECKLIST

	h	m	s
STEP 1:			
• GMT Time at Birth			
• Latitude/Longitude of Birth Place			
STEP 2:			
• Sidereal Time at Midnight (Noon)			
STEP 3:			
• Interval between Sidereal Time and Birth Time (+ or –)			
RESULT:			
STEP 4:			
• Acceleration on Interval (+ or –)			
STEP 5:			
• Sidereal Time at Greenwich at Birth			
• Longitude Equivalent in Time (+ or –)			
• Local Sidereal Time at Birth			
(subtract 24 hr if necessary)			

Use the checklist as a guide to completing Stage 2. A filled-in example is shown on the right.

TIME CALCULATION CHECKLIST

	h	m	s
STEP 1:			
• GMT Time at Birth		17	48
• Latitude/Longitude of Birth Place	48°50'N 2°20'E		
STEP 2:			
• Sidereal Time at Midnight (Noon)	2	12	21
STEP 3:			
• Interval between Sidereal Time and Birth Time (+ or –)	+5	48	00
RESULT:	8	00	21
STEP 4:			
• Acceleration on Interval (+ or –)	+0	00	58
STEP 5:			
• Sidereal Time at Greenwich at Birth	8	01	19
• Longitude Equivalent in Time (+ or –)	0	09	20
• Local Sidereal Time at Birth	8	10	39
(subtract 24 hr if necessary)			

STAGE 3

Find Ascendant

Step 1: Turn to your Table of Houses. Most Tables only give whole degrees of latitude, so pick the column that most nearly matches the Latitude of the Birth Place (eg for Paris, 48° 50'N = 49°N.) This will give you the Ascendant to within 20', accurate enough for most purposes.

Work down the column to find the Local Sidereal Times immediately **preceding** and **following** the Local Sidereal Time at Birth. Then, work across and note

---

the Ascendant and Midheaven degrees given for **both** times.

Step 2: Subtract the earlier Sidereal Time from the later one and convert the result to seconds. Call this **A**.

Example: 08 12 54
        − 08 08 44
        =   4 10 = 250sec

Step 3: Subtract the earlier Sidereal Time from the Local Sidereal Time at Birth and convert the result to seconds. Call this **B**.

Example: 08 10 34
        − 08 08 44
        =   2 55 = 175sec

Step 4: Subtract the earlier Ascendant degree from the later one and convert the result to minutes ('). Call this **C**.

Example: 24° 05' Libra
        − 23° 20' Libra
        = 0° 45' Libra

Step 5: Subtract the earlier Midheaven degree from the later one and convert the result to minutes (as the Midheaven is given a degree at a time, the result is always 60). Call this **D**.

Step 6: Using a calculator, multiply **B × C** and divide by **A**. Add the result to the earlier Ascendant degree (converted to minutes) to find the **approximate Ascendant degree at birth**.

Example (as above): If A = 250sec, B = 175sec and C = 45',
then 175(B)×45(C)/ 250(A) = 31.5' (say, 32'). Add this to the earlier Ascendant degree (23° 20' Libra) = Asc 23° 52'.

Step 7: Multiply **B×D** and divide by **A**. Add to the earlier Midheaven degree for the **exact Midheaven degree at Birth**.

Example (as above): 175(B)×60(D)/250(A) = 42°. Add this to the earlier Midheaven degree (0° Capricorn) = MC 5° 42' Capricorn.

Placing the Planets

O nce you have found the Ascendant and Midheaven degrees, all you need to complete the birthchart are the positions of the planets. You look these up against the Date of Birth (or the Adjusted Date of Birth, if you have had to adjust it after converting the time) in your Ephemeris. But because the planetary positions will be given for Midnight or Noon (depending on the Ephemeris), you must adjust them for the exact Time of Birth.

The outer planets, from Jupiter onwards, move so slowly that

these adjustments are hardly critical. But the inner planets – especially the Moon – move at a much faster rate, and their motions through the day must be worked out more carefully if the birthchart is to give a true picture.

The method shown here does not give the exact positions (which involves a lot of complicated maths) but is accurate to within a few minutes of a degree. The examples used are again based on our imaginary subject – for a Birth Time of 18.48 (17:48 GMT) on 25th April 1970 in Paris.

STAGE 4

To find a Planet's position

Step 1: Take a large sheet of paper and write down the Interval between the Time of Birth and Midnight (if you are using a Midnight Ephemeris) or Noon (for a Noon Ephemeris).

Step 2: Consult the page in the Ephemeris for the Date of Birth and write down each planet's position on that date. To avoid confusion, note whether they are for Midnight or Noon.

Step 3: So that you can work out how far each planet moves in one day, consult the Ephemeris again and write down the planets' positions for the following day.

> *Example – 25th April 1970:*
> ● *At Noon on 25th April the Moon was at 22° 47' Sagittarius*
> ● *At Noon on 26th April the Moon was at 6° 44' Capricorn*

Step 4: For each planet, subtract the higher figure from the lower one to find the planet's Daily Motion for the day (remember, there are 60 minutes to a degree). Add 30° if the Moon moves into an adjacent sign.

> *Continuing the example:*
> $$36° 44'$$
> $$- 22° 47'$$
> $$= 13° 57' \text{ (or 837')}$$

Step 5: Using a calculator, divide the planet's Daily Motion by 24 to find its Hourly Motion.

> *Continuing the example:*
> *837'/24 = 34.9' per hour*

Step 6: Using a calculator again, multiply the planet's Hourly Motion by the Interval between the Time of Birth and Midnight (Noon) to find its Motion During

---

PLANETARY POSITION CHECKLIST

Interval between Midnight (Noon) and Time of Birth   _____

_____'s position at End of Day (or Noon on day after/before birth)   _____

_____'s position at Start of Day (or Noon on day of birth)   _____

_____'s Daily Motion   _____

_____'s Hourly Motion   _____

Motion During interval   _____

Position at Start of Day (or Noon on Day of Birth)   _____

Position at Time of Birth   _____

Use this checklist as a guide (a sample for Venus is shown right).

the Interval. (To avoid complex sums, round off the interval to the nearest quarter of an hour – eg 22 min goes to 15min = 0.25hr; 23 min goes to 30 min = 0.5 hr).

> *Continuing the example:*
> ● *Interval = 5hr 48min (say, 5.75hr)*
> ● *Hourly motion = 34.9'*
> ● *Motion During Interval = 5.75 × 34.9 = 201' = 3° 21'*

Step 7: Returning to the planet's position for the Date of Birth, adjust it to allow for the Motion During the Interval. For a **Midnight** Ephemeris, **add** the Motion During the Interval; for a **Noon** Ephemeris, **subtract** it for a birth **before** noon, and **add** it for a birth after noon.

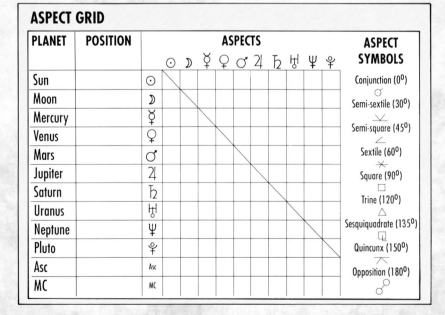

PLANETARY POSITION CHECKLIST

Continuing the example:
● *Position of the Moon at Noon on D.O.B. = 22° 47' Sagittarius*
● *Add Motion During Interval (3° 21') = 26° 08' Sagittarius at exact Time of Birth (17.48 GMT on 25th April 1970)*

Repeat for Mercury, Venus and Mars not forgetting that where the Ephemeris shows a planet to be retrograde, you work backwards through the sign instead of forwards. You will notice that the remaining planets move such a small distance in a day that for most purposes there is no need to work out their Motion During the Interval.

STAGE 5

Complete the Birthchart

Having found all the planets' positions, enter them on the birthchart. At the same time, it is a good idea to check the aspects between the planets and fill these in on an *aspect* grid (most blank birthcharts include one; if not, copy the one shown on the left). This helps to 'register' the aspects in your mind, which makes birthchart interpretation much easier to understand.

ASPECT GRID

PLANET	POSITION	ASPECTS	ASPECT SYMBOLS
		☉ ☽ ☿ ♀ ♂ ♃ ♄ ♅ ♆ ♇	
Sun		☉	Conjunction (0°) ☌
Moon		☽	Semi-sextile (30°) ⚺
Mercury		☿	Semi-square (45°) ∠
Venus		♀	Sextile (60°) ⚹
Mars		♂	Square (90°) □
Jupiter		♃	Trine (120°) △
Saturn		♄	Sesquiquadrate (135°) ⚼
Uranus		♅	Quincunx (150°) ⚻
Neptune		♆	Opposition (180°) ☍
Pluto		♇	
Asc		Asc	
MC		MC	

Copy this blank grid and use it to fill in the aspects.

Calculating Progressions

Learn how to work out the positions of progressed planets and Angles using the tried and tested Solar Arc method

Once you are familiar with the notion that, astrologically speaking, 24 hours equals one year, 'day-for-year' progressions are fairly easy to calculate.

STAGE 1

Progress the chart

Before you draw up a progressed chart for a particular year, you must establish the Progressed Date – the day equivalent to the year in question. For example, if you want to find the positions of the progressed planets for the 21st year (that is, between the 20th

and 21st birthday) of someone born on 25th April 1970, you convert the subject's age in years (20) into days (20) and then add them to the original date of birth to give a Progressed Date of 15th May 1970.

STAGE 2

Find Progressed Date

Once you have established the Progressed Date, the simplest way of calculating progressions by hand is to use a technique called the *Solar Arc Method*.

Step 1: Find Perpetual Date
Although the planetary positions

given in the Ephemeris for the Progressed Date apply to the year in question, unless you were born at Noon (Midnight) on that date, they do not correspond exactly to your birthday but to a date some time before or after (remember, in the day-for-year method 1 day = 1 year, so 1 hour of time = 15 days and 4 minutes = 1 day).

The simple way round this problem is to convert the GMT time interval between Noon (or Midnight, depending on the Ephemeris) on your birthday into days (see box below), then add or subtract the result from your birthday to find what astrologers call the *Perpetual Date*.

Having done this, you can look up the planetary positions given in the Ephemeris for Noon (or Midnight) on **any** Progressed Date, knowing exactly what date of the year (the Perpetual Date) these positions correspond to.

Example – to convert 17.48 GMT on 25th April to its Perpetual Noon Date:
Interval after Noon = 5hr 48min (Consulting table) 5hr = 75 days; 48min = 12 days
Total Difference = 87 days
For pm Birth Time, subtract from Birth Date (25th April) to give a Perpetual Noon Date of 28th January.

INTERVAL CONVERSION

Use the table below to convert the time interval between Noon (or Midnight) and the Time of Birth into months and days:

24 hours = 12 months
2 hours = 1 month
1 hour = 15 days
4 minutes = 1 day
1 minute = 6 hours

Remember, for a Birth Time **before** Noon, **add** the converted total to the Date of Birth to find the Perpetual Noon Date; for a Birth Time **after** Noon, **subtract** the total.

Step 2: Progress the Angles

Although the Perpetual Date takes care of the positions of the progressed planets, it does not progress the Angles. Using the Solar Arc Method, all you have to do is progress the Midheaven by the distance (*arc*) travelled by the Sun from its natal position to its noon position on the Progressed Date.

Example – to calculate the progressed MC and Ascendant for the twentieth year of someone born on 25th April 1970
Progressed Date = 15th May 1970
Sun's position at Noon GMT on 15th May 1970 = 24° 14' Taurus
Sun's position at Noon GMT on 25th April 1970 = 4° 51' Taurus
Difference = 19° 23'

Add the difference to the natal Midheaven degree to find the progressed Midheaven.

Now turn to your Table of Houses. Find the degree of the progressed Midheaven, and under the latitude of the Birth Place, read off the corresponding Ascendant degree. This is the progressed Ascendant for the year in question.

Step 3: Progress the Moon

The Moon covers between 12–14° in a day, which means that in a progressed year, it will make several aspects to both the natal and the progressed planets and Angles. To find out when these occur, you must calculate the Moon's average motion, month by month over the progressed year.

For example, to find the progressed Moon's monthly positions for the year in question:
- Enter the Moon's Noon position on 15th May 1970 = 16° 48' Virgo
- Enter the Moon's Noon position for the next day, 16th May 1970 = 28° 57' Virgo
- Subtract the first figure from the second to find the distance

ANOTHER METHOD

Another way of drawing up a progressed chart – known as the *Sidereal Time Method* – is to replace the Sidereal Time at Noon (or Midnight if you are using a Midnight Ephemeris) on your day of birth with the Sidereal Time at Noon (or Midnight) on the day of your Progressed Date and then draw up the chart as you would an ordinary birthchart.

This produces very detailed results, since it allows you to progress the house cusps, but it is extremely laborious to do by hand. Unless you have a computer, it is advisable to stick to the Solar Arc Method.

travelled by the Moon in one day (ie one year) = 12° 09'
- Convert the degrees to minutes = 729'
- Divide by 12 to find the Moon's average monthly motion: = 60.75'
= roughly 1° 01' per month.
- Bearing in mind that the Noon position of the Moon on 15th May 1970 corresponds to January 28th 1990, calculate its position for the 28th of each month by adding 1° 01' to each previous total: 28th January 1990: 16° 48' Virgo 28th February 1990: 17° 48' Virgo 28th March 1990: 18° 49' Virgo and so on through to 28th January 1991: 28° 57' Virgo.

Calculating the Aspects

Once you have worked out and entered the positions of the progressed planets and Angles on the birthchart, you can plot the aspects in the usual way. Remember, you are looking for aspects from progressed planets and Angles to other progressed planets, as well as aspects from progressed planets and Angles to their natal counterparts.

Calculating Transits

Learn how to plot planetary transits on the birthchart for a glimpse at what the future has waiting in store for you

There is no limit to the scope of transits. For example, they can be used to look at important one-off events such as a wedding, or the start-up of a business.

To find out what is in store, make a note of the exact time and place of the 'event' and draw up a chart as you would a birthchart. The new chart – which shows the positions of the transiting planets and house cusps – can be interpreted on its own, but it will be much more revealing if it is also compared with the birthcharts of the people involved.

If, on the other hand, you simply want to know how the transiting planets will affect you on a given day, simply make a note of their positions from the Ephemeris, then compare these with the planetary positions and Angles in the birthchart.

Since the Moon can move up to 14° each day, you may want to plot its position more accurately – especially if it changes sign during the day in question. In this case, simply repeat the procedure for working out its natal position (see pages 159–160).

Long-term Forecasting

Transits are also employed to look at long-term future trends. Single transits – when only one planet aspects a sensitive natal point – are not normally reliable indicators of major change. What you must look for are *complexes of transits* – build-ups of astrological activity around natal planets or Angles, over say, a period of about a year.

Over any 12-month period there will usually be several dates when this activity is at its most intense. These dates mark the times when significant events are most likely to occur.

However, in any single month, the transiting planets can make

The usual method of plotting transits is to draw them in on the outside of the birthchart wheel to see which houses are affected. Transits of the outer planets are held by astrologers to be the most significant.

anything from 30 to 40 aspects to the natal planets and Angles, and most of these – involving the inner planets – will be only fleeting. Since it is extremely time-consuming to work out all the transits for a year, the usual procedure is to plot the transits of the slower moving outer planets (from Jupiter to Pluto) and then see how transits from the inner planets tie in.

If you have a computer, all the commercial astrology programmes offer transit calculation as an optional – and indispensable – extra. Calculating transits by hand is not difficult, but it most certainly requires a fair amount of time and patience!

transit calculation

STEP 1

Turn to your Ephemeris and on a separate piece of paper note the distances travelled by the outer planets over the next 12 months. Many astrologers also mark the positions of the transiting planets on the outside of the birthchart wheel (writing the letter 'T' before their symbols), as this reminds them which houses the planets are transiting at any one time of the year.

Remember that when planets go retrograde, their positions at that moment may be further around the zodiac than at the end of the chosen 12-month period. Make a note if this is the case.

Example – movement of outer planets Jan – Dec 1991

♃ : 11° ♌ 56' – 14° ♍ 38'

♄ : 25° ♑ 43' – 5° ♒ 55'
(Retrograde 17 May @ 6° ♒ 50')

♅ : 9° ♑ 46' – 13° ♑ 43'
(Retrograde 18 April @ 13° ♑ 49')

♆ : 14° ♑ 8' – 16° ♑ 14'
(Retrograde 19 April @ 16° ♑ 46')

♇ : 19° ♏ 36' – 22° ♏ 6'

STEP 2

Work out the aspects that each transiting outer planet will make to the natal planets and Angles over this period. If you have a computer, you will be able to calculate the minor aspects as well; if not, concentrate on the major aspects and only turn to the minor ones if you need additional information.

Example – major aspects of transiting Saturn only
Jan – Dec 1991

T♄ : □ ♆ ;
☍ ♅ ;
☍ ♃ ;
△ ♇
then T♄ turns retrograde and returns to ☍ ♃

STEP 3

Returning to your Ephemeris, check through it to find out on which dates these aspects occur and how long they last. Allow an average orb of 1° each side of the exact aspect, but increase this slightly if several transiting planets combine to aspect a sensitive natal point at roughly the same time.

Example – dates of transiting Saturn's major aspects
Jan – Dec 1991

T♄ □ ♆ (22/12/90) – 8/1/91
T♄ ☍ ♅ (27/12/90) – 12/1/91
T♄ ☍ ♃ 8/2/91 – 27/2/91
T♄ △ ♇ 18/4/91 – 15/6/91
T♄ ℞ ☍ ♃ 13/8/91 – 27/9/91
T♄ D ☍ 12/10/91 – 24/11/91

nb ℞ = retrograde

STEP 4

By this stage you should have a clear picture of the general pattern and timing of outer planet transits to the birthchart. Now check your Ephemeris to see if any of the transiting inner planets join forces with the transiting outer planets during these times. Pay particular attention to the Sun and Mars, as these two seem to play a critical role in the precise timing of events.

Example – trigger aspects involving transiting Saturn for January 1991

Between Jan 1–2
T☽ : 25° – 26° ♋
T♀ : 25° – 26° ♑

T♀ ☌ T♄ □ ♆ ☍ ♅
[T☽ ☍ T♀
☍ T♄
☌ ♅] – □ ♆

Here, you can see that although transiting Saturn squares natal Neptune while opposing natal Uranus during early January, the critical time is the 1st, when the transiting Moon conjuncts natal Uranus, squares natal Neptune and opposes transiting Saturn, and is also joined by an opposition from transiting Venus. Pay close attention to events around this time. House positions and aspects natally and by transit should be carefully noted.

EPHEMERIS

Essential to every astrologer, an ephemeris contains lists of astronomical information. Our ephemeris has been slightly simplified for beginners, making it easy to use.

The first column gives the month and days. Reading across from the left, you will see that the second column is headed 'STime'. This refers to sidereal time, and must not be confused with Greenwich Mean Time. Sidereal time measures the rotation of the earth on its axis, and is calculated for noon each day. The measurement tells you how many hours and minutes have passed since the first point of Aries coincided with the Greenwich meridian. The

first point of Aries is where the ecliptic (or apparent path of the Sun around the Earth) and the equator intersect. At the vernal equinox the Sun sits exactly upon this point. If you look up the sidereal time it is listed as 0.02, because only two minutes have elapsed since the Sun was exactly conjunct the first point of Aries.

Reading across the next five columns you will find the daily noon position in degrees for the Sun, Moon, Mercury, Venus and Mars. When looking at the Moon's position, remember that its movement is swift, for it passes through all the signs of the zodiac in a month. Its average motion is approximately 13° a day - or

1° every two hours. Do not forget to take this notion into account for birth times before or after noon, adding (p.m.) or subtracting (a.m.) as necessary. You may find it has changed signs.

The final column contains the positions of the slower moving planets, Jupiter, Saturn, Uranus, Neptune and Pluto. Because these planets move fairly slowly, it is not necessary to give a daily position for each one.

For example, if you turn to 1 January 1983 you will find the following planetary positions: Jupiter 1° Sagittarius; Saturn 3° Scorpio; Uranus 7° Sagittarius; Neptune 27° Sagittarius; Pluto 29° Libra. One month later, on 1 February

1983 the positions are: Jupiter 6° Sagittarius; Saturn 4° Scorpio; Uranus 8° Sagittarius; Pluto still at 29° Libra. By the end of that year Pluto had moved into Scorpio, while the other planets were still in the same signs they had been in at the start of 1983, although they had moved on a little by degree. So, when using this column, simply take your positions from those given for the relevant week opposite your date of birth.

All planets, with the exception of the Sun and Moon, spend part of their transit through a sign in retrograde motion. This means that they are apparently going backwards in the heavens. Retrograde planets are marked with an 'R', and you will see the figures for their degree going backwards. When they turn direct once more, the 'R' is simply omitted. Such movements are quite important in transit and progression work, for they may indicate delays or blockages during the retrograde period, which will clear up once the planet turns to direct motion once more.

Jan	STime	☉	☽	☿	♀	♂	Plnts
1	18.39	9♑	9♉	20♐	26♏	16♎	♃17♌R
2	18.43	11	23	21	27	17	♄11♍R
3	18.47	12	8♊	23	29	17	♅29♒
4	18.51	13	23	24	0♐	18	♆11♌R
5	18.55	14	8♋	26	1	18	♇ 6♋R
6	18.59	15	23	27	2	19	♃16♌R
7	19.03	16	8♌	29	3	19	♄11♍R
8	19.07	17	22	0♑	5	20	♅29♒
9	19.11	18	6♍	2	6	20	♆10♌R
10	19.15	19	20	3	7	21	♇ 6♋R
11	19.19	20	2♎	5	8	21	♃16♌R
12	19.23	21	15	6	9	22	♄11♍R
13	19.27	22	27	8	10	22	♅29♒
14	19.31	23	9♏	9	12	23	♆10♌R
15	19.35	24	21	11	13	23	♇ 6♋R
16	19.39	25	3♐	12	14	23	♃15♌R
17	19.42	26	15	14	15	24	♄11♍R
18	19.46	27	26	15	16	24	♅29♒
19	19.50	28	8♑	17	18	25	♆10♌R
20	19.54	29	21	18	19	25	♇ 6♋R
21	19.58	0♒	3♒	20	20	26	♃15♌R
22	20.02	1	16	21	21	26	♄11♍R
23	20.06	2	28	23	22	26	♅ 0♓
24	20.10	3	11♓	25	24	27	♆10♌R
25	20.14	4	24	26	25	27	♇ 6♋R
26	20.18	5	8♈	28	26	28	♃14♌R
27	20.22	6	21	0♒	27	28	♄10♍R
28	20.26	7	5♉	1	28	28	♅ 0♓
29	20.30	8	19	3	0♑	29	♆10♌R
30	20.34	9	3♊	5	1	29	♇ 6♋R
31	20.38	10	18	6	2	0♏	♃13♌R

Feb	STime	☉	☽	☿	♀	♂	Plnts
1	20.42	11♒	2♋	8♒	3♑	0♏	♃13♌R
2	20.46	12	17	10	5	0	♄10♍R
3	20.49	13	1♌	11	6	1	♅ 0♓
4	20.53	14	16	13	7	1	♆10♌R
5	20.57	15	0♍	15	8	1	♇ 6♋R
6	21.01	16	14	17	9	2	♃12♌R
7	21.05	17	27	18	11	2	♄10♍R
8	21.09	18	10♎	20	12	2	♅ 1♓
9	21.13	19	23	22	13	3	♆10♌R
10	21.17	20	5♏	24	14	3	♇ 6♋R
11	21.21	21	17	26	15	3	♃12♌R
12	21.25	22	29	27	17	4	♄ 9♍R
13	21.29	23	11♐	29	18	4	♅ 1♓
14	21.33	24	23	1♓	19	4	♆ 9♌R
15	21.37	25	5♑	3	20	4	♇ 6♋R
16	21.41	26	17	5	22	5	♃11♌R
17	21.45	27	29	7	23	5	♄ 9♍R
18	21.49	28	12♒	8	24	5	♅ 1♓
19	21.53	29	24	10	25	6	♆ 9♌R
20	21.57	0♓	8♓	12	26	6	♇ 6♋R
21	22.00	1	21	14	28	6	♃11♌R
22	22.04	2	4♈	16	29	6	♄ 8♍R
23	22.08	3	18	17	0♒	6	♅ 1♓
24	22.12	4	2♉	19	1	7	♆ 9♌R
25	22.16	5	16	21	3	7	♇ 5♋R
26	22.20	6	0♊	22	4	7	♃10♌R
27	22.24	7	14	24	5	7	♄ 8♍R
28	22.28	8	28	25	6	7	♅ 2♓
29	22.32	9	12♋	27	7	8	♆ 9♌R

Mar	STime	☉	☽	☿	♀	♂	Plnts
1	22.36	10♓	27♋	28♓	9♒	8♏	♃10♌R
2	22.40	11	11♌	29	10	8	♄ 8♍R
3	22.44	12	25	0♈	11	8	♅ 2♓
4	22.48	13	9♍	1	12	8	♆ 9♌R
5	22.52	14	22	2	14	8	♇ 5♋
6	22.56	15	5♎	3	15	8	♃ 9♌R
7	23.00	16	18	4	16	8	♄ 7♍R
8	23.04	17	1♏	4	17	9	♅ 2♓
9	23.07	18	13	4	18	9	♆ 9♌R
10	23.11	19	25	4R	20	9	♇ 5♋R
11	23.15	20	7♐	4	21	9	♃ 9♌R
12	23.19	21	19	4	22	9	♄ 7♍R
13	23.23	22	0♑	4	23	9	♅ 3♓
14	23.27	23	12	3	25	9	♆ 9♌R
15	23.31	24	25	3	26	9R	♇ 5♋
16	23.35	25	7♒	2	27	9	♃ 8♌R
17	23.39	26	20	2	28	9	♄ 7♍R
18	23.43	27	3♓	1	0♓	9	♅ 3♓
19	23.47	28	16	0	1	9	♆ 9♌R
20	23.51	29	0♈	29♓	2	9	♇ 5♋
21	23.55	0♈	14	28	3	9	♃ 8♌R
22	23.59	1	28	27	4	8	♄ 6♍R
23	0.03	2	12♉	26	6	8	♅ 3♓
24	0.07	3	27	25	7	8	♆ 9♌R
25	0.11	4	11♊	25	8	8	♇ 5♋
26	0.14	5	25	24	9	8	♃ 8♌R
27	0.18	6	9♋	23	11	8	♄ 6♍R
28	0.22	7	23	23	12	8	♅ 3♓
29	0.26	8	7♌	22	13	8	♆ 9♌R
30	0.30	9	21	22	14	7	♇ 5♋
31	0.34	10	4♍	22	15	7	♃ 8♌R

Apr	STime	☉	☽	☿	♀	♂	Plnts
1	0.38	11♈	18♍	21♓	17♓	7♏	♃ 8♌
2	0.42	12	1♎	21D	18	7	♄ 6♍R
3	0.46	13	14	21	19	6	♅ 4♓
4	0.50	14	26	21	20	6	♆ 9♌R
5	0.54	15	9♏	22	22	6	♇ 5♋
6	0.58	16	21	22	23	6	♃ 8♌
7	1.02	17	3♐	22	24	5	♄ 5♍R
8	1.06	18	15	23	25	5	♅ 4♓
9	1.10	19	27	23	27	5	♆ 8♌
10	1.14	20	8♑	24	28	4	♇ 5♋
11	1.18	21	20	24	29	4	♃ 8♌
12	1.22	22	2♒	25	0♈	4	♄ 5♍R
13	1.25	23	15	26	1	3	♅ 4♓
14	1.29	24	28	27	3	3	♆ 8♌
15	1.33	25	11♓	28	4	3	♇ 6♋
16	1.37	26	24	28	5	2	♃ 8♌
17	1.41	27	8♈	29	6	2	♄ 5♍R
18	1.45	28	22	0♈	8	2	♅ 4♓
19	1.49	29	7♉	2	9	1	♆ 8♌
20	1.53	0♉	22	3	10	1	♇ 6♋
21	1.57	1	6♊	4	11	1	♃ 8♌
22	2.01	2	21	5	12	0	♄ 5♍R
23	2.05	3	6♋	6	14	0	♅ 4♓
24	2.09	4	20	7	15	29♎	♆ 8♌
25	2.13	5	4♌	9	16	29	♇ 6♋
26	2.17	6	18	10	17	29	♃ 9♌
27	2.21	7	1♍	12	19	28	♄ 5♍R
28	2.25	8	14	13	20	28	♅ 5♓
29	2.29	9	27	14	21	28	♆ 8♌
30	2.32	10	10♎	16	22	27	♇ 6♋

May	STime	☉	☽	☿	♀	♂	Plnts
1	2.36	10♉	23♎	17♈	24♈	27♎	♃ 9♌
2	2.40	11	5♏	19	25	27	♄ 5♍
3	2.44	12	17	20	26	26	♅ 5♓
4	2.48	13	29	22	27	26	♆ 9♌
5	2.52	14	11♐	24	28	26	♇ 6♋
6	2.56	15	23	25	0♉	25	♃ 9♌
7	3.00	16	5♑	27	1	25	♄ 5♍
8	3.04	17	17	29	2	25	♅ 5♓
9	3.08	18	29	1♉	3	24	♆ 9♌
10	3.12	19	11♒	2	5	24	♇ 6♋
11	3.16	20	23	4	6	24	♃10♌
12	3.20	21	6♓	6	7	24	♄ 5♍
13	3.24	22	19	8	8	23	♅ 5♓
14	3.28	23	2♈	10	9	23	♆ 9♌
15	3.32	24	16	12	11	23	♇ 6♋
16	3.36	25	1♉	14	12	23	♃10♌
17	3.40	26	15	16	13	22	♄ 5♍
18	3.43	27	0♊	18	14	22	♅ 5♓
19	3.47	28	15	20	16	22	♆ 9♌
20	3.51	29	0♋	22	17	22	♇ 6♋
21	3.55	0♊	15	24	18	22	♃11♌
22	3.59	1	0♌	26	19	22	♄ 5♍
23	4.03	2	14	29	20	21	♅ 5♓
24	4.07	3	28	1♊	22	21	♆ 9♌
25	4.11	4	11♍	3	23	21	♇ 6♋
26	4.15	5	24	5	24	21	♃12♌
27	4.19	6	7♎	7	25	21	♄ 5♍
28	4.23	7	20	10	27	21	♅ 5♓
29	4.27	7	2♏	12	28	21	♆ 9♌
30	4.31	8	14	14	29	21	♇ 6♋
31	4.35	9	26	16	0♊	21D	♃12♌

Jun	STime	☉	☽	☿	♀	♂	Plnts
1	4.39	10♊	8♐	18♊	2♊	21♎	♃13♌
2	4.43	11	20	20	3	21	♄ 5♍
3	4.47	12	2♑	22	4	21	♅ 5♓
4	4.50	13	13	24	5	21	♆ 9♌
5	4.54	14	25	26	6	21	♇ 6♋
6	4.58	15	7♒	28	8	21	♃13♌
7	5.02	16	20	0♋	9	21	♄ 5♍
8	5.06	17	2♓	2	10	21	♅ 5♓
9	5.10	18	15	4	11	21	♆ 9♌
10	5.14	19	28	6	13	22	♇ 7♋
11	5.18	20	11♈	8	14	22	♃14♌
12	5.22	21	25	10	15	22	♄ 6♍
13	5.26	22	9♉	11	16	22	♅ 5♓
14	5.30	23	24	13	17	22	♆ 9♌
15	5.34	24	9♊	15	19	22	♇ 7♋
16	5.38	25	24	16	20	22	♃15♌
17	5.42	26	9♋	18	21	23	♄ 6♍
18	5.46	27	24	19	22	23	♅ 5♓R
19	5.50	28	9♌	21	24	23	♆ 9♌
20	5.54	29	23	22	25	23	♇ 7♋
21	5.58	29	7♍	24	26	24	♃16♌
22	6.01	0♋	21	25	27	24	♄ 6♍
23	6.05	1	4♎	26	29	24	♅ 5♓R
24	6.09	2	17	27	0♋	24	♆10♌
25	6.13	3	29	29	1	25	♇ 7♋
26	6.17	4	11♏	0♌	2	25	♃17♌
27	6.21	5	23	1	3	25	♄ 7♍
28	6.25	6	5♐	2	5	25	♅ 5♓R
29	6.29	7	17	3	6	26	♆10♌
30	6.33	8	29	4	7	26	♇ 7♋

Jul	STime	☉	☽	☿	♀	♂	Plnts
1	6.37	9♋	11♑	5♌	8♋	26♎	♃18♌
2	6.41	10	22	5	10	27	♄ 7♍
3	6.45	11	4♒	6	11	27	♅ 5♓R
4	6.49	12	17	7	12	27	♆10♌
5	6.53	13	29	8	13	28	♇ 7♋
6	6.57	14	11♓	8	15	28	♃19♌
7	7.01	15	24	9	16	28	♄ 8♍
8	7.05	16	7♈	9	17	29	♅ 5♓R
9	7.08	17	20	9	18	29	♆10♌
10	7.12	18	4♉	10	19	0♏	♇ 7♋
11	7.16	19	18	10	21	0	♃20♌
12	7.20	20	2♊	10	22	0	♄ 8♍
13	7.24	20	17	10R	23	1	♅ 5♓R
14	7.28	21	2♋	10	24	1	♆10♌
15	7.32	22	17	10	26	2	♇ 7♋
16	7.36	23	2♌	10	27	2	♃21♌
17	7.40	24	17	9	28	3	♄ 9♍
18	7.44	25	2♍	9	29	3	♅ 5♓R
19	7.48	26	16	9	1♌	3	♆10♌
20	7.52	27	0♎	8	2	4	♇ 8♋
21	7.56	28	13	8	3	4	♃22♌
22	8.00	29	26	7	4	5	♄ 9♍
23	8.04	0♌	8♏	6	5	5	♅ 5♓R
24	8.08	1	20	6	7	6	♆11♌
25	8.12	2	2♐	5	8	6	♇ 8♋
26	8.15	3	14	4	9	7	♃23♌
27	8.19	4	26	4	10	7	♄10♍
28	8.23	5	7♑	3	12	8	♅ 5♓R
29	8.27	6	19	2	13	8	♆11♌
30	8.31	7	1♒	1	14	9	♇ 8♋
31	8.35	8	14	1	15	9	♃24♌

Aug	STime	☉	☽	☿	♀	♂	Plnts
1	8.39	9♌	26♒	0♌	17♌	10♏	♃24♌
2	8.43	10	8♓	0	18	10	♄10♍
3	8.47	11	21	0	19	11	♅ 4♓R
4	8.51	11	4♈	29♋	20	11	♆11♌
5	8.55	12	17	29	21	12	♇ 8♋
6	8.59	13	0♉	29D	23	12	♃25♌
7	9.03	14	14	29	24	13	♄11♍
8	9.07	15	28	29	25	13	♅ 4♓R
9	9.11	16	12♊	29	26	14	♆11♌
10	9.15	17	27	0♌	28	15	♇ 8♋
11	9.19	18	11♋	0	29	15	♃26♌
12	9.23	19	26	1	0♍	16	♄11♍
13	9.26	20	11♌	2	1	16	♅ 4♓R
14	9.30	21	26	2	3	17	♆11♌
15	9.34	22	10♍	3	4	17	♇ 8♋
16	9.38	23	24	4	5	18	♃27♌
17	9.42	24	8♎	6	6	19	♄12♍
18	9.46	25	21	7	7	19	♅ 4♓R
19	9.50	26	4♏	8	9	20	♆12♌
20	9.54	27	16	10	10	20	♇ 8♋
21	9.58	28	28	11	11	21	♃28♌
22	10.02	29	10♐	13	12	21	♄13♍
23	10.06	0♍	22	14	14	22	♅ 4♓R
24	10.10	1	4♑	16	15	23	♆12♌
25	10.14	2	16	18	16	23	♇ 8♋
26	10.18	3	28	20	17	24	♃ 0♍
27	10.22	4	10♒	22	19	24	♄13♍
28	10.26	5	22	23	20	25	♅ 3♓R
29	10.30	6	5♓	25	21	26	♆12♌
30	10.33	6	18	27	22	26	♇ 8♋
31	10.37	7	1♈	29	24	27	♃ 1♍

Sep	STime	☉	☽	☿	♀	♂	Plnts
1	10.41	8♍	14♈	1♍	25♍	28♏	♃ 1♍
2	10.45	9	27	3	26	28	♄14♍
3	10.49	10	11♉	5	27	29	♅ 3♓R
4	10.53	11	25	7	28	29	♆12♌
5	10.57	12	8♊	9	0♎	0♐	♇ 8♋
6	11.01	13	23	11	1	1	♃ 2♍
7	11.05	14	7♋	13	2	1	♄15♍
8	11.09	15	21	15	3	2	♅ 3♓R
9	11.13	16	6♌	17	5	3	♆12♌
10	11.17	17	20	18	6	3	♇ 8♋
11	11.21	18	5♍	20	7	4	♃ 3♍
12	11.25	19	19	22	8	5	♄15♍
13	11.29	20	2♎	24	10	5	♅ 3♓R
14	11.33	21	16	26	11	6	♆12♌
15	11.37	22	29	28	12	7	♇ 9♋
16	11.41	23	12♏	29	13	7	♃ 4♍
17	11.44	24	24	1♎	15	8	♄16♍
18	11.48	25	6♐	3	16	9	♅ 3♓R
19	11.52	26	18	5	17	9	♆13♌
20	11.56	27	0♑	6	18	10	♇ 9♋
21	12.00	28	12	8	19	11	♃ 5♍
22	12.04	29	24	10	21	11	♄17♍
23	12.08	0♎	6♒	11	22	12	♅ 2♓R
24	12.12	1	18	13	23	13	♆13♌
25	12.16	2	1♓	14	24	13	♇ 9♋
26	12.20	3	14	16	26	14	♃ 6♍
27	12.24	4	27	18	27	15	♄17♍
28	12.28	5	10♈	19	28	15	♅ 2♓R
29	12.32	6	23	21	29	16	♆13♌
30	12.36	7	7♉	22	1♏	17	♇ 9♋

Oct	STime	☉	☽	☿	♀	♂	Plnts
1	12.40	8♎	21♉	24♎	2♏	18♐	♃ 7♍
2	12.44	9	5♊	25	3	18	♄18♍
3	12.48	10	19	27	4	19	♅ 2♓R
4	12.51	11	4♋	28	5	20	♆13♌
5	12.55	12	18	0♏	7	20	♇ 9♋
6	12.59	13	2♌	1	8	21	♃ 8♍
7	13.03	14	16	3	9	22	♄18♍
8	13.07	15	0♍	4	10	22	♅ 2♓R
9	13.11	16	14	6	12	23	♆13♌
10	13.15	17	28	7	13	24	♇ 9♋
11	13.19	18	11♎	8	14	25	♃ 9♍
12	13.23	19	24	10	15	25	♄19♍
13	13.27	20	7♏	11	17	26	♅ 2♓R
14	13.31	21	20	12	18	27	♆13♌
15	13.35	22	2♐	14	19	27	♇ 9♋
16	13.39	23	14	15	20	28	♃10♍
17	13.43	24	26	16	21	29	♄19♍
18	13.47	25	8♑	18	23	0♑	♅ 2♓R
19	13.51	26	20	19	24	0	♆13♌
20	13.55	27	2♒	20	25	1	♇ 9♋R
21	13.59	27	14	21	26	2	♃11♍
22	14.02	28	26	22	28	3	♄20♍
23	14.06	29	9♓	23	29	3	♅ 2♓R
24	14.10	0♏	22	24	0♐	4	♆13♌
25	14.14	1	5♈	25	1	5	♇ 9♋R
26	14.18	2	18	26	3	6	♃12♍
27	14.22	3	2♉	27	4	6	♄21♍
28	14.26	4	16	28	5	7	♅ 2♓R
29	14.30	5	1♊	29	6	8	♆13♌
30	14.34	6	15	0♐	7	8	♇ 9♋
31	14.38	7	0♋	0	9	9	♃13♍

Nov	STime	☉	☽	☿	♀	♂	Plnts
1	14.42	8♏	14♋	1♐	10♐	10♑	♃13♍
2	14.46	9	29	1	11	11	♄21♍
3	14.50	10	13♌	2	12	11	♅ 1♓R
4	14.54	11	27	2	14	12	♆13♌
5	14.58	12	10♍	2R	15	13	♇ 8♋R
6	15.02	13	24	2	16	14	♃14♍
7	15.06	14	7♎	2	17	14	♄22♍
8	15.09	15	20	1	18	15	♅ 1♓
9	15.13	17	3♏	1	20	16	♆13♌
10	15.17	18	16	0	21	17	♇ 8♋R
11	15.21	19	28	29♏	22	17	♃14♍
12	15.25	20	10♐	28	23	18	♄22♍
13	15.29	21	22	27	25	19	♅ 1♓
14	15.33	22	4♑	26	26	20	♆13♌
15	15.37	23	16	24	27	20	♇ 8♋R
16	15.41	24	28	23	28	21	♃15♍
17	15.45	25	10♒	22	29	22	♄22♍
18	15.49	26	22	20	1♑	23	♅ 1♓
19	15.53	27	4♓	19	2	24	♆13♌
20	15.57	28	16	18	3	24	♇ 8♋R
21	16.01	29	29	17	4	25	♃16♍
22	16.05	0♐	12♈	17	6	26	♄23♍
23	16.09	1	26	16	7	27	♅ 2♓
24	16.13	2	10♉	16	8	27	♆13♌
25	16.16	3	25	16D	9	28	♇ 8♋R
26	16.20	4	10♊	16	10	29	♃16♍
27	16.24	5	25	16	12	0♒	♄23♍
28	16.28	6	10♋	17	13	0	♅ 2♓
29	16.32	7	24	17	14	1	♆13♌R
30	16.36	8	9♌	18	15	2	♇ 8♋R

Dec	STime	☉	☽	☿	♀	♂	Plnts
1	16.40	9♐	23♌	19♏	16♑	3♒	♃17♍
2	16.44	10	7♍	19	18	3	♄24♍
3	16.48	11	21	20	19	4	♅ 2♓
4	16.52	12	4♎	21	20	5	♆13♌R
5	16.56	13	17	23	21	6	♇ 8♋R
6	17.00	14	0♏	24	22	7	♃17♍
7	17.04	15	12	25	24	7	♄24♍
8	17.08	16	25	26	25	8	♅ 2♓
9	17.12	17	7♐	27	26	9	♆13♌R
10	17.16	18	19	29	27	10	♇ 8♋R
11	17.20	19	1♑	0♐	29	10	♃18♍
12	17.24	20	13	1	0♒	11	♄24♍
13	17.27	21	24	3	1	12	♅ 2♓
14	17.31	22	6♒	4	2	13	♆13♌R
15	17.35	23	18	6	3	14	♇ 8♋R
16	17.39	24	0♓	7	5	14	♃18♍
17	17.43	25	12	9	6	15	♄24♍
18	17.47	26	25	10	7	16	♅ 2♓
19	17.51	27	7♈	12	8	17	♆13♌R
20	17.55	28	20	13	9	17	♇ 8♋R
21	17.59	29	4♉	15	10	18	♃18♍
22	18.03	0♑	18	16	12	19	♄24♍
23	18.07	1	3♊	18	13	20	♅ 2♓
24	18.11	2	18	19	14	21	♆13♌R
25	18.15	3	3♋	21	15	21	♇ 8♋R
26	18.19	4	18	22	16	22	♃19♍
27	18.23	5	3♌	24	18	23	♄24♍
28	18.27	6	18	25	19	24	♅ 2♓
29	18.31	7	3♍	27	20	24	♆13♌R
30	18.34	8	17	28	21	25	♇ 8♋R
31	18.38	9	1♎	0♑	22	26	♃19♍

Jan	STime	☉	☽	☿	♀	♂	Plnts
1	18.42	10♑	14♎	1♑	23♒	27♒	♃19♍
2	18.46	11	27	3	25	28	♄24♍
3	18.50	12	9♏	4	26	28	♅ 3♓
4	18.54	13	22	6	27	29	♆13♌R
5	18.58	14	4♐	8	28	0♓	♇ 7♋R
6	19.02	15	16	9	29	1	♃19♍R
7	19.06	16	28	11	0♓	1	♄24♍R
8	19.10	17	9♑	12	2	2	♅ 3♓
9	19.14	18	21	14	3	3	♆13♌R
10	19.18	19	3♒	16	4	4	♇ 7♋R
11	19.22	20	15	17	5	4	♃19♍R
12	19.26	21	27	19	6	5	♄24♍R
13	19.30	22	9♓	20	7	6	♅ 3♓
14	19.34	24	21	22	8	7	♆13♌R
15	19.38	25	4♈	24	10	8	♇ 7♋R
16	19.42	26	16	25	11	8	♃18♍R
17	19.45	27	29	27	12	9	♄24♍R
18	19.49	28	13♉	29	13	10	♅ 3♓
19	19.53	29	27	0♒	14	11	♆12♌R
20	19.57	0♒	11♊	2	15	11	♇ 7♋R
21	20.01	1	26	4	16	12	♃18♍R
22	20.05	2	11♋	5	17	13	♄24♍R
23	20.09	3	26	7	19	14	♅ 4♓
24	20.13	4	11♌	9	20	15	♆12♌R
25	20.17	5	27	11	21	15	♇ 7♋R
26	20.21	6	11♍	12	22	16	♃18♍R
27	20.25	7	26	14	23	17	♄24♍R
28	20.29	8	10♎	16	24	18	♅ 4♓
29	20.33	9	23	18	25	18	♆12♌R
30	20.37	10	6♏	19	26	19	♇ 7♋R
31	20.41	11	18	21	27	20	♃17♍R

Feb	STime	☉	☽	☿	♀	♂	Plnts
1	20.45	12♒	1♐	23♒	28♓	21♓	♃17♍R
2	20.49	13	13	25	29	21	♄24♍R
3	20.52	14	25	26	0♈	22	♅ 4♓
4	20.56	15	6♑	28	2	23	♆12♌R
5	21.00	16	18	0♓	3	24	♇ 7♋R
6	21.04	17	0♒	2	4	25	♃17♍R
7	21.08	18	12	3	5	25	♄23♍R
8	21.12	19	24	5	6	26	♅ 4♓
9	21.16	20	6♓	6	7	27	♆12♌R
10	21.20	21	18	8	8	28	♇ 7♋R
11	21.24	22	1♈	9	9	28	♃16♍R
12	21.28	23	13	11	10	29	♄23♍R
13	21.32	24	26	12	11	0♈	♅ 5♓
14	21.36	25	9♉	13	12	1	♆12♌R
15	21.40	26	22	14	13	1	♇ 7♋R
16	21.44	27	6♊	15	14	2	♃16♍R
17	21.48	28	20	16	15	3	♄23♍R
18	21.52	29	5♋	16	15	4	♅ 5♓
19	21.56	0♓	19	17	16	4	♆12♌R
20	21.59	1	4♌	17	17	5	♇ 7♋R
21	22.03	2	19	17R	18	6	♃15♍R
22	22.07	3	4♍	17	19	7	♄23♍R
23	22.11	4	19	17	20	8	♅ 5♓
24	22.15	5	4♎	17	21	8	♆11♌R
25	22.19	6	18	16	22	9	♇ 7♋R
26	22.23	7	1♏	16	23	10	♃15♍R
27	22.27	8	14	15	24	11	♄22♍R
28	22.31	9	27	14	24	11	♅ 6♓

Mar	STime	☉	☽	☿	♀	♂	Plnts
1	22.35	10♓	9♐	13♓	25♈	12♈	♃14♍R
2	22.39	11	21	12	26	13	♄22♍R
3	22.43	12	3♑	11	27	14	♅ 6♓
4	22.47	13	15	10	28	14	♆11♌R
5	22.51	14	27	9	28	15	♇ 7♋R
6	22.55	15	9♒	8	29	16	♃13♍R
7	22.59	16	21	7	0♉	17	♄22♍R
8	23.03	17	3♓	6	0	17	♅ 6♓
9	23.07	18	15	6	1	18	♆11♌R
10	23.10	19	28	5	2	19	♇ 7♋
11	23.14	20	10♈	4	2	20	♃13♍R
12	23.18	21	23	4	3	20	♄21♍R
13	23.22	22	6♉	4	4	21	♅ 6♓
14	23.26	23	19	3	4	22	♆11♌R
15	23.30	24	3♊	3	5	22	♇ 7♋R
16	23.34	25	17	3D	5	23	♃12♍R
17	23.38	26	1♋	3	6	24	♄21♍R
18	23.42	27	15	3	6	25	♅ 7♓
19	23.46	28	29	4	7	25	♆11♌R
20	23.50	29	14♌	4	7	26	♇ 7♋
21	23.54	0♈	28	4	8	27	♃12♍R
22	23.58	1	13♍	5	8	28	♄20♍R
23	0.02	2	27	5	8	28	♅ 7♓
24	0.06	3	12♎	6	9	29	♆11♌R
25	0.10	4	25	7	9	0♉	♇ 7♋
26	0.14	5	9♏	8	9	1	♃11♍R
27	0.17	6	22	8	9	1	♄20♍R
28	0.21	7	5♐	9	10	2	♅ 7♓
29	0.25	8	17	10	10	3	♆11♌R
30	0.29	9	29	11	10	4	♇ 7♋
31	0.33	10	11♑	12	10	4	♃11♍R

Apr	STime	☉	☽	☿	♀	♂	Plnts
1	0.37	11♈	23♑	13♓	10♉	5♉	♃10♍R
2	0.41	12	5♒	14	10	6	♄20♍R
3	0.45	13	17	15	10	6	♅ 7♓
4	0.49	14	29	17	10	7	♆11♌R
5	0.53	15	11♓	18	10	8	♇ 7♋
6	0.57	16	24	19	9	9	♃10♍R
7	1.01	17	6♈	20	9	9	♄19♍R
8	1.05	18	19	22	9	10	♅ 8♓
9	1.09	19	2♉	23	9	11	♆11♌
10	1.13	20	16	24	8	12	♇ 7♋
11	1.17	21	0♊	26	8	12	♃10♍R
12	1.21	22	13	27	8	13	♄19♍R
13	1.25	23	27	29	7	14	♅ 8♓
14	1.28	24	11♋	0♈	7	14	♆11♌R
15	1.32	25	26	2	6	15	♇ 7♋
16	1.36	26	10♌	3	6	16	♃ 9♍R
17	1.40	27	24	5	5	17	♄19♍R
18	1.44	28	8♍	7	4	17	♅ 8♓
19	1.48	29	22	8	4	18	♆11♌
20	1.52	0♉	6♎	10	3	19	♇ 7♋
21	1.56	1	20	12	3	19	♃ 9♍R
22	2.00	2	4♏	13	2	20	♄18♍R
23	2.04	2	17	15	1	21	♅ 8♓
24	2.08	3	0♐	17	1	22	♆11♌
25	2.12	4	12	19	0	22	♇ 7♋
26	2.16	5	25	20	29♈	23	♃ 9♍R
27	2.20	6	7♑	22	29	24	♄18♍R
28	2.24	7	19	24	28	24	♅ 8♓
29	2.28	8	1♒	26	28	25	♆11♌
30	2.32	9	13	28	27	26	♇ 7♋

May	STime	☉	☽	☿	♀	♂	Plnts
1	2.35	10♉	25♒	0♉	27♈	26♉	♃ 9♍R
2	2.39	11	7♓	2	26	27	♄18♍R
3	2.43	12	19	4	26	28	♅ 9♓
4	2.47	13	2♈	6	25	29	♆11♌
5	2.51	14	15	8	25	29	♇ 7♋
6	2.55	15	28	10	25	0♊	♃ 9♍
7	2.59	16	11♉	13	24	1	♄18♍R
8	3.03	17	25	15	24	1	♅ 9♓
9	3.07	18	9♊	17	24	2	♆11♌
10	3.11	19	24	19	24	3	♇ 7♋
11	3.15	20	8♋	21	24	3	♃ 9♍
12	3.19	21	22	23	24	4	♄18♍R
13	3.23	22	7♌	26	24D	5	♅ 9♓
14	3.27	23	21	28	24	6	♆11♌
15	3.31	24	5♍	0♊	24	6	♇ 7♋
16	3.35	25	19	2	24	7	♃ 9♍
17	3.39	26	3♎	4	24	8	♄18♍R
18	3.43	27	16	6	24	8	♅ 9♓
19	3.46	28	0♏	8	24	9	♆11♌
20	3.50	29	13	10	24	10	♇ 7♋
21	3.54	0♊	26	12	25	10	♃ 9♍
22	3.58	1	8♐	14	25	11	♄18♍
23	4.02	1	21	16	25	12	♅ 9♓
24	4.06	2	3♑	18	26	12	♆11♌
25	4.10	3	15	20	26	13	♇ 7♋
26	4.14	4	27	22	26	14	♃ 9♍
27	4.18	5	9♒	24	27	15	♄18♍
28	4.22	6	21	25	27	15	♅ 9♓
29	4.26	7	3♓	27	28	16	♆11♌
30	4.30	8	15	29	28	17	♇ 7♋
31	4.34	9	27	0♋	29	17	♃10♍

Jun	STime	☉	☽	☿	♀	♂	Plnts
1	4.38	10♊	10♈	2♋	29♈	18♊	♃10♍
2	4.42	11	23	3	0♉	19	♄18♍
3	4.46	12	6♉	5	0	19	♅ 9♓
4	4.50	13	20	6	1	20	♆11♌
5	4.53	14	4♊	7	2	21	♇ 8♋
6	4.57	15	18	8	2	21	♃10♍
7	5.01	16	3♋	10	3	22	♄18♍
8	5.05	17	18	11	4	23	♅ 9♓
9	5.09	18	3♌	12	4	23	♆11♌
10	5.13	19	17	13	5	24	♇ 8♋
11	5.17	20	2♍	14	6	25	♃11♍
12	5.21	21	16	15	7	25	♄18♍
13	5.25	22	0♎	16	7	26	♅ 9♓
14	5.29	23	13	16	8	27	♆11♌
15	5.33	24	26	17	9	27	♇ 8♋
16	5.37	24	9♏	18	10	28	♃11♍
17	5.41	25	22	18	11	29	♄18♍
18	5.45	26	5♐	19	11	29	♅ 9♓
19	5.49	27	17	19	12	0♋	♆12♌
20	5.53	28	29	20	13	1	♇ 8♋
21	5.57	29	12♑	20	14	1	♃12♍
22	6.00	0♋	24	20	15	2	♄19♍
23	6.04	1	5♒	20	16	3	♅ 9♓R
24	6.08	2	17	21	17	3	♆12♌
25	6.12	3	29	21R	18	4	♇ 8♋
26	6.16	4	11♓	20	18	5	♃12♍
27	6.20	5	23	20	19	5	♄19♍
28	6.24	6	5♈	20	20	6	♅ 9♓R
29	6.28	7	18	20	21	7	♆12♌
30	6.32	8	1♉	19	22	7	♇ 8♋

Jul	STime	☉	☽	☿	♀	♂	Plnts
1	6.36	9♋	14♉	19♋	23♉	8♋	♃13♍
2	6.40	10	28	19	24	9	♄19♍
3	6.44	11	12♊	18	25	9	♅ 9♓R
4	6.48	12	27	17	26	10	♆12♌
5	6.52	13	12♋	17	27	11	♇ 8♋
6	6.56	14	27	16	28	11	♃14♍
7	7.00	15	12♌	16	29	12	♄20♍
8	7.04	15	27	15	0♊	13	♅ 9♓R
9	7.08	16	12♍	14	1	13	♆12♌
10	7.11	17	26	14	2	14	♇ 8♋
11	7.15	18	10♎	13	3	15	♃15♍
12	7.19	19	23	13	4	15	♄20♍
13	7.23	20	6♏	12	5	16	♅ 9♓R
14	7.27	21	19	12	6	17	♆12♌
15	7.31	22	2♐	11	7	17	♇ 8♋
16	7.35	23	14	11	8	18	♃15♍
17	7.39	24	26	11	9	19	♄20♍
18	7.43	25	8♑	11	10	19	♅ 9♓R
19	7.47	26	20	11D	11	20	♆13♌
20	7.51	27	2♒	11	12	21	♇ 9♋
21	7.55	28	14	11	13	21	♃16♍
22	7.59	29	26	11	14	22	♄21♍
23	8.03	0♌	8♓	12	15	23	♅ 9♓R
24	8.07	1	20	12	17	23	♆13♌
25	8.11	2	2♈	13	18	24	♇ 9♋
26	8.15	3	14	13	19	25	♃17♍
27	8.18	4	27	14	20	25	♄21♍
28	8.22	5	9♉	15	21	26	♅ 9♓R
29	8.26	6	23	16	22	26	♆13♌
30	8.30	6	6♊	17	23	27	♇ 9♋
31	8.34	7	20	18	24	28	♃18♍

Aug	STime	☉	☽	☿	♀	♂	Plnts
1	8.38	8♌	5♋	19♋	25♊	28♋	♃18♍
2	8.42	9	20	21	26	29	♄22♍
3	8.46	10	5♌	22	27	0♌	♅ 8♓R
4	8.50	11	21	23	28	0	♆13♌
5	8.54	12	6♍	25	0♋	1	♇ 9♋
6	8.58	13	21	27	1	2	♃19♍
7	9.02	14	5♎	28	2	2	♄22♍
8	9.06	15	19	0♌	3	3	♅ 8♓R
9	9.10	16	3♏	2	4	4	♆13♌
10	9.14	17	16	4	5	4	♇ 9♋
11	9.18	18	29	6	6	5	♃20♍
12	9.22	19	11♐	7	7	6	♄23♍
13	9.26	20	23	9	9	6	♅ 8♓R
14	9.29	21	5♑	11	10	7	♆13♌
15	9.33	22	17	13	11	7	♇ 9♋
16	9.37	23	29	15	12	8	♃21♍
17	9.41	24	11♒	17	13	9	♄23♍
18	9.45	25	23	20	14	9	♅ 8♓R
19	9.49	26	5♓	22	15	10	♆14♌
20	9.53	27	17	24	16	11	♇ 9♋
21	9.57	28	29	26	18	11	♃22♍
22	10.01	29	11♈	28	19	12	♄24♍
23	10.05	29	23	0♍	20	13	♅ 8♓R
24	10.09	0♍	6♉	2	21	13	♆14♌
25	10.13	1	19	3	22	14	♇ 9♋
26	10.17	2	2♊	5	23	14	♃23♍
27	10.21	3	16	7	25	15	♄25♍
28	10.25	4	0♋	9	26	16	♅ 7♓R
29	10.29	5	14	11	27	16	♆14♌
30	10.33	6	29	13	28	17	♇ 9♋
31	10.36	7	14♌	15	29	18	♃24♍

Sep	STime	☉	☽	☿	♀	♂	Plnts
1	10.40	8♍	29♌	17♍	0♌	18♌	♃24♍
2	10.44	9	14♍	18	2	19	♄25♍
3	10.48	10	29	20	3	20	♅ 7♓R
4	10.52	11	14♎	22	4	20	♆14♌
5	10.56	12	28	24	5	21	♇10♋
6	11.00	13	11♏	25	6	21	♃26♍
7	11.04	14	25	27	7	22	♄26♍
8	11.08	15	7♐	29	9	23	♅ 7♓R
9	11.12	16	20	0♎	10	23	♆14♌
10	11.16	17	2♑	2	11	24	♇10♋
11	11.20	18	14	4	12	25	♃27♍
12	11.24	19	26	5	13	25	♄27♍
13	11.28	20	8♒	7	15	26	♅ 7♓R
14	11.32	21	20	8	16	27	♆15♌
15	11.36	22	2♓	10	17	27	♇10♋
16	11.40	23	14	11	18	28	♃28♍
17	11.43	24	26	13	19	28	♄27♍
18	11.47	25	8♈	14	20	29	♅ 7♓R
19	11.51	26	20	16	22	0♍	♆15♌
20	11.55	27	3♉	17	23	0	♇10♋
21	11.59	28	16	19	24	1	♃29♍
22	12.03	29	29	20	25	2	♄28♍
23	12.07	0♎	12♊	22	26	2	♅ 6♓R
24	12.11	1	26	23	28	3	♆15♌
25	12.15	2	10♋	24	29	3	♇10♋
26	12.19	3	24	26	0♍	4	♃ 0♎
27	12.23	4	8♌	27	1	5	♄28♍
28	12.27	5	23	28	3	5	♅ 6♓R
29	12.31	5	8♍	29	4	6	♆15♌
30	12.35	6	23	1♏	5	7	♇10♋

Oct	STime	☉	☽	☿	♀	♂	Plnts
1	12.39	7♎	7♎	2♏	6♍	7♍	♃ 1♎
2	12.43	8	22	3	7	8	♄29♍
3	12.47	9	6♏	4	9	9	♅ 6♓R
4	12.51	10	19	5	10	9	♆15♌
5	12.54	11	3♐	7	11	10	♇10♋
6	12.58	12	16	8	12	10	♃ 2♎
7	13.02	13	28	9	13	11	♄ 0♎
8	13.06	14	11♑	10	15	12	♅ 6♓R
9	13.10	15	23	11	16	12	♆15♌
10	13.14	16	5♒	11	17	13	♇10♋
11	13.18	17	16	12	18	13	♃ 3♎
12	13.22	18	28	13	20	14	♄ 0♎
13	13.26	19	10♓	14	21	15	♅ 6♓R
14	13.30	20	22	14	22	15	♆15♌
15	13.34	21	5♈	15	23	16	♇10♋
16	13.38	22	17	15	24	17	♃ 4♎
17	13.42	23	0♉	16	26	17	♄ 1♎
18	13.46	24	13	16	27	18	♅ 6♓R
19	13.50	25	26	16	28	18	♆15♌
20	13.54	26	9♊	16R	29	19	♇10♋R
21	13.58	27	23	16	1♎	20	♃ 5♎
22	14.01	28	6♋	16	2	20	♄ 1♎
23	14.05	29	20	15	3	21	♅ 6♓R
24	14.09	0♏	4♌	15	4	22	♆15♌
25	14.13	1	19	14	6	22	♇10♋
26	14.17	2	3♍	13	7	23	♃ 6♎
27	14.21	3	17	12	8	23	♄ 2♎
28	14.25	4	2♎	11	9	24	♅ 6♓R
29	14.29	5	16	10	11	25	♆16♌
30	14.33	6	0♏	8	12	25	♇10♋R
31	14.37	7	14	7	13	26	♃ 7♎

Nov	STime	☉	☽	☿	♀	♂	Plnts
1	14.41	8♏	27♏	6♏	14♎	27♍	♃ 7♎
2	14.45	9	11♐	5	16	27	♄ 3♎
3	14.49	10	24	3	17	28	♅ 5♓R
4	14.53	11	6♑	2	18	28	♆16♌
5	14.57	12	18	2	19	29	♇10♋R
6	15.01	13	1♒	1	20	0♎	♃ 8♎
7	15.05	14	12	0	22	0	♄ 3♎
8	15.09	15	24	0	23	1	♅ 5♓R
9	15.12	16	6♓	0D	24	1	♆16♌
10	15.16	17	18	0	25	2	♇10♋R
11	15.20	18	0♈	0	27	3	♃ 9♎
12	15.24	19	13	1	28	3	♄ 4♎
13	15.28	20	25	2	29	4	♅ 5♓
14	15.32	21	8♉	2	0♏	4	♆16♌
15	15.36	22	21	3	2	5	♇10♋R
16	15.40	23	5♊	4	3	6	♃10♎
17	15.44	24	19	5	4	6	♄ 4♎
18	15.48	25	3♋	6	5	7	♅ 5♓
19	15.52	26	17	7	7	8	♆16♌
20	15.56	27	1♌	9	8	8	♇ 9♋R
21	16.00	28	15	10	9	9	♃11♎
22	16.04	29	0♍	11	10	9	♄ 5♎
23	16.08	0♐	14	13	12	10	♅ 5♓
24	16.12	1	28	14	13	11	♆16♌R
25	16.16	2	12♎	15	14	11	♇ 9♋R
26	16.19	3	25	17	15	12	♃12♎
27	16.23	4	9♏	18	17	12	♄ 5♎
28	16.27	5	22	20	18	13	♅ 5♓
29	16.31	6	6♐	21	19	14	♆16♌
30	16.35	7	19	23	21	14	♇ 9♋R

Dec	STime	☉	☽	☿	♀	♂	Plnts
1	16.39	8♐	2♑	24♏	22♏	15♎	♃13♎
2	16.43	9	14	26	23	15	♄ 5♎
3	16.47	11	26	27	24	16	♅ 6♓
4	16.51	12	8♒	29	26	17	♆16♌R
5	16.55	13	20	0♐	27	17	♇ 9♋R
6	16.59	14	2♓	2	28	18	♃14♎
7	17.03	15	14	4	29	18	♄ 6♎
8	17.07	16	26	5	1♐	19	♅ 6♓
9	17.11	17	8♈	7	2	20	♆16♌R
10	17.15	18	20	8	3	20	♇ 9♋R
11	17.19	19	3♉	10	4	21	♃14♎
12	17.23	20	16	11	6	21	♄ 6♎
13	17.27	21	0♊	13	7	22	♅ 6♓
14	17.30	22	14	14	8	23	♆15♌R
15	17.34	23	28	16	9	23	♇ 9♋R
16	17.38	24	12♋	17	11	24	♃15♎
17	17.42	25	27	19	12	24	♄ 6♎
18	17.46	26	12♌	21	13	25	♅ 6♓
19	17.50	27	26	22	14	26	♆15♌R
20	17.54	28	10♍	24	16	26	♇ 9♋R
21	17.58	29	25	25	17	27	♃16♎
22	18.02	0♑	8♎	27	18	27	♄ 7♎
23	18.06	1	22	28	19	28	♅ 6♓
24	18.10	2	6♏	0♑	21	29	♆15♌R
25	18.14	3	19	2	22	29	♇ 9♋R
26	18.18	4	2♐	3	23	0♏	♃16♎
27	18.22	5	15	5	24	0	♄ 7♎
28	18.26	6	27	6	26	1	♅ 6♓
29	18.30	7	10♑	8	27	1	♆15♌R
30	18.34	8	22	10	28	2	♇ 9♋R
31	18.37	9	4♒	11	29	3	♃17♎

Jan	STime	☉	☽	☿	♀	♂	Plnts
1	18.41	10♑	16♒	13♑	1♑	3♏	♃17♎
2	18.45	11	28	14	2	4	♄ 7♎
3	18.49	12	10♓	16	3	4	♅ 6♓
4	18.53	13	22	18	4	5	♆15♌R
5	18.57	14	4♈	19	6	6	♇ 9♋R
6	19.01	15	16	21	7	6	♃17♎
7	19.05	16	28	23	8	7	♄ 7♎
8	19.09	17	11♉	24	10	7	♅ 7♓
9	19.13	18	24	26	11	8	♆15♌R
10	19.17	19	7♊	28	12	8	♇ 9♋R
11	19.21	20	21	29	13	9	♃18♎
12	19.25	21	6♋	1♒	15	10	♄ 7♎
13	19.29	22	21	3	16	10	♅ 7♓
14	19.33	23	6♌	4	17	11	♆15♌R
15	19.37	24	21	6	18	11	♇ 8♋R
16	19.41	25	6♍	8	20	12	♃18♎
17	19.44	26	20	9	21	12	♄ 7♎
18	19.48	27	5♎	11	22	13	♅ 7♓
19	19.52	28	19	13	23	13	♆15♌R
20	19.56	29	3♏	14	25	14	♇ 8♋R
21	20.00	0♒	16	16	26	15	♃18♎
22	20.04	1	29	17	27	15	♄ 7♎R
23	20.08	2	12♐	19	28	16	♅ 7♓
24	20.12	3	24	20	0♒	16	♆15♌R
25	20.16	4	7♑	22	1	17	♇ 8♋R
26	20.20	5	19	23	2	17	♃19♎
27	20.24	6	1♒	25	3	18	♄ 7♎R
28	20.28	7	13	26	5	18	♅ 8♓
29	20.32	9	25	27	6	19	♆14♌R
30	20.36	10	7♓	28	7	20	♇ 8♋R
31	20.40	11	19	29	8	20	♃19♎

Feb	STime	☉	☽	☿	♀	♂	Plnts
1	20.44	12♒	0♈	0♓	10♒	21♏	♃19♎
2	20.48	13	12	0	11	21	♄ 7♎R
3	20.52	14	24	1	12	22	♅ 8♓
4	20.55	15	6♉	1	13	22	♆14♌R
5	20.59	16	19	1R	15	23	♇ 8♋R
6	21.03	17	2♊	1	16	23	♃19♎R
7	21.07	18	15	1	17	24	♄ 7♎R
8	21.11	19	29	0	18	24	♅ 8♓
9	21.15	20	14♋	29♒	20	25	♆14♌R
10	21.19	21	29	29	21	25	♇ 8♋R
11	21.23	22	14♌	28	22	26	♃18♎R
12	21.27	23	29	27	23	27	♄ 7♎R
13	21.31	24	14♍	26	25	27	♅ 8♓
14	21.35	25	29	25	26	28	♆14♌R
15	21.39	26	14♎	23	27	28	♇ 8♋R
16	21.43	27	28	22	28	29	♃18♎R
17	21.47	28	12♏	21	0♓	29	♄ 6♎R
18	21.51	29	26	20	1	0♐	♅ 9♓
19	21.55	0♓	9♐	19	2	0	♆14♌R
20	21.59	1	21	18	3	1	♇ 8♋R
21	22.02	2	4♑	18	5	1	♃18♎R
22	22.06	3	16	17	6	2	♄ 6♎R
23	22.10	4	28	16	7	2	♅ 9♓
24	22.14	5	10♒	16	9	3	♆14♌R
25	22.18	6	22	16	10	3	♇ 8♋R
26	22.22	7	4♓	16	11	4	♃18♎R
27	22.26	8	16	16D	12	4	♄ 6♎R
28	22.30	9	27	16	14	5	♅ 9♓

Mar	STime	☉	☽	☿	♀	♂	Plnts
1	22.34	10♓	9♈	16♒	15♓	5♐	♃18♎R
2	22.38	11	21	16	16	6	♄ 6♎R
3	22.42	12	3♉	17	17	6	♅ 9♓
4	22.46	13	16	17	19	6	♆14♌R
5	22.50	14	28	18	20	7	♇ 8♋R
6	22.54	15	11♊	18	21	7	♃17♎R
7	22.58	16	24	19	22	8	♄ 5♎R
8	23.02	17	8♋	20	23	8	♅10♓
9	23.06	18	22	21	25	9	♆13♌R
10	23.10	19	7♌	21	26	9	♇ 8♋R
11	23.13	20	22	22	27	10	♃17♎R
12	23.17	21	7♍	23	28	10	♄ 5♎R
13	23.21	22	22	24	0♈	11	♅10♓
14	23.25	23	7♎	25	1	11	♆13♌R
15	23.29	24	22	26	2	11	♇ 8♋
16	23.33	25	7♏	28	3	12	♃16♎R
17	23.37	26	21	29	5	12	♄ 5♎R
18	23.41	27	4♐	0♓	6	13	♅10♓
19	23.45	28	18	1	7	13	♆13♌R
20	23.49	29	0♑	2	8	13	♇ 8♋
21	23.53	0♈	13	4	10	14	♃15♎R
22	23.57	1	25	5	11	14	♄ 4♎R
23	0.01	2	7♒	6	12	15	♅11♓
24	0.05	3	19	8	13	15	♆13♌R
25	0.09	4	1♓	9	15	15	♇ 8♋
26	0.13	5	13	11	16	16	♃15♎R
27	0.17	6	24	12	17	16	♄ 4♎R
28	0.20	7	6♈	14	18	17	♅11♓
29	0.24	8	18	15	20	17	♆13♌R
30	0.28	9	0♉	17	21	17	♇ 8♋
31	0.32	10	13	18	22	18	♃14♎R

Apr	STime	☉	☽	☿	♀	♂	Plnts
1	0.36	11♈	25♉	20♓	23♈	18♐	♃14♎R
2	0.40	12	8♊	21	25	18	♄ 3♎R
3	0.44	13	21	23	26	19	♅11♓
4	0.48	14	4♋	25	27	19	♆13♌R
5	0.52	15	18	26	28	19	♇ 8♋
6	0.56	16	2♌	28	29	20	♃13♎R
7	1.00	17	16	0♈	1♉	20	♄ 3♎R
8	1.04	18	1♍	2	2	20	♅11♓
9	1.08	19	16	3	3	20	♆13♌R
10	1.12	20	1♎	5	4	21	♇ 8♋
11	1.16	21	16	7	6	21	♃13♎R
12	1.20	21	0♏	9	7	21	♄ 3♎R
13	1.24	22	15	11	8	22	♅12♓
14	1.28	23	29	13	9	22	♆13♌
15	1.31	24	13♐	15	11	22	♇ 8♋
16	1.35	25	26	16	12	22	♃12♎R
17	1.39	26	9♑	18	13	23	♄ 2♎R
18	1.43	27	21	20	14	23	♅12♓
19	1.47	28	4♒	23	16	23	♆13♌
20	1.51	29	16	25	17	23	♇ 8♋
21	1.55	0♉	27	27	18	23	♃12♎R
22	1.59	1	9♓	29	19	24	♄ 2♎R
23	2.03	2	21	1♉	20	24	♅12♓
24	2.07	3	3♈	3	22	24	♆13♌
25	2.11	4	15	5	23	24	♇ 8♋
26	2.15	5	27	7	24	24	♃11♎R
27	2.19	6	9♉	9	25	24	♄ 2♎R
28	2.23	7	22	12	27	24	♅12♓
29	2.27	8	5♊	14	28	25	♆13♌
30	2.31	9	18	16	29	25	♇ 8♋

May	STime	☉	☽	☿	♀	♂	Plnts
1	2.35	10♉	1♋	18♉	0♊	25♐	♃11♎R
2	2.38	11	15	20	1	25	♄ 1♎R
3	2.42	12	28	22	3	25	♅12♓
4	2.46	13	12♌	24	4	25	♆13♌
5	2.50	14	27	26	5	25	♇ 8♋
6	2.54	15	11♍	28	6	25	♃10♎R
7	2.58	16	25	0♊	8	25	♄ 1♎R
8	3.02	17	10♎	2	9	25R	♅13♓
9	3.06	18	24	4	10	25	♆13♌
10	3.10	19	9♏	6	11	25	♇ 8♋
11	3.14	20	23	7	12	25	♃10♎R
12	3.18	21	7♐	9	14	25	♄ 1♎R
13	3.22	22	21	11	15	25	♅13♓
14	3.26	23	4♑	12	16	25	♆13♌
15	3.30	24	17	14	17	25	♇ 8♋
16	3.34	25	29	15	19	25	♃ 9♎R
17	3.38	25	12♒	17	20	24	♄ 1♎R
18	3.42	26	24	18	21	24	♅13♓
19	3.45	27	5♓	19	22	24	♆13♌
20	3.49	28	17	21	23	24	♇ 8♋
21	3.53	29	29	22	25	24	♃ 9♎R
22	3.57	0♊	11♈	23	26	24	♄ 1♎R
23	4.01	1	23	24	27	24	♅13♓
24	4.05	2	5♉	25	28	23	♆13♌
25	4.09	3	18	26	29	23	♇ 8♋
26	4.13	4	1♊	26	1♋	23	♃ 9♎R
27	4.17	5	14	27	2	23	♄ 1♎R
28	4.21	6	28	28	3	22	♅13♓
29	4.25	7	11♋	28	4	22	♆13♌
30	4.29	8	25	29	5	22	♇ 8♋
31	4.33	9	9♌	29	7	22	♃ 9♎R

Jun	STime	☉	☽	☿	♀	♂	Plnts
1	4.37	10♊	23♌	0♋	8♋	21♐	♃ 9♎R
2	4.41	11	7♍	0	9	21	♄ 1♎
3	4.45	12	22	0	10	21	♅13♓
4	4.49	13	6♎	1	12	21	♆13♌
5	4.53	14	20	1R	13	20	♇ 9♋
6	4.56	15	4♏	1	14	20	♃ 9♎
7	5.00	16	18	1	15	20	♄ 1♎
8	5.04	17	2♐	0	16	19	♅13♓
9	5.08	18	16	0	18	19	♆13♌
10	5.12	19	29	0	19	19	♇ 9♋
11	5.16	19	12♑	0	20	18	♃ 9♎
12	5.20	20	25	29♊	21	18	♄ 1♎
13	5.24	21	7♒	29	22	18	♅13♓
14	5.28	22	19	28	24	17	♆14♌
15	5.32	23	1♓	28	25	17	♇ 9♋
16	5.36	24	13	27	26	17	♃ 9♎
17	5.40	25	25	27	27	16	♄ 1♎
18	5.44	26	7♈	26	28	16	♅13♓
19	5.48	27	19	25	29	16	♆14♌
20	5.52	28	1♉	25	1♌	15	♇ 9♋
21	5.56	29	14	24	2	15	♃ 9♎
22	6.00	0♋	26	24	3	15	♄ 1♎
23	6.03	1	10♊	23	4	14	♅13♓
24	6.07	2	23	23	5	14	♆14♌
25	6.11	3	7♋	23	7	14	♇ 9♋
26	6.15	4	21	22	8	14	♃ 9♎
27	6.19	5	5♌	22	9	13	♄ 1♎
28	6.23	6	20	22	10	13	♅13♓R
29	6.27	7	4♍	22D	11	13	♆14♌
30	6.31	8	18	22	13	13	♇ 9♋

Jul	STime	☉	☽	☿	♀	♂	Plnts
1	6.35	9♋	3♎	22♊	14♌	12♐	♃10♎
2	6.39	10	17	22	15	12	♄ 1♎
3	6.43	10	1♏	22	16	12	♅13♓R
4	6.47	11	14	23	17	12	♆14♌
5	6.51	12	28	23	18	12	♇ 9♋
6	6.55	13	11♐	24	20	12	♃10♎
7	6.59	14	25	24	21	11	♄ 1♎
8	7.03	15	8♑	25	22	11	♅13♓R
9	7.07	16	21	26	23	11	♆14♌
10	7.11	17	3♒	26	24	11	♇ 9♋
11	7.14	18	15	27	25	11	♃10♎
12	7.18	19	28	28	27	11	♄ 2♎
13	7.22	20	10♓	29	28	11	♅13♓R
14	7.26	21	21	0♋	29	11	♆14♌
15	7.30	22	3♈	2	0♍	11	♇10♋
16	7.34	23	15	3	1	11D	♃11♎
17	7.38	24	27	4	2	11	♄ 2♎
18	7.42	25	9♉	6	4	11	♅13♓R
19	7.46	26	22	7	5	11	♆15♌
20	7.50	27	4♊	9	6	11	♇10♋
21	7.54	28	18	10	7	11	♃12♎
22	7.58	29	1♋	12	8	11	♄ 2♎
23	8.02	0♌	16	14	9	11	♅13♓R
24	8.06	0	0♌	16	11	11	♆15♌
25	8.10	1	15	18	12	11	♇10♋
26	8.14	2	29	20	13	11	♃12♎
27	8.18	3	14♍	21	14	12	♄ 3♎
28	8.21	4	29	23	15	12	♅13♓R
29	8.25	5	13♎	25	16	12	♆15♌
30	8.29	6	27	28	17	12	♇10♋
31	8.33	7	11♏	0♌	19	12	♃13♎

Aug	STime	☉	☽	☿	♀	♂	Plnts
1	8.37	8♌	25♏	2♌	20♍	12♐	♃13♎
2	8.41	9	8♐	4	21	13	♄ 3♎
3	8.45	10	21	6	22	13	♅13♓R
4	8.49	11	4♑	8	23	13	♆15♌
5	8.53	12	17	10	24	13	♇10♋
6	8.57	13	0♒	12	25	14	♃14♎
7	9.01	14	12	14	26	14	♄ 4♎
8	9.05	15	24	16	28	14	♅12♓R
9	9.09	16	6♓	18	29	14	♆15♌
10	9.13	17	18	20	0♎	15	♇10♋
11	9.17	18	0♈	22	1	15	♃14♎
12	9.21	19	11	24	2	15	♄ 4♎
13	9.25	20	23	26	3	16	♅12♓R
14	9.28	21	5♉	28	4	16	♆16♌
15	9.32	22	17	0♍	5	16	♇10♋
16	9.36	23	0♊	2	6	17	♃15♎
17	9.40	23	13	4	8	17	♄ 5♎
18	9.44	24	26	6	9	17	♅12♓R
19	9.48	25	10♋	7	10	18	♆16♌
20	9.52	26	24	9	11	18	♇10♋
21	9.56	27	8♌	11	12	19	♃16♎
22	10.00	28	23	13	13	19	♄ 5♎
23	10.04	29	8♍	14	14	19	♅12♓R
24	10.08	0♍	23	16	15	20	♆16♌
25	10.12	1	8♎	18	16	20	♇10♋
26	10.16	2	23	19	17	21	♃17♎
27	10.20	3	7♏	21	18	21	♄ 6♎
28	10.24	4	21	23	19	22	♅12♓R
29	10.28	5	5♐	24	21	22	♆16♌
30	10.32	6	18	26	22	23	♇11♋
31	10.36	7	1♑	27	23	23	♃18♎

Sep	STime	☉	☽	☿	♀	♂	Plnts
1	10.39	8♍	14♑	29♍	24♎	23♐	♃18♎
2	10.43	9	27	0♎	25	24	♄ 7♎
3	10.47	10	9♒	2	26	24	♅11♓R
4	10.51	11	21	3	27	25	♆16♌
5	10.55	12	3♓	5	28	25	♇11♋
6	10.59	13	15	6	29	26	♃19♎
7	11.03	14	27	7	0♏	26	♄ 7♎
8	11.07	15	8♈	9	1	27	♅11♓R
9	11.11	16	20	10	2	28	♆17♌
10	11.15	17	2♉	11	3	28	♇11♋
11	11.19	18	14	13	4	29	♃20♎
12	11.23	19	26	14	5	29	♄ 8♎
13	11.27	20	9♊	15	6	0♑	♅11♓R
14	11.31	21	21	16	7	0	♆17♌
15	11.35	22	5♋	17	8	1	♇11♋
16	11.39	23	18	19	9	1	♃21♎
17	11.43	24	2♌	20	10	2	♄ 8♎
18	11.46	24	17	21	11	2	♅11♓R
19	11.50	25	1♍	22	12	3	♆17♌
20	11.54	26	17	23	13	4	♇11♋
21	11.58	27	2♎	24	14	4	♃22♎
22	12.02	28	17	25	15	5	♄ 9♎
23	12.06	29	2♏	25	15	5	♅11♓R
24	12.10	0♎	17	26	16	6	♆17♌
25	12.14	1	1♐	27	17	7	♇11♋
26	12.18	2	15	28	18	7	♃23♎
27	12.22	3	28	28	19	8	♄ 9♎
28	12.26	4	11♑	29	20	8	♅10♓R
29	12.30	5	24	29	21	9	♆17♌
30	12.34	6	6♒	29	22	10	♇11♋

Oct	STime	☉	☽	☿	♀	♂	Plnts
1	12.38	7♎	18♒	0♏	22♏	10♑	♃24♎
2	12.42	8	0♓	0	23	11	♄10♎
3	12.46	9	12	0R	24	12	♅10♓R
4	12.50	10	23	0	25	12	♆17♌
5	12.54	11	5♈	0	26	13	♇11♋
6	12.57	12	17	29♎	26	13	♃25♎
7	13.01	13	29	29	27	14	♄11♎
8	13.05	14	11♉	28	28	15	♅10♓R
9	13.09	15	23	27	29	15	♆17♌
10	13.13	16	5♊	27	29	16	♇11♋
11	13.17	17	18	26	0♐	17	♃26♎
12	13.21	18	1♋	25	1	17	♄11♎
13	13.25	19	14	23	1	18	♅10♓R
14	13.29	20	27	22	2	19	♆17♌
15	13.33	21	11♌	21	3	19	♇11♋
16	13.37	22	25	20	3	20	♃27♎
17	13.41	23	10♍	19	4	21	♄12♎
18	13.45	24	25	18	4	21	♅10♓R
19	13.49	25	10♎	17	5	22	♆18♌
20	13.53	26	25	16	5	23	♇11♋R
21	13.57	27	10♏	15	6	23	♃29♎
22	14.01	28	25	15	6	24	♄13♎
23	14.04	29	9♐	14	7	25	♅10♓R
24	14.08	0♏	23	14D	7	25	♆18♌
25	14.12	1	7♑	14	8	26	♇11♋R
26	14.16	2	20	15	8	27	♃ 0♏
27	14.20	3	2♒	15	8	27	♄13♎
28	14.24	4	15	16	9	28	♅10♓R
29	14.28	5	27	17	9	29	♆18♌
30	14.32	6	9♓	17	9	0♒	♇11♋R
31	14.36	7	20	18	9	0	♃ 1♏

Nov	STime	☉	☽	☿	♀	♂	Plnts
1	14.40	8♏	2♈	20♎	9♐	1♒	♃ 1♏
2	14.44	9	14	21	9	2	♄14♎
3	14.48	10	26	22	10	2	♅ 9♓R
4	14.52	11	8♉	23	10R	3	♆18♌
5	14.56	12	20	25	10	4	♇11♋R
6	15.00	13	3♊	26	9	4	♃ 2♏
7	15.04	14	15	28	9	5	♄14♎
8	15.08	15	28	29	9	6	♅ 9♓R
9	15.11	16	11♋	1♏	9	7	♆18♌
10	15.15	17	24	2	9	7	♇11♋R
11	15.19	18	8♌	4	9	8	♃ 3♏
12	15.23	19	21	5	8	9	♄15♎
13	15.27	20	5♍	7	8	9	♅ 9♓
14	15.31	21	19	8	8	10	♆18♌
15	15.35	22	4♎	10	7	11	♇11♋R
16	15.39	23	19	12	7	12	♃ 4♏
17	15.43	24	3♏	13	6	12	♄16♎
18	15.47	25	18	15	6	13	♅ 9♓
19	15.51	26	3♐	16	5	14	♆18♌
20	15.55	27	17	18	5	14	♇11♋R
21	15.59	28	1♑	19	4	15	♃ 5♏
22	16.03	29	15	21	4	16	♄16♎
23	16.07	0♐	28	23	3	17	♅ 9♓
24	16.11	1	10♒	24	2	17	♆18♌
25	16.15	2	23	26	2	18	♇11♋R
26	16.19	3	5♓	27	1	19	♃ 6♏
27	16.22	4	17	29	1	19	♄17♎
28	16.26	5	29	1♐	0	20	♅ 9♓
29	16.30	6	10♈	2	29♏	21	♆18♌R
30	16.34	7	22	4	29	22	♇10♋R

Dec	STime	☉	☽	☿	♀	♂	Plnts
1	16.38	8♐	4♉	5♐	28♏	22♒	♃ 7♏
2	16.42	9	16	7	28	23	♄17♎
3	16.46	10	29	8	27	24	♅ 9♓
4	16.50	11	12♊	10	27	25	♆18♌
5	16.54	12	24	12	26	25	♇10♋R
6	16.58	13	8♋	13	26	26	♃ 8♏
7	17.02	14	21	15	26	27	♄17♎
8	17.06	15	5♌	16	25	27	♅10♓
9	17.10	16	18	18	25	28	♆18♌R
10	17.14	17	2♍	19	25	29	♇10♋R
11	17.18	18	16	21	25	0♓	♃ 9♏
12	17.22	19	0♎	23	24	0	♄18♎
13	17.26	20	14	24	24	1	♅10♓
14	17.29	21	28	26	24	2	♆18♌R
15	17.33	22	13♏	27	24D	3	♇10♋R
16	17.37	23	27	29	24	3	♃10♏
17	17.41	24	11♐	0♑	24	4	♄18♎
18	17.45	25	25	2	24	5	♅10♓
19	17.49	27	9♑	4	24	6	♆18♌R
20	17.53	28	23	5	25	6	♇10♋R
21	17.57	29	6♒	7	25	7	♃11♏
22	18.01	0♑	18	8	25	8	♄19♎
23	18.05	1	1♓	10	25	8	♅10♓
24	18.09	2	13	12	26	9	♆18♌R
25	18.13	3	25	13	26	10	♇10♋R
26	18.17	4	6♈	15	26	11	♃12♏
27	18.21	5	18	16	27	11	♄19♎
28	18.25	6	0♉	18	27	12	♅10♓
29	18.29	7	12	20	28	13	♆17♌R
30	18.33	8	24	21	28	14	♇10♋R
31	18.37	9	7♊	23	29	14	♃13♏

1923

Jan	STime	☉	☽	☿	♀	♂	Plnts
1	18.40	10♑	20♊	24♑	29♏	15♓	♃13♏
2	18.44	11	3♋	26	0♐	16	♄19♎
3	18.48	12	17	27	0	17	♅10♓
4	18.52	13	1♌	29	1	17	♆17♌R
5	18.56	14	14	0♒	2	18	♇10♋R
6	19.00	15	29	2	2	19	♃14♏
7	19.04	16	13♍	3	3	20	♄19♎
8	19.08	17	27	5	4	20	♅10♓
9	19.12	18	11♎	6	4	21	♆17♌R
10	19.16	19	25	7	5	22	♇10♋R
11	19.20	20	9♏	9	6	22	♃15♏
12	19.24	21	23	10	7	23	♄20♎
13	19.28	22	7♐	11	7	24	♅11♓
14	19.32	23	21	12	8	25	♆17♌R
15	19.36	24	4♑	13	9	25	♇10♋R
16	19.40	25	18	13	10	26	♃15♏
17	19.44	26	1♒	14	11	27	♄20♎
18	19.47	27	14	14	12	28	♅11♓
19	19.51	28	26	15	12	28	♆17♌R
20	19.55	29	8♓	15R	13	29	♇ 9♋R
21	19.59	0♒	20	15	14	0♈	♃16♏
22	20.03	1	2♈	14	15	0	♄20♎
23	20.07	2	14	14	16	1	♅11♓
24	20.11	3	26	13	17	2	♆17♌R
25	20.15	4	8♉	12	18	3	♇ 9♋R
26	20.19	5	20	11	19	3	♃16♏
27	20.23	6	2♊	10	20	4	♄20♎
28	20.27	7	15	9	21	5	♅11♓
29	20.31	8	28	7	22	6	♆17♌R
30	20.35	9	11♋	6	23	6	♇ 9♋R
31	20.39	10	25	5	24	7	♃17♏

Feb	STime	☉	☽	☿	♀	♂	Plnts
1	20.43	11♒	9♌	4♒	25♐	8♈	♃17♏
2	20.47	12	24	3	26	9	♄20♎R
3	20.51	13	8♍	2	27	9	♅12♓
4	20.55	14	23	1	28	10	♆17♌R
5	20.58	15	7♎	0	29	11	♇ 9♋R
6	21.02	16	22	0	0♑	11	♃17♏
7	21.06	17	6♏	29♑	1	12	♄20♎R
8	21.10	18	20	29	2	13	♅12♓
9	21.14	19	4♐	29	3	14	♆16♌R
10	21.18	20	17	29D	4	14	♇ 9♋R
11	21.22	21	1♑	29	5	15	♃18♏
12	21.26	22	14	29	6	16	♄20♎R
13	21.30	23	27	0♒	7	16	♅12♓
14	21.34	24	10♒	0	8	17	♆16♌R
15	21.38	25	22	0	9	18	♇ 9♋R
16	21.42	26	4♓	1	10	19	♃18♏
17	21.46	28	17	2	11	19	♄20♎R
18	21.50	29	29	2	12	20	♅12♓
19	21.54	0♓	10♈	3	13	21	♆16♌R
20	21.58	1	22	4	14	21	♇ 9♋R
21	22.02	2	4♉	5	16	22	♃18♏
22	22.05	3	16	6	17	23	♄19♎R
23	22.09	4	28	7	18	24	♅13♓
24	22.13	5	10♊	8	19	24	♆16♌R
25	22.17	6	23	9	20	25	♇ 9♋R
26	22.21	7	6♋	10	21	26	♃19♏
27	22.25	8	19	11	22	26	♄19♎R
28	22.29	9	3♌	12	23	27	♅13♓

Mar	STime	☉	☽	☿	♀	♂	Plnts
1	22.33	10♓	17♌	14♒	24♑	28♈	♃19♏
2	22.37	11	2♍	15	25	29	♄19♎R
3	22.41	12	17	16	27	29	♅13♓
4	22.45	13	2♎	17	28	0♉	♆16♌R
5	22.49	14	17	19	29	1	♇ 9♋
6	22.53	15	1♏	20	0♒	1	♃19♏
7	22.57	16	16	22	1	2	♄19♎R
8	23.01	17	0♐	23	2	3	♅13♓
9	23.05	18	14	24	3	4	♆16♌R
10	23.09	19	28	26	5	4	♇ 9♋
11	23.12	20	11♑	27	6	5	♃19♏R
12	23.16	21	24	29	7	6	♄18♎R
13	23.20	22	6♒	0♓	8	6	♅14♓
14	23.24	23	19	2	9	7	♆16♌R
15	23.28	24	1♓	3	10	8	♇ 9♋
16	23.32	25	13	5	11	8	♃18♏R
17	23.36	26	25	7	13	9	♄18♎R
18	23.40	27	7♈	8	14	10	♅14♓
19	23.44	28	19	10	15	11	♆15♌R
20	23.48	29	1♉	11	16	11	♇ 9♋
21	23.52	0♈	12	13	17	12	♃18♏R
22	23.56	1	24	15	18	13	♄18♎R
23	0.00	2	6♊	17	20	13	♅14♓
24	0.04	3	19	18	21	14	♆15♌R
25	0.08	4	1♋	20	22	15	♇ 9♋
26	0.12	5	14	22	23	15	♃18♏R
27	0.16	6	27	24	24	16	♄17♎R
28	0.20	6	11♌	25	25	17	♅15♓
29	0.23	7	25	27	27	18	♆15♌R
30	0.27	8	10♍	29	28	18	♇ 9♋
31	0.31	9	25	1♈	29	19	♃18♏R

Apr	STime	☉	☽	☿	♀	♂	Plnts
1	0.35	10♈	10♎	3♈	0♓	20♉	♃18♏R
2	0.39	11	25	5	1	20	♄17♎R
3	0.43	12	10♏	7	2	21	♅15♓
4	0.47	13	25	9	4	22	♆15♌R
5	0.51	14	10♐	11	5	22	♇ 9♋
6	0.55	15	24	13	6	23	♃17♏R
7	0.59	16	7♑	15	7	24	♄16♎R
8	1.03	17	21	17	8	24	♅15♓
9	1.07	18	4♒	19	9	25	♆15♌R
10	1.11	19	16	21	11	26	♇ 9♋
11	1.15	20	28	23	12	27	♃17♏R
12	1.19	21	10♓	25	13	27	♄16♎R
13	1.23	22	22	28	14	28	♅15♓
14	1.27	23	4♈	0♉	15	29	♆15♌R
15	1.30	24	16	2	17	29	♇ 9♋
16	1.34	25	28	4	18	0♊	♃16♏R
17	1.38	26	9♉	6	19	1	♄16♎R
18	1.42	27	21	8	20	1	♅16♓
19	1.46	28	3♊	10	21	2	♆15♌
20	1.50	29	16	12	22	3	♇ 9♋
21	1.54	0♉	28	14	24	3	♃16♏R
22	1.58	1	10♋	16	25	4	♄15♎R
23	2.02	2	23	18	26	5	♅16♓
24	2.06	3	6♌	19	27	5	♆15♌R
25	2.10	4	20	21	28	6	♇ 9♋
26	2.14	5	4♍	23	0♈	7	♃15♏R
27	2.18	6	18	24	1	7	♄15♎R
28	2.22	7	3♎	26	2	8	♅16♓
29	2.26	8	18	27	3	9	♆15♌
30	2.30	9	3♏	29	4	9	♇ 9♋

May	STime	☉	☽	☿	♀	♂	Plnts
1	2.34	10♉	18♏	0♊	6♈	10♊	♃14♏R
2	2.38	11	3♐	1	7	11	♄15♎R
3	2.41	12	18	2	8	11	♅16♓
4	2.45	13	2♑	4	9	12	♆15♌
5	2.49	14	16	5	10	13	♇ 9♋
6	2.53	15	0♒	6	12	13	♃14♏R
7	2.57	16	13	6	13	14	♄14♎R
8	3.01	17	25	7	14	15	♅16♓
9	3.05	18	7♓	8	15	16	♆15♌
10	3.09	18	19	9	16	16	♇ 9♋
11	3.13	19	1♈	9	18	17	♃13♏R
12	3.17	20	13	10	19	18	♄14♎R
13	3.21	21	25	10	20	18	♅17♓
14	3.25	22	6♉	10	21	19	♆15♌
15	3.29	23	18	10	22	20	♇ 9♋
16	3.33	24	0♊	11	24	20	♃12♏R
17	3.37	25	13	11R	25	21	♄14♎R
18	3.41	26	25	11	26	22	♅17♓
19	3.45	27	8♋	10	27	22	♆15♌
20	3.48	28	20	10	28	23	♇ 9♋
21	3.52	29	3♌	10	0♉	23	♃12♏R
22	3.56	0♊	16	10	1	24	♄14♎R
23	4.00	1	0♍	9	2	25	♅17♓
24	4.04	2	14	9	3	25	♆15♌
25	4.08	3	28	8	4	26	♇ 9♋
26	4.12	4	12♎	8	6	27	♃11♏R
27	4.16	5	27	7	7	27	♄13♎R
28	4.20	6	12♏	7	8	28	♅17♓
29	4.24	7	27	6	9	29	♆15♌
30	4.28	8	12♐	6	10	29	♇10♋
31	4.32	9	26	5	12	0♋	♃11♏R

Jun	STime	☉	☽	☿	♀	♂	Plnts
1	4.36	10♊	11♑	5♊	13♉	1♋	♃11♏R
2	4.40	11	25	4	14	1	♄13♎R
3	4.44	12	8♒	4	15	2	♅17♓
4	4.48	13	21	3	16	3	♆15♌
5	4.52	13	3♓	3	18	3	♇10♋
6	4.56	14	16	3	19	4	♃10♏R
7	4.59	15	28	2	20	5	♄13♎R
8	5.03	16	10♈	2	21	5	♅17♓
9	5.07	17	21	2	22	6	♆16♌
10	5.11	18	3♉	2D	24	7	♇10♋
11	5.15	19	15	2	25	7	♃10♏R
12	5.19	20	27	2	26	8	♄13♎R
13	5.23	21	9♊	2	27	9	♅17♓
14	5.27	22	22	3	28	9	♆16♌
15	5.31	23	4♋	3	0♊	10	♇10♋
16	5.35	24	17	3	1	11	♃ 9♏R
17	5.39	25	0♌	4	2	11	♄13♎
18	5.43	26	13	4	3	12	♅17♓
19	5.47	27	27	5	5	13	♆16♌
20	5.51	28	10♍	6	6	13	♇10♋
21	5.55	29	24	7	7	14	♃ 9♏R
22	5.59	0♋	8♎	7	8	14	♄13♎
23	6.03	1	22	8	9	15	♅17♓R
24	6.06	2	7♏	9	11	16	♆16♌
25	6.10	3	21	10	12	16	♇10♋
26	6.14	4	6♐	12	13	17	♃ 9♏R
27	6.18	5	21	13	14	18	♄13♎
28	6.22	5	5♑	14	15	18	♅17♓
29	6.26	6	19	15	17	19	♆16♌
30	6.30	7	3♒	17	18	20	♇10♋

Jul	STime	☉	☽	☿	♀	♂	Plnts
1	6.34	8♋	16♒	18♊	19♊	20♋	♃ 9♏R
2	6.38	9	29	20	20	21	♄13♎
3	6.42	10	11♓	21	22	22	♅17♓R
4	6.46	11	24	23	23	22	♆16♌
5	6.50	12	6♈	24	24	23	♇10♋
6	6.54	13	18	26	25	24	♃ 9♏
7	6.58	14	29	28	26	24	♄13♎
8	7.02	15	11♉	0♋	28	25	♅17♓R
9	7.06	16	23	2	29	25	♆16♌
10	7.10	17	5♊	3	0♋	26	♇11♋
11	7.13	18	18	5	1	27	♃ 9♏
12	7.17	19	0♋	7	3	27	♄14♎
13	7.21	20	13	9	4	28	♅17♓R
14	7.25	21	26	11	5	29	♆17♌
15	7.29	22	10♌	14	6	29	♇11♋
16	7.33	23	23	16	7	0♌	♃ 9♏
17	7.37	24	7♍	18	9	1	♄14♎
18	7.41	25	21	20	10	1	♅17♓R
19	7.45	25	5♎	22	11	2	♆17♌
20	7.49	26	19	24	12	3	♇11♋
21	7.53	27	3♏	26	14	3	♃ 9♏
22	7.57	28	17	28	15	4	♄14♎
23	8.01	29	2♐	1♌	16	4	♅17♓R
24	8.05	0♌	16	3	17	5	♆17♌
25	8.09	1	0♑	5	18	6	♇11♋
26	8.13	2	14	7	20	6	♃ 9♏
27	8.17	3	28	9	21	7	♄14♎
28	8.21	4	11♒	11	22	8	♅17♓R
29	8.24	5	24	13	23	8	♆17♌
30	8.28	6	7♓	15	25	9	♇11♋
31	8.32	7	19	17	26	10	♃10♏

Aug	STime	☉	☽	☿	♀	♂	Plnts
1	8.36	8♌	2♈	19♌	27♋	10♌	♃10♏
2	8.40	9	14	21	28	11	♄15♎
3	8.44	10	26	22	29	12	♅17♓R
4	8.48	11	7♉	24	1♌	12	♆17♌
5	8.52	12	19	26	2	13	♇11♋
6	8.56	13	1♊	28	3	13	♃10♏
7	9.00	14	14	0♍	4	14	♄15♎
8	9.04	15	26	1	6	15	♅16♓R
9	9.08	16	9♋	3	7	15	♆18♌
10	9.12	17	22	5	8	16	♇11♋
11	9.16	17	5♌	6	9	17	♃11♏
12	9.20	18	19	8	11	17	♄16♎
13	9.24	19	3♍	10	12	18	♅16♓R
14	9.28	20	17	11	13	19	♆18♌
15	9.31	21	1♎	13	14	19	♇11♋
16	9.35	22	16	14	15	20	♃11♏
17	9.39	23	0♏	16	17	20	♄16♎
18	9.43	24	14	17	18	21	♅16♓R
19	9.47	25	28	19	19	22	♆18♌
20	9.51	26	12♐	20	20	22	♇12♋
21	9.55	27	26	21	22	23	♃12♏
22	9.59	28	10♑	23	23	24	♄16♎
23	10.03	29	24	24	24	24	♅16♓R
24	10.07	0♍	7♒	25	25	25	♆18♌
25	10.11	1	20	27	27	26	♇12♋
26	10.15	2	3♓	28	28	26	♃12♏
27	10.19	3	15	29	29	27	♄17♎
28	10.23	4	28	0♎	0♍	27	♅16♓R
29	10.27	5	10♈	2	2	28	♆18♌
30	10.31	6	22	3	3	29	♇12♋
31	10.35	7	4♉	4	4	29	♃13♏

Sep	STime	☉	☽	☿	♀	♂	Plnts
1	10.39	8♍	15♉	5♎	5♍	0♍	♃13♏
2	10.42	9	27	6	7	1	♄18♎
3	10.46	10	9♊	7	8	1	♅15♓R
4	10.50	11	21	8	9	2	♆18♌
5	10.54	12	4♋	8	10	3	♇12♋
6	10.58	13	17	9	11	3	♃14♏
7	11.02	14	0♌	10	13	4	♄18♎
8	11.06	15	13	11	14	4	♅15♓R
9	11.10	15	27	11	15	5	♆19♌
10	11.14	16	11♍	12	16	6	♇12♋
11	11.18	17	26	12	18	6	♃15♏
12	11.22	18	11♎	13	19	7	♄19♎
13	11.26	19	26	13	20	8	♅15♓R
14	11.30	20	10♏	13	21	8	♆19♌
15	11.34	21	25	13	23	9	♇12♋
16	11.38	22	9♐	13R	24	10	♃15♏
17	11.42	23	23	13	25	10	♄19♎
18	11.46	24	7♑	13	26	11	♅15♓R
19	11.49	25	20	13	28	11	♆19♌
20	11.53	26	4♒	13	29	12	♇12♋
21	11.57	27	16	12	0♎	13	♃16♏
22	12.01	28	29	11	1	13	♄20♎
23	12.05	29	12♓	11	3	14	♅15♓R
24	12.09	0♎	24	10	4	15	♆19♌
25	12.13	1	6♈	9	5	15	♇12♋
26	12.17	2	18	8	6	16	♃17♏
27	12.21	3	0♉	7	8	17	♄20♎
28	12.25	4	12	5	9	17	♅15♓R
29	12.29	5	24	4	10	18	♆19♌
30	12.33	6	6♊	3	11	18	♇12♋

Oct	STime	☉	☽	☿	♀	♂	Plnts
1	12.37	7♎	18♊	2♎	13♎	19♍	♃18♏
2	12.41	8	0♋	1	14	20	♄21♎
3	12.45	9	12	0	15	20	♅14♓R
4	12.49	10	25	0	16	21	♆19♌
5	12.53	11	8♌	29♍	18	22	♇12♋
6	12.56	12	21	29	19	22	♃19♏
7	13.00	13	5♍	29	20	23	♄22♎
8	13.04	14	20	29D	21	24	♅14♓R
9	13.08	15	4♎	29	23	24	♆20♌
10	13.12	16	19	29	24	25	♇12♋
11	13.16	17	4♏	29	25	25	♃20♏
12	13.20	18	20	0♎	26	26	♄22♎
13	13.24	19	5♐	1	28	27	♅14♓R
14	13.28	20	19	2	29	27	♆20♌
15	13.32	21	3♑	3	0♏	28	♇12♋
16	13.36	22	17	4	1	29	♃21♏
17	13.40	23	1♒	5	3	29	♄23♎
18	13.44	24	14	7	4	0♎	♅14♓R
19	13.48	25	26	8	5	1	♆20♌
20	13.52	26	9♓	9	6	1	♇12♋R
21	13.56	27	21	11	8	2	♃22♏
22	14.00	28	3♈	12	9	2	♄23♎
23	14.04	29	15	14	10	3	♅14♓R
24	14.07	0♏	27	16	11	4	♆20♌
25	14.11	1	9♉	17	13	4	♇12♋R
26	14.15	2	21	19	14	5	♃23♏
27	14.19	3	2♊	20	15	6	♄24♎
28	14.23	4	14	22	16	6	♅14♓R
29	14.27	5	26	24	18	7	♆20♌
30	14.31	6	8♋	25	19	8	♇12♋R
31	14.35	7	21	27	20	8	♃24♏

Nov	STime	☉	☽	☿	♀	♂	Plnts
1	14.39	8♏	3♌	29♎	21♏	9♎	♃25♏
2	14.43	9	16	0♏	23	9	♄25♎
3	14.47	10	0♍	2	24	10	♅14♓R
4	14.51	11	13	4	25	11	♆20♌
5	14.55	12	28	5	26	11	♇12♋
6	14.59	13	12♎	7	28	12	♃26♏
7	15.03	14	27	9	29	13	♄25♎
8	15.07	15	13♏	10	0♐	13	♅13♓R
9	15.11	16	28	12	1	14	♆20♌
10	15.14	17	13♐	13	3	15	♇12♋R
11	15.18	18	28	15	4	15	♃27♏
12	15.22	19	12♑	17	5	16	♄26♎
13	15.26	20	26	18	6	17	♅13♓R
14	15.30	21	10♒	20	8	17	♆20♌
15	15.34	22	23	21	9	18	♇12♋R
16	15.38	23	6♓	23	10	18	♃28♏
17	15.42	24	18	25	11	19	♄26♎
18	15.46	25	0♈	26	13	20	♅13♓R
19	15.50	26	12	28	14	20	♆20♌
20	15.54	27	24	29	15	21	♇12♋R
21	15.58	28	6♉	1♐	16	22	♃29♏
22	16.02	29	18	3	18	22	♄27♎
23	16.06	0♐	29	4	19	23	♅13♓
24	16.10	1	11♊	6	20	24	♆20♌
25	16.14	2	23	7	21	24	♇12♋R
26	16.18	3	6♋	9	23	25	♃ 0♐
27	16.22	4	18	10	24	25	♄28♎
28	16.25	5	0♌	12	25	26	♅13♓
29	16.29	6	13	13	26	27	♆20♌
30	16.33	7	26	15	28	27	♇12♋R

Dec	STime	☉	☽	☿	♀	♂	Plnts
1	16.37	8♐	9♍	17♐	29♐	28♎	♃ 1♐
2	16.41	9	23	18	0♑	29	♄28♎
3	16.45	10	7♎	20	1	29	♅13♓
4	16.49	11	21	21	2	0♏	♆20♌R
5	16.53	12	6♏	23	4	1	♇12♋R
6	16.57	13	21	24	5	1	♃ 2♐
7	17.01	14	6♐	26	6	2	♄29♎
8	17.05	15	21	27	7	3	♅13♓
9	17.09	16	6♑	29	9	3	♆20♌R
10	17.13	17	21	0♑	10	4	♇11♋R
11	17.17	18	5♒	2	11	4	♃ 3♐
12	17.21	19	18	3	12	5	♄29♎
13	17.25	20	2♓	5	14	6	♅13♓
14	17.29	21	14	7	15	6	♆20♌R
15	17.32	22	27	8	16	7	♇11♋R
16	17.36	23	9♈	10	17	8	♃ 5♐
17	17.40	24	21	11	19	8	♄29♎
18	17.44	25	2♉	12	20	9	♅14♓
19	17.48	26	14	14	21	10	♆20♌R
20	17.52	27	26	15	22	10	♇11♋R
21	17.56	28	8♊	17	24	11	♃ 6♐
22	18.00	29	20	18	25	12	♄ 0♏
23	18.04	0♑	2♋	19	26	12	♅14♓
24	18.08	1	15	21	27	13	♆20♌R
25	18.12	2	27	22	29	13	♇11♋R
26	18.16	3	10♌	23	0♒	14	♃ 7♐
27	18.20	4	23	24	1	15	♄ 0♏
28	18.24	5	6♍	25	2	15	♅14♓
29	18.28	6	19	26	4	16	♆20♌R
30	18.32	7	3♎	27	5	17	♇11♋R
31	18.36	8	16	27	6	17	♃ 8♐

1924

Jan	STime	☉	☽	☿	♀	♂	Plnts
1	18.40	10♑	1♏	28♑	7♒	18♏	♃ 8♐
2	18.43	11	15	28	9	19	♄ 1♏
3	18.47	12	0♐	29	10	19	♅14♓
4	18.51	13	15	29R	11	20	♆20♌R
5	18.55	14	29	28	12	21	♇11♋R
6	18.59	15	14♑	28	14	21	♃ 9♐
7	19.03	16	29	28	15	22	♄ 1♏
8	19.07	17	13♒	27	16	22	♅14♓
9	19.11	18	26	26	17	23	♆20♌R
10	19.15	19	9♓	25	18	24	♇11♋R
11	19.19	20	22	24	20	24	♃10♐
12	19.23	21	5♈	22	21	25	♄ 1♏
13	19.27	22	17	21	22	26	♅14♓
14	19.31	23	29	20	23	26	♆19♌R
15	19.35	24	11♉	18	25	27	♇11♋R
16	19.39	25	23	17	26	28	♃11♐
17	19.43	26	4♊	16	27	28	♄ 2♏
18	19.47	27	16	15	28	29	♅15♓
19	19.50	28	29	14	0♓	0♐	♆19♌R
20	19.54	29	11♋	14	1	0	♇11♋R
21	19.58	0♒	24	13	2	1	♃12♐
22	20.02	1	6♌	13	3	1	♄ 2♏
23	20.06	2	19	13	5	2	♅15♓
24	20.10	3	3♍	13D	6	3	♆19♌R
25	20.14	4	16	13	7	3	♇11♋R
26	20.18	5	0♎	13	8	4	♃13♐
27	20.22	6	13	13	9	5	♄ 2♏
28	20.26	7	27	13	11	5	♅15♓
29	20.30	8	11♏	14	12	6	♆19♌R
30	20.34	9	26	15	13	7	♇10♋R
31	20.38	10	10♐	15	14	7	♃14♐

Feb	STime	☉	☽	☿	♀	♂	Plnts
1	20.42	11♒	24♐	16♑	16♓	8♐	♃14♐
2	20.46	12	9♑	17	17	8	♄ 2♏
3	20.50	13	23	18	18	9	♅15♓
4	20.54	14	7♒	19	19	10	♆19♌R
5	20.57	15	21	20	20	10	♇10♋R
6	21.01	16	4♓	21	22	11	♃15♐
7	21.05	17	17	22	23	12	♄ 2♏
8	21.09	18	0♈	23	24	12	♅16♓
9	21.13	19	12	24	25	13	♆19♌R
10	21.17	20	25	25	26	14	♇10♋R
11	21.21	21	7♉	26	28	14	♃15♐
12	21.25	22	19	28	29	15	♄ 2♏
13	21.29	23	0♊	29	0♈	16	♅16♓
14	21.33	24	12	0♒	1	16	♆19♌R
15	21.37	25	24	1	2	17	♇10♋R
16	21.41	26	7♋	3	4	17	♃16♐
17	21.45	27	19	4	5	18	♄ 2♏R
18	21.49	28	2♌	6	6	19	♅16♓
19	21.53	29	15	7	7	19	♆18♌R
20	21.57	0♓	28	8	8	20	♇10♋R
21	22.01	1	12♍	10	10	21	♃17♐
22	22.05	2	26	11	11	21	♄ 2♏R
23	22.08	3	10♎	13	12	22	♅16♓
24	22.12	4	24	14	13	23	♆18♌R
25	22.16	5	8♏	16	14	23	♇10♋R
26	22.20	6	22	17	16	24	♃17♐
27	22.24	7	7♐	19	17	24	♄ 2♏R
28	22.28	8	21	20	18	25	♅17♓
29	22.32	9	5♑	22	19	26	♆18♌R

Mar	STime	☉	☽	☿	♀	♂	Plnts
1	22.36	10♓	19♑	24♒	20♈	26♐	♃18♐
2	22.40	11	2♒	25	22	27	♄ 2♏R
3	22.44	12	16	27	23	28	♅17♓
4	22.48	13	29	28	24	28	♆18♌R
5	22.52	14	12♓	0♓	25	29	♇10♋R
6	22.56	15	25	2	26	0♑	♃18♐
7	23.00	16	8♈	4	27	0	♄ 1♏R
8	23.04	17	20	5	29	1	♅17♓
9	23.08	18	2♉	7	0♉	1	♆18♌R
10	23.12	19	14	9	1	2	♇10♋R
11	23.15	20	26	11	2	3	♃19♐
12	23.19	21	8♊	12	3	3	♄ 1♏R
13	23.23	22	20	14	4	4	♅17♓
14	23.27	23	2♋	16	5	5	♆18♌R
15	23.31	24	14	18	7	5	♇10♋R
16	23.35	25	27	20	8	6	♃19♐
17	23.39	26	10♌	22	9	6	♄ 1♏R
18	23.43	27	23	24	10	7	♅18♓
19	23.47	28	6♍	25	11	8	♆18♌R
20	23.51	29	20	27	12	8	♇10♋
21	23.55	0♈	5♎	29	13	9	♃19♐
22	23.59	1	19	1♈	15	10	♄ 1♏R
23	0.03	2	4♏	3	16	10	♅18♓
24	0.07	3	18	5	17	11	♆18♌R
25	0.11	4	3♐	7	18	11	♇10♋
26	0.15	5	17	9	19	12	♃19♐
27	0.19	6	2♑	12	20	13	♄ 0♏R
28	0.23	7	16	14	21	13	♅18♓
29	0.26	8	29	16	22	14	♆18♌R
30	0.30	9	13♒	18	23	15	♇10♋
31	0.34	10	26	20	25	15	♃20♐

Apr	STime	☉	☽	☿	♀	♂	Plnts
1	0.38	11♈	9♓	22♈	26♉	16♑	♃20♐
2	0.42	12	21	24	27	16	♄ 0♏R
3	0.46	13	4♈	26	28	17	♅19♓
4	0.50	14	16	27	29	18	♆17♌R
5	0.54	15	29	29	0♊	18	♇10♋
6	0.58	16	11♉	1♉	1	19	♃20♐R
7	1.02	17	23	3	2	19	♄ 0♏R
8	1.06	18	5♊	5	3	20	♅19♓
9	1.10	19	16	6	4	21	♆17♌R
10	1.14	20	28	8	5	21	♇10♋
11	1.18	21	10♋	9	6	22	♃20♐R
12	1.22	22	22	11	7	22	♄29♎R
13	1.26	23	5♌	12	8	23	♅19♓
14	1.30	24	17	13	9	24	♆17♌
15	1.33	25	1♍	15	10	24	♇10♋
16	1.37	26	14	16	11	25	♃19♐R
17	1.41	27	28	17	12	25	♄29♎R
18	1.45	28	13♎	17	13	26	♅19♓
19	1.49	29	28	18	14	27	♆17♌
20	1.53	0♉	13♏	19	15	27	♇10♋
21	1.57	1	28	20	16	28	♃19♐R
22	2.01	2	13♐	20	17	28	♄28♎R
23	2.05	3	28	20	18	29	♅20♓
24	2.09	4	12♑	21	19	0♒	♆17♌
25	2.13	5	26	21	20	0	♇10♋
26	2.17	6	10♒	21	21	1	♃19♐R
27	2.21	7	23	21R	22	1	♄28♎R
28	2.25	8	6♓	21	23	2	♅20♓
29	2.29	9	18	21	24	2	♆17♌
30	2.33	10	1♈	21	25	3	♇10♋

May	STime	☉	☽	☿	♀	♂	Plnts
1	2.37	11♉	13♈	20♉	26♊	4♒	♃19♐R
2	2.40	11	25	20	27	4	♄28♎R
3	2.44	12	7♉	19	27	5	♅20♓
4	2.48	13	19	19	28	5	♆17♌
5	2.52	14	1♊	18	29	6	♇10♋
6	2.56	15	13	18	0♋	6	♃18♐R
7	3.00	16	25	17	1	7	♄27♎R
8	3.04	17	7♋	17	2	8	♅20♓
9	3.08	18	19	16	3	8	♆17♌
10	3.12	19	1♌	15	3	9	♇10♋
11	3.16	20	13	15	4	9	♃18♐R
12	3.20	21	26	14	5	10	♄27♎R
13	3.24	22	9♍	14	6	10	♅20♓
14	3.28	23	23	13	6	11	♆17♌
15	3.32	24	7♎	13	7	11	♇10♋
16	3.36	25	21	13	7	12	♃17♐R
17	3.40	26	6♏	12	8	13	♄27♎R
18	3.44	27	21	12	9	13	♅21♓
19	3.48	28	6♐	12	10	14	♆17♌
20	3.51	29	22	12D	10	14	♇11♋
21	3.55	0♊	7♑	12	11	15	♃17♐R
22	3.59	1	21	12	12	15	♄26♎R
23	4.03	2	5♒	12	12	16	♅21♓
24	4.07	3	19	12	13	16	♆17♌
25	4.11	4	3♓	13	13	17	♇11♋
26	4.15	5	15	13	14	17	♃16♐R
27	4.19	6	28	13	14	17	♄26♎R
28	4.23	7	10♈	14	14	18	♅21♓
29	4.27	8	22	14	15	18	♆18♌
30	4.31	8	4♉	15	15	19	♇11♋
31	4.35	9	16	16	16	20	♃15♐R

Jun	STime	☉	☽	☿	♀	♂	Plnts
1	4.39	10♊	28♉	17♉	16♋	20♒	♃15♐R
2	4.43	11	10♊	17	16	21	♄26♎R
3	4.47	12	22	18	16	21	♅21♓
4	4.51	13	4♋	19	17	22	♆18♌
5	4.55	14	16	20	17	22	♇11♋
6	4.58	15	28	21	17	22	♃15♐R
7	5.02	16	10♌	22	17	23	♄26♎R
8	5.06	17	23	24	17	23	♅21♓
9	5.10	18	5♍	25	17	24	♆18♌
10	5.14	19	18	26	17R	24	♇11♋
11	5.18	20	2♎	27	17	25	♃14♐R
12	5.22	21	15	29	17	25	♄26♎R
13	5.26	22	0♏	0♊	17	26	♅21♓
14	5.30	23	15	2	17	26	♆18♌
15	5.34	24	0♐	3	17	26	♇11♋
16	5.38	25	15	5	16	27	♃13♐R
17	5.42	26	0♑	7	16	27	♄25♎R
18	5.46	27	15	8	16	27	♅21♓
19	5.50	28	0♒	10	15	28	♆18♌
20	5.54	29	14	12	15	28	♇11♋
21	5.58	0♋	28	14	15	28	♃13♐R
22	6.02	0	11♓	15	14	29	♄25♎R
23	6.06	1	24	17	14	29	♅21♓
24	6.09	2	7♈	19	13	0♓	♆18♌
25	6.13	3	19	21	13	0	♇11♋
26	6.17	4	1♉	23	12	0	♃12♐R
27	6.21	5	13	25	12	1	♄25♎
28	6.25	6	25	27	11	1	♅21♓
29	6.29	7	7♊	0♋	10	1	♆18♌
30	6.33	8	19	2	10	1	♇12♋

Jul	STime	☉	☽	☿	♀	♂	Plnts
1	6.37	9♋	1♋	4♋	9♋	2♓	♃12♐R
2	6.41	10	13	6	8	2	♄25♎
3	6.45	11	25	8	8	2	♅21♓
4	6.49	12	7♌	10	7	3	♆18♌
5	6.53	13	20	13	7	3	♇12♋
6	6.57	14	2♍	15	6	3	♃11♐R
7	7.01	15	15	17	5	3	♄25♎
8	7.05	16	28	19	5	3	♅21♓R
9	7.09	17	12♎	21	4	4	♆19♌
10	7.13	18	25	23	4	4	♇12♋
11	7.16	19	9♏	25	3	4	♃11♐R
12	7.20	20	24	27	3	4	♄25♎
13	7.24	20	9♐	29	3	4	♅21♓R
14	7.28	21	24	1♌	2	4	♆19♌
15	7.32	22	9♑	3	2	4	♇12♋
16	7.36	23	23	5	2	5	♃10♐R
17	7.40	24	8♒	7	1	5	♄26♎
18	7.44	25	22	9	1	5	♅21♓R
19	7.48	26	6♓	11	1	5	♆19♌
20	7.52	27	20	13	1	5	♇12♋
21	7.56	28	3♈	15	1	5	♃10♐R
22	8.00	29	15	16	1D	5	♄26♎
23	8.04	0♌	28	18	1	5	♅21♓R
24	8.08	1	10♉	20	1	5R	♆19♌
25	8.12	2	22	21	1	5	♇12♋
26	8.16	3	4♊	23	1	5	♃10♐R
27	8.20	4	16	25	1	5	♄26♎
28	8.24	5	28	26	1	5	♅21♓R
29	8.27	6	10♋	28	2	5	♆19♌
30	8.31	7	22	29	2	5	♇12♋
31	8.35	8	4♌	1♍	2	5	♃10♐R

Aug	STime	☉	☽	☿	♀	♂	Plnts
1	8.39	9♌	16♌	2♍	2♋	5♓	♃10♐R
2	8.43	10	29	4	3	4	♄26♎
3	8.47	11	12♍	5	3	4	♅21♓R
4	8.51	12	25	7	3	4	♆19♌
5	8.55	12	8♎	8	4	4	♇12♋
6	8.59	13	22	9	4	4	♃10♐
7	9.03	14	6♏	11	5	4	♄27♎
8	9.07	15	20	12	5	4	♅21♓R
9	9.11	16	4♐	13	6	3	♆20♌
10	9.15	17	19	14	6	3	♇12♋
11	9.19	18	3♑	15	7	3	♃10♐
12	9.23	19	18	16	8	3	♄27♎
13	9.27	20	2♒	17	8	3	♅20♓R
14	9.31	21	17	18	9	3	♆20♌
15	9.34	22	1♓	19	9	2	♇13♋
16	9.38	23	14	20	10	2	♃10♐
17	9.42	24	28	21	11	2	♄27♎
18	9.46	25	11♈	22	11	2	♅20♓R
19	9.50	26	23	23	12	1	♆20♌
20	9.54	27	6♉	24	13	1	♇13♋
21	9.58	28	18	24	14	1	♃10♐
22	10.02	29	0♊	25	14	0	♄28♎
23	10.06	0♍	12	25	15	0	♅20♓R
24	10.10	1	24	26	16	0	♆20♌
25	10.14	2	6♋	26	17	29♒	♇13♋
26	10.18	3	18	26	18	29	♃10♐
27	10.22	4	0♌	27	19	29	♄28♎
28	10.26	5	13	27	19	29	♅20♓R
29	10.30	6	25	27R	20	28	♆20♌
30	10.34	7	8♍	27	21	28	♇13♋
31	10.38	7	21	26	22	28	♃11♐

Sep	STime	☉	☽	☿	♀	♂	Plnts
1	10.41	8♍	5♎	26♍	23♋	28♒	♃11♐
2	10.45	9	19	26	24	27	♄29♎
3	10.49	10	3♏	25	25	27	♅20♓R
4	10.53	11	17	25	26	27	♆21♌
5	10.57	12	1♐	24	26	27	♇13♋
6	11.01	13	15	23	27	27	♃11♐
7	11.05	14	29	22	28	26	♄29♎
8	11.09	15	13♑	21	29	26	♅19♓R
9	11.13	16	28	20	0♌	26	♆21♌
10	11.17	17	12♒	19	1	26	♇13♋
11	11.21	18	26	18	2	26	♃12♐
12	11.25	19	9♓	17	3	26	♄ 0♏
13	11.29	20	23	16	4	26	♅19♓R
14	11.33	21	6♈	15	5	25	♆21♌
15	11.37	22	19	15	6	25	♇13♋
16	11.41	23	1♉	14	7	25	♃12♐
17	11.45	24	14	13	8	25	♄ 0♏
18	11.49	25	26	13	9	25	♅19♓R
19	11.52	26	8♊	13	10	25	♆21♌
20	11.56	27	20	12D	11	25	♇13♋
21	12.00	28	2♋	12	12	25D	♃13♐
22	12.04	29	14	13	13	25	♄ 1♏
23	12.08	0♎	26	13	14	25	♅19♓R
24	12.12	1	8♌	14	15	25	♆21♌
25	12.16	2	21	14	17	25	♇13♋
26	12.20	3	3♍	15	18	25	♃13♐
27	12.24	4	17	16	19	25	♄ 1♏
28	12.28	5	0♎	17	20	25	♅19♓R
29	12.32	6	14	18	21	25	♆21♌
30	12.36	7	29	19	22	25	♇13♋

Oct	STime	☉	☽	☿	♀	♂	Plnts
1	12.40	8♎	13♏	21♍	23♌	26♒	♃14♐
2	12.44	9	27	22	24	26	♄ 2♏
3	12.48	10	12♐	24	25	26	♅18♓R
4	12.52	11	26	25	26	26	♆22♌
5	12.56	12	10♑	27	27	26	♇13♋
6	12.59	13	24	29	28	26	♃15♐
7	13.03	14	8♒	0♎	0♍	27	♄ 2♏
8	13.07	15	22	2	1	27	♅18♓R
9	13.11	16	5♓	4	2	27	♆22♌
10	13.15	17	18	5	3	27	♇13♋
11	13.19	18	2♈	7	4	27	♃16♐
12	13.23	19	14	9	5	28	♄ 3♏
13	13.27	20	27	11	6	28	♅18♓R
14	13.31	21	10♉	12	7	28	♆22♌
15	13.35	22	22	14	9	28	♇13♋
16	13.39	23	4♊	16	10	29	♃17♐
17	13.43	24	16	18	11	29	♄ 3♏
18	13.47	25	28	19	12	29	♅18♓R
19	13.51	26	10♋	21	13	0♓	♆22♌
20	13.55	27	22	23	14	0	♇13♋
21	13.59	28	4♌	24	16	0	♃17♐
22	14.03	29	16	26	17	1	♄ 4♏
23	14.07	0♏	28	28	18	1	♅18♓R
24	14.10	1	11♍	29	19	1	♆22♌
25	14.14	2	25	1♏	20	2	♇13♋
26	14.18	3	9♎	3	21	2	♃18♐
27	14.22	4	23	4	23	2	♄ 5♏
28	14.26	5	7♏	6	24	3	♅18♓R
29	14.30	6	22	8	25	3	♆22♌
30	14.34	7	7♐	9	26	4	♇13♋R
31	14.38	8	22	11	27	4	♃19♐

Nov	STime	☉	☽	☿	♀	♂	Plnts
1	14.42	9♏	7♑	12♏	28♍	4♓	♃20♐
2	14.46	10	21	14	0♎	5	♄ 5♏
3	14.50	11	5♒	16	1	5	♅18♓R
4	14.54	12	19	17	2	6	♆22♌
5	14.58	13	2♓	19	3	6	♇13♋R
6	15.02	14	15	20	4	7	♃21♐
7	15.06	15	28	22	6	7	♄ 6♏
8	15.10	16	11♈	24	7	7	♅17♓R
9	15.14	17	24	25	8	8	♆22♌
10	15.17	18	6♉	27	9	8	♇13♋R
11	15.21	19	18	28	10	9	♃22♐
12	15.25	20	0♊	0♐	12	9	♄ 7♏
13	15.29	21	12	1	13	10	♅17♓R
14	15.33	22	24	3	14	10	♆22♌
15	15.37	23	6♋	4	15	11	♇13♋R
16	15.41	24	18	6	16	11	♃23♐
17	15.45	25	0♌	7	18	12	♄ 7♏
18	15.49	26	12	9	19	12	♅17♓R
19	15.53	27	24	10	20	13	♆22♌
20	15.57	28	6♍	12	21	13	♇13♋R
21	16.01	29	19	13	22	14	♃24♐
22	16.05	0♐	3♎	15	24	14	♄ 8♏
23	16.09	1	16	16	25	15	♅17♓
24	16.13	2	1♏	18	26	15	♆22♌
25	16.17	3	15	19	27	16	♇13♋R
26	16.21	4	1♐	21	28	16	♃25♐
27	16.24	5	16	22	0♏	17	♄ 8♏
28	16.28	6	1♑	23	1	18	♅17♓
29	16.32	7	16	25	2	18	♆22♌
30	16.36	8	1♒	26	3	19	♇13♋R

Dec	STime	☉	☽	☿	♀	♂	Plnts
1	16.40	9♐	15♒	28♐	5♏	19♓	♃26♐
2	16.44	10	29	29	6	20	♄ 9♏
3	16.48	11	12♓	0♑	7	20	♅17♓
4	16.52	12	25	2	8	21	♆22♌R
5	16.56	13	8♈	3	10	22	♇13♋R
6	17.00	14	21	4	11	22	♃27♐
7	17.04	15	3♉	5	12	23	♄ 9♏
8	17.08	16	15	7	13	23	♅17♓
9	17.12	17	27	8	14	24	♆22♌R
10	17.16	18	9♊	9	16	24	♇13♋R
11	17.20	19	21	10	17	25	♃28♐
12	17.24	20	3♋	10	18	26	♄10♏
13	17.28	21	15	11	19	26	♅17♓
14	17.32	22	27	12	21	27	♆22♌R
15	17.35	23	9♌	12	22	27	♇13♋R
16	17.39	24	21	13	23	28	♃29♐
17	17.43	25	3♍	13	24	29	♄10♏
18	17.47	26	15	13R	26	29	♅17♓
19	17.51	27	28	13	27	0♈	♆22♌R
20	17.55	28	11♎	12	28	0	♇12♋R
21	17.59	29	25	12	29	1	♃ 0♑
22	18.03	0♑	9♏	11	1♐	2	♄11♏
23	18.07	1	24	10	2	2	♅18♓
24	18.11	2	9♐	9	3	3	♆22♌R
25	18.15	3	24	8	4	3	♇12♋R
26	18.19	4	9♑	6	6	4	♃ 2♑
27	18.23	5	24	5	7	5	♄11♏
28	18.27	6	9♒	4	8	5	♅18♓
29	18.31	7	24	2	9	6	♆22♌R
30	18.35	8	8♓	1	10	6	♇12♋R
31	18.39	9	21	0	12	7	♃ 3♑

Jan	STime	☉	☽	☿	♀	♂	Plnts
1	18.42	10♑	5♈	29♐	13♐	8♈	♃ 3♑
2	18.46	11	17	28	14	8	♄12♏
3	18.50	12	0♉	27	15	9	♅18♓
4	18.54	13	12	27	17	9	♆22♌R
5	18.58	14	24	27	18	10	♇12♋R
6	19.02	15	6♊	26D	19	11	♃ 4♑
7	19.06	16	18	26	20	11	♄12♏
8	19.10	17	0♋	27	22	12	♅18♓
9	19.14	18	12	27	23	13	♆22♌R
10	19.18	19	24	27	24	13	♇12♋R
11	19.22	20	6♌	28	25	14	♃ 5♑
12	19.26	21	18	28	27	14	♄13♏
13	19.30	23	0♍	29	28	15	♅18♓
14	19.34	24	12	0♑	29	16	♆22♌R
15	19.38	25	25	1	0♑	16	♇12♋R
16	19.42	26	7♎	2	2	17	♃ 6♑
17	19.46	27	21	3	3	18	♄13♏
18	19.50	28	4♏	4	4	18	♅18♓
19	19.53	29	18	5	5	19	♆22♌R
20	19.57	0♒	2♐	6	7	20	♇12♋R
21	20.01	1	17	7	8	20	♃ 7♑
22	20.05	2	2♑	8	9	21	♄13♏
23	20.09	3	17	9	10	21	♅19♓
24	20.13	4	2♒	10	12	22	♆21♌R
25	20.17	5	17	12	13	23	♇12♋R
26	20.21	6	2♓	13	14	23	♃ 9♑
27	20.25	7	16	14	15	24	♄13♏
28	20.29	8	0♈	16	17	25	♅19♓
29	20.33	9	13	17	18	25	♆21♌R
30	20.37	10	26	18	19	26	♇12♋R
31	20.41	11	9♉	20	20	27	♃10♑

Feb	STime	☉	☽	☿	♀	♂	Plnts
1	20.45	12♒	21♉	21♑	22♑	27♈	♃10♑
2	20.49	13	3♊	23	23	28	♄14♏
3	20.53	14	15	24	24	28	♅19♓
4	20.57	15	27	25	25	29	♆21♌R
5	21.00	16	8♋	27	27	0♉	♇12♋R
6	21.04	17	20	28	28	0	♃11♑
7	21.08	18	2♌	0♒	29	1	♄14♏
8	21.12	19	14	1	0♒	2	♅19♓
9	21.16	20	27	3	2	2	♆21♌R
10	21.20	21	9♍	4	3	3	♇11♋R
11	21.24	22	22	6	4	4	♃12♑
12	21.28	23	4♎	8	5	4	♄14♏
13	21.32	24	18	9	7	5	♅20♓
14	21.36	25	1♏	11	8	6	♆21♌R
15	21.40	26	14	12	9	6	♇11♋R
16	21.44	27	28	14	10	7	♃13♑
17	21.48	28	12♐	16	12	7	♄14♏
18	21.52	29	27	17	13	8	♅20♓
19	21.56	0♓	11♑	19	14	9	♆21♌R
20	22.00	1	26	21	15	9	♇11♋R
21	22.04	2	10♒	22	17	10	♃14♑
22	22.08	3	25	24	18	11	♄14♏
23	22.11	4	10♓	26	19	11	♅20♓
24	22.15	5	24	28	20	12	♆21♌R
25	22.19	6	8♈	29	22	13	♇11♋R
26	22.23	7	21	1♓	23	13	♃15♑
27	22.27	8	4♉	3	24	14	♄14♏R
28	22.31	9	17	5	25	15	♅20♓

Mar	STime	☉	☽	☿	♀	♂	Plnts
1	22.35	10♓	29♉	7♓	27♒	15♉	♃15♑
2	22.39	11	11♊	8	28	16	♄14♏R
3	22.43	12	23	10	29	16	♅21♓
4	22.47	13	5♋	12	0♓	17	♆20♌R
5	22.51	14	17	14	2	18	♇11♋R
6	22.55	15	29	16	3	18	♃16♑
7	22.59	16	11♌	18	4	19	♄14♏R
8	23.03	17	23	20	5	20	♅21♓
9	23.07	18	5♍	22	7	20	♆20♌R
10	23.11	19	18	24	8	21	♇11♋
11	23.15	20	1♎	26	9	22	♃17♑
12	23.18	21	14	28	10	22	♄14♏R
13	23.22	22	28	0♈	12	23	♅21♓
14	23.26	23	11♏	2	13	24	♆20♌R
15	23.30	24	25	4	14	24	♇11♋R
16	23.34	25	9♐	6	15	25	♃18♑
17	23.38	26	23	7	16	25	♄14♏R
18	23.42	27	7♑	9	18	26	♅21♓
19	23.46	28	21	11	19	27	♆20♌R
20	23.50	29	6♒	13	20	27	♇11♋
21	23.54	0♈	20	15	21	28	♃19♑
22	23.58	1	4♓	17	23	29	♄13♏R
23	0.02	2	18	18	24	29	♅22♓
24	0.06	3	2♈	20	25	0♊	♆20♌R
25	0.10	4	16	21	26	1	♇11♋
26	0.14	5	29	23	28	1	♃19♑
27	0.18	6	12♉	24	29	2	♄13♏R
28	0.22	7	24	26	0♈	3	♅22♓
29	0.25	8	7♊	27	1	3	♆20♌R
30	0.29	9	19	28	3	4	♇11♋
31	0.33	10	1♋	29	4	5	♃20♑

Apr	STime	☉	☽	☿	♀	♂	Plnts
1	0.37	11♈	13♋	0♉	5♈	5♊	♃20♑
2	0.41	12	25	0	6	6	♄13♏R
3	0.45	13	6♌	1	8	6	♅22♓
4	0.49	14	18	1	9	7	♆20♌R
5	0.53	15	1♍	2	10	8	♇11♋
6	0.57	16	13	2	11	8	♃20♑
7	1.01	17	26	2	13	9	♄12♏R
8	1.05	18	10♎	2R	14	10	♅23♓
9	1.09	19	23	2	15	10	♆20♌R
10	1.13	20	7♏	2	16	11	♇11♋
11	1.17	21	21	2	18	12	♃21♑
12	1.21	22	6♐	2	19	12	♄12♏R
13	1.25	23	20	1	20	13	♅23♓
14	1.29	24	4♑	1	21	13	♆20♌R
15	1.33	25	18	0	22	14	♇11♋
16	1.36	26	2♒	29♈	24	15	♃21♑
17	1.40	27	16	29	25	15	♄12♏R
18	1.44	28	0♓	28	26	16	♅23♓
19	1.48	29	14	27	27	17	♆20♌R
20	1.52	0♉	28	27	29	17	♇11♋
21	1.56	1	11♈	26	0♉	18	♃22♑
22	2.00	2	24	25	1	19	♄11♏R
23	2.04	3	7♉	25	2	19	♅23♓
24	2.08	3	20	24	4	20	♆20♌
25	2.12	4	3♊	23	5	21	♇11♋
26	2.16	5	15	23	6	21	♃22♑
27	2.20	6	27	23	7	22	♄11♏R
28	2.24	7	9♋	22	9	22	♅24♓
29	2.28	8	21	22	10	23	♆19♌
30	2.32	9	2♌	22	11	24	♇11♋

May	STime	☉	☽	☿	♀	♂	Plnts
1	2.36	10♉	14♌	22♈	12♉	24♊	♃22♑
2	2.40	11	26	22D	13	25	♄11♏R
3	2.43	12	9♍	22	15	26	♅24♓
4	2.47	13	21	22	16	26	♆20♌
5	2.51	14	4♎	22	17	27	♇11♋
6	2.55	15	18	22	18	28	♃22♑
7	2.59	16	2♏	23	20	28	♄10♏R
8	3.03	17	16	23	21	29	♅24♓
9	3.07	18	1♐	24	22	29	♆20♌
10	3.11	19	15	24	23	0♋	♇12♋
11	3.15	20	0♑	25	25	1	♃22♑R
12	3.19	21	15	26	26	1	♄10♏R
13	3.23	22	29	26	27	2	♅24♓
14	3.27	23	13♒	27	28	3	♆20♌
15	3.31	24	27	28	29	3	♇12♋
16	3.35	25	11♓	29	1♊	4	♃22♑R
17	3.39	26	24	0♉	2	4	♄10♏R
18	3.43	27	8♈	1	3	5	♅24♓
19	3.47	28	21	2	4	6	♆20♌
20	3.51	29	4♉	3	6	6	♇12♋
21	3.54	0♊	16	5	7	7	♃22♑R
22	3.58	1	29	6	8	8	♄ 9♏R
23	4.02	2	11♊	7	9	8	♅25♓
24	4.06	2	23	8	11	9	♆20♌
25	4.10	3	5♋	10	12	10	♇12♋
26	4.14	4	17	11	13	10	♃22♑R
27	4.18	5	29	13	14	11	♄ 9♏R
28	4.22	6	11♌	14	15	11	♅25♓
29	4.26	7	22	16	17	12	♆20♌
30	4.30	8	4♍	17	18	13	♇12♋
31	4.34	9	17	19	19	13	♃22♑R

Jun	STime	☉	☽	☿	♀	♂	Plnts
1	4.38	10♊	29♍	21♉	20♊	14♋	♃21♑R
2	4.42	11	13♎	22	22	15	♄ 9♏R
3	4.46	12	26	24	23	15	♅25♓
4	4.50	13	10♏	26	24	16	♆20♌
5	4.54	14	24	28	25	17	♇12♋
6	4.58	15	9♐	29	27	17	♃21♑R
7	5.01	16	24	1♊	28	18	♄ 8♏R
8	5.05	17	9♑	3	29	18	♅25♓
9	5.09	18	24	5	0♋	19	♆20♌
10	5.13	19	9♒	7	1	20	♇12♋
11	5.17	20	23	9	3	20	♃21♑R
12	5.21	21	7♓	11	4	21	♄ 8♏R
13	5.25	22	21	13	5	22	♅25♓
14	5.29	23	5♈	16	6	22	♆20♌
15	5.33	24	18	18	8	23	♇12♋
16	5.37	25	1♉	20	9	23	♃20♑R
17	5.41	25	13	22	10	24	♄ 8♏R
18	5.45	26	26	24	11	25	♅25♓
19	5.49	27	8♊	26	12	25	♆20♌
20	5.53	28	20	29	14	26	♇12♋
21	5.57	29	2♋	1♋	15	27	♃20♑R
22	6.01	0♋	14	3	16	27	♄ 8♏R
23	6.05	1	26	5	17	28	♅25♓
24	6.09	2	7♌	7	19	29	♆20♌
25	6.12	3	19	10	20	29	♇13♋
26	6.16	4	1♍	12	21	0♌	♃19♑R
27	6.20	5	13	14	22	0	♄ 7♏R
28	6.24	6	25	16	23	1	♅25♓
29	6.28	7	8♎	18	25	2	♆20♌
30	6.32	8	21	20	26	2	♇13♋

Jul	STime	☉	☽	☿	♀	♂	Plnts
1	6.36	9♋	5♏	22♋	27♋	3♌	♃18♑R
2	6.40	10	18	24	28	4	♄ 7♏R
3	6.44	11	3♐	26	0♌	4	♅25♓
4	6.48	12	18	27	1	5	♆21♌
5	6.52	13	3♑	29	2	5	♇13♋
6	6.56	14	18	1♌	3	6	♃18♑R
7	7.00	15	3♒	3	4	7	♄ 7♏
8	7.04	15	18	5	6	7	♅25♓R
9	7.08	16	3♓	6	7	8	♆21♌
10	7.12	17	17	8	8	9	♇13♋
11	7.16	18	1♈	10	9	9	♃17♑R
12	7.19	19	14	11	11	10	♄ 7♏
13	7.23	20	28	13	12	10	♅25♓R
14	7.27	21	10♉	14	13	11	♆21♌
15	7.31	22	23	16	14	12	♇13♋
16	7.35	23	5♊	17	15	12	♃17♑R
17	7.39	24	17	19	17	13	♄ 7♏
18	7.43	25	29	20	18	14	♅25♓R
19	7.47	26	11♋	21	19	14	♆21♌
20	7.51	27	23	23	20	15	♇13♋
21	7.55	28	4♌	24	22	16	♃16♑R
22	7.59	29	16	25	23	16	♄ 7♏
23	8.03	0♌	28	26	24	17	♅25♓R
24	8.07	1	10♍	28	25	17	♆21♌
25	8.11	2	22	29	26	18	♇13♋
26	8.15	3	5♎	0♍	28	19	♃15♑R
27	8.19	4	17	1	29	19	♄ 8♏
28	8.23	5	0♏	2	0♍	20	♅25♓R
29	8.26	6	14	3	1	21	♆21♌
30	8.30	6	27	4	2	21	♇13♋
31	8.34	7	12♐	4	4	22	♃15♑R

Aug	STime	☉	☽	☿	♀	♂	Plnts
1	8.38	8♌	26♐	5♍	5♍	22♌	♃15♑R
2	8.42	9	11♑	6	6	23	♄ 8♏
3	8.46	10	26	7	7	24	♅25♓R
4	8.50	11	11♒	7	9	24	♆22♌
5	8.54	12	26	8	10	25	♇14♋
6	8.58	13	11♓	8	11	26	♃14♑R
7	9.02	14	26	8	12	26	♄ 8♏
8	9.06	15	10♈	9	13	27	♅25♓R
9	9.10	16	23	9	15	28	♆22♌
10	9.14	17	7♉	9	16	28	♇14♋
11	9.18	18	19	9R	17	29	♃14♑R
12	9.22	19	2♊	9	18	29	♄ 8♏
13	9.26	20	14	9	19	0♍	♅24♓R
14	9.30	21	26	9	21	1	♆22♌
15	9.34	22	8♋	8	22	1	♇14♋
16	9.37	23	20	8	23	2	♃13♑R
17	9.41	24	1♌	8	24	3	♄ 8♏
18	9.45	25	13	7	25	3	♅24♓R
19	9.49	26	25	6	27	4	♆22♌
20	9.53	27	7♍	6	28	5	♇14♋
21	9.57	28	19	5	29	5	♃13♑R
22	10.01	29	2♎	4	0♎	6	♄ 9♏
23	10.05	0♍	14	3	1	6	♅24♓R
24	10.09	0	27	2	3	7	♆22♌
25	10.13	1	10♏	1	4	8	♇14♋
26	10.17	2	24	0	5	8	♃13♑R
27	10.21	3	7♐	0	6	9	♄ 9♏
28	10.25	4	21	29♌	7	10	♅24♓R
29	10.29	5	5♑	28	9	10	♆23♌
30	10.33	6	20	27	10	11	♇14♋
31	10.37	7	5♒	27	11	12	♃13♑R

Sep	STime	☉	☽	☿	♀	♂	Plnts
1	10.41	8♍	20♒	26♌	12♎	12♍	♃12♑R
2	10.44	9	5♓	26	13	13	♄ 9♏
3	10.48	10	19	26D	15	13	♅24♓R
4	10.52	11	4♈	26	16	14	♆23♌
5	10.56	12	18	26	17	15	♇14♋
6	11.00	13	2♉	26	18	15	♃12♑R
7	11.04	14	15	27	19	16	♄10♏
8	11.08	15	28	27	21	17	♅24♓R
9	11.12	16	10♊	28	22	17	♆23♌
10	11.16	17	22	29	23	18	♇14♋
11	11.20	18	4♋	0♍	24	19	♃12♑
12	11.24	19	16	1	25	19	♄10♏
13	11.28	20	28	2	27	20	♅23♓R
14	11.32	21	10♌	4	28	20	♆23♌
15	11.36	22	22	5	29	21	♇14♋
16	11.40	23	4♍	6	0♏	22	♃12♑
17	11.44	24	16	8	1	22	♄11♏
18	11.48	25	28	10	3	23	♅23♓R
19	11.52	26	11♎	11	4	24	♆23♌
20	11.55	27	24	13	5	24	♇14♋
21	11.59	28	7♏	15	6	25	♃13♑
22	12.03	29	21	17	7	26	♄11♏
23	12.07	0♎	4♐	18	8	26	♅23♓R
24	12.11	1	18	20	10	27	♆23♌
25	12.15	2	2♑	22	11	28	♇14♋
26	12.19	3	16	24	12	28	♃13♑
27	12.23	4	0♒	26	13	29	♄12♏
28	12.27	5	14	27	14	0♎	♅23♓R
29	12.31	6	29	29	16	0	♆24♌
30	12.35	7	13♓	1♎	17	1	♇14♋

Oct	STime	☉	☽	☿	♀	♂	Plnts
1	12.39	7♎	28♓	3♎	18♏	1♎	♃13♑
2	12.43	8	12♈	5	19	2	♄12♏
3	12.47	9	26	6	20	3	♅23♓R
4	12.51	10	10♉	8	21	3	♆24♌
5	12.55	11	23	10	23	4	♇14♋
6	12.59	12	6♊	12	24	5	♃14♑
7	13.02	13	18	14	25	5	♄13♏
8	13.06	14	0♋	15	26	6	♅22♓R
9	13.10	15	12	17	27	7	♆24♌
10	13.14	16	24	19	28	7	♇14♋
11	13.18	17	6♌	20	0♐	8	♃14♑
12	13.22	18	18	22	1	9	♄13♏
13	13.26	19	0♍	24	2	9	♅22♓R
14	13.30	20	12	25	3	10	♆24♌
15	13.34	21	24	27	4	11	♇14♋
16	13.38	22	7♎	29	5	11	♃15♑
17	13.42	23	20	0♏	7	12	♄14♏
18	13.46	24	3♏	2	8	13	♅22♓R
19	13.50	25	17	3	9	13	♆24♌
20	13.54	26	1♐	5	10	14	♇14♋
21	13.58	27	15	7	11	14	♃15♑
22	14.02	28	29	8	12	15	♄15♏
23	14.06	29	13♑	10	13	16	♅22♓R
24	14.09	0♏	27	11	15	16	♆24♌
25	14.13	1	11♒	13	16	17	♇14♋R
26	14.17	2	25	14	17	18	♃16♑
27	14.21	3	9♓	16	18	18	♄15♏
28	14.25	4	23	17	19	19	♅22♓R
29	14.29	5	7♈	19	20	20	♆24♌
30	14.33	6	21	20	21	20	♇14♋
31	14.37	7	5♉	22	23	21	♃16♑

Nov	STime	☉	☽	☿	♀	♂	Plnts
1	14.41	8♏	18♉	23♏	24♐	22♎	♃17♑
2	14.45	9	1♊	25	25	22	♄16♏
3	14.49	10	14	26	26	23	♅22♓R
4	14.53	11	26	28	27	24	♆24♌
5	14.57	12	8♋	29	28	24	♇14♋R
6	15.01	13	20	1♐	29	25	♃17♑
7	15.05	14	2♌	2	0♑	26	♄16♏
8	15.09	15	14	4	1	26	♅21♓R
9	15.13	16	26	5	3	27	♆24♌
10	15.17	17	8♍	6	4	28	♇14♋R
11	15.20	18	20	8	5	28	♃18♑
12	15.24	19	2♎	9	6	29	♄17♏
13	15.28	20	15	10	7	0♏	♅21♓R
14	15.32	21	29	12	8	0	♆24♌
15	15.36	22	12♏	13	9	1	♇14♋R
16	15.40	23	26	14	10	2	♃19♑
17	15.44	24	10♐	16	11	2	♄18♏
18	15.48	25	25	17	12	3	♅21♓R
19	15.52	26	9♑	18	13	4	♆24♌
20	15.56	27	23	19	14	4	♇14♋R
21	16.00	28	8♒	20	15	5	♃20♑
22	16.04	29	22	21	16	6	♄18♏
23	16.08	0♐	6♓	22	18	6	♅21♓
24	16.12	1	20	23	19	7	♆24♌
25	16.16	2	3♈	24	20	8	♇14♋R
26	16.20	3	17	25	21	8	♃21♑
27	16.24	4	0♉	25	22	9	♄19♏
28	16.27	5	14	26	23	10	♅21♓
29	16.31	6	27	26	24	10	♆24♌
30	16.35	7	9♊	27	25	11	♇14♋R

Dec	STime	☉	☽	☿	♀	♂	Plnts
1	16.39	8♐	22♊	27♐	26♑	12♏	♃22♑
2	16.43	10	4♋	27	27	12	♄19♏
3	16.47	11	16	27	28	13	♅21♓
4	16.51	12	28	26	29	14	♆24♌
5	16.55	13	10♌	26	0♒	14	♇14♋R
6	16.59	14	22	25	1	15	♃23♑
7	17.03	15	4♍	24	1	16	♄20♏
8	17.07	16	16	23	2	16	♅21♓
9	17.11	17	28	22	3	17	♆24♌
10	17.15	18	10♎	20	4	18	♇14♋R
11	17.19	19	23	19	5	18	♃24♑
12	17.23	20	6♏	18	6	19	♄21♏
13	17.27	21	20	16	7	20	♅21♓
14	17.31	22	4♐	15	8	20	♆24♌R
15	17.35	23	19	14	9	21	♇14♋R
16	17.38	24	3♑	13	10	22	♃25♑
17	17.42	25	18	12	10	23	♄21♏
18	17.46	26	3♒	11	11	23	♅21♓
19	17.50	27	18	11	12	24	♆24♌R
20	17.54	28	2♓	11	13	25	♇14♋R
21	17.58	29	16	11D	14	25	♃26♑
22	18.02	0♑	0♈	11	14	26	♄22♏
23	18.06	1	14	11	15	27	♅21♓
24	18.10	2	27	11	16	27	♆24♌R
25	18.14	3	10♉	12	17	28	♇14♋R
26	18.18	4	23	12	17	29	♃27♑
27	18.22	5	6♊	13	18	29	♄22♏
28	18.26	6	18	14	19	0♐	♅22♓
29	18.30	7	0♋	15	19	1	♆24♌R
30	18.34	8	13	16	20	1	♇13♋R
31	18.38	9	25	16	20	2	♃28♑

Jan	STime	☉	☽	☿	♀	♂	Plnts
1	18.42	10♑	6♌	18♐	21♒	3♐	♃29♑
2	18.45	11	18	19	21	3	♄23♏
3	18.49	12	0♍	20	22	4	♅22♓
4	18.53	13	12	21	22	5	♆24♌R
5	18.57	14	24	22	23	6	♇13♋R
6	19.01	15	6♎	23	23	6	♃ 0♒
7	19.05	16	18	25	24	7	♄23♏
8	19.09	17	1♏	26	24	8	♅22♓
9	19.13	18	14	27	24	8	♆24♌R
10	19.17	19	28	29	25	9	♇13♋R
11	19.21	20	12♐	0♑	25	10	♃ 1♒
12	19.25	21	27	1	25	10	♄24♏
13	19.29	22	11♑	3	25	11	♅22♓
14	19.33	23	26	4	26	12	♆24♌R
15	19.37	24	12♒	6	26	12	♇13♋R
16	19.41	25	27	7	26	13	♃ 2♒
17	19.45	26	12♓	8	26	14	♄24♏
18	19.49	27	26	10	26R	15	♅22♓
19	19.53	28	10♈	11	26	15	♆24♌R
20	19.56	29	24	13	26	16	♇13♋R
21	20.00	0♒	7♉	14	25	17	♃ 3♒
22	20.04	1	20	16	25	17	♄24♏
23	20.08	2	3♊	17	25	18	♅22♓
24	20.12	3	15	19	25	19	♆24♌R
25	20.16	4	27	20	25	19	♇13♋R
26	20.20	5	9♋	22	24	20	♃ 5♒
27	20.24	7	21	23	24	21	♄25♏
28	20.28	8	3♌	25	23	22	♅23♓
29	20.32	9	15	27	23	22	♆24♌R
30	20.36	10	27	28	23	23	♇13♋R
31	20.40	11	9♍	0♒	22	24	♃ 6♒

Feb	STime	☉	☽	☿	♀	♂	Plnts
1	20.44	12♒	21♍	1♒	21♒	24♐	♃ 6♒
2	20.48	13	3♎	3	21	25	♄25♏
3	20.52	14	15	5	20	26	♅23♓
4	20.56	15	27	6	20	26	♆23♌R
5	21.00	16	10♏	8	19	27	♇13♋R
6	21.03	17	23	10	19	28	♃ 7♒
7	21.07	18	6♐	11	18	29	♄25♏
8	21.11	19	20	13	17	29	♅23♓
9	21.15	20	5♑	15	17	0♑	♆23♌R
10	21.19	21	19	16	16	1	♇13♋R
11	21.23	22	4♒	18	15	1	♃ 8♒
12	21.27	23	20	20	15	2	♄25♏
13	21.31	24	5♓	22	14	3	♅23♓
14	21.35	25	20	24	14	3	♆23♌R
15	21.39	26	5♈	25	13	4	♇13♋R
16	21.43	27	19	27	13	5	♃ 9♒
17	21.47	28	3♉	29	12	6	♄26♏
18	21.51	29	17	1♓	12	6	♅24♓
19	21.55	0♓	0♊	3	12	7	♆23♌R
20	21.59	1	12	5	11	8	♇13♋R
21	22.03	2	24	6	11	8	♃11♒
22	22.07	3	6♋	8	11	9	♄26♏
23	22.10	4	18	10	10	10	♅24♓
24	22.14	5	0♌	12	10	11	♆23♌R
25	22.18	6	12	14	10	11	♇12♋R
26	22.22	7	24	16	10	12	♃12♒
27	22.26	8	6♍	18	10D	13	♄26♏
28	22.30	9	18	20	10	13	♅24♓

Mar	STime	☉	☽	☿	♀	♂	Plnts
1	22.34	10♓	0♎	21♓	10♒	14♑	♃12♒
2	22.38	11	12	23	10	15	♄26♏
3	22.42	12	24	25	10	16	♅24♓
4	22.46	13	7♏	27	10	16	♆23♌R
5	22.50	14	20	29	11	17	♇12♋R
6	22.54	15	3♐	0♈	11	18	♃14♒
7	22.58	16	16	2	11	18	♄26♏R
8	23.02	17	0♑	4	11	19	♅25♓
9	23.06	18	14	5	12	20	♆22♌R
10	23.10	19	28	6	12	21	♇12♋R
11	23.14	20	13♒	8	12	21	♃15♒
12	23.18	21	28	9	13	22	♄26♏R
13	23.21	22	13♓	10	13	23	♅25♓
14	23.25	23	28	11	14	23	♆22♌R
15	23.29	24	13♈	12	14	24	♇12♋
16	23.33	25	27	13	15	25	♃16♒
17	23.37	26	11♉	13	15	26	♄26♏R
18	23.41	27	25	14	16	26	♅25♓
19	23.45	28	8♊	14	16	27	♆22♌R
20	23.49	29	21	14	17	28	♇12♋
21	23.53	0♈	3♋	14R	18	28	♃17♒
22	23.57	1	15	14	18	29	♄26♏R
23	0.01	2	27	14	19	0♒	♅26♓
24	0.05	3	9♌	14	20	1	♆22♌R
25	0.09	4	21	13	20	1	♇12♋
26	0.13	5	2♍	13	21	2	♃18♒
27	0.17	6	14	12	22	3	♄25♏R
28	0.21	7	26	12	23	4	♅26♓
29	0.25	8	9♎	11	23	4	♆22♌R
30	0.28	9	21	10	24	5	♇12♋
31	0.32	10	4♏	9	25	6	♃19♒

Apr	STime	☉	☽	☿	♀	♂	Plnts
1	0.36	11♈	17♏	8♈	26♒	6♒	♃19♒
2	0.40	12	0♐	8	27	7	♄25♏R
3	0.44	13	13	7	27	8	♅26♓
4	0.48	14	26	6	28	9	♆22♌R
5	0.52	15	10♑	5	29	9	♇12♋
6	0.56	16	24	5	0♓	10	♃20♒
7	1.00	17	8♒	4	1	11	♄25♏R
8	1.04	18	22	4	2	11	♅26♓
9	1.08	19	7♓	3	3	12	♆22♌R
10	1.12	20	22	3	4	13	♇12♋
11	1.16	21	6♈	3	4	14	♃21♒
12	1.20	22	21	2	5	14	♄25♏R
13	1.24	22	5♉	2D	6	15	♅27♓
14	1.28	23	19	2	7	16	♆22♌R
15	1.32	24	3♊	2	8	17	♇12♋
16	1.36	25	16	3	9	17	♃21♒
17	1.39	26	29	3	10	18	♄24♏R
18	1.43	27	11♋	3	11	19	♅27♓
19	1.47	28	23	4	12	19	♆22♌R
20	1.51	29	5♌	4	13	20	♇12♋
21	1.55	0♉	17	5	14	21	♃22♒
22	1.59	1	29	5	15	22	♄24♏R
23	2.03	2	11♍	6	16	22	♅27♓
24	2.07	3	23	7	17	23	♆22♌
25	2.11	4	5♎	7	18	24	♇12♋
26	2.15	5	17	8	19	24	♃23♒
27	2.19	6	0♏	9	20	25	♄24♏R
28	2.23	7	13	10	21	26	♅27♓
29	2.27	8	26	11	22	27	♆22♌R
30	2.31	9	10♐	12	23	27	♇13♋

May	STime	☉	☽	☿	♀	♂	Plnts
1	2.35	10♉	23♐	13♈	24♓	28♒	♃24♒
2	2.39	11	7♑	15	25	29	♄23♏R
3	2.43	12	21	16	26	0♓	♅28♓
4	2.46	13	5♒	17	27	0	♆22♌
5	2.50	14	19	18	28	1	♇13♋
6	2.54	15	3♓	20	0♈	2	♃24♒
7	2.58	16	17	21	1	2	♄23♏R
8	3.02	17	2♈	22	2	3	♅28♓
9	3.06	18	16	24	3	4	♆22♌
10	3.10	19	0♉	25	4	5	♇13♋
11	3.14	20	14	27	5	5	♃25♒
12	3.18	21	28	28	6	6	♄23♏R
13	3.22	22	11♊	0♉	7	7	♅28♓
14	3.26	23	24	1	8	7	♆22♌
15	3.30	24	7♋	3	9	8	♇13♋
16	3.34	25	19	5	10	9	♃25♒
17	3.38	26	1♌	6	11	10	♄22♏R
18	3.42	26	13	8	13	10	♅28♓
19	3.46	27	25	10	14	11	♆22♌
20	3.50	28	7♍	12	15	12	♇13♋
21	3.53	29	19	14	16	12	♃26♒
22	3.57	0♊	1♎	15	17	13	♄22♏R
23	4.01	1	13	17	18	14	♅28♓
24	4.05	2	26	19	19	15	♆22♌
25	4.09	3	8♏	21	20	15	♇13♋
26	4.13	4	22	23	21	16	♃26♒
27	4.17	5	5♐	25	23	17	♄22♏R
28	4.21	6	19	27	24	17	♅29♓
29	4.25	7	3♑	0♊	25	18	♆22♌
30	4.29	8	17	2	26	19	♇13♋
31	4.33	9	1♒	4	27	20	♃26♒

Jun	STime	☉	☽	☿	♀	♂	Plnts
1	4.37	10♊	16♒	6♊	28♈	20♓	♃27♒
2	4.41	11	0♓	8	29	21	♄21♏R
3	4.45	12	14	10	0♉	22	♅29♓
4	4.49	13	28	13	2	22	♆22♌
5	4.53	14	12♈	15	3	23	♇13♋
6	4.57	15	26	17	4	24	♃27♒
7	5.01	16	10♉	19	5	24	♄21♏R
8	5.04	17	23	21	6	25	♅29♓
9	5.08	18	6♊	24	7	26	♆22♌
10	5.12	19	19	26	8	27	♇13♋
11	5.16	19	2♋	28	10	27	♃27♒
12	5.20	20	15	0♋	11	28	♄20♏R
13	5.24	21	27	2	12	29	♅29♓
14	5.28	22	9♌	4	13	29	♆22♌
15	5.32	23	21	6	14	0♈	♇13♋
16	5.36	24	3♍	8	15	1	♃27♒
17	5.40	25	15	10	16	1	♄20♏R
18	5.44	26	27	12	18	2	♅29♓
19	5.48	27	9♎	14	19	3	♆22♌
20	5.52	28	21	15	20	3	♇14♋
21	5.56	29	4♏	17	21	4	♃27♒R
22	6.00	0♋	17	19	22	5	♄20♏R
23	6.04	1	0♐	21	23	5	♅29♓
24	6.08	2	14	22	25	6	♆22♌
25	6.11	3	28	24	26	7	♇14♋
26	6.15	4	12♑	26	27	7	♃27♒R
27	6.19	5	27	27	28	8	♄20♏R
28	6.23	6	11♒	29	29	9	♅29♓
29	6.27	7	26	0♌	0♊	9	♆23♌
30	6.31	8	10♓	2	2	10	♇14♋

Jul	STime	☉	☽	☿	♀	♂	Plnts
1	6.35	9♋	25♓	3♌	3♊	11♈	♃27♒R
2	6.39	10	9♈	4	4	11	♄20♏R
3	6.43	10	23	6	5	12	♅29♓
4	6.47	11	6♉	7	6	13	♆23♌
5	6.51	12	20	8	7	13	♇14♋
6	6.55	13	3♊	9	9	14	♃26♒R
7	6.59	14	16	10	10	15	♄19♏R
8	7.03	15	29	12	11	15	♅29♓R
9	7.07	16	11♋	13	12	16	♆23♌
10	7.11	17	23	14	13	17	♇14♋
11	7.15	18	5♌	14	15	17	♃26♒R
12	7.19	19	17	15	16	18	♄19♏R
13	7.22	20	29	16	17	18	♅29♓
14	7.26	21	11♍	17	18	19	♆23♌
15	7.30	22	23	18	19	20	♇14♋
16	7.34	23	5♎	18	20	20	♃25♒R
17	7.38	24	17	19	22	21	♄19♏R
18	7.42	25	29	19	23	22	♅29♓R
19	7.46	26	12♏	20	24	22	♆23♌
20	7.50	27	25	20	25	23	♇14♋
21	7.54	28	8♐	21	26	23	♃25♒R
22	7.58	29	22	21	28	24	♄19♏
23	8.02	0♌	6♑	21	29	25	♅29♓R
24	8.06	1	21	21R	0♋	25	♆23♌
25	8.10	1	5♒	21	1	26	♇14♋
26	8.14	2	20	21	2	26	♃24♒R
27	8.18	3	5♓	21	4	27	♄19♏
28	8.22	4	20	20	5	28	♅29♓R
29	8.26	5	5♈	20	6	28	♆24♌
30	8.29	6	19	20	7	29	♇15♋
31	8.33	7	3♉	19	8	29	♃24♒R

Aug	STime	☉	☽	☿	♀	♂	Plnts
1	8.37	8♌	17♉	18♌	10♋	0♉	♃24♒R
2	8.41	9	0♊	18	11	0	♄19♏
3	8.45	10	13	17	12	1	♅29♓R
4	8.49	11	26	16	13	1	♆24♌
5	8.53	12	8♋	16	14	2	♇15♋
6	8.57	13	20	15	16	2	♃23♒R
7	9.01	14	2♌	14	17	3	♄19♏
8	9.05	15	14	13	18	4	♅29♓R
9	9.09	16	26	13	19	4	♆24♌
10	9.13	17	8♍	12	20	5	♇15♋
11	9.17	18	20	11	22	5	♃22♒R
12	9.21	19	1♎	11	23	6	♄19♏
13	9.25	20	13	10	24	6	♅29♓R
14	9.29	21	25	10	25	7	♆24♌
15	9.33	22	8♏	9	26	7	♇15♋
16	9.37	23	20	9	28	7	♃22♒R
17	9.40	24	3♐	9D	29	8	♄20♏
18	9.44	24	16	9	0♌	8	♅28♓R
19	9.48	25	0♑	9	1	9	♆24♌
20	9.52	26	14	10	3	9	♇15♋
21	9.56	27	29	10	4	10	♃21♒R
22	10.00	28	14♒	11	5	10	♄20♏
23	10.04	29	29	11	6	11	♅28♓R
24	10.08	0♍	14♓	12	7	11	♆24♌
25	10.12	1	29	13	9	11	♇15♋
26	10.16	2	14♈	14	10	12	♃21♒R
27	10.20	3	29	15	11	12	♄20♏
28	10.24	4	13♉	16	12	13	♅28♓R
29	10.28	5	27	18	13	13	♆25♌
30	10.32	6	10♊	19	15	13	♇15♋
31	10.36	7	23	21	16	14	♃20♒R

Sep	STime	☉	☽	☿	♀	♂	Plnts
1	10.40	8♍	5♋	22♌	17♌	14♉	♃20♒R
2	10.44	9	17	24	18	14	♄20♏
3	10.47	10	29	25	20	15	♅28♓R
4	10.51	11	11♌	27	21	15	♆25♌
5	10.55	12	23	29	22	15	♇15♋
6	10.59	13	5♍	1♍	23	16	♃19♒R
7	11.03	14	17	3	25	16	♄21♏
8	11.07	15	29	5	26	16	♅28♓R
9	11.11	16	10♎	7	27	16	♆25♌
10	11.15	17	23	8	28	17	♇15♋
11	11.19	18	5♏	10	29	17	♃19♒R
12	11.23	19	17	12	1♍	17	♄21♏
13	11.27	20	0♐	14	2	17	♅27♓R
14	11.31	21	12	16	3	18	♆25♌
15	11.35	22	25	18	4	18	♇15♋
16	11.39	23	9♑	20	6	18	♃18♒R
17	11.43	24	23	22	7	18	♄21♏
18	11.47	25	7♒	24	8	18	♅27♓R
19	11.51	25	22	25	9	18	♆25♌
20	11.54	26	7♓	27	11	19	♇16♋
21	11.58	27	22	29	12	19	♃18♒R
22	12.02	28	8♈	1♎	13	19	♄22♏
23	12.06	29	23	3	14	19	♅27♓R
24	12.10	0♎	7♉	4	16	19	♆26♌
25	12.14	1	22	6	17	19	♇16♋
26	12.18	2	5♊	8	18	19	♃18♒R
27	12.22	3	19	10	19	19	♄22♏
28	12.26	4	2♋	11	21	19	♅27♓R
29	12.30	5	14	13	22	19R	♆26♌
30	12.34	6	26	15	23	19	♇16♋

Oct	STime	☉	☽	☿	♀	♂	Plnts
1	12.38	7♎	8♌	16♎	24♍	19♉	♃17♒R
2	12.42	8	20	18	25	19	♄23♏
3	12.46	9	2♍	20	27	19	♅27♓R
4	12.50	10	14	21	28	19	♆26♌
5	12.54	11	25	23	29	19	♇16♋
6	12.58	12	7♎	24	0♎	19	♃17♒R
7	13.02	13	20	26	2	19	♄23♏
8	13.05	14	2♏	28	3	19	♅26♓R
9	13.09	15	14	29	4	18	♆26♌
10	13.13	16	27	1♏	5	18	♇16♋
11	13.17	17	9♐	2	7	18	♃17♒R
12	13.21	18	22	4	8	18	♄24♏
13	13.25	19	5♑	5	9	18	♅26♓R
14	13.29	20	19	7	10	17	♆26♌
15	13.33	21	3♒	8	12	17	♇16♋
16	13.37	22	17	10	13	17	♃17♒
17	13.41	23	1♓	11	14	17	♄24♏
18	13.45	24	16	12	15	16	♅26♓R
19	13.49	25	1♈	14	17	16	♆26♌
20	13.53	26	16	15	18	16	♇16♋
21	13.57	27	1♉	17	19	16	♃17♒
22	14.01	28	16	18	20	15	♄25♏
23	14.05	29	0♊	19	22	15	♅26♓R
24	14.09	0♏	14	21	23	15	♆26♌
25	14.12	1	27	22	24	14	♇16♋
26	14.16	2	10♋	23	25	14	♃17♒
27	14.20	3	22	25	27	14	♄25♏
28	14.24	4	4♌	26	28	13	♅26♓R
29	14.28	5	16	27	29	13	♆26♌
30	14.32	6	28	29	0♏	13	♇16♋R
31	14.36	7	10♍	0♐	2	12	♃18♒

Nov	STime	☉	☽	☿	♀	♂	Plnts
1	14.40	8♏	22♍	1♐	3♏	12♉	♃18♒
2	14.44	9	4♎	2	4	12	♄26♏
3	14.48	10	16	3	6	11	♅26♓R
4	14.52	11	28	4	7	11	♆27♌
5	14.56	12	11♏	5	8	11	♇16♋R
6	15.00	13	23	6	9	10	♃18♒
7	15.04	14	6♐	7	11	10	♄27♏
8	15.08	15	19	8	12	10	♅26♓R
9	15.12	16	2♑	9	13	9	♆27♌
10	15.16	17	16	9	14	9	♇16♋R
11	15.20	18	29	10	16	9	♃18♒
12	15.23	19	13♒	10	17	8	♄27♏
13	15.27	20	27	11	18	8	♅25♓R
14	15.31	21	11♓	11	19	8	♆27♌
15	15.35	22	26	11R	21	7	♇15♋R
16	15.39	23	10♈	11	22	7	♃19♒
17	15.43	24	25	11	23	7	♄28♏
18	15.47	25	9♉	10	24	7	♅25♓R
19	15.51	26	24	10	26	6	♆27♌
20	15.55	27	8♊	9	27	6	♇15♋R
21	15.59	28	21	8	28	6	♃19♒
22	16.03	29	5♋	7	29	6	♄28♏
23	16.07	0♐	18	6	1♐	5	♅25♓R
24	16.11	1	0♌	5	2	5	♆27♌
25	16.15	2	12	3	3	5	♇15♋R
26	16.19	3	24	2	4	5	♃20♒
27	16.23	4	6♍	1	6	5	♄29♏
28	16.27	5	18	29♏	7	5	♅25♓
29	16.30	6	0♎	28	8	5	♆27♌
30	16.34	7	12	27	9	5	♇15♋R

Dec	STime	☉	☽	☿	♀	♂	Plnts
1	16.38	8♐	24♎	26♏	11♐	4♉	♃21♒
2	16.42	9	7♏	26	12	4	♄ 0♐
3	16.46	10	19	25	13	4	♅25♓
4	16.50	11	2♐	25	14	4	♆27♌R
5	16.54	12	15	25D	16	4	♇15♋R
6	16.58	13	29	25	17	4D	♃21♒
7	17.02	14	12♑	25	18	4	♄ 0♐
8	17.06	15	26	26	19	4	♅25♓
9	17.10	16	10♒	26	21	4	♆27♌R
10	17.14	17	24	27	22	4	♇15♋R
11	17.18	18	8♓	28	23	4	♃22♒
12	17.22	19	22	28	25	4	♄ 1♐
13	17.26	20	6♈	29	26	4	♅25♓
14	17.30	21	21	0♐	27	5	♆27♌R
15	17.34	22	5♉	1	28	5	♇15♋R
16	17.38	23	19	3	0♑	5	♃23♒
17	17.41	25	3♊	4	1	5	♄ 1♐
18	17.45	26	16	5	2	5	♅25♓
19	17.49	27	0♋	6	3	5	♆27♌R
20	17.53	28	13	7	5	5	♇15♋R
21	17.57	29	25	9	6	6	♃24♒
22	18.01	0♑	8♌	10	7	6	♄ 2♐
23	18.05	1	20	11	8	6	♅25♓
24	18.09	2	2♍	13	10	6	♆27♌R
25	18.13	3	14	14	11	6	♇15♋R
26	18.17	4	26	16	12	7	♃25♒
27	18.21	5	8♎	17	13	7	♄ 2♐
28	18.25	6	20	18	15	7	♅25♓
29	18.29	7	2♏	20	16	7	♆26♌R
30	18.33	8	14	21	17	7	♇15♋R
31	18.37	9	27	23	18	8	♃26♒

Jan	STime	☉	☽	☿	♀	♂	Plnts
1	18.41	10♑	10♐	24♐	20♑	8♉	♃26♒
2	18.45	11	24	26	21	8	♄ 3♐
3	18.48	12	7♑	27	22	9	♅26♓
4	18.52	13	21	29	23	9	♆26♌R
5	18.56	14	6♒	0♑	25	9	♇15♋R
6	19.00	15	20	2	26	9	♃27♒
7	19.04	16	5♓	3	27	10	♄ 4♐
8	19.08	17	19	5	28	10	♅26♓
9	19.12	18	3♈	6	0♒	10	♆26♌R
10	19.16	19	17	8	1	11	♇14♋R
11	19.20	20	1♉	10	2	11	♃28♒
12	19.24	21	15	11	3	12	♄ 4♐
13	19.28	22	29	13	5	12	♅26♓
14	19.32	23	12♊	14	6	12	♆26♌R
15	19.36	24	25	16	7	13	♇14♋R
16	19.40	25	8♋	17	8	13	♃29♒
17	19.44	26	21	19	10	13	♄ 5♐
18	19.48	27	4♌	21	11	14	♅26♓
19	19.52	28	16	22	12	14	♆26♌R
20	19.55	29	28	24	14	15	♇14♋R
21	19.59	0♒	10♍	25	15	15	♃ 0♓
22	20.03	1	22	27	16	15	♄ 5♐
23	20.07	2	4♎	29	17	16	♅26♓
24	20.11	3	16	0♒	19	16	♆26♌R
25	20.15	4	28	2	20	17	♇14♋R
26	20.19	5	10♏	4	21	17	♃ 2♓
27	20.23	6	22	6	22	17	♄ 5♐
28	20.27	7	5♐	7	24	18	♅26♓
29	20.31	8	18	9	25	18	♆26♌R
30	20.35	9	1♑	11	26	19	♇14♋R
31	20.39	10	15	12	27	19	♃ 3♓

Feb	STime	☉	☽	☿	♀	♂	Plnts
1	20.43	11♒	29♑	14♒	29♒	20♉	♃ 3♓
2	20.47	12	14♒	16	0♓	20	♄ 6♐
3	20.51	13	29	18	1	21	♅27♓
4	20.55	14	14♓	19	2	21	♆26♌R
5	20.59	15	29	21	4	22	♇14♋R
6	21.03	16	14♈	23	5	22	♃ 4♓
7	21.06	17	28	25	6	22	♄ 6♐
8	21.10	18	12♉	27	7	23	♅27♓
9	21.14	19	26	28	9	23	♆25♌R
10	21.18	20	9♊	0♓	10	24	♇14♋R
11	21.22	21	22	2	11	24	♃ 5♓
12	21.26	22	5♋	4	12	25	♄ 6♐
13	21.30	23	18	6	13	25	♅27♓
14	21.34	25	0♌	7	15	26	♆25♌R
15	21.38	26	12	9	16	26	♇14♋R
16	21.42	27	25	11	17	27	♃ 6♓
17	21.46	28	7♍	13	18	27	♄ 7♐
18	21.50	29	19	14	20	28	♅27♓
19	21.54	0♓	0♎	16	21	28	♆25♌R
20	21.58	1	12	17	22	29	♇14♋R
21	22.02	2	24	19	23	29	♃ 8♓
22	22.06	3	6♏	20	25	0♊	♄ 7♐
23	22.10	4	18	21	26	0	♅28♓
24	22.13	5	0♐	23	27	1	♆25♌R
25	22.17	6	13	24	28	1	♇14♋R
26	22.21	7	26	25	0♈	2	♃ 9♓
27	22.25	8	9♑	25	1	3	♄ 7♐
28	22.29	9	23	26	2	3	♅28♓

Mar	STime	☉	☽	☿	♀	♂	Plnts
1	22.33	10♓	7♒	27♓	3♈	4♊	♃10♓
2	22.37	11	22	27	5	4	♄ 7♐
3	22.41	12	7♓	27	6	5	♅28♓
4	22.45	13	23	27R	7	5	♆25♌R
5	22.49	14	8♈	27	8	6	♇14♋R
6	22.53	15	23	27	10	6	♃11♓
7	22.57	16	8♉	26	11	7	♄ 7♐
8	23.01	17	22	26	12	7	♅28♓
9	23.05	18	6♊	25	13	8	♆25♌R
10	23.09	19	19	25	14	8	♇14♋R
11	23.13	20	2♋	24	16	9	♃12♓
12	23.17	21	15	23	17	10	♄ 7♐
13	23.21	22	27	22	18	10	♅29♓
14	23.24	23	9♌	21	19	11	♆25♌R
15	23.28	24	21	20	21	11	♇14♋
16	23.32	25	3♍	19	22	12	♃13♓
17	23.36	26	15	18	23	12	♄ 7♐
18	23.40	27	27	17	24	13	♅29♓
19	23.44	28	9♎	16	25	13	♆24♌R
20	23.48	29	21	16	27	14	♇13♋
21	23.52	0♈	3♏	15	28	15	♃14♓
22	23.56	1	15	15	29	15	♄ 7♐
23	0.00	2	27	14	0♉	16	♅29♓
24	0.04	3	9♐	14	2	16	♆24♌R
25	0.08	4	22	14	3	17	♇13♋
26	0.12	5	5♑	14	4	17	♃16♓
27	0.16	6	18	14D	5	18	♄ 7♐R
28	0.20	7	2♒	14	6	18	♅ 0♈
29	0.24	8	16	14	8	19	♆24♌R
30	0.28	8	0♓	14	9	20	♇13♋
31	0.31	9	15	14	10	20	♃17♓

Apr	STime	☉	☽	☿	♀	♂	Plnts
1	0.35	10♈	1♈	15♓	11♉	21♊	♃17♓
2	0.39	11	16	15	13	21	♄ 7♐R
3	0.43	12	1♉	16	14	22	♅ 0♈
4	0.47	13	16	17	15	22	♆24♌R
5	0.51	14	1♊	17	16	23	♇13♋
6	0.55	15	15	18	17	24	♃18♓
7	0.59	16	28	19	19	24	♄ 7♐R
8	1.03	17	11♋	20	20	25	♅ 0♈
9	1.07	18	24	21	21	25	♆24♌R
10	1.11	19	6♌	22	22	26	♇14♋
11	1.15	20	19	23	23	26	♃19♓
12	1.19	21	1♍	24	25	27	♄ 7♐R
13	1.23	22	12	25	26	28	♅ 0♈
14	1.27	23	24	26	27	28	♆24♌R
15	1.31	24	6♎	27	28	29	♇14♋
16	1.35	25	18	28	29	29	♃20♓
17	1.38	26	0♏	0♈	1♊	0♋	♄ 7♐R
18	1.42	27	12	1	2	1	♅ 1♈
19	1.46	28	24	2	3	1	♆24♌R
20	1.50	29	6♐	4	4	2	♇14♋
21	1.54	0♉	19	5	5	2	♃21♓
22	1.58	1	1♑	7	6	3	♄ 6♐R
23	2.02	2	14	8	8	3	♅ 1♈
24	2.06	3	28	9	9	4	♆24♌R
25	2.10	4	11♒	11	10	5	♇14♋
26	2.14	5	25	13	11	5	♃22♓
27	2.18	6	10♓	14	12	6	♄ 6♐R
28	2.22	7	24	16	14	6	♅ 1♈
29	2.26	8	9♈	17	15	7	♆24♌
30	2.30	9	24	19	16	8	♇14♋

May	STime	☉	☽	☿	♀	♂	Plnts
1	2.34	10♉	9♉	21♈	17♊	8♋	♃24♓
2	2.38	11	24	22	18	9	♄ 6♐R
3	2.42	12	9♊	24	19	9	♅ 1♈
4	2.46	13	23	26	21	10	♆24♌
5	2.49	14	7♋	28	22	11	♇14♋
6	2.53	15	20	0♉	23	11	♃24♓
7	2.57	16	3♌	2	24	12	♄ 5♐R
8	3.01	17	15	4	25	12	♅ 2♈
9	3.05	18	27	5	26	13	♆24♌
10	3.09	19	9♍	7	28	14	♇14♋
11	3.13	19	21	9	29	14	♃25♓
12	3.17	20	3♎	12	0♋	15	♄ 5♐R
13	3.21	21	15	14	1	15	♅ 2♈
14	3.25	22	27	16	2	16	♆24♌
15	3.29	23	9♏	18	3	16	♇14♋
16	3.33	24	21	20	4	17	♃26♓
17	3.37	25	3♐	22	6	18	♄ 5♐R
18	3.41	26	16	24	7	18	♅ 2♈
19	3.45	27	29	26	8	19	♆24♌
20	3.49	28	11♑	29	9	19	♇14♋
21	3.53	29	25	1♊	10	20	♃27♓
22	3.56	0♊	8♒	3	11	21	♄ 4♐R
23	4.00	1	22	5	12	21	♅ 2♈
24	4.04	2	6♓	7	14	22	♆24♌
25	4.08	3	20	10	15	22	♇14♋
26	4.12	4	4♈	12	16	23	♃28♓
27	4.16	5	19	14	17	24	♄ 4♐R
28	4.20	6	3♉	16	18	24	♅ 2♈
29	4.24	7	18	18	19	25	♆24♌
30	4.28	8	3♊	20	20	25	♇14♋
31	4.32	9	17	22	21	26	♃29♓

Jun	STime	☉	☽	☿	♀	♂	Plnts
1	4.36	10♊	1♋	24♊	22♋	27♋	♃29♓
2	4.40	11	15	26	24	27	♄ 4♐R
3	4.44	12	28	28	25	28	♅ 3♈
4	4.48	13	11♌	0♋	26	29	♆24♌
5	4.52	14	23	1	27	29	♇14♋
6	4.56	14	5♍	3	28	0♌	♃ 0♈
7	5.00	15	17	5	29	0	♄ 3♐R
8	5.04	16	29	6	0♌	1	♅ 3♈
9	5.07	17	11♎	8	1	2	♆24♌
10	5.11	18	23	10	2	2	♇14♋
11	5.15	19	5♏	11	3	3	♃ 0♈
12	5.19	20	17	13	4	3	♄ 3♐R
13	5.23	21	0♐	14	5	4	♅ 3♈
14	5.27	22	12	16	7	5	♆24♌
15	5.31	23	25	17	8	5	♇15♋
16	5.35	24	8♑	18	9	6	♃ 1♈
17	5.39	25	21	19	10	6	♄ 3♐R
18	5.43	26	5♒	21	11	7	♅ 3♈
19	5.47	27	18	22	12	8	♆24♌
20	5.51	28	2♓	23	13	8	♇15♋
21	5.55	29	16	24	14	9	♃ 2♈
22	5.59	0♋	1♈	25	15	9	♄ 2♐R
23	6.03	1	15	26	16	10	♅ 3♈
24	6.07	2	29	27	17	11	♆25♌
25	6.11	3	13♉	27	18	11	♇15♋
26	6.14	4	28	28	19	12	♃ 2♈
27	6.18	5	12♊	29	20	13	♄ 2♐R
28	6.22	5	26	0♌	21	13	♅ 3♈
29	6.26	6	9♋	0	22	14	♆25♌
30	6.30	7	23	1	23	14	♇15♋

Jul	STime	☉	☽	☿	♀	♂	Plnts
1	6.34	8♋	6♌	1♌	24♌	15♌	♃ 2♈
2	6.38	9	19	1	25	16	♄ 2♐R
3	6.42	10	1♍	2	26	16	♅ 3♈
4	6.46	11	13	2	27	17	♆25♌
5	6.50	12	25	2	28	17	♇15♋
6	6.54	13	7♎	2R	29	18	♃ 3♈
7	6.58	14	19	2	29	19	♄ 1♐R
8	7.02	15	1♏	2	0♍	19	♅ 3♈
9	7.06	16	13	2	1	20	♆25♌
10	7.10	17	25	1	2	21	♇15♋
11	7.14	18	8♐	1	3	21	♃ 3♈
12	7.18	19	20	1	4	22	♄ 1♐R
13	7.21	20	3♑	0	5	22	♅ 3♈R
14	7.25	21	17	0	6	23	♆25♌
15	7.29	22	1♒	29♋	6	24	♇15♋
16	7.33	23	15	28	7	24	♃ 3♈
17	7.37	24	29	28	8	25	♄ 1♐R
18	7.41	25	13♓	27	9	25	♅ 3♈R
19	7.45	26	27	26	10	26	♆25♌
20	7.49	26	12♈	26	11	27	♇15♋
21	7.53	27	26	25	11	27	♃ 3♈
22	7.57	28	10♉	24	12	28	♄ 1♐R
23	8.01	29	24	24	13	29	♅ 3♈R
24	8.05	0♌	8♊	23	14	29	♆25♌
25	8.09	1	22	23	14	0♍	♇16♋
26	8.13	2	5♋	22	15	0	♃ 3♈R
27	8.17	3	18	22	16	1	♄ 1♐R
28	8.21	4	1♌	22	16	2	♅ 3♈R
29	8.25	5	14	22	17	2	♆26♌
30	8.29	6	27	21D	18	3	♇16♋
31	8.32	7	9♍	21	18	4	♃ 3♈R

Aug	STime	☉	☽	☿	♀	♂	Plnts
1	8.36	8♌	21♍	22♋	19♍	4♍	♃ 3♈R
2	8.40	9	3♎	22	19	5	♄ 1♐R
3	8.44	10	15	22	20	5	♅ 3♈R
4	8.48	11	27	23	20	6	♆26♌
5	8.52	12	9♏	23	21	7	♇16♋
6	8.56	13	21	24	21	7	♃ 3♈R
7	9.00	14	3♐	25	22	8	♄ 1♐
8	9.04	15	16	26	22	9	♅ 3♈R
9	9.08	16	28	27	23	9	♆26♌
10	9.12	17	12♑	28	23	10	♇16♋
11	9.16	18	25	29	23	10	♃ 3♈R
12	9.20	18	9♒	0♌	24	11	♄ 1♐
13	9.24	19	24	2	24	12	♅ 3♈R
14	9.28	20	8♓	3	24	12	♆26♌
15	9.32	21	23	5	24	13	♇16♋
16	9.36	22	8♈	6	24	14	♃ 2♈R
17	9.39	23	22	8	25	14	♄ 1♐
18	9.43	24	7♉	10	25	15	♅ 3♈R
19	9.47	25	21	11	25	16	♆26♌
20	9.51	26	5♊	13	25R	16	♇16♋
21	9.55	27	18	15	25	17	♃ 2♈R
22	9.59	28	2♋	17	25	17	♄ 1♐
23	10.03	29	15	19	25	18	♅ 2♈R
24	10.07	0♍	28	21	24	19	♆27♌
25	10.11	1	10♌	23	24	19	♇16♋
26	10.15	2	23	25	24	20	♃ 2♈R
27	10.19	3	5♍	27	24	21	♄ 1♐
28	10.23	4	18	29	23	21	♅ 2♈R
29	10.27	5	0♎	1♍	23	22	♆27♌
30	10.31	6	12	3	23	23	♇16♋
31	10.35	7	24	5	22	23	♃ 1♈R

Sep	STime	☉	☽	☿	♀	♂	Plnts
1	10.39	8♍	5♏	7♍	22♍	24♍	♃ 1♈R
2	10.43	9	17	9	21	24	♄ 1♐
3	10.47	10	29	11	21	25	♅ 2♈R
4	10.50	11	11♐	12	20	26	♆27♌
5	10.54	12	24	14	20	26	♇16♋
6	10.58	13	6♑	16	19	27	♃ 0♈R
7	11.02	14	20	18	19	28	♄ 2♐
8	11.06	15	3♒	20	18	28	♅ 2♈R
9	11.10	16	17	22	17	29	♆27♌
10	11.14	16	2♓	23	17	0♎	♇17♋
11	11.18	17	17	25	16	0	♃ 0♈R
12	11.22	18	2♈	27	16	1	♄ 2♐
13	11.26	19	17	29	15	2	♅ 2♈R
14	11.30	20	2♉	0♎	14	2	♆27♌
15	11.34	21	17	2	14	3	♇17♋
16	11.38	22	1♊	4	13	4	♃29♓R
17	11.42	23	15	5	13	4	♄ 2♐
18	11.46	24	29	7	12	5	♅ 1♈R
19	11.50	25	12♋	9	12	5	♆27♌
20	11.54	26	25	10	11	6	♇17♋
21	11.57	27	7♌	12	11	7	♃28♓R
22	12.01	28	20	14	10	7	♄ 3♐
23	12.05	29	2♍	15	10	8	♅ 1♈R
24	12.09	0♎	14	17	10	9	♆28♌
25	12.13	1	26	18	9	9	♇17♋
26	12.17	2	8♎	20	9	10	♃28♓R
27	12.21	3	20	21	9	11	♄ 3♐
28	12.25	4	2♏	23	9	11	♅ 1♈R
29	12.29	5	14	24	9	12	♆28♌
30	12.33	6	26	26	9	13	♇17♋

Oct	STime	☉	☽	☿	♀	♂	Plnts
1	12.37	7♎	8♐	27♎	9♍	13♎	♃27♓R
2	12.41	8	20	28	9D	14	♄ 3♐
3	12.45	9	2♑	0♏	9	15	♅ 1♈R
4	12.49	10	15	1	9	15	♆28♌
5	12.53	11	28	3	9	16	♇17♋
6	12.57	12	12♒	4	9	17	♃26♓R
7	13.01	13	26	5	9	17	♄ 4♐
8	13.05	14	10♓	7	9	18	♅ 1♈R
9	13.08	15	25	8	10	19	♆28♌
10	13.12	16	10♈	9	10	19	♇17♋
11	13.16	17	26	10	10	20	♃26♓R
12	13.20	18	11♉	12	11	21	♄ 4♐
13	13.24	19	26	13	11	21	♅ 0♈R
14	13.28	20	10♊	14	11	22	♆28♌
15	13.32	21	25	15	12	23	♇17♋
16	13.36	22	8♋	16	12	23	♃25♓R
17	13.40	23	22	17	13	24	♄ 5♐
18	13.44	24	4♌	18	13	25	♅ 0♈R
19	13.48	25	17	19	14	25	♆28♌
20	13.52	26	29	20	14	26	♇17♋
21	13.56	27	11♍	21	15	27	♃25♓R
22	14.00	28	23	22	16	27	♄ 5♐
23	14.04	29	5♎	23	16	28	♅ 0♈R
24	14.08	0♏	17	23	17	29	♆28♌
25	14.12	1	29	24	18	29	♇17♋
26	14.15	2	11♏	24	18	0♏	♃24♓R
27	14.19	3	23	25	19	1	♄ 6♐
28	14.23	4	5♐	25	20	1	♅ 0♈R
29	14.27	5	17	25	20	2	♆29♌
30	14.31	6	29	25R	21	3	♇17♋
31	14.35	7	11♑	25	22	3	♃24♓R

Nov	STime	☉	☽	☿	♀	♂	Plnts
1	14.39	8♏	24♑	25♏	23♍	4♏	♃24♓R
2	14.43	9	7♒	24	24	5	♄ 6♐
3	14.47	10	21	24	24	5	♅ 0♈R
4	14.51	11	4♓	23	25	6	♆29♌
5	14.55	12	19	22	26	7	♇17♋R
6	14.59	13	3♈	21	27	8	♃24♓R
7	15.03	14	19	20	28	8	♄ 7♐
8	15.07	15	4♉	19	29	9	♅ 0♈R
9	15.11	16	19	18	0♎	10	♆29♌
10	15.15	17	4♊	16	1	10	♇17♋R
11	15.19	18	19	15	1	11	♃23♓R
12	15.22	19	3♋	14	2	12	♄ 7♐
13	15.26	20	17	12	3	12	♅29♓R
14	15.30	21	0♌	11	4	13	♆29♌
15	15.34	22	13	11	5	14	♇17♋R
16	15.38	23	26	10	6	14	♃23♓R
17	15.42	24	8♍	10	7	15	♄ 8♐
18	15.46	25	20	9	8	16	♅29♓R
19	15.50	26	2♎	9D	9	16	♆29♌
20	15.54	27	14	9	10	17	♇17♋R
21	15.58	28	26	10	11	18	♃23♓
22	16.02	29	8♏	10	12	19	♄ 9♐
23	16.06	0♐	20	11	13	19	♅29♓R
24	16.10	1	2♐	11	14	20	♆29♌
25	16.14	2	14	12	15	21	♇17♋R
26	16.18	3	26	13	16	21	♃23♓
27	16.22	4	8♑	14	17	22	♄ 9♐
28	16.26	5	21	15	18	23	♅29♓R
29	16.30	6	4♒	16	20	23	♆29♌
30	16.33	7	17	18	21	24	♇17♋R

Dec	STime	☉	☽	☿	♀	♂	Plnts
1	16.37	8♐	0♓	19♏	22♎	25♏	♃24♓
2	16.41	9	14	20	23	26	♄10♐
3	16.45	10	28	21	24	26	♅29♓
4	16.49	11	13♈	23	25	27	♆29♌
5	16.53	12	27	24	26	28	♇16♋R
6	16.57	13	12♉	26	27	28	♃24♓
7	17.01	14	27	27	28	29	♄10♐
8	17.05	15	12♊	28	29	0♐	♅29♓
9	17.09	16	27	0♐	0♏	0	♆29♌R
10	17.13	17	11♋	1	1	1	♇16♋R
11	17.17	18	25	3	3	2	♃24♓
12	17.21	19	8♌	4	4	3	♄11♐
13	17.25	20	21	6	5	3	♅29♓
14	17.29	21	4♍	7	6	4	♆29♌R
15	17.33	22	17	9	7	5	♇16♋R
16	17.37	23	29	10	8	5	♃25♓
17	17.40	24	11♎	12	9	6	♄12♐
18	17.44	25	23	13	11	7	♅29♓
19	17.48	26	4♏	15	12	8	♆29♌R
20	17.52	27	16	16	13	8	♇16♋R
21	17.56	28	28	18	14	9	♃25♓
22	18.00	29	10♐	19	15	10	♄12♐
23	18.04	0♑	23	21	16	10	♅29♓
24	18.08	1	5♑	23	17	11	♆29♌R
25	18.12	2	18	24	19	12	♇16♋R
26	18.16	3	1♒	26	20	13	♃26♓
27	18.20	4	14	27	21	13	♄13♐
28	18.24	5	27	29	22	14	♅29♓
29	18.28	6	11♓	0♑	23	15	♆29♌R
30	18.32	7	25	2	24	15	♇16♋R
31	18.36	9	9♈	4	26	16	♃26♓

Jan	STime	☉	☽	☿	♀	♂	Plnts
1	18.40	10♑	23♈	5♑	27♏	17♐	♃26♓
2	18.44	11	7♉	7	28	18	♄13♐
3	18.48	12	22	8	29	18	♅29♓
4	18.51	13	6♊	10	0♐	19	♆29♌R
5	18.55	14	20	11	1	20	♇16♋R
6	18.59	15	5♋	13	3	20	♃27♓
7	19.03	16	19	15	4	21	♄14♐
8	19.07	17	3♌	16	5	22	♅ 0♈
9	19.11	18	16	18	6	23	♆29♌R
10	19.15	19	29	20	7	23	♇16♋R
11	19.19	20	12♍	21	9	24	♃28♓
12	19.23	21	24	23	10	25	♄14♐
13	19.27	22	7♎	25	11	26	♅ 0♈
14	19.31	23	19	26	12	26	♆28♌R
15	19.35	24	0♏	28	13	27	♇16♋R
16	19.39	25	12	0♒	15	28	♃29♓
17	19.43	26	24	1	16	29	♄15♐
18	19.47	27	6♐	3	17	29	♅ 0♈
19	19.51	28	18	5	18	0♑	♆28♌R
20	19.55	29	1♑	6	19	1	♇16♋R
21	19.58	0♒	14	8	21	1	♃29♓
22	20.02	1	27	10	22	2	♄15♐
23	20.06	2	10♒	12	23	3	♅ 0♈
24	20.10	3	24	13	24	4	♆28♌R
25	20.14	4	8♓	15	25	4	♇15♋R
26	20.18	5	22	17	27	5	♃ 0♈
27	20.22	6	6♈	18	28	6	♄16♐
28	20.26	7	20	20	29	7	♅ 0♈
29	20.30	8	4♉	22	0♑	7	♆28♌R
30	20.34	9	18	23	1	8	♇15♋R
31	20.38	10	2♊	25	3	9	♃ 1♈

Feb	STime	☉	☽	☿	♀	♂	Plnts
1	20.42	11♒	16♊	27♒	4♑	10♑	♃ 1♈
2	20.46	12	0♋	28	5	10	♄16♐
3	20.50	13	14	0♓	6	11	♅ 0♈
4	20.54	14	28	1	8	12	♆28♌R
5	20.58	15	11♌	3	9	13	♇15♋R
6	21.02	16	24	4	10	13	♃ 2♈
7	21.06	17	7♍	5	11	14	♄17♐
8	21.09	18	20	6	12	15	♅ 1♈
9	21.13	19	2♎	7	14	16	♆28♌R
10	21.17	20	14	8	15	16	♇15♋R
11	21.21	21	26	9	16	17	♃ 3♈
12	21.25	22	8♏	10	17	18	♄17♐
13	21.29	23	20	10	18	19	♅ 1♈
14	21.33	24	2♐	10	20	19	♆28♌R
15	21.37	25	14	10R	21	20	♇15♋R
16	21.41	26	26	10	22	21	♃ 5♈
17	21.45	27	9♑	10	23	22	♄18♐
18	21.49	28	22	10	25	22	♅ 1♈
19	21.53	29	5♒	9	26	23	♆27♌R
20	21.57	0♓	19	8	27	24	♇15♋R
21	22.01	1	3♓	8	28	25	♃ 6♈
22	22.05	2	17	7	29	25	♄18♐
23	22.09	3	1♈	6	1♒	26	♅ 1♈
24	22.13	4	16	5	2	27	♆27♌R
25	22.16	5	0♉	4	3	28	♇15♋R
26	22.20	6	15	2	4	28	♃ 7♈
27	22.24	7	29	1	6	29	♄18♐
28	22.28	8	13♊	0	7	0♒	♅ 2♈
29	22.32	9	27	29♒	8	1	♆27♌R

Mar	STime	☉	☽	☿	♀	♂	Plnts
1	22.36	10♓	10♋	29♒	9♒	1♒	♃ 8♈
2	22.40	11	24	28	11	2	♄18♐
3	22.44	12	7♌	27	12	3	♅ 2♈
4	22.48	13	20	27	13	4	♆27♌R
5	22.52	14	3♍	26	14	4	♇15♋R
6	22.56	15	16	26	15	5	♃ 9♈
7	23.00	16	28	26	17	6	♄18♐
8	23.04	17	10♎	26D	18	7	♅ 2♈
9	23.08	18	22	26	19	7	♆27♌R
10	23.12	19	4♏	26	20	8	♇15♋R
11	23.16	20	16	26	22	9	♃10♈
12	23.20	21	28	26	23	10	♄19♐
13	23.23	22	10♐	27	24	11	♅ 2♈
14	23.27	23	22	27	25	11	♆27♌R
15	23.31	24	4♑	28	26	12	♇15♋R
16	23.35	25	17	29	28	13	♃11♈
17	23.39	26	29	29	29	14	♄19♐
18	23.43	27	13♒	0♓	0♓	14	♅ 3♈
19	23.47	28	27	1	1	15	♆27♌R
20	23.51	29	11♓	2	3	16	♇15♋R
21	23.55	0♈	25	3	4	17	♃12♈
22	23.59	1	10♈	4	5	17	♄19♐
23	0.03	2	25	5	6	18	♅ 3♈
24	0.07	3	10♉	6	8	19	♆27♌R
25	0.11	4	25	7	9	20	♇15♋
26	0.15	5	9♊	8	10	20	♃14♈
27	0.19	6	24	9	11	21	♄19♐
28	0.23	7	7♋	10	12	22	♅ 3♈
29	0.27	8	21	12	14	23	♆26♌R
30	0.31	9	4♌	13	15	23	♇15♋
31	0.34	10	17	14	16	24	♃15♈

Apr	STime	☉	☽	☿	♀	♂	Plnts
1	0.38	11♈	0♍	15♓	17♓	25♒	♃15♈
2	0.42	12	12	17	19	26	♄19♐R
3	0.46	13	25	18	20	27	♅ 4♈
4	0.50	14	7♎	20	21	27	♆26♌R
5	0.54	15	19	21	22	28	♇15♋
6	0.58	16	1♏	23	23	29	♃16♈
7	1.02	17	13	24	25	0♓	♄19♐R
8	1.06	18	25	26	26	0	♅ 4♈
9	1.10	19	6♐	27	27	1	♆26♌R
10	1.14	20	18	29	28	2	♇15♋
11	1.18	21	0♑	0♈	0♈	3	♃17♈
12	1.22	22	12	2	1	3	♄19♐R
13	1.26	23	25	4	2	4	♅ 4♈
14	1.30	24	8♒	5	3	5	♆26♌R
15	1.34	25	21	7	5	6	♇15♋
16	1.38	26	5♓	9	6	7	♃19♈
17	1.41	27	19	11	7	7	♄19♐R
18	1.45	28	4♈	12	8	8	♅ 4♈
19	1.49	29	19	14	9	9	♆26♌R
20	1.53	0♉	4♉	16	11	10	♇15♋
21	1.57	1	19	18	12	10	♃20♈
22	2.01	2	4♊	20	13	11	♄18♐R
23	2.05	3	19	22	14	12	♅ 5♈
24	2.09	4	3♋	24	16	13	♆26♌R
25	2.13	5	17	26	17	13	♇15♋
26	2.17	6	1♌	28	18	14	♃21♈
27	2.21	7	14	0♉	19	15	♄18♐R
28	2.25	8	27	2	20	16	♅ 5♈
29	2.29	9	9♍	4	22	16	♆26♌R
30	2.33	10	22	6	23	17	♇15♋

May	STime	☉	☽	☿	♀	♂	Plnts
1	2.37	11♉	4♎	8♉	24♈	18♓	♃22♈
2	2.41	12	16	10	25	19	♄18♐R
3	2.45	12	28	12	27	20	♅ 5♈
4	2.49	13	10♏	15	28	20	♆26♌
5	2.52	14	22	17	29	21	♇15♋
6	2.56	15	3♐	19	0♉	22	♃23♈
7	3.00	16	15	21	2	23	♄18♐R
8	3.04	17	27	23	3	23	♅ 5♈
9	3.08	18	9♑	25	4	24	♆26♌
10	3.12	19	21	28	5	25	♇15♋
11	3.16	20	4♒	0♊	6	26	♃25♈
12	3.20	21	17	2	8	26	♄17♐R
13	3.24	22	0♓	4	9	27	♅ 6♈
14	3.28	23	14	6	10	28	♆26♌
15	3.32	24	28	8	11	29	♇15♋
16	3.36	25	12♈	10	13	29	♃26♈
17	3.40	26	27	12	14	0♈	♄17♐R
18	3.44	27	12♉	13	15	1	♅ 6♈
19	3.48	28	27	15	16	2	♆26♌
20	3.52	29	12♊	17	17	2	♇15♋
21	3.56	0♊	27	19	19	3	♃27♈
22	3.59	1	12♋	20	20	4	♄17♐R
23	4.03	2	26	22	21	5	♅ 6♈
24	4.07	3	10♌	23	22	5	♆26♌
25	4.11	4	23	25	24	6	♇15♋
26	4.15	5	6♍	26	25	7	♃28♈
27	4.19	6	19	28	26	8	♄16♐R
28	4.23	7	1♎	29	27	8	♅ 6♈
29	4.27	8	13	0♋	29	9	♆26♌
30	4.31	9	25	2	0♊	10	♇15♋
31	4.35	9	7♏	3	1	11	♃29♈

Jun	STime	☉	☽	☿	♀	♂	Plnts
1	4.39	10♊	19♏	4♋	2♊	11♈	♃29♈
2	4.43	11	0♐	5	3	12	♄16♐R
3	4.47	12	12	6	5	13	♅ 6♈
4	4.51	13	24	7	6	14	♆26♌
5	4.55	14	6♑	8	7	14	♇16♋
6	4.59	15	18	8	8	15	♃ 0♉
7	5.03	16	1♒	9	10	16	♄15♐R
8	5.06	17	14	10	11	17	♅ 7♈
9	5.10	18	26	10	12	17	♆26♌
10	5.14	19	10♓	11	13	18	♇16♋
11	5.18	20	23	11	14	19	♃ 1♉
12	5.22	21	7♈	12	16	20	♄15♐R
13	5.26	22	21	12	17	20	♅ 7♈
14	5.30	23	6♉	12	18	21	♆26♌
15	5.34	24	21	12	19	22	♇16♋
16	5.38	25	6♊	12R	21	23	♃ 2♉
17	5.42	26	21	12	22	23	♄15♐R
18	5.46	27	6♋	12	23	24	♅ 7♈
19	5.50	28	20	12	24	25	♆27♌
20	5.54	29	4♌	12	26	25	♇16♋
21	5.58	0♋	18	11	27	26	♃ 3♉
22	6.02	0	2♍	11	28	27	♄14♐R
23	6.06	1	15	11	29	28	♅ 7♈
24	6.10	2	27	10	0♋	28	♆27♌
25	6.14	3	10♎	10	2	29	♇16♋
26	6.17	4	22	9	3	0♉	♃ 4♉
27	6.21	5	4♏	8	4	1	♄14♐R
28	6.25	6	15	8	5	1	♅ 7♈
29	6.29	7	27	7	7	2	♆27♌
30	6.33	8	9♐	7	8	3	♇16♋

Jul	STime	☉	☽	☿	♀	♂	Plnts
1	6.37	9♋	21♐	6♋	9♋	3♉	♃ 5♉
2	6.41	10	3♑	6	10	4	♄14♐R
3	6.45	11	15	5	11	5	♅ 7♈
4	6.49	12	28	5	13	6	♆27♌
5	6.53	13	11♒	4	14	6	♇16♋
6	6.57	14	23	4	15	7	♃ 6♉
7	7.01	15	7♓	3	16	8	♄13♐R
8	7.05	16	20	3	18	8	♅ 7♈
9	7.09	17	4♈	3	19	9	♆27♌
10	7.13	18	17	3D	20	10	♇16♋
11	7.17	19	2♉	3	21	10	♃ 6♉
12	7.21	20	16	3	23	11	♄13♐R
13	7.24	21	0♊	3	24	12	♅ 7♈
14	7.28	21	15	4	25	13	♆27♌
15	7.32	22	0♋	4	26	13	♇17♋
16	7.36	23	14	4	27	14	♃ 7♉
17	7.40	24	28	5	29	15	♄13♐R
18	7.44	25	13♌	6	0♌	15	♅ 7♈
19	7.48	26	26	6	1	16	♆27♌
20	7.52	27	10♍	7	2	17	♇17♋
21	7.56	28	23	8	4	17	♃ 8♉
22	8.00	29	5♎	9	5	18	♄13♐R
23	8.04	0♌	18	10	6	19	♅ 7♈R
24	8.08	1	0♏	11	7	19	♆28♌
25	8.12	2	12	13	9	20	♇17♋
26	8.16	3	24	14	10	21	♃ 8♉
27	8.20	4	5♐	15	11	21	♄13♐R
28	8.24	5	17	17	12	22	♅ 7♈R
29	8.28	6	29	18	13	23	♆28♌
30	8.32	7	12♑	20	15	23	♇17♋
31	8.35	8	24	22	16	24	♃ 9♉

Aug	STime	☉	☽	☿	♀	♂	Plnts
1	8.39	9♌	7♒	23♋	17♌	25♉	♃ 9♉
2	8.43	10	20	25	18	25	♄12♐R
3	8.47	11	3♓	27	20	26	♅ 7♈R
4	8.51	12	17	29	21	27	♆28♌
5	8.55	12	1♈	1♌	22	27	♇17♋
6	8.59	13	14	3	23	28	♃ 9♉
7	9.03	14	28	5	25	29	♄12♐R
8	9.07	15	12♉	7	26	29	♅ 7♈R
9	9.11	16	27	9	27	0♊	♆28♌
10	9.15	17	11♊	11	28	1	♇17♋
11	9.19	18	25	13	0♍	1	♃10♉
12	9.23	19	9♋	15	1	2	♄12♐R
13	9.27	20	23	17	2	2	♅ 7♈R
14	9.31	21	7♌	19	3	3	♆28♌
15	9.35	22	21	21	4	4	♇17♋
16	9.39	23	5♍	23	6	4	♃10♉
17	9.42	24	18	25	7	5	♄12♐
18	9.46	25	1♎	27	8	6	♅ 7♈R
19	9.50	26	13	29	9	6	♆29♌
20	9.54	27	26	1♍	11	7	♇17♋
21	9.58	28	8♏	3	12	7	♃10♉
22	10.02	29	20	5	13	8	♄12♐
23	10.06	0♍	1♐	7	14	9	♅ 6♈R
24	10.10	1	13	9	16	9	♆29♌
25	10.14	2	25	11	17	10	♇18♋
26	10.18	3	7♑	12	18	10	♃10♉
27	10.22	4	20	14	19	11	♄12♐
28	10.26	5	2♒	16	21	12	♅ 6♈R
29	10.30	6	15	18	22	12	♆29♌
30	10.34	7	29	19	23	13	♇18♋
31	10.38	8	13♓	21	24	13	♃10♉R

Sep	STime	☉	☽	☿	♀	♂	Plnts
1	10.42	8♍	26♓	23♍	25♍	14♊	♃10♉R
2	10.46	9	11♈	25	27	14	♄12♐
3	10.50	10	25	26	28	15	♅ 6♈R
4	10.53	11	9♉	28	29	16	♆29♌
5	10.57	12	23	29	0♎	16	♇18♋
6	11.01	13	8♊	1♎	2	17	♃10♉R
7	11.05	14	22	3	3	17	♄13♐
8	11.09	15	6♋	4	4	18	♅ 6♈R
9	11.13	16	19	6	5	18	♆29♌
10	11.17	17	3♌	7	7	19	♇18♋
11	11.21	18	17	9	8	19	♃10♉R
12	11.25	19	0♍	10	9	20	♄13♐
13	11.29	20	13	12	10	20	♅ 6♈R
14	11.33	21	26	13	11	21	♆29♌
15	11.37	22	9♎	14	13	21	♇18♋
16	11.41	23	22	16	14	22	♃10♉R
17	11.45	24	4♏	17	15	23	♄13♐
18	11.49	25	16	18	16	23	♅ 6♈R
19	11.53	26	28	20	18	24	♆ 0♍
20	11.57	27	9♐	21	19	24	♇18♋
21	12.00	28	21	22	20	24	♃ 9♉R
22	12.04	29	3♑	24	21	25	♄13♐
23	12.08	0♎	15	25	23	25	♅ 5♈R
24	12.12	1	28	26	24	26	♆ 0♍
25	12.16	2	10♒	27	25	26	♇18♋
26	12.20	3	23	28	26	27	♃ 9♉R
27	12.24	4	7♓	29	27	27	♄14♐
28	12.28	5	21	0♏	29	28	♅ 5♈R
29	12.32	6	5♈	2	0♏	28	♆ 0♍
30	12.36	7	20	2	1	29	♇18♋

Oct	STime	☉	☽	☿	♀	♂	Plnts
1	12.40	8♎	5♉	3♏	2♏	29♊	♃ 8♉R
2	12.44	9	19	4	4	29	♄14♐
3	12.48	10	4♊	5	5	0♋	♅ 5♈R
4	12.52	11	18	6	6	0	♆ 0♍
5	12.56	12	2♋	7	7	1	♇18♋
6	13.00	13	16	7	9	1	♃ 8♉R
7	13.04	14	0♌	8	10	1	♄14♐
8	13.07	15	14	8	11	2	♅ 5♈R
9	13.11	16	27	9	12	2	♆ 0♍
10	13.15	17	10♍	9	13	3	♇18♋
11	13.19	18	23	9	15	3	♃ 7♉R
12	13.23	19	5♎	9R	16	3	♄15♐
13	13.27	20	18	9	17	4	♅ 5♈R
14	13.31	21	0♏	9	18	4	♆ 0♍
15	13.35	22	12	9	20	4	♇18♋
16	13.39	23	24	8	21	5	♃ 7♉R
17	13.43	24	6♐	8	22	5	♄15♐
18	13.47	25	17	7	23	5	♅ 4♈R
19	13.51	26	29	6	25	5	♆ 1♍
20	13.55	27	11♑	5	26	6	♇18♋
21	13.59	28	23	4	27	6	♃ 6♉R
22	14.03	29	6♒	3	28	6	♄16♐
23	14.07	0♏	18	1	29	6	♅ 4♈R
24	14.11	1	1♓	0	1♐	7	♆ 1♍
25	14.15	2	15	29♎	2	7	♇18♋
26	14.18	3	29	28	3	7	♃ 5♉R
27	14.22	4	13♈	27	4	7	♄16♐
28	14.26	5	28	26	6	8	♅ 4♈R
29	14.30	6	13♉	25	7	8	♆ 1♍
30	14.34	7	28	24	8	8	♇18♋
31	14.38	8	13♊	24	9	8	♃ 5♉R

Nov	STime	☉	☽	☿	♀	♂	Plnts
1	14.42	9♏	28♊	24♎	10♐	8♋	♃ 5♉R
2	14.46	10	13♋	24D	12	8	♄17♐
3	14.50	11	27	24	13	8	♅ 4♈R
4	14.54	12	10♌	24	14	9	♆ 1♍
5	14.58	13	24	24	15	9	♇18♋R
6	15.02	14	7♍	25	17	9	♃ 4♉R
7	15.06	15	20	26	18	9	♄17♐
8	15.10	16	2♎	27	19	9	♅ 4♈R
9	15.14	17	15	28	20	9	♆ 1♍
10	15.18	18	27	29	21	9	♇18♋R
11	15.22	19	9♏	0♏	23	9	♃ 3♉R
12	15.25	20	21	1	24	9R	♄18♐
13	15.29	21	2♐	2	25	9	♅ 4♈R
14	15.33	22	14	4	26	9	♆ 1♍
15	15.37	23	26	5	28	9	♇18♋R
16	15.41	24	8♑	6	29	9	♃ 3♉R
17	15.45	25	20	8	0♑	9	♄18♐
18	15.49	26	2♒	9	1	9	♅ 3♈R
19	15.53	27	14	11	2	9	♆ 1♍
20	15.57	28	27	12	4	9	♇18♋R
21	16.01	29	10♓	14	5	8	♃ 2♉R
22	16.05	0♐	23	15	6	8	♄19♐
23	16.09	1	7♈	17	7	8	♅ 3♈R
24	16.13	2	21	18	9	8	♆ 1♍
25	16.17	3	6♉	20	10	8	♇18♋R
26	16.21	4	21	22	11	8	♃ 2♉R
27	16.25	5	6♊	23	12	7	♄19♐
28	16.29	6	22	25	13	7	♅ 3♈R
29	16.33	7	7♋	26	15	7	♆ 1♍
30	16.36	8	22	28	16	7	♇18♋R

Dec	STime	☉	☽	☿	♀	♂	Plnts
1	16.40	9♐	6♌	29♏	17♑	6♋	♃ 1♉R
2	16.44	10	20	1♐	18	6	♄20♐
3	16.48	11	3♍	3	19	6	♅ 3♈R
4	16.52	12	17	4	21	5	♆ 1♍
5	16.56	13	29	6	22	5	♇18♋R
6	17.00	14	12♎	7	23	5	♃ 1♉R
7	17.04	15	24	9	24	5	♄21♐
8	17.08	16	6♏	10	25	4	♅ 3♈R
9	17.12	17	18	12	27	4	♆ 1♍R
10	17.16	18	29	13	28	3	♇18♋R
11	17.20	19	11♐	15	29	3	♃ 0♉R
12	17.24	20	23	17	0♒	3	♄21♐
13	17.28	21	5♑	18	1	2	♅ 3♈
14	17.32	22	17	20	3	2	♆ 1♍R
15	17.36	23	29	21	4	2	♇17♋R
16	17.40	24	11♒	23	5	1	♃ 0♉R
17	17.43	25	23	24	6	1	♄22♐
18	17.47	26	6♓	26	7	0	♅ 3♈
19	17.51	27	19	28	9	0	♆ 1♍R
20	17.55	28	2♈	29	10	0	♇17♋R
21	17.59	29	16	1♑	11	29♊	♃ 0♉R
22	18.03	0♑	0♉	2	12	29	♄22♐
23	18.07	1	14	4	13	28	♅ 3♈
24	18.11	2	29	6	15	28	♆ 1♍R
25	18.15	3	14♊	7	16	28	♇17♋R
26	18.19	4	0♋	9	17	27	♃ 0♉
27	18.23	5	15	10	18	27	♄23♐
28	18.27	6	0♌	12	19	27	♅ 3♈
29	18.31	7	14	14	20	26	♆ 1♍R
30	18.35	8	28	15	22	26	♇17♋R
31	18.39	9	12♍	17	23	25	♃ 0♉

1 9 2 9

Jan	STime	☉	☽	☿	♀	♂	Plnts
1	18.43	10♑	25♍	18♑	24♒	25♊	♃ 0♉
2	18.47	11	8♎	20	25	25	♄24♐
3	18.51	12	21	22	26	25	♅ 3♈
4	18.54	13	3♏	23	27	24	♆ 1♍R
5	18.58	14	15	25	29	24	♇17♋R
6	19.02	15	26	27	0♓	24	♃ 0♉
7	19.06	16	8♐	28	1	23	♄24♐
8	19.10	17	20	0♒	2	23	♅ 3♈
9	19.14	18	2♑	2	3	23	♆ 1♍R
10	19.18	19	14	3	4	23	♇17♋R
11	19.22	21	26	5	5	22	♃ 1♉
12	19.26	22	8♒	6	7	22	♄25♐
13	19.30	23	21	8	8	22	♅ 4♈
14	19.34	24	3♓	10	9	22	♆ 1♍R
15	19.38	25	16	11	10	22	♇17♋R
16	19.42	26	29	13	11	21	♃ 1♉
17	19.46	27	12♈	14	12	21	♄25♐
18	19.50	28	26	15	13	21	♅ 4♈
19	19.54	29	10♉	17	14	21	♆ 1♍R
20	19.58	0♒	24	18	16	21	♇17♋R
21	20.01	1	8♊	19	17	21	♃ 1♉
22	20.05	2	23	20	18	21	♄26♐
23	20.09	3	8♋	21	19	21	♅ 4♈
24	20.13	4	23	22	20	21	♆ 0♍R
25	20.17	5	8♌	23	21	21	♇17♋R
26	20.21	6	22	23	22	21	♃ 2♉
27	20.25	7	6♍	24	23	21D	♄26♐
28	20.29	8	20	24	24	21	♅ 4♈
29	20.33	9	3♎	24R	25	21	♆ 0♍R
30	20.37	10	16	24	26	21	♇17♋R
31	20.41	11	29	24	27	21	♃ 2♉

Feb	STime	☉	☽	☿	♀	♂	Plnts
1	20.45	12♒	11♏	23♒	29♓	21♊	♃ 2♉
2	20.49	13	23	22	0♈	21	♄27♐
3	20.53	14	5♐	22	1	21	♅ 4♈
4	20.57	15	16	21	2	21	♆ 0♍R
5	21.01	16	28	20	3	21	♇16♋R
6	21.05	17	10♑	18	4	21	♃ 3♉
7	21.08	18	22	17	5	21	♄27♐
8	21.12	19	5♒	16	6	22	♅ 5♈
9	21.16	20	17	15	7	22	♆ 0♍R
10	21.20	21	0♓	14	8	22	♇16♋R
11	21.24	22	13	13	9	22	♃ 4♉
12	21.28	23	26	12	10	22	♄28♐
13	21.32	24	9♈	11	11	22	♅ 5♈
14	21.36	25	23	10	12	23	♆ 0♍R
15	21.40	26	7♉	10	13	23	♇16♋R
16	21.44	27	20	9	14	23	♃ 5♉
17	21.48	28	4♊	9	14	23	♄28♐
18	21.52	29	19	9	15	23	♅ 5♈
19	21.56	0♓	3♋	9D	16	24	♆ 0♍R
20	22.00	1	17	9	17	24	♇16♋R
21	22.04	2	2♌	9	18	24	♃ 5♉
22	22.08	3	16	9	19	24	♄29♐
23	22.12	4	0♍	9	20	25	♅ 5♈
24	22.16	5	14	10	21	25	♆ 0♍R
25	22.19	6	28	10	22	25	♇16♋R
26	22.23	7	11♎	11	22	26	♃ 6♉
27	22.27	8	24	12	23	26	♄29♐
28	22.31	9	6♏	12	24	26	♅ 5♈

Mar	STime	☉	☽	☿	♀	♂	Plnts
1	22.35	10♓	19♏	13♒	25♈	26♊	♃ 7♉
2	22.39	11	1♐	14	26	27	♄29♐
3	22.43	12	13	15	26	27	♅ 6♈
4	22.47	13	24	16	27	27	♆29♌R
5	22.51	14	6♑	17	28	28	♇16♋R
6	22.55	15	18	18	28	28	♃ 8♉
7	22.59	16	0♒	19	29	28	♄29♐
8	23.03	17	13	20	0♉	29	♅ 6♈
9	23.07	18	26	21	0	29	♆29♌R
10	23.11	19	9♓	23	1	0♋	♇16♋R
11	23.15	20	22	24	2	0	♃ 9♉
12	23.19	21	5♈	25	2	0	♄ 0♑
13	23.23	22	19	26	3	1	♅ 6♈
14	23.26	23	3♉	28	3	1	♆29♌R
15	23.30	24	17	29	4	1	♇16♋R
16	23.34	25	1♊	0♓	4	2	♃10♉
17	23.38	26	15	2	5	2	♄ 0♑
18	23.42	27	29	3	5	3	♅ 6♈
19	23.46	28	14♋	5	6	3	♆29♌R
20	23.50	29	28	6	6	3	♇16♋
21	23.54	0♈	12♌	8	6	4	♃11♉
22	23.58	1	26	9	7	4	♄ 0♑
23	0.02	2	9♍	11	7	5	♅ 7♈
24	0.06	3	23	12	7	5	♆29♌R
25	0.10	4	6♎	14	7	6	♇16♋
26	0.14	5	19	15	7	6	♃12♉
27	0.18	6	2♏	17	8	6	♄ 0♑
28	0.22	7	14	19	8	7	♅ 7♈
29	0.26	8	26	20	8	7	♆29♌R
30	0.30	9	8♐	22	8R	8	♇16♋
31	0.34	10	20	24	8	8	♃13♉

Apr	STime	☉	☽	☿	♀	♂	Plnts
1	0.37	11♈	2♑	25♓	8♉	9♋	♃13♉
2	0.41	12	14	27	8	9	♄ 0♑
3	0.45	13	26	29	7	10	♅ 7♈
4	0.49	14	8♒	1♈	7	10	♆29♌R
5	0.53	15	21	3	7	11	♇16♋
6	0.57	16	4♓	5	7	11	♃14♉
7	1.01	17	17	6	6	11	♄ 0♑
8	1.05	18	0♈	8	6	12	♅ 8♈
9	1.09	19	14	10	6	12	♆29♌R
10	1.13	20	28	12	5	13	♇16♋
11	1.17	21	13♉	14	5	13	♃15♉
12	1.21	22	27	16	4	14	♄ 0♑R
13	1.25	23	12♊	18	4	14	♅ 8♈
14	1.29	24	26	20	3	15	♆28♌R
15	1.33	25	10♋	22	3	15	♇16♋
16	1.37	26	25	24	2	16	♃16♉
17	1.41	27	8♌	26	1	16	♄ 0♑R
18	1.44	28	22	29	1	17	♅ 8♈
19	1.48	29	6♍	1♉	0	17	♆28♌R
20	1.52	0♉	19	3	29♈	18	♇16♋
21	1.56	1	2♎	5	29	18	♃17♉
22	2.00	2	15	7	28	19	♄ 0♑R
23	2.04	3	28	9	28	19	♅ 9♈
24	2.08	4	10♏	11	27	20	♆28♌R
25	2.12	4	23	13	26	20	♇16♋
26	2.16	5	5♐	16	26	21	♃19♉
27	2.20	6	16	18	25	21	♄ 0♑R
28	2.24	7	28	20	25	22	♅ 9♈
29	2.28	8	10♑	22	24	22	♆28♌
30	2.32	9	22	23	24	23	♇16♋

May	STime	☉	☽	☿	♀	♂	Plnts
1	2.36	10♉	4♒	25♉	23♈	24♋	♃20♉
2	2.40	11	16	27	23	24	♄ 0♑R
3	2.44	12	29	29	23	25	♅ 9♈
4	2.48	13	12♓	1♊	22	25	♆28♌
5	2.51	14	25	2	22	26	♇16♋
6	2.55	15	8♈	4	22	26	♃21♉
7	2.59	16	22	6	22	27	♄ 0♑R
8	3.03	17	7♉	7	22	27	♅ 9♈
9	3.07	18	21	9	21	28	♆28♌
10	3.11	19	6♊	10	21	28	♇16♋
11	3.15	20	21	11	21D	29	♃22♉
12	3.19	21	6♋	12	21	29	♄29♐R
13	3.23	22	21	14	21	0♌	♅ 9♈
14	3.27	23	5♌	15	22	0	♆28♌
15	3.31	24	19	16	22	1	♇16♋
16	3.35	25	3♍	17	22	2	♃23♉
17	3.39	26	16	18	22	2	♄29♐R
18	3.43	27	29	18	22	3	♅10♈
19	3.47	28	12♎	19	22	3	♆28♌
20	3.51	29	25	20	23	4	♇16♋
21	3.55	0♊	7♏	20	23	4	♃25♉
22	3.59	1	19	21	23	5	♄29♐R
23	4.02	2	1♐	21	24	5	♅10♈
24	4.06	3	13	22	24	6	♆28♌
25	4.10	3	25	22	25	7	♇17♋
26	4.14	4	7♑	22	25	7	♃26♉
27	4.18	5	19	22	26	8	♄29♐R
28	4.22	6	1♒	22R	26	8	♅10♈
29	4.26	7	13	22	27	9	♆28♌
30	4.30	8	25	22	27	9	♇17♋
31	4.34	9	7♓	22	28	10	♃27♉

Jun	STime	☉	☽	☿	♀	♂	Plnts
1	4.38	10♊	20♓	22♊	28♈	10♌	♃27♉
2	4.42	11	3♈	21	29	11	♄28♐R
3	4.46	12	17	21	0♉	12	♅10♈
4	4.50	13	1♉	20	0	12	♆28♌
5	4.54	14	15	20	1	13	♇17♋
6	4.58	15	0♊	19	2	13	♃28♉
7	5.02	16	15	19	3	14	♄28♐R
8	5.06	17	0♋	18	3	14	♅10♈
9	5.09	18	15	18	4	15	♆29♌
10	5.13	19	0♌	17	5	16	♇17♋
11	5.17	20	15	17	6	16	♃29♉
12	5.21	21	29	16	6	17	♄27♐R
13	5.25	22	13♍	16	7	17	♅11♈
14	5.29	23	26	15	8	18	♆29♌
15	5.33	24	9♎	15	9	19	♇17♋
16	5.37	25	22	14	10	19	♃ 1♊
17	5.41	25	4♏	14	10	20	♄27♐R
18	5.45	26	16	14	11	20	♅11♈
19	5.49	27	28	14	12	21	♆29♌
20	5.53	28	10♐	14	13	21	♇17♋
21	5.57	29	22	14D	14	22	♃ 2♊
22	6.01	0♋	4♑	14	15	23	♄27♐R
23	6.05	1	16	14	16	23	♅11♈
24	6.09	2	27	14	17	24	♆29♌
25	6.13	3	9♒	14	18	24	♇17♋
26	6.17	4	22	15	18	25	♃ 3♊
27	6.20	5	4♓	15	19	26	♄26♐R
28	6.24	6	16	16	20	26	♅11♈
29	6.28	7	29	16	21	27	♆29♌
30	6.32	8	12♈	17	22	27	♇17♋

Jul	STime	☉	☽	☿	♀	♂	Plnts
1	6.36	9♋	25♈	18♊	23♉	28♌	♃ 4♊
2	6.40	10	9♉	18	24	29	♄26♐R
3	6.44	11	24	19	25	29	♅11♈
4	6.48	12	8♊	20	26	0♍	♆29♌
5	6.52	13	23	21	27	0	♇17♋
6	6.56	14	8♋	22	28	1	♃ 5♊
7	7.00	15	24	24	29	2	♄26♐R
8	7.04	16	9♌	25	0♊	2	♅11♈
9	7.08	16	24	26	1	3	♆29♌
10	7.12	17	8♍	28	2	3	♇18♋
11	7.16	18	22	29	3	4	♃ 6♊
12	7.20	19	5♎	1♋	4	5	♄25♐R
13	7.24	20	18	2	5	5	♅11♈
14	7.27	21	1♏	4	6	6	♆29♌
15	7.31	22	13	6	7	6	♇18♋
16	7.35	23	25	7	8	7	♃ 7♊
17	7.39	24	7♐	9	9	8	♄25♐R
18	7.43	25	19	11	10	8	♅11♈
19	7.47	26	1♑	13	12	9	♆ 0♍
20	7.51	27	13	15	13	9	♇18♋
21	7.55	28	25	17	14	10	♃ 8♊
22	7.59	29	7♒	19	15	11	♄25♐R
23	8.03	0♌	19	21	16	11	♅11♈R
24	8.07	1	1♓	23	17	12	♆ 0♍
25	8.11	2	13	25	18	13	♇18♋
26	8.15	3	26	27	19	13	♃ 9♊
27	8.19	4	9♈	29	20	14	♄24♐R
28	8.23	5	22	2♌	21	14	♅11♈R
29	8.27	6	5♉	4	22	15	♆ 0♍
30	8.31	7	19	6	23	16	♇18♋
31	8.34	7	3♊	8	24	16	♃10♊

Aug	STime	☉	☽	☿	♀	♂	Plnts
1	8.38	8♌	17♊	10♌	26♊	17♍	♃10♊
2	8.42	9	2♋	12	27	17	♄24♐R
3	8.46	10	17	14	28	18	♅11♈R
4	8.50	11	2♌	16	29	19	♆ 0♍
5	8.54	12	17	18	0♋	19	♇18♋
6	8.58	13	2♍	20	1	20	♃11♊
7	9.02	14	16	22	2	21	♄24♐R
8	9.06	15	0♎	24	3	21	♅11♈R
9	9.10	16	14	26	4	22	♆ 0♍
10	9.14	17	27	28	6	22	♇18♋
11	9.18	18	9♏	29	7	23	♃12♊
12	9.22	19	22	1♍	8	24	♄24♐R
13	9.26	20	4♐	3	9	24	♅11♈R
14	9.30	21	16	5	10	25	♆ 0♍
15	9.34	22	28	7	11	26	♇19♋
16	9.38	23	9♑	8	12	26	♃12♊
17	9.42	24	21	10	14	27	♄24♐R
18	9.45	25	3♒	12	15	28	♅11♈R
19	9.49	26	15	13	16	28	♆ 1♍
20	9.53	27	28	15	17	29	♇19♋
21	9.57	28	10♓	17	18	29	♃13♊
22	10.01	29	23	18	19	0♎	♄24♐R
23	10.05	0♍	6♈	20	20	1	♅11♈R
24	10.09	1	19	21	22	1	♆ 1♍
25	10.13	1	2♉	23	23	2	♇19♋
26	10.17	2	15	24	24	3	♃14♊
27	10.21	3	29	26	25	3	♄24♐
28	10.25	4	13♊	27	26	4	♅10♈R
29	10.29	5	27	29	27	5	♆ 1♍
30	10.33	6	12♋	0♎	29	5	♇19♋
31	10.37	7	26	1	0♌	6	♃14♊

Sep	STime	☉	☽	☿	♀	♂	Plnts
1	10.41	8♍	11♌	3♎	1♌	7♎	♃14♊
2	10.45	9	26	4	2	7	♄24♐
3	10.49	10	10♍	5	3	8	♅10♈R
4	10.52	11	25	7	4	8	♆ 1♍
5	10.56	12	8♎	8	6	9	♇19♋
6	11.00	13	22	9	7	10	♃15♊
7	11.04	14	5♏	10	8	10	♄24♐
8	11.08	15	18	11	9	11	♅10♈R
9	11.12	16	0♐	13	10	12	♆ 1♍
10	11.16	17	12	14	12	12	♇19♋
11	11.20	18	24	15	13	13	♃15♊
12	11.24	19	6♑	16	14	14	♄24♐
13	11.28	20	18	17	15	14	♅10♈R
14	11.32	21	0♒	17	16	15	♆ 2♍
15	11.36	22	12	18	17	16	♇19♋
16	11.40	23	24	19	19	16	♃16♊
17	11.44	24	6♓	20	20	17	♄24♐
18	11.48	25	19	21	21	18	♅10♈R
19	11.52	26	2♈	21	22	18	♆ 2♍
20	11.56	27	15	22	23	19	♇19♋
21	12.00	28	29	22	25	20	♃16♊
22	12.03	29	12♉	23	26	20	♄24♐
23	12.07	0♎	26	23	27	21	♅ 9♈R
24	12.11	1	10♊	23	28	22	♆ 2♍
25	12.15	2	24	23R	29	22	♇19♋
26	12.19	3	8♋	23	1♍	23	♃16♊
27	12.23	4	22	23	2	24	♄24♐
28	12.27	5	7♌	23	3	24	♅ 9♈R
29	12.31	6	21	22	4	25	♆ 2♍
30	12.35	7	5♍	22	6	26	♇19♋

Oct	STime	☉	☽	☿	♀	♂	Plnts
1	12.39	8♎	19♍	21♎	7♍	26♎	♃16♊
2	12.43	9	3♎	20	8	27	♄25♐
3	12.47	9	17	19	9	28	♅ 9♈R
4	12.51	10	0♏	18	10	28	♆ 2♍
5	12.55	11	13	17	12	29	♇19♋
6	12.59	12	25	16	13	0♏	♃16♊R
7	13.03	13	8♐	15	14	0	♄25♐
8	13.07	14	20	14	15	1	♅ 9♈R
9	13.10	15	2♑	13	17	2	♆ 2♍
10	13.14	16	14	12	18	2	♇19♋
11	13.18	17	25	11	19	3	♃16♊R
12	13.22	18	7♒	10	20	4	♄25♐
13	13.26	19	20	9	21	4	♅ 9♈R
14	13.30	20	2♓	8	23	5	♆ 3♍
15	13.34	21	15	8	24	6	♇19♋
16	13.38	22	27	8	25	7	♃16♊R
17	13.42	23	11♈	8D	26	7	♄26♐
18	13.46	24	24	8	28	8	♅ 8♈R
19	13.50	25	8♉	8	29	9	♆ 3♍
20	13.54	26	22	9	0♎	9	♇19♋
21	13.58	27	6♊	9	1	10	♃16♊R
22	14.02	28	21	10	3	11	♄26♐
23	14.06	29	5♋	11	4	11	♅ 8♈R
24	14.10	0♏	19	12	5	12	♆ 3♍
25	14.14	1	3♌	13	6	13	♇19♋R
26	14.18	2	17	14	7	13	♃15♊R
27	14.21	3	1♍	16	9	14	♄26♐
28	14.25	4	15	17	10	15	♅ 8♈R
29	14.29	5	29	18	11	16	♆ 3♍
30	14.33	6	12♎	20	12	16	♇19♋
31	14.37	7	25	21	14	17	♃15♊R

Nov	STime	☉	☽	☿	♀	♂	Plnts
1	14.41	8♏	8♏	23♎	15♎	18♏	♃15♊R
2	14.45	9	21	24	16	18	♄27♐
3	14.49	10	3♐	26	17	19	♅ 8♈R
4	14.53	11	16	28	19	20	♆ 3♍
5	14.57	12	28	29	20	20	♇19♋R
6	15.01	13	10♑	1♏	21	21	♃14♊R
7	15.05	14	21	2	22	22	♄27♐
8	15.09	15	3♒	4	24	23	♅ 8♈R
9	15.13	16	15	6	25	23	♆ 3♍
10	15.17	17	27	7	26	24	♇19♋
11	15.21	18	10♓	9	27	25	♃14♊R
12	15.25	19	22	11	29	25	♄28♐
13	15.28	20	5♈	12	0♏	26	♅ 8♈R
14	15.32	21	19	14	1	27	♆ 3♍
15	15.36	22	2♉	15	2	28	♇19♋R
16	15.40	23	17	17	4	28	♃13♊R
17	15.44	24	1♊	19	5	29	♄28♐
18	15.48	25	16	20	6	0♐	♅ 7♈R
19	15.52	26	0♋	22	7	0	♆ 3♍
20	15.56	27	15	23	9	1	♇19♋R
21	16.00	28	0♌	25	10	2	♃13♊R
22	16.04	29	14	27	11	3	♄29♐
23	16.08	0♐	28	28	12	3	♅ 7♈R
24	16.12	1	12♍	0♐	14	4	♆ 3♍
25	16.16	2	26	1	15	5	♇19♋R
26	16.20	3	9♎	3	16	5	♃12♊R
27	16.24	4	22	4	17	6	♄29♐
28	16.28	5	5♏	6	19	7	♅ 7♈R
29	16.32	7	17	8	20	8	♆ 3♍
30	16.35	8	0♐	9	21	8	♇19♋R

Dec	STime	☉	☽	☿	♀	♂	Plnts
1	16.39	9♐	12♐	11♐	22♏	9♐	♃11♊R
2	16.43	10	24	12	24	10	♄ 0♑
3	16.47	11	6♑	14	25	10	♅ 7♈R
4	16.51	12	18	15	26	11	♆ 3♍
5	16.55	13	0♒	17	27	12	♇19♋R
6	16.59	14	12	19	29	13	♃11♊R
7	17.03	15	23	20	0♐	13	♄ 1♑
8	17.07	16	6♓	22	1	14	♅ 7♈
9	17.11	17	18	23	2	15	♆ 3♍
10	17.15	18	0♈	25	4	16	♇19♋R
11	17.19	19	13	26	5	16	♃10♊R
12	17.23	20	26	28	6	17	♄ 1♑
13	17.27	21	10♉	0♑	7	18	♅ 7♈
14	17.31	22	24	1	9	19	♆ 3♍R
15	17.35	23	9♊	3	10	19	♇19♋R
16	17.39	24	24	4	11	20	♃ 9♊R
17	17.43	25	9♋	6	13	21	♄ 2♑
18	17.46	26	24	7	14	22	♅ 7♈
19	17.50	27	9♌	9	15	22	♆ 3♍R
20	17.54	28	24	11	16	23	♇19♋R
21	17.58	29	8♍	12	18	24	♃ 9♊R
22	18.02	0♑	22	14	19	24	♄ 2♑
23	18.06	1	6♎	15	20	25	♅ 7♈
24	18.10	2	19	17	21	26	♆ 3♍R
25	18.14	3	2♏	18	23	27	♇19♋R
26	18.18	4	14	20	24	27	♃ 8♊R
27	18.22	5	27	21	25	28	♄ 3♑
28	18.26	6	9♐	23	26	29	♅ 7♈
29	18.30	7	21	24	28	0♑	♆ 3♍R
30	18.34	8	3♑	26	29	0	♇18♋R
31	18.38	9	15	27	0♑	1	♃ 8♊R

Jan	STime	☉	☽	☿	♀	♂	Plnts
1	18.42	10♑	26♑	28♑	1♑	2♑	♃ 8♊R
2	18.46	11	8♒	0♒	3	3	♄ 4♑
3	18.50	12	20	1	4	3	♅ 7♈
4	18.53	13	2♓	2	5	4	♆ 3♍R
5	18.57	14	14	3	6	5	♇18♋R
6	19.01	15	26	4	8	6	♃ 7♊R
7	19.05	16	9♈	5	9	7	♄ 4♑
8	19.09	17	21	6	10	7	♅ 7♈
9	19.13	18	5♉	7	11	8	♆ 3♍R
10	19.17	19	18	7	13	9	♇18♋R
11	19.21	20	2♊	8	14	10	♃ 7♊R
12	19.25	21	17	8	15	10	♄ 5♑
13	19.29	22	2♋	8R	16	11	♅ 7♈
14	19.33	23	17	8	18	12	♆ 3♍R
15	19.37	24	2♌	7	19	13	♇18♋R
16	19.41	25	18	7	20	13	♃ 6♊R
17	19.45	26	3♍	6	22	14	♄ 5♑
18	19.49	27	17	5	23	15	♅ 8♈
19	19.53	28	2♎	4	24	16	♆ 3♍R
20	19.57	29	15	3	25	16	♇18♋R
21	20.01	0♒	28	2	27	17	♃ 6♊R
22	20.04	1	11♏	0	28	18	♄ 6♑
23	20.08	2	24	29♑	29	19	♅ 8♈
24	20.12	3	6♐	28	0♒	19	♆ 3♍R
25	20.16	5	18	27	2	20	♇18♋R
26	20.20	6	0♑	26	3	21	♃ 6♊R
27	20.24	7	12	25	4	22	♄ 6♑
28	20.28	8	23	24	5	23	♅ 8♈
29	20.32	9	5♒	23	7	23	♆ 3♍R
30	20.36	10	17	23	8	24	♇18♋R
31	20.40	11	29	22	9	25	♃ 6♊

Feb	STime	☉	☽	☿	♀	♂	Plnts
1	20.44	12♒	11♓	22♑	10♒	26♑	♃ 6♊
2	20.48	13	23	22D	12	26	♄ 7♑
3	20.52	14	6♈	22	13	27	♅ 8♈
4	20.56	15	18	22	14	28	♆ 2♍R
5	21.00	16	1♉	22	15	29	♇18♋R
6	21.04	17	14	23	17	29	♃ 6♊
7	21.08	18	27	23	18	0♒	♄ 8♑
8	21.11	19	11♊	24	19	1	♅ 8♈
9	21.15	20	26	24	20	2	♆ 2♍R
10	21.19	21	10♋	25	22	3	♇18♋R
11	21.23	22	25	26	23	3	♃ 6♊
12	21.27	23	11♌	27	24	4	♄ 8♑
13	21.31	24	26	28	25	5	♅ 9♈
14	21.35	25	11♍	29	27	6	♆ 2♍R
15	21.39	26	26	0♒	28	6	♇18♋R
16	21.43	27	10♎	1	29	7	♃ 6♊
17	21.47	28	24	2	0♓	8	♄ 9♑
18	21.51	29	7♏	3	2	9	♅ 9♈
19	21.55	0♓	20	4	3	10	♆ 2♍R
20	21.59	1	2♐	5	4	10	♇17♋R
21	22.03	2	15	6	5	11	♃ 7♊
22	22.07	3	27	8	7	12	♄ 9♑
23	22.11	4	8♑	9	8	13	♅ 9♈
24	22.15	5	20	10	9	13	♆ 2♍R
25	22.18	6	2♒	11	10	14	♇17♋R
26	22.22	7	14	13	12	15	♃ 7♊
27	22.26	8	26	14	13	16	♄ 9♑
28	22.30	9	8♓	16	14	17	♅ 9♈

Mar	STime	☉	☽	☿	♀	♂	Plnts
1	22.34	10♓	20♓	17♒	15♓	17♒	♃ 7♊
2	22.38	11	3♈	18	17	18	♄10♑
3	22.42	12	15	20	18	19	♅ 9♈
4	22.46	13	28	21	19	20	♆ 2♍R
5	22.50	14	11♉	23	20	20	♇17♋R
6	22.54	15	24	24	22	21	♃ 8♊
7	22.58	16	7♊	26	23	22	♄10♑
8	23.02	17	21	27	24	23	♅10♈
9	23.06	18	5♋	29	25	24	♆ 1♍R
10	23.10	19	20	1♓	27	24	♇17♋R
11	23.14	20	4♌	2	28	25	♃ 9♊
12	23.18	21	19	4	29	26	♄10♑
13	23.22	22	4♍	5	0♈	27	♅10♈
14	23.26	23	19	7	2	28	♆ 1♍R
15	23.29	24	3♎	9	3	28	♇17♋
16	23.33	25	18	11	4	29	♃ 9♊
17	23.37	26	2♏	12	5	0♓	♄11♑
18	23.41	27	15	14	7	1	♅10♈
19	23.45	28	28	16	8	1	♆ 1♍R
20	23.49	29	10♐	18	9	2	♇17♋
21	23.53	0♈	23	19	10	3	♃10♊
22	23.57	1	5♑	21	12	4	♄11♑
23	0.01	2	17	23	13	5	♅11♈
24	0.05	3	29	25	14	5	♆ 1♍R
25	0.09	4	11♒	27	15	6	♇17♋R
26	0.13	5	22	29	17	7	♃11♊
27	0.17	6	5♓	1♈	18	8	♄11♑
28	0.21	7	17	3	19	8	♅11♈
29	0.25	8	29	5	20	9	♆ 1♍R
30	0.29	9	12♈	7	22	10	♇17♋
31	0.33	10	25	9	23	11	♃11♊

Apr	STime	☉	☽	☿	♀	♂	Plnts
1	0.36	11♈	8♉	11♈	24♈	12♓	♃12♊
2	0.40	12	21	13	25	12	♄11♑
3	0.44	13	4♊	15	26	13	♅11♈
4	0.48	14	18	17	28	14	♆ 1♍R
5	0.52	15	2♋	19	29	15	♇17♋
6	0.56	16	16	21	0♉	16	♃12♊
7	1.00	17	0♌	23	1	16	♄11♑
8	1.04	18	15	25	3	17	♅11♈
9	1.08	19	29	27	4	18	♆ 1♍R
10	1.12	20	13♍	29	5	19	♇17♋
11	1.16	21	28	1♉	6	19	♃13♊
12	1.20	22	12♎	3	8	20	♄12♑
13	1.24	23	26	5	9	21	♅12♈
14	1.28	24	9♏	7	10	22	♆ 1♍R
15	1.32	24	23	9	11	23	♇17♋
16	1.36	25	6♐	11	12	23	♃14♊
17	1.40	26	18	13	14	24	♄12♑
18	1.44	27	1♑	14	15	25	♅12♈
19	1.47	28	13	16	16	26	♆ 1♍R
20	1.51	29	25	18	17	26	♇17♋
21	1.55	0♉	7♒	19	19	27	♃15♊
22	1.59	1	19	21	20	28	♄12♑
23	2.03	2	1♓	22	21	29	♅12♈
24	2.07	3	13	23	22	0♈	♆ 1♍R
25	2.11	4	25	24	24	0	♇17♋
26	2.15	5	7♈	26	25	1	♃16♊
27	2.19	6	20	27	26	2	♄12♑R
28	2.23	7	3♉	28	27	3	♅13♈
29	2.27	8	17	28	28	3	♆ 1♍R
30	2.31	9	1♊	29	0♊	4	♇17♋

May	STime	☉	☽	☿	♀	♂	Plnts
1	2.35	10♉	15♊	0♊	1♊	5♈	♃17♊
2	2.39	11	29	0	2	6	♄11♑R
3	2.43	12	13♋	1	3	6	♅13♈
4	2.47	13	27	1	5	7	♆ 1♍R
5	2.51	14	11♌	2	6	8	♇17♋
6	2.54	15	25	2	7	9	♃18♊
7	2.58	16	10♍	2	8	10	♄11♑R
8	3.02	17	24	2R	9	10	♅13♈
9	3.06	18	7♎	2	11	11	♆ 0♍
10	3.10	19	21	2	12	12	♇17♋
11	3.14	20	5♏	2	13	13	♃19♊
12	3.18	21	18	2	14	13	♄11♑R
13	3.22	22	1♐	1	16	14	♅13♈
14	3.26	23	14	1	17	15	♆ 0♍
15	3.30	24	26	1	18	16	♇18♋
16	3.34	25	9♑	0	19	16	♃20♊
17	3.38	26	21	0	20	17	♄11♑R
18	3.42	27	3♒	29♉	22	18	♅14♈
19	3.46	27	15	29	23	19	♆ 1♍
20	3.50	28	26	28	24	19	♇18♋
21	3.54	29	8♓	27	25	20	♃21♊
22	3.58	0♊	21	27	26	21	♄11♑R
23	4.02	1	3♈	26	28	22	♅14♈
24	4.05	2	15	26	29	22	♆ 1♍
25	4.09	3	28	25	0♋	23	♇18♋
26	4.13	4	12♉	25	1	24	♃23♊
27	4.17	5	26	24	2	25	♄11♑R
28	4.21	6	10♊	24	4	25	♅14♈
29	4.25	7	24	24	5	26	♆ 1♍
30	4.29	8	9♋	24	6	27	♇18♋
31	4.33	9	23	24	7	28	♃24♊

Jun	STime	☉	☽	☿	♀	♂	Plnts
1	4.37	10♊	8♌	24♉	9♋	28♈	♃24♊
2	4.41	11	22	24	10	29	♄10♑R
3	4.45	12	6♍	24	11	0♉	♅14♈
4	4.49	13	20	24	12	1	♆ 1♍
5	4.53	14	4♎	24	13	1	♇18♋
6	4.57	15	18	24	15	2	♃25♊
7	5.01	16	1♏	25	16	3	♄10♑R
8	5.05	17	14	25	17	4	♅14♈
9	5.09	18	27	26	18	4	♆ 1♍
10	5.12	19	10♐	26	19	5	♇18♋
11	5.16	20	22	27	21	6	♃26♊
12	5.20	20	5♑	28	22	7	♄10♑R
13	5.24	21	17	29	23	7	♅15♈
14	5.28	22	29	29	24	8	♆ 1♍
15	5.32	23	11♒	0♊	25	9	♇18♋
16	5.36	24	23	1	26	10	♃27♊
17	5.40	25	5♓	2	28	10	♄ 9♑R
18	5.44	26	17	3	29	11	♅15♈
19	5.48	27	29	5	0♌	12	♆ 1♍
20	5.52	28	11♈	6	1	13	♇18♋
21	5.56	29	23	7	2	13	♃28♊
22	6.00	0♋	6♉	9	4	14	♄ 9♑R
23	6.04	1	20	10	5	15	♅15♈
24	6.08	2	4♊	11	6	15	♆ 1♍
25	6.12	3	18	13	7	16	♇18♋
26	6.16	4	3♋	14	8	17	♃ 0♋
27	6.19	5	18	16	10	18	♄ 9♑R
28	6.23	6	3♌	18	11	18	♅15♈
29	6.27	7	18	20	12	19	♆ 1♍
30	6.31	8	2♍	21	13	20	♇19♋

Jul	STime	☉	☽	☿	♀	♂	Plnts
1	6.35	9♋	17♍	23♊	14♌	20♉	♃ 1♋
2	6.39	10	1♎	25	15	21	♄ 8♑R
3	6.43	11	15	27	17	22	♅15♈
4	6.47	11	28	29	18	23	♆ 1♍
5	6.51	12	11♏	1♋	19	23	♇19♋
6	6.55	13	24	3	20	24	♃ 2♋
7	6.59	14	7♐	5	21	25	♄ 8♑R
8	7.03	15	19	7	22	25	♅15♈
9	7.07	16	1♑	9	24	26	♆ 1♍
10	7.11	17	13	11	25	27	♇19♋
11	7.15	18	26	13	26	28	♃ 3♋
12	7.19	19	7♒	16	27	28	♄ 7♑R
13	7.23	20	19	18	28	29	♅15♈
14	7.27	21	1♓	20	29	0♊	♆ 2♍
15	7.30	22	13	22	1♍	0	♇19♋
16	7.34	23	25	24	2	1	♃ 4♋
17	7.38	24	7♈	26	3	2	♄ 7♑R
18	7.42	25	19	28	4	2	♅15♈
19	7.46	26	2♉	1♌	5	3	♆ 2♍
20	7.50	27	15	3	6	4	♇19♋
21	7.54	28	28	5	8	5	♃ 5♋
22	7.58	29	12♊	7	9	5	♄ 7♑R
23	8.02	0♌	26	9	10	6	♅15♈
24	8.06	1	11♋	11	11	7	♆ 2♍
25	8.10	2	26	13	12	7	♇19♋
26	8.14	2	12♌	14	13	8	♃ 6♋
27	8.18	3	27	16	14	9	♄ 6♑R
28	8.22	4	12♍	18	16	9	♅15♈R
29	8.26	5	26	20	17	10	♆ 2♍
30	8.30	6	11♎	22	18	11	♇19♋
31	8.34	7	25	24	19	11	♃ 7♋

Aug	STime	☉	☽	☿	♀	♂	Plnts
1	8.37	8♌	8♏	25♌	20♍	12♊	♃ 8♋
2	8.41	9	21	27	21	13	♄ 6♑R
3	8.45	10	4♐	29	22	13	♅15♈R
4	8.49	11	16	0♍	24	14	♆ 2♍
5	8.53	12	28	2	25	15	♇19♋
6	8.57	13	10♑	4	26	15	♃ 9♋
7	9.01	14	22	5	27	16	♄ 6♑R
8	9.05	15	4♒	7	28	17	♅15♈R
9	9.09	16	16	8	29	17	♆ 2♍
10	9.13	17	28	10	0♎	18	♇20♋
11	9.17	18	10♓	11	1	19	♃10♋
12	9.21	19	22	13	2	19	♄ 6♑R
13	9.25	20	4♈	14	4	20	♅15♈R
14	9.29	21	16	15	5	21	♆ 3♍
15	9.33	22	28	17	6	21	♇20♋
16	9.37	23	11♉	18	7	22	♃11♋
17	9.41	24	24	19	8	23	♄ 5♑R
18	9.45	25	7♊	21	9	23	♅15♈R
19	9.48	25	21	22	10	24	♆ 3♍
20	9.52	26	5♋	23	11	25	♇20♋
21	9.56	27	20	24	12	25	♃12♋
22	10.00	28	5♌	25	13	26	♄ 5♑R
23	10.04	29	20	26	14	27	♅15♈R
24	10.08	0♍	5♍	27	15	27	♆ 3♍
25	10.12	1	20	29	17	28	♇20♋
26	10.16	2	5♎	29	18	28	♃13♋
27	10.20	3	20	0♎	19	29	♄ 5♑R
28	10.24	4	4♏	1	20	0♋	♅15♈R
29	10.28	5	17	2	21	0	♆ 3♍
30	10.32	6	0♐	3	22	1	♇20♋
31	10.36	7	13	4	23	2	♃13♋

Sep	STime	☉	☽	☿	♀	♂	Plnts
1	10.40	8♍	25♐	4♎	24♎	2♋	♃14♋
2	10.44	9	7♑	5	25	3	♄ 5♑R
3	10.48	10	19	5	26	3	♅14♈R
4	10.52	11	1♒	6	27	4	♆ 3♍
5	10.55	12	13	6	28	5	♇20♋
6	10.59	13	25	6	29	5	♃14♋
7	11.03	14	7♓	6	0♏	6	♄ 5♑R
8	11.07	15	19	6R	1	7	♅14♈R
9	11.11	16	1♈	6	2	7	♆ 4♍
10	11.15	17	13	6	3	8	♇20♋
11	11.19	18	25	6	4	8	♃15♋
12	11.23	19	8♉	6	5	9	♄ 5♑
13	11.27	20	21	5	6	10	♅14♈R
14	11.31	21	3♊	5	7	10	♆ 4♍
15	11.35	22	17	4	8	11	♇20♋
16	11.39	23	0♋	3	9	11	♃16♋
17	11.43	24	14	2	10	12	♄ 5♑
18	11.47	25	29	1	11	12	♅14♈R
19	11.51	26	14♌	0	12	13	♆ 4♍
20	11.55	26	29	29♍	13	14	♇20♋
21	11.59	27	14♍	28	13	14	♃17♋
22	12.03	28	29	27	14	15	♄ 5♑
23	12.06	29	13♎	26	15	15	♅14♈R
24	12.10	0♎	28	25	16	16	♆ 4♍
25	12.14	1	12♏	24	17	17	♇20♋
26	12.18	2	26	23	18	17	♃17♋
27	12.22	3	9♐	23	19	18	♄ 5♑
28	12.26	4	21	22	20	18	♅13♈R
29	12.30	5	4♑	22	20	19	♆ 4♍
30	12.34	6	16	22D	21	19	♇20♋

Oct	STime	☉	☽	☿	♀	♂	Plnts
1	12.38	7♎	28♑	22♍	22♏	20♋	♃18♋
2	12.42	8	10♒	22	23	20	♄ 5♑
3	12.46	9	22	22	24	21	♅13♈R
4	12.50	10	4♓	23	24	21	♆ 4♍
5	12.54	11	16	24	25	22	♇21♋
6	12.58	12	28	24	26	23	♃19♋
7	13.02	13	10♈	25	27	23	♄ 6♑
8	13.06	14	22	26	27	24	♅13♈R
9	13.10	15	5♉	28	28	24	♆ 5♍
10	13.13	16	18	29	29	25	♇21♋
11	13.17	17	1♊	0♎	29	25	♃19♋
12	13.21	18	14	2	0♐	26	♄ 6♑
13	13.25	19	27	3	1	26	♅13♈R
14	13.29	20	11♋	5	1	27	♆ 5♍
15	13.33	21	25	6	2	27	♇21♋
16	13.37	22	9♌	8	2	28	♃19♋
17	13.41	23	23	9	3	28	♄ 6♑
18	13.45	24	8♍	11	3	29	♅13♈R
19	13.49	25	23	13	4	29	♆ 5♍
20	13.53	26	7♎	14	4	0♌	♇21♋
21	13.57	27	22	16	5	0	♃20♋
22	14.01	28	6♏	18	5	1	♄ 6♑
23	14.05	29	20	19	5	1	♅12♈R
24	14.09	0♏	3♐	21	6	2	♆ 5♍
25	14.13	1	17	23	6	2	♇21♋
26	14.17	2	29	24	6	2	♃20♋
27	14.20	3	12♑	26	6	3	♄ 7♑
28	14.24	4	24	28	7	3	♅12♈R
29	14.28	5	6♒	0♏	7	4	♆ 5♍
30	14.32	6	18	1	7	4	♇21♋R
31	14.36	7	0♓	3	7	5	♃20♋

Nov	STime	☉	☽	☿	♀	♂	Plnts
1	14.40	8♏	12♓	5♏	7♐	5♌	♃20♋
2	14.44	9	24	6	7R	5	♄ 7♑
3	14.48	10	6♈	8	7	6	♅12♈R
4	14.52	11	18	9	7	6	♆ 5♍
5	14.56	12	1♉	11	7	7	♇21♋R
6	15.00	13	14	13	7	7	♃20♋
7	15.04	14	27	14	7	8	♄ 8♑
8	15.08	15	10♊	16	6	8	♅12♈R
9	15.12	16	24	18	6	8	♆ 5♍
10	15.16	17	8♋	19	6	9	♇21♋R
11	15.20	18	22	21	5	9	♃20♋R
12	15.24	19	6♌	22	5	9	♄ 8♑
13	15.28	20	20	24	5	10	♅12♈R
14	15.31	21	4♍	25	4	10	♆ 5♍
15	15.35	22	18	27	4	10	♇20♋R
16	15.39	23	2♎	29	3	11	♃20♋R
17	15.43	24	16	0♐	3	11	♄ 9♑
18	15.47	25	0♏	2	2	11	♅12♈R
19	15.51	26	14	3	1	12	♆ 5♍
20	15.55	27	28	5	1	12	♇20♋R
21	15.59	28	11♐	6	0	12	♃20♋R
22	16.03	29	24	8	0	13	♄ 9♑
23	16.07	0♐	7♑	9	29♏	13	♅11♈R
24	16.11	1	20	11	28	13	♆ 5♍
25	16.15	2	2♒	12	28	13	♇20♋R
26	16.19	3	14	14	27	14	♃20♋R
27	16.23	4	26	16	27	14	♄10♑
28	16.27	5	8♓	17	26	14	♅11♈R
29	16.31	6	20	19	26	14	♆ 5♍
30	16.35	7	2♈	20	25	15	♇20♋R

Dec	STime	☉	☽	☿	♀	♂	Plnts
1	16.38	8♐	14♈	22♐	25♏	15♌	♃19♋R
2	16.42	9	26	23	24	15	♄10♑
3	16.46	10	9♉	25	24	15	♅11♈R
4	16.50	11	22	26	23	15	♆ 5♍
5	16.54	12	6♊	28	23	15	♇20♋R
6	16.58	13	19	29	23	16	♃19♋R
7	17.02	14	4♋	1♑	22	16	♄11♑
8	17.06	15	18	2	22	16	♅11♈R
9	17.10	16	2♌	4	22	16	♆ 5♍
10	17.14	17	17	5	22	16	♇20♋R
11	17.18	18	1♍	6	22	16	♃18♋R
12	17.22	19	15	8	22	16	♄11♑
13	17.26	20	29	9	22D	16	♅11♈R
14	17.30	21	13♎	11	22	16	♆ 5♍R
15	17.34	22	27	12	22	16	♇20♋R
16	17.38	24	10♏	13	22	16	♃18♋R
17	17.42	25	24	14	22	17	♄12♑
18	17.46	26	7♐	16	22	17	♅11♈
19	17.49	27	20	17	23	17R	♆ 5♍
20	17.53	28	3♑	18	23	16	♇20♋R
21	17.57	29	15	19	23	16	♃17♋R
22	18.01	0♑	28	20	23	16	♄12♑
23	18.05	1	10♒	20	24	16	♅11♈
24	18.09	2	22	21	24	16	♆ 5♍R
25	18.13	3	4♓	21	25	16	♇20♋R
26	18.17	4	16	22	25	16	♃17♋R
27	18.21	5	27	22	25	16	♄13♑
28	18.25	6	9♈	22R	26	16	♅11♈
29	18.29	7	22	22	26	16	♆ 5♍R
30	18.33	8	4♉	21	27	16	♇20♋R
31	18.37	9	17	21	28	15	♃16♋R

1 9 3 1

Jan	STime	☉	☽	☿	♀	♂	Plnts
1	18.41	10♑	0♊	20♑	28♏	15♌	♃16♋R
2	18.45	11	14	19	29	15	♄14♑
3	18.49	12	28	18	29	15	♅11♈
4	18.53	13	12♋	17	0♐	15	♆ 5♍R
5	18.56	14	27	15	1	14	♇20♋R
6	19.00	15	12♌	14	2	14	♃15♋R
7	19.04	16	27	13	2	14	♄14♑
8	19.08	17	11♍	11	3	14	♅11♈
9	19.12	18	26	10	4	13	♆ 5♍R
10	19.16	19	10♎	9	5	13	♇20♋R
11	19.20	20	24	8	5	13	♃15♋R
12	19.24	21	7♏	7	6	12	♄15♑
13	19.28	22	20	7	7	12	♅11♈
14	19.32	23	4♐	6	8	12	♆ 5♍R
15	19.36	24	16	6	9	11	♇19♋R
16	19.40	25	29	6	9	11	♃14♋R
17	19.44	26	12♑	6D	10	11	♄15♑
18	19.48	27	24	6	11	10	♅11♈
19	19.52	28	6♒	6	12	10	♆ 5♍R
20	19.56	29	18	6	13	10	♇19♋R
21	20.00	0♒	0♓	7	14	9	♃13♋R
22	20.03	1	12	8	15	9	♄16♑
23	20.07	2	24	8	16	8	♅12♈
24	20.11	3	6♈	9	17	8	♆ 5♍R
25	20.15	4	18	10	18	8	♇19♋R
26	20.19	5	0♉	11	19	7	♃13♋R
27	20.23	6	12	11	20	7	♄17♑
28	20.27	7	25	12	21	6	♅12♈
29	20.31	8	8♊	13	22	6	♆ 5♍R
30	20.35	9	21	15	23	6	♇19♋R
31	20.39	10	6♋	16	24	5	♃12♋R

Feb	STime	☉	☽	☿	♀	♂	Plnts
1	20.43	11♒	20♋	17♑	25♐	5♌	♃12♋R
2	20.47	12	5♌	18	26	4	♄17♑
3	20.51	13	20	19	27	4	♅12♈
4	20.55	14	5♍	20	28	4	♆ 5♍R
5	20.59	15	20	22	29	3	♇19♋R
6	21.03	16	5♎	23	0♑	3	♃11♋R
7	21.07	17	20	24	1	3	♄18♑
8	21.11	18	4♏	26	2	2	♅12♈
9	21.14	19	17	27	3	2	♆ 5♍R
10	21.18	20	1♐	28	4	1	♇19♋R
11	21.22	22	14	0♒	5	1	♃11♋R
12	21.26	23	26	1	6	1	♄18♑
13	21.30	24	9♑	3	7	1	♅12♈
14	21.34	25	21	4	8	0	♆ 4♍R
15	21.38	26	3♒	5	9	0	♇19♋R
16	21.42	27	15	7	10	0	♃11♋R
17	21.46	28	27	8	11	29♋	♄19♑
18	21.50	29	9♓	10	12	29	♅13♈
19	21.54	0♓	21	11	14	29	♆ 4♍R
20	21.58	1	2♈	13	15	29	♇19♋R
21	22.02	2	14	15	16	29	♃10♋R
22	22.06	3	26	16	17	28	♄19♑
23	22.10	4	8♉	18	18	28	♅13♈
24	22.14	5	21	19	19	28	♆ 4♍R
25	22.18	6	3♊	21	20	28	♇19♋R
26	22.21	7	16	23	21	28	♃10♋R
27	22.25	8	0♋	24	22	28	♄20♑
28	22.29	9	14	26	24	28	♅13♈

Mar	STime	☉	☽	☿	♀	♂	Plnts
1	22.33	10♓	28♋	28♒	25♑	27♋	♃10♋R
2	22.37	11	13♌	29	26	27	♄20♑
3	22.41	12	28	1♓	27	27	♅13♈
4	22.45	13	13♍	3	28	27	♆ 4♍R
5	22.49	14	29	5	29	27	♇19♋R
6	22.53	15	14♎	6	0♒	27	♃10♋
7	22.57	16	28	8	2	27	♄20♑
8	23.01	17	13♏	10	3	27D	♅13♈
9	23.05	18	27	12	4	27	♆ 4♍R
10	23.09	19	10♐	14	5	27	♇18♋
11	23.13	20	23	15	6	27	♃10♋
12	23.17	21	6♑	17	7	27	♄21♑
13	23.21	22	18	19	8	27	♅14♈
14	23.25	23	0♒	21	10	27	♆ 4♍R
15	23.29	24	12	23	11	27	♇18♋
16	23.32	25	24	25	12	28	♃10♋
17	23.36	26	6♓	27	13	28	♄21♑
18	23.40	27	18	29	14	28	♅14♈
19	23.44	28	0♈	1♈	15	28	♆ 3♍R
20	23.48	29	11	3	16	28	♇18♋
21	23.52	0♈	23	5	18	28	♃10♋
22	23.56	1	5♉	7	19	28	♄22♑
23	0.00	2	18	9	20	28	♅14♈
24	0.04	3	0♊	11	21	29	♆ 3♍R
25	0.08	4	13	13	22	29	♇18♋
26	0.12	5	26	15	23	29	♃11♋
27	0.16	6	9♋	17	25	29	♄22♑
28	0.20	7	23	19	26	29	♅15♈
29	0.24	8	7♌	21	27	0♌	♆ 3♍R
30	0.28	9	22	23	28	0	♇18♋
31	0.32	10	7♍	25	29	0	♃11♋

Apr	STime	☉	☽	☿	♀	♂	Plnts
1	0.36	11♈	22♍	26♈	1♓	0♌	♃11♋
2	0.39	11	7♎	28	2	1	♄22♑
3	0.43	12	22	0♉	3	1	♅15♈
4	0.47	13	7♏	1	4	1	♆ 3♍R
5	0.51	14	21	3	5	1	♇18♋
6	0.55	15	5♐	4	6	2	♃12♋
7	0.59	16	19	5	8	2	♄22♑
8	1.03	17	2♑	6	9	2	♅15♈
9	1.07	18	14	8	10	2	♆ 3♍R
10	1.11	19	27	9	11	3	♇18♋
11	1.15	20	9♒	10	12	3	♃12♋
12	1.19	21	21	10	14	3	♄23♑
13	1.23	22	3♓	11	15	4	♅15♈
14	1.27	23	15	12	16	4	♆ 3♍R
15	1.31	24	26	12	17	4	♇18♋
16	1.35	25	8♈	13	18	5	♃13♋
17	1.39	26	20	13	19	5	♄23♑
18	1.43	27	2♉	13	21	5	♅16♈
19	1.47	28	15	13R	22	6	♆ 3♍R
20	1.50	29	27	13	23	6	♇18♋
21	1.54	0♉	10♊	13	24	6	♃13♋
22	1.58	1	23	13	25	7	♄23♑
23	2.02	2	6♋	12	27	7	♅16♈
24	2.06	3	19	12	28	8	♆ 3♍R
25	2.10	4	3♌	12	29	8	♇19♋
26	2.14	5	17	11	0♈	8	♃14♋
27	2.18	6	1♍	11	1	9	♄23♑
28	2.22	7	16	10	3	9	♅16♈
29	2.26	8	1♎	9	4	10	♆ 3♍R
30	2.30	9	15	9	5	10	♇19♋

May	STime	☉	☽	☿	♀	♂	Plnts
1	2.34	10♉	0♏	8♉	6♈	10♌	♃15♋
2	2.38	11	15	7	7	11	♄23♑
3	2.42	12	29	7	9	11	♅17♈
4	2.46	13	13♐	6	10	12	♆ 3♍
5	2.50	14	27	6	11	12	♇19♋
6	2.54	15	10♑	5	12	13	♃15♋
7	2.57	16	23	5	13	13	♄23♑R
8	3.01	17	5♒	4	15	13	♅17♈
9	3.05	18	17	4	16	14	♆ 3♍
10	3.09	19	29	4	17	14	♇19♋
11	3.13	20	11♓	3	18	15	♃16♋
12	3.17	20	23	3	19	15	♄23♑R
13	3.21	21	5♈	3D	21	16	♅17♈
14	3.25	22	17	3	22	16	♆ 3♍
15	3.29	23	29	3	23	17	♇19♋
16	3.33	24	11♉	4	24	17	♃17♋
17	3.37	25	24	4	25	18	♄23♑R
18	3.41	26	6♊	4	27	18	♅17♈
19	3.45	27	19	5	28	18	♆ 3♍
20	3.49	28	3♋	5	29	19	♇19♋
21	3.53	29	16	6	0♉	19	♃18♋
22	3.57	0♊	0♌	6	1	20	♄23♑R
23	4.01	1	14	7	3	20	♅18♈
24	4.04	2	28	8	4	21	♆ 3♍
25	4.08	3	12♍	8	5	21	♇19♋
26	4.12	4	26	9	6	22	♃19♋
27	4.16	5	10♎	10	7	22	♄23♑R
28	4.20	6	25	11	9	23	♅18♈
29	4.24	7	9♏	12	10	23	♆ 3♍
30	4.28	8	23	13	11	24	♇19♋
31	4.32	9	7♐	14	12	24	♃20♋

Jun	STime	☉	☽	☿	♀	♂	Plnts
1	4.36	10♊	21♐	16♉	13♉	25♌	♃20♋
2	4.40	11	5♑	17	15	25	♄22♑R
3	4.44	12	18	18	16	26	♅18♈
4	4.48	13	1♒	19	17	26	♆ 3♍
5	4.52	14	13	21	18	27	♇19♋
6	4.56	15	25	22	19	28	♃21♋
7	5.00	15	7♓	24	21	28	♄22♑R
8	5.04	16	19	25	22	29	♅18♈
9	5.08	17	1♈	27	23	29	♆ 3♍
10	5.12	18	13	28	24	0♍	♇19♋
11	5.15	19	25	0♊	26	0	♃22♋
12	5.19	20	7♉	2	27	1	♄22♑R
13	5.23	21	19	3	28	1	♅18♈
14	5.27	22	2♊	5	29	2	♆ 3♍
15	5.31	23	15	7	0♊	2	♇19♋
16	5.35	24	29	9	2	3	♃23♋
17	5.39	25	12♋	11	3	3	♄21♑R
18	5.43	26	26	13	4	4	♅19♈
19	5.47	27	10♌	15	5	5	♆ 3♍
20	5.51	28	25	17	6	5	♇20♋
21	5.55	29	9♍	19	8	6	♃24♋
22	5.59	0♋	23	21	9	6	♄21♑R
23	6.03	1	7♎	23	10	7	♅19♈
24	6.07	2	21	25	11	7	♆ 3♍
25	6.11	3	5♏	27	12	8	♇20♋
26	6.15	4	19	0♋	14	8	♃25♋
27	6.19	5	3♐	2	15	9	♄21♑R
28	6.22	6	17	4	16	10	♅19♈
29	6.26	6	0♑	6	17	10	♆ 3♍
30	6.30	7	13	8	19	11	♇20♋

Jul	STime	☉	☽	☿	♀	♂	Plnts
1	6.34	8♋	26♑	10♋	20♊	11♍	♃26♋
2	6.38	9	9♒	13	21	12	♄20♑R
3	6.42	10	21	15	22	12	♅19♈
4	6.46	11	3♓	17	23	13	♆ 3♍
5	6.50	12	15	19	25	14	♇20♋
6	6.54	13	27	21	26	14	♃27♋
7	6.58	14	9♈	23	27	15	♄20♑R
8	7.02	15	21	25	28	15	♅19♈
9	7.06	16	3♉	27	0♋	16	♆ 3♍
10	7.10	17	15	29	1	16	♇20♋
11	7.14	18	27	1♌	2	17	♃28♋
12	7.18	19	10♊	3	3	18	♄20♑R
13	7.22	20	24	5	4	18	♅19♈
14	7.26	21	7♋	7	6	19	♆ 4♍
15	7.30	22	22	8	7	19	♇20♋
16	7.33	23	6♌	10	8	20	♃ 0♌
17	7.37	24	20	12	9	21	♄19♑R
18	7.41	25	5♍	14	11	21	♅19♈
19	7.45	26	19	15	12	22	♆ 4♍
20	7.49	27	4♎	17	13	22	♇20♋
21	7.53	27	18	19	14	23	♃ 1♌
22	7.57	28	2♏	20	15	24	♄19♑R
23	8.01	29	16	22	17	24	♅19♈
24	8.05	0♌	0♐	23	18	25	♆ 4♍
25	8.09	1	13	25	19	25	♇20♋
26	8.13	2	26	26	20	26	♃ 2♌
27	8.17	3	9♑	28	22	27	♄19♑R
28	8.21	4	22	29	23	27	♅19♈R
29	8.25	5	5♒	0♍	24	28	♆ 4♍
30	8.29	6	17	2	25	28	♇21♋
31	8.33	7	29	3	26	29	♃ 3♌

Aug	STime	☉	☽	☿	♀	♂	Plnts
1	8.37	8♌	11♓	4♍	28♋	0♎	♃ 3♌
2	8.40	9	23	6	29	0	♄18♑R
3	8.44	10	5♈	7	0♌	1	♅19♈R
4	8.48	11	17	8	1	1	♆ 4♍
5	8.52	12	29	9	3	2	♇21♋
6	8.56	13	11♉	10	4	3	♃ 4♌
7	9.00	14	23	11	5	3	♄18♑R
8	9.04	15	6♊	12	6	4	♅19♈R
9	9.08	16	18	13	8	5	♆ 4♍
10	9.12	17	2♋	14	9	5	♇21♋
11	9.16	18	16	15	10	6	♃ 5♌
12	9.20	19	0♌	15	11	6	♄18♑R
13	9.24	19	15	16	12	7	♅19♈R
14	9.28	20	29	17	14	8	♆ 5♍
15	9.32	21	14♍	17	15	8	♇21♋
16	9.36	22	29	18	16	9	♃ 6♌
17	9.40	23	14♎	18	17	10	♄17♑R
18	9.44	24	28	19	19	10	♅19♈R
19	9.48	25	13♏	19	20	11	♆ 5♍
20	9.51	26	26	19	21	11	♇21♋
21	9.55	27	10♐	19	22	12	♃ 7♌
22	9.59	28	23	19R	24	13	♄17♑R
23	10.03	29	6♑	19	25	13	♅19♈R
24	10.07	0♍	19	19	26	14	♆ 5♍
25	10.11	1	1♒	19	27	15	♇21♋
26	10.15	2	14	19	29	15	♃ 9♌
27	10.19	3	26	18	0♍	16	♄17♑R
28	10.23	4	8♓	18	1	17	♅19♈R
29	10.27	5	20	17	2	17	♆ 5♍
30	10.31	6	2♈	16	3	18	♇21♋
31	10.35	7	13	15	5	19	♃10♌

Sep	STime	☉	☽	☿	♀	♂	Plnts
1	10.39	8♍	25♈	15♍	6♍	19♎	♃10♌
2	10.43	9	7♉	14	7	20	♄17♑R
3	10.47	10	19	13	8	21	♅18♈R
4	10.51	11	1♊	12	10	21	♆ 5♍
5	10.55	12	14	11	11	22	♇21♋
6	10.58	13	27	10	12	22	♃11♌
7	11.02	14	10♋	9	13	23	♄17♑R
8	11.06	15	24	8	15	24	♅18♈R
9	11.10	16	8♌	7	16	24	♆ 6♍
10	11.14	17	23	7	17	25	♇21♋
11	11.18	17	8♍	6	18	26	♃12♌
12	11.22	18	23	6	20	26	♄16♑R
13	11.26	19	8♎	6	21	27	♅18♈R
14	11.30	20	23	6D	22	28	♆ 6♍
15	11.34	21	8♏	6	23	28	♇22♋
16	11.38	22	22	6	25	29	♃13♌
17	11.42	23	6♐	6	26	0♏	♄16♑R
18	11.46	24	20	7	27	0	♅18♈R
19	11.50	25	3♑	8	28	1	♆ 6♍
20	11.54	26	16	8	0♎	2	♇22♋
21	11.58	27	29	9	1	2	♃14♌
22	12.02	28	11♒	10	2	3	♄16♑
23	12.05	29	23	12	3	4	♅18♈R
24	12.09	0♎	5♓	13	5	5	♆ 6♍
25	12.13	1	17	14	6	5	♇22♋
26	12.17	2	29	16	7	6	♃15♌
27	12.21	3	10♈	17	8	7	♄16♑
28	12.25	4	22	19	10	7	♅18♈R
29	12.29	5	4♉	21	11	8	♆ 6♍
30	12.33	6	16	22	12	9	♇22♋

Oct	STime	☉	☽	☿	♀	♂	Plnts
1	12.37	7♎	28♉	24♍	13♎	9♏	♃16♌
2	12.41	8	10♊	26	15	10	♄16♑
3	12.45	9	23	27	16	11	♅17♈R
4	12.49	10	6♋	29	17	11	♆ 6♍
5	12.53	11	19	1♎	18	12	♇22♋
6	12.57	12	3♌	3	20	13	♃16♌
7	13.01	13	17	5	21	13	♄17♑
8	13.05	14	1♍	6	22	14	♅17♈R
9	13.09	15	16	8	23	15	♆ 7♍
10	13.13	16	1♎	10	25	16	♇22♋
11	13.16	17	16	12	26	16	♃17♌
12	13.20	18	1♏	13	27	17	♄17♑
13	13.24	19	16	15	28	18	♅17♈R
14	13.28	20	1♐	17	0♏	18	♆ 7♍
15	13.32	21	15	19	1	19	♇22♋
16	13.36	22	29	20	2	20	♃18♌
17	13.40	23	12♑	22	3	20	♄17♑
18	13.44	24	25	24	5	21	♅17♈R
19	13.48	25	8♒	25	6	22	♆ 7♍
20	13.52	26	20	27	7	23	♇22♋
21	13.56	27	2♓	29	8	23	♃19♌
22	14.00	28	14	0♏	9	24	♄17♑
23	14.04	29	26	2	11	25	♅17♈R
24	14.08	0♏	7♈	4	12	25	♆ 7♍
25	14.12	1	19	5	13	26	♇22♋
26	14.16	2	1♉	7	14	27	♃19♌
27	14.20	3	13	8	16	28	♄17♑
28	14.23	4	25	10	17	28	♅16♈R
29	14.27	5	8♊	12	18	29	♆ 7♍
30	14.31	6	20	13	19	0♐	♇22♋R
31	14.35	7	3♋	15	21	0	♃20♌

Nov	STime	☉	☽	☿	♀	♂	Plnts
1	14.39	8♏	16♋	16♏	22♏	1♐	♃20♌
2	14.43	9	29	18	23	2	♄18♑
3	14.47	10	12♌	20	24	3	♅16♈R
4	14.51	11	26	21	26	3	♆ 7♍
5	14.55	12	10♍	23	27	4	♇22♋
6	14.59	13	25	24	28	5	♃21♌
7	15.03	14	10♎	26	29	5	♄18♑
8	15.07	15	24	27	1♐	6	♅16♈R
9	15.11	16	9♏	29	2	7	♆ 7♍
10	15.15	17	24	0♐	3	8	♇22♋
11	15.19	18	9♐	2	4	8	♃21♌
12	15.23	19	23	3	6	9	♄18♑
13	15.27	20	7♑	5	7	10	♅16♈R
14	15.31	21	21	6	8	11	♆ 7♍
15	15.34	22	4♒	8	9	11	♇22♋R
16	15.38	23	16	9	11	12	♃21♌
17	15.42	24	28	11	12	13	♄19♑
18	15.46	25	10♓	12	13	14	♅16♈R
19	15.50	26	22	13	14	14	♆ 8♍
20	15.54	27	4♈	15	16	15	♇22♋R
21	15.58	28	16	16	17	16	♃22♌
22	16.02	29	28	18	18	16	♄19♑
23	16.06	0♐	10♉	19	19	17	♅16♈R
24	16.10	1	22	20	21	18	♆ 8♍
25	16.14	2	4♊	22	22	19	♇22♋R
26	16.18	3	17	23	23	19	♃22♌
27	16.22	4	0♋	24	24	20	♄20♑
28	16.26	5	13	26	26	21	♅15♈R
29	16.30	6	26	27	27	22	♆ 8♍
30	16.34	7	9♌	28	28	22	♇22♋R

Dec	STime	☉	☽	☿	♀	♂	Plnts
1	16.38	8♐	23♌	29♐	29♐	23♐	♃22♌
2	16.41	9	6♍	0♑	1♑	24	♄20♑
3	16.45	10	20	1	2	25	♅15♈R
4	16.49	11	5♎	2	3	25	♆ 8♍
5	16.53	12	19	3	4	26	♇22♋R
6	16.57	13	3♏	4	6	27	♃22♌
7	17.01	14	18	5	7	28	♄21♑
8	17.05	15	3♐	5	8	28	♅15♈R
9	17.09	16	17	6	9	29	♆ 8♍
10	17.13	17	1♑	6	11	0♑	♇21♋R
11	17.17	18	15	6R	12	1	♃22♌
12	17.21	19	28	6	13	1	♄21♑
13	17.25	20	12♒	6	14	2	♅15♈R
14	17.29	21	24	5	16	3	♆ 8♍
15	17.33	22	6♓	5	17	4	♇21♋R
16	17.37	23	18	4	18	5	♃22♌R
17	17.41	24	0♈	3	19	5	♄22♑
18	17.45	25	12	2	21	6	♅15♈R
19	17.48	26	24	1	22	7	♆ 8♍R
20	17.52	27	6♉	29♐	23	8	♇21♋R
21	17.56	28	18	28	24	8	♃22♌R
22	18.00	29	0♊	27	26	9	♄22♑
23	18.04	0♑	13	25	27	10	♅15♈
24	18.08	1	26	24	28	11	♆ 8♍R
25	18.12	2	9♋	23	29	11	♇21♋R
26	18.16	3	22	22	1♒	12	♃22♌R
27	18.20	4	6♌	21	2	13	♄23♑
28	18.24	5	20	21	3	14	♅15♈
29	18.28	7	3♍	20	4	15	♆ 8♍R
30	18.32	8	17	20	6	15	♇21♋R
31	18.36	9	1♎	20D	7	16	♃22♌R

Jan	STime	☉	☽	☿	♀	♂	Plnts
1	18.40	10♑	15♎	20♐	8♒	17♑	♃22♌R
2	18.44	11	29	20	9	18	♄24♑
3	18.48	12	14♏	20	10	18	♅15♈
4	18.52	13	28	21	12	19	♆ 8♍R
5	18.56	14	12♐	21	13	20	♇21♋R
6	18.59	15	26	22	14	21	♃21♌R
7	19.03	16	10♑	23	15	21	♄24♑
8	19.07	17	23	24	17	22	♅15♈
9	19.11	18	6♒	24	18	23	♆ 7♍R
10	19.15	19	19	25	19	24	♇21♋R
11	19.19	20	2♓	26	20	25	♃21♌R
12	19.23	21	14	27	22	25	♄25♑
13	19.27	22	26	29	23	26	♅15♈
14	19.31	23	8♈	0♑	24	27	♆ 7♍R
15	19.35	24	20	1	25	28	♇21♋R
16	19.39	25	2♉	2	27	29	♃20♌R
17	19.43	26	14	3	28	29	♄25♑
18	19.47	27	26	5	29	0♒	♅15♈
19	19.51	28	8♊	6	0♓	1	♆ 7♍R
20	19.55	29	21	7	1	2	♇21♋R
21	19.59	0♒	4♋	8	3	2	♃20♌R
22	20.03	1	17	10	4	3	♄26♑
23	20.06	2	1♌	11	5	4	♅15♈
24	20.10	3	15	13	6	5	♆ 7♍R
25	20.14	4	29	14	8	6	♇20♋R
26	20.18	5	14♍	15	9	6	♃19♌R
27	20.22	6	28	17	10	7	♄27♑
28	20.26	7	12♎	18	11	8	♅16♈
29	20.30	8	26	20	12	9	♆ 7♍R
30	20.34	9	10♏	21	14	9	♇20♋R
31	20.38	10	24	23	15	10	♃18♌R

Feb	STime	☉	☽	☿	♀	♂	Plnts
1	20.42	11♒	8♐	24♑	16♓	11♒	♃18♌R
2	20.46	12	22	26	17	12	♄27♑
3	20.50	13	5♑	27	19	13	♅16♈
4	20.54	14	19	29	20	13	♆ 7♍R
5	20.58	15	2♒	0♒	21	14	♇20♋R
6	21.02	16	15	2	22	15	♃18♌R
7	21.06	17	27	3	23	16	♄28♑
8	21.10	18	10♓	5	25	17	♅16♈
9	21.14	19	22	7	26	17	♆ 7♍R
10	21.17	20	4♈	8	27	18	♇20♋R
11	21.21	21	16	10	28	19	♃17♌R
12	21.25	22	28	12	29	20	♄28♑
13	21.29	23	9♉	13	1♈	21	♅16♈
14	21.33	24	21	15	2	21	♆ 7♍R
15	21.37	25	4♊	17	3	22	♇20♋R
16	21.41	26	16	18	4	23	♃16♌R
17	21.45	27	29	20	5	24	♄29♑
18	21.49	28	12♋	22	7	24	♅16♈
19	21.53	29	25	23	8	25	♆ 7♍R
20	21.57	0♓	9♌	25	9	26	♇20♋R
21	22.01	1	23	27	10	27	♃16♌R
22	22.05	2	8♍	29	11	28	♄ 0♒
23	22.09	3	23	1♓	13	28	♅17♈
24	22.13	4	7♎	2	14	29	♆ 6♍R
25	22.17	5	22	4	15	0♓	♇20♋R
26	22.21	6	7♏	6	16	1	♃15♌R
27	22.24	7	21	8	17	2	♄ 0♒
28	22.28	8	5♐	10	19	2	♅17♈
29	22.32	9	19	12	20	3	♆ 6♍R

Mar	STime	☉	☽	☿	♀	♂	Plnts
1	22.36	10♓	2♑	14♓	21♈	4♓	♃15♌R
2	22.40	11	16	16	22	5	♄ 0♒
3	22.44	12	29	17	23	6	♅17♈
4	22.48	13	11♒	19	24	6	♆ 6♍R
5	22.52	14	24	21	26	7	♇20♋R
6	22.56	15	6♓	23	27	8	♃14♌R
7	23.00	16	18	25	28	9	♄ 1♒
8	23.04	17	0♈	27	29	9	♅17♈
9	23.08	18	12	29	0♉	10	♆ 6♍R
10	23.12	19	24	1♈	1	11	♇20♋R
11	23.16	20	6♉	3	2	12	♃14♌R
12	23.20	21	18	5	4	13	♄ 1♒
13	23.24	22	0♊	6	5	13	♅18♈
14	23.28	23	12	8	6	14	♆ 6♍R
15	23.31	24	24	10	7	15	♇20♋
16	23.35	25	7♋	12	8	16	♃13♌R
17	23.39	26	20	13	9	17	♄ 2♒
18	23.43	27	3♌	15	10	17	♅18♈
19	23.47	28	17	16	12	18	♆ 6♍R
20	23.51	29	1♍	17	13	19	♇20♋
21	23.55	0♈	16	19	14	20	♃13♌R
22	23.59	1	1♎	20	15	20	♄ 2♒
23	0.03	2	16	21	16	21	♅18♈
24	0.07	3	1♏	22	17	22	♆ 6♍R
25	0.11	4	16	23	18	23	♇20♋
26	0.15	5	1♐	23	19	24	♃13♌R
27	0.19	6	15	24	20	24	♄ 3♒
28	0.23	7	29	24	22	25	♅18♈
29	0.27	8	13♑	25	23	26	♆ 5♍R
30	0.31	9	26	25	24	27	♇20♋
31	0.35	10	8♒	25R	25	28	♃12♌R

Apr	STime	☉	☽	☿	♀	♂	Plnts
1	0.39	11♈	21♒	25♈	26♉	28♓	♃12♌R
2	0.42	12	3♓	24	27	29	♄ 3♒
3	0.46	13	15	24	28	0♈	♅19♈
4	0.50	14	27	24	29	1	♆ 5♍R
5	0.54	15	9♈	23	0♊	1	♇20♋
6	0.58	16	21	23	1	2	♃12♌
7	1.02	17	3♉	22	2	3	♄ 3♒
8	1.06	18	15	21	3	4	♅19♈
9	1.10	19	26	21	4	5	♆ 5♍R
10	1.14	20	8♊	20	5	5	♇20♋
11	1.18	21	21	19	6	6	♃12♌
12	1.22	22	3♋	18	8	7	♄ 4♒
13	1.26	23	15	18	9	8	♅19♈
14	1.30	24	28	17	10	8	♆ 5♍R
15	1.34	25	12♌	16	11	9	♇20♋
16	1.38	26	25	16	12	10	♃12♌
17	1.42	27	10♍	15	13	11	♄ 4♒
18	1.46	28	24	15	14	11	♅20♈
19	1.49	29	9♎	14	15	12	♆ 5♍R
20	1.53	0♉	24	14	15	13	♇20♋
21	1.57	1	10♏	14	16	14	♃13♌
22	2.01	2	25	14	17	15	♄ 4♒
23	2.05	3	10♐	13D	18	15	♅20♈
24	2.09	4	24	13	19	16	♆ 5♍R
25	2.13	5	8♑	14	20	17	♇20♋
26	2.17	6	22	14	21	18	♃13♌
27	2.21	7	5♒	14	22	18	♄ 4♒
28	2.25	8	18	14	23	19	♅20♈
29	2.29	9	0♓	15	24	20	♆ 5♍
30	2.33	10	12	15	25	21	♇20♋

May	STime	☉	☽	☿	♀	♂	Plnts
1	2.37	11♉	24♓	16♈	26♊	21♈	♃13♌
2	2.41	12	6♈	16	26	22	♄ 4♒
3	2.45	13	18	17	27	23	♅20♈
4	2.49	13	0♉	18	28	24	♆ 5♍R
5	2.53	14	12	18	29	24	♇20♋
6	2.57	15	24	19	0♋	25	♃13♌
7	3.00	16	6♊	20	1	26	♄ 4♒
8	3.04	17	18	21	1	27	♅21♈
9	3.08	18	0♋	22	2	27	♆ 5♍
10	3.12	19	12	23	3	28	♇20♋
11	3.16	20	25	24	4	29	♃14♌
12	3.20	21	8♌	25	4	0♉	♄ 4♒
13	3.24	22	21	27	5	0	♅21♈
14	3.28	23	5♍	28	6	1	♆ 5♍
15	3.32	24	19	29	6	2	♇20♋
16	3.36	25	3♎	0♉	7	3	♃14♌
17	3.40	26	18	2	8	3	♄ 4♒R
18	3.44	27	3♏	3	8	4	♅21♈
19	3.48	28	18	5	9	5	♆ 5♍
20	3.52	29	3♐	6	10	6	♇20♋
21	3.56	0♊	18	8	10	6	♃15♌
22	4.00	1	3♑	9	11	7	♄ 4♒R
23	4.04	2	17	11	11	8	♅21♈
24	4.07	3	1♒	12	12	9	♆ 5♍
25	4.11	4	14	14	12	9	♇20♋
26	4.15	5	27	16	12	10	♃16♌
27	4.19	6	9♓	18	13	11	♄ 4♒R
28	4.23	7	21	19	13	12	♅22♈
29	4.27	8	3♈	21	14	12	♆ 5♍
30	4.31	9	15	23	14	13	♇20♋
31	4.35	10	27	25	14	14	♃16♌

Jun	STime	☉	☽	☿	♀	♂	Plnts
1	4.39	10♊	8♉	27♉	14♋	15♉	♃16♌
2	4.43	11	20	29	15	15	♄ 4♒R
3	4.47	12	2♊	1♊	15	16	♅22♈
4	4.51	13	15	3	15	17	♆ 5♍
5	4.55	14	27	5	15	17	♇20♋
6	4.59	15	9♋	7	15	18	♃17♌
7	5.03	16	22	9	15R	19	♄ 4♒R
8	5.07	17	5♌	11	15	20	♅22♈
9	5.11	18	18	13	15	20	♆ 5♍
10	5.15	19	1♍	16	15	21	♇21♋
11	5.18	20	15	18	15	22	♃18♌
12	5.22	21	29	20	15	23	♄ 4♒R
13	5.26	22	13♎	22	14	23	♅22♈
14	5.30	23	27	24	14	24	♆ 5♍
15	5.34	24	12♏	27	14	25	♇21♋
16	5.38	25	27	29	14	25	♃19♌
17	5.42	26	12♐	1♋	13	26	♄ 4♒R
18	5.46	27	26	3	13	27	♅22♈
19	5.50	28	11♑	5	12	28	♆ 5♍
20	5.54	29	25	7	12	28	♇21♋
21	5.58	0♋	9♒	9	11	29	♃20♌
22	6.02	1	22	11	11	0♊	♄ 3♒R
23	6.06	1	5♓	13	10	0	♅23♈
24	6.10	2	17	15	10	1	♆ 5♍
25	6.14	3	29	17	9	2	♇21♋
26	6.18	4	11♈	19	9	3	♃20♌
27	6.22	5	23	21	8	3	♄ 3♒R
28	6.25	6	5♉	23	7	4	♅23♈
29	6.29	7	17	25	7	5	♆ 5♍
30	6.33	8	29	27	6	5	♇21♋

Jul	STime	☉	☽	☿	♀	♂	Plnts
1	6.37	9♋	11♊	28♋	5♋	6♊	♃21♌
2	6.41	10	23	0♌	5	7	♄ 3♒R
3	6.45	11	6♋	2	4	8	♅23♈
4	6.49	12	19	3	4	8	♆ 6♍
5	6.53	13	2♌	5	3	9	♇21♋
6	6.57	14	15	6	3	10	♃22♌
7	7.01	15	28	8	2	10	♄ 2♒R
8	7.05	16	12♍	9	2	11	♅23♈
9	7.09	17	26	11	1	12	♆ 6♍
10	7.13	18	9♎	12	1	12	♇21♋
11	7.17	19	24	14	0	13	♃23♌
12	7.21	20	8♏	15	0	14	♄ 2♒R
13	7.25	21	22	16	0	15	♅23♈
14	7.29	22	7♐	18	29♊	15	♆ 6♍
15	7.32	22	21	19	29	16	♇21♋
16	7.36	23	5♑	20	29	17	♃24♌
17	7.40	24	19	21	29	17	♄ 2♒R
18	7.44	25	3♒	22	29	18	♅23♈
19	7.48	26	17	23	29	19	♆ 6♍
20	7.52	27	0♓	24	29D	19	♇22♋
21	7.56	28	13	25	29	20	♃25♌
22	8.00	29	25	26	29	21	♄ 1♒R
23	8.04	0♌	7♈	27	29	21	♅23♈
24	8.08	1	19	28	29	22	♆ 6♍
25	8.12	2	1♉	28	29	23	♇22♋
26	8.16	3	13	29	29	23	♃26♌
27	8.20	4	25	0♍	29	24	♄ 1♒R
28	8.24	5	7♊	0	0♋	25	♅23♈
29	8.28	6	19	0	0	25	♆ 6♍
30	8.32	7	2♋	1	0	26	♇22♋
31	8.36	8	14	1	1	27	♃27♌

Aug	STime	☉	☽	☿	♀	♂	Plnts
1	8.40	9♌	28♋	1♍	1♋	27♊	♃28♌
2	8.43	10	11♌	2	1	28	♄ 0♒R
3	8.47	11	24	2R	2	29	♅23♈
4	8.51	12	8♍	2	2	29	♆ 6♍
5	8.55	13	22	1	3	0♋	♇22♋
6	8.59	13	6♎	1	3	1	♃29♌
7	9.03	14	20	1	4	1	♄ 0♒R
8	9.07	15	5♏	1	4	2	♅23♈R
9	9.11	16	19	0	5	3	♆ 7♍
10	9.15	17	3♐	0	6	3	♇22♋
11	9.19	18	17	29♌	6	4	♃ 0♍
12	9.23	19	1♑	28	7	5	♄ 0♒R
13	9.27	20	15	28	8	5	♅23♈R
14	9.31	21	29	27	8	6	♆ 7♍
15	9.35	22	12♒	26	9	7	♇22♋
16	9.39	23	25	25	10	7	♃ 1♍
17	9.43	24	8♓	24	10	8	♄29♑R
18	9.47	25	21	23	11	9	♅23♈R
19	9.50	26	3♈	23	12	9	♆ 7♍
20	9.54	27	15	22	13	10	♇22♋
21	9.58	28	27	21	13	11	♃ 2♍
22	10.02	29	9♉	20	14	11	♄29♑R
23	10.06	0♍	21	20	15	12	♅23♈R
24	10.10	1	3♊	20	16	13	♆ 7♍
25	10.14	2	15	19	17	13	♇22♋
26	10.18	3	27	19	17	14	♃ 3♍
27	10.22	4	10♋	19D	18	15	♄29♑R
28	10.26	5	23	19	19	15	♅23♈R
29	10.30	6	6♌	19	20	16	♆ 7♍
30	10.34	7	19	20	21	16	♇23♋
31	10.38	8	3♍	20	22	17	♃ 4♍

Sep	STime	☉	☽	☿	♀	♂	Plnts
1	10.42	9♍	17♍	21♌	23♋	18♋	♃ 4♍
2	10.46	9	2♎	22	24	18	♄29♑R
3	10.50	10	16	22	25	19	♅23♈R
4	10.54	11	1♏	23	26	20	♆ 8♍
5	10.58	12	15	25	27	20	♇23♋
6	11.01	13	0♐	26	27	21	♃ 5♍
7	11.05	14	14	27	28	21	♄28♑R
8	11.09	15	28	29	29	22	♅22♈R
9	11.13	16	12♑	0♍	0♌	23	♆ 8♍
10	11.17	17	25	2	1	23	♇23♋
11	11.21	18	8♒	3	2	24	♃ 6♍
12	11.25	19	21	5	3	25	♄28♑R
13	11.29	20	4♓	7	4	25	♅22♈R
14	11.33	21	17	8	5	26	♆ 8♍
15	11.37	22	29	10	6	26	♇23♋
16	11.41	23	11♈	12	7	27	♃ 8♍
17	11.45	24	23	14	8	28	♄28♑R
18	11.49	25	5♉	16	9	28	♅22♈R
19	11.53	26	17	18	10	29	♆ 8♍
20	11.57	27	29	19	12	0♌	♇23♋
21	12.01	28	11♊	21	13	0	♃ 9♍
22	12.05	29	23	23	14	1	♄28♑R
23	12.08	0♎	5♋	25	15	1	♅22♈R
24	12.12	1	18	27	16	2	♆ 8♍
25	12.16	2	0♌	29	17	3	♇23♋
26	12.20	3	14	1♎	18	3	♃10♍
27	12.24	4	27	2	19	4	♄28♑R
28	12.28	5	11♍	4	20	4	♅22♈R
29	12.32	6	26	6	21	5	♆ 8♍
30	12.36	7	11♎	8	22	5	♇23♋

Oct	STime	☉	☽	☿	♀	♂	Plnts
1	12.40	8♎	25♎	9♎	23♌	6♌	♃11♍
2	12.44	9	10♏	11	24	7	♄28♑
3	12.48	10	25	13	26	7	♅22♈R
4	12.52	11	10♐	15	27	8	♆ 9♍
5	12.56	12	24	16	28	8	♇23♋
6	13.00	13	8♑	18	29	9	♃12♍
7	13.04	14	22	20	0♍	10	♄28♑
8	13.08	15	5♒	21	1	10	♅21♈R
9	13.12	16	18	23	2	11	♆ 9♍
10	13.15	17	1♓	25	3	11	♇23♋
11	13.19	18	14	26	5	12	♃13♍
12	13.23	19	26	28	6	12	♄28♑
13	13.27	20	8♈	29	7	13	♅21♈R
14	13.31	21	20	1♏	8	14	♆ 9♍
15	13.35	22	2♉	3	9	14	♇23♋
16	13.39	23	14	4	10	15	♃14♍
17	13.43	24	26	6	11	15	♄28♑
18	13.47	25	8♊	7	13	16	♅21♈R
19	13.51	26	19	9	14	16	♆ 9♍
20	13.55	27	2♋	10	15	17	♇23♋
21	13.59	28	14	12	16	18	♃15♍
22	14.03	29	26	13	17	18	♄28♑
23	14.07	0♏	9♌	15	18	19	♅21♈R
24	14.11	1	22	16	19	19	♆ 9♍
25	14.15	2	5♍	18	21	20	♇23♋R
26	14.19	3	19	19	22	20	♃16♍
27	14.23	4	4♎	21	23	21	♄28♑
28	14.26	5	19	22	24	21	♅21♈R
29	14.30	6	4♏	24	25	22	♆ 9♍
30	14.34	7	19	25	27	22	♇23♋
31	14.38	8	4♐	26	28	23	♃16♍

Nov	STime	☉	☽	☿	♀	♂	Plnts
1	14.42	9♏	19♐	28♏	29♍	23♌	♃17♍
2	14.46	10	4♑	29	0♎	24	♄29♑
3	14.50	11	18	1♐	1	24	♅20♈R
4	14.54	12	2♒	2	2	25	♆ 9♍
5	14.58	13	15	3	4	26	♇23♋R
6	15.02	14	28	5	5	26	♃17♍
7	15.06	15	11♓	6	6	27	♄29♑
8	15.10	16	23	7	7	27	♅20♈R
9	15.14	17	5♈	8	8	28	♆10♍
10	15.18	18	17	10	10	28	♇23♋R
11	15.22	19	29	11	11	29	♃18♍
12	15.26	20	11♉	12	12	29	♄29♑
13	15.30	21	23	13	13	0♍	♅20♈R
14	15.33	22	5♊	14	14	0	♆10♍
15	15.37	23	16	15	16	0	♇23♋R
16	15.41	24	28	16	17	1	♃19♍
17	15.45	25	11♋	17	18	1	♄ 0♒
18	15.49	26	23	18	19	2	♅20♈R
19	15.53	27	5♌	18	21	2	♆10♍
20	15.57	28	18	19	22	3	♇23♋R
21	16.01	29	1♍	20	23	3	♃20♍
22	16.05	0♐	14	20	24	4	♄ 0♒
23	16.09	1	28	20	25	4	♅20♈R
24	16.13	2	12♎	20R	27	5	♆10♍
25	16.17	3	27	20	28	5	♇23♋R
26	16.21	4	12♏	20	29	6	♃20♍
27	16.25	5	27	20	0♏	6	♄ 0♒
28	16.29	6	12♐	19	2	6	♅20♈R
29	16.33	7	28	18	3	7	♆10♍
30	16.37	8	12♑	17	4	7	♇23♋R

Dec	STime	☉	☽	☿	♀	♂	Plnts
1	16.41	9♐	27♑	16♐	5♏	8♍	♃21♍
2	16.44	10	11♒	15	6	8	♄ 1♒
3	16.48	11	24	14	8	9	♅19♈R
4	16.52	12	7♓	12	9	9	♆10♍
5	16.56	13	20	11	10	9	♇23♋R
6	17.00	14	2♈	10	11	10	♃21♍
7	17.04	15	14	8	13	10	♄ 1♒
8	17.08	16	26	7	14	11	♅19♈R
9	17.12	17	8♉	6	15	11	♆10♍
10	17.16	18	20	5	16	11	♇23♋R
11	17.20	19	1♊	5	18	12	♃22♍
12	17.24	20	13	4	19	12	♄ 2♒
13	17.28	21	25	4	20	12	♅19♈R
14	17.32	22	8♋	4D	21	13	♆10♍
15	17.36	23	20	4	22	13	♇23♋R
16	17.40	24	2♌	4	24	13	♃22♍
17	17.44	25	15	5	25	14	♄ 2♒
18	17.48	26	27	5	26	14	♅19♈R
19	17.51	27	10♍	6	27	14	♆10♍R
20	17.55	28	24	7	29	15	♇23♋R
21	17.59	29	7♎	7	0♐	15	♃22♍
22	18.03	0♑	21	8	1	15	♄ 3♒
23	18.07	1	6♏	9	2	16	♅19♈R
24	18.11	2	21	10	4	16	♆10♍R
25	18.15	3	6♐	11	5	16	♇22♋R
26	18.19	4	21	13	6	16	♃23♍
27	18.23	5	6♑	14	7	17	♄ 3♒
28	18.27	6	20	15	9	17	♅19♈
29	18.31	7	5♒	16	10	17	♆10♍R
30	18.35	8	19	17	11	17	♇22♋R
31	18.39	9	2♓	19	12	18	♃23♍

1933

Jan	STime	☉	☽	☿	♀	♂	Plnts
1	18.43	10♑	15♓	20♐	14♐	18♍	♃23♍
2	18.47	11	28	21	15	18	♄ 4♒
3	18.51	12	10♈	23	16	18	♅19♈
4	18.55	13	22	24	17	18	♆10♍R
5	18.59	14	4♉	26	19	19	♇22♋R
6	19.02	15	16	27	20	19	♃23♍
7	19.06	16	28	28	21	19	♄ 4♒
8	19.10	17	10♊	0♑	22	19	♅19♈
9	19.14	18	22	1	24	19	♆10♍R
10	19.18	20	4♋	3	25	19	♇22♋R
11	19.22	21	16	4	26	19	♃23♍R
12	19.26	22	29	6	27	20	♄ 5♒
13	19.30	23	12♌	7	29	20	♅19♈
14	19.34	24	24	9	0♑	20	♆10♍R
15	19.38	25	7♍	10	1	20	♇22♋R
16	19.42	26	21	12	2	20	♃23♍R
17	19.46	27	4♎	13	4	20	♄ 6♒
18	19.50	28	18	15	5	20	♅19♈
19	19.54	29	2♏	16	6	20	♆10♍R
20	19.58	0♒	16	18	7	20	♇22♋R
21	20.02	1	0♐	19	9	20R	♃23♍R
22	20.06	2	15	21	10	20	♄ 6♒
23	20.09	3	29	23	11	20	♅19♈
24	20.13	4	14♑	24	12	20	♆ 9♍R
25	20.17	5	29	26	14	20	♇22♋R
26	20.21	6	13♒	27	15	20	♃22♍R
27	20.25	7	27	29	16	20	♄ 7♒
28	20.29	8	10♓	1♒	17	20	♅20♈
29	20.33	9	23	2	19	20	♆ 9♍R
30	20.37	10	6♈	4	20	19	♇22♋R
31	20.41	11	18	6	21	19	♃22♍R

Feb	STime	☉	☽	☿	♀	♂	Plnts
1	20.45	12♒	0♉	7♒	22♑	19♍	♃22♍R
2	20.49	13	12	9	24	19	♄ 8♒
3	20.53	14	24	11	25	19	♅20♈
4	20.57	15	6♊	12	26	19	♆ 9♍R
5	21.01	16	18	14	27	18	♇22♋R
6	21.05	17	0♋	16	29	18	♃22♍R
7	21.09	18	12	18	0♒	18	♄ 8♒
8	21.13	19	25	19	1	18	♅20♈
9	21.16	20	8♌	21	2	18	♆ 9♍R
10	21.20	21	21	23	4	17	♇21♋R
11	21.24	22	4♍	25	5	17	♃21♍R
12	21.28	23	17	27	6	17	♄ 9♒
13	21.32	24	1♎	28	7	16	♅20♈
14	21.36	25	15	0♓	9	16	♆ 9♍R
15	21.40	26	29	2	10	16	♇21♋R
16	21.44	27	13♏	4	11	15	♃21♍R
17	21.48	28	27	6	12	15	♄ 9♒
18	21.52	29	11♐	8	14	15	♅20♈
19	21.56	0♓	25	9	15	14	♆ 9♍R
20	22.00	1	9♑	11	16	14	♇21♋R
21	22.04	2	24	13	17	14	♃20♍R
22	22.08	3	7♒	15	18	13	♄10♒
23	22.12	4	21	17	20	13	♅20♈
24	22.16	5	5♓	19	21	13	♆ 9♍R
25	22.20	6	18	20	22	12	♇21♋R
26	22.24	7	1♈	22	23	12	♃19♍R
27	22.27	8	14	24	25	11	♄10♒
28	22.31	9	26	25	26	11	♅21♈

Mar	STime	☉	☽	☿	♀	♂	Plnts
1	22.35	10♓	8♉	27♓	27♒	11♍	♃19♍R
2	22.39	11	20	28	28	10	♄11♒
3	22.43	12	2♊	0♈	0♓	10	♅21♈
4	22.47	13	14	1	1	9	♆ 8♍R
5	22.51	14	26	2	2	9	♇21♋R
6	22.55	15	8♋	3	3	9	♃18♍R
7	22.59	16	20	4	5	8	♄11♒
8	23.03	17	3♌	5	6	8	♅21♈
9	23.07	18	16	6	7	8	♆ 8♍R
10	23.11	19	29	6	8	7	♇21♋R
11	23.15	20	12♍	7	10	7	♃18♍R
12	23.19	21	26	7	11	6	♄12♒
13	23.23	22	10♎	7R	12	6	♅21♈
14	23.27	23	25	7	13	6	♆ 8♍R
15	23.31	24	9♏	7	15	5	♇21♋
16	23.34	25	24	7	16	5	♃17♍R
17	23.38	26	8♐	6	17	5	♄12♒
18	23.42	27	22	6	18	4	♅22♈
19	23.46	28	6♑	5	20	4	♆ 8♍R
20	23.50	29	20	4	21	4	♇21♋R
21	23.54	0♈	4♒	4	22	4	♃16♍R
22	23.58	1	17	3	23	3	♄13♒
23	0.02	2	1♓	2	25	3	♅22♈
24	0.06	3	14	1	26	3	♆ 8♍R
25	0.10	4	27	0	27	3	♇21♋
26	0.14	5	9♈	29♓	28	2	♃16♍R
27	0.18	6	22	28	0♈	2	♄13♒
28	0.22	7	4♉	28	1	2	♅22♈
29	0.26	8	16	27	2	2	♆ 8♍R
30	0.30	9	28	26	3	2	♇21♋
31	0.34	10	10♊	26	5	1	♃15♍R

Apr	STime	☉	☽	☿	♀	♂	Plnts
1	0.38	11♈	22♊	25♓	6♈	1♍	♃15♍R
2	0.42	12	4♋	25	7	1	♄14♒
3	0.45	13	16	25	8	1	♅22♈
4	0.49	14	28	24	10	1	♆ 8♍R
5	0.53	15	11♌	24D	11	1	♇21♋
6	0.57	16	23	24	12	1	♃15♍R
7	1.01	17	7♍	24	13	1	♄14♒
8	1.05	18	20	25	14	1	♅23♈
9	1.09	19	4♎	25	16	1	♆ 8♍R
10	1.13	20	19	25	17	1	♇21♋
11	1.17	21	4♏	26	18	1D	♃14♍R
12	1.21	22	19	26	19	1	♄14♒
13	1.25	23	3♐	27	21	1	♅23♈
14	1.29	24	18	27	22	1	♆ 7♍R
15	1.33	25	3♑	28	23	1	♇21♋
16	1.37	26	17	29	24	1	♃14♍R
17	1.41	27	1♒	0♈	26	1	♄15♒
18	1.45	28	14	0	27	1	♅23♈
19	1.49	29	28	1	28	1	♆ 7♍R
20	1.52	0♉	11♓	2	29	1	♇21♋
21	1.56	1	23	3	1♉	1	♃14♍R
22	2.00	2	6♈	4	2	1	♄15♒
23	2.04	3	18	6	3	1	♅24♈
24	2.08	4	0♉	7	4	1	♆ 7♍R
25	2.12	5	13	8	6	2	♇21♋
26	2.16	5	25	9	7	2	♃13♍R
27	2.20	6	6♊	10	8	2	♄15♒
28	2.24	7	18	12	9	2	♅24♈
29	2.28	8	0♋	13	10	2	♆ 7♍R
30	2.32	9	12	14	12	2	♇21♋

May	STime	☉	☽	☿	♀	♂	Plnts
1	2.36	10♉	24♋	16♈	13♉	3♍	♃13♍R
2	2.40	11	6♌	17	14	3	♄16♒
3	2.44	12	19	19	15	3	♅24♈
4	2.48	13	1♍	20	17	3	♆ 7♍
5	2.52	14	15	22	18	4	♇21♋
6	2.56	15	28	23	19	4	♃13♍R
7	3.00	16	13♎	25	20	4	♄16♒
8	3.03	17	27	27	22	4	♅24♈
9	3.07	18	12♏	28	23	5	♆ 7♍
10	3.11	19	27	0♉	24	5	♇21♋
11	3.15	20	13♐	2	25	5	♃13♍
12	3.19	21	28	4	26	5	♄16♒
13	3.23	22	12♑	5	28	6	♅25♈
14	3.27	23	27	7	29	6	♆ 7♍
15	3.31	24	11♒	9	0♊	6	♇21♋
16	3.35	25	24	11	1	7	♃13♍
17	3.39	26	8♓	13	3	7	♄16♒
18	3.43	27	20	15	4	7	♅25♈
19	3.47	28	3♈	17	5	8	♆ 7♍
20	3.51	29	15	19	6	8	♇21♋
21	3.55	0♊	27	21	8	8	♃13♍
22	3.59	1	9♉	23	9	9	♄16♒
23	4.03	2	21	25	10	9	♅25♈
24	4.07	3	3♊	27	11	9	♆ 7♍
25	4.10	4	15	29	12	10	♇21♋
26	4.14	4	27	2♊	14	10	♃13♍
27	4.18	5	9♋	4	15	11	♄16♒
28	4.22	6	21	6	16	11	♅25♈
29	4.26	7	3♌	8	17	11	♆ 7♍
30	4.30	8	15	10	19	12	♇22♋
31	4.34	9	28	13	20	12	♃14♍

Jun	STime	☉	☽	☿	♀	♂	Plnts
1	4.38	10♊	10♍	15♊	21♊	13♍	♃14♍
2	4.42	11	23	17	22	13	♄16♒R
3	4.46	12	7♎	19	24	13	♅26♈
4	4.50	13	21	21	25	14	♆ 7♍
5	4.54	14	6♏	23	26	14	♇22♋
6	4.58	15	21	25	27	15	♃14♍
7	5.02	16	6♐	28	28	15	♄16♒R
8	5.06	17	21	0♋	0♋	16	♅26♈
9	5.10	18	6♑	2	1	16	♆ 7♍
10	5.14	19	21	3	2	17	♇22♋
11	5.17	20	6♒	5	3	17	♃14♍
12	5.21	21	20	7	5	17	♄16♒R
13	5.25	22	4♓	9	6	18	♅26♈
14	5.29	23	17	11	7	18	♆ 7♍
15	5.33	24	0♈	13	8	19	♇22♋
16	5.37	25	12	14	9	19	♃15♍
17	5.41	26	25	16	11	20	♄16♒R
18	5.45	26	7♉	18	12	20	♅26♈
19	5.49	27	19	19	13	21	♆ 7♍
20	5.53	28	0♊	21	14	21	♇22♋
21	5.57	29	12	22	16	22	♃16♍
22	6.01	0♋	24	24	17	22	♄16♒R
23	6.05	1	6♋	25	18	23	♅26♈
24	6.09	2	18	26	19	23	♆ 7♍
25	6.13	3	0♌	28	20	24	♇22♋
26	6.17	4	12	29	22	24	♃16♍
27	6.21	5	24	0♌	23	25	♄15♒R
28	6.25	6	7♍	1	24	25	♅27♈
29	6.28	7	20	3	25	26	♆ 8♍
30	6.32	8	3♎	4	27	26	♇22♋

Jul	STime	☉	☽	☿	♀	♂	Plnts
1	6.36	9♋	16♎	5♌	28♋	27♍	♃17♍
2	6.40	10	0♏	6	29	27	♄15♒R
3	6.44	11	15	7	0♌	28	♅27♈
4	6.48	12	29	8	1	28	♆ 8♍
5	6.52	13	14♐	8	3	29	♇22♋
6	6.56	14	0♑	9	4	29	♃17♍
7	7.00	15	15	10	5	0♎	♄15♒R
8	7.04	16	0♒	10	6	1	♅27♈
9	7.08	17	14	11	8	1	♆ 8♍
10	7.12	17	28	12	9	2	♇23♋
11	7.16	18	12♓	12	10	2	♃18♍
12	7.20	19	26	12	11	3	♄14♒R
13	7.24	20	8♈	13	12	3	♅27♈
14	7.28	21	21	13	14	4	♆ 8♍
15	7.32	22	3♉	13	15	4	♇23♋
16	7.35	23	15	13R	16	5	♃19♍
17	7.39	24	27	13	17	6	♄14♒R
18	7.43	25	9♊	13	19	6	♅27♈
19	7.47	26	21	13	20	7	♆ 8♍
20	7.51	27	3♋	12	21	7	♇23♋
21	7.55	28	15	12	22	8	♃20♍
22	7.59	29	27	12	23	8	♄14♒R
23	8.03	0♌	9♌	11	25	9	♅27♈
24	8.07	1	22	11	26	10	♆ 8♍
25	8.11	2	4♍	10	27	10	♇23♋
26	8.15	3	17	9	28	11	♃21♍
27	8.19	4	0♎	9	29	11	♄13♒R
28	8.23	5	13	8	1♍	12	♅27♈
29	8.27	6	27	7	2	13	♆ 8♍
30	8.31	7	11♏	7	3	13	♇23♋
31	8.35	8	25	6	4	14	♃22♍

Aug	STime	☉	☽	☿	♀	♂	Plnts
1	8.39	8♌	9♐	5♌	6♍	14♎	♃22♍
2	8.43	9	24	4	7	15	♄13♒R
3	8.46	10	9♑	4	8	15	♅27♈
4	8.50	11	23	3	9	16	♆ 9♍
5	8.54	12	8♒	3	10	17	♇23♋
6	8.58	13	22	2	12	17	♃23♍
7	9.02	14	7♓	2	13	18	♄13♒R
8	9.06	15	20	2	14	19	♅27♈
9	9.10	16	4♈	2D	15	19	♆ 9♍
10	9.14	17	17	2	16	20	♇23♋
11	9.18	18	29	2	18	20	♃24♍
12	9.22	19	12♉	2	19	21	♄12♒R
13	9.26	20	24	3	20	22	♅27♈R
14	9.30	21	6♊	3	21	22	♆ 9♍
15	9.34	22	18	4	22	23	♇23♋
16	9.38	23	29	4	24	23	♃25♍
17	9.42	24	11♋	5	25	24	♄12♒R
18	9.46	25	23	6	26	25	♅27♈R
19	9.50	26	6♌	7	27	25	♆ 9♍
20	9.53	27	18	8	28	26	♇24♋
21	9.57	28	1♍	10	0♎	27	♃26♍
22	10.01	29	14	11	1	27	♄12♒R
23	10.05	0♍	27	12	2	28	♅27♈R
24	10.09	1	10♎	14	3	29	♆ 9♍
25	10.13	2	24	16	4	29	♇24♋
26	10.17	2	7♏	17	6	0♏	♃27♍
27	10.21	3	21	19	7	0	♄11♒R
28	10.25	4	5♐	21	8	1	♅27♈R
29	10.29	5	20	23	9	2	♆ 9♍
30	10.33	6	4♑	24	10	2	♇24♋
31	10.37	7	18	26	12	3	♃28♍

Sep	STime	☉	☽	☿	♀	♂	Plnts
1	10.41	8♍	3♒	28♌	13♎	4♏	♃28♍
2	10.45	9	17	0♍	14	4	♄11♒R
3	10.49	10	1♓	2	15	5	♅27♈R
4	10.53	11	15	4	16	6	♆10♍
5	10.57	12	28	6	18	6	♇24♋
6	11.00	13	12♈	8	19	7	♃29♍
7	11.04	14	25	10	20	8	♄11♒R
8	11.08	15	7♉	12	21	8	♅27♈R
9	11.12	16	20	14	22	9	♆10♍
10	11.16	17	2♊	16	24	10	♇24♋
11	11.20	18	14	18	25	10	♃ 0♎
12	11.24	19	26	19	26	11	♄10♒R
13	11.28	20	7♋	21	27	12	♅26♈R
14	11.32	21	19	23	28	12	♆10♍
15	11.36	22	1♌	25	0♏	13	♇24♋
16	11.40	23	14	27	1	14	♃ 1♎
17	11.44	24	26	29	2	14	♄10♒R
18	11.48	25	9♍	0♎	3	15	♅26♈R
19	11.52	26	22	2	4	16	♆10♍
20	11.56	27	6♎	4	5	16	♇24♋
21	12.00	28	20	6	7	17	♃ 2♎
22	12.04	29	4♏	7	8	18	♄10♒R
23	12.08	0♎	18	9	9	19	♅26♈R
24	12.11	1	2♐	11	10	19	♆10♍
25	12.15	2	16	12	11	20	♇24♋
26	12.19	3	1♑	14	13	21	♃ 3♎
27	12.23	4	15	16	14	21	♄10♒R
28	12.27	5	29	17	15	22	♅26♈R
29	12.31	6	13♒	19	16	23	♆11♍
30	12.35	7	27	20	17	23	♇24♋

Oct	STime	☉	☽	☿	♀	♂	Plnts
1	12.39	8♎	10♓	22♎	18♏	24♏	♃ 4♎
2	12.43	9	24	23	20	25	♄10♒R
3	12.47	10	7♈	25	21	25	♅26♈R
4	12.51	11	20	27	22	26	♆11♍
5	12.55	11	3♉	28	23	27	♇24♋
6	12.59	12	15	0♏	24	28	♃ 5♎
7	13.03	13	28	1	25	28	♄ 9♒R
8	13.07	14	10♊	2	27	29	♅26♈R
9	13.11	15	22	4	28	0♐	♆11♍
10	13.15	16	3♋	5	29	0	♇24♋
11	13.18	17	15	7	0♐	1	♃ 6♎
12	13.22	18	27	8	1	2	♄ 9♒
13	13.26	19	9♌	10	2	3	♅25♈R
14	13.30	20	22	11	4	3	♆11♍
15	13.34	21	4♍	12	5	4	♇24♋
16	13.38	22	17	14	6	5	♃ 8♎
17	13.42	23	1♎	15	7	5	♄ 9♒
18	13.46	24	15	16	8	6	♅25♈R
19	13.50	25	29	18	9	7	♆11♍
20	13.54	26	13♏	19	10	8	♇24♋
21	13.58	27	28	20	12	8	♃ 9♎
22	14.02	28	13♐	21	13	9	♄ 9♒
23	14.06	29	27	23	14	10	♅25♈R
24	14.10	0♏	12♑	24	15	11	♆11♍
25	14.14	1	26	25	16	11	♇24♋
26	14.18	2	10♒	26	17	12	♃10♎
27	14.22	3	23	27	18	13	♄10♒
28	14.26	4	7♓	28	19	13	♅25♈R
29	14.29	5	20	29	21	14	♆11♍
30	14.33	6	3♈	0♐	22	15	♇24♋R
31	14.37	7	16	1	23	16	♃11♎

Nov	STime	☉	☽	☿	♀	♂	Plnts
1	14.41	8♏	29♈	2♐	24♐	16♐	♃11♎
2	14.45	9	11♉	2	25	17	♄10♒
3	14.49	10	24	3	26	18	♅24♈R
4	14.53	11	6♊	3	27	19	♆12♍
5	14.57	12	18	4	28	19	♇24♋R
6	15.01	13	0♋	4	0♑	20	♃12♎
7	15.05	14	11	4	1	21	♄10♒
8	15.09	15	23	4R	2	22	♅24♈R
9	15.13	16	5♌	4	3	22	♆12♍
10	15.17	17	17	4	4	23	♇24♋
11	15.21	18	29	4	5	24	♃13♎
12	15.25	19	12♍	3	6	25	♄10♒
13	15.29	20	25	2	7	25	♅24♈R
14	15.33	21	9♎	1	8	26	♆12♍
15	15.36	22	23	0	9	27	♇24♋R
16	15.40	23	7♏	29♏	10	28	♃14♎
17	15.44	24	22	28	11	28	♄10♒
18	15.48	25	7♐	27	12	29	♅24♈R
19	15.52	26	22	25	13	0♑	♆12♍
20	15.56	27	7♑	24	15	1	♇24♋R
21	16.00	28	22	23	16	1	♃15♎
22	16.04	29	6♒	22	17	2	♄11♒
23	16.08	0♐	20	21	18	3	♅24♈R
24	16.12	1	4♓	20	19	4	♆12♍
25	16.16	2	17	19	20	4	♇24♋R
26	16.20	3	0♈	19	21	5	♃16♎
27	16.24	5	13	18	22	6	♄11♒
28	16.28	6	25	18D	23	7	♅24♈R
29	16.32	7	8♉	18	24	7	♆12♍
30	16.36	8	20	19	25	8	♇24♋R

Dec	STime	☉	☽	☿	♀	♂	Plnts
1	16.40	9♐	2♊	19♏	26♑	9♑	♃17♎
2	16.44	10	14	20	27	10	♄11♒
3	16.47	11	26	20	28	11	♅24♈R
4	16.51	12	8♋	21	29	11	♆12♍
5	16.55	13	20	22	29	12	♇24♋R
6	16.59	14	2♌	23	0♒	13	♃17♎
7	17.03	15	14	24	1	14	♄12♒
8	17.07	16	26	25	2	14	♅23♈R
9	17.11	17	8♍	26	3	15	♆12♍
10	17.15	18	20	28	4	16	♇24♋R
11	17.19	19	3♎	29	5	17	♃18♎
12	17.23	20	17	0♐	6	17	♄12♒
13	17.27	21	1♏	1	7	18	♅23♈R
14	17.31	22	15	3	7	19	♆12♍
15	17.35	23	0♐	4	8	20	♇24♋R
16	17.39	24	15	6	9	21	♃19♎
17	17.43	25	0♑	7	10	21	♄13♒
18	17.47	26	15	8	11	22	♅23♈R
19	17.51	27	0♒	10	11	23	♆12♍
20	17.54	28	15	11	12	24	♇24♋R
21	17.58	29	0♓	13	13	24	♃20♎
22	18.02	0♑	13	14	14	25	♄13♒
23	18.06	1	27	16	14	26	♅23♈
24	18.10	2	10♈	17	15	27	♆12♍
25	18.14	3	23	19	16	28	♇24♋R
26	18.18	4	5♉	20	16	28	♃20♎
27	18.22	5	17	22	17	29	♄14♒
28	18.26	6	29	23	18	0♒	♅23♈
29	18.30	7	11♊	25	18	1	♆12♍R
30	18.34	8	23	26	19	2	♇24♋R
31	18.38	9	5♋	28	19	2	♃21♎

Jan	STime	☉	☽	☿	♀	♂	Plnts
1	18.42	10♑	17♋	29♐	20♒	3♒	♃21♎
2	18.46	11	29	1♑	20	4	♄14♒
3	18.50	12	11♌	2	21	5	♅23♈
4	18.54	13	23	4	21	5	♆12♍R
5	18.58	14	5♍	5	21	6	♇24♋R
6	19.01	15	17	7	22	7	♃21♎
7	19.05	16	29	9	22	8	♄15♒
8	19.09	17	12♎	10	22	9	♅23♈
9	19.13	18	26	12	23	9	♆12♍R
10	19.17	19	9♏	13	23	10	♇23♋R
11	19.21	20	23	15	23	11	♃22♎
12	19.25	21	8♐	17	23	12	♄15♒
13	19.29	22	23	18	23	13	♅23♈
14	19.33	23	8♑	20	23	13	♆12♍R
15	19.37	24	23	21	23R	14	♇23♋R
16	19.41	25	9♒	23	23	15	♃22♎
17	19.45	26	23	25	23	16	♄16♒
18	19.49	27	8♓	26	23	17	♅23♈
19	19.53	28	22	28	23	17	♆12♍R
20	19.57	29	6♈	0♒	23	18	♇23♋R
21	20.01	0♒	19	1	23	19	♃22♎
22	20.05	1	2♉	3	22	20	♄17♒
23	20.09	3	14	5	22	20	♅23♈
24	20.12	4	26	7	22	21	♆12♍R
25	20.16	5	8♊	8	21	22	♇23♋R
26	20.20	6	20	10	21	23	♃23♎
27	20.24	7	2♋	12	20	24	♄17♒
28	20.28	8	14	13	20	24	♅23♈
29	20.32	9	26	15	19	25	♆12♍R
30	20.36	10	8♌	17	19	26	♇23♋R
31	20.40	11	20	19	18	27	♃23♎

Feb	STime	☉	☽	☿	♀	♂	Plnts
1	20.44	12♒	2♍	20♒	18♒	28♒	♃23♎
2	20.48	13	14	22	17	28	♄18♒
3	20.52	14	27	24	16	29	♅24♈
4	20.56	15	9♎	26	16	0♓	♆11♍R
5	21.00	16	22	28	15	1	♇23♋R
6	21.04	17	6♏	29	15	2	♃23♎
7	21.08	18	19	1♓	14	2	♄18♒
8	21.12	19	3♐	3	13	3	♅24♈
9	21.16	20	17	4	13	4	♆11♍R
10	21.19	21	2♑	6	12	5	♇23♋R
11	21.23	22	17	8	12	5	♃23♎R
12	21.27	23	2♒	9	11	6	♄19♒
13	21.31	24	16	11	11	7	♅24♈
14	21.35	25	1♓	12	10	8	♆11♍R
15	21.39	26	16	14	10	9	♇23♋R
16	21.43	27	0♈	15	9	9	♃23♎R
17	21.47	28	14	16	9	10	♄20♒
18	21.51	29	27	17	9	11	♅24♈
19	21.55	0♓	10♉	18	8	12	♆11♍R
20	21.59	1	22	19	8	13	♇23♋R
21	22.03	2	5♊	19	8	13	♃23♎R
22	22.07	3	17	20	8	14	♄20♒
23	22.11	4	29	20	8	15	♅24♈
24	22.15	5	10♋	20R	8	16	♆11♍R
25	22.19	6	22	20	8D	17	♇23♋R
26	22.23	7	4♌	20	8	17	♃22♎R
27	22.27	8	16	20	8	18	♄21♒
28	22.30	9	28	19	8	19	♅25♈

Mar	STime	☉	☽	☿	♀	♂	Plnts
1	22.34	10♓	11♍	18♓	8♒	20♓	♃22♎R
2	22.38	11	23	18	8	20	♄21♒
3	22.42	12	6♎	17	8	21	♅25♈
4	22.46	13	19	16	9	22	♆11♍R
5	22.50	14	3♏	15	9	23	♇22♋R
6	22.54	15	16	14	9	24	♃22♎R
7	22.58	16	0♐	13	9	24	♄22♒
8	23.02	17	14	12	10	25	♅25♈
9	23.06	18	28	11	10	26	♆11♍R
10	23.10	19	12♑	10	11	27	♇22♋R
11	23.14	20	26	9	11	27	♃21♎R
12	23.18	21	11♒	8	12	28	♄22♒
13	23.22	22	25	8	12	29	♅25♈
14	23.26	23	10♓	7	13	0♈	♆10♍R
15	23.30	24	24	7	13	1	♇22♋R
16	23.34	25	8♈	6	14	1	♃21♎R
17	23.37	26	21	6	14	2	♄23♒
18	23.41	27	5♉	6	15	3	♅25♈
19	23.45	28	18	6D	16	4	♆10♍R
20	23.49	29	0♊	6	16	4	♇22♋
21	23.53	0♈	13	6	17	5	♃20♎R
22	23.57	1	25	6	18	6	♄23♒
23	0.01	2	7♋	7	18	7	♅26♈
24	0.05	3	18	7	19	8	♆10♍R
25	0.09	4	0♌	8	20	8	♇22♋
26	0.13	5	12	8	21	9	♃20♎R
27	0.17	6	24	9	21	10	♄24♒
28	0.21	7	7♍	10	22	11	♅26♈
29	0.25	8	19	10	23	11	♆10♍R
30	0.29	9	2♎	11	24	12	♇22♋R
31	0.33	10	15	12	25	13	♃19♎R

Apr	STime	☉	☽	☿	♀	♂	Plnts
1	0.37	11♈	29♎	13♓	25♒	14♈	♃19♎R
2	0.41	12	13♏	14	26	14	♄24♒
3	0.45	13	26	15	27	15	♅26♈
4	0.48	14	10♐	16	28	16	♆10♍R
5	0.52	15	25	17	29	17	♇22♋
6	0.56	16	9♑	18	0♓	17	♃18♎R
7	1.00	17	23	19	1	18	♄25♒
8	1.04	18	7♒	21	2	19	♅27♈
9	1.08	19	21	22	3	20	♆10♍R
10	1.12	20	5♓	23	3	21	♇22♋
11	1.16	21	19	25	4	21	♃18♎R
12	1.20	22	3♈	26	5	22	♄25♒
13	1.24	23	16	27	6	23	♅27♈
14	1.28	24	0♉	29	7	24	♆10♍R
15	1.32	25	13	0♈	8	24	♇22♋
16	1.36	26	26	2	9	25	♃17♎R
17	1.40	26	8♊	3	10	26	♄26♒
18	1.44	27	20	5	11	27	♅27♈
19	1.48	28	2♋	6	12	27	♆10♍R
20	1.52	29	14	8	13	28	♇22♋
21	1.55	0♉	26	9	14	29	♃16♎R
22	1.59	1	8♌	11	15	0♉	♄26♒
23	2.03	2	20	13	16	0	♅27♈
24	2.07	3	2♍	14	17	1	♆ 9♍R
25	2.11	4	14	16	18	2	♇22♋
26	2.15	5	27	18	19	3	♃16♎R
27	2.19	6	10♎	20	20	3	♄26♒
28	2.23	7	24	22	21	4	♅28♈
29	2.27	8	8♏	23	22	5	♆ 9♍R
30	2.31	9	22	25	23	6	♇22♋

May	STime	☉	☽	☿	♀	♂	Plnts
1	2.35	10♉	6♐	27♈	25♓	6♉	♃15♎R
2	2.39	11	21	29	26	7	♄27♒
3	2.43	12	5♑	1♉	27	8	♅28♈
4	2.47	13	20	3	28	9	♆ 9♍R
5	2.51	14	4♒	5	29	9	♇22♋
6	2.55	15	18	7	0♈	10	♃15♎R
7	2.59	16	2♓	9	1	11	♄27♒
8	3.02	17	15	11	2	11	♅28♈
9	3.06	18	29	13	3	12	♆ 9♍R
10	3.10	19	12♈	16	4	13	♇22♋
11	3.14	20	26	18	5	14	♃14♎R
12	3.18	21	9♉	20	6	14	♄27♒
13	3.22	22	21	22	7	15	♅29♈
14	3.26	23	4♊	24	9	16	♆ 9♍
15	3.30	24	16	26	10	17	♇23♋
16	3.34	25	29	29	11	17	♃14♎R
17	3.38	26	11♋	1♊	12	18	♄27♒
18	3.42	27	22	3	13	19	♅29♈
19	3.46	28	4♌	5	14	19	♆ 9♍
20	3.50	28	16	7	15	20	♇23♋
21	3.54	29	28	9	16	21	♃14♎R
22	3.58	0♊	10♍	11	17	22	♄28♒
23	4.02	1	22	13	19	22	♅29♈
24	4.06	2	5♎	15	20	23	♆ 9♍
25	4.10	3	18	17	21	24	♇23♋
26	4.13	4	2♏	19	22	25	♃13♎R
27	4.17	5	16	21	23	25	♄28♒
28	4.21	6	1♐	23	24	26	♅29♈
29	4.25	7	15	25	25	27	♆ 9♍
30	4.29	8	0♑	27	26	27	♇23♋
31	4.33	9	15	28	28	28	♃13♎R

Jun	STime	☉	☽	☿	♀	♂	Plnts
1	4.37	10♊	0♒	0♋	29♈	29♉	♃13♎R
2	4.41	11	14	2	0♉	0♊	♄28♒
3	4.45	12	28	3	1	0	♅ 0♉
4	4.49	13	12♓	5	2	1	♆ 9♍
5	4.53	14	26	6	3	2	♇23♋
6	4.57	15	9♈	7	4	2	♃13♎R
7	5.01	16	23	9	5	3	♄28♒
8	5.05	17	5♉	10	7	4	♅ 0♉
9	5.09	18	18	11	8	5	♆ 9♍
10	5.13	19	1♊	13	9	5	♇23♋
11	5.17	20	13	14	10	6	♃13♎
12	5.20	21	25	15	11	7	♄28♒
13	5.24	21	7♋	16	12	7	♅ 0♉
14	5.28	22	19	17	14	8	♆ 9♍
15	5.32	23	1♌	18	15	9	♇23♋
16	5.36	24	12	19	16	9	♃13♎
17	5.40	25	24	19	17	10	♄28♒R
18	5.44	26	6♍	20	18	11	♅ 0♉
19	5.48	27	18	21	19	12	♆10♍
20	5.52	28	1♎	21	20	12	♇23♋
21	5.56	29	13	22	22	13	♃13♎
22	6.00	0♋	27	22	23	14	♄28♒R
23	6.04	1	10♏	23	24	14	♅ 0♉
24	6.08	2	24	23	25	15	♆10♍
25	6.12	3	9♐	23	26	16	♇23♋
26	6.16	4	24	24	27	16	♃13♎
27	6.20	5	9♑	24	29	17	♄28♒R
28	6.24	6	24	24R	0♊	18	♅ 1♉
29	6.28	7	9♒	24	1	19	♆10♍
30	6.31	8	24	24	2	19	♇24♋

Jul	STime	☉	☽	☿	♀	♂	Plnts
1	6.35	9♋	8♓	23♋	3♊	20♊	♃14♎
2	6.39	10	22	23	5	21	♄27♒R
3	6.43	11	6♈	23	6	21	♅ 1♉
4	6.47	12	19	22	7	22	♆10♍
5	6.51	12	3♉	22	8	23	♇24♋
6	6.55	13	15	21	9	23	♃14♎
7	6.59	14	28	21	10	24	♄27♒R
8	7.03	15	10♊	20	12	25	♅ 1♉
9	7.07	16	22	19	13	25	♆10♍
10	7.11	17	4♋	19	14	26	♇24♋
11	7.15	18	16	18	15	27	♃14♎
12	7.19	19	28	18	16	27	♄27♒R
13	7.23	20	9♌	17	17	28	♅ 1♉
14	7.27	21	21	16	19	29	♆10♍
15	7.31	22	3♍	16	20	29	♇24♋
16	7.35	23	15	15	21	0♋	♃15♎
17	7.38	24	27	15	22	1	♄27♒R
18	7.42	25	10♎	15	23	1	♅ 1♉
19	7.46	26	22	14	25	2	♆10♍
20	7.50	27	5♏	14	26	3	♇24♋
21	7.54	28	19	14	27	3	♃15♎
22	7.58	29	3♐	14D	28	4	♄26♒R
23	8.02	0♌	17	14	29	5	♅ 1♉
24	8.06	1	2♑	14	1♋	5	♆10♍
25	8.10	2	17	14	2	6	♇24♋
26	8.14	3	2♒	15	3	7	♃16♎
27	8.18	3	18	15	4	7	♄26♒R
28	8.22	4	3♓	16	5	8	♅ 1♉
29	8.26	5	17	16	7	9	♆10♍
30	8.30	6	2♈	17	8	9	♇24♋
31	8.34	7	15	18	9	10	♃17♎

Aug	STime	☉	☽	☿	♀	♂	Plnts
1	8.38	8♌	29♈	19♋	10♋	11♋	♃17♎
2	8.42	9	12♉	20	11	11	♄26♒R
3	8.45	10	25	21	13	12	♅ 1♉
4	8.49	11	7♊	22	14	13	♆11♍
5	8.53	12	19	24	15	13	♇25♋
6	8.57	13	1♋	25	16	14	♃17♎
7	9.01	14	13	26	17	15	♄25♒R
8	9.05	15	25	28	19	15	♅ 1♉R
9	9.09	16	7♌	0♌	20	16	♆11♍
10	9.13	17	18	1	21	17	♇25♋
11	9.17	18	0♍	3	22	17	♃18♎
12	9.21	19	12	5	23	18	♄25♒R
13	9.25	20	24	7	25	19	♅ 1♉R
14	9.29	21	7♎	9	26	19	♆11♍
15	9.33	22	19	11	27	20	♇25♋
16	9.37	23	2♏	12	28	21	♃19♎
17	9.41	24	15	14	0♌	21	♄25♒R
18	9.45	25	28	16	1	22	♅ 1♉R
19	9.49	26	12♐	18	2	23	♆11♍
20	9.53	26	26	20	3	23	♇25♋
21	9.56	27	11♑	23	4	24	♃20♎
22	10.00	28	26	25	6	25	♄24♒R
23	10.04	29	11♒	27	7	25	♅ 1♉R
24	10.08	0♍	26	29	8	26	♆11♍
25	10.12	1	11♓	1♍	9	26	♇25♋
26	10.16	2	26	2	10	27	♃21♎
27	10.20	3	10♈	4	12	28	♄24♒R
28	10.24	4	24	6	13	28	♅ 1♉R
29	10.28	5	8♉	8	14	29	♆12♍
30	10.32	6	21	10	15	0♌	♇25♋
31	10.36	7	3♊	12	17	0	♃22♎

Sep	STime	☉	☽	☿	♀	♂	Plnts
1	10.40	8♍	16♊	14♍	18♌	1♌	♃22♎
2	10.44	9	28	16	19	2	♄23♒R
3	10.48	10	10♋	18	20	2	♅ 1♉R
4	10.52	11	22	19	22	3	♆12♍
5	10.56	12	3♌	21	23	3	♇25♋
6	11.00	13	15	23	24	4	♃23♎
7	11.03	14	27	25	25	5	♄23♒R
8	11.07	15	9♍	26	26	5	♅ 1♉R
9	11.11	16	21	28	28	6	♆12♍
10	11.15	17	4♎	0♎	29	7	♇25♋
11	11.19	18	16	1	0♍	7	♃24♎
12	11.23	19	29	3	1	8	♄23♒R
13	11.27	20	12♏	5	3	9	♅ 1♉R
14	11.31	21	25	6	4	9	♆12♍
15	11.35	22	9♐	8	5	10	♇25♋
16	11.39	23	22	9	6	10	♃25♎
17	11.43	24	6♑	11	8	11	♄22♒R
18	11.47	25	21	13	9	12	♅ 0♉R
19	11.51	26	5♒	14	10	12	♆12♍
20	11.55	27	20	16	11	13	♇25♋
21	11.59	28	4♓	17	13	13	♃26♎
22	12.03	28	19	18	14	14	♄22♒R
23	12.07	29	4♈	20	15	15	♅ 0♉R
24	12.11	0♎	18	21	16	15	♆13♍
25	12.14	1	2♉	23	17	16	♇26♋
26	12.18	2	16	24	19	17	♃27♎
27	12.22	3	29	26	20	17	♄22♒R
28	12.26	4	12♊	27	21	18	♅ 0♉R
29	12.30	5	24	28	22	18	♆13♍
30	12.34	6	6♋	0♏	24	19	♇26♋

Oct	STime	☉	☽	☿	♀	♂	Plnts
1	12.38	7♎	18♋	1♏	25♍	20♌	♃28♎
2	12.42	8	0♌	2	26	20	♄22♒R
3	12.46	9	12	3	27	21	♅ 0♉R
4	12.50	10	23	5	29	21	♆13♍
5	12.54	11	5♍	6	0♎	22	♇26♋
6	12.58	12	18	7	1	23	♃29♎
7	13.02	13	0♎	8	2	23	♄22♒R
8	13.06	14	13	9	4	24	♅ 0♉R
9	13.10	15	26	10	5	24	♆13♍
10	13.14	16	9♏	11	6	25	♇26♋
11	13.18	17	22	12	7	26	♃ 0♏
12	13.21	18	6♐	13	9	26	♄21♒R
13	13.25	19	19	14	10	27	♅ 0♉R
14	13.29	20	3♑	15	11	27	♆13♍
15	13.33	21	17	16	12	28	♇26♋
16	13.37	22	1♒	16	14	29	♃ 1♏
17	13.41	23	15	17	15	29	♄21♒R
18	13.45	24	0♓	17	16	0♍	♅29♈R
19	13.49	25	14	18	17	0	♆13♍
20	13.53	26	28	18	19	1	♇26♋
21	13.57	27	12♈	18	20	2	♃ 2♏
22	14.01	28	26	19R	21	2	♄21♒
23	14.05	29	10♉	19	22	3	♅29♈R
24	14.09	0♏	24	18	24	3	♆13♍
25	14.13	1	7♊	18	25	4	♇26♋
26	14.17	2	19	18	26	5	♃ 3♏
27	14.21	3	2♋	17	27	5	♄21♒
28	14.25	4	14	16	29	6	♅29♈R
29	14.29	5	26	15	0♏	6	♆14♍
30	14.32	6	8♌	14	1	7	♇26♋
31	14.36	7	20	13	2	7	♃ 4♏

Nov	STime	☉	☽	☿	♀	♂	Plnts
1	14.40	8♏	1♍	12♏	4♏	8♍	♃ 4♏
2	14.44	9	13	11	5	9	♄21♒
3	14.48	10	26	9	6	9	♅29♈R
4	14.52	11	8♎	8	7	10	♆14♍
5	14.56	12	21	7	9	10	♇26♋
6	15.00	13	4♏	6	10	11	♃ 5♏
7	15.04	14	18	5	11	11	♄21♒
8	15.08	15	2♐	4	12	12	♅29♈R
9	15.12	16	16	3	14	13	♆14♍
10	15.16	17	0♑	3	15	13	♇26♋R
11	15.20	18	14	3	16	14	♃ 7♏
12	15.24	19	28	3D	18	14	♄21♒
13	15.28	20	12♒	3	19	15	♅28♈R
14	15.32	21	26	3	20	15	♆14♍
15	15.36	22	10♓	4	21	16	♇26♋R
16	15.39	23	24	4	23	17	♃ 8♏
17	15.43	24	8♈	5	24	17	♄22♒
18	15.47	25	22	6	25	18	♅28♈R
19	15.51	26	5♉	7	26	18	♆14♍
20	15.55	27	19	8	28	19	♇26♋R
21	15.59	28	2♊	9	29	19	♃ 9♏
22	16.03	29	15	10	0♐	20	♄22♒
23	16.07	0♐	27	11	1	20	♅28♈R
24	16.11	1	10♋	13	3	21	♆14♍
25	16.15	2	22	14	4	21	♇26♋R
26	16.19	3	4♌	15	5	22	♃10♏
27	16.23	4	15	17	6	22	♄22♒
28	16.27	5	27	18	8	23	♅28♈R
29	16.31	6	9♍	20	9	24	♆14♍
30	16.35	7	21	21	10	24	♇26♋R

Dec	STime	☉	☽	☿	♀	♂	Plnts
1	16.39	8♐	3♎	23♏	11♐	25♍	♃11♏
2	16.43	9	16	24	13	25	♄22♒
3	16.46	10	29	25	14	26	♅28♈R
4	16.50	11	12♏	27	15	26	♆14♍
5	16.54	12	26	29	16	27	♇25♋R
6	16.58	13	10♐	0♐	18	27	♃12♏
7	17.02	14	25	2	19	28	♄23♒
8	17.06	15	9♑	3	20	28	♅28♈R
9	17.10	16	24	5	21	29	♆14♍
10	17.14	17	8♒	6	23	29	♇25♋R
11	17.18	18	23	8	24	0♎	♃13♏
12	17.22	19	7♓	9	25	0	♄23♒
13	17.26	20	21	11	26	1	♅27♈R
14	17.30	22	5♈	12	28	1	♆14♍
15	17.34	23	19	14	29	2	♇25♋R
16	17.38	24	2♉	15	0♑	2	♃14♏
17	17.42	25	15	17	1	3	♄23♒
18	17.46	26	28	19	3	3	♅27♈R
19	17.50	27	11♊	20	4	4	♆14♍
20	17.54	28	23	22	5	4	♇25♋R
21	17.57	29	6♋	23	7	5	♃15♏
22	18.01	0♑	18	25	8	5	♄24♒
23	18.05	1	0♌	26	9	6	♅27♈R
24	18.09	2	12	28	10	6	♆14♍
25	18.13	3	24	29	12	6	♇25♋R
26	18.17	4	5♍	1♑	13	7	♃16♏
27	18.21	5	17	3	14	7	♄24♒
28	18.25	6	29	4	15	8	♅27♈R
29	18.29	7	11♎	6	17	8	♆14♍
30	18.33	8	24	7	18	9	♇25♋R
31	18.37	9	7♏	9	19	9	♃16♏

1935

Jan	STime	☉	☽	☿	♀	♂	Plnts
1	18.41	10♑	20♏	11♑	20♑	10♎	♃17♏
2	18.45	11	4♐	12	22	10	♄25♒
3	18.49	12	18	14	23	10	♅27♈
4	18.53	13	3♑	16	24	11	♆14♍R
5	18.57	14	18	17	25	11	♇25♋R
6	19.01	15	3♒	19	27	12	♃17♏
7	19.04	16	18	20	28	12	♄25♒
8	19.08	17	3♓	22	29	13	♅27♈
9	19.12	18	17	24	0♒	13	♆14♍R
10	19.16	19	1♈	25	2	13	♇25♋R
11	19.20	20	15	27	3	14	♃18♏
12	19.24	21	29	29	4	14	♄26♒
13	19.28	22	12♉	0♒	5	15	♅27♈
14	19.32	23	25	2	7	15	♆14♍R
15	19.36	24	8♊	4	8	15	♇25♋R
16	19.40	25	20	5	9	16	♃19♏
17	19.44	26	2♋	7	10	16	♄26♒
18	19.48	27	15	9	12	16	♅27♈
19	19.52	28	26	11	13	17	♆14♍R
20	19.56	29	8♌	12	14	17	♇25♋R
21	20.00	0♒	20	14	15	17	♃20♏
22	20.04	1	2♍	16	17	18	♄27♒
23	20.08	2	14	17	18	18	♅27♈
24	20.12	3	26	19	19	18	♆14♍R
25	20.15	4	8♎	20	20	19	♇24♋R
26	20.19	5	20	22	22	19	♃20♏
27	20.23	6	2♏	23	23	19	♄28♒
28	20.27	7	15	25	24	20	♅27♈
29	20.31	8	28	26	25	20	♆14♍R
30	20.35	9	12♐	27	27	20	♇24♋R
31	20.39	10	26	29	28	20	♃21♏

Feb	STime	☉	☽	☿	♀	♂	Plnts
1	20.43	11♒	11♑	0♓	29♒	21♎	♃21♏
2	20.47	12	26	1	0♓	21	♄28♒
3	20.51	13	11♒	2	2	21	♅28♈
4	20.55	14	26	2	3	21	♆14♍R
5	20.59	15	11♓	3	4	22	♇24♋R
6	21.03	16	26	3	5	22	♃21♏
7	21.07	17	11♈	4	7	22	♄29♒
8	21.11	19	25	4R	8	22	♅28♈
9	21.15	20	9♉	3	9	22	♆14♍R
10	21.19	21	22	3	10	23	♇24♋R
11	21.22	22	5♊	3	12	23	♃22♏
12	21.26	23	17	2	13	23	♄29♒
13	21.30	24	29	1	14	23	♅28♈
14	21.34	25	12♋	0	15	23	♆13♍R
15	21.38	26	23	29♒	17	23	♇24♋R
16	21.42	27	5♌	28	18	24	♃22♏
17	21.46	28	17	27	19	24	♄ 0♓
18	21.50	29	29	26	20	24	♅28♈
19	21.54	0♓	11♍	25	22	24	♆13♍R
20	21.58	1	23	24	23	24	♇24♋R
21	22.02	2	5♎	23	24	24	♃23♏
22	22.06	3	17	22	25	24	♄ 1♓
23	22.10	4	29	21	27	24	♅28♈
24	22.14	5	12♏	20	28	24	♆13♍R
25	22.18	6	24	20	29	24	♇24♋R
26	22.22	7	8♐	19	0♈	24	♃23♏
27	22.26	8	21	19	2	24R	♄ 1♓
28	22.29	9	5♑	19	3	24	♅28♈

Mar	STime	☉	☽	☿	♀	♂	Plnts
1	22.33	10♓	19♑	19♒	4♈	24♎	♃23♏
2	22.37	11	4♒	18D	5	24	♄ 2♓
3	22.41	12	19	19	6	24	♅28♈
4	22.45	13	4♓	19	8	24	♆13♍R
5	22.49	14	19	19	9	24	♇24♋R
6	22.53	15	4♈	19	10	24	♃23♏
7	22.57	16	19	20	11	24	♄ 2♓
8	23.01	17	3♉	20	13	24	♅29♈
9	23.05	18	17	21	14	24	♆13♍R
10	23.09	19	1♊	22	15	24	♇24♋R
11	23.13	20	14	23	16	23	♃23♏R
12	23.17	21	26	23	18	23	♄ 3♓
13	23.21	22	8♋	24	19	23	♅29♈
14	23.25	23	20	25	20	23	♆13♍R
15	23.29	24	2♌	26	21	23	♇24♋R
16	23.33	25	14	27	22	22	♃23♏R
17	23.37	26	26	28	24	22	♄ 3♓
18	23.40	27	8♍	29	25	22	♅29♈
19	23.44	28	20	0♓	26	22	♆13♍R
20	23.48	29	2♎	2	27	21	♇24♋R
21	23.52	0♈	14	3	29	21	♃23♏R
22	23.56	1	26	4	0♉	21	♄ 4♓
23	0.00	2	9♏	5	1	21	♅29♈
24	0.04	3	21	7	2	20	♆12♍R
25	0.08	4	4♐	8	3	20	♇24♋R
26	0.12	5	17	9	5	20	♃23♏R
27	0.16	6	1♑	11	6	19	♄ 5♓
28	0.20	7	15	12	7	19	♅ 0♉
29	0.24	8	29	13	8	19	♆12♍R
30	0.28	9	13♒	15	9	18	♇24♋R
31	0.32	10	28	16	11	18	♃22♏R

Apr	STime	☉	☽	☿	♀	♂	Plnts
1	0.36	11♈	13♓	18♓	12♉	18♎	♃22♏R
2	0.40	12	28	19	13	17	♄ 5♓
3	0.44	13	12♈	21	14	17	♅ 0♉
4	0.47	13	27	23	16	17	♆12♍R
5	0.51	14	11♉	24	17	16	♇24♋R
6	0.55	15	25	26	18	16	♃22♏R
7	0.59	16	9♊	28	19	15	♄ 6♓
8	1.03	17	22	29	20	15	♅ 0♉
9	1.07	18	4♋	1♈	22	15	♆12♍R
10	1.11	19	17	3	23	14	♇24♋
11	1.15	20	29	4	24	14	♃21♏R
12	1.19	21	11♌	6	25	13	♄ 6♓
13	1.23	22	22	8	26	13	♅ 1♉
14	1.27	23	4♍	10	28	13	♆12♍R
15	1.31	24	16	12	29	12	♇24♋
16	1.35	25	28	14	0♊	12	♃21♏R
17	1.39	26	10♎	16	1	12	♄ 7♓
18	1.43	27	23	17	2	11	♅ 1♉
19	1.47	28	5♏	19	3	11	♆12♍R
20	1.51	29	18	21	5	11	♇24♋
21	1.55	0♉	1♐	23	6	10	♃20♏R
22	1.58	1	14	26	7	10	♄ 7♓
23	2.02	2	28	28	8	10	♅ 1♉
24	2.06	3	11♑	0♉	9	9	♆12♍R
25	2.10	4	25	2	11	9	♇24♋
26	2.14	5	9♒	4	12	9	♃20♏R
27	2.18	6	23	6	13	8	♄ 8♓
28	2.22	7	8♓	8	14	8	♅ 1♉
29	2.26	8	22	10	15	8	♆12♍R
30	2.30	9	7♈	12	16	8	♇24♋

May	STime	☉	☽	☿	♀	♂	Plnts
1	2.34	10♉	21♈	15♉	18♊	8♎	♃19♏R
2	2.38	11	6♉	17	19	7	♄ 8♓
3	2.42	12	20	19	20	7	♅ 2♉
4	2.46	13	3♊	21	21	7	♆12♍R
5	2.50	14	17	23	22	7	♇24♋
6	2.54	15	0♋	25	23	7	♃19♏R
7	2.58	16	12	27	25	6	♄ 8♓
8	3.02	17	25	29	26	6	♅ 2♉
9	3.05	18	7♌	1♊	27	6	♆12♍R
10	3.09	19	19	3	28	6	♇24♋
11	3.13	20	0♍	5	29	6	♃18♏R
12	3.17	21	12	7	0♋	6	♄ 9♓
13	3.21	21	24	9	2	6	♅ 2♉
14	3.25	22	6♎	10	3	6	♆12♍R
15	3.29	23	19	12	4	6	♇24♋
16	3.33	24	1♏	14	5	6	♃17♏R
17	3.37	25	14	15	6	6D	♄ 9♓
18	3.41	26	27	17	7	6	♅ 3♉
19	3.45	27	11♐	18	8	6	♆12♍
20	3.49	28	24	20	9	6	♇24♋
21	3.53	29	8♑	21	11	6	♃17♏R
22	3.57	0♊	22	22	12	6	♄ 9♓
23	4.01	1	6♒	24	13	6	♅ 3♉
24	4.05	2	20	25	14	6	♆11♍
25	4.09	3	4♓	26	15	6	♇24♋
26	4.13	4	18	27	16	6	♃16♏R
27	4.16	5	3♈	28	17	6	♄ 9♓
28	4.20	6	17	29	18	6	♅ 3♉
29	4.24	7	1♉	29	20	7	♆12♍
30	4.28	8	15	0♋	21	7	♇24♋
31	4.32	9	28	1	22	7	♃16♏R

Jun	STime	☉	☽	☿	♀	♂	Plnts
1	4.36	10♊	12♊	2♋	23♋	7♎	♃15♏R
2	4.40	11	25	2	24	7	♄10♓
3	4.44	12	8♋	3	25	7	♅ 3♉
4	4.48	13	20	3	26	8	♆12♍
5	4.52	14	3♌	3	27	8	♇24♋
6	4.56	15	15	4	28	8	♃15♏R
7	5.00	16	26	4	29	8	♄10♓
8	5.04	16	8♍	4	0♌	8	♅ 4♉
9	5.08	17	20	4R	2	9	♆12♍
10	5.12	18	2♎	4	3	9	♇24♋
11	5.16	19	14	4	4	9	♃14♏R
12	5.20	20	27	3	5	10	♄10♓
13	5.23	21	9♏	3	6	10	♅ 4♉
14	5.27	22	22	3	7	10	♆12♍
15	5.31	23	6♐	2	8	10	♇24♋
16	5.35	24	20	2	9	11	♃14♏R
17	5.39	25	4♑	1	10	11	♄10♓
18	5.43	26	18	1	11	11	♅ 4♉
19	5.47	27	2♒	0	12	12	♆12♍
20	5.51	28	17	0	13	12	♇25♋
21	5.55	29	1♓	29♊	14	12	♃14♏R
22	5.59	0♋	15	29	15	13	♄10♓R
23	6.03	1	29	28	16	13	♅ 4♉
24	6.07	2	14♈	28	17	13	♆12♍
25	6.11	3	27	27	18	14	♇25♋
26	6.15	4	11♉	27	19	14	♃13♏R
27	6.19	5	25	26	20	15	♄10♓R
28	6.23	6	8♊	26	21	15	♅ 4♉
29	6.27	7	21	25	22	15	♆12♍
30	6.30	7	4♋	25	23	16	♇25♋

Jul	STime	☉	☽	☿	♀	♂	Plnts
1	6.34	8♋	16♋	25♊	24♌	16♎	♃13♏R
2	6.38	9	29	25	25	17	♄10♓R
3	6.42	10	11♌	25D	26	17	♅ 5♉
4	6.46	11	23	25	27	17	♆12♍
5	6.50	12	5♍	25	28	18	♇25♋
6	6.54	13	16	25	28	18	♃13♏R
7	6.58	14	28	26	29	19	♄10♓R
8	7.02	15	10♎	26	0♍	19	♅ 5♉
9	7.06	16	22	27	1	20	♆12♍
10	7.10	17	5♏	27	2	20	♇25♋
11	7.14	18	17	28	3	20	♃13♏
12	7.18	19	1♐	29	4	21	♄10♓R
13	7.22	20	14	29	5	21	♅ 5♉
14	7.26	21	28	0♋	5	22	♆12♍
15	7.30	22	12♑	1	6	22	♇25♋
16	7.34	23	27	2	7	23	♃13♏
17	7.38	24	11♒	3	8	23	♄ 9♓R
18	7.41	25	26	5	9	24	♅ 5♉
19	7.45	26	11♓	6	9	24	♆12♍
20	7.49	27	26	7	10	25	♇25♋
21	7.53	27	10♈	9	11	25	♃13♏
22	7.57	28	24	10	12	26	♄ 9♓R
23	8.01	29	8♉	12	12	26	♅ 5♉
24	8.05	0♌	22	13	13	27	♆12♍
25	8.09	1	5♊	15	14	27	♇25♋
26	8.13	2	18	17	14	28	♃13♏
27	8.17	3	0♋	19	15	28	♄ 9♓R
28	8.21	4	13	21	16	29	♅ 5♉
29	8.25	5	25	23	16	0♏	♆13♍
30	8.29	6	7♌	25	17	0	♇26♋
31	8.33	7	19	27	17	1	♃14♏

Aug	STime	☉	☽	☿	♀	♂	Plnts
1	8.37	8♌	1♍	29♋	18♍	1♏	♃14♏
2	8.41	9	13	1♌	18	2	♄ 9♓R
3	8.45	10	25	3	19	2	♅ 5♉
4	8.48	11	7♎	5	19	3	♆13♍
5	8.52	12	19	7	20	3	♇26♋
6	8.56	13	1♏	9	20	4	♃14♏
7	9.00	14	13	11	20	5	♄ 8♓R
8	9.04	15	26	13	21	5	♅ 5♉
9	9.08	16	9♐	15	21	6	♆13♍
10	9.12	17	22	17	21	6	♇26♋
11	9.16	18	6♑	19	22	7	♃15♏
12	9.20	19	20	21	22	7	♄ 8♓R
13	9.24	20	5♒	23	22	8	♅ 5♉
14	9.28	20	20	25	22	9	♆13♍
15	9.32	21	5♓	27	22	9	♇26♋
16	9.36	22	20	29	22	10	♃15♏
17	9.40	23	5♈	1♍	22	10	♄ 8♓R
18	9.44	24	20	3	22R	11	♅ 5♉
19	9.48	25	4♉	5	22	12	♆13♍
20	9.52	26	18	7	22	12	♇26♋
21	9.56	27	2♊	8	22	13	♃16♏
22	9.59	28	15	10	22	14	♄ 7♓R
23	10.03	29	27	12	22	14	♅ 5♉R
24	10.07	0♍	10♋	14	22	15	♆13♍
25	10.11	1	22	15	21	15	♇26♋
26	10.15	2	4♌	17	21	16	♃16♏
27	10.19	3	16	19	21	17	♄ 7♓R
28	10.23	4	28	20	20	17	♅ 5♉R
29	10.27	5	10♍	22	20	18	♆14♍
30	10.31	6	22	24	19	19	♇26♋
31	10.35	7	4♎	25	19	19	♃17♏

Sep	STime	☉	☽	☿	♀	♂	Plnts
1	10.39	8♍	16♎	27♍	18♍	20♏	♃17♏
2	10.43	9	28	28	18	20	♄ 6♓R
3	10.47	10	10♏	0♎	17	21	♅ 5♉R
4	10.51	11	22	1	17	22	♆14♍
5	10.55	12	5♐	3	16	22	♇27♋
6	10.59	13	17	4	16	23	♃18♏
7	11.03	14	1♑	6	15	24	♄ 6♓R
8	11.06	15	14	7	14	24	♅ 5♉R
9	11.10	16	29	9	14	25	♆14♍
10	11.14	17	13♒	10	13	26	♇27♋
11	11.18	18	28	11	13	26	♃18♏
12	11.22	18	14♓	13	12	27	♄ 6♓R
13	11.26	19	29	14	11	28	♅ 5♉R
14	11.30	20	14♈	15	11	28	♆14♍
15	11.34	21	29	16	10	29	♇27♋
16	11.38	22	13♉	18	10	0♐	♃19♏
17	11.42	23	27	19	9	0	♄ 5♓R
18	11.46	24	11♊	20	9	1	♅ 5♉R
19	11.50	25	24	21	8	2	♆14♍
20	11.54	26	7♋	22	8	2	♇27♋
21	11.58	27	19	23	8	3	♃20♏
22	12.02	28	1♌	24	7	4	♄ 5♓R
23	12.06	29	13	25	7	4	♅ 4♉R
24	12.10	0♎	25	26	7	5	♆15♍
25	12.14	1	7♍	27	7	6	♇27♋
26	12.17	2	19	28	7	7	♃21♏
27	12.21	3	1♎	29	6	7	♄ 5♓R
28	12.25	4	13	0♏	6	8	♅ 4♉R
29	12.29	5	25	0	6D	9	♆15♍
30	12.33	6	7♏	1	6	9	♇27♋

Oct	STime	☉	☽	☿	♀	♂	Plnts
1	12.37	7♎	19♏	1♏	6♍	10♐	♃22♏
2	12.41	8	1♐	2	6	11	♄ 4♓R
3	12.45	9	14	2	7	11	♅ 4♉R
4	12.49	10	27	2	7	12	♆15♍
5	12.53	11	10♑	2	7	13	♇27♋
6	12.57	12	24	3R	7	14	♃23♏
7	13.01	13	8♒	2	7	14	♄ 4♓R
8	13.05	14	22	2	8	15	♅ 4♉R
9	13.09	15	7♓	2	8	16	♆15♍
10	13.13	16	22	1	8	16	♇27♋
11	13.17	17	7♈	1	9	17	♃24♏
12	13.21	18	22	0	9	18	♄ 4♓R
13	13.24	19	7♉	29♎	10	19	♅ 4♉R
14	13.28	20	22	28	10	19	♆15♍
15	13.32	21	6♊	27	11	20	♇27♋
16	13.36	22	20	26	11	21	♃25♏
17	13.40	23	3♋	25	12	21	♄ 4♓R
18	13.44	24	15	23	12	22	♅ 4♉R
19	13.48	25	28	22	13	23	♆15♍
20	13.52	26	10♌	21	14	24	♇27♋
21	13.56	27	22	20	14	24	♃26♏
22	14.00	28	4♍	19	15	25	♄ 3♓R
23	14.04	29	16	18	16	26	♅ 3♉R
24	14.08	0♏	27	18	16	27	♆16♍
25	14.12	1	9♎	17	17	27	♇27♋
26	14.16	2	21	17	18	28	♃27♏
27	14.20	3	4♏	17D	18	29	♄ 3♓R
28	14.24	4	16	17	19	29	♅ 3♉R
29	14.28	5	29	17	20	0♑	♆16♍
30	14.31	6	11♐	18	21	1	♇27♋
31	14.35	7	24	19	22	2	♃28♏

Nov	STime	☉	☽	☿	♀	♂	Plnts
1	14.39	8♏	7♑	19♎	22♍	2♑	♃28♏
2	14.43	9	20	20	23	3	♄ 3♓
3	14.47	10	4♒	21	24	4	♅ 3♉R
4	14.51	11	18	22	25	5	♆16♍
5	14.55	12	2♓	24	26	5	♇27♋
6	14.59	13	16	25	27	6	♃29♏
7	15.03	14	1♈	26	28	7	♄ 3♓
8	15.07	15	16	27	29	8	♅ 3♉R
9	15.11	16	1♉	29	0♎	8	♆16♍
10	15.15	17	15	0♏	0	9	♇27♋
11	15.19	18	0♊	2	1	10	♃ 0♐
12	15.23	19	14	3	2	11	♄ 3♓
13	15.27	20	27	5	3	11	♅ 3♉R
14	15.31	21	11♋	6	4	12	♆16♍
15	15.35	22	24	8	5	13	♇27♋R
16	15.39	23	6♌	10	6	14	♃ 1♐
17	15.42	24	18	11	7	15	♄ 3♓
18	15.46	25	0♍	13	8	15	♅ 2♉R
19	15.50	26	12	14	9	16	♆16♍
20	15.54	27	24	16	10	17	♇27♋R
21	15.58	28	6♎	17	11	18	♃ 2♐
22	16.02	29	18	19	12	18	♄ 3♓
23	16.06	0♐	0♏	21	13	19	♅ 2♉R
24	16.10	1	12	22	14	20	♆16♍
25	16.14	2	25	24	15	21	♇27♋R
26	16.18	3	8♐	25	17	21	♃ 4♐
27	16.22	4	21	27	18	22	♄ 4♓
28	16.26	5	4♑	28	19	23	♅ 2♉R
29	16.30	6	17	0♐	20	24	♆16♍
30	16.34	7	1♒	2	21	25	♇27♋R

Dec	STime	☉	☽	☿	♀	♂	Plnts
1	16.38	8♐	15♒	3♐	22♎	25♑	♃ 5♐
2	16.42	9	29	5	23	26	♄ 4♓
3	16.46	10	13♓	6	24	27	♅ 2♉R
4	16.49	11	27	8	25	28	♆16♍
5	16.53	12	11♈	9	26	28	♇27♋R
6	16.57	13	25	11	27	29	♃ 6♐
7	17.01	14	10♉	13	28	0♒	♄ 4♓
8	17.05	15	24	14	0♏	1	♅ 2♉R
9	17.09	16	8♊	16	1	1	♆16♍
10	17.13	17	22	17	2	2	♇27♋R
11	17.17	18	5♋	19	3	3	♃ 7♐
12	17.21	19	18	20	4	4	♄ 4♓
13	17.25	20	1♌	22	5	5	♅ 2♉R
14	17.29	21	14	24	6	5	♆16♍
15	17.33	22	26	25	7	6	♇27♋R
16	17.37	23	8♍	27	9	7	♃ 8♐
17	17.41	24	20	28	10	8	♄ 5♓
18	17.45	25	2♎	0♑	11	8	♅ 1♉R
19	17.49	26	14	2	12	9	♆16♍
20	17.53	27	26	3	13	10	♇27♋R
21	17.57	28	8♏	5	14	11	♃ 9♐
22	18.00	29	20	6	16	12	♄ 5♓
23	18.04	0♑	3♐	8	17	12	♅ 1♉R
24	18.08	1	16	9	18	13	♆16♍
25	18.12	2	29	11	19	14	♇26♋R
26	18.16	3	13♑	13	20	15	♃10♐
27	18.20	5	27	14	21	16	♄ 5♓
28	18.24	6	11♒	16	23	16	♅ 1♉R
29	18.28	7	25	18	24	17	♆16♍
30	18.32	8	9♓	19	25	18	♇26♋R
31	18.36	9	24	21	26	19	♃11♐

Jan	STime	☉	☽	☿	♀	♂	Plnts
1	18.40	10♑	8♈	22♑	27♏	19♒	♃11♐
2	18.44	11	22	24	28	20	♄ 6♓
3	18.48	12	6♉	26	0♐	21	♅ 1♉R
4	18.52	13	20	27	1	22	♆16♍R
5	18.56	14	4♊	29	2	23	♇26♋R
6	19.00	15	17	0♒	3	23	♃13♐
7	19.04	16	1♋	2	4	24	♄ 6♓
8	19.07	17	14	3	6	25	♅ 1♉
9	19.11	18	26	5	7	26	♆16♍R
10	19.15	19	9♌	6	8	26	♇26♋R
11	19.19	20	21	8	9	27	♃14♐
12	19.23	21	4♍	9	10	28	♄ 7♓
13	19.27	22	16	10	12	29	♅ 1♉
14	19.31	23	28	12	13	0♓	♆16♍R
15	19.35	24	10♎	13	14	0	♇26♋R
16	19.39	25	21	14	15	1	♃15♐
17	19.43	26	3♏	15	16	2	♄ 7♓
18	19.47	27	16	15	18	3	♅ 1♉
19	19.51	28	28	16	19	4	♆16♍R
20	19.55	29	11♐	17	20	4	♇26♋R
21	19.59	0♒	24	17	21	5	♃15♐
22	20.03	1	7♑	17	22	6	♄ 8♓
23	20.07	2	21	17R	24	7	♅ 1♉
24	20.11	3	6♒	17	25	7	♆16♍R
25	20.14	4	20	17	26	8	♇26♋R
26	20.18	5	5♓	16	27	9	♃16♐
27	20.22	6	20	15	28	10	♄ 8♓
28	20.26	7	4♈	15	0♑	11	♅ 1♉
29	20.30	8	19	13	1	11	♆16♍R
30	20.34	9	3♉	12	2	12	♇26♋R
31	20.38	10	17	11	3	13	♃17♐

Feb	STime	☉	☽	☿	♀	♂	Plnts
1	20.42	11♒	0♊	10♒	4♑	14♓	♃17♐
2	20.46	12	14	9	6	14	♄ 9♓
3	20.50	13	27	7	7	15	♅ 1♉
4	20.54	14	10♋	6	8	16	♆16♍R
5	20.58	15	23	5	9	17	♇26♋R
6	21.02	16	5♌	4	11	18	♃18♐
7	21.06	17	18	4	12	18	♄ 9♓
8	21.10	18	0♍	3	13	19	♅ 2♉
9	21.14	19	12	2	14	20	♆16♍R
10	21.18	20	24	2	15	21	♇25♋R
11	21.22	21	6♎	2	17	21	♃19♐
12	21.25	22	18	2	18	22	♄10♓
13	21.29	23	0♏	2D	19	23	♅ 2♉
14	21.33	24	11	2	20	24	♆16♍R
15	21.37	25	24	2	22	25	♇25♋R
16	21.41	26	6♐	2	23	25	♃20♐
17	21.45	27	19	3	24	26	♄11♓
18	21.49	28	2♑	3	25	27	♅ 2♉
19	21.53	29	15	4	26	28	♆16♍R
20	21.57	0♓	29	4	28	28	♇25♋R
21	22.01	1	14♒	5	29	29	♃21♐
22	22.05	2	29	6	0♒	0♈	♄11♓
23	22.09	3	14♓	7	1	1	♅ 2♉
24	22.13	4	29	8	3	1	♆15♍R
25	22.17	5	14♈	9	4	2	♇25♋R
26	22.21	6	29	10	5	3	♃21♐
27	22.25	7	13♉	11	6	4	♄12♓
28	22.29	8	27	12	7	5	♅ 2♉
29	22.32	9	11♊	13	9	5	♆15♍R

Mar	STime	☉	☽	☿	♀	♂	Plnts
1	22.36	10♓	24♊	14♒	10♒	6♈	♃22♐
2	22.40	11	7♋	15	11	7	♄12♓
3	22.44	12	20	16	12	8	♅ 2♉
4	22.48	13	2♌	18	14	8	♆15♍R
5	22.52	14	14	19	15	9	♇25♋R
6	22.56	15	26	20	16	10	♃22♐
7	23.00	16	9♍	22	17	11	♄13♓
8	23.04	17	21	23	18	11	♅ 3♉
9	23.08	18	2♎	24	20	12	♆15♍R
10	23.12	19	14	26	21	13	♇25♋R
11	23.16	20	26	27	22	14	♃23♐
12	23.20	21	8♏	29	23	14	♄14♓
13	23.24	22	20	0♓	25	15	♅ 3♉
14	23.28	23	2♐	2	26	16	♆15♍R
15	23.32	24	14	3	27	17	♇25♋R
16	23.36	25	27	5	28	17	♃23♐
17	23.40	26	10♑	6	0♓	18	♄14♓
18	23.43	27	23	8	1	19	♅ 3♉
19	23.47	28	7♒	9	2	20	♆15♍R
20	23.51	29	22	11	3	20	♇25♋R
21	23.55	0♈	7♓	13	4	21	♃23♐
22	23.59	1	22	14	6	22	♄15♓
23	0.03	2	7♈	16	7	23	♅ 3♉
24	0.07	3	22	18	8	23	♆15♍R
25	0.11	4	7♉	19	9	24	♇25♋
26	0.15	5	22	21	11	25	♃24♐
27	0.19	6	6♊	23	12	26	♄15♓
28	0.23	7	20	25	13	26	♅ 4♉
29	0.27	8	4♋	27	14	27	♆14♍R
30	0.31	9	17	28	16	28	♇25♋
31	0.35	10	29	0♈	17	29	♃24♐

Apr	STime	☉	☽	☿	♀	♂	Plnts
1	0.39	11♈	11♌	2♈	18♓	29♈	♃24♐
2	0.43	12	24	4	19	0♉	♄16♓
3	0.47	13	6♍	6	20	1	♅ 4♉
4	0.50	14	18	8	22	2	♆14♍R
5	0.54	15	29	10	23	2	♇25♋
6	0.58	16	11♎	12	24	3	♃24♐
7	1.02	17	23	14	25	4	♄17♓
8	1.06	18	5♏	16	27	5	♅ 4♉
9	1.10	19	17	18	28	5	♆14♍R
10	1.14	20	29	20	29	6	♇25♋
11	1.18	21	11♐	22	0♈	7	♃24♐
12	1.22	22	24	24	2	8	♄17♓
13	1.26	23	6♑	26	3	8	♅ 4♉
14	1.30	24	19	28	4	9	♆14♍R
15	1.34	25	3♒	1♉	5	10	♇25♋
16	1.38	26	16	3	6	10	♃24♐R
17	1.42	27	1♓	5	8	11	♄18♓
18	1.46	28	15	7	9	12	♅ 5♉
19	1.50	29	0♈	9	10	13	♆14♍R
20	1.54	0♉	15	11	11	13	♇25♋
21	1.58	1	1♉	13	13	14	♃24♐R
22	2.01	2	16	15	14	15	♄18♓
23	2.05	3	0♊	17	15	15	♅ 5♉
24	2.09	4	15	19	16	16	♆14♍R
25	2.13	5	29	21	17	17	♇25♋
26	2.17	6	12♋	22	19	18	♃24♐R
27	2.21	7	25	24	20	18	♄19♓
28	2.25	8	8♌	26	21	19	♅ 5♉
29	2.29	9	20	27	22	20	♆14♍R
30	2.33	10	2♍	29	24	21	♇25♋

May	STime	☉	☽	☿	♀	♂	Plnts
1	2.37	11♉	14♍	0♊	25♈	21♉	♃23♐R
2	2.41	12	26	2	26	22	♄19♓
3	2.45	13	8♎	3	27	23	♅ 6♉
4	2.49	14	20	4	29	23	♆14♍R
5	2.53	14	2♏	5	0♉	24	♇25♋
6	2.57	15	14	7	1	25	♃23♐R
7	3.01	16	26	8	2	26	♄20♓
8	3.05	17	8♐	9	3	26	♅ 6♉
9	3.08	18	21	9	5	27	♆14♍R
10	3.12	19	3♑	10	6	28	♇25♋
11	3.16	20	16	11	7	28	♃23♐R
12	3.20	21	29	12	8	29	♄20♓
13	3.24	22	13♒	12	10	0♊	♅ 6♉
14	3.28	23	26	13	11	0	♆14♍R
15	3.32	24	10♓	13	12	1	♇25♋
16	3.36	25	25	13	13	2	♃22♐R
17	3.40	26	9♈	14	14	3	♄20♓
18	3.44	27	24	14	16	3	♅ 6♉
19	3.48	28	9♉	14R	17	4	♆14♍R
20	3.52	29	24	14	18	5	♇25♋
21	3.56	0♊	9♊	14	19	5	♃22♐R
22	4.00	1	23	13	21	6	♄21♓
23	4.04	2	7♋	13	22	7	♅ 7♉
24	4.08	3	21	13	23	8	♆14♍
25	4.12	4	4♌	13	24	8	♇25♋
26	4.15	5	16	12	26	9	♃21♐R
27	4.19	6	29	12	27	10	♄21♓
28	4.23	7	11♍	11	28	10	♅ 7♉
29	4.27	8	23	11	29	11	♆14♍
30	4.31	9	5♎	10	0♊	12	♇25♋
31	4.35	10	17	10	2	12	♃21♐R

Jun	STime	☉	☽	☿	♀	♂	Plnts
1	4.39	10♊	29♎	9♊	3♊	13♊	♃20♐R
2	4.43	11	11♏	8	4	14	♄21♓
3	4.47	12	23	8	5	14	♅ 7♉
4	4.51	13	5♐	7	7	15	♆14♍
5	4.55	14	17	7	8	16	♇26♋
6	4.59	15	0♑	7	9	17	♃20♐R
7	5.03	16	13	6	10	17	♄22♓
8	5.07	17	26	6	11	18	♅ 8♉
9	5.11	18	10♒	6	13	19	♆14♍
10	5.15	19	23	5	14	19	♇26♋
11	5.19	20	7♓	5	15	20	♃19♐R
12	5.23	21	21	5D	16	21	♄22♓
13	5.26	22	5♈	5	18	21	♅ 8♉
14	5.30	23	20	5	19	22	♆14♍
15	5.34	24	4♉	6	20	23	♇26♋
16	5.38	25	19	6	21	23	♃19♐R
17	5.42	26	3♊	6	23	24	♄22♓
18	5.46	27	17	6	24	25	♅ 8♉
19	5.50	28	1♋	7	25	25	♆14♍
20	5.54	29	15	8	26	26	♇26♋
21	5.58	0♋	29	8	27	27	♃18♐R
22	6.02	1	12♌	9	29	27	♄22♓
23	6.06	2	24	10	0♋	28	♅ 8♉
24	6.10	2	7♍	10	1	29	♆14♍
25	6.14	3	19	11	2	29	♇26♋
26	6.18	4	1♎	12	4	0♋	♃17♐R
27	6.22	5	13	13	5	1	♄22♓
28	6.26	6	25	14	6	1	♅ 8♉
29	6.30	7	7♏	16	7	2	♆14♍
30	6.33	8	19	17	8	3	♇26♋

Jul	STime	☉	☽	☿	♀	♂	Plnts
1	6.37	9♋	1♐	18♊	10♋	3♋	♃17♐R
2	6.41	10	13	20	11	4	♄22♓
3	6.45	11	26	21	12	5	♅ 9♉
4	6.49	12	9♑	23	13	5	♆14♍
5	6.53	13	22	24	15	6	♇26♋
6	6.57	14	6♒	26	16	7	♃16♐R
7	7.01	15	20	27	17	7	♄22♓
8	7.05	16	4♓	29	18	8	♅ 9♉
9	7.09	17	18	1♋	20	9	♆14♍
10	7.13	18	2♈	3	21	9	♇26♋
11	7.17	19	16	5	22	10	♃16♐R
12	7.21	20	0♉	6	23	11	♄22♓R
13	7.25	21	15	8	24	11	♅ 9♉
14	7.29	22	29	10	26	12	♆14♍
15	7.33	22	13♊	12	27	13	♇27♋
16	7.37	23	27	15	28	13	♃15♐R
17	7.41	24	10♋	17	29	14	♄22♓R
18	7.44	25	24	19	1♌	15	♅ 9♉
19	7.48	26	7♌	21	2	15	♆14♍
20	7.52	27	20	23	3	16	♇27♋
21	7.56	28	2♍	25	4	17	♃15♐R
22	8.00	29	15	27	6	17	♄22♓R
23	8.04	0♌	27	29	7	18	♅ 9♉
24	8.08	1	9♎	1♌	8	19	♆15♍
25	8.12	2	21	4	9	19	♇27♋
26	8.16	3	3♏	6	10	20	♃15♐R
27	8.20	4	15	8	12	21	♄22♓R
28	8.24	5	27	10	13	21	♅ 9♉
29	8.28	6	9♐	12	14	22	♆15♍
30	8.32	7	21	14	15	23	♇27♋
31	8.36	8	4♑	16	17	23	♃14♐R

Aug	STime	☉	☽	☿	♀	♂	Plnts
1	8.40	9♌	18♑	18♌	18♌	24♋	♃14♐R
2	8.44	10	1♒	20	19	25	♄22♓R
3	8.48	11	15	22	20	25	♅ 9♉
4	8.51	12	29	23	22	26	♆15♍
5	8.55	13	14♓	25	23	27	♇27♋
6	8.59	14	28	27	24	27	♃14♐R
7	9.03	14	13♈	29	25	28	♄21♓R
8	9.07	15	27	1♍	27	28	♅ 9♉
9	9.11	16	11♉	2	28	29	♆15♍
10	9.15	17	25	4	29	0♌	♇27♋
11	9.19	18	9♊	6	0♍	0	♃14♐
12	9.23	19	23	7	1	1	♄21♓R
13	9.27	20	6♋	9	3	2	♅ 9♉
14	9.31	21	20	11	4	2	♆15♍
15	9.35	22	3♌	12	5	3	♇27♋
16	9.39	23	16	14	6	4	♃14♐
17	9.43	24	28	15	8	4	♄21♓R
18	9.47	25	11♍	17	9	5	♅ 9♉R
19	9.51	26	23	18	10	6	♆15♍
20	9.55	27	5♎	20	11	6	♇27♋
21	9.58	28	17	21	13	7	♃14♐
22	10.02	29	29	23	14	7	♄20♓R
23	10.06	0♍	11♏	24	15	8	♅ 9♉R
24	10.10	1	23	25	16	9	♆16♍
25	10.14	2	5♐	27	17	9	♇28♋
26	10.18	3	17	28	19	10	♃15♐
27	10.22	4	29	29	20	11	♄20♓R
28	10.26	5	12♑	1♎	21	11	♅ 9♉R
29	10.30	6	26	2	22	12	♆16♍
30	10.34	7	9♒	3	24	13	♇28♋
31	10.38	8	24	4	25	13	♃15♐

Sep	STime	☉	☽	☿	♀	♂	Plnts
1	10.42	9♍	8♓	5♎	26♍	14♌	♃15♐
2	10.46	10	23	6	27	15	♄20♓R
3	10.50	10	8♈	7	29	15	♅ 9♉R
4	10.54	11	23	8	0♎	16	♆16♍
5	10.58	12	8♉	9	1	16	♇28♋
6	11.02	13	22	10	2	17	♃15♐
7	11.06	14	6♊	11	4	18	♄19♓R
8	11.09	15	20	12	5	18	♅ 9♉R
9	11.13	16	3♋	13	6	19	♆16♍
10	11.17	17	17	13	7	20	♇28♋
11	11.21	18	0♌	14	8	20	♃16♐
12	11.25	19	12	15	10	21	♄19♓R
13	11.29	20	25	15	11	21	♅ 9♉R
14	11.33	21	7♍	15	12	22	♆16♍
15	11.37	22	19	16	13	23	♇28♋
16	11.41	23	2♎	16	15	23	♃16♐
17	11.45	24	14	16	16	24	♄18♓R
18	11.49	25	26	16R	17	25	♅ 9♉R
19	11.53	26	7♏	16	18	25	♆17♍
20	11.57	27	19	16	20	26	♇28♋
21	12.01	28	1♐	16	21	26	♃17♐
22	12.05	29	13	15	22	27	♄18♓R
23	12.09	0♎	25	15	23	28	♅ 9♉R
24	12.13	1	8♑	14	24	28	♆17♍
25	12.16	2	20	13	26	29	♇28♋
26	12.20	3	4♒	12	27	0♍	♃17♐
27	12.24	4	17	11	28	0	♄18♓R
28	12.28	5	2♓	10	29	1	♅ 9♉R
29	12.32	6	16	9	1♏	1	♆17♍
30	12.36	7	1♈	8	2	2	♇28♋

Oct	STime	☉	☽	☿	♀	♂	Plnts
1	12.40	8♎	17♈	7♎	3♏	3♍	♃18♐
2	12.44	9	2♉	6	4	3	♄17♓R
3	12.48	10	17	5	6	4	♅ 8♉R
4	12.52	11	2♊	4	7	5	♆17♍
5	12.56	12	16	3	8	5	♇28♋
6	13.00	13	0♋	2	9	6	♃19♐
7	13.04	14	14	2	10	6	♄17♓R
8	13.08	15	27	1	12	7	♅ 8♉R
9	13.12	16	9♌	1D	13	8	♆17♍
10	13.16	17	22	1	14	8	♇28♋
11	13.20	18	4♍	1	15	9	♃20♐
12	13.24	19	16	2	17	10	♄17♓R
13	13.27	20	29	2	18	10	♅ 8♉R
14	13.31	21	10♎	3	19	11	♆17♍
15	13.35	22	22	4	20	11	♇28♋
16	13.39	23	4♏	5	21	12	♃20♐
17	13.43	24	16	6	23	13	♄16♓R
18	13.47	25	28	7	24	13	♅ 8♉R
19	13.51	26	10♐	8	25	14	♆18♍
20	13.55	27	22	9	26	14	♇28♋
21	13.59	28	4♑	11	28	15	♃21♐
22	14.03	29	16	12	29	16	♄16♓R
23	14.07	0♏	29	14	0♐	16	♅ 8♉R
24	14.11	1	12♒	15	1	17	♆18♍
25	14.15	2	26	17	3	18	♇28♋
26	14.19	3	10♓	18	4	18	♃22♐
27	14.23	4	25	20	5	19	♄16♓R
28	14.27	5	10♈	22	6	19	♅ 7♉R
29	14.31	6	25	23	7	20	♆18♍
30	14.34	7	10♉	25	9	21	♇28♋
31	14.38	8	25	26	10	21	♃23♐

Nov	STime	☉	☽	☿	♀	♂	Plnts
1	14.42	9♏	10♊	28♎	11♐	22♍	♃23♐
2	14.46	10	25	0♏	12	22	♄16♓R
3	14.50	11	9♋	1	14	23	♅ 7♉R
4	14.54	12	23	3	15	24	♆18♍
5	14.58	13	6♌	5	16	24	♇28♋
6	15.02	14	19	6	17	25	♃24♐
7	15.06	15	1♍	8	18	25	♄16♓R
8	15.10	16	13	10	20	26	♅ 7♉R
9	15.14	17	26	11	21	27	♆18♍
10	15.18	18	8♎	13	22	27	♇28♋
11	15.22	19	19	15	23	28	♃25♐
12	15.26	20	1♏	16	24	28	♄16♓R
13	15.30	21	13	18	26	29	♅ 7♉R
14	15.34	22	25	19	27	0♎	♆18♍
15	15.38	23	7♐	21	28	0	♇28♋R
16	15.41	24	19	23	29	1	♃26♐
17	15.45	25	1♑	24	1♑	1	♄15♓
18	15.49	26	13	26	2	2	♅ 7♉R
19	15.53	27	26	27	3	3	♆18♍
20	15.57	28	9♒	29	4	3	♇28♋R
21	16.01	29	22	0♐	5	4	♃27♐
22	16.05	0♐	5♓	2	7	4	♄15♓
23	16.09	1	19	4	8	5	♅ 6♉R
24	16.13	2	4♈	5	9	6	♆18♍
25	16.17	3	18	7	10	6	♇28♋R
26	16.21	4	3♉	8	11	7	♃28♐
27	16.25	5	18	10	13	7	♄16♓
28	16.29	6	3♊	11	14	8	♅ 6♉R
29	16.33	7	18	13	15	9	♆19♍
30	16.37	8	3♋	15	16	9	♇28♋R

Dec	STime	☉	☽	☿	♀	♂	Plnts
1	16.41	9♐	17♋	16♐	18♑	10♎	♃ 0♑
2	16.45	10	1♌	18	19	10	♄16♓
3	16.49	11	14	19	20	11	♅ 6♉R
4	16.52	12	27	21	21	11	♆19♍
5	16.56	13	10♍	22	22	12	♇28♋R
6	17.00	14	22	24	24	13	♃ 1♑
7	17.04	15	4♎	25	25	13	♄16♓
8	17.08	16	16	27	26	14	♅ 6♉R
9	17.12	17	28	28	27	14	♆19♍
10	17.16	18	10♏	0♑	28	15	♇28♋R
11	17.20	19	22	2	0♒	15	♃ 2♑
12	17.24	20	4♐	3	1	16	♄16♓
13	17.28	21	16	5	2	17	♅ 6♉R
14	17.32	22	28	6	3	17	♆19♍
15	17.36	23	10♑	8	4	18	♇28♋R
16	17.40	24	23	9	6	18	♃ 3♑
17	17.44	25	6♒	11	7	19	♄16♓
18	17.48	26	19	12	8	19	♅ 6♉R
19	17.52	27	2♓	14	9	20	♆19♍
20	17.56	28	16	15	10	21	♇28♋R
21	17.59	29	29	17	11	21	♃ 4♑
22	18.03	0♑	13♈	18	13	22	♄16♓
23	18.07	1	28	19	14	22	♅ 6♉R
24	18.11	2	12♉	21	15	23	♆19♍
25	18.15	3	27	22	16	23	♇28♋R
26	18.19	4	12♊	23	17	24	♃ 5♑
27	18.23	5	26	25	19	25	♄17♓
28	18.27	6	11♋	26	20	25	♅ 5♉R
29	18.31	7	25	27	21	26	♆19♍R
30	18.35	8	9♌	28	22	26	♇28♋R
31	18.39	9	22	29	23	27	♃ 6♑

1 9 3 7

Jan	STime	☉	☽	☿	♀	♂	Plnts
1	18.43	10♑	5♍	0♒	24♒	27♎	♃ 7♑
2	18.47	11	18	0	25	28	♄17♓
3	18.51	12	0♎	1	27	28	♅ 5♉R
4	18.55	13	12	1	28	29	♆19♍R
5	18.59	14	24	1R	29	0♏	♇28♋R
6	19.03	15	6♏	1	0♓	0	♃ 8♑
7	19.07	16	18	1	1	1	♄18♓
8	19.10	18	0♐	1	2	1	♅ 5♉
9	19.14	19	12	0	4	2	♆19♍R
10	19.18	20	24	29♑	5	2	♇28♋R
11	19.22	21	7♑	28	6	3	♃ 9♑
12	19.26	22	19	27	7	3	♄18♓
13	19.30	23	2♒	26	8	4	♅ 5♉
14	19.34	24	15	25	9	4	♆19♍R
15	19.38	25	29	23	10	5	♇27♋R
16	19.42	26	13♓	22	11	5	♃10♑
17	19.46	27	26	21	13	6	♄18♓
18	19.50	28	10♈	20	14	6	♅ 5♉
19	19.54	29	24	19	15	7	♆18♍R
20	19.58	0♒	8♉	18	16	7	♇27♋R
21	20.02	1	23	17	17	8	♃11♑
22	20.06	2	7♊	16	18	8	♄19♓
23	20.10	3	21	16	19	9	♅ 5♉
24	20.14	4	5♋	15	20	9	♆18♍R
25	20.17	5	19	15	21	10	♇27♋R
26	20.21	6	3♌	15D	22	10	♃12♑
27	20.25	7	17	15	23	11	♄19♓
28	20.29	8	0♍	15	25	11	♅ 5♉
29	20.33	9	13	16	26	12	♆18♍R
30	20.37	10	26	16	27	12	♇27♋R
31	20.41	11	8♎	17	28	13	♃13♑

Feb	STime	☉	☽	☿	♀	♂	Plnts
1	20.45	12♒	20♎	17♑	29♓	13♏	♃14♑
2	20.49	13	2♏	18	0♈	14	♄20♓
3	20.53	14	14	19	1	14	♅ 5♉
4	20.57	15	26	20	2	15	♆18♍R
5	21.01	16	8♐	20	3	15	♇27♋R
6	21.05	17	20	21	4	16	♃15♑
7	21.09	18	2♑	22	5	16	♄21♓
8	21.13	19	15	23	6	17	♅ 6♉
9	21.17	20	27	24	7	17	♆18♍R
10	21.21	21	11♒	26	8	18	♇27♋R
11	21.25	22	24	27	9	18	♃16♑
12	21.28	23	8♓	28	10	19	♄21♓
13	21.32	24	22	29	11	19	♅ 6♉
14	21.36	25	7♈	0♒	12	19	♆18♍R
15	21.40	26	21	2	13	20	♇27♋R
16	21.44	27	5♉	3	13	20	♃17♑
17	21.48	28	19	4	14	21	♄22♓
18	21.52	29	4♊	5	15	21	♅ 6♉
19	21.56	0♓	17	7	16	22	♆18♍R
20	22.00	1	1♋	8	17	22	♇27♋R
21	22.04	2	15	10	18	23	♃18♑
22	22.08	3	29	11	19	23	♄22♓
23	22.12	4	12♌	12	20	23	♅ 6♉
24	22.16	5	25	14	20	24	♆18♍R
25	22.20	6	8♍	15	21	24	♇27♋R
26	22.24	7	21	17	22	25	♃19♑
27	22.28	8	4♎	18	23	25	♄23♓
28	22.32	9	16	20	24	25	♅ 6♉

Mar	STime	☉	☽	☿	♀	♂	Plnts
1	22.35	10♓	28♎	22♒	24♈	26♏	♃19♑
2	22.39	11	10♏	23	25	26	♄23♓
3	22.43	12	22	25	26	26	♅ 6♉
4	22.47	13	4♐	26	26	27	♆17♍R
5	22.51	14	15	28	27	27	♇26♋R
6	22.55	15	27	0♓	28	28	♃20♑
7	22.59	16	10♑	1	28	28	♄24♓
8	23.03	17	22	3	29	28	♅ 7♉
9	23.07	18	5♒	5	0♉	29	♆17♍R
10	23.11	19	19	6	0	29	♇26♋R
11	23.15	20	3♓	8	1	29	♃21♑
12	23.19	21	17	10	1	29	♄24♓
13	23.23	22	2♈	12	2	0♐	♅ 7♉
14	23.27	23	16	13	2	0	♆17♍R
15	23.31	24	1♉	15	3	0	♇26♋R
16	23.35	25	16	17	3	1	♃22♑
17	23.39	26	0♊	19	4	1	♄25♓
18	23.42	27	14	21	4	1	♅ 7♉
19	23.46	28	28	23	4	2	♆17♍R
20	23.50	29	12♋	25	4	2	♇26♋R
21	23.54	0♈	25	26	5	2	♃23♑
22	23.58	1	9♌	28	5	2	♄26♓
23	0.02	2	22	0♈	5	3	♅ 7♉
24	0.06	3	5♍	2	5	3	♆17♍R
25	0.10	4	17	4	5	3	♇26♋
26	0.14	5	0♎	6	5	3	♃23♑
27	0.18	6	12	8	6	3	♄26♓
28	0.22	7	24	10	6R	4	♅ 7♉
29	0.26	8	6♏	13	5	4	♆17♍R
30	0.30	9	18	15	5	4	♇26♋R
31	0.34	10	0♐	17	5	4	♃24♑

Apr	STime	☉	☽	☿	♀	♂	Plnts
1	0.38	11♈	12♐	19♈	5♉	4♐	♃24♑
2	0.42	12	24	21	5	4	♄27♓
3	0.46	13	6♑	23	5	4	♅ 8♉
4	0.50	14	18	25	4	5	♆17♍R
5	0.53	15	0♒	27	4	5	♇26♋
6	0.57	16	13	29	4	5	♃25♑
7	1.01	17	27	1♉	3	5	♄28♓
8	1.05	18	11♓	2	3	5	♅ 8♉
9	1.09	19	25	4	2	5	♆16♍R
10	1.13	20	10♈	6	2	5	♇26♋
11	1.17	21	25	8	1	5	♃25♑
12	1.21	22	10♉	9	1	5	♄28♓
13	1.25	23	25	11	0	5	♅ 8♉
14	1.29	24	10♊	12	29♈	5R	♆16♍R
15	1.33	25	24	14	29	5	♇26♋
16	1.37	26	8♋	15	28	5	♃26♑
17	1.41	27	22	16	28	5	♄29♓
18	1.45	28	6♌	17	27	5	♅ 9♉
19	1.49	29	19	19	26	5	♆16♍R
20	1.53	0♉	2♍	20	26	5	♇26♋
21	1.57	1	14	20	25	5	♃26♑
22	2.00	2	27	21	25	5	♄29♓
23	2.04	3	9♎	22	24	5	♅ 9♉
24	2.08	4	21	23	23	5	♆16♍R
25	2.12	5	3♏	23	23	4	♇26♋
26	2.16	6	15	23	22	4	♃26♑
27	2.20	6	27	24	22	4	♄ 0♈
28	2.24	7	9♐	24	21	4	♅ 9♉
29	2.28	8	20	24	21	4	♆16♍R
30	2.32	9	2♑	24R	21	4	♇26♋

May	STime	☉	☽	☿	♀	♂	Plnts
1	2.36	10♉	14♑	24♉	20♈	3♐	♃27♑
2	2.40	11	26	24	20	3	♄ 0♈
3	2.44	12	9♒	24	20	3	♅ 9♉
4	2.48	13	22	23	20	3	♆16♍R
5	2.52	14	5♓	23	19	3	♇26♋
6	2.56	15	19	23	19	2	♃27♑
7	3.00	16	3♈	22	19	2	♄ 1♈
8	3.04	17	18	22	19	2	♅10♉
9	3.08	18	3♉	21	19D	1	♆16♍R
10	3.11	19	18	21	19	1	♇26♋
11	3.15	20	3♊	20	19	1	♃27♑
12	3.19	21	19	19	19	0	♄ 1♈
13	3.23	22	3♋	19	19	0	♅10♉
14	3.27	23	18	18	20	0	♆16♍
15	3.31	24	2♌	18	20	0	♇26♋
16	3.35	25	15	17	20	29♏	♃27♑
17	3.39	26	28	17	20	29	♄ 2♈
18	3.43	27	11♍	16	21	28	♅10♉
19	3.47	28	24	16	21	28	♆16♍R
20	3.51	29	6♎	16	21	28	♇27♋
21	3.55	0♊	18	15	22	27	♃27♑R
22	3.59	1	0♏	15	22	27	♄ 2♈
23	4.03	2	12	15	23	27	♅11♉
24	4.07	3	24	15D	23	26	♆16♍
25	4.11	4	6♐	15	24	26	♇27♋
26	4.15	5	17	15	24	26	♃27♑R
27	4.18	5	29	15	25	25	♄ 3♈
28	4.22	6	11♑	16	25	25	♅11♉
29	4.26	7	23	16	26	25	♆16♍
30	4.30	8	6♒	16	27	24	♇27♋
31	4.34	9	18	17	27	24	♃27♑R

Jun	STime	☉	☽	☿	♀	♂	Plnts
1	4.38	10♊	1♓	18♉	28♈	24♏	♃27♑R
2	4.42	11	15	18	28	23	♄ 3♈
3	4.46	12	28	19	29	23	♅11♉
4	4.50	13	12♈	20	0♉	23	♆16♍
5	4.54	14	27	20	1	22	♇27♋
6	4.58	15	12♉	21	1	22	♃26♑R
7	5.02	16	27	22	2	22	♄ 4♈
8	5.06	17	12♊	23	3	22	♅11♉
9	5.10	18	27	24	4	21	♆16♍
10	5.14	19	12♋	25	4	21	♇27♋
11	5.18	20	26	27	5	21	♃26♑R
12	5.22	21	10♌	28	6	21	♄ 4♈
13	5.26	22	24	29	7	21	♅12♉
14	5.29	23	7♍	0♊	8	20	♆16♍
15	5.33	24	20	2	9	20	♇27♋
16	5.37	25	3♎	3	9	20	♃25♑R
17	5.41	26	15	5	10	20	♄ 4♈
18	5.45	27	27	6	11	20	♅12♉
19	5.49	27	9♏	8	12	20	♆16♍
20	5.53	28	21	10	13	20	♇27♋
21	5.57	29	2♐	11	14	19	♃25♑R
22	6.01	0♋	14	13	15	19	♄ 4♈
23	6.05	1	26	15	16	19	♅12♉
24	6.09	2	8♑	17	17	19	♆16♍
25	6.13	3	20	18	18	19	♇27♋
26	6.17	4	3♒	20	18	19D	♃24♑R
27	6.21	5	15	22	19	19	♄ 5♈
28	6.25	6	28	24	20	19	♅12♉
29	6.29	7	11♓	26	21	19	♆16♍
30	6.33	8	25	28	22	19	♇27♋

Jul	STime	☉	☽	☿	♀	♂	Plnts
1	6.36	9♋	8♈	1♋	23♉	19♏	♃24♑R
2	6.40	10	22	3	24	19	♄ 5♈
3	6.44	11	6♉	5	25	19	♅13♉
4	6.48	12	21	7	26	20	♆16♍
5	6.52	13	6♊	9	27	20	♇28♋
6	6.56	14	21	11	28	20	♃23♑R
7	7.00	15	5♋	13	29	20	♄ 5♈
8	7.04	16	20	16	0♊	20	♅13♉
9	7.08	17	4♌	18	1	20	♆16♍
10	7.12	17	19	20	2	20	♇28♋
11	7.16	18	2♍	22	3	21	♃23♑R
12	7.20	19	16	24	4	21	♄ 5♈
13	7.24	20	29	26	5	21	♅13♉
14	7.28	21	11♎	28	7	21	♆16♍
15	7.32	22	23	0♌	8	21	♇28♋
16	7.36	23	5♏	2	9	22	♃22♑R
17	7.40	24	17	4	10	22	♄ 5♈
18	7.43	25	29	6	11	22	♅13♉
19	7.47	26	11♐	8	12	22	♆17♍
20	7.51	27	23	10	13	23	♇28♋
21	7.55	28	5♑	12	14	23	♃21♑R
22	7.59	29	17	14	15	23	♄ 5♈R
23	8.03	0♌	29	16	16	23	♅13♉
24	8.07	1	12♒	17	17	24	♆17♍
25	8.11	2	25	19	18	24	♇28♋
26	8.15	3	8♓	21	19	24	♃21♑R
27	8.19	4	22	23	20	25	♄ 5♈R
28	8.23	5	5♈	24	22	25	♅13♉
29	8.27	6	19	26	23	26	♆17♍
30	8.31	7	3♉	28	24	26	♇28♋
31	8.35	8	17	29	25	26	♃20♑R

Aug	STime	☉	☽	☿	♀	♂	Plnts
1	8.39	9♌	1♊	1♍	26♊	27♏	♃20♑R
2	8.43	9	16	2	27	27	♄ 5♈R
3	8.47	10	0♋	4	28	27	♅13♉
4	8.51	11	14	5	29	28	♆17♍
5	8.54	12	29	7	0♋	28	♇28♋
6	8.58	13	13♌	8	2	29	♃19♑R
7	9.02	14	27	9	3	29	♄ 4♈R
8	9.06	15	11♍	11	4	0♐	♅13♉
9	9.10	16	24	12	5	0	♆17♍
10	9.14	17	7♎	13	6	0	♇29♋
11	9.18	18	19	15	7	1	♃19♑R
12	9.22	19	1♏	16	8	1	♄ 4♈R
13	9.26	20	13	17	9	2	♅13♉
14	9.30	21	25	18	11	2	♆17♍
15	9.34	22	7♐	19	12	3	♇29♋
16	9.38	23	19	20	13	3	♃18♑R
17	9.42	24	1♑	21	14	4	♄ 4♈R
18	9.46	25	13	22	15	4	♅13♉
19	9.50	26	25	23	16	5	♆18♍
20	9.54	27	8♒	24	17	5	♇29♋
21	9.58	28	21	25	19	6	♃18♑R
22	10.01	29	4♓	26	20	6	♄ 4♈R
23	10.05	0♍	18	26	21	7	♅13♉
24	10.09	1	2♈	27	22	7	♆18♍
25	10.13	2	16	27	23	8	♇29♋
26	10.17	3	0♉	28	24	8	♃18♑R
27	10.21	3	14	28	26	9	♄ 3♈R
28	10.25	4	28	29	27	9	♅13♉R
29	10.29	5	12♊	29	28	10	♆18♍
30	10.33	6	26	29	29	11	♇29♋
31	10.37	7	10♋	29	0♌	11	♃17♑R

Sep	STime	☉	☽	☿	♀	♂	Plnts
1	10.41	8♍	24♋	29♍	1♌	12♐	♃17♑R
2	10.45	9	8♌	29	3	12	♄ 3♈R
3	10.49	10	22	29	4	13	♅13♉R
4	10.53	11	6♍	29	5	13	♆18♍
5	10.57	12	19	28	6	14	♇29♋
6	11.01	13	2♎	28	7	15	♃17♑R
7	11.05	14	15	27	9	15	♄ 3♈R
8	11.09	15	27	27	10	16	♅13♉R
9	11.12	16	9♏	26	11	16	♆18♍
10	11.16	17	21	25	12	17	♇29♋
11	11.20	18	3♐	24	13	18	♃17♑R
12	11.24	19	15	23	14	18	♄ 2♈R
13	11.28	20	27	22	16	19	♅13♉R
14	11.32	21	9♑	21	17	19	♆19♍
15	11.36	22	21	20	18	20	♇29♋
16	11.40	23	3♒	19	19	21	♃17♑
17	11.44	24	16	18	20	21	♄ 2♈R
18	11.48	25	29	17	22	22	♅13♉R
19	11.52	26	13♓	16	23	23	♆19♍
20	11.56	27	27	16	24	23	♇29♋
21	12.00	28	11♈	15	25	24	♃17♑
22	12.04	29	26	15	26	25	♄ 2♈R
23	12.08	0♎	10♉	15D	28	25	♅13♉R
24	12.12	1	24	15	29	26	♆19♍
25	12.16	2	9♊	15	0♍	26	♇ 0♌
26	12.19	3	23	16	1	27	♃17♑
27	12.23	4	7♋	16	3	28	♄ 1♈R
28	12.27	5	21	17	4	28	♅13♉R
29	12.31	6	5♌	18	5	29	♆19♍
30	12.35	7	18	19	6	0♑	♇ 0♌

Oct	STime	☉	☽	☿	♀	♂	Plnts
1	12.39	8♎	2♍	20♍	7♍	0♑	♃18♑
2	12.43	9	15	21	9	1	♄ 1♈R
3	12.47	10	28	22	10	2	♅13♉R
4	12.51	11	11♎	24	11	2	♆19♍
5	12.55	12	23	25	12	3	♇ 0♌
6	12.59	13	5♏	27	13	4	♃18♑
7	13.03	14	17	28	15	4	♄ 0♈R
8	13.07	14	29	0♎	16	5	♅12♉R
9	13.11	15	11♐	1	17	6	♆19♍
10	13.15	16	23	3	18	7	♇ 0♌
11	13.19	17	5♑	5	20	7	♃18♑
12	13.23	18	17	7	21	8	♄ 0♈R
13	13.26	19	29	8	22	9	♅12♉R
14	13.30	20	11♒	10	23	9	♆20♍
15	13.34	21	24	12	25	10	♇ 0♌
16	13.38	22	7♓	13	26	11	♃19♑
17	13.42	23	21	15	27	11	♄ 0♈R
18	13.46	24	5♈	17	28	12	♅12♉R
19	13.50	25	20	19	29	13	♆20♍
20	13.54	26	4♉	20	1♎	14	♇ 0♌
21	13.58	27	19	22	2	14	♃19♑
22	14.02	28	4♊	24	3	15	♄29♓R
23	14.06	29	19	25	4	16	♅12♉R
24	14.10	0♏	3♋	27	6	16	♆20♍
25	14.14	1	18	29	7	17	♇ 0♌
26	14.18	2	2♌	0♏	8	18	♃20♑
27	14.22	3	15	2	9	19	♄29♓R
28	14.26	4	29	4	11	19	♅12♉R
29	14.30	5	12♍	5	12	20	♆20♍
30	14.34	6	25	7	13	21	♇ 0♌
31	14.37	7	7♎	9	14	21	♃21♑

Nov	STime	☉	☽	☿	♀	♂	Plnts
1	14.41	8♏	20♎	10♏	16♎	22♑	♃21♑
2	14.45	9	2♏	12	17	23	♄29♓R
3	14.49	10	14	14	18	24	♅11♉R
4	14.53	11	26	15	19	24	♆20♍
5	14.57	12	8♐	17	21	25	♇ 0♌
6	15.01	13	19	18	22	26	♃21♑
7	15.05	14	1♑	20	23	27	♄29♓R
8	15.09	15	13	21	24	27	♅11♉R
9	15.13	16	25	23	26	28	♆20♍
10	15.17	17	7♒	25	27	29	♇ 0♌R
11	15.21	18	20	26	28	29	♃22♑
12	15.25	19	2♓	28	29	0♒	♄28♓R
13	15.29	20	15	29	1♏	1	♅11♉R
14	15.33	21	29	1♐	2	2	♆20♍
15	15.37	22	13♈	2	3	2	♇ 0♌
16	15.41	23	28	4	4	3	♃23♑
17	15.44	24	13♉	5	6	4	♄28♓R
18	15.48	25	28	7	7	5	♅11♉R
19	15.52	26	13♊	8	8	5	♆21♍
20	15.56	27	28	10	9	6	♇ 0♌R
21	16.00	28	13♋	11	11	7	♃24♑
22	16.04	29	27	13	12	8	♄28♓R
23	16.08	0♐	12♌	14	13	8	♅11♉R
24	16.12	2	25	16	14	9	♆21♍
25	16.16	3	9♍	17	16	10	♇ 0♌R
26	16.20	4	22	19	17	11	♃25♑
27	16.24	5	4♎	20	18	11	♄28♓
28	16.28	6	17	22	19	12	♅10♉R
29	16.32	7	29	23	21	13	♆21♍
30	16.36	8	11♏	25	22	14	♇ 0♌R

Dec	STime	☉	☽	☿	♀	♂	Plnts
1	16.40	9♐	23♏	26♐	23♏	14♒	♃26♑
2	16.44	10	5♐	28	24	15	♄28♓
3	16.48	11	16	29	26	16	♅10♉R
4	16.52	12	28	0♑	27	17	♆21♍
5	16.55	13	10♑	2	28	17	♇ 0♌R
6	16.59	14	22	3	29	18	♃27♑
7	17.03	15	4♒	4	1♐	19	♄28♓
8	17.07	16	16	6	2	20	♅10♉R
9	17.11	17	28	7	3	20	♆21♍
10	17.15	18	11♓	8	4	21	♇ 0♌R
11	17.19	19	24	9	6	22	♃28♑
12	17.23	20	8♈	10	7	23	♄28♓
13	17.27	21	21	11	8	23	♅10♉R
14	17.31	22	6♉	12	9	24	♆21♍
15	17.35	23	21	13	11	25	♇29♋R
16	17.39	24	6♊	14	12	26	♃29♑
17	17.43	25	21	14	13	26	♄28♓
18	17.47	26	6♋	15	14	27	♅10♉R
19	17.51	27	21	15	16	28	♆21♍
20	17.55	28	6♌	15R	17	29	♇29♋R
21	17.59	29	20	15	18	0♓	♃ 0♒
22	18.02	0♑	4♍	15	19	0	♄28♓
23	18.06	1	18	15	21	1	♅10♉R
24	18.10	2	1♎	14	22	2	♆21♍
25	18.14	3	13	13	23	3	♇29♋R
26	18.18	4	26	12	25	3	♃ 1♒
27	18.22	5	8♏	11	26	4	♄29♓
28	18.26	6	20	10	27	5	♅10♉R
29	18.30	7	2♐	9	28	6	♆21♍
30	18.34	8	13	7	0♑	6	♇29♋R
31	18.38	9	25	6	1	7	♃ 2♒

Jan	STime	☉	☽	☿	♀	♂	Plnts
1	18.42	10♑	7♑	5♑	2♑	8♓	♃ 2♒
2	18.46	11	19	3	3	9	♄29♓
3	18.50	12	1♒	2	5	9	♅10♉R
4	18.54	13	13	1	6	10	♆21♍
5	18.58	14	25	1	7	11	♇29♋R
6	19.02	15	8♓	0	8	12	♃ 4♒
7	19.06	16	21	29♐	10	12	♄29♓
8	19.10	17	4♈	29	11	13	♅ 9♉
9	19.13	18	17	29D	12	14	♆21♍R
10	19.17	19	1♉	29	13	15	♇29♋R
11	19.21	20	15	29	15	15	♃ 5♒
12	19.25	21	29	0♑	16	16	♄ 0♈
13	19.29	22	14♊	0	17	17	♅ 9♉
14	19.33	23	29	0	18	18	♆21♍R
15	19.37	24	14♋	1	20	18	♇29♋R
16	19.41	25	29	2	21	19	♃ 6♒
17	19.45	26	14♌	3	22	20	♄ 0♈
18	19.49	27	28	3	23	21	♅ 9♉
19	19.53	28	12♍	4	25	21	♆21♍R
20	19.57	29	26	5	26	22	♇29♋R
21	20.01	1♒	9♎	6	27	23	♃ 7♒
22	20.05	2	22	7	28	24	♄ 0♈
23	20.09	3	4♏	8	0♒	24	♅ 9♉
24	20.13	4	16	10	1	25	♆21♍R
25	20.17	5	28	11	2	26	♇29♋R
26	20.20	6	10♐	12	4	27	♃ 8♒
27	20.24	7	22	13	5	27	♄ 1♈
28	20.28	8	4♑	14	6	28	♅ 9♉
29	20.32	9	16	16	7	29	♆20♍R
30	20.36	10	28	17	9	0♈	♇28♋R
31	20.40	11	10♒	18	10	0	♃ 9♒

Feb	STime	☉	☽	☿	♀	♂	Plnts
1	20.44	12♒	22♒	20♑	11♒	1♈	♃10♒
2	20.48	13	5♓	21	12	2	♄ 1♈
3	20.52	14	18	22	14	3	♅10♉
4	20.56	15	1♈	24	15	3	♆20♍R
5	21.00	16	14	25	16	4	♇28♋R
6	21.04	17	27	27	17	5	♃11♒
7	21.08	18	11♉	28	19	6	♄ 2♈
8	21.12	19	25	0♒	20	6	♅10♉
9	21.16	20	9♊	1	21	7	♆20♍R
10	21.20	21	23	3	22	8	♇28♋R
11	21.24	22	8♋	4	24	9	♃12♒
12	21.27	23	23	6	25	9	♄ 2♈
13	21.31	24	7♌	7	26	10	♅10♉
14	21.35	25	22	9	27	11	♆20♍R
15	21.39	26	6♍	10	29	12	♇28♋R
16	21.43	27	20	12	0♓	12	♃13♒
17	21.47	28	4♎	13	1	13	♄ 3♈
18	21.51	29	17	15	2	14	♅10♉
19	21.55	0♓	0♏	17	4	15	♆20♍R
20	21.59	1	12	18	5	15	♇28♋R
21	22.03	2	24	20	6	16	♃14♒
22	22.07	3	6♐	22	7	17	♄ 3♈
23	22.11	4	18	23	9	17	♅10♉
24	22.15	5	0♑	25	10	18	♆20♍R
25	22.19	6	12	27	11	19	♇28♋R
26	22.23	7	24	29	12	20	♃16♒
27	22.27	8	6♒	0♓	14	20	♄ 4♈
28	22.31	9	18	2	15	21	♅10♉

Mar	STime	☉	☽	☿	♀	♂	Plnts
1	22.35	10♓	1♓	4♓	16♓	22♈	♃16♒
2	22.38	11	14	6	17	23	♄ 4♈
3	22.42	12	27	8	19	23	♅10♉
4	22.46	13	11♈	9	20	24	♆20♍R
5	22.50	14	24	11	21	25	♇28♋R
6	22.54	15	8♉	13	22	25	♃17♒
7	22.58	16	22	15	24	26	♄ 5♈
8	23.02	17	6♊	17	25	27	♅10♉
9	23.06	18	20	19	26	28	♆20♍R
10	23.10	19	4♋	21	27	28	♇28♋R
11	23.14	20	18	23	29	29	♃19♒
12	23.18	21	2♌	25	0♈	0♉	♄ 6♈
13	23.22	22	17	27	1	1	♅11♉
14	23.26	23	1♍	29	2	1	♆19♍R
15	23.30	24	15	1♈	4	2	♇28♋R
16	23.34	25	28	3	5	3	♃20♒
17	23.38	26	12♎	5	6	3	♄ 6♈
18	23.42	27	25	7	7	4	♅11♉
19	23.45	28	8♏	9	9	5	♆19♍R
20	23.49	29	20	11	10	6	♇28♋R
21	23.53	0♈	2♐	12	11	6	♃21♒
22	23.57	1	14	14	12	7	♄ 7♈
23	0.01	2	26	16	14	8	♅11♉
24	0.05	3	8♑	18	15	8	♆19♍R
25	0.09	4	20	20	16	9	♇28♋R
26	0.13	5	2♒	21	17	10	♃22♒
27	0.17	6	14	23	18	11	♄ 7♈
28	0.21	7	27	24	20	11	♅11♉
29	0.25	8	9♓	26	21	12	♆19♍R
30	0.29	9	23	27	22	13	♇28♋R
31	0.33	10	6♈	28	23	13	♃23♒

Apr	STime	☉	☽	☿	♀	♂	Plnts
1	0.37	11♈	20♈	0♉	25♈	14♉	♃23♒
2	0.41	12	4♉	1	26	15	♄ 8♈
3	0.45	13	18	2	27	16	♅12♉
4	0.49	14	2♊	2	28	16	♆19♍R
5	0.53	15	17	3	0♉	17	♇28♋R
6	0.56	16	1♋	4	1	18	♃24♒
7	1.00	17	15	4	2	18	♄ 9♈
8	1.04	18	29	5	3	19	♅12♉
9	1.08	19	13♌	5	5	20	♆19♍R
10	1.12	20	27	5	6	20	♇28♋
11	1.16	21	11♍	5R	7	21	♃25♒
12	1.20	22	24	5	8	22	♄ 9♈
13	1.24	23	7♎	5	9	23	♅12♉
14	1.28	24	20	5	11	23	♆19♍R
15	1.32	25	3♏	5	12	24	♇28♋
16	1.36	26	16	4	13	25	♃26♒
17	1.40	27	28	4	14	25	♄10♈
18	1.44	27	10♐	3	16	26	♅12♉
19	1.48	28	22	2	17	27	♆18♍R
20	1.52	29	4♑	2	18	27	♇28♋
21	1.56	0♉	16	1	19	28	♃27♒
22	2.00	1	28	0	21	29	♄11♈
23	2.03	2	10♒	0	22	0♊	♅13♉
24	2.07	3	22	29♈	23	0	♆18♍R
25	2.11	4	4♓	28	24	1	♇28♋
26	2.15	5	17	28	25	2	♃27♒
27	2.19	6	1♈	27	27	2	♄11♈
28	2.23	7	14	27	28	3	♅13♉
29	2.27	8	28	26	29	4	♆18♍R
30	2.31	9	13♉	26	0♊	4	♇28♋

May	STime	☉	☽	☿	♀	♂	Plnts
1	2.35	10♉	27♉	25♈	2♊	5♊	♃28♒
2	2.39	11	12♊	25	3	6	♄12♈
3	2.43	12	27	25	4	6	♅13♉
4	2.47	13	11♋	25	5	7	♆18♍R
5	2.51	14	26	25D	6	8	♇28♋
6	2.55	15	10♌	25	8	8	♃29♒
7	2.59	16	24	25	9	9	♄12♈
8	3.03	17	7♍	25	10	10	♅14♉
9	3.07	18	21	26	11	10	♆18♍R
10	3.10	19	4♎	26	13	11	♇28♋
11	3.14	20	17	26	14	12	♃29♒
12	3.18	21	0♏	27	15	13	♄13♈
13	3.22	22	12	27	16	13	♅14♉
14	3.26	23	24	28	17	14	♆18♍R
15	3.30	24	6♐	29	19	15	♇28♋
16	3.34	25	18	0♉	20	15	♃ 0♓
17	3.38	26	0♑	0	21	16	♄13♈
18	3.42	27	12	1	22	17	♅14♉
19	3.46	28	24	2	23	17	♆18♍
20	3.50	29	6♒	3	25	18	♇28♋
21	3.54	29	18	4	26	19	♃ 0♓
22	3.58	0♊	0♓	5	27	19	♄14♈
23	4.02	1	13	6	28	20	♅14♉
24	4.06	2	26	8	0♋	21	♆18♍
25	4.10	3	9♈	9	1	21	♇28♋
26	4.14	4	22	10	2	22	♃ 1♓
27	4.18	5	7♉	11	3	23	♄14♈
28	4.21	6	21	13	4	23	♅15♉
29	4.25	7	6♊	14	6	24	♆18♍
30	4.29	8	21	16	7	25	♇28♋
31	4.33	9	6♋	17	8	25	♃ 1♓

Jun	STime	☉	☽	☿	♀	♂	Plnts
1	4.37	10♊	21♋	19♉	9♋	26♊	♃ 1♓
2	4.41	11	6♌	20	10	27	♄15♈
3	4.45	12	20	22	12	27	♅15♉
4	4.49	13	4♍	24	13	28	♆18♍
5	4.53	14	18	25	14	29	♇28♋
6	4.57	15	1♎	27	15	29	♃ 2♓
7	5.01	16	14	29	16	0♋	♄15♈
8	5.05	17	27	1♊	18	1	♅15♉
9	5.09	18	9♏	2	19	1	♆18♍
10	5.13	19	21	4	20	2	♇28♋
11	5.17	20	3♐	6	21	3	♃ 2♓
12	5.21	21	15	8	22	3	♄16♈
13	5.25	22	27	10	24	4	♅16♉
14	5.28	22	9♑	12	25	5	♆18♍
15	5.32	23	21	14	26	5	♇28♋
16	5.36	24	3♒	17	27	6	♃ 2♓
17	5.40	25	15	19	28	7	♄16♈
18	5.44	26	27	21	29	7	♅16♉
19	5.48	27	9♓	23	1♌	8	♆18♍
20	5.52	28	21	25	2	9	♇29♋
21	5.56	29	4♈	27	3	9	♃ 2♓
22	6.00	0♋	17	0♋	4	10	♄17♈
23	6.04	1	1♉	2	5	11	♅16♉
24	6.08	2	15	4	7	11	♆18♍
25	6.12	3	29	6	8	12	♇29♋
26	6.16	4	14♊	8	9	13	♃ 2♓R
27	6.20	5	29	10	10	13	♄17♈
28	6.24	6	15♋	13	11	14	♅16♉
29	6.28	7	0♌	15	12	14	♆18♍
30	6.32	8	15	17	14	15	♇29♋

Jul	STime	☉	☽	☿	♀	♂	Plnts
1	6.36	9♋	29♌	19♋	15♌	16♋	♃ 2♓R
2	6.39	10	14♍	21	16	16	♄17♈
3	6.43	11	27	23	17	17	♅16♉
4	6.47	12	11♎	25	18	18	♆18♍
5	6.51	12	24	27	20	18	♇29♋
6	6.55	13	6♏	29	21	19	♃ 2♓R
7	6.59	14	18	0♌	22	20	♄17♈
8	7.03	15	0♐	2	23	20	♅17♉
9	7.07	16	12	4	24	21	♆18♍
10	7.11	17	24	6	25	22	♇29♋
11	7.15	18	6♑	7	27	22	♃ 1♓R
12	7.19	19	18	9	28	23	♄17♈
13	7.23	20	0♒	11	29	24	♅17♉
14	7.27	21	12	12	0♍	24	♆19♍
15	7.31	22	24	14	1	25	♇29♋
16	7.35	23	6♓	16	2	26	♃ 1♓R
17	7.39	24	18	17	3	26	♄18♈
18	7.43	25	1♈	19	5	27	♅17♉
19	7.46	26	13	20	6	27	♆19♍
20	7.50	27	27	21	7	28	♇29♋
21	7.54	28	10♉	23	8	29	♃ 1♓R
22	7.58	29	24	24	9	29	♄18♈
23	8.02	0♌	8♊	25	10	0♌	♅17♉
24	8.06	1	23	27	12	1	♆19♍
25	8.10	2	8♋	28	13	1	♇29♋
26	8.14	3	23	29	14	2	♃ 0♓R
27	8.18	3	8♌	0♍	15	3	♄18♈
28	8.22	4	23	1	16	3	♅17♉
29	8.26	5	8♍	3	17	4	♆19♍
30	8.30	6	22	4	18	5	♇ 0♌
31	8.34	7	6♎	5	19	5	♃ 0♓R

Aug	STime	☉	☽	☿	♀	♂	Plnts
1	8.38	8♌	20♎	5♍	21♍	6♌	♃29♒R
2	8.42	9	2♏	6	22	7	♄18♈R
3	8.46	10	15	7	23	7	♅17♉
4	8.50	11	27	8	24	8	♆19♍
5	8.54	12	9♐	9	25	8	♇ 0♌
6	8.57	13	21	9	26	9	♃29♒R
7	9.01	14	3♑	10	27	10	♄18♈R
8	9.05	15	15	10	28	10	♅17♉
9	9.09	16	27	11	29	11	♆19♍
10	9.13	17	9♒	11	1♎	12	♇ 0♌
11	9.17	18	21	12	2	12	♃28♒R
12	9.21	19	3♓	12	3	13	♄18♈R
13	9.25	20	15	12	4	14	♅17♉
14	9.29	21	28	12R	5	14	♆19♍
15	9.33	22	11♈	12	6	15	♇ 0♌
16	9.37	23	23	12	7	15	♃28♒R
17	9.41	24	7♉	12	8	16	♄17♈R
18	9.45	25	20	11	9	17	♅17♉
19	9.49	26	4♊	11	10	17	♆20♍
20	9.53	27	18	10	11	18	♇ 0♌
21	9.57	27	2♋	10	13	19	♃27♒R
22	10.01	28	17	9	14	19	♄17♈R
23	10.04	29	2♌	8	15	20	♅18♉
24	10.08	0♍	17	8	16	21	♆20♍
25	10.12	1	2♍	7	17	21	♇ 0♌
26	10.16	2	16	6	18	22	♃26♒R
27	10.20	3	1♎	5	19	22	♄17♈R
28	10.24	4	14	4	20	23	♅18♉R
29	10.28	5	28	3	21	24	♆20♍
30	10.32	6	11♏	2	22	24	♇ 0♌
31	10.36	7	23	1	23	25	♃26♒R

Sep	STime	☉	☽	☿	♀	♂	Plnts
1	10.40	8♍	6♐	1♍	24♎	26♌	♃26♒R
2	10.44	9	18	0	25	26	♄17♈R
3	10.48	10	29	0	26	27	♅17♉R
4	10.52	11	11♑	29♌	27	28	♆20♍
5	10.56	12	23	29	28	28	♇ 1♌
6	11.00	13	5♒	29D	29	29	♃25♒R
7	11.04	14	17	29	0♏	29	♄17♈R
8	11.08	15	29	29	1	0♍	♅17♉R
9	11.11	16	12♓	29	2	1	♆20♍
10	11.15	17	25	0♍	3	1	♇ 1♌
11	11.19	18	7♈	0	4	2	♃24♒R
12	11.23	19	20	1	5	3	♄16♈R
13	11.27	20	4♉	2	6	3	♅17♉R
14	11.31	21	17	3	7	4	♆21♍
15	11.35	22	1♊	4	8	5	♇ 1♌
16	11.39	23	14	5	9	5	♃24♒R
17	11.43	24	28	7	10	6	♄16♈R
18	11.47	25	13♋	8	11	6	♅17♉R
19	11.51	26	27	9	12	7	♆21♍
20	11.55	27	12♌	11	12	8	♇ 1♌
21	11.59	28	26	13	13	8	♃23♒R
22	12.03	29	10♍	14	14	9	♄16♈R
23	12.07	0♎	25	16	15	10	♅17♉R
24	12.11	0	9♎	18	16	10	♆21♍
25	12.15	1	23	19	17	11	♇ 1♌
26	12.19	2	6♏	21	18	12	♃23♒R
27	12.22	3	19	23	18	12	♄15♈R
28	12.26	4	1♐	25	19	13	♅17♉R
29	12.30	5	13	27	20	13	♆21♍
30	12.34	6	25	28	21	14	♇ 1♌

Oct	STime	☉	☽	☿	♀	♂	Plnts
1	12.38	7♎	7♑	0♎	22♏	15♍	♃23♒R
2	12.42	8	19	2	22	15	♄15♈R
3	12.46	9	1♒	4	23	16	♅17♉R
4	12.50	10	13	6	24	17	♆21♍
5	12.54	11	25	7	25	17	♇ 1♌
6	12.58	12	8♓	9	25	18	♃22♒R
7	13.02	13	20	11	26	18	♄14♈R
8	13.06	14	3♈	13	27	19	♅17♉R
9	13.10	15	16	15	27	20	♆22♍
10	13.14	16	0♉	16	28	20	♇ 1♌
11	13.18	17	13	18	28	21	♃22♒R
12	13.22	18	27	20	29	22	♄14♈R
13	13.26	19	11♊	21	0♐	22	♅17♉R
14	13.29	20	25	23	0	23	♆22♍
15	13.33	21	9♋	25	1	24	♇ 1♌
16	13.37	22	24	26	1	24	♃22♒R
17	13.41	23	8♌	28	2	25	♄14♈R
18	13.45	24	22	0♏	2	25	♅16♉R
19	13.49	25	6♍	1	2	26	♆22♍
20	13.53	26	20	3	3	27	♇ 1♌
21	13.57	27	4♎	5	3	27	♃22♒
22	14.01	28	17	6	3	28	♄13♈R
23	14.05	29	1♏	8	4	29	♅16♉R
24	14.09	0♏	14	9	4	29	♆22♍
25	14.13	1	27	11	4	0♎	♇ 1♌
26	14.17	2	9♐	12	4	0	♃22♒
27	14.21	3	21	14	4	1	♄13♈R
28	14.25	4	3♑	15	5	2	♅16♉R
29	14.29	5	15	17	5	2	♆22♍
30	14.33	6	27	19	5R	3	♇ 1♌
31	14.37	7	9♒	20	5	4	♃22♒

Nov	STime	☉	☽	☿	♀	♂	Plnts
1	14.40	8♏	21♒	22♏	5♐	4♎	♃22♒
2	14.44	9	3♓	23	4	5	♄12♈R
3	14.48	10	16	25	4	6	♅16♉R
4	14.52	11	28	26	4	6	♆22♍
5	14.56	12	11♈	28	4	7	♇ 1♌
6	15.00	13	25	29	4	7	♃23♒
7	15.04	14	8♉	0♐	3	8	♄12♈R
8	15.08	15	23	2	3	9	♅16♉R
9	15.12	16	7♊	3	3	9	♆22♍
10	15.16	17	21	5	2	10	♇ 1♌
11	15.20	18	6♋	6	2	11	♃23♒
12	15.24	19	20	8	1	11	♄12♈R
13	15.28	20	5♌	9	1	12	♅15♉R
14	15.32	21	19	10	0	12	♆23♍
15	15.36	22	3♍	12	0	13	♇ 1♌R
16	15.40	23	17	13	29♏	14	♃23♒
17	15.44	24	0♎	14	29	14	♄12♈R
18	15.47	25	14	16	28	15	♅15♉R
19	15.51	26	27	17	27	16	♆23♍
20	15.55	27	10♏	18	27	16	♇ 1♌
21	15.59	28	22	20	26	17	♃24♒
22	16.03	29	5♐	21	26	17	♄11♈R
23	16.07	0♐	17	22	25	18	♅15♉R
24	16.11	1	29	23	24	19	♆23♍
25	16.15	2	11♑	24	24	19	♇ 1♌R
26	16.19	3	23	25	23	20	♃24♒
27	16.23	4	5♒	26	23	21	♄11♈R
28	16.27	5	17	27	22	21	♅15♉R
29	16.31	6	29	27	22	22	♆23♍
30	16.35	7	11♓	28	21	23	♇ 1♌R

Dec	STime	☉	☽	☿	♀	♂	Plnts
1	16.39	8♐	23♓	29♐	21♏	23♎	♃25♒
2	16.43	9	6♈	29	21	24	♄11♈R
3	16.47	10	19	29	20	24	♅15♉R
4	16.51	11	3♉	29R	20	25	♆23♍
5	16.54	12	16	29	20	26	♇ 1♌R
6	16.58	13	1♊	29	20	26	♃26♒
7	17.02	14	15	29	20	27	♄11♈R
8	17.06	15	0♋	28	19	28	♅14♉R
9	17.10	16	15	27	19	28	♆23♍
10	17.14	17	0♌	26	19D	29	♇ 1♌R
11	17.18	18	15	25	19	29	♃27♒
12	17.22	20	29	24	19	0♏	♄11♈R
13	17.26	21	13♍	23	19	1	♅14♉R
14	17.30	22	27	21	20	1	♆23♍
15	17.34	23	11♎	20	20	2	♇ 1♌R
16	17.38	24	24	19	20	3	♃27♒
17	17.42	25	6♏	17	20	3	♄11♈
18	17.46	26	19	16	20	4	♅14♉R
19	17.50	27	1♐	15	21	4	♆23♍
20	17.54	28	14	15	21	5	♇ 1♌R
21	17.58	29	26	14	21	6	♃28♒
22	18.02	0♑	8♑	13	22	6	♄11♈
23	18.05	1	20	13	22	7	♅14♉R
24	18.09	2	2♒	13D	23	8	♆23♍
25	18.13	3	14	13	23	8	♇ 1♌R
26	18.17	4	25	13	24	9	♃29♒
27	18.21	5	7♓	14	24	9	♄11♈
28	18.25	6	19	14	25	10	♅14♉R
29	18.29	7	2♈	15	25	11	♆23♍
30	18.33	8	14	16	26	11	♇ 1♌R
31	18.37	9	27	16	27	12	♃ 0♓

1 9 3 9

Jan	STime	☉	☽	☿	♀	♂	Plnts
1	18.41	10♑	10♉	17♐	27♏	13♏	♃ 0♓
2	18.45	11	24	18	28	13	♄11♈
3	18.49	12	9♊	19	29	14	♅14♉R
4	18.53	13	23	20	29	14	♆23♍
5	18.57	14	8♋	21	0♐	15	♇ 0♌R
6	19.01	15	24	22	1	16	♃ 1♓
7	19.05	16	9♌	24	2	16	♄11♈
8	19.09	17	24	25	2	17	♅14♉R
9	19.12	18	9♍	26	3	17	♆23♍R
10	19.16	19	23	27	4	18	♇ 0♌R
11	19.20	20	7♎	29	5	19	♃ 2♓
12	19.24	21	21	0♑	6	19	♄12♈
13	19.28	22	4♏	1	7	20	♅14♉R
14	19.32	23	16	3	7	21	♆23♍R
15	19.36	24	29	4	8	21	♇ 0♌R
16	19.40	25	11♐	5	9	22	♃ 3♓
17	19.44	26	23	7	10	22	♄12♈
18	19.48	27	5♑	8	11	23	♅14♉
19	19.52	28	17	10	12	24	♆23♍R
20	19.56	29	29	11	13	24	♇ 0♌R
21	20.00	0♒	10♒	13	14	25	♃ 4♓
22	20.04	1	22	14	15	25	♄12♈
23	20.08	2	4♓	15	16	26	♅14♉
24	20.12	3	16	17	17	27	♆23♍R
25	20.16	4	28	18	18	27	♇ 0♌R
26	20.20	5	11♈	20	19	28	♃ 6♓
27	20.23	6	23	22	20	29	♄13♈
28	20.27	7	6♉	23	21	29	♅14♉
29	20.31	8	19	25	22	0♐	♆23♍R
30	20.35	9	3♊	26	23	0	♇ 0♌R
31	20.39	10	17	28	24	1	♃ 7♓

Feb	STime	☉	☽	☿	♀	♂	Plnts
1	20.43	11♒	1♋	29♑	25♐	2♐	♃ 7♓
2	20.47	12	16	1♒	26	2	♄13♈
3	20.51	13	2♌	2	27	3	♅14♉
4	20.55	14	17	4	28	3	♆23♍R
5	20.59	15	2♍	6	29	4	♇ 0♌R
6	21.03	17	17	7	0♑	5	♃ 8♓
7	21.07	18	2♎	9	1	5	♄14♈
8	21.11	19	16	11	2	6	♅14♉
9	21.15	20	0♏	12	3	6	♆22♍R
10	21.19	21	13	14	4	7	♇ 0♌R
11	21.23	22	25	16	5	8	♃ 9♓
12	21.27	23	8♐	18	6	8	♄14♈
13	21.30	24	20	19	7	9	♅14♉
14	21.34	25	2♑	21	8	9	♆22♍R
15	21.38	26	14	23	9	10	♇ 0♌R
16	21.42	27	26	25	11	11	♃10♓
17	21.46	28	7♒	26	12	11	♄14♈
18	21.50	29	19	28	13	12	♅14♉
19	21.54	0♓	1♓	0♓	14	12	♆22♍R
20	21.58	1	13	2	15	13	♇29♋R
21	22.02	2	25	4	16	14	♃12♓
22	22.06	3	8♈	6	17	14	♄15♈
23	22.10	4	20	7	18	15	♅14♉
24	22.14	5	3♉	9	19	15	♆22♍R
25	22.18	6	16	11	21	16	♇29♋R
26	22.22	7	29	13	22	17	♃13♓
27	22.26	8	12♊	15	23	17	♄15♈
28	22.30	9	26	17	24	18	♅14♉

Mar	STime	☉	☽	☿	♀	♂	Plnts
1	22.34	10♓	10♋	19♓	25♑	18♐	♃14♓
2	22.38	11	25	21	26	19	♄16♈
3	22.41	12	10♌	23	27	19	♅14♉
4	22.45	13	25	24	28	20	♆22♍R
5	22.49	14	10♍	26	0♒	21	♇29♋R
6	22.53	15	25	28	1	21	♃15♓
7	22.57	16	10♎	0♈	2	22	♄16♈
8	23.01	17	24	2	3	22	♅14♉
9	23.05	18	8♏	3	4	23	♆22♍R
10	23.09	19	21	5	5	24	♇29♋R
11	23.13	20	4♐	7	7	24	♃16♓
12	23.17	21	16	8	8	25	♄17♈
13	23.21	22	28	9	9	25	♅15♉
14	23.25	23	10♑	11	10	26	♆22♍R
15	23.29	24	22	12	11	26	♇29♋R
16	23.33	25	4♒	13	12	27	♃17♓
17	23.37	26	16	14	13	28	♄18♈
18	23.41	27	28	15	15	28	♅15♉
19	23.45	28	10♓	16	16	29	♆22♍R
20	23.48	29	22	16	17	29	♇29♋R
21	23.52	0♈	5♈	17	18	0♑	♃18♓
22	23.56	1	17	17	19	0	♄18♈
23	0.00	2	0♉	17	20	1	♅15♉
24	0.04	3	13	17R	22	1	♆21♍R
25	0.08	4	26	17	23	2	♇29♋
26	0.12	5	9♊	17	24	3	♃20♓
27	0.16	6	23	17	25	3	♄19♈
28	0.20	7	6♋	16	26	4	♅15♉
29	0.24	8	21	16	28	4	♆21♍R
30	0.28	9	5♌	15	29	5	♇29♋R
31	0.32	10	20	15	0♓	5	♃21♓

Apr	STime	☉	☽	☿	♀	♂	Plnts
1	0.36	11♈	4♍	14♈	1♓	6♑	♃21♓
2	0.40	12	19	13	2	6	♄20♈
3	0.44	13	3♎	12	3	7	♅16♉
4	0.48	14	18	11	5	7	♆21♍R
5	0.52	15	2♏	11	6	8	♇29♋
6	0.55	15	15	10	7	9	♃22♓
7	0.59	16	29	9	8	9	♄20♈
8	1.03	17	12♐	8	9	10	♅16♉
9	1.07	18	24	8	11	10	♆21♍R
10	1.11	19	6♑	7	12	11	♇29♋
11	1.15	20	18	7	13	11	♃23♓
12	1.19	21	0♒	6	14	12	♄21♈
13	1.23	22	12	6	15	12	♅16♉
14	1.27	23	24	6	16	13	♆21♍R
15	1.31	24	6♓	5	18	13	♇29♋
16	1.35	25	18	5D	19	14	♃24♓
17	1.39	26	1♈	5	20	14	♄21♈
18	1.43	27	13	5	21	15	♅16♉
19	1.47	28	26	6	22	15	♆21♍R
20	1.51	29	9♉	6	24	16	♇29♋
21	1.55	0♉	22	6	25	16	♃26♓
22	1.59	1	6♊	7	26	17	♄22♈
23	2.03	2	19	7	27	17	♅17♉
24	2.06	3	3♋	8	28	18	♆21♍R
25	2.10	4	17	8	0♈	18	♇29♋
26	2.14	5	2♌	9	1	18	♃27♓
27	2.18	6	16	10	2	19	♄23♈
28	2.22	7	0♍	10	3	19	♅17♉
29	2.26	8	14	11	4	20	♆21♍R
30	2.30	9	28	12	6	20	♇29♋

May	STime	☉	☽	☿	♀	♂	Plnts
1	2.34	10♉	13♎	13♈	7♈	21♑	♃28♓
2	2.38	11	26	14	8	21	♄23♈
3	2.42	12	10♏	15	9	22	♅17♉
4	2.46	13	24	16	10	22	♆20♍R
5	2.50	14	7♐	17	12	22	♇29♋
6	2.54	15	19	19	13	23	♃29♓
7	2.58	16	2♑	20	14	23	♄24♈
8	3.02	17	14	21	15	24	♅17♉
9	3.06	18	26	22	16	24	♆20♍R
10	3.10	19	8♒	24	18	25	♇29♋
11	3.13	20	20	25	19	25	♃ 0♈
12	3.17	21	2♓	27	20	25	♄25♈
13	3.21	22	14	28	21	26	♅18♉
14	3.25	22	26	0♉	22	26	♆20♍R
15	3.29	23	9♈	1	24	26	♇29♋
16	3.33	24	21	3	25	27	♃ 1♈
17	3.37	25	4♉	4	26	27	♄25♈
18	3.41	26	18	6	27	28	♅18♉
19	3.45	27	1♊	8	28	28	♆20♍
20	3.49	28	15	9	0♉	28	♇29♋
21	3.53	29	29	11	1	29	♃ 2♈
22	3.57	0♊	14♋	13	2	29	♄26♈
23	4.01	1	28	15	3	29	♅18♉
24	4.05	2	13♌	17	4	0♒	♆20♍
25	4.09	3	27	18	6	0	♇29♋
26	4.13	4	11♍	20	7	0	♃ 2♈
27	4.17	5	25	22	8	0	♄26♈
28	4.21	6	9♎	24	9	1	♅19♉
29	4.24	7	22	26	10	1	♆20♍
30	4.28	8	6♏	28	12	1	♇29♋
31	4.32	9	19	1♊	13	1	♃ 3♈

Jun	STime	☉	☽	☿	♀	♂	Plnts
1	4.36	10♊	2♐	3♊	14♉	2♒	♃ 3♈
2	4.40	11	15	5	15	2	♄27♈
3	4.44	12	28	7	16	2	♅19♉
4	4.48	13	10♑	9	18	2	♆20♍
5	4.52	14	22	11	19	3	♇ 0♌
6	4.56	15	4♒	13	20	3	♃ 4♈
7	5.00	16	16	16	21	3	♄27♈
8	5.04	17	28	18	23	3	♅19♉
9	5.08	17	10♓	20	24	3	♆20♍
10	5.12	18	22	22	25	3	♇ 0♌
11	5.16	19	4♈	24	26	4	♃ 5♈
12	5.20	20	17	27	27	4	♄28♈
13	5.24	21	29	29	29	4	♅19♉
14	5.28	22	12♉	1♋	0♊	4	♆20♍
15	5.31	23	26	3	1	4	♇ 0♌
16	5.35	24	10♊	5	2	4	♃ 6♈
17	5.39	25	24	7	3	4	♄28♈
18	5.43	26	9♋	9	5	4	♅20♉
19	5.47	27	24	11	6	4	♆20♍
20	5.51	28	8♌	13	7	4	♇ 0♌
21	5.55	29	23	15	8	4	♃ 6♈
22	5.59	0♋	8♍	17	9	4R	♄29♈
23	6.03	1	22	18	11	4	♅20♉
24	6.07	2	6♎	20	12	4	♆20♍
25	6.11	3	19	22	13	4	♇ 0♌
26	6.15	4	3♏	24	14	4	♃ 7♈
27	6.19	5	16	25	16	4	♄29♈
28	6.23	6	29	27	17	4	♅20♉
29	6.27	7	12♐	28	18	4	♆20♍
30	6.31	8	24	0♌	19	4	♇ 0♌

Jul	STime	☉	☽	☿	♀	♂	Plnts
1	6.35	8♋	6♑	2♌	20♊	4♒	♃ 7♈
2	6.39	9	19	3	22	4	♄29♈
3	6.42	10	1♒	4	23	4	♅20♉
4	6.46	11	13	6	24	4	♆21♍
5	6.50	12	25	7	25	3	♇ 0♌
6	6.54	13	6♓	8	27	3	♃ 8♈
7	6.58	14	18	10	28	3	♄ 0♉
8	7.02	15	0♈	11	29	3	♅21♉
9	7.06	16	12	12	0♋	3	♆21♍
10	7.10	17	25	13	1	3	♇ 0♌
11	7.14	18	7♉	14	3	2	♃ 8♈
12	7.18	19	21	15	4	2	♄ 0♉
13	7.22	20	4♊	16	5	2	♅21♉
14	7.26	21	18	17	6	2	♆21♍
15	7.30	22	3♋	18	8	1	♇ 1♌
16	7.34	23	17	19	9	1	♃ 8♈
17	7.38	24	2♌	20	10	1	♄ 0♉
18	7.42	25	18	21	11	1	♅21♉
19	7.46	26	3♍	21	12	0	♆21♍
20	7.49	27	17	22	14	0	♇ 1♌
21	7.53	28	2♎	22	15	0	♃ 8♈
22	7.57	28	16	23	16	0	♄ 1♉
23	8.01	29	0♏	23	17	29♑	♅21♉
24	8.05	0♌	13	23	19	29	♆21♍
25	8.09	1	26	24	20	29	♇ 1♌
26	8.13	2	9♐	24	21	28	♃ 8♈
27	8.17	3	21	24R	22	28	♄ 1♉
28	8.21	4	3♑	24	23	28	♅21♉
29	8.25	5	15	24	25	28	♆21♍
30	8.29	6	28	24	26	27	♇ 1♌
31	8.33	7	10♒	23	27	27	♃ 9♈R

Aug	STime	☉	☽	☿	♀	♂	Plnts
1	8.37	8♌	21♒	23♌	28♋	27♑	♃ 8♈R
2	8.41	9	3♓	23	0♌	27	♄ 1♉
3	8.45	10	15	22	1	26	♅21♉
4	8.49	11	27	21	2	26	♆21♍
5	8.53	12	9♈	21	3	26	♇ 1♌
6	8.56	13	21	20	5	26	♃ 8♈R
7	9.00	14	3♉	19	6	25	♄ 1♉
8	9.04	15	16	19	7	25	♅21♉
9	9.08	16	29	18	8	25	♆21♍
10	9.12	17	13♊	17	9	25	♇ 1♌
11	9.16	18	27	16	11	25	♃ 8♈R
12	9.20	19	11♋	15	12	25	♄ 1♉
13	9.24	20	26	15	13	24	♅22♉
14	9.28	21	11♌	14	14	24	♆22♍
15	9.32	21	26	13	16	24	♇ 1♌
16	9.36	22	12♍	13	17	24	♃ 8♈R
17	9.40	23	27	12	18	24	♄ 1♉
18	9.44	24	11♎	12	19	24	♅22♉
19	9.48	25	25	12	21	24	♆22♍
20	9.52	26	9♏	12D	22	24	♇ 2♌
21	9.56	27	23	12	23	24	♃ 8♈R
22	10.00	28	5♐	12	24	24	♄ 1♉R
23	10.04	29	18	12	26	24D	♅22♉
24	10.07	0♍	0♑	13	27	24	♆22♍
25	10.11	1	13	13	28	24	♇ 2♌
26	10.15	2	25	14	29	24	♃ 7♈R
27	10.19	3	7♒	15	0♍	24	♄ 1♉R
28	10.23	4	18	16	2	24	♅22♉
29	10.27	5	0♓	17	3	24	♆22♍
30	10.31	6	12	18	4	24	♇ 2♌
31	10.35	7	24	19	5	24	♃ 7♈R

Sep	STime	☉	☽	☿	♀	♂	Plnts
1	10.39	8♍	6♈	21♌	7♍	24♑	♃ 7♈R
2	10.43	9	18	22	8	24	♄ 1♉R
3	10.47	10	0♉	23	9	24	♅22♉
4	10.51	11	13	25	10	25	♆22♍
5	10.55	12	25	27	12	25	♇ 2♌
6	10.59	13	8♊	28	13	25	♃ 6♈R
7	11.03	14	22	0♍	14	25	♄ 0♉R
8	11.07	15	6♋	2	15	25	♅22♉R
9	11.11	16	20	4	17	25	♆22♍
10	11.14	17	5♌	6	18	26	♇ 2♌
11	11.18	18	19	8	19	26	♃ 6♈R
12	11.22	19	5♍	9	20	26	♄ 0♉R
13	11.26	19	20	11	22	26	♅22♉R
14	11.30	20	5♎	13	23	27	♆23♍
15	11.34	21	20	15	24	27	♇ 2♌
16	11.38	22	4♏	17	25	27	♃ 5♈R
17	11.42	23	18	19	27	28	♄ 0♉R
18	11.46	24	1♐	21	28	28	♅21♉R
19	11.50	25	14	23	29	28	♆23♍
20	11.54	26	27	25	0♎	28	♇ 2♌
21	11.58	27	9♑	26	2	29	♃ 4♈R
22	12.02	28	21	28	3	29	♄ 0♉R
23	12.06	29	3♒	0♎	4	0♒	♅21♉R
24	12.10	0♎	15	2	5	0	♆23♍
25	12.14	1	27	4	7	0	♇ 2♌
26	12.18	2	9♓	5	8	1	♃ 4♈R
27	12.22	3	21	7	9	1	♄29♈R
28	12.25	4	3♈	9	10	1	♅21♉R
29	12.29	5	15	11	11	2	♆23♍
30	12.33	6	27	12	13	2	♇ 2♌

Oct	STime	☉	☽	☿	♀	♂	Plnts
1	12.37	7♎	10♉	14♎	14♎	3♒	♃ 3♈R
2	12.41	8	22	16	15	3	♄29♈R
3	12.45	9	5♊	17	16	4	♅21♉R
4	12.49	10	18	19	18	4	♆23♍
5	12.53	11	2♋	21	19	4	♇ 2♌
6	12.57	12	16	22	20	5	♃ 2♈R
7	13.01	13	0♌	24	21	5	♄29♈R
8	13.05	14	14	25	23	6	♅21♉R
9	13.09	15	29	27	24	6	♆24♍
10	13.13	16	13♍	29	25	7	♇ 2♌
11	13.17	17	28	0♏	26	7	♃ 2♈R
12	13.21	18	13♎	2	28	8	♄28♈R
13	13.25	19	28	3	29	8	♅21♉R
14	13.29	20	12♏	5	0♏	9	♆24♍
15	13.32	21	26	6	1	9	♇ 3♌
16	13.36	22	9♐	8	3	10	♃ 1♈R
17	13.40	23	23	9	4	10	♄28♈R
18	13.44	24	5♑	11	5	11	♅21♉R
19	13.48	25	18	12	6	11	♆24♍
20	13.52	26	0♒	14	8	12	♇ 3♌
21	13.56	27	12	15	9	12	♃ 1♈R
22	14.00	28	24	17	10	13	♄27♈R
23	14.04	29	6♓	18	11	14	♅20♉R
24	14.08	0♏	17	19	13	14	♆24♍
25	14.12	1	29	21	14	15	♇ 3♌
26	14.16	2	12♈	22	15	15	♃ 0♈R
27	14.20	3	24	23	16	16	♄27♈R
28	14.24	4	6♉	25	18	16	♅20♉R
29	14.28	5	19	26	19	17	♆24♍
30	14.32	6	2♊	27	20	17	♇ 3♌
31	14.36	7	15	29	21	18	♃ 0♈R

Nov	STime	☉	☽	☿	♀	♂	Plnts
1	14.39	8♏	29♊	0♐	23♏	19♒	♃ 0♈R
2	14.43	9	12♋	1	24	19	♄27♈R
3	14.47	10	26	2	25	20	♅20♉R
4	14.51	11	10♌	4	26	20	♆24♍
5	14.55	12	24	5	28	21	♇ 3♌
6	14.59	13	9♍	6	29	22	♃29♓R
7	15.03	14	23	7	0♐	22	♄26♈R
8	15.07	15	7♎	8	1	23	♅20♉R
9	15.11	16	22	9	3	23	♆25♍
10	15.15	17	6♏	10	4	24	♇ 3♌
11	15.19	18	20	11	5	25	♃29♓R
12	15.23	19	4♐	11	6	25	♄26♈R
13	15.27	20	17	12	8	26	♅20♉R
14	15.31	21	0♑	13	9	26	♆25♍
15	15.35	22	13	13	10	27	♇ 3♌R
16	15.39	23	26	13	11	28	♃29♓R
17	15.43	24	8♒	14	13	28	♄26♈R
18	15.47	25	20	14R	14	29	♅19♉R
19	15.50	26	2♓	14	15	0♓	♆25♍
20	15.54	27	14	13	16	0	♇ 3♌R
21	15.58	28	25	13	18	1	♃29♓R
22	16.02	29	7♈	12	19	1	♄25♈R
23	16.06	0♐	20	12	20	2	♅19♉R
24	16.10	1	2♉	11	21	3	♆25♍
25	16.14	2	15	9	23	3	♇ 3♌R
26	16.18	3	28	8	24	4	♃29♓
27	16.22	4	11♊	7	25	5	♄25♈R
28	16.26	5	25	6	26	5	♅19♉R
29	16.30	6	9♋	4	28	6	♆25♍
30	16.34	7	23	3	29	7	♇ 2♌R

Dec	STime	☉	☽	☿	♀	♂	Plnts
1	16.38	8♐	7♌	2♐	0♑	7♓	♃29♓
2	16.42	9	21	1	1	8	♄25♈R
3	16.46	10	5♍	0	3	9	♅19♉R
4	16.50	11	19	29♏	4	9	♆25♍
5	16.54	12	4♎	28	5	10	♇ 2♌R
6	16.57	13	18	28	6	11	♃29♓
7	17.01	14	1♏	27	8	11	♄24♈R
8	17.05	15	15	27D	9	12	♅19♉R
9	17.09	16	29	28	10	13	♆25♍
10	17.13	17	12♐	28	11	13	♇ 2♌R
11	17.17	18	25	28	13	14	♃29♓
12	17.21	19	8♑	29	14	15	♄24♈R
13	17.25	20	21	29	15	15	♅18♉R
14	17.29	21	3♒	0♐	16	16	♆25♍
15	17.33	22	16	1	18	17	♇ 2♌R
16	17.37	23	28	2	19	17	♃29♓
17	17.41	24	9♓	3	20	18	♄24♈R
18	17.45	25	21	4	21	19	♅18♉R
19	17.49	26	3♈	5	22	19	♆25♍
20	17.53	27	15	6	24	20	♇ 2♌R
21	17.57	28	27	8	25	21	♃ 0♈
22	18.01	29	10♉	9	26	21	♄24♈R
23	18.05	0♑	23	10	27	22	♅18♉R
24	18.08	1	6♊	11	29	23	♆25♍
25	18.12	2	20	13	0♒	23	♇ 2♌R
26	18.16	4	4♋	14	1	24	♃ 0♈
27	18.20	5	18	16	2	25	♄24♈
28	18.24	6	3♌	17	4	25	♅18♉R
29	18.28	7	17	18	5	26	♆25♍
30	18.32	8	2♍	20	6	27	♇ 2♌R
31	18.36	9	16	21	7	27	♃ 1♈

Jan	STime	☉	☽	☿	♀	♂	Plnts
1	18.40	10♑	0♎	23♐	9♒	28♓	♃ 1♈
2	18.44	11	14	24	10	29	♄24♈
3	18.48	12	28	26	11	29	♅18♉R
4	18.52	13	12♏	27	12	0♈	♆25♍
5	18.56	14	25	28	14	1	♇ 2♌R
6	19.00	15	8♐	0♑	15	1	♃ 2♈
7	19.04	16	21	1	16	2	♄24♈
8	19.08	17	4♑	3	17	3	♅18♉R
9	19.12	18	17	4	19	3	♆25♍R
10	19.15	19	29	6	20	4	♇ 2♌R
11	19.19	20	12♒	8	21	5	♃ 2♈
12	19.23	21	24	9	22	5	♄24♈
13	19.27	22	6♓	11	23	6	♅18♉R
14	19.31	23	17	12	25	7	♆25♍R
15	19.35	24	29	14	26	8	♇ 2♌R
16	19.39	25	11♈	15	27	8	♃ 3♈
17	19.43	26	23	17	28	9	♄24♈
18	19.47	27	5♉	18	0♓	10	♅18♉R
19	19.51	28	18	20	1	10	♆25♍R
20	19.55	29	0♊	22	2	11	♇ 2♌R
21	19.59	0♒	14	23	3	12	♃ 4♈
22	20.03	1	28	25	5	12	♄25♈
23	20.07	2	12♋	27	6	13	♅18♉
24	20.11	3	26	28	7	14	♆25♍R
25	20.15	4	11♌	0♒	8	14	♇ 1♌R
26	20.19	5	26	1	9	15	♃ 5♈
27	20.23	6	11♍	3	11	16	♄25♈
28	20.26	7	26	5	12	16	♅18♉
29	20.30	8	11♎	7	13	17	♆25♍R
30	20.34	9	25	8	14	18	♇ 1♌R
31	20.38	10	9♏	10	15	18	♃ 6♈

Feb	STime	☉	☽	☿	♀	♂	Plnts
1	20.42	11♒	22♏	12♒	17♓	19♈	♃ 6♈
2	20.46	12	5♐	13	18	20	♄25♈
3	20.50	13	18	15	19	20	♅18♉
4	20.54	14	1♑	17	20	21	♆25♍R
5	20.58	15	14	19	22	22	♇ 1♌R
6	21.02	16	26	21	23	23	♃ 7♈
7	21.06	17	8♒	22	24	23	♄26♈
8	21.10	18	20	24	25	24	♅18♉
9	21.14	19	2♓	26	26	25	♆25♍R
10	21.18	20	14	28	28	25	♇ 1♌R
11	21.22	21	26	0♓	29	26	♃ 8♈
12	21.26	22	8♈	1	0♈	27	♄26♈
13	21.30	23	19	3	1	27	♅18♉
14	21.33	24	1♉	5	2	28	♆25♍R
15	21.37	25	13	7	4	29	♇ 1♌R
16	21.41	26	26	9	5	29	♃ 9♈
17	21.45	27	9♊	10	6	0♉	♄26♈
18	21.49	28	22	12	7	1	♅18♉
19	21.53	29	6♋	14	8	1	♆25♍R
20	21.57	0♓	20	16	10	2	♇ 1♌R
21	22.01	1	4♌	17	11	3	♃10♈
22	22.05	2	19	19	12	3	♄27♈
23	22.09	3	5♍	20	13	4	♅18♉
24	22.13	4	20	22	14	5	♆24♍R
25	22.17	5	5♎	23	15	5	♇ 1♌R
26	22.21	6	20	24	17	6	♃11♈
27	22.25	7	4♏	26	18	7	♄27♈
28	22.29	8	18	27	19	7	♅18♉
29	22.33	9	2♐	27	20	8	♆24♍R

Mar	STime	☉	☽	☿	♀	♂	Plnts
1	22.37	10♓	15♐	28♓	21♈	9♉	♃12♈
2	22.40	11	28	29	23	9	♄28♈
3	22.44	12	11♑	29	24	10	♅18♉
4	22.48	13	23	0♈	25	11	♆24♍R
5	22.52	14	5♒	0	26	11	♇ 1♌R
6	22.56	15	17	0R	27	12	♃13♈
7	23.00	16	29	0	28	13	♄28♈
8	23.04	17	11♓	0	29	13	♅18♉
9	23.08	18	23	29♓	1♉	14	♆24♍R
10	23.12	19	5♈	29	2	15	♇ 1♌R
11	23.16	20	16	28	3	15	♃14♈
12	23.20	21	28	27	4	16	♄29♈
13	23.24	22	10♉	26	5	17	♅19♉
14	23.28	23	23	26	6	18	♆24♍R
15	23.32	24	5♊	25	7	18	♇ 0♌R
16	23.36	25	18	24	9	19	♃15♈
17	23.40	26	1♋	23	10	20	♄29♈
18	23.44	27	14	22	11	20	♅19♉
19	23.48	28	28	21	12	21	♆24♍R
20	23.51	29	13♌	20	13	22	♇ 0♌R
21	23.55	0♈	28	19	14	22	♃16♈
22	23.59	1	13♍	19	15	23	♄ 0♉
23	0.03	2	28	18	16	24	♅19♉
24	0.07	3	13♎	18	18	24	♆24♍R
25	0.11	4	28	17	19	25	♇ 0♌R
26	0.15	5	13♏	17	20	26	♃18♈
27	0.19	6	27	17	21	26	♄ 1♉
28	0.23	7	11♐	17	22	27	♅19♉
29	0.27	8	24	17D	23	28	♆23♍R
30	0.31	9	7♑	17	24	28	♇ 0♌R
31	0.35	10	20	17	25	29	♃19♈

Apr	STime	☉	☽	☿	♀	♂	Plnts
1	0.39	11♈	2♒	17♓	26♉	0♊	♃19♈
2	0.43	12	14	17	27	0	♄ 1♉
3	0.47	13	26	18	28	1	♅20♉
4	0.51	14	8♓	18	29	1	♆23♍R
5	0.55	15	20	19	0♊	2	♇ 0♌
6	0.58	16	2♈	20	2	3	♃20♈
7	1.02	17	13	20	3	3	♄ 2♉
8	1.06	18	25	21	4	4	♅20♉
9	1.10	19	7♉	22	5	5	♆23♍R
10	1.14	20	20	23	6	5	♇ 0♌
11	1.18	21	2♊	24	7	6	♃21♈
12	1.22	22	15	25	8	7	♄ 3♉
13	1.26	23	27	26	9	7	♅20♉
14	1.30	24	11♋	27	10	8	♆23♍R
15	1.34	25	24	28	11	9	♇ 0♌
16	1.38	26	8♌	29	12	9	♃23♈
17	1.42	27	22	0♈	13	10	♄ 3♉
18	1.46	28	7♍	1	14	11	♅20♉
19	1.50	29	21	3	15	11	♆23♍R
20	1.54	0♉	6♎	4	16	12	♇ 0♌
21	1.58	1	21	5	16	13	♃24♈
22	2.02	2	6♏	7	17	13	♄ 4♉
23	2.06	3	21	8	18	14	♅21♉
24	2.09	4	5♐	9	19	15	♆23♍R
25	2.13	5	19	11	20	15	♇ 0♌
26	2.17	6	3♑	12	21	16	♃25♈
27	2.21	7	16	14	22	17	♄ 4♉
28	2.25	8	28	15	23	17	♅21♉
29	2.29	9	11♒	17	24	18	♆23♍R
30	2.33	10	23	19	25	19	♇ 0♌

May	STime	☉	☽	☿	♀	♂	Plnts
1	2.37	11♉	5♓	20♈	25♊	19♊	♃26♈
2	2.41	12	17	22	26	20	♄ 5♉
3	2.45	13	28	24	27	21	♅21♉
4	2.49	14	10♈	25	28	21	♆23♍R
5	2.53	15	22	27	29	22	♇ 0♌
6	2.57	15	4♉	29	29	22	♃27♈
7	3.01	16	16	1♉	0♋	23	♄ 6♉
8	3.05	17	29	3	1	24	♅21♉
9	3.09	18	12♊	5	2	24	♆23♍R
10	3.13	19	24	7	2	25	♇ 0♌
11	3.16	20	8♋	8	3	26	♃29♈
12	3.20	21	21	10	4	26	♄ 6♉
13	3.24	22	5♌	12	5	27	♅22♉
14	3.28	23	18	15	5	28	♆23♍R
15	3.32	24	2♍	17	6	28	♇ 1♌
16	3.36	25	17	19	6	29	♃ 0♉
17	3.40	26	1♎	21	7	0♋	♄ 7♉
18	3.44	27	16	23	8	0	♅22♉
19	3.48	28	0♏	25	8	1	♆22♍R
20	3.52	29	15	27	9	2	♇ 1♌
21	3.56	0♊	29	0♊	9	2	♃ 1♉
22	4.00	1	13♐	2	10	3	♄ 8♉
23	4.04	2	27	4	10	4	♅22♉
24	4.08	3	11♑	6	10	4	♆22♍
25	4.12	4	24	8	11	5	♇ 1♌
26	4.16	5	6♒	10	11	5	♃ 2♉
27	4.20	6	19	13	12	6	♄ 8♉
28	4.24	7	1♓	15	12	7	♅23♉
29	4.27	8	13	17	12	7	♆22♍
30	4.31	9	25	19	12	8	♇ 1♌
31	4.35	10	6♈	21	13	9	♃ 3♉

Jun	STime	☉	☽	☿	♀	♂	Plnts
1	4.39	11♊	18♈	23♊	13♋	9♋	♃ 3♉
2	4.43	11	0♉	25	13	10	♄ 9♉
3	4.47	12	13	27	13	11	♅23♉
4	4.51	13	25	29	13	11	♆22♍
5	4.55	14	8♊	1♋	13R	12	♇ 1♌
6	4.59	15	21	3	13	13	♃ 4♉
7	5.03	16	4♋	4	13	13	♄ 9♉
8	5.07	17	18	6	13	14	♅23♉
9	5.11	18	1♌	8	13	14	♆22♍
10	5.15	19	15	9	12	15	♇ 1♌
11	5.19	20	29	11	12	16	♃ 5♉
12	5.23	21	13♍	13	12	16	♄10♉
13	5.27	22	27	14	12	17	♅23♉
14	5.31	23	12♎	16	11	18	♆22♍
15	5.34	24	26	17	11	18	♇ 1♌
16	5.38	25	10♏	18	11	19	♃ 6♉
17	5.42	26	24	20	10	20	♄10♉
18	5.46	27	8♐	21	10	20	♅24♉
19	5.50	28	22	22	9	21	♆23♍
20	5.54	29	5♑	24	9	21	♇ 1♌
21	5.58	0♋	19	25	8	22	♃ 7♉
22	6.02	1	2♒	26	7	23	♄11♉
23	6.06	2	14	27	7	23	♅24♉
24	6.10	3	27	28	6	24	♆23♍
25	6.14	3	9♓	29	6	25	♇ 1♌
26	6.18	4	21	0♌	5	25	♃ 8♉
27	6.22	5	3♈	0	4	26	♄11♉
28	6.26	6	14	1	4	27	♅24♉
29	6.30	7	26	2	3	27	♆23♍
30	6.34	8	8♉	3	3	28	♇ 1♌

Jul	STime	☉	☽	☿	♀	♂	Plnts
1	6.38	9♋	21♉	3♌	2♋	28♋	♃ 9♉
2	6.41	10	3♊	4	1	29	♄12♉
3	6.45	11	16	4	1	0♌	♅24♉
4	6.49	12	0♋	4	0	0	♆23♍
5	6.53	13	13	5	0	1	♇ 2♌
6	6.57	14	27	5	29♊	2	♃10♉
7	7.01	15	11♌	5	29	2	♄12♉
8	7.05	16	26	5R	28	3	♅25♉
9	7.09	17	10♍	5	28	4	♆23♍
10	7.13	18	24	5	28	4	♇ 2♌
11	7.17	19	9♎	5	27	5	♃11♉
12	7.21	20	23	4	27	5	♄13♉
13	7.25	21	7♏	4	27	6	♅25♉
14	7.29	22	20	4	27	7	♆23♍
15	7.33	23	4♐	3	27	7	♇ 2♌
16	7.37	23	18	3	27	8	♃12♉
17	7.41	24	1♑	2	27	9	♄13♉
18	7.45	25	14	1	26D	9	♅25♉
19	7.49	26	27	1	27	10	♆23♍
20	7.52	27	10♒	0	27	11	♇ 2♌
21	7.56	28	23	29♋	27	11	♃12♉
22	8.00	29	5♓	29	27	12	♄13♉
23	8.04	0♌	17	28	27	12	♅25♉
24	8.08	1	29	27	27	13	♆23♍
25	8.12	2	11♈	27	27	14	♇ 2♌
26	8.16	3	22	26	28	14	♃13♉
27	8.20	4	4♉	26	28	15	♄14♉
28	8.24	5	16	25	28	16	♅25♉
29	8.28	6	29	25	29	16	♆23♍
30	8.32	7	11♊	25	29	17	♇ 2♌
31	8.36	8	24	24	29	18	♃13♉

Aug	STime	☉	☽	☿	♀	♂	Plnts
1	8.40	9♌	8♋	24♋	0♋	18♌	♃14♉
2	8.44	10	22	24	0	19	♄14♉
3	8.48	11	6♌	25	1	19	♅25♉
4	8.52	12	21	25	1	20	♆23♍
5	8.56	13	5♍	25	2	21	♇ 2♌
6	8.59	14	20	26	2	21	♃14♉
7	9.03	15	5♎	26	3	22	♄14♉
8	9.07	15	19	27	4	23	♅26♉
9	9.11	16	3♏	28	4	23	♆24♍
10	9.15	17	17	28	5	24	♇ 3♌
11	9.19	18	1♐	29	6	25	♃14♉
12	9.23	19	15	1♌	6	25	♄14♉
13	9.27	20	28	2	7	26	♅26♉
14	9.31	21	11♑	3	8	26	♆24♍
15	9.35	22	24	4	8	27	♇ 3♌
16	9.39	23	6♒	6	9	28	♃15♉
17	9.43	24	19	7	10	28	♄14♉
18	9.47	25	1♓	9	11	29	♅26♉
19	9.51	26	13	11	11	0♍	♆24♍
20	9.55	27	25	13	12	0	♇ 3♌
21	9.59	28	7♈	14	13	1	♃15♉
22	10.03	29	19	16	14	2	♄14♉
23	10.07	0♍	1♉	18	15	2	♅26♉
24	10.10	1	12	20	16	3	♆24♍
25	10.14	2	24	22	16	3	♇ 3♌
26	10.18	3	7♊	24	17	4	♃15♉
27	10.22	4	19	26	18	5	♄14♉R
28	10.26	5	3♋	28	19	5	♅26♉
29	10.30	6	16	0♍	20	6	♆24♍
30	10.34	7	0♌	2	21	7	♇ 3♌
31	10.38	8	14	4	22	7	♃15♉

Sep	STime	☉	☽	☿	♀	♂	Plnts
1	10.42	9♍	29♌	6♍	23♋	8♍	♃15♉
2	10.46	10	14♍	8	24	9	♄14♉R
3	10.50	11	29	10	25	9	♅26♉
4	10.54	11	14♎	11	26	10	♆24♍
5	10.58	12	29	13	27	10	♇ 3♌
6	11.02	13	13♏	15	28	11	♃15♉R
7	11.06	14	28	17	29	12	♄14♉R
8	11.10	15	11♐	19	0♌	12	♅26♉
9	11.14	16	25	21	0	13	♆25♍
10	11.17	17	8♑	23	1	14	♇ 3♌
11	11.21	18	21	24	2	14	♃15♉R
12	11.25	19	3♒	26	4	15	♄14♉R
13	11.29	20	16	28	5	16	♅26♉R
14	11.33	21	28	0♎	6	16	♆25♍
15	11.37	22	10♓	1	7	17	♇ 4♌
16	11.41	23	22	3	8	17	♃15♉R
17	11.45	24	4♈	5	9	18	♄14♉R
18	11.49	25	16	7	10	19	♅26♉R
19	11.53	26	27	8	11	19	♆25♍
20	11.57	27	9♉	10	12	20	♇ 4♌
21	12.01	28	21	11	13	21	♃15♉R
22	12.05	29	3♊	13	14	21	♄14♉R
23	12.09	0♎	15	15	15	22	♅26♉R
24	12.13	1	28	16	16	23	♆25♍
25	12.17	2	11♋	18	17	23	♇ 4♌
26	12.21	3	24	19	18	24	♃15♉R
27	12.24	4	8♌	21	19	25	♄14♉R
28	12.28	5	23	22	20	25	♅26♉R
29	12.32	6	7♍	24	22	26	♆25♍
30	12.36	7	22	25	23	26	♇ 4♌

Oct	STime	☉	☽	☿	♀	♂	Plnts
1	12.40	8♎	7♎	27♎	24♌	27♍	♃14♉R
2	12.44	9	23	28	25	28	♄13♉R
3	12.48	10	8♏	0♏	26	28	♅25♉R
4	12.52	11	22	1	27	29	♆26♍
5	12.56	12	7♐	3	28	0♎	♇ 4♌
6	13.00	13	21	4	29	0	♃14♉R
7	13.04	14	5♑	5	0♍	1	♄13♉R
8	13.08	15	18	7	2	2	♅25♉R
9	13.12	16	0♒	8	3	2	♆26♍
10	13.16	17	13	9	4	3	♇ 4♌
11	13.20	18	25	11	5	4	♃13♉R
12	13.24	19	7♓	12	6	4	♄13♉R
13	13.28	20	19	13	7	5	♅25♉R
14	13.32	21	1♈	14	8	5	♆26♍
15	13.35	22	13	16	10	6	♇ 4♌
16	13.39	23	24	17	11	7	♃13♉R
17	13.43	24	6♉	18	12	7	♄12♉R
18	13.47	25	18	19	13	8	♅25♉R
19	13.51	26	0♊	20	14	9	♆26♍
20	13.55	27	12	21	15	9	♇ 4♌
21	13.59	28	25	22	16	10	♃12♉R
22	14.03	29	7♋	23	18	11	♄12♉R
23	14.07	0♏	20	24	19	11	♅25♉R
24	14.11	1	4♌	25	20	12	♆26♍
25	14.15	2	17	25	21	13	♇ 4♌
26	14.19	3	1♍	26	22	13	♃11♉R
27	14.23	4	16	27	24	14	♄12♉R
28	14.27	5	1♎	27	25	15	♅25♉R
29	14.31	6	16	27	26	15	♆26♍
30	14.35	7	1♏	28	27	16	♇ 4♌
31	14.39	8	16	28	28	16	♃11♉R

Nov	STime	☉	☽	☿	♀	♂	Plnts
1	14.42	9♏	1♐	28♏	29♍	17♎	♃11♉R
2	14.46	10	15	28	1♎	18	♄11♉R
3	14.50	11	29	27	2	18	♅24♉R
4	14.54	12	13♑	27	3	19	♆27♍
5	14.58	13	26	26	4	20	♇ 4♌
6	15.02	14	9♒	26	5	20	♃10♉R
7	15.06	15	22	25	7	21	♄11♉R
8	15.10	16	4♓	24	8	22	♅24♉R
9	15.14	17	16	22	9	22	♆27♍
10	15.18	18	28	21	10	23	♇ 4♌R
11	15.22	19	9♈	20	11	24	♃ 9♉R
12	15.26	20	21	18	13	24	♄10♉R
13	15.30	21	3♉	17	14	25	♅24♉R
14	15.34	22	15	16	15	26	♆27♍
15	15.38	23	27	15	16	26	♇ 4♌R
16	15.42	24	9♊	14	17	27	♃ 9♉R
17	15.46	25	22	13	19	28	♄10♉R
18	15.50	26	5♋	12	20	28	♅24♉R
19	15.53	27	17	12	21	29	♆27♍
20	15.57	28	0♌	12	22	0♏	♇ 4♌R
21	16.01	29	14	12D	24	0	♃ 8♉R
22	16.05	0♐	27	12	25	1	♄10♉R
23	16.09	1	11♍	12	26	2	♅24♉R
24	16.13	2	25	13	27	2	♆27♍
25	16.17	3	10♎	13	28	3	♇ 4♌R
26	16.21	4	24	14	0♏	4	♃ 7♉R
27	16.25	5	9♏	15	1	4	♄ 9♉R
28	16.29	6	24	16	2	5	♅23♉R
29	16.33	7	9♐	17	3	5	♆27♍
30	16.37	8	23	18	5	6	♇ 4♌R

Dec	STime	☉	☽	☿	♀	♂	Plnts
1	16.41	9♐	7♑	19♏	6♏	7♏	♃ 7♉R
2	16.45	10	21	20	7	7	♄ 9♉R
3	16.49	11	5♒	21	8	8	♅23♉R
4	16.53	12	17	23	10	9	♆27♍
5	16.57	13	0♓	24	11	9	♇ 4♌R
6	17.00	14	12	25	12	10	♃ 6♉R
7	17.04	15	24	27	13	11	♄ 9♉R
8	17.08	16	6♈	28	14	11	♅23♉R
9	17.12	17	18	0♐	16	12	♆27♍
10	17.16	18	29	1	17	13	♇ 4♌R
11	17.20	19	11♉	3	18	13	♃ 6♉R
12	17.24	20	23	4	19	14	♄ 8♉R
13	17.28	21	6♊	5	21	15	♅23♉R
14	17.32	22	18	7	22	15	♆27♍
15	17.36	23	1♋	8	23	16	♇ 4♌R
16	17.40	24	14	10	24	17	♃ 6♉R
17	17.44	25	27	11	26	17	♄ 8♉R
18	17.48	26	11♌	13	27	18	♅23♉R
19	17.52	27	24	14	28	19	♆27♍
20	17.56	28	8♍	16	29	19	♇ 4♌R
21	18.00	29	22	18	1♐	20	♃ 6♉R
22	18.04	0♑	6♎	19	2	21	♄ 8♉R
23	18.08	1	20	21	3	21	♅22♉R
24	18.11	2	4♏	22	4	22	♆27♍
25	18.15	3	19	24	6	23	♇ 4♌R
26	18.19	4	3♐	25	7	23	♃ 5♉R
27	18.23	5	17	27	8	24	♄ 8♉R
28	18.27	6	1♑	28	9	25	♅22♉R
29	18.31	7	15	0♑	11	25	♆27♍
30	18.35	8	29	1	12	26	♇ 3♌R
31	18.39	9	12♒	3	13	27	♃ 5♉

1 9 4 1

Jan	STime	☉	☽	☿	♀	♂	Plnts
1	18.43	10♑	25♒	5♑	14♐	27♏	♃ 5♉
2	18.47	11	8♓	6	15	28	♄ 8♉R
3	18.51	12	20	8	17	29	♅22♉R
4	18.55	13	2♈	9	18	29	♆27♍
5	18.59	14	14	11	19	0♐	♇ 3♌R
6	19.03	15	25	13	20	1	♃ 5♉
7	19.07	17	7♉	14	22	2	♄ 8♉
8	19.11	18	19	16	23	2	♅22♉R
9	19.15	19	1♊	17	24	3	♆27♍R
10	19.18	20	14	19	25	4	♇ 3♌R
11	19.22	21	27	21	27	4	♃ 6♉
12	19.26	22	10♋	22	28	5	♄ 8♉
13	19.30	23	23	24	29	6	♅22♉R
14	19.34	24	7♌	26	0♑	6	♆27♍R
15	19.38	25	21	27	2	7	♇ 3♌R
16	19.42	26	5♍	29	3	8	♃ 6♉
17	19.46	27	19	1♒	4	8	♄ 8♉
18	19.50	28	3♎	2	5	9	♅22♉R
19	19.54	29	17	4	7	10	♆27♍R
20	19.58	0♒	1♏	6	8	10	♇ 3♌R
21	20.02	1	15	7	9	11	♃ 6♉
22	20.06	2	29	9	10	12	♄ 8♉
23	20.10	3	13♐	11	12	12	♅22♉R
24	20.14	4	27	13	13	13	♆27♍R
25	20.18	5	11♑	14	14	14	♇ 3♌R
26	20.22	6	24	16	15	14	♃ 7♉
27	20.25	7	7♒	18	17	15	♄ 8♉
28	20.29	8	20	20	18	16	♅22♉
29	20.33	9	3♓	21	19	16	♆27♍R
30	20.37	10	15	23	20	17	♇ 3♌R
31	20.41	11	28	25	22	18	♃ 7♉

Feb	STime	☉	☽	☿	♀	♂	Plnts
1	20.45	12♒	10♈	26♒	23♑	18♐	♃ 7♉
2	20.49	13	21	28	24	19	♄ 8♉
3	20.53	14	3♉	0♓	25	20	♅22♉
4	20.57	15	15	1	27	20	♆27♍R
5	21.01	16	27	3	28	21	♇ 3♌R
6	21.05	17	9♊	4	29	22	♃ 8♉
7	21.09	18	22	6	0♒	23	♄ 8♉
8	21.13	19	5♋	7	2	23	♅22♉
9	21.17	20	18	8	3	24	♆27♍R
10	21.21	21	1♌	9	4	25	♇ 3♌R
11	21.25	22	15	10	5	25	♃ 8♉
12	21.29	23	29	11	7	26	♄ 9♉
13	21.33	24	14♍	12	8	27	♅22♉
14	21.36	25	28	12	9	27	♆27♍R
15	21.40	26	13♎	13	10	28	♇ 2♌R
16	21.44	27	27	13	12	29	♃ 9♉
17	21.48	28	12♏	13R	13	29	♄ 9♉
18	21.52	29	26	13	14	0♑	♅22♉
19	21.56	0♓	10♐	13	15	1	♆27♍R
20	22.00	1	23	12	17	1	♇ 2♌R
21	22.04	2	7♑	12	18	2	♃10♉
22	22.08	3	20	11	19	3	♄ 9♉
23	22.12	4	3♒	10	20	3	♅22♉
24	22.16	5	16	9	22	4	♆27♍R
25	22.20	6	29	8	23	5	♇ 2♌R
26	22.24	7	11♓	7	24	6	♃11♉
27	22.28	8	24	6	25	6	♄10♉
28	22.32	9	6♈	5	27	7	♅22♉

Mar	STime	☉	☽	☿	♀	♂	Plnts
1	22.36	10♓	18♈	4♓	28♒	8♑	♃11♉
2	22.40	11	29	3	29	8	♄10♉
3	22.43	12	11♉	2	0♓	9	♅22♉
4	22.47	13	23	1	2	10	♆26♍R
5	22.51	14	5♊	1	3	10	♇ 2♌R
6	22.55	15	17	0	4	11	♃12♉
7	22.59	16	0♋	0	5	12	♄10♉
8	23.03	17	12	29♒	7	12	♅22♉
9	23.07	18	26	29	8	13	♆26♍R
10	23.11	19	9♌	29	9	14	♇ 2♌R
11	23.15	20	23	29D	10	14	♃13♉
12	23.19	21	8♍	29	12	15	♄11♉
13	23.23	22	22	29	13	16	♅23♉
14	23.27	23	7♎	29	14	17	♆26♍R
15	23.31	24	22	29	15	17	♇ 2♌R
16	23.35	25	7♏	0♓	17	18	♃14♉
17	23.39	26	22	0	18	19	♄11♉
18	23.43	27	6♐	1	19	19	♅23♉
19	23.47	28	20	1	20	20	♆26♍R
20	23.51	29	4♑	2	22	21	♇ 2♌R
21	23.54	0♈	17	3	23	21	♃15♉
22	23.58	1	0♒	4	24	22	♄12♉
23	0.02	2	13	4	25	23	♅23♉
24	0.06	3	26	5	27	23	♆26♍R
25	0.10	4	8♓	6	28	24	♇ 2♌R
26	0.14	5	20	7	29	25	♃16♉
27	0.18	6	2♈	8	0♈	26	♄12♉
28	0.22	7	14	10	2	26	♅23♉
29	0.26	8	26	11	3	27	♆26♍R
30	0.30	9	8♉	12	4	28	♇ 2♌R
31	0.34	10	20	13	5	28	♃17♉

Apr	STime	☉	☽	☿	♀	♂	Plnts
1	0.38	11♈	2♊	14♓	6♈	29♑	♃17♉
2	0.42	12	14	16	8	0♒	♄13♉
3	0.46	13	26	17	9	0	♅23♉
4	0.50	14	8♋	18	10	1	♆26♍R
5	0.54	15	21	20	11	2	♇ 2♌
6	0.58	16	4♌	21	13	2	♃18♉
7	1.01	17	17	22	14	3	♄14♉
8	1.05	18	1♍	24	15	4	♅24♉
9	1.09	19	16	25	16	5	♆25♍R
10	1.13	20	0♎	27	18	5	♇ 2♌
11	1.17	21	15	28	19	6	♃19♉
12	1.21	22	1♏	0♈	20	7	♄14♉
13	1.25	23	16	2	21	7	♅24♉
14	1.29	24	1♐	3	23	8	♆25♍R
15	1.33	25	16	5	24	9	♇ 2♌
16	1.37	26	0♑	7	25	9	♃20♉
17	1.41	27	14	8	26	10	♄15♉
18	1.45	28	27	10	28	11	♅24♉
19	1.49	29	10♒	12	29	11	♆25♍R
20	1.53	0♉	23	14	0♉	12	♇ 2♌
21	1.57	1	5♓	15	1	13	♃21♉
22	2.01	2	17	17	2	14	♄16♉
23	2.05	3	29	19	4	14	♅25♉
24	2.08	4	11♈	21	5	15	♆25♍R
25	2.12	5	23	23	6	16	♇ 2♌
26	2.16	6	5♉	25	7	16	♃23♉
27	2.20	7	17	27	9	17	♄16♉
28	2.24	7	29	29	10	18	♅25♉
29	2.28	8	11♊	1♉	11	18	♆25♍R
30	2.32	9	23	3	12	19	♇ 2♌

May	STime	☉	☽	☿	♀	♂	Plnts
1	2.36	10♉	5♋	5♉	14♉	20♒	♃24♉
2	2.40	11	17	7	15	20	♄17♉
3	2.44	12	0♌	9	16	21	♅25♉
4	2.48	13	13	11	17	22	♆25♍R
5	2.52	14	26	13	19	22	♇ 2♌
6	2.56	15	10♍	16	20	23	♃25♉
7	3.00	16	24	18	21	24	♄18♉
8	3.04	17	9♎	20	22	24	♅25♉
9	3.08	18	24	22	23	25	♆25♍R
10	3.12	19	9♏	24	25	26	♇ 2♌
11	3.16	20	24	26	26	27	♃26♉
12	3.19	21	9♐	29	27	27	♄18♉
13	3.23	22	24	1♊	28	28	♅26♉
14	3.27	23	9♑	3	0♊	29	♆25♍R
15	3.31	24	23	5	1	29	♇ 2♌
16	3.35	25	6♒	7	2	0♓	♃27♉
17	3.39	26	19	9	3	1	♄19♉
18	3.43	27	2♓	11	5	1	♅26♉
19	3.47	28	14	13	6	2	♆25♍R
20	3.51	29	26	15	7	3	♇ 2♌
21	3.55	0♊	8♈	17	8	3	♃29♉
22	3.59	1	20	18	9	4	♄19♉
23	4.03	2	2♉	20	11	5	♅26♉
24	4.07	3	14	22	12	5	♆25♍R
25	4.11	4	26	23	13	6	♇ 2♌
26	4.15	5	8♊	25	14	7	♃ 0♊
27	4.19	5	20	26	16	7	♄20♉
28	4.23	6	2♋	28	17	8	♅27♉
29	4.26	7	14	29	18	9	♆25♍
30	4.30	8	27	1♋	19	9	♇ 2♌
31	4.34	9	10♌	2	21	10	♃ 1♊

Jun	STime	☉	☽	☿	♀	♂	Plnts
1	4.38	10♊	23♌	3♋	22♊	11♓	♃ 1♊
2	4.42	11	6♍	5	23	11	♄21♉
3	4.46	12	20	6	24	12	♅27♉
4	4.50	13	4♎	7	25	13	♆25♍
5	4.54	14	18	8	27	13	♇ 2♌
6	4.58	15	3♏	9	28	14	♃ 2♊
7	5.02	16	18	10	29	14	♄21♉
8	5.06	17	3♐	11	0♋	15	♅27♉
9	5.10	18	18	11	2	16	♆25♍
10	5.14	19	2♑	12	3	16	♇ 2♌
11	5.18	20	17	13	4	17	♃ 3♊
12	5.22	21	1♒	13	5	18	♄22♉
13	5.26	22	15	14	6	18	♅27♉
14	5.30	23	28	14	8	19	♆25♍
15	5.34	24	10♓	15	9	20	♇ 3♌
16	5.37	25	23	15	10	20	♃ 5♊
17	5.41	26	5♈	15	11	21	♄23♉
18	5.45	27	17	15	13	21	♅28♉
19	5.49	27	29	15R	14	22	♆25♍
20	5.53	28	10♉	15	15	23	♇ 3♌
21	5.57	29	22	15	16	23	♃ 6♊
22	6.01	0♋	4♊	15	17	24	♄23♉
23	6.05	1	16	15	19	25	♅28♉
24	6.09	2	29	15	20	25	♆25♍
25	6.13	3	11♋	14	21	26	♇ 3♌
26	6.17	4	24	14	22	26	♃ 7♊
27	6.21	5	7♌	13	24	27	♄24♉
28	6.25	6	20	13	25	28	♅28♉
29	6.29	7	3♍	12	26	28	♆25♍
30	6.33	8	16	12	27	29	♇ 3♌

Jul	STime	☉	☽	☿	♀	♂	Plnts
1	6.37	9♋	0♎	11♋	28♋	29♓	♃ 8♊
2	6.41	10	14	11	0♌	0♈	♄24♉
3	6.44	11	28	10	1	0	♅28♉
4	6.48	12	13♏	9	2	1	♆25♍
5	6.52	13	27	9	3	2	♇ 3♌
6	6.56	14	12♐	8	5	2	♃ 9♊
7	7.00	15	26	8	6	3	♄25♉
8	7.04	16	11♑	7	7	3	♅29♉
9	7.08	17	25	7	8	4	♆25♍
10	7.12	18	9♒	7	9	4	♇ 3♌
11	7.16	18	23	6	11	5	♃10♊
12	7.20	19	6♓	6	12	5	♄25♉
13	7.24	20	19	6	13	6	♅29♉
14	7.28	21	1♈	6D	14	7	♆25♍
15	7.32	22	13	6	16	7	♇ 3♌
16	7.36	23	25	6	17	8	♃11♊
17	7.40	24	7♉	7	18	8	♄26♉
18	7.44	25	19	7	19	9	♅29♉
19	7.48	26	1♊	7	20	9	♆25♍
20	7.51	27	13	8	22	10	♇ 3♌
21	7.55	28	25	9	23	10	♃12♊
22	7.59	29	7♋	9	24	11	♄26♉
23	8.03	0♌	20	10	25	11	♅29♉
24	8.07	1	3♌	11	26	12	♆25♍
25	8.11	2	16	12	28	12	♇ 4♌
26	8.15	3	0♍	13	29	12	♃13♊
27	8.19	4	13	14	0♍	13	♄26♉
28	8.23	5	27	16	1	13	♅29♉
29	8.27	6	11♎	17	3	14	♆25♍
30	8.31	7	25	18	4	14	♇ 4♌
31	8.35	8	9♏	20	5	15	♃14♊

Aug	STime	☉	☽	☿	♀	♂	Plnts
1	8.39	9♌	23♏	21♋	6♍	15♈	♃14♊
2	8.43	9	8♐	23	7	16	♄27♉
3	8.47	10	22	25	9	16	♅ 0♊
4	8.51	11	6♑	26	10	16	♆26♍
5	8.55	12	20	28	11	17	♇ 4♌
6	8.59	13	4♒	0♌	12	17	♃15♊
7	9.02	14	18	2	13	17	♄27♉
8	9.06	15	1♓	4	15	18	♅ 0♊
9	9.10	16	14	6	16	18	♆26♍
10	9.14	17	26	8	17	19	♇ 4♌
11	9.18	18	9♈	10	18	19	♃16♊
12	9.22	19	21	12	19	19	♄27♉
13	9.26	20	3♉	14	21	19	♅ 0♊
14	9.30	21	15	16	22	20	♆26♍
15	9.34	22	27	18	23	20	♇ 4♌
16	9.38	23	9♊	20	24	20	♃17♊
17	9.42	24	21	22	25	21	♄28♉
18	9.46	25	3♋	24	27	21	♅ 0♊
19	9.50	26	16	26	28	21	♆26♍
20	9.54	27	28	28	29	21	♇ 4♌
21	9.58	28	12♌	0♍	0♎	22	♃17♊
22	10.02	29	25	2	1	22	♄28♉
23	10.06	0♍	9♍	4	3	22	♅ 0♊
24	10.09	1	23	6	4	22	♆26♍
25	10.13	2	7♎	8	5	22	♇ 4♌
26	10.17	3	22	10	6	23	♃18♊
27	10.21	4	6♏	12	7	23	♄28♉
28	10.25	4	20	13	9	23	♅ 0♊
29	10.29	5	4♐	15	10	23	♆26♍
30	10.33	6	18	17	11	23	♇ 5♌
31	10.37	7	2♑	19	12	23	♃19♊

Sep	STime	☉	☽	☿	♀	♂	Plnts
1	10.41	8♍	16♑	21♍	13♎	23♈	♃19♊
2	10.45	9	0♒	22	15	23	♄28♉
3	10.49	10	13	24	16	23	♅ 0♊
4	10.53	11	27	26	17	23	♆27♍
5	10.57	12	9♓	27	18	23	♇ 5♌
6	11.01	13	22	29	19	23R	♃19♊
7	11.05	14	5♈	1♎	21	23	♄28♉
8	11.09	15	17	2	22	23	♅ 0♊
9	11.13	16	29	4	23	23	♆27♍
10	11.17	17	11♉	5	24	23	♇ 5♌
11	11.20	18	23	7	25	23	♃20♊
12	11.24	19	5♊	8	27	23	♄28♉
13	11.28	20	17	10	28	23	♅ 0♊R
14	11.32	21	29	11	29	23	♆27♍
15	11.36	22	11♋	13	0♏	23	♇ 5♌
16	11.40	23	24	14	1	23	♃20♊
17	11.44	24	6♌	16	2	23	♄28♉R
18	11.48	25	20	17	4	22	♅ 0♊R
19	11.52	26	3♍	18	5	22	♆27♍
20	11.56	27	18	20	6	22	♇ 5♌
21	12.00	28	2♎	21	7	22	♃21♊
22	12.04	29	17	22	8	22	♄28♉R
23	12.08	0♎	1♏	24	10	21	♅ 0♊R
24	12.12	1	16	25	11	21	♆27♍
25	12.16	2	1♐	26	12	21	♇ 5♌
26	12.20	3	15	27	13	21	♃21♊
27	12.24	4	29	29	14	20	♄28♉R
28	12.27	5	13♑	0♏	15	20	♅ 0♊R
29	12.31	6	27	1	17	20	♆27♍
30	12.35	7	10♒	2	18	20	♇ 5♌

Oct	STime	☉	☽	☿	♀	♂	Plnts
1	12.39	8♎	23♒	3♏	19♏	19♈	♃21♊
2	12.43	9	6♓	4	20	19	♄28♉R
3	12.47	10	19	5	21	19	♅ 0♊R
4	12.51	11	1♈	6	22	18	♆28♍
5	12.55	12	13	7	24	18	♇ 5♌
6	12.59	13	25	8	25	18	♃21♊
7	13.03	14	7♉	9	26	17	♄28♉R
8	13.07	15	19	9	27	17	♅ 0♊R
9	13.11	16	1♊	10	28	17	♆28♍
10	13.15	16	13	10	29	17	♇ 5♌
11	13.19	17	25	11	1♐	16	♃21♊
12	13.23	18	7♋	11	2	16	♄27♉R
13	13.27	19	19	12	3	16	♅29♉R
14	13.31	20	2♌	12	4	15	♆28♍
15	13.35	21	14	12R	5	15	♇ 5♌
16	13.38	22	28	12	6	15	♃21♊R
17	13.42	23	11♍	12	7	14	♄27♉R
18	13.46	24	26	11	9	14	♅29♉R
19	13.50	25	10♎	11	10	14	♆28♍
20	13.54	26	25	10	11	14	♇ 5♌
21	13.58	27	10♏	9	12	13	♃21♊R
22	14.02	28	25	8	13	13	♄27♉R
23	14.06	29	10♐	7	14	13	♅29♉R
24	14.10	0♏	25	6	15	13	♆28♍
25	14.14	1	9♑	5	16	12	♇ 5♌
26	14.18	2	23	4	18	12	♃21♊R
27	14.22	3	7♒	3	19	12	♄26♉R
28	14.26	4	20	1	20	12	♅29♉R
29	14.30	5	3♓	0	21	12	♆28♍
30	14.34	6	16	29♎	22	12	♇ 5♌
31	14.38	7	28	28	23	11	♃20♊R

Nov	STime	☉	☽	☿	♀	♂	Plnts
1	14.42	8♏	10♈	27♎	24♐	11♈	♃20♊R
2	14.45	9	22	27	25	11	♄26♉R
3	14.49	10	4♉	26	26	11	♅29♉R
4	14.53	11	16	26	28	11	♆29♍
5	14.57	12	28	26D	29	11	♇ 5♌
6	15.01	13	10♊	26	0♑	11	♃20♊R
7	15.05	14	22	27	1	11	♄26♉R
8	15.09	15	3♋	27	2	11	♅29♉R
9	15.13	16	16	28	3	11	♆29♍
10	15.17	17	28	28	4	11D	♇ 5♌
11	15.21	18	10♌	29	5	11	♃19♊R
12	15.25	19	23	0♏	6	11	♄25♉R
13	15.29	20	6♍	1	7	11	♅28♉R
14	15.33	21	20	3	8	11	♆29♍
15	15.37	22	4♎	4	9	11	♇ 5♌
16	15.41	23	18	5	10	11	♃19♊R
17	15.45	24	3♏	6	12	11	♄25♉R
18	15.49	25	18	8	13	11	♅28♉R
19	15.52	26	4♐	9	14	11	♆29♍
20	15.56	27	19	11	15	11	♇ 5♌R
21	16.00	28	4♑	12	16	12	♃18♊R
22	16.04	0♐	19	14	17	12	♄24♉R
23	16.08	1	3♒	15	18	12	♅28♉R
24	16.12	2	16	17	19	12	♆29♍
25	16.16	3	0♓	18	20	12	♇ 5♌
26	16.20	4	12	20	21	12	♃18♊R
27	16.24	5	25	21	22	13	♄24♉R
28	16.28	6	7♈	23	23	13	♅28♉R
29	16.32	7	19	24	24	13	♆29♍
30	16.36	8	1♉	26	25	13	♇ 5♌R

Dec	STime	☉	☽	☿	♀	♂	Plnts
1	16.40	9♐	13♉	27♏	26♑	14♈	♃17♊R
2	16.44	10	25	29	26	14	♄24♉R
3	16.48	11	7♊	0♐	27	14	♅28♉R
4	16.52	12	19	2	28	14	♆29♍
5	16.56	13	1♋	4	29	15	♇ 5♌R
6	17.00	14	13	5	0♒	15	♃16♊R
7	17.03	15	25	7	1	15	♄23♉R
8	17.07	16	7♌	8	2	15	♅27♉R
9	17.11	17	20	10	3	16	♆29♍
10	17.15	18	2♍	11	4	16	♇ 5♌R
11	17.19	19	15	13	5	16	♃16♊R
12	17.23	20	29	15	5	17	♄23♉R
13	17.27	21	13♎	16	6	17	♅27♉R
14	17.31	22	27	18	7	17	♆29♍
15	17.35	23	11♏	19	8	18	♇ 5♌R
16	17.39	24	26	21	9	18	♃15♊R
17	17.43	25	12♐	22	9	19	♄23♉R
18	17.47	26	27	24	10	19	♅27♉R
19	17.51	27	12♑	25	11	19	♆ 0♎
20	17.55	28	27	27	12	20	♇ 5♌R
21	17.59	29	11♒	29	12	20	♃14♊R
22	18.03	0♑	25	0♑	13	20	♄22♉R
23	18.07	1	8♓	2	14	21	♅27♉R
24	18.10	2	21	3	14	21	♆ 0♎
25	18.14	3	4♈	5	15	22	♇ 5♌R
26	18.18	4	16	7	15	22	♃14♊R
27	18.22	5	28	8	16	23	♄22♉R
28	18.26	6	10♉	10	16	23	♅27♉R
29	18.30	7	22	11	17	23	♆ 0♎
30	18.34	8	3♊	13	17	24	♇ 5♌R
31	18.38	9	15	15	18	24	♃13♊R

Jan	STime	☉	☽	☿	♀	♂	Plnts
1	18.42	10♑	27♊	16♑	18♒	25♈	♃13♊R
2	18.46	11	9♋	18	19	25	♄22♉R
3	18.50	12	22	20	19	26	♅26♉R
4	18.54	13	4♌	21	19	26	♆ 0♎R
5	18.58	14	17	23	20	27	♇ 5♌R
6	19.02	15	29	25	20	27	♃13♊R
7	19.06	16	12♍	26	20	28	♄22♉R
8	19.10	17	25	28	20	28	♅26♉R
9	19.14	18	9♎	29	21	29	♆ 0♎
10	19.18	19	22	1♒	21	29	♇ 5♌R
11	19.21	20	7♏	3	21	29	♃12♊R
12	19.25	21	21	4	21	0♉	♄21♉R
13	19.29	22	6♐	6	21R	0	♅26♉R
14	19.33	23	20	8	21	1	♆ 0♎R
15	19.37	24	5♑	9	21	1	♇ 5♌R
16	19.41	25	20	11	21	2	♃12♊R
17	19.45	26	5♒	12	20	2	♄21♉R
18	19.49	27	19	14	20	3	♅26♉R
19	19.53	28	3♓	15	20	4	♆29♍R
20	19.57	0♒	16	17	20	4	♇ 4♌R
21	20.01	1	29	18	19	5	♃11♊R
22	20.05	2	12♈	20	19	5	♄21♉
23	20.09	3	24	21	19	6	♅26♉R
24	20.13	4	6♉	22	18	6	♆29♍R
25	20.17	5	18	23	18	7	♇ 4♌R
26	20.21	6	0♊	24	17	7	♃11♊R
27	20.25	7	12	25	17	8	♄21♉
28	20.28	8	24	26	16	8	♅26♉
29	20.32	9	6♋	26	16	9	♆29♍R
30	20.36	10	18	26	15	9	♇ 4♌R
31	20.40	11	0♌	27	14	10	♃11♊R

Feb	STime	☉	☽	☿	♀	♂	Plnts
1	20.44	12♒	13♌	27♒	14♒	10♉	♃11♊R
2	20.48	13	26	27	13	11	♄21♉
3	20.52	14	9♍	26	12	12	♅26♉
4	20.56	15	22	26	12	12	♆29♍R
5	21.00	16	6♎	25	11	13	♇ 4♌R
6	21.04	17	19	24	11	13	♃11♊
7	21.08	18	3♏	23	10	14	♄22♉
8	21.12	19	17	22	10	14	♅26♉
9	21.16	20	1♐	21	9	15	♆29♍R
10	21.20	21	16	20	8	15	♇ 4♌R
11	21.24	22	0♑	18	8	16	♃11♊
12	21.28	23	14	17	8	17	♄22♉
13	21.32	24	29	16	7	17	♅26♉
14	21.36	25	13♒	15	7	18	♆29♍R
15	21.39	26	27	14	6	18	♇ 4♌R
16	21.43	27	11♓	14	6	19	♃11♊
17	21.47	28	24	13	6	19	♄22♉
18	21.51	29	7♈	12	6	20	♅26♉
19	21.55	0♓	19	12	6	21	♆29♍R
20	21.59	1	2♉	12	5	21	♇ 4♌R
21	22.03	2	14	11	5	22	♃12♊
22	22.07	3	26	11D	5	22	♄22♉
23	22.11	4	8♊	11	5D	23	♅26♉
24	22.15	5	20	12	5	23	♆29♍R
25	22.19	6	2♋	12	5	24	♇ 4♌R
26	22.23	7	14	12	5	25	♃12♊
27	22.27	8	26	13	6	25	♄22♉
28	22.31	9	9♌	13	6	26	♅26♉

Mar	STime	☉	☽	☿	♀	♂	Plnts
1	22.35	10♓	21♌	14♒	6♒	26♉	♃12♊
2	22.39	11	5♍	14	6	27	♄23♉
3	22.43	12	18	15	7	27	♅26♉
4	22.46	13	2♎	16	7	28	♆29♍R
5	22.50	14	16	17	7	29	♇ 4♌R
6	22.54	15	0♏	18	8	29	♃12♊
7	22.58	16	14	19	8	0♊	♄23♉
8	23.02	17	28	20	8	0	♅27♉
9	23.06	18	12♐	21	9	1	♆28♍R
10	23.10	19	27	22	9	2	♇ 3♌R
11	23.14	20	11♑	23	10	2	♃13♊
12	23.18	21	25	24	10	3	♄23♉
13	23.22	22	9♒	25	11	3	♅27♉
14	23.26	23	22	26	12	4	♆28♍R
15	23.30	24	6♓	28	12	5	♇ 3♌R
16	23.34	25	19	29	13	5	♃14♊
17	23.38	26	2♈	0♓	13	6	♄24♉
18	23.42	27	15	2	14	6	♅27♉
19	23.46	28	27	3	15	7	♆28♍R
20	23.50	29	10♉	4	16	8	♇ 3♌R
21	23.53	0♈	22	6	16	8	♃14♊
22	23.57	1	4♊	7	17	9	♄24♉
23	0.01	2	16	9	18	9	♅27♉
24	0.05	3	27	10	19	10	♆28♍R
25	0.09	4	9♋	12	19	10	♇ 3♌R
26	0.13	5	22	13	20	11	♃15♊
27	0.17	6	4♌	15	21	12	♄25♉
28	0.21	7	16	17	22	12	♅27♉
29	0.25	8	29	18	23	13	♆28♍R
30	0.29	9	13♍	20	23	14	♇ 3♌R
31	0.33	10	26	21	24	14	♃16♊

Apr	STime	☉	☽	☿	♀	♂	Plnts
1	0.37	11♈	11♎	23♓	25♒	15♊	♃16♊
2	0.41	12	25	25	26	15	♄25♉
3	0.45	13	10♏	27	27	16	♅27♉
4	0.49	14	24	28	28	17	♆28♍R
5	0.53	15	9♐	0♈	29	17	♇ 3♌
6	0.57	16	23	2	0♓	18	♃17♊
7	1.01	17	8♑	4	1	18	♄26♉
8	1.04	18	22	6	2	19	♅28♉
9	1.08	19	5♒	7	2	20	♆28♍R
10	1.12	20	19	9	3	20	♇ 3♌
11	1.16	21	2♓	11	4	21	♃17♊
12	1.20	22	15	13	5	21	♄26♉
13	1.24	23	28	15	6	22	♅28♉
14	1.28	24	11♈	17	7	23	♆28♍R
15	1.32	25	23	19	8	23	♇ 3♌
16	1.36	26	6♉	21	9	24	♃18♊
17	1.40	27	18	23	10	24	♄27♉
18	1.44	28	0♊	25	11	25	♅28♉
19	1.48	28	12	27	12	26	♆27♍R
20	1.52	29	24	0♉	13	26	♇ 3♌
21	1.56	0♉	6♋	2	14	27	♃19♊
22	2.00	1	17	4	15	27	♄28♉
23	2.04	2	0♌	6	16	28	♅28♉
24	2.08	3	12	8	17	29	♆27♍R
25	2.11	4	24	10	18	29	♇ 3♌
26	2.15	5	7♍	12	19	0♋	♃20♊
27	2.19	6	21	14	21	0	♄28♉
28	2.23	7	4♎	17	22	1	♅29♉
29	2.27	8	19	19	23	2	♆27♍R
30	2.31	9	3♏	21	24	2	♇ 3♌

May	STime	☉	☽	☿	♀	♂	Plnts
1	2.35	10♉	18♏	23♉	25♓	3♋	♃21♊
2	2.39	11	3♐	25	26	4	♄29♉
3	2.43	12	18	27	27	4	♅29♉
4	2.47	13	3♑	28	28	5	♆27♍R
5	2.51	14	18	0♊	29	5	♇ 3♌
6	2.55	15	2♒	2	0♈	6	♃22♊
7	2.59	16	16	4	1	7	♄ 0♊
8	3.03	17	29	5	2	7	♅29♉
9	3.07	18	12♓	7	3	8	♆27♍R
10	3.11	19	25	9	4	8	♇ 3♌
11	3.15	20	8♈	10	6	9	♃23♊
12	3.19	21	20	12	7	10	♄ 0♊
13	3.22	22	2♉	13	8	10	♅ 0♊
14	3.26	23	15	14	9	11	♆27♍R
15	3.30	24	27	15	10	11	♇ 3♌
16	3.34	25	9♊	17	11	12	♃24♊
17	3.38	26	20	18	12	13	♄ 1♊
18	3.42	27	2♋	19	13	13	♅ 0♊
19	3.46	28	14	20	14	14	♆27♍R
20	3.50	29	26	21	16	15	♇ 3♌
21	3.54	29	8♌	21	17	15	♃25♊
22	3.58	0♊	20	22	18	16	♄ 1♊
23	4.02	1	3♍	23	19	16	♅ 0♊
24	4.06	2	16	23	20	17	♆27♍R
25	4.10	3	29	24	21	18	♇ 3♌
26	4.14	4	13♎	24	22	18	♃26♊
27	4.18	5	27	25	23	19	♄ 2♊
28	4.22	6	12♏	25	25	19	♅ 0♊
29	4.26	7	27	25	26	20	♆27♍R
30	4.29	8	12♐	25	27	21	♇ 4♌
31	4.33	9	27	25R	28	21	♃27♊

Jun	STime	☉	☽	☿	♀	♂	Plnts
1	4.37	10♊	12♑	25♊	29♈	22♋	♃28♊
2	4.41	11	27	25	0♉	23	♄ 3♊
3	4.45	12	12♒	25	1	23	♅ 1♊
4	4.49	13	26	25	3	24	♆27♍R
5	4.53	14	9♓	25	4	24	♇ 4♌
6	4.57	15	22	24	5	25	♃29♊
7	5.01	16	5♈	24	6	26	♄ 4♊
8	5.05	17	17	23	7	26	♅ 1♊
9	5.09	18	0♉	23	8	27	♆27♍
10	5.13	19	12	22	9	27	♇ 4♌
11	5.17	20	24	22	11	28	♃ 0♋
12	5.21	21	6♊	21	12	29	♄ 4♊
13	5.25	22	17	21	13	29	♅ 1♊
14	5.29	22	29	20	14	0♌	♆27♍
15	5.33	23	11♋	19	15	1	♇ 4♌
16	5.36	24	23	19	16	1	♃ 1♋
17	5.40	25	5♌	18	18	2	♄ 5♊
18	5.44	26	17	18	19	2	♅ 2♊
19	5.48	27	29	18	20	3	♆27♍
20	5.52	28	12♍	17	21	4	♇ 4♌
21	5.56	29	25	17	22	4	♃ 2♋
22	6.00	0♋	8♎	17	23	5	♄ 5♊
23	6.04	1	22	17	25	5	♅ 2♊
24	6.08	2	6♏	17D	26	6	♆27♍
25	6.12	3	20	17	27	7	♇ 4♌
26	6.16	4	5♐	17	28	7	♃ 3♋
27	6.20	5	20	17	29	8	♄ 6♊
28	6.24	6	6♑	17	0♊	9	♅ 2♊
29	6.28	7	21	18	2	9	♆27♍
30	6.32	8	6♒	18	3	10	♇ 4♌

Jul	STime	☉	☽	☿	♀	♂	Plnts
1	6.36	9♋	20♒	19♊	4♊	10♌	♃ 5♋
2	6.40	10	4♓	19	5	11	♄ 7♊
3	6.44	11	18	20	6	12	♅ 2♊
4	6.47	12	1♈	21	7	12	♆27♍
5	6.51	13	14	21	9	13	♇ 4♌
6	6.55	13	26	22	10	14	♃ 6♋
7	6.59	14	9♉	23	11	14	♄ 7♊
8	7.03	15	21	24	12	15	♅ 3♊
9	7.07	16	3♊	25	13	15	♆27♍
10	7.11	17	14	27	15	16	♇ 5♌
11	7.15	18	26	28	16	17	♃ 7♋
12	7.19	19	8♋	29	17	17	♄ 8♊
13	7.23	20	20	1♋	18	18	♅ 3♊
14	7.27	21	2♌	2	19	19	♆27♍
15	7.31	22	14	4	20	19	♇ 5♌
16	7.35	23	27	5	22	20	♃ 8♋
17	7.39	24	9♍	7	23	20	♄ 8♊
18	7.43	25	22	9	24	21	♅ 3♊
19	7.47	26	5♎	10	25	22	♆27♍
20	7.51	27	18	12	26	22	♇ 5♌
21	7.54	28	1♏	14	28	23	♃ 9♋
22	7.58	29	15	16	29	24	♄ 9♊
23	8.02	0♌	0♐	18	0♋	24	♅ 3♊
24	8.06	1	14	20	1	25	♆27♍
25	8.10	2	29	22	2	25	♇ 5♌
26	8.14	3	14♑	24	4	26	♃10♋
27	8.18	4	29	26	5	27	♄ 9♊
28	8.22	4	14♒	28	6	27	♅ 3♊
29	8.26	5	29	0♌	7	28	♆27♍
30	8.30	6	13♓	2	8	29	♇ 5♌
31	8.34	7	26	5	10	29	♃11♋

Aug	STime	☉	☽	☿	♀	♂	Plnts
1	8.38	8♌	10♈	7♌	11♋	0♍	♃11♋
2	8.42	9	22	9	12	0	♄10♊
3	8.46	10	5♉	11	13	1	♅ 4♊
4	8.50	11	17	13	14	2	♆28♍
5	8.54	12	29	15	16	2	♇ 5♌
6	8.58	13	11♊	17	17	3	♃12♋
7	9.02	14	23	19	18	4	♄10♊
8	9.05	15	5♋	21	19	4	♅ 4♊
9	9.09	16	17	23	20	5	♆28♍
10	9.13	17	29	25	22	5	♇ 5♌
11	9.17	18	11♌	27	23	6	♃14♋
12	9.21	19	23	29	24	7	♄11♊
13	9.25	20	6♍	0♍	25	7	♅ 4♊
14	9.29	21	19	2	27	8	♆28♍
15	9.33	22	2♎	4	28	9	♇ 6♌
16	9.37	23	15	6	29	9	♃15♋
17	9.41	24	28	8	0♌	10	♄11♊
18	9.45	25	12♏	9	1	11	♅ 4♊
19	9.49	26	26	11	3	11	♆28♍
20	9.53	27	10♐	13	4	12	♇ 6♌
21	9.57	27	24	14	5	12	♃16♋
22	10.01	28	9♑	16	6	13	♄11♊
23	10.05	29	24	18	7	14	♅ 4♊
24	10.09	0♍	8♒	19	9	14	♆28♍
25	10.12	1	23	21	10	15	♇ 6♌
26	10.16	2	7♓	22	11	16	♃16♋
27	10.20	3	21	24	12	16	♄11♊
28	10.24	4	4♈	26	14	17	♅ 4♊
29	10.28	5	18	27	15	18	♆28♍
30	10.32	6	0♉	28	16	18	♇ 6♌
31	10.36	7	13	0♎	17	19	♃17♋

Sep	STime	☉	☽	☿	♀	♂	Plnts
1	10.40	8♍	25♉	1♎	18♌	19♍	♃18♋
2	10.44	9	7♊	3	20	20	♄12♊
3	10.48	10	19	4	21	21	♅ 4♊
4	10.52	11	1♋	5	22	21	♆29♍
5	10.56	12	13	7	23	22	♇ 6♌
6	11.00	13	25	8	25	23	♃18♋
7	11.04	14	7♌	9	26	23	♄12♊
8	11.08	15	19	11	27	24	♅ 4♊
9	11.12	16	2♍	12	28	25	♆29♍
10	11.16	17	15	13	0♍	25	♇ 6♌
11	11.20	18	28	14	1	26	♃19♋
12	11.23	19	11♎	15	2	27	♄12♊
13	11.27	20	25	16	3	27	♅ 4♊
14	11.31	21	9♏	17	5	28	♆29♍
15	11.35	22	23	18	6	28	♇ 6♌
16	11.39	23	7♐	19	7	29	♃20♋
17	11.43	24	21	20	8	0♎	♄12♊
18	11.47	25	5♑	21	9	0	♅ 4♊R
19	11.51	26	19	22	11	1	♆29♍
20	11.55	27	4♒	23	12	2	♇ 6♌
21	11.59	28	18	23	13	2	♃21♋
22	12.03	29	2♓	24	14	3	♄12♊
23	12.07	0♎	16	24	16	4	♅ 4♊R
24	12.11	1	29	25	17	4	♆29♍
25	12.15	1	13♈	25	18	5	♇ 7♌
26	12.19	2	26	25	19	6	♃22♋
27	12.23	3	8♉	26	21	6	♄12♊
28	12.27	4	21	26R	22	7	♅ 4♊R
29	12.30	5	3♊	26	23	8	♆ 0♎
30	12.34	6	15	26	24	8	♇ 7♌

Oct	STime	☉	☽	☿	♀	♂	Plnts
1	12.38	7♎	27♊	25♎	26♍	9♎	♃22♋
2	12.42	8	9♋	25	27	10	♄12♊R
3	12.46	9	21	24	28	10	♅ 4♊R
4	12.50	10	3♌	24	29	11	♆ 0♎
5	12.54	11	15	23	1♎	11	♇ 7♌
6	12.58	12	27	22	2	12	♃23♋
7	13.02	13	10♍	21	3	13	♄12♊R
8	13.06	14	23	20	4	13	♅ 4♊R
9	13.10	15	7♎	19	6	14	♆ 0♎
10	13.14	16	20	17	7	15	♇ 7♌
11	13.18	17	5♏	16	8	15	♃23♋
12	13.22	18	19	15	9	16	♄12♊R
13	13.26	19	3♐	14	11	17	♅ 4♊R
14	13.30	20	18	13	12	17	♆ 0♎
15	13.34	21	2♑	12	13	18	♇ 7♌
16	13.37	22	16	11	14	19	♃24♋
17	13.41	23	0♒	11	16	19	♄12♊R
18	13.45	24	14	11	17	20	♅ 4♊R
19	13.49	25	28	10	18	21	♆ 0♎
20	13.53	26	12♓	10D	19	21	♇ 7♌
21	13.57	27	25	11	21	22	♃24♋
22	14.01	28	8♈	11	22	23	♄12♊R
23	14.05	29	21	11	23	23	♅ 4♊R
24	14.09	0♏	4♉	12	24	24	♆ 0♎
25	14.13	1	17	13	26	25	♇ 7♌
26	14.17	2	29	14	27	25	♃24♋
27	14.21	3	11♊	15	28	26	♄11♊R
28	14.25	4	23	16	29	27	♅ 3♊R
29	14.29	5	5♋	17	1♏	27	♆ 1♎
30	14.33	6	17	18	2	28	♇ 7♌
31	14.37	7	29	20	3	29	♃25♋

Nov	STime	☉	☽	☿	♀	♂	Plnts
1	14.41	8♏	11♌	21♎	4♏	29♎	♃25♋
2	14.45	9	23	23	6	0♏	♄11♊R
3	14.48	10	5♍	24	7	1	♅ 3♊R
4	14.52	11	18	26	8	1	♆ 1♎
5	14.56	12	1♎	27	9	2	♇ 7♌
6	15.00	13	15	29	11	3	♃25♋
7	15.04	14	29	0♏	12	3	♄11♊R
8	15.08	15	13♏	2	13	4	♅ 3♊R
9	15.12	16	28	4	14	5	♆ 1♎
10	15.16	17	13♐	5	16	5	♇ 7♌
11	15.20	18	28	7	17	6	♃25♋
12	15.24	19	12♑	8	18	7	♄10♊R
13	15.28	20	27	10	19	8	♅ 3♊R
14	15.32	21	11♒	12	21	8	♆ 1♎
15	15.36	22	25	13	22	9	♇ 7♌
16	15.40	23	8♓	15	23	10	♃25♋R
17	15.44	24	22	16	24	10	♄10♊R
18	15.48	25	5♈	18	26	11	♅ 3♊R
19	15.52	26	18	20	27	12	♆ 1♎
20	15.55	27	0♉	21	28	12	♇ 7♌R
21	15.59	28	13	23	29	13	♃25♋R
22	16.03	29	25	24	1♐	14	♄10♊R
23	16.07	0♐	8♊	26	2	14	♅ 2♊R
24	16.11	1	20	28	3	15	♆ 1♎
25	16.15	2	2♋	29	5	16	♇ 7♌R
26	16.19	3	13	1♐	6	16	♃25♋R
27	16.23	4	25	2	7	17	♄ 9♊R
28	16.27	5	7♌	4	8	18	♅ 2♊R
29	16.31	6	19	5	10	18	♆ 1♎
30	16.35	7	1♍	7	11	19	♇ 7♌

Dec	STime	☉	☽	☿	♀	♂	Plnts
1	16.39	8♐	13♍	9♐	12♐	20♏	♃24♋R
2	16.43	9	26	10	13	21	♄ 9♊R
3	16.47	10	9♎	12	15	21	♅ 2♊R
4	16.51	11	23	13	16	22	♆ 2♎
5	16.55	12	7♏	15	17	23	♇ 7♌R
6	16.59	13	21	16	18	23	♃24♋R
7	17.03	14	6♐	18	20	24	♄ 8♊R
8	17.06	15	21	20	21	25	♅ 2♊R
9	17.10	16	7♑	21	22	25	♆ 2♎
10	17.14	18	22	23	23	26	♇ 7♌R
11	17.18	19	6♒	24	25	27	♃24♋R
12	17.22	20	21	26	26	27	♄ 8♊R
13	17.26	21	5♓	27	27	28	♅ 2♊R
14	17.30	22	19	29	28	29	♆ 2♎
15	17.34	23	2♈	1♑	0♑	0♐	♇ 7♌R
16	17.38	24	15	2	1	0	♃23♋R
17	17.42	25	27	4	2	1	♄ 7♊R
18	17.46	26	10♉	5	3	2	♅ 1♊R
19	17.50	27	22	7	5	2	♆ 2♎
20	17.54	28	4♊	8	6	3	♇ 7♌R
21	17.58	29	16	10	7	4	♃23♋R
22	18.02	0♑	28	12	8	4	♄ 7♊R
23	18.06	1	10♋	13	10	5	♅ 1♊R
24	18.10	2	22	15	11	6	♆ 2♎
25	18.13	3	4♌	16	12	7	♇ 7♌R
26	18.17	4	16	18	13	7	♃22♋R
27	18.21	5	28	19	15	8	♄ 7♊R
28	18.25	6	10♍	21	16	9	♅ 1♊R
29	18.29	7	22	23	17	9	♆ 2♎
30	18.33	8	5♎	24	19	10	♇ 6♌R
31	18.37	9	18	26	20	11	♃21♋R

Jan	STime	☉	☽	☿	♀	♂	Plnts
1	18.41	10♑	1♏	27♑	21♑	12♐	♃21♋R
2	18.45	11	15	28	22	12	♄ 6♊R
3	18.49	12	29	0♒	24	13	♅ 1♊R
4	18.53	13	14♐	1	25	14	♆ 2♎
5	18.57	14	29	3	26	14	♇ 6♌R
6	19.01	15	15♑	4	27	15	♃21♋R
7	19.05	16	0♒	5	29	16	♄ 6♊R
8	19.09	17	15	6	0♒	17	♅ 1♊R
9	19.13	18	0♓	7	1	17	♆ 2♎
10	19.17	19	14	8	2	18	♇ 6♌R
11	19.21	20	28	9	4	19	♃20♋R
12	19.24	21	11♈	10	5	19	♄ 6♊R
13	19.28	22	24	10	6	20	♅ 1♊R
14	19.32	23	7♉	10	7	21	♆ 2♎R
15	19.36	24	19	11R	9	22	♇ 6♌R
16	19.40	25	1♊	10	10	22	♃19♋R
17	19.44	26	13	10	11	23	♄ 6♊R
18	19.48	27	25	10	12	24	♅ 0♊R
19	19.52	28	7♋	9	14	24	♆ 2♎R
20	19.56	29	19	8	15	25	♇ 6♌R
21	20.00	0♒	1♌	8	16	26	♃19♋R
22	20.04	1	13	6	17	27	♄ 6♊R
23	20.08	2	25	5	19	27	♅ 0♊R
24	20.12	3	7♍	4	20	28	♆ 2♎R
25	20.16	4	19	3	21	29	♇ 6♌R
26	20.20	5	1♎	1	22	29	♃18♋R
27	20.24	6	14	0	24	0♑	♄ 5♊R
28	20.28	7	27	29♑	25	1	♅ 0♊R
29	20.31	8	10♏	28	26	2	♆ 2♎R
30	20.35	9	24	27	27	2	♇ 6♌R
31	20.39	10	8♐	26	29	3	♃17♋R

Feb	STime	☉	☽	☿	♀	♂	Plnts
1	20.43	11♒	23♐	26♑	0♓	4♑	♃17♋R
2	20.47	12	8♑	25	1	5	♄ 5♊
3	20.51	13	23	25	2	5	♅ 0♊
4	20.55	15	8♒	25	4	6	♆ 1♎R
5	20.59	16	23	25D	5	7	♇ 6♌R
6	21.03	17	8♓	25	6	8	♃17♋R
7	21.07	18	22	25	7	8	♄ 5♊
8	21.11	19	6♈	25	9	9	♅ 0♊
9	21.15	20	20	25	10	10	♆ 1♎R
10	21.19	21	3♉	26	11	10	♇ 5♌R
11	21.23	22	16	27	12	11	♃16♋R
12	21.27	23	28	27	14	12	♄ 5♊
13	21.31	24	10♊	28	15	13	♅ 0♊
14	21.35	25	22	29	16	13	♆ 1♎R
15	21.38	26	4♋	29	17	14	♇ 5♌R
16	21.42	27	16	0♒	19	15	♃16♋R
17	21.46	28	28	1	20	16	♄ 5♊
18	21.50	29	9♌	2	21	16	♅ 0♊
19	21.54	0♓	21	3	22	17	♆ 1♎R
20	21.58	1	4♍	4	24	18	♇ 5♌R
21	22.02	2	16	5	25	19	♃15♋R
22	22.06	3	28	7	26	19	♄ 6♊
23	22.10	4	11♎	8	27	20	♅ 0♊
24	22.14	5	24	9	28	21	♆ 1♎R
25	22.18	6	7♏	10	0♈	21	♇ 5♌R
26	22.22	7	21	12	1	22	♃15♋R
27	22.26	8	4♐	13	2	23	♄ 6♊
28	22.30	9	18	14	3	24	♅ 0♊

Mar	STime	☉	☽	☿	♀	♂	Plnts
1	22.34	10♓	2♑	15♒	5♈	24♑	♃15♋R
2	22.38	11	17	17	6	25	♄ 6♊
3	22.42	12	2♒	18	7	26	♅ 1♊
4	22.46	13	16	20	8	27	♆ 1♎R
5	22.49	14	1♓	21	10	27	♇ 5♌R
6	22.53	15	16	23	11	28	♃15♋R
7	22.57	16	0♈	24	12	29	♄ 6♊
8	23.01	17	14	26	13	0♒	♅ 1♊
9	23.05	18	28	27	14	0	♆ 1♎R
10	23.09	19	11♉	29	16	1	♇ 5♌R
11	23.13	20	24	0♓	17	2	♃15♋
12	23.17	21	6♊	2	18	3	♄ 6♊
13	23.21	22	18	3	19	3	♅ 1♊
14	23.25	23	0♋	5	21	4	♆ 1♎R
15	23.29	24	12	7	22	5	♇ 5♌R
16	23.33	25	24	8	23	6	♃15♋
17	23.37	26	6♌	10	24	6	♄ 7♊
18	23.41	27	18	12	26	7	♅ 1♊
19	23.45	28	0♍	13	27	8	♆ 0♎R
20	23.49	29	12	15	28	9	♇ 5♌R
21	23.53	0♈	25	17	29	9	♃15♋
22	23.56	1	8♎	19	0♉	10	♄ 7♊
23	0.00	2	21	20	2	11	♅ 1♊
24	0.04	3	4♏	22	3	12	♆ 0♎R
25	0.08	4	17	24	4	12	♇ 5♌R
26	0.12	5	1♐	26	5	13	♃15♋
27	0.16	6	15	28	6	14	♄ 7♊
28	0.20	7	29	0♈	8	15	♅ 1♊
29	0.24	8	13♑	2	9	15	♆ 0♎R
30	0.28	9	27	4	10	16	♇ 5♌R
31	0.32	10	12♒	6	11	17	♃15♋

Apr	STime	☉	☽	☿	♀	♂	Plnts
1	0.36	11♈	26♒	8♈	13♉	18♒	♃16♋
2	0.40	12	10♓	10	14	18	♄ 8♊
3	0.44	13	24	12	15	19	♅ 2♊
4	0.48	14	8♈	14	16	20	♆ 0♎R
5	0.52	15	22	16	17	21	♇ 5♌
6	0.56	16	5♉	18	19	21	♃16♋
7	1.00	16	19	20	20	22	♄ 8♊
8	1.04	17	1♊	22	21	23	♅ 2♊
9	1.07	18	14	24	22	24	♆ 0♎R
10	1.11	19	26	26	23	24	♇ 5♌
11	1.15	20	8♋	28	25	25	♃16♋
12	1.19	21	20	0♉	26	26	♄ 9♊
13	1.23	22	2♌	2	27	27	♅ 2♊
14	1.27	23	14	4	28	27	♆ 0♎R
15	1.31	24	26	6	29	28	♇ 5♌
16	1.35	25	8♍	8	0♊	29	♃17♋
17	1.39	26	20	10	2	0♓	♄ 9♊
18	1.43	27	3♎	12	3	1	♅ 2♊
19	1.47	28	16	14	4	1	♆ 0♎R
20	1.51	29	0♏	16	5	2	♇ 5♌
21	1.55	0♉	13	17	6	3	♃17♋
22	1.59	1	27	19	8	4	♄10♊
23	2.03	2	12♐	21	9	4	♅ 2♊
24	2.07	3	26	22	10	5	♆ 0♎R
25	2.11	4	10♑	24	11	6	♇ 5♌
26	2.14	5	24	25	12	7	♃18♋
27	2.18	6	8♒	26	13	7	♄11♊
28	2.22	7	22	27	15	8	♅ 3♊
29	2.26	8	6♓	28	16	9	♆29♍R
30	2.30	9	20	0♊	17	10	♇ 5♌

May	STime	☉	☽	☿	♀	♂	Plnts
1	2.34	10♉	4♈	0♊	18♊	10♓	♃19♋
2	2.38	11	17	1	19	11	♄11♊
3	2.42	12	1♉	2	20	12	♅ 3♊
4	2.46	13	14	3	22	13	♆29♍R
5	2.50	14	27	3	23	13	♇ 5♌
6	2.54	15	10♊	4	24	14	♃19♋
7	2.58	16	22	4	25	15	♄12♊
8	3.02	17	4♋	5	26	16	♅ 3♊
9	3.06	18	16	5	27	16	♆29♍R
10	3.10	19	28	5	29	17	♇ 5♌
11	3.14	20	10♌	5	0♋	18	♃20♋
12	3.18	21	22	5R	1	19	♄12♊
13	3.21	22	4♍	5	2	19	♅ 4♊
14	3.25	23	16	5	3	20	♆29♍R
15	3.29	23	28	5	4	21	♇ 5♌
16	3.33	24	11♎	5	5	22	♃21♋
17	3.37	25	24	4	7	22	♄13♊
18	3.41	26	8♏	4	8	23	♅ 4♊
19	3.45	27	22	4	9	24	♆29♍R
20	3.49	28	7♐	3	10	25	♇ 5♌
21	3.53	29	21	2	11	25	♃22♋
22	3.57	0♊	6♑	2	12	26	♄14♊
23	4.01	1	20	1	13	27	♅ 4♊
24	4.05	2	5♒	1	14	28	♆29♍R
25	4.09	3	19	0	16	28	♇ 5♌
26	4.13	4	3♓	0	17	29	♃23♋
27	4.17	5	17	29♉	18	0♈	♄14♊
28	4.21	6	1♈	29	19	1	♅ 4♊
29	4.25	7	14	28	20	1	♆29♍R
30	4.29	8	27	28	21	2	♇ 5♌
31	4.32	9	10♉	27	22	3	♃24♋

Jun	STime	☉	☽	☿	♀	♂	Plnts
1	4.36	10♊	23♉	27♉	23♋	3♈	♃24♋
2	4.40	11	6♊	27	24	4	♄15♊
3	4.44	12	18	27	25	5	♅ 5♊
4	4.48	13	0♋	27D	26	6	♆29♍
5	4.52	14	12	27	28	6	♇ 5♌
6	4.56	15	24	27	29	7	♃25♋
7	5.00	16	6♌	27	0♌	8	♄16♊
8	5.04	17	18	27	1	9	♅ 5♊
9	5.08	17	0♍	27	2	9	♆29♍
10	5.12	18	12	28	3	10	♇ 5♌
11	5.16	19	24	28	4	11	♃26♋
12	5.20	20	6♎	29	5	12	♄16♊
13	5.24	21	19	29	6	12	♅ 5♊
14	5.28	22	3♏	0♊	7	13	♆29♍
15	5.32	23	16	1	8	14	♇ 5♌
16	5.36	24	1♐	2	9	14	♃27♋
17	5.39	25	15	2	10	15	♄17♊
18	5.43	26	0♑	3	11	16	♅ 6♊
19	5.47	27	15	4	12	17	♆29♍
20	5.51	28	0♒	5	13	17	♇ 5♌
21	5.55	29	15	6	14	18	♃28♋
22	5.59	0♋	29	8	15	19	♄18♊
23	6.03	1	14♓	9	16	19	♅ 6♊
24	6.07	2	27	10	17	20	♆29♍
25	6.11	3	11♈	11	18	21	♇ 6♌
26	6.15	4	24	13	19	22	♃29♋
27	6.19	5	7♉	14	20	22	♄18♊
28	6.23	6	20	16	21	23	♅ 6♊
29	6.27	7	3♊	17	22	24	♆29♍
30	6.31	8	15	19	23	24	♇ 6♌

Jul	STime	☉	☽	☿	♀	♂	Plnts
1	6.35	8♋	27♊	21♊	24♌	25♈	♃ 0♌
2	6.39	9	9♋	23	25	26	♄19♊
3	6.43	10	21	24	26	27	♅ 6♊
4	6.47	11	3♌	26	27	27	♆29♍
5	6.50	12	15	28	27	28	♇ 6♌
6	6.54	13	26	0♋	28	29	♃ 1♌
7	6.58	14	8♍	2	29	29	♄20♊
8	7.02	15	20	4	0♍	0♉	♅ 7♊
9	7.06	16	2♎	6	1	1	♆29♍
10	7.10	17	15	8	2	1	♇ 6♌
11	7.14	18	28	10	3	2	♃ 2♌
12	7.18	19	11♏	12	4	3	♄20♊
13	7.22	20	25	14	4	4	♅ 7♊
14	7.26	21	9♐	17	5	4	♆29♍
15	7.30	22	23	19	6	5	♇ 6♌
16	7.34	23	8♑	21	7	6	♃ 3♌
17	7.38	24	23	23	7	6	♄21♊
18	7.42	25	9♒	25	8	7	♅ 7♊
19	7.46	26	24	27	9	8	♆29♍
20	7.50	27	9♓	29	10	8	♇ 6♌
21	7.54	28	23	1♌	10	9	♃ 4♌
22	7.57	29	7♈	4	11	10	♄21♊
23	8.01	29	21	6	12	10	♅ 7♊
24	8.05	0♌	4♉	8	12	11	♆29♍
25	8.09	1	17	10	13	12	♇ 6♌
26	8.13	2	0♊	12	14	12	♃ 5♌
27	8.17	3	12	14	14	13	♄22♊
28	8.21	4	24	15	15	14	♅ 8♊
29	8.25	5	6♋	17	15	14	♆ 0♎
30	8.29	6	18	19	16	15	♇ 7♌
31	8.33	7	0♌	21	16	15	♃ 6♌

Aug	STime	☉	☽	☿	♀	♂	Plnts
1	8.37	8♌	12♌	23♌	17♍	16♉	♃ 7♌
2	8.41	9	23	25	17	17	♄22♊
3	8.45	10	5♍	26	18	17	♅ 8♊
4	8.49	11	17	28	18	18	♆ 0♎
5	8.53	12	29	0♍	18	19	♇ 7♌
6	8.57	13	12♎	1	19	19	♃ 8♌
7	9.01	14	24	3	19	20	♄23♊
8	9.04	15	7♏	5	19	20	♅ 8♊
9	9.08	16	20	6	20	21	♆ 0♎
10	9.12	17	4♐	8	20	22	♇ 7♌
11	9.16	18	18	9	20	22	♃ 9♌
12	9.20	19	2♑	11	20	23	♄23♊
13	9.24	20	17	12	20	24	♅ 8♊
14	9.28	21	2♒	14	20	24	♆ 0♎
15	9.32	21	17	15	20R	25	♇ 7♌
16	9.36	22	2♓	17	20	25	♃10♌
17	9.40	23	17	18	20	26	♄24♊
18	9.44	24	2♈	19	20	27	♅ 8♊
19	9.48	25	16	21	20	27	♆ 0♎
20	9.52	26	0♉	22	20	28	♇ 7♌
21	9.56	27	13	23	20	28	♃11♌
22	10.00	28	26	25	19	29	♄24♊
23	10.04	29	9♊	26	19	29	♅ 8♊
24	10.08	0♍	21	27	19	0♊	♆ 0♎
25	10.12	1	3♋	28	18	1	♇ 7♌
26	10.15	2	15	29	18	1	♃12♌
27	10.19	3	27	0♎	18	2	♄25♊
28	10.23	4	9♌	1	17	2	♅ 8♊
29	10.27	5	20	2	17	3	♆ 1♎
30	10.31	6	2♍	3	16	3	♇ 7♌
31	10.35	7	14	4	16	4	♃13♌

Sep	STime	☉	☽	☿	♀	♂	Plnts
1	10.39	8♍	26♍	5♎	15♍	4♊	♃13♌
2	10.43	9	9♎	6	14	5	♄25♊
3	10.47	10	21	6	14	5	♅ 8♊
4	10.51	11	4♏	7	13	6	♆ 1♎
5	10.55	12	17	7	13	6	♇ 8♌
6	10.59	13	0♐	8	12	7	♃14♌
7	11.03	14	13	8	11	7	♄25♊
8	11.07	15	27	9	11	8	♅ 9♊
9	11.11	16	11♑	9	10	8	♆ 1♎
10	11.15	17	26	9	9	9	♇ 8♌
11	11.19	18	11♒	9R	9	9	♃15♌
12	11.22	19	25	9	8	10	♄26♊
13	11.26	20	10♓	9	8	10	♅ 9♊
14	11.30	20	25	9	7	11	♆ 1♎
15	11.34	21	10♈	8	7	11	♇ 8♌
16	11.38	22	24	8	6	12	♃16♌
17	11.42	23	8♉	7	6	12	♄26♊
18	11.46	24	22	7	6	12	♅ 9♊
19	11.50	25	5♊	6	5	13	♆ 1♎
20	11.54	26	17	5	5	13	♇ 8♌
21	11.58	27	0♋	4	5	14	♃17♌
22	12.02	28	12	3	5	14	♄26♊
23	12.06	29	24	2	4	14	♅ 9♊R
24	12.10	0♎	5♌	1	4	15	♆ 1♎
25	12.14	1	17	0	4	15	♇ 8♌
26	12.18	2	29	29♍	4	16	♃18♌
27	12.22	3	11♍	28	4D	16	♄26♊
28	12.26	4	23	27	4	16	♅ 8♊R
29	12.30	5	5♎	26	4	17	♆ 2♎
30	12.33	6	18	25	4	17	♇ 8♌

Oct	STime	☉	☽	☿	♀	♂	Plnts
1	12.37	7♎	1♏	25♍	4♍	17♊	♃19♌
2	12.41	8	14	25	5	18	♄26♊
3	12.45	9	27	24D	5	18	♅ 8♊R
4	12.49	10	10♐	24	5	18	♆ 2♎
5	12.53	11	24	25	5	19	♇ 8♌
6	12.57	12	8♑	25	6	19	♃20♌
7	13.01	13	22	26	6	19	♄26♊
8	13.05	14	6♒	26	6	19	♅ 8♊R
9	13.09	15	20	27	7	20	♆ 2♎
10	13.13	16	5♓	28	7	20	♇ 8♌
11	13.17	17	19	29	8	20	♃21♌
12	13.21	18	4♈	0♎	8	20	♄26♊R
13	13.25	19	18	2	9	20	♅ 8♊R
14	13.29	20	2♉	3	9	21	♆ 2♎
15	13.33	21	16	4	10	21	♇ 8♌
16	13.37	22	0♊	6	10	21	♃22♌
17	13.40	23	13	7	11	21	♄26♊R
18	13.44	24	25	9	12	21	♅ 8♊R
19	13.48	25	8♋	11	12	21	♆ 2♎
20	13.52	26	20	12	13	22	♇ 8♌
21	13.56	27	2♌	14	14	22	♃23♌
22	14.00	28	13	15	14	22	♄26♊R
23	14.04	29	25	17	15	22	♅ 8♊R
24	14.08	0♏	7♍	19	16	22	♆ 3♎
25	14.12	1	19	20	16	22	♇ 8♌
26	14.16	2	1♎	22	17	22	♃23♌
27	14.20	3	14	24	18	22	♄26♊R
28	14.24	4	27	26	19	22R	♅ 8♊R
29	14.28	5	10♏	27	20	22	♆ 3♎
30	14.32	6	23	29	20	22	♇ 8♌
31	14.36	7	7♐	1♏	21	22	♃24♌

Nov	STime	☉	☽	☿	♀	♂	Plnts
1	14.40	8♏	21♐	2♏	22♍	22♊	♃24♌
2	14.44	9	5♑	4	23	22	♄26♊R
3	14.48	10	19	6	24	22	♅ 8♊R
4	14.51	11	3♒	7	25	22	♆ 3♎
5	14.55	12	17	9	26	21	♇ 8♌
6	14.59	13	1♓	10	27	21	♃25♌
7	15.03	14	15	12	28	21	♄26♊R
8	15.07	15	29	14	29	21	♅ 7♊R
9	15.11	16	13♈	15	29	21	♆ 3♎
10	15.15	17	27	17	0♎	21	♇ 8♌
11	15.19	18	11♉	19	1	20	♃25♌
12	15.23	19	24	20	2	20	♄25♊R
13	15.27	20	8♊	22	3	20	♅ 7♊R
14	15.31	21	21	23	4	20	♆ 3♎
15	15.35	22	3♋	25	5	19	♇ 8♌
16	15.39	23	15	26	6	19	♃26♌
17	15.43	24	27	28	7	19	♄25♊R
18	15.47	25	9♌	0♐	8	19	♅ 7♊R
19	15.51	26	21	1	9	18	♆ 3♎
20	15.55	27	3♍	3	10	18	♇ 8♌
21	15.58	28	15	4	11	18	♃26♌
22	16.02	29	27	6	12	17	♄25♊R
23	16.06	0♐	9♎	7	14	17	♅ 7♊R
24	16.10	1	22	9	15	17	♆ 3♎
25	16.14	2	5♏	10	16	16	♇ 8♌
26	16.18	3	18	12	17	16	♃26♌
27	16.22	4	2♐	14	18	16	♄24♊R
28	16.26	5	16	15	19	15	♅ 7♊R
29	16.30	6	0♑	17	20	15	♆ 4♎
30	16.34	7	15	18	21	14	♇ 8♌

Dec	STime	☉	☽	☿	♀	♂	Plnts
1	16.38	8♐	29♑	20♐	22♎	14♊	♃27♌
2	16.42	9	13♒	21	23	14	♄24♊R
3	16.46	10	28	23	24	13	♅ 6♊R
4	16.50	11	12♓	24	25	13	♆ 4♎
5	16.54	12	26	26	27	13	♇ 8♌R
6	16.58	13	9♈	27	28	12	♃27♌
7	17.02	14	23	29	29	12	♄24♊R
8	17.05	15	7♉	0♑	0♏	11	♅ 6♊R
9	17.09	16	20	2	1	11	♆ 4♎
10	17.13	17	3♊	3	2	11	♇ 8♌R
11	17.17	18	16	5	3	10	♃27♌
12	17.21	19	29	6	4	10	♄23♊R
13	17.25	20	11♋	8	6	10	♅ 6♊R
14	17.29	21	23	9	7	9	♆ 4♎
15	17.33	22	5♌	11	8	9	♇ 8♌R
16	17.37	23	17	12	9	9	♃27♌R
17	17.41	24	29	13	10	8	♄23♊R
18	17.45	25	11♍	15	11	8	♅ 6♊R
19	17.49	26	23	16	12	8	♆ 4♎
20	17.53	27	5♎	17	14	7	♇ 8♌R
21	17.57	28	17	18	15	7	♃27♌R
22	18.01	29	0♏	19	16	7	♄22♊R
23	18.05	0♑	13	20	17	7	♅ 6♊R
24	18.09	2	26	21	18	6	♆ 4♎
25	18.13	3	10♐	22	19	6	♇ 8♌R
26	18.16	4	25	23	21	6	♃27♌R
27	18.20	5	9♑	24	22	6	♄22♊R
28	18.24	6	24	24	23	6	♅ 5♊R
29	18.28	7	9♒	24	24	5	♆ 4♎
30	18.32	8	23	25R	25	5	♇ 8♌R
31	18.36	9	8♓	24	27	5	♃26♌R

Jan	STime	☉	☽	☿	♀	♂	Plnts
1	18.40	10♑	22♓	24♑	28♏	5♊	♃26♌R
2	18.44	11	6♈	24	29	5	♄21♊R
3	18.48	12	20	23	0♐	5	♅ 5♊R
4	18.52	13	4♉	22	1	5	♆ 4♎
5	18.56	14	17	21	2	5	♇ 8♌R
6	19.00	15	0♊	20	4	5	♃26♌R
7	19.04	16	13	19	5	5	♄21♊R
8	19.08	17	25	18	6	5	♅ 5♊R
9	19.12	18	7♋	16	7	5	♆ 4♎
10	19.16	19	20	15	8	5D	♇ 8♌R
11	19.20	20	2♌	14	10	5	♃25♌R
12	19.23	21	14	13	11	5	♄21♊R
13	19.27	22	25	12	12	5	♅ 5♊R
14	19.31	23	7♍	11	13	5	♆ 4♎R
15	19.35	24	19	10	14	5	♇ 8♌R
16	19.39	25	1♎	9	16	5	♃25♌R
17	19.43	26	13	9	17	5	♄20♊R
18	19.47	27	25	8	18	5	♅ 5♊R
19	19.51	28	8♏	8D	19	5	♆ 4♎R
20	19.55	29	21	8	20	5	♇ 7♌R
21	19.59	0♒	4♐	8	22	5	♃24♌R
22	20.03	1	18	9	23	5	♄20♊R
23	20.07	2	2♑	9	24	6	♅ 5♊R
24	20.11	3	17	10	25	6	♆ 4♎R
25	20.15	4	2♒	10	26	6	♇ 7♌R
26	20.19	5	17	11	28	6	♃24♌R
27	20.23	6	2♓	12	29	6	♄20♊R
28	20.27	7	17	12	0♑	7	♅ 5♊R
29	20.31	8	2♈	13	1	7	♆ 4♎R
30	20.34	9	16	14	3	7	♇ 7♌R
31	20.38	10	0♉	15	4	7	♃23♌R

Feb	STime	☉	☽	☿	♀	♂	Plnts
1	20.42	11♒	14♉	16♑	5♑	7♊	♃23♌R
2	20.46	12	27	17	6	8	♄20♊R
3	20.50	13	10♊	18	7	8	♅ 5♊R
4	20.54	14	22	19	9	8	♆ 4♎R
5	20.58	15	4♋	21	10	8	♇ 7♌R
6	21.02	16	17	22	11	9	♃22♌R
7	21.06	17	29	23	12	9	♄20♊R
8	21.10	18	10♌	24	14	9	♅ 5♊
9	21.14	19	22	26	15	10	♆ 4♎R
10	21.18	20	4♍	27	16	10	♇ 7♌R
11	21.22	21	16	28	17	10	♃22♌R
12	21.26	22	28	0♒	18	11	♄19♊R
13	21.30	23	10♎	1	20	11	♅ 5♊
14	21.34	24	22	2	21	11	♆ 4♎R
15	21.38	25	4♏	4	22	12	♇ 7♌R
16	21.41	26	17	5	23	12	♃21♌R
17	21.45	27	0♐	7	25	12	♄19♊
18	21.49	28	13	8	26	13	♅ 5♊
19	21.53	29	26	10	27	13	♆ 3♎R
20	21.57	0♓	11♑	11	28	13	♇ 7♌R
21	22.01	1	25	13	29	14	♃21♌R
22	22.05	2	10♒	14	1♒	14	♄19♊
23	22.09	3	25	16	2	14	♅ 5♊
24	22.13	4	10♓	17	3	15	♆ 3♎R
25	22.17	5	26	19	4	15	♇ 7♌R
26	22.21	6	11♈	20	6	16	♃20♌R
27	22.25	7	25	22	7	16	♄19♊
28	22.29	8	9♉	24	8	16	♅ 5♊
29	22.33	9	23	25	9	17	♆ 3♎R

Mar	STime	☉	☽	☿	♀	♂	Plnts
1	22.37	10♓	6♊	27♒	11♒	17♊	♃19♌R
2	22.41	11	19	29	12	18	♄20♊
3	22.45	12	1♋	0♓	13	18	♅ 5♊
4	22.48	13	14	2	14	19	♆ 3♎R
5	22.52	14	26	4	15	19	♇ 7♌R
6	22.56	15	7♌	6	17	19	♃19♌R
7	23.00	16	19	7	18	20	♄20♊
8	23.04	17	1♍	9	19	20	♅ 5♊
9	23.08	18	13	11	20	21	♆ 3♎R
10	23.12	19	25	13	22	21	♇ 6♌R
11	23.16	20	7♎	15	23	22	♃18♌R
12	23.20	21	19	16	24	22	♄20♊
13	23.24	22	1♏	18	25	23	♅ 5♊
14	23.28	23	14	20	26	23	♆ 3♎R
15	23.32	24	26	22	28	23	♇ 6♌R
16	23.36	25	9♐	24	29	24	♃18♌R
17	23.40	26	22	26	0♓	24	♄20♊
18	23.44	27	6♑	28	1	25	♅ 5♊
19	23.48	28	20	0♈	3	25	♆ 3♎R
20	23.52	29	4♒	2	4	26	♇ 6♌R
21	23.56	0♈	19	4	5	26	♃18♌R
22	23.59	1	4♓	6	6	27	♄20♊
23	0.03	2	19	8	8	27	♅ 5♊
24	0.07	3	4♈	10	9	28	♆ 3♎R
25	0.11	4	19	12	10	28	♇ 6♌R
26	0.15	5	3♉	14	11	29	♃17♌R
27	0.19	6	18	16	12	29	♄21♊
28	0.23	7	1♊	18	14	0♋	♅ 5♊
29	0.27	8	15	20	15	0	♆ 2♎R
30	0.31	9	28	22	16	1	♇ 6♌R
31	0.35	10	10♋	24	17	1	♃17♌R

Apr	STime	☉	☽	☿	♀	♂	Plnts
1	0.39	11♈	22♋	26♈	19♓	2♋	♃17♌R
2	0.43	12	4♌	28	20	2	♄21♊
3	0.47	13	16	29	21	3	♅ 6♊
4	0.51	14	28	1♉	22	3	♆ 2♎R
5	0.55	15	10♍	3	24	4	♇ 6♌R
6	0.59	16	22	4	25	4	♃17♌R
7	1.03	17	4♎	6	26	5	♄21♊
8	1.06	18	16	7	27	5	♅ 6♊
9	1.10	19	28	8	28	6	♆ 2♎R
10	1.14	20	11♏	9	0♈	6	♇ 6♌
11	1.18	21	23	11	1	7	♃17♌R
12	1.22	22	6♐	12	2	7	♄22♊
13	1.26	23	19	12	3	8	♅ 6♊
14	1.30	24	2♑	13	5	9	♆ 2♎R
15	1.34	25	16	14	6	9	♇ 6♌
16	1.38	26	0♒	15	7	10	♃17♌
17	1.42	27	14	15	8	10	♄22♊
18	1.46	28	28	16	10	11	♅ 6♊
19	1.50	29	13♓	16	11	11	♆ 2♎R
20	1.54	0♉	28	16	12	12	♇ 6♌
21	1.58	1	12♈	16	13	12	♃17♌
22	2.02	2	27	16R	14	13	♄23♊
23	2.06	3	11♉	16	16	13	♅ 7♊
24	2.10	4	26	16	17	14	♆ 2♎R
25	2.14	5	9♊	16	18	14	♇ 6♌
26	2.17	6	23	15	19	15	♃17♌
27	2.21	7	6♋	15	21	16	♄23♊
28	2.25	8	18	14	22	16	♅ 7♊
29	2.29	9	0♌	14	23	17	♆ 2♎R
30	2.33	10	12	13	24	17	♇ 6♌

May	STime	☉	☽	☿	♀	♂	Plnts
1	2.37	11♉	24♌	13♉	25♈	18♋	♃17♌
2	2.41	12	6♍	12	27	18	♄24♊
3	2.45	13	18	11	28	19	♅ 7♊
4	2.49	14	0♎	11	29	19	♆ 2♎R
5	2.53	15	12	10	0♉	20	♇ 6♌
6	2.57	16	24	9	2	21	♃18♌
7	3.01	16	7♏	9	3	21	♄24♊
8	3.05	17	20	8	4	22	♅ 7♊
9	3.09	18	3♐	8	5	22	♆ 1♎R
10	3.13	19	16	8	7	23	♇ 6♌
11	3.17	20	29	7	8	23	♃18♌
12	3.21	21	13♑	7	9	24	♄25♊
13	3.24	22	27	7	10	25	♅ 8♊
14	3.28	23	11♒	7	11	25	♆ 1♎R
15	3.32	24	25	6D	13	26	♇ 6♌
16	3.36	25	9♓	6	14	26	♃18♌
17	3.40	26	23	7	15	27	♄25♊
18	3.44	27	7♈	7	16	27	♅ 8♊
19	3.48	28	22	7	18	28	♆ 1♎R
20	3.52	29	6♉	7	19	29	♇ 6♌
21	3.56	0♊	20	8	20	29	♃19♌
22	4.00	1	4♊	8	21	0♌	♄26♊
23	4.04	2	18	9	23	0	♅ 8♊
24	4.08	3	1♋	9	24	1	♆ 1♎R
25	4.12	4	14	10	25	1	♇ 6♌
26	4.16	5	26	11	26	2	♃19♌
27	4.20	6	8♌	11	27	3	♄27♊
28	4.24	7	20	12	29	3	♅ 9♊
29	4.28	8	2♍	13	0♊	4	♆ 1♎R
30	4.32	9	14	14	1	4	♇ 6♌
31	4.35	10	26	15	2	5	♃20♌

Jun	STime	☉	☽	☿	♀	♂	Plnts
1	4.39	11♊	8♎	16♉	4♊	5♌	♃20♌
2	4.43	12	20	17	5	6	♄27♊
3	4.47	12	3♏	19	6	7	♅ 9♊
4	4.51	13	15	20	7	7	♆ 1♎
5	4.55	14	28	21	8	8	♇ 7♌
6	4.59	15	12♐	22	10	8	♃21♌
7	5.03	16	25	24	11	9	♄28♊
8	5.07	17	9♑	25	12	10	♅ 9♊
9	5.11	18	23	27	13	10	♆ 1♎
10	5.15	19	7♒	28	15	11	♇ 7♌
11	5.19	20	21	0♊	16	11	♃22♌
12	5.23	21	6♓	1	17	12	♄29♊
13	5.27	22	20	3	18	12	♅ 9♊
14	5.31	23	4♈	5	20	13	♆ 1♎
15	5.35	24	18	6	21	14	♇ 7♌
16	5.39	25	2♉	8	22	14	♃22♌
17	5.42	26	16	10	23	15	♄29♊
18	5.46	27	0♊	12	24	15	♅10♊
19	5.50	28	13	14	26	16	♆ 1♎
20	5.54	29	26	16	27	17	♇ 7♌
21	5.58	0♋	9♋	18	28	17	♃23♌
22	6.02	1	22	20	29	18	♄ 0♋
23	6.06	2	4♌	22	1♋	18	♅10♊
24	6.10	3	16	24	2	19	♆ 1♎
25	6.14	3	28	26	3	20	♇ 7♌
26	6.18	4	10♍	28	4	20	♃24♌
27	6.22	5	22	0♋	5	21	♄ 1♋
28	6.26	6	4♎	3	7	21	♅10♊
29	6.30	7	16	5	8	22	♆ 1♎
30	6.34	8	28	7	9	23	♇ 7♌

Jul	STime	☉	☽	☿	♀	♂	Plnts
1	6.38	9♋	11♏	9♋	10♋	23♌	♃25♌
2	6.42	10	23	11	12	24	♄ 1♋
3	6.46	11	7♐	14	13	24	♅11♊
4	6.49	12	20	16	14	25	♆ 1♎
5	6.53	13	4♑	18	15	26	♇ 7♌
6	6.57	14	18	20	17	26	♃26♌
7	7.01	15	3♒	22	18	27	♄ 2♋
8	7.05	16	17	24	19	28	♅11♊
9	7.09	17	2♓	26	20	28	♆ 1♎
10	7.13	18	16	28	21	29	♇ 7♌
11	7.17	19	1♈	0♌	23	29	♃27♌
12	7.21	20	15	2	24	0♍	♄ 3♋
13	7.25	21	29	4	25	1	♅11♊
14	7.29	22	13♉	6	26	1	♆ 1♎
15	7.33	23	26	8	28	2	♇ 8♌
16	7.37	24	10♊	9	29	2	♃28♌
17	7.41	24	23	11	0♌	3	♄ 3♋
18	7.45	25	5♋	13	1	4	♅11♊
19	7.49	26	18	15	3	4	♆ 2♎
20	7.53	27	0♌	16	4	5	♇ 8♌
21	7.57	28	12	18	5	5	♃29♌
22	8.00	29	24	20	6	6	♄ 4♋
23	8.04	0♌	6♍	21	7	7	♅12♊
24	8.08	1	18	23	9	7	♆ 2♎
25	8.12	2	0♎	25	10	8	♇ 8♌
26	8.16	3	12	26	11	9	♃ 0♍
27	8.20	4	24	28	12	9	♄ 4♋
28	8.24	5	6♏	29	14	10	♅12♊
29	8.28	6	19	0♍	15	10	♆ 2♎
30	8.32	7	1♐	2	16	11	♇ 8♌
31	8.36	8	15	3	17	12	♃ 1♍

Aug	STime	☉	☽	☿	♀	♂	Plnts
1	8.40	9♌	28♐	5♍	19♌	12♍	♃ 1♍
2	8.44	10	12♑	6	20	13	♄ 5♋
3	8.48	11	27	7	21	14	♅12♊
4	8.52	12	11♒	8	22	14	♆ 2♎
5	8.56	13	26	9	23	15	♇ 8♌
6	9.00	14	11♓	11	25	15	♃ 2♍
7	9.04	15	26	12	26	16	♄ 6♋
8	9.07	15	11♈	13	27	17	♅12♊
9	9.11	16	25	14	28	17	♆ 2♎
10	9.15	17	9♉	15	0♍	18	♇ 8♌
11	9.19	18	23	16	1	19	♃ 3♍
12	9.23	19	7♊	17	2	19	♄ 6♋
13	9.27	20	20	17	3	20	♅12♊
14	9.31	21	2♋	18	5	20	♆ 2♎
15	9.35	22	15	19	6	21	♇ 8♌
16	9.39	23	27	20	7	22	♃ 4♍
17	9.43	24	9♌	20	8	22	♄ 7♋
18	9.47	25	21	21	10	23	♅12♊
19	9.51	26	3♍	21	11	24	♆ 2♎
20	9.55	27	15	22	12	24	♇ 9♌
21	9.59	28	27	22	13	25	♃ 5♍
22	10.03	29	9♎	22	14	26	♄ 7♋
23	10.07	0♍	21	22	16	26	♅13♊
24	10.11	1	3♏	22R	17	27	♆ 2♎
25	10.15	2	15	22	18	27	♇ 9♌
26	10.18	3	27	22	19	28	♃ 6♍
27	10.22	4	10♐	22	21	29	♄ 8♋
28	10.26	5	23	21	22	29	♅13♊
29	10.30	6	6♑	21	23	0♎	♆ 3♎
30	10.34	7	20	20	24	1	♇ 9♌
31	10.38	8	5♒	20	26	1	♃ 7♍

Sep	STime	☉	☽	☿	♀	♂	Plnts
1	10.42	9♍	20♒	19♍	27♍	2♎	♃ 8♍
2	10.46	10	5♓	18	28	3	♄ 8♋
3	10.50	11	20	17	29	3	♅13♊
4	10.54	12	5♈	16	0♎	4	♆ 3♎
5	10.58	12	20	15	2	5	♇ 9♌
6	11.02	13	5♉	14	3	5	♃ 9♍
7	11.06	14	19	13	4	6	♄ 9♋
8	11.10	15	3♊	12	5	6	♅13♊
9	11.14	16	16	11	7	7	♆ 3♎
10	11.18	17	29	11	8	8	♇ 9♌
11	11.22	18	12♋	10	9	8	♃10♍
12	11.25	19	24	9	10	9	♄ 9♋
13	11.29	20	6♌	9	12	10	♅13♊
14	11.33	21	18	8	13	10	♆ 3♎
15	11.37	22	0♍	8	14	11	♇ 9♌
16	11.41	23	12	8D	15	12	♃11♍
17	11.45	24	24	8	16	12	♄ 9♋
18	11.49	25	6♎	9	18	13	♅13♊
19	11.53	26	18	9	19	14	♆ 3♎
20	11.57	27	0♏	10	20	14	♇ 9♌
21	12.01	28	12	10	21	15	♃12♍
22	12.05	29	24	11	23	16	♄10♋
23	12.09	0♎	6♐	12	24	16	♅13♊R
24	12.13	1	19	13	25	17	♆ 4♎
25	12.17	2	2♑	15	26	18	♇ 9♌
26	12.21	3	15	16	28	18	♃13♍
27	12.25	4	29	17	29	19	♄10♋
28	12.29	5	13♒	19	0♏	20	♅13♊R
29	12.33	6	28	20	1	20	♆ 4♎
30	12.36	7	13♓	22	2	21	♇10♌

Oct	STime	☉	☽	☿	♀	♂	Plnts
1	12.40	8♎	28♓	24♍	4♏	22♎	♃14♍
2	12.44	9	13♈	25	5	22	♄10♋
3	12.48	10	29	27	6	23	♅13♊R
4	12.52	11	13♉	29	7	24	♆ 4♎
5	12.56	12	28	0♎	9	24	♇10♌
6	13.00	13	12♊	2	10	25	♃15♍
7	13.04	14	25	4	11	26	♄10♋
8	13.08	15	8♋	6	12	26	♅13♊R
9	13.12	16	21	7	14	27	♆ 4♎
10	13.16	17	3♌	9	15	28	♇10♌
11	13.20	18	15	11	16	28	♃16♍
12	13.24	19	27	13	17	29	♄10♋
13	13.28	20	9♍	14	18	0♏	♅13♊R
14	13.32	21	21	16	20	0	♆ 4♎
15	13.36	22	3♎	18	21	1	♇10♌
16	13.40	23	15	20	22	2	♃17♍
17	13.43	24	27	21	23	2	♄10♋
18	13.47	25	9♏	23	25	3	♅12♊R
19	13.51	26	21	25	26	4	♆ 5♎
20	13.55	27	3♐	26	27	4	♇10♌
21	13.59	28	16	28	28	5	♃18♍
22	14.03	29	29	0♏	29	6	♄10♋
23	14.07	0♏	12♑	1	1♐	7	♅12♊R
24	14.11	1	25	3	2	7	♆ 5♎
25	14.15	2	9♒	5	3	8	♇10♌
26	14.19	3	23	6	4	9	♃19♍
27	14.23	4	7♓	8	6	9	♄10♋R
28	14.27	5	22	10	7	10	♅12♊R
29	14.31	6	7♈	11	8	11	♆ 5♎
30	14.35	7	22	13	9	11	♇10♌
31	14.39	8	7♉	14	10	12	♃20♍

Nov	STime	☉	☽	☿	♀	♂	Plnts
1	14.43	9♏	21♉	16♏	12♐	13♏	♃20♍
2	14.47	10	6♊	17	13	13	♄10♋R
3	14.50	11	20	19	14	14	♅12♊R
4	14.54	12	4♋	21	15	15	♆ 5♎
5	14.58	13	17	22	17	16	♇10♌
6	15.02	14	29	24	18	16	♃21♍
7	15.06	15	12♌	25	19	17	♄10♋R
8	15.10	16	24	27	20	18	♅12♊R
9	15.14	17	6♍	28	21	18	♆ 5♎
10	15.18	18	17	0♐	23	19	♇10♌
11	15.22	19	29	1	24	20	♃22♍
12	15.26	20	11♎	3	25	20	♄10♋R
13	15.30	21	23	4	26	21	♅12♊R
14	15.34	22	5♏	6	27	22	♆ 5♎
15	15.38	23	18	7	29	23	♇10♌R
16	15.42	24	0♐	9	0♑	23	♃23♍
17	15.46	25	13	10	1	24	♄10♋R
18	15.50	26	26	12	2	25	♅11♊R
19	15.54	27	9♑	13	4	25	♆ 5♎
20	15.58	28	22	15	5	26	♇10♌
21	16.01	29	5♒	16	6	27	♃23♍
22	16.05	0♐	19	17	7	27	♄10♋R
23	16.09	1	3♓	19	8	28	♅11♊R
24	16.13	2	17	20	10	29	♆ 6♎
25	16.17	3	2♈	22	11	0♐	♇10♌
26	16.21	4	16	23	12	0	♃24♍
27	16.25	5	1♉	24	13	1	♄ 9♋R
28	16.29	6	15	26	14	2	♅11♊R
29	16.33	7	0♊	27	16	2	♆ 6♎
30	16.37	8	14	28	17	3	♇10♌R

Dec	STime	☉	☽	☿	♀	♂	Plnts
1	16.41	9♐	28♊	0♑	18♑	4♐	♃25♍
2	16.45	10	11♋	1	19	5	♄ 9♋R
3	16.49	11	24	2	20	5	♅11♊R
4	16.53	12	7♌	3	22	6	♆ 6♎
5	16.57	13	20	4	23	7	♇10♌R
6	17.01	14	2♍	5	24	7	♃25♍
7	17.05	15	14	6	25	8	♄ 9♋R
8	17.08	16	25	7	26	9	♅11♊R
9	17.12	17	7♎	7	28	10	♆ 6♎
10	17.16	18	19	8	29	10	♇10♌R
11	17.20	19	1♏	8	0♒	11	♃26♍
12	17.24	20	14	9	1	12	♄ 8♋R
13	17.28	21	26	9R	2	13	♅10♊R
14	17.32	22	9♐	9	4	13	♆ 6♎
15	17.36	23	22	8	5	14	♇10♌R
16	17.40	24	5♑	8	6	15	♃26♍
17	17.44	25	18	7	7	15	♄ 8♋R
18	17.48	26	2♒	6	8	16	♅10♊R
19	17.52	27	16	5	10	17	♆ 6♎
20	17.56	28	0♓	4	11	18	♇10♌R
21	18.00	29	14	3	12	18	♃26♍
22	18.04	0♑	28	2	13	19	♄ 8♋R
23	18.08	1	12♈	0	14	20	♅10♊R
24	18.12	2	26	29♐	15	21	♆ 6♎
25	18.16	3	11♉	28	17	21	♇10♌R
26	18.19	4	25	26	18	22	♃27♍
27	18.23	5	9♊	25	19	23	♄ 7♋R
28	18.27	6	22	24	20	24	♅10♊R
29	18.31	7	6♋	24	21	24	♆ 6♎
30	18.35	8	19	23	22	25	♇ 9♌R
31	18.39	9	2♌	23	24	26	♃27♍

Jan	STime	☉	☽	☿	♀	♂	Plnts
1	18.43	10♑	15♌	22♐	25♒	27♐	♃27♍
2	18.47	11	27	22D	26	27	♄ 7♋R
3	18.51	12	9♍	22	27	28	♅10♊R
4	18.55	13	21	23	28	29	♆ 6♎
5	18.59	15	3♎	23	29	29	♇ 9♌R
6	19.03	16	15	23	0♓	0♑	♃27♍
7	19.07	17	27	24	2	1	♄ 6♋R
8	19.11	18	9♏	25	3	2	♅ 9♊R
9	19.15	19	21	25	4	2	♆ 6♎
10	19.19	20	4♐	26	5	3	♇ 9♌R
11	19.23	21	17	27	6	4	♃27♍
12	19.26	22	0♑	28	7	5	♄ 6♋R
13	19.30	23	14	29	8	5	♅ 9♊R
14	19.34	24	27	0♑	10	6	♆ 6♎
15	19.38	25	12♒	1	11	7	♇ 9♌R
16	19.42	26	26	2	12	8	♃27♍R
17	19.46	27	10♓	3	13	8	♄ 5♋R
18	19.50	28	25	5	14	9	♅ 9♊R
19	19.54	29	9♈	6	15	10	♆ 6♎
20	19.58	0♒	23	7	16	11	♇ 9♌R
21	20.02	1	7♉	8	17	11	♃27♍R
22	20.06	2	21	10	18	12	♄ 5♋R
23	20.10	3	5♊	11	19	13	♅ 9♊R
24	20.14	4	19	12	20	14	♆ 6♎R
25	20.18	5	2♋	14	22	15	♇ 9♌R
26	20.22	6	15	15	23	15	♃27♍R
27	20.26	7	28	17	24	16	♄ 5♋R
28	20.30	8	10♌	18	25	17	♅ 9♊R
29	20.33	9	23	19	26	18	♆ 6♎R
30	20.37	10	5♍	21	27	18	♇ 9♌R
31	20.41	11	17	22	28	19	♃27♍R

Feb	STime	☉	☽	☿	♀	♂	Plnts
1	20.45	12♒	29♍	24♑	29♓	20♑	♃27♍R
2	20.49	13	11♎	25	0♈	21	♄ 4♋R
3	20.53	14	23	27	1	21	♅ 9♊R
4	20.57	15	5♏	28	2	22	♆ 6♎R
5	21.01	16	17	0♒	3	23	♇ 9♌R
6	21.05	17	29	1	4	24	♃26♍R
7	21.09	18	12♐	3	5	24	♄ 4♋R
8	21.13	19	25	5	6	25	♅ 9♊R
9	21.17	20	8♑	6	7	26	♆ 6♎R
10	21.21	21	21	8	8	27	♇ 9♌R
11	21.25	22	6♒	9	9	27	♃26♍R
12	21.29	23	20	11	10	28	♄ 4♋R
13	21.33	24	5♓	13	11	29	♅ 9♊R
14	21.37	25	20	14	11	0♒	♆ 6♎R
15	21.41	26	5♈	16	12	1	♇ 8♌R
16	21.44	27	19	18	13	1	♃25♍R
17	21.48	28	4♉	19	14	2	♄ 4♋R
18	21.52	29	18	21	15	3	♅ 9♊
19	21.56	0♓	2♊	23	16	4	♆ 6♎R
20	22.00	1	16	24	17	4	♇ 8♌R
21	22.04	2	29	26	18	5	♃25♍R
22	22.08	3	12♋	28	18	6	♄ 4♋R
23	22.12	4	24	0♓	19	7	♅ 9♊
24	22.16	5	7♌	2	20	7	♆ 6♎R
25	22.20	6	19	3	21	8	♇ 8♌R
26	22.24	7	2♍	5	22	9	♃24♍R
27	22.28	8	14	7	22	10	♄ 4♋R
28	22.32	9	26	9	23	11	♅ 9♊

Mar	STime	☉	☽	☿	♀	♂	Plnts
1	22.36	10♓	8♎	11♓	24♈	11♒	♃24♍R
2	22.40	11	20	13	24	12	♄ 4♋
3	22.44	12	1♏	15	25	13	♅ 9♊
4	22.48	13	13	17	26	14	♆ 5♎R
5	22.51	14	25	18	26	14	♇ 8♌R
6	22.55	15	7♐	20	27	15	♃23♍R
7	22.59	16	20	22	28	16	♄ 4♋
8	23.03	17	3♑	24	28	17	♅ 9♊
9	23.07	18	16	26	29	18	♆ 5♎R
10	23.11	19	29	28	29	18	♇ 8♌R
11	23.15	20	13♒	0♈	0♉	19	♃23♍R
12	23.19	21	28	2	0	20	♄ 4♋
13	23.23	22	13♓	4	1	21	♅ 9♊
14	23.27	23	28	6	1	21	♆ 5♎R
15	23.31	24	13♈	8	1	22	♇ 8♌R
16	23.35	25	28	10	2	23	♃22♍R
17	23.39	26	13♉	11	2	24	♄ 4♋
18	23.43	27	28	13	2	25	♅ 9♊
19	23.47	28	12♊	15	3	25	♆ 5♎R
20	23.51	29	26	16	3	26	♇ 8♌R
21	23.55	0♈	9♋	18	3	27	♃21♍R
22	23.59	1	22	19	3	28	♄ 4♋
23	0.02	2	4♌	20	3	28	♅ 9♊
24	0.06	3	16	22	3	29	♆ 5♎R
25	0.10	4	29	23	3R	0♓	♇ 8♌R
26	0.14	5	11♍	24	3	1	♃21♍R
27	0.18	6	23	25	3	2	♄ 4♋
28	0.22	7	5♎	25	3	2	♅10♊
29	0.26	8	16	26	3	3	♆ 5♎R
30	0.30	9	28	27	3	4	♇ 8♌R
31	0.34	10	10♏	27	3	5	♃20♍R

Apr	STime	☉	☽	☿	♀	♂	Plnts
1	0.38	11♈	22♏	27♈	2♉	5♓	♃20♍R
2	0.42	12	4♐	28	2	6	♄ 4♋
3	0.46	13	16	28R	2	7	♅10♊
4	0.50	14	29	28	1	8	♆ 5♎R
5	0.54	15	11♑	27	1	9	♇ 8♌R
6	0.58	16	24	27	0	9	♃19♍R
7	1.02	17	8♒	27	0	10	♄ 5♋
8	1.06	18	22	26	29♈	11	♅10♊
9	1.09	19	6♓	26	29	12	♆ 4♎R
10	1.13	20	21	25	28	12	♇ 8♌
11	1.17	21	6♈	25	28	13	♃19♍R
12	1.21	22	22	24	27	14	♄ 5♋
13	1.25	23	7♉	23	26	15	♅10♊
14	1.29	24	22	22	26	16	♆ 4♎R
15	1.33	25	7♊	22	25	16	♇ 8♌R
16	1.37	26	21	21	25	17	♃18♍R
17	1.41	27	5♋	20	24	18	♄ 5♋
18	1.45	28	18	20	23	19	♅10♊
19	1.49	29	1♌	19	23	19	♆ 4♎R
20	1.53	0♉	13	18	22	20	♇ 8♌
21	1.57	1	26	18	22	21	♃18♍R
22	2.01	2	8♍	17	21	22	♄ 6♋
23	2.05	3	20	17	20	22	♅11♊
24	2.09	4	2♎	17	20	23	♆ 4♎R
25	2.13	5	13	17	20	24	♇ 8♌
26	2.17	6	25	17	19	25	♃18♍R
27	2.20	7	7♏	17D	19	26	♄ 6♋
28	2.24	8	19	17	18	26	♅11♊
29	2.28	8	1♐	17	18	27	♆ 4♎R
30	2.32	9	13	17	18	28	♇ 8♌

May	STime	☉	☽	☿	♀	♂	Plnts
1	2.36	10♉	26♐	17♈	17♈	29♓	♃17♍R
2	2.40	11	8♑	18	17	29	♄ 6♋
3	2.44	12	21	18	17	0♈	♅11♊
4	2.48	13	4♒	19	17	1	♆ 4♎R
5	2.52	14	17	19	17	2	♇ 8♌
6	2.56	15	1♓	20	17D	3	♃17♍R
7	3.00	16	15	21	17	3	♄ 7♋
8	3.04	17	0♈	21	17	4	♅11♊
9	3.08	18	15	22	17	5	♆ 4♎R
10	3.12	19	0♉	23	17	6	♇ 8♌
11	3.16	20	15	24	17	6	♃17♍R
12	3.20	21	0♊	25	17	7	♄ 7♋
13	3.24	22	15	26	18	8	♅12♊
14	3.27	23	29	27	18	9	♆ 4♎R
15	3.31	24	13♋	28	18	9	♇ 8♌
16	3.35	25	26	0♉	19	10	♃17♍
17	3.39	26	9♌	1	19	11	♄ 8♋
18	3.43	27	22	2	19	12	♅12♊
19	3.47	28	4♍	3	20	12	♆ 4♎R
20	3.51	29	16	5	20	13	♇ 8♌
21	3.55	0♊	28	6	21	14	♃17♍
22	3.59	1	10♎	8	21	15	♄ 8♋
23	4.03	2	22	9	22	15	♅12♊
24	4.07	3	4♏	11	22	16	♆ 3♎R
25	4.11	4	16	12	23	17	♇ 8♌
26	4.15	5	28	14	23	18	♃17♍
27	4.19	6	10♐	15	24	18	♄ 9♋
28	4.23	6	23	17	25	19	♅13♊
29	4.27	7	5♑	19	25	20	♆ 3♎
30	4.31	8	18	20	26	21	♇ 8♌
31	4.34	9	1♒	22	26	22	♃18♍

Jun	STime	☉	☽	☿	♀	♂	Plnts
1	4.38	10♊	14♒	24♉	27♈	22♈	♃18♍
2	4.42	11	28	26	28	23	♄10♋
3	4.46	12	12♓	28	29	24	♅13♊
4	4.50	13	26	0♊	29	24	♆ 3♎
5	4.54	14	10♈	2	0♉	25	♇ 8♌
6	4.58	15	25	4	1	26	♃18♍
7	5.02	16	9♉	6	2	27	♄10♋
8	5.06	17	24	8	2	27	♅13♊
9	5.10	18	9♊	10	3	28	♆ 3♎
10	5.14	19	23	12	4	29	♇ 8♌
11	5.18	20	7♋	14	5	0♉	♃18♍
12	5.22	21	21	17	6	0	♄11♋
13	5.26	22	4♌	19	7	1	♅13♊
14	5.30	23	17	21	7	2	♆ 3♎
15	5.34	24	0♍	23	8	3	♇ 8♌
16	5.38	25	12	25	9	3	♃19♍
17	5.42	26	25	27	10	4	♄12♋
18	5.45	27	7♎	0♋	11	5	♅14♊
19	5.49	28	18	2	12	6	♆ 3♎
20	5.53	28	0♏	4	13	6	♇ 8♌
21	5.57	29	12	6	14	7	♃19♍
22	6.01	0♋	24	8	15	8	♄12♋
23	6.05	1	7♐	10	16	9	♅14♊
24	6.09	2	19	12	17	9	♆ 3♎
25	6.13	3	2♑	14	18	10	♇ 9♌
26	6.17	4	15	16	19	11	♃20♍
27	6.21	5	28	18	20	11	♄13♋
28	6.25	6	11♒	20	20	12	♅14♊
29	6.29	7	25	22	21	13	♆ 3♎
30	6.33	8	8♓	24	22	14	♇ 9♌

Jul	STime	☉	☽	☿	♀	♂	Plnts
1	6.37	9♋	22♓	26♋	23♉	14♉	♃20♍
2	6.41	10	6♈	28	24	15	♄14♋
3	6.45	11	21	29	25	16	♅15♊
4	6.49	12	5♉	1♌	26	16	♆ 3♎
5	6.52	13	19	3	27	17	♇ 9♌
6	6.56	14	4♊	5	28	18	♃21♍
7	7.00	15	18	6	0♊	19	♄14♋
8	7.04	16	2♋	8	1	19	♅15♊
9	7.08	17	16	9	2	20	♆ 4♎
10	7.12	18	29	11	3	21	♇ 9♌
11	7.16	19	13♌	12	4	21	♃22♍
12	7.20	19	25	14	5	22	♄15♋
13	7.24	20	8♍	15	6	23	♅15♊
14	7.28	21	20	16	7	24	♆ 4♎
15	7.32	22	3♎	18	8	24	♇ 9♌
16	7.36	23	15	19	9	25	♃23♍
17	7.40	24	26	20	10	26	♄15♋
18	7.44	25	8♏	22	11	26	♅15♊
19	7.48	26	20	23	12	27	♆ 4♎
20	7.52	27	2♐	24	13	28	♇ 9♌
21	7.56	28	15	25	14	28	♃23♍
22	8.00	29	27	26	15	29	♄16♋
23	8.03	0♌	10♑	27	16	0♊	♅16♊
24	8.07	1	23	28	18	0	♆ 4♎
25	8.11	2	7♒	29	19	1	♇ 9♌
26	8.15	3	21	0♍	20	2	♃24♍
27	8.19	4	5♓	0	21	3	♄17♋
28	8.23	5	19	1	22	3	♅16♊
29	8.27	6	3♈	2	23	4	♆ 4♎
30	8.31	7	17	2	24	5	♇ 9♌
31	8.35	8	2♉	3	25	5	♃25♍

Aug	STime	☉	☽	☿	♀	♂	Plnts
1	8.39	9♌	16♉	3♍	26♊	6♊	♃25♍
2	8.43	10	0♊	4	28	7	♄17♋
3	8.47	10	14	4	29	7	♅16♊
4	8.51	11	28	4	0♋	8	♆ 4♎
5	8.55	12	11♋	4	1	9	♇10♌
6	8.59	13	25	5R	2	9	♃26♍
7	9.03	14	8♌	4	3	10	♄18♋
8	9.07	15	21	4	4	11	♅16♊
9	9.10	16	4♍	4	5	11	♆ 4♎
10	9.14	17	16	4	7	12	♇10♌
11	9.18	18	28	4	8	13	♃27♍
12	9.22	19	11♎	3	9	13	♄19♋
13	9.26	20	23	2	10	14	♅16♊
14	9.30	21	4♏	2	11	15	♆ 4♎
15	9.34	22	16	1	12	15	♇10♌
16	9.38	23	28	0	13	16	♃28♍
17	9.42	24	10♐	0	15	16	♄19♋
18	9.46	25	23	29♌	16	17	♅17♊
19	9.50	26	5♑	28	17	18	♆ 4♎
20	9.54	27	18	27	18	18	♇10♌
21	9.58	28	2♒	26	19	19	♃29♍
22	10.02	29	15	25	20	20	♄20♋
23	10.06	0♍	0♓	25	21	20	♅17♊
24	10.10	1	14	24	23	21	♆ 5♎
25	10.14	2	29	23	24	22	♇10♌
26	10.18	3	13♈	23	25	22	♃ 0♎
27	10.21	4	28	22	26	23	♄20♋
28	10.25	5	13♉	22	27	23	♅17♊
29	10.29	5	27	22	28	24	♆ 5♎
30	10.33	6	11♊	22D	0♌	25	♇10♌
31	10.37	7	25	22	1	25	♃ 1♎

Sep	STime	☉	☽	☿	♀	♂	Plnts
1	10.41	8♍	8♋	22♌	2♌	26♊	♃ 1♎
2	10.45	9	21	22	3	26	♄21♋
3	10.49	10	4♌	23	4	27	♅17♊
4	10.53	11	17	24	6	28	♆ 5♎
5	10.57	12	0♍	24	7	28	♇11♌
6	11.01	13	12	25	8	29	♃ 2♎
7	11.05	14	25	26	9	29	♄22♋
8	11.09	15	7♎	27	10	0♋	♅17♊
9	11.13	16	19	29	11	1	♆ 5♎
10	11.17	17	1♏	0♍	13	1	♇11♌
11	11.21	18	13	1	14	2	♃ 3♎
12	11.25	19	24	3	15	2	♄22♋
13	11.28	20	6♐	5	16	3	♅17♊
14	11.32	21	18	6	17	4	♆ 5♎
15	11.36	22	1♑	8	19	4	♇11♌
16	11.40	23	13	10	20	5	♃ 4♎
17	11.44	24	26	11	21	5	♄22♋
18	11.48	25	10♒	13	22	6	♅17♊
19	11.52	26	24	15	23	6	♆ 6♎
20	11.56	27	8♓	17	25	7	♇11♌
21	12.00	28	23	19	26	8	♃ 5♎
22	12.04	29	8♈	20	27	8	♄23♋
23	12.08	0♎	23	22	28	9	♅17♊
24	12.12	1	8♉	24	29	9	♆ 6♎
25	12.16	2	23	26	1♍	10	♇11♌
26	12.20	3	7♊	28	2	10	♃ 6♎
27	12.24	4	21	0♎	3	11	♄23♋
28	12.28	5	5♋	2	4	11	♅17♊
29	12.32	6	18	3	6	12	♆ 6♎
30	12.35	7	1♌	5	7	12	♇11♌

Oct	STime	☉	☽	☿	♀	♂	Plnts
1	12.39	8♎	14♌	7♎	8♍	13♋	♃ 8♎
2	12.43	9	27	9	9	13	♄23♋
3	12.47	10	9♍	10	10	14	♅17♊R
4	12.51	11	21	12	12	14	♆ 6♎
5	12.55	12	4♎	14	13	15	♇11♌
6	12.59	13	16	16	14	15	♃ 9♎
7	13.03	14	28	17	15	16	♄24♋
8	13.07	15	9♏	19	17	16	♅17♊R
9	13.11	16	21	21	18	17	♆ 6♎
10	13.15	17	3♐	22	19	17	♇11♌
11	13.19	18	15	24	20	18	♃10♎
12	13.23	19	27	26	21	18	♄24♋
13	13.27	19	9♑	27	23	19	♅17♊R
14	13.31	20	22	29	24	19	♆ 6♎
15	13.35	21	5♒	0♏	25	20	♇11♌
16	13.39	22	18	2	26	20	♃11♎
17	13.43	23	2♓	4	28	21	♄24♋
18	13.46	24	16	5	29	21	♅17♊R
19	13.50	25	1♈	7	0♎	21	♆ 7♎
20	13.54	26	16	8	1	22	♇11♌
21	13.58	27	1♉	10	3	22	♃12♎
22	14.02	28	16	11	4	23	♄24♋
23	14.06	29	2♊	13	5	23	♅17♊R
24	14.10	0♏	16	14	6	24	♆ 7♎
25	14.14	1	1♋	16	8	24	♇11♌
26	14.18	2	15	17	9	24	♃13♎
27	14.22	3	28	19	10	25	♄25♋
28	14.26	4	11♌	20	11	25	♅17♊R
29	14.30	5	24	22	13	25	♆ 7♎
30	14.34	6	6♍	23	14	26	♇11♌
31	14.38	7	19	25	15	26	♃14♎

Nov	STime	☉	☽	☿	♀	♂	Plnts
1	14.42	8♏	1♎	26♏	16♎	27♋	♃14♎
2	14.46	9	13	28	17	27	♄25♋
3	14.50	10	25	29	19	27	♅16♊R
4	14.53	11	6♏	0♐	20	28	♆ 7♎
5	14.57	12	18	2	21	28	♇12♌
6	15.01	13	0♐	3	22	28	♃15♎
7	15.05	14	12	5	24	28	♄25♋
8	15.09	15	24	6	25	29	♅16♊R
9	15.13	16	6♑	7	26	29	♆ 7♎
10	15.17	17	18	9	27	29	♇12♌
11	15.21	18	1♒	10	29	0♌	♃16♎
12	15.25	19	14	11	0♏	0	♄25♋R
13	15.29	20	27	12	1	0	♅16♊R
14	15.33	21	11♓	13	2	0	♆ 7♎
15	15.37	22	25	15	4	1	♇12♌
16	15.41	23	9♈	16	5	1	♃17♎
17	15.45	24	24	17	6	1	♄24♋R
18	15.49	25	9♉	18	7	1	♅16♊R
19	15.53	27	25	19	9	1	♆ 8♎
20	15.57	28	10♊	20	10	2	♇12♌R
21	16.01	29	25	20	11	2	♃18♎
22	16.04	0♐	9♋	21	12	2	♄24♋R
23	16.08	1	23	22	14	2	♅16♊R
24	16.12	2	7♌	22	15	2	♆ 8♎
25	16.16	3	20	23	16	2	♇11♌R
26	16.20	4	3♍	23	17	2	♃19♎
27	16.24	5	15	23R	19	3	♄24♋R
28	16.28	6	28	23	20	3	♅16♊R
29	16.32	7	10♎	22	21	3	♆ 8♎
30	16.36	8	21	22	23	3	♇11♌R

Dec	STime	☉	☽	☿	♀	♂	Plnts
1	16.40	9♐	3♏	21♐	24♏	3♌	♃20♎
2	16.44	10	15	21	25	3	♄24♋R
3	16.48	11	27	20	26	3	♅15♊R
4	16.52	12	9♐	19	28	3	♆ 8♎
5	16.56	13	21	17	29	3R	♇11♌R
6	17.00	14	3♑	16	0♐	3	♃21♎
7	17.04	15	15	15	1	3	♄24♋R
8	17.08	16	28	13	3	3	♅15♊R
9	17.11	17	11♒	12	4	3	♆ 8♎
10	17.15	18	23	11	5	3	♇11♌R
11	17.19	19	7♓	10	6	3	♃22♎
12	17.23	20	20	9	8	3	♄23♋R
13	17.27	21	4♈	8	9	2	♅15♊R
14	17.31	22	18	7	10	2	♆ 8♎
15	17.35	23	3♉	7	11	2	♇11♌R
16	17.39	24	18	7	13	2	♃22♎
17	17.43	25	3♊	7D	14	2	♄23♋R
18	17.47	26	18	7	15	2	♅15♊R
19	17.51	27	2♋	7	16	1	♆ 8♎
20	17.55	28	17	7	18	1	♇11♌R
21	17.59	29	1♌	8	19	1	♃23♎
22	18.03	0♑	15	9	20	1	♄23♋R
23	18.07	1	28	9	21	1	♅14♊R
24	18.11	2	11♍	10	23	0	♆ 8♎
25	18.15	3	24	11	24	0	♇11♌R
26	18.18	4	6♎	12	25	0	♃24♎
27	18.22	5	18	13	26	29♋	♄22♋R
28	18.26	6	0♏	14	28	29	♅14♊R
29	18.30	7	12	15	29	29	♆ 8♎
30	18.34	8	24	16	0♑	28	♇11♌R
31	18.38	9	5♐	18	1	28	♃24♎

Jan	STime	☉	☽	☿	♀	♂	Plnts
1	18.42	10♑	17♐	19♐	3♑	28♋	♃25♎
2	18.46	11	0♑	20	4	27	♄22♋R
3	18.50	12	12	21	5	27	♅14♊R
4	18.54	13	25	23	7	27	♆ 8♎
5	18.58	14	7♒	24	8	26	♇11♌R
6	19.02	15	20	25	9	26	♃25♎
7	19.06	16	4♓	27	10	26	♄22♋R
8	19.10	17	17	28	12	25	♅14♊R
9	19.14	18	1♈	0♑	13	25	♆ 8♎
10	19.18	19	15	1	14	24	♇11♌R
11	19.22	20	29	2	15	24	♃26♎
12	19.26	21	13♉	4	17	24	♄21♋R
13	19.29	22	27	5	18	23	♅14♊R
14	19.33	23	12♊	7	19	23	♆ 8♎R
15	19.37	24	26	8	20	22	♇11♌R
16	19.41	25	11♋	10	22	22	♃26♎
17	19.45	26	25	11	23	22	♄21♋R
18	19.49	27	9♌	13	24	21	♅14♊R
19	19.53	29	23	14	25	21	♆ 8♎R
20	19.57	0♒	6♍	16	27	20	♇11♌R
21	20.01	1	19	17	28	20	♃26♎
22	20.05	2	2♎	19	29	20	♄20♋R
23	20.09	3	14	20	0♒	19	♅13♊R
24	20.13	4	26	22	2	19	♆ 8♎R
25	20.17	5	8♏	24	3	19	♇10♌R
26	20.21	6	20	25	4	18	♃27♎
27	20.25	7	1♐	27	5	18	♄20♋R
28	20.29	8	13	28	7	18	♅13♊R
29	20.33	9	25	0♒	8	17	♆ 8♎R
30	20.36	10	8♑	2	9	17	♇10♌R
31	20.40	11	20	3	10	17	♃27♎

Feb	STime	☉	☽	☿	♀	♂	Plnts
1	20.44	12♒	3♒	5♒	12♒	17♋	♃27♎
2	20.48	13	16	7	13	16	♄19♋R
3	20.52	14	0♓	8	14	16	♅13♊R
4	20.56	15	14	10	15	16	♆ 8♎R
5	21.00	16	28	12	17	16	♇10♌R
6	21.04	17	12♈	13	18	15	♃27♎
7	21.08	18	26	15	19	15	♄19♋R
8	21.12	19	10♉	17	20	15	♅13♊R
9	21.16	20	24	19	22	15	♆ 8♎R
10	21.20	21	8♊	20	23	15	♇10♌R
11	21.24	22	22	22	24	14	♃27♎R
12	21.28	23	6♋	24	26	14	♄19♋R
13	21.32	24	20	26	27	14	♅13♊R
14	21.36	25	4♌	28	28	14	♆ 8♎R
15	21.40	26	17	29	29	14	♇10♌R
16	21.44	27	1♍	1♓	1♓	14	♃27♎R
17	21.47	28	14	3	2	14	♄19♋R
18	21.51	29	27	5	3	14	♅13♊
19	21.55	0♓	9♎	7	4	14	♆ 8♎R
20	21.59	1	22	9	6	14	♇10♌R
21	22.03	2	4♏	11	7	14D	♃27♎R
22	22.07	3	16	12	8	14	♄18♋R
23	22.11	4	27	14	9	14	♅13♊
24	22.15	5	9♐	16	11	14	♆ 8♎R
25	22.19	6	21	18	12	14	♇10♌R
26	22.23	7	3♑	20	13	14	♃27♎R
27	22.27	8	16	22	14	14	♄18♋R
28	22.31	9	28	23	16	14	♅13♊

Mar	STime	☉	☽	☿	♀	♂	Plnts
1	22.35	10♓	11♒	25♓	17♓	14♋	♃27♎R
2	22.39	11	25	27	18	14	♄18♋R
3	22.43	12	9♓	28	19	14	♅13♊
4	22.47	13	23	0♈	21	14	♆ 8♎R
5	22.51	14	7♈	1	22	15	♇10♌R
6	22.54	15	22	3	23	15	♃26♎R
7	22.58	16	6♉	4	24	15	♄18♋R
8	23.02	17	21	5	26	15	♅13♊
9	23.06	18	5♊	6	27	15	♆ 7♎R
10	23.10	19	19	7	28	15	♇10♌R
11	23.14	20	3♋	8	29	15	♃26♎R
12	23.18	21	17	9	1♈	16	♄18♋R
13	23.22	22	0♌	9	2	16	♅13♊
14	23.26	23	13	10	3	16	♆ 7♎R
15	23.30	24	27	10	4	16	♇ 9♌R
16	23.34	25	10♍	10R	5	17	♃25♎R
17	23.38	26	22	10	7	17	♄18♋R
18	23.42	27	5♎	10	8	17	♅13♊
19	23.46	28	17	9	9	17	♆ 7♎R
20	23.50	29	0♏	9	10	18	♇ 9♌R
21	23.54	0♈	12	8	12	18	♃25♎R
22	23.58	1	24	8	13	18	♄18♋
23	0.02	2	5♐	7	14	18	♅14♊
24	0.05	3	17	6	15	19	♆ 7♎R
25	0.09	4	29	6	17	19	♇ 9♌R
26	0.13	5	11♑	5	18	19	♃24♎R
27	0.17	6	23	4	19	20	♄18♋
28	0.21	7	6♒	3	20	20	♅14♊
29	0.25	8	19	2	22	20	♆ 7♎R
30	0.29	9	3♓	1	23	21	♇ 9♌R
31	0.33	10	17	1	24	21	♃24♎R

Apr	STime	☉	☽	☿	♀	♂	Plnts
1	0.37	11♈	1♈	0♈	25♈	21♋	♃24♎R
2	0.41	12	16	29♓	27	22	♄18♋
3	0.45	13	1♉	29	28	22	♅14♊
4	0.49	14	16	28	29	22	♆ 7♎R
5	0.53	15	1♊	28	0♉	23	♇ 9♌R
6	0.57	16	15	28	1	23	♃23♎R
7	1.01	17	0♋	27	3	23	♄18♋
8	1.05	18	13	27D	4	24	♅14♊
9	1.09	19	27	27	5	24	♆ 7♎R
10	1.12	20	10♌	27	6	25	♇ 9♌R
11	1.16	21	24	28	8	25	♃22♎R
12	1.20	22	6♍	28	9	25	♄18♋
13	1.24	23	19	28	10	26	♅14♊
14	1.28	24	2♎	29	11	26	♆ 7♎R
15	1.32	25	14	29	13	27	♇ 9♌R
16	1.36	26	26	0♈	14	27	♃22♎R
17	1.40	27	8♏	0	15	27	♄18♋
18	1.44	28	20	1	16	28	♅14♊
19	1.48	29	2♐	2	18	28	♆ 6♎R
20	1.52	29	14	2	19	29	♇ 9♌
21	1.56	0♉	26	3	20	29	♃21♎R
22	2.00	1	7♑	4	21	0♌	♄19♋
23	2.04	2	19	5	22	0	♅15♊
24	2.08	3	2♒	6	24	0	♆ 6♎R
25	2.12	4	14	7	25	1	♇ 9♌
26	2.16	5	28	8	26	1	♃20♎R
27	2.19	6	11♓	10	27	2	♄19♋
28	2.23	7	25	11	29	2	♅15♊
29	2.27	8	10♈	12	0♊	3	♆ 6♎R
30	2.31	9	24	13	1	3	♇ 9♌

May	STime	☉	☽	☿	♀	♂	Plnts
1	2.35	10♉	9♉	15♈	2♊	4♌	♃20♎R
2	2.39	11	25	16	3	4	♄19♋
3	2.43	12	10♊	17	5	5	♅15♊
4	2.47	13	25	19	6	5	♆ 6♎R
5	2.51	14	9♋	20	7	6	♇ 9♌
6	2.55	15	23	22	8	6	♃19♎R
7	2.59	16	7♌	23	10	6	♄20♋
8	3.03	17	20	25	11	7	♅15♊
9	3.07	18	4♍	26	12	7	♆ 6♎R
10	3.11	19	16	28	13	8	♇ 9♌
11	3.15	20	29	0♉	14	8	♃19♎R
12	3.19	21	11♎	1	16	9	♄20♋
13	3.23	22	23	3	17	9	♅16♊
14	3.27	23	5♏	5	18	10	♆ 6♎R
15	3.30	24	17	6	19	10	♇ 9♌
16	3.34	25	29	8	20	11	♃18♎R
17	3.38	26	11♐	10	22	11	♄21♋
18	3.42	27	22	12	23	12	♅16♊
19	3.46	28	4♑	14	24	12	♆ 6♎R
20	3.50	29	16	16	25	13	♇ 9♌
21	3.54	0♊	28	18	27	13	♃18♎R
22	3.58	0	11♒	20	28	14	♄21♋
23	4.02	1	23	22	29	15	♅16♊
24	4.06	2	6♓	24	0♋	15	♆ 6♎R
25	4.10	3	20	26	1	16	♇ 9♌
26	4.14	4	4♈	28	3	16	♃18♎R
27	4.18	5	18	0♊	4	17	♄22♋
28	4.22	6	3♉	3	5	17	♅17♊
29	4.26	7	18	5	6	18	♆ 6♎
30	4.30	8	3♊	7	7	18	♇ 9♌
31	4.34	9	18	9	9	19	♃17♎R

Jun	STime	☉	☽	☿	♀	♂	Plnts
1	4.37	10♊	3♋	11♊	10♋	19♌	♃17♎R
2	4.41	11	18	14	11	20	♄22♋
3	4.45	12	2♌	16	12	20	♅17♊
4	4.49	13	16	18	13	21	♆ 6♎
5	4.53	14	0♍	20	15	21	♇10♌
6	4.57	15	13	22	16	22	♃17♎R
7	5.01	16	26	24	17	23	♄23♋
8	5.05	17	8♎	26	18	23	♅17♊
9	5.09	18	20	29	19	24	♆ 6♎R
10	5.13	19	2♏	1♋	21	24	♇10♌
11	5.17	20	14	3	22	25	♃17♎
12	5.21	21	26	5	23	25	♄23♋
13	5.25	22	8♐	6	24	26	♅18♊
14	5.29	23	19	8	25	26	♆ 6♎
15	5.33	23	1♑	10	26	27	♇10♌
16	5.37	24	13	12	27	28	♃17♎
17	5.41	25	25	14	29	28	♄24♋
18	5.45	26	8♒	16	0♌	29	♅18♊
19	5.48	27	20	17	1	29	♆ 6♎
20	5.52	28	3♓	19	2	0♍	♇10♌
21	5.56	29	16	20	4	0	♃17♎
22	6.00	0♋	29	22	5	1	♄24♋
23	6.04	1	13♈	24	6	1	♅18♊
24	6.08	2	27	25	7	2	♆ 6♎
25	6.12	3	12♉	27	8	3	♇10♌
26	6.16	4	27	28	10	3	♃17♎
27	6.20	5	11♊	29	11	4	♄25♋
28	6.24	6	26	1♌	12	4	♅18♊
29	6.28	7	11♋	2	13	5	♆ 6♎
30	6.32	8	26	3	14	6	♇10♌

Jul	STime	☉	☽	☿	♀	♂	Plnts
1	6.36	9♋	11♌	4♌	15♌	6♍	♃18♎
2	6.40	10	25	5	17	7	♄26♋
3	6.44	11	8♍	7	18	7	♅19♊
4	6.48	12	21	8	19	8	♆ 6♎
5	6.52	13	4♎	9	20	8	♇10♌
6	6.55	14	17	10	21	9	♃18♎
7	6.59	14	29	10	22	10	♄26♋
8	7.03	15	11♏	11	24	10	♅19♊
9	7.07	16	23	12	25	11	♆ 6♎
10	7.11	17	4♐	13	26	11	♇10♌
11	7.15	18	16	13	27	12	♃18♎
12	7.19	19	28	14	28	12	♄27♋
13	7.23	20	10♑	15	29	13	♅19♊
14	7.27	21	22	15	1♍	14	♆ 6♎
15	7.31	22	5♒	15	2	14	♇11♌
16	7.35	23	17	16	3	15	♃19♎
17	7.39	24	0♓	16	4	15	♄28♋
18	7.43	25	13	16	5	16	♅19♊
19	7.47	26	26	16R	6	17	♆ 6♎
20	7.51	27	10♈	16	7	17	♇11♌
21	7.55	28	24	16	9	18	♃19♎
22	7.59	29	8♉	16	10	19	♄28♋
23	8.03	0♌	22	16	11	19	♅20♊
24	8.06	1	6♊	15	12	20	♆ 6♎
25	8.10	2	21	15	13	20	♇11♌
26	8.14	3	5♋	14	14	21	♃20♎
27	8.18	4	20	14	15	22	♄29♋
28	8.22	5	5♌	13	16	22	♅20♊
29	8.26	5	19	12	18	23	♆ 6♎
30	8.30	6	3♍	12	19	23	♇11♌
31	8.34	7	16	11	20	24	♃20♎

Aug	STime	☉	☽	☿	♀	♂	Plnts
1	8.38	8♌	0♎	10♌	21♍	25♍	♃20♎
2	8.42	9	12	9	23	25	♄ 0♌
3	8.46	10	25	9	24	26	♅20♊
4	8.50	11	7♏	8	24	27	♆ 6♎
5	8.54	12	19	7	25	27	♇11♌
6	8.58	13	1♐	7	27	28	♃21♎
7	9.02	14	13	6	28	28	♄ 0♌
8	9.06	15	25	6	29	29	♅20♊
9	9.10	16	6♑	5	0♎	0♎	♆ 6♎
10	9.13	17	19	5	1	0	♇11♌
11	9.17	18	1♒	5	2	1	♃22♎
12	9.21	19	14	5D	3	2	♄ 1♌
13	9.25	20	27	5	4	2	♅21♊
14	9.29	21	10♓	5	5	3	♆ 6♎
15	9.33	22	23	5	6	3	♇11♌
16	9.37	23	7♈	5	7	4	♃22♎
17	9.41	24	20	6	9	5	♄ 2♌
18	9.45	25	4♉	6	10	5	♅21♊
19	9.49	26	18	7	11	6	♆ 7♎
20	9.53	27	2♊	8	12	6	♇12♌
21	9.57	28	17	9	13	7	♃23♎
22	10.01	28	1♋	10	14	8	♄ 2♌
23	10.05	29	15	11	15	8	♅21♊
24	10.09	0♍	29	13	16	9	♆ 7♎
25	10.13	1	13♌	14	17	10	♇12♌
26	10.17	2	27	15	18	10	♃24♎
27	10.20	3	11♍	17	19	11	♄ 3♌
28	10.24	4	25	19	20	12	♅21♊
29	10.28	5	8♎	20	21	12	♆ 7♎
30	10.32	6	20	22	22	13	♇12♌
31	10.36	7	3♏	24	23	14	♃25♎

Sep	STime	☉	☽	☿	♀	♂	Plnts
1	10.40	8♍	15♏	26♌	24♎	14♎	♃25♎
2	10.44	9	27	27	25	15	♄ 3♌
3	10.48	10	9♐	29	26	16	♅21♊
4	10.52	11	21	1♍	27	16	♆ 7♎
5	10.56	12	2♑	3	28	17	♇12♌
6	11.00	13	14	5	29	18	♃26♎
7	11.04	14	27	7	0♏	18	♄ 4♌
8	11.08	15	9♒	9	1	19	♅21♊
9	11.12	16	22	11	2	19	♆ 7♎
10	11.16	17	5♓	13	3	20	♇12♌
11	11.20	18	19	15	4	21	♃27♎
12	11.24	19	3♈	17	5	21	♄ 5♌
13	11.28	20	17	19	6	22	♅21♊
14	11.31	21	1♉	20	7	23	♆ 7♎
15	11.35	22	15	22	8	24	♇12♌
16	11.39	23	29	24	9	24	♃28♎
17	11.43	24	13♊	26	10	25	♄ 5♌
18	11.47	25	28	28	10	25	♅21♊
19	11.51	26	12♋	0♎	11	26	♆ 8♎
20	11.55	27	26	1	12	27	♇12♌
21	11.59	28	9♌	3	13	28	♃29♎
22	12.03	29	23	5	14	28	♄ 6♌
23	12.07	0♎	7♍	7	15	29	♅21♊
24	12.11	1	20	8	16	0♏	♆ 8♎
25	12.15	2	3♎	10	16	0	♇13♌
26	12.19	2	16	12	17	1	♃ 0♏
27	12.23	3	29	13	18	2	♄ 6♌
28	12.27	4	11♏	15	19	2	♅22♊
29	12.31	5	23	17	20	3	♆ 8♎
30	12.35	6	5♐	18	20	4	♇13♌

Oct	STime	☉	☽	☿	♀	♂	Plnts
1	12.38	7♎	17♐	20♎	21♏	4♏	♃ 1♏
2	12.42	8	28	21	22	5	♄ 6♌
3	12.46	9	10♑	23	22	6	♅21♊R
4	12.50	10	22	25	23	6	♆ 8♎
5	12.54	11	5♒	26	24	7	♇13♌
6	12.58	12	17	28	24	8	♃ 2♏
7	13.02	13	0♓	29	25	8	♄ 7♌
8	13.06	14	14	1♏	26	9	♅21♊R
9	13.10	15	27	2	26	10	♆ 8♎
10	13.14	16	11♈	4	27	10	♇13♌
11	13.18	17	26	5	27	11	♃ 3♏
12	13.22	18	10♉	7	28	12	♄ 7♌
13	13.26	19	25	8	28	13	♅21♊R
14	13.30	20	10♊	9	29	13	♆ 9♎
15	13.34	21	24	11	29	14	♇13♌
16	13.38	22	8♋	12	0♐	15	♃ 4♏
17	13.42	23	22	14	0	15	♄ 8♌
18	13.45	24	6♌	15	0	16	♅21♊R
19	13.49	25	20	16	1	17	♆ 9♎
20	13.53	26	3♍	18	1	17	♇13♌
21	13.57	27	16	19	1	18	♃ 5♏
22	14.01	28	29	20	2	19	♄ 8♌
23	14.05	29	12♎	22	2	20	♅21♊R
24	14.09	0♏	25	23	2	20	♆ 9♎
25	14.13	1	7♏	24	2	21	♇13♌
26	14.17	2	19	25	2	22	♃ 6♏
27	14.21	3	1♐	26	2	22	♄ 8♌
28	14.25	4	13	28	2R	23	♅21♊R
29	14.29	5	25	29	2	24	♆ 9♎
30	14.33	6	7♑	0♐	2	25	♇13♌
31	14.37	7	18	1	2	25	♃ 7♏

Nov	STime	☉	☽	☿	♀	♂	Plnts
1	14.41	8♏	0♒	2♐	2♐	26♏	♃ 8♏
2	14.45	9	13	3	2	27	♄ 8♌
3	14.49	10	25	3	1	27	♅21♊R
4	14.53	11	8♓	4	1	28	♆ 9♎
5	14.56	12	21	5	1	29	♇13♌
6	15.00	13	5♈	6	0	0♐	♃ 9♏
7	15.04	14	19	6	0	0	♄ 8♌
8	15.08	15	4♉	7	29♏	1	♅21♊R
9	15.12	16	19	7	29	2	♆ 9♎
10	15.16	17	4♊	7	29	2	♇13♌
11	15.20	18	19	7R	28	3	♃10♏
12	15.24	19	4♋	7	28	4	♄ 9♌
13	15.28	20	18	7	27	5	♅21♊R
14	15.32	21	3♌	6	27	5	♆10♎
15	15.36	22	17	6	26	6	♇13♌
16	15.40	23	0♍	5	25	7	♃11♏
17	15.44	24	13	4	25	7	♄ 9♌
18	15.48	25	26	3	24	8	♅20♊R
19	15.52	26	9♎	2	24	9	♆10♎
20	15.56	27	22	0	23	10	♇13♌R
21	16.00	28	4♏	29♏	22	10	♃12♏
22	16.03	29	16	27	22	11	♄ 9♌R
23	16.07	0♐	28	26	21	12	♅20♊R
24	16.11	1	10♐	25	21	13	♆10♎
25	16.15	2	21	24	20	13	♇13♌R
26	16.19	3	3♑	23	20	14	♃13♏
27	16.23	4	15	22	19	15	♄ 9♌R
28	16.27	5	27	21	19	16	♅20♊R
29	16.31	6	9♒	21	18	16	♆10♎
30	16.35	7	21	21	18	17	♇13♌R

Dec	STime	☉	☽	☿	♀	♂	Plnts
1	16.39	8♐	4♓	21♏	18♏	18♐	♃14♏
2	16.43	9	16	21	18	18	♄ 8♌R
3	16.47	10	0♈	21	17	19	♅20♊R
4	16.51	11	13	22	17	20	♆10♎
5	16.55	12	27	22	17	21	♇13♌R
6	16.59	13	12♉	23	17	21	♃15♏
7	17.03	14	27	24	17	22	♄ 8♌R
8	17.07	16	12♊	25	17D	23	♅20♊R
9	17.11	17	27	26	17	23	♆10♎
10	17.14	18	12♋	27	17	24	♇13♌R
11	17.18	19	27	28	17	25	♃16♏
12	17.22	20	12♌	29	17	25	♄ 8♌R
13	17.26	21	26	0♐	17	27	♅19♊R
14	17.30	22	10♍	2	18	27	♆10♎
15	17.34	23	23	3	18	28	♇13♌R
16	17.38	24	6♎	4	18	29	♃17♏
17	17.42	25	19	5	18	0♑	♄ 8♌R
18	17.46	26	1♏	7	19	0	♅19♊R
19	17.50	27	13	8	19	1	♆10♎
20	17.54	28	25	10	20	2	♇13♌R
21	17.58	29	7♐	11	20	3	♃18♏
22	18.02	0♑	18	12	20	4	♄ 8♌R
23	18.06	1	0♑	14	21	5	♅19♊R
24	18.10	2	12	15	22	5	♆10♎
25	18.14	3	24	17	22	6	♇13♌R
26	18.18	4	6♒	18	23	7	♃19♏
27	18.21	5	18	20	23	7	♄ 7♌R
28	18.25	6	0♓	21	24	8	♅19♊R
29	18.29	7	13	23	25	9	♆10♎
30	18.33	8	26	24	25	10	♇13♌R
31	18.37	9	9♈	26	26	10	♃20♏

1 9 4 7

Jan	STime	☉	☽	☿	♀	♂	Plnts
1	18.41	10♑	22♈	27♐	27♏	11♑	♃20♏
2	18.45	11	6♉	29	27	12	♄ 7♌R
3	18.49	12	20	0♑	28	13	♅19♊R
4	18.53	13	5♊	2	29	13	♆10♎
5	18.57	14	20	3	0♐	14	♇13♌R
6	19.01	15	5♋	5	0	15	♃21♏
7	19.05	16	20	7	1	16	♄ 7♌R
8	19.09	17	5♌	8	2	17	♅18♊R
9	19.13	18	20	10	3	17	♆11♎
10	19.17	19	5♍	11	4	18	♇12♌R
11	19.21	20	19	13	4	19	♃22♏
12	19.25	21	2♎	14	5	20	♄ 6♌R
13	19.29	22	15	16	6	20	♅18♊R
14	19.32	23	28	18	7	21	♆11♎
15	19.36	24	10♏	19	8	22	♇12♌R
16	19.40	25	22	21	9	23	♃23♏
17	19.44	26	4♐	22	10	23	♄ 6♌R
18	19.48	27	15	24	11	24	♅18♊R
19	19.52	28	27	26	12	25	♆10♎
20	19.56	29	9♑	27	13	26	♇12♌R
21	20.00	0♒	21	29	14	27	♃23♏
22	20.04	1	3♒	1♒	15	27	♄ 5♌R
23	20.08	2	15	2	16	28	♅18♊R
24	20.12	3	27	4	17	29	♆10♎R
25	20.16	4	10♓	6	18	0♒	♇12♌R
26	20.20	5	23	8	19	0	♃24♏
27	20.24	6	6♈	9	20	1	♄ 5♌R
28	20.28	7	19	11	21	2	♅18♊R
29	20.32	8	2♉	13	22	3	♆10♎R
30	20.36	9	16	14	23	4	♇12♌R
31	20.39	10	0♊	16	24	4	♃25♏

Feb	STime	☉	☽	☿	♀	♂	Plnts
1	20.43	11♒	14♊	18♒	25♐	5♒	♃25♏
2	20.47	13	29	20	26	6	♄ 5♌R
3	20.51	14	14♋	22	27	7	♅18♊R
4	20.55	15	28	23	28	8	♆10♎R
5	20.59	16	13♌	25	29	8	♇12♌R
6	21.03	17	28	27	0♑	9	♃25♏
7	21.07	18	12♍	29	1	10	♄ 4♌R
8	21.11	19	26	0♓	2	11	♅18♊R
9	21.15	20	10♎	2	3	11	♆10♎R
10	21.19	21	23	4	4	12	♇12♌R
11	21.23	22	6♏	6	5	13	♃26♏
12	21.27	23	18	7	6	14	♄ 4♌R
13	21.31	24	0♐	9	8	15	♅18♊R
14	21.35	25	12	11	9	15	♆10♎R
15	21.39	26	24	12	10	16	♇12♌R
16	21.43	27	5♑	14	11	17	♃26♏
17	21.46	28	17	15	12	18	♄ 3♌R
18	21.50	29	29	16	13	19	♅17♊
19	21.54	0♓	12♒	18	14	19	♆10♎R
20	21.58	1	24	19	15	20	♇11♌R
21	22.02	2	7♓	20	16	21	♃27♏
22	22.06	3	19	21	18	22	♄ 3♌R
23	22.10	4	2♈	21	19	22	♅17♊R
24	22.14	5	16	22	20	23	♆10♎R
25	22.18	6	29	22	21	24	♇11♌R
26	22.22	7	13♉	23	22	25	♃27♏
27	22.26	8	26	23R	23	26	♄ 3♌R
28	22.30	9	10♊	23	24	26	♅17♊

Mar	STime	☉	☽	☿	♀	♂	Plnts
1	22.34	10♓	24♊	23♓	25♑	27♒	♃27♏
2	22.38	11	9♋	22	27	28	♄ 3♌R
3	22.42	12	23	22	28	29	♅17♊
4	22.46	13	8♌	21	29	0♓	♆10♎R
5	22.50	14	22	20	0♒	0	♇11♌R
6	22.54	15	6♍	20	1	1	♃27♏
7	22.57	16	21	19	2	2	♄ 2♌R
8	23.01	17	4♎	18	3	3	♅18♊
9	23.05	18	18	17	5	3	♆10♎R
10	23.09	19	1♏	16	6	4	♇11♌R
11	23.13	20	14	15	7	5	♃27♏
12	23.17	21	26	14	8	6	♄ 2♌R
13	23.21	22	8♐	13	9	7	♅18♊
14	23.25	23	20	12	10	7	♆10♎R
15	23.29	24	2♑	11	12	8	♇11♌R
16	23.33	25	13	11	13	9	♃27♏
17	23.37	26	25	10	14	10	♄ 2♌R
18	23.41	27	7♒	10	15	11	♅18♊
19	23.45	28	20	9	16	11	♆ 9♎R
20	23.49	29	2♓	9	17	12	♇11♌R
21	23.53	0♈	15	9	19	13	♃27♏R
22	23.57	1	28	9D	20	14	♄ 2♌R
23	0.01	2	12♈	9	21	14	♅18♊
24	0.04	3	25	9	22	15	♆ 9♎R
25	0.08	4	9♉	9	23	16	♇11♌R
26	0.12	5	23	10	24	17	♃27♏R
27	0.16	6	7♊	10	26	18	♄ 2♌R
28	0.20	7	21	11	27	18	♅18♊
29	0.24	8	5♋	11	28	19	♆ 9♎R
30	0.28	9	19	12	29	20	♇11♌R
31	0.32	10	4♌	12	0♓	21	♃27♏R

Apr	STime	☉	☽	☿	♀	♂	Plnts
1	0.36	11♈	18♌	13♓	2♓	22♓	♃27♏R
2	0.40	12	2♍	14	3	22	♄ 2♌
3	0.44	13	16	15	4	23	♅18♊
4	0.48	14	29	16	5	24	♆ 9♎R
5	0.52	15	13♎	17	6	25	♇11♌R
6	0.56	16	26	18	7	25	♃26♏R
7	1.00	17	9♏	19	9	26	♄ 2♌
8	1.04	18	21	20	10	27	♅18♊
9	1.08	18	4♐	21	11	28	♆ 9♎R
10	1.12	19	16	22	12	29	♇11♌
11	1.15	20	28	24	13	29	♃26♏R
12	1.19	21	9♑	25	15	0♈	♄ 2♌
13	1.23	22	21	26	16	1	♅18♊
14	1.27	23	3♒	27	17	2	♆ 9♎R
15	1.31	24	15	29	18	2	♇11♌
16	1.35	25	28	0♈	19	3	♃26♏R
17	1.39	26	10♓	2	21	4	♄ 2♌
18	1.43	27	23	3	22	5	♅19♊
19	1.47	28	7♈	4	23	6	♆ 9♎R
20	1.51	29	20	6	24	6	♇11♌R
21	1.55	0♉	4♉	8	25	7	♃25♏R
22	1.59	1	19	9	27	8	♄ 2♌
23	2.03	2	3♊	11	28	9	♅19♊
24	2.07	3	17	12	29	9	♆ 8♎R
25	2.11	4	2♋	14	0♈	10	♇11♌
26	2.15	5	16	16	1	11	♃25♏R
27	2.19	6	0♌	17	3	12	♄ 2♌
28	2.22	7	15	19	4	13	♅19♊
29	2.26	8	28	21	5	13	♆ 8♎R
30	2.30	9	12♍	23	6	14	♇11♌

May	STime	☉	☽	☿	♀	♂	Plnts
1	2.34	10♉	26♍	25♈	7♈	15♈	♃24♏R
2	2.38	11	9♎	26	9	16	♄ 2♌
3	2.42	12	22	28	10	16	♅19♊
4	2.46	13	5♏	0♉	11	17	♆ 8♎R
5	2.50	14	17	2	12	18	♇11♌
6	2.54	15	0♐	4	13	19	♃23♏R
7	2.58	16	12	6	15	19	♄ 3♌
8	3.02	17	24	8	16	20	♅20♊
9	3.06	18	6♑	10	17	21	♆ 8♎R
10	3.10	19	17	12	18	22	♇11♌
11	3.14	20	29	14	19	22	♃23♏R
12	3.18	21	11♒	17	21	23	♄ 3♌
13	3.22	22	23	19	22	24	♅20♊
14	3.26	23	6♓	21	23	25	♆ 8♎R
15	3.29	24	18	23	24	25	♇11♌
16	3.33	24	1♈	25	25	26	♃22♏R
17	3.37	25	15	27	27	27	♄ 3♌
18	3.41	26	29	0♊	28	28	♅20♊
19	3.45	27	13♉	2	29	28	♆ 8♎R
20	3.49	28	27	4	0♉	29	♇11♌
21	3.53	29	12♊	6	1	0♉	♃21♏R
22	3.57	0♊	27	8	3	1	♄ 4♌
23	4.01	1	12♋	10	4	1	♅20♊
24	4.05	2	26	12	5	2	♆ 8♎R
25	4.09	3	11♌	14	6	3	♇11♌
26	4.13	4	25	17	7	4	♃21♏R
27	4.17	5	9♍	19	9	4	♄ 4♌
28	4.21	6	23	20	10	5	♅21♊
29	4.25	7	6♎	22	11	6	♆ 8♎R
30	4.29	8	19	24	12	7	♇11♌
31	4.33	9	1♏	26	13	7	♃20♏R

Jun	STime	☉	☽	☿	♀	♂	Plnts
1	4.37	10♊	14♏	28♊	15♉	8♉	♃20♏R
2	4.40	11	26	0♋	16	9	♄ 5♌
3	4.44	12	8♐	1	17	10	♅21♊
4	4.48	13	20	3	18	10	♆ 8♎R
5	4.52	14	2♑	5	20	11	♇11♌
6	4.56	15	14	6	21	12	♃20♏R
7	5.00	16	26	8	22	13	♄ 5♌
8	5.04	17	8♒	9	23	13	♅21♊
9	5.08	18	20	10	24	14	♆ 8♎R
10	5.12	18	2♓	12	26	15	♇11♌
11	5.16	19	14	13	27	16	♃19♏R
12	5.20	20	27	14	28	16	♄ 6♌
13	5.24	21	10♈	16	29	17	♅22♊
14	5.28	22	23	17	0♊	18	♆ 8♎R
15	5.32	23	7♉	18	2	18	♇11♌
16	5.36	24	21	19	3	19	♃19♏R
17	5.40	25	6♊	20	4	20	♄ 6♌
18	5.44	26	21	21	5	21	♅22♊
19	5.47	27	6♋	22	6	21	♆ 8♎
20	5.51	28	21	22	8	22	♇11♌
21	5.55	29	6♌	23	9	23	♃18♏R
22	5.59	0♋	21	24	10	24	♄ 7♌
23	6.03	1	5♍	24	11	24	♅22♊
24	6.07	2	19	25	13	25	♆ 8♎
25	6.11	3	3♎	26	14	26	♇12♌
26	6.15	4	16	26	15	26	♃18♏R
27	6.19	5	29	26	16	27	♄ 7♌
28	6.23	6	11♏	27	17	28	♅22♊
29	6.27	7	23	27	19	29	♆ 8♎
30	6.31	8	5♐	27	20	29	♇12♌

Jul	STime	☉	☽	☿	♀	♂	Plnts
1	6.35	9♋	17♐	27♋	21♊	0♊	♃18♏R
2	6.39	9	29	27	22	1	♄ 8♌
3	6.43	10	11♑	27	24	1	♅23♊
4	6.47	11	23	26	25	2	♆ 8♎
5	6.51	12	5♒	26	26	3	♇12♌
6	6.55	13	17	26	27	3	♃18♏R
7	6.58	14	29	25	28	4	♄ 8♌
8	7.02	15	11♓	25	0♋	5	♅23♊
9	7.06	16	23	24	1	6	♆ 8♎
10	7.10	17	6♈	24	2	6	♇12♌
11	7.14	18	19	23	3	7	♃17♏R
12	7.18	19	2♉	23	5	8	♄ 9♌
13	7.22	20	15	22	6	8	♅23♊
14	7.26	21	0♊	21	7	9	♆ 8♎
15	7.30	22	14	21	8	10	♇12♌
16	7.34	23	29	20	9	10	♃17♏
17	7.38	24	14♋	19	11	11	♄10♌
18	7.42	25	29	19	12	12	♅24♊
19	7.46	26	15♌	18	13	13	♆ 8♎
20	7.50	27	29	18	14	13	♇12♌
21	7.54	28	14♍	18	16	14	♃17♏
22	7.58	29	28	17	17	15	♄10♌
23	8.02	29	12♎	17	18	15	♅24♊
24	8.05	0♌	25	17	19	16	♆ 8♎
25	8.09	1	8♏	17D	20	17	♇12♌
26	8.13	2	20	17	22	17	♃18♏
27	8.17	3	2♐	17	23	18	♄11♌
28	8.21	4	14	17	24	19	♅24♊
29	8.25	5	26	18	25	19	♆ 8♎
30	8.29	6	8♑	18	27	20	♇12♌
31	8.33	7	20	18	28	21	♃18♏

Aug	STime	☉	☽	☿	♀	♂	Plnts
1	8.37	8♌	2♒	19♋	29♋	21♊	♃18♏
2	8.41	9	14	20	0♌	22	♄12♌
3	8.45	10	26	21	1	23	♅24♊
4	8.49	11	8♓	22	3	23	♆ 8♎
5	8.53	12	20	23	4	24	♇13♌
6	8.57	13	3♈	24	5	25	♃18♏
7	9.01	14	15	25	6	25	♄12♌
8	9.05	15	28	26	8	26	♅25♊
9	9.09	16	11♉	28	9	27	♆ 8♎
10	9.13	17	25	29	10	27	♇13♌
11	9.16	18	9♊	1♌	11	28	♃18♏
12	9.20	19	23	3	13	29	♄13♌
13	9.24	20	8♋	4	14	29	♅25♊
14	9.28	21	23	6	15	0♋	♆ 9♎
15	9.32	22	8♌	8	16	1	♇13♌
16	9.36	22	23	10	18	1	♃19♏
17	9.40	23	8♍	12	19	2	♄14♌
18	9.44	24	22	14	20	3	♅25♊
19	9.48	25	7♎	15	21	3	♆ 9♎
20	9.52	26	20	17	22	4	♇13♌
21	9.56	27	4♏	19	24	5	♃19♏
22	10.00	28	16	21	25	5	♄14♌
23	10.04	29	29	23	26	6	♅25♊
24	10.08	0♍	11♐	25	27	7	♆ 9♎
25	10.12	1	23	27	29	7	♇13♌
26	10.16	2	5♑	29	0♍	8	♃20♏
27	10.20	3	17	1♍	1	9	♄15♌
28	10.23	4	29	3	2	9	♅25♊
29	10.27	5	10♒	5	4	10	♆ 9♎
30	10.31	6	23	7	5	10	♇13♌
31	10.35	7	5♓	9	6	11	♃20♏

Sep	STime	☉	☽	☿	♀	♂	Plnts
1	10.39	8♍	17♓	11♍	7♍	12♋	♃21♏
2	10.43	9	0♈	13	9	12	♄16♌
3	10.47	10	12	15	10	13	♅26♊
4	10.51	11	25	17	11	14	♆ 9♎
5	10.55	12	8♉	19	12	14	♇14♌
6	10.59	13	22	20	14	15	♃21♏
7	11.03	14	5♊	22	15	15	♄16♌
8	11.07	15	19	24	16	16	♅26♊
9	11.11	16	3♋	26	17	17	♆ 9♎
10	11.15	17	18	27	19	17	♇14♌
11	11.19	18	2♌	29	20	18	♃22♏
12	11.23	19	17	1♎	21	19	♄17♌
13	11.27	20	2♍	2	22	19	♅26♊
14	11.30	21	16	4	23	20	♆10♎
15	11.34	22	1♎	6	25	20	♇14♌
16	11.38	22	15	7	26	21	♃23♏
17	11.42	23	28	9	27	22	♄17♌
18	11.46	24	12♏	11	28	22	♅26♊
19	11.50	25	25	12	0♎	23	♆10♎
20	11.54	26	7♐	14	1	23	♇14♌
21	11.58	27	19	15	2	24	♃24♏
22	12.02	28	1♑	17	3	25	♄18♌
23	12.06	29	13	18	5	25	♅26♊
24	12.10	0♎	25	20	6	26	♆10♎
25	12.14	1	7♒	21	7	26	♇14♌
26	12.18	2	19	23	8	27	♃24♏
27	12.22	3	1♓	24	10	28	♄18♌
28	12.26	4	13	25	11	28	♅26♊
29	12.30	5	26	27	12	29	♆10♎
30	12.34	6	9♈	28	13	29	♇14♌

Oct	STime	☉	☽	☿	♀	♂	Plnts
1	12.38	7♎	22♈	0♏	15♎	0♌	♃25♏
2	12.41	8	5♉	1	16	1	♄19♌
3	12.45	9	19	2	17	1	♅26♊
4	12.49	10	2♊	3	18	2	♆10♎
5	12.53	11	16	5	20	2	♇14♌
6	12.57	12	0♋	6	21	3	♃26♏
7	13.01	13	14	7	22	3	♄19♌
8	13.05	14	28	8	23	4	♅26♊R
9	13.09	15	12♌	10	25	4	♆10♎
10	13.13	16	27	11	26	5	♇14♌
11	13.17	17	11♍	12	27	6	♃27♏
12	13.21	18	25	13	28	6	♄20♌
13	13.25	19	9♎	14	0♏	7	♅26♊R
14	13.29	20	23	15	1	7	♆11♎
15	13.33	21	7♏	16	2	8	♇14♌
16	13.37	22	20	17	3	8	♃28♏
17	13.41	23	2♐	17	5	9	♄20♌
18	13.45	24	15	18	6	9	♅26♊R
19	13.48	25	27	19	7	10	♆11♎
20	13.52	26	9♑	20	8	11	♇14♌
21	13.56	27	21	20	10	11	♃29♏
22	14.00	28	3♒	21	11	12	♄21♌
23	14.04	29	15	21	12	12	♅26♊R
24	14.08	0♏	27	21	13	13	♆11♎
25	14.12	1	9♓	21R	15	13	♇15♌
26	14.16	2	21	21	16	14	♃ 0♐
27	14.20	3	4♈	21	17	14	♄21♌
28	14.24	4	17	21	18	15	♅26♊R
29	14.28	5	1♉	20	20	15	♆11♎
30	14.32	6	14	19	21	16	♇15♌
31	14.36	7	28	19	22	16	♃ 1♐

Nov	STime	☉	☽	☿	♀	♂	Plnts
1	14.40	8♏	12♊	18♏	23♏	17♌	♃ 1♐
2	14.44	9	26	17	25	17	♄21♌
3	14.48	10	11♋	16	26	18	♅25♊R
4	14.52	11	25	14	27	18	♆11♎
5	14.56	12	9♌	13	28	19	♇15♌
6	14.59	13	23	12	0♐	19	♃ 3♐
7	15.03	14	7♍	10	1	20	♄22♌
8	15.07	15	21	9	2	20	♅25♊R
9	15.11	16	5♎	8	3	21	♆12♎
10	15.15	17	19	7	5	21	♇15♌
11	15.19	18	2♏	6	6	21	♃ 4♐
12	15.23	19	15	6	7	22	♄22♌
13	15.27	20	28	5	8	22	♅25♊R
14	15.31	21	10♐	5D	10	23	♆12♎
15	15.35	22	23	5	11	23	♇15♌
16	15.39	23	5♑	5	12	24	♃ 5♐
17	15.43	24	17	6	13	24	♄22♌
18	15.47	25	29	6	15	25	♅25♊R
19	15.51	26	11♒	7	16	25	♆12♎
20	15.55	27	23	8	17	25	♇15♌
21	15.59	28	5♓	8	18	26	♃ 6♐
22	16.03	29	17	9	19	26	♄22♌
23	16.06	0♐	29	11	21	27	♅25♊R
24	16.10	1	12♈	12	22	27	♆12♎
25	16.14	2	25	13	23	27	♇15♌
26	16.18	3	9♉	14	24	28	♃ 7♐
27	16.22	4	23	15	26	28	♄22♌
28	16.26	5	7♊	17	27	29	♅25♊R
29	16.30	6	21	18	28	29	♆12♎
30	16.34	7	6♋	19	29	29	♇15♌

Dec	STime	☉	☽	☿	♀	♂	Plnts
1	16.38	8♐	21♋	21♏	1♑	0♍	♃ 8♐
2	16.42	9	5♌	22	2	0	♄22♌
3	16.46	10	20	24	3	0	♅24♊R
4	16.50	11	4♍	25	4	1	♆12♎
5	16.54	12	18	27	6	1	♇15♌R
6	16.58	13	2♎	28	7	1	♃ 9♐
7	17.02	14	15	0♐	8	2	♄22♌R
8	17.06	15	28	1	9	2	♅24♊R
9	17.10	16	11♏	3	11	2	♆12♎
10	17.14	17	24	4	12	3	♇15♌R
11	17.17	18	7♐	6	13	3	♃10♐
12	17.21	19	19	7	14	3	♄22♌R
13	17.25	20	1♑	9	16	3	♅24♊R
14	17.29	21	13	10	17	4	♆12♎
15	17.33	22	25	12	18	4	♇14♌R
16	17.37	23	7♒	13	19	4	♃11♐
17	17.41	24	19	15	21	5	♄22♌R
18	17.45	25	1♓	16	22	5	♅24♊R
19	17.49	26	13	18	23	5	♆12♎
20	17.53	27	25	20	24	5	♇14♌R
21	17.57	28	7♈	21	26	5	♃13♐
22	18.01	29	20	23	27	6	♄22♌R
23	18.05	1♑	3♉	24	28	6	♅24♊R
24	18.09	2	16	26	29	6	♆13♎
25	18.13	3	0♊	27	1♒	6	♇14♌R
26	18.17	4	15	29	2	6	♃14♐
27	18.21	5	0♋	1♑	3	6	♄22♌R
28	18.24	6	15	2	4	7	♅23♊R
29	18.28	7	0♌	4	6	7	♆13♎
30	18.32	8	15	5	7	7	♇14♌R
31	18.36	9	0♍	7	8	7	♃15♐

Jan	STime	☉	☽	☿	♀	♂	Plnts
1	18.40	10♑	14♍	8♑	9♒	7♍	♃15♐
2	18.44	11	28	10	10	7	♄22♌R
3	18.48	12	12♎	12	12	7	♅23♊R
4	18.52	13	25	13	13	7	♆13♎
5	18.56	14	8♏	15	14	7	♇14♌R
6	19.00	15	21	17	15	7	♃16♐
7	19.04	16	3♐	18	17	7	♄21♌R
8	19.08	17	16	20	18	7	♅23♊R
9	19.12	18	28	21	19	7R	♆13♎
10	19.16	19	10♑	23	20	7	♇14♌R
11	19.20	20	22	25	22	7	♃17♐
12	19.24	21	4♒	26	23	7	♄21♌R
13	19.28	22	16	28	24	7	♅23♊R
14	19.31	23	27	0♒	25	7	♆13♎
15	19.35	24	9♓	2	27	7	♇14♌R
16	19.39	25	21	3	28	7	♃18♐
17	19.43	26	3♈	5	29	7	♄21♌R
18	19.47	27	16	7	0♓	7	♅23♊R
19	19.51	28	28	8	1	7	♆13♎R
20	19.55	29	11♉	10	3	6	♇14♌R
21	19.59	0♒	25	12	4	6	♃19♐
22	20.03	1	8♊	13	5	6	♄20♌R
23	20.07	2	23	15	6	6	♅22♊R
24	20.11	3	8♋	17	8	6	♆13♎R
25	20.15	4	23	18	9	5	♇14♌R
26	20.19	5	8♌	20	10	5	♃20♐
27	20.23	6	23	22	11	5	♄20♌R
28	20.27	7	8♍	23	12	5	♅22♊R
29	20.31	8	23	25	14	4	♆13♎R
30	20.35	9	8♎	26	15	4	♇14♌R
31	20.39	10	22	28	16	4	♃21♐

Feb	STime	☉	☽	☿	♀	♂	Plnts
1	20.42	11♒	5♏	29♒	17♓	4♍	♃21♐
2	20.46	12	18	0♓	18	3	♄19♌R
3	20.50	13	1♐	1	20	3	♅22♊R
4	20.54	14	13	3	21	3	♆13♎R
5	20.58	15	25	4	22	2	♇13♌R
6	21.02	16	7♑	4	23	2	♃22♐
7	21.06	17	19	5	25	2	♄19♌R
8	21.10	18	1♒	6	26	1	♅22♊R
9	21.14	19	13	6	27	1	♆13♎R
10	21.18	20	24	6	28	0	♇13♌R
11	21.22	21	6♓	6R	29	0	♃23♐
12	21.26	22	18	6	1♈	0	♄19♌R
13	21.30	23	0♈	6	2	29♌	♅22♊R
14	21.34	24	13	5	3	29	♆12♎R
15	21.38	25	25	5	4	28	♇13♌R
16	21.42	26	7♉	4	5	28	♃24♐
17	21.46	27	20	3	7	28	♄18♌R
18	21.49	28	4♊	2	8	27	♅22♊R
19	21.53	29	17	1	9	27	♆12♎R
20	21.57	0♓	1♋	0	10	27	♇13♌R
21	22.01	1	16	29♒	11	26	♃24♐
22	22.05	2	1♌	27	12	26	♄18♌R
23	22.09	3	16	26	14	25	♅22♊R
24	22.13	4	1♍	25	15	25	♆12♎R
25	22.17	5	17	24	16	25	♇13♌R
26	22.21	7	1♎	24	17	24	♃25♐
27	22.25	8	16	23	18	24	♄17♌R
28	22.29	9	0♏	22	20	23	♅22♊
29	22.33	10	14	22	21	23	♆12♎R

Mar	STime	☉	☽	☿	♀	♂	Plnts
1	22.37	11♓	27♏	22♒	22♈	23♌	♃26♐
2	22.41	12	9♐	21	23	22	♄17♌R
3	22.45	13	22	21D	24	22	♅22♊
4	22.49	14	4♑	21	25	22	♆12♎R
5	22.53	15	16	21	26	21	♇13♌R
6	22.57	16	28	22	28	21	♃26♐
7	23.00	17	9♒	22	29	21	♄17♌R
8	23.04	18	21	22	0♉	21	♅22♊
9	23.08	19	3♓	23	1	20	♆12♎R
10	23.12	20	15	23	2	20	♇13♌R
11	23.16	21	27	24	3	20	♃27♐
12	23.20	22	10♈	25	4	20	♄17♌R
13	23.24	23	22	25	6	19	♅22♊
14	23.28	24	5♉	26	7	19	♆12♎R
15	23.32	25	17	27	8	19	♇13♌R
16	23.36	26	0♊	28	9	19	♃27♐
17	23.40	27	14	29	10	19	♄16♌R
18	23.44	27	27	0♓	11	19	♅22♊
19	23.48	28	11♋	1	12	18	♆12♎R
20	23.52	29	25	2	13	18	♇13♌R
21	23.56	0♈	10♌	3	15	18	♃28♐
22	0.00	1	25	4	16	18	♄16♌R
23	0.04	2	10♍	5	17	18	♅22♊
24	0.07	3	25	7	18	18	♆12♎R
25	0.11	4	9♎	8	19	18	♇12♌R
26	0.15	5	24	9	20	18	♃28♐
27	0.19	6	8♏	11	21	18	♄16♌R
28	0.23	7	22	12	22	18D	♅22♊
29	0.27	8	5♐	13	23	18	♆11♎R
30	0.31	9	17	15	24	18	♇12♌R
31	0.35	10	0♑	16	25	18	♃28♐

Apr	STime	☉	☽	☿	♀	♂	Plnts
1	0.39	11♈	12♑	18♓	27♉	18♌	♃28♐
2	0.43	12	24	19	28	18	♄16♌R
3	0.47	13	6♒	21	29	18	♅22♊
4	0.51	14	18	22	0♊	18	♆11♎R
5	0.55	15	0♓	24	1	18	♇12♌R
6	0.59	16	12	25	2	18	♃29♐
7	1.03	17	24	27	3	18	♄16♌R
8	1.07	18	6♈	29	4	18	♅22♊
9	1.11	19	19	0♈	5	19	♆11♎R
10	1.15	20	1♉	2	6	19	♇12♌R
11	1.18	21	14	4	7	19	♃29♐
12	1.22	22	27	6	8	19	♄15♌R
13	1.26	23	11♊	7	9	19	♅23♊
14	1.30	24	24	9	10	19	♆11♎R
15	1.34	25	8♋	11	11	19	♇12♌
16	1.38	26	22	13	12	20	♃29♐R
17	1.42	27	6♌	15	13	20	♄15♌
18	1.46	28	20	17	14	20	♅23♊
19	1.50	29	5♍	18	15	20	♆11♎R
20	1.54	0♉	19	20	16	20	♇12♌
21	1.58	1	4♎	22	16	21	♃29♐R
22	2.02	2	18	24	17	21	♄15♌
23	2.06	3	2♏	26	18	21	♅23♊
24	2.10	4	16	29	19	21	♆11♎R
25	2.14	5	29	1♉	20	22	♇12♌
26	2.18	6	13♐	3	21	22	♃28♐R
27	2.22	7	25	5	22	22	♄16♌
28	2.25	8	8♑	7	23	23	♅23♊
29	2.29	9	20	9	24	23	♆11♎R
30	2.33	10	2♒	11	24	23	♇12♌

May	STime	☉	☽	☿	♀	♂	Plnts
1	2.37	11♉	14♒	13♉	25♊	23♌	♃28♐R
2	2.41	12	26	16	26	24	♄16♌
3	2.45	13	8♓	18	27	24	♅23♊
4	2.49	14	20	20	28	24	♆10♎R
5	2.53	15	2♈	22	28	25	♇12♌
6	2.57	16	14	24	29	25	♃28♐R
7	3.01	17	27	26	0♋	25	♄16♌
8	3.05	17	10♉	28	1	26	♅24♊
9	3.09	18	23	0♊	1	26	♆10♎R
10	3.13	19	7♊	2	2	26	♇12♌
11	3.17	20	21	4	3	27	♃28♐R
12	3.21	21	5♋	6	3	27	♄16♌
13	3.25	22	19	8	4	28	♅24♊
14	3.29	23	3♌	10	4	28	♆10♎R
15	3.32	24	17	12	5	28	♇12♌
16	3.36	25	1♍	13	6	29	♃27♐R
17	3.40	26	15	15	6	29	♄16♌
18	3.44	27	0♎	17	7	0♍	♅24♊
19	3.48	28	14	18	7	0	♆10♎R
20	3.52	29	27	20	8	0	♇12♌
21	3.56	0♊	11♏	21	8	1	♃27♐R
22	4.00	1	25	23	8	1	♄17♌
23	4.04	2	8♐	24	9	2	♅25♊
24	4.08	3	21	25	9	2	♆10♎R
25	4.12	4	3♑	26	10	2	♇12♌
26	4.16	5	16	28	10	3	♃26♐R
27	4.20	6	28	29	10	3	♄17♌
28	4.24	7	10♒	0♋	10	4	♅25♊
29	4.28	8	22	1	10	4	♆10♎R
30	4.32	9	4♓	2	11	5	♇13♌
31	4.36	10	16	2	11	5	♃26♐R

Jun	STime	☉	☽	☿	♀	♂	Plnts
1	4.40	11♊	28♓	3♋	11♋	6♍	♃25♐R
2	4.43	12	10♈	4	11	6	♄17♌
3	4.47	12	22	5	11R	7	♅25♊
4	4.51	13	5♉	5	11	7	♆10♎R
5	4.55	14	18	6	11	8	♇13♌
6	4.59	15	2♊	6	11	8	♃25♐R
7	5.03	16	16	6	10	8	♄18♌
8	5.07	17	0♋	7	10	9	♅25♊
9	5.11	18	14	7	10	9	♆10♎R
10	5.15	19	29	7	10	10	♇13♌
11	5.19	20	14♌	7R	9	10	♃24♐R
12	5.23	21	28	7	9	11	♄18♌
13	5.27	22	12♍	7	9	11	♅26♊
14	5.31	23	26	7	8	12	♆10♎R
15	5.35	24	10♎	6	8	12	♇13♌
16	5.39	25	24	6	7	13	♃24♐R
17	5.43	26	7♏	6	7	13	♄19♌
18	5.47	27	21	5	6	14	♅26♊
19	5.50	28	4♐	5	6	14	♆10♎
20	5.54	29	17	4	5	15	♇13♌
21	5.58	0♋	29	4	5	15	♃23♐R
22	6.02	1	12♑	3	4	16	♄19♌
23	6.06	2	24	3	3	17	♅26♊
24	6.10	3	6♒	2	3	17	♆10♎
25	6.14	4	18	1	2	18	♇13♌
26	6.18	4	0♓	1	1	18	♃22♐R
27	6.22	5	12	0	1	19	♄20♌
28	6.26	6	24	0	0	19	♅27♊
29	6.30	7	6♈	29♊	0	20	♆10♎
30	6.34	8	18	29	29♊	20	♇13♌

Jul	STime	☉	☽	☿	♀	♂	Plnts
1	6.38	9♋	0♉	29♊	29♊	21♍	♃22♐R
2	6.42	10	13	28	28	21	♄20♌
3	6.46	11	26	28	27	22	♅27♊
4	6.50	12	10♊	28	27	22	♆10♎
5	6.54	13	24	28D	27	23	♇13♌
6	6.58	14	9♋	28	26	24	♃21♐R
7	7.01	15	24	28	26	24	♄21♌
8	7.05	16	8♌	28	26	25	♅27♊
9	7.09	17	23	29	25	25	♆10♎
10	7.13	18	8♍	29	25	26	♇13♌
11	7.17	19	23	0♋	25	26	♃21♐R
12	7.21	20	7♎	0	25	27	♄21♌
13	7.25	21	21	1	24	28	♅28♊
14	7.29	22	4♏	1	24	28	♆10♎
15	7.33	23	18	2	24D	29	♇14♌
16	7.37	24	1♐	3	24	29	♃20♐R
17	7.41	24	13	4	24	0♎	♄22♌
18	7.45	25	26	5	24	0	♅28♊
19	7.49	26	8♑	6	25	1	♆10♎
20	7.53	27	21	8	25	2	♇14♌
21	7.57	28	3♒	9	25	2	♃20♐R
22	8.01	29	15	10	25	3	♄22♌
23	8.05	0♌	27	12	25	3	♅28♊
24	8.08	1	9♓	13	26	4	♆10♎
25	8.12	2	20	15	26	5	♇14♌
26	8.16	3	2♈	16	26	5	♃19♐R
27	8.20	4	14	18	27	6	♄23♌
28	8.24	5	26	20	27	6	♅28♊
29	8.28	6	9♉	22	27	7	♆10♎
30	8.32	7	21	24	28	8	♇14♌
31	8.36	8	5♊	26	28	8	♃19♐R

Aug	STime	☉	☽	☿	♀	♂	Plnts
1	8.40	9♌	18♊	28♋	29♊	9♎	♃19♐R
2	8.44	10	3♋	0♌	29	9	♄24♌
3	8.48	11	17	2	0♋	10	♅29♊
4	8.52	12	2♌	4	1	11	♆10♎
5	8.56	13	17	6	1	11	♇14♌
6	9.00	14	2♍	8	2	12	♃19♐R
7	9.04	15	18	10	2	12	♄24♌
8	9.08	16	2♎	12	3	13	♅29♊
9	9.12	16	17	14	4	14	♆11♎
10	9.15	17	1♏	16	4	14	♇14♌
11	9.19	18	14	18	5	15	♃19♐R
12	9.23	19	28	20	6	16	♄25♌
13	9.27	20	11♐	22	6	16	♅29♊
14	9.31	21	23	24	7	17	♆11♎
15	9.35	22	5♑	26	8	17	♇15♌
16	9.39	23	18	28	9	18	♃19♐
17	9.43	24	0♒	0♍	10	19	♄26♌
18	9.47	25	12	2	10	19	♅29♊
19	9.51	26	24	4	11	20	♆11♎
20	9.55	27	5♓	6	12	21	♇15♌
21	9.59	28	17	7	13	21	♃19♐
22	10.03	29	29	9	14	22	♄26♌
23	10.07	0♍	11♈	11	15	23	♅29♊
24	10.11	1	23	13	15	23	♆11♎
25	10.15	2	5♉	15	16	24	♇15♌
26	10.19	3	18	16	17	24	♃19♐
27	10.23	4	0♊	18	18	25	♄27♌
28	10.26	5	14	20	19	26	♅ 0♋
29	10.30	6	27	21	20	26	♆11♎
30	10.34	7	11♋	23	21	27	♇15♌
31	10.38	8	26	25	22	28	♃19♐

Sep	STime	☉	☽	☿	♀	♂	Plnts
1	10.42	9♍	11♌	26♍	23♋	28♎	♃19♐
2	10.46	10	26	28	24	29	♄28♌
3	10.50	11	11♍	29	25	0♏	♅ 0♋
4	10.54	12	26	1♎	26	0	♆11♎
5	10.58	13	11♎	3	27	1	♇15♌
6	11.02	13	26	4	28	2	♃19♐
7	11.06	14	10♏	6	29	2	♄28♌
8	11.10	15	24	7	0♌	3	♅ 0♋
9	11.14	16	7♐	8	1	4	♆11♎
10	11.18	17	20	10	2	4	♇15♌
11	11.22	18	2♑	11	3	5	♃20♐
12	11.26	19	15	13	4	6	♄29♌
13	11.30	20	27	14	5	6	♅ 0♋
14	11.33	21	9♒	15	6	7	♆12♎
15	11.37	22	21	17	7	8	♇15♌
16	11.41	23	2♓	18	8	8	♃20♐
17	11.45	24	14	19	9	9	♄ 0♍
18	11.49	25	26	20	10	10	♅ 0♋
19	11.53	26	8♈	22	11	10	♆12♎
20	11.57	27	20	23	12	11	♇16♌
21	12.01	28	2♉	24	13	12	♃21♐
22	12.05	29	15	25	14	12	♄ 0♍
23	12.09	0♎	27	26	15	13	♅ 0♋
24	12.13	1	10♊	27	16	14	♆12♎
25	12.17	2	23	28	17	14	♇16♌
26	12.21	3	7♋	29	19	15	♃21♐
27	12.25	4	20	0♏	20	16	♄ 1♍
28	12.29	5	5♌	1	21	17	♅ 0♋
29	12.33	6	19	2	22	17	♆12♎
30	12.37	7	4♍	2	23	18	♇16♌

Oct	STime	☉	☽	☿	♀	♂	Plnts
1	12.41	8♎	19♍	3♏	24♌	19♏	♃22♐
2	12.44	9	4♎	3	25	19	♄ 1♍
3	12.48	10	19	4	26	20	♅ 0♋
4	12.52	11	4♏	4	27	21	♆12♎
5	12.56	12	18	5	29	21	♇16♌
6	13.00	13	2♐	5	0♍	22	♃23♐
7	13.04	14	15	5	1	23	♄ 2♍
8	13.08	15	28	5R	2	24	♅ 0♋
9	13.12	16	11♑	5	3	24	♆13♎
10	13.16	17	23	5	4	25	♇16♌
11	13.20	18	5♒	4	5	26	♃23♐
12	13.24	19	17	4	7	26	♄ 2♍
13	13.28	20	29	3	8	27	♅ 0♋R
14	13.32	21	11♓	2	9	28	♆13♎
15	13.36	22	23	1	10	28	♇16♌
16	13.40	23	5♈	0	11	29	♃24♐
17	13.44	24	17	29♎	12	0♐	♄ 3♍
18	13.48	25	29	28	13	1	♅ 0♋R
19	13.51	26	12♉	27	15	1	♆13♎
20	13.55	27	24	26	16	2	♇16♌
21	13.59	28	7♊	24	17	3	♃25♐
22	14.03	29	20	23	18	3	♄ 3♍
23	14.07	0♏	3♋	22	19	4	♅ 0♋R
24	14.11	1	17	21	20	5	♆13♎
25	14.15	2	1♌	21	22	6	♇16♌
26	14.19	3	15	20	23	6	♃26♐
27	14.23	4	29	20	24	7	♄ 4♍
28	14.27	5	14♍	19D	25	8	♅ 0♋R
29	14.31	6	28	19	26	9	♆13♎
30	14.35	7	13♎	20	28	9	♇16♌
31	14.39	8	28	20	29	10	♃27♐

Nov	STime	☉	☽	☿	♀	♂	Plnts
1	14.43	9♏	12♏	21♎	0♎	11♐	♃27♐
2	14.47	10	26	21	1	11	♄ 4♍
3	14.51	11	10♐	22	2	12	♅ 0♋R
4	14.55	12	23	23	4	13	♆13♎
5	14.59	13	6♑	24	5	14	♇16♌
6	15.02	14	19	25	6	14	♃28♐
7	15.06	15	1♒	26	7	15	♄ 5♍
8	15.10	16	13	28	8	16	♅ 0♋R
9	15.14	17	25	29	10	17	♆14♎
10	15.18	18	7♓	0♏	11	17	♇16♌
11	15.22	19	19	2	12	18	♃29♐
12	15.26	20	1♈	3	13	19	♄ 5♍
13	15.30	21	13	5	14	20	♅ 0♋R
14	15.34	22	25	6	16	20	♆14♎
15	15.38	23	8♉	8	17	21	♇16♌
16	15.42	24	21	9	18	22	♃ 0♑
17	15.46	25	3♊	11	19	23	♄ 5♍
18	15.50	26	17	12	20	23	♅ 0♋R
19	15.54	27	0♋	14	22	24	♆14♎
20	15.58	28	14	15	23	25	♇16♌
21	16.02	29	28	17	24	26	♃ 1♑
22	16.06	0♐	12♌	18	25	26	♄ 5♍
23	16.09	1	26	20	27	27	♅29♊R
24	16.13	2	10♍	22	28	28	♆14♎
25	16.17	3	24	23	29	29	♇16♌
26	16.21	4	8♎	25	0♏	29	♃ 2♑
27	16.25	5	22	26	2	0♑	♄ 6♍
28	16.29	6	7♏	28	3	1	♅29♊R
29	16.33	7	21	29	4	2	♆14♎
30	16.37	8	4♐	1♐	5	2	♇16♌R

Dec	STime	☉	☽	☿	♀	♂	Plnts
1	16.41	9♐	18♐	3♐	6♏	3♑	♃ 3♑
2	16.45	10	1♑	4	8	4	♄ 6♍
3	16.49	11	14	6	9	5	♅29♊R
4	16.53	12	27	7	10	5	♆14♎
5	16.57	13	9♒	9	11	6	♇16♌R
6	17.01	14	21	10	13	7	♃ 4♑
7	17.05	15	3♓	12	14	8	♄ 6♍
8	17.09	16	15	14	15	9	♅29♊R
9	17.13	17	27	15	16	9	♆14♎
10	17.16	18	9♈	17	18	10	♇16♌R
11	17.20	19	21	18	19	11	♃ 5♑
12	17.24	20	3♉	20	20	12	♄ 6♍
13	17.28	21	16	21	21	12	♅29♊R
14	17.32	22	29	23	22	13	♆15♎
15	17.36	23	12♊	25	24	14	♇16♌R
16	17.40	24	26	26	25	15	♃ 6♑
17	17.44	25	10♋	28	26	15	♄ 6♍R
18	17.48	26	24	29	27	16	♅28♊R
19	17.52	27	8♌	1♑	29	17	♆15♎
20	17.56	28	22	3	0♐	18	♇16♌R
21	18.00	29	7♍	4	1	19	♃ 8♑
22	18.04	0♑	21	6	2	19	♄ 6♍R
23	18.08	1	5♎	7	4	20	♅28♊R
24	18.12	2	19	9	5	21	♆15♎
25	18.16	3	3♏	11	6	22	♇16♌R
26	18.20	4	16	12	7	22	♃ 9♑
27	18.24	5	0♐	14	9	23	♄ 6♍R
28	18.27	6	13	15	10	24	♅28♊R
29	18.31	7	27	17	11	25	♆15♎
30	18.35	8	10♑	19	12	26	♇16♌R
31	18.39	9	22	20	14	26	♃10♑

Jan	STime	☉	☽	☿	♀	♂	Plnts
1	18.43	10♑	5♒	22♑	15♐	27♑	♃10♑
2	18.47	11	17	23	16	28	♄ 6♍R
3	18.51	12	29	25	17	29	♅28♊R
4	18.55	14	11♓	27	19	29	♆15♎
5	18.59	15	23	28	20	0♒	♇16♌R
6	19.03	16	5♈	0♒	21	1	♃11♑
7	19.07	17	17	1	22	2	♄ 5♍R
8	19.11	18	29	3	24	3	♅27♊R
9	19.15	19	11♉	5	25	3	♆15♎
10	19.19	20	23	6	26	4	♇16♌R
11	19.23	21	6♊	8	27	5	♃12♑
12	19.27	22	20	9	29	6	♄ 5♍R
13	19.31	23	4♋	10	0♑	7	♅27♊R
14	19.34	24	18	12	1	7	♆15♎
15	19.38	25	3♌	13	2	8	♇16♌R
16	19.42	26	17	14	4	9	♃14♑
17	19.46	27	2♍	15	5	10	♄ 5♍R
18	19.50	28	17	17	6	11	♅27♊R
19	19.54	29	1♎	17	7	11	♆15♎
20	19.58	0♒	16	18	9	12	♇15♌R
21	20.02	1	0♏	19	10	13	♃15♑
22	20.06	2	13	19	11	14	♄ 5♍R
23	20.10	3	27	20	12	14	♅27♊R
24	20.14	4	10♐	20R	14	15	♆15♎R
25	20.18	5	23	20	15	16	♇15♌R
26	20.22	6	6♑	20	16	17	♃16♑
27	20.26	7	19	19	17	18	♄ 4♍R
28	20.30	8	1♒	19	19	18	♅27♊R
29	20.34	9	13	18	20	19	♆15♎R
30	20.38	10	25	17	21	20	♇15♌R
31	20.42	11	7♓	16	22	21	♃17♑

Apr	STime	☉	☽	☿	♀	♂	Plnts
1	0.38	11♈	12♉	29♓	7♈	8♈	♃28♑
2	0.42	12	25	1♈	8	9	♄ 0♍R
3	0.46	13	7♊	3	10	9	♅27♊
4	0.50	14	19	5	11	10	♆14♎R
5	0.54	15	2♋	7	12	11	♇14♌R
6	0.58	16	15	9	13	12	♃29♑
7	1.02	17	29	11	15	13	♄ 0♍R
8	1.06	18	13♌	13	16	13	♅27♊
9	1.10	19	28	15	17	14	♆13♎R
10	1.14	20	12♍	17	18	15	♇14♌R
11	1.17	21	27	19	20	16	♃ 0♒
12	1.21	22	12♎	21	21	16	♄29♌R
13	1.25	23	28	23	22	17	♅27♊
14	1.29	24	12♏	25	23	18	♆13♎R
15	1.33	25	27	27	25	19	♇14♌R
16	1.37	26	11♐	29	26	19	♃ 0♒
17	1.41	27	25	2♉	27	20	♄29♌R
18	1.45	28	8♑	4	28	21	♅27♊
19	1.49	29	21	6	29	22	♆13♎R
20	1.53	0♉	4♒	8	1♉	22	♇14♌R
21	1.57	1	16	10	2	23	♃ 1♒
22	2.01	2	28	12	3	24	♄29♌R
23	2.05	3	10♓	14	4	25	♅27♊
24	2.09	4	22	16	6	25	♆13♎R
25	2.13	5	4♈	18	7	26	♇14♌
26	2.17	6	15	20	8	27	♃ 1♒
27	2.21	7	27	22	9	28	♄29♌R
28	2.25	8	9♉	24	11	28	♅27♊
29	2.28	9	22	25	12	29	♆13♎R
30	2.32	9	4♊	27	13	0♉	♇14♌

Jul	STime	☉	☽	☿	♀	♂	Plnts
1	6.37	9♋	15♍	17♊	29♋	15♊	♃29♑R
2	6.41	10	29	19	0♌	16	♄ 2♍
3	6.45	11	13♎	20	2	16	♅ 1♋
4	6.49	12	27	21	3	17	♆12♎
5	6.53	13	11♏	23	4	18	♇15♌
6	6.57	14	25	24	5	18	♃29♑R
7	7.00	15	9♐	25	6	19	♄ 3♍
8	7.04	16	23	27	8	20	♅ 1♋
9	7.08	17	6♑	29	9	20	♆12♎
10	7.12	18	20	0♋	10	21	♇15♌
11	7.16	19	3♒	2	11	22	♃28♑R
12	7.20	19	16	4	13	22	♄ 3♍
13	7.24	20	28	6	14	23	♅ 2♋
14	7.28	21	10♓	8	15	24	♆12♎
15	7.32	22	22	10	16	24	♇15♌
16	7.36	23	4♈	11	17	25	♃27♑R
17	7.40	24	16	13	19	26	♄ 4♍
18	7.44	25	28	16	20	26	♅ 2♋
19	7.48	26	10♉	18	21	27	♆12♎
20	7.52	27	22	20	22	28	♇15♌
21	7.56	28	4♊	22	23	29	♃27♑R
22	8.00	29	17	24	25	29	♄ 4♍
23	8.04	0♌	0♋	26	26	0♋	♅ 2♋
24	8.08	1	14	28	27	1	♆12♎
25	8.11	2	28	0♌	28	1	♇15♌
26	8.15	3	12♌	2	0♍	2	♃26♑R
27	8.19	4	26	5	1	3	♄ 5♍
28	8.23	5	11♍	7	2	3	♅ 3♋
29	8.27	6	25	9	3	4	♆12♎
30	8.31	7	10♎	11	4	5	♇16♌
31	8.35	8	24	13	6	5	♃26♑R

Oct	STime	☉	☽	☿	♀	♂	Plnts
1	12.40	8♎	5♒	13♎	19♏	15♌	♃22♑
2	12.44	9	18	12	21	15	♄13♍
3	12.47	10	0♓	10	22	16	♅ 5♋
4	12.51	11	12	9	23	17	♆14♎
5	12.55	12	24	8	24	17	♇17♌
6	12.59	13	6♈	7	25	17	♃23♑
7	13.03	14	18	6	26	18	♄14♍
8	13.07	15	29	5	27	19	♅ 5♋
9	13.11	16	11♉	5	29	20	♆15♎
10	13.15	17	23	4	0♐	20	♇18♌
11	13.19	18	5♊	4	1	21	♃23♑
12	13.23	19	17	4D	2	21	♄14♍
13	13.27	20	0♋	4	3	22	♅ 5♋R
14	13.31	21	12	4	4	22	♆15♎
15	13.35	22	25	4	6	23	♇18♌
16	13.39	22	9♌	5	7	24	♃23♑
17	13.43	23	23	6	8	24	♄15♍
18	13.47	24	7♍	6	9	25	♅ 5♋
19	13.51	25	22	7	10	25	♆15♎
20	13.54	26	7♎	8	11	26	♇18♌
21	13.58	27	22	10	12	27	♃24♑
22	14.02	28	7♏	11	13	27	♄15♍
23	14.06	29	22	12	15	28	♅ 5♋R
24	14.10	0♏	7♐	14	16	28	♆15♎
25	14.14	1	21	15	17	29	♇18♌
26	14.18	2	5♑	16	18	29	♃24♑
27	14.22	3	19	18	19	0♍	♄16♍
28	14.26	4	2♒	20	20	1	♅ 5♋R
29	14.30	5	15	21	21	1	♆15♎
30	14.34	6	27	23	22	2	♇18♌
31	14.38	7	9♓	24	23	2	♃25♑

Feb	STime	☉	☽	☿	♀	♂	Plnts
1	20.45	12♒	19♓	15♒	24♑	22♒	♃17♑
2	20.49	13	1♈	14	25	22	♄ 4♍R
3	20.53	14	13	12	26	23	♅27♊R
4	20.57	15	25	11	27	24	♆15♎R
5	21.01	16	7♉	10	29	25	♇15♌R
6	21.05	17	19	9	0♒	26	♃18♑
7	21.09	18	1♊	8	1	26	♄ 4♍R
8	21.13	19	14	7	2	27	♅26♊R
9	21.17	20	28	6	4	28	♆15♎R
10	21.21	21	12♋	6	5	29	♇15♌R
11	21.25	22	26	5	6	29	♃19♑
12	21.29	23	11♌	5	7	0♓	♄ 3♍R
13	21.33	24	26	4	9	1	♅26♊R
14	21.37	25	11♍	4D	10	2	♆15♎R
15	21.41	26	26	4	11	3	♇15♌R
16	21.45	27	11♎	4	12	3	♃20♑
17	21.49	28	26	5	14	4	♄ 3♍R
18	21.52	29	10♏	5	15	5	♅26♊R
19	21.56	0♓	24	5	16	6	♆15♎R
20	22.00	1	7♐	6	17	7	♇15♌R
21	22.04	2	20	6	19	7	♃22♑
22	22.08	3	3♑	7	20	8	♄ 2♍R
23	22.12	4	16	8	21	9	♅26♊R
24	22.16	5	28	9	22	10	♆14♎R
25	22.20	6	10♒	9	24	11	♇15♌R
26	22.24	7	22	10	25	11	♃23♑
27	22.28	8	4♓	11	26	12	♄ 2♍R
28	22.32	9	16	12	27	13	♅26♊R

May	STime	☉	☽	☿	♀	♂	Plnts
1	2.36	10♉	16♊	29♉	14♉	1♉	♃ 1♒
2	2.40	11	29	0♊	16	1	♄29♌
3	2.44	12	12♋	2	17	2	♅28♊
4	2.48	13	26	3	18	3	♆13♎R
5	2.52	14	9♌	5	19	4	♇14♌
6	2.56	15	23	6	20	4	♃ 2♒
7	3.00	16	7♍	7	22	5	♄29♌
8	3.04	17	22	8	23	6	♅28♊
9	3.08	18	6♎	10	24	7	♆13♎R
10	3.12	19	21	11	25	7	♇14♌
11	3.16	20	6♏	12	27	8	♃ 2♒
12	3.20	21	21	12	28	9	♄29♌
13	3.24	22	5♐	13	29	10	♅28♊
14	3.28	23	19	14	0♊	11	♆13♎R
15	3.32	24	3♑	15	2	11	♇14♌
16	3.35	25	17	15	3	12	♃ 2♒
17	3.39	26	0♒	16	4	13	♄29♌
18	3.43	27	12	16	5	13	♅28♊
19	3.47	28	24	16	6	14	♆12♎R
20	3.51	29	6♓	17	8	15	♇14♌
21	3.55	0♊	18	17	9	16	♃ 2♒R
22	3.59	1	0♈	17	10	16	♄29♌
23	4.03	2	12	17R	11	17	♅29♊
24	4.07	3	24	17	13	18	♆12♎R
25	4.11	4	6♉	17	14	18	♇14♌
26	4.15	5	18	16	15	19	♃ 2♒R
27	4.19	6	0♊	16	16	20	♄ 0♍
28	4.23	7	13	16	18	21	♅29♊
29	4.27	7	26	15	19	21	♆12♎R
30	4.31	8	9♋	15	20	22	♇14♌
31	4.35	9	23	15	21	23	♃ 2♒R

Aug	STime	☉	☽	☿	♀	♂	Plnts
1	8.39	9♌	8♏	15♌	7♍	6♋	♃25♑R
2	8.43	10	22	17	8	7	♄ 5♍
3	8.47	11	6♐	19	9	7	♅ 3♋
4	8.51	11	19	21	10	8	♆13♎
5	8.55	12	3♑	23	11	9	♇16♌
6	8.59	13	16	24	13	9	♃25♑R
7	9.03	14	29	26	14	10	♄ 6♍
8	9.07	15	12♒	28	15	11	♅ 3♋
9	9.11	16	24	0♍	16	11	♆13♎
10	9.15	17	6♓	2	18	12	♇16♌
11	9.18	18	19	3	19	13	♃24♑R
12	9.22	19	1♈	5	20	13	♄ 7♍
13	9.26	20	12	7	21	14	♅ 3♋
14	9.30	21	24	9	22	14	♆13♎
15	9.34	22	6♉	10	24	15	♇16♌
16	9.38	23	18	12	25	16	♃24♑R
17	9.42	24	0♊	13	26	16	♄ 7♍
18	9.46	25	12	15	27	17	♅ 4♋
19	9.50	26	25	17	28	18	♆13♎
20	9.54	27	8♋	18	0♎	18	♇16♌
21	9.58	28	22	20	1	19	♃23♑R
22	10.02	29	6♌	21	2	20	♄ 8♍
23	10.06	0♍	21	23	3	20	♅ 4♋
24	10.10	1	5♍	24	4	21	♆13♎
25	10.14	2	20	25	6	22	♇16♌
26	10.18	3	5♎	27	7	22	♃23♑R
27	10.22	4	20	28	8	23	♄ 9♍
28	10.26	5	4♏	29	9	24	♅ 4♋
29	10.29	6	19	1♎	10	24	♆13♎
30	10.33	6	3♐	2	12	25	♇17♌
31	10.37	7	16	3	13	25	♃23♑R

Nov	STime	☉	☽	☿	♀	♂	Plnts
1	14.42	8♏	21♓	26♎	25♐	3♍	♃25♑
2	14.46	9	3♈	28	26	3	♄16♍
3	14.50	10	15	29	27	4	♅ 4♋R
4	14.54	11	26	1♏	28	4	♆16♎
5	14.58	12	8♉	3	29	5	♇18♌
6	15.01	13	20	4	0♑	6	♃26♑
7	15.05	14	2♊	6	1	6	♄17♍
8	15.09	15	14	7	2	7	♅ 4♋R
9	15.13	16	27	9	3	7	♆16♎
10	15.17	17	9♋	11	4	8	♇18♌
11	15.21	18	22	12	5	8	♃26♑
12	15.25	19	5♌	14	6	9	♄17♍
13	15.29	20	18	16	7	9	♅ 4♋R
14	15.33	21	2♍	17	9	10	♆16♎
15	15.37	23	16	19	10	10	♇18♌
16	15.41	24	1♎	20	11	11	♃27♑
17	15.45	25	15	22	12	11	♄18♍
18	15.49	26	0♏	24	13	12	♅ 4♋R
19	15.53	27	15	25	14	13	♆16♎
20	15.57	28	0♐	27	15	13	♇18♌
21	16.01	29	15	28	16	14	♃28♑
22	16.05	0♐	29	0♐	17	14	♄18♍
23	16.09	1	14♑	1	18	15	♅ 4♋R
24	16.12	2	27	3	19	15	♆16♎
25	16.16	3	10♒	5	20	16	♇18♌
26	16.20	4	23	6	21	16	♃29♑
27	16.24	5	6♓	8	22	17	♄18♍
28	16.28	6	18	9	23	17	♅ 4♋R
29	16.32	7	0♈	11	24	18	♆16♎
30	16.36	8	11	12	24	18	♇18♌

Mar	STime	☉	☽	☿	♀	♂	Plnts
1	22.36	10♓	28♓	13♒	29♒	14♓	♃23♑
2	22.40	11	10♈	14	0♓	14	♄ 2♍R
3	22.44	12	22	16	1	15	♅26♊
4	22.48	13	3♉	17	2	16	♆14♎R
5	22.52	14	15	18	4	17	♇14♌R
6	22.56	15	28	19	5	18	♃24♑
7	23.00	16	10♊	20	6	18	♄ 1♍R
8	23.03	17	23	22	7	19	♅26♊
9	23.07	18	6♋	23	9	20	♆14♎R
10	23.11	19	20	24	10	21	♇14♌R
11	23.15	20	4♌	26	11	22	♃25♑
12	23.19	21	19	27	12	22	♄ 1♍R
13	23.23	22	4♍	28	14	23	♅26♊
14	23.27	23	19	0♓	15	24	♆14♎R
15	23.31	24	4♎	1	16	25	♇14♌R
16	23.35	25	19	3	17	25	♃26♑
17	23.39	26	4♏	4	19	26	♄ 1♍R
18	23.43	27	19	6	20	27	♅26♊
19	23.47	28	3♐	7	21	28	♆14♎R
20	23.51	29	16	9	22	29	♇14♌R
21	23.55	0♈	0♑	10	23	29	♃27♑
22	23.59	1	12	12	25	0♈	♄ 0♍R
23	0.03	2	25	14	26	1	♅26♊
24	0.07	3	7♒	15	27	2	♆14♎R
25	0.10	4	19	17	28	2	♇14♌R
26	0.14	5	1♓	19	0♈	3	♃27♑
27	0.18	6	13	20	1	4	♄ 0♍R
28	0.22	7	25	22	2	5	♅26♊
29	0.26	8	7♈	24	3	6	♆14♎R
30	0.30	9	19	26	5	6	♇14♌R
31	0.34	10	0♉	28	6	7	♃28♑

Jun	STime	☉	☽	☿	♀	♂	Plnts
1	4.39	10♊	6♌	14♊	22♊	24♉	♃ 2♒R
2	4.43	11	20	13	24	24	♄ 0♍
3	4.46	12	4♍	13	25	25	♅29♊
4	4.50	13	18	12	26	26	♆12♎R
5	4.54	14	2♎	12	27	26	♇14♌
6	4.58	15	16	12	29	27	♃ 1♒R
7	5.02	16	1♏	11	0♋	28	♄ 0♍
8	5.06	17	15	10	1	29	♅ 0♋
9	5.10	18	29	10	2	29	♆12♎R
10	5.14	19	14♐	9	3	0♊	♇14♌
11	5.18	20	28	9	5	1	♃ 1♒R
12	5.22	21	11♑	9	6	1	♄ 1♍
13	5.26	22	25	9	7	2	♅ 0♋
14	5.30	23	8♒	8	8	3	♆12♎R
15	5.34	24	20	8D	10	4	♇14♌
16	5.38	25	2♓	8	11	4	♃ 1♒R
17	5.42	26	14	8	12	5	♄ 1♍
18	5.46	27	26	9	13	6	♅ 0♋
19	5.50	28	8♈	9	14	6	♆12♎
20	5.53	29	20	9	16	7	♇15♌
21	5.57	29	2♉	10	17	8	♃ 0♒R
22	6.01	0♋	14	10	18	9	♄ 1♍
23	6.05	1	26	11	19	9	♅ 0♋
24	6.09	2	9♊	11	21	10	♆12♎
25	6.13	3	22	12	22	11	♇15♌
26	6.17	4	5♋	13	23	11	♃ 0♒R
27	6.21	5	19	13	24	12	♄ 2♍
28	6.25	6	3♌	14	25	13	♅ 1♋
29	6.29	7	17	15	27	13	♆12♎
30	6.33	8	1♍	16	28	14	♇15♌

Sep	STime	☉	☽	☿	♀	♂	Plnts
1	10.41	8♍	0♑	5♎	14♎	26♋	♃23♑R
2	10.45	9	13	6	15	27	♄ 9♍
3	10.49	10	26	7	16	27	♅ 4♋
4	10.53	11	8♒	8	18	28	♆13♎
5	10.57	12	21	9	19	29	♇17♌
6	11.01	13	3♓	10	20	29	♃22♑R
7	11.05	14	15	11	21	0♌	♄10♍
8	11.09	15	27	12	22	1	♅ 4♋
9	11.13	16	9♈	13	24	1	♆14♎
10	11.17	17	21	14	25	2	♇17♌
11	11.21	18	3♉	15	26	2	♃22♑R
12	11.25	19	14	15	27	3	♄11♍
13	11.29	20	26	16	28	4	♅ 4♋
14	11.33	21	8♊	17	29	4	♆14♎
15	11.36	22	21	17	1♏	5	♇17♌
16	11.40	23	4♋	18	2	6	♃22♑R
17	11.44	24	17	18	3	6	♄11♍
18	11.48	25	0♌	18	4	7	♅ 4♋
19	11.52	26	14	19	5	7	♆14♎
20	11.56	27	29	19	7	8	♇17♌
21	12.00	28	14♍	19R	8	9	♃22♑
22	12.04	29	29	19	9	9	♄12♍
23	12.08	0♎	14♎	19	10	10	♅ 5♋
24	12.12	1	29	18	11	10	♆14♎
25	12.16	2	14♏	18	12	11	♇17♌
26	12.20	3	28	17	14	12	♃22♑
27	12.24	4	12♐	16	15	12	♄12♍
28	12.28	5	26	16	16	13	♅ 5♋
29	12.32	6	10♑	15	17	14	♆14♎
30	12.36	7	23	14	18	14	♇17♌

Dec	STime	☉	☽	☿	♀	♂	Plnts
1	16.40	9♐	23♈	14♐	25♑	19♍	♃ 0♒
2	16.44	10	5♉	16	26	19	♄18♍
3	16.48	11	17	17	27	20	♅ 4♋R
4	16.52	12	29	19	28	20	♆16♎
5	16.56	13	11♊	20	29	21	♇18♌R
6	17.00	14	24	22	0♒	21	♃ 1♒
7	17.04	15	6♋	23	1	22	♄19♍
8	17.08	16	19	25	2	22	♅ 3♋R
9	17.12	17	2♌	26	2	22	♆17♎
10	17.16	18	15	28	3	23	♇18♌R
11	17.19	19	29	0♑	4	23	♃ 2♒
12	17.23	20	12♍	1	5	24	♄19♍
13	17.27	21	26	3	6	24	♅ 3♋R
14	17.31	22	10♎	4	6	25	♆17♎
15	17.35	23	25	6	7	25	♇18♌R
16	17.39	24	9♏	7	8	26	♃ 3♒
17	17.43	25	24	9	9	26	♄19♍
18	17.47	26	9♐	10	9	26	♅ 3♋R
19	17.51	27	23	12	10	27	♆17♎
20	17.55	28	7♑	13	11	27	♇18♌R
21	17.59	29	21	15	11	28	♃ 4♒
22	18.03	0♑	5♒	16	12	28	♄19♍
23	18.07	1	18	18	13	29	♅ 3♋R
24	18.11	2	1♓	19	13	29	♆17♎
25	18.15	3	14	21	14	29	♇18♌R
26	18.19	4	26	22	14	0♎	♃ 5♒
27	18.23	5	8♈	24	15	0	♄19♍
28	18.27	6	19	25	15	1	♅ 3♋R
29	18.30	7	1♉	26	16	1	♆17♎
30	18.34	8	13	27	16	1	♇18♌R
31	18.38	9	25	29	16	2	♃ 6♒

Jan	STime	☉	☽	☿	♀	♂	Plnts
1	18.42	10♑	7♊	0♒	17♒	2♎	♃ 6♒
2	18.46	11	20	1	17	2	♄19♍R
3	18.50	12	2♋	2	17	3	♅ 2♋R
4	18.54	13	15	2	18	3	♆17♎
5	18.58	14	29	3	18	4	♇17♌R
6	19.02	15	12♌	3	18	4	♃ 7♒
7	19.06	16	26	4	18	4	♄19♍R
8	19.10	17	9♍	4R	18	5	♅ 2♋R
9	19.14	18	23	4	18	5	♆17♎
10	19.18	19	7♎	4	18R	5	♇17♌R
11	19.22	20	21	3	18	5	♃ 9♒
12	19.26	21	5♏	2	18	6	♄19♍R
13	19.30	22	19	2	18	6	♅ 2♋R
14	19.34	23	4♐	1	18	6	♆17♎
15	19.37	24	18	29♑	18	7	♇17♌R
16	19.41	25	2♑	28	18	7	♃10♒
17	19.45	27	16	27	17	7	♄19♍R
18	19.49	28	0♒	26	17	7	♅ 2♋R
19	19.53	29	13	24	17	8	♆17♎
20	19.57	0♒	26	23	16	8	♇17♌R
21	20.01	1	9♓	22	16	8	♃11♒
22	20.05	2	21	21	16	8	♄19♍R
23	20.09	3	3♈	20	15	9	♅ 1♋R
24	20.13	4	15	19	15	9	♆17♎R
25	20.17	5	27	19	14	9	♇17♌R
26	20.21	6	9♉	18	13	9	♃12♒
27	20.25	7	21	18	13	9	♄18♍R
28	20.29	8	3♊	18	12	9	♅ 1♋R
29	20.33	9	15	18D	12	10	♆17♎
30	20.37	10	28	18	11	10	♇17♌R
31	20.41	11	11♋	18	10	10	♃13♒

Feb	STime	☉	☽	☿	♀	♂	Plnts
1	20.44	12♒	24♋	18♑	10♒	10♎	♃14♒
2	20.48	13	7♌	19	9	10	♄18♍R
3	20.52	14	21	19	9	10	♅ 1♋R
4	20.56	15	5♍	20	8	10	♆17♎R
5	21.00	16	19	21	7	10	♇17♌R
6	21.04	17	4♎	21	7	11	♃15♒
7	21.08	18	18	22	6	11	♄18♍R
8	21.12	19	2♏	23	6	11	♅ 1♋R
9	21.16	20	16	24	5	11	♆17♎R
10	21.20	21	0♐	25	5	11	♇17♌R
11	21.24	22	14	26	5	11	♃16♒
12	21.28	23	28	27	4	11R	♄17♍R
13	21.32	24	12♑	28	4	11	♅ 1♋R
14	21.36	25	25	29	4	11	♆17♎R
15	21.40	26	9♒	1♒	3	11	♇16♌R
16	21.44	27	22	2	3	11	♃17♒
17	21.48	28	4♓	3	3	11	♄17♍R
18	21.52	29	17	4	3	10	♅ 1♋R
19	21.55	0♓	29	6	3	10	♆17♎R
20	21.59	1	11♈	7	3D	10	♇16♌R
21	22.03	2	23	8	3	10	♃18♒
22	22.07	3	5♉	10	3	10	♄17♍R
23	22.11	4	17	11	3	10	♅ 1♋R
24	22.15	5	29	12	3	10	♆17♎R
25	22.19	6	11♊	14	3	10	♇16♌R
26	22.23	7	23	15	3	9	♃19♒
27	22.27	8	5♋	17	4	9	♄16♍R
28	22.31	9	18	18	4	9	♅ 1♋R

Mar	STime	☉	☽	☿	♀	♂	Plnts
1	22.35	10♓	2♌	20♒	4♒	9♎	♃20♒
2	22.39	11	15	21	5	9	♄16♍R
3	22.43	12	29	23	5	8	♅ 1♋
4	22.47	13	14♍	24	5	8	♆17♎R
5	22.51	14	28	26	6	8	♇16♌R
6	22.55	15	13♎	27	6	8	♃21♒
7	22.59	16	28	29	7	7	♄16♍R
8	23.02	17	13♏	1♓	7	7	♅ 1♋
9	23.06	18	27	2	8	7	♆16♎R
10	23.10	19	11♐	4	8	6	♇16♌R
11	23.14	20	25	6	9	6	♃22♒
12	23.18	21	9♑	7	9	6	♄15♍R
13	23.22	22	22	9	10	5	♅ 1♋
14	23.26	23	5♒	11	11	5	♆16♎R
15	23.30	24	18	13	11	5	♇16♌R
16	23.34	25	1♓	14	12	4	♃24♒
17	23.38	26	13	16	13	4	♄15♍R
18	23.42	27	25	18	13	4	♅ 1♋
19	23.46	28	8♈	20	14	3	♆16♎R
20	23.50	29	20	22	15	3	♇16♌R
21	23.54	0♈	1♉	24	16	2	♃25♒
22	23.58	1	13	26	17	2	♄15♍R
23	0.02	2	25	27	17	2	♅ 1♋
24	0.06	3	7♊	29	18	1	♆16♎R
25	0.10	4	19	1♈	19	1	♇16♌R
26	0.13	5	1♋	3	20	0	♃26♒
27	0.17	6	14	5	21	0	♄14♍R
28	0.21	7	26	7	21	0	♅ 1♋
29	0.25	8	10♌	9	22	29♍	♆16♎R
30	0.29	9	23	11	23	29	♇16♌R
31	0.33	10	7♍	13	24	29	♃27♒

Apr	STime	☉	☽	☿	♀	♂	Plnts
1	0.37	11♈	22♍	16♈	25♒	28♍	♃27♒
2	0.41	12	7♎	18	26	28	♄14♍R
3	0.45	13	22	20	27	27	♅ 1♋
4	0.49	14	7♏	22	28	27	♆16♎R
5	0.53	15	22	24	29	27	♇16♌R
6	0.57	16	7♐	26	0♓	26	♃28♒
7	1.01	17	21	28	1	26	♄13♍R
8	1.05	18	5♑	0♉	1	26	♅ 1♋
9	1.09	19	19	2	2	25	♆16♎R
10	1.13	20	2♒	4	3	25	♇16♌R
11	1.17	21	15	5	4	25	♃29♒
12	1.20	22	28	7	5	25	♄13♍R
13	1.24	23	10♓	9	6	24	♅ 1♋
14	1.28	24	22	11	7	24	♆15♎R
15	1.32	25	4♈	12	8	24	♇16♌R
16	1.36	26	16	14	9	24	♃ 0♓
17	1.40	27	28	15	10	23	♄13♍R
18	1.44	28	10♉	17	11	23	♅ 1♋
19	1.48	29	22	18	12	23	♆15♎R
20	1.52	0♉	4♊	19	13	23	♇15♌
21	1.56	1	16	20	14	23	♃ 1♓
22	2.00	1	28	22	16	23	♄13♍R
23	2.04	2	10♋	22	17	22	♅ 2♋
24	2.08	3	22	23	18	22	♆15♎R
25	2.12	4	5♌	24	19	22	♇15♌
26	2.16	5	18	25	20	22	♃ 2♓
27	2.20	6	2♍	25	21	22	♄13♍R
28	2.24	7	16	26	22	22	♅ 2♋
29	2.27	8	0♎	26	23	22	♆15♎R
30	2.31	9	15	27	24	22	♇15♌

May	STime	☉	☽	☿	♀	♂	Plnts
1	2.35	10♉	0♏	27♉	25♓	22♍	♃ 2♓
2	2.39	11	15	27	26	22D	♄12♍R
3	2.43	12	0♐	27R	27	22	♅ 2♋
4	2.47	13	15	27	28	22	♆15♎R
5	2.51	14	0♑	27	29	22	♇15♌
6	2.55	15	14	27	0♈	22	♃ 3♓
7	2.59	16	28	27	2	22	♄12♍R
8	3.03	17	12♒	26	3	22	♅ 2♋
9	3.07	18	25	26	4	22	♆15♎R
10	3.11	19	7♓	25	5	22	♇16♌
11	3.15	20	19	25	6	22	♃ 4♓
12	3.19	21	2♈	24	7	22	♄12♍R
13	3.23	22	13	24	8	22	♅ 2♋
14	3.27	23	25	23	9	22	♆15♎R
15	3.31	24	7♉	23	10	23	♇16♌
16	3.35	25	19	22	12	23	♃ 5♓
17	3.38	26	1♊	21	13	23	♄12♍
18	3.42	27	13	21	14	23	♅ 3♋
19	3.46	28	25	20	15	23	♆15♎R
20	3.50	29	7♋	20	16	23	♇16♌
21	3.54	0♊	19	19	17	24	♃ 5♓
22	3.58	1	2♌	19	18	24	♄12♍
23	4.02	1	14	19	19	24	♅ 3♋
24	4.06	2	28	19	20	24	♆15♎R
25	4.10	3	11♍	18	22	24	♇16♌
26	4.14	4	25	18	23	25	♃ 6♓
27	4.18	5	9♎	18D	24	25	♄12♍
28	4.22	6	24	18	25	25	♅ 3♋
29	4.26	7	8♏	18	26	25	♆14♎R
30	4.30	8	24	19	27	26	♇16♌
31	4.34	9	9♐	19	28	26	♃ 6♓

Jun	STime	☉	☽	☿	♀	♂	Plnts
1	4.38	10♊	24♐	19♉	0♉	26♍	♃ 6♓
2	4.42	11	9♑	20	1	27	♄13♍
3	4.45	12	23	20	2	27	♅ 3♋
4	4.49	13	7♒	21	3	27	♆14♎R
5	4.53	14	20	21	4	28	♇16♌
6	4.57	15	3♓	22	5	28	♃ 6♓
7	5.01	16	16	23	6	28	♄13♍
8	5.05	17	28	23	8	29	♅ 4♋
9	5.09	18	10♈	24	9	29	♆14♎R
10	5.13	19	22	25	10	29	♇16♌
11	5.17	20	4♉	26	11	0♎	♃ 7♓
12	5.21	21	16	27	12	0	♄13♍
13	5.25	22	28	28	13	0	♅ 4♋
14	5.29	23	10♊	0♊	15	1	♆14♎
15	5.33	24	22	1	16	1	♇16♌
16	5.37	24	4♋	2	17	1	♃ 7♓
17	5.41	25	16	3	18	2	♄13♍
18	5.45	26	29	5	19	2	♅ 4♋
19	5.49	27	12♌	6	20	3	♆14♎
20	5.53	28	24	8	22	3	♇16♌
21	5.56	29	8♍	9	23	4	♃ 7♓
22	6.00	0♋	21	11	24	4	♄14♍
23	6.04	1	5♎	13	25	4	♅ 5♋
24	6.08	2	19	14	26	5	♆14♎
25	6.12	3	3♏	16	27	5	♇16♌
26	6.16	4	18	18	29	6	♃ 7♓
27	6.20	5	3♐	20	0♊	6	♄14♍
28	6.24	6	17	21	1	7	♅ 5♋
29	6.28	7	2♑	23	2	7	♆14♎
30	6.32	8	17	25	3	7	♇16♌

Jul	STime	☉	☽	☿	♀	♂	Plnts
1	6.36	9♋	1♒	27♊	4♊	8♎	♃ 7♓R
2	6.40	10	15	29	6	8	♄14♍
3	6.44	11	29	2♋	7	9	♅ 5♋
4	6.48	12	12♓	4	8	9	♆14♎
5	6.52	13	24	6	9	10	♇16♌
6	6.56	14	7♈	8	10	10	♃ 7♓R
7	7.00	14	19	10	12	11	♄15♍
8	7.03	15	1♉	12	13	11	♅ 6♋
9	7.07	16	12	14	14	12	♆14♎
10	7.11	17	24	17	15	12	♇17♌
11	7.15	18	6♊	19	16	13	♃ 7♓R
12	7.19	19	18	21	17	13	♄15♍
13	7.23	20	0♋	23	19	14	♅ 6♋
14	7.27	21	13	25	20	14	♆14♎
15	7.31	22	25	27	21	15	♇17♌
16	7.35	23	8♌	29	22	15	♃ 7♓R
17	7.39	24	21	1♌	23	16	♄15♍
18	7.43	25	5♍	3	25	17	♅ 6♋
19	7.47	26	18	5	26	17	♆14♎
20	7.51	27	2♎	7	27	18	♇17♌
21	7.55	28	15	9	28	18	♃ 6♓R
22	7.59	29	29	11	29	19	♄16♍
23	8.03	0♌	14♏	13	1♋	19	♅ 6♋
24	8.07	1	28	15	2	20	♆14♎
25	8.11	2	12♐	17	3	20	♇17♌
26	8.14	3	27	19	4	21	♃ 6♓R
27	8.18	4	11♑	20	5	21	♄16♍
28	8.22	5	26	22	7	22	♅ 7♋
29	8.26	5	10♒	24	8	23	♆15♎
30	8.30	6	23	25	9	23	♇17♌
31	8.34	7	7♓	27	10	24	♃ 5♓R

Aug	STime	☉	☽	☿	♀	♂	Plnts
1	8.38	8♌	20♓	29♌	11♋	24♎	♃ 5♓R
2	8.42	9	2♈	0♍	13	25	♄17♍
3	8.46	10	15	2	14	25	♅ 7♋
4	8.50	11	27	3	15	26	♆15♎
5	8.54	12	9♉	5	16	27	♇17♌
6	8.58	13	20	6	17	27	♃ 5♓R
7	9.02	14	2♊	8	19	28	♄18♍
8	9.06	15	14	9	20	28	♅ 7♋
9	9.10	16	26	11	21	29	♆15♎
10	9.14	17	9♋	12	22	0♏	♇18♌
11	9.18	18	21	13	24	0	♃ 4♓R
12	9.21	19	4♌	15	25	1	♄18♍
13	9.25	20	17	16	26	1	♅ 8♋
14	9.29	21	1♍	17	27	2	♆15♎
15	9.33	22	14	18	28	3	♇18♌
16	9.37	23	28	20	0♌	3	♃ 3♓R
17	9.41	24	12♎	21	1	4	♄19♍
18	9.45	25	26	22	2	4	♅ 8♋
19	9.49	26	10♏	23	3	5	♆15♎
20	9.53	27	25	24	4	6	♇18♌
21	9.57	28	9♐	25	6	6	♃ 3♓R
22	10.01	29	23	26	7	7	♄19♍
23	10.05	29	7♑	27	8	8	♅ 8♋
24	10.09	0♍	21	28	9	8	♆15♎
25	10.13	1	5♒	28	11	9	♇18♌
26	10.17	2	19	29	12	9	♃ 2♓R
27	10.21	3	2♓	0♎	13	10	♄20♍
28	10.25	4	15	0	14	11	♅ 8♋
29	10.28	5	28	1	15	11	♆15♎
30	10.32	6	10♈	1	17	12	♇18♌
31	10.36	7	22	2	18	13	♃ 1♓R

Sep	STime	☉	☽	☿	♀	♂	Plnts
1	10.40	8♍	5♉	2♎	19♌	13♏	♃ 1♓R
2	10.44	9	16	2	20	14	♄21♍
3	10.48	10	28	2	22	15	♅ 8♋
4	10.52	11	10♊	2R	23	15	♆16♎
5	10.56	12	22	2	24	16	♇18♌
6	11.00	13	4♋	2	25	17	♃ 1♓R
7	11.04	14	17	2	27	17	♄21♍
8	11.08	15	29	1	28	18	♅ 9♋
9	11.12	16	12♌	1	29	19	♆16♎
10	11.16	17	26	0	0♍	19	♇18♌
11	11.20	18	9♍	29♍	1	20	♃ 0♓R
12	11.24	19	23	28	3	21	♄22♍
13	11.28	20	8♎	27	4	21	♅ 9♋
14	11.32	21	22	26	5	22	♆16♎
15	11.36	22	7♏	25	6	23	♇19♌
16	11.39	23	21	24	8	23	♃ 0♓R
17	11.43	24	6♐	23	9	24	♄23♍
18	11.47	25	20	22	10	25	♅ 9♋
19	11.51	26	4♑	21	11	25	♆16♎
20	11.55	27	18	20	13	26	♇19♌
21	11.59	28	1♒	20	14	27	♃29♒R
22	12.03	29	15	19	15	27	♄23♍
23	12.07	0♎	28	18	16	28	♅ 9♋
24	12.11	1	11♓	18	18	29	♆16♎
25	12.15	2	24	18	19	29	♇19♌
26	12.19	3	6♈	18D	20	0♐	♃29♒R
27	12.23	4	18	18	21	1	♄24♍
28	12.27	4	1♉	18	23	2	♅ 9♋
29	12.31	5	13	18	24	2	♆16♎
30	12.35	6	25	19	25	3	♇19♌

Oct	STime	☉	☽	☿	♀	♂	Plnts
1	12.39	7♎	6♊	20♍	26♍	4♐	♃28♒R
2	12.43	8	18	21	28	4	♄24♍
3	12.46	9	0♋	22	29	5	♅ 9♋
4	12.50	10	12	23	0♎	6	♆17♎
5	12.54	11	25	24	1	6	♇19♌
6	12.58	12	7♌	25	3	7	♃28♒R
7	13.02	13	20	27	4	8	♄25♍
8	13.06	14	4♍	28	5	9	♅ 9♋
9	13.10	15	18	0♎	6	9	♆17♎
10	13.14	16	2♎	1	8	10	♇19♌
11	13.18	17	16	3	9	11	♃28♒R
12	13.22	18	1♏	4	10	11	♄26♍
13	13.26	19	16	6	11	12	♅ 9♋
14	13.30	20	1♐	8	13	13	♆17♎
15	13.34	21	16	9	14	14	♇19♌
16	13.38	22	0♑	11	15	14	♃27♒R
17	13.42	23	15	13	16	15	♄26♍
18	13.46	24	28	14	18	16	♅ 9♋R
19	13.50	25	12♒	16	19	17	♆17♎
20	13.54	26	25	18	20	17	♇19♌
21	13.57	27	8♓	20	21	18	♃27♒R
22	14.01	28	20	21	23	19	♄27♍
23	14.05	29	3♈	23	24	19	♅ 9♋
24	14.09	0♏	15	25	25	20	♆17♎
25	14.13	1	27	26	26	21	♇19♌
26	14.17	2	9♉	28	28	22	♃27♒
27	14.21	3	21	0♏	29	22	♄27♍
28	14.25	4	3♊	1	0♏	23	♅ 9♋R
29	14.29	5	15	3	1	24	♆17♎
30	14.33	6	27	5	3	25	♇19♌
31	14.37	7	9♋	6	4	25	♃27♒

Nov	STime	☉	☽	☿	♀	♂	Plnts
1	14.41	8♏	21♋	8♏	5♏	26♐	♃27♒
2	14.45	9	3♌	10	6	27	♄28♍
3	14.49	10	16	11	8	28	♅ 9♋R
4	14.53	11	28	13	9	28	♆18♎
5	14.57	12	12♍	15	10	29	♇20♌
6	15.01	13	25	16	11	0♑	♃28♒
7	15.04	14	10♎	18	13	1	♄28♍
8	15.08	15	24	19	14	1	♅ 9♋R
9	15.12	16	9♏	21	15	2	♆18♎
10	15.16	17	25	22	16	3	♇20♌
11	15.20	18	10♐	24	18	4	♃28♒
12	15.24	19	25	26	19	4	♄29♍
13	15.28	20	10♑	27	20	5	♅ 9♋R
14	15.32	21	24	29	21	6	♆18♎
15	15.36	22	8♒	0♐	23	7	♇20♌
16	15.40	23	22	2	24	7	♃28♒
17	15.44	24	5♓	3	25	8	♄29♍
18	15.48	25	17	5	26	9	♅ 9♋R
19	15.52	26	0♈	6	28	10	♆18♎
20	15.56	27	12	8	29	10	♇20♌
21	16.00	28	24	9	0♐	11	♃29♒
22	16.04	29	6♉	11	1	12	♄ 0♎
23	16.08	0♐	18	13	3	13	♅ 9♋R
24	16.12	1	0♊	14	4	14	♆18♎
25	16.15	2	12	16	5	14	♇20♌
26	16.19	3	24	17	6	15	♃29♒
27	16.23	4	6♋	19	8	16	♄ 0♎
28	16.27	5	18	20	9	17	♅ 8♋R
29	16.31	6	0♌	22	10	17	♆18♎
30	16.35	7	12	23	11	18	♇20♌

Dec	STime	☉	☽	☿	♀	♂	Plnts
1	16.39	8♐	24♌	25♐	13♐	19♑	♃ 0♓
2	16.43	9	7♍	26	14	20	♄ 1♎
3	16.47	10	20	27	15	20	♅ 8♋R
4	16.51	11	4♎	29	17	21	♆19♎
5	16.55	12	18	0♑	18	22	♇20♌R
6	16.59	14	3♏	2	19	23	♃ 0♓
7	17.03	15	18	3	20	24	♄ 1♎
8	17.07	16	3♐	4	22	24	♅ 8♋R
9	17.11	17	18	6	23	25	♆19♎
10	17.15	18	3♑	7	24	26	♇19♌R
11	17.19	19	18	8	25	27	♃ 1♓
12	17.22	20	3♒	10	27	27	♄ 1♎
13	17.26	21	17	11	28	28	♅ 8♋R
14	17.30	22	1♓	12	29	29	♆19♎
15	17.34	23	14	13	0♑	0♒	♇19♌R
16	17.38	24	27	14	2	1	♃ 2♓
17	17.42	25	9♈	15	3	1	♄ 1♎
18	17.46	26	21	16	4	2	♅ 8♋R
19	17.50	27	3♉	16	5	3	♆19♎
20	17.54	28	15	17	7	4	♇19♌R
21	17.58	29	27	17	8	4	♃ 3♓
22	18.02	0♑	9♊	18	9	5	♄ 2♎
23	18.06	1	21	18R	10	6	♅ 7♋R
24	18.10	2	3♋	18	12	7	♆19♎
25	18.14	3	15	18	13	8	♇19♌R
26	18.18	4	27	17	14	8	♃ 3♓
27	18.22	5	9♌	16	15	9	♄ 2♎
28	18.26	6	21	16	17	10	♅ 7♋R
29	18.29	7	4♍	15	18	11	♆19♎
30	18.33	8	17	13	19	12	♇19♌R
31	18.37	9	0♎	12	20	12	♃ 4♓

Jan	STime	☉	☽	☿	♀	♂	Plnts
1	18.41	10♑	14♎	11♑	22♑	13♒	♃ 4♓
2	18.45	11	27	9	23	14	♄ 2♎
3	18.49	12	12♏	8	24	15	♅ 7♋R
4	18.53	13	26	7	25	15	♆19♎
5	18.57	14	11♐	6	27	16	♇19♌R
6	19.01	15	26	5	28	17	♃ 5♓
7	19.05	16	11♑	4	29	18	♄ 2♎
8	19.09	17	26	3	0♒	19	♅ 7♋R
9	19.13	18	11♒	2	2	19	♆19♎
10	19.17	19	25	2	3	20	♇19♌R
11	19.21	20	9♓	2	4	21	♃ 6♓
12	19.25	21	22	2D	5	22	♄ 2♎
13	19.29	22	5♈	2	7	23	♅ 7♋R
14	19.33	23	17	2	8	23	♆19♎
15	19.37	24	0♉	2	9	24	♇19♌R
16	19.40	25	12	3	11	25	♃ 7♓
17	19.44	26	23	3	12	26	♄ 2♎R
18	19.48	27	5♊	4	13	27	♅ 6♋R
19	19.52	28	17	4	14	27	♆19♎
20	19.56	29	29	5	16	28	♇19♌R
21	20.00	0♒	11♋	6	17	29	♃ 9♓
22	20.04	1	23	7	18	0♓	♄ 2♎R
23	20.08	2	6♌	8	19	0	♅ 6♋R
24	20.12	3	18	9	21	1	♆19♎
25	20.16	4	1♍	10	22	2	♇19♌R
26	20.20	5	14	11	23	3	♃10♓
27	20.24	6	27	12	24	4	♄ 2♎R
28	20.28	7	10♎	13	26	4	♅ 6♋R
29	20.32	8	24	15	27	5	♆19♎R
30	20.36	9	8♏	16	28	6	♇19♌R
31	20.40	11	22	17	29	7	♃11♓

Feb	STime	☉	☽	☿	♀	♂	Plnts
1	20.44	12♒	6♐	18♑	1♓	8♓	♃11♓
2	20.47	13	21	20	2	8	♄ 2♎R
3	20.51	14	5♑	21	3	9	♅ 6♋R
4	20.55	15	20	22	4	10	♆19♎R
5	20.59	16	4♒	24	6	11	♇18♌R
6	21.03	17	19	25	7	11	♃12♓
7	21.07	18	3♓	26	8	12	♄ 1♎R
8	21.11	19	17	28	9	13	♅ 6♋R
9	21.15	20	0♈	29	10	14	♆19♎R
10	21.19	21	13	1♒	12	15	♇18♌R
11	21.23	22	25	2	13	15	♃13♓
12	21.27	23	8♉	4	14	16	♄ 1♎R
13	21.31	24	20	5	15	17	♅ 5♋R
14	21.35	25	1♊	7	17	18	♆19♎R
15	21.39	26	13	8	18	18	♇18♌R
16	21.43	27	25	10	19	19	♃14♓
17	21.47	28	7♋	11	20	20	♄ 1♎R
18	21.51	29	19	13	22	21	♅ 5♋R
19	21.55	0♓	2♌	15	23	22	♆19♎R
20	21.58	1	14	16	24	22	♇18♌R
21	22.02	2	27	18	25	23	♃16♓
22	22.06	3	10♍	19	27	24	♄ 1♎R
23	22.10	4	24	21	28	25	♅ 5♋R
24	22.14	5	7♎	23	29	25	♆19♎R
25	22.18	6	21	24	0♈	26	♇18♌R
26	22.22	7	5♏	26	2	27	♃17♓
27	22.26	8	19	28	3	28	♄ 0♎R
28	22.30	9	3♐	0♓	4	29	♅ 5♋R

Mar	STime	☉	☽	☿	♀	♂	Plnts
1	22.34	10♓	17♐	1♓	5♈	29♓	♃18♓
2	22.38	11	1♑	3	7	0♈	♄ 0♎R
3	22.42	12	15	5	8	1	♅ 5♋R
4	22.46	13	0♒	7	9	2	♆19♎R
5	22.50	14	14	9	10	2	♇18♌R
6	22.54	15	28	10	11	3	♃19♓
7	22.58	16	11♓	12	13	4	♄ 0♎R
8	23.02	17	25	14	14	5	♅ 5♋R
9	23.05	18	8♈	16	15	6	♆19♎R
10	23.09	19	20	18	16	6	♇18♌R
11	23.13	20	3♉	20	18	7	♃20♓
12	23.17	21	15	22	19	8	♄29♍R
13	23.21	22	27	24	20	9	♅ 5♋
14	23.25	23	9♊	26	21	9	♆19♎R
15	23.29	24	21	28	22	10	♇18♌R
16	23.33	25	3♋	0♈	24	11	♃21♓
17	23.37	26	15	2	25	12	♄29♍R
18	23.41	27	27	4	26	12	♅ 5♋
19	23.45	28	10♌	6	27	13	♆18♎R
20	23.49	29	22	8	29	14	♇17♌R
21	23.53	0♈	5♍	10	0♉	15	♃22♓
22	23.57	1	19	12	1	15	♄29♍R
23	0.01	2	2♎	14	2	16	♅ 5♋
24	0.05	3	16	15	3	17	♆18♎R
25	0.09	4	1♏	17	5	18	♇17♌R
26	0.12	5	15	19	6	19	♃24♓
27	0.16	6	29	21	7	19	♄28♍R
28	0.20	7	14♐	23	8	20	♅ 5♋
29	0.24	8	28	24	9	21	♆18♎R
30	0.28	9	12♑	26	11	22	♇17♌R
31	0.32	10	26	27	12	22	♃25♓

Apr	STime	☉	☽	☿	♀	♂	Plnts
1	0.36	11♈	10♒	29♈	13♉	23♈	♃25♓
2	0.40	12	24	0♉	14	24	♄28♍R
3	0.44	13	7♓	1	16	25	♅ 5♋
4	0.48	14	20	3	17	25	♆18♎R
5	0.52	15	3♈	4	18	26	♇17♌R
6	0.56	16	16	5	19	27	♃26♓
7	1.00	17	29	5	20	28	♄27♍R
8	1.04	18	11♉	6	22	28	♅ 5♋
9	1.08	19	23	7	23	29	♆18♎R
10	1.12	20	5♊	7	24	0♉	♇17♌
11	1.16	20	17	8	25	1	♃27♓
12	1.20	21	29	8	26	1	♄27♍R
13	1.23	22	11♋	8	27	2	♅ 6♋
14	1.27	23	23	8R	29	3	♆18♎R
15	1.31	24	5♌	8	0♊	3	♇17♌R
16	1.35	25	17	8	1	4	♃29♓
17	1.39	26	0♍	8	2	5	♄27♍R
18	1.43	27	13	8	3	6	♅ 6♋
19	1.47	28	27	7	5	6	♆18♎R
20	1.51	29	11♎	7	6	7	♇17♌R
21	1.55	0♉	25	6	7	8	♃ 0♈
22	1.59	1	10♏	6	8	9	♄26♍R
23	2.03	2	24	5	9	9	♅ 6♋
24	2.07	3	9♐	4	10	10	♆17♎R
25	2.11	4	24	4	12	11	♇17♌
26	2.15	5	9♑	3	13	12	♃ 1♈
27	2.19	6	23	2	14	12	♄26♍R
28	2.23	7	7♒	2	15	13	♅ 6♋
29	2.27	8	21	1	16	14	♆17♎R
30	2.30	9	4♓	0	18	14	♇17♌

May	STime	☉	☽	☿	♀	♂	Plnts
1	2.34	10♉	17♓	0♉	19♊	15♉	♃ 2♈
2	2.38	11	0♈	29♈	20	16	♄26♍R
3	2.42	12	13	29	21	17	♅ 6♋
4	2.46	13	25	29	22	17	♆17♎R
5	2.50	14	7♉	28	23	18	♇17♌
6	2.54	15	20	28	24	19	♃ 3♈
7	2.58	16	2♊	28	26	20	♄26♍R
8	3.02	17	14	28D	27	20	♅ 6♋
9	3.06	18	26	28	28	21	♆17♎R
10	3.10	19	8♋	28	29	22	♇17♌
11	3.14	20	19	28	0♋	22	♃ 4♈
12	3.18	21	1♌	29	1	23	♄25♍R
13	3.22	22	13	29	2	24	♅ 7♋
14	3.26	23	26	29	4	25	♆17♎R
15	3.30	24	8♍	0♉	5	25	♇17♌
16	3.34	25	21	0	6	26	♃ 5♈
17	3.38	25	5♎	1	7	27	♄25♍R
18	3.41	26	19	2	8	27	♅ 7♋
19	3.45	27	3♏	3	9	28	♆17♎R
20	3.49	28	18	3	10	29	♇17♌
21	3.53	29	3♐	4	11	0♊	♃ 6♈
22	3.57	0♊	18	5	13	0	♄25♍R
23	4.01	1	3♑	6	14	1	♅ 7♋
24	4.05	2	18	7	15	2	♆17♎R
25	4.09	3	3♒	8	16	2	♇17♌
26	4.13	4	17	9	17	3	♃ 7♈
27	4.17	5	1♓	11	18	4	♄25♍
28	4.21	6	14	12	19	5	♅ 7♋
29	4.25	7	27	13	20	5	♆17♎R
30	4.29	8	10♈	14	21	6	♇17♌
31	4.33	9	22	16	22	7	♃ 8♈

Jun	STime	☉	☽	☿	♀	♂	Plnts
1	4.37	10♊	5♉	17♉	24♋	7♊	♃ 8♈
2	4.41	11	17	19	25	8	♄25♍
3	4.45	12	29	20	26	9	♅ 8♋
4	4.48	13	11♊	22	27	9	♆17♎R
5	4.52	14	23	23	28	10	♇17♌
6	4.56	15	4♋	25	29	11	♃ 9♈
7	5.00	16	16	26	0♌	12	♄25♍
8	5.04	17	28	28	1	12	♅ 8♋
9	5.08	18	10♌	0♊	2	13	♆17♎R
10	5.12	19	22	2	3	14	♇18♌
11	5.16	19	4♍	4	4	14	♃10♈
12	5.20	20	17	5	5	15	♄25♍
13	5.24	21	0♎	7	6	16	♅ 8♋
14	5.28	22	13	9	7	16	♆17♎R
15	5.32	23	27	11	8	17	♇18♌
16	5.36	24	12♏	13	9	18	♃10♈
17	5.40	25	26	15	10	18	♄26♍
18	5.44	26	11♐	18	11	19	♅ 9♋
19	5.48	27	27	20	12	20	♆16♎R
20	5.52	28	12♑	22	13	21	♇18♌
21	5.56	29	27	24	14	21	♃11♈
22	5.59	0♋	12♒	26	15	22	♄26♍
23	6.03	1	26	28	16	23	♅ 9♋
24	6.07	2	10♓	1♋	17	23	♆16♎
25	6.11	3	24	3	18	24	♇18♌
26	6.15	4	7♈	5	19	25	♃12♈
27	6.19	5	19	7	20	25	♄26♍
28	6.23	6	2♉	9	21	26	♅ 9♋
29	6.27	7	14	11	22	27	♆16♎
30	6.31	8	26	14	23	27	♇18♌

Jul	STime	☉	☽	☿	♀	♂	Plnts
1	6.35	9♋	8♊	16♋	24♌	28♊	♃12♈
2	6.39	10	20	18	25	29	♄26♍
3	6.43	10	1♋	20	26	29	♅ 9♋
4	6.47	11	13	22	27	0♋	♆16♎
5	6.51	12	25	24	27	1	♇18♌
6	6.55	13	7♌	26	28	1	♃13♈
7	6.59	14	19	28	29	2	♄27♍
8	7.03	15	1♍	0♌	0♍	3	♅10♋
9	7.06	16	14	1	1	3	♆16♎
10	7.10	17	26	3	2	4	♇18♌
11	7.14	18	9♎	5	2	5	♃13♈
12	7.18	19	23	7	3	5	♄27♍
13	7.22	20	6♏	9	4	6	♅10♋
14	7.26	21	21	10	5	7	♆17♎
15	7.30	22	5♐	12	6	7	♇18♌
16	7.34	23	20	14	6	8	♃13♈
17	7.38	24	5♑	15	7	9	♄27♍
18	7.42	25	20	17	8	9	♅10♋
19	7.46	26	5♒	18	8	10	♆17♎
20	7.50	27	20	20	9	11	♇18♌
21	7.54	28	5♓	21	10	11	♃14♈
22	7.58	29	19	23	10	12	♄28♍
23	8.02	0♌	2♈	24	11	13	♅11♋
24	8.06	0	15	26	12	13	♆17♎
25	8.10	1	28	27	12	14	♇19♌
26	8.13	2	10♉	28	13	15	♃14♈
27	8.17	3	23	0♍	13	15	♄28♍
28	8.21	4	5♊	1	14	16	♅11♋
29	8.25	5	16	2	14	17	♆17♎
30	8.29	6	28	3	15	17	♇19♌
31	8.33	7	10♋	4	15	18	♃14♈

Aug	STime	☉	☽	☿	♀	♂	Plnts
1	8.37	8♌	22♋	5♍	16♍	19♋	♃14♈
2	8.41	9	4♌	6	16	19	♄29♍
3	8.45	10	16	7	16	20	♅11♋
4	8.49	11	29	8	17	21	♆17♎
5	8.53	12	11♍	9	17	21	♇19♌
6	8.57	13	24	10	17	22	♃14♈R
7	9.01	14	6♎	11	17	23	♄29♍
8	9.05	15	19	11	18	23	♅12♋
9	9.09	16	3♏	12	18	24	♆17♎
10	9.13	17	17	13	18	25	♇19♌
11	9.17	18	1♐	13	18	25	♃14♈R
12	9.21	19	15	14	18	26	♄ 0♎
13	9.24	20	0♑	14	18R	27	♅12♋
14	9.28	21	14	14	18	27	♆17♎
15	9.32	22	29	15	18	28	♇19♌
16	9.36	23	14♒	15	18	28	♃14♈R
17	9.40	23	29	15R	18	29	♄ 0♎
18	9.44	24	13♓	15	18	0♌	♅12♋
19	9.48	25	27	15	17	0	♆17♎
20	9.52	26	10♈	14	17	1	♇19♌
21	9.56	27	24	14	17	2	♃13♈R
22	10.00	28	6♉	14	16	2	♄ 1♎
23	10.04	29	19	13	16	3	♅12♋
24	10.08	0♍	1♊	13	16	4	♆17♎
25	10.12	1	13	12	15	4	♇20♌
26	10.16	2	25	11	15	5	♃13♈R
27	10.20	3	7♋	10	14	6	♄ 1♎
28	10.24	4	19	9	14	6	♅12♋
29	10.28	5	1♌	9	13	7	♆17♎
30	10.31	6	13	8	13	7	♇20♌
31	10.35	7	25	7	12	8	♃13♈R

Sep	STime	☉	☽	☿	♀	♂	Plnts
1	10.39	8♍	8♍	6♍	11♍	9♌	♃13♈R
2	10.43	9	20	5	11	9	♄ 2♎
3	10.47	10	3♎	4	10	10	♅13♋
4	10.51	11	16	3	9	11	♆18♎
5	10.55	12	0♏	3	9	11	♇20♌
6	10.59	13	13	2	8	12	♃12♈R
7	11.03	14	27	2	8	13	♄ 2♎
8	11.07	15	11♐	1	7	13	♅13♋
9	11.11	16	25	1D	6	14	♆18♎
10	11.15	17	10♑	1	6	14	♇20♌
11	11.19	18	24	2	5	15	♃12♈R
12	11.23	19	9♒	2	5	16	♄ 3♎
13	11.27	20	23	2	4	16	♅13♋
14	11.31	21	7♓	3	4	17	♆18♎
15	11.35	22	21	4	4	18	♇20♌
16	11.39	23	5♈	5	3	18	♃11♈R
17	11.42	23	18	6	3	19	♄ 4♎
18	11.46	24	1♉	7	3	19	♅13♋
19	11.50	25	14	8	2	20	♆18♎
20	11.54	26	27	9	2	21	♇20♌
21	11.58	27	9♊	11	2	21	♃10♈R
22	12.02	28	21	12	2	22	♄ 4♎
23	12.06	29	3♋	14	2	23	♅13♋
24	12.10	0♎	15	15	2	23	♆18♎
25	12.14	1	27	17	2D	24	♇20♌
26	12.18	2	9♌	19	2	24	♃10♈R
27	12.22	3	21	21	2	25	♄ 5♎
28	12.26	4	3♍	22	2	26	♅13♋
29	12.30	5	16	24	2	26	♆18♎
30	12.34	6	29	26	2	27	♇21♌

Oct	STime	☉	☽	☿	♀	♂	Plnts
1	12.38	7♎	12♎	28♍	3♍	28♌	♃ 9♈R
2	12.42	8	26	0♎	3	28	♄ 6♎
3	12.46	9	10♏	1	3	29	♅14♋
4	12.49	10	24	3	3	29	♆19♎
5	12.53	11	8♐	5	4	0♍	♇21♌
6	12.57	12	22	7	4	1	♃ 8♈R
7	13.01	13	7♑	8	5	1	♄ 6♎
8	13.05	14	21	10	5	2	♅14♋
9	13.09	15	5♒	12	6	2	♆19♎
10	13.13	16	19	14	6	3	♇21♌
11	13.17	17	3♓	16	7	4	♃ 8♈R
12	13.21	18	16	17	7	4	♄ 7♎
13	13.25	19	0♈	19	8	5	♅14♋
14	13.29	20	13	21	8	6	♆19♎
15	13.33	21	27	22	9	6	♇21♌
16	13.37	22	10♉	24	9	7	♃ 7♈R
17	13.41	23	22	26	10	7	♄ 7♎
18	13.45	24	5♊	27	11	8	♅14♋
19	13.49	25	17	29	12	9	♆19♎
20	13.53	26	29	1♏	12	9	♇21♌
21	13.56	27	11♋	2	13	10	♃ 6♈R
22	14.00	28	23	4	14	10	♄ 8♎
23	14.04	29	4♌	6	14	11	♅14♋
24	14.08	0♏	16	7	15	12	♆19♎
25	14.12	1	29	9	16	12	♇21♌
26	14.16	2	11♍	10	17	13	♃ 6♈R
27	14.20	3	24	12	18	13	♄ 9♎
28	14.24	4	7♎	13	19	14	♅14♋R
29	14.28	5	21	15	19	15	♆20♎
30	14.32	6	5♏	17	20	15	♇21♌
31	14.36	7	19	18	21	16	♃ 5♈R

Nov	STime	☉	☽	☿	♀	♂	Plnts
1	14.40	8♏	4♐	20♏	22♍	16♍	♃ 5♈R
2	14.44	9	18	21	23	17	♄ 9♎
3	14.48	10	3♑	23	24	18	♅14♋R
4	14.52	11	17	24	25	18	♆20♎
5	14.56	12	2♒	26	26	19	♇21♌
6	15.00	13	16	27	27	19	♃ 5♈R
7	15.04	14	29	29	28	20	♄10♎
8	15.07	15	13♓	0♐	28	21	♅14♋R
9	15.11	16	26	2	29	21	♆20♎
10	15.15	17	10♈	3	0♎	22	♇21♌
11	15.19	18	23	5	1	22	♃ 5♈R
12	15.23	19	5♉	6	2	23	♄10♎
13	15.27	20	18	7	3	23	♅13♋R
14	15.31	21	1♊	9	4	24	♆20♎
15	15.35	22	13	10	5	25	♇21♌
16	15.39	23	25	12	6	25	♃ 4♈R
17	15.43	24	7♋	13	7	26	♄11♎
18	15.47	25	19	14	8	26	♅13♋R
19	15.51	26	1♌	16	10	27	♆20♎
20	15.55	27	12	17	11	28	♇21♌
21	15.59	28	24	18	12	28	♃ 4♈R
22	16.03	29	7♍	20	13	29	♄11♎
23	16.07	0♐	19	21	14	29	♅13♋R
24	16.11	1	2♎	22	15	0♎	♆20♎
25	16.14	2	15	23	16	0	♇21♌
26	16.18	3	29	25	17	1	♃ 4♈R
27	16.22	4	13♏	26	18	2	♄12♎
28	16.26	5	28	27	19	2	♅13♋R
29	16.30	6	13♐	28	20	3	♆21♎
30	16.34	7	28	29	21	3	♇21♌

Dec	STime	☉	☽	☿	♀	♂	Plnts
1	16.38	8♐	13♑	29♐	22♎	4♎	♃ 4♈
2	16.42	9	27	0♑	24	4	♄12♎
3	16.46	10	12♒	1	25	5	♅13♋R
4	16.50	11	26	1	26	6	♆21♎
5	16.54	12	10♓	2	27	6	♇21♌R
6	16.58	13	23	2	28	7	♃ 4♈
7	17.02	14	7♈	2R	29	7	♄13♎
8	17.06	15	20	2	0♏	8	♅13♋R
9	17.10	16	2♉	2	1	8	♆21♎
10	17.14	17	15	1	3	9	♇21♌R
11	17.18	18	27	1	4	9	♃ 4♈
12	17.22	19	9♊	0	5	10	♄13♎
13	17.25	20	21	29♐	6	11	♅13♋R
14	17.29	21	3♋	28	7	11	♆21♎
15	17.33	22	15	26	8	12	♇21♌R
16	17.37	23	27	25	9	12	♃ 4♈
17	17.41	24	9♌	24	11	13	♄13♎
18	17.45	25	21	22	12	13	♅12♋R
19	17.49	26	3♍	21	13	14	♆21♎
20	17.53	27	15	20	14	14	♇21♌R
21	17.57	29	27	19	15	15	♃ 5♈
22	18.01	0♑	10♎	18	16	15	♄14♎
23	18.05	1	23	17	18	16	♅12♋R
24	18.09	2	7♏	16	19	16	♆21♎
25	18.13	3	21	16	20	17	♇21♌R
26	18.17	4	6♐	16	21	17	♃ 5♈
27	18.21	5	21	16D	22	18	♄14♎
28	18.25	6	6♑	16	23	19	♅12♋R
29	18.29	7	21	16	25	19	♆21♎
30	18.32	8	6♒	16	26	20	♇21♌R
31	18.36	9	21	17	27	20	♃ 6♈

Jan	STime	☉	☽	☿	♀	♂	Plnts
1	18.40	10♑	6♓	18♐	28♏	21♎	♃ 6♈
2	18.44	11	20	18	29	21	♄14♎
3	18.48	12	3♈	19	1♐	22	♅12♋R
4	18.52	13	16	20	2	22	♆21♎
5	18.56	14	29	21	3	23	♇21♌R
6	19.00	15	12♉	22	4	23	♃ 6♈
7	19.04	16	24	23	5	24	♄14♎
8	19.08	17	6♊	24	7	24	♅11♋R
9	19.12	18	18	25	8	25	♆21♎
10	19.16	19	0♋	26	9	25	♇21♌R
11	19.20	20	12	27	10	26	♃ 7♈
12	19.24	21	24	29	11	26	♄15♎
13	19.28	22	6♌	0♑	13	27	♅11♋R
14	19.32	23	18	1	14	27	♆21♎
15	19.36	24	0♍	3	15	28	♇21♌R
16	19.39	25	12	4	16	28	♃ 8♈
17	19.43	26	24	5	17	29	♄15♎
18	19.47	27	6♎	7	19	29	♅11♋R
19	19.51	28	19	8	20	29	♆21♎
20	19.55	29	2♏	9	21	0♏	♇21♌R
21	19.59	0♒	16	11	22	0	♃ 8♈
22	20.03	1	29	12	23	1	♄15♎
23	20.07	2	14♐	14	25	1	♅11♋R
24	20.11	3	29	15	26	2	♆21♎
25	20.15	4	14♑	17	27	2	♇20♌R
26	20.19	5	29	18	28	3	♃ 9♈
27	20.23	6	14♒	20	29	3	♄15♎R
28	20.27	7	29	21	1♑	3	♅11♋R
29	20.31	8	14♓	23	2	4	♆21♎
30	20.35	9	28	24	3	4	♇20♌R
31	20.39	10	12♈	26	4	5	♃10♈

Feb	STime	☉	☽	☿	♀	♂	Plnts
1	20.43	11♒	25♈	27♑	6♑	5♏	♃10♈
2	20.47	12	8♉	29	7	6	♄15♎R
3	20.50	13	21	0♒	8	6	♅10♋R
4	20.54	14	3♊	2	9	6	♆21♎
5	20.58	15	15	4	10	7	♇20♌R
6	21.02	16	27	5	12	7	♃11♈
7	21.06	17	9♋	7	13	8	♄15♎R
8	21.10	18	21	8	14	8	♅10♋R
9	21.14	19	3♌	10	15	8	♆21♎R
10	21.18	20	15	12	17	9	♇20♌R
11	21.22	21	27	13	18	9	♃12♈
12	21.26	22	9♍	15	19	9	♄14♎R
13	21.30	23	21	17	20	10	♅10♋R
14	21.34	24	3♎	19	21	10	♆21♎R
15	21.38	25	16	20	23	11	♇20♌R
16	21.42	26	29	22	24	11	♃13♈
17	21.46	27	12♏	24	25	11	♄14♎R
18	21.50	28	25	26	26	12	♅10♋R
19	21.54	29	9♐	27	28	12	♆21♎R
20	21.57	0♓	23	29	29	12	♇20♌R
21	22.01	2	8♑	1♓	0♒	13	♃14♈
22	22.05	3	22	3	1	13	♄14♎R
23	22.09	4	7♒	5	3	13	♅10♋R
24	22.13	5	22	7	4	13	♆21♎R
25	22.17	6	7♓	8	5	14	♇20♌R
26	22.21	7	22	10	6	14	♃15♈
27	22.25	8	6♈	12	7	14	♄14♎R
28	22.29	9	20	14	9	15	♅10♋R
29	22.33	10	4♉	16	10	15	♆21♎R

Mar	STime	☉	☽	☿	♀	♂	Plnts
1	22.37	11♓	17♉	18♓	11♒	15♏	♃16♈
2	22.41	12	29	20	12	15	♄13♎R
3	22.45	13	12♊	22	14	15	♅10♋R
4	22.49	14	24	24	15	16	♆21♎R
5	22.53	15	6♋	26	16	16	♇19♌R
6	22.57	16	18	27	17	16	♃17♈
7	23.01	17	29	29	19	16	♄13♎R
8	23.05	18	11♌	1♈	20	17	♅10♋R
9	23.08	19	23	3	21	17	♆21♎R
10	23.12	20	5♍	5	22	17	♇19♌R
11	23.16	21	18	6	23	17	♃18♈
12	23.20	22	0♎	8	25	17	♄13♎R
13	23.24	23	13	10	26	17	♅10♋
14	23.28	24	26	11	27	17	♆21♎R
15	23.32	25	9♏	12	28	18	♇19♌R
16	23.36	26	22	14	0♓	18	♃19♈
17	23.40	27	6♐	15	1	18	♄12♎R
18	23.44	28	20	16	2	18	♅10♋
19	23.48	29	4♑	17	3	18	♆21♎R
20	23.52	0♈	18	18	5	18	♇19♌R
21	23.56	1	2♒	18	6	18	♃21♈
22	0.00	2	17	19	7	18	♄12♎R
23	0.04	3	1♓	20	8	18	♅10♋
24	0.08	3	16	20	9	18	♆21♎R
25	0.12	4	0♈	20	11	18R	♇19♌R
26	0.15	5	14	20R	12	18	♃22♈
27	0.19	6	28	20	13	18	♄12♎R
28	0.23	7	11♉	20	14	18	♅10♋
29	0.27	8	25	20	16	18	♆20♎R
30	0.31	9	7♊	19	17	18	♇19♌R
31	0.35	10	20	19	18	18	♃23♈

Apr	STime	☉	☽	☿	♀	♂	Plnts
1	0.39	11♈	2♋	18♈	19♓	18♏	♃23♈
2	0.43	12	14	17	21	18	♄11♎R
3	0.47	13	26	17	22	18	♅10♋
4	0.51	14	8♌	16	23	18	♆20♎R
5	0.55	15	19	15	24	17	♇19♌R
6	0.59	16	1♍	14	25	17	♃24♈
7	1.03	17	14	14	27	17	♄11♎R
8	1.07	18	26	13	28	17	♅10♋
9	1.11	19	9♎	12	29	17	♆20♎R
10	1.15	20	22	11	0♈	17	♇19♌R
11	1.19	21	5♏	11	2	16	♃26♈
12	1.23	22	19	10	3	16	♄10♎R
13	1.26	23	3♐	10	4	16	♅10♋
14	1.30	24	16	9	5	16	♆20♎R
15	1.34	25	0♑	9	7	15	♇19♌R
16	1.38	26	15	9	8	15	♃27♈
17	1.42	27	29	8	9	15	♄10♎R
18	1.46	28	13♒	8	10	15	♅10♋
19	1.50	29	27	8D	11	14	♆20♎R
20	1.54	0♉	11♓	8	13	14	♇19♌R
21	1.58	1	25	9	14	14	♃28♈
22	2.02	2	9♈	9	15	13	♄10♎R
23	2.06	3	23	9	16	13	♅10♋
24	2.10	4	6♉	10	18	13	♆20♎R
25	2.14	5	20	10	19	12	♇19♌
26	2.18	6	3♊	11	20	12	♃29♈
27	2.22	7	15	11	21	12	♄ 9♎R
28	2.26	8	28	12	22	11	♅10♋
29	2.30	9	10♋	13	24	11	♆20♎R
30	2.33	10	22	13	25	11	♇19♌

May	STime	☉	☽	☿	♀	♂	Plnts
1	2.37	11♉	4♌	14♈	26♈	10♏	♃ 0♉
2	2.41	12	15	15	27	10	♄ 9♎R
3	2.45	13	27	16	29	9	♅11♋
4	2.49	14	9♍	17	0♉	9	♆19♎R
5	2.53	15	22	18	1	9	♇19♌
6	2.57	16	4♎	19	2	8	♃ 2♉
7	3.01	17	17	20	4	8	♄ 9♎R
8	3.05	18	0♏	22	5	8	♅11♋
9	3.09	18	14	23	6	7	♆19♎R
10	3.13	19	28	24	7	7	♇19♌
11	3.17	20	12♐	25	8	6	♃ 3♉
12	3.21	21	27	27	10	6	♄ 9♎R
13	3.25	22	11♑	28	11	6	♅11♋
14	3.29	23	25	0♉	12	5	♆19♎R
15	3.33	24	10♒	1	13	5	♇19♌
16	3.37	25	24	2	15	5	♃ 4♉
17	3.40	26	8♓	4	16	5	♄ 8♎R
18	3.44	27	22	6	17	4	♅11♋
19	3.48	28	5♈	7	18	4	♆19♎R
20	3.52	29	19	9	19	4	♇19♌
21	3.56	0♊	2♉	11	21	3	♃ 5♉
22	4.00	1	15	12	22	3	♄ 8♎R
23	4.04	2	28	14	23	3	♅11♋
24	4.08	3	11♊	16	24	3	♆19♎R
25	4.12	4	23	18	26	2	♇19♌
26	4.16	5	6♋	20	27	2	♃ 6♉
27	4.20	6	18	21	28	2	♄ 8♎R
28	4.24	7	0♌	23	29	2	♅12♋
29	4.28	8	12	25	1♊	2	♆19♎R
30	4.32	9	23	27	2	2	♇19♌
31	4.36	10	5♍	29	3	1	♃ 7♉

Jun	STime	☉	☽	☿	♀	♂	Plnts
1	4.40	11♊	17♍	1♊	4♊	1♏	♃ 7♉
2	4.44	12	29	4	5	1	♄ 8♎R
3	4.48	13	12♎	6	7	1	♅12♋
4	4.51	13	25	8	8	1	♆19♎R
5	4.55	14	9♏	10	9	1	♇19♌
6	4.59	15	22	12	10	1	♃ 9♉
7	5.03	16	7♐	14	12	1	♄ 8♎R
8	5.07	17	21	17	13	1	♅12♋
9	5.11	18	6♑	19	14	1D	♆19♎R
10	5.15	19	21	21	15	1	♇19♌
11	5.19	20	6♒	23	17	1	♃10♉
12	5.23	21	20	25	18	1	♄ 8♎
13	5.27	22	4♓	28	19	1	♅13♋
14	5.31	23	18	0♋	20	1	♆19♎R
15	5.35	24	2♈	2	21	1	♇19♌
16	5.39	25	16	4	23	1	♃11♉
17	5.43	26	29	6	24	1	♄ 8♎
18	5.47	27	12♉	8	25	1	♅13♋
19	5.51	28	25	10	26	1	♆19♎
20	5.55	29	8♊	12	28	2	♇19♌
21	5.58	0♋	20	14	29	2	♃12♉
22	6.02	1	2♋	16	0♋	2	♄ 8♎
23	6.06	2	14	18	1	2	♅13♋
24	6.10	3	26	20	2	2	♆19♎
25	6.14	4	8♌	21	4	2	♇19♌
26	6.18	5	20	23	5	3	♃13♉
27	6.22	5	2♍	25	6	3	♄ 8♎
28	6.26	6	13	27	7	3	♅13♋
29	6.30	7	25	28	9	3	♆19♎
30	6.34	8	8♎	0♌	10	3	♇20♌

Jul	STime	☉	☽	☿	♀	♂	Plnts
1	6.38	9♋	20♎	1♌	11♋	4♏	♃14♉
2	6.42	10	3♏	3	12	4	♄ 8♎
3	6.46	11	17	4	14	4	♅14♋
4	6.50	12	1♐	6	15	4	♆19♎
5	6.54	13	15	7	16	5	♇20♌
6	6.58	14	0♑	9	17	5	♃14♉
7	7.02	15	15	10	18	5	♄ 8♎
8	7.06	16	0♒	11	20	6	♅14♋
9	7.09	17	15	13	21	6	♆19♎
10	7.13	18	0♓	14	22	6	♇20♌
11	7.17	19	14	15	23	7	♃15♉
12	7.21	20	29	16	25	7	♄ 9♎
13	7.25	21	12♈	17	26	7	♅14♋
14	7.29	22	26	18	27	8	♆19♎
15	7.33	23	9♉	19	28	8	♇20♌
16	7.37	24	22	20	0♌	8	♃16♉
17	7.41	25	5♊	21	1	9	♄ 9♎
18	7.45	25	17	22	2	9	♅15♋
19	7.49	26	29	23	3	10	♆19♎
20	7.53	27	11♋	23	4	10	♇20♌
21	7.57	28	23	24	6	10	♃17♉
22	8.01	29	5♌	25	7	11	♄ 9♎
23	8.05	0♌	17	25	8	11	♅15♋
24	8.09	1	29	26	9	12	♆19♎
25	8.13	2	10♍	26	11	12	♇20♌
26	8.16	3	22	26	12	13	♃17♉
27	8.20	4	4♎	27	13	13	♄10♎
28	8.24	5	17	27	14	14	♅15♋
29	8.28	6	29	27R	16	14	♆19♎
30	8.32	7	12♏	27	17	14	♇20♌
31	8.36	8	25	27	18	15	♃18♉

Aug	STime	☉	☽	☿	♀	♂	Plnts
1	8.40	9♌	9♐	27♌	19♌	15♏	♃18♉
2	8.44	10	23	26	20	16	♄10♎
3	8.48	11	8♑	26	22	16	♅16♋
4	8.52	12	23	26	23	17	♆19♎
5	8.56	13	8♒	25	24	17	♇21♌
6	9.00	14	23	24	25	18	♃19♉
7	9.04	15	8♓	24	27	18	♄11♎
8	9.08	16	23	23	28	19	♅16♋
9	9.12	17	8♈	22	29	19	♆19♎
10	9.16	17	22	21	0♍	20	♇21♌
11	9.20	18	5♉	21	2	20	♃19♉
12	9.24	19	19	20	3	21	♄11♎
13	9.27	20	1♊	19	4	22	♅16♋
14	9.31	21	14	18	5	22	♆19♎
15	9.35	22	26	18	6	23	♇21♌
16	9.39	23	8♋	17	8	23	♃20♉
17	9.43	24	20	16	9	24	♄11♎
18	9.47	25	2♌	16	10	24	♅16♋
19	9.51	26	14	15	11	25	♆19♎
20	9.55	27	26	15	13	25	♇21♌
21	9.59	28	7♍	15	14	26	♃20♉
22	10.03	29	19	15D	15	27	♄12♎
23	10.07	0♍	1♎	15	16	27	♅17♋
24	10.11	1	14	15	18	28	♆19♎
25	10.15	2	26	15	19	28	♇21♌
26	10.19	3	9♏	16	20	29	♃20♉
27	10.23	4	22	16	21	0♐	♄12♎
28	10.27	5	5♐	17	23	0	♅17♋
29	10.31	6	18	18	24	1	♆20♎
30	10.34	7	2♑	19	25	1	♇21♌
31	10.38	8	17	20	26	2	♃21♉

Sep	STime	☉	☽	☿	♀	♂	Plnts
1	10.42	9♍	2♒	21♌	27♍	3♐	♃21♉
2	10.46	10	17	22	29	3	♄13♎
3	10.50	11	2♓	23	0♎	4	♅17♋
4	10.54	12	17	25	1	4	♆20♎
5	10.58	13	2♈	26	2	5	♇22♌
6	11.02	14	16	28	4	6	♃21♉
7	11.06	14	0♉	0♍	5	6	♄14♎
8	11.10	15	14	1	6	7	♅17♋
9	11.14	16	27	3	7	8	♆20♎
10	11.18	17	10♊	5	9	8	♇22♌
11	11.22	18	23	7	10	9	♃21♉R
12	11.26	19	5♋	9	11	9	♄14♎
13	11.30	20	17	11	12	10	♅17♋
14	11.34	21	29	12	13	11	♆20♎
15	11.38	22	11♌	14	15	11	♇22♌
16	11.41	23	22	16	16	12	♃21♉R
17	11.45	24	4♍	18	17	13	♄15♎
18	11.49	25	16	20	18	13	♅18♋
19	11.53	26	28	22	20	14	♆20♎
20	11.57	27	11♎	24	21	15	♇22♌
21	12.01	28	23	26	22	15	♃20♉R
22	12.05	29	6♏	27	23	16	♄15♎
23	12.09	0♎	19	29	25	17	♅18♋
24	12.13	1	2♐	1♎	26	17	♆20♎
25	12.17	2	15	3	27	18	♇22♌
26	12.21	3	28	5	28	19	♃20♉R
27	12.25	4	12♑	6	29	19	♄16♎
28	12.29	5	26	8	1♏	20	♅18♋
29	12.33	6	11♒	10	2	21	♆21♎
30	12.37	7	25	12	3	21	♇22♌

Oct	STime	☉	☽	☿	♀	♂	Plnts
1	12.41	8♎	10♓	13♎	4♏	22♐	♃20♉R
2	12.45	9	25	15	6	23	♄17♎
3	12.49	10	10♈	17	7	24	♅18♋
4	12.52	11	24	18	8	24	♆21♎
5	12.56	12	8♉	20	9	25	♇22♌
6	13.00	13	22	22	10	26	♃20♉R
7	13.04	14	6♊	23	12	26	♄17♎
8	13.08	15	19	25	13	27	♅18♋
9	13.12	16	1♋	26	14	28	♆21♎
10	13.16	17	13	28	15	28	♇22♌
11	13.20	18	25	0♏	17	29	♃19♉R
12	13.24	19	7♌	1	18	0♑	♄18♎
13	13.28	20	19	3	19	1	♅18♋
14	13.32	21	1♍	4	20	1	♆21♎
15	13.36	22	13	6	21	2	♇23♌
16	13.40	23	25	7	23	3	♃19♉R
17	13.44	24	7♎	9	24	3	♄18♎
18	13.48	25	20	10	25	4	♅18♋
19	13.52	26	2♏	12	26	5	♆21♎
20	13.56	27	15	13	28	6	♇23♌
21	13.59	28	28	15	29	6	♃18♉R
22	14.03	29	12♐	16	0♐	7	♄19♎
23	14.07	0♏	25	18	1	8	♅18♋
24	14.11	1	9♑	19	3	9	♆22♎
25	14.15	2	23	21	4	9	♇23♌
26	14.19	3	7♒	22	5	10	♃17♉R
27	14.23	4	21	23	6	11	♄20♎
28	14.27	5	5♓	25	7	11	♅18♋R
29	14.31	6	20	26	9	12	♆22♎
30	14.35	7	4♈	27	10	13	♇23♌
31	14.39	8	18	29	11	14	♃17♉R

Nov	STime	☉	☽	☿	♀	♂	Plnts
1	14.43	9♏	3♉	0♐	12♐	14♑	♃17♉R
2	14.47	10	17	1	13	15	♄20♎
3	14.51	11	0♊	3	15	16	♅18♋R
4	14.55	12	14	4	16	17	♆22♎
5	14.59	13	26	5	17	17	♇23♌
6	15.03	14	9♋	6	18	18	♃16♉R
7	15.07	15	21	7	20	19	♄21♎
8	15.10	16	3♌	8	21	20	♅18♋R
9	15.14	17	15	10	22	20	♆22♎
10	15.18	18	27	11	23	21	♇23♌
11	15.22	19	9♍	12	24	22	♃15♉R
12	15.26	20	21	12	26	23	♄21♎
13	15.30	21	3♎	13	27	23	♅18♋R
14	15.34	22	15	14	28	24	♆22♎
15	15.38	23	28	15	29	25	♇23♌
16	15.42	24	11♏	15	1♑	26	♃15♉R
17	15.46	25	24	16	2	26	♄22♎
18	15.50	26	8♐	16	3	27	♅18♋R
19	15.54	27	22	16	4	28	♆22♎
20	15.58	28	6♑	16R	5	29	♇23♌
21	16.02	29	20	16	7	29	♃14♉R
22	16.06	0♐	4♒	16	8	0♒	♄23♎
23	16.10	1	18	15	9	1	♅18♋R
24	16.14	2	2♓	15	10	2	♆23♎
25	16.17	3	16	14	11	2	♇23♌
26	16.21	4	0♈	13	13	3	♃13♉R
27	16.25	5	14	12	14	4	♄23♎
28	16.29	6	28	11	15	5	♅18♋R
29	16.33	7	12♉	9	16	6	♆23♎
30	16.37	8	25	8	17	6	♇23♌

Dec	STime	☉	☽	☿	♀	♂	Plnts
1	16.41	9♐	9♊	6♐	19♑	7♒	♃13♉R
2	16.45	10	22	5	20	8	♄24♎
3	16.49	11	4♋	4	21	9	♅18♋R
4	16.53	12	17	3	22	9	♆23♎
5	16.57	13	29	2	23	10	♇23♌R
6	17.01	14	11♌	1	25	11	♃12♉R
7	17.05	15	23	1	26	12	♄24♎
8	17.09	16	5♍	0	27	12	♅17♋R
9	17.13	17	16	0	28	13	♆23♎
10	17.17	18	28	0D	29	14	♇23♌R
11	17.21	19	11♎	0	1♒	15	♃12♉R
12	17.24	20	23	0	2	16	♄25♎
13	17.28	21	6♏	1	3	16	♅17♋R
14	17.32	22	19	1	4	17	♆23♎
15	17.36	23	3♐	2	5	18	♇23♌R
16	17.40	24	16	3	6	19	♃11♉R
17	17.44	25	1♑	4	8	19	♄25♎
18	17.48	26	15	5	9	20	♅17♋R
19	17.52	27	0♒	6	10	21	♆23♎
20	17.56	28	14	7	11	22	♇23♌R
21	18.00	29	29	8	12	22	♃11♉R
22	18.04	0♑	13♓	9	14	23	♄25♎
23	18.08	1	27	10	15	24	♅17♋R
24	18.12	2	11♈	12	16	25	♆23♎
25	18.16	3	25	13	17	26	♇23♌R
26	18.20	4	8♉	14	18	26	♃11♉R
27	18.24	5	22	15	19	27	♄26♎
28	18.28	6	5♊	17	21	28	♅17♋R
29	18.32	7	18	18	22	29	♆23♎
30	18.35	8	0♋	20	23	29	♇23♌R
31	18.39	9	13	21	24	0♓	♃11♉R

Jan	STime	☉	☽	☿	♀	♂	Plnts
1	18.43	10♑	25♋	22♐	25♒	1♓	♃11♉R
2	18.47	12	7♌	24	26	2	♄26♎
3	18.51	13	19	25	27	2	♅16♋R
4	18.55	14	1♍	27	29	3	♆23♎
5	18.59	15	13	28	0♓	4	♇23♌R
6	19.03	16	24	0♑	1	5	♃11♉
7	19.07	17	6♎	1	2	6	♄26♎
8	19.11	18	18	3	3	6	♅16♋R
9	19.15	19	1♏	4	4	7	♆24♎
10	19.19	20	14	6	5	8	♇22♌R
11	19.23	21	27	7	6	9	♃11♉
12	19.27	22	10♐	9	8	9	♄27♎
13	19.31	23	24	10	9	10	♅16♋R
14	19.35	24	9♑	12	10	11	♆24♎
15	19.39	25	24	13	11	12	♇22♌R
16	19.42	26	8♒	15	12	12	♃11♉
17	19.46	27	23	16	13	13	♄27♎
18	19.50	28	8♓	18	14	14	♅16♋R
19	19.54	29	23	20	15	15	♆24♎
20	19.58	0♒	7♈	21	16	16	♇22♌R
21	20.02	1	21	23	17	16	♃11♉
22	20.06	2	5♉	24	19	17	♄27♎
23	20.10	3	19	26	20	18	♅15♋R
24	20.14	4	2♊	28	21	19	♆24♎
25	20.18	5	14	29	22	19	♇22♌R
26	20.22	6	27	1♒	23	20	♃11♉
27	20.26	7	9♋	3	24	21	♄27♎
28	20.30	8	22	4	25	22	♅15♋R
29	20.34	9	4♌	6	26	22	♆24♎
30	20.38	10	16	8	27	23	♇22♌R
31	20.42	11	27	9	28	24	♃12♉

Apr	STime	☉	☽	☿	♀	♂	Plnts
1	0.38	11♈	3♏	19♓	29♈	9♉	♃21♉
2	0.42	12	16	20	29	9	♄25♎R
3	0.46	13	28	20	28	10	♅14♋
4	0.50	14	11♐	20	28	11	♆22♎R
5	0.54	15	24	20	27	11	♇21♌R
6	0.58	16	7♑	21	27	12	♃22♉
7	1.02	17	21	21	26	13	♄24♎R
8	1.06	18	5♒	22	26	14	♅14♋
9	1.10	19	19	22	25	14	♆22♎R
10	1.14	20	3♓	23	25	15	♇21♌R
11	1.18	21	18	24	24	16	♃23♉
12	1.22	22	3♈	25	23	16	♄24♎R
13	1.25	23	18	26	23	17	♅14♋
14	1.29	24	3♉	26	22	18	♆22♎R
15	1.33	25	18	27	21	19	♇21♌R
16	1.37	26	2♊	28	21	19	♃24♉
17	1.41	27	15	29	20	20	♄23♎R
18	1.45	28	29	1♈	20	21	♅14♋
19	1.49	29	11♋	2	19	21	♆22♎R
20	1.53	0♉	24	3	19	22	♇21♌
21	1.57	1	6♌	4	18	23	♃26♉
22	2.01	2	18	5	18	24	♄23♎R
23	2.05	3	0♍	7	17	24	♅15♋
24	2.09	4	12	8	17	25	♆22♎R
25	2.13	5	23	9	16	26	♇21♌
26	2.17	6	5♎	11	16	26	♃27♉
27	2.21	7	17	12	16	27	♄23♎R
28	2.25	8	0♏	14	15	28	♅15♋
29	2.29	9	12	15	15	28	♆22♎R
30	2.33	10	25	17	15	29	♇21♌

Jul	STime	☉	☽	☿	♀	♂	Plnts
1	6.37	9♋	7♓	4♌	24♉	11♋	♃12♊
2	6.41	10	21	5	25	12	♄20♎
3	6.45	11	5♈	6	26	13	♅18♋
4	6.49	12	20	6	27	13	♆21♎
5	6.53	13	4♉	7	28	14	♇21♌
6	6.57	14	17	7	29	15	♃13♊
7	7.01	15	1♊	7	0♊	15	♄20♎
8	7.05	16	14	8	1	16	♅18♋
9	7.09	17	28	8	2	16	♆21♎
10	7.12	18	11♋	8	3	17	♇22♌
11	7.16	19	23	8R	4	18	♃14♊
12	7.20	20	6♌	8	5	18	♄21♎
13	7.24	20	18	8	6	19	♅19♋
14	7.28	21	0♍	8	7	20	♆21♎
15	7.32	22	12	8	8	20	♇22♌
16	7.36	23	24	7	9	21	♃15♊
17	7.40	24	6♎	7	10	22	♄21♎
18	7.44	25	18	6	11	22	♅19♋
19	7.48	26	0♏	6	13	23	♆21♎
20	7.52	27	12	5	14	24	♇22♌
21	7.56	28	24	5	15	24	♃16♊
22	8.00	29	7♐	4	16	25	♄21♎
23	8.04	0♌	21	3	17	26	♅19♋
24	8.08	1	4♑	2	18	26	♆21♎
25	8.12	2	18	2	19	27	♇22♌
26	8.16	3	3♒	1	20	28	♃17♊
27	8.19	4	17	0	21	28	♄21♎
28	8.23	5	2♓	0	22	29	♅20♋
29	8.27	6	17	29♋	24	0♌	♆21♎
30	8.31	7	2♈	29	25	0	♇22♌
31	8.35	8	16	28	26	1	♃18♊

Oct	STime	☉	☽	☿	♀	♂	Plnts
1	12.40	8♎	26♋	25♎	9♍	10♍	♃26♊
2	12.44	9	8♌	26	10	11	♄27♎
3	12.48	10	20	28	11	12	♅23♋
4	12.52	11	2♍	29	12	12	♆23♎
5	12.55	12	14	1♏	14	13	♇24♌
6	12.59	13	26	2	15	13	♃26♊
7	13.03	14	8♎	4	16	14	♄28♎
8	13.07	15	20	5	17	15	♅23♋
9	13.11	16	2♏	7	18	15	♆23♎
10	13.15	17	14	8	20	16	♇24♌
11	13.19	18	26	9	21	17	♃26♊
12	13.23	19	8♐	11	22	17	♄28♎
13	13.27	20	21	12	23	18	♅23♋
14	13.31	21	4♑	13	25	18	♆23♎
15	13.35	22	17	14	26	19	♇24♌
16	13.39	23	0♒	16	27	20	♃26♊
17	13.43	24	14	17	28	20	♄29♎
18	13.47	25	28	18	0♎	21	♅23♋
19	13.51	26	13♓	19	1	22	♆23♎
20	13.55	27	28	20	2	22	♇24♌
21	13.59	28	13♈	22	3	23	♃26♊R
22	14.02	28	28	23	4	23	♄ 0♏
23	14.06	29	13♉	24	6	24	♅23♋
24	14.10	0♏	28	25	7	25	♆24♎
25	14.14	1	12♊	26	8	25	♇24♌
26	14.18	2	26	26	9	26	♃26♊R
27	14.22	3	9♋	27	11	27	♄ 0♏
28	14.26	4	22	28	12	27	♅23♋
29	14.30	5	5♌	29	13	28	♆24♎
30	14.34	6	17	29	14	28	♇25♌
31	14.38	7	29	0♐	16	29	♃26♊R

Feb	STime	☉	☽	☿	♀	♂	Plnts
1	20.46	12♒	9♍	11♒	29♓	25♓	♃12♉
2	20.50	13	21	13	0♈	25	♄27♎
3	20.53	14	3♎	14	1	26	♅15♋R
4	20.57	15	15	16	2	27	♆24♎R
5	21.01	16	27	18	3	28	♇22♌R
6	21.05	17	9♏	20	4	29	♃12♉
7	21.09	18	22	22	5	29	♄27♎
8	21.13	19	5♐	23	6	0♈	♅15♋R
9	21.17	20	18	25	7	1	♆24♎R
10	21.21	21	2♑	27	8	2	♇22♌R
11	21.25	22	17	29	9	2	♃13♉
12	21.29	23	1♒	1♓	10	3	♄27♎R
13	21.33	24	16	2	10	4	♅15♋R
14	21.37	25	2♓	4	11	5	♆23♎R
15	21.41	26	17	6	12	5	♇22♌R
16	21.45	27	2♈	8	13	6	♃14♉
17	21.49	28	17	10	14	7	♄27♎R
18	21.53	29	1♉	12	15	8	♅15♋R
19	21.57	0♓	15	13	16	8	♆23♎R
20	22.00	1	28	15	16	9	♇22♌R
21	22.04	2	11♊	17	17	10	♃14♉
22	22.08	3	24	19	18	11	♄27♎R
23	22.12	4	7♋	20	19	11	♅14♋R
24	22.16	5	19	22	20	12	♆23♎R
25	22.20	6	1♌	23	20	13	♇21♌R
26	22.24	7	13	25	21	14	♃15♉
27	22.28	8	24	26	22	14	♄27♎R
28	22.32	9	6♍	27	22	15	♅14♋R

May	STime	☉	☽	☿	♀	♂	Plnts
1	2.36	11♉	8♐	18♈	15♈	0♊	♃28♉
2	2.40	11	21	20	15	1	♄22♎R
3	2.44	12	4♑	22	15	1	♅15♋
4	2.48	13	18	23	15D	2	♆22♎R
5	2.52	14	1♒	25	15	3	♇21♌
6	2.56	15	15	27	15	3	♃29♉
7	3.00	16	29	28	15	4	♄22♎R
8	3.04	17	14♓	0♉	15	5	♅15♋
9	3.08	18	28	2	15	5	♆22♎R
10	3.12	19	13♈	4	15	6	♇21♌
11	3.16	20	27	6	16	7	♃ 0♊
12	3.20	21	12♉	8	16	8	♄22♎R
13	3.24	22	26	10	16	8	♅15♋
14	3.28	23	10♊	11	16	9	♆21♎R
15	3.32	24	23	13	17	10	♇21♌
16	3.36	25	7♋	16	17	10	♃ 1♊
17	3.40	26	19	18	18	11	♄21♎R
18	3.43	27	2♌	20	18	12	♅15♋
19	3.47	28	14	22	19	12	♆21♎R
20	3.51	29	26	24	19	13	♇21♌
21	3.55	0♊	8♍	26	20	14	♃ 2♊
22	3.59	1	20	28	20	14	♄21♎R
23	4.03	2	2♎	0♊	21	15	♅16♋
24	4.07	3	14	3	21	16	♆21♎R
25	4.11	4	26	5	22	16	♇21♌
26	4.15	5	8♏	7	23	17	♃ 4♊
27	4.19	6	21	9	23	18	♄21♎R
28	4.23	7	4♐	11	24	18	♅16♋
29	4.27	8	17	14	25	19	♆21♎R
30	4.31	8	1♑	16	25	20	♇21♌
31	4.35	9	14	18	26	21	♃ 5♊

Aug	STime	☉	☽	☿	♀	♂	Plnts
1	8.39	9♌	0♉	28♋	27♊	1♌	♃18♊
2	8.43	10	14	28	28	2	♄22♎
3	8.47	11	28	27	29	3	♅20♋
4	8.51	12	11♊	27D	0♋	3	♆21♎
5	8.55	12	24	27	1	4	♇22♌
6	8.59	13	7♋	27	2	5	♃19♊
7	9.03	14	20	28	4	5	♄22♎
8	9.07	15	2♌	28	5	6	♅20♋
9	9.11	16	14	28	6	7	♆21♎
10	9.15	17	26	29	7	7	♇22♌
11	9.19	18	8♍	0♌	8	8	♃20♊
12	9.23	19	20	0	9	9	♄22♎
13	9.26	20	2♎	1	10	9	♅20♋
14	9.30	21	14	2	12	10	♆21♎
15	9.34	22	26	3	13	10	♇23♌
16	9.38	23	8♏	5	14	11	♃21♊
17	9.42	24	20	6	15	12	♄23♎
18	9.46	25	3♐	7	16	12	♅21♋
19	9.50	26	15	9	17	13	♆21♎
20	9.54	27	29	10	19	14	♇23♌
21	9.58	28	12♑	12	20	14	♃22♊
22	10.02	29	26	14	21	15	♄23♎
23	10.06	0♍	11♒	16	22	16	♅21♋
24	10.10	1	26	17	23	16	♆22♎
25	10.14	2	11♓	19	24	17	♇23♌
26	10.18	3	26	21	26	17	♃22♊
27	10.22	4	11♈	23	27	18	♄23♎
28	10.26	5	26	25	28	19	♅21♋
29	10.30	6	10♉	27	29	19	♆22♎
30	10.34	7	24	29	0♌	20	♇23♌
31	10.37	7	8♊	1♍	1	21	♃23♊

Nov	STime	☉	☽	☿	♀	♂	Plnts
1	14.42	8♏	11♍	0♐	17♎	0♎	♃26♊R
2	14.46	9	23	0	18	0	♄ 1♏
3	14.50	10	5♎	0R	19	1	♅23♋
4	14.54	11	17	0	21	2	♆24♎
5	14.58	12	29	0	22	2	♇25♌
6	15.02	13	11♏	0	23	3	♃25♊R
7	15.06	14	23	29♏	24	3	♄ 2♏
8	15.10	15	5♐	29	26	4	♅23♋R
9	15.13	17	18	28	27	5	♆24♎
10	15.17	18	1♑	27	28	5	♇25♌
11	15.21	19	14	26	29	6	♃25♊R
12	15.25	20	27	25	1♏	6	♄ 2♏
13	15.29	21	10♒	23	2	7	♅23♋R
14	15.33	22	24	22	3	8	♆24♎
15	15.37	23	8♓	21	4	8	♇25♌
16	15.41	24	22	19	6	9	♃24♊R
17	15.45	25	7♈	18	7	10	♄ 3♏
18	15.49	26	21	17	8	10	♅23♋R
19	15.53	27	6♉	16	9	11	♆25♎
20	15.57	28	21	15	11	11	♇25♌
21	16.01	29	6♊	15	12	12	♃24♊R
22	16.05	0♐	20	14	13	13	♄ 3♏
23	16.09	1	4♋	14D	14	13	♅23♋R
24	16.13	2	17	14	16	14	♆25♎
25	16.17	3	0♌	15	17	14	♇25♌
26	16.20	4	13	15	18	15	♃23♊R
27	16.24	5	25	15	19	16	♄ 4♏
28	16.28	6	7♍	16	21	16	♅22♋R
29	16.32	7	19	17	22	17	♆25♎
30	16.36	8	1♎	18	23	18	♇25♌

Mar	STime	☉	☽	☿	♀	♂	Plnts
1	22.36	10♓	18♍	28♓	23♈	16♈	♃15♉
2	22.40	11	0♎	29	24	17	♄26♎R
3	22.44	12	12	0♈	24	17	♅14♋R
4	22.48	13	24	1	25	18	♆23♎R
5	22.52	14	6♏	2	26	19	♇21♌R
6	22.56	15	18	2	26	20	♃16♉
7	23.00	16	1♐	2	27	20	♄26♎R
8	23.04	17	14	3	27	21	♅14♋R
9	23.08	18	27	3R	28	22	♆23♎R
10	23.11	19	11♑	3	28	23	♇21♌R
11	23.15	20	25	2	29	23	♃17♉
12	23.19	21	10♒	2	29	24	♄26♎R
13	23.23	22	25	1	29	25	♅14♋
14	23.27	23	10♓	1	0♉	25	♆23♎R
15	23.31	24	25	0	0	26	♇21♌R
16	23.35	25	10♈	29♓	0	27	♃18♉
17	23.39	26	25	28	0	28	♄26♎R
18	23.43	27	10♉	27	1	28	♅14♋
19	23.47	28	24	27	1	29	♆23♎R
20	23.51	29	7♊	26	1	0♉	♇21♌R
21	23.55	0♈	20	25	1	1	♃19♉
22	23.59	1	3♋	24	1	1	♄25♎R
23	0.03	2	15	23	1R	2	♅14♋
24	0.07	3	28	22	1	3	♆23♎R
25	0.11	4	9♌	22	1	4	♇21♌R
26	0.15	5	21	21	1	4	♃20♉
27	0.18	6	3♍	21	1	5	♄25♎R
28	0.22	7	15	20	0	6	♅14♋
29	0.26	8	27	20	0	6	♆23♎R
30	0.30	9	9♎	20	0	7	♇21♌R
31	0.34	10	21	20	0	8	♃21♉

Jun	STime	☉	☽	☿	♀	♂	Plnts
1	4.39	10♊	28♑	20♊	27♈	21♊	♃ 5♊
2	4.43	11	12♒	22	27	22	♄21♎R
3	4.47	12	26	24	28	23	♅16♋
4	4.51	13	10♓	26	29	23	♆21♎R
5	4.54	14	24	28	0♉	24	♇21♌
6	4.58	15	9♈	0♋	1	25	♃ 6♊
7	5.02	16	23	2	1	25	♄20♎R
8	5.06	17	7♉	4	2	26	♅17♋
9	5.10	18	21	6	3	27	♆21♎R
10	5.14	19	5♊	7	4	27	♇21♌
11	5.18	20	18	9	5	28	♃ 7♊
12	5.22	21	2♋	11	6	29	♄20♎R
13	5.26	22	15	12	6	29	♅17♋
14	5.30	23	27	14	7	0♋	♆21♎R
15	5.34	24	10♌	16	8	1	♇21♌
16	5.38	25	22	17	9	1	♃ 9♊
17	5.42	26	4♍	19	10	2	♄20♎R
18	5.46	27	16	20	11	3	♅17♋
19	5.50	28	28	21	12	3	♆21♎R
20	5.54	29	9♎	23	13	4	♇21♌
21	5.58	0♋	22	24	14	5	♃10♊
22	6.01	0	4♏	25	15	5	♄20♎
23	6.05	1	16	26	16	6	♅17♋
24	6.09	2	29	28	17	7	♆21♎R
25	6.13	3	12♐	29	18	7	♇21♌
26	6.17	4	26	0♌	19	8	♃11♊
27	6.21	5	10♑	1	20	9	♄20♎
28	6.25	6	24	2	21	9	♅18♋
29	6.29	7	8♒	3	22	10	♆21♎
30	6.33	8	22	3	23	11	♇21♌

Sep	STime	☉	☽	☿	♀	♂	Plnts
1	10.41	8♍	21♊	3♍	3♌	21♌	♃23♊
2	10.45	9	4♋	5	4	22	♄24♎
3	10.49	10	17	7	5	23	♅21♋
4	10.53	11	29	9	6	23	♆22♎
5	10.57	12	11♌	11	7	24	♇23♌
6	11.01	13	23	12	9	24	♃24♊
7	11.05	14	5♍	14	10	25	♄25♎
8	11.09	15	17	16	11	26	♅22♋
9	11.13	16	29	18	12	26	♆22♎
10	11.17	17	11♎	20	13	27	♇23♌
11	11.21	18	23	22	14	28	♃24♊
12	11.25	19	5♏	24	16	28	♄25♎
13	11.29	20	17	25	17	29	♅22♋
14	11.33	21	29	27	18	0♍	♆22♎
15	11.37	22	11♐	29	19	0	♇24♌
16	11.41	23	24	1♎	20	1	♃25♊
17	11.44	24	7♑	2	22	1	♄26♎
18	11.48	25	21	4	23	2	♅22♋
19	11.52	26	5♒	6	24	3	♆22♎
20	11.56	27	19	8	25	3	♇24♌
21	12.00	28	4♓	9	26	4	♃25♊
22	12.04	29	19	11	28	5	♄26♎
23	12.08	0♎	4♈	12	29	5	♅22♋
24	12.12	1	20	14	0♍	6	♆22♎
25	12.16	2	5♉	16	1	6	♇24♌
26	12.20	3	19	17	3	7	♃26♊
27	12.24	4	4♊	19	4	8	♄27♎
28	12.28	5	18	20	5	8	♅22♋
29	12.32	6	1♋	22	6	9	♆23♎
30	12.36	7	14	23	7	10	♇24♌

Dec	STime	☉	☽	☿	♀	♂	Plnts
1	16.40	9♐	13♎	19♏	24♏	18♎	♃23♊R
2	16.44	10	25	20	26	19	♄ 4♏
3	16.48	11	7♏	21	27	19	♅22♋R
4	16.52	12	19	22	28	20	♆25♎
5	16.56	13	2♐	23	29	21	♇25♌R
6	17.00	14	14	24	1♐	21	♃22♊R
7	17.04	15	27	25	2	22	♄ 5♏
8	17.08	16	10♑	27	3	22	♅22♋R
9	17.12	17	24	28	5	23	♆25♎
10	17.16	18	7♒	0♐	6	24	♇25♌R
11	17.20	19	21	1	7	24	♃21♊R
12	17.24	20	4♓	2	8	25	♄ 5♏
13	17.27	21	18	4	10	25	♅22♋R
14	17.31	22	3♈	5	11	26	♆25♎
15	17.35	23	17	7	12	27	♇25♌R
16	17.39	24	1♉	8	13	27	♃21♊R
17	17.43	25	16	10	15	28	♄ 6♏
18	17.47	26	0♊	11	16	29	♅22♋R
19	17.51	27	14	13	17	29	♆25♎
20	17.55	28	28	14	18	0♏	♇25♌R
21	17.59	29	12♋	16	20	0	♃20♊R
22	18.03	0♑	25	17	21	1	♄ 6♏
23	18.07	1	8♌	19	22	2	♅22♋R
24	18.11	2	21	20	23	2	♆25♎
25	18.15	3	3♍	22	25	3	♇25♌R
26	18.19	4	15	23	26	3	♃19♊R
27	18.23	5	27	25	27	4	♄ 7♏
28	18.27	6	9♎	26	28	5	♅21♋R
29	18.31	7	21	28	0♑	5	♆26♎
30	18.35	8	3♏	29	1	6	♇24♌R
31	18.38	9	15	1♑	2	6	♃19♊R

Jan	STime	☉	☽	☿	♀	♂	Plnts
1	18.42	10♑	27♏	2♑	3♑	7♏	♃19♊R
2	18.46	11	10♐	4	5	8	♄ 7♏
3	18.50	12	23	6	6	8	♅21♋R
4	18.54	13	6♑	7	7	9	♆26♎
5	18.58	14	19	9	8	9	♇24♌R
6	19.02	15	3♒	10	10	10	♃18♊R
7	19.06	16	17	12	11	10	♄ 8♏
8	19.10	17	1♓	14	12	11	♅21♋R
9	19.14	18	15	15	13	12	♆26♎
10	19.18	19	29	17	15	12	♇24♌R
11	19.22	20	14♈	18	16	13	♃18♊R
12	19.26	21	28	20	17	13	♄ 8♏
13	19.30	22	12♉	22	19	14	♅21♋R
14	19.34	23	26	23	20	15	♆26♎
15	19.38	25	10♊	25	21	15	♇24♌R
16	19.42	26	23	27	22	16	♃17♊R
17	19.45	27	7♋	28	24	16	♄ 8♏
18	19.49	28	20	0♒	25	17	♅20♋R
19	19.53	29	3♌	2	26	18	♆26♎
20	19.57	0♒	16	3	27	18	♇24♌R
21	20.01	1	29	5	29	19	♃17♊R
22	20.05	2	11♍	7	0♒	19	♄ 8♏
23	20.09	3	23	9	1	20	♅20♋R
24	20.13	4	5♎	10	2	20	♆26♎
25	20.17	5	17	12	4	21	♇24♌R
26	20.21	6	29	14	5	22	♃16♊R
27	20.25	7	11♏	15	6	22	♄ 9♏
28	20.29	8	23	17	7	23	♅20♋R
29	20.33	9	5♐	19	9	23	♆26♎
30	20.37	10	18	21	10	24	♇24♌R
31	20.41	11	1♑	22	11	24	♃16♊R

Feb	STime	☉	☽	☿	♀	♂	Plnts
1	20.45	12♒	14♑	24♒	12♒	25♏	♃16♊R
2	20.49	13	28	26	14	26	♄ 9♏
3	20.53	14	12♒	28	15	26	♅20♋R
4	20.56	15	26	29	16	27	♆26♎R
5	21.00	16	11♓	1♓	17	27	♇24♌R
6	21.04	17	25	3	19	28	♃16♊R
7	21.08	18	10♈	4	20	28	♄ 9♏
8	21.12	19	24	6	21	29	♅20♋R
9	21.16	20	9♉	7	22	0♐	♆26♎R
10	21.20	21	23	8	24	0	♇24♌R
11	21.24	22	7♊	10	25	1	♃16♊
12	21.28	23	20	11	26	1	♄ 9♏
13	21.32	24	3♋	12	27	2	♅19♋R
14	21.36	25	16	13	29	2	♆26♎R
15	21.40	26	29	14	0♓	3	♇23♌R
16	21.44	27	12♌	15	1	3	♃16♊
17	21.48	28	25	15	2	4	♄ 9♏
18	21.52	29	7♍	16	4	4	♅19♋R
19	21.56	0♓	19	16	5	5	♆26♎R
20	22.00	1	1♎	16R	6	6	♇23♌R
21	22.03	2	13	16	7	6	♃16♊
22	22.07	3	25	15	9	7	♄ 9♏R
23	22.11	4	7♏	15	10	7	♅19♋R
24	22.15	5	19	14	11	8	♆26♎R
25	22.19	6	1♐	14	12	8	♇23♌R
26	22.23	7	13	13	14	9	♃17♊
27	22.27	8	25	12	15	9	♄ 9♏R
28	22.31	9	8♑	11	16	10	♅19♋R

Mar	STime	☉	☽	☿	♀	♂	Plnts
1	22.35	10♓	22♑	10♓	17♓	10♐	♃17♊
2	22.39	11	5♒	9	19	11	♄ 9♏R
3	22.43	12	20	8	20	11	♅19♋R
4	22.47	13	4♓	7	21	12	♆25♎R
5	22.51	14	19	6	22	12	♇23♌R
6	22.55	15	4♈	5	24	13	♃17♊
7	22.59	16	19	4	25	13	♄ 9♏R
8	23.03	17	4♉	3	26	14	♅19♋R
9	23.07	18	19	3	27	14	♆25♎R
10	23.10	19	3♊	2	29	15	♇23♌R
11	23.14	20	17	2	0♈	15	♃17♊
12	23.18	21	0♋	2	1	16	♄ 9♏R
13	23.22	22	14	1	2	16	♅19♋R
14	23.26	23	26	1D	4	17	♆25♎R
15	23.30	24	9♌	1	5	17	♇23♌R
16	23.34	25	21	2	6	18	♃18♊
17	23.38	26	4♍	2	7	18	♄ 8♏R
18	23.42	27	16	2	9	19	♅19♋R
19	23.46	28	28	3	10	19	♆25♎R
20	23.50	29	10♎	3	11	20	♇23♌R
21	23.54	0♈	22	4	12	20	♃19♊
22	23.58	1	3♏	4	14	21	♄ 8♏R
23	0.02	2	15	5	15	21	♅19♋R
24	0.06	3	27	6	16	22	♆25♎R
25	0.10	4	9♐	6	17	22	♇23♌R
26	0.14	5	21	7	19	23	♃19♊
27	0.18	6	4♑	8	20	23	♄ 8♏R
28	0.21	7	17	9	21	23	♅19♋
29	0.25	8	0♒	10	22	24	♆25♎R
30	0.29	9	14	11	24	24	♇23♌R
31	0.33	10	28	12	25	25	♃20♊

Apr	STime	☉	☽	☿	♀	♂	Plnts
1	0.37	11♈	12♓	13♓	26♈	25♐	♃20♊
2	0.41	12	27	15	27	26	♄ 7♏R
3	0.45	13	13♈	16	28	26	♅19♋
4	0.49	14	28	17	0♉	26	♆25♎R
5	0.53	15	13♉	18	1	27	♇22♌R
6	0.57	16	28	20	2	27	♃21♊
7	1.01	17	13♊	21	3	28	♄ 7♏R
8	1.05	18	27	22	5	28	♅19♋
9	1.09	19	10♋	24	6	28	♆25♎R
10	1.13	20	23	25	7	29	♇22♌R
11	1.17	21	6♌	27	8	29	♃21♊
12	1.21	22	18	28	10	0♑	♄ 7♏R
13	1.25	23	1♍	0♈	11	0	♅19♋
14	1.28	24	13	1	12	0	♆24♎R
15	1.32	25	25	3	14	1	♇22♌R
16	1.36	26	7♎	4	15	1	♃22♊
17	1.40	27	19	6	16	1	♄ 6♏R
18	1.44	28	0♏	8	17	2	♅19♋
19	1.48	29	12	9	18	2	♆24♎R
20	1.52	0♉	24	11	19	2	♇22♌R
21	1.56	1	6♐	13	21	3	♃23♊
22	2.00	2	18	15	22	3	♄ 6♏R
23	2.04	2	1♑	16	23	3	♅19♋
24	2.08	3	13	18	24	4	♆24♎R
25	2.12	4	26	20	26	4	♇22♌
26	2.16	5	9♒	22	27	4	♃24♊
27	2.20	6	23	24	28	4	♄ 6♏R
28	2.24	7	7♓	26	29	5	♅19♋
29	2.28	8	21	28	0♊	5	♆24♎R
30	2.32	9	6♈	0♉	2	5	♇22♌R

May	STime	☉	☽	☿	♀	♂	Plnts
1	2.36	10♉	21♈	2♉	3♊	5♑	♃25♊
2	2.39	11	6♉	4	4	6	♄ 5♏R
3	2.43	12	21	6	5	6	♅19♋
4	2.47	13	6♊	8	7	6	♆24♎R
5	2.51	14	21	10	8	6	♇22♌
6	2.55	15	5♋	12	9	7	♃26♊
7	2.59	16	19	14	10	7	♄ 5♏R
8	3.03	17	2♌	17	11	7	♅19♋
9	3.07	18	15	19	13	7	♆24♎R
10	3.11	19	27	21	14	7	♇22♌
11	3.15	20	10♍	23	15	7	♃27♊
12	3.19	21	22	25	16	7	♄ 5♏R
13	3.23	22	4♎	27	17	8	♅20♋
14	3.27	23	15	0♊	19	8	♆24♎R
15	3.31	24	27	2	20	8	♇22♌
16	3.35	25	9♏	4	21	8	♃28♊
17	3.39	26	21	6	22	8	♄ 4♏R
18	3.43	27	3♐	8	24	8	♅20♋
19	3.46	28	15	10	25	8	♆24♎R
20	3.50	29	28	12	26	8	♇22♌
21	3.54	0♊	10♑	14	27	8	♃29♊
22	3.58	1	23	16	28	8	♄ 4♏R
23	4.02	2	6♒	18	0♋	8R	♅20♋
24	4.06	2	19	20	1	8	♆23♎R
25	4.10	3	2♓	21	2	8	♇22♌
26	4.14	4	16	23	3	8	♃ 0♋
27	4.18	5	1♈	25	4	8	♄ 4♏R
28	4.22	6	15	26	6	8	♅20♋
29	4.26	7	0♉	28	7	8	♆23♎R
30	4.30	8	15	29	8	8	♇22♌
31	4.34	9	0♊	1♋	9	8	♃ 1♋

Jun	STime	☉	☽	☿	♀	♂	Plnts
1	4.38	10♊	15♊	2♋	10♋	8♑	♃ 2♋
2	4.42	11	29	4	12	8	♄ 3♏R
3	4.46	12	13♋	5	13	7	♅21♋
4	4.50	13	27	6	14	7	♆23♎R
5	4.54	14	10♌	8	15	7	♇22♌
6	4.57	15	23	9	16	7	♃ 3♋
7	5.01	16	6♍	10	18	7	♄ 3♏R
8	5.05	17	18	11	19	7	♅21♋
9	5.09	18	0♎	12	20	6	♆23♎R
10	5.13	19	12	13	21	6	♇23♌
11	5.17	20	24	14	22	6	♃ 4♋
12	5.21	21	6♏	14	24	6	♄ 3♏R
13	5.25	22	18	15	25	6	♅21♋
14	5.29	23	0♐	16	26	5	♆23♎R
15	5.33	24	12	16	27	5	♇23♌
16	5.37	25	24	17	28	5	♃ 5♋
17	5.41	25	7♑	17	29	4	♄ 3♏R
18	5.45	26	20	18	1♌	4	♅21♋
19	5.49	27	3♒	18	2	4	♆23♎R
20	5.53	28	16	18	3	4	♇23♌
21	5.57	29	29	18	4	3	♃ 6♋
22	6.01	0♋	13♓	19	5	3	♄ 3♏R
23	6.04	1	27	19R	7	3	♅22♋
24	6.08	2	11♈	18	8	2	♆23♎R
25	6.12	3	25	18	9	2	♇23♌
26	6.16	4	10♉	18	10	2	♃ 7♋
27	6.20	5	24	18	11	1	♄ 2♏R
28	6.24	6	9♊	17	12	1	♅22♋
29	6.28	7	23	17	14	1	♆23♎R
30	6.32	8	8♋	17	15	0	♇23♌

Jul	STime	☉	☽	☿	♀	♂	Plnts
1	6.36	9♋	22♋	16♋	16♌	0♑	♃ 8♋
2	6.40	10	5♌	16	17	0	♄ 2♏R
3	6.44	11	18	15	18	0	♅22♋
4	6.48	12	1♍	14	19	29♐	♆23♎
5	6.52	13	14	14	21	29	♇23♌
6	6.56	14	26	13	22	29	♃ 9♋
7	7.00	15	8♎	13	23	28	♄ 2♏
8	7.04	15	20	12	24	28	♅23♋
9	7.08	16	2♏	11	25	28	♆23♎
10	7.11	17	14	11	26	28	♇23♌
11	7.15	18	26	10	28	27	♃11♋
12	7.19	19	8♐	10	29	27	♄ 2♏
13	7.23	20	20	10	0♍	27	♅23♋
14	7.27	21	3♑	9	1	27	♆23♎
15	7.31	22	16	9	2	27	♇23♌
16	7.35	23	29	9	3	26	♃12♋
17	7.39	24	12♒	9D	4	26	♄ 2♏
18	7.43	25	26	9	6	26	♅23♋
19	7.47	26	10♓	9	7	26	♆23♎
20	7.51	27	24	9	8	26	♇23♌
21	7.55	28	8♈	10	9	26	♃13♋
22	7.59	29	22	10	10	26	♄ 3♏
23	8.03	0♌	6♉	11	11	26	♅23♋
24	8.07	1	20	11	12	25	♆23♎
25	8.11	2	5♊	12	14	25	♇24♌
26	8.15	3	19	13	15	25	♃14♋
27	8.19	4	3♋	14	16	25	♄ 3♏
28	8.22	5	17	15	17	25	♅24♋
29	8.26	6	0♌	16	18	25D	♆23♎
30	8.30	6	14	17	19	25	♇24♌
31	8.34	7	27	18	20	25	♃15♋

Aug	STime	☉	☽	☿	♀	♂	Plnts
1	8.38	8♌	9♍	20♋	21♍	25♐	♃15♋
2	8.42	9	22	21	23	25	♄ 3♏
3	8.46	10	4♎	23	24	25	♅24♋
4	8.50	11	16	24	25	25	♆23♎
5	8.54	12	28	26	26	26	♇24♌
6	8.58	13	10♏	28	27	26	♃16♋
7	9.02	14	22	29	28	26	♄ 3♏
8	9.06	15	4♐	1♌	29	26	♅24♋
9	9.10	16	16	3	0♎	26	♆23♎
10	9.14	17	28	5	1	26	♇24♌
11	9.18	18	11♑	7	2	26	♃17♋
12	9.22	19	24	9	3	27	♄ 3♏
13	9.26	20	8♒	11	5	27	♅25♋
14	9.29	21	21	13	6	27	♆23♎
15	9.33	22	5♓	15	7	27	♇24♌
16	9.37	23	20	17	8	27	♃18♋
17	9.41	24	4♈	19	9	28	♄ 4♏
18	9.45	25	19	21	10	28	♅25♋
19	9.49	26	3♉	23	11	28	♆24♎
20	9.53	27	17	25	12	28	♇24♌
21	9.57	28	1♊	27	13	29	♃19♋
22	10.01	29	15	29	14	29	♄ 4♏
23	10.05	0♍	29	1♍	15	29	♅25♋
24	10.09	0	13♋	3	16	0♑	♆24♎
25	10.13	1	26	5	17	0	♇25♌
26	10.17	2	9♌	7	18	0	♃20♋
27	10.21	3	22	9	19	1	♄ 4♏
28	10.25	4	5♍	11	20	1	♅26♋
29	10.29	5	18	13	21	1	♆24♎
30	10.33	6	0♎	14	22	2	♇25♌
31	10.37	7	12	16	23	2	♃21♋

Sep	STime	☉	☽	☿	♀	♂	Plnts
1	10.40	8♍	24♎	18♍	24♎	3♑	♃21♋
2	10.44	9	6♏	20	25	3	♄ 5♏
3	10.48	10	18	22	26	3	♅26♋
4	10.52	11	0♐	23	27	4	♆24♎
5	10.56	12	12	25	28	4	♇25♌
6	11.00	13	24	27	29	5	♃22♋
7	11.04	14	6♑	28	0♏	5	♄ 5♏
8	11.08	15	19	0♎	1	5	♅26♋
9	11.12	16	2♒	2	2	6	♆24♎
10	11.16	17	16	3	3	6	♇25♌
11	11.20	18	0♓	5	4	7	♃23♋
12	11.24	19	14	6	5	7	♄ 6♏
13	11.28	20	29	8	6	8	♅26♋
14	11.32	21	14♈	9	7	8	♆24♎
15	11.36	22	29	11	8	9	♇25♌
16	11.40	23	13♉	12	9	9	♃24♋
17	11.44	24	28	14	9	10	♄ 6♏
18	11.47	25	12♊	15	10	10	♅26♋
19	11.51	26	26	17	11	11	♆24♎
20	11.55	27	10♋	18	12	11	♇25♌
21	11.59	28	23	20	13	12	♃25♋
22	12.03	29	6♌	21	14	12	♄ 7♏
23	12.07	0♎	19	22	14	13	♅27♋
24	12.11	1	2♍	24	15	13	♆25♎
25	12.15	2	14	25	16	14	♇26♌
26	12.19	3	27	26	17	15	♃26♋
27	12.23	4	9♎	28	18	15	♄ 7♏
28	12.27	5	21	29	18	16	♅27♋
29	12.31	6	3♏	0♏	19	16	♆25♎
30	12.35	6	15	1	20	17	♇26♌

Oct	STime	☉	☽	☿	♀	♂	Plnts
1	12.39	7♎	26♏	2♏	20♏	17♑	♃26♋
2	12.43	8	8♐	4	21	18	♄ 8♏
3	12.47	9	20	5	22	19	♅27♋
4	12.51	10	2♑	6	22	19	♆25♎
5	12.54	11	14	7	23	20	♇26♌
6	12.58	12	27	8	24	20	♃27♋
7	13.02	13	10♒	9	24	21	♄ 8♏
8	13.06	14	24	10	25	22	♅27♋
9	13.10	15	8♓	10	25	22	♆25♎
10	13.14	16	22	11	26	23	♇26♌
11	13.18	17	7♈	12	26	23	♃28♋
12	13.22	18	22	13	27	24	♄ 9♏
13	13.26	19	8♉	13	27	25	♅27♋
14	13.30	20	23	14	27	25	♆25♎
15	13.34	21	8♊	14	28	26	♇26♌
16	13.38	22	22	14	28	26	♃28♋
17	13.42	23	6♋	14	29	27	♄10♏
18	13.46	24	20	14R	29	28	♅27♋
19	13.50	25	3♌	14	29	28	♆25♎
20	13.54	26	16	14	29	29	♇26♌
21	13.58	27	29	14	29	0♒	♃29♋
22	14.02	28	11♍	13	0♐	1	♄10♏
23	14.05	29	23	13	0	1	♅27♋
24	14.09	0♏	6♎	12	0	2	♆26♎
25	14.13	1	18	11	0R	2	♇26♌
26	14.17	2	0♏	10	0	3	♃29♋
27	14.21	3	11	9	0	4	♄11♏
28	14.25	4	23	7	0	4	♅27♋
29	14.29	5	5♐	6	29♏	5	♆26♎
30	14.33	6	17	5	29	6	♇26♌
31	14.37	7	29	4	29	6	♃29♋

Nov	STime	☉	☽	☿	♀	♂	Plnts
1	14.41	8♏	11♑	2♏	29♏	7♒	♃29♋
2	14.45	9	23	1	29	8	♄11♏
3	14.49	10	6♒	0	28	8	♅27♋
4	14.53	11	19	0	28	9	♆26♎
5	14.57	12	2♓	29♎	27	10	♇26♌
6	15.01	13	16	29	27	10	♃29♋
7	15.05	14	1♈	29D	27	11	♄12♏
8	15.09	15	15	29	26	12	♅27♋
9	15.12	16	0♉	29	25	12	♆26♎
10	15.16	17	16	29	25	13	♇26♌
11	15.20	18	1♊	0♏	24	14	♃ 0♌
12	15.24	19	16	0	24	14	♄13♏
13	15.28	20	1♋	1	23	15	♅27♋R
14	15.32	21	15	2	23	16	♆26♎
15	15.36	22	29	3	22	16	♇26♌
16	15.40	23	13♌	4	21	17	♃ 0♌
17	15.44	24	26	5	21	18	♄13♏
18	15.48	25	8♍	7	20	18	♅27♋R
19	15.52	26	21	8	20	19	♆27♎
20	15.56	27	3♎	9	19	20	♇26♌
21	16.00	28	15	11	18	20	♃ 0♌R
22	16.04	29	27	12	18	21	♄14♏
23	16.08	0♐	9♏	13	17	22	♅27♋R
24	16.12	1	20	15	17	23	♆27♎
25	16.16	2	2♐	16	17	23	♇26♌
26	16.20	3	14	18	16	24	♃ 0♌R
27	16.23	4	26	19	16	25	♄14♏
28	16.27	5	8♑	21	16	26	♅27♋R
29	16.31	6	20	22	15	26	♆27♎
30	16.35	7	3♒	24	15	27	♇27♌

Dec	STime	☉	☽	☿	♀	♂	Plnts
1	16.39	8♐	15♒	25♏	15♏	28♒	♃29♋R
2	16.43	9	28	27	15	28	♄15♏
3	16.47	10	12♓	28	14	29	♅27♋R
4	16.51	11	25	0♐	14	0♓	♆27♎
5	16.55	13	9♈	2	14D	1	♇26♌R
6	16.59	14	24	3	14	1	♃29♋R
7	17.03	15	9♉	5	14	2	♄16♏
8	17.07	16	24	6	15	3	♅27♋R
9	17.11	17	9♊	8	15	3	♆27♎
10	17.15	18	24	9	15	4	♇26♌
11	17.19	19	9♋	11	15	5	♃29♋R
12	17.23	20	23	12	15	5	♄16♏
13	17.27	21	7♌	14	15	6	♅27♋R
14	17.30	22	21	16	16	7	♆27♎
15	17.34	23	4♍	17	16	8	♇26♌R
16	17.38	24	17	19	17	8	♃28♋R
17	17.42	25	29	20	17	9	♄17♏
18	17.46	26	11♎	22	17	10	♅27♋R
19	17.50	27	23	23	18	11	♆27♎
20	17.54	28	5♏	25	18	11	♇26♌R
21	17.58	29	17	27	19	12	♃28♋R
22	18.02	0♑	29	28	19	13	♄17♏
23	18.06	1	11♐	0♑	20	13	♅26♋R
24	18.10	2	23	1	20	14	♆28♎
25	18.14	3	5♑	3	21	15	♇26♌R
26	18.18	4	17	4	22	15	♃27♋R
27	18.22	5	0♒	6	22	16	♄18♏
28	18.26	6	12	8	23	17	♅26♋R
29	18.30	7	25	9	24	18	♆28♎
30	18.34	8	8♓	11	24	18	♇26♌R
31	18.38	9	22	12	25	19	♃27♋R

1 9 5 5

Jan	STime	☉	☽	☿	♀	♂	Plnts
1	18.41	10♑	5♈	14♑	26♏	20♓	♃26♋R
2	18.45	11	19	16	27	21	♄18♏
3	18.49	12	4♉	17	27	21	♅26♋R
4	18.53	13	18	19	28	22	♆28♎
5	18.57	14	3♊	21	29	23	♇26♌R
6	19.01	15	17	22	0♐	23	♃26♋R
7	19.05	16	2♋	24	1	24	♄19♏
8	19.09	17	17	26	2	25	♅26♋R
9	19.13	18	1♌	27	2	26	♆28♎
10	19.17	19	15	29	3	26	♇26♌R
11	19.21	20	29	1♒	4	27	♃25♋R
12	19.25	21	12♍	2	5	28	♄19♏
13	19.29	22	25	4	6	28	♅26♋R
14	19.33	23	7♎	6	7	29	♆28♎
15	19.37	24	20	7	8	0♈	♇26♌R
16	19.41	25	2♏	9	9	1	♃25♋R
17	19.45	26	13	10	10	1	♄19♏
18	19.48	27	25	12	11	2	♅25♋R
19	19.52	28	7♐	14	12	3	♆28♎
20	19.56	29	19	15	13	3	♇26♌R
21	20.00	0♒	1♑	17	14	4	♃24♋R
22	20.04	1	13	18	15	5	♄20♏
23	20.08	2	26	20	16	6	♅25♋R
24	20.12	3	9♒	21	17	6	♆28♎
25	20.16	4	22	22	18	7	♇26♌R
26	20.20	5	5♓	24	19	8	♃23♋R
27	20.24	6	19	25	20	9	♄20♏
28	20.28	7	2♈	26	21	9	♅25♋R
29	20.32	9	16	27	22	10	♆28♎
30	20.36	10	0♉	28	23	11	♇26♌R
31	20.40	11	14	28	24	11	♃23♋R

Feb	STime	☉	☽	☿	♀	♂	Plnts
1	20.44	12♒	28♉	29♒	25♐	12♈	♃22♋R
2	20.48	13	13♊	29	26	13	♄20♏
3	20.52	14	27	29R	27	13	♅25♋R
4	20.55	15	11♋	29	28	14	♆28♎
5	20.59	16	25	29	29	15	♇26♌R
6	21.03	17	9♌	29	0♑	16	♃22♋R
7	21.07	18	23	28	1	16	♄20♏
8	21.11	19	7♍	27	2	17	♅24♋R
9	21.15	20	20	27	3	18	♆28♎R
10	21.19	21	3♎	26	5	18	♇25♌R
11	21.23	22	15	24	6	19	♃21♋R
12	21.27	23	27	23	7	20	♄21♏
13	21.31	24	9♏	22	8	21	♅24♋R
14	21.35	25	21	21	9	21	♆28♎R
15	21.39	26	3♐	20	10	22	♇25♌R
16	21.43	27	15	19	11	23	♃21♋R
17	21.47	28	27	18	12	23	♄21♏
18	21.51	29	9♑	17	13	24	♅24♋R
19	21.55	0♓	21	16	15	25	♆28♎R
20	21.59	1	4♒	16	16	26	♇25♌R
21	22.03	2	17	15	17	26	♃20♋R
22	22.06	3	1♓	15	18	27	♄21♏
23	22.10	4	14	14	19	28	♅24♋R
24	22.14	5	28	14	20	28	♆28♎R
25	22.18	6	13♈	14D	21	29	♇25♌R
26	22.22	7	27	14	22	0♉	♃20♋R
27	22.26	8	11♉	14	24	0	♄21♏
28	22.30	9	25	15	25	1	♅24♋R

Mar	STime	☉	☽	☿	♀	♂	Plnts
1	22.34	10♓	9♊	15♒	26♑	2♉	♃20♋R
2	22.38	11	23	15	27	3	♄21♏
3	22.42	12	7♋	16	28	3	♅24♋R
4	22.46	13	21	16	29	4	♆28♎R
5	22.50	14	5♌	17	0♒	5	♇25♌R
6	22.54	15	18	18	2	5	♃20♋R
7	22.58	16	2♍	19	3	6	♄21♏R
8	23.02	17	15	20	4	7	♅24♋R
9	23.06	18	28	20	5	7	♆28♎R
10	23.10	19	11♎	21	6	8	♇25♌R
11	23.13	20	23	22	7	9	♃20♋R
12	23.17	21	5♏	23	9	9	♄21♏R
13	23.21	22	17	25	10	10	♅23♋R
14	23.25	23	29	26	11	11	♆27♎R
15	23.29	24	11♐	27	12	12	♇25♌R
16	23.33	25	23	28	13	12	♃20♋
17	23.37	26	5♑	29	14	13	♄21♏R
18	23.41	27	17	0♓	16	14	♅23♋R
19	23.45	28	29	2	17	14	♆27♎R
20	23.49	29	12♒	3	18	15	♇25♌R
21	23.53	0♈	25	4	19	16	♃20♋
22	23.57	1	9♓	6	20	16	♄21♏R
23	0.01	2	23	7	21	17	♅23♋R
24	0.05	3	7♈	9	23	18	♆27♎R
25	0.09	4	22	10	24	18	♇24♌R
26	0.13	5	7♉	12	25	19	♃20♋
27	0.17	6	21	13	26	20	♄20♏R
28	0.21	7	6♊	15	27	21	♅23♋
29	0.24	8	20	16	29	21	♆27♎R
30	0.28	9	4♋	18	0♓	22	♇24♌R
31	0.32	10	18	19	1	23	♃20♋

Apr	STime	☉	☽	☿	♀	♂	Plnts
1	0.36	11♈	2♌	21♓	2♓	23♉	♃20♋
2	0.40	12	15	23	3	24	♄20♏R
3	0.44	13	28	24	4	25	♅23♋
4	0.48	14	11♍	26	6	25	♆27♎R
5	0.52	15	24	28	7	26	♇24♌R
6	0.56	16	7♎	29	8	27	♃20♋
7	1.00	17	19	1♈	9	27	♄20♏R
8	1.04	18	1♏	3	10	28	♅23♋
9	1.08	19	13	5	12	29	♆27♎R
10	1.12	20	25	7	13	29	♇24♌R
11	1.16	21	7♐	8	14	0♊	♃21♋
12	1.20	22	19	10	15	1	♄19♏R
13	1.24	22	1♑	12	16	1	♅23♋
14	1.28	23	13	14	18	2	♆27♎R
15	1.31	24	25	16	19	3	♇24♌R
16	1.35	25	7♒	18	20	3	♃21♋
17	1.39	26	20	20	21	4	♄19♏R
18	1.43	27	3♓	22	22	5	♅23♋
19	1.47	28	17	24	24	5	♆27♎R
20	1.51	29	1♈	26	25	6	♇24♌R
21	1.55	0♉	16	28	26	7	♃22♋
22	1.59	1	1♉	0♉	27	7	♄19♏R
23	2.03	2	16	3	28	8	♅24♋
24	2.07	3	1♊	5	0♈	9	♆26♎R
25	2.11	4	16	7	1	9	♇24♌R
26	2.15	5	0♋	9	2	10	♃22♋
27	2.19	6	15	11	3	11	♄18♏R
28	2.23	7	28	13	4	11	♅24♋
29	2.27	8	12♌	15	6	12	♆26♎R
30	2.31	9	25	18	7	13	♇24♌R

May	STime	☉	☽	☿	♀	♂	Plnts
1	2.35	10♉	8♍	20♉	8♈	13♊	♃23♋
2	2.38	11	21	22	9	14	♄18♏R
3	2.42	12	4♎	24	10	15	♅24♋
4	2.46	13	16	26	12	15	♆26♎R
5	2.50	14	28	28	13	16	♇24♌
6	2.54	15	10♏	0♊	14	17	♃23♋
7	2.58	16	22	1	15	17	♄18♏R
8	3.02	17	4♐	3	16	18	♅24♋
9	3.06	18	16	5	18	19	♆26♎R
10	3.10	19	28	7	19	19	♇24♌
11	3.14	20	9♑	8	20	20	♃24♋
12	3.18	21	21	10	21	21	♄17♏R
13	3.22	22	4♒	12	22	21	♅24♋
14	3.26	23	16	13	24	22	♆26♎R
15	3.30	24	29	14	25	23	♇24♌
16	3.34	25	12♓	16	26	23	♃25♋
17	3.38	26	25	17	27	24	♄17♏R
18	3.42	26	10♈	18	28	25	♅24♋
19	3.46	27	24	20	0♉	25	♆26♎R
20	3.49	28	9♉	21	1	26	♇24♌
21	3.53	29	24	22	2	27	♃26♋
22	3.57	0♊	9♊	23	3	27	♄17♏R
23	4.01	1	24	24	4	28	♅24♋
24	4.05	2	9♋	24	6	29	♆26♎R
25	4.09	3	24	25	7	29	♇24♌
26	4.13	4	8♌	26	8	0♋	♃26♋
27	4.17	5	22	26	9	1	♄16♏R
28	4.21	6	5♍	27	10	1	♅25♋
29	4.25	7	18	27	12	2	♆26♎R
30	4.29	8	1♎	28	13	3	♇24♌
31	4.33	9	13	28	14	3	♃27♋

Jun	STime	☉	☽	☿	♀	♂	Plnts
1	4.37	10♊	25♎	28♊	15♉	4♋	♃28♋
2	4.41	11	7♏	28	17	5	♄16♏R
3	4.45	12	19	29R	18	5	♅25♋
4	4.49	13	1♐	29	19	6	♆25♎R
5	4.53	14	13	28	20	7	♇24♌
6	4.56	15	25	28	21	7	♃28♋
7	5.00	16	6♑	28	23	8	♄16♏R
8	5.04	17	18	28	24	8	♅25♋
9	5.08	18	0♒	27	25	9	♆25♎R
10	5.12	19	13	27	26	10	♇24♌
11	5.16	19	25	27	27	10	♃29♋
12	5.20	20	8♓	26	29	11	♄15♏R
13	5.24	21	21	26	0♊	12	♅25♋
14	5.28	22	5♈	25	1	12	♆25♎R
15	5.32	23	18	24	2	13	♇24♌
16	5.36	24	3♉	24	4	14	♃ 0♌
17	5.40	25	17	23	5	14	♄15♏R
18	5.44	26	2♊	23	6	15	♅26♋
19	5.48	27	18	22	7	16	♆25♎R
20	5.52	28	3♋	22	8	16	♇24♌
21	5.56	29	18	21	10	17	♃ 1♌
22	6.00	0♋	2♌	21	11	18	♄15♏R
23	6.04	1	17	21	12	18	♅26♋
24	6.07	2	1♍	20	13	19	♆25♎R
25	6.11	3	14	20	14	19	♇25♌
26	6.15	4	27	20	16	20	♃ 2♌
27	6.19	5	10♎	20D	17	21	♄15♏R
28	6.23	6	22	20	18	21	♅26♋
29	6.27	7	4♏	20	19	22	♆25♎
30	6.31	8	16	20	21	23	♇25♌

Jul	STime	☉	☽	☿	♀	♂	Plnts
1	6.35	9♋	28♏	20♊	22♊	23♋	♃ 3♌
2	6.39	10	10♐	21	23	24	♄14♏R
3	6.43	10	22	21	24	25	♅27♋
4	6.47	11	3♑	22	25	25	♆25♎
5	6.51	12	15	22	27	26	♇25♌
6	6.55	13	27	23	28	27	♃ 5♌
7	6.59	14	10♒	24	29	27	♄14♏R
8	7.03	15	22	24	0♋	28	♅27♋
9	7.07	16	5♓	25	2	28	♆25♎
10	7.11	17	18	26	3	29	♇25♌
11	7.14	18	1♈	27	4	0♌	♃ 6♌
12	7.18	19	15	28	5	0	♄14♏R
13	7.22	20	28	0♋	6	1	♅27♋
14	7.26	21	12♉	1	8	2	♆25♎
15	7.30	22	27	2	9	2	♇25♌
16	7.34	23	11♊	4	10	3	♃ 7♌
17	7.38	24	26	5	11	4	♄14♏R
18	7.42	25	11♋	7	13	4	♅27♋
19	7.46	26	26	8	14	5	♆25♎
20	7.50	27	11♌	10	15	6	♇25♌
21	7.54	28	25	12	16	6	♃ 8♌
22	7.58	29	9♍	13	17	7	♄14♏
23	8.02	0♌	22	15	19	7	♅28♋
24	8.06	1	5♎	17	20	8	♆25♎
25	8.10	1	18	19	21	9	♇25♌
26	8.14	2	1♏	21	22	9	♃ 9♌
27	8.18	3	13	23	24	10	♄14♏
28	8.22	4	25	25	25	11	♅28♋
29	8.25	5	6♐	27	26	11	♆25♎
30	8.29	6	18	29	27	12	♇26♌
31	8.33	7	0♑	1♌	28	13	♃10♌

Aug	STime	☉	☽	☿	♀	♂	Plnts
1	8.37	8♌	12♑	3♌	0♌	13♌	♃10♌
2	8.41	9	24	6	1	14	♄14♏
3	8.45	10	6♒	8	2	14	♅28♋
4	8.49	11	19	10	3	15	♆25♎
5	8.53	12	2♓	12	5	16	♇26♌
6	8.57	13	15	14	6	16	♃11♌
7	9.01	14	28	16	7	17	♄15♏
8	9.05	15	11♈	18	8	18	♅29♋
9	9.09	16	25	20	10	18	♆25♎
10	9.13	17	9♉	22	11	19	♇26♌
11	9.17	18	23	24	12	20	♃12♌
12	9.21	19	7♊	26	13	20	♄15♏
13	9.25	20	21	28	15	21	♅29♋
14	9.29	21	6♋	0♍	16	21	♆26♎
15	9.32	22	20	1	17	22	♇26♌
16	9.36	23	5♌	3	18	23	♃13♌
17	9.40	24	19	5	19	23	♄15♏
18	9.44	24	3♍	7	21	24	♅29♋
19	9.48	25	17	9	22	25	♆26♎
20	9.52	26	1♎	10	23	25	♇26♌
21	9.56	27	14	12	24	26	♃15♌
22	10.00	28	26	14	26	27	♄15♏
23	10.04	29	9♏	16	27	27	♅ 0♌
24	10.08	0♍	21	17	28	28	♆26♎
25	10.12	1	3♐	19	29	28	♇26♌
26	10.16	2	14	20	1♍	29	♃16♌
27	10.20	3	26	22	2	0♍	♄15♏
28	10.24	4	8♑	24	3	0	♅ 0♌
29	10.28	5	20	25	4	1	♆26♎
30	10.32	6	2♒	27	6	2	♇27♌
31	10.36	7	15	28	7	2	♃17♌

Sep	STime	☉	☽	☿	♀	♂	Plnts
1	10.39	8♍	28♒	0♎	8♍	3♍	♃17♌
2	10.43	9	11♓	1	9	4	♄16♏
3	10.47	10	24	3	11	4	♅ 0♌
4	10.51	11	8♈	4	12	5	♆26♎
5	10.55	12	22	5	13	5	♇27♌
6	10.59	13	6♉	7	14	6	♃18♌
7	11.03	14	20	8	15	7	♄16♏
8	11.07	15	4♊	9	17	7	♅ 0♌
9	11.11	16	18	11	18	8	♆26♎
10	11.15	17	2♋	12	19	9	♇27♌
11	11.19	18	16	13	20	9	♃19♌
12	11.23	19	0♌	14	22	10	♄17♏
13	11.27	20	14	16	23	11	♅ 1♌
14	11.31	21	28	17	24	11	♆26♎
15	11.35	22	12♍	18	25	12	♇27♌
16	11.39	23	26	19	27	12	♃20♌
17	11.43	24	9♎	20	28	13	♄17♏
18	11.47	25	22	21	29	14	♅ 1♌
19	11.50	25	4♏	22	0♎	14	♆27♎
20	11.54	26	17	23	2	15	♇27♌
21	11.58	27	29	24	3	16	♃21♌
22	12.02	28	10♐	24	4	16	♄17♏
23	12.06	29	22	25	5	17	♅ 1♌
24	12.10	0♎	4♑	26	7	18	♆27♎
25	12.14	1	16	26	8	18	♇27♌
26	12.18	2	28	27	9	19	♃22♌
27	12.22	3	10♒	27	10	20	♄18♏
28	12.26	4	23	28	12	20	♅ 1♌
29	12.30	5	6♓	28	13	21	♆27♎
30	12.34	6	20	28	14	21	♇27♌

Oct	STime	☉	☽	☿	♀	♂	Plnts
1	12.38	7♎	3♈	28♎	15♎	22♍	♃23♌
2	12.42	8	17	28	17	23	♄18♏
3	12.46	9	2♉	28	18	23	♅ 1♌
4	12.50	10	16	28	19	24	♆27♎
5	12.54	11	0♊	27	20	25	♇28♌
6	12.57	12	15	27	22	25	♃24♌
7	13.01	13	29	26	23	26	♄19♏
8	13.05	14	13♋	25	24	27	♅ 2♌
9	13.09	15	27	24	25	27	♆27♎
10	13.13	16	11♌	23	27	28	♇28♌
11	13.17	17	24	22	28	28	♃25♌
12	13.21	18	8♍	21	29	29	♄19♏
13	13.25	19	21	20	0♏	0♎	♅ 2♌
14	13.29	20	4♎	19	2	0	♆27♎
15	13.33	21	17	18	3	1	♇28♌
16	13.37	22	0♏	16	4	2	♃26♌
17	13.41	23	12	15	5	2	♄20♏
18	13.45	24	25	15	7	3	♅ 2♌
19	13.49	25	7♐	14	8	4	♆28♎
20	13.53	26	18	13	9	4	♇28♌
21	13.57	27	0♑	13	10	5	♃26♌
22	14.01	28	12	13D	12	5	♄21♏
23	14.05	29	24	13	13	6	♅ 2♌
24	14.08	0♏	6♒	13	14	7	♆28♎
25	14.12	1	18	14	15	7	♇28♌
26	14.16	2	1♓	14	17	8	♃27♌
27	14.20	3	14	15	18	9	♄21♏
28	14.24	4	28	16	19	9	♅ 2♌
29	14.28	5	11♈	17	20	10	♆28♎
30	14.32	6	26	18	21	11	♇28♌
31	14.36	7	10♉	19	23	11	♃28♌

Nov	STime	☉	☽	☿	♀	♂	Plnts
1	14.40	8♏	25♉	20♎	24♏	12♎	♃28♌
2	14.44	9	10♊	21	25	13	♄22♏
3	14.48	10	25	23	26	13	♅ 2♌
4	14.52	11	9♋	24	28	14	♆28♎
5	14.56	12	24	26	29	14	♇28♌
6	15.00	13	8♌	27	0♐	15	♃29♌
7	15.04	14	21	29	1	16	♄22♏
8	15.08	15	5♍	0♏	3	16	♅ 2♌
9	15.12	16	18	2	4	17	♆28♎
10	15.15	17	1♎	3	5	18	♇28♌
11	15.19	18	14	5	6	18	♃29♌
12	15.23	19	26	6	8	19	♄23♏
13	15.27	20	9♏	8	9	20	♅ 2♌
14	15.31	21	21	9	10	20	♆29♎
15	15.35	22	3♐	11	11	21	♇28♌
16	15.39	23	15	13	13	22	♃ 0♍
17	15.43	24	27	14	14	22	♄24♏
18	15.47	25	9♑	16	15	23	♅ 2♌R
19	15.51	26	20	17	16	24	♆29♎
20	15.55	27	2♒	19	18	24	♇28♌
21	15.59	28	14	21	19	25	♃ 0♍
22	16.03	29	26	22	20	25	♄24♏
23	16.07	0♐	9♓	24	21	26	♅ 2♌R
24	16.11	1	22	25	23	27	♆29♎
25	16.15	2	5♈	27	24	27	♇28♌
26	16.19	3	19	29	25	28	♃ 0♍
27	16.23	4	4♉	0♐	26	29	♄25♏
28	16.26	5	18	2	28	29	♅ 2♌R
29	16.30	6	3♊	3	29	0♏	♆29♎
30	16.34	7	18	5	0♑	1	♇28♌

Dec	STime	☉	☽	☿	♀	♂	Plnts
1	16.38	8♐	4♋	6♐	1♑	1♏	♃ 1♍
2	16.42	9	19	8	3	2	♄25♏
3	16.46	10	3♌	10	4	3	♅ 2♌R
4	16.50	11	18	11	5	3	♆29♎
5	16.54	12	2♍	13	6	4	♇28♌
6	16.58	13	15	14	8	5	♃ 1♍
7	17.02	14	28	16	9	5	♄26♏
8	17.06	15	11♎	17	10	6	♅ 2♌R
9	17.10	16	24	19	11	6	♆29♎
10	17.14	17	6♏	21	13	7	♇28♌R
11	17.18	18	18	22	14	8	♃ 1♍
12	17.22	19	0♐	24	15	8	♄27♏
13	17.26	20	12	25	16	9	♅ 2♌R
14	17.30	21	24	27	18	10	♆29♎
15	17.33	22	5♑	28	19	10	♇28♌R
16	17.37	23	17	0♑	20	11	♃ 1♍
17	17.41	24	29	2	21	12	♄27♏
18	17.45	25	11♒	3	23	12	♅ 1♌R
19	17.49	27	23	5	24	13	♆ 0♏
20	17.53	28	5♓	6	25	14	♇28♌R
21	17.57	29	18	8	26	14	♃ 1♍R
22	18.01	0♑	1♈	10	27	15	♄28♏
23	18.05	1	14	11	29	16	♅ 1♌R
24	18.09	2	28	13	0♒	16	♆ 0♏
25	18.13	3	12♉	14	1	17	♇28♌R
26	18.17	4	26	16	2	18	♃ 1♍R
27	18.21	5	11♊	18	4	18	♄28♏
28	18.25	6	26	19	5	19	♅ 1♌R
29	18.29	7	12♋	21	6	20	♆ 0♏
30	18.33	8	27	22	7	20	♇28♌R
31	18.37	9	12♌	24	9	21	♃ 1♍R

Jan	STime	☉	☽	☿	♀	♂	Plnts
1	18.40	10♑	26♌	25♑	10♒	21♏	♃ 1♍R
2	18.44	11	11♍	27	11	22	♄29♏
3	18.48	12	24	28	12	23	♅ 1♌R
4	18.52	13	8♎	0♒	14	23	♆ 0♏
5	18.56	14	20	1	15	24	♇28♌R
6	19.00	15	3♏	3	16	25	♃ 1♍R
7	19.04	16	15	4	17	25	♄29♏
8	19.08	17	27	5	19	26	♅ 1♌R
9	19.12	18	9♐	7	20	27	♆ 0♏
10	19.16	19	21	8	21	27	♇28♌R
11	19.20	20	2♑	9	22	28	♃ 0♍R
12	19.24	21	14	10	23	29	♄ 0♐
13	19.28	22	26	11	25	29	♅ 0♌R
14	19.32	23	8♒	12	26	0♐	♆ 0♏
15	19.36	24	20	12	27	1	♇28♌R
16	19.40	25	2♓	13	28	1	♃ 0♍R
17	19.44	26	15	13	0♓	2	♄ 0♐
18	19.48	27	27	13R	1	3	♅ 0♌R
19	19.51	28	10♈	13	2	3	♆ 0♏
20	19.55	29	23	13	3	4	♇28♌R
21	19.59	0♒	7♉	12	4	5	♃29♌R
22	20.03	1	21	12	6	5	♄ 1♐
23	20.07	2	5♊	11	7	6	♅ 0♌R
24	20.11	3	20	10	8	7	♆ 0♏
25	20.15	4	5♋	9	9	7	♇28♌R
26	20.19	5	20	8	11	8	♃29♌R
27	20.23	6	5♌	6	12	8	♄ 1♐
28	20.27	7	20	5	13	9	♅ 0♌R
29	20.31	8	4♍	4	14	10	♆ 0♏
30	20.35	9	19	3	15	10	♇28♌R
31	20.39	10	3♎	2	17	11	♃28♌R

Feb	STime	☉	☽	☿	♀	♂	Plnts
1	20.43	11♒	16♎	1♒	18♓	12♐	♃28♌R
2	20.47	12	29	0	19	12	♄ 1♐
3	20.51	13	11♏	29♑	20	13	♅29♋R
4	20.55	14	24	28	21	14	♆ 0♏R
5	20.58	15	6♐	28	23	14	♇27♌R
6	21.02	16	17	28	24	15	♃28♌R
7	21.06	17	29	27	25	16	♄ 2♐
8	21.10	18	11♑	27D	26	16	♅29♋R
9	21.14	19	23	27	28	17	♆ 0♏
10	21.18	20	5♒	28	29	18	♇27♌R
11	21.22	21	17	28	0♈	18	♃27♌R
12	21.26	22	29	28	1	19	♄ 2♐
13	21.30	23	12♓	29	2	20	♅29♋R
14	21.34	24	24	29	3	20	♆ 0♏R
15	21.38	25	7♈	0♒	5	21	♇27♌R
16	21.42	26	20	1	6	22	♃26♌R
17	21.46	28	4♉	1	7	22	♄ 2♐
18	21.50	29	17	2	8	23	♅29♋R
19	21.54	0♓	1♊	3	9	24	♆ 0♏R
20	21.58	1	15	4	11	24	♇27♌R
21	22.02	2	29	5	12	25	♃26♌R
22	22.06	3	14♋	6	13	26	♄ 2♐
23	22.09	4	28	7	14	26	♅29♋R
24	22.13	5	13♌	8	15	27	♆ 0♏R
25	22.17	6	28	9	16	28	♇27♌R
26	22.21	7	12♍	11	18	28	♃25♌R
27	22.25	8	27	12	19	29	♄ 2♐
28	22.29	9	10♎	13	20	29	♅29♋R
29	22.33	10	24	14	21	0♑	♆ 0♏R

Mar	STime	☉	☽	☿	♀	♂	Plnts
1	22.37	11♓	7♏	16♒	22♈	1♑	♃24♌R
2	22.41	12	19	17	23	1	♄ 2♐
3	22.45	13	2♐	18	25	2	♅28♋R
4	22.49	14	14	20	26	3	♆ 0♏R
5	22.53	15	25	21	27	3	♇27♌R
6	22.57	16	7♑	22	28	4	♃24♌R
7	23.01	17	19	24	29	5	♄ 3♐
8	23.05	18	1♒	25	0♉	5	♅28♋R
9	23.09	19	13	27	2	6	♆ 0♏R
10	23.13	20	25	28	3	7	♇27♌R
11	23.16	21	8♓	0♓	4	7	♃23♌R
12	23.20	22	21	1	5	8	♄ 3♐
13	23.24	23	4♈	3	6	9	♅28♋R
14	23.28	24	17	4	7	9	♆ 0♏R
15	23.32	25	1♉	6	8	10	♇26♌R
16	23.36	26	14	8	9	11	♃23♌R
17	23.40	27	28	9	11	11	♄ 2♐R
18	23.44	28	12♊	11	12	12	♅28♋R
19	23.48	29	26	13	13	13	♆ 0♏R
20	23.52	0♈	10♋	14	14	13	♇26♌R
21	23.56	1	24	16	15	14	♃22♌R
22	0.00	2	8♌	18	16	15	♄ 2♐R
23	0.04	3	23	20	17	15	♅28♋R
24	0.08	4	7♍	21	18	16	♆29♎R
25	0.12	5	21	23	19	16	♇26♌R
26	0.16	6	5♎	25	20	17	♃22♌R
27	0.20	7	18	27	21	18	♄ 2♐R
28	0.23	7	2♏	29	23	18	♅28♋
29	0.27	8	15	1♈	24	19	♆29♎R
30	0.31	9	27	3	25	20	♇26♌R
31	0.35	10	9♐	5	26	20	♃22♌R

Apr	STime	☉	☽	☿	♀	♂	Plnts
1	0.39	11♈	21♐	7♈	27♉	21♑	♃22♌R
2	0.43	12	3♑	9	28	22	♄ 2♐R
3	0.47	13	15	11	29	22	♅28♋
4	0.51	14	27	13	0♊	23	♆29♎R
5	0.55	15	9♒	15	1	24	♇26♌R
6	0.59	16	21	17	2	24	♃21♌R
7	1.03	17	4♓	19	3	25	♄ 2♐R
8	1.07	18	16	21	4	26	♅28♋
9	1.11	19	29	23	5	26	♆29♎R
10	1.15	20	13♈	25	6	27	♇26♌R
11	1.19	21	26	27	7	27	♃21♌R
12	1.23	22	10♉	29	8	28	♄ 2♐R
13	1.27	23	24	1♉	9	29	♅28♋
14	1.31	24	8♊	3	10	29	♆29♎R
15	1.34	25	22	5	11	0♒	♇26♌R
16	1.38	26	7♋	7	12	1	♃21♌
17	1.42	27	21	9	13	1	♄ 1♐R
18	1.46	28	5♌	11	14	2	♅28♋
19	1.50	29	19	13	15	3	♆29♎R
20	1.54	0♉	3♍	15	16	3	♇26♌
21	1.58	1	17	17	16	4	♃21♌
22	2.02	2	0♎	19	17	4	♄ 1♐R
23	2.06	3	14	20	18	5	♅28♋
24	2.10	4	27	22	19	6	♆29♎R
25	2.14	5	10♏	24	20	6	♇26♌R
26	2.18	6	23	25	21	7	♃21♌
27	2.22	7	5♐	27	22	8	♄ 1♐R
28	2.26	8	17	28	22	8	♅28♋
29	2.30	9	29	29	23	9	♆28♎R
30	2.34	10	11♑	0♊	24	10	♇26♌R

May	STime	☉	☽	☿	♀	♂	Plnts
1	2.38	11♉	23♑	1♊	25♊	10♒	♃21♌
2	2.41	12	5♒	3	26	11	♄ 1♐R
3	2.45	13	17	3	26	11	♅28♋
4	2.49	14	29	4	27	12	♆28♎R
5	2.53	15	11♓	5	28	13	♇26♌
6	2.57	16	24	6	29	13	♃22♌
7	3.01	17	7♈	7	29	14	♄ 0♐R
8	3.05	18	21	7	0♋	14	♅28♋
9	3.09	19	5♉	8	1	15	♆28♎R
10	3.13	19	19	8	1	16	♇26♌
11	3.17	20	3♊	8	2	16	♃22♌
12	3.21	21	18	8	2	17	♄ 0♐R
13	3.25	22	3♋	9	3	18	♅29♋
14	3.29	23	17	9R	4	18	♆28♎R
15	3.33	24	2♌	9	4	19	♇26♌
16	3.37	25	16	8	5	19	♃22♌
17	3.41	26	0♍	8	5	20	♄29♏R
18	3.45	27	14	8	6	21	♅29♋
19	3.49	28	27	8	6	21	♆28♎R
20	3.52	29	10♎	7	6	22	♇26♌
21	3.56	0♊	24	7	7	22	♃23♌
22	4.00	1	6♏	6	7	23	♄29♏R
23	4.04	2	19	6	7	24	♅29♋
24	4.08	3	1♐	5	8	24	♆28♎R
25	4.12	4	14	5	8	25	♇26♌
26	4.16	5	26	4	8	25	♃23♌
27	4.20	6	8♑	4	8	26	♄29♏R
28	4.24	7	19	3	9	26	♅29♋
29	4.28	8	1♒	2	9	27	♆28♎R
30	4.32	9	13	2	9	28	♇26♌
31	4.36	10	25	2	9R	28	♃24♌

Jun	STime	☉	☽	☿	♀	♂	Plnts
1	4.40	11♊	7♓	1♊	9♋	29♒	♃24♌
2	4.44	12	20	1	9	29	♄28♏R
3	4.48	13	2♈	0	9	0♓	♅29♋
4	4.52	14	15	0	8	0	♆28♎R
5	4.56	14	29	0	8	1	♇26♌
6	4.59	15	13♉	0	8	1	♃25♌
7	5.03	16	27	0D	8	2	♄28♏R
8	5.07	17	12♊	0	8	3	♅ 0♌
9	5.11	18	27	0	7	3	♆28♎R
10	5.15	19	12♋	0	7	4	♇26♌
11	5.19	20	27	1	6	4	♃25♌
12	5.23	21	12♌	1	6	5	♄28♏R
13	5.27	22	26	1	6	5	♅ 0♌
14	5.31	23	10♍	2	5	6	♆28♎R
15	5.35	24	24	2	5	6	♇26♌
16	5.39	25	8♎	3	4	7	♃26♌
17	5.43	26	21	4	3	7	♄27♏R
18	5.47	27	3♏	5	3	8	♅ 0♌
19	5.51	28	16	5	2	8	♆27♎R
20	5.55	29	28	6	2	9	♇26♌
21	5.59	0♋	10♐	7	1	9	♃27♌
22	6.03	1	22	8	0	10	♄27♏R
23	6.06	2	4♑	9	0	10	♅ 0♌
24	6.10	3	16	11	29♊	11	♆27♎
25	6.14	4	28	12	28	11	♇26♌
26	6.18	5	10♒	13	28	12	♃28♌
27	6.22	5	22	14	27	12	♄27♏R
28	6.26	6	4♓	16	27	12	♅ 1♌
29	6.30	7	16	17	26	13	♆27♎
30	6.34	8	28	19	26	13	♇26♌

Jul	STime	☉	☽	☿	♀	♂	Plnts
1	6.38	9♋	11♈	20♊	25♊	14♓	♃29♌
2	6.42	10	24	22	25	14	♄26♏R
3	6.46	11	7♉	24	24	15	♅ 1♌
4	6.50	12	21	26	24	15	♆27♎
5	6.54	13	5♊	27	24	15	♇27♌
6	6.58	14	20	29	23	16	♃29♌
7	7.02	15	5♋	1♋	23	16	♄26♏R
8	7.06	16	20	3	23	17	♅ 1♌
9	7.10	17	6♌	5	23	17	♆27♎
10	7.14	18	21	7	22	17	♇27♌
11	7.17	19	5♍	9	22	18	♃ 0♍
12	7.21	20	20	11	22	18	♄26♏R
13	7.25	21	4♎	13	22D	18	♅ 2♌
14	7.29	22	17	15	22	19	♆27♎
15	7.33	23	0♏	17	22	19	♇27♌
16	7.37	24	13	20	22	19	♃ 1♍
17	7.41	25	25	22	22	20	♄26♏R
18	7.45	26	7♐	24	23	20	♅ 2♌
19	7.49	26	19	26	23	20	♆27♎
20	7.53	27	1♑	28	23	20	♇27♌
21	7.57	28	13	0♌	23	21	♃ 2♍
22	8.01	29	25	2	24	21	♄26♏R
23	8.05	0♌	7♒	4	24	21	♅ 2♌
24	8.09	1	19	7	24	21	♆27♎
25	8.13	2	1♓	9	25	22	♇27♌
26	8.17	3	13	11	25	22	♃ 3♍
27	8.21	4	25	13	25	22	♄26♏R
28	8.24	5	8♈	14	26	22	♅ 3♌
29	8.28	6	20	16	26	22	♆27♎
30	8.32	7	3♉	18	27	23	♇27♌
31	8.36	8	16	20	27	23	♃ 4♍

Aug	STime	☉	☽	☿	♀	♂	Plnts
1	8.40	9♌	0♊	22♌	28♊	23♓	♃ 5♍
2	8.44	10	14	24	29	23	♄26♏
3	8.48	11	29	26	29	23	♅ 3♌
4	8.52	12	14♋	27	0♋	23	♆28♎
5	8.56	13	29	29	0	23	♇27♌
6	9.00	14	14♌	1♍	1	23	♃ 6♍
7	9.04	15	29	3	2	23	♄26♏
8	9.08	16	14♍	4	2	23	♅ 3♌
9	9.12	17	29	6	3	23	♆28♎
10	9.16	18	13♎	8	4	23R	♇28♌
11	9.20	18	26	9	5	23	♃ 7♍
12	9.24	19	9♏	11	5	23	♄26♏
13	9.28	20	22	12	6	23	♅ 3♌
14	9.32	21	4♐	14	7	23	♆28♎
15	9.35	22	16	15	8	23	♇28♌
16	9.39	23	28	17	8	23	♃ 8♍
17	9.43	24	10♑	18	9	23	♄26♏
18	9.47	25	22	19	10	23	♅ 4♌
19	9.51	26	4♒	21	11	23	♆28♎
20	9.55	27	16	22	12	23	♇28♌
21	9.59	28	28	24	13	23	♃ 9♍
22	10.03	29	10♓	25	14	22	♄26♏
23	10.07	0♍	22	26	14	22	♅ 4♌
24	10.11	1	5♈	27	15	22	♆28♎
25	10.15	2	17	28	16	22	♇28♌
26	10.19	3	0♉	0♎	17	22	♃10♍
27	10.23	4	13	1	18	22	♄26♏
28	10.27	5	26	2	19	21	♅ 4♌
29	10.31	6	10♊	3	20	21	♆28♎
30	10.35	7	24	4	21	21	♇28♌
31	10.39	8	8♋	5	22	21	♃11♍

Sep	STime	☉	☽	☿	♀	♂	Plnts
1	10.42	9♍	23♋	6♎	23♋	20♓	♃11♍
2	10.46	10	8♌	7	24	20	♄27♏
3	10.50	11	23	7	25	20	♅ 5♌
4	10.54	12	8♍	8	26	20	♆28♎
5	10.58	13	22	9	27	19	♇28♌
6	11.02	14	7♎	10	28	19	♃12♍
7	11.06	15	21	10	29	19	♄27♏
8	11.10	16	4♏	11	0♌	19	♅ 5♌
9	11.14	16	18	11	1	18	♆28♎
10	11.18	17	0♐	11	2	18	♇29♌
11	11.22	18	13	12	3	18	♃13♍
12	11.26	19	25	12	4	17	♄27♏
13	11.30	20	7♑	12R	5	17	♅ 5♌
14	11.34	21	19	12	6	17	♆28♎
15	11.38	22	0♒	12	7	17	♇29♌
16	11.42	23	12	11	8	16	♃14♍
17	11.46	24	24	11	9	16	♄28♏
18	11.50	25	7♓	11	10	16	♅ 5♌
19	11.53	26	19	10	11	16	♆29♎
20	11.57	27	1♈	9	12	15	♇29♌
21	12.01	28	14	8	13	15	♃15♍
22	12.05	29	27	7	15	15	♄28♏
23	12.09	0♎	10♉	6	16	15	♅ 6♌
24	12.13	1	23	5	17	15	♆29♎
25	12.17	2	7♊	4	18	14	♇29♌
26	12.21	3	20	3	19	14	♃16♍
27	12.25	4	4♋	2	20	14	♄29♏
28	12.29	5	18	1	21	14	♅ 6♌
29	12.33	6	3♌	0	22	14	♆29♎
30	12.37	7	17	29♍	23	14	♇29♌

Oct	STime	☉	☽	☿	♀	♂	Plnts
1	12.41	8♎	2♍	28♍	24♌	13♓	♃18♍
2	12.45	9	16	28	26	13	♄29♏
3	12.49	10	1♎	27	27	13	♅ 6♌
4	12.53	11	15	27	28	13	♆29♎
5	12.57	12	29	27D	29	13	♇29♌
6	13.00	13	12♏	27	0♍	13	♃19♍
7	13.04	14	26	27	1	13	♄29♏
8	13.08	15	8♐	28	2	13	♅ 6♌
9	13.12	16	21	28	4	13	♆29♎
10	13.16	17	3♑	29	5	13D	♇29♌
11	13.20	18	15	0♎	6	13	♃20♍
12	13.24	19	27	1	7	13	♄ 0♐
13	13.28	20	8♒	2	8	13	♅ 6♌
14	13.32	21	20	3	9	13	♆ 0♏
15	13.36	22	3♓	4	10	13	♇ 0♍
16	13.40	23	15	6	12	13	♃21♍
17	13.44	24	27	7	13	13	♄ 0♐
18	13.48	25	10♈	9	14	13	♅ 6♌
19	13.52	26	23	10	15	13	♆ 0♏
20	13.56	27	6♉	12	16	14	♇ 0♍
21	14.00	28	20	13	17	14	♃22♍
22	14.04	29	3♊	15	19	14	♄ 1♐
23	14.07	0♏	17	17	20	14	♅ 7♌
24	14.11	1	1♋	18	21	14	♆ 0♏
25	14.15	2	15	20	22	14	♇ 0♍
26	14.19	3	29	22	23	15	♃23♍
27	14.23	4	14♌	23	25	15	♄ 1♐
28	14.27	5	28	25	26	15	♅ 7♌
29	14.31	6	12♍	27	27	15	♆ 0♏
30	14.35	7	26	28	28	15	♇ 0♍
31	14.39	8	10♎	0♏	29	16	♃23♍

Nov	STime	☉	☽	☿	♀	♂	Plnts
1	14.43	9♏	24♎	2♏	1♎	16♓	♃24♍
2	14.47	10	7♏	3	2	16	♄ 2♐
3	14.51	11	21	5	3	16	♅ 7♌
4	14.55	12	3♐	7	4	17	♆ 0♏
5	14.59	13	16	8	5	17	♇ 0♍
6	15.03	14	28	10	7	17	♃25♍
7	15.07	15	11♑	11	8	18	♄ 3♐
8	15.11	16	23	13	9	18	♅ 7♌
9	15.15	17	4♒	15	10	18	♆ 0♏
10	15.18	18	16	16	11	19	♇ 0♍
11	15.22	19	28	18	13	19	♃25♍
12	15.26	20	10♓	20	14	19	♄ 3♐
13	15.30	21	23	21	15	20	♅ 7♌
14	15.34	22	5♈	23	16	20	♆ 1♏
15	15.38	23	18	24	17	20	♇ 0♍
16	15.42	24	1♉	26	19	21	♃26♍
17	15.46	25	15	27	20	21	♄ 4♐
18	15.50	26	29	29	21	22	♅ 7♌
19	15.54	27	13♊	1♐	22	22	♆ 1♏
20	15.58	28	27	2	24	22	♇ 0♍
21	16.02	29	12♋	4	25	23	♃27♍
22	16.06	0♐	26	5	26	23	♄ 4♐
23	16.10	1	10♌	7	27	24	♅ 7♌R
24	16.14	2	25	8	28	24	♆ 1♏
25	16.18	3	9♍	10	0♏	25	♇ 0♍
26	16.22	4	23	12	1	25	♃28♍
27	16.25	5	6♎	13	2	25	♄ 5♐
28	16.29	6	20	15	3	26	♅ 7♌R
29	16.33	7	3♏	16	5	26	♆ 1♏
30	16.37	8	16	18	6	27	♇ 0♍

Dec	STime	☉	☽	☿	♀	♂	Plnts
1	16.41	9♐	29♏	19♐	7♏	27♓	♃28♍
2	16.45	10	12♐	21	8	28	♄ 6♐
3	16.49	11	24	22	10	28	♅ 6♌R
4	16.53	12	6♑	24	11	29	♆ 1♏
5	16.57	13	19	25	12	29	♇ 0♍
6	17.01	14	1♒	27	13	0♈	♃29♍
7	17.05	15	12	28	14	0	♄ 6♐
8	17.09	16	24	0♑	16	1	♅ 6♌R
9	17.13	17	6♓	2	17	1	♆ 1♏
10	17.17	18	18	3	18	2	♇ 0♍
11	17.21	19	0♈	5	19	2	♃ 0♎
12	17.25	20	13	6	21	3	♄ 7♐
13	17.29	21	26	8	22	3	♅ 6♌R
14	17.33	22	9♉	9	23	4	♆ 2♏
15	17.36	23	23	10	24	4	♇ 0♍R
16	17.40	24	7♊	12	26	5	♃ 0♎
17	17.44	25	21	13	27	5	♄ 7♐
18	17.48	26	6♋	15	28	6	♅ 6♌R
19	17.52	27	21	16	29	6	♆ 2♏
20	17.56	28	6♌	17	1♐	7	♇ 0♍R
21	18.00	29	21	19	2	8	♃ 0♎
22	18.04	0♑	5♍	20	3	8	♄ 8♐
23	18.08	1	19	21	4	9	♅ 6♌R
24	18.12	2	3♎	22	6	9	♆ 2♏
25	18.16	3	17	23	7	10	♇ 0♍R
26	18.20	4	0♏	24	8	10	♃ 1♎
27	18.24	5	13	25	9	11	♄ 9♐
28	18.28	6	26	26	11	11	♅ 6♌R
29	18.32	7	8♐	26	12	12	♆ 2♏
30	18.36	8	21	27	13	13	♇ 0♍R
31	18.40	10	3♑	27	14	13	♃ 1♎

1 9 5 7

Jan	STime	☉	☽	☿	♀	♂	Plnts
1	18.43	11♑	15♑	27♑	16♐	14♈	♃ 1♎
2	18.47	12	27	27	17	14	♄ 9♐
3	18.51	13	9♒	27	18	15	♅ 6♌R
4	18.55	14	21	26	19	15	♆ 2♏
5	18.59	15	3♓	26	21	16	♇ 0♍R
6	19.03	16	15	25	22	17	♃ 1♎
7	19.07	17	26	24	23	17	♄10♐
8	19.11	18	9♈	23	24	18	♅ 5♌R
9	19.15	19	21	21	26	18	♆ 2♏
10	19.19	20	4♉	20	27	19	♇ 0♍R
11	19.23	21	17	19	28	19	♃ 1♎
12	19.27	22	0♊	17	29	20	♄10♐
13	19.31	23	14	16	1♑	21	♅ 5♌R
14	19.35	24	29	15	2	21	♆ 2♏
15	19.39	25	14♋	14	3	22	♇ 0♍R
16	19.43	26	29	13	4	22	♃ 2♎
17	19.47	27	14♌	12	6	23	♄11♐
18	19.51	28	0♍	12	7	24	♅ 5♌R
19	19.54	29	15	11	8	24	♆ 2♏
20	19.58	0♒	29	11	9	25	♇ 0♍R
21	20.02	1	13♎	11D	11	25	♃ 1♎R
22	20.06	2	27	11	12	26	♄11♐
23	20.10	3	10♏	11	13	27	♅ 5♌R
24	20.14	4	23	11	14	27	♆ 2♏
25	20.18	5	5♐	12	16	28	♇29♌R
26	20.22	6	18	12	17	28	♃ 1♎R
27	20.26	7	0♑	13	18	29	♄12♐
28	20.30	8	12	14	19	0♉	♅ 5♌R
29	20.34	9	24	14	21	0	♆ 2♏
30	20.38	10	6♒	15	22	1	♇29♌R
31	20.42	11	18	16	23	1	♃ 1♎R

Feb	STime	☉	☽	☿	♀	♂	Plnts
1	20.46	12♒	0♓	17♑	24♑	2♉	♃ 1♎R
2	20.50	13	11	18	26	3	♄12♐
3	20.54	14	23	19	27	3	♅ 4♌R
4	20.58	15	5♈	20	28	4	♆ 2♏
5	21.01	16	18	21	29	5	♇29♌R
6	21.05	17	0♉	22	1♒	5	♃ 1♎R
7	21.09	18	12	23	2	6	♄12♐
8	21.13	19	25	24	3	6	♅ 4♌R
9	21.17	20	9♊	26	4	7	♆ 2♏R
10	21.21	21	23	27	6	8	♇29♌R
11	21.25	22	7♋	28	7	8	♃ 0♎R
12	21.29	23	22	0♒	8	9	♄13♐
13	21.33	24	7♌	1	9	9	♅ 4♌R
14	21.37	25	23	2	11	10	♆ 2♏R
15	21.41	26	8♍	4	12	11	♇29♌R
16	21.45	27	23	5	13	11	♃ 0♎R
17	21.49	28	8♎	6	14	12	♄13♐
18	21.53	29	22	8	16	13	♅ 4♌R
19	21.57	0♓	6♏	9	17	13	♆ 2♏R
20	22.01	1	19	11	18	14	♇29♌R
21	22.05	2	2♐	12	19	14	♃ 0♎R
22	22.08	3	15	14	21	15	♄13♐
23	22.12	4	27	15	22	16	♅ 3♌R
24	22.16	5	9♑	17	23	16	♆ 2♏R
25	22.20	6	21	18	24	17	♇29♌R
26	22.24	7	3♒	20	25	18	♃29♍R
27	22.28	8	15	22	27	18	♄14♐
28	22.32	9	27	23	28	19	♅ 3♌R

Mar	STime	☉	☽	☿	♀	♂	Plnts
1	22.36	10♓	8♓	25♒	29♒	19♉	♃29♍R
2	22.40	11	20	26	0♓	20	♄14♐
3	22.44	12	2♈	28	2	21	♅ 3♌R
4	22.48	13	15	0♓	3	21	♆ 2♏R
5	22.52	14	27	1	4	22	♇29♌R
6	22.56	15	9♉	3	5	23	♃28♍R
7	23.00	16	22	5	7	23	♄14♐
8	23.04	17	5♊	7	8	24	♅ 3♌R
9	23.08	18	18	8	9	24	♆ 2♏R
10	23.12	19	2♋	10	10	25	♇28♌R
11	23.16	20	16	12	12	26	♃27♍R
12	23.19	21	1♌	14	13	26	♄14♐
13	23.23	22	16	16	14	27	♅ 3♌R
14	23.27	23	1♍	17	15	28	♆ 2♏R
15	23.31	24	16	19	17	28	♇28♌R
16	23.35	25	1♎	21	18	29	♃27♍R
17	23.39	26	16	23	19	29	♄14♐
18	23.43	27	0♏	25	20	0♊	♅ 3♌R
19	23.47	28	14	27	22	1	♆ 2♏R
20	23.51	29	28	29	23	1	♇28♌R
21	23.55	0♈	11♐	1♈	24	2	♃26♍R
22	23.59	1	23	3	25	3	♄14♐
23	0.03	2	6♑	5	27	3	♅ 3♌R
24	0.07	3	18	7	28	4	♆ 2♏R
25	0.11	4	0♒	9	29	4	♇28♌R
26	0.15	5	11	11	0♈	5	♃25♍R
27	0.19	6	23	13	2	6	♄14♐R
28	0.23	7	5♓	15	3	6	♅ 3♌R
29	0.26	8	17	17	4	7	♆ 2♏R
30	0.30	9	29	19	5	8	♇28♌R
31	0.34	10	11♈	21	7	8	♃25♍R

Apr	STime	☉	☽	☿	♀	♂	Plnts
1	0.38	11♈	24♈	23♈	8♈	9♊	♃25♍R
2	0.42	12	6♉	25	9	10	♄14♐R
3	0.46	13	19	27	10	10	♅ 3♌
4	0.50	14	2♊	29	12	11	♆ 1♏R
5	0.54	15	15	1♉	13	11	♇28♌R
6	0.58	16	29	2	14	12	♃24♍R
7	1.02	17	13♋	4	15	13	♄14♐R
8	1.06	18	26	6	17	13	♅ 3♌R
9	1.10	19	11♌	7	18	14	♆ 1♏R
10	1.14	20	25	9	19	15	♇28♌R
11	1.18	21	10♍	10	20	15	♃24♍R
12	1.22	22	25	11	21	16	♄14♐R
13	1.26	23	9♎	12	23	16	♅ 3♌
14	1.30	24	24	13	24	17	♆ 1♏R
15	1.34	25	8♏	15	25	18	♇28♌R
16	1.37	26	22	15	26	18	♃23♍R
17	1.41	27	5♐	16	28	19	♄14♐R
18	1.45	28	18	17	29	20	♅ 3♌
19	1.49	29	1♑	18	0♉	20	♆ 1♏R
20	1.53	0♉	14	18	1	21	♇28♌R
21	1.57	1	26	18	3	21	♃23♍R
22	2.01	2	8♒	19	4	22	♄13♐R
23	2.05	3	20	19	5	23	♅ 3♌
24	2.09	4	2♓	19	6	23	♆ 1♏R
25	2.13	5	13	19R	8	24	♇28♌R
26	2.17	6	25	19	9	25	♃22♍R
27	2.21	7	8♈	19	10	25	♄13♐R
28	2.25	8	20	19	11	26	♅ 3♌
29	2.29	9	3♉	18	12	26	♆ 1♏R
30	2.33	10	16	18	14	27	♇28♌

May	STime	☉	☽	☿	♀	♂	Plnts
1	2.37	11♉	29♉	18♉	15♉	28♊	♃22♍R
2	2.41	12	12♊	17	16	28	♄13♐R
3	2.44	12	26	16	17	29	♅ 3♌
4	2.48	13	9♋	16	19	0♋	♆ 1♏R
5	2.52	14	23	15	20	0	♇28♌
6	2.56	15	7♌	15	21	1	♃22♍R
7	3.00	16	22	14	22	1	♄13♐R
8	3.04	17	6♍	13	24	2	♅ 3♌
9	3.08	18	20	13	25	3	♆ 0♏R
10	3.12	19	4♎	12	26	3	♇28♌
11	3.16	20	19	12	27	4	♃22♍R
12	3.20	21	3♏	11	29	5	♄12♐R
13	3.24	22	17	11	0♊	5	♅ 3♌
14	3.28	23	0♐	10	1	6	♆ 0♏R
15	3.32	24	13	10	2	7	♇28♌
16	3.36	25	26	10	3	7	♃22♍
17	3.40	26	9♑	10	5	8	♄12♐R
18	3.44	27	21	10D	6	8	♅ 3♌
19	3.48	28	4♒	10	7	9	♆ 0♏R
20	3.51	29	16	10	8	10	♇28♌
21	3.55	0♊	28	10	10	10	♃22♍
22	3.59	1	9♓	10	11	11	♄11♐R
23	4.03	2	21	10	12	12	♅ 3♌
24	4.07	3	3♈	11	13	12	♆ 0♏R
25	4.11	4	16	11	15	13	♇28♌
26	4.15	5	28	12	16	13	♃22♍
27	4.19	6	11♉	12	17	14	♄11♐R
28	4.23	7	24	13	18	15	♅ 4♌
29	4.27	8	8♊	14	19	15	♆ 0♏R
30	4.31	9	21	14	21	16	♇28♌
31	4.35	9	6♋	15	22	17	♃22♍

Jun	STime	☉	☽	☿	♀	♂	Plnts
1	4.39	10♊	20♋	16♉	23♊	17♋	♃22♍
2	4.43	11	4♌	17	24	18	♄11♐R
3	4.47	12	18	18	26	18	♅ 4♌
4	4.51	13	3♍	19	27	19	♆ 0♏R
5	4.55	14	17	20	28	20	♇28♌
6	4.59	15	1♎	22	29	20	♃22♍
7	5.02	16	15	23	0♋	21	♄10♐R
8	5.06	17	29	24	2	22	♅ 4♌
9	5.10	18	12♏	25	3	22	♆ 0♏R
10	5.14	19	26	27	4	23	♇28♌
11	5.18	20	9♐	28	5	23	♃22♍
12	5.22	21	22	0♊	7	24	♄10♐R
13	5.26	22	5♑	1	8	25	♅ 4♌
14	5.30	23	17	3	9	25	♆ 0♏R
15	5.34	24	29	4	10	26	♇28♌
16	5.38	25	12♒	6	11	27	♃23♍
17	5.42	26	24	8	13	27	♄10♐R
18	5.46	27	6♓	9	14	28	♅ 5♌
19	5.50	28	17	11	15	28	♆ 0♏R
20	5.54	29	29	13	16	29	♇28♌
21	5.58	0♋	11♈	15	18	0♌	♃23♍
22	6.02	0	24	17	19	0	♄ 9♐R
23	6.06	1	6♉	19	20	1	♅ 5♌
24	6.09	2	19	21	21	2	♆ 0♏
25	6.13	3	2♊	23	22	2	♇28♌
26	6.17	4	16	25	24	3	♃24♍
27	6.21	5	0♋	27	25	3	♄ 9♐R
28	6.25	6	15	29	26	4	♅ 5♌
29	6.29	7	29	1♋	27	5	♆ 0♏R
30	6.33	8	14♌	4	29	5	♇28♌

Jul	STime	☉	☽	☿	♀	♂	Plnts
1	6.37	9♋	29♌	6♋	0♌	6♌	♃24♍
2	6.41	10	13♍	8	1	7	♄ 9♐R
3	6.45	11	28	10	2	7	♅ 5♌
4	6.49	12	12♎	12	3	8	♆ 0♏
5	6.53	13	26	14	5	8	♇28♌
6	6.57	14	9♏	17	6	9	♃25♍
7	7.01	15	22	19	7	10	♄ 8♐R
8	7.05	16	5♐	21	8	10	♅ 6♌
9	7.09	17	18	23	10	11	♆ 0♏
10	7.13	18	1♑	25	11	12	♇28♌
11	7.17	19	13	27	12	12	♃25♍
12	7.20	20	26	29	13	13	♄ 8♐R
13	7.24	21	8♒	1♌	14	13	♅ 6♌
14	7.28	21	20	3	16	14	♆ 0♏
15	7.32	22	2♓	5	17	15	♇29♌
16	7.36	23	14	7	18	15	♃26♍
17	7.40	24	26	9	19	16	♄ 8♐R
18	7.44	25	8♈	11	20	17	♅ 6♌
19	7.48	26	20	12	22	17	♆ 0♏
20	7.52	27	2♉	14	23	18	♇29♌
21	7.56	28	14	16	24	19	♃27♍
22	8.00	29	27	18	25	19	♄ 8♐R
23	8.04	0♌	11♊	19	27	20	♅ 7♌
24	8.08	1	24	21	28	20	♆ 0♏
25	8.12	2	9♋	23	29	21	♇29♌
26	8.16	3	23	24	0♍	22	♃28♍
27	8.20	4	8♌	26	1	22	♄ 8♐R
28	8.24	5	23	27	3	23	♅ 7♌
29	8.27	6	8♍	29	4	24	♆ 0♏
30	8.31	7	23	0♍	5	24	♇29♌
31	8.35	8	8♎	2	6	25	♃29♍

Aug	STime	☉	☽	☿	♀	♂	Plnts
1	8.39	9♌	22♎	3♍	7♍	25♌	♃29♍
2	8.43	10	6♏	5	9	26	♄ 7♐R
3	8.47	11	19	6	10	27	♅ 7♌
4	8.51	12	3♐	7	11	27	♆ 0♏
5	8.55	12	15	9	12	28	♇29♌
6	8.59	13	28	10	13	29	♃ 0♎
7	9.03	14	10♑	11	15	29	♄ 7♐R
8	9.07	15	23	12	16	0♍	♅ 8♌
9	9.11	16	5♒	13	17	1	♆ 0♏
10	9.15	17	17	14	18	1	♇29♌
11	9.19	18	29	16	19	2	♃ 1♎
12	9.23	19	11♓	17	21	2	♄ 7♐
13	9.27	20	22	18	22	3	♅ 8♌
14	9.31	21	4♈	18	23	4	♆ 0♏
15	9.34	22	16	19	24	4	♇ 0♍
16	9.38	23	28	20	25	5	♃ 1♎
17	9.42	24	10♉	21	27	6	♄ 7♐
18	9.46	25	23	22	28	6	♅ 8♌
19	9.50	26	6♊	22	29	7	♆ 0♏
20	9.54	27	19	23	0♎	7	♇ 0♍
21	9.58	28	3♋	23	1	8	♃ 2♎
22	10.02	29	17	24	3	9	♄ 7♐
23	10.06	0♍	2♌	24	4	9	♅ 8♌
24	10.10	1	17	25	5	10	♆ 0♏
25	10.14	2	2♍	25	6	11	♇ 0♍
26	10.18	3	17	25	7	11	♃ 3♎
27	10.22	4	2♎	25R	9	12	♄ 8♐
28	10.26	5	17	25	10	13	♅ 9♌
29	10.30	6	2♏	25	11	13	♆ 0♏
30	10.34	7	16	24	12	14	♇ 0♍
31	10.38	8	29	24	13	14	♃ 4♎

Sep	STime	☉	☽	☿	♀	♂	Plnts
1	10.42	8♍	12♐	24♍	15♎	15♍	♃ 5♎
2	10.45	9	25	23	16	16	♄ 8♐
3	10.49	10	7♑	22	17	16	♅ 9♌
4	10.53	11	20	22	18	17	♆ 0♏
5	10.57	12	2♒	21	19	18	♇ 0♍
6	11.01	13	14	20	21	18	♃ 6♎
7	11.05	14	26	19	22	19	♄ 8♐
8	11.09	15	8♓	18	23	20	♅ 9♌
9	11.13	16	19	17	24	20	♆ 0♏
10	11.17	17	1♈	16	25	21	♇ 0♍
11	11.21	18	13	15	26	22	♃ 7♎
12	11.25	19	25	14	28	22	♄ 8♐
13	11.29	20	7♉	13	29	23	♅10♌
14	11.33	21	20	13	0♏	23	♆ 1♏
15	11.37	22	2♊	12	1	24	♇ 1♍
16	11.41	23	15	11	2	25	♃ 8♎
17	11.45	24	28	11	4	25	♄ 8♐
18	11.49	25	12♋	11	5	26	♅10♌
19	11.52	26	26	11D	6	27	♆ 1♏
20	11.56	27	10♌	11	7	27	♇ 1♍
21	12.00	28	25	11	8	28	♃ 9♎
22	12.04	29	10♍	12	9	29	♄ 9♐
23	12.08	0♎	26	12	11	29	♅10♌
24	12.12	1	11♎	13	12	0♎	♆ 1♏
25	12.16	2	26	14	13	1	♇ 1♍
26	12.20	3	10♏	15	14	1	♃10♎
27	12.24	4	24	16	15	2	♄ 9♐
28	12.28	5	8♐	17	16	2	♅10♌
29	12.32	6	21	19	18	3	♆ 1♏
30	12.36	7	4♑	20	19	4	♇ 1♍

Oct	STime	☉	☽	☿	♀	♂	Plnts
1	12.40	8♎	16♑	22♍	20♏	4♎	♃11♎
2	12.44	9	29	23	21	5	♄ 9♐
3	12.48	10	11♒	25	22	6	♅10♌
4	12.52	11	23	26	23	6	♆ 1♏
5	12.56	12	4♓	28	24	7	♇ 1♍
6	13.00	13	16	0♎	26	8	♃12♎
7	13.03	14	28	1	27	8	♄10♐
8	13.07	15	10♈	3	28	9	♅11♌
9	13.11	16	22	5	29	10	♆ 1♏
10	13.15	17	4♉	7	0♐	10	♇ 1♍
11	13.19	18	17	8	1	11	♃13♎
12	13.23	19	29	10	2	12	♄10♐
13	13.27	20	12♊	12	4	12	♅11♌
14	13.31	21	25	14	5	13	♆ 2♏
15	13.35	22	8♋	15	6	14	♇ 1♍
16	13.39	23	22	17	7	14	♃14♎
17	13.43	24	6♌	19	8	15	♄11♐
18	13.47	25	20	21	9	16	♅11♌
19	13.51	26	4♍	22	10	16	♆ 2♏
20	13.55	27	19	24	12	17	♇ 2♍
21	13.59	28	4♎	26	13	18	♃15♎
22	14.03	29	19	27	14	18	♄11♐
23	14.07	0♏	4♏	29	15	19	♅11♌
24	14.10	1	18	1♏	16	20	♆ 2♏
25	14.14	2	2♐	2	17	20	♇ 2♍
26	14.18	3	16	4	18	21	♃16♎
27	14.22	4	29	6	19	21	♄12♐
28	14.26	5	12♑	7	20	22	♅11♌
29	14.30	6	25	9	22	23	♆ 2♏
30	14.34	7	7♒	11	23	23	♇ 2♍
31	14.38	8	19	12	24	24	♃17♎

Nov	STime	☉	☽	☿	♀	♂	Plnts
1	14.42	9♏	1♓	14♏	25♐	25♎	♃18♎
2	14.46	10	13	15	26	25	♄12♐
3	14.50	11	25	17	27	26	♅11♌
4	14.54	12	7♈	18	28	27	♆ 2♏
5	14.58	13	19	20	29	27	♇ 2♍
6	15.02	14	1♉	22	0♑	28	♃19♎
7	15.06	15	13	23	1	29	♄13♐
8	15.10	16	26	25	2	29	♅11♌
9	15.14	17	9♊	26	3	0♏	♆ 3♏
10	15.18	18	22	28	4	1	♇ 2♍
11	15.21	19	5♋	29	6	1	♃20♎
12	15.25	20	19	1♐	7	2	♄13♐
13	15.29	21	2♌	2	8	3	♅11♌
14	15.33	22	16	4	9	3	♆ 3♏
15	15.37	23	0♍	5	10	4	♇ 2♍
16	15.41	24	14	7	11	5	♃21♎
17	15.45	25	29	8	12	5	♄14♐
18	15.49	26	13♎	10	13	6	♅11♌R
19	15.53	27	28	11	14	7	♆ 3♏
20	15.57	28	12♏	13	15	7	♇ 2♍
21	16.01	29	26	14	16	8	♃22♎
22	16.05	0♐	10♐	16	17	9	♄15♐
23	16.09	1	24	17	18	10	♅11♌R
24	16.13	2	7♑	19	19	10	♆ 3♏
25	16.17	3	20	20	20	11	♇ 2♍
26	16.21	4	3♒	22	21	12	♃23♎
27	16.25	5	15	23	22	12	♄15♐
28	16.28	6	27	24	22	13	♅11♌R
29	16.32	7	9♓	26	23	14	♆ 3♏
30	16.36	8	21	27	24	14	♇ 2♍

Dec	STime	☉	☽	☿	♀	♂	Plnts
1	16.40	9♐	3♈	28♐	25♑	15♏	♃24♎
2	16.44	10	15	0♑	26	16	♄16♐
3	16.48	11	27	1	27	16	♅11♌R
4	16.52	12	9♉	2	28	17	♆ 3♏
5	16.56	13	22	3	29	18	♇ 2♍
6	17.00	14	5♊	5	0♒	18	♃24♎
7	17.04	15	18	6	0	19	♄16♐
8	17.08	16	1♋	7	1	20	♅11♌R
9	17.12	17	15	8	2	20	♆ 4♏
10	17.16	18	29	9	3	21	♇ 2♍
11	17.20	19	13♌	9	4	22	♃25♎
12	17.24	20	27	10	4	22	♄17♐
13	17.28	21	11♍	10	5	23	♅11♌R
14	17.32	22	25	11	6	24	♆ 4♏
15	17.36	23	9♎	11	7	24	♇ 2♍
16	17.39	24	23	11R	7	25	♃26♎
17	17.43	25	7♏	11	8	26	♄17♐
18	17.47	26	21	11	9	27	♅11♌R
19	17.51	27	5♐	10	9	27	♆ 4♏
20	17.55	28	19	10	10	28	♇ 2♍R
21	17.59	29	2♑	9	10	29	♃27♎
22	18.03	0♑	15	8	11	29	♄18♐
23	18.07	1	28	7	12	0♐	♅11♌R
24	18.11	2	10♒	5	12	1	♆ 4♏
25	18.15	3	23	4	13	1	♇ 2♍R
26	18.19	4	5♓	3	13	2	♃28♎
27	18.23	5	17	1	13	3	♄19♐
28	18.27	6	29	0	14	3	♅11♌R
29	18.31	7	10♈	29♐	14	4	♆ 4♏
30	18.35	8	22	28	15	5	♇ 2♍R
31	18.39	9	4♉	27	15	6	♃28♎

Jan	STime	☉	☽	☿	♀	♂	Plnts
1	18.43	10♑	17♉	26♐	15♒	6♐	♃28♎
2	18.46	11	29	26	15	7	♄19♐
3	18.50	12	13♊	25	16	8	♅10♌R
4	18.54	13	26	25	16	8	♆ 4♏
5	18.58	14	10♋	25D	16	9	♇ 2♍R
6	19.02	15	24	25	16	10	♃29♎
7	19.06	16	9♌	25	16	10	♄20♐
8	19.10	17	23	26	16R	11	♅10♌R
9	19.14	18	8♍	26	16	12	♆ 4♏
10	19.18	19	22	27	16	13	♇ 2♍R
11	19.22	20	6♎	27	16	13	♃29♎
12	19.26	21	20	28	16	14	♄20♐
13	19.30	23	4♏	29	15	15	♅10♌R
14	19.34	24	18	0♑	15	15	♆ 4♏
15	19.38	25	1♐	1	15	16	♇ 2♍R
16	19.42	26	15	2	15	17	♃ 0♏
17	19.46	27	28	3	14	17	♄21♐
18	19.50	28	11♑	4	14	18	♅10♌R
19	19.53	29	24	5	13	19	♆ 4♏
20	19.57	0♒	6♒	6	13	20	♇ 2♍R
21	20.01	1	19	7	12	20	♃ 0♏
22	20.05	2	1♓	9	12	21	♄21♐
23	20.09	3	13	10	11	22	♅10♌R
24	20.13	4	25	11	11	22	♆ 4♏
25	20.17	5	7♈	12	10	23	♇ 1♍R
26	20.21	6	18	14	10	24	♃ 1♏
27	20.25	7	0♉	15	9	25	♄22♐
28	20.29	8	12	16	8	25	♅ 9♌R
29	20.33	9	25	18	8	26	♆ 4♏
30	20.37	10	7♊	19	7	27	♇ 1♍R
31	20.41	11	20	21	6	27	♃ 1♏

Apr	STime	☉	☽	☿	♀	♂	Plnts
1	0.37	11♈	3♍	29♈	25♒	11♒	♃28♎R
2	0.41	12	18	0♉	26	12	♄25♐
3	0.45	13	4♎	0	27	12	♅ 7♌R
4	0.49	14	19	0	28	13	♆ 4♏R
5	0.53	15	4♏	0	29	14	♇ 0♍R
6	0.57	16	19	1R	0♓	15	♃28♎R
7	1.01	17	3♐	0	1	15	♄25♐
8	1.05	18	17	0	1	16	♅ 7♌
9	1.09	19	1♑	0	2	17	♆ 4♏R
10	1.13	20	14	0	3	17	♇ 0♍R
11	1.17	21	27	29♈	4	18	♃27♎R
12	1.21	22	9♒	29	5	19	♄25♐R
13	1.25	23	21	28	6	20	♅ 7♌
14	1.29	24	3♓	28	7	20	♆ 3♏R
15	1.33	25	15	27	8	21	♇ 0♍R
16	1.36	26	27	26	9	22	♃27♎R
17	1.40	27	9♈	25	11	23	♄25♐R
18	1.44	28	21	25	12	23	♅ 7♌
19	1.48	29	3♉	24	13	24	♆ 3♏R
20	1.52	0♉	15	23	14	25	♇ 0♍R
21	1.56	1	27	23	15	26	♃26♎R
22	2.00	2	9♊	22	16	26	♄25♐R
23	2.04	3	21	22	17	27	♅ 7♌
24	2.08	3	4♋	21	18	28	♆ 3♏R
25	2.12	4	17	21	19	29	♇ 0♍R
26	2.16	5	0♌	20	20	29	♃25♎R
27	2.20	6	14	20	21	0♓	♄25♐R
28	2.24	7	28	20	22	1	♅ 7♌
29	2.28	8	12♍	20	23	1	♆ 3♏R
30	2.32	9	27	20D	24	2	♇ 0♍R

Jul	STime	☉	☽	☿	♀	♂	Plnts
1	6.36	9♋	12♑	23♋	5♊	17♈	♃22♎
2	6.40	10	25	25	6	17	♄21♐R
3	6.44	11	9♒	27	7	18	♅10♌
4	6.48	12	21	29	9	19	♆ 2♏
5	6.52	13	4♓	1♌	10	19	♇ 0♍
6	6.56	14	16	2	11	20	♃22♎
7	7.00	15	28	4	12	21	♄20♐R
8	7.04	16	10♈	6	13	21	♅10♌
9	7.08	16	22	7	15	22	♆ 2♏
10	7.12	17	4♉	9	16	23	♇ 0♍
11	7.16	18	16	11	17	23	♃22♎
12	7.19	19	28	12	18	24	♄20♐R
13	7.23	20	10♊	14	19	25	♅10♌
14	7.27	21	23	15	20	25	♆ 2♏
15	7.31	22	6♋	17	22	26	♇ 0♍
16	7.35	23	20	18	23	27	♃23♎
17	7.39	24	3♌	19	24	27	♄20♐R
18	7.43	25	17	21	25	28	♅11♌
19	7.47	26	2♍	22	26	29	♆ 2♏
20	7.51	27	16	23	28	29	♇ 1♍
21	7.55	28	0♎	24	29	0♉	♃23♎
22	7.59	29	14	26	0♋	0	♄20♐R
23	8.03	0♌	29	27	1	1	♅11♌
24	8.07	1	13♏	28	2	2	♆ 2♏
25	8.11	2	27	29	4	2	♇ 1♍
26	8.15	3	10♐	0♍	5	3	♃23♎
27	8.19	4	24	1	6	4	♄19♐R
28	8.23	5	8♑	2	7	4	♅11♌
29	8.27	6	21	2	8	5	♆ 2♏
30	8.30	7	4♒	3	10	5	♇ 1♍
31	8.34	7	17	4	11	6	♃24♎

Oct	STime	☉	☽	☿	♀	♂	Plnts
1	12.39	8♎	16♉	4♎	27♍	2♊	♃ 4♏
2	12.43	8	28	6	28	2	♄20♐
3	12.47	9	10♊	8	29	2	♅15♌
4	12.51	10	22	10	1♎	2	♆ 3♏
5	12.55	11	5♋	11	2	2	♇ 3♍
6	12.59	12	18	13	3	2	♃ 5♏
7	13.03	13	1♌	15	4	2	♄20♐
8	13.06	14	15	17	6	2	♅15♌
9	13.10	15	29	18	7	2	♆ 4♏
10	13.14	16	13♍	20	8	2R	♇ 3♍
11	13.18	17	28	22	9	2	♃ 6♏
12	13.22	18	13♎	23	11	2	♄21♐
13	13.26	19	28	25	12	2	♅15♌
14	13.30	20	13♏	27	13	2	♆ 4♏
15	13.34	21	28	28	14	2	♇ 3♍
16	13.38	22	13♐	0♏	16	2	♃ 8♏
17	13.42	23	27	2	17	2	♄21♐
18	13.46	24	11♑	3	18	2	♅16♌
19	13.50	25	24	5	19	2	♆ 4♏
20	13.54	26	7♒	6	21	2	♇ 3♍
21	13.58	27	20	8	22	1	♃ 9♏
22	14.02	28	2♓	9	23	1	♄21♐
23	14.06	29	14	11	24	1	♅16♌
24	14.10	0♏	26	12	26	1	♆ 4♏
25	14.13	1	8♈	14	27	1	♇ 3♍
26	14.17	2	20	16	28	0	♃10♏
27	14.21	3	2♉	17	29	0	♄22♐
28	14.25	4	13	19	1♏	0	♅16♌
29	14.29	5	25	20	2	0	♆ 4♏
30	14.33	6	7♊	22	3	29♉	♇ 4♍
31	14.37	7	19	23	4	29	♃11♏

Feb	STime	☉	☽	☿	♀	♂	Plnts
1	20.45	12♒	4♋	22♑	6♒	28♐	♃ 1♏
2	20.49	13	18	24	5	29	♄22♐
3	20.53	14	2♌	25	5	29	♅ 9♌R
4	20.57	15	17	26	4	0♑	♆ 4♏
5	21.01	16	2♍	28	4	1	♇ 1♍R
6	21.04	17	17	29	3	2	♃ 1♏
7	21.08	18	2♎	1♒	3	2	♄23♐
8	21.12	19	17	3	2	3	♅ 9♌R
9	21.16	20	1♏	4	2	4	♆ 4♏
10	21.20	21	15	6	2	5	♇ 1♍R
11	21.24	22	28	7	1	5	♃ 1♏
12	21.28	23	12♐	9	1	6	♄23♐
13	21.32	24	25	10	1	7	♅ 9♌R
14	21.36	25	8♑	12	1	7	♆ 4♏R
15	21.40	26	20	14	1	8	♇ 1♍R
16	21.44	27	3♒	15	0	9	♃ 1♏R
17	21.48	28	15	17	0	10	♄24♐
18	21.52	29	27	19	0D	10	♅ 8♌R
19	21.56	0♓	9♓	20	0	11	♆ 4♏R
20	22.00	1	21	22	0	12	♇ 1♍R
21	22.04	2	3♈	24	1	12	♃ 1♏R
22	22.08	3	15	25	1	13	♄24♐
23	22.11	4	27	27	1	14	♅ 8♌R
24	22.15	5	9♉	29	1	15	♆ 4♏R
25	22.19	6	21	1♓	1	15	♇ 1♍R
26	22.23	7	3♊	3	2	16	♃ 1♏R
27	22.27	8	15	4	2	17	♄24♐
28	22.31	9	28	6	2	17	♅ 8♌R

May	STime	☉	☽	☿	♀	♂	Plnts
1	2.36	10♉	12♎	20♈	25♓	3♓	♃25♎R
2	2.40	11	27	20	26	4	♄25♐R
3	2.44	12	12♏	20	28	4	♅ 7♌
4	2.47	13	27	20	29	5	♆ 3♏R
5	2.51	14	11♐	21	0♈	6	♇29♌R
6	2.55	15	25	21	1	7	♃24♎R
7	2.59	16	9♑	22	2	7	♄25♐R
8	3.03	17	22	22	3	8	♅ 7♌
9	3.07	18	5♒	23	4	9	♆ 3♏R
10	3.11	19	18	24	5	10	♇29♌
11	3.15	20	0♓	24	6	10	♃24♎R
12	3.19	21	12	25	7	11	♄24♐R
13	3.23	22	24	26	9	12	♅ 8♌
14	3.27	23	6♈	27	10	12	♆ 3♏R
15	3.31	24	17	28	11	13	♇29♌
16	3.35	25	29	29	12	14	♃23♎R
17	3.39	26	11♉	0♉	13	15	♄24♐R
18	3.43	27	23	1	14	15	♅ 8♌
19	3.47	28	6♊	2	15	16	♆ 2♏R
20	3.51	29	18	4	16	17	♇ 0♍
21	3.54	0♊	1♋	5	18	18	♃23♎R
22	3.58	1	14	6	19	18	♄24♐R
23	4.02	2	27	8	20	19	♅ 8♌
24	4.06	3	11♌	9	21	20	♆ 2♏R
25	4.10	3	24	10	22	21	♇ 0♍
26	4.14	4	8♍	12	23	21	♃22♎R
27	4.18	5	23	13	24	22	♄23♐R
28	4.22	6	7♎	15	25	23	♅ 8♌
29	4.26	7	21	17	27	23	♆ 2♏R
30	4.30	8	6♏	18	28	24	♇ 0♍
31	4.34	9	21	20	29	25	♃22♎R

Aug	STime	☉	☽	☿	♀	♂	Plnts
1	8.38	8♌	0♓	5♍	12♋	7♉	♃24♎
2	8.42	9	12	5	13	7	♄19♐R
3	8.46	10	24	6	14	8	♅12♌
4	8.50	11	6♈	6	16	8	♆ 2♏
5	8.54	12	18	7	17	9	♇ 1♍
6	8.58	13	0♉	7	18	10	♃25♎
7	9.02	14	12	7	19	10	♄19♐R
8	9.06	15	24	7	21	11	♅12♌
9	9.10	16	6♊	7R	22	11	♆ 2♏
10	9.14	17	18	7	23	12	♇ 1♍
11	9.18	18	1♋	7	24	12	♃25♎
12	9.22	19	14	7	25	13	♄19♐R
13	9.26	20	28	7	27	13	♅12♌
14	9.30	21	12♌	6	28	14	♆ 2♏
15	9.34	22	27	6	29	15	♇ 1♍
16	9.37	23	11♍	5	0♌	15	♃26♎
17	9.41	24	26	5	1	16	♄19♐R
18	9.45	25	11♎	4	3	16	♅13♌
19	9.49	26	25	3	4	17	♆ 2♏
20	9.53	27	9♏	2	5	17	♇ 2♍
21	9.57	28	23	2	6	18	♃27♎
22	10.01	29	7♐	1	8	18	♄19♐
23	10.05	0♍	21	0	9	19	♅13♌
24	10.09	1	4♑	29♌	10	19	♆ 2♏
25	10.13	1	18	28	11	20	♇ 2♍
26	10.17	2	1♒	27	12	20	♃28♎
27	10.21	3	13	27	14	21	♄19♐
28	10.25	4	26	26	15	21	♅13♌
29	10.29	5	8♓	25	16	22	♆ 2♏
30	10.33	6	20	25	17	22	♇ 2♍
31	10.37	7	2♈	25	19	22	♃28♎

Nov	STime	☉	☽	☿	♀	♂	Plnts
1	14.41	8♏	2♋	24♏	6♏	29♉	♃11♏
2	14.45	9	14	26	7	28	♄22♐
3	14.49	10	27	27	8	28	♅16♌
4	14.53	11	10♌	29	10	28	♆ 4♏
5	14.57	12	23	0♐	11	27	♇ 4♍
6	15.01	13	7♍	2	12	27	♃12♏
7	15.05	14	22	3	13	27	♄23♐
8	15.09	15	6♎	4	15	26	♅16♌
9	15.13	16	21	6	16	26	♆ 5♏
10	15.17	17	6♏	7	17	26	♇ 4♍
11	15.20	18	21	9	18	25	♃13♏
12	15.24	19	7♐	10	20	25	♄23♐
13	15.28	20	21	11	21	25	♅16♌
14	15.32	21	6♑	12	22	24	♆ 5♏
15	15.36	22	20	14	23	24	♇ 4♍
16	15.40	23	3♒	15	25	24	♃14♏
17	15.44	24	16	16	26	23	♄24♐
18	15.48	25	29	17	27	23	♅16♌
19	15.52	26	11♓	18	28	22	♆ 5♏
20	15.56	27	23	19	0♐	22	♇ 4♍
21	16.00	28	5♈	20	1	22	♃15♏
22	16.04	29	17	21	2	21	♄25♐
23	16.08	0♐	28	22	3	21	♅16♌
24	16.12	1	10♉	23	5	21	♆ 5♏
25	16.16	2	22	24	6	20	♇ 4♍
26	16.20	3	4♊	24	7	20	♃16♏
27	16.24	4	16	25	8	20	♄25♐
28	16.28	5	29	25	10	20	♅16♌R
29	16.31	6	11♋	25	11	19	♆ 5♏
30	16.35	7	24	25R	12	19	♇ 4♍

Mar	STime	☉	☽	☿	♀	♂	Plnts
1	22.35	10♓	12♋	8♓	3♒	18♑	♃ 1♏R
2	22.39	11	26	10	3	19	♄24♐
3	22.43	12	10♌	12	4	20	♅ 8♌R
4	22.47	13	25	14	4	20	♆ 4♏R
5	22.51	14	10♍	16	5	21	♇ 0♍R
6	22.55	15	26	18	5	22	♃ 1♏R
7	22.59	16	11♎	19	6	23	♄25♐
8	23.03	17	26	21	6	23	♅ 8♌R
9	23.07	18	10♏	23	7	24	♆ 4♏R
10	23.11	19	25	25	7	25	♇ 0♍R
11	23.15	20	8♐	27	8	25	♃ 0♏R
12	23.18	21	22	29	9	26	♄25♐
13	23.22	22	5♑	1♈	9	27	♅ 8♌R
14	23.26	23	18	3	10	28	♆ 4♏R
15	23.30	24	0♒	5	11	28	♇ 0♍R
16	23.34	25	12	7	11	29	♃ 0♏R
17	23.38	26	24	9	12	0♒	♄25♐
18	23.42	27	6♓	11	13	1	♅ 8♌R
19	23.46	28	18	13	14	1	♆ 4♏R
20	23.50	29	0♈	14	14	2	♇ 0♍R
21	23.54	0♈	12	16	15	3	♃ 0♏R
22	23.58	1	24	18	16	4	♄25♐
23	0.02	2	5♉	19	17	4	♅ 7♌R
24	0.06	3	17	21	18	5	♆ 4♏R
25	0.10	4	29	22	19	6	♇ 0♍R
26	0.14	5	12♊	23	19	6	♃29♎R
27	0.18	6	24	25	20	7	♄25♐
28	0.22	7	7♋	26	21	8	♅ 7♌R
29	0.26	8	21	27	22	9	♆ 4♏R
30	0.29	9	4♌	28	23	9	♇ 0♍R
31	0.33	10	19	28	24	10	♃29♎R

Jun	STime	☉	☽	☿	♀	♂	Plnts
1	4.38	10♊	5♐	22♉	0♉	26♓	♃22♎R
2	4.42	11	20	23	1	26	♄23♐R
3	4.46	12	4♑	25	2	27	♅ 8♌
4	4.50	13	17	27	4	28	♆ 2♏R
5	4.54	14	0♒	29	5	28	♇ 0♍
6	4.58	15	13	1♊	6	29	♃22♎R
7	5.02	16	26	3	7	0♈	♄23♐R
8	5.05	17	8♓	5	8	1	♅ 8♌
9	5.09	18	20	7	9	1	♆ 2♏R
10	5.13	19	2♈	9	10	2	♇ 0♍
11	5.17	20	14	11	12	3	♃22♎R
12	5.21	21	26	13	13	3	♄22♐R
13	5.25	22	8♉	15	14	4	♅ 9♌
14	5.29	23	20	17	15	5	♆ 2♏R
15	5.33	24	2♊	20	16	6	♇ 0♍
16	5.37	25	15	22	17	6	♃21♎R
17	5.41	25	27	24	19	7	♄22♐R
18	5.45	26	11♋	26	20	8	♅ 9♌
19	5.49	27	24	28	21	8	♆ 2♏R
20	5.53	28	8♌	1♋	22	9	♇ 0♍
21	5.57	29	21	3	23	10	♃21♎
22	6.01	0♋	5♍	5	24	10	♄21♐R
23	6.05	1	19	7	26	11	♅ 9♌
24	6.09	2	3♎	9	27	12	♆ 2♏R
25	6.12	3	18	11	28	13	♇ 0♍
26	6.16	4	2♏	13	29	13	♃22♎
27	6.20	5	16	15	0♊	14	♄21♐R
28	6.24	6	0♐	17	2	15	♅ 9♌
29	6.28	7	14	19	3	15	♆ 2♏
30	6.32	8	28	21	4	16	♇ 0♍

Sep	STime	☉	☽	☿	♀	♂	Plnts
1	10.41	8♍	14♈	24♌	20♌	23♉	♃29♎
2	10.45	9	26	24D	21	23	♄19♐
3	10.48	10	8♉	24	22	24	♅13♌
4	10.52	11	20	25	24	24	♆ 2♏
5	10.56	12	2♊	25	25	25	♇ 2♍
6	11.00	13	14	26	26	25	♃ 0♏
7	11.04	14	26	26	27	25	♄19♐
8	11.08	15	9♋	27	28	26	♅14♌
9	11.12	16	22	28	0♍	26	♆ 3♏
10	11.16	17	6♌	29	1	26	♇ 2♍
11	11.20	18	20	0♍	2	27	♃ 0♏
12	11.24	19	5♍	2	3	27	♄19♐
13	11.28	20	20	3	5	27	♅14♌
14	11.32	21	5♎	4	6	28	♆ 3♏
15	11.36	22	20	6	7	28	♇ 2♍
16	11.40	23	5♏	7	8	28	♃ 1♏
17	11.44	24	19	9	10	29	♄19♐
18	11.48	25	4♐	11	11	29	♅14♌
19	11.52	26	18	13	12	29	♆ 3♏
20	11.55	27	1♑	14	13	0♊	♇ 3♍
21	11.59	28	15	16	15	0	♃ 2♏
22	12.03	29	28	18	16	0	♄19♐
23	12.07	0♎	10♒	20	17	0	♅15♌
24	12.11	1	23	22	18	0	♆ 3♏
25	12.15	2	5♓	23	19	1	♇ 3♍
26	12.19	3	17	25	21	1	♃ 3♏
27	12.23	4	29	27	22	1	♄20♐
28	12.27	5	11♈	29	23	1	♅15♌
29	12.31	6	23	1♎	24	1	♆ 3♏
30	12.35	7	5♉	3	26	2	♇ 3♍

Dec	STime	☉	☽	☿	♀	♂	Plnts
1	16.39	8♐	7♌	25♐	13♐	19♉	♃18♏
2	16.43	10	20	25	15	18	♄26♐
3	16.47	11	3♍	24	16	18	♅16♌R
4	16.51	12	17	24	17	18	♆ 6♏
5	16.55	13	1♎	23	18	18	♇ 4♍
6	16.59	14	15	22	20	18	♃19♏
7	17.03	15	0♏	21	21	17	♄26♐
8	17.07	16	15	20	22	17	♅16♌R
9	17.11	17	0♐	18	23	17	♆ 6♏
10	17.15	18	15	17	25	17	♇ 4♍
11	17.19	19	29	15	26	17	♃20♏
12	17.23	20	14♑	14	27	17	♄27♐
13	17.27	21	28	13	28	17	♅16♌R
14	17.31	22	11♒	12	0♑	17	♆ 6♏
15	17.35	23	24	11	1	16	♇ 4♍R
16	17.38	24	7♓	10	2	16	♃21♏
17	17.42	25	19	10	4	16	♄27♐
18	17.46	26	1♈	9	5	16	♅16♌R
19	17.50	27	13	9	6	16	♆ 6♏
20	17.54	28	25	9D	7	16D	♇ 4♍R
21	17.58	29	7♉	9	9	16	♃22♏
22	18.02	0♑	19	10	10	16	♄28♐
23	18.06	1	1♊	10	11	16	♅16♌R
24	18.10	2	13	11	12	16	♆ 6♏
25	18.14	3	25	11	14	16	♇ 4♍R
26	18.18	4	8♋	12	15	17	♃23♏
27	18.22	5	21	13	16	17	♄29♐
28	18.26	6	4♌	14	17	17	♅15♌R
29	18.30	7	17	15	19	17	♆ 6♏
30	18.34	8	0♍	16	20	17	♇ 4♍R
31	18.38	9	14	17	21	17	♃24♏

Jan	STime	☉	☽	☿	♀	♂	Plnts
1	18.42	10♑	28♍	18♐	22♑	17♉	♃24♏
2	18.46	11	12♎	19	24	17	♄29♐
3	18.49	12	26	20	25	18	♅15♌R
4	18.53	13	10♏	21	26	18	♆ 6♏
5	18.57	14	24	23	27	18	♇ 4♍R
6	19.01	15	9♐	24	29	18	♃25♏
7	19.05	16	23	25	0♒	18	♄ 0♑
8	19.09	17	8♑	27	1	19	♅15♌R
9	19.13	18	22	28	2	19	♆ 6♏
10	19.17	19	5♒	29	4	19	♇ 4♍R
11	19.21	20	19	1♑	5	19	♃26♏
12	19.25	21	2♓	2	6	19	♄ 0♑
13	19.29	22	15	4	7	20	♅15♌R
14	19.33	23	27	5	9	20	♆ 7♏
15	19.37	24	9♈	6	10	20	♇ 4♍R
16	19.41	25	21	8	11	21	♃26♏
17	19.45	26	3♉	9	12	21	♄ 1♑
18	19.49	27	15	11	14	21	♅15♌R
19	19.53	28	27	12	15	21	♆ 7♏
20	19.56	29	9♊	14	16	22	♇ 3♍R
21	20.00	0♒	21	15	17	22	♃27♏
22	20.04	1	4♋	17	19	22	♄ 2♑
23	20.08	2	16	18	20	23	♅15♌R
24	20.12	3	0♌	20	21	23	♆ 7♏
25	20.16	4	13	22	22	23	♇ 3♍R
26	20.20	5	27	23	24	24	♃28♏
27	20.24	7	11♍	25	25	24	♄ 2♑
28	20.28	8	25	26	26	24	♅14♌R
29	20.32	9	9♎	28	27	25	♆ 7♏
30	20.36	10	23	29	29	25	♇ 3♍R
31	20.40	11	7♏	1♒	0♓	26	♃29♏

Feb	STime	☉	☽	☿	♀	♂	Plnts
1	20.44	12♒	21♏	3♒	1♓	26♉	♃29♏
2	20.48	13	5♐	4	2	26	♄ 3♑
3	20.52	14	19	6	4	27	♅14♌R
4	20.56	15	3♑	8	5	27	♆ 7♏
5	21.00	16	17	9	6	28	♇ 3♍R
6	21.03	17	0♒	11	7	28	♃29♏
7	21.07	18	14	13	9	28	♄ 3♑
8	21.11	19	27	14	10	29	♅14♌R
9	21.15	20	10♓	16	11	29	♆ 7♏
10	21.19	21	23	18	12	0♊	♇ 3♍R
11	21.23	22	5♈	20	14	0	♃ 0♐
12	21.27	23	17	21	15	1	♄ 4♑
13	21.31	24	29	23	16	1	♅14♌R
14	21.35	25	11♉	25	17	1	♆ 7♏R
15	21.39	26	22	27	19	2	♇ 3♍R
16	21.43	27	4♊	29	20	2	♃ 0♐
17	21.47	28	16	0♓	21	3	♄ 4♑
18	21.51	29	29	2	22	3	♅13♌R
19	21.55	0♓	11♋	4	24	4	♆ 7♏R
20	21.59	1	24	6	25	4	♇ 3♍R
21	22.03	2	8♌	8	26	5	♃ 1♐
22	22.07	3	21	10	27	5	♄ 5♑
23	22.11	4	6♍	12	29	6	♅13♌R
24	22.14	5	20	14	0♈	6	♆ 7♏R
25	22.18	6	4♎	15	1	7	♇ 3♍R
26	22.22	7	19	17	2	7	♃ 1♐
27	22.26	8	3♏	19	3	8	♄ 5♑
28	22.30	9	18	21	5	8	♅13♌R

Mar	STime	☉	☽	☿	♀	♂	Plnts
1	22.34	10♓	2♐	23♓	6♈	8♊	♃ 1♐
2	22.38	11	16	25	7	9	♄ 5♑
3	22.42	12	0♑	26	8	9	♅13♌R
4	22.46	13	13	28	10	10	♆ 6♏R
5	22.50	14	27	0♈	11	10	♇ 2♍R
6	22.54	15	10♒	1	12	11	♃ 1♐
7	22.58	16	23	3	13	11	♄ 5♑
8	23.02	17	6♓	4	15	12	♅13♌R
9	23.06	18	18	6	16	13	♆ 6♏R
10	23.10	19	1♈	7	17	13	♇ 2♍R
11	23.14	20	13	8	18	14	♃ 2♐
12	23.18	21	25	9	19	14	♄ 6♑
13	23.21	22	7♉	10	21	15	♅13♌R
14	23.25	23	19	11	22	15	♆ 6♏R
15	23.29	24	0♊	11	23	16	♇ 2♍R
16	23.33	25	12	12	24	16	♃ 2♐
17	23.37	26	24	12	26	17	♄ 6♑
18	23.41	27	7♋	13	27	17	♅12♌R
19	23.45	28	19	13R	28	18	♆ 6♏R
20	23.49	29	2♌	13	29	18	♇ 2♍R
21	23.53	0♈	16	13	0♉	19	♃ 2♐R
22	23.57	1	29	12	2	19	♄ 6♑
23	0.01	2	14♍	12	3	20	♅12♌R
24	0.05	3	28	11	4	20	♆ 6♏R
25	0.09	4	13♎	11	5	21	♇ 2♍R
26	0.13	5	28	10	6	21	♃ 2♐R
27	0.17	6	13♏	9	8	22	♄ 6♑
28	0.21	7	28	8	9	23	♅12♌R
29	0.25	8	12♐	8	10	23	♆ 6♏R
30	0.29	9	26	7	11	24	♇ 2♍R
31	0.32	10	10♑	6	13	24	♃ 1♐R

Apr	STime	☉	☽	☿	♀	♂	Plnts
1	0.36	11♈	24♑	5♈	14♉	25♊	♃ 1♐R
2	0.40	12	7♒	4	15	25	♄ 7♑
3	0.44	13	20	4	16	26	♅12♌R
4	0.48	14	3♓	3	17	26	♆ 6♏R
5	0.52	15	15	2	19	27	♇ 2♍R
6	0.56	16	27	2	20	28	♃ 1♐R
7	1.00	17	10♈	1	21	28	♄ 7♑
8	1.04	18	21	1	22	29	♅12♌R
9	1.08	19	3♉	1	23	29	♆ 6♏R
10	1.12	20	15	0	24	0♋	♇ 2♍R
11	1.16	21	27	0	26	0	♃ 1♐R
12	1.20	22	9♊	0D	27	1	♄ 7♑
13	1.24	23	21	0	28	1	♅12♌
14	1.28	23	3♋	1	29	2	♆ 6♏R
15	1.32	24	15	1	0♊	3	♇ 2♍R
16	1.36	25	28	1	2	3	♃ 0♐R
17	1.39	26	10♌	2	3	4	♄ 7♑
18	1.43	27	24	2	4	4	♅12♌
19	1.47	28	7♍	3	5	5	♆ 5♏R
20	1.51	29	22	3	6	5	♇ 2♍R
21	1.55	0♉	6♎	4	8	6	♃ 0♐R
22	1.59	1	21	5	9	7	♄ 7♑R
23	2.03	2	6♏	5	10	7	♅12♌
24	2.07	3	22	6	11	8	♆ 5♏R
25	2.11	4	7♐	7	12	8	♇ 1♍R
26	2.15	5	21	8	13	9	♃ 0♐R
27	2.19	6	6♑	9	15	9	♄ 7♑R
28	2.23	7	20	10	16	10	♅12♌
29	2.27	8	4♒	11	17	11	♆ 5♏R
30	2.31	9	17	12	18	11	♇ 1♍R

May	STime	☉	☽	☿	♀	♂	Plnts
1	2.35	10♉	0♓	14♈	19♊	12♋	♃29♏R
2	2.39	11	12	15	20	12	♄ 7♑R
3	2.43	12	24	16	21	13	♅12♌
4	2.47	13	7♈	17	23	13	♆ 5♏R
5	2.50	14	18	19	24	14	♇ 1♍
6	2.54	15	0♉	20	25	15	♃28♏R
7	2.58	16	12	22	26	15	♄ 6♑R
8	3.02	17	24	23	27	16	♅12♌
9	3.06	18	6♊	25	28	16	♆ 5♏R
10	3.10	19	18	26	0♋	17	♇ 1♍
11	3.14	20	0♋	28	1	18	♃28♏R
12	3.18	21	12	29	2	18	♄ 6♑R
13	3.22	22	24	1♉	3	19	♅12♌
14	3.26	23	7♌	2	4	19	♆ 5♏R
15	3.30	24	19	4	5	20	♇ 1♍
16	3.34	25	3♍	6	6	20	♃27♏R
17	3.38	26	16	8	7	21	♄ 6♑R
18	3.42	26	0♎	9	9	22	♅12♌
19	3.46	27	15	11	10	22	♆ 5♏R
20	3.50	28	0♏	13	11	23	♇ 1♍
21	3.54	29	15	15	12	23	♃26♏R
22	3.57	0♊	0♐	17	13	24	♄ 6♑R
23	4.01	1	15	19	14	25	♅12♌
24	4.05	2	0♑	21	15	25	♆ 5♏R
25	4.09	3	15	23	16	26	♇ 1♍
26	4.13	4	29	25	17	26	♃26♏R
27	4.17	5	13♒	27	19	27	♄ 5♑R
28	4.21	6	26	29	20	28	♅13♌
29	4.25	7	9♓	1♊	21	28	♆ 4♏R
30	4.29	8	21	3	22	29	♇ 1♍
31	4.33	9	4♈	6	23	29	♃25♏R

Jun	STime	☉	☽	☿	♀	♂	Plnts
1	4.37	10♊	16♈	8♊	24♋	0♌	♃25♏R
2	4.41	11	27	10	25	1	♄ 5♑R
3	4.45	12	9♉	12	26	1	♅13♌
4	4.49	13	21	14	27	2	♆ 4♏R
5	4.53	14	3♊	17	28	2	♇ 1♍
6	4.57	15	15	19	29	3	♃25♏R
7	5.01	16	27	21	0♌	4	♄ 5♑R
8	5.04	17	9♋	23	1	4	♅13♌
9	5.08	18	21	25	2	5	♆ 4♏R
10	5.12	19	4♌	27	3	5	♇ 2♍
11	5.16	20	16	0♋	4	6	♃24♏R
12	5.20	20	29	2	5	7	♄ 4♑R
13	5.24	21	12♍	4	6	7	♅13♌
14	5.28	22	26	6	7	8	♆ 4♏R
15	5.32	23	10♎	8	9	8	♇ 2♍
16	5.36	24	24	9	10	9	♃23♏R
17	5.40	25	9♏	11	11	10	♄ 4♑R
18	5.44	26	23	13	12	10	♅13♌
19	5.48	27	8♐	15	12	11	♆ 4♏R
20	5.52	28	23	17	13	11	♇ 2♍
21	5.56	29	8♑	18	14	12	♃23♏R
22	6.00	0♋	23	20	15	13	♄ 4♑R
23	6.04	1	7♒	22	16	13	♅14♌
24	6.08	2	21	23	17	14	♆ 4♏R
25	6.12	3	5♓	25	18	14	♇ 2♍
26	6.15	4	17	27	19	15	♃23♏R
27	6.19	5	0♈	28	20	16	♄ 3♑R
28	6.23	6	12	29	21	16	♅14♌
29	6.27	7	24	1♌	22	17	♆ 4♏R
30	6.31	8	6♉	2	23	17	♇ 2♍

Jul	STime	☉	☽	☿	♀	♂	Plnts
1	6.35	9♋	18♉	4♌	24♌	18♌	♃22♏R
2	6.39	10	0♊	5	25	19	♄ 3♑R
3	6.43	11	12	6	25	19	♅14♌
4	6.47	11	24	7	26	20	♆ 4♏R
5	6.51	12	6♋	8	27	20	♇ 2♍
6	6.55	13	18	9	28	21	♃22♏R
7	6.59	14	1♌	11	29	22	♄ 3♑R
8	7.03	15	13	12	0♍	22	♅14♌
9	7.07	16	26	12	1	23	♆ 4♏
10	7.11	17	9♍	13	1	24	♇ 2♍
11	7.15	18	23	14	2	24	♃22♏R
12	7.19	19	6♎	15	3	25	♄ 2♑R
13	7.22	20	20	16	4	25	♅15♌
14	7.26	21	4♏	16	4	26	♆ 4♏
15	7.30	22	18	17	5	27	♇ 2♍
16	7.34	23	3♐	17	6	27	♃22♏R
17	7.38	24	18	18	6	28	♄ 2♑R
18	7.42	25	2♑	18	7	28	♅15♌
19	7.46	26	17	19	8	29	♆ 4♏
20	7.50	27	1♒	19	8	0♍	♇ 2♍
21	7.54	28	16	19	9	0	♃22♏
22	7.58	29	29	19R	10	1	♄ 2♑R
23	8.02	0♌	13♓	19	10	2	♅15♌
24	8.06	1	26	19	11	2	♆ 4♏
25	8.10	2	8♈	19	11	3	♇ 3♍
26	8.14	2	20	19	12	3	♃22♏
27	8.18	3	2♉	18	12	4	♄ 1♑R
28	8.22	4	14	18	13	5	♅16♌
29	8.26	5	26	17	13	5	♆ 4♏
30	8.30	6	8♊	17	13	6	♇ 3♍
31	8.33	7	20	16	14	7	♃22♏

Aug	STime	☉	☽	☿	♀	♂	Plnts
1	8.37	8♌	2♋	15♌	14♍	7♍	♃22♏
2	8.41	9	14	15	15	8	♄ 1♑R
3	8.45	10	27	14	15	8	♅16♌
4	8.49	11	10♌	13	15	9	♆ 4♏
5	8.53	12	23	12	15	10	♇ 3♍
6	8.57	13	6♍	12	15	10	♃22♏
7	9.01	14	20	11	16	11	♄ 1♑R
8	9.05	15	3♎	10	16	12	♅16♌
9	9.09	16	17	10	16	12	♆ 4♏
10	9.13	17	1♏	9	16	13	♇ 3♍
11	9.17	18	15	8	16R	13	♃23♏
12	9.21	19	29	8	16	14	♄ 1♑R
13	9.25	20	13♐	8	16	15	♅17♌
14	9.29	21	28	8	16	15	♆ 4♏
15	9.33	22	12♑	7D	15	16	♇ 3♍
16	9.37	23	26	7	15	17	♃23♏
17	9.40	24	10♒	8	15	17	♄ 0♑R
18	9.44	25	24	8	15	18	♅17♌
19	9.48	25	8♓	8	14	19	♆ 4♏
20	9.52	26	21	9	14	19	♇ 3♍
21	9.56	27	3♈	9	14	20	♃23♏
22	10.00	28	16	10	13	20	♄ 0♑R
23	10.04	29	28	11	13	21	♅17♌
24	10.08	0♍	10♉	12	12	22	♆ 4♏
25	10.12	1	22	13	12	22	♇ 4♍
26	10.16	2	4♊	14	11	23	♃24♏
27	10.20	3	16	15	11	24	♄ 0♑R
28	10.24	4	28	17	10	24	♅18♌
29	10.28	5	10♋	18	9	25	♆ 4♏
30	10.32	6	23	20	9	26	♇ 4♍
31	10.36	7	5♌	22	8	26	♃24♏

Sep	STime	☉	☽	☿	♀	♂	Plnts
1	10.40	8♍	18♌	23♌	8♍	27♍	♃25♏
2	10.44	9	2♍	25	7	27	♄ 0♑
3	10.48	10	15	27	6	28	♅18♌
4	10.51	11	29	29	6	29	♆ 5♏
5	10.55	12	13♎	0♍	5	29	♇ 4♍
6	10.59	13	27	2	5	0♎	♃25♏
7	11.03	14	12♏	4	4	1	♄ 0♑
8	11.07	15	26	6	4	1	♅18♌
9	11.11	16	10♐	8	3	2	♆ 5♏
10	11.15	17	24	10	3	3	♇ 4♍
11	11.19	18	8♑	12	2	3	♃26♏
12	11.23	19	22	14	2	4	♄ 0♑
13	11.27	20	6♒	16	1	5	♅18♌
14	11.31	21	20	18	1	5	♆ 5♏
15	11.35	22	3♓	19	1	6	♇ 4♍
16	11.39	23	16	21	0	7	♃27♏
17	11.43	24	29	23	0	7	♄ 0♑
18	11.47	25	12♈	25	0	8	♅19♌
19	11.51	26	24	27	0	9	♆ 5♏
20	11.55	26	6♉	29	0	9	♇ 4♍
21	11.58	27	18	0♎	0	10	♃27♏
22	12.02	28	0♊	2	0D	10	♄ 0♑
23	12.06	29	12	4	0	11	♅19♌
24	12.10	0♎	24	6	0	12	♆ 5♏
25	12.14	1	6♋	8	0	12	♇ 5♍
26	12.18	2	18	9	0	13	♃28♏
27	12.22	3	0♌	11	0	14	♄ 1♑
28	12.26	4	13	13	0	14	♅19♌
29	12.30	5	26	14	0	15	♆ 5♏
30	12.34	6	10♍	16	1	16	♇ 5♍

Oct	STime	☉	☽	☿	♀	♂	Plnts
1	12.38	7♎	24♍	18♎	1♍	16♎	♃29♏
2	12.42	8	8♎	19	1	17	♄ 1♑
3	12.46	9	22	21	2	18	♅19♌
4	12.50	10	7♏	22	2	18	♆ 5♏
5	12.54	11	22	24	3	19	♇ 5♍
6	12.58	12	6♐	26	3	20	♃ 0♐
7	13.02	13	21	27	3	20	♄ 1♑
8	13.05	14	5♑	29	4	21	♅20♌
9	13.09	15	19	0♏	4	22	♆ 6♏
10	13.13	16	3♒	2	5	22	♇ 5♍
11	13.17	17	16	3	6	23	♃ 1♐
12	13.21	18	0♓	5	6	24	♄ 1♑
13	13.25	19	13	6	7	24	♅20♌
14	13.29	20	25	8	7	25	♆ 6♏
15	13.33	21	8♈	9	8	26	♇ 5♍
16	13.37	22	20	11	9	26	♃ 2♐
17	13.41	23	2♉	12	10	27	♄ 2♑
18	13.45	24	14	13	10	28	♅20♌
19	13.49	25	26	15	11	28	♆ 6♏
20	13.53	26	8♊	16	12	29	♇ 5♍
21	13.57	27	20	18	12	0♏	♃ 3♐
22	14.01	28	2♋	19	13	0	♄ 2♑
23	14.05	29	14	20	14	1	♅20♌
24	14.09	0♏	26	22	15	2	♆ 6♏
25	14.13	1	8♌	23	16	2	♇ 5♍
26	14.16	2	21	24	17	3	♃ 4♐
27	14.20	3	4♍	25	17	4	♄ 2♑
28	14.24	4	18	27	18	5	♅20♌
29	14.28	5	2♎	28	19	5	♆ 6♏
30	14.32	6	16	29	20	6	♇ 5♍
31	14.36	7	1♏	0♐	21	7	♃ 5♐

Nov	STime	☉	☽	☿	♀	♂	Plnts
1	14.40	8♏	16♏	1♐	22♍	7♏	♃ 5♐
2	14.44	9	1♐	2	23	8	♄ 3♑
3	14.48	10	16	3	24	9	♅21♌
4	14.52	11	1♑	4	25	9	♆ 7♏
5	14.56	12	15	5	26	10	♇ 6♍
6	15.00	13	0♒	6	27	11	♃ 6♐
7	15.04	14	13	7	27	11	♄ 3♑
8	15.08	15	27	8	28	12	♅21♌
9	15.12	16	10♓	8	29	13	♆ 7♏
10	15.16	17	22	9	0♎	13	♇ 6♍
11	15.20	18	5♈	9	1	14	♃ 7♐
12	15.23	19	17	9	2	15	♄ 4♑
13	15.27	20	29	10	3	16	♅21♌
14	15.31	21	11♉	10R	4	16	♆ 7♏
15	15.35	22	23	9	6	17	♇ 6♍
16	15.39	23	5♊	9	7	18	♃ 8♐
17	15.43	24	17	9	8	18	♄ 4♑
18	15.47	25	29	8	9	19	♅21♌
19	15.51	26	11♋	7	10	20	♆ 7♏
20	15.55	27	23	6	11	20	♇ 6♍
21	15.59	28	5♌	5	12	21	♃ 9♐
22	16.03	29	17	4	13	22	♄ 5♑
23	16.07	0♐	0♍	2	14	22	♅21♌
24	16.11	1	13	1	15	23	♆ 7♏
25	16.15	2	26	0	16	24	♇ 6♍
26	16.19	3	10♎	28♏	17	25	♃10♐
27	16.23	4	24	27	18	25	♄ 5♑
28	16.27	5	9♏	26	19	26	♅21♌R
29	16.31	6	24	25	21	27	♆ 7♏
30	16.34	7	9♐	24	22	27	♇ 6♍

Dec	STime	☉	☽	☿	♀	♂	Plnts
1	16.38	8♐	24♐	24♏	23♎	28♏	♃12♐
2	16.42	9	10♑	24	24	29	♄ 6♑
3	16.46	10	24	23D	25	0♐	♅21♌R
4	16.50	11	9♒	23	26	0	♆ 8♏
5	16.54	12	23	24	27	1	♇ 6♍
6	16.58	13	6♓	24	28	2	♃13♐
7	17.02	14	19	24	29	2	♄ 6♑
8	17.06	15	2♈	25	1♏	3	♅21♌R
9	17.10	16	14	26	2	4	♆ 8♏
10	17.14	17	26	27	3	4	♇ 6♍
11	17.18	18	8♉	28	4	5	♃14♐
12	17.22	19	20	28	5	6	♄ 7♑
13	17.26	20	2♊	0♐	6	7	♅21♌R
14	17.30	21	14	1	8	7	♆ 8♏
15	17.34	22	26	2	9	8	♇ 6♍
16	17.38	23	8♋	3	10	9	♃15♐
17	17.41	24	20	4	11	10	♄ 7♑
18	17.45	26	2♌	6	12	10	♅21♌R
19	17.49	27	14	7	13	11	♆ 8♏
20	17.53	28	26	8	14	12	♇ 6♍R
21	17.57	29	9♍	10	16	12	♃16♐
22	18.01	0♑	22	11	17	13	♄ 8♑
23	18.05	1	5♎	12	18	14	♅20♌R
24	18.09	2	19	14	19	15	♆ 8♏
25	18.13	3	3♏	15	20	15	♇ 6♍R
26	18.17	4	17	17	22	16	♃17♐
27	18.21	5	2♐	18	23	17	♄ 9♑
28	18.25	6	17	19	24	17	♅20♌R
29	18.29	7	2♑	21	25	18	♆ 8♏
30	18.33	8	18	22	26	19	♇ 6♍R
31	18.37	9	3♒	24	27	20	♃18♐

Jan	STime	☉	☽	☿	♀	♂	Plnts
1	18.41	10♑	17♒	25♐	29♏	20♐	♃19♐
2	18.45	11	1♓	27	0♐	21	♄ 9♑
3	18.48	12	15	28	1	22	♅20♌R
4	18.52	13	28	0♑	2	23	♆ 8♏
5	18.56	14	11♈	1	3	23	♇ 6♍R
6	19.00	15	23	3	5	24	♃20♐
7	19.04	16	5♉	4	6	25	♄10♑
8	19.08	17	17	6	7	25	♅20♌R
9	19.12	18	29	8	8	26	♆ 9♏
10	19.16	19	11♊	9	9	27	♇ 6♍R
11	19.20	20	23	11	11	28	♃21♐
12	19.24	21	5♋	12	12	28	♄11♑
13	19.28	22	17	14	13	29	♅20♌R
14	19.32	23	29	15	14	0♑	♆ 9♏
15	19.36	24	11♌	17	15	1	♇ 6♍R
16	19.40	25	23	19	17	1	♃22♐
17	19.44	26	6♍	20	18	2	♄11♑
18	19.48	27	19	22	19	3	♅20♌R
19	19.52	28	2♎	23	20	4	♆ 9♏
20	19.56	29	15	25	22	4	♇ 5♍R
21	19.59	0♒	29	27	23	5	♃23♐
22	20.03	1	12♏	28	24	6	♄12♑
23	20.07	2	27	0♒	25	7	♅19♌R
24	20.11	3	11♐	2	26	7	♆ 9♏
25	20.15	4	26	3	28	8	♇ 5♍R
26	20.19	5	11♑	5	29	9	♃24♐
27	20.23	6	26	7	0♑	10	♄12♑
28	20.27	7	11♒	9	1	10	♅19♌R
29	20.31	8	25	10	3	11	♆ 9♏
30	20.35	9	9♓	12	4	12	♇ 5♍R
31	20.39	10	23	14	5	13	♃25♐

Feb	STime	☉	☽	☿	♀	♂	Plnts
1	20.43	11♒	6♈	16♒	6♑	13♑	♃25♐
2	20.47	12	19	17	7	14	♄13♑
3	20.51	13	1♉	19	9	15	♅19♌R
4	20.55	14	13	21	10	16	♆ 9♏
5	20.59	15	25	23	11	16	♇ 5♍R
6	21.03	16	7♊	24	12	17	♃26♐
7	21.06	17	19	26	14	18	♄13♑
8	21.10	18	1♋	28	15	19	♅19♌R
9	21.14	19	13	0♓	16	19	♆ 9♏
10	21.18	20	25	2	17	20	♇ 5♍R
11	21.22	21	7♌	3	18	21	♃27♐
12	21.26	22	20	5	20	22	♄14♑
13	21.30	23	3♍	7	21	22	♅19♌R
14	21.34	24	16	9	22	23	♆ 9♏
15	21.38	26	29	10	23	24	♇ 5♍R
16	21.42	27	12♎	12	25	25	♃28♐
17	21.46	28	26	14	26	25	♄14♑
18	21.50	29	9♏	15	27	26	♅18♌R
19	21.54	0♓	23	17	28	27	♆ 9♏
20	21.58	1	7♐	18	29	28	♇ 5♍R
21	22.02	2	21	19	1♒	28	♃28♐
22	22.06	3	6♑	21	2	29	♄15♑
23	22.10	4	20	22	3	0♒	♅18♌R
24	22.14	5	5♒	23	4	1	♆ 9♏R
25	22.17	6	19	23	6	1	♇ 5♍R
26	22.21	7	3♓	24	7	2	♃29♐
27	22.25	8	17	25	8	3	♄15♑
28	22.29	9	0♈	25	9	4	♅18♌R
29	22.33	10	14	25	11	5	♆ 9♏R

Mar	STime	☉	☽	☿	♀	♂	Plnts
1	22.37	11♓	26♈	26♓	12♒	5♒	♃ 0♑
2	22.41	12	9♉	25	13	6	♄16♑
3	22.45	13	21	25	14	7	♅18♌R
4	22.49	14	3♊	25	15	8	♆ 9♏R
5	22.53	15	15	24	17	8	♇ 4♍R
6	22.57	16	27	24	18	9	♃ 0♑
7	23.01	17	9♋	23	19	10	♄16♑
8	23.05	18	21	22	20	11	♅18♌R
9	23.09	19	3♌	21	22	11	♆ 9♏R
10	23.13	20	16	20	23	12	♇ 4♍R
11	23.17	21	28	19	24	13	♃ 1♑
12	23.21	22	11♍	18	25	14	♄16♑
13	23.24	23	24	17	27	14	♅17♌R
14	23.28	24	8♎	17	28	15	♆ 9♏R
15	23.32	25	22	16	29	16	♇ 4♍R
16	23.36	26	6♏	15	0♓	17	♃ 1♑
17	23.40	27	20	14	1	18	♄17♑
18	23.44	28	4♐	14	3	18	♅17♌R
19	23.48	29	18	13	4	19	♆ 8♏R
20	23.52	0♈	2♑	13	5	20	♇ 4♍R
21	23.56	1	17	12	6	21	♃ 2♑
22	0.00	2	1♒	12	8	21	♄17♑
23	0.04	3	15	12	9	22	♅17♌R
24	0.08	4	28	12D	10	23	♆ 8♏R
25	0.12	5	12♓	12	11	24	♇ 4♍R
26	0.16	6	26	12	13	24	♃ 2♑
27	0.20	7	9♈	12	14	25	♄17♑
28	0.24	8	22	13	15	26	♅17♌R
29	0.28	9	4♉	13	16	27	♆ 8♏R
30	0.31	9	17	13	17	28	♇ 4♍R
31	0.35	10	29	14	19	28	♃ 3♑

Apr	STime	☉	☽	☿	♀	♂	Plnts
1	0.39	11♈	11♊	15♓	20♓	29♒	♃ 3♑
2	0.43	12	23	15	21	0♓	♄18♑
3	0.47	13	5♋	16	22	1	♅17♌R
4	0.51	14	17	17	24	1	♆ 8♏R
5	0.55	15	29	18	25	2	♇ 4♍R
6	0.59	16	11♌	19	26	3	♃ 3♑
7	1.03	17	23	20	27	4	♄18♑
8	1.07	18	6♍	21	29	4	♅17♌R
9	1.11	19	19	22	0♈	5	♆ 8♏R
10	1.15	20	3♎	23	1	6	♇ 4♍R
11	1.19	21	17	24	2	7	♃ 3♑
12	1.23	22	1♏	25	3	8	♄18♑
13	1.27	23	15	26	5	8	♅17♌R
14	1.31	24	0♐	28	6	9	♆ 8♏R
15	1.35	25	15	29	7	10	♇ 3♍R
16	1.39	26	29	0♈	8	11	♃ 3♑
17	1.42	27	13♑	2	10	11	♄18♑
18	1.46	28	28	3	11	12	♅17♌
19	1.50	29	12♒	4	12	13	♆ 8♏R
20	1.54	0♉	25	6	13	14	♇ 3♍R
21	1.58	1	9♓	7	15	15	♃ 3♑R
22	2.02	2	22	9	16	15	♄18♑
23	2.06	3	5♈	10	17	16	♅17♌
24	2.10	4	18	12	18	17	♆ 8♏R
25	2.14	5	0♉	14	19	18	♇ 3♍R
26	2.18	6	13	15	21	18	♃ 3♑R
27	2.22	7	25	17	22	19	♄18♑
28	2.26	8	7♊	19	23	20	♅17♌
29	2.30	9	19	20	24	21	♆ 7♏R
30	2.34	10	1♋	22	26	21	♇ 3♍R

May	STime	☉	☽	☿	♀	♂	Plnts
1	2.38	11♉	13♋	24♈	27♈	22♓	♃ 3♑R
2	2.42	12	25	26	28	23	♄18♑R
3	2.46	13	7♌	27	29	24	♅17♌
4	2.49	14	19	29	1♉	24	♆ 7♏R
5	2.53	15	1♍	1♉	2	25	♇ 3♍R
6	2.57	16	14	3	3	26	♃ 3♑R
7	3.01	17	27	5	4	27	♄18♑R
8	3.05	18	11♎	7	5	28	♅17♌
9	3.09	19	25	9	7	28	♆ 7♏R
10	3.13	20	9♏	11	8	29	♇ 3♍
11	3.17	20	24	13	9	0♈	♃ 3♑R
12	3.21	21	9♐	15	10	1	♄18♑R
13	3.25	22	24	17	12	1	♅17♌
14	3.29	23	9♑	20	13	2	♆ 7♏R
15	3.33	24	24	22	14	3	♇ 3♍
16	3.37	25	8♒	24	15	4	♃ 2♑R
17	3.41	26	22	26	16	4	♄18♑R
18	3.45	27	6♓	28	18	5	♅17♌
19	3.49	28	19	0♊	19	6	♆ 7♏R
20	3.53	29	2♈	3	20	7	♇ 3♍
21	3.57	0♊	15	5	21	7	♃ 2♑R
22	4.00	1	27	7	23	8	♄18♑R
23	4.04	2	9♉	9	24	9	♅17♌
24	4.08	3	22	11	25	10	♆ 7♏R
25	4.12	4	4♊	13	26	10	♇ 3♍
26	4.16	5	16	16	28	11	♃ 1♑R
27	4.20	6	28	18	29	12	♄17♑R
28	4.24	7	10♋	20	0♊	13	♅17♌
29	4.28	8	21	22	1	13	♆ 7♏R
30	4.32	9	3♌	23	2	14	♇ 3♍
31	4.36	10	15	25	4	15	♃ 1♑R

Jun	STime	☉	☽	☿	♀	♂	Plnts
1	4.40	11♊	27♌	27♊	5♊	16♈	♃ 1♑R
2	4.44	12	10♍	29	6	16	♄17♑R
3	4.48	13	22	1♋	7	17	♅17♌
4	4.52	14	5♎	3	9	18	♆ 7♏R
5	4.56	15	19	4	10	19	♇ 3♍
6	5.00	15	3♏	6	11	19	♃ 0♑R
7	5.04	16	18	7	12	20	♄17♑R
8	5.07	17	3♐	9	14	21	♅18♌
9	5.11	18	18	11	15	22	♆ 6♏R
10	5.15	19	3♑	12	16	22	♇ 3♍
11	5.19	20	18	13	17	23	♃ 0♑R
12	5.23	21	3♒	15	18	24	♄17♑R
13	5.27	22	18	16	20	25	♅18♌
14	5.31	23	2♓	17	21	25	♆ 6♏R
15	5.35	24	16	18	22	26	♇ 4♍
16	5.39	25	29	20	23	27	♃29♐R
17	5.43	26	12♈	21	25	28	♄16♑R
18	5.47	27	24	22	26	28	♅18♌
19	5.51	28	7♉	23	27	29	♆ 6♏R
20	5.55	29	19	24	28	0♉	♇ 4♍
21	5.59	0♋	1♊	25	29	1	♃28♐R
22	6.03	1	13	25	1♋	1	♄16♑R
23	6.07	2	25	26	2	2	♅18♌
24	6.11	3	7♋	27	3	3	♆ 6♏R
25	6.15	4	18	27	4	3	♇ 4♍
26	6.18	5	0♌	28	6	4	♃28♐R
27	6.22	6	12	29	7	5	♄16♑R
28	6.26	6	24	29	8	6	♅18♌
29	6.30	7	6♍	29	9	6	♆ 6♏R
30	6.34	8	19	0♌	11	7	♇ 4♍

Jul	STime	☉	☽	☿	♀	♂	Plnts
1	6.38	9♋	1♎	0♌	12♋	8♉	♃27♐R
2	6.42	10	14	0	13	8	♄15♑R
3	6.46	11	28	0R	14	9	♅19♌
4	6.50	12	12♏	0	15	10	♆ 6♏R
5	6.54	13	26	0	17	11	♇ 4♍
6	6.58	14	11♐	0	18	11	♃26♐R
7	7.02	15	26	29♋	19	12	♄15♑R
8	7.06	16	11♑	29	20	13	♅19♌
9	7.10	17	27	29	22	13	♆ 6♏R
10	7.14	18	12♒	28	23	14	♇ 4♍
11	7.18	19	26	28	24	15	♃26♐R
12	7.22	20	11♓	27	25	16	♄14♑R
13	7.25	21	25	26	27	16	♅19♌
14	7.29	22	8♈	26	28	17	♆ 6♏
15	7.33	23	21	25	29	18	♇ 4♍
16	7.37	24	3♉	24	0♌	18	♃25♐R
17	7.41	25	16	24	1	19	♄14♑R
18	7.45	26	28	23	3	20	♅19♌
19	7.49	26	10♊	23	4	20	♆ 6♏
20	7.53	27	22	22	5	21	♇ 4♍
21	7.57	28	4♋	21	6	22	♃25♐R
22	8.01	29	15	21	8	22	♄14♑R
23	8.05	0♌	27	21	9	23	♅20♌
24	8.09	1	9♌	20	10	24	♆ 6♏
25	8.13	2	21	20	11	25	♇ 4♍
26	8.17	3	4♍	20	13	25	♃24♐R
27	8.21	4	16	20D	14	26	♄13♑R
28	8.25	5	28	20	15	27	♅20♌
29	8.29	6	11♎	20	16	27	♆ 6♏
30	8.33	7	24	20	17	28	♇ 5♍
31	8.36	8	8♏	20	19	29	♃24♐R

Aug	STime	☉	☽	☿	♀	♂	Plnts
1	8.40	9♌	21♏	21♋	20♌	29♉	♃24♐R
2	8.44	10	6♐	21	21	0♊	♄13♑R
3	8.48	11	20	22	22	1	♅20♌
4	8.52	12	5♑	23	24	1	♆ 6♏
5	8.56	13	20	24	25	2	♇ 5♍
6	9.00	14	5♒	25	26	3	♃24♐R
7	9.04	15	20	26	27	3	♄13♑R
8	9.08	16	5♓	27	29	4	♅21♌
9	9.12	17	19	28	0♍	5	♆ 6♏
10	9.16	18	3♈	29	1	5	♇ 5♍
11	9.20	19	16	1♌	2	6	♃24♐R
12	9.24	19	29	2	3	6	♄12♑R
13	9.28	20	12♉	4	5	7	♅21♌
14	9.32	21	24	6	6	8	♆ 6♏
15	9.36	22	6♊	7	7	8	♇ 5♍
16	9.40	23	18	9	8	9	♃24♐R
17	9.43	24	0♋	11	10	10	♄12♑R
18	9.47	25	12	13	11	10	♅21♌
19	9.51	26	24	15	12	11	♆ 6♏
20	9.55	27	6♌	17	13	12	♇ 5♍
21	9.59	28	18	19	15	12	♃23♐
22	10.03	29	0♍	20	16	13	♄12♑R
23	10.07	0♍	13	22	17	13	♅22♌
24	10.11	1	25	24	18	14	♆ 6♏
25	10.15	2	8♎	26	19	15	♇ 5♍
26	10.19	3	21	28	21	15	♃24♐
27	10.23	4	5♏	0♍	22	16	♄12♑R
28	10.27	5	18	2	23	16	♅22♌
29	10.31	6	2♐	4	24	17	♆ 7♏
30	10.35	7	16	6	26	18	♇ 6♍
31	10.39	8	0♑	8	27	18	♃24♐

Sep	STime	☉	☽	☿	♀	♂	Plnts
1	10.43	9♍	15♑	10♍	28♍	19♊	♃24♐
2	10.47	10	29	12	29	19	♄12♑R
3	10.50	11	14♒	14	1♎	20	♅22♌
4	10.54	12	29	16	2	21	♆ 7♏
5	10.58	13	13♓	18	3	21	♇ 6♍
6	11.02	14	27	20	4	22	♃24♐
7	11.06	15	11♈	21	5	22	♄12♑R
8	11.10	16	24	23	7	23	♅23♌
9	11.14	17	7♉	25	8	23	♆ 7♏
10	11.18	17	20	27	9	24	♇ 6♍
11	11.22	18	2♊	28	10	25	♃24♐
12	11.26	19	15	0♎	12	25	♄12♑
13	11.30	20	27	2	13	26	♅23♌
14	11.34	21	9♋	3	14	26	♆ 7♏
15	11.38	22	20	5	15	27	♇ 6♍
16	11.42	23	2♌	7	17	27	♃25♐
17	11.46	24	14	8	18	28	♄12♑
18	11.50	25	27	10	19	28	♅23♌
19	11.54	26	9♍	12	20	29	♆ 7♏
20	11.58	27	22	13	21	29	♇ 6♍
21	12.01	28	5♎	15	23	0♋	♃25♐
22	12.05	29	18	16	24	0	♄12♑
23	12.09	0♎	1♏	18	25	1	♅23♌
24	12.13	1	15	19	26	1	♆ 7♏
25	12.17	2	29	21	28	2	♇ 6♍
26	12.21	3	13♐	22	29	2	♃26♐
27	12.25	4	27	24	0♏	3	♄12♑
28	12.29	5	11♑	25	1	3	♅24♌
29	12.33	6	25	27	3	4	♆ 7♏
30	12.37	7	9♒	28	4	4	♇ 7♍

Oct	STime	☉	☽	☿	♀	♂	Plnts
1	12.41	8♎	24♒	29♎	5♏	5♋	♃26♐
2	12.45	9	8♓	1♏	6	5	♄12♑
3	12.49	10	22	2	7	6	♅24♌
4	12.53	11	6♈	3	9	6	♆ 8♏
5	12.57	12	19	5	10	7	♇ 7♍
6	13.01	13	2♉	6	11	7	♃27♐
7	13.05	14	15	7	12	7	♄12♑
8	13.08	15	28	9	14	8	♅24♌
9	13.12	16	10♊	10	15	8	♆ 8♏
10	13.16	17	23	11	16	9	♇ 7♍
11	13.20	18	5♋	12	17	9	♃27♐
12	13.24	19	16	13	18	10	♄12♑
13	13.28	20	28	14	20	10	♅24♌
14	13.32	21	10♌	15	21	10	♆ 8♏
15	13.36	22	22	17	22	11	♇ 7♍
16	13.40	23	5♍	18	23	11	♃28♐
17	13.44	24	17	18	25	11	♄12♑
18	13.48	25	0♎	19	26	12	♅25♌
19	13.52	26	13	20	27	12	♆ 8♏
20	13.56	27	27	21	28	13	♇ 7♍
21	14.00	28	11♏	22	29	13	♃29♐
22	14.04	29	25	22	1♐	13	♄13♑
23	14.08	0♏	9♐	23	2	14	♅25♌
24	14.12	1	23	23	3	14	♆ 8♏
25	14.15	2	8♑	23	4	14	♇ 7♍
26	14.19	3	22	24	6	14	♃ 0♑
27	14.23	4	6♒	24R	7	15	♄13♑
28	14.27	5	20	24	8	15	♅25♌
29	14.31	6	4♓	23	9	15	♆ 8♏
30	14.35	7	18	23	10	16	♇ 7♍
31	14.39	8	1♈	23	12	16	♃ 1♑

Nov	STime	☉	☽	☿	♀	♂	Plnts
1	14.43	9♏	15♈	22♏	13♐	16♋	♃ 1♑
2	14.47	10	28	21	14	16	♄13♑
3	14.51	11	11♉	20	15	16	♅25♌
4	14.55	12	24	19	16	17	♆ 9♏
5	14.59	13	6♊	18	18	17	♇ 8♍
6	15.03	14	18	17	19	17	♃ 2♑
7	15.07	15	1♋	15	20	17	♄14♑
8	15.11	16	12	14	21	17	♅25♌
9	15.15	17	24	13	23	18	♆ 9♏
10	15.19	18	6♌	11	24	18	♇ 8♍
11	15.23	19	18	10	25	18	♃ 3♑
12	15.26	20	0♍	10	26	18	♄14♑
13	15.30	21	12	9	27	18	♅25♌
14	15.34	22	25	8	29	18	♆ 9♏
15	15.38	23	8♎	8	0♑	18	♇ 8♍
16	15.42	24	21	8D	1	18	♃ 4♑
17	15.46	25	5♏	8	2	18	♄15♑
18	15.50	26	19	8	3	18	♅25♌
19	15.54	27	4♐	8	5	18	♆ 9♏
20	15.58	28	19	9	6	18R	♇ 8♍
21	16.02	29	3♑	10	7	18	♃ 5♑
22	16.06	0♐	18	10	8	18	♄15♑
23	16.10	1	3♒	11	10	18	♅25♌
24	16.14	2	17	12	11	18	♆ 9♏
25	16.18	3	1♓	13	12	18	♇ 8♍
26	16.22	4	15	14	13	18	♃ 6♑
27	16.26	5	28	16	14	18	♄15♑
28	16.30	6	11♈	17	16	18	♅26♌
29	16.33	7	24	18	17	18	♆10♏
30	16.37	8	7♉	19	18	18	♇ 8♍

Dec	STime	☉	☽	☿	♀	♂	Plnts
1	16.41	9♐	20♉	21♏	19♑	18♋	♃ 7♑
2	16.45	10	2♊	22	20	17	♄16♑
3	16.49	11	15	24	22	17	♅26♌
4	16.53	12	27	25	23	17	♆10♏
5	16.57	13	9♋	26	24	17	♇ 8♍
6	17.01	14	21	28	25	17	♃ 8♑
7	17.05	15	3♌	29	26	16	♄17♑
8	17.09	16	14	1♐	27	16	♅25♌R
9	17.13	17	26	2	29	16	♆10♏
10	17.17	18	8♍	4	0♒	16	♇ 8♍
11	17.21	19	20	5	1	15	♃ 9♑
12	17.25	20	3♎	7	2	15	♄17♑
13	17.29	21	16	8	3	15	♅25♌R
14	17.33	22	29	10	5	14	♆10♏
15	17.37	23	13♏	11	6	14	♇ 8♍
16	17.41	24	27	13	7	14	♃10♑
17	17.44	25	12♐	14	8	13	♄18♑
18	17.48	26	27	16	9	13	♅25♌R
19	17.52	27	12♑	18	10	13	♆10♏
20	17.56	28	27	19	12	12	♇ 8♍R
21	18.00	29	12♒	21	13	12	♃11♑
22	18.04	0♑	27	22	14	12	♄18♑
23	18.08	1	11♓	24	15	11	♅25♌R
24	18.12	2	25	25	16	11	♆10♏
25	18.16	3	8♈	27	17	10	♇ 8♍R
26	18.20	4	21	28	19	10	♃13♑
27	18.24	5	4♉	0♑	20	10	♄19♑
28	18.28	6	17	2	21	9	♅25♌R
29	18.32	7	29	3	22	9	♆10♏
30	18.36	9	11♊	5	23	8	♇ 8♍R
31	18.40	10	24	6	24	8	♃14♑

Jan	STime	☉	☽	☿	♀	♂	Plnts
1	18.44	11♑	6♋	8♑	26♒	8♋	♃14♑
2	18.48	12	17	10	27	7	♄19♑
3	18.51	13	29	11	28	7	♅25♌R
4	18.55	14	11♌	13	29	6	♆11♏
5	18.59	15	23	14	0♓	6	♇ 8♍R
6	19.03	16	5♍	16	1	6	♃15♑
7	19.07	17	17	18	2	5	♄20♑
8	19.11	18	29	19	3	5	♅25♌R
9	19.15	19	11♎	21	5	5	♆11♏
10	19.19	20	24	23	6	4	♇ 8♍R
11	19.23	21	7♏	24	7	4	♃16♑
12	19.27	22	21	26	8	4	♄21♑
13	19.31	23	5♐	28	9	3	♅25♌R
14	19.35	24	20	29	10	3	♆11♏
15	19.39	25	5♑	1♒	11	3	♇ 8♍R
16	19.43	26	20	3	12	3	♃17♑
17	19.47	27	5♒	4	13	2	♄21♑
18	19.51	28	21	6	14	2	♅25♌R
19	19.55	29	6♓	8	16	2	♆11♏
20	19.59	0♒	20	9	17	2	♇ 7♍R
21	20.02	1	4♈	11	18	1	♃19♑
22	20.06	2	18	13	19	1	♄22♑
23	20.10	3	1♉	15	20	1	♅24♌R
24	20.14	4	14	16	21	1	♆11♏
25	20.18	5	26	18	22	1	♇ 7♍R
26	20.22	6	8♊	20	23	0	♃20♑
27	20.26	7	21	21	24	0	♄22♑
28	20.30	8	2♋	23	25	0	♅24♌R
29	20.34	9	14	25	26	0	♆11♏
30	20.38	10	26	26	27	0	♇ 7♍R
31	20.42	11	8♌	28	28	0	♃21♑

Feb	STime	☉	☽	☿	♀	♂	Plnts
1	20.46	12♒	20♌	29♒	29♓	0♋	♃21♑
2	20.50	13	2♍	1♓	0♈	0	♄23♑
3	20.54	14	14	2	1	0	♅24♌R
4	20.58	15	26	3	2	0	♆11♏
5	21.02	16	8♎	4	3	0D	♇ 7♍R
6	21.06	17	21	5	4	0	♃22♑
7	21.09	18	4♏	6	5	0	♄24♑
8	21.13	19	17	7	6	0	♅24♌R
9	21.17	20	0♐	8	7	0	♆11♏
10	21.21	21	14	8	8	0	♇ 7♍R
11	21.25	22	29	9	8	0	♃23♑
12	21.29	23	13♑	9	9	0	♄24♑
13	21.33	24	28	9R	10	0	♅23♌R
14	21.37	25	13♒	9	11	0	♆11♏
15	21.41	26	29	8	12	0	♇ 7♍R
16	21.45	27	13♓	8	13	0	♃24♑
17	21.49	28	28	7	14	0	♄25♑
18	21.53	29	12♈	6	14	1	♅23♌R
19	21.57	0♓	26	5	15	1	♆11♏R
20	22.01	1	9♉	4	16	1	♇ 7♍R
21	22.05	2	22	3	17	1	♃25♑
22	22.09	3	5♊	2	18	1	♄25♑
23	22.13	4	17	1	18	1	♅23♌R
24	22.16	5	29	0	19	2	♆11♏R
25	22.20	6	11♋	29♒	20	2	♇ 7♍R
26	22.24	7	23	28	20	2	♃26♑
27	22.28	8	5♌	27	21	2	♄26♑
28	22.32	9	17	26	22	3	♅23♌R

Mar	STime	☉	☽	☿	♀	♂	Plnts
1	22.36	10♓	29♌	26♒	22♈	3♋	♃27♑
2	22.40	11	11♍	25	23	3	♄26♑
3	22.44	12	23	25	23	3	♅23♌R
4	22.48	13	5♎	24	24	4	♆11♏R
5	22.52	14	18	24	25	4	♇ 6♍R
6	22.56	15	1♏	24D	25	4	♃28♑
7	23.00	16	14	24	26	4	♄27♑
8	23.04	17	27	24	26	5	♅22♌R
9	23.08	18	10♐	24	26	5	♆11♏R
10	23.12	19	24	25	27	5	♇ 6♍R
11	23.16	20	8♑	25	27	6	♃29♑
12	23.20	21	23	26	27	6	♄27♑
13	23.24	22	7♒	26	28	6	♅22♌R
14	23.27	23	22	27	28	7	♆11♏R
15	23.31	24	7♓	27	28	7	♇ 6♍R
16	23.35	25	22	28	28	7	♃ 0♒
17	23.39	26	6♈	29	29	8	♄27♑
18	23.43	27	20	0♓	29	8	♅22♌R
19	23.47	28	4♉	1	29	8	♆11♏R
20	23.51	29	17	2	29R	9	♇ 6♍R
21	23.55	0♈	0♊	3	29	9	♃ 1♒
22	23.59	1	13	4	29	9	♄28♑
23	0.03	2	25	5	29	10	♅22♌R
24	0.07	3	8♋	6	29	10	♆11♏R
25	0.11	4	19	7	28	11	♇ 6♍R
26	0.15	5	1♌	8	28	11	♃ 2♒
27	0.19	6	13	10	28	11	♄28♑
28	0.23	7	25	11	28	12	♅22♌R
29	0.27	8	7♍	12	27	12	♆10♏R
30	0.31	9	19	13	27	13	♇ 6♍R
31	0.34	10	2♎	15	26	13	♃ 2♒

Apr	STime	☉	☽	☿	♀	♂	Plnts
1	0.38	11♈	14♎	16♓	26♈	13♋	♃ 3♒
2	0.42	12	27	18	26	14	♄28♑
3	0.46	13	10♏	19	25	14	♅22♌R
4	0.50	14	24	20	24	15	♆10♏R
5	0.54	15	7♐	22	24	15	♇ 6♍R
6	0.58	16	21	24	23	15	♃ 3♒
7	1.02	17	5♑	25	23	16	♄29♑
8	1.06	18	19	27	22	16	♅22♌R
9	1.10	19	3♒	28	22	17	♆10♏R
10	1.14	20	17	0♈	21	17	♇ 6♍R
11	1.18	21	2♓	2	20	18	♃ 4♒
12	1.22	22	16	3	20	18	♄29♑
13	1.26	23	0♈	5	19	19	♅21♌R
14	1.30	24	14	7	18	19	♆10♏R
15	1.34	25	28	8	18	20	♇ 5♍R
16	1.38	26	12♉	10	17	20	♃ 5♒
17	1.42	27	25	12	17	21	♄29♑.
18	1.45	28	8♊	14	16	21	♅21♌R
19	1.49	29	21	16	16	21	♆10♏R
20	1.53	0♉	3♋	18	15	22	♇ 5♍R
21	1.57	1	15	20	15	22	♃ 5♒
22	2.01	2	27	21	14	23	♄29♑
23	2.05	3	9♌	23	14	23	♅21♌R
24	2.09	4	21	25	14	24	♆10♏R
25	2.13	5	3♍	27	13	24	♇ 5♍R
26	2.17	6	15	29	13	25	♃ 6♒
27	2.21	7	27	2♉	13	25	♄29♑
28	2.25	8	10♎	4	13	26	♅21♌
29	2.29	9	23	6	13	26	♆10♏R
30	2.33	10	6♏	8	13	27	♇ 5♍

May	STime	☉	☽	☿	♀	♂	Plnts
1	2.37	11♉	20♏	10♉	12♈	27♋	♃ 6♒
2	2.41	12	4♐	12	12	28	♄ 0♒
3	2.45	13	18	14	12	28	♅21♌
4	2.49	13	2♑	16	13	29	♆10♏R
5	2.52	14	16	19	13	29	♇ 5♍R
6	2.56	15	0♒	21	13	0♌	♃ 6♒
7	3.00	16	14	23	13	0	♄ 0♒
8	3.04	17	28	25	13	1	♅21♌
9	3.08	18	12♓	27	13	1	♆ 9♏R
10	3.12	19	26	29	14	2	♇ 5♍
11	3.16	20	10♈	1♊	14	3	♃ 7♒
12	3.20	21	24	3	14	3	♄ 0♒
13	3.24	22	7♉	5	15	4	♅21♌
14	3.28	23	21	7	15	4	♆ 9♏R
15	3.32	24	4♊	9	16	5	♇ 5♍
16	3.36	25	17	11	16	5	♃ 7♒
17	3.40	26	29	13	17	6	♄ 0♒R
18	3.44	27	11♋	15	17	6	♅22♌
19	3.48	28	23	16	18	7	♆ 9♏R
20	3.52	29	5♌	18	18	7	♇ 5♍
21	3.56	0♊	17	20	19	8	♃ 7♒
22	4.00	1	29	21	19	8	♄29♑R
23	4.03	2	11♍	23	20	9	♅22♌
24	4.07	3	23	24	21	10	♆ 9♏R
25	4.11	4	5♎	26	21	10	♇ 5♍
26	4.15	5	18	27	22	11	♃ 7♒R
27	4.19	6	1♏	28	23	11	♄29♑R
28	4.23	7	15	29	23	12	♅22♌
29	4.27	8	28	1♋	24	12	♆ 9♏R
30	4.31	9	13♐	2	25	13	♇ 5♍
31	4.35	9	27	3	25	13	♃ 7♒R

Jun	STime	☉	☽	☿	♀	♂	Plnts
1	4.39	10♊	12♑	4♋	26♈	14♌	♃ 7♒R
2	4.43	11	26	5	27	14	♄29♑R
3	4.47	12	11♒	5	28	15	♅22♌
4	4.51	13	25	6	29	16	♆ 9♏R
5	4.55	14	9♓	7	29	16	♇ 5♍
6	4.59	15	23	8	0♉	17	♃ 7♒R
7	5.03	16	7♈	8	1	17	♄29♑R
8	5.07	17	20	9	2	18	♅22♌
9	5.10	18	4♉	9	3	18	♆ 9♏R
10	5.14	19	17	9	4	19	♇ 5♍
11	5.18	20	0♊	10	5	20	♃ 6♒R
12	5.22	21	13	10	5	20	♄29♑R
13	5.26	22	25	10	6	21	♅22♌
14	5.30	23	7♋	10R	7	21	♆ 9♏R
15	5.34	24	20	10	8	22	♇ 5♍
16	5.38	25	2♌	10	9	22	♃ 6♒R
17	5.42	26	13	10	10	23	♄28♑R
18	5.46	27	25	10	11	24	♅22♌
19	5.50	28	7♍	9	12	24	♆ 8♏R
20	5.54	29	19	9	13	25	♇ 6♍
21	5.58	0♋	1♎	9	14	25	♃ 6♒R
22	6.02	1	13	8	15	26	♄28♑R
23	6.06	1	26	8	16	26	♅23♌
24	6.10	2	9♏	7	17	27	♆ 8♏R
25	6.14	3	23	6	18	28	♇ 6♍
26	6.17	4	7♐	6	19	28	♃ 5♒R
27	6.21	5	21	5	20	29	♄28♑R
28	6.25	6	6♑	5	21	29	♅23♌
29	6.29	7	21	4	22	0♍	♆ 8♏R
30	6.33	8	6♒	4	23	1	♇ 6♍

Jul	STime	☉	☽	☿	♀	♂	Plnts
1	6.37	9♋	21♒	3♋	24♉	1♍	♃ 5♒R
2	6.41	10	5♓	3	25	2	♄27♑R
3	6.45	11	20	2	26	2	♅23♌
4	6.49	12	4♈	2	27	3	♆ 8♏R
5	6.53	13	17	2	28	4	♇ 6♍
6	6.57	14	1♉	1	29	4	♃ 4♒R
7	7.01	15	14	1	0♊	5	♄27♑R
8	7.05	16	27	1D	1	5	♅23♌
9	7.09	17	9♊	1	2	6	♆ 8♏R
10	7.13	18	22	1	3	7	♇ 6♍
11	7.17	19	4♋	1	4	7	♃ 4♒R
12	7.21	20	16	2	5	8	♄27♑R
13	7.25	21	28	2	6	8	♅24♌
14	7.28	21	10♌	2	7	9	♆ 8♏
15	7.32	22	22	3	9	10	♇ 6♍
16	7.36	23	4♍	4	10	10	♃ 3♒R
17	7.40	24	15	4	11	11	♄26♑R
18	7.44	25	27	5	12	11	♅24♌
19	7.48	26	9♎	6	13	12	♆ 8♏
20	7.52	27	22	7	14	13	♇ 6♍
21	7.56	28	4♏	8	15	13	♃ 2♒R
22	8.00	29	18	9	16	14	♄26♑R
23	8.04	0♌	1♐	10	17	14	♅24♌
24	8.08	1	15	12	18	15	♆ 8♏
25	8.12	2	29	13	19	16	♇ 6♍
26	8.16	3	14♑	15	21	16	♃ 2♒R
27	8.20	4	29	16	22	17	♄26♑R
28	8.24	5	14♒	18	23	17	♅25♌
29	8.28	6	0♓	19	24	18	♆ 8♏
30	8.32	7	14	21	25	19	♇ 7♍
31	8.35	8	29	23	26	19	♃ 1♒R

Aug	STime	☉	☽	☿	♀	♂	Plnts
1	8.39	9♌	13♈	25♋	27♊	20♍	♃ 1♒R
2	8.43	10	27	27	28	21	♄25♑R
3	8.47	11	11♉	29	0♋	21	♅25♌
4	8.51	12	24	1♌	1	22	♆ 8♏
5	8.55	13	7♊	3	2	22	♇ 7♍
6	8.59	13	19	5	3	23	♃ 0♒R
7	9.03	14	1♋	7	4	24	♄25♑R
8	9.07	15	13	9	5	24	♅25♌
9	9.11	16	25	11	6	25	♆ 8♏
10	9.15	17	7♌	13	8	26	♇ 7♍
11	9.19	18	19	15	9	26	♃ 0♒R
12	9.23	19	1♍	17	10	27	♄25♑R
13	9.27	20	12	19	11	27	♅25♌
14	9.31	21	24	21	12	28	♆ 8♏
15	9.35	22	6♎	23	13	29	♇ 7♍
16	9.39	23	18	25	14	29	♃29♑R
17	9.43	24	1♏	27	16	0♎	♄24♑R
18	9.46	25	14	29	17	1	♅26♌
19	9.50	26	27	1♍	18	1	♆ 8♏
20	9.54	27	10♐	3	19	2	♇ 7♍
21	9.58	28	24	5	20	3	♃29♑R
22	10.02	29	8♑	7	21	3	♄24♑R
23	10.06	0♍	23	8	23	4	♅26♌
24	10.10	1	8♒	10	24	4	♆ 9♏
25	10.14	2	23	12	25	5	♇ 7♍
26	10.18	3	8♓	14	26	6	♃28♑R
27	10.22	4	23	16	27	6	♄24♑R
28	10.26	5	8♈	17	28	7	♅26♌
29	10.30	6	22	19	0♌	8	♆ 9♏
30	10.34	7	6♉	21	1	8	♇ 8♍
31	10.38	8	20	23	2	9	♃28♑R

Sep	STime	☉	☽	☿	♀	♂	Plnts
1	10.42	9♍	3♊	24♍	3♌	10♎	♃28♑R
2	10.46	9	16	26	4	10	♄23♑R
3	10.50	10	28	27	6	11	♅27♌
4	10.53	11	10♋	29	7	12	♆ 9♏
5	10.57	12	22	1♎	8	12	♇ 8♍
6	11.01	13	4♌	2	9	13	♃27♑R
7	11.05	14	16	4	10	14	♄23♑R
8	11.09	15	28	5	11	14	♅27♌
9	11.13	16	10♍	7	13	15	♆ 9♏
10	11.17	17	21	8	14	15	♇ 8♍
11	11.21	18	3♎	10	15	16	♃27♑R
12	11.25	19	16	11	16	17	♄23♑R
13	11.29	20	28	12	17	17	♅27♌
14	11.33	21	10♏	14	19	18	♆ 9♏
15	11.37	22	23	15	20	19	♇ 8♍
16	11.41	23	6♐	17	21	19	♃27♑R
17	11.45	24	20	18	22	20	♄23♑R
18	11.49	25	3♑	19	23	21	♅28♌
19	11.53	26	17	20	25	21	♆ 9♏
20	11.57	27	2♒	22	26	22	♇ 8♍
21	12.00	28	16	23	27	23	♃27♑R
22	12.04	29	1♓	24	28	23	♄23♑R
23	12.08	0♎	16	25	0♍	24	♅28♌
24	12.12	1	1♈	26	1	25	♆ 9♏
25	12.16	2	16	28	2	25	♇ 8♍
26	12.20	3	0♉	29	3	26	♃27♑
27	12.24	4	15	0♏	4	27	♄23♑
28	12.28	5	28	1	6	27	♅28♌
29	12.32	6	12♊	2	7	28	♆ 9♏
30	12.36	7	24	3	8	29	♇ 9♍

Oct	STime	☉	☽	☿	♀	♂	Plnts
1	12.40	8♎	7♋	3♏	9♍	29♎	♃27♑
2	12.44	9	19	4	10	0♏	♄23♑
3	12.48	10	1♌	5	12	1	♅28♌
4	12.52	11	13	6	13	2	♆10♏
5	12.56	12	24	6	14	2	♇ 9♍
6	13.00	13	6♍	7	15	3	♃27♑
7	13.04	14	18	7	17	4	♄23♑
8	13.08	15	0♎	7	18	4	♅29♌
9	13.11	16	12	8	19	5	♆10♏
10	13.15	17	25	8	20	6	♇ 9♍
11	13.19	18	7♏	8R	22	6	♃28♑
12	13.23	19	20	8	23	7	♄23♑
13	13.27	20	3♐	7	24	8	♅29♌
14	13.31	21	17	7	25	8	♆10♏
15	13.35	22	0♑	6	26	9	♇ 9♍
16	13.39	23	14	6	28	10	♃28♑
17	13.43	24	28	5	29	10	♄23♑
18	13.47	25	12♒	4	0♎	11	♅29♌
19	13.51	26	26	3	1	12	♆10♏
20	13.55	27	10♓	2	3	12	♇ 9♍
21	13.59	28	25	0	4	13	♃28♑
22	14.03	29	10♈	29♎	5	14	♄23♑
23	14.07	0♏	24	28	6	15	♅29♌
24	14.11	1	9♉	27	8	15	♆10♏
25	14.15	2	23	26	9	16	♇ 9♍
26	14.18	3	6♊	25	10	17	♃29♑
27	14.22	4	19	24	11	17	♄24♑
28	14.26	5	2♋	23	13	18	♅ 0♍
29	14.30	6	15	22	14	19	♆11♏
30	14.34	7	27	22	15	19	♇ 9♍
31	14.38	8	9♌	22D	16	20	♃29♑

Nov	STime	☉	☽	☿	♀	♂	Plnts
1	14.42	9♏	21♌	22♎	18♎	21♏	♃29♑
2	14.46	10	3♍	22	19	22	♄24♑
3	14.50	11	14	23	20	22	♅ 0♍
4	14.54	12	26	23	21	23	♆11♏
5	14.58	13	8♎	24	23	24	♇ 9♍
6	15.02	14	21	25	24	24	♃ 0♒
7	15.06	15	4♏	26	25	25	♄24♑
8	15.10	16	17	27	26	26	♅ 0♍
9	15.14	17	0♐	28	28	27	♆11♏
10	15.18	18	13	29	29	27	♇10♍
11	15.22	19	27	0♏	0♏	28	♃ 1♒
12	15.26	20	11♑	2	1	29	♄25♑
13	15.29	21	25	3	3	29	♅ 0♍
14	15.33	22	8♒	4	4	0♐	♆11♏
15	15.37	23	22	6	5	1	♇10♍
16	15.41	24	7♓	7	6	2	♃ 1♒
17	15.45	25	21	9	8	2	♄25♑
18	15.49	26	5♈	10	9	3	♅ 0♍
19	15.53	27	19	12	10	4	♆11♏
20	15.57	28	3♉	13	11	4	♇10♍
21	16.01	29	17	15	13	5	♃ 2♒
22	16.05	0♐	1♊	16	14	6	♄25♑
23	16.09	1	14	18	15	7	♅ 0♍
24	16.13	2	27	20	16	7	♆12♏
25	16.17	3	10♋	21	18	8	♇10♍
26	16.21	4	23	23	19	9	♃ 3♒
27	16.25	5	5♌	24	20	10	♄26♑
28	16.29	6	17	26	21	10	♅ 0♍
29	16.33	7	28	27	23	11	♆12♏
30	16.36	8	10♍	29	24	12	♇10♍

Dec	STime	☉	☽	☿	♀	♂	Plnts
1	16.40	9♐	22♍	1♐	25♏	12♐	♃ 4♒
2	16.44	10	4♎	2	26	13	♄26♑
3	16.48	11	16	4	28	14	♅ 0♍
4	16.52	12	29	5	29	15	♆12♏
5	16.56	13	12♏	7	0♐	15	♇10♍
6	17.00	14	25	8	1	16	♃ 5♒
7	17.04	15	8♐	10	3	17	♄27♑
8	17.08	16	22	12	4	18	♅ 0♍R
9	17.12	17	6♑	13	5	18	♆12♏
10	17.16	18	21	15	6	19	♇10♍
11	17.20	19	5♒	16	8	20	♃ 6♒
12	17.24	20	19	18	9	21	♄27♑
13	17.28	21	3♓	19	10	21	♅ 0♍
14	17.32	22	18	21	11	22	♆12♏
15	17.36	23	2♈	23	13	23	♇10♍
16	17.40	24	16	24	14	24	♃ 7♒
17	17.44	25	29	26	15	24	♄28♑
18	17.47	26	13♉	27	16	25	♅ 0♍R
19	17.51	27	26	29	18	26	♆12♏
20	17.55	28	10♊	0♑	19	27	♇10♍
21	17.59	29	23	2	20	27	♃ 8♒
22	18.03	0♑	6♋	4	22	28	♄28♑
23	18.07	1	18	5	23	29	♅ 0♍R
24	18.11	2	1♌	7	24	0♑	♆12♏
25	18.15	3	13	8	25	0	♇10♍
26	18.19	4	25	10	27	1	♃ 9♒
27	18.23	5	6♍	12	28	2	♄29♑
28	18.27	6	18	13	29	3	♅ 0♍R
29	18.31	7	0♎	15	0♑	3	♆13♏
30	18.35	8	12	16	2	4	♇10♍R
31	18.39	9	24	18	3	5	♃10♒

Jan	STime	☉	☽	☿	♀	♂	Plnts
1	18.43	10♑	7♏	20♑	4♑	6♑	♃10♒
2	18.47	11	20	21	5	6	♄ 0♒
3	18.51	12	3♐	23	7	7	♅ 0♍R
4	18.54	13	17	25	8	8	♆13♏
5	18.58	14	1♑	26	9	9	♇10♍R
6	19.02	15	15	28	10	9	♃11♒
7	19.06	16	0♒	29	12	10	♄ 0♒
8	19.10	17	14	1♒	13	11	♅ 0♍R
9	19.14	18	29	3	14	12	♆13♏
10	19.18	19	14♓	4	15	12	♇10♍R
11	19.22	20	28	6	17	13	♃13♒
12	19.26	22	12♈	7	18	14	♄ 1♒
13	19.30	23	26	9	19	15	♅ 0♍R
14	19.34	24	10♉	10	20	15	♆13♏
15	19.38	25	23	12	22	16	♇10♍R
16	19.42	26	6♊	13	23	17	♃14♒
17	19.46	27	19	15	24	18	♄ 1♒
18	19.50	28	2♋	16	25	19	♅29♌R
19	19.54	29	14	17	27	19	♆13♏
20	19.58	0♒	27	18	28	20	♇ 9♍R
21	20.01	1	9♌	19	29	21	♃15♒
22	20.05	2	21	20	1♒	22	♄ 2♒
23	20.09	3	3♍	21	2	22	♅29♌R
24	20.13	4	15	22	3	23	♆13♏
25	20.17	5	26	22	4	24	♇ 9♍R
26	20.21	6	8♎	22	6	25	♃16♒
27	20.25	7	20	23R	7	25	♄ 2♒
28	20.29	8	2♏	22	8	26	♅29♌R
29	20.33	9	15	22	9	27	♆13♏
30	20.37	10	28	22	11	28	♇ 9♍R
31	20.41	11	11♐	21	12	29	♃17♒

Feb	STime	☉	☽	☿	♀	♂	Plnts
1	20.45	12♒	24♐	20♒	13♒	29♑	♃17♒
2	20.49	13	8♑	19	14	0♒	♄ 3♒
3	20.53	14	23	18	16	1	♅29♌R
4	20.57	15	8♒	17	17	2	♆13♏
5	21.01	16	23	16	18	2	♇ 9♍R
6	21.05	17	8♓	15	19	3	♃19♒
7	21.09	18	23	14	21	4	♄ 4♒
8	21.12	19	8♈	12	22	5	♅29♌R
9	21.16	20	22	11	23	6	♆13♏
10	21.20	21	6♉	10	24	6	♇ 9♍R
11	21.24	22	20	10	26	7	♃20♒
12	21.28	23	3♊	9	27	8	♄ 4♒
13	21.32	24	16	8	28	9	♅28♌R
14	21.36	25	29	8	29	9	♆13♏
15	21.40	26	11♋	7	1♓	10	♇ 9♍R
16	21.44	27	24	7	2	11	♃21♒
17	21.48	28	6♌	7D	3	12	♄ 5♒
18	21.52	29	18	7	4	13	♅28♌R
19	21.56	0♓	29	7	6	13	♆13♏
20	22.00	1	11♍	7	7	14	♇ 9♍R
21	22.04	2	23	8	8	15	♃22♒
22	22.08	3	5♎	8	9	16	♄ 6♒
23	22.12	4	17	9	11	16	♅28♌R
24	22.16	5	29	9	12	17	♆13♏R
25	22.19	6	11♏	10	13	18	♇ 9♍R
26	22.23	7	24	11	14	19	♃23♒
27	22.27	8	6♐	11	16	20	♄ 6♒
28	22.31	9	19	12	17	20	♅28♌R

Mar	STime	☉	☽	☿	♀	♂	Plnts
1	22.35	10♓	3♑	13♒	18♓	21♒	♃24♒
2	22.39	11	17	14	19	22	♄ 6♒
3	22.43	12	1♒	15	21	23	♅28♌R
4	22.47	13	16	16	22	24	♆13♏R
5	22.51	14	1♓	17	23	24	♇ 8♍R
6	22.55	15	16	18	24	25	♃25♒
7	22.59	16	1♈	19	26	26	♄ 7♒
8	23.03	17	16	21	27	27	♅27♌R
9	23.07	18	1♉	22	28	27	♆13♏R
10	23.11	19	15	23	29	28	♇ 8♍R
11	23.15	20	29	24	1♈	29	♃26♒
12	23.19	21	13♊	26	2	0♓	♄ 7♒
13	23.23	22	26	27	3	1	♅27♌R
14	23.27	23	8♋	28	4	1	♆13♏R
15	23.30	24	21	0♓	6	2	♇ 8♍R
16	23.34	25	3♌	1	7	3	♃28♒
17	23.38	26	15	3	8	4	♄ 8♒
18	23.42	27	26	4	9	5	♅27♌R
19	23.46	28	8♍	5	11	5	♆13♏R
20	23.50	29	20	7	12	6	♇ 8♍R
21	23.54	0♈	2♎	9	13	7	♃29♒
22	23.58	1	14	10	14	8	♄ 8♒
23	0.02	2	26	12	16	8	♅27♌R
24	0.06	3	8♏	13	17	9	♆13♏R
25	0.10	4	20	15	18	10	♇ 8♍R
26	0.14	5	3♐	16	19	11	♃ 0♓
27	0.18	6	16	18	20	12	♄ 9♒
28	0.22	7	29	20	22	12	♅27♌R
29	0.26	8	12♑	22	23	13	♆13♏R
30	0.30	9	26	23	24	14	♇ 8♍R
31	0.34	10	10♒	25	25	15	♃ 1♓

Apr	STime	☉	☽	☿	♀	♂	Plnts
1	0.37	11♈	24♒	27♓	27♈	16♓	♃ 1♓
2	0.41	12	9♓	29	28	16	♄ 9♒
3	0.45	13	24	0♈	29	17	♅27♌R
4	0.49	14	9♈	2	0♉	18	♆13♏R
5	0.53	15	24	4	2	19	♇ 8♍R
6	0.57	16	9♉	6	3	19	♃ 2♓
7	1.01	17	24	8	4	20	♄10♒
8	1.05	18	8♊	10	5	21	♅26♌R
9	1.09	19	21	12	7	22	♆12♏R
10	1.13	20	4♋	14	8	23	♇ 8♍R
11	1.17	21	17	16	9	23	♃ 3♓
12	1.21	22	29	18	10	24	♄10♒
13	1.25	23	11♌	20	11	25	♅26♌R
14	1.29	24	23	22	13	26	♆12♏R
15	1.33	25	5♍	24	14	26	♇ 8♍R
16	1.37	26	17	26	15	27	♃ 4♓
17	1.41	27	29	28	16	28	♄10♒
18	1.45	28	11♎	0♉	18	29	♅26♌R
19	1.48	29	23	3	19	0♈	♆12♏R
20	1.52	0♉	5♏	5	20	0	♇ 7♍R
21	1.56	1	17	7	21	1	♃ 5♓
22	2.00	2	0♐	9	22	2	♄10♒
23	2.04	3	13	11	24	3	♅26♌R
24	2.08	4	26	13	25	3	♆12♏R
25	2.12	4	9♑	15	26	4	♇ 7♍R
26	2.16	5	22	17	27	5	♃ 6♓
27	2.20	6	6♒	19	29	6	♄11♒
28	2.24	7	20	21	0♊	7	♅26♌R
29	2.28	8	4♓	23	1	7	♆12♏R
30	2.32	9	19	25	2	8	♇ 7♍R

May	STime	☉	☽	☿	♀	♂	Plnts
1	2.36	10♉	3♈	27♉	3♊	9♈	♃ 7♓
2	2.40	11	18	28	5	10	♄11♒
3	2.44	12	3♉	0♊	6	10	♅26♌
4	2.48	13	18	2	7	11	♆12♏R
5	2.52	14	2♊	3	8	12	♇ 7♍R
6	2.55	15	16	5	10	13	♃ 8♓
7	2.59	16	29	6	11	13	♄11♒
8	3.03	17	13♋	8	12	14	♅26♌
9	3.07	18	25	9	13	15	♆12♏R
10	3.11	19	8♌	10	14	16	♇ 7♍R
11	3.15	20	20	11	16	16	♃ 8♓
12	3.19	21	2♍	13	17	17	♄11♒
13	3.23	22	13	14	18	18	♅26♌
14	3.27	23	25	15	19	19	♆12♏R
15	3.31	24	7♎	15	21	20	♇ 7♍
16	3.35	25	19	16	22	20	♃ 9♓
17	3.39	26	1♏	17	23	21	♄11♒
18	3.43	27	14	18	24	22	♅26♌
19	3.47	28	26	18	25	23	♆11♏R
20	3.51	29	9♐	19	27	23	♇ 7♍
21	3.55	0♊	22	19	28	24	♃10♓
22	3.59	1	6♑	20	29	25	♄11♒
23	4.02	2	19	20	0♋	26	♅26♌
24	4.06	3	3♒	20	1	26	♆11♏R
25	4.10	3	17	20	3	27	♇ 7♍
26	4.14	4	1♓	20R	4	28	♃10♓
27	4.18	5	15	20	5	29	♄11♒R
28	4.22	6	29	20	6	29	♅26♌
29	4.26	7	13♈	20	7	0♉	♆11♏R
30	4.30	8	28	19	9	1	♇ 7♍
31	4.34	9	12♉	19	10	2	♃11♓

Jun	STime	☉	☽	☿	♀	♂	Plnts
1	4.38	10♊	26♉	19♊	11♋	2♉	♃11♓
2	4.42	11	10♊	18	12	3	♄11♒R
3	4.46	12	24	18	13	4	♅27♌
4	4.50	13	7♋	17	15	5	♆11♏R
5	4.54	14	21	17	16	5	♇ 7♍
6	4.58	15	3♌	16	17	6	♃11♓
7	5.02	16	15	16	18	7	♄11♒R
8	5.06	17	28	15	19	8	♅27♌
9	5.10	18	10♍	15	21	8	♆11♏R
10	5.13	19	21	14	22	9	♇ 7♍
11	5.17	20	3♎	14	23	10	♃12♓
12	5.21	21	15	13	24	10	♄11♒R
13	5.25	22	27	13	25	11	♅27♌
14	5.29	23	10♏	12	26	12	♆11♏R
15	5.33	24	22	12	28	13	♇ 7♍
16	5.37	25	5♐	12	29	13	♃12♓
17	5.41	26	18	12	0♌	14	♄11♒R
18	5.45	26	2♑	12	1	15	♅27♌
19	5.49	27	15	12D	2	16	♆11♏R
20	5.53	28	29	12	4	16	♇ 7♍
21	5.57	29	13♒	12	5	17	♃12♓
22	6.01	0♋	27	12	6	18	♄10♒R
23	6.05	1	12♓	12	7	18	♅27♌
24	6.09	2	26	13	8	19	♆11♏R
25	6.13	3	10♈	13	9	20	♇ 8♍
26	6.17	4	24	14	11	21	♃12♓
27	6.20	5	8♉	14	12	21	♄10♒R
28	6.24	6	22	15	13	22	♅27♌
29	6.28	7	6♊	16	14	23	♆11♏R
30	6.32	8	20	16	15	24	♇ 8♍

Jul	STime	☉	☽	☿	♀	♂	Plnts
1	6.36	9♋	3♋	17♊	16♌	24♉	♃12♓
2	6.40	10	16	18	18	25	♄10♒R
3	6.44	11	29	19	19	26	♅28♌
4	6.48	12	11♌	20	20	26	♆11♏R
5	6.52	13	23	22	21	27	♇ 8♍
6	6.56	14	5♍	23	22	28	♃12♓R
7	7.00	15	17	24	23	29	♄ 9♒R
8	7.04	16	29	25	25	29	♅28♌
9	7.08	16	11♎	27	26	0♊	♆10♏R
10	7.12	17	23	28	27	1	♇ 8♍
11	7.16	18	5♏	0♋	28	1	♃12♓R
12	7.20	19	18	2	29	2	♄ 9♒R
13	7.24	20	0♐	3	0♍	3	♅28♌
14	7.28	21	13	5	1	3	♆10♏R
15	7.31	22	27	7	3	4	♇ 8♍
16	7.35	23	10♑	9	4	5	♃12♓R
17	7.39	24	24	11	5	6	♄ 9♒R
18	7.43	25	9♒	13	6	6	♅28♌
19	7.47	26	23	15	7	7	♆10♏
20	7.51	27	8♓	17	8	8	♇ 8♍
21	7.55	28	22	19	9	8	♃12♓R
22	7.59	29	7♈	21	11	9	♄ 8♒R
23	8.03	0♌	21	23	12	10	♅29♌
24	8.07	1	5♉	25	13	10	♆10♏
25	8.11	2	19	27	14	11	♇ 8♍
26	8.15	3	3♊	29	15	12	♃11♓R
27	8.19	4	16	1♌	16	12	♄ 8♒R
28	8.23	5	29	3	17	13	♅29♌
29	8.27	6	12♋	5	18	14	♆10♏
30	8.31	7	25	8	20	14	♇ 8♍
31	8.35	7	7♌	10	21	15	♃11♓R

Aug	STime	☉	☽	☿	♀	♂	Plnts
1	8.38	8♌	20♌	12♌	22♍	16♊	♃11♓R
2	8.42	9	2♍	14	23	17	♄ 8♒R
3	8.46	10	14	16	24	17	♅29♌
4	8.50	11	26	18	25	18	♆10♏
5	8.54	12	7♎	20	26	19	♇ 9♍
6	8.58	13	19	22	27	19	♃10♓R
7	9.02	14	1♏	24	28	20	♄ 7♒R
8	9.06	15	13	25	29	21	♅ 0♍
9	9.10	16	26	27	1♎	21	♆11♏
10	9.14	17	8♐	29	2	22	♇ 9♍
11	9.18	18	21	1♍	3	23	♃10♓R
12	9.22	19	5♑	3	4	23	♄ 7♒R
13	9.26	20	18	5	5	24	♅ 0♍
14	9.30	21	3♒	6	6	25	♆11♏
15	9.34	22	17	8	7	25	♇ 9♍
16	9.38	23	2♓	10	8	26	♃ 9♓R
17	9.42	24	17	11	9	26	♄ 7♒R
18	9.45	25	2♈	13	10	27	♅ 0♍
19	9.49	26	17	15	11	28	♆11♏
20	9.53	27	1♉	16	12	28	♇ 9♍
21	9.57	28	16	18	13	29	♃ 9♓R
22	10.01	29	29	19	14	0♋	♄ 6♒R
23	10.05	0♍	13♊	21	15	0	♅ 1♍
24	10.09	1	26	22	16	1	♆11♏
25	10.13	2	9♋	24	17	2	♇ 9♍
26	10.17	2	22	25	18	2	♃ 8♓R
27	10.21	3	4♌	27	19	3	♄ 6♒R
28	10.25	4	16	28	20	4	♅ 1♍
29	10.29	5	28	29	21	4	♆11♏
30	10.33	6	10♍	1♎	22	5	♇ 9♍
31	10.37	7	22	2	23	5	♃ 7♓R

Sep	STime	☉	☽	☿	♀	♂	Plnts
1	10.41	8♍	4♎	3♎	24♎	6♋	♃ 7♓R
2	10.45	9	16	5	25	7	♄ 6♒R
3	10.49	10	28	6	26	7	♅ 1♍
4	10.53	11	10♏	7	27	8	♆11♏
5	10.56	12	22	8	28	9	♇10♍
6	11.00	13	4♐	10	29	9	♃ 7♓R
7	11.04	14	17	11	0♏	10	♄ 5♒R
8	11.08	15	29	12	1	10	♅ 2♍
9	11.12	16	13♑	13	2	11	♆11♏
10	11.16	17	27	14	3	12	♇10♍
11	11.20	18	11♒	15	4	12	♃ 6♓R
12	11.24	19	25	16	5	13	♄ 5♒R
13	11.28	20	10♓	17	6	13	♅ 2♍
14	11.32	21	26	17	7	14	♆11♏
15	11.36	22	11♈	18	7	15	♇10♍
16	11.40	23	26	19	8	15	♃ 5♓R
17	11.44	24	11♉	19	9	16	♄ 5♒R
18	11.48	25	25	20	10	16	♅ 2♍
19	11.52	26	9♊	20	11	17	♆11♏
20	11.56	27	23	21	12	18	♇10♍
21	12.00	28	6♋	21	12	18	♃ 5♓R
22	12.03	29	19	21	13	19	♄ 5♒R
23	12.07	0♎	1♌	21	14	19	♅ 2♍
24	12.11	1	13	21R	15	20	♆11♏
25	12.15	2	25	21	15	21	♇10♍
26	12.19	3	7♍	21	16	21	♃ 4♓R
27	12.23	4	19	21	17	22	♄ 5♒R
28	12.27	5	1♎	20	18	22	♅ 3♍
29	12.31	6	13	20	18	23	♆12♏
30	12.35	7	25	19	19	23	♇10♍

Oct	STime	☉	☽	☿	♀	♂	Plnts
1	12.39	8♎	7♏	18♎	20♏	24♋	♃ 4♓R
2	12.43	9	19	17	20	25	♄ 5♒R
3	12.47	9	1♐	16	21	25	♅ 3♍
4	12.51	10	13	15	21	26	♆12♏
5	12.55	11	26	14	22	26	♇11♍
6	12.59	12	8♑	13	23	27	♃ 3♓R
7	13.03	13	22	12	23	27	♄ 4♒
8	13.07	14	5♒	11	24	28	♅ 3♍
9	13.11	15	19	9	24	28	♆12♏
10	13.14	16	4♓	9	24	29	♇11♍
11	13.18	17	19	8	25	29	♃ 3♓R
12	13.22	18	4♈	7	25	0♌	♄ 4♒
13	13.26	19	19	7	26	1	♅ 3♍
14	13.30	20	4♉	6	26	1	♆12♏
15	13.34	21	19	6D	26	2	♇11♍
16	13.38	22	4♊	6	26	2	♃ 3♓R
17	13.42	23	18	7	27	3	♄ 5♒
18	13.46	24	2♋	7	27	3	♅ 4♍
19	13.50	25	15	8	27	4	♆12♏
20	13.54	26	28	8	27	4	♇11♍
21	13.58	27	10♌	9	27	5	♃ 3♓R
22	14.02	28	22	10	27	5	♄ 5♒
23	14.06	29	4♍	11	27R	6	♅ 4♍
24	14.10	0♏	16	12	27	6	♆12♏
25	14.14	1	28	14	27	7	♇11♍
26	14.18	2	10♎	15	27	7	♃ 3♓R
27	14.21	3	22	16	27	8	♄ 5♒
28	14.25	4	4♏	18	27	8	♅ 4♍
29	14.29	5	16	19	27	8	♆13♏
30	14.33	6	28	21	26	9	♇11♍
31	14.37	7	10♐	22	26	9	♃ 3♓

Nov	STime	☉	☽	☿	♀	♂	Plnts
1	14.41	8♏	23♐	24♎	26♏	10♌	♃ 3♓
2	14.45	9	5♑	26	25	10	♄ 5♒
3	14.49	10	18	27	25	11	♅ 4♍
4	14.53	11	1♒	29	24	11	♆13♏
5	14.57	12	15	0♏	24	12	♇11♍
6	15.01	13	29	2	23	12	♃ 3♓
7	15.05	14	13♓	4	23	13	♄ 5♒
8	15.09	15	27	5	22	13	♅ 5♍
9	15.13	16	12♈	7	22	13	♆13♏
10	15.17	17	27	8	21	14	♇12♍
11	15.21	18	12♉	10	20	14	♃ 3♓
12	15.25	19	27	12	20	15	♄ 5♒
13	15.29	20	12♊	13	19	15	♅ 5♍
14	15.32	21	26	15	19	15	♆13♏
15	15.36	22	10♋	17	18	16	♇12♍
16	15.40	23	23	18	17	16	♃ 3♓
17	15.44	24	6♌	20	17	16	♄ 6♒
18	15.48	25	19	21	16	17	♅ 5♍
19	15.52	26	1♍	23	16	17	♆13♏
20	15.56	27	13	25	15	18	♇12♍
21	16.00	28	25	26	15	18	♃ 3♓
22	16.04	29	7♎	28	14	18	♄ 6♒
23	16.08	0♐	18	29	14	19	♅ 5♍
24	16.12	1	0♏	1♐	14	19	♆14♏
25	16.16	2	13	2	13	19	♇12♍
26	16.20	3	25	4	13	20	♃ 4♓
27	16.24	4	7♐	6	13	20	♄ 6♒
28	16.28	5	20	7	12	20	♅ 5♍
29	16.32	6	2♑	9	12	20	♆14♏
30	16.36	8	15	10	12	21	♇12♍

Dec	STime	☉	☽	☿	♀	♂	Plnts
1	16.39	9♐	28♑	12♐	12♏	21♌	♃ 4♓
2	16.43	10	12♒	13	12	21	♄ 7♒
3	16.47	11	25	15	12D	21	♅ 5♍
4	16.51	12	9♓	17	12	22	♆14♏
5	16.55	13	23	18	12	22	♇12♍
6	16.59	14	7♈	20	12	22	♃ 5♓
7	17.03	15	22	21	12	22	♄ 7♒
8	17.07	16	6♉	23	12	23	♅ 5♍
9	17.11	17	21	24	13	23	♆14♏
10	17.15	18	6♊	26	13	23	♇12♍
11	17.19	19	20	28	13	23	♃ 6♓
12	17.23	20	4♋	29	13	23	♄ 8♒
13	17.27	21	18	1♑	14	24	♅ 5♍
14	17.31	22	1♌	2	14	24	♆14♏
15	17.35	23	14	4	15	24	♇12♍
16	17.39	24	27	5	15	24	♃ 6♓
17	17.43	25	9♍	7	16	24	♄ 8♒
18	17.46	26	21	8	16	24	♅ 5♍R
19	17.50	27	3♎	10	17	24	♆14♏
20	17.54	28	15	12	17	24	♇12♍
21	17.58	29	27	13	18	24	♃ 7♓
22	18.02	0♑	9♏	15	18	24	♄ 9♒
23	18.06	1	21	16	19	24	♅ 5♍R
24	18.10	2	3♐	18	20	24	♆15♏
25	18.14	3	16	19	20	24	♇12♍R
26	18.18	4	28	21	21	24R	♃ 8♓
27	18.22	5	12♑	22	22	24	♄ 9♒
28	18.26	6	25	24	22	24	♅ 5♍R
29	18.30	7	8♒	25	23	24	♆15♏
30	18.34	8	22	26	24	24	♇12♍
31	18.38	9	6♓	28	25	24	♃ 9♓

1 9 6 3

January – July – October (top band)

Jan	STime	☉	☽	☿	♀	♂	Plnts		Apr	STime	☉	☽	☿	♀	♂	Plnts		Jul	STime	☉	☽	☿	♀	♂	Plnts		Oct	STime	☉	☽	☿	♀	♂	Plnts
1	18.42	10♑	20♓	29♒	25♑	24♌	♃9♓		1	0.37	11♈	15♌	12♈	3♓	6♌	♃29♓		1	6.35	9♋	8♏	25♊	22♊	15♌	♃17♈		1	12.38	7♎	14♓	21♍	16♎	13♍	♃15♈R
2	18.46	11	4♈	0♒	26	24	♄10♒		2	0.40	12	28	14	4	7	♄20♒		2	6.39	10	20	26	24	15	♄22♒R		2	12.42	8	29	21	17	13	♄16♒R
3	18.50	12	18	1	27	24	♅5♏		3	0.44	13	11♍	17	5	7	♅1♏R		3	6.43	11	2♐	28	25	16	♅2♏		3	12.46	9	13♈	22	18	14	♅7♏
4	18.54	13	2♉	2	28	24	♆15♏R		4	0.48	14	23	19	6	7	♆15♏R		4	6.47	12	14	0♋	26	16	♆13♏R		4	12.50	10	29	22	20	15	♆14♏
5	18.57	14	17	3	29	24	♇12♏R		5	0.52	15	6♎	21	7	7	♇10♏R		5	6.51	13	27	3	27	17	♇10♏		5	12.54	11	14♉	23	21	16	♇13♏
6	19.01	15	1♊	4	0♒	24	♃10♈		6	0.56	16	18	23	9	7	♃0♈		6	6.55	14	9♑	5	29	18	♃17♈		6	12.58	12	28	24	22	16	♃15♈R
7	19.05	16	15	5	0	24	♄10♒		7	1.00	17	0♏	25	10	8	♄20♒		7	6.59	14	21	7	0♋	18	♄22♒R		7	13.02	13	13♊	25	23	17	♄16♒R
8	19.09	17	29	6	2	23	♅5♏		8	1.04	18	12	27	11	8	♅1♏R		8	7.03	15	4♒	9	1	19	♅2♏R		8	13.06	14	27	27	25	18	♅7♏
9	19.13	18	12♋	6	2	23	♆15♏R		9	1.08	19	24	29	12	8	♆15♏R		9	7.07	16	17	11	3	20	♆13♏R		9	13.10	15	11♋	28	26	18	♆13♏
10	19.17	19	26	6	3	23	♇12♏R		10	1.12	20	6♐	1♉	13	8	♇10♏R		10	7.11	17	1♓	13	3	20	♇10♏		10	13.14	16	25	29	27	19	♇13♏
11	19.21	20	9♌	6R	4	23	♃11♈		11	1.16	21	17	3	15	9	♃1♈		11	7.15	18	13	15	5	20	♃18♈		11	13.17	17	8♌	1♎	28	20	♃16♈R
12	19.25	21	22	6	5	23	♄11♒		12	1.20	22	29	5	16	9	♄21♒		12	7.19	19	28	17	6	21	♄22♒R		12	13.21	18	21	2	0♏	20	♄16♒R
13	19.29	22	4♏	6	6	22	♅5♏		13	1.24	23	11♑	7	17	9	♅1♏R		13	7.23	20	12♈	20	7	22	♅2♏R		13	13.25	19	4♍	4	1	21	♅7♏
14	19.33	23	17	6	7	22	♆15♏R		14	1.28	24	23	9	18	9	♆15♏R		14	7.27	21	27	22	8	22	♆13♏R		14	13.29	20	16	6	2	22	♆13♏
15	19.37	24	29	5	8	22	♇12♏R		15	1.32	24	6♒	10	19	10	♇10♏R		15	7.30	22	11♉	24	10	23	♇10♏		15	13.33	21	28	7	3	22	♇13♏
16	19.41	25	11♐	5	10	21	♃12♈		16	1.36	25	18	12	21	10	♃3♈		16	7.34	23	25	26	11	23	♃18♈		16	13.37	22	11♎	9	5	23	♃16♈R
17	19.45	26	22	3	10	21	♄12♒		17	1.40	26	1♓	14	22	10	♄21♒		17	7.38	24	10♊	28	11	24	♄21♒R		17	13.41	23	23	11	6	24	♅7♏
18	19.49	27	4♑	1	12	21	♅5♏		18	1.44	27	14	15	23	11	♅1♏R		18	7.42	25	24	0♋	13	25	♆13♏R		18	13.45	24	5♏	12	7	25	♆8♏
19	19.53	28	16	1	12	21	♆15♏R		19	1.47	28	28	17	24	11	♆14♏R		19	7.46	26	8♋	2	14	25	♇10♏		19	13.49	25	17	14	8	25	♇13♏
20	19.57	29	29	29♑	13	20	♇12♏R		20	1.51	29	12♓	18	25	11	♇9♏R		20	7.50	27	22	4	16	26	♃18♈		20	13.53	26	28	16	10	26	♃16♈R
21	20.01	0♒	11♒	28	15	20	♃13♈		21	1.55	0♉	25	19	27	12	♃4♈		21	7.54	28	6♌	6	18	27	♄21♒R		21	13.57	27	10♐	17	11	27	♄16♒R
22	20.04	1	24	27	15	20	♄12♒		22	1.59	1	12♈	21	28	12	♄21♒		22	7.58	29	19	8	18	27	♅2♏R		22	14.01	28	22	19	12	27	♅7♏
23	20.08	2	7♓	26	16	19	♅4♏R		23	2.03	2	27	22	29	12	♅1♏R		23	8.02	0♌	2♍	10	19	27	♆13♏R		23	14.05	29	4♑	21	13	28	♆8♏
24	20.12	3	19	26	18	19	♆15♏R		24	2.07	3	13♉	24	0♈	13	♆14♏R		24	8.06	1	15	12	21	28	♇10♏		24	14.09	0♏	16	22	15	0♎	♇13♏
25	20.16	4	4♒	25	18	19	♇11♏R		25	2.11	4	28	24	1	13	♇9♏R		25	8.10	2	10♎	16	22	29	♃19♈		25	14.13	1	28	24	16	0	♃13♈R
26	20.20	6	18	23	19	18	♃14♈		26	2.15	5	13♊	25	3	13	♃5♈		26	8.14	2	10♎	16	23	29	♄21♒R		26	14.17	2	11♒	26	17	0	♃12♈R
27	20.24	7	2♈	22	20	18	♄13♒		27	2.19	6	27	27	4	14	♄22♒		27	8.18	3	22	18	25	0♎	♅2♏R		27	14.21	3	24	27	18	1	♅16♏
28	20.28	8	16	21	21	17	♅4♏R		28	2.23	7	11♋	27	5	14	♅1♏R		28	8.22	4	4♏	20	25	0	♆13♏R		28	14.24	4	8♓	29	20	2	♆9♏
29	20.32	9	0♈	21	22	17	♆15♏R		29	2.27	8	25	28	6	14	♆14♏R		29	8.26	5	16	22	27	1	♇10♏		29	14.28	5	22	1♏	21	2	♇13♏
30	20.36	10	14	21	23	17	♇11♏R		30	2.31	9	8♌	29	7	15	♇9♏R		30	8.30	6	28	23	29	2	♃19♈		30	14.32	6	7♈	1	22	3	♄15♒R
31	20.40	11	29	20	24	16	♃15♓											31	8.34	7	10♐	25	29	2	♃19♈		31	14.36	7	22	4	23	4	♃11♈R

February – May – August – November (middle band)

Feb	STime	☉	☽	☿	♀	♂	Plnts		May	STime	☉	☽	☿	♀	♂	Plnts		Aug	STime	☉	☽	☿	♀	♂	Plnts		Nov	STime	☉	☽	☿	♀	♂	Plnts
1	20.44	12♒	13♉	20♑	25♒	16♌	♃15♓		1	2.35	10♉	20♌	29♉	9♈	15♌	♃6♈		1	8.38	8♌	22♐	27♋	0♌	3♎	♃19♈		1	14.40	8♏	7♉	6♏	25♎	5♎	♃11♈R
2	20.48	13	27	21	26	15	♄13♒		2	2.39	11	3♍	29	10	15	♄20♒		2	8.41	9	4♑	28	2	4	♄20♒R		2	14.44	9	22	7	26	5	♄16♒R
3	20.52	14	11♊	21	26	15	♅4♏R		3	2.43	12	15	0♊	11	16	♅1♏R		3	8.45	10	17	0♌	3	4	♅4♏		3	14.48	10	7♊	7	27	6	♅7♏
4	20.56	15	25	22	28	15	♆15♏R		4	2.47	13	27	2	12	16	♆14♏R		4	8.49	11	0♒	1	5	5	♆13♏		4	14.52	11	22	8	28	7	♆15♏
5	21.00	16	8♋	22	29	14	♇16♏R		5	2.51	14	9♎	5	14	17	♃7♈		5	8.53	12	13	3	5	5	♇13♏		5	14.56	12	7♋	8	0♐	7	♇13♏
6	21.04	17	21	21	0♓	14	♃16♓		6	2.55	15	21	0R	15	17	♄22♒		6	8.57	13	27	5	7	5	♃19♈		6	15.00	13	21	7R	2	8	♃11♈R
7	21.08	18	4♌	23	1	13	♄14♒		7	2.58	16	3♏	0	16	17	♄22♒		7	9.01	14	11♓	6	8	7	♄20♒R		7	15.04	14	5♌	6	2	9	♄16♒R
8	21.12	19	17	24	4	13	♅4♏R		8	3.02	17	14	0	17	18	♅1♏R		8	9.05	15	25	8	9	7	♅4♏		8	15.08	15	19	5	3	10	♅7♏
9	21.15	20	0♍	24	4	13	♆15♏R		9	3.06	18	26	0	18	18	♆14♏R		9	9.09	16	9♈	10	10	8	♆13♏		9	15.12	16	1♍	4	5	10	♆15♏
10	21.19	21	12	25	6	12	♇16♏R		10	3.10	19	8♐	0	19	18	♇9♏R		10	9.13	17	23	11	11	8	♇13♏		10	15.16	17	13	3	6	11	♃14♏
11	21.23	22	24	26	6	12	♃17♓		11	3.14	20	20	29♉	21	19	♃8♈		11	9.17	18	8♉	12	13	9	♃19♈		11	15.20	18	8♎	3	8	11	♃11♈R
12	21.27	23	7♎	27	7	12	♄15♒		12	3.18	21	3♑	29	22	19	♄22♒R		12	9.21	19	22	13	14	10	♄20♒R		12	15.24	19	8♌	2	8	13	♄17♒R
13	21.31	24	19	28	8	11	♅3♏R		13	3.22	22	15	29	24	20	♅1♏R		13	9.25	20	6♊	15	15	10	♅4♏		13	15.28	20	20	1	11	14	♅7♏
14	21.35	25	0♍	29	9	11	♆15♏R		14	3.26	23	28	28	24	20	♆14♏R		14	9.29	21	20	16	16	11	♆13♏		14	15.31	20	2♍	27	11	14	♆16♏
15	21.39	26	12	0♒	10	10	♇11♏R		15	3.30	24	11♒	28	25	21	♇9♏R		15	9.33	22	4♎	17	18	12	♇11♏		15	15.35	22	14	28	12	15	♃14♏
16	21.43	27	24	1	11	10	♃18♓		16	3.34	25	24	27	27	21	♃9♈		16	9.37	23	18	19	19	12	♃19♈		16	15.39	23	25	0♎	13	16	♃10♈R
17	21.47	28	6♏	2	13	10	♄15♒		17	3.38	26	7♓	27	28	22	♄23♒R		17	9.41	24	1♏	20	20	14	♄19♒R		17	15.43	24	7♎	1	15	16	♅7♏
18	21.51	29	19	3	14	9	♅15♏		18	3.42	27	21	26	29	22	♅14♏R		18	9.45	25	15	21	21	14	♅5♏		18	15.47	25	19	3	16	17	♆9♏
19	21.55	0♓	1♐	4	15	9	♆15♏R		19	3.46	28	6♈	25	0♉	23	♆9♏R		19	9.48	26	28	22	22	14	♇11♏		19	15.51	26	1♏	4	17	17	♇9♏
20	21.59	1	14	6	16	9	♇11♏R		20	3.50	28	21	25	1	23	♇9♏R		20	9.52	26	11♍	23	24	15	♃11♏		20	15.55	27	13	6	18	19	♃14♏
21	22.03	2	27	7	18	9	♃20♓		21	3.54	29	6♉	24	4	23	♄10♈		21	9.56	27	23	25	25	15	♄19♒R		21	16.03	29	25	7	20	19	♄17♒R
22	22.07	3	12♑	8	18	8	♅16♏		22	3.58	0♊	21	24	4	24	♅1♏		22	10.00	28	6♏	26	26	15	♅19♏R		22	16.03	29	7♐	9	21	20	♅7♏
23	22.11	4	26	10	19	8	♆3♏R		23	4.02	1	6♊	23	5	24	♆1♏R		23	10.04	29	19	28	28	17	♆5♏		23	16.07	0♐	20	11	22	21	♃10♏
24	22.15	5	11♓	11	21	8	♅15♏		24	4.05	2	21	23	6	24	♅9♏R		24	10.08	0♍	0♏	29	28	17	♇11♏		24	16.11	1	3♓	14	23	22	♃14♏
25	22.19	6	25	13	22	7	♇11♏R		25	4.09	3	5♋	22	7	25	♇9♏R		25	10.12	1	12	29	0♍	19	♃19♈		25	16.15	2	17	15	25	22	♄14♏
26	22.22	7	10♈	14	23	7	♃21♓		26	4.13	4	19	22	9	26	♃11♈		26	10.16	2	24	29	1	19	♄18♒R		26	16.19	3	1♈	17	25	23	♃9♈R
27	22.26	8	25	16	23	7	♅16♏		27	4.17	5	3♌	22	10	26	♄23♒R		27	10.20	3	6♐	0♍	2	19	♅18♏R		27	16.23	4	15	18	26	24	♅7♏
28	22.30	9	10♉	16	25	7	♆3♏R		28	4.21	6	16	21	11	27	♅1♏R		28	10.24	4	18	1	4	20	♆5♏		28	16.27	5	0♉	18	28	24	♆10♏
									29	4.25	7	29	21	12	27	♆13♏R		29	10.28	5	0♑	2	5	21	♇11♏		29	16.31	6	15	20	0♐	25	♃16♏
									30	4.29	8	11♍	21D	14	28	♇9♏R		30	10.32	6	12	2	6	21	♄11♏		30	16.35	6	0♊	21	1	26	♃14♏
									31	4.33	9	24	21	15	28	♃12♈		31	10.36	7	25	3	7	22	♃18♈R									

March – June – September – December (bottom band)

Mar	STime	☉	☽	☿	♀	♂	Plnts		Jun	STime	☉	☽	☿	♀	♂	Plnts		Sep	STime	☉	☽	☿	♀	♂	Plnts		Dec	STime	☉	☽	☿	♀	♂	Plnts
1	22.34	10♓	24♉	18♒	26♓	7♌	♃22♓		1	4.37	10♊	6♎	22♉	16♉	29♌	♃12♈		1	10.40	8♍	8♒	3♍	9♍	23♎	♃18♈R		1	16.39	8♐	15♊	23♐	2♐	27♎	♃9♈R
2	22.38	11	8♊	19	27	6	♄17♒		2	4.41	11	18	22	17	29	♄1♏		2	10.44	9	20	4	10	23	♄18♒R		2	16.42	9	0♋	24	3	28	♄18♒R
3	22.42	12	22	21	29	6	♅3♏R		3	4.45	12	0♏	22	18	0♍	♅1♏R		3	10.48	10	6♓	4	11	24	♅6♏		3	16.46	10	14	25	5	28	♅7♏
4	22.46	13	5♋	22	0♈	6	♆15♏R		4	4.49	13	11♏	22	20	0	♆13♏R		4	10.52	11	19	5	12	24	♆13♏		4	16.50	11	29	27	6	29	♆16♏
5	22.50	14	18	24	1	6	♇10♏R		5	4.53	14	23	23	21	1	♇10♏R		5	10.56	12	5♈	5	14	25	♇12♏		5	16.58	12	13♋	28	8	0♐	♇13♏
6	22.54	15	1♌	25	2	6	♃23♓		6	4.57	15	5♐	23	22	1	♃13♈		6	10.59	13	19	5	15	25	♃18♈R		6	16.58	13	27	0♑	9	1	♃9♈R
7	22.58	16	14	27	3	6	♄17♒		7	5.01	16	17	24	23	2	♄23♒R		7	11.03	14	4♉	5R	16	26	♄18♒R		7	17.02	14	10♌	2	11	1	♄18♒R
8	23.02	17	26	28	6	5	♅2♏R		8	5.05	18	0♑	24	26	3	♅1♏R		8	11.07	15	18	5	17	27	♅6♏		8	17.06	16	24	3	12	2	♅7♏
9	23.06	18	9♍	0♓	6	5	♆15♏R		9	5.09	18	12	25	26	3	♆13♏R		9	11.11	16	3♊	5	18	27	♆13♏		9	17.10	16	5♍	4	12	3	♆16♏
10	23.10	19	21	2	7	5	♇10♏R		10	5.13	19	25	26	28	4	♇10♏R		10	11.15	17	17	4	20	28	♇12♏		10	17.14	17	17	6	13	4	♃14♏
11	23.14	20	3♎	3	9	5	♃24♓		11	5.16	20	8♒	26	28	4	♃14♈		11	11.19	18	1♋	4	20	29	♃17♈R		11	17.18	18	11♎	7	15	4	♃9♈R
12	23.18	21	15	5	9	5	♄18♒		12	5.20	21	21	27	0♊	4	♄23♒R		12	11.23	19	14	3	22	0♍	♄17♒R		12	17.22	19	11♍	9	16	5	♄18♒R
13	23.22	22	27	7	11	5	♅2♏R		13	5.24	22	4♓	29	1♊	4	♅1♏		13	11.27	20	28	3	23	0	♅17♏R		13	17.26	20	23	11	17	6	♅7♏
14	23.26	23	9♏	8	11	5	♆15♏R		14	5.28	22	17	29	2	5	♆13♏R		14	11.31	21	11♌	2	25	1	♆13♏		14	17.30	21	4♐	11	18	6	♆16♏
15	23.30	24	21	10	13	5	♇10♏R		15	5.32	23	2♈	0♊	3	6	♇10♏R		15	11.35	22	24	1	26	1	♇12♏R		15	17.34	22	16	12	19	7	♇14♏
16	23.33	25	2♐	12	14	5D	♃25♓		16	5.36	24	16	1	4	7	♃15♈		16	11.39	23	7♍	0♍	27	2	♃17♈R		16	17.38	24	28	14	21	7	♃9♈R
17	23.37	26	15	14	15	5	♄18♒		17	5.40	25	0♉	3	5	7	♄23♒R		17	11.43	24	19	29♌	29	2	♄17♒R		17	17.42	25	10♑	15	22	8	♃9♈R
18	23.41	27	27	15	17	5	♅1♏R		18	5.44	26	15	4	6	8	♅1♏R		18	11.47	25	2♎	28	0♎	3	♅7♏R		18	17.46	26	22	16	23	9	♅7♏
19	23.45	28	9♑	17	17	5	♆15♏R		19	5.48	26	0♊	5	8	8	♆13♏R		19	11.51	26	14	27	1	4	♆13♏		19	17.49	28	5♒	18	24	10	♆16♏
20	23.49	29	22	19	18	5	♇10♏R		20	5.52	28	15	6	9	9	♇9♏R		20	11.55	27	26	26	2	4	♇12♏R		20	17.53	28	17	19	26	11	♃14♏
21	23.53	0♈	6♒	21	21	5	♃26♓		21	5.56	29	29	8♊	11	10	♄23♒R		21	12.03	28	8♏	24	4	5	♃16♈R		21	18.01	0♑	13	21	27	12	♃10♏
22	23.57	1	20	23	21	5	♄19♒		22	6.00	0♋	14♊	9	11	10	♄23♒R		22	12.03	28	20	23	5	5	♄17♒R		22	18.05	1	26	22	29	13	♄18♒R
23	0.01	2	4♓	25	22	5	♅1♏R		23	6.04	1	28	11	13	10	♅1♏R		23	12.06	29	2♐	23	6	6	♅17♏R		23	18.05	1	26	24	29	14	♃10♏R
24	0.05	3	18	26	23	5	♆15♏R		24	6.08	2	12♋	13	14	11	♆13♏R		24	12.14	1	26	21	9	7	♆13♏		24	18.09	2	9♈	24	0♑	14	♅7♏
25	0.09	4	2♈	28	24	6	♇9♏R		25	6.12	3	26	15	15	11	♇10♏R		25	12.14	1	26	21	9	7	♄17♒R		25	18.13	3	24	24	1	14	♃14♏
26	0.13	5	16	0♈	25	6	♃28♓		26	6.20	4	10♌	17	16	11	♃16♈		26	12.18	2	8♑	21	10	7	♅17♏R		26	18.17	4	9♉	26	3	16	♃9♈R
27	0.17	6	0♉	2	27	6	♄19♒		27	6.20	5	24	19	17	12	♄22♒R		27	12.22	3	20	20	12	8	♆13♏		27	18.21	5	23	27	4	16	♄17♒R
28	0.21	7	14	4	28	6	♅1♏R		28	6.23	6	8♍	19	19	13	♅1♏R		28	12.26	4	3♒	20	12	9	♇12♏R		28	18.25	6	8♊	0♑	5	17	♅7♏
29	0.25	8	4♊	6	29	6	♆15♏R		29	6.27	7	20	21	20	13	♆13♏R		29	12.30	5	15	20D	14	9	♃16♈R		29	18.29	7	23	1	6	18	♆17♏
30	0.29	9	18	8	0♈	6	♇10♏R		30	6.31	8	3♏	22	21	14	♇10♏R		30	12.34	6	27	20	15	12	♇12♏R		30	18.33	8	8♋	3	8	18	♃9♈R
31	0.33	10	2♋	10	1	6	♃29♓																				31	18.37	9	23	4	9	19	♃10♏R

Jan	STime	☉	☽	☿	♀	♂	Plnts
1	18.41	10♑	7♌	17♑	10♒	21♑	♃10♈
2	18.45	11	21	16	12	21	♄20♒
3	18.49	12	5♍	14	13	22	♅10♍R
4	18.53	13	18	13	14	23	♆17♏
5	18.57	14	1♎	12	15	24	♇14♍R
6	19.00	15	13	10	17	24	♃11♈
7	19.04	16	25	9	18	25	♄21♒
8	19.08	17	7♏	8	19	26	♅10♍R
9	19.12	18	19	7	20	27	♆17♏
10	19.16	19	1♐	6	22	28	♇14♍R
11	19.20	20	13	5	23	28	♃12♈
12	19.24	21	25	5	24	29	♄21♒
13	19.28	22	7♑	4	25	0♒	♅ 9♍R
14	19.32	23	19	4	26	1	♆17♏
15	19.36	24	1♒	4D	28	1	♇14♍R
16	19.40	25	14	4	29	2	♃12♈
17	19.44	26	27	4	0♓	3	♄22♒
18	19.48	27	10♓	5	1	4	♅ 9♍R
19	19.52	28	23	5	3	5	♆17♏
20	19.56	29	7♈	6	4	5	♇14♍R
21	20.00	0♒	21	6	5	6	♃13♈
22	20.04	1	5♉	7	6	7	♄22♒
23	20.07	2	19	8	7	8	♅ 9♍R
24	20.11	3	3♊	9	9	9	♆17♏
25	20.15	4	18	10	10	9	♇14♍R
26	20.19	5	2♋	11	11	10	♃14♈
27	20.23	6	17	12	12	11	♄23♒
28	20.27	7	1♌	13	14	12	♅ 9♍R
29	20.31	8	15	14	15	12	♆17♏
30	20.35	9	29	15	16	13	♇13♍R
31	20.39	10	13♍	16	17	14	♃14♈

Feb	STime	☉	☽	☿	♀	♂	Plnts
1	20.43	11♒	26♍	17♑	18♓	15♒	♃15♈
2	20.47	12	9♎	18	20	16	♄24♒
3	20.51	13	21	20	21	16	♅ 9♍R
4	20.55	14	3♏	21	22	17	♆17♏
5	20.59	15	15	22	23	18	♇13♍R
6	21.03	16	27	24	24	19	♃15♈
7	21.07	17	9♐	25	26	20	♄24♒
8	21.11	18	21	26	27	20	♅ 9♍R
9	21.14	19	3♑	28	28	21	♆18♏
10	21.18	20	15	29	29	22	♇13♍R
11	21.22	21	27	1♒	0♈	23	♃16♈
12	21.26	23	10♒	2	2	24	♄25♒
13	21.30	24	23	3	3	24	♅ 8♍R
14	21.34	25	6♓	5	4	25	♆18♏
15	21.38	26	20	6	5	26	♇13♍R
16	21.42	27	4♈	8	6	27	♃17♈
17	21.46	28	18	9	8	27	♄26♒
18	21.50	29	2♉	11	9	28	♅ 8♍R
19	21.54	0♓	16	13	10	29	♆18♏
20	21.58	1	0♊	14	11	0♓	♇13♍R
21	22.02	2	14	16	12	1	♃18♈
22	22.06	3	28	17	13	1	♄26♒
23	22.10	4	12♋	19	15	2	♅ 8♍R
24	22.14	5	26	21	16	3	♆18♏R
25	22.18	6	10♌	22	17	4	♇13♍R
26	22.22	7	24	24	18	5	♃19♈
27	22.25	8	7♍	26	19	5	♄27♒
28	22.29	9	21	27	20	6	♅ 8♍R
29	22.33	10	4♎	29	22	7	♆18♏

Mar	STime	☉	☽	☿	♀	♂	Plnts
1	22.37	11♓	16♎	1♓	23♈	8♓	♃20♈
2	22.41	12	29	2	24	9	♄27♒
3	22.45	13	11♏	4	25	9	♅ 8♍R
4	22.49	14	23	6	26	10	♆17♏R
5	22.53	15	5♐	8	27	11	♇13♍R
6	22.57	16	17	10	29	12	♃21♈
7	23.01	17	28	11	0♉	12	♄28♒
8	23.05	18	10♑	13	1	13	♅ 7♍R
9	23.09	19	23	15	2	14	♆17♏R
10	23.13	20	5♒	17	3	15	♇12♍R
11	23.17	21	18	19	4	16	♃22♈
12	23.21	22	1♓	21	5	16	♄28♒
13	23.25	23	15	23	6	17	♅ 7♍R
14	23.29	24	29	25	8	18	♆17♏R
15	23.32	25	13♈	27	9	19	♇12♍R
16	23.36	26	28	29	10	20	♃23♈
17	23.40	27	12♉	1♈	11	20	♄29♒
18	23.44	28	26	3	12	21	♅ 7♍R
19	23.48	29	11♊	5	13	22	♆17♏R
20	23.52	0♈	25	7	14	23	♇12♍R
21	23.56	1	9♋	9	15	23	♃25♈
22	0.00	2	23	11	16	24	♄ 0♓
23	0.04	3	6♌	13	17	25	♅ 7♍R
24	0.08	4	20	15	19	26	♆17♏R
25	0.12	5	3♍	17	20	27	♇12♍R
26	0.16	6	16	18	21	27	♃26♈
27	0.20	7	29	20	22	28	♄ 0♓
28	0.24	8	12♎	22	23	29	♅ 7♍R
29	0.28	9	25	24	24	0♈	♆17♏R
30	0.32	10	7♏	26	25	1	♇12♍R
31	0.36	11	19	27	26	1	♃27♈

Apr	STime	☉	☽	☿	♀	♂	Plnts
1	0.40	11♈	1♐	29♈	27♉	2♈	♃27♈
2	0.43	12	13	0♉	28	3	♄ 1♓
3	0.47	13	24	2	29	4	♅ 6♍R
4	0.51	14	6♑	3	0♊	4	♆17♏R
5	0.55	15	18	4	1	5	♇12♍R
6	0.59	16	1♒	5	2	6	♃28♈
7	1.03	17	13	7	3	7	♄ 1♓
8	1.07	18	26	7	4	7	♅ 6♍R
9	1.11	19	9♓	8	5	8	♆17♏R
10	1.15	20	23	9	6	9	♇12♍R
11	1.19	21	7♈	10	7	10	♃ 0♉
12	1.23	22	22	10	8	11	♄ 2♓
13	1.27	23	7♉	11	9	11	♅ 6♍R
14	1.31	24	22	11	10	12	♆17♏R
15	1.35	25	6♊	11	11	13	♇12♍R
16	1.39	26	21	11R	12	14	♃ 1♉
17	1.43	27	5♋	11	13	14	♄ 2♓
18	1.47	28	20	11	14	15	♅ 6♍R
19	1.50	29	3♌	11	15	16	♆17♏R
20	1.54	0♉	17	11	15	17	♇12♍R
21	1.58	1	0♍	10	16	17	♃ 2♉
22	2.02	2	13	10	17	18	♄ 2♓
23	2.06	3	26	9	18	19	♅ 6♍R
24	2.10	4	9♎	9	19	20	♆17♏R
25	2.14	5	21	8	20	21	♇11♍R
26	2.18	6	3♏	7	21	21	♃ 3♉
27	2.22	7	15	7	21	22	♄ 3♓
28	2.26	8	27	6	22	23	♅ 6♍R
29	2.30	9	9♐	5	23	24	♆16♏R
30	2.34	10	21	5	24	24	♇11♍R

May	STime	☉	☽	☿	♀	♂	Plnts
1	2.38	11♉	3♑	4♉	24♊	25♈	♃ 4♉
2	2.42	12	15	4	25	26	♄ 3♓
3	2.46	13	27	3	26	27	♅ 6♍R
4	2.50	14	9♒	3	27	27	♆16♏R
5	2.54	15	21	2	27	28	♇11♍
6	2.57	16	4♓	2	28	29	♃ 5♉
7	3.01	17	17	2	29	0♉	♄ 4♓
8	3.05	18	1♈	1	29	0	♅ 6♍R
9	3.09	19	16	1	0♋	1	♆16♏R
10	3.13	20	0♉	1D	1	2	♇11♍R
11	3.17	21	15	1	1	3	♃ 7♉
12	3.21	21	0♊	1	2	3	♄ 4♓
13	3.25	22	15	2	2	4	♅ 6♍
14	3.29	23	0♋	2	3	5	♆16♏R
15	3.33	24	15	2	3	6	♇11♍
16	3.37	25	29	3	4	6	♃ 8♉
17	3.41	26	13♌	3	4	7	♄ 4♓
18	3.45	27	27	4	4	8	♅ 6♍
19	3.49	28	10♍	4	5	9	♆16♏R
20	3.53	29	23	5	5	9	♇11♍
21	3.57	0♊	6♎	6	5	10	♃ 9♉
22	4.01	1	18	6	6	11	♄ 4♓
23	4.05	2	0♏	7	6	12	♅ 6♍
24	4.08	3	12	8	6	12	♆16♏R
25	4.12	4	24	9	6	13	♇11♍
26	4.16	5	6♐	10	6	14	♃10♉
27	4.20	6	18	11	7	14	♄ 4♓
28	4.24	7	0♑	12	7	15	♅ 6♍
29	4.28	8	12	13	7R	16	♆16♏R
30	4.32	9	23	15	7	17	♇11♍
31	4.36	10	5♒	16	6	17	♃11♉

Jun	STime	☉	☽	☿	♀	♂	Plnts
1	4.40	11♊	18♒	17♉	6♋	18♉	♃12♉
2	4.44	12	0♓	19	6	19	♄ 5♓
3	4.48	13	13	20	6	20	♅ 6♍
4	4.52	14	26	21	6	20	♆15♏R
5	4.56	15	10♈	23	6	21	♇11♍
6	5.00	15	24	25	5	22	♃13♉
7	5.04	16	9♉	26	5	23	♄ 5♓
8	5.08	17	24	28	5	23	♅ 6♍
9	5.12	18	9♊	29	4	24	♆15♏R
10	5.15	19	24	1♊	4	25	♇11♍
11	5.19	20	9♋	3	3	25	♃14♉
12	5.23	21	24	5	3	26	♄ 5♓
13	5.27	22	8♌	7	2	27	♅ 6♍
14	5.31	23	23	8	2	28	♆15♏R
15	5.35	24	6♍	10	1	28	♇11♍
16	5.39	25	20	12	0	29	♃15♉
17	5.43	26	2♎	14	0	0♊	♄ 5♓R
18	5.47	27	15	16	29♊	0	♅ 6♍
19	5.51	28	27	19	29	1	♆15♏R
20	5.55	29	9♏	21	28	2	♇12♍
21	5.59	0♋	21	23	27	3	♃16♉
22	6.03	1	3♐	25	27	3	♄ 5♓R
23	6.07	2	15	27	26	4	♅ 6♍
24	6.11	3	27	29	26	5	♆15♏R
25	6.15	4	9♑	1♋	25	5	♇12♍
26	6.19	5	21	4	24	6	♃17♉
27	6.23	6	3♒	6	24	7	♄ 5♓R
28	6.26	7	15	8	23	8	♅ 7♍
29	6.30	7	27	10	23	8	♆15♏R
30	6.34	8	10♓	12	22	9	♇12♍

Jul	STime	☉	☽	☿	♀	♂	Plnts
1	6.38	9♋	23♓	14♋	22♊	10♊	♃18♉
2	6.42	10	6♈	17	22	10	♄ 4♓R
3	6.46	11	19	19	21	11	♅ 7♍
4	6.50	12	3♉	21	21	12	♆15♏R
5	6.54	13	18	23	21	12	♇12♍
6	6.58	14	2♊	25	21	13	♃19♉
7	7.02	15	17	27	20	14	♄ 4♓R
8	7.06	16	2♋	29	20	15	♅ 7♍
9	7.10	17	17	1♌	20	15	♆15♏
10	7.14	18	2♌	2	20	16	♇12♍
11	7.18	19	17	4	20D	17	♃20♉
12	7.22	20	1♍	6	20	17	♄ 4♓R
13	7.26	21	15	8	20	18	♅ 7♍
14	7.30	22	28	10	20	19	♆15♏
15	7.33	23	11♎	11	20	19	♇12♍
16	7.37	24	24	13	21	20	♃20♉
17	7.41	25	6♏	15	21	21	♄ 4♓R
18	7.45	26	18	16	21	21	♅ 7♍
19	7.49	27	0♐	18	21	22	♆15♏R
20	7.53	27	12	20	22	23	♇12♍
21	7.57	28	24	21	22	23	♃21♉
22	8.01	29	5♑	23	22	24	♄ 4♓R
23	8.05	0♌	17	24	23	25	♅ 8♍
24	8.09	1	29	26	23	25	♆15♏
25	8.13	2	12♒	27	23	26	♇12♍
26	8.17	3	24	28	24	27	♃22♉
27	8.21	4	7♓	0♍	24	28	♄ 3♓R
28	8.25	5	20	1	25	28	♅ 8♍
29	8.29	6	3♈	2	25	29	♆15♏
30	8.33	7	16	4	26	0♋	♇12♍
31	8.37	8	0♉	5	27	0	♃23♉

Aug	STime	☉	☽	☿	♀	♂	Plnts
1	8.41	9♌	14♉	6♍	27♊	1♋	♃23♉
2	8.44	10	28	7	28	2	♄ 3♓R
3	8.48	11	12♊	8	28	2	♅ 8♍
4	8.52	12	26	9	29	3	♆15♏
5	8.56	13	11♋	10	0♋	4	♇13♍
6	9.00	14	26	11	0	4	♃23♉
7	9.04	15	11♌	12	1	5	♄ 3♓R
8	9.08	16	25	13	2	6	♅ 9♍
9	9.12	17	9♍	14	3	6	♆15♏
10	9.16	18	23	14	3	7	♇13♍
11	9.20	19	6♎	15	4	8	♃24♉
12	9.24	19	19	16	5	8	♄ 2♓R
13	9.28	20	2♏	16	6	9	♅ 9♍
14	9.32	21	14	17	7	9	♆15♏
15	9.36	22	26	17	7	10	♇13♍
16	9.40	23	8♐	17	8	11	♃24♉
17	9.44	24	20	17	9	11	♄ 2♓R
18	9.48	25	2♑	18	10	12	♅ 9♍
19	9.51	26	14	18R	11	13	♆15♏
20	9.55	27	26	18	12	13	♇13♍
21	9.59	28	8♒	17	13	14	♃25♉
22	10.03	29	21	17	14	15	♄ 2♓R
23	10.07	0♍	3♓	17	14	15	♅ 9♍
24	10.11	1	16	17	15	16	♆15♏
25	10.15	2	0♈	16	16	17	♇13♍
26	10.19	3	13	15	17	17	♃25♉
27	10.23	4	27	15	18	18	♄ 1♓R
28	10.27	5	10♉	14	19	19	♅10♍
29	10.31	6	24	13	20	19	♆15♏
30	10.35	7	8♊	12	21	20	♇13♍
31	10.39	8	22	11	22	20	♃25♉

Sep	STime	☉	☽	☿	♀	♂	Plnts
1	10.43	9♍	7♋	10♍	23♋	21♋	♃26♉
2	10.47	10	21	9	24	22	♄ 1♓R
3	10.51	11	5♌	8	25	22	♅10♍
4	10.55	12	20	8	26	23	♆15♏
5	10.59	13	4♍	7	27	24	♇14♍
6	11.02	14	18	6	28	24	♃26♉
7	11.06	15	1♎	5	29	25	♄ 0♓R
8	11.10	16	15	5	0♌	26	♅10♍
9	11.14	17	27	4	1	26	♆15♏
10	11.18	17	10♏	4	2	27	♇14♍
11	11.22	18	22	4D	3	27	♃26♉
12	11.26	19	4♐	4	4	28	♄ 0♓R
13	11.30	20	16	4	5	29	♅11♍
14	11.34	21	28	5	6	29	♆15♏
15	11.38	22	10♑	5	7	0♌	♇14♍
16	11.42	23	22	6	8	0	♃26♉R
17	11.46	24	4♒	7	9	1	♄ 0♓R
18	11.50	25	16	7	11	2	♅11♍
19	11.54	26	29	8	12	2	♆16♏
20	11.58	27	12♓	10	13	3	♇14♍
21	12.02	28	25	11	14	4	♃26♉R
22	12.06	29	9♈	12	15	4	♄29♒R
23	12.09	0♎	23	14	16	5	♅11♍
24	12.13	1	7♉	15	17	5	♆16♏
25	12.17	2	21	17	18	6	♇14♍
26	12.21	3	5♊	18	19	7	♃26♉R
27	12.25	4	19	20	20	7	♄29♒R
28	12.29	5	3♋	22	22	8	♅12♍
29	12.33	6	17	23	23	8	♆16♏
30	12.37	7	2♌	25	24	9	♇15♍

Oct	STime	☉	☽	☿	♀	♂	Plnts
1	12.41	8♎	15♌	27♍	25♌	10♌	♃25♉R
2	12.45	9	29	29	26	10	♄29♒R
3	12.49	10	13♍	1♎	27	11	♅12♍
4	12.53	11	26	2	28	11	♆16♏
5	12.57	12	10♎	4	29	12	♇15♍
6	13.01	13	23	6	1♍	13	♃25♉R
7	13.05	14	6♏	8	2	13	♄29♒R
8	13.09	15	18	9	3	14	♅12♍
9	13.13	16	0♐	11	4	14	♆16♏
10	13.16	17	12	13	5	15	♇15♍
11	13.20	18	24	15	6	15	♃25♉R
12	13.24	19	6♑	17	7	16	♄28♒R
13	13.28	20	18	18	9	17	♅13♍
14	13.32	21	0♒	20	10	17	♆16♏
15	13.36	22	12	22	11	18	♇15♍
16	13.40	23	24	23	12	18	♃24♉R
17	13.44	24	7♓	25	13	19	♄28♒R
18	13.48	25	20	27	14	19	♅13♍
19	13.52	26	4♈	28	16	20	♆16♏
20	13.56	27	18	0♏	17	21	♇15♍
21	14.00	28	2♉	2	18	21	♃24♉R
22	14.04	29	16	3	19	22	♄28♒R
23	14.08	0♏	1♊	5	20	22	♅13♍
24	14.12	1	15	7	22	23	♆17♏
25	14.16	2	0♋	8	23	23	♇15♍
26	14.20	3	14	10	24	24	♃23♉R
27	14.24	4	28	11	25	25	♄28♒R
28	14.27	5	12♌	13	26	25	♅13♍
29	14.31	6	26	14	27	26	♆17♏
30	14.35	7	10♍	16	29	26	♇15♍
31	14.39	8	23	18	0♎	27	♃22♉R

Nov	STime	☉	☽	☿	♀	♂	Plnts
1	14.43	9♏	6♎	19♏	1♎	27♌	♃22♉R
2	14.47	10	19	21	2	28	♄28♒
3	14.51	11	2♏	22	3	28	♅14♍
4	14.55	12	14	24	5	29	♆17♏
5	14.59	13	26	25	6	29	♇16♍
6	15.03	14	8♐	27	7	0♍	♃22♉R
7	15.07	15	20	28	8	0	♄28♒
8	15.11	16	2♑	0♐	9	1	♅14♍
9	15.15	17	14	1	11	1	♆17♏
10	15.19	18	26	3	12	2	♇16♍
11	15.23	19	8♒	4	13	2	♃21♉R
12	15.27	20	20	6	14	3	♄28♒
13	15.31	21	2♓	7	16	4	♅14♍
14	15.34	22	15	9	17	4	♆17♏
15	15.38	23	28	10	18	5	♇16♍
16	15.42	24	11♈	11	19	5	♃20♉R
17	15.46	25	26	13	20	6	♄28♒
18	15.50	26	10♉	14	22	6	♅14♍
19	15.54	27	25	16	23	7	♆18♏
20	15.58	28	10♊	17	24	7	♇16♍
21	16.02	29	25	18	25	7	♃20♉R
22	16.06	0♐	10♋	20	27	8	♄28♒
23	16.10	1	24	21	28	8	♅14♍
24	16.14	2	9♌	22	29	9	♆18♏
25	16.18	3	23	24	0♏	9	♇16♍
26	16.22	4	7♍	25	1	10	♃19♉R
27	16.26	5	20	26	3	10	♄29♒
28	16.30	6	3♎	27	4	11	♅14♍
29	16.34	7	16	28	5	11	♆18♏
30	16.38	8	28	29	6	12	♇16♍

Dec	STime	☉	☽	☿	♀	♂	Plnts
1	16.42	9♐	11♏	0♑	8♏	12♍	♃18♉R
2	16.45	10	23	1	9	13	♄29♒
3	16.49	11	5♐	2	10	13	♅14♍
4	16.53	12	17	3	11	13	♆18♏
5	16.57	13	29	3	13	14	♇16♍
6	17.01	14	11♑	4	14	14	♃18♉R
7	17.05	15	22	4	15	15	♄29♒
8	17.09	16	4♒	5	16	15	♅14♍
9	17.13	17	16	5R	18	16	♆18♏
10	17.17	18	28	4	19	16	♇16♍
11	17.21	19	10♓	4	20	16	♃17♉R
12	17.25	20	23	4	21	17	♄29♒
13	17.29	21	6♈	3	23	17	♅15♍
14	17.33	22	20	2	24	18	♆19♏
15	17.37	23	3♉	1	25	18	♇16♍
16	17.41	24	18	0	26	18	♃17♉R
17	17.45	25	3♊	29♐	27	19	♄ 0♓
18	17.49	26	18	27	29	19	♅15♍
19	17.52	27	3♋	26	0♐	19	♆19♏
20	17.56	28	18	24	1	20	♇16♍
21	18.00	29	3♌	23	2	20	♃16♉R
22	18.04	0♑	18	22	4	21	♄ 0♓
23	18.08	1	2♍	21	5	21	♅15♍
24	18.12	2	16	20	6	21	♆19♏
25	18.16	3	0♎	19	7	22	♇16♍R
26	18.20	4	13	19	9	22	♃16♉R
27	18.24	5	25	18	10	22	♄ 1♓
28	18.28	6	8♏	18	11	22	♅15♍R
29	18.32	8	20	18D	12	23	♆19♏
30	18.36	9	2♐	18	14	23	♇16♍
31	18.40	10	14	19	15	23	♃16♉R

1965

Jan	STime	☉	☽	☿	♀	♂	Plnts
1	18.44	11♑	26♐	19♐	16♐	24♍	♃16♉R
2	18.48	12	7♑	20	17	24	♄ 1♓
3	18.52	13	19	20	19	24	♅14♍R
4	18.56	14	1♒	21	20	24	♆19♏
5	18.59	15	13	22	21	25	♇16♍R
6	19.03	16	25	23	22	25	♃16♉R
7	19.07	17	7♓	24	24	25	♄ 2♓
8	19.11	18	20	25	25	25	♅14♍R
9	19.15	19	2♈	26	26	26	♆19♏
10	19.19	20	15	27	27	26	♇16♍R
11	19.23	21	28	28	29	26	♃16♉
12	19.27	22	12♉	29	0♑	26	♄ 2♓
13	19.31	23	26	0♑	1	26	♅14♍R
14	19.35	24	11♊	1	2	27	♆19♏
15	19.39	25	26	3	4	27	♇16♍R
16	19.43	26	11♋	4	5	27	♃16♉
17	19.47	27	26	5	6	27	♄ 3♓
18	19.51	28	11♌	7	7	27	♅14♍R
19	19.55	29	26	8	9	27	♆19♏
20	19.59	0♒	11♍	9	10	27	♇16♍R
21	20.03	1	25	11	11	27	♃16♉
22	20.07	2	9♎	12	12	28	♄ 3♓
23	20.10	3	22	13	14	28	♅14♍R
24	20.14	4	4♏	15	15	28	♆20♏
25	20.18	5	17	16	16	28	♇16♍R
26	20.22	6	29	18	17	28	♃16♉
27	20.26	7	11♐	19	19	28	♄ 4♓
28	20.30	8	23	21	20	28	♅14♍R
29	20.34	9	4♑	22	21	28R	♆20♏
30	20.38	10	16	24	22	28	♇16♍R
31	20.42	11	28	25	24	28	♃17♉

Feb	STime	☉	☽	☿	♀	♂	Plnts
1	20.46	12♒	10♒	27♑	25♑	28♍	♃17♉
2	20.50	13	22	28	26	28	♄ 4♓
3	20.54	14	4♓	0♒	27	28	♅14♍R
4	20.58	15	17	1	29	27	♆20♏
5	21.02	16	29	3	0♒	27	♇15♍R
6	21.06	17	12♈	5	1	27	♃17♉
7	21.10	18	25	6	2	27	♄ 5♓
8	21.14	19	8♉	8	4	27	♅13♍R
9	21.17	20	22	9	5	27	♆20♏
10	21.21	21	6♊	11	6	27	♇15♍R
11	21.25	22	20	13	7	27	♃18♉
12	21.29	23	4♋	14	9	26	♄ 6♓
13	21.33	24	19	16	10	26	♅13♍R
14	21.37	25	4♌	18	11	26	♆20♏
15	21.41	26	19	20	12	26	♇15♍R
16	21.45	27	4♍	21	14	26	♃18♉
17	21.49	28	19	23	15	25	♄ 6♓
18	21.53	29	3♎	25	16	25	♅13♍R
19	21.57	0♓	17	27	17	25	♆20♏
20	22.01	1	0♏	28	19	24	♇15♍R
21	22.05	2	13	0♓	20	24	♃19♉
22	22.09	3	25	2	21	24	♄ 7♓
23	22.13	4	7♐	4	22	24	♅13♍R
24	22.17	5	19	6	24	23	♆20♏
25	22.21	6	1♑	8	25	23	♇15♍R
26	22.25	7	13	9	26	23	♃19♉
27	22.28	8	25	11	27	22	♄ 7♓
28	22.32	9	7♒	13	29	22	♅13♍R

Mar	STime	☉	☽	☿	♀	♂	Plnts
1	22.36	10♓	19♒	15♓	0♓	22♍	♃20♉
2	22.40	11	1♓	17	1	21	♄ 8♓
3	22.44	12	13	19	2	21	♅13♍R
4	22.48	13	26	21	4	20	♆20♏R
5	22.52	14	9♈	23	5	20	♇15♍R
6	22.56	15	22	25	6	20	♃21♉
7	23.00	16	5♉	27	7	19	♄ 8♓
8	23.04	17	19	29	9	19	♅12♍R
9	23.08	18	2♊	0♈	10	18	♆20♏R
10	23.12	19	16	2	11	18	♇15♍R
11	23.16	20	0♋	4	12	18	♃21♉
12	23.20	21	14	6	14	17	♄ 9♓
13	23.24	22	29	8	15	17	♅12♍R
14	23.28	23	13♌	9	16	16	♆20♏R
15	23.32	24	28	11	17	16	♇14♍R
16	23.35	25	12♍	12	19	16	♃22♉
17	23.39	26	27	14	20	15	♄10♓
18	23.43	27	11♎	15	21	15	♅12♍R
19	23.47	28	24	17	22	15	♆20♏R
20	23.51	29	8♏	18	24	14	♇14♍R
21	23.55	0♈	21	19	25	14	♃23♉
22	23.59	1	3♐	20	26	14	♄10♓
23	0.03	2	15	21	27	13	♅12♍R
24	0.07	3	27	21	29	13	♆19♏R
25	0.11	4	9♑	22	0♈	13	♇14♍R
26	0.15	5	21	22	1	12	♃24♉
27	0.19	6	3♒	23	2	12	♄11♓
28	0.23	7	15	23	4	12	♅11♍R
29	0.27	8	27	23R	5	11	♆19♏R
30	0.31	9	9♓	23	6	11	♇14♍R
31	0.35	10	22	23	7	11	♃25♉

Apr	STime	☉	☽	☿	♀	♂	Plnts
1	0.39	11♈	5♈	22♈	9♈	11♍	♃25♉
2	0.42	12	18	22	10	10	♄11♓
3	0.46	13	2♉	22	11	10	♅11♍R
4	0.50	14	15	21	12	10	♆19♏R
5	0.54	15	29	20	13	10	♇14♍R
6	0.58	16	13♊	20	15	10	♃26♉
7	1.02	17	27	19	16	9	♄12♓
8	1.06	18	11♋	18	17	9	♅11♍R
9	1.10	19	25	17	18	9	♆19♏R
10	1.14	20	9♌	17	20	9	♇14♍R
11	1.18	21	24	16	21	9	♃27♉
12	1.22	22	8♍	15	22	9	♄13♓
13	1.26	23	22	15	23	9	♅11♍R
14	1.30	24	6♎	14	25	9	♆19♏R
15	1.34	25	19	13	26	9	♇14♍R
16	1.38	26	3♏	13	27	8	♃28♉
17	1.42	27	16	12	28	8	♄13♓
18	1.46	28	28	12	0♉	8	♅11♍R
19	1.50	29	11♐	12	1	8D	♆19♏R
20	1.53	0♉	23	12	2	8	♇14♍R
21	1.57	1	5♑	11	3	8	♃29♉
22	2.01	2	17	11D	5	8	♄14♓
23	2.05	3	29	12	6	9	♅11♍R
24	2.09	4	11♒	12	7	9	♆19♏R
25	2.13	5	23	12	8	9	♇14♍R
26	2.17	6	5♓	12	9	9	♃ 1♊
27	2.21	7	17	13	11	9	♄14♓
28	2.25	8	0♈	13	12	9	♅11♍R
29	2.29	9	13	14	13	9	♆19♏R
30	2.33	10	27	14	14	9	♇14♍R

May	STime	☉	☽	☿	♀	♂	Plnts
1	2.37	11♉	11♉	15♈	16♉	9♍	♃ 2♊
2	2.41	12	25	16	17	9	♄14♓
3	2.45	13	9♊	16	18	10	♅11♍R
4	2.49	13	23	17	19	10	♆18♏R
5	2.53	14	8♋	18	21	10	♇13♍R
6	2.57	15	22	19	22	10	♃ 3♊
7	3.00	16	6♌	20	23	10	♄15♓
8	3.04	17	20	21	24	10	♅10♍R
9	3.08	18	4♍	22	25	11	♆18♏R
10	3.12	19	18	23	27	11	♇13♍
11	3.16	20	2♎	24	28	11	♃ 4♊
12	3.20	21	15	26	29	11	♄15♓
13	3.24	22	29	27	0♊	12	♅10♍R
14	3.28	23	11♏	28	2	12	♆18♏R
15	3.32	24	24	0♉	3	12	♇13♍
16	3.36	25	7♐	1	4	12	♃ 5♊
17	3.40	26	19	2	5	13	♄16♓
18	3.44	27	1♑	4	7	13	♅10♍
19	3.48	28	13	5	8	13	♆18♏R
20	3.52	29	25	7	9	13	♇13♍
21	3.56	0♊	7♒	9	10	14	♃ 6♊
22	4.00	1	19	10	11	14	♄16♓
23	4.04	2	1♓	12	13	14	♅10♍
24	4.08	3	13	13	14	15	♆18♏R
25	4.11	4	25	15	15	15	♇13♍
26	4.15	5	8♈	17	16	15	♃ 7♊
27	4.19	6	21	19	18	16	♄16♓
28	4.23	7	5♉	21	19	16	♅10♍
29	4.27	8	19	23	20	16	♆18♏R
30	4.31	9	3♊	24	21	17	♇13♍
31	4.35	10	18	26	23	17	♃ 9♊

Jun	STime	☉	☽	☿	♀	♂	Plnts
1	4.39	10♊	3♋	28♉	24♊	18♍	♃ 9♊
2	4.43	11	18	0♊	25	18	♄16♓
3	4.47	12	2♌	2	26	18	♅11♍
4	4.51	13	17	5	27	19	♆18♏R
5	4.55	14	1♍	7	29	19	♇13♍
6	4.59	15	15	9	0♋	19	♃10♊
7	5.03	16	29	11	1	20	♄17♓
8	5.07	17	12♎	13	2	20	♅11♍
9	5.11	18	25	15	4	21	♆18♏R
10	5.15	19	8♏	17	5	21	♇13♍
11	5.18	20	21	20	6	22	♃11♊
12	5.22	21	3♐	22	7	22	♄17♓
13	5.26	22	15	24	8	22	♅11♍
14	5.30	23	28	26	10	23	♆17♏R
15	5.34	24	9♑	28	11	23	♇14♍
16	5.38	25	21	1♋	12	24	♃12♊
17	5.42	26	3♒	3	13	24	♄17♓
18	5.46	27	15	5	15	25	♅11♍
19	5.50	28	27	7	16	25	♆17♏R
20	5.54	29	9♓	9	17	26	♇14♍
21	5.58	0♋	21	11	18	26	♃14♊
22	6.02	1	4♈	13	19	27	♄17♓
23	6.06	2	16	15	21	27	♅11♍
24	6.10	2	0♉	17	22	27	♆17♏R
25	6.14	3	13	19	23	28	♇14♍
26	6.18	4	27	21	24	28	♃15♊
27	6.22	5	12♊	23	26	29	♄17♓
28	6.26	6	26	24	27	29	♅11♍
29	6.29	7	11♋	26	28	0♎	♆17♏R
30	6.33	8	27	28	29	0	♇14♍

Jul	STime	☉	☽	☿	♀	♂	Plnts
1	6.37	9♋	12♌	29♋	0♌	1♎	♃16♊
2	6.41	10	26	1♌	2	1	♄17♓R
3	6.45	11	11♍	3	3	2	♅11♍
4	6.49	12	25	4	4	2	♆17♏R
5	6.53	13	9♎	6	5	3	♇14♍
6	6.57	14	22	7	7	4	♃17♊
7	7.01	15	5♏	9	8	4	♄17♓R
8	7.05	16	18	10	9	5	♅12♍
9	7.09	17	0♐	12	10	5	♆17♏R
10	7.13	18	12	13	11	6	♇14♍
11	7.17	19	24	14	13	6	♃18♊
12	7.21	20	6♑	15	14	7	♄17♓R
13	7.25	21	18	17	15	7	♅12♍
14	7.29	22	0♒	18	16	8	♆17♏
15	7.33	22	12	19	17	8	♇14♍
16	7.36	23	24	20	19	9	♃19♊
17	7.40	24	6♓	21	20	9	♄17♓R
18	7.44	25	18	22	21	10	♅12♍
19	7.48	26	0♈	23	22	11	♆17♏
20	7.52	27	13	24	24	11	♇14♍
21	7.56	28	25	25	25	12	♃20♊
22	8.00	29	8♉	26	26	12	♄16♓R
23	8.04	0♌	22	26	27	13	♅12♍
24	8.08	1	6♊	27	28	13	♆17♏
25	8.12	2	20	28	0♍	14	♇14♍
26	8.16	3	5♋	28	1	15	♃21♊
27	8.20	4	20	29	2	15	♄16♓R
28	8.24	5	5♌	29	3	16	♅12♍
29	8.28	6	20	29	4	16	♆17♏
30	8.32	7	5♍	0♍	6	17	♇14♍
31	8.36	8	20	0	7	17	♃22♊

Aug	STime	☉	☽	☿	♀	♂	Plnts
1	8.40	9♌	4♎	0♍	8♍	18♎	♃22♊
2	8.43	10	18	0	9	19	♄16♓R
3	8.47	11	2♏	0	10	19	♅13♍
4	8.51	12	15	0	12	20	♆17♏
5	8.55	13	27	29♌	13	20	♇15♍
6	8.59	14	10♐	29	14	21	♃23♊
7	9.03	14	22	28	15	22	♄16♓R
8	9.07	15	3♑	28	16	22	♅13♍
9	9.11	16	15	27	18	23	♆17♏
10	9.15	17	27	27	19	23	♇15♍
11	9.19	18	9♒	26	20	24	♃24♊
12	9.23	19	21	25	21	25	♄15♓R
13	9.27	20	3♓	24	22	25	♅13♍
14	9.31	21	15	24	24	26	♆17♏
15	9.35	22	27	23	25	27	♇15♍
16	9.39	23	10♈	22	26	27	♃25♊
17	9.43	24	22	21	27	28	♄15♓R
18	9.47	25	5♉	20	28	28	♅14♍
19	9.51	26	18	20	0♎	29	♆17♏
20	9.54	27	1♊	19	1	0♏	♇15♍
21	9.58	28	15	18	2	0	♃26♊
22	10.02	29	29	18	3	1	♄15♓R
23	10.06	0♍	14♋	18	4	2	♅14♍
24	10.10	1	28	17	6	2	♆17♏
25	10.14	2	14♌	17D	7	3	♇15♍
26	10.18	3	29	17	8	4	♃27♊
27	10.22	4	14♍	18	9	4	♄14♓R
28	10.26	5	29	18	10	5	♅14♍
29	10.30	6	13♎	18	12	5	♆17♏
30	10.34	7	27	19	13	6	♇15♍
31	10.38	8	10♏	20	14	7	♃27♊

Sep	STime	☉	☽	☿	♀	♂	Plnts
1	10.42	9♍	23♏	20♌	15♎	7♏	♃27♊
2	10.46	10	6♐	21	16	8	♄14♓R
3	10.50	10	18	22	18	9	♅15♍
4	10.54	11	0♑	24	19	9	♆17♏
5	10.58	12	12	25	20	10	♇16♍
6	11.01	13	24	26	21	11	♃28♊
7	11.05	14	6♒	28	22	11	♄13♓R
8	11.09	15	18	29	23	12	♅15♍
9	11.13	16	0♓	1♍	25	13	♆17♏
10	11.17	17	12	3	26	13	♇16♍
11	11.21	18	24	4	27	14	♃29♊
12	11.25	19	7♈	6	28	15	♄13♓R
13	11.29	20	19	8	29	15	♅15♍
14	11.33	21	2♉	10	0♏	16	♆18♏
15	11.37	22	15	12	2	17	♇16♍
16	11.41	23	28	13	3	17	♃29♊
17	11.45	24	11♊	15	4	18	♄13♓R
18	11.49	25	25	17	5	19	♅16♍
19	11.53	26	9♋	19	6	19	♆18♏
20	11.57	27	23	21	8	20	♇16♍
21	12.01	28	8♌	23	9	21	♃ 0♋
22	12.05	29	23	25	10	21	♄12♓R
23	12.09	0♎	7♍	27	11	22	♅16♍
24	12.12	1	22	28	12	23	♆18♏
25	12.16	2	7♎	0♎	13	24	♇16♍
26	12.20	3	21	2	15	24	♃ 0♋
27	12.24	4	5♏	4	16	25	♄12♓R
28	12.28	5	18	6	17	26	♅16♍
29	12.32	6	1♐	7	18	26	♆18♏
30	12.36	7	14	9	19	27	♇17♍

Oct	STime	☉	☽	☿	♀	♂	Plnts
1	12.40	8♎	26♐	11♎	20♏	28♏	♃ 0♋
2	12.44	9	8♑	13	21	28	♄12♓R
3	12.48	10	20	14	23	29	♅17♍
4	12.52	11	2♒	16	24	0♐	♆18♏
5	12.56	12	14	18	25	1	♇17♍
6	13.00	13	26	19	26	1	♃ 1♋
7	13.04	14	8♓	21	27	2	♄11♓R
8	13.08	15	20	23	28	3	♅17♍
9	13.12	16	3♈	24	29	3	♆18♏
10	13.16	17	16	26	1♐	4	♇17♍
11	13.19	18	28	27	2	5	♃ 1♋
12	13.23	19	12♉	29	3	6	♄11♓R
13	13.27	20	25	1♏	4	6	♅17♍
14	13.31	21	8♊	2	5	7	♆18♏
15	13.35	22	22	4	6	8	♇17♍
16	13.39	23	6♋	5	7	8	♃ 1♋
17	13.43	24	20	7	9	9	♄11♓R
18	13.47	25	4♌	8	10	10	♅17♍
19	13.51	26	18	10	11	11	♆19♏
20	13.55	27	3♍	11	12	11	♇17♍
21	13.59	28	17	13	13	12	♃ 1♋R
22	14.03	29	1♎	14	14	13	♄11♓R
23	14.07	0♏	15	16	15	13	♅18♍
24	14.11	1	29	17	16	14	♆19♏
25	14.15	2	13♏	19	17	15	♇17♍
26	14.19	3	26	20	19	16	♃ 1♋R
27	14.23	4	9♐	22	20	16	♄10♓R
28	14.26	5	22	23	21	17	♅18♍
29	14.30	6	4♑	25	22	18	♆19♏
30	14.34	7	16	26	23	19	♇17♍
31	14.38	8	28	27	24	19	♃ 1♋R

Nov	STime	☉	☽	☿	♀	♂	Plnts
1	14.42	9♏	10♒	29♏	25♐	20♐	♃ 1♋R
2	14.46	10	22	0♐	26	21	♄10♓R
3	14.50	11	4♓	1	27	22	♅18♍
4	14.54	12	16	3	28	22	♆19♏
5	14.58	13	28	4	29	23	♇18♍
6	15.02	14	11♈	5	0♑	24	♃ 0♋R
7	15.06	15	24	6	1	25	♄10♓R
8	15.10	16	7♉	8	3	25	♅18♍
9	15.14	17	21	9	4	26	♆19♏
10	15.18	18	4♊	10	5	27	♇18♍
11	15.22	19	18	11	6	28	♃ 0♋R
12	15.26	20	2♋	12	7	28	♄10♓
13	15.30	21	17	13	8	29	♅19♍
14	15.34	22	1♌	14	9	0♑	♆20♏
15	15.37	23	15	15	10	1	♇18♍
16	15.41	24	29	16	11	1	♃ 0♋R
17	15.45	25	13♍	17	12	2	♄10♓
18	15.49	26	27	17	13	3	♅19♍
19	15.53	27	11♎	18	14	4	♆20♏
20	15.57	28	25	18	15	4	♇18♍
21	16.01	29	8♏	19	16	5	♃29♊R
22	16.05	0♐	22	19	17	6	♄10♓
23	16.09	1	5♐	19R	18	7	♅19♍
24	16.13	2	17	19	19	7	♆20♏
25	16.17	3	0♑	18	19	8	♇18♍
26	16.21	4	12	18	20	9	♃29♊R
27	16.25	5	24	17	21	10	♄10♓
28	16.29	6	6♒	16	22	10	♅19♍
29	16.33	7	18	15	23	11	♆20♏
30	16.37	8	0♓	14	24	12	♇18♍

Dec	STime	☉	☽	☿	♀	♂	Plnts
1	16.41	9♐	12♓	13♐	25♑	13♑	♃28♊R
2	16.44	10	24	11	26	14	♄10♓
3	16.48	11	6♈	10	27	14	♅19♍
4	16.52	12	19	9	27	15	♆20♏
5	16.56	13	2♉	7	28	16	♇18♍
6	17.00	14	15	6	29	17	♃28♊R
7	17.04	15	29	5	0♒	17	♄11♓
8	17.08	16	13♊	4	1	18	♅19♍
9	17.12	17	27	4	1	19	♆20♏
10	17.16	18	12♋	3	2	20	♇18♍
11	17.20	19	27	3	3	21	♃27♊R
12	17.24	20	11♌	3D	4	21	♄11♓
13	17.28	21	26	3	4	22	♅19♍
14	17.32	22	10♍	3	5	23	♆21♏
15	17.36	23	24	3	6	24	♇18♍
16	17.40	24	8♎	4	6	24	♃26♊R
17	17.44	25	22	4	7	25	♄11♓
18	17.48	26	5♏	5	8	26	♅19♍
19	17.52	27	18	6	8	27	♆21♏
20	17.55	28	1♐	6	9	28	♇18♍
21	17.59	29	13	7	9	28	♃26♊R
22	18.03	0♑	26	8	10	29	♄11♓
23	18.07	1	8♑	10	10	0♒	♅19♍
24	18.11	2	20	11	11	1	♆21♏
25	18.15	3	2♒	12	11	1	♇18♍R
26	18.19	4	14	13	12	2	♃25♊R
27	18.23	5	26	14	12	3	♄12♓
28	18.27	6	8♓	16	12	4	♅19♍
29	18.31	7	20	17	13	5	♆21♏
30	18.35	8	2♈	18	13	5	♇18♍R
31	18.39	9	14	19	13	6	♃24♊R

Jan	STime	☉	☽	☿	♀	♂	Plnts
1	18.43	10♑	27♈	21♐	13♒	7♒	♃24♊R
2	18.47	11	10♉	22	13	8	♄12♓
3	18.51	12	23	24	13	9	♅19♍R
4	18.55	13	7♊	25	14	9	♆21♏
5	18.59	14	21	26	14R	10	♇18♍R
6	19.02	15	5♋	28	14	11	♃23♊R
7	19.06	16	20	29	13	12	♄13♓
8	19.10	17	5♌	1♑	13	12	♅19♍R
9	19.14	18	21	2	13	13	♆21♏
10	19.18	19	6♍	4	13	14	♇18♍R
11	19.22	21	20	5	13	15	♃23♊R
12	19.26	22	4♎	7	13	16	♄13♓
13	19.30	23	18	8	12	16	♅19♍R
14	19.34	24	2♏	10	12	17	♆21♏
15	19.38	25	15	11	12	18	♇18♍R
16	19.42	26	28	13	11	19	♃22♊R
17	19.46	27	10♐	14	11	20	♄14♓
18	19.50	28	23	16	10	20	♅19♍R
19	19.54	29	5♑	17	10	21	♆22♏
20	19.58	0♒	17	19	9	22	♇18♍R
21	20.02	1	29	21	9	23	♃22♊R
22	20.06	2	11♒	22	8	24	♄14♓
23	20.10	3	23	24	7	24	♅19♍R
24	20.13	4	5♓	25	7	25	♆22♏
25	20.17	5	16	27	6	26	♇18♍R
26	20.21	6	28	29	6	27	♃22♊R
27	20.25	7	10♈	0♒	5	27	♄15♓
28	20.29	8	23	2	4	28	♅19♍R
29	20.33	9	5♉	4	4	29	♆22♏
30	20.37	10	18	5	3	0♓	♇18♍R
31	20.41	11	1♊	7	3	1	♃21♊R

Feb	STime	☉	☽	☿	♀	♂	Plnts
1	20.45	12♒	15♊	9♒	2♒	1♓	♃21♊R
2	20.49	13	29	10	2	2	♄15♓
3	20.53	14	13♋	12	1	3	♅19♍R
4	20.57	15	28	14	1	4	♆22♏
5	21.01	16	14♌	15	0	5	♇18♍R
6	21.05	17	29	17	0	5	♃21♊R
7	21.09	18	14♍	19	29♑	6	♄16♓
8	21.13	19	29	21	29	7	♅18♍R
9	21.17	20	14♎	23	29	8	♆22♏
10	21.20	21	28	24	29	9	♇18♍R
11	21.24	22	11♏	26	28	9	♃21♊R
12	21.28	23	25	28	28	10	♄16♓
13	21.32	24	7♐	0♓	28	11	♅18♍R
14	21.36	25	20	2	28	12	♆22♏
15	21.40	26	2♑	4	28D	12	♇17♍R
16	21.44	27	14	5	28	13	♃21♊
17	21.48	28	26	7	28	14	♄17♓
18	21.52	29	8♒	9	28	15	♅18♍R
19	21.56	0♓	20	11	28	16	♆22♏
20	22.00	1	2♓	13	28	16	♇17♍R
21	22.04	2	14	15	29	17	♃21♊
22	22.08	3	25	16	29	18	♄18♓
23	22.12	4	7♈	18	29	19	♅18♍R
24	22.16	5	20	20	29	20	♆22♏
25	22.20	6	2♉	21	0♒	20	♇17♍R
26	22.24	7	14	23	0	21	♃21♊
27	22.27	8	27	25	0	22	♄18♓
28	22.31	9	10♊	26	1	23	♅18♍R

Mar	STime	☉	☽	☿	♀	♂	Plnts
1	22.35	10♓	23♊	28♓	1♒	23♓	♃21♊
2	22.39	11	7♋	29	2	24	♄19♓
3	22.43	12	22	0♈	2	25	♅18♍R
4	22.47	13	7♌	1	3	26	♆22♏
5	22.51	14	22	2	3	27	♇17♍R
6	22.55	15	7♍	3	4	27	♃22♊
7	22.59	16	22	4	5	28	♄19♓
8	23.03	17	7♎	4	5	29	♅17♍R
9	23.07	18	22	5	6	0♈	♆22♏R
10	23.11	19	6♏	5	7	0	♇17♍R
11	23.15	20	20	5	7	1	♃22♊
12	23.19	21	3♐	5R	8	2	♄20♓
13	23.23	22	16	5	9	3	♅17♍R
14	23.27	23	29	5	9	4	♆22♏R
15	23.31	24	11♑	5	10	4	♇17♍R
16	23.35	25	23	4	11	5	♃22♊
17	23.38	26	5♒	3	12	6	♄20♓
18	23.42	27	17	3	12	7	♅17♍R
19	23.46	28	29	2	13	7	♆22♏R
20	23.50	29	10♓	1	14	8	♇17♍R
21	23.54	0♈	22	0	15	9	♃23♊
22	23.58	1	4♈	29♓	16	10	♄21♓
23	0.02	2	17	28	17	10	♅17♍R
24	0.06	3	29	28	17	11	♆22♏R
25	0.10	4	11♉	27	18	12	♇16♍R
26	0.14	5	24	26	19	13	♃23♊
27	0.18	6	7♊	25	20	14	♄22♓
28	0.22	7	20	25	21	14	♅16♍R
29	0.26	8	3♋	24	22	15	♆22♏R
30	0.30	9	17	23	23	16	♇16♍R
31	0.34	10	1♌	23	24	17	♃24♊

Apr	STime	☉	☽	☿	♀	♂	Plnts
1	0.38	11♈	16♌	23♓	25♒	17♈	♃24♊
2	0.42	12	1♍	23	26	18	♄22♓
3	0.45	13	16	22	27	19	♅16♍R
4	0.49	14	1♎	22D	28	20	♆21♏R
5	0.53	15	15	23	29	20	♇16♍R
6	0.57	16	0♏	23	0♓	21	♃25♊
7	1.01	17	14	23	1	22	♄23♓
8	1.05	18	28	23	2	23	♅16♍R
9	1.09	19	11♐	24	3	23	♆21♏R
10	1.13	20	24	24	4	24	♇16♍R
11	1.17	21	7♑	25	5	25	♃26♊
12	1.21	22	19	25	6	26	♄23♓
13	1.25	23	1♒	26	7	26	♅16♍R
14	1.29	24	13	27	8	27	♆21♏R
15	1.33	25	25	28	9	28	♇16♍R
16	1.37	26	7♓	28	10	29	♃26♊
17	1.41	27	19	29	11	29	♄24♓
18	1.45	28	1♈	0♈	12	0♉	♅16♍R
19	1.49	29	13	1	13	1	♆21♏R
20	1.53	0♉	26	2	14	2	♇16♍R
21	1.56	1	8♉	3	15	2	♃27♊
22	2.00	2	21	5	16	3	♄25♓
23	2.04	3	4♊	6	17	4	♅16♍R
24	2.08	4	17	7	18	5	♆21♏R
25	2.12	5	0♋	8	19	5	♇16♍R
26	2.16	5	14	10	20	6	♃28♊
27	2.20	6	28	11	21	7	♄25♓
28	2.24	7	12♌	12	22	8	♅15♍R
29	2.28	8	26	14	23	8	♆21♏R
30	2.32	9	11♍	15	25	9	♇16♍R

May	STime	☉	☽	☿	♀	♂	Plnts
1	2.36	10♉	25♍	17♈	26♓	10♉	♃29♊
2	2.40	11	10♎	18	27	11	♄26♓
3	2.44	12	24	20	28	11	♅15♍R
4	2.48	13	8♏	21	29	12	♆21♏R
5	2.52	14	22	23	0♈	13	♇16♍R
6	2.56	15	6♐	24	1	13	♃ 0♋
7	3.00	16	19	26	2	14	♄26♓
8	3.03	17	2♑	28	3	15	♅15♍R
9	3.07	18	15	29	4	16	♆21♏R
10	3.11	19	27	1♉	6	16	♇16♍R
11	3.15	20	9♒	3	7	17	♃ 1♋
12	3.19	21	21	5	8	18	♄27♓
13	3.23	22	3♓	7	9	19	♅15♍R
14	3.27	23	15	9	10	19	♆20♏R
15	3.31	24	27	11	11	20	♇16♍
16	3.35	25	9♈	13	12	21	♃ 2♋
17	3.39	26	21	14	13	21	♄27♓
18	3.43	27	4♉	17	15	22	♅15♍R
19	3.47	28	17	19	16	23	♆20♏R
20	3.51	29	0♊	21	17	24	♇16♍
21	3.55	0♊	13	23	18	24	♃ 3♋
22	3.59	1	27	25	19	25	♄27♓
23	4.03	2	11♋	27	20	26	♅15♍
24	4.07	3	25	29	21	27	♆20♏R
25	4.11	4	9♌	1♊	23	27	♇16♍
26	4.14	4	23	4	24	28	♃ 4♋
27	4.18	5	7♍	6	25	29	♄28♓
28	4.22	6	21	8	26	29	♅15♍
29	4.26	7	6♎	10	27	0♊	♆20♏R
30	4.30	8	20	12	28	1	♇16♍
31	4.34	9	4♏	14	29	2	♃ 5♋

Jun	STime	☉	☽	☿	♀	♂	Plnts
1	4.38	10♊	17♏	17♊	1♉	2♊	♃ 5♋
2	4.42	11	1♐	19	2	3	♄28♓
3	4.46	12	14	21	3	4	♅15♍
4	4.50	13	27	23	4	4	♆20♏R
5	4.54	14	10♑	25	5	5	♇16♍
6	4.58	15	23	27	6	6	♃ 6♋
7	5.02	16	5♒	29	7	6	♄28♓
8	5.06	17	17	1♋	9	7	♅15♍
9	5.10	18	29	3	10	8	♆20♏R
10	5.14	19	11♓	5	11	9	♇16♍
11	5.18	20	23	7	12	9	♃ 7♋
12	5.21	21	5♈	9	13	10	♄29♓
13	5.25	22	17	10	14	11	♅15♍
14	5.29	23	29	12	16	11	♆20♏R
15	5.33	24	12♉	14	17	12	♇16♍
16	5.37	25	25	15	18	13	♃ 9♋
17	5.41	26	8♊	17	19	13	♄29♓
18	5.45	27	22	18	20	14	♅15♍
19	5.49	27	6♋	20	21	15	♆20♏R
20	5.53	28	20	21	23	16	♇16♍
21	5.57	29	5♌	23	24	16	♃10♋
22	6.01	0♋	19	24	25	17	♄29♓
23	6.05	1	4♍	26	26	18	♅15♍
24	6.09	2	18	27	27	18	♆19♏R
25	6.13	3	2♎	28	29	19	♇16♍
26	6.17	4	16	29	0♊	20	♃11♋
27	6.21	5	0♏	1♌	1	20	♄29♓
28	6.25	6	14	2	2	21	♅16♍
29	6.28	7	27	3	3	22	♆19♏R
30	6.32	8	10♐	4	4	22	♇16♍

Jul	STime	☉	☽	☿	♀	♂	Plnts
1	6.36	9♋	23♐	5♌	6♊	23♊	♃12♋
2	6.40	10	6♑	5	7	24	♄29♓
3	6.44	11	19	6	8	25	♅16♍
4	6.48	12	1♒	7	9	25	♆19♏R
5	6.52	13	13	8	10	26	♇16♍
6	6.56	14	25	8	12	27	♃13♋
7	7.00	15	7♓	9	13	27	♄29♓
8	7.04	16	19	10	14	28	♅16♍
9	7.08	17	1♈	10	15	29	♆19♏R
10	7.12	17	13	10	16	29	♇16♍
11	7.16	18	25	11	17	0♋	♃14♋
12	7.20	19	7♉	11	19	1	♄29♓
13	7.24	20	20	11	20	1	♅16♍
14	7.28	21	3♊	11R	21	2	♆19♏R
15	7.32	22	17	11	22	3	♇16♍
16	7.36	23	0♋	11	23	3	♃15♋
17	7.39	24	15	11	25	4	♄29♓R
18	7.43	25	29	11	26	5	♅17♍
19	7.47	26	14♌	10	27	5	♆19♏R
20	7.51	27	29	10	28	6	♇16♍
21	7.55	28	14♍	9	29	7	♃16♋
22	7.59	29	29	9	1♋	7	♄29♓R
23	8.03	0♌	13♎	8	2	8	♅17♍
24	8.07	1	27	8	3	9	♆19♏
25	8.11	2	11♏	7	4	9	♇16♍
26	8.15	3	24	6	5	10	♃17♋
27	8.19	4	7♐	6	7	11	♄29♓R
28	8.23	5	20	5	8	11	♅17♍
29	8.27	6	3♑	4	9	12	♆19♏
30	8.31	7	15	3	10	13	♇17♍
31	8.35	8	28	3	11	13	♃19♋

Aug	STime	☉	☽	☿	♀	♂	Plnts
1	8.39	8♌	10♒	2♌	13♋	14♋	♃19♋
2	8.43	9	22	2	14	15	♄29♓R
3	8.46	10	4♓	1	15	15	♅17♍
4	8.50	11	16	1	16	16	♆19♏
5	8.54	12	28	0	18	17	♇17♍
6	8.58	13	10♈	0	19	17	♃20♋
7	9.02	14	21	0D	20	18	♄29♓R
8	9.06	15	3♉	0	21	19	♅18♍
9	9.10	16	16	0	22	19	♆19♏
10	9.14	17	28	0	24	20	♇17♍
11	9.18	18	11♊	1	25	21	♃21♋
12	9.22	19	25	1	26	21	♄29♓R
13	9.26	20	9♋	2	27	22	♅18♍
14	9.30	21	23	2	28	22	♆19♏
15	9.34	22	8♌	3	0♌	23	♇17♍
16	9.38	23	23	4	1	24	♃22♋
17	9.42	24	8♍	5	2	24	♄28♓R
18	9.46	25	23	6	3	25	♅18♍
19	9.50	26	8♎	8	5	26	♆19♏
20	9.54	27	23	9	6	26	♇17♍
21	9.57	28	7♏	10	7	27	♃23♋
22	10.01	29	21	12	8	28	♄28♓R
23	10.05	0♍	4♐	13	9	28	♅18♍
24	10.09	1	17	15	11	29	♆19♏
25	10.13	2	0♑	17	12	0♌	♇17♍
26	10.17	3	12	19	13	0	♃24♋
27	10.21	3	25	20	14	1	♄28♓R
28	10.25	4	7♒	22	16	2	♅19♍
29	10.29	5	19	24	17	2	♆19♏
30	10.33	6	1♓	26	18	3	♇18♍
31	10.37	7	13	28	19	3	♃25♋

Sep	STime	☉	☽	☿	♀	♂	Plnts
1	10.41	8♍	25♓	0♍	20♌	4♌	♃25♋
2	10.45	9	6♈	2	22	5	♄27♓R
3	10.49	10	18	4	23	5	♅19♍
4	10.53	11	0♉	6	24	6	♆19♏
5	10.57	12	12	8	25	7	♇18♍
6	11.01	13	25	10	27	7	♃26♋
7	11.04	14	7♊	11	28	8	♄27♓R
8	11.08	15	20	13	29	8	♅19♍
9	11.12	16	3♋	15	0♍	9	♆20♏
10	11.16	17	17	17	2	10	♇18♍
11	11.20	18	2♌	19	3	10	♃27♋
12	11.24	19	16	21	4	11	♄27♓R
13	11.28	20	1♍	23	5	11	♅20♍
14	11.32	21	17	25	7	12	♆20♏
15	11.36	22	2♎	26	8	13	♇18♍
16	11.40	23	17	28	9	14	♃28♋
17	11.44	24	2♏	0♎	10	14	♄26♓R
18	11.48	25	16	2	11	15	♅20♍
19	11.52	26	0♐	3	13	15	♆20♏
20	11.56	27	14	5	14	16	♇18♍
21	12.00	28	27	7	15	17	♃29♋
22	12.04	29	9♑	9	16	17	♄26♓R
23	12.08	0♎	22	10	18	18	♅20♍
24	12.11	1	4♒	12	19	19	♆20♏
25	12.15	2	16	14	20	19	♇18♍
26	12.19	3	28	15	21	20	♃ 0♌
27	12.23	4	10♓	17	23	20	♄25♓R
28	12.27	5	22	18	24	21	♅21♍
29	12.31	6	3♈	20	25	22	♆20♏
30	12.35	7	15	21	26	22	♇19♍

Oct	STime	☉	☽	☿	♀	♂	Plnts
1	12.39	8♎	27♈	23♎	28♍	23♌	♃ 0♌
2	12.43	9	9♉	25	29	23	♄25♓R
3	12.47	10	22	26	0♎	24	♅21♍
4	12.51	11	4♊	28	1	25	♆20♏
5	12.55	11	17	29	3	25	♇19♍
6	12.59	12	0♋	1♏	4	26	♃ 1♌
7	13.03	13	13	2	5	27	♄25♓R
8	13.07	14	27	3	6	27	♅21♍
9	13.11	15	11♌	5	8	28	♆20♏
10	13.15	16	25	6	9	28	♇19♍
11	13.19	17	10♍	8	10	29	♃ 2♌
12	13.22	18	25	9	11	0♍	♄24♓R
13	13.26	19	10♎	10	13	0	♅22♍
14	13.30	20	25	12	14	1	♆20♏
15	13.34	21	10♏	13	15	1	♇19♍
16	13.38	22	24	14	16	2	♃ 2♌
17	13.42	23	8♐	16	18	3	♄24♓R
18	13.46	24	22	17	19	3	♅22♍
19	13.50	25	5♑	18	20	4	♆21♏
20	13.54	26	18	20	21	4	♇19♍
21	13.58	27	0♒	21	23	5	♃ 3♌
22	14.02	28	13	22	24	6	♄24♓R
23	14.06	29	25	23	25	6	♅22♍
24	14.10	0♏	6♓	24	26	7	♆21♏
25	14.14	1	18	25	28	7	♇19♍
26	14.18	2	0♈	26	29	8	♃ 3♌
27	14.22	3	12	27	0♏	8	♄23♓R
28	14.26	4	24	28	1	9	♅22♍
29	14.29	5	6♉	29	3	10	♆21♏
30	14.33	6	19	0♐	4	10	♇20♍
31	14.37	7	1♊	1	5	11	♃ 3♌

Nov	STime	☉	☽	☿	♀	♂	Plnts
1	14.41	8♏	14♊	1♐	6♏	11♍	♃ 4♌
2	14.45	9	27	2	8	12	♄23♓R
3	14.49	10	10♋	2	9	13	♅23♍
4	14.53	11	23	3	10	13	♆21♏
5	14.57	12	7♌	3	11	14	♇20♍
6	15.01	13	21	3R	13	14	♃ 4♌
7	15.05	14	5♍	3	14	15	♄23♓R
8	15.09	15	19	3	15	15	♅23♍
9	15.13	16	4♎	3	16	16	♆21♏
10	15.17	17	19	2	18	17	♇20♍
11	15.21	18	3♏	1	19	17	♃ 4♌
12	15.25	19	18	0	20	18	♄23♓R
13	15.29	20	2♐	29♏	21	18	♅23♍
14	15.33	21	16	28	23	19	♆22♏
15	15.37	22	0♑	27	24	19	♇20♍
16	15.40	23	13	26	25	20	♃ 4♌
17	15.44	24	26	24	27	21	♄23♓R
18	15.48	25	8♒	23	28	21	♅23♍
19	15.52	26	21	22	29	22	♆22♏
20	15.56	27	3♓	20	0♐	22	♇20♍
21	16.00	28	15	19	2	23	♃ 4♌
22	16.04	29	26	19	3	23	♄23♓R
23	16.08	0♐	8♈	18	4	24	♅24♍
24	16.12	1	20	17	5	25	♆22♏
25	16.16	2	2♉	17	7	25	♇20♍
26	16.20	3	15	17D	8	26	♃ 4♌R
27	16.24	4	27	17	9	26	♄23♓
28	16.28	6	10♊	17	10	27	♅24♍
29	16.32	7	23	17	12	27	♆22♏
30	16.36	8	7♋	18	13	28	♇20♍

Dec	STime	☉	☽	☿	♀	♂	Plnts
1	16.40	9♐	20♋	19♏	14♐	28♍	♃ 4♌R
2	16.44	10	4♌	19	15	29	♄23♓
3	16.47	11	18	20	17	29	♅24♍
4	16.51	12	2♍	21	18	0♎	♆22♏
5	16.55	13	16	22	19	0	♇20♍
6	16.59	14	0♎	23	20	1	♃ 4♌R
7	17.03	15	14	24	22	1	♄23♓
8	17.07	16	28	26	23	2	♅24♍
9	17.11	17	13♏	27	24	2	♆23♏
10	17.15	18	27	28	25	3	♇20♍
11	17.19	19	11♐	0♐	27	4	♃ 4♌R
12	17.23	20	24	1	28	4	♄23♓
13	17.27	21	8♑	2	29	4	♅24♍
14	17.31	22	21	4	0♑	5	♆23♏
15	17.35	23	4♒	4	2	6	♇20♍
16	17.39	24	16	6	3	6	♃ 3♌R
17	17.43	25	29	8	4	7	♄23♓
18	17.47	26	11♓	9	5	7	♅24♍
19	17.51	27	22	11	7	8	♆23♏
20	17.54	28	4♈	12	8	8	♇20♍
21	17.58	29	16	14	9	9	♃ 3♌R
22	18.02	0♑	28	15	10	9	♄23♓
23	18.06	1	10♉	17	12	10	♅24♍
24	18.10	2	23	18	13	10	♆23♏
25	18.14	3	5♊	20	14	11	♇20♍
26	18.18	4	19	21	15	11	♃ 2♌R
27	18.22	5	2♋	23	17	12	♄23♓
28	18.26	6	16	24	18	12	♅24♍
29	18.30	7	0♌	26	19	13	♆23♏
30	18.34	8	14	27	21	13	♇20♍R
31	18.38	9	28	29	22	14	♃ 2♌R

1 9 6 7

Jan	STime	☉	☽	☿	♀	♂	Plnts
1	18.42	10♑	12♏	0♑	23♐	14♑	♃ 2♏R
2	18.46	11	27	2	24	15	♄24♏
3	18.50	12	11♎	4	26	15	♅24♏
4	18.54	13	25	5	27	15	Ψ23♏
5	18.58	14	9♏	7	28	16	♇20♏
6	19.02	15	23	8	29	16	♃ 1♏R
7	19.05	16	6♐	10	1♑	17	♄24♏
8	19.09	17	20	11	2	17	♅24♏
9	19.13	18	3♑	13	4	18	Ψ23♏
10	19.17	19	16	15	4	18	♇20♏R
11	19.21	20	29	16	6	19	♃ 0♏R
12	19.25	21	12♒	18	7	19	♄25♏
13	19.29	22	24	19	8	19	♅24♏
14	19.33	23	6♓	21	9	20	Ψ24♏
15	19.37	24	18	23	11	20	♃ 0♏R
16	19.41	25	0♈	24	12	21	♄25♏
17	19.45	26	12	26	13	21	♅25♏
18	19.49	27	24	28	14	22	Ψ24♏
19	19.53	28	6♉	29	16	22	♇20♏
20	19.57	29	18	1♒	17	22	♃29♈R
21	20.01	0♒	0♊	3	18	23	♄25♓
22	20.05	1	13	4	19	23	♅25♏
23	20.09	2	26	6	21	24	Ψ24♏
24	20.12	4	10♋	8	22	24	♇20♏
25	20.16	5	24	10	23	24	♇20♏
26	20.20	6	9♌	11	24	24	♃28♈R
27	20.24	7	23	13	26	25	♄26♓
28	20.28	8	8♍	15	27	25	♅25♏
29	20.32	9	23	17	28	26	Ψ24♏
30	20.36	10	7♎	18	29	26	♇20♏R
31	20.40	11	22	20	1♓	26	♃28♈R

Feb	STime	☉	☽	☿	♀	♂	Plnts
1	20.44	12♒	6♏	22♒	2♓	27♑	♃28♈R
2	20.48	13	20	24	4	27	♄26♓
3	20.52	14	3♐	25	4	27	♅24♏
4	20.56	15	16	27	6	27	Ψ23♏
5	21.00	16	0♑	29	7	28	♇20♏
6	21.04	17	13	1♓	8	28	♃27♈R
7	21.08	18	25	2	9	28	♄27♓
8	21.12	19	8♒	4	11	28	♅23♏
9	21.16	20	20	5	12	29	Ψ23♏
10	21.20	21	3♓	7	13	29	♇20♏
11	21.23	22	15	8	14	29	♃26♈R
12	21.27	23	27	10	16	0♒	♄27♓
13	21.31	24	8♈	11	17	0	♅23♏R
14	21.35	25	20	13	18	0	Ψ24♏
15	21.39	26	2♉	14	19	0	♇20♏
16	21.43	27	14	15	20	1	♃26♈R
17	21.47	28	26	17	23	1	♄28♓
18	21.51	29	8♊	17	23	1	♅23♏R
19	21.55	0♓	21	17	24	1	Ψ24♏
20	21.59	1	4♋	18	25	1	♇20♏
21	22.03	2	18	18	27	2	♃25♈R
22	22.07	3	2♌	17	28	2	♄29♓
23	22.11	4	17	18R	29	2	♅23♏R
24	22.15	5	2♍	18	0♈	2	Ψ24♏
25	22.19	6	17	17	2	2	♇19♏
26	22.23	7	2♎	18	3	2	♃25♈R
27	22.27	8	17	17	4	2	♄29♓
28	22.30	9	1♏	16	5	3	♅23♏R

Mar	STime	☉	☽	☿	♀	♂	Plnts
1	22.34	10♓	16♏	15♒	7♈	3♒	♃25♈R
2	22.38	11	0♐	15	8	3	♄ 0♈
3	22.42	12	13	14	9	3	♅23♏R
4	22.46	13	26	13	10	3	Ψ19♏R
5	22.50	14	10♑	13	11	3	♇19♏
6	22.54	15	22	13	13	3	♃24♈R
7	22.58	16	5♒	13	14	3	♄ 0♈
8	23.02	17	17	13	15	3	♅22♏R
9	23.06	18	29	14	16	3R	Ψ19♏R
10	23.10	19	11♓	14	18	3	♇19♏
11	23.14	20	23	15	19	3	♃24♈R
12	23.18	21	5♈	16	20	3	♄ 1♈
13	23.22	22	17	17	21	3	♅22♏R
14	23.26	23	29	18	22	3	Ψ19♏R
15	23.30	24	11♉	18	24	3	♇19♏
16	23.34	25	23	4	25	3	♃24♈R
17	23.38	26	5♊	4D	26	2	♄ 1♈
18	23.41	27	17	4	27	2	♅22♏R
19	23.45	28	0♋	4	29	2	Ψ19♏R
20	23.49	29	13	5	0♉	2	♇19♏
21	23.53	0♈	26	5	1	2	♃24♈
22	23.57	1	10♌	5	2	2	♄ 2♈
23	0.01	2	25	5	3	2	♅22♏R
24	0.05	3	10♍	6	5	2	Ψ19♏R
25	0.09	4	25	6	6	2	♃24♈
26	0.13	5	10♎	6	7	1	♄ 2♈
27	0.17	6	25	7	8	1	♅ 3♈
28	0.21	7	10♏	9	9	1	♄21♏R
29	0.25	8	25	10	11	0	Ψ24♏
30	0.29	9	9♐	11	12	0	♇19♏R
31	0.33	10	23	12	13	0	♃24♈

Apr	STime	☉	☽	☿	♀	♂	Plnts
1	0.37	11♈	6♑	13♓	14♉	29♑	♃24♈
2	0.41	12	19	14	15	29	♄ 3♈
3	0.45	13	2♒	15	17	29	♅21♏R
4	0.48	14	14	16	18	28	Ψ22♏R
5	0.52	15	26	17	19	28	♇18♏
6	0.56	16	8♓	19	20	28	♃25♈
7	1.00	17	20	21	23	27	♄ 4♈
8	1.04	18	2♈	21	23	27	♅21♏R
9	1.08	19	14	23	24	27	Ψ22♏R
10	1.12	20	26	24	26	26	♇18♏
11	1.16	21	8♉	25	26	26	♃25♈
12	1.20	22	20	27	27	26	♄ 5♈
13	1.24	23	2♊	28	29	25	♅21♏R
14	1.28	24	14	0♈	0♊	25	Ψ23♏R
15	1.32	25	26	1	1	25	♇18♏
16	1.36	26	9♋	3	2	24	♃25♈
17	1.40	27	22	4	3	24	♄ 5♈
18	1.44	28	5♌	6	5	23	♅21♏R
19	1.48	29	19	7	6	23	Ψ23♏R
20	1.52	29	3♍	9	8	22	♇18♏
21	1.55	0♉	18	11	9	22	♃26♈
22	1.59	1	3♎	12	9	22	♄ 6♈
23	2.03	2	18	14	11	22	♅21♏R
24	2.07	3	3♏	16	12	21	Ψ23♏R
25	2.11	4	18	18	13	21	♇18♏
26	2.15	5	3♐	19	14	20	♃26♈
27	2.19	6	17	21	15	20	♄ 6♈
28	2.23	7	1♑	23	16	20	Ψ20♏R
29	2.27	8	15	25	17	19	Ψ23♏R
30	2.31	9	28	27	19	19	♇18♏R

May	STime	☉	☽	☿	♀	♂	Plnts
1	2.35	10♉	11♒	11♈	29♊	20♉	19♍	♃27♈
2	2.39	11	23	18	21	18	♄ 7♈
3	2.43	12	5♓	3	22	18	♅20♏R
4	2.47	13	17	5	23	18	Ψ23♏R
5	2.51	14	29	7	24	18	♇18♏
6	2.55	15	11♈	9	25	17	♃27♈
7	2.59	16	23	11	27	17	♄ 7♈
8	3.03	17	5♉	13	28	17	♅20♏R
9	3.06	18	16	15	29	17	Ψ23♏R
10	3.10	19	29	17	0♋	16	♇18♏
11	3.14	20	11♊	20	1	16	♃28♈
12	3.18	21	23	22	3	16	♄ 8♈
13	3.22	22	6♋	24	4	16	♅20♏R
14	3.26	23	19	26	6	16	Ψ23♏R
15	3.30	24	2♌	28	7	15	♇18♏
16	3.34	25	15	0♊	7	15	♃29♈
17	3.38	26	29	3	9	15	♄ 8♈
18	3.42	27	13♍	5	9	15	Ψ23♏R
19	3.46	28	27	8	10	15	♇18♏
20	3.50	29	12♎	9	11	15	♃29♈
21	3.54	29	27	11	13	15	♄ 9♈
22	3.58	0♊	12♏	13	13	15	♅19♏R
23	4.02	1	27	15	15	15	Ψ22♏R
24	4.06	2	11♐	17	16	15D	♇18♏
25	4.10	3	26	19	18	15	♃ 0♉
26	4.13	4	10♑	21	19	15	♄ 9♈
27	4.17	5	23	23	19	15	Ψ22♏R
28	4.21	6	6♒	25	21	15	♇18♏
29	4.25	7	19	26	22	15	♃ 1♉
30	4.29	8	2♓	28	24	15	♄ 0♈
31	4.33	9	14	29	23	15	♃ 1♍

Jun	STime	☉	☽	☿	♀	♂	Plnts
1	4.37	10♊	26♓	1♋	24♋	15♉	♃ 1♍
2	4.41	11	8♈	2	25	15	♄10♈
3	4.45	12	19	4	26	15	♅20♏
4	4.49	13	1♉	5	28	15	♇18♏
5	4.53	14	13	7	29	15	♃ 2♍
6	4.57	15	25	8	29	15	♄10♈
7	5.01	16	7♊	9	1♌	16	♅20♏
8	5.05	17	20	10	2	16	Ψ22♏R
9	5.09	18	3♋	11	4	16	♇18♏
10	5.13	19	16	13	4	16	♃ 3♍
11	5.17	20	29	14	5	16	♄11♈
12	5.21	21	12♌	16	7	17	♅20♏
13	5.24	22	26	16	8	17	Ψ22♏R
14	5.28	22	10♍	17	9	17	♃ 4♍
15	5.32	23	24	17	11	17	♄11♈
16	5.36	24	8♎	18	10	18	♅20♏
17	5.40	25	22	19	11	18	Ψ22♏R
18	5.44	26	7♏	18	12	18	♇18♏
19	5.48	27	21	20	14	18	♃ 5♍
20	5.52	28	6♐	20	14	19	♄11♈
21	5.56	29	21	21	16	19	♅20♏
22	6.00	0♋	4♑	21	18	19	♄11♈
23	6.04	1	18	21	19	19	Ψ22♏R
24	6.08	2	1♒	21	20	20	♃ 6♍
25	6.12	3	14	21	22R	20	♄12♈
26	6.16	4	27	22	22	20	♅20♏
27	6.20	5	10♓	22	24	20	♃12♈
28	6.24	6	22	21	23	21	Ψ22♏R
29	6.28	7	4♈	21	21	21	♇18♏
30	6.31	8	16	21	23	22	♇18♏

Jul	STime	☉	☽	☿	♀	♂	Plnts
1	6.35	9♋	27♈	21♋	24♌	22♉	♃ 7♍
2	6.39	10	9♉	20	24	22	♄12♈
3	6.43	11	21	20	25	23	♅21♏
4	6.47	12	3♊	19	26	23	Ψ22♏R
5	6.51	13	16	19	27	23	♇18♏
6	6.55	13	29	18	28	24	♃ 8♍
7	6.59	14	12♋	18	29	24	♄12♈
8	7.03	16	25	18	1♍	25	♅21♏
9	7.07	16	9♌	18	0♍	25	Ψ21♏R
10	7.11	17	23	16	1	25	♇18♏
11	7.15	18	7♍	15	2	26	♃ 9♍
12	7.19	19	21	14	2	26	♄12♈
13	7.23	20	5♎	14	3	27	♅21♏
14	7.27	21	19	13	4	27	Ψ21♏R
15	7.31	22	3♏	13	5	28	♃10♍
16	7.35	23	17	13	5	28	♄12♈
17	7.39	24	1♐	13	6	29	♅21♏
18	7.42	25	15	12	7	29	Ψ21♏R
19	7.46	26	29	12	7	29	♇18♏
20	7.50	27	13♑	12D	8	0♊	♇18♏
21	7.54	28	26	12	8	0	♃11♍
22	7.58	29	10♒	12	9	1	♄12♈
23	8.02	0♌	23	12	9	1	♅21♏
24	8.06	1	5♓	13	10	2	Ψ21♏R
25	8.10	2	18	13	10	2	♇18♏
26	8.14	3	0♈	14	11	3	♃12♍
27	8.18	3	12	14	11	4	♄12♈
28	8.22	4	23	15	11	4	♅21♏
29	8.26	5	5♉	16	12	5	Ψ21♏R
30	8.30	6	17	17	12	5	♇19♏
31	8.34	7	29	18	12	6	♃13♍

Aug	STime	☉	☽	☿	♀	♂	Plnts
1	8.38	8♌	11♊	19♌	13♍	6♊	♃14♍
2	8.42	9	24	20	13	7	♄12♈R
3	8.46	10	7♋	21	13	7	♅22♏
4	8.49	11	20	23	13	8	Ψ21♏R
5	8.53	13	4♌	24	13	9	♇19♏
6	8.57	13	18	26	14	9	♃15♍
7	9.01	14	2♍	28	14	10	♄12♈R
8	9.05	15	17	29	14R	10	♅22♏
9	9.09	16	1♎	1♍	14	10	Ψ21♏R
10	9.13	17	16	2	14	11	♇19♏
11	9.17	18	0♏	4	13	12	♃16♍
12	9.21	19	14	6	13	12	♄12♈R
13	9.25	20	28	8	13	13	♅22♏
14	9.29	21	12♐	10	13	13	Ψ21♏R
15	9.33	22	26	12	13	14	♇19♏
16	9.37	23	9♑	14	12	15	♃17♍
17	9.41	24	22	16	12	15	♄12♈R
18	9.45	25	6♒	18	11	16	Ψ23♏
19	9.49	26	18	20	11	16	Ψ21♏R
20	9.53	26	1♓	24	10	17	♇18♏
21	9.56	28	14	24	10	18	♃18♍
22	10.00	28	26	26	10	18	♄12♈R
23	10.04	29	8♈	28	9	19	♅21♏
24	10.08	0♍	20	0♎	9	19	Ψ21♏R
25	10.12	1	2♉	2	8	20	♇19♏
26	10.16	2	13	4	8	20	♃19♍
27	10.20	3	25	6	7	21	♄11♈R
28	10.24	4	7♊	8	6	22	♅23♏
29	10.28	5	19	10	6	22	Ψ21♏R
30	10.32	6	2♋	12	5	23	♇20♏
31	10.36	7	15	14	5	24	♃20♌

Sep	STime	☉	☽	☿	♀	♂	Plnts
1	10.40	8♍	29♋	15♍	4♍	24♊	♃20♍
2	10.44	9	12♌	17	3	25	♄11♈R
3	10.48	10	27	19	3	25	♅24♏
4	10.52	11	11♍	21	2	26	Ψ22♏
5	10.56	12	26	23	2	26	♇20♏
6	11.00	13	11♎	24	1	27	♃21♍
7	11.04	14	26	26	1	27	♄11♈R
8	11.07	15	10♏	28	0	29	♅24♏
9	11.11	16	25	29	0	29	Ψ22♏
10	11.15	17	9♐	1♎	29♌	0♋	♇20♏
11	11.19	18	23	3	29	1	♃23♍
12	11.23	19	6♑	4	28	1	♄10♈R
13	11.27	20	19	6	28	2	♅24♏
14	11.31	21	2♒	7	28	3	Ψ22♏
15	11.35	22	15	9	28	3	♇20♏
16	11.39	23	28	10	28	4	♃24♍
17	11.43	24	10♈	11	28	5	♄10♈R
18	11.47	25	22	13	27	5	♅25♏
19	11.51	26	4♉	15	27	27D	Ψ22♏
20	11.55	27	16	17	28	7	♃25♍
21	11.59	28	28	18	27	7	♄10♈R
22	12.03	28	10♊	19	27	8	♅25♏
23	12.07	28	22	21	27	8	Ψ22♏
24	12.11	0♎	3♊	22	27	9	♇20♏
25	12.14	1	16	24	28	10	♃26♍
26	12.18	2	28	25	28	10	♄ 9♈R
27	12.22	3	10♌	26	28	11	♅25♏
28	12.26	4	24	27	29	12	Ψ22♏
29	12.30	5	7♍	29	29	12	♇21♏
30	12.34	6	20	0♏	29	14	♃27♍

Oct	STime	☉	☽	☿	♀	♂	Plnts
1	12.38	7♎	5♏	1♏	0♎	14♋	♃27♍
2	12.42	8	19	3	0	15	♄ 9♈R
3	12.46	9	4♎	4	0	16	♅25♏
4	12.50	10	19	5	1	17	♇21♏
5	12.54	11	5♏	6	1	17	♇21♏
6	12.58	12	20	7	2	18	♃27♍
7	13.02	13	4♐	8	3	19	♄ 8♈R
8	13.06	14	19	9	3	19	♅26♏
9	13.10	15	3♑	10	4	20	Ψ21♏
10	13.14	16	16	11	4	21	♇21♏
11	13.18	17	29	12	5	21	♃28♍
12	13.22	18	12♒	13	5	22	♄ 8♈R
13	13.25	19	25	14	6	23	♅26♏
14	13.29	20	7♓	15	7	23	Ψ21♏
15	13.33	21	20	15	8	24	♃29♍
16	13.37	22	1♈	16	8	25	♃29♍
17	13.41	23	13	16	9	26	♄ 8♈R
18	13.45	25	25	17	10	26	♅26♏
19	13.49	25	7♉	17	10	27	Ψ21♏
20	13.53	26	18	17	11	28	♇21♏
21	13.57	27	0♊	17R	12	29	♃ 0♎
22	14.01	28	12	17	13	29	♄ 7♈R
23	14.05	29	24	16	14	0♌	♅26♏
24	14.09	0♏	7♋	16	15	1	Ψ23♏
25	14.13	1	19	16	15	1	♇22♏
26	14.17	2	3♌	15	16	2	♃ 1♎
27	14.21	2	15	14	17	2	♄ 7♈R
28	14.25	4	29	13	18	2	♅27♏
29	14.29	5	13♍	12	19	4	Ψ23♏
30	14.32	6	28	11	20	5	♇22♏
31	14.36	7	12♎	10	21	6	♃ 2♎

Nov	STime	☉	☽	☿	♀	♂	Plnts
1	14.40	8♏	27♎	8♏	22♎	7♌	♃ 2♎
2	14.44	9	13♏	7	23	7	♄ 7♈R
3	14.48	10	28	6	24	8	♅27♏
4	14.52	11	13♐	5	25	9	♇22♏
5	14.56	12	27	4	26	10	♃ 2♎
6	15.00	13	12♑	3	27	10	♄ 7♈R
7	15.04	14	25	2	28	11	♅27♏
8	15.08	15	9♒	2	29	12	Ψ23♏
9	15.12	16	22	1D	0♏	13	♇23♏
10	15.16	17	4♓	1	1	13	♃ 3♎
11	15.20	18	16	1	2	14	♄ 7♈R
12	15.24	19	28	2	4	15	♅28♏
13	15.28	20	10♈	2	4	16	Ψ24♏
14	15.32	21	22	4	5	16	♇23♏
15	15.36	22	4♉	4	7	18	♃ 4♎
16	15.40	23	15	6	7	18	♄ 6♈R
17	15.43	24	27	7	8	19	♅28♏
18	15.47	26	9♊	9	10	20	Ψ24♏
19	15.51	26	21	7	10	20	♇23♏
20	15.55	27	2♋	10	11	22	♃ 4♎
21	15.59	28	16	11	13	22	♄ 6♈R
22	16.03	29	29	11	13	23	♅28♏
23	16.07	0♐	12♌	13	15	24	Ψ24♏
24	16.11	1	26	14	15	24	♃ 4♎
25	16.15	2	8♍	15	17	25	♄ 6♈R
26	16.19	3	22	16	18	26	♅ 4♏
27	16.23	4	6♎	18	19	27	♄ 5♈R
28	16.27	5	21	19	20	27	Ψ28♏
29	16.31	6	6♏	21	21	29	Ψ24♏
30	16.35	7	21	22	22	29	♇22♏

Dec	STime	☉	☽	☿	♀	♂	Plnts
1	16.39	8♐	6♐	24♏	23♏	29♌	♃ 5♎
2	16.43	9	21	25	24	0♍	♄ 5♈R
3	16.47	10	6♑	27	25	1	♅28♏
4	16.50	11	20	28	26	2	♇22♏
5	16.54	12	4♒	0♐	28	3	♇22♏
6	16.58	13	17	1	29	3	♃ 5♎
7	17.02	14	0♓	3	0♐	4	♄ 5♈R
8	17.06	15	13	4	1	5	♅29♏
9	17.10	16	25	6	2	6	♇22♏
10	17.14	17	7♈	7	3	6	♃ 6♎
11	17.18	18	19	9	4	7	♄ 5♈R
12	17.22	19	0♉	10	6	8	♅29♏
13	17.26	20	12	12	7	8	♃29♍
14	17.30	22	24	13	8	9	Ψ25♏
15	17.34	24	6♊	15	9	10	♇22♏
16	17.38	24	18	15	11	10	♃ 5♎
17	17.42	25	0♋	18	12	11	♄ 5♈
18	17.46	26	13	19	13	12	Ψ25♏
19	17.50	27	26	21	14	13	Ψ25♏
20	17.53	28	9♌	23	16	13	♇22♏
21	17.57	29	23	24	16	15	♃ 6♎
22	18.01	0♑	5♍	26	17	16	♄ 6♈
23	18.05	1	19	28	18	17	♅29♏
24	18.09	2	2♎	29	20	17	Ψ25♏
25	18.13	3	16	1♑	21	18	Ψ23♏
26	18.17	4	0♏	2	22	19	♇22♏
27	18.21	5	15	4	23	20	♃ 6♎
28	18.25	6	29	6	24	21	♄ 6♈
29	18.29	7	14	7	26	21	Ψ25♏
30	18.33	8	29	9	27	22	Ψ23♏
31	18.37	9	14♏	10	28	23	♃ 5♎R

Jan	STime	☉	☽	☿	♀	♂	Plnts
1	18.41	10♑	28♑	12♑	29♏	24♒	♃ 5♍R
2	18.45	11	12♒	14	0♐	24	♄ 6♈
3	18.49	12	25	15	2	25	♅29♍
4	18.53	13	8♓	17	3	26	♆25♏
5	18.57	14	21	18	4	27	♇23♍
6	19.01	15	3♈	20	5	27	♃ 5♍R
7	19.05	16	15	22	6	28	♄ 6♈
8	19.08	17	27	23	8	29	♅29♍R
9	19.12	18	8♉	25	9	0♓	♆26♏
10	19.16	19	20	27	10	1	♇23♍R
11	19.20	20	2♊	28	11	1	♃ 5♍R
12	19.24	21	14	0♒	12	2	♄ 6♈
13	19.28	22	27	2	14	3	♅29♍R
14	19.32	23	9♋	3	15	4	♆26♏
15	19.36	24	22	5	16	4	♇22♍R
16	19.40	25	5♌	7	17	5	♃ 5♍R
17	19.44	26	18	8	18	6	♄ 7♈
18	19.48	27	2♍	10	20	7	♅29♍R
19	19.52	28	16	12	21	8	♆26♏
20	19.56	29	29	13	22	8	♇22♍R
21	20.00	0♒	13♎	15	23	9	♃ 4♍R
22	20.04	1	27	17	25	10	♄ 7♈
23	20.08	2	11♏	18	26	11	♅29♍R
24	20.12	3	25	20	27	11	♆26♏
25	20.15	4	10♐	21	28	12	♇22♍R
26	20.19	5	24	23	29	13	♃ 4♍R
27	20.23	6	8♑	24	1♑	14	♄ 7♈
28	20.27	7	22	25	2	15	♅29♍R
29	20.31	8	6♒	27	3	15	♆26♏
30	20.35	9	20	28	4	16	♇22♍R
31	20.39	10	3♓	29	6	17	♃ 3♍R

Feb	STime	☉	☽	☿	♀	♂	Plnts
1	20.43	11♒	16♓	0♓	7♑	18♓	♃ 3♍R
2	20.47	12	28	0	8	18	♄ 8♈
3	20.51	13	11♈	1	9	19	♅29♍R
4	20.55	14	23	2	10	20	♆26♏
5	20.59	15	4♉	2	12	21	♇22♍R
6	21.03	16	16	2R	13	22	♃ 2♍R
7	21.07	17	28	2	14	22	♄ 8♈
8	21.11	18	10♊	2	15	23	♅28♍R
9	21.15	20	22	1	17	24	♆26♏
10	21.19	21	5♋	1	18	25	♇22♍R
11	21.23	22	17	0	19	25	♃ 2♍R
12	21.26	23	0♌	29♒	20	26	♄ 9♈
13	21.30	24	14	28	21	27	♅28♍R
14	21.34	25	27	27	23	28	♆26♏
15	21.38	26	11♍	26	24	28	♇22♍R
16	21.42	27	25	25	25	29	♃ 1♍R
17	21.46	28	10♎	24	26	0♈	♄ 9♈
18	21.50	29	24	22	28	1	♅28♍R
19	21.54	0♓	8♏	21	29	1	♆26♏
20	21.58	1	22	20	0♒	2	♇22♍R
21	22.02	2	6♐	20	1	3	♃ 0♍R
22	22.06	3	20	19	3	4	♄10♈
23	22.10	4	4♑	18	4	5	♅28♍R
24	22.14	5	18	18	5	5	♆26♏
25	22.18	6	2♒	17	6	6	♇22♍R
26	22.22	7	15	17	7	7	♃ 0♍R
27	22.26	8	28	17	9	8	♄10♈
28	22.30	9	11♓	17D	10	8	♅28♍R
29	22.33	10	24	17	11	9	♆26♏

Mar	STime	☉	☽	☿	♀	♂	Plnts
1	22.37	11♓	6♈	17♒	12♒	10♈	♃29♌R
2	22.41	12	18	17	14	11	♄11♈
3	22.45	13	0♉	18	15	11	♅27♍R
4	22.49	14	12	18	16	12	♆26♏
5	22.53	15	24	19	17	13	♇21♍R
6	22.57	16	6♊	19	19	14	♃29♌R
7	23.01	17	18	20	20	14	♄12♈
8	23.05	18	0♋	21	21	15	♅27♍R
9	23.09	19	12	21	22	16	♆26♏R
10	23.13	20	25	22	23	17	♇21♍R
11	23.17	21	8♌	23	25	17	♃28♌R
12	23.21	22	22	24	26	18	♄12♈
13	23.25	23	6♍	25	27	19	♅27♍R
14	23.29	24	20	26	28	20	♆26♏R
15	23.33	25	4♎	27	0♓	20	♇21♍R
16	23.37	26	19	28	1	21	♃28♌R
17	23.40	27	4♏	0♓	2	22	♄13♈
18	23.44	28	18	1	3	23	♅27♍R
19	23.48	29	3♐	2	5	23	♆26♏R
20	23.52	0♈	17	3	6	24	♇21♍R
21	23.56	1	1♑	5	7	25	♃27♌R
22	0.00	2	15	6	8	26	♄13♈
23	0.04	3	28	7	9	26	♅27♍R
24	0.08	4	12♒	9	11	27	♆26♏R
25	0.12	5	25	10	12	28	♇21♍R
26	0.16	6	8♓	11	13	29	♃27♌R
27	0.20	7	20	13	14	29	♄14♈
28	0.24	8	2♈	14	16	0♉	♅26♍R
29	0.28	9	15	16	17	1	♆26♏R
30	0.32	10	27	17	18	2	♇21♍R
31	0.36	11	9♉	19	19	2	♃26♌R

Apr	STime	☉	☽	☿	♀	♂	Plnts
1	0.40	12♈	21♉	21♓	21♓	3♉	♃26♌R
2	0.44	13	2♊	22	22	4	♄15♈
3	0.48	13	14	24	23	4	♅26♍R
4	0.51	14	26	25	24	5	♆26♏R
5	0.55	15	8♋	27	25	6	♇21♍R
6	0.59	16	20	29	27	7	♃26♌R
7	1.03	17	3♌	0♈	28	7	♄15♈
8	1.07	18	16	2	29	8	♅26♍R
9	1.11	19	0♍	4	0♈	9	♆26♏R
10	1.15	20	14	6	2	10	♇21♍R
11	1.19	21	28	8	3	10	♃26♌R
12	1.23	22	13♎	9	4	11	♄16♈
13	1.27	23	28	11	5	12	♅26♍R
14	1.31	24	13♏	13	7	12	♆26♏R
15	1.35	25	28	15	8	13	♇20♍R
16	1.39	26	12♐	17	9	14	♃26♌R
17	1.43	27	27	19	10	15	♄17♈
18	1.47	28	11♑	21	12	15	♅26♍R
19	1.51	29	25	23	13	16	♆26♏R
20	1.55	0♉	9♒	25	14	17	♇20♍R
21	1.58	1	22	27	15	18	♃26♌
22	2.02	2	5♓	29	16	18	♄17♈
23	2.06	3	17	1♉	18	19	♅25♍R
24	2.10	4	29	4	19	20	♆25♏R
25	2.14	5	12♈	6	20	20	♇20♍R
26	2.18	6	24	8	21	21	♃26♌
27	2.22	7	5♉	10	23	22	♄18♈
28	2.26	8	17	12	24	23	♅25♍R
29	2.30	9	29	14	25	23	♆25♏R
30	2.34	10	11♊	16	26	24	♇20♍R

May	STime	☉	☽	☿	♀	♂	Plnts
1	2.38	11♉	23♊	19♉	27♈	25♉	♃26♌
2	2.42	12	5♋	21	29	25	♄18♈
3	2.46	13	17	23	0♉	26	♅25♍R
4	2.50	14	29	25	1	27	♆25♏R
5	2.54	15	12♌	27	2	28	♇20♍R
6	2.58	16	25	29	4	28	♃26♌
7	3.02	17	8♍	1♊	5	29	♄19♈
8	3.06	18	22	3	6	0♊	♅25♍R
9	3.09	19	6♎	5	7	0	♆25♏R
10	3.13	20	21	6	9	1	♇20♍R
11	3.17	21	6♏	8	10	2	♃26♌
12	3.21	22	21	10	11	2	♄20♈
13	3.25	22	6♐	11	12	3	♅25♍R
14	3.29	23	21	13	13	4	♆25♏R
15	3.33	24	6♑	15	15	5	♇20♍R
16	3.37	25	21	16	16	5	♃26♌
17	3.41	26	5♒	17	17	6	♄20♈
18	3.45	27	18	19	18	7	♅25♍R
19	3.49	28	1♓	20	20	7	♆25♏R
20	3.53	29	14	21	21	8	♇20♍
21	3.57	0♊	27	23	22	9	♃27♌
22	4.01	1	9♈	24	23	9	♄21♈
23	4.05	2	21	25	25	10	♅25♍
24	4.09	3	3♉	26	26	11	♆25♏R
25	4.13	4	14	27	27	11	♇20♍
26	4.16	5	26	27	28	12	♃27♌
27	4.20	6	8♊	28	29	13	♄21♈
28	4.24	7	20	29	1♊	14	♅25♍
29	4.28	8	2♋	29	2	14	♆25♏R
30	4.32	9	14	0♋	3	15	♇20♍
31	4.36	10	26	0	4	16	♃28♌

Jun	STime	☉	☽	☿	♀	♂	Plnts
1	4.40	11♊	9♌	1♋	6♊	16♊	♃28♌
2	4.44	12	21	1	7	17	♄22♈
3	4.48	13	4♍	1	8	18	♅25♍
4	4.52	14	17	2	9	18	♆24♏R
5	4.56	15	1♎	2	10	19	♇20♍
6	5.00	16	15	2R	12	20	♃28♌
7	5.04	16	29	2	13	20	♄22♈
8	5.08	17	14♏	2	14	21	♅25♍
9	5.12	18	29	1	15	22	♆24♏R
10	5.16	19	15♐	1	17	22	♇20♍
11	5.20	20	0♑	1	18	23	♃29♌
12	5.24	21	15	0	19	24	♄23♈
13	5.27	22	29	0	20	24	♅25♍
14	5.31	23	13♒	29♊	22	25	♆24♏R
15	5.35	24	27	29	23	26	♇20♍
16	5.39	25	10♓	28	24	27	♃ 0♍
17	5.43	26	23	28	25	27	♄23♈
18	5.47	27	5♈	27	26	28	♅25♍
19	5.51	28	18	27	28	29	♆24♏R
20	5.55	29	29	26	29	29	♇20♍
21	5.59	0♋	11♉	26	0♋	0♋	♃ 1♍
22	6.03	1	23	25	1	1	♄24♈
23	6.07	2	5♊	25	3	1	♅25♍
24	6.11	3	17	24	4	2	♆24♏R
25	6.15	4	29	24	5	3	♇20♍
26	6.19	5	11♋	24	6	3	♃ 1♍
27	6.23	6	23	23	8	4	♄24♈
28	6.27	7	6♌	23	9	5	♅25♍
29	6.31	7	18	23	10	5	♆24♏R
30	6.34	8	1♍	23D	11	6	♇20♍

Jul	STime	☉	☽	☿	♀	♂	Plnts
1	6.38	9♋	14♍	23♊	12♋	7♋	♃ 2♍
2	6.42	10	27	23	14	7	♄24♈
3	6.46	11	11♎	23	15	8	♅25♍
4	6.50	12	25	24	16	9	♆24♏R
5	6.54	13	9♏	24	17	9	♇20♍
6	6.58	14	24	25	19	10	♃ 3♍
7	7.02	15	8♐	25	20	11	♄24♈
8	7.06	16	23	26	21	11	♅25♍
9	7.10	17	8♑	26	22	12	♆24♏R
10	7.14	18	23	27	24	13	♇20♍
11	7.18	19	7♒	28	25	13	♃ 4♍
12	7.22	20	22	29	26	14	♄25♈
13	7.26	21	5♓	0♋	27	15	♅26♍
14	7.30	22	19	1	28	15	♆24♏R
15	7.34	23	1♈	2	0♌	16	♇20♍
16	7.38	24	14	4	1	17	♃ 5♍
17	7.41	25	26	5	2	17	♄25♈
18	7.45	26	8♉	7	3	18	♅26♍
19	7.49	27	20	8	5	18	♆24♏R
20	7.53	28	2♊	10	6	19	♇21♍
21	7.57	28	13	11	7	20	♃ 6♍
22	8.01	29	25	13	8	20	♄25♈
23	8.05	0♌	8♋	15	10	21	♅26♍
24	8.09	1	20	16	11	22	♆24♏R
25	8.13	2	2♌	18	12	22	♇21♍
26	8.17	3	15	20	13	23	♃ 7♍
27	8.21	4	28	22	14	24	♄25♈
28	8.25	5	11♍	24	16	24	♅26♍
29	8.29	6	24	26	17	25	♆23♏
30	8.33	7	8♎	28	18	26	♇21♍
31	8.37	8	22	0♌	19	26	♃ 8♍

Aug	STime	☉	☽	☿	♀	♂	Plnts
1	8.41	9♌	5♏	2♌	21♌	27♋	♃ 8♍
2	8.45	10	20	4	22	28	♄25♈
3	8.49	11	4♐	6	23	28	♅26♍
4	8.52	12	18	9	24	29	♆23♏
5	8.56	13	3♑	11	26	0♌	♇21♍
6	9.00	14	17	13	27	0	♃ 9♍
7	9.04	15	2♒	15	28	1	♄25♈R
8	9.08	16	16	17	29	2	♅27♍
9	9.12	17	0♓	19	0♍	2	♆23♏
10	9.16	18	13	21	2	3	♇21♍
11	9.20	19	27	23	3	3	♃10♍
12	9.24	20	9♈	25	4	4	♄25♈R
13	9.28	20	22	27	5	5	♅27♍
14	9.32	21	4♉	29	7	5	♆23♏
15	9.36	22	16	1♍	8	6	♇21♍
16	9.40	23	28	2	9	7	♃11♍
17	9.44	24	10♊	4	10	7	♄25♈R
18	9.48	25	22	6	12	8	♅27♍
19	9.52	26	4♋	8	13	9	♆24♏
20	9.56	27	16	10	14	9	♇21♍
21	9.59	28	28	12	15	10	♃12♍
22	10.03	29	11♌	13	16	11	♄25♈R
23	10.07	0♍	24	15	18	11	♅27♍
24	10.11	1	7♍	17	19	12	♆24♏
25	10.15	2	21	18	20	12	♇22♍
26	10.19	3	4♎	20	21	13	♃13♍
27	10.23	4	18	22	23	14	♄25♈R
28	10.27	5	2♏	23	24	14	♅28♍
29	10.31	6	16	25	25	15	♆24♏
30	10.35	7	1♐	26	26	16	♇22♍
31	10.39	8	15	28	28	16	♃14♍

Sep	STime	☉	☽	☿	♀	♂	Plnts
1	10.43	9♍	29♐	29♍	29♍	17♌	♃14♍
2	10.47	10	13♑	1♎	0♎	18	♄25♈R
3	10.51	11	27	2	1	18	♅28♍
4	10.55	12	11♒	4	2	19	♆24♏
5	10.59	13	25	5	4	19	♇22♍
6	11.03	14	8♓	7	5	20	♃16♍
7	11.07	15	22	8	6	21	♄24♈R
8	11.10	16	5♈	9	7	21	♅28♍
9	11.14	17	17	11	9	22	♆24♏
10	11.18	18	0♉	12	10	23	♇22♍
11	11.22	19	12	13	11	23	♃17♍
12	11.26	19	24	15	12	24	♄24♈R
13	11.30	20	6♊	16	14	24	♅29♍
14	11.34	21	18	17	15	25	♆24♏
15	11.38	22	29	18	16	26	♇22♍
16	11.42	23	12♋	19	17	26	♃18♍
17	11.46	24	24	20	18	27	♄24♈R
18	11.50	25	6♌	22	20	28	♅29♍
19	11.54	26	19	23	21	28	♆24♏
20	11.58	27	2♍	24	22	29	♇23♍
21	12.02	28	16	25	23	0♍	♃19♍
22	12.06	29	0♎	25	25	0	♄24♈R
23	12.10	0♎	14	26	26	1	♅29♍
24	12.14	1	28	27	27	1	♆24♏
25	12.17	2	13♏	28	28	2	♇23♍
26	12.21	3	27	29	29	3	♃20♍
27	12.25	4	11♐	29	1♏	3	♄23♈R
28	12.29	5	26	0♏	2	4	♅ 0♎
29	12.33	6	10♑	0	3	5	♆24♏
30	12.37	7	24	0	4	5	♇23♍

Oct	STime	☉	☽	☿	♀	♂	Plnts
1	12.41	8♎	8♒	1♏	6♏	6♍	♃21♍
2	12.45	9	21	1	7	6	♄23♈R
3	12.49	10	4♓	1R	8	7	♅ 0♎
4	12.53	11	18	1	9	8	♆24♏
5	12.57	12	0♈	1	10	8	♇23♍
6	13.01	13	13	0	12	9	♃22♍
7	13.05	14	26	0	13	10	♄22♈R
8	13.09	15	8♉	29♎	14	10	♅ 0♎
9	13.13	16	20	29	15	11	♆25♏
10	13.17	17	2♊	28	17	11	♇23♍
11	13.21	18	14	27	18	12	♃23♍
12	13.24	19	26	26	19	13	♄22♈R
13	13.28	20	7♋	25	20	13	♅ 1♎
14	13.32	21	19	23	22	14	♆25♏
15	13.36	22	2♌	22	23	15	♇23♍
16	13.40	23	14	21	24	15	♃24♍
17	13.44	24	27	20	25	16	♄22♈R
18	13.48	25	10♍	19	26	16	♅ 1♎
19	13.52	26	24	18	28	17	♆25♏
20	13.56	27	8♎	17	29	18	♇24♍
21	14.00	28	22	16	0♐	18	♃25♍
22	14.04	29	7♏	16	1	19	♄21♈R
23	14.08	0♏	22	16	2	19	♅ 1♎
24	14.12	1	7♐	15D	4	20	♆25♏
25	14.16	2	22	15	5	21	♇24♍
26	14.20	3	6♑	16	6	21	♃26♍
27	14.24	4	21	16	7	22	♄21♈R
28	14.28	5	5♒	17	9	23	♅ 1♎
29	14.32	6	18	17	10	23	♆25♏
30	14.35	7	1♓	18	11	24	♇24♍
31	14.39	8	14	19	12	24	♃27♍

Nov	STime	☉	☽	☿	♀	♂	Plnts
1	14.43	9♏	27♓	20♎	13♐	25♍	♃27♍
2	14.47	10	10♈	22	15	26	♄20♈R
3	14.51	11	22	23	16	26	♅ 2♎
4	14.55	12	4♉	24	17	27	♆25♏
5	14.59	13	16	25	18	27	♇24♍
6	15.03	14	28	27	20	28	♃28♍
7	15.07	15	10♊	28	21	29	♄20♈R
8	15.11	16	22	0♏	22	29	♅ 2♎
9	15.15	17	4♋	1	23	0♎	♆26♏
10	15.19	18	16	3	24	0	♇24♍
11	15.23	19	28	4	26	1	♃29♍
12	15.27	20	10♌	6	27	2	♄20♈R
13	15.31	21	22	7	28	2	♅ 2♎
14	15.35	22	5♍	9	29	3	♆26♏
15	15.39	23	18	11	0♑	3	♇24♍
16	15.42	24	2♎	12	2	4	♃ 0♎
17	15.46	25	16	14	3	5	♄19♈R
18	15.50	26	0♏	15	4	5	♅ 3♎
19	15.54	27	15	17	5	6	♆26♏
20	15.58	28	0♐	19	6	7	♇24♍
21	16.02	29	16	20	8	7	♃ 1♎
22	16.06	0♐	1♑	22	9	8	♄19♈R
23	16.10	1	16	23	10	8	♅ 3♎
24	16.14	2	0♒	25	11	9	♆26♏
25	16.18	3	14	26	12	10	♇25♍
26	16.22	4	28	28	14	10	♃ 1♎
27	16.26	5	11♓	0♐	15	11	♄19♈R
28	16.30	6	24	1	16	11	♅ 3♎
29	16.34	7	7♈	3	17	12	♆26♏
30	16.38	8	19	4	18	13	♇25♍

Dec	STime	☉	☽	☿	♀	♂	Plnts
1	16.42	9♐	1♉	6♐	20♑	13♎	♃ 2♎
2	16.46	10	13	8	21	14	♄19♈R
3	16.50	11	25	9	22	14	♅ 3♎
4	16.53	12	7♊	11	23	15	♆27♏
5	16.57	13	19	12	24	15	♇25♍
6	17.01	14	1♋	14	26	16	♃ 3♎
7	17.05	15	13	15	27	17	♄19♈R
8	17.09	16	25	17	28	17	♅ 3♎
9	17.13	17	7♌	19	29	18	♆27♏
10	17.17	18	19	20	0♒	18	♇25♍
11	17.21	19	1♍	22	2	19	♃ 3♎
12	17.25	20	14	23	3	20	♄18♈R
13	17.29	21	27	25	4	20	♅ 3♎
14	17.33	22	10♎	26	5	21	♆27♏
15	17.37	23	24	28	6	21	♇25♍
16	17.41	24	8♏	0♑	7	22	♃ 4♎
17	17.45	25	23	1	9	23	♄18♈
18	17.49	26	8♐	3	10	23	♅ 4♎
19	17.53	27	24	4	11	24	♆27♏
20	17.57	28	9♑	6	12	24	♇25♍
21	18.00	29	24	7	13	25	♃ 4♎
22	18.04	0♑	9♒	9	14	25	♄18♈
23	18.08	1	23	11	16	26	♅ 4♎
24	18.12	2	7♓	12	17	27	♆27♏
25	18.16	3	21	14	18	27	♇25♍
26	18.20	4	3♈	15	19	28	♃ 5♎
27	18.24	6	16	17	20	28	♄18♈
28	18.28	7	28	19	21	29	♅ 4♎
29	18.32	8	10♉	20	22	29	♆27♏
30	18.36	9	22	22	24	0♏	♇25♍
31	18.40	10	4♊	23	25	1	♃ 5♎

1 9 6 9

Jan	STime	☉	☽	☿	♀	♂	Plnts
1	18.44	11♑	16♊	25♑	26♒	1♏	♃ 5♎
2	18.48	12	28	27	27	2	♄19♈
3	18.52	13	10♋	28	28	2	♅ 4♎
4	18.56	14	22	0♒	29	3	♆28♏
5	19.00	15	4♌	1	0♓	3	♇25♍
6	19.04	16	16	3	2	4	♃ 5♎
7	19.08	17	28	4	3	5	♄19♈
8	19.11	18	11♍	6	4	5	♅ 4♎
9	19.15	19	23	7	5	6	♆28♏
10	19.19	20	6♎	8	6	6	♇25♍R
11	19.23	21	20	9	7	7	♃ 6♎
12	19.27	22	3♏	11	8	7	♄19♈
13	19.31	23	18	12	9	8	♅ 4♎R
14	19.35	24	2♐	13	10	8	♆28♏
15	19.39	25	17	14	11	9	♇25♍R
16	19.43	26	2♑	14	13	10	♃ 6♎
17	19.47	27	17	15	14	10	♄19♈
18	19.51	28	2♒	15	15	11	♅ 4♎R
19	19.55	29	17	16	16	11	♆28♏
20	19.59	0♒	1♓	16R	17	12	♇25♍R
21	20.03	1	15	16	18	12	♃ 6♎
22	20.07	2	29	15	19	13	♄19♈
23	20.11	3	12♈	15	20	13	♅ 4♎R
24	20.15	4	24	14	21	14	♆28♏
25	20.18	5	7♉	13	22	14	♇25♍R
26	20.22	6	19	12	23	15	♃ 6♎R
27	20.26	7	1♊	11	24	15	♄20♈
28	20.30	8	13	10	25	16	♅ 4♎R
29	20.34	9	24	9	26	17	♆28♏
30	20.38	10	6♋	8	27	17	♇25♍R
31	20.42	11	18	6	28	18	♃ 6♎R

Feb	STime	☉	☽	☿	♀	♂	Plnts
1	20.46	12♒	1♌	5♒	29♓	18♏	♃ 6♎R
2	20.50	13	13	4	0♈	19	♄20♈
3	20.54	14	25	3	1	19	♅ 3♎R
4	20.58	15	8♍	2	2	20	♆28♏
5	21.02	16	21	2	3	20	♇24♍R
6	21.06	17	4♎	1	4	21	♃ 5♎R
7	21.10	18	17	0	5	21	♄20♈
8	21.14	19	0♏	0	6	22	♅ 3♎R
9	21.18	20	14	0	7	22	♆28♏
10	21.22	21	28	0D	7	23	♇24♍R
11	21.25	22	12♐	0	8	23	♃ 5♎R
12	21.29	23	26	0	9	24	♄21♈
13	21.33	24	11♑	0	10	24	♅ 3♎R
14	21.37	25	26	1	11	25	♆28♏
15	21.41	26	10♒	1	12	25	♇24♍R
16	21.45	27	25	2	12	26	♃ 5♎R
17	21.49	28	9♓	3	13	26	♄21♈
18	21.53	29	23	3	14	27	♅ 3♎R
19	21.57	0♓	6♈	4	15	27	♆28♏
20	22.01	1	20	5	16	28	♇24♍R
21	22.05	2	2♉	6	16	28	♃ 4♎R
22	22.09	3	15	7	17	28	♄22♈
23	22.13	4	27	8	18	29	♅ 3♎R
24	22.17	5	9♊	9	18	29	♆28♏
25	22.21	6	21	10	19	0♐	♇24♍R
26	22.25	7	3♋	11	20	0	♃ 4♎R
27	22.29	8	15	12	20	1	♄22♈
28	22.33	9	27	13	21	1	♅ 3♎R

Mar	STime	☉	☽	☿	♀	♂	Plnts
1	22.36	10♓	9♌	14♒	21♈	2♐	♃ 3♎R
2	22.40	11	21	16	22	2	♄23♈
3	22.44	12	4♍	17	22	2	♅ 2♎R
4	22.48	13	17	18	23	3	♆28♏R
5	22.52	14	0♎	20	23	3	♇24♍R
6	22.56	15	13	21	24	4	♃ 3♎R
7	23.00	16	27	22	24	4	♄23♈
8	23.04	17	11♏	24	25	5	♅ 2♎R
9	23.08	18	25	25	25	5	♆28♏R
10	23.12	19	9♐	27	25	5	♇24♍R
11	23.16	20	23	28	26	6	♃ 2♎R
12	23.20	21	7♑	29	26	6	♄24♈
13	23.24	22	21	1♓	26	7	♅ 2♎R
14	23.28	23	5♒	3	26	7	♆28♏R
15	23.32	24	20	4	26	7	♇23♍R
16	23.36	25	4♓	6	26	8	♃ 2♎R
17	23.40	26	18	7	27	8	♄24♈
18	23.43	27	1♈	9	27R	8	♅ 2♎R
19	23.47	28	14	10	27	9	♆28♏R
20	23.51	29	27	12	26	9	♇23♍R
21	23.55	0♈	10♉	14	26	9	♃ 1♎R
22	23.59	1	22	16	26	10	♄25♈
23	0.03	2	5♊	17	26	10	♅ 2♎R
24	0.07	3	17	19	26	10	♆28♏R
25	0.11	4	29	21	26	11	♇23♍R
26	0.15	5	10♋	23	25	11	♃ 0♎R
27	0.19	6	22	24	25	11	♄25♈
28	0.23	7	4♌	26	24	12	♅ 1♎R
29	0.27	8	17	28	24	12	♆28♏R
30	0.31	9	29	0♈	24	12	♇23♍R
31	0.35	10	12♍	2	23	13	♃ 0♎R

Apr	STime	☉	☽	☿	♀	♂	Plnts
1	0.39	11♈	25♍	4♈	23♈	13♐	♃ 0♎R
2	0.43	12	9♎	6	22	13	♄26♈
3	0.47	13	23	8	21	13	♅ 1♎R
4	0.51	14	7♏	10	21	14	♆28♏R
5	0.54	15	21	12	20	14	♇23♍R
6	0.58	16	5♐	14	20	14	♃29♍R
7	1.02	17	19	16	19	14	♄27♈
8	1.06	18	4♑	18	18	14	♅ 1♎R
9	1.10	19	18	20	18	15	♆28♏R
10	1.14	20	2♒	22	17	15	♇23♍R
11	1.18	21	16	24	17	15	♃28♍R
12	1.22	22	0♓	26	16	15	♄27♈
13	1.26	23	13	28	15	15	♅ 1♎R
14	1.30	24	27	0♉	15	15	♆28♏R
15	1.34	25	10♈	2	14	16	♇23♍R
16	1.38	26	23	4	14	16	♃28♍R
17	1.42	27	6♉	6	13	16	♄28♈
18	1.46	28	18	9	13	16	♅ 1♎R
19	1.50	29	0♊	11	12	16	♆28♏R
20	1.54	0♉	13	13	12	16	♇23♍R
21	1.58	1	25	14	12	16	♃27♍R
22	2.01	2	7♋	16	11	16	♄29♈
23	2.05	3	18	18	11	16	♅ 0♎R
24	2.09	4	0♌	20	11	16	♆28♏R
25	2.13	5	12	22	11	16	♇22♍R
26	2.17	6	25	23	10	16	♃27♍R
27	2.21	7	7♍	25	10	16	♄29♈
28	2.25	8	20	27	10	16R	♅ 0♎R
29	2.29	9	3♎	28	10D	16	♆28♏R
30	2.33	10	17	0♊	10	16	♇22♍R

May	STime	☉	☽	☿	♀	♂	Plnts
1	2.37	11♉	1♏	1♊	10♈	16♐	♃27♍R
2	2.41	12	15	2	10	16	♄ 0♉
3	2.45	13	0♐	3	10	16	♅ 0♎R
4	2.49	14	15	4	11	16	♆27♏R
5	2.53	15	0♑	5	11	16	♇22♍R
6	2.57	15	14	6	11	16	♃26♍R
7	3.01	16	29	7	11	16	♄ 1♉
8	3.05	17	13♒	8	12	16	♅ 0♎R
9	3.08	18	27	9	12	16	♆27♏R
10	3.12	19	10♓	10	12	15	♇22♍R
11	3.16	20	24	10	13	15	♃26♍R
12	3.20	21	7♈	11	13	15	♄ 1♉
13	3.24	22	19	11	14	15	♅ 0♎R
14	3.28	23	2♉	11	14	15	♆27♏R
15	3.32	24	14	12	14	14	♇22♍R
16	3.36	25	27	12	15	14	♃26♍R
17	3.40	26	9♊	12R	16	14	♄ 2♉
18	3.44	27	21	12	16	14	♅ 0♎R
19	3.48	28	3♋	12	17	13	♆27♏R
20	3.52	29	15	11	17	13	♇22♍R
21	3.56	0♊	27	11	18	13	♃26♍R
22	4.00	1	9♌	11	19	13	♄ 2♉
23	4.04	2	21	11	19	12	♅ 0♎R
24	4.08	3	3♍	10	20	12	♆27♏R
25	4.12	4	15	10	21	12	♇22♍
26	4.16	5	28	9	21	11	♃26♍
27	4.19	6	11♎	9	22	11	♄ 3♉
28	4.23	7	25	8	23	11	♅ 0♎R
29	4.27	8	9♏	8	24	10	♆27♏R
30	4.31	9	24	7	24	10	♇22♍
31	4.35	10	9♐	6	25	10	♃26♍

Jun	STime	☉	☽	☿	♀	♂	Plnts
1	4.39	11♊	24♐	6♊	26♈	9♐	♃26♍
2	4.43	11	9♑	5	27	9	♄ 4♉
3	4.47	12	24	5	28	9	♅ 0♎
4	4.51	13	9♒	4	28	8	♆27♏R
5	4.55	14	23	4	29	8	♇22♍
6	4.59	15	7♓	4	0♉	8	♃26♍
7	5.03	16	21	3	1	7	♄ 4♉
8	5.07	17	4♈	3	2	7	♅ 0♎
9	5.11	18	17	3	3	7	♆26♏R
10	5.15	19	29	3D	4	6	♇22♍
11	5.19	20	11♉	3	4	6	♃26♍
12	5.23	21	24	3	5	6	♄ 5♉
13	5.26	22	6♊	3	6	5	♅ 0♎
14	5.30	23	18	4	7	5	♆26♏R
15	5.34	24	0♋	4	8	5	♇22♍
16	5.38	25	12	4	9	5	♃27♍
17	5.42	26	24	5	10	4	♄ 5♉
18	5.46	27	5♌	5	11	4	♅ 0♎
19	5.50	28	17	6	12	4	♆26♏R
20	5.54	29	29	7	13	4	♇22♍
21	5.58	0♋	11♍	8	14	3	♃27♍
22	6.02	1	24	8	15	3	♄ 6♉
23	6.06	2	7♎	9	16	3	♅ 0♎
24	6.10	2	20	10	17	3	♆26♏R
25	6.14	3	3♏	11	18	3	♇22♍
26	6.18	4	18	12	19	2	♃27♍
27	6.22	5	2♐	14	20	2	♄ 6♉
28	6.26	6	17	15	21	2	♅ 0♎
29	6.30	7	2♑	16	22	2	♆26♏R
30	6.34	8	18	17	23	2	♇22♍

Jul	STime	☉	☽	☿	♀	♂	Plnts
1	6.37	9♋	3♒	19♊	24♉	2♐	♃28♍
2	6.41	10	18	20	25	2	♄ 7♉
3	6.45	11	2♓	22	26	2	♅ 0♎
4	6.49	12	16	23	27	2	♆26♏R
5	6.53	13	0♈	25	28	1	♇22♍
6	6.57	14	13	27	29	1	♃29♍
7	7.01	15	26	29	0♊	1	♄ 7♉
8	7.05	16	9♉	0♋	1	1D	♅ 0♎
9	7.09	17	21	2	2	1	♆26♏R
10	7.13	18	3♊	4	4	1	♇22♍
11	7.17	19	15	6	5	1	♃29♍
12	7.21	20	27	8	6	2	♄ 7♉
13	7.25	21	9♋	10	7	2	♅ 0♎
14	7.29	22	21	12	8	2	♆26♏R
15	7.33	23	2♌	14	9	2	♇23♍
16	7.37	23	14	16	10	2	♃ 0♎
17	7.41	24	26	18	11	2	♄ 8♉
18	7.44	25	8♍	21	12	2	♅ 0♎
19	7.48	26	21	23	13	2	♆26♏R
20	7.52	27	3♎	25	14	2	♇23♍
21	7.56	28	16	27	15	3	♃ 1♎
22	8.00	29	29	29	17	3	♄ 8♉
23	8.04	0♌	13♏	1♌	18	3	♅ 0♎
24	8.08	1	27	3	19	3	♆26♏
25	8.12	2	11♐	5	20	3	♇23♍
26	8.16	3	26	7	21	4	♃ 1♎
27	8.20	4	11♑	9	22	4	♄ 8♉
28	8.24	5	26	11	23	4	♅ 1♎
29	8.28	6	11♒	13	24	4	♆26♏
30	8.32	7	26	15	26	5	♇23♍
31	8.36	8	11♓	17	27	5	♃ 2♎

Aug	STime	☉	☽	☿	♀	♂	Plnts
1	8.40	9♌	25♓	19♌	28♊	5♐	♃ 2♎
2	8.44	10	9♈	21	29	6	♄ 8♉
3	8.48	11	22	23	0♋	6	♅ 1♎
4	8.52	12	5♉	25	1	6	♆26♏
5	8.55	13	18	27	2	6	♇23♍
6	8.59	14	0♊	29	3	7	♃ 3♎
7	9.03	15	12	0♍	5	7	♄ 8♉
8	9.07	15	24	2	6	8	♅ 1♎
9	9.11	16	6♋	4	7	8	♆26♏
10	9.15	17	18	5	8	8	♇23♍
11	9.19	18	29	7	9	9	♃ 4♎
12	9.23	19	11♌	9	10	9	♄ 9♉
13	9.27	20	23	10	11	9	♅ 1♎
14	9.31	21	6♍	12	13	10	♆26♏
15	9.35	22	18	13	14	10	♇23♍
16	9.39	23	0♎	15	15	11	♃ 5♎
17	9.43	24	13	16	16	11	♄ 9♉
18	9.47	25	26	18	17	12	♅ 2♎
19	9.51	26	9♏	19	18	12	♆26♏
20	9.55	27	23	21	20	12	♇24♍
21	9.59	28	7♐	22	21	13	♃ 6♎
22	10.02	29	21	24	22	13	♄ 9♉
23	10.06	0♍	5♑	25	23	14	♅ 2♎
24	10.10	1	20	26	24	14	♆26♏
25	10.14	2	5♒	27	25	15	♇24♍
26	10.18	3	20	29	27	15	♃ 7♎
27	10.22	4	5♓	0♎	28	16	♄ 9♉R
28	10.26	5	19	1	29	16	♅ 2♎
29	10.30	6	3♈	2	0♌	17	♆26♏
30	10.34	7	17	3	1	17	♇24♍
31	10.38	8	0♉	5	3	18	♃ 8♎

Sep	STime	☉	☽	☿	♀	♂	Plnts
1	10.42	9♍	13♉	6♎	4♌	18♐	♃ 8♎
2	10.46	10	26	7	5	19	♄ 9♉R
3	10.50	11	8♊	8	6	19	♅ 3♎
4	10.54	11	20	8	7	20	♆26♏
5	10.58	12	2♋	9	8	21	♇24♍
6	11.02	13	14	10	10	21	♃ 9♎
7	11.06	14	26	11	11	22	♄ 8♉R
8	11.09	15	8♌	12	12	22	♅ 3♎
9	11.13	16	20	12	13	23	♆26♏
10	11.17	17	2♍	13	14	23	♇24♍
11	11.21	18	14	13	16	24	♃10♎
12	11.25	19	27	14	17	24	♄ 8♉R
13	11.29	20	10♎	14	18	25	♅ 3♎
14	11.33	21	23	14	19	26	♆26♏
15	11.37	22	6♏	15	20	26	♇25♍
16	11.41	23	20	15R	22	27	♃11♎
17	11.45	24	3♐	15	23	27	♄ 8♉R
18	11.49	25	17	14	24	28	♅ 4♎
19	11.53	26	1♑	14	25	29	♆26♏
20	11.57	27	16	14	26	29	♇25♍
21	12.01	28	0♒	13	28	0♑	♃12♎
22	12.05	29	14	13	29	0	♄ 8♉R
23	12.09	0♎	29	12	0♍	1	♅ 4♎
24	12.13	1	13♓	11	1	2	♆26♏
25	12.17	2	27	10	3	2	♇25♍
26	12.20	3	11♈	9	4	3	♃13♎
27	12.24	4	25	8	5	4	♄ 7♉R
28	12.28	5	8♉	7	6	4	♅ 4♎
29	12.32	6	21	6	7	5	♆26♏
30	12.36	7	4♊	5	9	6	♇25♍

Oct	STime	☉	☽	☿	♀	♂	Plnts
1	12.40	8♎	16♊	3♎	10♍	6♑	♃14♎
2	12.44	9	28	3	11	7	♄ 7♉R
3	12.48	10	10♋	2	12	7	♅ 4♎
4	12.52	11	22	1	14	8	♆27♏
5	12.56	12	4♌	0	15	9	♇25♍
6	13.00	13	16	0	16	9	♃15♎
7	13.04	14	28	0	17	10	♄ 7♉R
8	13.08	15	10♍	0D	18	11	♅ 5♎
9	13.12	16	23	0	20	11	♆27♏
10	13.16	17	6♎	0	21	12	♇25♍
11	13.20	18	19	0	22	13	♃16♎
12	13.24	19	2♏	1	23	13	♄ 6♉R
13	13.27	20	16	2	25	14	♅ 5♎
14	13.31	21	0♐	3	26	15	♆27♏
15	13.35	22	14	4	27	15	♇26♍
16	13.39	23	28	5	28	16	♃18♎
17	13.43	24	12♑	6	0♎	17	♄ 6♉R
18	13.47	25	27	7	1	18	♅ 5♎
19	13.51	26	11♒	9	2	18	♆27♏
20	13.55	27	25	10	3	19	♇26♍
21	13.59	28	9♓	12	5	20	♃19♎
22	14.03	29	23	13	6	20	♄ 6♉R
23	14.07	0♏	6♈	15	7	21	♅ 6♎
24	14.11	1	20	16	8	22	♆27♏
25	14.15	2	3♉	18	10	22	♇26♍
26	14.19	3	16	19	11	23	♃20♎
27	14.23	4	29	21	12	24	♄ 5♉R
28	14.27	5	12♊	23	13	25	♅ 6♎
29	14.31	6	24	24	14	25	♆27♏
30	14.35	7	6♋	26	16	26	♇26♍
31	14.38	8	18	28	17	27	♃21♎

Nov	STime	☉	☽	☿	♀	♂	Plnts
1	14.42	9♏	0♌	29♎	18♎	27♑	♃21♎
2	14.46	10	12	1♏	19	28	♄ 5♉R
3	14.50	11	24	3	21	29	♅ 6♎
4	14.54	12	6♍	4	22	29	♆28♏
5	14.58	13	18	6	23	0♒	♇26♍
6	15.02	14	1♎	8	24	1	♃22♎
7	15.06	15	14	9	26	2	♄ 4♉R
8	15.10	16	27	11	27	2	♅ 7♎
9	15.14	17	11♏	13	28	3	♆28♏
10	15.18	18	25	14	29	4	♇26♍
11	15.22	19	10♐	16	1♏	5	♃23♎
12	15.26	20	24	17	2	5	♄ 4♉R
13	15.30	21	9♑	19	3	6	♅ 7♎
14	15.34	22	23	21	4	7	♆28♏
15	15.38	23	7♒	22	6	7	♇27♍
16	15.42	24	22	24	7	8	♃24♎
17	15.45	25	6♓	25	8	9	♄ 4♉R
18	15.49	26	19	27	9	10	♅ 7♎
19	15.53	27	3♈	29	11	10	♆28♏
20	15.57	28	16	0♐	12	11	♇27♍
21	16.01	29	29	2	13	12	♃25♎
22	16.05	0♐	12♉	3	14	13	♄ 3♉R
23	16.09	1	25	5	16	13	♅ 7♎
24	16.13	2	8♊	6	17	14	♆28♏
25	16.17	3	20	8	18	15	♇27♍
26	16.21	4	2♋	9	20	16	♃26♎
27	16.25	5	14	11	21	16	♄ 3♉R
28	16.29	6	26	13	22	17	♅ 8♎
29	16.33	7	8♌	14	23	18	♆28♏
30	16.37	8	20	16	25	18	♇27♍

Dec	STime	☉	☽	☿	♀	♂	Plnts
1	16.41	9♐	2♍	17♐	26♏	19♒	♃27♎
2	16.45	10	14	19	27	20	♄ 3♉R
3	16.49	11	26	20	28	21	♅ 8♎
4	16.53	12	9♎	22	0♐	21	♆29♏
5	16.56	13	22	23	1	22	♇27♍
6	17.00	14	5♏	25	2	23	♃28♎
7	17.04	15	19	27	3	24	♄ 2♉R
8	17.08	16	4♐	28	5	24	♅ 8♎
9	17.12	17	18	0♑	6	25	♆29♏
10	17.16	18	3♑	1	7	26	♇27♍
11	17.20	19	18	3	8	27	♃29♎
12	17.24	20	3♒	4	10	27	♄ 2♉R
13	17.28	21	18	6	11	28	♅ 8♎
14	17.32	22	2♓	7	12	29	♆29♏
15	17.36	23	16	9	13	0♓	♇27♍
16	17.40	24	0♈	10	15	0	♃ 0♏
17	17.44	25	13	12	16	1	♄ 2♉R
18	17.48	26	26	13	17	2	♅ 8♎
19	17.52	27	9♉	15	18	3	♆29♏
20	17.56	28	22	16	20	3	♇27♍
21	18.00	29	4♊	17	21	4	♃ 0♏
22	18.03	0♑	16	19	22	5	♄ 2♉R
23	18.07	1	29	20	23	6	♅ 8♎
24	18.11	2	11♋	21	25	6	♆29♏
25	18.15	3	23	23	26	7	♇27♍
26	18.19	4	4♌	24	27	8	♃ 1♏
27	18.23	5	16	25	28	9	♄ 2♉R
28	18.27	6	28	26	0♑	9	♅ 8♎
29	18.31	7	10♍	27	1	10	♆ 0♐
30	18.35	8	22	28	2	11	♇27♍
31	18.39	9	4♎	28	4	12	♃ 2♏

Jan	STime	☉	☽	☿	♀	♂	Plnts
1	18.43	10♑	17♎	29♑	5♑	12♓	♃ 2♏
2	18.47	11	0♏	29	6	13	♄ 2♉
3	18.51	12	13	0♒	7	14	♅ 8♎
4	18.55	13	27	0R	9	15	♆ 0♐
5	18.59	14	11♐	0	10	15	♇27♍R
6	19.03	15	26	29♑	11	16	♃ 3♏
7	19.07	16	11♑	29	12	17	♄ 2♉
8	19.10	17	27	28	14	18	♅ 8♎
9	19.14	19	12♒	27	15	18	♆ 0♐
10	19.18	20	27	26	16	19	♇27♍
11	19.22	21	12♓	25	17	20	♃ 3♏
12	19.26	22	26	24	19	21	♄ 2♉
13	19.30	23	10♈	22	20	21	♅ 8♎
14	19.34	24	23	21	21	22	♆ 0♐
15	19.38	25	6♉	20	22	23	♇27♍R
16	19.42	26	19	18	24	23	♃ 4♏
17	19.46	27	1♊	17	25	24	♄ 2♉
18	19.50	28	13	16	26	25	♅ 8♎R
19	19.54	29	26	16	27	26	♆ 0♐
20	19.58	0♒	8♋	15	29	26	♇27♍R
21	20.02	1	19	14	0♒	27	♃ 4♏
22	20.06	2	1♌	14	1	28	♄ 2♉
23	20.10	3	13	14	2	29	♅ 8♎R
24	20.14	4	25	14D	4	29	♆ 0♐
25	20.18	5	7♍	14	5	0♈	♇27♍R
26	20.21	6	19	14	6	1	♃ 5♏
27	20.25	7	1♎	14	7	2	♄ 2♉
28	20.29	8	13	14	9	2	♅ 8♎R
29	20.33	9	26	15	10	3	♆ 0♐
30	20.37	10	9♏	16	11	4	♇27♍R
31	20.41	11	22	16	12	5	♃ 5♏

Feb	STime	☉	☽	☿	♀	♂	Plnts
1	20.45	12♒	6♐	17♑	14♒	5♈	♃ 5♏
2	20.49	13	20	18	15	6	♄ 3♉
3	20.53	14	4♑	19	16	7	♅ 8♎R
4	20.57	15	19	19	18	8	♆ 0♐
5	21.01	16	5♒	20	19	8	♇27♍R
6	21.05	17	20	21	20	9	♃ 5♏
7	21.09	18	5♓	23	21	10	♄ 3♉
8	21.13	19	20	24	23	10	♅ 8♎R
9	21.17	20	4♈	25	24	11	♆ 0♐
10	21.21	21	18	26	25	12	♇27♍R
11	21.25	22	2♉	27	26	13	♃ 6♏
12	21.28	23	15	28	28	13	♄ 3♉
13	21.32	24	28	0♒	29	14	♅ 8♎R
14	21.36	25	10♊	1	0♓	15	♆ 1♐
15	21.40	26	23	2	1	16	♇27♍R
16	21.44	27	5♋	4	3	16	♃ 6♏
17	21.48	28	16	5	4	17	♄ 4♉
18	21.52	29	28	6	5	18	♅ 8♎R
19	21.56	0♓	10♌	8	6	18	♆ 1♐
20	22.00	1	22	9	8	19	♇26♍R
21	22.04	2	4♍	11	9	20	♃ 6♏R
22	22.08	3	16	12	10	21	♄ 4♉
23	22.12	4	28	13	11	21	♅ 8♎R
24	22.16	5	10♎	15	13	22	♆ 1♐
25	22.20	6	23	16	14	23	♇26♍R
26	22.24	7	5♏	18	15	24	♃ 6♏R
27	22.28	8	18	20	16	24	♄ 4♉
28	22.32	9	2♐	21	18	25	♅ 8♎R

Mar	STime	☉	☽	☿	♀	♂	Plnts
1	22.36	10♓	15♐	23♒	19♓	26♈	♃ 6♏R
2	22.39	11	29	24	20	26	♄ 5♉
3	22.43	12	13♑	26	21	27	♅ 7♎R
4	22.47	13	28	27	23	28	♆ 1♐
5	22.51	14	13♒	29	24	29	♇26♍R
6	22.55	15	28	1♓	25	29	♃ 5♏R
7	22.59	16	13♓	2	26	0♉	♄ 5♉
8	23.03	17	28	4	28	1	♅ 7♎R
9	23.07	18	12♈	6	29	1	♆ 1♐
10	23.11	19	26	8	0♈	2	♇26♍R
11	23.15	20	10♉	9	1	3	♃ 5♏R
12	23.19	21	23	11	3	4	♄ 6♉
13	23.23	22	6♊	13	4	4	♅ 7♎R
14	23.27	23	19	15	5	5	♆ 1♐R
15	23.31	24	1♋	17	6	6	♇26♍R
16	23.35	25	13	18	8	6	♃ 5♏R
17	23.39	26	25	20	9	7	♄ 6♉
18	23.43	27	7♌	22	10	8	♅ 7♎R
19	23.46	28	19	24	11	9	♆ 1♐R
20	23.50	29	0♍	26	12	9	♇26♍R
21	23.54	0♈	12	28	14	10	♃ 4♏R
22	23.58	1	25	0♈	15	11	♄ 7♉
23	0.02	2	7♎	2	16	11	♅ 7♎R
24	0.06	3	20	4	17	12	♆ 0♐R
25	0.10	4	2♏	6	19	13	♇26♍R
26	0.14	5	15	8	20	13	♃ 4♏R
27	0.18	6	29	10	21	14	♄ 7♉
28	0.22	7	12♐	12	22	15	♅ 6♎R
29	0.26	8	26	14	24	16	♆ 0♐R
30	0.30	9	10♑	16	25	16	♇25♍R
31	0.34	10	24	18	26	17	♃ 3♏R

Apr	STime	☉	☽	☿	♀	♂	Plnts
1	0.38	11♈	8♒	20♈	27♈	18♉	♃ 3♏R
2	0.42	12	22	22	29	18	♄ 8♉
3	0.46	13	7♓	24	0♉	19	♅ 6♎R
4	0.50	14	22	26	1	20	♆ 0♐R
5	0.53	15	6♈	28	2	20	♇25♍R
6	0.57	16	20	0♉	3	21	♃ 3♏R
7	1.01	17	4♉	2	5	22	♄ 9♉
8	1.05	18	18	4	6	23	♅ 6♎R
9	1.09	19	1♊	5	7	23	♆ 0♐R
10	1.13	20	14	7	8	24	♇25♍R
11	1.17	21	27	9	10	25	♃ 2♏R
12	1.21	22	9♋	10	11	25	♄ 9♉
13	1.25	23	21	12	12	26	♅ 6♎R
14	1.29	24	3♌	13	13	27	♆ 0♐R
15	1.33	25	15	14	15	27	♇25♍R
16	1.37	26	27	15	16	28	♃ 1♏R
17	1.41	27	9♍	16	17	29	♄10♉
18	1.45	28	21	17	18	29	♅ 6♎R
19	1.49	29	3♎	18	19	0♊	♆ 0♐R
20	1.53	0♉	16	19	21	1	♇25♍R
21	1.57	1	28	20	22	2	♃ 1♏R
22	2.01	2	12♏	21	23	2	♄10♉
23	2.04	3	25	21	24	3	♅ 5♎R
24	2.08	4	9♐	21	26	4	♆ 0♐R
25	2.12	5	23	22	27	4	♇25♍R
26	2.16	6	6♑	22	28	5	♃ 0♏R
27	2.20	7	20	22	29	6	♄11♉
28	2.24	7	5♒	22R	0♊	6	♅ 5♎R
29	2.28	8	19	22	2	7	♆ 0♐R
30	2.32	9	3♓	22	3	8	♇25♍R

May	STime	☉	☽	☿	♀	♂	Plnts
1	2.36	10♉	17♓	22♉	4♊	8♊	♃ 0♏R
2	2.40	11	1♈	21	5	9	♄12♉
3	2.44	12	15	21	7	10	♅ 5♎R
4	2.48	13	29	21	8	10	♆ 0♐R
5	2.52	14	13♉	20	9	11	♇25♍R
6	2.56	15	26	20	10	12	♃29♎R
7	3.00	16	9♊	19	11	12	♄12♉
8	3.04	17	22	19	13	13	♅ 5♎R
9	3.08	18	5♋	18	14	14	♆ 0♐R
10	3.11	19	17	17	15	14	♇25♍R
11	3.15	20	29	17	16	15	♃28♎R
12	3.19	21	11♌	16	18	16	♄13♉
13	3.23	22	23	16	19	17	♅ 5♎R
14	3.27	23	5♍	15	20	17	♆29♏R
15	3.31	24	17	15	21	18	♇24♍R
16	3.35	25	29	14	22	19	♃28♎R
17	3.39	26	11♎	14	24	19	♄14♉
18	3.43	27	24	13	25	20	♅ 5♎R
19	3.47	28	7♏	13	26	21	♆29♏R
20	3.51	29	20	13	27	21	♇24♍R
21	3.55	0♊	4♐	13	28	22	♃27♎R
22	3.59	1	18	13D	0♋	23	♄14♉
23	4.03	2	3♑	13	1	23	♅ 5♎R
24	4.07	3	17	13	2	24	♆29♏R
25	4.11	4	1♒	13	3	25	♇24♍
26	4.15	5	16	14	4	25	♃27♎R
27	4.19	5	0♓	14	6	26	♄15♉
28	4.22	6	14	14	7	27	♅ 4♎R
29	4.26	7	28	15	8	27	♆29♏R
30	4.30	8	11♈	15	9	28	♇24♍
31	4.34	9	25	16	10	29	♃27♎R

Jun	STime	☉	☽	☿	♀	♂	Plnts
1	4.38	10♊	9♉	17♉	12♋	29♊	♃26♎R
2	4.42	11	22	17	13	0♋	♄16♉
3	4.46	12	5♊	18	14	1	♅ 4♎R
4	4.50	13	18	19	15	1	♆29♏R
5	4.54	14	1♋	20	16	2	♇24♍
6	4.58	15	13	21	18	2	♃26♎R
7	5.02	16	25	22	19	3	♄16♉
8	5.06	17	7♌	23	20	4	♅ 4♎
9	5.10	18	19	24	21	4	♆29♏R
10	5.14	19	1♍	26	22	5	♇24♍
11	5.18	20	12	27	23	6	♃26♎R
12	5.22	21	24	28	25	6	♄17♉
13	5.26	22	7♎	0♊	26	7	♅ 4♎
14	5.29	23	19	1	27	8	♆29♏R
15	5.33	24	2♏	3	28	8	♇24♍
16	5.37	25	15	4	29	9	♃26♎R
17	5.41	26	29	6	1♌	10	♄17♉
18	5.45	27	13♐	7	2	10	♅ 4♎
19	5.49	27	27	9	3	11	♆28♏R
20	5.53	28	12♑	11	4	12	♇24♍
21	5.57	29	27	12	5	12	♃26♎R
22	6.01	0♋	11♒	14	6	13	♄18♉
23	6.05	1	26	16	8	14	♅ 4♎
24	6.09	2	10♓	18	9	14	♆28♏R
25	6.13	3	25	20	10	15	♇24♍
26	6.17	4	8♈	22	11	16	♃26♎
27	6.21	5	22	24	12	16	♄18♉
28	6.25	6	5♉	26	14	17	♅ 4♎
29	6.29	7	19	28	15	18	♆28♏R
30	6.33	8	2♊	0♋	16	18	♇25♍

Jul	STime	☉	☽	☿	♀	♂	Plnts
1	6.36	9♋	14♊	2♋	17♌	19♋	♃26♎
2	6.40	10	27	4	18	19	♄19♉
3	6.44	11	9♋	7	19	20	♅ 5♎
4	6.48	12	22	9	20	21	♆28♏R
5	6.52	13	3♌	11	22	21	♇25♍
6	6.56	14	15	13	23	22	♃26♎
7	7.00	15	27	15	24	23	♄19♉
8	7.04	16	9♍	17	25	23	♅ 5♎
9	7.08	17	21	20	26	24	♆28♏R
10	7.12	18	3♎	22	27	25	♇25♍
11	7.16	18	15	24	29	25	♃26♎
12	7.20	19	27	26	0♍	26	♄20♉
13	7.24	20	10♏	28	1	27	♅ 5♎
14	7.28	21	23	0♌	2	27	♆28♏R
15	7.32	22	7♐	2	3	28	♇25♍
16	7.36	23	21	4	4	29	♃27♎
17	7.40	24	6♑	6	5	29	♄20♉
18	7.44	25	20	8	7	0♌	♅ 5♎
19	7.47	26	5♒	10	8	0	♆28♏R
20	7.51	27	21	12	9	1	♇25♍
21	7.55	28	6♓	13	10	2	♃27♎
22	7.59	29	20	15	11	2	♄21♉
23	8.03	0♌	5♈	17	12	3	♅ 5♎
24	8.07	1	19	19	13	4	♆28♏R
25	8.11	2	2♉	20	14	4	♇25♍
26	8.15	3	16	22	16	5	♃27♎
27	8.19	4	29	24	17	6	♄21♉
28	8.23	5	11♊	25	18	6	♅ 5♎
29	8.27	6	24	27	19	7	♆28♏R
30	8.31	7	6♋	29	20	8	♇25♍
31	8.35	8	18	0♍	21	8	♃28♎

Aug	STime	☉	☽	☿	♀	♂	Plnts
1	8.39	9♌	0♌	2♍	22♍	9♌	♃28♎
2	8.43	9	12	3	23	9	♄21♉
3	8.47	10	24	5	24	10	♅ 6♎
4	8.51	11	6♍	6	25	11	♆28♏
5	8.54	12	18	7	27	11	♇25♍
6	8.58	13	29	9	28	12	♃29♎
7	9.02	14	11♎	10	29	13	♄22♉
8	9.06	15	24	11	0♎	13	♅ 6♎
9	9.10	16	6♏	13	1	14	♆28♏
10	9.14	17	19	14	2	15	♇25♍
11	9.18	18	2♐	15	3	15	♃29♎
12	9.22	19	15	16	4	16	♄22♉
13	9.26	20	29	17	5	17	♅ 6♎
14	9.30	21	14♑	18	6	17	♆28♏
15	9.34	22	29	19	7	18	♇26♍
16	9.38	23	14♒	20	8	18	♃ 0♏
17	9.42	24	29	21	9	19	♄22♉
18	9.46	25	14♓	22	10	20	♅ 6♎
19	9.50	26	29	23	11	20	♆28♏
20	9.54	27	14♈	24	12	21	♇26♍
21	9.58	28	28	24	13	22	♃ 1♏
22	10.02	29	12♉	25	15	22	♄22♉
23	10.05	0♍	25	26	16	23	♅ 6♎
24	10.09	1	8♊	26	17	24	♆28♏
25	10.13	2	21	27	18	24	♇26♍
26	10.17	3	3♋	27	19	25	♃ 1♏
27	10.21	4	15	27	20	25	♄22♉
28	10.25	4	27	28	21	26	♅ 7♎
29	10.29	5	9♌	28	22	27	♆28♏
30	10.33	6	21	28R	23	27	♇26♍
31	10.37	7	3♍	28	23	28	♃ 2♏

Sep	STime	☉	☽	☿	♀	♂	Plnts
1	10.41	8♍	15♍	27♍	24♎	29♌	♃ 2♏
2	10.45	9	27	27	25	29	♄22♉
3	10.49	10	8♎	27	26	0♍	♅ 7♎
4	10.53	11	21	26	27	1	♆28♏
5	10.57	12	3♏	26	28	1	♇26♍
6	11.01	13	15	25	29	2	♃ 3♏
7	11.05	14	28	24	0♏	2	♄22♉R
8	11.09	15	11♐	23	1	3	♅ 7♎
9	11.12	16	25	23	2	4	♆28♏
10	11.16	17	8♑	22	3	4	♇27♍
11	11.20	18	23	21	4	5	♃ 4♏
12	11.24	19	7♒	20	5	6	♄22♉R
13	11.28	20	22	19	5	6	♅ 8♎
14	11.32	21	7♓	18	6	7	♆28♏
15	11.36	22	22	17	7	8	♇27♍
16	11.40	23	7♈	16	8	8	♃ 5♏
17	11.44	24	22	15	9	9	♄22♉R
18	11.48	25	7♉	14	10	9	♅ 8♎
19	11.52	26	21	14	10	10	♆28♏
20	11.56	27	4♊	14	11	11	♇27♍
21	12.00	28	17	14D	12	11	♃ 6♏
22	12.04	29	0♋	14	13	12	♄22♉R
23	12.08	0♎	12	14	13	13	♅ 8♎
24	12.12	1	24	14	14	13	♆28♏
25	12.16	2	6♌	14	15	14	♇27♍
26	12.20	3	18	15	16	14	♃ 7♏
27	12.23	4	0♍	16	16	15	♄22♉R
28	12.27	5	12	17	17	16	♅ 9♎
29	12.31	6	23	18	18	16	♆28♏
30	12.35	7	5♎	19	18	17	♇27♍

Oct	STime	☉	☽	☿	♀	♂	Plnts
1	12.39	8♎	18♎	20♍	19♏	18♍	♃ 8♏
2	12.43	9	0♏	22	19	18	♄22♉R
3	12.47	10	12	23	20	19	♅ 9♎
4	12.51	11	25	25	20	20	♆29♏
5	12.55	12	8♐	26	21	20	♇27♍
6	12.59	13	21	28	21	21	♃ 9♏
7	13.03	14	5♑	29	22	21	♄21♉R
8	13.07	14	18	1♎	22	22	♅ 9♎
9	13.11	15	2♒	3	23	23	♆29♏
10	13.15	16	17	4	23	23	♇28♍
11	13.19	17	1♓	6	23	24	♃10♏
12	13.23	18	16	8	24	25	♄21♉R
13	13.27	19	1♈	10	24	25	♅10♎
14	13.30	20	16	11	24	26	♆29♏
15	13.34	21	0♉	13	24	27	♇28♍
16	13.38	22	15	15	25	27	♃11♏
17	13.42	23	29	16	25	28	♄21♉R
18	13.46	24	12♊	18	25	28	♅10♎
19	13.50	25	25	20	25	29	♆29♏
20	13.54	26	8♋	22	25R	0♎	♇28♍
21	13.58	27	21	23	25	0	♃12♏
22	14.02	28	3♌	25	25	1	♄20♉R
23	14.06	29	15	27	25	2	♅10♎
24	14.10	0♏	26	28	25	2	♆29♏
25	14.14	1	8♍	0♏	24	3	♇28♍
26	14.18	2	20	2	24	4	♃13♏
27	14.22	3	2♎	3	24	4	♄20♉R
28	14.26	4	14	5	24	5	♅10♎
29	14.30	5	26	7	23	5	♆29♏
30	14.34	6	9♏	8	23	6	♇28♍
31	14.37	7	22	10	23	7	♃14♏

Nov	STime	☉	☽	☿	♀	♂	Plnts
1	14.41	8♏	5♐	12♏	22♏	7♎	♃14♏
2	14.45	9	18	13	22	8	♄20♉R
3	14.49	10	2♑	15	21	9	♅11♎
4	14.53	11	15	16	21	9	♆ 0♐
5	14.57	12	29	18	20	10	♇29♍
6	15.01	13	13♒	20	20	11	♃16♏
7	15.05	14	27	21	19	11	♄19♉R
8	15.09	15	11♓	23	18	12	♅11♎
9	15.13	16	26	24	18	12	♆ 0♐
10	15.17	17	10♈	26	17	13	♇29♍
11	15.21	18	24	27	17	14	♃17♏
12	15.25	19	9♉	29	16	14	♄19♉R
13	15.29	20	23	0♐	15	15	♅11♎
14	15.33	21	7♊	2	15	16	♆ 0♐
15	15.37	22	20	3	14	16	♇29♍
16	15.41	23	3♋	5	14	17	♃18♏
17	15.45	24	16	6	13	18	♄18♉R
18	15.48	25	28	8	13	18	♅12♎
19	15.52	26	10♌	10	12	19	♆ 0♐
20	15.56	27	22	11	12	19	♇29♍
21	16.00	28	4♍	13	11	20	♃19♏
22	16.04	29	16	14	11	21	♄18♉R
23	16.08	0♐	28	15	11	21	♅12♎
24	16.12	1	10♎	17	10	22	♆ 0♐
25	16.16	3	22	18	10	23	♇29♍
26	16.20	4	5♏	20	10	23	♃20♏
27	16.24	5	18	21	10	24	♄18♉R
28	16.28	6	1♐	23	10	25	♅12♎
29	16.32	7	14	24	10	25	♆ 1♐
30	16.36	8	28	26	9D	26	♇29♍

Dec	STime	☉	☽	☿	♀	♂	Plnts
1	16.40	9♐	12♑	27♐	9♏	26♎	♃21♏
2	16.44	10	26	28	10	27	♄17♉R
3	16.48	11	10♒	0♑	10	28	♅12♎
4	16.52	12	24	1	10	28	♆ 1♐
5	16.55	13	8♓	2	10	29	♇29♍
6	16.59	14	22	4	10	0♏	♃22♏
7	17.03	15	6♈	5	10	0	♄17♉R
8	17.07	16	20	6	11	1	♅13♎
9	17.11	17	4♉	7	11	1	♆ 1♐
10	17.15	18	18	8	11	2	♇29♍
11	17.19	19	2♊	9	12	3	♃23♏
12	17.23	20	15	10	12	3	♄17♉R
13	17.27	21	28	11	12	4	♅13♎
14	17.31	22	11♋	12	13	5	♆ 1♐
15	17.35	23	24	13	13	5	♇29♍
16	17.39	24	6♌	13	14	6	♃24♏
17	17.43	25	18	14	14	7	♄16♉R
18	17.47	26	0♍	14	15	7	♅13♎
19	17.51	27	12	14R	16	8	♆ 1♐
20	17.55	28	24	14	16	8	♇29♍
21	17.59	29	6♎	13	17	9	♃25♏
22	18.03	0♑	18	13	17	10	♄16♉R
23	18.06	1	0♏	12	18	10	♅13♎
24	18.10	2	13	11	19	11	♆ 1♐
25	18.14	3	26	10	19	12	♇29♍
26	18.18	4	9♐	9	20	12	♃26♏
27	18.22	5	23	8	21	13	♄16♉R
28	18.26	6	7♑	6	22	14	♅13♎
29	18.30	7	21	5	22	14	♆ 2♐
30	18.34	8	5♒	4	23	15	♇29♍
31	18.38	9	20	2	24	15	♃27♏

Jan	STime	☉	☽	☿	♀	♂	Plnts
1	18.42	10♑	4♓	1♑	25♏	16♏	♃27♏
2	18.46	11	19	0	26	17	♄16♉R
3	18.50	12	3♈	29♐	27	17	♅13♎
4	18.54	13	17	29	27	18	♆ 2♐
5	18.58	14	1♉	28	28	19	♇29♍
6	19.02	15	14	28	29	19	♃28♏
7	19.06	16	28	28	0♐	20	♄15♉R
8	19.10	17	11♊	28D	1	21	♅13♎
9	19.13	18	24	28	2	21	♆ 2♐
10	19.17	19	7♋	28	3	22	♇29♍
11	19.21	20	20	28	4	22	♃29♏
12	19.25	21	2♌	29	5	23	♄15♉R
13	19.29	22	14	29	6	24	♅13♎
14	19.33	23	26	0♑	7	24	♆ 2♐
15	19.37	24	8♍	1	8	25	♇29♍R
16	19.41	25	20	2	9	26	♃ 0♐
17	19.45	26	2♎	2	10	26	♄15♉
18	19.49	27	14	3	11	27	♅13♎R
19	19.53	28	26	4	12	27	♆ 2♐
20	19.57	29	8♏	5	13	28	♇29♍R
21	20.01	0♒	20	7	14	29	♃ 1♐
22	20.05	2	3♐	8	15	29	♄15♉
23	20.09	3	17	9	16	0♐	♅13♎
24	20.13	4	1♑	10	17	1	♆ 2♐
25	20.17	5	15	11	18	1	♇29♍R
26	20.21	6	29	13	19	2	♃ 2♐
27	20.24	7	14♒	14	20	2	♄15♉
28	20.28	8	29	15	21	3	♅13♎R
29	20.32	9	14♓	16	22	4	♆ 2♐
30	20.36	10	29	18	23	4	♇29♍R
31	20.40	11	13♈	19	24	5	♃ 2♐

Feb	STime	☉	☽	☿	♀	♂	Plnts
1	20.44	12♒	28♈	21♑	25♐	6♐	♃ 3♐
2	20.48	13	11♉	22	26	6	♄16♉
3	20.52	14	25	23	27	7	♅13♎R
4	20.56	15	8♊	25	28	8	♆ 3♐
5	21.00	16	21	26	0♑	8	♇29♍R
6	21.04	17	4♋	28	1	9	♃ 3♐
7	21.08	18	16	29	2	9	♄16♉
8	21.12	19	29	1♒	3	10	♅13♎R
9	21.16	20	11♌	2	4	11	♆ 3♐
10	21.20	21	23	4	5	11	♇29♍R
11	21.24	22	5♍	5	6	12	♃ 4♐
12	21.28	23	16	7	7	13	♄16♉
13	21.31	24	28	8	8	13	♅13♎R
14	21.35	25	10♎	10	10	14	♆ 3♐
15	21.39	26	22	11	11	14	♇29♍R
16	21.43	27	4♏	13	12	15	♃ 4♐
17	21.47	28	16	15	13	16	♄16♉
18	21.51	29	29	16	14	16	♅13♎R
19	21.55	0♓	12♐	18	15	17	♆ 3♐
20	21.59	1	25	20	16	17	♇29♍R
21	22.03	2	9♑	21	17	18	♃ 5♐
22	22.07	3	23	23	19	19	♄17♉
23	22.11	4	7♒	25	20	19	♅13♎R
24	22.15	5	22	26	21	20	♆ 3♐
25	22.19	6	7♓	28	22	21	♇29♍R
26	22.23	7	22	0♓	23	21	♃ 5♐
27	22.27	8	8♈	2	24	22	♄17♉
28	22.31	9	22	4	26	22	♅13♎R

Mar	STime	☉	☽	☿	♀	♂	Plnts
1	22.35	10♓	7♉	5♓	27♑	23♐	♃ 5♐
2	22.38	11	21	7	28	24	♄17♉
3	22.42	12	5♊	9	29	24	♅12♎R
4	22.46	13	18	11	0♒	25	♆ 3♐
5	22.50	14	1♋	13	1	25	♇28♍R
6	22.54	15	13	15	2	26	♃ 6♐
7	22.58	16	26	17	4	27	♄18♉
8	23.02	17	8♌	19	5	27	♅12♎R
9	23.06	18	20	20	6	28	♆ 3♐
10	23.10	19	2♍	22	7	29	♇28♍R
11	23.14	20	13	24	8	29	♃ 6♐
12	23.18	21	25	26	10	0♑	♄18♉
13	23.22	22	7♎	28	11	0	♅12♎R
14	23.26	23	19	0♈	12	1	♆ 3♐
15	23.30	24	1♏	2	13	2	♇28♍R
16	23.34	25	13	4	14	2	♃ 6♐
17	23.38	26	25	6	15	3	♄18♉
18	23.42	27	8♐	8	17	3	♅12♎R
19	23.46	28	21	10	18	4	♆ 3♐R
20	23.49	29	4♑	12	19	5	♇28♍R
21	23.53	0♈	17	14	20	5	♃ 6♐
22	23.57	1	1♒	16	21	6	♄19♉
23	0.01	2	16	17	22	6	♅12♎R
24	0.05	3	0♓	19	24	7	♆ 3♐R
25	0.09	4	15	21	25	8	♇28♍R
26	0.13	5	1♈	22	26	8	♃ 6♐R
27	0.17	6	16	24	27	9	♄19♉
28	0.21	7	1♉	25	28	9	♅11♎R
29	0.25	8	16	26	0♓	10	♆ 3♐R
30	0.29	9	0♊	28	1	11	♇28♍R
31	0.33	10	14	29	2	11	♃ 6♐R

Apr	STime	☉	☽	☿	♀	♂	Plnts
1	0.37	11♈	27♊	0♉	3♓	12♑	♃ 6♐R
2	0.41	12	10♋	0	4	12	♄20♉
3	0.45	13	23	1	6	13	♅11♎R
4	0.49	14	5♌	2	7	13	♆ 3♐R
5	0.53	15	17	2	8	14	♇28♍R
6	0.56	16	29	3	9	15	♃ 6♐R
7	1.00	17	10♍	3	10	15	♄21♉
8	1.04	18	22	3	12	16	♅11♎R
9	1.08	19	4♎	3R	13	16	♆ 2♐R
10	1.12	20	16	3	14	17	♇28♍R
11	1.16	21	28	3	15	17	♃ 6♐R
12	1.20	22	10♏	3	16	18	♄21♉
13	1.24	23	22	3	18	19	♅11♎R
14	1.28	24	5♐	2	19	19	♆ 2♐R
15	1.32	25	18	2	20	20	♇27♍R
16	1.36	26	0♑	1	21	20	♃ 5♐R
17	1.40	27	14	1	22	21	♄22♉
18	1.44	27	27	0	24	21	♅11♎R
19	1.48	28	11♒	29♈	25	22	♆ 2♐R
20	1.52	29	25	29	26	23	♇27♍R
21	1.56	0♉	9♓	28	27	23	♃ 5♐R
22	2.00	1	24	27	28	24	♄22♉
23	2.04	2	9♈	27	0♈	24	♅10♎R
24	2.07	3	24	26	1	25	♆ 2♐R
25	2.11	4	9♉	25	2	25	♇27♍R
26	2.15	5	24	25	3	26	♃ 4♐R
27	2.19	6	8♊	24	4	26	♄23♉
28	2.23	7	22	24	6	27	♅10♎R
29	2.27	8	5♋	23	7	27	♆ 2♐R
30	2.31	9	18	23	8	28	♇27♍R

May	STime	☉	☽	☿	♀	♂	Plnts
1	2.35	10♉	1♌	23♈	9♈	28♑	♃ 4♐R
2	2.39	11	13	23	10	29	♄24♉
3	2.43	12	25	23D	12	29	♅10♎R
4	2.47	13	7♍	23	13	0♒	♆ 2♐R
5	2.51	14	19	23	14	1	♇27♍R
6	2.55	15	1♎	23	15	1	♃ 3♐R
7	2.59	16	13	23	16	2	♄24♉
8	3.03	17	25	24	18	2	♅10♎R
9	3.07	18	7♏	24	19	3	♆ 2♐R
10	3.11	19	19	25	20	3	♇27♍R
11	3.14	20	2♐	25	21	4	♃ 3♐R
12	3.18	21	14	26	22	4	♄25♉
13	3.22	22	27	27	24	5	♅10♎R
14	3.26	23	11♑	27	25	5	♆ 2♐R
15	3.30	24	24	28	26	5	♇27♍R
16	3.34	25	7♒	29	27	6	♃ 2♐R
17	3.38	26	21	0♉	28	6	♄26♉
18	3.42	27	5♓	1	0♉	7	♅10♎R
19	3.46	28	19	2	1	7	♆ 2♐R
20	3.50	29	4♈	3	2	8	♇27♍R
21	3.54	29	18	4	3	8	♃ 2♐R
22	3.58	0♊	3♉	5	4	9	♄26♉
23	4.02	1	18	7	6	9	♅ 9♎R
24	4.06	2	2♊	8	7	10	♆ 1♐R
25	4.10	3	16	9	8	10	♇27♍R
26	4.14	4	0♋	11	9	10	♃ 1♐R
27	4.18	5	13	12	11	11	♄27♉
28	4.21	6	26	13	12	11	♅ 9♎R
29	4.25	7	9♌	15	13	12	♆ 1♐R
30	4.29	8	21	16	14	12	♇27♍
31	4.33	9	3♍	18	15	13	♃ 0♐R

Jun	STime	☉	☽	☿	♀	♂	Plnts
1	4.37	10♊	15♍	20♉	17♉	13♒	♃ 0♐R
2	4.41	11	27	21	18	13	♄28♉
3	4.45	12	9♎	23	19	14	♅ 9♎R
4	4.49	13	21	25	20	14	♆ 1♐R
5	4.53	14	3♏	26	21	14	♇27♍
6	4.57	15	15	28	23	15	♃ 0♐R
7	5.01	16	28	0♊	24	15	♄28♉
8	5.05	17	11♐	2	25	16	♅ 9♎R
9	5.09	18	24	4	26	16	♆ 1♐R
10	5.13	19	7♑	6	28	16	♇27♍
11	5.17	20	21	8	29	17	♃29♏R
12	5.21	21	4♒	10	0♊	17	♄29♉
13	5.25	22	18	12	1	17	♅ 9♎
14	5.29	22	2♓	14	2	17	♆ 1♐R
15	5.32	23	16	16	4	18	♇27♍
16	5.36	24	0♈	18	5	18	♃28♏R
17	5.40	25	14	21	6	18	♄ 0♊
18	5.44	26	29	23	7	19	♅ 9♎
19	5.48	27	13♉	25	8	19	♆ 1♐R
20	5.52	28	27	27	10	19	♇27♍
21	5.56	29	11♊	29	11	19	♃28♏R
22	6.00	0♋	25	1♋	12	20	♄ 0♊
23	6.04	1	8♋	4	13	20	♅ 9♎
24	6.08	2	22	6	15	20	♆ 1♐R
25	6.12	3	4♌	8	16	20	♇27♍
26	6.16	4	17	10	17	20	♃27♏R
27	6.20	5	29	12	18	20	♄ 1♊
28	6.24	6	11♍	14	19	21	♅ 9♎
29	6.28	7	23	16	21	21	♆ 0♐R
30	6.32	8	5♎	18	22	21	♇27♍

Jul	STime	☉	☽	☿	♀	♂	Plnts
1	6.36	9♋	17♎	20♋	23♊	21♒	♃27♏R
2	6.39	10	29	22	24	21	♄ 1♊
3	6.43	11	11♏	24	26	21	♅ 9♎
4	6.47	12	23	26	27	21	♆ 0♐R
5	6.51	13	6♐	28	28	21	♇27♍
6	6.55	13	19	0♌	29	22	♃27♏R
7	6.59	14	2♑	2	0♋	22	♄ 2♊
8	7.03	15	16	4	2	22	♅ 9♎
9	7.07	16	0♒	5	3	22	♆ 0♐R
10	7.11	17	14	7	4	22	♇27♍
11	7.15	18	28	9	5	22R	♃27♏R
12	7.19	19	13♓	10	7	22	♄ 2♊
13	7.23	20	27	12	8	22	♅ 9♎
14	7.27	21	11♈	13	9	22	♆ 0♐R
15	7.31	22	25	15	10	22	♇27♍
16	7.35	23	10♉	16	11	21	♃26♏R
17	7.39	24	23	18	13	21	♄ 3♊
18	7.43	25	7♊	19	14	21	♅10♎
19	7.47	26	21	21	15	21	♆ 0♐R
20	7.50	27	4♋	22	16	21	♇27♍
21	7.54	28	17	23	18	21	♃26♏R
22	7.58	29	0♌	25	19	21	♄ 3♊
23	8.02	0♌	13	26	20	21	♅10♎
24	8.06	1	25	27	21	21	♆ 0♐R
25	8.10	2	7♍	28	22	20	♇27♍
26	8.14	3	19	29	24	20	♃26♏
27	8.18	4	1♎	1♍	25	20	♄ 4♊
28	8.22	4	13	2	26	20	♅10♎
29	8.26	5	25	3	27	20	♆ 0♐R
30	8.30	6	7♏	4	29	19	♇27♍
31	8.34	7	19	4	0♌	19	♃26♏

Aug	STime	☉	☽	☿	♀	♂	Plnts
1	8.38	8♌	1♐	5♍	1♌	19♒	♃26♏
2	8.42	9	14	6	2	19	♄ 4♊
3	8.46	10	27	7	4	18	♅10♎
4	8.50	11	11♑	7	5	18	♆ 0♐
5	8.54	12	24	8	6	18	♇28♍
6	8.57	13	9♒	9	7	18	♃27♏
7	9.01	14	23	9	8	17	♄ 5♊
8	9.05	15	8♓	9	10	17	♅10♎
9	9.09	16	23	10	11	17	♆ 0♐
10	9.13	17	7♈	10	12	17	♇28♍
11	9.17	18	22	10	13	16	♃27♏
12	9.21	19	6♉	10R	15	16	♄ 5♊
13	9.25	20	20	10	16	16	♅11♎
14	9.29	21	4♊	10	17	16	♆ 0♐
15	9.33	22	18	10	18	15	♇28♍
16	9.37	23	1♋	10	20	15	♃27♏
17	9.41	24	14	9	21	15	♄ 5♊
18	9.45	25	27	9	22	15	♅11♎
19	9.49	26	9♌	8	23	14	♆ 0♐
20	9.53	27	21	8	25	14	♇28♍
21	9.57	27	4♍	7	26	14	♃27♏
22	10.01	28	16	6	27	14	♄ 6♊
23	10.04	29	28	5	28	13	♅11♎
24	10.08	0♍	9♎	4	29	13	♆ 0♐
25	10.12	1	21	3	1♍	13	♇28♍
26	10.16	2	3♏	3	2	13	♃28♏
27	10.20	3	15	2	3	13	♄ 6♊
28	10.24	4	27	1	4	13	♅11♎
29	10.28	5	10♐	0	6	12	♆ 0♐
30	10.32	6	22	29♌	7	12	♇28♍
31	10.36	7	5♑	29	8	12	♃28♏

Sep	STime	☉	☽	☿	♀	♂	Plnts
1	10.40	8♍	19♑	28♌	9♍	12♒	♃28♏
2	10.44	9	3♒	28	11	12	♄ 6♊
3	10.48	10	17	27	12	12	♅12♎
4	10.52	11	2♓	27	13	12	♆ 0♐
5	10.56	12	17	27D	14	12	♇29♍
6	11.00	13	2♈	27	16	12	♃29♏
7	11.04	14	17	27	17	12	♄ 6♊
8	11.08	15	2♉	28	18	12D	♅12♎
9	11.12	16	16	28	19	12	♆ 0♐
10	11.15	17	1♊	29	21	12	♇29♍
11	11.19	18	14	0♍	22	12	♃ 0♐
12	11.23	19	28	1	23	12	♄ 6♊
13	11.27	20	11♋	2	24	12	♅12♎
14	11.31	21	24	3	26	12	♆ 0♐
15	11.35	22	6♌	4	27	12	♇29♍
16	11.39	23	18	6	28	12	♃ 0♐
17	11.43	24	0♍	7	29	12	♄ 6♊
18	11.47	25	12	9	1♎	12	♅12♎
19	11.51	26	24	10	2	12	♆ 0♐
20	11.55	27	6♎	12	3	12	♇29♍
21	11.59	28	18	14	4	13	♃ 1♐
22	12.03	29	0♏	15	5	13	♄ 6♊R
23	12.07	0♎	12	17	7	13	♅13♎
24	12.11	0	24	19	8	13	♆ 0♐
25	12.15	1	6♐	21	9	13	♇29♍
26	12.19	2	18	23	10	13	♃ 2♐
27	12.22	3	1♑	24	12	14	♄ 6♊R
28	12.26	4	14	26	13	14	♅13♎
29	12.30	5	27	28	14	14	♆ 1♐
30	12.34	6	11♒	0♎	15	14	♇ 0♎

Oct	STime	☉	☽	☿	♀	♂	Plnts
1	12.38	7♎	25♒	2♎	17♎	15♒	♃ 3♐
2	12.42	8	10♓	4	18	15	♄ 6♊R
3	12.46	9	25	5	19	15	♅13♎
4	12.50	10	10♈	7	20	16	♆ 1♐
5	12.54	11	25	9	22	16	♇ 0♎
6	12.58	12	11♉	11	23	16	♃ 4♐
7	13.02	13	25	12	24	16	♄ 6♊R
8	13.06	14	10♊	14	25	17	♅14♎
9	13.10	15	24	16	27	17	♆ 1♐
10	13.14	16	7♋	18	28	18	♇ 0♎
11	13.18	17	20	19	29	18	♃ 4♐
12	13.22	18	3♌	21	0♏	18	♄ 6♊R
13	13.26	19	15	23	2	19	♅14♎
14	13.30	20	28	24	3	19	♆ 1♐
15	13.33	21	10♍	26	4	19	♇ 0♎
16	13.37	22	21	28	5	20	♃ 5♐
17	13.41	23	3♎	29	7	20	♄ 6♊R
18	13.45	24	15	1♏	8	21	♅14♎
19	13.49	25	27	3	9	21	♆ 1♐
20	13.53	26	9♏	4	10	21	♇ 0♎
21	13.57	27	21	6	12	22	♃ 6♐
22	14.01	28	3♐	7	13	22	♄ 5♊R
23	14.05	29	15	9	14	23	♅15♎
24	14.09	0♏	28	10	15	23	♆ 1♐
25	14.13	1	10♑	12	17	24	♇ 0♎
26	14.17	2	23	14	18	24	♃ 7♐
27	14.21	3	6♒	15	19	25	♄ 5♊R
28	14.25	4	20	17	20	25	♅15♎
29	14.29	5	4♓	18	22	26	♆ 2♐
30	14.33	6	18	20	23	26	♇ 1♎
31	14.37	7	3♈	21	24	27	♃ 8♐

Nov	STime	☉	☽	☿	♀	♂	Plnts
1	14.40	8♏	18♈	23♏	25♏	27♒	♃ 9♐
2	14.44	9	4♉	24	27	28	♄ 5♊R
3	14.48	10	19	26	28	28	♅15♎
4	14.52	11	4♊	27	29	29	♆ 2♐
5	14.56	12	18	29	0♐	29	♇ 1♎
6	15.00	13	2♋	0♐	2	0♓	♃10♐
7	15.04	14	16	1	3	0	♄ 4♊R
8	15.08	15	29	3	4	1	♅16♎
9	15.12	16	12♌	4	5	1	♆ 2♐
10	15.16	17	24	6	7	2	♇ 1♎
11	15.20	18	6♍	7	8	2	♃11♐
12	15.24	19	18	8	9	3	♄ 4♊R
13	15.28	20	0♎	10	10	3	♅16♎
14	15.32	21	12	11	12	4	♆ 2♐
15	15.36	22	24	13	13	5	♇ 1♎
16	15.40	23	6♏	14	14	5	♃12♐
17	15.44	24	18	15	15	6	♄ 3♊R
18	15.48	25	0♐	16	16	6	♅16♎
19	15.51	26	12	18	18	7	♆ 2♐
20	15.55	27	25	19	19	7	♇ 1♎
21	15.59	28	7♑	20	20	8	♃13♐
22	16.03	29	20	21	21	9	♄ 3♊R
23	16.07	0♐	3♒	22	23	9	♅16♎
24	16.11	1	16	23	24	10	♆ 2♐
25	16.15	2	0♓	24	25	10	♇ 1♎
26	16.19	3	14	25	26	11	♃14♐
27	16.23	4	28	26	28	12	♄ 3♊R
28	16.27	5	12♈	26	29	12	♅17♎
29	16.31	6	27	27	0♑	13	♆ 3♐
30	16.35	7	12♉	27	1	13	♇ 1♎

Dec	STime	☉	☽	☿	♀	♂	Plnts
1	16.39	8♐	27♉	28♐	3♑	14♓	♃15♐
2	16.43	9	12♊	28	4	15	♄ 2♊R
3	16.47	10	26	28R	5	15	♅17♎
4	16.51	11	10♋	28	6	16	♆ 3♐
5	16.55	12	24	27	8	16	♇ 2♎
6	16.58	13	7♌	27	9	17	♃16♐
7	17.02	14	20	26	10	18	♄ 2♊R
8	17.06	15	2♍	25	11	18	♅17♎
9	17.10	16	15	24	13	19	♆ 3♐
10	17.14	17	27	23	14	19	♇ 2♎
11	17.18	18	8♎	22	15	20	♃17♐
12	17.22	20	20	20	16	21	♄ 1♊R
13	17.26	21	2♏	19	18	21	♅17♎
14	17.30	22	14	18	19	22	♆ 3♐
15	17.34	23	26	16	20	23	♇ 2♎
16	17.38	24	9♐	15	21	23	♃19♐
17	17.42	25	21	14	23	24	♄ 1♊R
18	17.46	26	4♑	13	24	24	♅17♎
19	17.50	27	17	13	25	25	♆ 3♐
20	17.54	28	0♒	12	26	26	♇ 2♎
21	17.58	29	13	12	28	26	♃20♐
22	18.02	0♑	27	12D	29	27	♄ 1♊R
23	18.06	1	10♓	12	0♒	28	♅18♎
24	18.09	2	24	12	1	28	♆ 4♐
25	18.13	3	8♈	12	2	29	♇ 2♎
26	18.17	4	23	13	4	0♈	♃21♐
27	18.21	5	7♉	13	5	0	♄ 0♊R
28	18.25	6	21	14	6	1	♅18♎
29	18.29	7	6♊	15	7	1	♆ 4♐
30	18.33	8	20	15	9	2	♇ 2♎
31	18.37	9	4♋	16	10	3	♃22♐

Jan	STime	☉	☽	☿	♀	♂	Plnts
1	18.41	10♑	18♋	17♐	11♒	3♈	♃22♐
2	18.45	11	2♌	18	12	4	♄ 0♊R
3	18.49	12	15	19	14	5	♅18♎
4	18.53	13	28	21	15	5	♆ 4♐
5	18.57	14	10♍	22	16	6	♇ 2♎
6	19.01	15	22	23	17	7	♃23♐
7	19.05	16	4♎	24	18	7	♄ 0♊R
8	19.09	17	16	25	20	8	♅18♎
9	19.13	18	28	27	21	9	♆ 4♐
10	19.16	19	10♏	28	22	9	♇ 2♎
11	19.20	20	22	29	23	10	♃24♐
12	19.24	21	4♐	1♑	25	11	♄ 0♊R
13	19.28	22	17	2	26	11	♅18♎
14	19.32	23	29	3	27	12	♆ 4♐
15	19.36	24	12♑	5	28	13	♇ 2♎R
16	19.40	25	26	6	0♓	13	♃25♐
17	19.44	26	9♒	8	1	14	♄29♉R
18	19.48	27	23	9	2	14	♅18♎
19	19.52	28	7♓	11	3	15	♆ 4♐
20	19.56	29	21	12	4	16	♇ 2♎R
21	20.00	0♒	5♈	14	6	16	♃26♐
22	20.04	1	19	15	7	17	♄29♉R
23	20.08	2	4♉	17	8	18	♅18♎
24	20.12	3	18	18	9	18	♆ 4♐
25	20.16	4	2♊	20	11	19	♇ 2♎R
26	20.20	5	16	21	12	20	♃27♐
27	20.23	6	0♋	23	13	20	♄29♉R
28	20.27	7	13	24	14	21	♅18♎
29	20.31	8	27	26	15	22	♆ 5♐
30	20.35	9	10♌	27	17	22	♇ 2♎R
31	20.39	10	23	29	18	23	♃28♐

Feb	STime	☉	☽	☿	♀	♂	Plnts
1	20.43	11♒	6♍	1♒	19♓	24♈	♃29♐
2	20.47	12	18	2	20	24	♄29♉
3	20.51	13	0♎	4	21	25	♅18♎R
4	20.55	14	12	5	23	26	♆ 5♐
5	20.59	15	24	7	24	26	♇ 1♎R
6	21.03	16	6♏	9	25	27	♃ 0♑
7	21.07	18	18	10	26	28	♄29♉
8	21.11	19	0♐	12	27	28	♅18♎R
9	21.15	20	12	14	29	29	♆ 5♐
10	21.19	21	25	15	0♈	0♉	♇ 1♎R
11	21.23	22	7♑	17	1	0	♃ 1♑
12	21.27	23	20	19	2	1	♄29♉
13	21.31	24	4♒	21	3	2	♅18♎R
14	21.34	25	18	22	5	2	♆ 5♐
15	21.38	26	2♓	24	6	3	♇ 1♎R
16	21.42	27	16	26	7	4	♃ 1♑
17	21.46	28	1♈	28	8	4	♄ 0♊
18	21.50	29	16	0♓	9	5	♅18♎R
19	21.54	0♓	0♉	1	10	6	♆ 5♐
20	21.58	1	15	3	12	6	♇ 1♎R
21	22.02	2	29	5	13	7	♃ 2♑
22	22.06	3	13♊	7	14	8	♄ 0♊
23	22.10	4	26	9	15	8	♅18♎R
24	22.14	5	10♋	11	16	9	♆ 5♐
25	22.18	6	23	13	17	10	♇ 1♎R
26	22.22	7	6♌	15	19	10	♃ 3♑
27	22.26	8	19	16	20	11	♄ 0♊
28	22.30	9	1♍	18	21	12	♅17♎R
29	22.34	10	14	20	22	12	♆ 5♐

Mar	STime	☉	☽	☿	♀	♂	Plnts
1	22.38	11♓	26♍	22♓	23♈	13♉	♃ 4♑
2	22.41	12	8♎	24	24	13	♄ 0♊
3	22.45	13	20	26	26	14	♅17♎R
4	22.49	14	2♏	28	27	15	♆ 5♐
5	22.53	15	14	29	28	15	♇ 1♎R
6	22.57	16	26	1♈	29	16	♃ 4♑
7	23.01	17	8♐	3	0♉	17	♄ 0♊
8	23.05	18	20	4	1	17	♅17♎R
9	23.09	19	2♑	6	2	18	♆ 5♐R
10	23.13	20	15	7	3	19	♇ 1♎R
11	23.17	21	28	9	5	19	♃ 5♑
12	23.21	22	12♒	10	6	20	♄ 1♊
13	23.25	23	26	11	7	21	♅17♎R
14	23.29	24	10♓	12	8	21	♆ 5♐
15	23.33	25	25	13	9	22	♇ 1♎R
16	23.37	26	10♈	14	10	23	♃ 6♑
17	23.41	27	25	14	11	23	♄ 1♊
18	23.45	28	10♉	15	12	24	♅17♎R
19	23.48	29	25	15	13	25	♆ 5♐R
20	23.52	0♈	9♊	15	15	25	♇ 0♎R
21	23.56	1	23	16R	16	26	♃ 6♑
22	0.00	2	7♋	16	17	27	♄ 2♊
23	0.04	3	20	15	18	27	♅17♎R
24	0.08	4	3♌	15	19	28	♆ 5♐
25	0.12	5	16	15	20	29	♇ 0♎R
26	0.16	6	28	14	21	29	♃ 7♑
27	0.20	7	11♍	14	22	0♊	♄ 2♊
28	0.24	8	23	13	23	1	♅16♎R
29	0.28	9	5♎	12	24	1	♆ 5♐R
30	0.32	10	17	11	25	2	♇ 0♎R
31	0.36	11	29	11	26	3	♃ 7♑

Apr	STime	☉	☽	☿	♀	♂	Plnts
1	0.40	12♈	11♏	10♈	27♉	3♊	♃ 7♑
2	0.44	13	23	9	28	4	♄ 3♊
3	0.48	14	4♐	8	29	4	♅16♎R
4	0.52	15	16	7	0♊	5	♆ 5♐R
5	0.56	16	28	7	1	6	♇ 0♎R
6	0.59	16	11♑	6	2	6	♃ 7♑
7	1.03	17	23	5	3	7	♄ 3♊
8	1.07	18	6♒	5	4	8	♅16♎R
9	1.11	19	20	4	5	8	♆ 5♐R
10	1.15	20	4♓	4	6	9	♇ 0♎R
11	1.19	21	18	4	7	10	♃ 8♑
12	1.23	22	3♈	3	8	10	♄ 4♊
13	1.27	23	18	3	9	11	♅16♎R
14	1.31	24	4♉	3D	10	12	♆ 5♐R
15	1.35	25	19	3	11	12	♇ 0♎R
16	1.39	26	4♊	4	12	13	♃ 8♑
17	1.43	27	18	4	13	14	♄ 4♊
18	1.47	28	3♋	4	14	14	♅15♎R
19	1.51	29	16	5	14	15	♆ 4♐R
20	1.55	0♉	0♌	5	15	16	♇ 0♎R
21	1.59	1	13	6	16	16	♃ 8♑
22	2.03	2	25	6	17	17	♄ 5♊
23	2.06	3	8♍	7	18	17	♅15♎R
24	2.10	4	20	8	19	18	♆ 4♐R
25	2.14	5	2♎	8	19	19	♇ 0♎R
26	2.18	6	14	9	20	19	♃ 8♑R
27	2.22	7	26	10	21	20	♄ 5♊
28	2.26	8	8♏	11	22	21	♅15♎R
29	2.30	9	20	12	23	21	♆ 4♐R
30	2.34	10	1♐	13	23	22	♇29♍R

May	STime	☉	☽	☿	♀	♂	Plnts
1	2.38	11♉	13♐	14♈	24♊	23♊	♃ 8♑R
2	2.42	12	25	15	25	23	♄ 6♊
3	2.46	13	8♑	17	25	24	♅15♎R
4	2.50	14	20	18	26	25	♆ 4♐R
5	2.54	15	3♒	19	27	25	♇29♍R
6	2.58	16	15	20	27	26	♃ 8♑R
7	3.02	17	29	22	28	26	♄ 7♊
8	3.06	18	13♓	23	29	27	♅15♎R
9	3.10	19	27	24	29	28	♆ 4♐R
10	3.14	20	12♈	26	0♋	28	♇29♍R
11	3.17	21	27	27	0	29	♃ 8♑R
12	3.21	22	12♉	29	1	0♋	♄ 7♊
13	3.25	23	27	0♉	1	0	♅15♎R
14	3.29	23	12♊	2	2	1	♆ 4♐R
15	3.33	24	27	4	2	2	♇29♍R
16	3.37	25	11♋	5	2	2	♃ 7♑R
17	3.41	26	25	7	3	3	♄ 8♊
18	3.45	27	9♌	9	3	4	♅14♎R
19	3.49	28	22	11	3	4	♆ 4♐R
20	3.53	29	4♍	12	4	5	♇29♍R
21	3.57	0♊	17	14	4	5	♃ 7♑R
22	4.01	1	29	16	4	6	♄ 9♊
23	4.05	2	11♎	18	4	7	♅14♎R
24	4.09	3	23	20	4	7	♆ 4♐R
25	4.13	4	5♏	22	4	8	♇29♍R
26	4.17	5	17	24	4	9	♃ 7♑R
27	4.21	6	28	26	4R	9	♄ 9♊
28	4.24	7	10♐	28	4	10	♅14♎R
29	4.28	8	23	0♊	4	11	♆ 3♐R
30	4.32	9	5♑	2	4	11	♇29♍
31	4.36	10	17	4	4	12	♃ 6♑R

Jun	STime	☉	☽	☿	♀	♂	Plnts
1	4.40	11♊	0♒	7♊	4♋	12♋	♃ 6♑R
2	4.44	12	12	9	4	13	♄10♊
3	4.48	13	25	11	3	14	♅14♎R
4	4.52	14	9♓	13	3	14	♆ 3♐R
5	4.56	15	22	15	3	15	♇29♍
6	5.00	16	7♈	18	2	16	♃ 5♑R
7	5.04	17	21	20	2	16	♄11♊
8	5.08	17	6♉	22	1	17	♅14♎R
9	5.12	18	21	24	1	18	♆ 3♐R
10	5.16	19	6♊	26	0	18	♇29♍
11	5.20	20	21	28	0	19	♃ 5♑R
12	5.24	21	5♋	0♋	29♊	19	♄11♊
13	5.28	22	20	3	29	20	♅14♎
14	5.32	23	4♌	5	28	21	♆ 3♐R
15	5.35	24	17	7	28	21	♇29♍
16	5.39	25	0♍	9	27	22	♃ 4♑R
17	5.43	26	13	11	26	23	♄12♊
18	5.47	27	25	12	26	23	♅14♎
19	5.51	28	7♎	14	25	24	♆ 3♐R
20	5.55	29	19	16	24	25	♇29♍
21	5.59	0♋	1♏	18	24	25	♃ 4♑R
22	6.03	1	13	20	23	26	♄13♊
23	6.07	2	25	21	23	26	♅14♎
24	6.11	3	7♐	23	22	27	♆ 3♐R
25	6.15	4	19	25	22	28	♇29♍
26	6.19	5	1♑	26	21	28	♃ 3♑R
27	6.23	6	14	28	21	29	♄13♊
28	6.27	7	26	29	20	0♌	♅14♎
29	6.31	8	9♒	1♌	20	0	♆ 3♐R
30	6.35	8	22	2	19	1	♇29♍

Jul	STime	☉	☽	☿	♀	♂	Plnts
1	6.39	9♋	6♓	4♌	19♊	1♌	♃ 2♑R
2	6.42	10	19	5	19	2	♄14♊
3	6.46	11	3♈	6	19	3	♅14♎
4	6.50	12	17	8	18	3	♆ 3♐R
5	6.54	13	1♉	9	18	4	♇29♍
6	6.58	14	16	10	18	5	♃ 2♑R
7	7.02	15	0♊	11	18	5	♄14♊
8	7.06	16	15	12	18D	6	♅14♎
9	7.10	17	29	13	18	7	♆ 3♐R
10	7.14	18	14♋	14	18	7	♇29♍
11	7.18	19	28	15	18	8	♃ 1♑R
12	7.22	20	12♌	16	18	8	♄15♊
13	7.26	21	25	17	18	9	♅14♎
14	7.30	22	8♍	18	18	10	♆ 2♐R
15	7.34	23	21	19	19	10	♇29♍
16	7.38	24	3♎	19	19	11	♃ 1♑R
17	7.42	25	16	20	19	12	♄15♊
18	7.46	26	28	20	19	12	♅14♎
19	7.49	27	9♏	21	20	13	♆ 2♐R
20	7.53	28	21	21	20	14	♇29♍
21	7.57	29	3♐	22	21	14	♃ 0♑R
22	8.01	29	15	22	21	15	♄16♊
23	8.05	0♌	28	22	21	15	♅14♎
24	8.09	1	10♑	22	22	16	♆ 2♐R
25	8.13	2	23	22R	22	17	♇ 0♎
26	8.17	3	6♒	22	23	17	♃ 0♑R
27	8.21	4	19	22	23	18	♄17♊
28	8.25	5	2♓	22	24	19	♅14♎
29	8.29	6	16	21	25	19	♆ 2♐R
30	8.33	7	0♈	21	25	20	♇ 0♎
31	8.37	8	14	20	26	20	♃29♐R

Aug	STime	☉	☽	☿	♀	♂	Plnts
1	8.41	9♌	28♈	20♌	27♊	21♌	♃29♐R
2	8.45	10	12♉	19	27	22	♄17♊
3	8.49	11	26	18	28	22	♅15♎
4	8.53	12	11♊	18	29	23	♆ 2♐
5	8.57	13	25	17	29	24	♇ 0♎
6	9.00	14	9♋	16	0♋	24	♃29♐R
7	9.04	15	23	15	1	25	♄18♊
8	9.08	16	7♌	15	2	26	♅15♎
9	9.12	17	20	14	2	26	♆ 2♐
10	9.16	18	3♍	13	3	27	♇ 0♎
11	9.20	19	16	12	4	27	♃28♐R
12	9.24	20	29	12	5	28	♄18♊
13	9.28	21	11♎	11	6	29	♅15♎
14	9.32	21	23	11	6	29	♆ 2♐
15	9.36	22	6♏	11	7	0♍	♇ 0♎
16	9.40	23	17	10	8	1	♃28♐R
17	9.44	24	29	10D	9	1	♄18♊
18	9.48	25	11♐	10	10	2	♅15♎
19	9.52	26	23	10	11	3	♆ 2♐
20	9.56	27	6♑	11	12	3	♇ 0♎
21	10.00	28	18	11	13	4	♃28♐R
22	10.04	29	1♒	11	13	4	♄19♊
23	10.07	0♍	14	12	14	5	♅16♎
24	10.11	1	28	13	15	6	♆ 2♐
25	10.15	2	12♓	14	16	6	♇ 0♎
26	10.19	3	26	15	17	7	♃28♐
27	10.23	4	10♈	16	18	8	♄19♊
28	10.27	5	24	17	19	8	♅16♎
29	10.31	6	9♉	18	20	9	♆ 2♐
30	10.35	7	23	20	21	10	♇ 1♎
31	10.39	8	7♊	21	22	10	♃28♐

Sep	STime	☉	☽	☿	♀	♂	Plnts
1	10.43	9♍	21♊	23♌	23♋	11♍	♃28♐
2	10.47	10	5♋	25	24	11	♄19♊
3	10.51	11	19	26	25	12	♅16♎
4	10.55	12	3♌	28	26	13	♆ 2♐
5	10.59	13	16	0♍	27	13	♇ 1♎
6	11.03	14	29	2	28	14	♃28♐
7	11.07	15	12♍	3	29	15	♄20♊
8	11.11	16	25	5	0♌	15	♅16♎
9	11.15	17	7♎	7	1	16	♆ 2♐
10	11.18	18	19	9	2	17	♇ 1♎
11	11.22	19	2♏	11	3	17	♃29♐
12	11.26	20	14	13	4	18	♄20♊
13	11.30	20	25	15	6	18	♅17♎
14	11.34	21	7♐	17	7	19	♆ 2♐
15	11.38	22	19	19	8	20	♇ 1♎
16	11.42	23	1♑	20	9	20	♃29♐
17	11.46	24	13	22	10	21	♄20♊
18	11.50	25	26	24	11	22	♅17♎
19	11.54	26	9♒	26	12	22	♆ 3♐
20	11.58	27	22	28	13	23	♇ 1♎
21	12.02	28	6♓	0♎	14	24	♃29♐
22	12.06	29	20	1	15	24	♄20♊
23	12.10	0♎	5♈	3	16	25	♅17♎
24	12.14	1	19	5	17	26	♆ 3♐
25	12.18	2	4♉	7	19	26	♇ 2♎
26	12.22	3	19	9	20	27	♃ 0♑
27	12.25	4	4♊	10	21	27	♄20♊
28	12.29	5	18	12	22	28	♅18♎
29	12.33	6	2♋	14	23	29	♆ 3♐
30	12.37	7	16	15	24	29	♇ 2♎

Oct	STime	☉	☽	☿	♀	♂	Plnts
1	12.41	8♎	29♋	17♎	25♌	0♎	♃ 0♑
2	12.45	9	13♌	19	26	1	♄20♊
3	12.49	10	26	20	28	1	♅18♎
4	12.53	11	8♍	22	29	2	♆ 3♐
5	12.57	12	21	23	0♍	3	♇ 2♎
6	13.01	13	4♎	25	1	3	♃ 1♑
7	13.05	14	16	27	2	4	♄20♊R
8	13.09	15	28	28	3	5	♅18♎
9	13.13	16	10♏	0♏	4	5	♆ 3♐
10	13.17	17	22	1	6	6	♇ 2♎
11	13.21	18	4♐	3	7	7	♃ 1♑
12	13.25	19	16	4	8	7	♄20♊R
13	13.29	20	27	6	9	8	♅19♎
14	13.33	21	9♑	7	10	8	♆ 3♐
15	13.36	22	21	9	11	9	♇ 2♎
16	13.40	23	4♒	10	13	10	♃ 2♑
17	13.44	24	17	12	14	10	♄20♊R
18	13.48	25	0♓	13	15	11	♅19♎
19	13.52	26	14	15	16	12	♆ 3♐
20	13.56	27	28	16	17	12	♇ 3♎
21	14.00	28	13♈	17	19	13	♃ 3♑
22	14.04	29	28	19	20	14	♄20♊R
23	14.08	0♏	13♉	20	21	14	♅19♎
24	14.12	1	28	22	22	15	♆ 3♐
25	14.16	2	13♊	23	23	16	♇ 3♎
26	14.20	3	28	24	24	16	♃ 4♑
27	14.24	4	12♋	26	26	17	♄20♊R
28	14.28	5	26	27	27	18	♅19♎
29	14.32	6	10♌	28	28	18	♆ 4♐
30	14.36	7	23	29	29	19	♇ 3♎
31	14.40	8	6♍	1♐	0♎	20	♃ 5♑

Nov	STime	☉	☽	☿	♀	♂	Plnts
1	14.43	9♏	18♍	2♐	2♎	20♎	♃ 5♑
2	14.47	10	0♎	3	3	21	♄19♊R
3	14.51	11	13	4	4	22	♅20♎
4	14.55	12	25	5	5	22	♆ 4♐
5	14.59	13	7♏	6	6	23	♇ 3♎
6	15.03	14	19	7	8	23	♃ 6♑
7	15.07	15	1♐	8	9	24	♄19♊R
8	15.11	16	12	9	10	25	♅20♎
9	15.15	17	24	10	11	25	♆ 4♐
10	15.19	18	6♑	10	13	26	♇ 3♎
11	15.23	19	18	11	14	27	♃ 7♑
12	15.27	20	0♒	11	15	27	♄19♊R
13	15.31	21	13	12	16	28	♅20♎
14	15.35	22	25	12	17	29	♆ 4♐
15	15.39	23	9♓	12R	19	29	♇ 3♎
16	15.43	24	22	12	20	0♏	♃ 8♑
17	15.47	25	6♈	12	21	1	♄19♊R
18	15.50	26	21	12	22	1	♅21♎
19	15.54	27	6♉	11	23	2	♆ 4♐
20	15.58	28	21	10	25	3	♇ 4♎
21	16.02	29	7♊	9	26	3	♃ 9♑
22	16.06	0♐	22	8	27	4	♄18♊R
23	16.10	1	7♋	7	28	5	♅21♎
24	16.14	2	21	6	0♏	5	♆ 5♐
25	16.18	3	5♌	5	1	6	♇ 4♎
26	16.22	4	19	3	2	7	♃10♑
27	16.26	5	2♍	2	3	7	♄18♊R
28	16.30	6	15	1	5	8	♅21♎
29	16.34	7	28	29♏	6	9	♆ 5♐
30	16.38	8	10♎	28	7	9	♇ 4♎

Dec	STime	☉	☽	☿	♀	♂	Plnts
1	16.42	9♐	22♎	28♏	8♏	10♏	♃11♑
2	16.46	10	4♏	27	10	11	♄17♊R
3	16.50	11	16	26	11	11	♅21♎
4	16.54	12	28	26	12	12	♆ 5♐
5	16.58	13	9♐	26D	13	13	♇ 4♎
6	17.01	14	21	26	14	13	♃12♑
7	17.05	15	3♑	26	16	14	♄17♊R
8	17.09	16	15	27	17	15	♅22♎
9	17.13	17	27	27	18	15	♆ 5♐
10	17.17	18	9♒	28	19	16	♇ 4♎
11	17.21	19	22	28	21	17	♃13♑
12	17.25	20	5♓	29	22	17	♄17♊R
13	17.29	21	18	0♐	23	18	♅22♎
14	17.33	22	1♈	1	24	19	♆ 5♐
15	17.37	23	15	2	26	19	♇ 4♎
16	17.41	24	0♉	3	27	20	♃14♑
17	17.45	25	14	5	28	21	♄16♊R
18	17.49	26	29	6	29	21	♅22♎
19	17.53	27	15♊	7	1♐	22	♆ 6♐
20	17.57	28	0♋	8	2	23	♇ 4♎
21	18.01	29	15	10	3	23	♃15♑
22	18.05	0♑	29	11	4	24	♄16♊R
23	18.08	1	14♌	12	6	25	♅22♎
24	18.12	2	27	14	7	26	♆ 6♐
25	18.16	4	11♍	15	8	26	♇ 4♎
26	18.20	5	24	16	9	27	♃16♑
27	18.24	6	6♎	18	11	28	♄15♊R
28	18.28	7	19	19	12	28	♅22♎
29	18.32	8	1♏	21	13	29	♆ 6♐
30	18.36	9	13	22	14	0♐	♇ 4♎
31	18.40	10	24	24	16	0	♃17♑

1 9 7 3

Jan	STime	☉	☽	☿	♀	♂	Plnts
1	18.44	11♑	6♐	25♐	17♐	1♐	♃18♑
2	18.48	12	18	27	18	2	♄15♊R
3	18.52	13	0♑	28	19	2	♅23♎
4	18.56	14	12	0♑	21	3	♆ 6♐
5	19.00	15	24	1	22	4	♇ 4♎
6	19.04	16	7♒	3	23	4	♃19♑
7	19.08	17	19	4	24	5	♄15♊R
8	19.12	18	2♓	6	26	6	♅23♎
9	19.16	19	15	7	27	6	♆ 6♐
10	19.19	20	28	9	28	7	♇ 4♎
11	19.23	21	12♈	10	29	8	♃20♑
12	19.27	22	25	12	1♑	8	♄14♊R
13	19.31	23	9♉	13	2	9	♅23♎
14	19.35	24	24	15	3	10	♆ 6♐
15	19.39	25	8♊	16	4	11	♇ 4♎R
16	19.43	26	23	18	6	11	♃21♑
17	19.47	27	8♋	20	7	12	♄14♊R
18	19.51	28	23	21	8	13	♅23♎
19	19.55	29	7♌	23	9	13	♆ 6♐
20	19.59	0♒	21	25	11	14	♇ 4♎R
21	20.03	1	5♍	26	12	15	♃22♑
22	20.07	2	19	28	13	15	♄14♊R
23	20.11	3	2♎	29	14	16	♅23♎
24	20.15	4	14	1♒	16	17	♆ 7♐
25	20.19	5	27	3	17	17	♇ 4♎R
26	20.23	6	9♏	4	18	18	♃23♑
27	20.26	7	21	6	19	19	♄14♊R
28	20.30	8	3♐	8	21	19	♅23♎
29	20.34	9	14	10	22	20	♆ 7♐
30	20.38	10	26	11	23	21	♇ 4♎R
31	20.42	11	8♑	13	24	22	♃25♑

Feb	STime	☉	☽	☿	♀	♂	Plnts
1	20.46	12♒	20♑	15♒	26♑	22♐	♃25♑
2	20.50	13	3♒	17	27	23	♄13♊R
3	20.54	14	15	18	28	24	♅23♎R
4	20.58	15	28	20	29	24	♆ 7♐
5	21.02	16	12♓	22	1♒	25	♇ 4♎R
6	21.06	17	25	24	2	26	♃26♑
7	21.10	18	9♈	26	3	26	♄13♊R
8	21.14	19	22	27	4	27	♅23♎R
9	21.18	20	6♉	29	6	28	♆ 7♐
10	21.22	21	20	1♓	7	28	♇ 4♎R
11	21.26	22	4♊	3	8	29	♃27♑
12	21.30	23	19	5	9	0♑	♄13♊
13	21.33	24	3♋	6	11	1	♅23♎R
14	21.37	25	17	8	12	1	♆ 7♐
15	21.41	26	1♌	10	13	2	♇ 4♎R
16	21.45	27	15	12	14	3	♃28♑
17	21.49	28	29	13	16	3	♄13♊
18	21.53	29	13♍	15	17	4	♅23♎R
19	21.57	0♓	26	17	18	5	♆ 7♐
20	22.01	1	9♎	18	19	5	♇ 4♎R
21	22.05	2	22	20	21	6	♃29♑
22	22.09	3	5♏	21	22	7	♄13♊
23	22.13	4	17	22	23	8	♅22♎R
24	22.17	5	29	23	24	8	♆ 7♐
25	22.21	6	10♐	25	26	9	♇ 3♎R
26	22.25	7	22	25	27	10	♃ 0♒
27	22.29	8	4♑	26	28	10	♄14♊
28	22.33	9	16	27	29	11	♅22♎R

Mar	STime	☉	☽	☿	♀	♂	Plnts
1	22.37	10♓	28♑	28♓	1♓	12♑	♃ 1♒
2	22.41	11	11♒	28	2	12	♄14♊
3	22.44	12	24	28	3	13	♅22♎R
4	22.48	13	7♓	28R	4	14	♆ 7♐
5	22.52	14	21	28	6	15	♇ 3♎R
6	22.56	15	5♈	28	7	15	♃ 2♒
7	23.00	16	19	28	8	16	♄14♊
8	23.04	17	3♉	27	9	17	♅22♎R
9	23.08	18	17	27	11	17	♆ 7♐
10	23.12	19	1♊	26	12	18	♇ 3♎R
11	23.16	20	15	25	13	19	♃ 3♒
12	23.20	21	29	24	14	20	♄14♊
13	23.24	22	13♋	23	16	20	♅22♎R
14	23.28	23	27	22	17	21	♆ 7♐
15	23.32	24	11♌	21	18	22	♇ 3♎R
16	23.36	25	25	20	19	22	♃ 4♒
17	23.40	26	8♍	19	21	23	♄14♊
18	23.44	27	22	19	22	24	♅22♎R
19	23.48	28	5♎	18	23	24	♆ 7♐
20	23.51	29	18	17	24	25	♇ 3♎R
21	23.55	0♈	0♏	16	26	26	♃ 5♒
22	23.59	1	12	16	27	27	♄15♊
23	0.03	2	25	15	28	27	♅22♎R
24	0.07	3	6♐	15	29	28	♆ 7♐R
25	0.11	4	18	15	1♈	29	♇ 3♎R
26	0.15	5	0♑	15	2	29	♃ 6♒
27	0.19	6	12	15D	3	0♒	♄15♊
28	0.23	7	24	15	4	1	♅21♎R
29	0.27	8	6♒	15	5	2	♆ 7♐R
30	0.31	9	19	15	7	2	♇ 3♎R
31	0.35	10	2♓	15	8	3	♃ 7♒

Apr	STime	☉	☽	☿	♀	♂	Plnts
1	0.39	11♈	15♓	16♓	9♈	4♒	♃ 7♒
2	0.43	12	29	16	10	4	♄15♊
3	0.47	13	13♈	17	12	5	♅21♎R
4	0.51	14	28	18	13	6	♆ 7♐R
5	0.55	15	12♉	18	14	7	♇ 2♎R
6	0.59	16	27	19	15	7	♃ 7♒
7	1.02	17	12♊	20	17	8	♄16♊
8	1.06	18	26	21	18	9	♅21♎R
9	1.10	19	10♋	22	19	9	♆ 7♐R
10	1.14	20	24	23	20	10	♇ 2♎R
11	1.18	21	8♌	24	22	11	♃ 8♒
12	1.22	22	21	25	23	12	♄16♊
13	1.26	23	5♍	26	24	12	♅21♎R
14	1.30	24	18	27	25	13	♆ 7♐R
15	1.34	25	1♎	28	27	14	♇ 2♎R
16	1.38	26	14	29	28	14	♃ 9♒
17	1.42	27	26	0♈	29	15	♄17♊
18	1.46	28	9♏	2	0♉	16	♅20♎R
19	1.50	29	21	3	1	16	♆ 7♐R
20	1.54	0♉	3♐	4	3	17	♇ 2♎R
21	1.58	1	15	6	4	18	♃ 9♒
22	2.02	2	26	7	5	19	♄17♊
23	2.06	3	8♑	9	6	19	♅20♎R
24	2.09	4	20	10	8	20	♆ 7♐R
25	2.13	5	2♒	12	9	21	♇ 2♎R
26	2.17	6	14	13	10	21	♃10♒
27	2.21	7	27	15	11	22	♄18♊
28	2.25	8	10♓	16	13	23	♅20♎R
29	2.29	9	23	18	14	24	♆ 6♐R
30	2.33	10	7♈	20	15	24	♇ 2♎R

May	STime	☉	☽	☿	♀	♂	Plnts
1	2.37	11♉	22♈	21♈	16♉	25♒	♃10♒
2	2.41	12	6♉	23	18	26	♄18♊
3	2.45	13	21	25	19	26	♅20♎R
4	2.49	14	6♊	27	20	27	♆ 6♐R
5	2.53	15	21	29	21	28	♇ 2♎R
6	2.57	16	6♋	0♉	22	29	♃11♒
7	3.01	16	20	2	24	29	♄19♊
8	3.05	17	5♌	4	25	0♓	♅20♎R
9	3.09	18	18	6	26	1	♆ 6♐R
10	3.13	19	2♍	8	27	1	♇ 2♎R
11	3.17	20	15	10	29	2	♃11♒
12	3.20	21	28	12	0♊	3	♄20♊
13	3.24	22	10♎	14	1	3	♅19♎R
14	3.28	23	23	16	2	4	♆ 6♐R
15	3.32	24	5♏	18	4	5	♇ 2♎R
16	3.36	25	17	21	5	6	♃11♒
17	3.40	26	29	23	6	6	♄20♊
18	3.44	27	11♐	25	7	7	♅19♎R
19	3.48	28	23	27	8	8	♆ 6♐R
20	3.52	29	5♑	29	10	8	♇ 2♎R
21	3.56	0♊	17	1♊	11	9	♃12♒
22	4.00	1	29	4	12	10	♄21♊
23	4.04	2	11♒	6	13	10	♅19♎R
24	4.08	3	23	8	15	11	♆ 6♐R
25	4.12	4	5♓	10	16	12	♇ 1♎R
26	4.16	5	18	12	17	13	♃12♒
27	4.20	6	2♈	14	18	13	♄21♊
28	4.24	7	16	17	20	14	♅19♎R
29	4.27	8	0♉	19	21	15	♆ 6♐R
30	4.31	9	15	21	22	15	♇ 1♎R
31	4.35	10	0♊	23	23	16	♃12♒

Jun	STime	☉	☽	☿	♀	♂	Plnts
1	4.39	11♊	15♊	25♊	24♊	17♓	♃12♒R
2	4.43	12	0♋	27	26	17	♄22♊
3	4.47	12	15	28	27	18	♅19♎R
4	4.51	13	0♌	0♋	28	19	♆ 6♐R
5	4.55	14	14	2	29	19	♇ 1♎
6	4.59	15	28	4	1♋	20	♃12♒R
7	5.03	16	12♍	6	2	21	♄23♊
8	5.07	17	25	7	3	21	♅19♎R
9	5.11	18	8♎	9	4	22	♆ 5♐R
10	5.15	19	20	10	5	23	♇ 1♎
11	5.19	20	2♏	12	7	23	♃12♒R
12	5.23	21	14	13	8	24	♄23♊
13	5.27	22	26	15	9	25	♅19♎R
14	5.31	23	8♐	16	10	25	♆ 5♐R
15	5.34	24	20	18	12	26	♇ 1♎
16	5.38	25	2♑	19	13	27	♃11♒R
17	5.42	26	14	20	14	27	♄24♊
18	5.46	27	26	21	15	28	♅19♎R
19	5.50	28	8♒	23	16	29	♆ 5♐R
20	5.54	29	20	24	18	29	♇ 1♎
21	5.58	0♋	2♓	25	19	0♈	♃11♒R
22	6.02	1	15	26	20	1	♄25♊
23	6.06	2	28	27	21	1	♅19♎
24	6.10	3	11♈	28	23	2	♆ 5♐R
25	6.14	3	25	28	24	3	♇ 1♎
26	6.18	4	9♉	29	25	3	♃11♒R
27	6.22	5	23	0♌	26	4	♄25♊
28	6.26	6	8♊	0	27	5	♅19♎
29	6.30	7	23	1	29	5	♆ 5♐R
30	6.34	8	8♋	2	0♌	6	♇ 1♎

Jul	STime	☉	☽	☿	♀	♂	Plnts
1	6.38	9♋	24♋	2♌	1♌	7♈	♃10♒R
2	6.42	10	8♌	2	2	7	♄26♊
3	6.45	11	23	3	4	8	♅19♎
4	6.49	12	7♍	3	5	8	♆ 5♐R
5	6.53	13	21	3	6	9	♇ 2♎
6	6.57	14	4♎	3R	7	10	♃10♒R
7	7.01	15	17	3	8	10	♄27♊
8	7.05	16	29	3	10	11	♅19♎
9	7.09	17	11♏	3	11	12	♆ 5♐R
10	7.13	18	23	3	12	12	♇ 2♎
11	7.17	19	5♐	2	13	13	♃ 9♒R
12	7.21	20	17	2	14	13	♄27♊
13	7.25	21	29	1	16	14	♅19♎
14	7.29	22	11♑	1	17	15	♆ 5♐R
15	7.33	23	23	0	18	15	♇ 2♎
16	7.37	24	5♒	0	19	16	♃ 9♒R
17	7.41	24	17	29♋	21	16	♄28♊
18	7.45	25	29	28	22	17	♅19♎
19	7.49	26	12♓	28	23	17	♆ 5♐R
20	7.52	27	24	27	24	18	♇ 2♎
21	7.56	28	7♈	26	25	19	♃ 8♒R
22	8.00	29	21	26	27	19	♄29♊
23	8.04	0♌	4♉	25	28	20	♅19♎
24	8.08	1	18	24	29	20	♆ 5♐R
25	8.12	2	3♊	24	0♍	21	♇ 2♎
26	8.16	3	17	23	1	21	♃ 7♒R
27	8.20	4	2♋	23	3	22	♄29♊
28	8.24	5	17	23	4	22	♅19♎
29	8.28	6	2♌	23	5	23	♆ 4♐
30	8.32	7	17	23D	6	23	♇ 2♎
31	8.36	8	1♍	23	7	24	♃ 7♒R

Aug	STime	☉	☽	☿	♀	♂	Plnts
1	8.40	9♌	15♍	23♋	9♍	24♈	♃ 7♒R
2	8.44	10	29	23	10	25	♄ 0♋
3	8.48	11	12♎	23	11	25	♅19♎
4	8.52	12	25	24	12	26	♆ 4♐R
5	8.56	13	8♏	24	13	26	♇ 2♎
6	9.00	14	20	25	15	27	♃ 6♒R
7	9.03	15	2♐	26	16	27	♄ 0♋
8	9.07	15	14	26	17	28	♅19♎
9	9.11	16	26	27	18	28	♆ 4♐
10	9.15	17	7♑	29	19	29	♇ 2♎
11	9.19	18	19	0♌	21	29	♃ 5♒R
12	9.23	19	1♒	1	22	0♉	♄ 1♋
13	9.27	20	13	2	23	0	♅20♎
14	9.31	21	26	4	24	0	♆ 4♐
15	9.35	22	9♓	5	25	1	♇ 2♎
16	9.39	23	21	7	27	1	♃ 5♒R
17	9.43	24	4♈	9	28	2	♄ 1♋
18	9.47	25	18	10	29	2	♅20♎
19	9.51	26	1♉	12	0♎	2	♆ 4♐
20	9.55	27	15	14	1	3	♇ 3♎
21	9.59	28	29	16	3	3	♃ 4♒R
22	10.03	29	13♊	18	4	4	♄ 2♋
23	10.07	0♍	27	20	5	4	♅20♎
24	10.10	1	12♋	22	6	4	♆ 4♐
25	10.14	2	26	23	7	5	♇ 3♎
26	10.18	3	11♌	25	9	5	♃ 4♒R
27	10.22	4	25	27	10	5	♄ 2♋
28	10.26	5	9♍	29	11	6	♅20♎
29	10.30	6	23	1♍	12	6	♆ 4♐
30	10.34	7	7♎	3	13	6	♇ 3♎
31	10.38	8	20	5	15	6	♃ 3♒R

Sep	STime	☉	☽	☿	♀	♂	Plnts
1	10.42	9♍	3♏	7♍	16♎	7♉	♃ 3♒R
2	10.46	10	16	9	17	7	♄ 3♋
3	10.50	11	28	11	18	7	♅21♎
4	10.54	12	10♐	13	19	7	♆ 4♐
5	10.58	12	22	15	20	7	♇ 3♎
6	11.02	13	4♑	17	22	8	♃ 3♒R
7	11.06	14	15	19	23	8	♄ 3♋
8	11.10	15	27	21	24	8	♅21♎
9	11.14	16	10♒	22	25	8	♆ 5♐
10	11.18	17	22	24	26	8	♇ 3♎
11	11.21	18	5♓	26	27	8	♃ 2♒R
12	11.25	19	18	28	29	9	♄ 3♋
13	11.29	20	1♈	29	0♏	9	♅21♎
14	11.33	21	14	1♎	1	9	♆ 5♐
15	11.37	22	28	3	2	9	♇ 4♎
16	11.41	23	12♉	5	3	9	♃ 2♒R
17	11.45	24	26	6	5	9	♄ 4♋
18	11.49	25	10♊	8	6	9	♅21♎
19	11.53	26	24	9	7	9	♆ 5♐
20	11.57	27	8♋	11	8	9R	♇ 4♎
21	12.01	28	22	13	9	9	♃ 2♒R
22	12.05	29	6♌	14	10	9	♄ 4♋
23	12.09	0♎	20	16	12	9	♅22♎
24	12.13	1	4♍	17	13	9	♆ 5♐
25	12.17	2	18	19	14	9	♇ 4♎
26	12.21	3	2♎	20	15	9	♃ 2♒R
27	12.25	4	15	22	16	9	♄ 4♋
28	12.28	5	28	23	17	8	♅22♎
29	12.32	6	11♏	25	18	8	♆ 5♐
30	12.36	7	24	26	20	8	♇ 4♎

Oct	STime	☉	☽	☿	♀	♂	Plnts
1	12.40	8♎	6♐	28♎	21♏	8♉	♃ 2♒
2	12.44	9	18	29	22	8	♄ 4♋
3	12.48	10	0♑	1♏	23	8	♅22♎
4	12.52	11	11	2	24	7	♆ 5♐
5	12.56	12	23	3	25	7	♇ 4♎
6	13.00	13	5♒	5	26	7	♃ 2♒
7	13.04	14	18	6	28	7	♄ 4♋
8	13.08	15	0♓	7	29	6	♅23♎
9	13.12	16	13	9	0♐	6	♆ 5♐
10	13.16	17	26	10	1	6	♇ 4♎
11	13.20	18	10♈	11	2	6	♃ 2♒
12	13.24	19	23	12	3	5	♄ 4♋
13	13.28	20	8♉	14	4	5	♅23♎
14	13.32	21	22	15	6	5	♆ 5♐
15	13.35	22	6♊	16	7	4	♇ 5♎
16	13.39	23	20	17	8	4	♃ 3♒
17	13.43	24	5♋	18	9	4	♄ 4♋
18	13.47	25	19	19	10	4	♅23♎
19	13.51	26	3♌	20	11	3	♆ 5♐
20	13.55	27	17	21	12	3	♇ 5♎
21	13.59	28	1♍	22	13	3	♃ 3♒
22	14.03	29	14	23	14	2	♄ 4♋R
23	14.07	0♏	28	24	16	2	♅24♎
24	14.11	1	11♎	24	17	1	♆ 6♐
25	14.15	2	24	25	18	1	♇ 5♎
26	14.19	3	7♏	25	19	1	♃ 3♒
27	14.23	4	19	26	20	0	♄ 4♋R
28	14.27	5	2♐	26	21	0	♅24♎
29	14.31	6	14	26	22	0	♆ 6♐
30	14.35	7	26	26R	23	0	♇ 5♎
31	14.39	8	8♑	26	24	29♈	♃ 4♒

Nov	STime	☉	☽	☿	♀	♂	Plnts
1	14.43	9♏	19♑	26♏	25♐	29♈	♃ 4♒
2	14.46	10	1♒	26	26	29	♄ 4♋R
3	14.50	11	13	25	27	28	♅24♎
4	14.54	12	25	24	28	28	♆ 6♐
5	14.58	13	8♓	24	0♑	28	♇ 5♎
6	15.02	14	21	23	1	28	♃ 4♒
7	15.06	15	4♈	21	2	27	♄ 4♋R
8	15.10	16	18	20	3	27	♅25♎
9	15.14	17	2♉	19	4	27	♆ 6♐
10	15.18	18	16	18	5	27	♇ 6♎
11	15.22	19	1♊	16	6	26	♃ 5♒
12	15.26	20	16	15	7	26	♄ 4♋R
13	15.30	21	0♋	14	8	26	♅25♎
14	15.34	22	15	13	9	26	♆ 6♐
15	15.38	23	0♌	12	10	26	♇ 6♎
16	15.42	24	14	11	11	26	♃ 6♒
17	15.46	25	28	11	12	25	♄ 4♋R
18	15.50	26	11♍	10	13	25	♅25♎
19	15.53	27	25	10D	14	25	♆ 6♐
20	15.57	28	8♎	10	15	25	♇ 6♎
21	16.01	29	21	11	16	25	♃ 6♒
22	16.05	0♐	3♏	11	17	25	♄ 3♋R
23	16.09	1	16	12	17	25	♅25♎
24	16.13	2	28	12	18	25	♆ 7♐
25	16.17	3	10♐	13	19	25D	♇ 6♎
26	16.21	4	22	14	20	25	♃ 7♒
27	16.25	5	4♑	15	21	25	♄ 3♋R
28	16.29	6	16	16	22	25	♅26♎
29	16.33	7	28	17	23	25	♆ 7♐
30	16.37	8	9♒	18	24	25	♇ 6♎

Dec	STime	☉	☽	☿	♀	♂	Plnts
1	16.41	9♐	21♒	20♏	25♑	25♈	♃ 8♒
2	16.45	10	3♓	21	25	25	♄ 3♋R
3	16.49	11	16	22	26	25	♅26♎
4	16.53	12	29	23	27	25	♆ 7♐
5	16.57	13	12♈	25	28	26	♇ 6♎
6	17.01	14	26	26	29	26	♃ 9♒
7	17.04	15	10♉	28	29	26	♄ 2♋R
8	17.08	16	24	29	0♒	26	♅26♎
9	17.12	17	9♊	1♐	1	26	♆ 7♐
10	17.16	18	24	2	2	26	♇ 6♎
11	17.20	19	9♋	4	2	27	♃10♒
12	17.24	20	24	5	3	27	♄ 2♋R
13	17.28	21	9♌	7	4	27	♅26♎
14	17.32	22	24	8	4	27	♆ 7♐
15	17.36	23	8♍	10	5	27	♇ 6♎
16	17.40	24	21	11	5	28	♃11♒
17	17.44	25	5♎	13	6	28	♄ 1♋R
18	17.48	26	18	14	7	28	♅27♎
19	17.52	27	0♏	16	7	28	♆ 8♐
20	17.56	28	13	17	8	29	♇ 6♎
21	18.00	29	25	19	8	29	♃12♒
22	18.04	0♑	7♐	20	8	29	♄ 1♋R
23	18.08	1	19	22	9	29	♅27♎
24	18.11	2	1♑	23	9	0♉	♆ 8♐
25	18.15	3	13	25	10	0	♇ 6♎
26	18.19	4	24	26	10	0	♃13♒
27	18.23	5	6♒	28	10	1	♄ 1♋R
28	18.27	6	18	29	10	1	♅27♎
29	18.31	7	0♓	1♑	11	1	♆ 8♐
30	18.35	8	12	3	11	2	♇ 7♎
31	18.39	9	25	4	11	2	♃14♒

January

Jan	STime	☉	☽	☿	♀	♂	Plnts
1	18.43	10♑	7♈	6♑	11≈	28	♃14≈
2	18.47	11	20	7	11	3	♄0♋R
3	18.51	12	4♉	9	11R	3	♅26♎
4	18.55	13	18	11	11	4	♆8♐
5	18.59	14	2♊	12	11	4	♇7♎
6	19.03	15	17	14	11	4	♃15≈
7	19.07	17	2♋	15	11	5	♄0♋R
8	19.11	18	17	17	11	5	♅27♎
9	19.15	19	2♌	19	10	6	♆8♐
10	19.18	20	18	20	10	6	♇7♎
11	19.22	21	2♍	22	10	6	♃16≈
12	19.26	22	17	24	9	7	♄29♊R
13	19.30	23	1♎	25	9	7	♅27♎
14	19.34	24	14	27	8	8	♆9♐
15	19.38	25	27	29	8	8	♇7♎
16	19.42	26	10♏	0≈	8	8	♃18≈
17	19.46	27	22	2	7	9	♄29♊R
18	19.50	28	4♐	4	6	9	♅27♎
19	19.54	29	16	5	6	10	♆9♐
20	19.58	0≈	28	7	5	10	♇7♎R
21	20.02	1	10♑	9	5	11	♃19≈
22	20.06	2	21	10	4	11	♄29♊R
23	20.10	3	3≈	12	3	12	♅27♎
24	20.14	4	15	14	3	12	♆9♐
25	20.18	5	27	16	2	13	♇7♎R
26	20.22	6	9♓	17	1	13	♃20≈
27	20.26	7	22	19	1	14	♄28♊R
28	20.29	8	4♈	21	0	14	♅27♎
29	20.33	9	17	22	0	15	♆9♐
30	20.37	10	0♉	24	29♑	15	♇6♎R
31	20.41	11	13	26	29	16	♃21≈

February

Feb	STime	☉	☽	☿	♀	♂	Plnts
1	20.45	12≈	27♉	27≈	28♑	16♑	♃21≈
2	20.49	13	11♊	29	28	17	♄28♊R
3	20.53	14	25	1♓	27	18	♅27♎
4	20.57	15	10♋	2	27	18	♆9♐
5	21.01	16	25	3	27	18	♇6♎R
6	21.05	17	10♌	5	26	19	♃23≈
7	21.09	18	25	6	26	19	♄28♊R
8	21.13	19	10♍	7	26	20	♅27♎
9	21.17	20	25	8	26	20	♆9♐
10	21.21	21	9♎	9	26	21	♇6♎R
11	21.25	22	23	10	26	21	♃24≈
12	21.29	23	6♏	11	26	22	♄28♊R
13	21.33	24	18	11	26D	22	♅27♎
14	21.36	25	1♐	12R	26	23	♆9♐
15	21.40	26	13	12	26	24	♇6♎R
16	21.44	27	25	11	26	24	♃25≈
17	21.48	28	6♑	11	26	25	♄28♊R
18	21.52	29	18	11	26	25	♅27♎
19	21.56	0♓	0≈	10	27	26	♆9♐
20	22.00	1	12	9	27	26	♇6♎R
21	22.04	2	24	9	27	26	♃26≈
22	22.08	3	6♓	8	27	27	♄28♊R
23	22.12	4	19	7	27	27	♅27♎
24	22.16	5	1♈	6	28	28	♆9♐R
25	22.20	6	14	5	28	28	♇6♎R
26	22.24	7	27	4	29	29	♃27≈
27	22.28	8	10♉	3	29	0♈	♄27♊R
28	22.32	9	23	0≈	0	0	♅27♎

March

Mar	STime	☉	☽	☿	♀	♂	Plnts
1	22.36	10♓	7♊	1♓	0≈	1♊	♃28≈
2	22.40	11	21	0	1	1	♄28♊R
3	22.44	12	5♋	29≈	1	2	♅27♎
4	22.47	13	19	28	2	3	♆9♐
5	22.51	14	4♌	28	2	3	♇6♎R
6	22.55	15	19	27	3	4	♃29≈
7	22.59	16	4♍	27	4	4	♄28♊R
8	23.03	17	18	27	4	5	♅27♎R
9	23.07	18	3♎	27D	5	5	♆9♐R
10	23.11	19	17	27	6	6	♇6♎R
11	23.15	20	0♏	27	7	7	♃0♓
12	23.19	21	14	27	7	8	♄28♊R
13	23.23	22	26	27	8	8	♅27♎R
14	23.27	23	9♐	27	9	9	♆9♐R
15	23.31	24	21	28	10	9	♇5♎R
16	23.35	25	3♑	29	10	9	♃2♓
17	23.39	26	15	29	11	10	♄28♊R
18	23.43	27	26	0♓	12	10	♅27♎R
19	23.47	28	8≈	1	13	11	♆9♐R
20	23.51	29	20	2	14	12	♇5♎R
21	23.54	0♈	2♓	3	15	12	♃3♓
22	23.58	1	15	5	16	13	♄28♊R
23	0.02	2	28	6	16	13	♅26♎R
24	0.06	3	10♈	7	17	14	♆9♐R
25	0.10	4	24	8	19	15	♇5♎R
26	0.14	5	7♉	8	19	15	♃4♓
27	0.18	6	20	9	20	16	♄28♊R
28	0.22	7	4♊	10	21	16	♅26♎R
29	0.26	8	18	11	22	17	♆9♐R
30	0.30	9	2♋	12	23	17	♇5♎R
31	0.34	10	16	14	24	18	♃5♓

April

Apr	STime	☉	☽	☿	♀	♂	Plnts
1	0.38	11♈	0♌	15♓	25≈	19♊	♃5♓
2	0.42	12	14	16	26	19	♄29♊R
3	0.46	13	29	18	27	20	♅26♎R
4	0.50	14	13♍	19	28	21	♆9♐R
5	0.54	15	27	20	29	21	♇5♎R
6	0.58	16	11♎	22	0♓	22	♃6♓
7	1.01	17	25	23	1	22	♄29♊R
8	1.05	18	8♏	25	2	23	♅26♎R
9	1.09	19	21	26	3	23	♆9♐R
10	1.13	20	4♐	28	4	24	♇5♎R
11	1.17	21	17	29	5	24	♃7♓
12	1.21	22	29	1♈	6	25	♄29♊R
13	1.25	23	11♑	3	7	26	♅26♎R
14	1.29	24	23	4	9	27	♆9♐R
15	1.33	25	4≈	6	9	27	♇5♎R
16	1.37	26	16	8	10	27	♃8♓
17	1.41	27	28	10	11	28	♄0♋
18	1.45	28	11♓	11	12	29	♅25♎R
19	1.49	29	23	13	13	29	♆9♐R
20	1.53	0♉	6♈	15	14	0♋	♇5♎R
21	1.57	1	19	17	15	0	♃9♓
22	2.01	2	3♉	19	16	1	♄0♋
23	2.05	3	16	21	17	2	♅25♎R
24	2.09	4	0♊	22	18	2	♆9♐R
25	2.12	5	14	24	19	3	♇5♎R
26	2.16	6	28	26	21	3	♃10♓
27	2.20	7	13♋	28	22	4	♄0♋
28	2.24	8	27	0♉	23	4	♅25♎R
29	2.28	9	11♌	3	24	5	♆9♐R
30	2.32	10	25	5	25	5	♇4♎R

May

May	STime	☉	☽	☿	♀	♂	Plnts
1	2.36	10♉	9♍	7♉	26♓	6♋	♃11♓
2	2.40	11	23	9	27	7	♄1♋
3	2.44	12	7♎	11	28	7	♅25♎R
4	2.48	13	20	13	29	8	♆9♐R
5	2.52	14	4♏	15	0♈	9	♇4♎R
6	2.56	15	17	17	2	9	♃12♓
7	3.00	16	0♐	20	3	10	♄1♋
8	3.04	17	12	22	4	11	♅25♎R
9	3.08	18	24	24	5	11	♆9♐R
10	3.12	19	7♑	26	6	12	♇4♎R
11	3.16	20	19	28	7	12	♃13♓
12	3.19	21	0≈	0♊	8	13	♄2♋
13	3.23	22	12	2	9	14	♅24♎R
14	3.27	23	24	4	11	14	♆9♐R
15	3.31	24	6♓	6	12	15	♇4♎R
16	3.35	25	19	8	13	15	♃13♓
17	3.39	26	1♈	10	14	16	♄2♋
18	3.43	27	14	12	15	17	♄24♎R
19	3.47	28	27	14	16	17	♆8♐R
20	3.51	29	11♉	15	17	18	♇4♎R
21	3.55	0♊	25	18	18	18	♃14♓
22	3.59	1	9♊	19	19	19	♄3♋
23	4.03	2	24	21	21	20	♅24♎R
24	4.07	3	8♋	23	22	20	♆8♐R
25	4.11	4	23	24	23	21	♇4♎R
26	4.15	5	7♌	26	24	21	♃15♓
27	4.19	6	21	28	25	22	♄4♋
28	4.23	7	6♍	29	26	23	♅24♎R
29	4.27	7	20	0♋	28	23	♆8♐R
30	4.30	8	3♎	1	29	24	♇4♎R
31	4.34	9	17	2	0♉	25	♃15♓

June

Jun	STime	☉	☽	☿	♀	♂	Plnts
1	4.38	10♊	0♏	4♋	1♉	25♋	♃16♓
2	4.42	11	13	5	2	26	♄4♋
3	4.46	12	26	6	3	26	♅24♎R
4	4.50	13	8♐	7	5	27	♆8♐R
5	4.54	14	21	8	6	27	♇4♎R
6	4.58	15	3♑	9	7	28	♃17♓
7	5.02	16	15	9	8	29	♄5♋
8	5.06	17	27	10	9	29	♅24♎R
9	5.10	18	9≈	11	10	0♌	♆8♐R
10	5.14	19	21	11	11	1	♇4♎R
11	5.18	20	2♓	11	13	1	♃16♓
12	5.22	21	14	12	14	2	♄6♋
13	5.26	22	27	13	15	3	♅24♎R
14	5.30	23	9♈	13	16	4	♆8♐R
15	5.34	24	22	13	17	4	♇4♎R
16	5.37	25	5♉	13	19	5	♃17♓
17	5.41	26	19	13R	20	5	♄6♋
18	5.45	27	3♊	13	21	6	♅23♎R
19	5.49	28	18	13	22	6	♆8♐R
20	5.53	28	3♋	13	23	7	♇4♎R
21	5.57	29	18	13	24	7	♃17♓
22	6.01	0♋	2♌	13	25	8	♄7♋
23	6.05	1	17	12	26	8	♅23♎R
24	6.09	2	2♍	12	28	9	♆7♐R
25	6.13	3	16	11	29	9	♇4♎R
26	6.17	4	0♎	11	0♊	10	♃17♓
27	6.21	5	14	10	1	11	♄8♋
28	6.25	6	27	10	3	12	♅23♎R
29	6.29	7	10♏	9	4	12	♆7♐R
30	6.33	8	23	9	5	13	♇4♎R

July

Jul	STime	☉	☽	☿	♀	♂	Plnts
1	6.37	9♋	5♐	8♋	6♊	13♌	♃18♓
2	6.41	10	17	7	7	14	♄8♋
3	6.45	11	0♑	7	9	15	♅23♎R
4	6.48	12	12	6	10	16	♆7♐R
5	6.52	13	23	6	11	16	♇4♎R
6	6.56	14	5≈	5	13	17	♃18♓
7	7.00	15	17	5	14	18	♄9♋
8	7.04	16	29	5	15	18	♅23♎R
9	7.08	17	11♓	4	16	19	♆7♐R
10	7.12	18	23	4	17	19	♇4♎R
11	7.16	19	5♈	4	19	20	♃18♓R
12	7.20	19	18	4D	19	20	♄10♋
13	7.24	20	1♉	4	20	21	♅23♎R
14	7.28	21	14	4	22	22	♆7♐R
15	7.32	22	27	5	23	22	♇4♎R
16	7.36	23	12♊	5	24	23	♃17♓R
17	7.40	24	26	5	25	23	♄10♋
18	7.44	25	11♋	6	26	24	♅23♎R
19	7.48	26	26	7	29	25	♆7♐R
20	7.52	27	11♌	7	29	25	♇4♎R
21	7.55	28	26	8	0♋	26	♃17♓R
22	7.59	29	10♍	9	1	27	♄11♋
23	8.03	0♌	26	10	2	27	♅24♎R
24	8.07	1	10♎	11	4	28	♆7♐R
25	8.11	2	24	12	5	28	♇4♎R
26	8.15	3	11♏	13	6	29	♃17♓R
27	8.19	4	20	15	7	0♍	♄11♋
28	8.23	5	2♐	15	8	0	♅24♎R
29	8.27	6	15	18	10	1	♆7♐R
30	8.31	7	27	19	11	2	♇4♎R
31	8.35	8	9♑	21	12	2	♃17♓R

August

Aug	STime	☉	☽	☿	♀	♂	Plnts
1	8.39	9♌	20♑	22♋	13♋	3♍	♃17♓R
2	8.43	10	2≈	24	15	3	♄12♋
3	8.47	10	14	26	16	4	♅25♎R
4	8.51	11	26	28	17	5	♆7♐R
5	8.55	12	8♓	0♌	18	5	♇4♎R
6	8.59	13	20	2	19	6	♃16♓R
7	9.03	14	2♈	4	21	7	♄13♋
8	9.06	15	14	6	22	7	♅25♎R
9	9.10	16	27	8	23	8	♆7♐R
10	9.14	17	10♉	10	24	8	♇5♎
11	9.18	18	23	12	26	9	♃16♓R
12	9.22	19	6♊	14	27	10	♄13♋
13	9.26	20	20	16	28	10	♅25♎R
14	9.30	21	5♋	18	29	0♏	♆7♐R
15	9.34	22	19	20	0♌	12	♇5♎
16	9.38	23	4♌	22	2	12	♃15♓R
17	9.42	24	20	24	3	13	♄14♋
18	9.46	25	5♍	26	4	14	♅25♎R
19	9.50	26	20	28	5	15	♆7♐R
20	9.54	27	5♎	0♍	6	15	♇5♎
21	9.58	28	19	2	8	15	♃15♓R
22	10.02	29	3♏	3	9	16	♄14♋
23	10.06	0♍	16	6	10	17	♅25♎R
24	10.10	1	29	8	11	17	♆7♐R
25	10.13	2	11♐	8	13	17	♇5♎
26	10.17	3	24	11	14	19	♃14♓R
27	10.21	4	6♑	13	15	19	♄15♋
28	10.25	5	17	15	17	20	♅25♎R
29	10.29	5	29	17	18	21	♆7♐R
30	10.33	6	11≈	18	19	21	♇5♎
31	10.37	7	23	20	20	22	♃13♓R

September

Sep	STime	☉	☽	☿	♀	♂	Plnts
1	10.41	8♍	5♓	22♍	21♌	22♏	♃13♓R
2	10.45	9	17	24	23	23	♄16♋
3	10.49	10	29	25	24	24	♅25♎R
4	10.53	11	12♈	27	25	24	♆7♐R
5	10.57	12	24	29	26	25	♇5♎
6	11.01	13	7♉	0♎	27	26	♃12♓R
7	11.05	14	20	2	29	26	♄16♋
8	11.09	15	3♊	3	0♍	27	♅25♎R
9	11.13	16	16	5	1	28	♆7♐R
10	11.17	17	0♋	6	2	28	♇6♎
11	11.20	18	14	8	3	29	♃12♓R
12	11.24	19	28	9	5	0♐	♄16♋
13	11.28	20	13♌	11	6	0	♅26♎R
14	11.32	21	28	12	7	1	♆7♐R
15	11.36	22	13♍	14	8	1	♇6♎
16	11.40	23	28	15	10	2	♃11♓R
17	11.44	24	13♎	17	11	3	♄17♋
18	11.48	25	27	18	12	3	♅26♎R
19	11.52	26	11♏	20	13	4	♆6♐R
20	11.56	27	24	21	15	5	♇6♎
21	12.00	28	7♐	22	16	5	♃11♓R
22	12.04	29	20	23	17	6	♄17♋
23	12.08	0♎	2♑	24	18	7	♅26♎R
24	12.12	1	14	25	20	7	♆6♐R
25	12.16	2	26	25	21	8	♇6♎
26	12.20	3	8≈	26	22	9	♃10♓R
27	12.24	4	20	26R	23	9	♄18♋
28	12.28	5	2♓	26	25	10	♅26♎R
29	12.31	6	14	26	26	11	♆6♐R
30	12.35	7	26	27	27	11	♇6♎

October

Oct	STime	☉	☽	☿	♀	♂	Plnts
1	12.39	8♎	8♈	3♎	28♍	12♐	♃9♓R
2	12.43	9	21	4	0♎	13	♄18♋
3	12.47	10	4♉	5	1	13	♅27♎
4	12.51	11	17	6	3	14	♆7♐
5	12.55	12	0♊	7	3	15	♇6♎
6	12.59	13	13	8	5	15	♃9♓R
7	13.03	14	27	8	6	16	♄18♋
8	13.07	15	10♋	9	7	16	♅27♎
9	13.11	16	24	9	8	17	♆7♐
10	13.15	17	9♌	10	10	18	♇6♎
11	13.19	17	23	10	11	18	♃9♓R
12	13.23	18	8♍	10	12	19	♄18♋
13	13.27	19	22	10R	13	20	♅27♎
14	13.31	20	7♎	10	15	20	♆7♐
15	13.35	21	21	10	16	21	♇7♎
16	13.38	22	5♏	10	17	22	♃8♓R
17	13.42	23	19	9	19	22	♄18♋
18	13.46	24	2♐	9	20	23	♅28♎
19	13.50	25	15	8	21	24	♆8♐
20	13.54	25	28	8	22	24	♇7♎
21	13.58	27	10♑	8	23	25	♃8♓R
22	14.02	28	22	8	25	26	♄19♋
23	14.06	29	4≈	8	26	26	♅28♎
24	14.10	0♏	16	8	27	27	♆8♐
25	14.14	1	28	9	28	27	♇7♎
26	14.18	2	10♓	0	0♏	28	♃8♓R
27	14.22	3	22	29♍	1	29	♄19♋
28	14.26	4	4♈	29D	2	0♑	♅28♎
29	14.30	5	17	29	3	1	♆8♐
30	14.34	6	0♉	0♎	5	1	♇8♎
31	14.38	7	13	0	6	2	♃8♓R

November

Nov	STime	☉	☽	☿	♀	♂	Plnts
1	14.42	8♏	26♉	25♎	7♏	3♑	♃8♓R
2	14.45	9	10♊	25	8	3	♄19♋
3	14.49	10	23	25D	10	4	♅29♎
4	14.53	11	7♋	25	11	5	♆8♐
5	14.57	12	21	25	12	6	♇8♎
6	15.01	13	5♌	26	13	6	♃8♓R
7	15.05	14	19	26	15	7	♄19♋R
8	15.09	15	4♍	27	16	7	♅29♎
9	15.13	16	18	28	17	8	♆8♐
10	15.17	17	2♎	28	18	9	♇8♎
11	15.21	18	16	0♏	20	9	♃8♓R
12	15.25	19	0♏	1	21	10	♄19♋R
13	15.29	20	14	2	22	11	♅29♎
14	15.33	21	27	4	23	11	♆8♐
15	15.37	22	10♐	5	25	12	♇8♎
16	15.41	23	23	6	26	13	♃8♓R
17	15.45	24	6♑	8	27	14	♄18♋R
18	15.49	25	18	9	28	14	♅0♏
19	15.53	26	0≈	10	0♐	15	♆9♐
20	15.56	27	12	12	1	16	♇8♎
21	16.00	28	24	13	2	16	♃8♓R
22	16.04	0♐	6♓	14	3	17	♄18♋R
23	16.08	1	18	16	5	18	♅0♏
24	16.12	1	0♈	18	6	18	♆9♐
25	16.16	2	12	19	7	19	♇8♎
26	16.20	4	25	21	8	20	♃9♓R
27	16.24	5	8♉	22	10	20	♄18♋R
28	16.28	6	21	23	11	21	♅0♏
29	16.32	7	5♊	25	12	22	♆9♐
30	16.36	8	19	26	14	22	♇8♎

December

Dec	STime	☉	☽	☿	♀	♂	Plnts
1	16.40	9♐	3♋	29♐	15♐	23♑	♃9♓
2	16.44	10	17	0♑	16	24	♄18♋R
3	16.48	11	1♌	2	17	25	♅0♏
4	16.52	12	16	3	19	25	♆9♐
5	16.56	13	0♍	5	20	26	♇9♎
6	17.00	14	15	6	21	27	♃9♓
7	17.03	15	29	8	22	27	♄17♋R
8	17.07	16	13♎	9	24	28	♅1♏
9	17.11	17	26	11	25	29	♆9♐
10	17.15	18	10♏	13	26	29	♇9♎
11	17.19	19	23	14	27	0♒	♃10♓
12	17.23	20	6♐	16	29	1	♄17♋R
13	17.27	21	19	17	0♑	1	♅1♏
14	17.31	22	1♑	18	1	2	♆9♐
15	17.35	24	14	20	2	3	♇9♎
16	17.39	25	26	22	4	4	♃11♓
17	17.43	26	8♒	23	5	4	♄17♋R
18	17.47	27	20	25	6	5	♅1♏
19	17.51	28	2♓	27	7	6	♆10♐
20	17.55	28	13	28	9	7	♇9♎
21	17.59	29	25	0♒	10	8	♃11♓
22	18.03	0♑	7♈	1	11	8	♄16♋R
23	18.07	1	20	2	12	9	♅1♏
24	18.11	2	2♉	2	14	9	♆10♐
25	18.14	3	16	2	15	10	♇9♎
26	18.18	4	29	1	16	11	♃12♓
27	18.22	5	13♊	9	17	11	♄16♋R
28	18.26	6	27	0♑	19	12	♅1♏
29	18.30	7	12♋	28♐	20	13	♆10♐
30	18.34	9	26	28	21	14	♇9♎
31	18.38	10	11♌	16	22	14	♃13♓

Jan	STime	☉	☽	☿	♀	♂	Plnts
1	18.42	10♑	26♌	18♑	24♑	15♐	♃13♓
2	18.46	11	11♍	19	25	16	♄15♋R
3	18.50	12	25	21	26	16	♅ 2♏
4	18.54	13	9♎	22	27	17	♆10♐
5	18.58	14	23	24	29	18	♇ 9♎
6	19.02	15	7♏	26	0♒	19	♃14♓
7	19.06	16	20	27	1	19	♄15♋R
8	19.10	17	3♐	29	2	20	♅ 2♏
9	19.14	18	15	1♒	4	21	♆10♐
10	19.18	19	28	2	5	21	♇ 9♎
11	19.21	20	10♑	4	6	22	♃15♓
12	19.25	21	22	6	8	23	♄15♋R
13	19.29	22	4♒	7	9	24	♅ 2♏
14	19.33	23	16	9	10	24	♆11♐
15	19.37	24	28	10	11	25	♇ 9♎
16	19.41	25	10♓	12	13	26	♃16♓
17	19.45	26	22	13	14	27	♄14♋R
18	19.49	27	4♈	15	15	27	♅ 2♏
19	19.53	28	16	16	16	28	♆11♐
20	19.57	0♒	28	18	18	29	♇ 9♎
21	20.01	1	11♉	19	19	29	♃17♓
22	20.05	2	23	20	20	0♑	♄14♋R
23	20.09	3	7♊	21	21	1	♅ 2♏
24	20.13	4	21	22	23	2	♆11♐
25	20.17	5	5♋	23	24	2	♇ 9♎R
26	20.21	6	20	24	25	3	♃18♓
27	20.25	7	5♌	24	26	4	♄13♋R
28	20.29	8	20	25	28	5	♅ 2♏
29	20.32	9	5♍	25	29	5	♆11♐
30	20.36	10	20	25R	0♓	6	♇ 9♎R
31	20.40	11	5♎	25	1	7	♃19♓

Feb	STime	☉	☽	☿	♀	♂	Plnts
1	20.44	12♒	19♎	25♒	3♓	8♑	♃19♓
2	20.48	13	3♏	24	4	8	♄13♋R
3	20.52	14	17	24	5	9	♅ 2♏
4	20.56	15	0♐	23	6	10	♆11♐
5	21.00	16	12	22	7	11	♇ 9♎R
6	21.04	17	25	21	9	11	♃20♓
7	21.08	18	7♑	20	10	12	♄13♋R
8	21.12	19	19	19	11	13	♅ 2♏
9	21.16	20	1♒	17	12	13	♆11♐
10	21.20	21	13	16	14	14	♇ 9♎R
11	21.24	22	25	15	15	15	♃21♓
12	21.28	23	7♓	14	16	16	♄12♋R
13	21.32	24	19	13	17	16	♅ 2♏R
14	21.36	25	1♈	12	19	17	♆11♐
15	21.39	26	12	11	20	18	♇ 9♎R
16	21.43	27	25	11	21	19	♃23♓
17	21.47	28	7♉	10	22	19	♄12♋R
18	21.51	29	19	10	24	20	♅ 2♏R
19	21.55	0♓	2♊	10	25	21	♆11♐
20	21.59	1	15	10D	26	22	♇ 9♎R
21	22.03	2	29	10	27	22	♃24♓
22	22.07	3	13♋	10	29	23	♄12♋R
23	22.11	4	28	10	0♈	24	♅ 2♏R
24	22.15	5	13♌	10	1	25	♆11♐
25	22.19	6	28	11	2	25	♇ 8♎R
26	22.23	7	13♍	11	4	26	♃25♓
27	22.27	8	29	12	5	27	♄12♋R
28	22.31	9	14♎	13	6	28	♅ 2♏R

Mar	STime	☉	☽	☿	♀	♂	Plnts
1	22.35	10♓	28♎	13♒	7♈	28♑	♃26♓
2	22.39	11	12♏	14	8	29	♄12♋R
3	22.43	12	26	15	10	0♒	♅ 2♏R
4	22.46	13	9♐	16	11	1	♆11♐
5	22.50	14	22	17	12	1	♇ 8♎R
6	22.54	15	4♑	18	13	2	♃27♓
7	22.58	16	16	19	15	3	♄12♋R
8	23.02	17	28	20	16	4	♅ 2♏R
9	23.06	18	10♒	21	17	4	♆11♐
10	23.10	19	22	22	18	5	♇ 8♎R
11	23.14	20	4♓	23	19	6	♃28♓
12	23.18	21	16	25	21	7	♄12♋R
13	23.22	22	28	26	22	7	♅ 2♏R
14	23.26	23	10♈	27	23	8	♆12♐
15	23.30	24	22	28	24	9	♇ 8♎R
16	23.34	25	4♉	0♓	26	10	♃29♓
17	23.38	26	16	1	27	10	♄12♋
18	23.42	27	29	2	28	11	♅ 1♏R
19	23.46	28	12♊	4	29	12	♆11♐
20	23.50	29	25	5	0♉	13	♇ 8♎R
21	23.54	0♈	8♋	7	2	14	♃ 0♈
22	23.57	1	22	8	3	14	♄12♋
23	0.01	2	7♌	10	4	15	♅ 1♏R
24	0.05	3	21	11	5	16	♆11♐R
25	0.09	4	6♍	13	6	17	♇ 8♎R
26	0.13	5	22	14	8	17	♃ 2♈
27	0.17	6	7♎	16	9	18	♄12♋
28	0.21	7	22	18	10	19	♅ 1♏R
29	0.25	8	6♏	19	11	20	♆11♐R
30	0.29	9	20	21	12	20	♇ 8♎R
31	0.33	10	4♐	23	14	21	♃ 3♈

Apr	STime	☉	☽	☿	♀	♂	Plnts
1	0.37	11♈	17♐	24♓	15♉	22♒	♃ 3♈
2	0.41	12	0♑	26	16	23	♄12♋
3	0.45	13	13	28	17	23	♅ 1♏R
4	0.49	14	25	0♈	18	24	♆11♐R
5	0.53	15	7♒	1	20	25	♇ 7♎R
6	0.57	16	19	3	21	26	♃ 4♈
7	1.01	17	1♓	5	22	26	♄12♋
8	1.04	18	12	7	23	27	♅ 1♏R
9	1.08	19	24	9	24	28	♆11♐R
10	1.12	20	6♈	11	26	29	♇ 7♎R
11	1.16	21	19	13	27	29	♃ 5♈
12	1.20	22	1♉	15	28	0♓	♄12♋
13	1.24	23	13	17	29	1	♅ 0♏R
14	1.28	24	26	19	0♊	2	♆11♐R
15	1.32	25	9♊	21	2	3	♇ 7♎R
16	1.36	26	22	23	3	3	♃ 7♈
17	1.40	27	5♋	25	4	4	♄13♋
18	1.44	28	19	27	5	5	♅ 0♏R
19	1.48	29	2♌	29	6	6	♆11♐R
20	1.52	29	17	1♉	7	6	♇ 7♎R
21	1.56	0♉	1♍	3	9	7	♃ 8♈
22	2.00	1	16	6	10	8	♄13♋
23	2.04	2	1♎	8	11	9	♅ 0♏R
24	2.08	3	15	10	12	9	♆11♐R
25	2.12	4	0♏	12	13	10	♇ 7♎R
26	2.15	5	14	14	14	11	♃ 9♈
27	2.19	6	28	16	16	12	♄13♋
28	2.23	7	12♐	18	17	12	♅ 0♏R
29	2.27	8	25	20	18	13	♆11♐R
30	2.31	9	8♑	22	19	14	♇ 7♎R

May	STime	☉	☽	☿	♀	♂	Plnts
1	2.35	10♉	21♑	24♉	20♊	15♓	♃10♈
2	2.39	11	3♒	26	21	15	♄14♋
3	2.43	12	15	28	22	16	♅ 0♏R
4	2.47	13	27	0♊	24	17	♆11♐R
5	2.51	14	9♓	1	25	18	♇ 7♎R
6	2.55	15	21	3	26	18	♃11♈
7	2.59	16	3♈	5	27	19	♄14♋
8	3.03	17	15	6	28	20	♅29♎R
9	3.07	18	27	8	29	21	♆11♐R
10	3.11	19	10♉	9	0♋	22	♇ 7♎R
11	3.15	20	22	11	2	22	♃12♈
12	3.19	21	5♊	12	3	23	♄15♋
13	3.22	22	18	13	4	24	♅29♎R
14	3.26	23	2♋	14	5	25	♆11♐R
15	3.30	24	16	16	6	25	♇ 6♎R
16	3.34	25	29	17	7	26	♃13♈
17	3.38	26	13♌	18	8	27	♄15♋
18	3.42	27	27	18	9	28	♅29♎R
19	3.46	28	12♍	19	10	28	♆10♐R
20	3.50	29	26	20	12	29	♇ 6♎R
21	3.54	0♊	10♎	21	13	0♈	♃14♈
22	3.58	0	25	21	14	1	♄16♋
23	4.02	1	9♏	22	15	1	♅29♎R
24	4.06	2	23	22	16	2	♆10♐R
25	4.10	3	7♐	23	17	3	♇ 6♎R
26	4.14	4	20	23	18	4	♃15♈
27	4.18	5	3♑	23	19	4	♄16♋
28	4.22	6	16	23	20	5	♅29♎R
29	4.26	7	29	23R	21	6	♆10♐R
30	4.30	8	11♒	23	22	7	♇ 6♎R
31	4.33	9	23	23	23	7	♃16♈

Jun	STime	☉	☽	☿	♀	♂	Plnts
1	4.37	10♊	5♓	23♊	25♋	8♈	♃17♈
2	4.41	11	17	23	26	9	♄17♋
3	4.45	12	29	22	27	10	♅29♎R
4	4.49	13	11♈	22	28	10	♆10♐R
5	4.53	14	23	22	29	11	♇ 6♎R
6	4.57	15	5♉	21	0♌	12	♃17♈
7	5.01	16	18	21	1	13	♄17♋
8	5.05	17	1♊	20	2	13	♅28♎R
9	5.09	18	14	20	3	14	♆10♐R
10	5.13	19	28	19	4	15	♇ 6♎
11	5.17	20	12♋	19	5	15	♃18♈
12	5.21	21	26	18	6	16	♄18♋
13	5.25	22	10♌	17	7	17	♅28♎R
14	5.29	23	24	17	8	18	♆10♐R
15	5.33	23	9♍	16	9	18	♇ 6♎
16	5.37	24	23	16	10	19	♃19♈
17	5.40	25	7♎	16	11	20	♄19♋
18	5.44	26	21	15	12	21	♅28♎R
19	5.48	27	5♏	15	13	21	♆10♐R
20	5.52	28	19	15	14	22	♇ 6♎
21	5.56	29	2♐	15	15	23	♃20♈
22	6.00	0♋	16	15D	15	23	♄19♋
23	6.04	1	29	15	16	24	♅28♎R
24	6.08	2	12♑	15	17	25	♆10♐R
25	6.12	3	24	15	18	26	♇ 6♎
26	6.16	4	7♒	15	19	26	♃21♈
27	6.20	5	19	16	20	27	♄20♋
28	6.24	6	1♓	16	21	28	♅28♎R
29	6.28	7	13	17	22	29	♆ 9♐R
30	6.32	8	25	17	23	29	♇ 6♎

Jul	STime	☉	☽	☿	♀	♂	Plnts
1	6.36	9♋	7♈	18♊	23♌	0♉	♃21♈
2	6.40	10	19	19	24	1	♄21♋
3	6.44	11	1♉	19	25	1	♅28♎
4	6.47	12	13	20	26	2	♆ 9♐R
5	6.51	13	26	21	27	3	♇ 6♎
6	6.55	14	9♊	22	27	3	♃22♈
7	6.59	14	23	23	28	4	♄21♋
8	7.03	15	6♋	25	29	5	♅28♎
9	7.07	16	21	26	0♍	6	♆ 9♐R
10	7.11	17	5♌	27	0	6	♇ 6♎
11	7.15	18	20	28	1	7	♃23♈
12	7.19	19	5♍	0♋	2	8	♄22♋
13	7.23	20	19	1	3	8	♅28♎
14	7.27	21	4♎	3	3	9	♆ 9♐R
15	7.31	22	18	5	4	10	♇ 6♎
16	7.35	23	2♏	6	4	10	♃23♈
17	7.39	24	15	8	5	11	♄22♋
18	7.43	25	29	10	6	12	♅28♎
19	7.47	26	12♐	12	6	13	♆ 9♐R
20	7.51	27	25	14	7	13	♇ 6♎
21	7.55	28	8♑	16	7	14	♃23♈
22	7.58	29	20	18	8	15	♄23♋
23	8.02	0♌	3♒	20	8	15	♅28♎
24	8.06	1	15	22	9	16	♆ 9♐R
25	8.10	2	27	24	9	17	♇ 7♎
26	8.14	3	9♓	26	9	17	♃24♈
27	8.18	4	21	28	10	18	♄24♋
28	8.22	5	3♈	0♌	10	19	♅28♎
29	8.26	5	15	2	10	19	♆ 9♐R
30	8.30	6	27	4	11	20	♇ 7♎
31	8.34	7	9♉	6	11	21	♃24♈

Aug	STime	☉	☽	☿	♀	♂	Plnts
1	8.38	8♌	21♉	8♌	11♍	21♉	♃24♈
2	8.42	9	4♊	11	11	22	♄25♋
3	8.46	10	17	13	11	22	♅28♎
4	8.50	11	1♋	15	11	23	♆ 9♐R
5	8.54	12	15	17	11	24	♇ 7♎
6	8.58	13	29	19	11R	24	♃24♈
7	9.02	14	14♌	21	11	25	♄25♋
8	9.05	15	29	23	11	26	♅29♎
9	9.09	16	14♍	25	11	26	♆ 9♐
10	9.13	17	29	26	11	27	♇ 7♎
11	9.17	18	14♎	28	11	28	♃24♈
12	9.21	19	28	0♍	11	28	♄26♋
13	9.25	20	12♏	2	10	29	♅29♎
14	9.29	21	26	4	10	29	♆ 9♐R
15	9.33	22	9♐	6	10	0♊	♇ 7♎
16	9.37	23	22	7	9	1	♃24♈R
17	9.41	24	5♑	9	9	1	♄26♋
18	9.45	25	17	11	8	2	♅29♎
19	9.49	26	0♒	12	8	3	♆ 9♐
20	9.53	27	12	14	7	3	♇ 7♎
21	9.57	28	24	16	7	4	♃24♈R
22	10.01	28	6♓	17	6	4	♄27♋
23	10.05	29	18	19	6	5	♅29♎
24	10.09	0♍	0♈	20	5	6	♆ 9♐
25	10.13	1	12	22	5	6	♇ 7♎
26	10.16	2	23	24	4	7	♃24♈R
27	10.20	3	5♉	25	3	7	♄28♋
28	10.24	4	17	27	3	8	♅29♎
29	10.28	5	0♊	28	2	8	♆ 9♐
30	10.32	6	12	29	2	9	♇ 8♎
31	10.36	7	25	1♎	1	10	♃24♈R

Sep	STime	☉	☽	☿	♀	♂	Plnts
1	10.40	8♍	9♋	2♎	0♍	10♊	♃24♈R
2	10.44	9	23	4	0	11	♄28♋
3	10.48	10	8♌	5	29♌	11	♅29♎
4	10.52	11	22	6	29	12	♆ 9♐
5	10.56	12	8♍	7	28	12	♇ 8♎
6	11.00	13	23	9	28	13	♃24♈R
7	11.04	14	8♎	10	27	13	♄29♋
8	11.08	15	23	11	27	14	♅ 0♏
9	11.12	16	8♏	12	27	14	♆ 9♐
10	11.16	17	22	13	26	15	♇ 8♎
11	11.20	18	6♐	14	26	15	♃23♈R
12	11.23	19	19	15	26	16	♄29♋
13	11.27	20	2♑	16	26	16	♅ 0♏
14	11.31	21	14	17	25	17	♆ 9♐
15	11.35	22	27	18	25	17	♇ 8♎
16	11.39	23	9♒	19	25	18	♃23♈R
17	11.43	24	21	20	25D	18	♄ 0♌
18	11.47	25	3♓	21	25	19	♅ 0♏
19	11.51	26	15	21	25	19	♆ 9♐
20	11.55	27	27	22	25	20	♇ 8♎
21	11.59	28	9♈	23	25	20	♃22♈R
22	12.03	29	20	23	26	21	♄ 0♌
23	12.07	0♎	2♉	23	26	21	♅ 1♏
24	12.11	1	14	24	26	22	♆ 9♐
25	12.15	2	27	24	26	22	♇ 9♎
26	12.19	2	9♊	24	26	23	♃22♈R
27	12.23	3	22	24R	27	23	♄ 1♌
28	12.27	4	5♋	24	27	23	♅ 1♏
29	12.30	5	18	24	28	24	♆ 9♐
30	12.34	6	2♌	23	28	24	♇ 9♎

Oct	STime	☉	☽	☿	♀	♂	Plnts
1	12.38	7♎	16♌	23♎	28♌	25♊	♃21♈R
2	12.42	8	1♍	22	29	25	♄ 1♌
3	12.46	9	16	22	29	25	♅ 1♏
4	12.50	10	1♎	21	0♍	26	♆ 9♐
5	12.54	11	16	20	0	26	♇ 9♎
6	12.58	12	1♏	19	1	26	♃20♈R
7	13.02	13	16	18	2	27	♄ 1♌
8	13.06	14	1♐	16	2	27	♅ 1♏
9	13.10	15	14	15	3	27	♆ 9♐
10	13.14	16	28	14	3	28	♇ 9♎
11	13.18	17	11♑	13	4	28	♃20♈R
12	13.22	18	23	12	5	28	♄ 2♌
13	13.26	19	6♒	11	6	29	♅ 2♏
14	13.30	20	18	10	6	29	♆ 9♐
15	13.34	21	0♓	10	7	29	♇ 9♎
16	13.38	22	12	9	8	29	♃19♈R
17	13.41	23	24	9	9	0♋	♄ 2♌
18	13.45	24	5♈	9D	9	0	♅ 2♏
19	13.49	25	17	9	10	0	♆10♐
20	13.53	26	29	9	11	0	♇10♎
21	13.57	27	11♉	10	12	1	♃18♈R
22	14.01	28	24	10	13	1	♄ 2♌
23	14.05	29	6♊	11	13	1	♅ 2♏
24	14.09	0♏	19	12	14	1	♆10♐
25	14.13	1	1♋	13	15	1	♇10♎
26	14.17	2	14	14	16	2	♃18♈R
27	14.21	3	28	15	17	2	♄ 2♌
28	14.25	4	12♌	16	18	2	♅ 3♏
29	14.29	5	26	18	19	2	♆10♐
30	14.33	6	10♍	19	20	2	♇10♎
31	14.37	7	25	21	21	2	♃17♈R

Nov	STime	☉	☽	☿	♀	♂	Plnts
1	14.41	8♏	10♎	22♎	22♍	2♋	♃17♈R
2	14.45	9	25	24	23	2	♄ 3♌
3	14.48	10	9♏	25	24	2	♅ 3♏
4	14.52	11	24	27	25	2	♆10♐
5	14.56	12	9♐	28	26	2	♇10♎
6	15.00	13	22	0♏	27	2	♃16♈R
7	15.04	14	6♑	2	28	2R	♄ 3♌
8	15.08	15	19	3	29	2	♅ 3♏
9	15.12	16	2♒	5	0♎	2	♆10♐
10	15.16	17	14	6	1	2	♇10♎
11	15.20	18	26	8	2	2	♃16♈R
12	15.24	19	8♓	10	3	2	♄ 3♌
13	15.28	20	20	11	4	2	♅ 4♏
14	15.32	21	2♈	13	5	2	♆10♐
15	15.36	22	14	14	6	2	♇10♎
16	15.40	23	26	16	7	2	♃15♈R
17	15.44	24	8♉	18	8	2	♄ 3♌R
18	15.48	25	20	19	9	1	♅ 4♏
19	15.52	26	3♊	21	10	1	♆11♐
20	15.56	27	15	22	11	1	♇11♎
21	15.59	28	28	24	12	1	♃15♈R
22	16.03	29	11♋	26	13	1	♄ 3♌R
23	16.07	0♐	25	27	15	0	♅ 4♏
24	16.11	1	8♌	29	16	0	♆11♐
25	16.15	2	22	0♐	17	0	♇11♎
26	16.19	3	6♍	2	18	0	♃15♈R
27	16.23	4	20	4	19	29♊	♄ 3♌R
28	16.27	5	5♎	5	20	29	♅ 5♏
29	16.31	6	19	7	21	29	♆11♐
30	16.35	7	3♏	8	22	28	♇11♎

Dec	STime	☉	☽	☿	♀	♂	Plnts
1	16.39	8♐	18♏	10♐	23♎	28♊	♃15♈R
2	16.43	9	2♐	11	25	28	♄ 2♌R
3	16.47	10	16	13	26	27	♅ 5♏
4	16.51	11	0♑	15	27	27	♆11♐
5	16.55	12	14	16	28	27	♇11♎
6	16.59	13	27	18	29	26	♃14♈R
7	17.03	14	10♒	19	0♏	26	♄ 2♌R
8	17.06	15	22	21	1	25	♅ 5♏
9	17.10	16	4♓	22	3	25	♆11♐
10	17.14	17	16	24	4	25	♇11♎
11	17.18	19	28	25	5	24	♃14♈
12	17.22	20	10♈	27	6	24	♄ 2♌R
13	17.26	21	22	29	7	24	♅ 5♏
14	17.30	22	4♉	0♑	8	23	♆12♐
15	17.34	23	16	2	10	23	♇11♎
16	17.38	24	29	3	11	22	♃15♈
17	17.42	25	11♊	5	12	22	♄ 2♌R
18	17.46	26	24	6	13	22	♅ 6♏
19	17.50	27	8♋	8	14	21	♆12♐
20	17.54	28	21	10	15	21	♇11♎
21	17.58	29	5♌	11	17	20	♃15♈
22	18.02	0♑	19	13	18	20	♄ 1♌R
23	18.06	1	3♍	14	19	20	♅ 6♏
24	18.10	2	17	16	20	19	♆12♐
25	18.14	3	1♎	17	21	19	♇11♎
26	18.17	4	15	19	23	19	♃15♈
27	18.21	5	29	21	24	18	♄ 1♌R
28	18.25	6	13♏	22	25	18	♅ 6♏
29	18.29	7	27	24	26	18	♆12♐
30	18.33	8	11♐	25	27	17	♇11♎
31	18.37	9	25	26	28	17	♃15♈

Jan	STime	☉	☽	☿	♀	♂	Plnts
1	18.41	10♑	9♑	28♑	0♐	17♊	♃15♈
2	18.45	11	22	29	1	17	♄ 1♌R
3	18.49	12	5♒	1♒	2	16	♅ 6♏
4	18.53	13	17	2	3	16	♆12♐
5	18.57	14	0♓	3	5	16	♇11♎
6	19.01	15	12	4	6	16	♃16♈
7	19.05	16	24	5	7	16	♄ 0♌R
8	19.09	17	6♈	6	8	15	♅ 6♏
9	19.13	18	18	7	9	15	♆13♐
10	19.17	19	0♉	8	11	15	♇11♎
11	19.21	20	12	8	12	15	♃16♈
12	19.24	21	24	9	13	15	♄ 0♌R
13	19.28	22	6♊	9	14	15	♅ 6♏
14	19.32	23	19	9R	15	15	♆13♐
15	19.36	24	2♋	9	17	15	♇11♎
16	19.40	25	16	9	18	15	♃17♈
17	19.44	26	0♌	8	19	15	♄29♋R
18	19.48	27	14	7	20	14	♅ 7♏
19	19.52	28	29	6	21	14	♆13♐
20	19.56	29	13♍	5	23	14D	♇11♎R
21	20.00	0♒	28	4	24	14	♃17♈
22	20.04	1	12♎	3	25	14	♄29♋R
23	20.08	2	26	2	26	14	♅ 7♏
24	20.12	3	10♏	0	28	15	♆13♐
25	20.16	4	24	29♑	29	15	♇11♎
26	20.20	5	8♐	28	0♑	15	♃18♈
27	20.24	6	21	27	1	15	♄29♋R
28	20.28	7	4♑	26	2	15	♅ 7♏
29	20.31	8	18	25	4	15	♆13♐
30	20.35	9	0♒	24	5	15	♇11♎R
31	20.39	10	13	24	6	15	♃19♈

Feb	STime	☉	☽	☿	♀	♂	Plnts
1	20.43	11♒	26♒	23♑	7♑	15♊	♃19♈
2	20.47	12	8♓	23	9	15	♄28♋R
3	20.51	13	20	23D	10	16	♅ 7♏
4	20.55	14	2♈	23	11	16	♆13♐
5	20.59	16	14	23	12	16	♇11♎R
6	21.03	17	26	23	13	16	♃20♈
7	21.07	18	7♉	24	15	16	♄28♋R
8	21.11	19	19	24	16	16	♅ 7♏
9	21.15	20	2♊	25	17	17	♆13♐
10	21.19	21	14	25	18	17	♇11♎R
11	21.23	22	27	26	20	17	♃21♈
12	21.27	23	10♋	27	21	17	♄27♋R
13	21.31	24	24	28	22	18	♅ 7♏
14	21.35	25	8♌	28	23	18	♆13♐
15	21.39	26	23	29	25	18	♇11♎R
16	21.42	27	8♍	0♒	26	18	♃21♈
17	21.46	28	23	1	27	19	♄27♋R
18	21.50	29	8♎	2	28	19	♅ 7♏R
19	21.54	0♓	22	4	29	19	♆13♐
20	21.58	1	7♏	5	1♒	20	♇11♎R
21	22.02	2	21	6	2	20	♃22♈
22	22.06	3	5♐	7	3	20	♄27♋R
23	22.10	4	18	8	4	20	♅ 7♏R
24	22.14	5	1♑	10	6	21	♆14♐
25	22.18	6	14	11	7	21	♇11♎R
26	22.22	7	27	12	8	21	♃23♈
27	22.26	8	10♒	14	9	22	♄27♋R
28	22.30	9	22	15	11	22	♅ 7♏R
29	22.34	10	4♓	16	12	22	♆14♐

Mar	STime	☉	☽	☿	♀	♂	Plnts
1	22.38	11♓	17♓	18♒	13♒	23♊	♃24♈
2	22.42	12	29	19	14	23	♄26♋R
3	22.46	13	10♈	21	15	24	♅ 7♏R
4	22.49	14	22	22	17	24	♆14♐
5	22.53	15	4♉	24	18	24	♇11♎R
6	22.57	16	16	25	19	25	♃25♈
7	23.01	17	28	27	20	25	♄26♋R
8	23.05	18	10♊	28	22	26	♅ 7♏R
9	23.09	19	22	0♓	23	26	♆14♐
10	23.13	20	5♋	1	24	26	♇11♎R
11	23.17	21	18	3	25	27	♃26♈
12	23.21	22	2♌	5	27	27	♄26♋R
13	23.25	23	16	6	28	28	♅ 6♏R
14	23.29	24	1♍	8	29	28	♆14♐
15	23.33	25	16	10	0♓	28	♇10♎R
16	23.37	26	1♎	11	1	29	♃27♈
17	23.41	27	16	13	3	29	♄26♋R
18	23.45	28	1♏	15	4	0♋	♅ 6♏R
19	23.49	29	16	16	5	0	♆14♐
20	23.53	0♈	1♐	18	6	1	♇10♎R
21	23.57	1	15	20	8	1	♃29♈
22	0.00	2	28	22	9	1	♄26♋R
23	0.04	3	11♑	24	10	2	♅ 6♏R
24	0.08	4	24	26	11	2	♆14♐
25	0.12	5	7♒	27	13	3	♇10♎R
26	0.16	6	19	29	14	3	♃ 0♉
27	0.20	7	1♓	1♈	15	4	♄26♋
28	0.24	8	14	3	16	4	♅ 6♏R
29	0.28	9	25	5	18	5	♆14♐R
30	0.32	10	7♈	7	19	5	♇10♎R
31	0.36	11	19	9	20	6	♃ 1♉

Apr	STime	☉	☽	☿	♀	♂	Plnts
1	0.40	12♈	1♉	11♈	21♓	6♋	♃ 1♉
2	0.44	13	13	13	22	7	♄26♋
3	0.48	14	25	15	24	7	♅ 6♏R
4	0.52	15	7♊	17	25	8	♆14♐R
5	0.56	16	19	20	26	8	♇10♎R
6	1.00	17	1♋	22	27	9	♃ 2♉
7	1.04	17	14	24	29	9	♄26♋
8	1.07	18	27	26	0♈	10	♅ 6♏R
9	1.11	19	11♌	28	1	10	♆14♐R
10	1.15	20	25	0♉	2	11	♇10♎R
11	1.19	21	9♍	2	4	11	♃ 3♉
12	1.23	22	24	4	5	12	♄26♋
13	1.27	23	9♎	6	6	12	♅ 5♏R
14	1.31	24	24	8	7	13	♆13♐R
15	1.35	25	10♏	10	8	13	♇10♎R
16	1.39	26	25	12	10	14	♃ 5♉
17	1.43	27	9♐	13	11	14	♄26♋
18	1.47	28	23	15	12	15	♅ 5♏R
19	1.51	29	7♑	17	13	15	♆13♐R
20	1.55	0♉	21	18	15	16	♇ 9♎R
21	1.59	1	4♒	20	16	16	♃ 6♉
22	2.03	2	16	21	17	17	♄26♋
23	2.07	3	28	23	18	17	♅ 5♏R
24	2.11	4	11♓	24	20	18	♆13♐R
25	2.14	5	22	25	21	18	♇ 9♎R
26	2.18	6	4♈	26	22	19	♃ 7♉
27	2.22	7	16	27	23	19	♄27♋
28	2.26	8	28	28	24	20	♅ 5♏R
29	2.30	9	10♉	29	26	20	♆13♐R
30	2.34	10	22	0♊	27	21	♇ 9♎R

May	STime	☉	☽	☿	♀	♂	Plnts
1	2.38	11♉	4♊	1♊	28♈	21♋	♃ 8♉
2	2.42	12	16	1	29	22	♄27♋
3	2.46	13	28	2	1♉	23	♅ 4♏R
4	2.50	14	11♋	2	2	23	♆13♐R
5	2.54	15	24	3	3	24	♇ 9♎R
6	2.58	16	7♌	3	4	24	♃ 9♉
7	3.02	17	20	3	6	25	♄27♋
8	3.06	18	4♍	3	7	25	♅ 4♏R
9	3.10	19	18	3R	8	26	♆13♐R
10	3.14	20	3♎	3	9	26	♇ 9♎R
11	3.18	21	18	3	10	27	♃11♉
12	3.22	22	3♏	3	12	28	♄28♋
13	3.25	23	18	3	13	28	♅ 4♏R
14	3.29	24	3♐	2	14	29	♆13♐R
15	3.33	24	17	2	15	29	♇ 9♎R
16	3.37	25	2♑	1	17	0♌	♃12♉
17	3.41	26	16	1	18	0	♄28♋
18	3.45	27	29	0	19	1	♅ 4♏R
19	3.49	28	12♒	0	20	1	♆13♐R
20	3.53	29	25	29♉	22	2	♇ 9♎R
21	3.57	0♊	7♓	29	23	3	♃13♉
22	4.01	1	19	28	24	3	♄28♋
23	4.05	2	1♈	28	25	4	♅ 4♏R
24	4.09	3	13	27	26	4	♆13♐R
25	4.13	4	25	27	28	5	♇ 9♎R
26	4.17	5	7♉	26	29	5	♃14♉
27	4.21	6	18	26	0♊	6	♄29♋
28	4.25	7	0♊	25	1	7	♅ 4♏R
29	4.29	8	13	25	3	7	♆12♐R
30	4.32	9	25	25	4	8	♇ 9♎R
31	4.36	10	8♋	25	5	8	♃15♉

Jun	STime	☉	☽	☿	♀	♂	Plnts
1	4.40	11♊	21♋	25♉	6♊	9♌	♃15♉
2	4.44	12	4♌	25	7	9	♄29♋
3	4.48	13	17	25	9	10	♅ 3♏R
4	4.52	14	1♍	25	10	11	♆12♐R
5	4.56	15	14	25	11	11	♇ 9♎
6	5.00	16	28	25	12	12	♃17♉
7	5.04	17	13♎	26	14	12	♄ 0♌
8	5.08	18	27	26	15	13	♅ 3♏R
9	5.12	18	12♏	27	16	13	♆12♐R
10	5.16	19	27	27	17	14	♇ 9♎
11	5.20	20	11♐	28	19	15	♃18♉
12	5.24	21	26	29	20	15	♄ 0♌
13	5.28	22	10♑	29	21	16	♅ 3♏R
14	5.32	23	24	0♊	22	16	♆12♐R
15	5.36	24	7♒	1	23	17	♇ 9♎
16	5.40	25	20	2	25	18	♃19♉
17	5.43	26	3♓	3	26	18	♄ 1♌
18	5.47	27	15	4	27	19	♅ 3♏R
19	5.51	28	27	5	28	19	♆12♐R
20	5.55	29	9♈	7	0♋	20	♇ 9♎
21	5.59	0♋	21	8	1	20	♃20♉
22	6.03	1	3♉	9	2	21	♄ 2♌
23	6.07	2	15	11	3	22	♅ 3♏R
24	6.11	3	27	12	5	22	♆12♐R
25	6.15	4	9♊	14	6	23	♇ 9♎
26	6.19	5	22	15	7	23	♃21♉
27	6.23	6	4♋	17	8	24	♄ 2♌
28	6.27	7	17	18	9	25	♅ 3♏R
29	6.31	8	0♌	20	11	25	♆12♐R
30	6.35	9	14	22	12	26	♇ 9♎

Jul	STime	☉	☽	☿	♀	♂	Plnts
1	6.39	9♋	28♌	24♊	13♋	26♌	♃22♉
2	6.43	10	11♍	26	14	27	♄ 3♌
3	6.47	11	25	28	16	28	♅ 3♏
4	6.50	12	9♎	0♋	17	28	♆12♐R
5	6.54	13	23	2	18	29	♇ 9♎
6	6.58	14	8♏	4	19	29	♃23♉
7	7.02	15	22	6	21	0♍	♄ 3♌
8	7.06	16	6♐	8	22	1	♅ 3♏
9	7.10	17	20	10	23	1	♆11♐R
10	7.14	18	5♑	12	24	2	♇ 9♎
11	7.18	19	18	14	25	2	♃24♉
12	7.22	20	2♒	16	27	3	♄ 4♌
13	7.26	21	15	18	28	4	♅ 3♏
14	7.30	22	28	21	29	4	♆11♐R
15	7.34	23	11♓	23	0♌	5	♇ 9♎
16	7.38	24	23	25	2	5	♃25♉
17	7.42	25	5♈	27	3	6	♄ 5♌
18	7.46	26	17	29	4	7	♅ 3♏
19	7.50	27	29	1♌	5	7	♆11♐R
20	7.54	28	11♉	3	6	8	♇ 9♎
21	7.58	29	23	5	8	9	♃25♉
22	8.01	29	5♊	7	9	9	♄ 5♌
23	8.05	0♌	17	9	10	10	♅ 3♏
24	8.09	1	0♋	11	11	10	♆11♐R
25	8.13	2	13	13	13	11	♇ 9♎
26	8.17	3	26	15	14	12	♃26♉
27	8.21	4	10♌	17	15	12	♄ 6♌
28	8.25	5	24	19	16	13	♅ 3♏
29	8.29	6	8♍	21	18	13	♆11♐R
30	8.33	7	22	22	19	14	♇ 9♎
31	8.37	8	6♎	24	20	15	♃27♉

Aug	STime	☉	☽	☿	♀	♂	Plnts
1	8.41	9♌	20♎	26♌	21♌	15♍	♃27♉
2	8.45	10	4♏	28	22	16	♄ 7♌
3	8.49	11	19	29	24	17	♅ 3♏
4	8.53	12	3♐	1♍	25	17	♆11♐R
5	8.57	13	16	3	26	18	♇ 9♎
6	9.01	14	0♑	4	27	18	♃28♉
7	9.05	15	14	6	29	19	♄ 7♌
8	9.08	16	28	7	0♍	20	♅ 3♏
9	9.12	17	11♒	9	1	20	♆11♐R
10	9.16	18	24	10	2	21	♇ 9♎
11	9.20	19	7♓	12	4	22	♃28♉
12	9.24	20	19	13	5	22	♄ 8♌
13	9.28	21	1♈	15	6	23	♅ 3♏
14	9.32	22	13	16	7	24	♆11♐R
15	9.36	22	25	18	8	24	♇10♎
16	9.40	23	7♉	19	10	25	♃29♉
17	9.44	24	19	20	11	25	♄ 9♌
18	9.48	25	1♊	21	12	26	♅ 3♏
19	9.52	26	13	23	13	27	♆11♐
20	9.56	27	25	24	15	27	♇10♎
21	10.00	28	8♋	25	16	28	♃ 0♊
22	10.04	29	21	26	17	29	♄ 9♌
23	10.08	0♍	5♌	27	18	29	♅ 4♏
24	10.12	1	18	28	20	0♎	♆11♐
25	10.15	2	3♍	29	21	1	♇10♎
26	10.19	3	17	0♎	22	1	♃ 0♊
27	10.23	4	2♎	1	23	2	♄10♌
28	10.27	5	16	2	24	2	♅ 4♏
29	10.31	6	1♏	3	26	3	♆11♐
30	10.35	7	15	4	27	4	♇10♎
31	10.39	8	29	4	28	4	♃ 0♊

Sep	STime	☉	☽	☿	♀	♂	Plnts
1	10.43	9♍	13♐	5♎	29♍	5♎	♃ 0♊
2	10.47	10	27	6	1♎	6	♄11♌
3	10.51	11	11♑	6	2	6	♅ 4♏
4	10.55	12	24	7	3	7	♆11♐
5	10.59	13	7♒	7	4	8	♇10♎
6	11.03	14	20	7	6	8	♃ 1♊
7	11.07	15	3♓	7	7	9	♄11♌
8	11.11	16	15	8R	8	10	♅ 4♏
9	11.15	17	28	8	9	10	♆11♐
10	11.19	18	10♈	7	10	11	♇10♎
11	11.23	19	22	7	12	12	♃ 1♊
12	11.26	20	3♉	7	13	12	♄12♌
13	11.30	21	15	6	14	13	♅ 4♏
14	11.34	21	27	6	15	13	♆11♐
15	11.38	22	9♊	5	17	14	♇11♎
16	11.42	23	21	4	18	15	♃ 1♊
17	11.46	24	3♋	4	19	15	♄12♌
18	11.50	25	16	3	20	16	♅ 5♏
19	11.54	26	29	2	22	17	♆11♐
20	11.58	27	13♌	1	23	17	♇11♎
21	12.02	28	27	29♍	24	18	♃ 1♊R
22	12.06	29	11♍	28	25	19	♄13♌
23	12.10	0♎	26	27	26	19	♅ 5♏
24	12.14	1	11♎	26	28	20	♆11♐
25	12.18	2	26	25	29	21	♇11♎
26	12.22	3	11♏	25	0♏	21	♃ 1♊R
27	12.26	4	25	24	1	22	♄13♌
28	12.30	5	10♐	23	3	23	♅ 5♏
29	12.33	6	24	23	4	23	♆11♐
30	12.37	7	8♑	23	5	24	♇11♎

Oct	STime	☉	☽	☿	♀	♂	Plnts
1	12.41	8♎	21♑	23♍	6♏	25♎	♃ 1♊R
2	12.45	9	4♒	23	7	25	♄14♌
3	12.49	10	17	23	9	26	♅ 6♏
4	12.53	11	0♓	24	10	27	♆11♐
5	12.57	12	12	24	11	27	♇11♎
6	13.01	13	24	25	12	28	♃ 0♊R
7	13.05	14	6♈	26	14	29	♄14♌
8	13.09	15	18	27	15	29	♅ 6♏
9	13.13	16	0♉	28	16	0♏	♆11♐
10	13.17	17	12	0♎	17	1	♇12♎
11	13.21	18	24	1	18	2	♃ 0♊R
12	13.25	19	5♊	2	20	2	♄15♌
13	13.29	20	17	4	21	3	♅ 6♏
14	13.33	21	29	5	22	4	♆12♐
15	13.37	22	12♋	7	23	4	♇12♎
16	13.41	23	24	8	25	5	♃ 0♊R
17	13.44	24	7♌	10	26	6	♄15♌
18	13.48	25	21	12	27	6	♅ 6♏
19	13.52	26	5♍	13	28	7	♆12♐
20	13.56	27	19	15	29	8	♇12♎
21	14.00	28	4♎	17	1♐	8	♃29♉R
22	14.04	29	19	18	2	9	♄15♌
23	14.08	0♏	4♏	20	3	10	♅ 7♏
24	14.12	1	19	22	4	10	♆12♐
25	14.16	2	4♐	23	6	11	♇12♎
26	14.20	3	19	25	7	12	♃29♉R
27	14.24	4	3♑	27	8	12	♄16♌
28	14.28	5	17	29	9	13	♅ 7♏
29	14.32	6	1♒	0♏	10	14	♆12♐
30	14.36	7	14	2	12	15	♇12♎
31	14.40	8	27	4	13	15	♃28♉R

Nov	STime	☉	☽	☿	♀	♂	Plnts
1	14.44	9♏	9♓	5♏	14♐	16♏	♃28♉R
2	14.48	10	21	7	15	17	♄16♌
3	14.51	11	3♈	8	16	17	♅ 7♏
4	14.55	12	15	10	18	18	♆12♐
5	14.59	13	27	12	19	19	♇13♎
6	15.03	14	9♉	13	20	19	♃27♉R
7	15.07	15	21	15	21	20	♄16♌
8	15.11	16	2♊	17	23	21	♅ 8♏
9	15.15	17	14	18	24	22	♆12♐
10	15.19	18	26	20	25	22	♇13♎
11	15.23	19	9♋	21	26	23	♃27♉R
12	15.27	20	21	23	27	24	♄16♌
13	15.31	21	4♌	25	29	24	♅ 8♏
14	15.35	22	17	26	0♑	25	♆13♐
15	15.39	23	0♍	28	1	26	♇13♎
16	15.43	24	13	29	2	27	♃26♉R
17	15.47	25	28	1♐	3	27	♄16♌
18	15.51	26	12♎	2	5	28	♅ 8♏
19	15.55	27	27	4	6	29	♆13♐
20	15.59	28	12♏	5	7	29	♇13♎
21	16.02	29	27	7	8	0♐	♃25♉R
22	16.06	0♐	12♐	9	9	1	♄17♌
23	16.10	1	27	10	11	1	♅ 9♏
24	16.14	2	12♑	12	12	2	♆13♐
25	16.18	3	26	13	13	3	♇13♎
26	16.22	4	10♒	15	14	4	♃25♉R
27	16.26	5	23	16	15	4	♄17♌
28	16.30	6	6♓	18	17	5	♅ 9♏
29	16.34	7	18	19	18	6	♆13♐
30	16.38	8	0♈	21	19	7	♇13♎

Dec	STime	☉	☽	☿	♀	♂	Plnts
1	16.42	9♐	12♈	22♐	20♑	7♐	♃24♉R
2	16.46	10	24	24	21	8	♄17♌R
3	16.50	11	6♉	25	23	9	♅ 9♏
4	16.54	12	18	27	24	9	♆13♐
5	16.58	13	29	28	25	10	♇13♎
6	17.02	14	11♊	0♑	26	11	♃23♉R
7	17.06	15	23	1	27	12	♄17♌R
8	17.09	16	6♋	3	28	12	♅ 9♏
9	17.13	17	18	4	0♒	13	♆14♐
10	17.17	18	1♌	6	1	14	♇14♎
11	17.21	19	13	7	2	15	♃23♉R
12	17.25	20	26	9	3	15	♄16♌R
13	17.29	21	10♍	10	4	16	♅10♏
14	17.33	22	23	11	6	17	♆14♐
15	17.37	23	7♎	13	7	17	♇14♎
16	17.41	24	21	14	8	18	♃22♉R
17	17.45	25	6♏	15	9	19	♄16♌R
18	17.49	26	20	16	10	20	♅10♏
19	17.53	27	5♐	17	11	20	♆14♐
20	17.57	28	20	19	13	21	♇14♎
21	18.01	29	5♑	20	14	22	♃22♉R
22	18.05	0♑	20	20	15	23	♄16♌R
23	18.09	1	4♒	21	16	23	♅10♏
24	18.13	3	18	22	17	24	♆14♐
25	18.16	4	1♓	22	18	25	♇14♎
26	18.20	5	14	23	19	26	♃22♉R
27	18.24	6	26	23	21	26	♄16♌R
28	18.28	7	9♈	23R	22	27	♅10♏
29	18.32	8	20	23	23	28	♆14♐
30	18.36	9	2♉	23	24	29	♇14♎
31	18.40	10	14	22	25	29	♃21♉R

Jan	STime	☉	☽	☿	♀	♂	Plnts
1	18.44	11♑	26♉	21♉	26♒	0♑	♃21♉R
2	18.48	12	8♊	20	27	1	♄15♎R
3	18.52	13	20	19	29	2	♅11♏
4	18.56	14	2♊	18	0♓	2	♆14♐
5	19.00	15	15	17	1	3	♇14♎
6	19.04	16	27	15	2	4	♃21♉R
7	19.08	17	10♌	14	3	5	♄15♎R
8	19.12	18	23	13	4	6	♅11♏
9	19.16	19	7♍	12	5	6	♆15♐
10	19.20	20	20	10	6	7	♇14♎
11	19.24	21	4♎	9	7	8	♃21♉R
12	19.27	22	18	9	8	8	♄15♎R
13	19.31	23	2♏	8	9	9	♅11♏
14	19.35	24	16	7	11	10	♆15♐
15	19.39	25	0♐	7	11	10	♇14♎
16	19.43	26	15	7	13	11	♇14♎
17	19.47	27	29	7�D	14	12	♄14♎R
18	19.51	28	14♑	7	15	13	♅11♏
19	19.55	29	28	7	16	14	♆15♐
20	19.59	0♒	12♒	7	17	14	♇14♎
21	20.03	1	25	8	19	16	♃21♉R
22	20.07	2	9♓	8	19	16	♄14♎R
23	20.11	3	22	9	20	17	♅11♏
24	20.15	4	4♈	11	21	18	♆15♐
25	20.19	5	16	11	23	18	♇14♎
26	20.23	6	28	13	23	19	♃21♉R
27	20.27	7	10♉	14	24	20	♄14♎R
28	20.31	8	22	15	25	20	♅11♏
29	20.34	9	4♊	16	27	21	♆15♐
30	20.38	10	16	18	28	22	♇14♎
31	20.42	11	28	20	28	23	♃21♉

Feb	STime	☉	☽	☿	♀	♂	Plnts
1	20.46	12♒	10♊	18♓	29♓	24♑	♃21♉
2	20.50	13	23	19	0♈	24	♄15♎R
3	20.54	14	6♌	20	1	25	♅11♏
4	20.58	15	19	21	2	26	♆15♐R
5	21.02	16	3♍	22	3	27	♃22♉R
6	21.06	17	17	24	4	27	♇13♎R
7	21.10	18	1♎	25	5	28	♅11♏
8	21.14	19	14	26	6	29	♆15♐
9	21.18	20	28	28	6	0♒	♇15♐
10	21.22	21	13♏	29	7	0	♇14♎R
11	21.26	22	27	0♒	8	1	♃22♉R
12	21.30	23	11♐	2	9	2	♄12♎R
13	21.34	24	25	3	10	4	♅11♏R
14	21.38	25	9♑	5	10	4	♆16♐
15	21.42	26	23	6	11	5	♇14♎R
16	21.45	27	7♒	8	12	5	♃23♉
17	21.49	28	20	9	13	6	♄12♎R
18	21.53	29	4♓	11	14	7	♅11♏R
19	21.57	0♓	17	12	14	7	♆16♐
20	22.01	1	0♈	14	15	8	♇14♎R
21	22.05	2	12	15	16	9	♃23♉
22	22.09	3	24	17	16	10	♄12♎R
23	22.13	4	6♉	18	17	11	♅11♏R
24	22.17	5	18	20	17	11	♆16♐
25	22.21	6	0♊	22	18	12	♇13♎R
26	22.25	7	12	23	19	13	♃24♉
27	22.29	8	24	25	19	14	♄11♎R
28	22.33	9	6♌	27	20	14	♅11♏R

Mar	STime	☉	☽	☿	♀	♂	Plnts
1	22.37	10♓	18♌	28♒	20♈	15♒	♃24♉
2	22.41	11	1♍	0♈	21	17	♄11♎R
3	22.45	12	14	2	21	17	♅11♏R
4	22.49	13	28	3	22	18	♆16♐R
5	22.52	14	12♍	5	22	19	♇13♎R
6	22.56	15	26	7	23	19	♃25♉
7	23.00	16	10♎	8	23	20	♄11♎R
8	23.04	18	25	11	23	21	♅11♏R
9	23.08	19	9♏	12	24	21	♆16♐R
10	23.12	20	23	14	24	22	♇13♎R
11	23.16	21	8♐	16	24	23	♃26♉
12	23.20	21	22	18	24	24	♄10♎R
13	23.24	22	6♑	20	24	25	♅11♏R
14	23.28	23	19	22	24	25	♆16♐R
15	23.32	24	3♒	24	24	26	♇13♎R
16	23.36	25	16	26	24R	27	♃26♉
17	23.40	26	0♓	28	24	28	♄10♎R
18	23.44	27	13	0♈	24	29	♅11♏R
19	23.48	28	25	2	24	29	♆16♐R
20	23.52	29	8♈	4	24	0♓	♇13♎R
21	23.56	0♈	20	6	24	1	♃27♉
22	0.00	1	2♉	8	23	2	♄10♎R
23	0.03	2	14	10	23	2	♅11♏R
24	0.07	3	26	12	23	3	♆16♐R
25	0.11	4	8♊	14	22	4	♇13♎R
26	0.15	5	20	16	22	5	♃28♉
27	0.19	6	2♌	18	22	5	♄10♎R
28	0.23	7	14	20	21	6	♅11♏R
29	0.27	8	26	22	21	7	♆16♐R
30	0.31	9	9♌	23	20	8	♇13♎R
31	0.35	10	22	25	20	9	♃29♉

Apr	STime	☉	☽	☿	♀	♂	Plnts
1	0.39	11♈	6♍	27♈	19♈	9♓	♃29♉
2	0.43	12	20	29	18	10	♄15♎R
3	0.47	13	4♎	0♉	18	11	♅11♏R
4	0.51	14	19	2	17	12	♆16♐R
5	0.55	15	4♏	3	17	12	♇12♎R
6	0.59	16	19	5	16	13	♃0♊
7	1.03	17	3♐	6	15	14	♄10♎R
8	1.07	18	18	7	15	15	♅10♏R
9	1.10	19	2♑	8	14	16	♆16♐R
10	1.14	20	16	9	13	16	♇12♎R
11	1.18	21	0♒	10	13	17	♃1♊
12	1.22	22	13	11	12	18	♄10♎R
13	1.26	23	27	12	11	18	♅10♏R
14	1.30	24	9♓	13	11	19	♆16♐R
15	1.34	25	22	13	11	20	♇12♎R
16	1.38	26	4♈	14	11	21	♃2♊
17	1.42	27	17	14	10	22	♄10♎R
18	1.46	28	29	14	10	23	♅10♏R
19	1.50	29	11♉	14	9	23	♆16♐R
20	1.54	0♉	22	14R	9	24	♇12♎R
21	1.58	1	4♊	14	9	25	♃3♊
22	2.02	2	16	14	8	26	♄10♎R
23	2.06	3	28	14	8	26	♅10♏R
24	2.10	4	10♌	13	8	27	♆15♐R
25	2.14	5	22	13	8	28	♇12♎R
26	2.17	6	5♌	12	8	29	♃4♊
27	2.21	7	17	12	8�D	0♈	♄10♎R
28	2.25	8	0♍	11	8	0	♅10♏R
29	2.29	9	14	11	8	1	♆15♐R
30	2.33	10	27	10	8	2	♇12♎R

May	STime	☉	☽	☿	♀	♂	Plnts
1	2.37	11♉	12♍	9♉	8♈	3♈	♃6♊
2	2.41	12	27	9	8	3	♄10♎R
3	2.45	13	12♎	9	9	4	♅9♏R
4	2.49	14	27	8	9	5	♆15♐R
5	2.53	15	12♏	7	9	6	♃7♊
6	2.57	16	27	7	9	6	♇12♎R
7	3.01	17	12♐	6	10	7	♃7♊
8	3.05	18	26	6	10	8	♅9♏R
9	3.09	19	10♑	5	11	9	♆15♐R
10	3.13	20	24	5	11	10	♇11♎R
11	3.17	21	6♒	5	11	10	♃8♊
12	3.21	22	20	4	12	11	♄10♎R
13	3.25	23	2♈	4♍	12	12	♅9♏R
14	3.28	24	14	4	13	12	♆15♐R
15	3.32	25	26	5	14	13	♇11♎R
16	3.36	26	8♉	5	14	14	♃9♊
17	3.40	27	19	5	15	15	♄11♎R
18	3.44	28	1♊	5	15	16	♅9♏R
19	3.48	29	13	6	16	17	♆15♐R
20	3.52	29	25	6	17	17	♇11♎R
21	3.56	0♊	7♌	7	18	19	♃11♊
22	4.00	1	19	7	18	19	♄11♎R
23	4.04	2	1♍	8	19	20	♅9♏R
24	4.08	3	14	9	19	20	♆15♐R
25	4.12	4	26	9	20	21	♇11♎R
26	4.16	5	9♍	10	21	22	♃11♊
27	4.20	6	23	11	22	22	♄11♎R
28	4.24	7	6♎	12	22	23	♅8♏R
29	4.28	8	21	13	23	24	♆15♐R
30	4.32	9	5♏	14	24	25	♇11♎R
31	4.35	10	20	15	25	25	♃12♊

Jun	STime	☉	☽	☿	♀	♂	Plnts
1	4.39	11♊	6♐	16♉	26♈	26♈	♃13♊
2	4.43	12	21	18	27	28	♄11♎R
3	4.47	13	6♑	19	27	28	♅8♏R
4	4.51	14	21	20	28	28	♆15♐R
5	4.55	15	5♒	22	29	29	♃14♊
6	4.59	15	19	23	0♉	0♉	♇11♎R
7	5.03	16	3♈	25	1	1	♃15♊
8	5.07	17	16	26	2	1	♅8♏R
9	5.11	18	28	27	3	2	♆14♐R
10	5.15	19	11♉	29	4	3	♇11♎R
11	5.19	20	23	1♊	4	3	♃15♊
12	5.23	21	5♊	2	5	4	♄13♎
13	5.27	22	17	4	6	5	♅8♏R
14	5.31	23	28	6	7	6	♆14♐R
15	5.35	24	10♌	8	8	7	♇11♎R
16	5.39	25	22	10	9	7	♃16♊
17	5.43	26	4♍	12	10	8	♄13♎
18	5.46	27	16	15	11	8	♅8♏R
19	5.50	28	28	15	12	10	♆14♐R
20	5.54	29	11♍	17	13	10	♇11♎R
21	5.58	0♋	24	19	14	11	♃17♊
22	6.02	1	6♎	22	15	12	♄14♎
23	6.06	2	19	24	16	12	♅8♏R
24	6.10	3	2♏	26	17	13	♆14♐R
25	6.14	4	16	28	18	14	♇11♎R
26	6.18	5	0♐	0♋	20	15	♃18♊
27	6.22	5	14	2	20	15	♄14♎
28	6.26	6	29	5	21	16	♅8♏R
29	6.30	7	14♐	7	22	17	♆14♐R
30	6.34	8	29	9	23	18	♇11♎R

Jul	STime	☉	☽	☿	♀	♂	Plnts
1	6.38	9♋	14♑	11♋	24♉	18♉	♃20♊
2	6.42	10	29	13	25	19	♄15♎
3	6.46	11	14♒	15	26	20	♅7♏R
4	6.50	12	28	17	27	20	♆14♐R
5	6.53	13	11♈	19	29	21	♃21♊
6	6.57	14	24	22	0♊	22	♃21♊
7	7.01	15	7♉	24	1	23	♅7♏R
8	7.05	16	19	26	2	23	♆14♐R
9	7.09	17	1♊	28	3	24	♇11♎R
10	7.13	18	13	0♌	4	25	♃22♊
11	7.17	19	25	2	5	25	♄16♎
12	7.21	20	7♌	4	6	26	♅7♏R
13	7.25	21	19	6	7	27	♆14♐R
14	7.29	22	1♍	8	7	28	♇11♎R
15	7.33	23	13	9	9	29	♃23♊
16	7.37	24	25	11	10	29	♄17♎
17	7.41	24	8♎	13	11	0♊	♅7♏R
18	7.45	25	20	14	13	0	♆13♐R
19	7.49	26	3♏	16	14	1	♇11♎R
20	7.53	27	16	18	15	2	♃24♊
21	7.57	28	29	19	16	2	♄17♎
22	8.00	29	12♐	21	17	3	♅7♏R
23	8.04	0♌	26	22	18	4	♆13♐R
24	8.08	1	10♑	24	19	4	♇11♎R
25	8.12	2	24	25	20	5	♃25♊
26	8.16	3	9♒	27	21	6	♄18♎
27	8.20	4	23	23	23	7	♅7♏R
28	8.24	5	8♈	24	24	7	♆13♐R
29	8.28	6	23	1	25	8	♇11♎R
30	8.32	7	8♉	3	26	9	♃26♊
31	8.36	8	22	4	27	9	♃26♊

Aug	STime	☉	☽	☿	♀	♂	Plnts
1	8.40	9♌	6♊	5♌	28♊	10♊	♃26♊
2	8.44	10	19	6	29	11	♄19♎
3	8.48	11	2♈	1♌	0♋	11	♅8♏
4	8.52	12	15	9	2	12	♆13♐R
5	8.56	13	27	10	3	13	♃27♊
6	9.00	14	10♌	11	4	13	♄19♎
7	9.04	15	21	12	5	15	♅8♏
8	9.08	16	3♍	13	6	15	♆13♐R
9	9.11	16	15	14	7	15	♇12♎R
10	9.15	17	27	15	9	16	♃28♊
11	9.19	18	9♍	16	10	17	♄20♎
12	9.23	19	21	16	11	17	♅8♏
13	9.27	20	4♎	17	12	18	♆13♐R
14	9.31	21	17	18	14	19	♇12♎R
15	9.35	22	0♏	19	15	19	♃29♊
16	9.39	23	13♍	19	16	20	♄21♎
17	9.43	24	26	19	17	21	♅8♏
18	9.47	25	9♏	20	18	21	♆13♐R
19	9.51	26	23	20	19	22	♇13♐
20	9.55	27	7♏	20	20	23	♃0♋
21	9.59	28	21	20	22	23	♄21♎
22	10.03	29	5♑	20R	22	24	♅8♏
23	10.07	0♍	20	20	24	24	♆13♐R
24	10.11	1	4♒	20	25	25	♇12♎R
25	10.15	1	18	19	26	25	♃1♋
26	10.18	2	2♈	20	27	27	♄22♎
27	10.22	4	16	19	28	28	♅9♏
28	10.26	5	0♉	19	0♌	28	♆13♐R
29	10.30	6	14	18	1	29	♇12♎R
30	10.34	7	27	18	2	29	♃2♋
31	10.38	8	10♌	17	3	29	♃2♋

Sep	STime	☉	☽	☿	♀	♂	Plnts
1	10.42	9♍	23♌	16♍	4♌	0♋	♃2♋
2	10.46	10	5♎	16	5	1	♄23♎
3	10.50	11	17	14	7	1	♅8♏
4	10.54	12	29	13	8	2	♆13♐
5	10.58	13	11♍	11	9	2	♇13♐
6	11.02	13	23	11	10	2	♃3♋
7	11.06	14	5♏	10	11	4	♄23♎
8	11.10	15	17	9	13	5	♅9♏
9	11.14	16	0♎	9	14	5	♆13♐
10	11.18	17	12	8	15	5	♇13♐
11	11.22	18	25	7	16	6	♃3♋
12	11.26	19	8♍	7	17	7	♄24♎
13	11.29	20	22	7	18	8	♅9♏
14	11.33	21	5♑	7♐	20	8	♆13♐
15	11.37	21	19	7	21	8	♇13♐
16	11.41	23	3♒	7	22	9	♃4♋
17	11.45	24	18	7	23	9	♄24♎
18	11.49	25	2♈	8	25	11	♅9♏
19	11.53	26	16	8	26	11	♆13♐
20	11.57	27	0♉	9	27	12	♇13♐
21	12.01	28	14	10	28	12	♃4♋
22	12.05	29	28	11	0♍	12	♄25♎
23	12.09	0♎	12♊	12♏	1	13	♅9♏
24	12.13	1	26	13	3	14	♆13♐
25	12.17	2	10♌	15	3	14	♇13♐
26	12.21	3	23	16	5	16	♃5♋
27	12.25	4	6♈	18	6	16	♄26♎
28	12.29	5	19	20	7	16	♅10♏
29	12.33	6	1♍	21	9	17	♆13♐
30	12.36	7	13	23	9	17	♇14♎

Oct	STime	☉	☽	☿	♀	♂	Plnts
1	12.40	8♎	25♍	25♏	11♍	17♍	♃5♋
2	12.44	9	7♏	26	12	18	♅10♏
3	12.48	10	19	28	13	18	♅10♏
4	12.52	11	1♍	0♐	14	19	♆14♐
5	12.56	12	13	2	15	20	♃5♋
6	13.00	13	25	3	17	20	♄27♎
7	13.04	14	7♌	5	18	21	♅10♏
8	13.08	15	20	7	19	21	♆14♐
9	13.12	16	3♍	9	20	22	♇14♎
10	13.16	17	16	11	22	23	♃6♋
11	13.20	18	0♎	12	23	23	♄27♎
12	13.24	19	14	14	24	23	♄27♎
13	13.28	20	28	16	25	24	♅10♏
14	13.32	21	13♍	18	27	24	♆14♐
15	13.36	22	28	19	28	25	♇14♎
16	13.40	23	12♐	21	29	25	♃7♋
17	13.44	24	27	23	0♎	26	♄28♎
18	13.47	25	11♑	25	1	26	♅11♏
19	13.51	26	25	26	3	26	♆14♐
20	13.55	27	9♒	28	4	27	♇14♎
21	13.59	28	23	29	5	28	♃7♋
22	14.03	29	6♓	1♑	6	28	♄28♎
23	14.07	0♏	19	3	8	28	♅11♏
24	14.11	1	2♈	5	9	29	♆14♐
25	14.15	1	15	6	10	29	♇14♎
26	14.19	3	27	8	11	0♎	♃8♋
27	14.23	4	9♉	9	13	0	♄28♎
28	14.27	5	22	11	14	0	♅11♏
29	14.31	6	4♊	13	15	1	♆14♐
30	14.35	7	16	14	16	1	♇15♎
31	14.39	8	27	16	18	2	♃9♋

Nov	STime	☉	☽	☿	♀	♂	Plnts
1	14.43	9♏	9♌	17♑	19♎	2♎	♃9♋R
2	14.47	10	21	19	20	2	♄29♎
3	14.51	11	3♍	20	21	3	♆14♐
4	14.54	12	15	22	23	3	♇15♎
5	15.02	14	28	23	24	4	♃9♋R
6	15.06	15	24	25	26	4	♄29♎
7	15.10	16	8♎	28	28	5	♅12♏
8	15.14	17	22	29	29	5	♆15♐
9	15.22	19	7♏	1♒	0♏	6	♃9♋R
10	15.26	20	7♐	4	3	6	♄29♎
11	15.30	21	22	5	5	7	♅12♏
12	15.34	22	7♑	7	5	7	♆15♐
13	15.38	23	21	8	6	7	♇15♎
14	15.42	24	6♒	10	8	8	♃9♋R
15	15.46	25	20	11	9	9	♄0♏
16	15.50	26	3♈	13	11	10	♅13♏
17	15.54	27	16	14	11	11	♆15♐
18	15.58	28	29	16	13	11	♇15♎
19	16.01	0♐	12♉	18	14	9	♃9♋R
20	16.05	0	24	19	16	9	♄0♏
21	16.09	1	6♊	20	16	9	♅13♏
22	16.13	2	18	22	18	10	♆15♐
23	16.17	3	0♌	23	19	9	♇16♎
24	16.21	4	12	25	21	10	♃8♋R
25	16.25	5	24	25	22	10	♄0♏
26	16.29	6	6♍	26	24	10	♅13♏
27	16.33	7	18	28	24	10	♆15♐
28	16.37	8	0♎	29	29	10	♇16♎

Dec	STime	☉	☽	☿	♀	♂	Plnts
1	16.41	9♐	12♎	0♒	26♏	10♎	♃8♋R
2	16.45	10	24	1	28	11	♄0♏
3	16.49	11	6♏	2	29	11	♅14♏
4	16.53	12	19	3	0♐	11	♆15♐
5	16.57	13	2♐	3	2	11	♇16♎
6	17.01	14	16	5	3	11	♃7♋R
7	17.05	15	0♑	5	5	11	♄0♏
8	17.09	16	15	6	6	11	♅14♏
9	17.12	17	0♒	7	7	11	♆16♐
10	17.16	18	15	7	9	11	♃7♋R
11	17.20	19	0♓	8	10	11	♄0♏
12	17.24	20	15	7R	10	11	♄0♏
13	17.28	21	0♈	7	13	11R	♅14♏
14	17.32	22	14	7	15	11	♆16♐
15	17.36	23	29	6	15	11	♇16♎
16	17.40	24	13♉	5	15	11	♃6♋R
17	17.44	25	26	4	17	11	♄0♏R
18	17.48	26	9♊	2	19	11	♅14♏
19	17.52	27	21	2	19	11	♆16♐
20	17.56	28	3♌	3♒	20	11	♇16♎
21	18.00	29	15	29♑	23	11	♃5♋R
22	18.04	0♑	27	29	23	11	♄0♏R
23	18.08	1	9♍	27	24	11	♅15♏
24	18.12	2	21	28	26	11	♆16♐
25	18.16	3	3♎	24	27	10	♇16♎
26	18.19	4	15	24	28	10	♃5♋R
27	18.23	5	27	24	29	10	♄0♏R
28	18.27	6	9♍	22	0♑	10	♅15♏
29	18.31	7	21	22	1	9	♆16♐
30	18.35	8	3♏	21	3	9	♇16♎
31	18.39	9	16	21♑	4	9	♃0♋R

Jan	STime	☉	☽	☿	♀	♂	Plnts
1	18.43	10♑	28♍	21♐	5♑	9♌	♃ 0♋R
2	18.47	11	11♎	21	7	8	♄ 0♍R
3	18.51	12	25	21	8	8	♅15♏
4	18.55	13	9♏	22	9	8	♆17♐
5	18.59	14	23	22	10	7	♇16♎
6	19.03	16	8♐	23	12	7	♃29♊R
7	19.07	17	23	24	13	7	♄ 0♍R
8	19.11	18	8♑	24	14	6	♅15♏
9	19.15	19	23	25	16	6	♆17♐
10	19.19	20	8♒	26	17	6	♇16♎
11	19.23	21	23	27	18	5	♃28♊R
12	19.27	22	7♓	28	19	5	♄29♌R
13	19.30	23	21	29	21	5	♅15♏
14	19.34	24	5♈	0♑	22	4	♆17♐
15	19.38	25	17	2	23	4	♇16♎
16	19.42	26	0♉	3	24	4	♃28♊R
17	19.46	27	12	4	26	3	♄29♌R
18	19.50	28	24	5	27	3	♅16♏
19	19.54	29	6♊	7	28	2	♆17♐
20	19.58	0♒	18	8	29	2	♇16♎
21	20.02	1	0♋	9	1♒	2	♃27♊R
22	20.06	2	12	11	2	1	♄29♌R
23	20.10	3	24	12	3	1	♅16♏
24	20.14	4	6♌	13	4	0	♆17♐
25	20.18	5	18	15	6	0	♇16♎
26	20.22	6	0♍	16	7	0	♃27♊R
27	20.26	7	13	18	8	29♋	♄28♌R
28	20.30	8	25	19	9	29	♅16♏
29	20.34	9	8♎	20	11	28	♆17♐
30	20.37	10	21	22	12	28	♇16♎R
31	20.41	11	5♏	23	13	28	♃26♊R

Feb	STime	☉	☽	☿	♀	♂	Plnts
1	20.45	12♒	18♏	25♑	14♒	27♋	♃26♊R
2	20.49	13	3♐	26	16	27	♄28♌R
3	20.53	14	17	28	17	27	♅16♏
4	20.57	15	2♑	29	18	26	♆17♐
5	21.01	16	17	1♒	19	26	♇16♎R
6	21.05	17	2♒	3	21	26	♃26♊R
7	21.09	18	16	4	22	25	♄28♌R
8	21.13	19	1♓	6	23	25	♅16♏
9	21.17	20	15	7	24	25	♆18♐
10	21.21	21	29	9	26	25	♇16♎R
11	21.25	22	13♈	11	27	24	♃26♊R
12	21.29	23	26	12	28	24	♄27♌R
13	21.33	24	8♉	14	29	24	♅16♏
14	21.37	25	20	16	1♓	24	♆18♐
15	21.41	26	2♊	17	2	23	♇16♎R
16	21.45	27	14	19	3	23	♃26♊R
17	21.48	28	26	21	4	23	♄27♌R
18	21.52	29	8♋	22	6	23	♅16♏
19	21.56	0♓	20	24	7	23	♆18♐
20	22.00	1	2♌	26	8	23	♇16♎R
21	22.04	2	14	28	9	22	♃26♊
22	22.08	3	27	29	11	22	♄26♌R
23	22.12	4	9♍	1♓	12	22	♅16♏
24	22.16	5	22	3	13	22	♆18♐
25	22.20	6	5♎	5	14	22	♇16♎R
26	22.24	7	18	7	16	22	♃26♊
27	22.28	8	2♏	9	17	22	♄26♌R
28	22.32	9	15	10	18	22	♅16♏R

Mar	STime	☉	☽	☿	♀	♂	Plnts
1	22.36	10♓	29♏	12♓	19♓	22♋	♃26♊
2	22.40	11	13♐	14	21	22	♄26♌R
3	22.44	12	27	16	22	22	♅16♏R
4	22.48	13	12♑	18	23	22	♆18♐
5	22.52	14	26	20	24	22	♇16♎R
6	22.55	15	11♒	22	26	22	♃26♊
7	22.59	16	25	24	27	22	♄25♌R
8	23.03	17	9♓	26	28	22	♅16♏R
9	23.07	18	23	28	29	22	♆18♐
10	23.11	19	7♈	0♈	1♈	22	♇16♎R
11	23.15	20	20	2	2	22	♃26♊
12	23.19	21	3♉	3	3	23	♄25♌R
13	23.23	22	16	5	4	23	♅16♏R
14	23.27	23	28	7	6	23	♆18♐
15	23.31	24	10♊	9	7	23	♇16♎R
16	23.35	25	22	11	8	23	♃27♊
17	23.39	26	4♋	12	9	23	♄25♌R
18	23.43	27	16	14	11	23	♅16♏R
19	23.47	28	28	15	12	24	♆18♐
20	23.51	29	10♌	17	13	24	♇15♎R
21	23.55	0♈	23	18	14	24	♃27♊
22	23.59	1	5♍	20	16	24	♄24♌R
23	0.02	2	18	21	17	24	♅16♏R
24	0.06	3	1♎	22	18	25	♆18♐
25	0.10	4	14	23	19	25	♇15♎R
26	0.14	5	28	23	21	25	♃28♊
27	0.18	6	12♏	24	22	25	♄24♌R
28	0.22	7	26	25	23	26	♅16♏R
29	0.26	8	10♐	25	24	26	♆18♐
30	0.30	9	24	26	26	26	♇15♎R
31	0.34	10	8♑	26	27	26	♃28♊

Apr	STime	☉	☽	☿	♀	♂	Plnts
1	0.38	11♈	23♑	26♈	28♈	27♋	♃28♊
2	0.42	12	7♒	26	29	27	♄24♌R
3	0.46	13	21	26	0♉	27	♅15♏R
4	0.50	14	5♓	25	2	28	♆18♐
5	0.54	15	18	25	3	28	♇15♎R
6	0.58	16	2♈	25	4	28	♃29♊
7	1.02	17	15	24	5	29	♄24♌R
8	1.06	18	28	23	7	29	♅15♏R
9	1.10	19	11♉	23	8	29	♆18♐R
10	1.13	20	24	22	9	0♌	♇15♎R
11	1.17	21	6♊	21	10	0	♃ 0♋
12	1.21	22	18	21	12	0	♄24♌R
13	1.25	23	0♋	20	13	1	♅15♏R
14	1.29	24	12	19	14	1	♆18♐R
15	1.33	25	24	18	15	1	♇15♎R
16	1.37	26	6♌	18	16	2	♃ 0♋
17	1.41	27	18	17	18	2	♄23♌R
18	1.45	28	0♍	16	19	3	♅15♏R
19	1.49	29	13	16	20	3	♆18♐R
20	1.53	0♉	26	16	21	3	♇15♎R
21	1.57	1	9♎	15	23	4	♃ 1♋
22	2.01	2	23	15	24	4	♄23♌
23	2.05	3	7♏	15	25	5	♅15♏R
24	2.09	4	21	15	26	5	♆18♐R
25	2.13	5	6♐	15D	27	5	♇14♎R
26	2.17	6	20	15	29	6	♃ 2♋
27	2.20	7	5♑	15	0♊	6	♄23♌
28	2.24	8	19	15	1	7	♅14♏R
29	2.28	9	4♒	15	2	7	♆18♐R
30	2.32	9	18	16	4	7	♇14♎R

May	STime	☉	☽	☿	♀	♂	Plnts
1	2.36	10♉	1♓	16♈	5♊	8♌	♃ 3♋
2	2.40	11	15	17	6	8	♄23♌
3	2.44	12	28	17	7	9	♅14♏R
4	2.48	13	11♈	18	8	9	♆18♐R
5	2.52	14	24	19	10	10	♇14♎R
6	2.56	15	7♉	19	11	10	♃ 4♋
7	3.00	16	20	20	12	11	♄23♌
8	3.04	17	2♊	21	13	11	♅14♏R
9	3.08	18	14	22	15	12	♆17♐R
10	3.12	19	26	23	16	12	♇14♎R
11	3.16	20	8♋	24	17	12	♃ 5♋
12	3.20	21	20	25	18	13	♄24♌
13	3.24	22	2♌	26	19	13	♅14♏R
14	3.27	23	14	27	21	14	♆17♐R
15	3.31	24	26	29	22	14	♇14♎R
16	3.35	25	8♍	0♉	23	15	♃ 6♋
17	3.39	26	21	1	24	15	♄24♌
18	3.43	27	4♎	3	25	16	♅14♏R
19	3.47	28	17	4	27	16	♆17♐R
20	3.51	29	1♏	5	28	17	♇14♎R
21	3.55	0♊	15	7	29	17	♃ 7♋
22	3.59	1	0♐	8	0♋	18	♄24♌
23	4.03	2	15	10	1	18	♅13♏R
24	4.07	3	0♑	11	3	19	♆17♐R
25	4.11	4	15	13	4	19	♇14♎R
26	4.15	5	0♒	15	5	20	♃ 8♋
27	4.19	6	14	16	6	20	♄24♌
28	4.23	7	28	18	7	21	♅13♏R
29	4.27	7	12♓	20	9	21	♆17♐R
30	4.31	8	25	22	10	22	♇14♎R
31	4.35	9	8♈	24	11	22	♃ 9♋

Jun	STime	☉	☽	☿	♀	♂	Plnts
1	4.38	10♊	21♈	26♉	12♋	23♌	♃ 9♋
2	4.42	11	4♉	27	13	23	♄25♌
3	4.46	12	16	29	15	24	♅13♏R
4	4.50	13	29	1♊	16	25	♆17♐R
5	4.54	14	11♊	3	17	25	♇14♎R
6	4.58	15	23	6	18	26	♃10♋
7	5.02	16	5♋	8	19	26	♄25♌
8	5.06	17	17	10	21	27	♅13♏R
9	5.10	18	29	12	22	27	♆17♐R
10	5.14	19	11♌	14	23	28	♇14♎R
11	5.18	20	22	16	24	28	♃11♋
12	5.22	21	4♍	18	25	29	♄25♌
13	5.26	22	17	21	26	29	♅13♏R
14	5.30	23	29	23	28	0♍	♆16♐R
15	5.34	24	12♎	25	29	0	♇14♎R
16	5.38	25	25	27	0♌	1	♃12♋
17	5.42	26	9♏	29	1	2	♄26♌
18	5.45	27	24	2♋	2	2	♅12♏R
19	5.49	28	8♐	4	4	3	♆16♐R
20	5.53	29	23	6	5	3	♇14♎
21	5.57	29	9♑	8	6	4	♃13♋
22	6.01	0♋	24	10	7	4	♄26♌
23	6.05	1	9♒	12	8	5	♅12♏R
24	6.09	2	24	14	9	5	♆16♐R
25	6.13	3	8♓	16	11	6	♇14♎
26	6.17	4	22	18	12	7	♃14♋
27	6.21	5	5♈	20	13	7	♄27♌
28	6.25	6	18	22	14	8	♅12♏R
29	6.29	7	1♉	24	15	8	♆16♐R
30	6.33	8	14	25	16	9	♇14♎

Jul	STime	☉	☽	☿	♀	♂	Plnts
1	6.37	9♋	26♉	27♋	18♌	9♍	♃16♋
2	6.41	10	8♊	29	19	10	♄27♌
3	6.45	11	20	1♌	20	11	♅12♏R
4	6.49	12	2♋	2	21	11	♆16♐R
5	6.53	13	14	4	22	12	♇14♎
6	6.56	14	26	6	23	12	♃17♋
7	7.00	15	7♌	7	24	13	♄28♌
8	7.04	16	19	9	26	14	♅12♏R
9	7.08	17	1♍	10	27	14	♆16♐R
10	7.12	18	13	12	28	15	♇14♎
11	7.16	19	26	13	29	15	♃18♋
12	7.20	19	8♎	14	0♍	16	♄28♌
13	7.24	20	21	16	1	16	♅12♏
14	7.28	21	4♏	17	2	17	♆16♐R
15	7.32	22	18	18	4	18	♇14♎
16	7.36	23	2♐	20	5	18	♃19♋
17	7.40	24	17	21	6	19	♄29♌
18	7.44	25	2♑	22	7	19	♅12♏
19	7.48	26	17	23	8	20	♆16♐R
20	7.52	27	2♒	24	9	21	♇14♎
21	7.56	28	18	25	10	21	♃20♋
22	8.00	29	2♓	26	11	22	♄29♌
23	8.03	0♌	17	27	13	22	♅12♏
24	8.07	1	1♈	28	14	23	♆16♐R
25	8.11	2	15	28	15	24	♇14♎
26	8.15	3	28	29	16	24	♃21♋
27	8.19	4	10♉	0♍	17	25	♄ 0♍
28	8.23	5	23	0	18	25	♅12♏
29	8.27	6	5♊	1	19	26	♆15♐R
30	8.31	7	17	1	20	27	♇14♎
31	8.35	8	29	2	21	27	♃22♋

Aug	STime	☉	☽	☿	♀	♂	Plnts
1	8.39	9♌	11♋	2♍	23♍	28♍	♃22♋
2	8.43	10	23	2	24	29	♄ 1♍
3	8.47	11	5♌	3	25	29	♅12♏
4	8.51	11	16	3R	26	0♎	♆15♐R
5	8.55	12	28	3	27	0	♇14♎
6	8.59	13	11♍	3	28	1	♃24♋
7	9.03	14	23	2	29	2	♄ 1♍
8	9.07	15	5♎	2	0♎	2	♅12♏
9	9.11	16	18	2	1	3	♆15♐R
10	9.14	17	1♏	1	2	4	♇14♎
11	9.18	18	14	1	3	4	♃25♋
12	9.22	19	28	0	4	5	♄ 2♍
13	9.26	20	12♐	0	5	5	♅12♏
14	9.30	21	26	29♌	6	6	♆15♐R
15	9.34	22	11♑	28	7	7	♇14♎
16	9.38	23	26	27	9	7	♃26♋
17	9.42	24	11♒	26	10	8	♄ 2♍
18	9.46	25	26	26	11	9	♅12♏
19	9.50	26	11♓	25	12	9	♆15♐R
20	9.54	27	25	24	13	10	♇14♎
21	9.58	28	9♈	23	14	10	♃27♋
22	10.02	29	23	22	15	11	♄ 3♍
23	10.06	0♍	6♉	22	16	12	♅12♏
24	10.10	1	19	21	17	12	♆15♐
25	10.14	2	1♊	21	18	13	♇15♎
26	10.18	3	14	20	19	14	♃28♋
27	10.21	4	26	20	20	14	♄ 4♍
28	10.25	5	8♋	20D	21	15	♅13♏
29	10.29	5	20	20	22	16	♆15♐
30	10.33	6	1♌	20	23	16	♇15♎
31	10.37	7	13	21	23	17	♃29♋

Sep	STime	☉	☽	☿	♀	♂	Plnts
1	10.41	8♍	25♌	21♌	24♎	18♎	♃29♋
2	10.45	9	7♍	22	25	18	♄ 4♍
3	10.49	10	20	22	26	19	♅13♏
4	10.53	11	2♎	23	27	20	♆15♐
5	10.57	12	15	24	28	20	♇15♎
6	11.01	13	28	25	29	21	♃ 0♌
7	11.05	14	11♏	27	0♏	21	♄ 5♍
8	11.09	15	24	28	1	22	♅13♏
9	11.13	16	8♐	29	2	23	♆15♐
10	11.17	17	22	1♍	3	23	♇15♎
11	11.21	18	6♑	2	3	24	♃ 1♌
12	11.25	19	20	4	4	25	♄ 6♍
13	11.29	20	5♒	6	5	25	♅13♏
14	11.32	21	20	7	6	26	♆15♐
15	11.36	22	4♓	9	7	27	♇15♎
16	11.40	23	19	11	8	27	♃ 2♌
17	11.44	24	3♈	13	8	28	♄ 6♍
18	11.48	25	17	15	9	29	♅13♏
19	11.52	26	1♉	16	10	29	♆15♐
20	11.56	27	14	18	11	0♏	♇16♎
21	12.00	28	27	20	11	1	♃ 3♌
22	12.04	29	10♊	22	12	1	♄ 7♍
23	12.08	0♎	22	24	13	2	♅14♏
24	12.12	1	4♋	26	13	3	♆15♐
25	12.16	2	16	28	14	4	♇16♎
26	12.20	3	28	29	15	4	♃ 3♌
27	12.24	4	10♌	1♎	15	5	♄ 8♍
28	12.28	5	22	3	16	6	♅14♏
29	12.32	6	4♍	5	17	6	♆16♐
30	12.36	7	16	7	17	7	♇16♎

Oct	STime	☉	☽	☿	♀	♂	Plnts
1	12.39	8♎	28♍	8♎	18♏	8♏	♃ 4♌
2	12.43	9	11♎	10	18	8	♄ 8♍
3	12.47	10	24	12	19	9	♅14♏
4	12.51	11	8♏	14	19	10	♆16♐
5	12.55	12	21	15	20	10	♇16♎
6	12.59	13	5♐	17	20	11	♃ 5♌
7	13.03	14	19	19	20	12	♄ 9♍
8	13.07	15	3♑	20	21	12	♅14♏
9	13.11	16	17	22	21	13	♆16♐
10	13.15	17	1♒	24	21	14	♇16♎
11	13.19	18	15	25	22	14	♃ 6♌
12	13.23	19	0♓	27	22	15	♄ 9♍
13	13.27	20	14	29	22	16	♅15♏
14	13.31	20	28	0♏	22	17	♆16♐
15	13.35	21	12♈	2	22	17	♇17♎
16	13.39	22	26	3	22	18	♃ 6♌
17	13.43	23	9♉	5	22	19	♄10♍
18	13.46	24	22	6	22R	19	♅15♏
19	13.50	25	5♊	8	22	20	♆16♐
20	13.54	26	17	10	22	21	♇17♎
21	13.58	27	0♋	11	22	21	♃ 7♌
22	14.02	28	12	13	22	22	♄10♍
23	14.06	29	24	14	22	23	♅15♏
24	14.10	0♏	6♌	16	22	24	♆16♐
25	14.14	1	18	17	21	24	♇17♎
26	14.18	2	29	19	21	25	♃ 7♌
27	14.22	3	12♍	20	21	26	♄11♍
28	14.26	4	24	21	20	26	♅16♏
29	14.30	5	7♎	23	20	27	♆16♐
30	14.34	6	20	24	20	28	♇17♎
31	14.38	7	3♏	26	19	29	♃ 8♌

Nov	STime	☉	☽	☿	♀	♂	Plnts
1	14.42	8♏	17♏	27♏	19♏	29♏	♃ 8♌
2	14.46	9	1♐	29	18	0♐	♄11♍
3	14.50	10	15	0♐	17	1	♅16♏
4	14.54	11	29	1	17	1	♆16♐
5	14.57	12	14♑	3	16	2	♇17♎
6	15.01	13	28	4	16	3	♃ 8♌
7	15.05	14	12♒	5	15	4	♄12♍
8	15.09	15	26	7	14	4	♅16♏
9	15.13	16	10♓	8	14	5	♆17♐
10	15.17	17	24	9	13	6	♇18♎
11	15.21	18	7♈	10	13	7	♃ 8♌
12	15.25	19	21	12	12	7	♄12♍
13	15.29	20	4♉	13	12	8	♅17♏
14	15.33	21	17	14	11	9	♆17♐
15	15.37	22	0♊	15	10	9	♇18♎
16	15.41	23	13	16	10	10	♃ 9♌
17	15.45	24	25	17	10	11	♄12♍
18	15.49	25	8♋	18	9	12	♅17♏
19	15.53	27	20	19	9	12	♆17♐
20	15.57	28	2♌	19	8	13	♇18♎
21	16.01	29	13	20	8	14	♃ 9♌
22	16.04	0♐	25	20	8	15	♄13♍
23	16.08	1	7♍	21	8	15	♅17♏
24	16.12	2	19	21	7	16	♆17♐
25	16.16	3	2♎	21R	7	17	♇18♎
26	16.20	4	14	21	7	18	♃ 9♌R
27	16.24	5	28	21	7	18	♄13♍
28	16.28	6	11♏	21	7D	19	♅18♏
29	16.32	7	25	20	7	20	♆17♐
30	16.36	8	10♐	19	7	21	♇18♎

Dec	STime	☉	☽	☿	♀	♂	Plnts
1	16.40	9♐	24♐	19♐	7♏	21♐	♃ 9♌R
2	16.44	10	9♑	18	7	22	♄13♍
3	16.48	11	24	16	8	23	♅18♏
4	16.52	12	8♒	15	8	24	♆18♐
5	16.56	13	23	14	8	24	♇18♎
6	17.00	14	7♓	12	8	25	♃ 9♌R
7	17.04	15	21	11	9	26	♄13♍
8	17.08	16	4♈	10	9	27	♅18♏
9	17.12	17	18	8	9	27	♆18♐
10	17.15	18	1♉	7	10	28	♇18♎
11	17.19	19	14	7	10	29	♃ 8♌R
12	17.23	20	27	6	11	0♑	♄14♍
13	17.27	21	9♊	5	11	0	♅18♏
14	17.31	22	22	5	12	1	♆18♐
15	17.35	23	4♋	5D	12	2	♇19♎
16	17.39	24	16	5	13	3	♃ 8♌R
17	17.43	25	28	5	13	3	♄14♍
18	17.47	26	10♌	6	14	4	♅19♏
19	17.51	27	22	6	15	5	♆18♐
20	17.55	28	3♍	7	15	6	♇19♎
21	17.59	29	15	7	16	6	♃ 8♌R
22	18.03	0♑	27	8	17	7	♄14♍
23	18.07	1	10♎	9	17	8	♅19♏
24	18.11	2	22	10	18	9	♆18♐
25	18.15	3	5♏	11	19	9	♇19♎
26	18.19	4	19	12	20	10	♃ 7♌R
27	18.22	5	3♐	13	20	11	♄14♍
28	18.26	6	18	14	21	12	♅19♏
29	18.30	7	3♑	16	22	12	♆18♐
30	18.34	8	18	17	23	13	♇19♎
31	18.38	9	3♒	18	24	14	♃ 7♌R

1 9 7 9

Jan	STime	☉	☽	☿	♀	♂	Plnts
1	18.42	10♑	18♒	19♐	25♏	15♑	♃ 7♌R
2	18.46	11	3♓	21	25	16	♄14♍R
3	18.50	12	17	22	26	16	♅20♏
4	18.54	13	1♈	23	27	17	♆19♐
5	18.58	14	15	25	28	18	♇19♎
6	19.02	15	28	26	29	19	♃ 6♌R
7	19.06	16	11♉	28	0♐	19	♄13♍R
8	19.10	17	24	29	1	20	♅20♏
9	19.14	18	6♊	0♑	2	21	♆19♐
10	19.18	19	18	2	3	22	♇19♎
11	19.22	20	1♋	3	4	23	♃ 5♌R
12	19.26	21	13	5	5	23	♄13♍R
13	19.29	22	25	6	6	24	♅20♏
14	19.33	23	7♌	8	7	25	♆19♐
15	19.37	24	18	9	8	26	♇19♎
16	19.41	25	0♍	11	9	26	♃ 5♌R
17	19.45	26	12	12	10	27	♄13♍R
18	19.49	27	24	14	11	28	♅20♏
19	19.53	29	6♎	15	12	29	♆19♐
20	19.57	0♒	18	17	13	0♒	♇19♎
21	20.01	1	1♏	18	14	0	♃ 4♌R
22	20.05	2	14	20	15	1	♄13♍R
23	20.09	3	27	22	16	2	♅20♏
24	20.13	4	11♐	23	17	3	♆19♐
25	20.17	5	26	25	18	3	♇19♎
26	20.21	6	11♑	26	19	4	♃ 3♌R
27	20.25	7	26	28	20	5	♄13♍R
28	20.29	8	11♒	0♒	21	6	♅20♏
29	20.33	9	26	1	22	7	♆19♐
30	20.37	10	11♓	3	23	7	♇19♎
31	20.40	11	26	5	24	8	♃ 3♌R

Feb	STime	☉	☽	☿	♀	♂	Plnts
1	20.44	12♒	10♈	6♒	25♐	9♒	♃ 3♌R
2	20.48	13	24	8	27	10	♄12♍R
3	20.52	14	7♉	10	28	11	♅21♏
4	20.56	15	20	11	29	11	♆20♐
5	21.00	16	3♊	13	0♑	12	♇19♎R
6	21.04	17	15	15	1	13	♃ 2♌R
7	21.08	18	28	17	2	14	♄12♍R
8	21.12	19	10♋	18	3	14	♅21♏
9	21.16	20	22	20	4	15	♆20♐
10	21.20	21	3♌	22	5	16	♇19♎R
11	21.24	22	15	24	7	17	♃ 1♌R
12	21.28	23	27	25	8	18	♄12♍R
13	21.32	24	9♍	27	9	18	♅21♏
14	21.36	25	21	29	10	19	♆20♐
15	21.40	26	3♎	1♓	11	20	♇19♎R
16	21.44	27	15	3	12	21	♃ 1♌R
17	21.47	28	27	5	13	22	♄11♍R
18	21.51	29	10♏	6	14	22	♅21♏
19	21.55	0♓	23	8	16	23	♆20♐
20	21.59	1	6♐	10	17	24	♇19♎R
21	22.03	2	20	12	18	25	♃ 0♌R
22	22.07	3	4♑	14	19	25	♄11♍R
23	22.11	4	19	16	20	26	♅21♏
24	22.15	5	4♒	17	21	27	♆20♐
25	22.19	6	19	19	22	28	♇19♎R
26	22.23	7	4♓	21	24	29	♃ 0♌R
27	22.27	8	19	23	25	29	♄10♍R
28	22.31	9	4♈	24	26	0♓	♅21♏

Mar	STime	☉	☽	☿	♀	♂	Plnts
1	22.35	10♓	18♈	26♓	27♑	1♓	♃ 0♌R
2	22.39	11	3♉	28	28	2	♄10♍R
3	22.43	12	16	29	29	3	♅21♏R
4	22.47	13	29	1♈	1♒	3	♆20♐
5	22.51	14	12♊	2	2	4	♇18♎R
6	22.55	15	24	3	3	5	♃29♋R
7	22.58	16	6♋	4	4	6	♄10♍R
8	23.02	17	18	5	5	7	♅21♏R
9	23.06	18	0♌	6	6	7	♆20♐
10	23.10	19	12	7	8	8	♇18♎R
11	23.14	20	24	7	9	9	♃29♋R
12	23.18	21	6♍	8	10	10	♄ 9♍R
13	23.22	22	18	8	11	10	♅21♏R
14	23.26	23	0♎	8	12	11	♆20♐
15	23.30	24	12	8R	14	12	♇18♎R
16	23.34	25	25	8	15	13	♃29♋R
17	23.38	26	7♏	8	16	14	♄ 9♍R
18	23.42	27	20	7	17	14	♅20♏R
19	23.46	28	3♐	7	18	15	♆20♐
20	23.50	29	17	6	19	16	♇18♎R
21	23.54	0♈	0♑	6	21	17	♃29♋R
22	23.58	1	14	5	22	18	♄ 9♍R
23	0.02	2	29	4	23	18	♅20♏R
24	0.05	3	13♒	3	24	19	♆20♐
25	0.09	4	28	2	25	20	♇18♎R
26	0.13	5	13♓	1	27	21	♃29♋
27	0.17	6	27	0	28	21	♄ 8♍R
28	0.21	7	12♈	0	29	22	♅20♏R
29	0.25	8	26	29♓	0♓	23	♆20♐R
30	0.29	9	10♉	28	1	24	♇18♎R
31	0.33	10	24	28	3	25	♃29♋

Apr	STime	☉	☽	☿	♀	♂	Plnts
1	0.37	11♈	7♊	27♓	4♓	25♓	♃29♋
2	0.41	12	20	26	5	26	♄ 8♍R
3	0.45	13	3♋	26	6	27	♅20♏R
4	0.49	14	15	26	7	28	♆20♐R
5	0.53	15	27	26	8	28	♇18♎R
6	0.57	16	9♌	25	10	29	♃29♋
7	1.01	17	20	25D	11	0♈	♄ 8♍R
8	1.05	18	2♍	25	12	1	♅20♏R
9	1.09	19	14	26	13	2	♆20♐R
10	1.13	20	26	26	14	2	♇18♎R
11	1.16	21	9♎	26	16	3	♃29♋
12	1.20	22	21	27	17	4	♄ 7♍R
13	1.24	23	4♏	27	18	5	♅20♏R
14	1.28	24	17	28	19	5	♆20♐R
15	1.32	25	0♐	28	20	6	♇17♎R
16	1.36	26	14	29	22	7	♃29♋
17	1.40	27	27	0♈	23	8	♄ 7♍R
18	1.44	28	11♑	0	24	9	♅20♏R
19	1.48	29	25	1	25	9	♆20♐R
20	1.52	0♉	9♒	2	26	10	♇17♎R
21	1.56	0	23	3	28	11	♃ 0♌
22	2.00	1	8♓	4	29	12	♄ 7♍R
23	2.04	2	22	5	0♈	12	♅19♏R
24	2.08	3	6♈	6	1	13	♆20♐R
25	2.12	4	21	7	3	14	♇17♎R
26	2.16	5	5♉	9	4	15	♃ 0♌
27	2.20	6	19	10	5	16	♄ 7♍R
28	2.23	7	2♊	11	6	16	♅19♏R
29	2.27	8	15	12	7	17	♆20♐R
30	2.31	9	28	14	9	18	♇17♎R

May	STime	☉	☽	☿	♀	♂	Plnts
1	2.35	10♉	10♋	15♈	10♈	19♈	♃ 1♌
2	2.39	11	23	17	11	19	♄ 7♍R
3	2.43	12	5♌	18	12	20	♅19♏R
4	2.47	13	17	19	13	21	♆20♐R
5	2.51	14	28	21	15	22	♇17♎R
6	2.55	15	10♍	22	16	22	♃ 1♌
7	2.59	16	22	24	17	23	♄ 7♍
8	3.03	17	4♎	26	18	24	♅19♏R
9	3.07	18	17	27	19	25	♆20♐R
10	3.11	19	0♏	29	21	25	♇17♎R
11	3.15	20	13	1♉	22	26	♃ 2♌
12	3.19	21	26	2	23	27	♄ 7♍
13	3.23	22	10♐	4	24	28	♅19♏R
14	3.27	23	24	6	25	28	♆20♐R
15	3.30	24	8♑	8	27	29	♇17♎R
16	3.34	25	22	10	28	0♉	♃ 3♌
17	3.38	26	6♒	12	29	1	♄ 7♍
18	3.42	27	20	14	0♉	1	♅18♏R
19	3.46	28	4♓	16	1	2	♆19♐R
20	3.50	29	18	18	3	3	♇17♎R
21	3.54	0♊	2♈	20	4	4	♃ 3♌
22	3.58	1	16	22	5	4	♄ 7♍
23	4.02	1	0♉	24	6	5	♅18♏R
24	4.06	2	14	26	8	6	♆19♐R
25	4.10	3	27	28	9	7	♇16♎R
26	4.14	4	10♊	0♊	10	7	♃ 4♌
27	4.18	5	23	2	11	8	♄ 7♍
28	4.22	6	6♋	4	12	9	♅18♏R
29	4.26	7	18	7	14	10	♆19♐R
30	4.30	8	1♌	9	15	10	♇16♎R
31	4.34	9	13	11	16	11	♃ 5♌

Jun	STime	☉	☽	☿	♀	♂	Plnts
1	4.38	10♊	24♌	13♊	17♉	12♉	♃ 5♌
2	4.41	11	6♍	15	18	13	♄ 7♍
3	4.45	12	18	18	20	13	♅18♏R
4	4.49	13	0♎	20	21	14	♆19♐R
5	4.53	14	12	22	22	15	♇16♎R
6	4.57	15	25	24	23	16	♃ 6♌
7	5.01	16	8♏	26	25	16	♄ 7♍
8	5.05	17	21	28	26	17	♅18♏R
9	5.09	18	5♐	0♋	27	18	♆19♐R
10	5.13	19	19	2	28	18	♇16♎R
11	5.17	20	3♑	4	29	19	♃ 7♌
12	5.21	21	17	6	1♊	20	♄ 8♍
13	5.25	22	2♒	8	2	21	♅17♏R
14	5.29	23	17	10	3	21	♆19♐R
15	5.33	24	1♓	12	4	22	♇16♎R
16	5.37	24	15	13	5	23	♃ 8♌
17	5.41	25	29	15	7	24	♄ 8♍
18	5.45	26	13♈	17	8	24	♅17♏R
19	5.48	27	27	18	9	25	♆19♐R
20	5.52	28	10♉	20	10	26	♇16♎
21	5.56	29	23	21	12	26	♃ 9♌
22	6.00	0♋	7♊	23	13	27	♄ 8♍
23	6.04	1	19	24	14	28	♅17♏R
24	6.08	2	2♋	26	15	29	♆18♐R
25	6.12	3	15	27	16	29	♇16♎
26	6.16	4	27	29	18	0♊	♃10♌
27	6.20	5	9♌	0♌	19	1	♄ 9♍
28	6.24	6	21	1	20	1	♅17♏R
29	6.28	7	3♍	2	21	2	♆18♐R
30	6.32	8	14	3	23	3	♇16♎

Jul	STime	☉	☽	☿	♀	♂	Plnts
1	6.36	9♋	26♍	5♌	24♊	4♊	♃11♌
2	6.40	10	8♎	6	25	4	♄ 9♍
3	6.44	11	20	7	26	5	♅17♏R
4	6.48	12	3♏	8	27	6	♆18♐R
5	6.52	13	16	8	29	6	♇16♎
6	6.56	14	29	9	0♋	7	♃12♌
7	6.59	14	13♐	10	1	8	♄10♍
8	7.03	15	27	11	2	8	♅17♏R
9	7.07	16	12♑	11	4	9	♆18♐R
10	7.11	17	27	12	5	10	♇16♎
11	7.15	18	11♒	13	6	11	♃13♌
12	7.19	19	26	13	7	11	♄10♍
13	7.23	20	11♓	13	8	12	♅17♏R
14	7.27	21	26	14	10	13	♆18♐R
15	7.31	22	10♈	14	11	13	♇16♎
16	7.35	23	24	14	12	14	♃14♌
17	7.39	24	7♉	14R	13	15	♄11♍
18	7.43	25	20	14	15	15	♅17♏R
19	7.47	26	3♊	14	16	16	♆18♐R
20	7.51	27	16	14	17	17	♇16♎
21	7.55	28	29	14	18	17	♃15♌
22	7.59	29	11♋	13	19	18	♄11♍
23	8.03	0♌	23	13	21	19	♅17♏
24	8.06	1	5♌	12	22	20	♆18♐R
25	8.10	2	17	12	23	20	♇16♎
26	8.14	3	29	11	24	21	♃16♌
27	8.18	4	11♍	11	26	22	♄12♍
28	8.22	5	23	10	27	22	♅17♏
29	8.26	5	5♎	9	28	23	♆18♐R
30	8.30	6	17	9	29	24	♇16♎
31	8.34	7	29	8	1♌	24	♃17♌

Aug	STime	☉	☽	☿	♀	♂	Plnts
1	8.38	8♌	11♏	7♌	2♌	25♊	♃17♌
2	8.42	9	24	6	3	26	♄12♍
3	8.46	10	7♐	6	4	26	♅17♏
4	8.50	11	21	5	5	27	♆18♐R
5	8.54	12	5♑	4	7	28	♇17♎
6	8.58	13	20	4	8	28	♃18♌
7	9.02	14	5♒	4	9	29	♄13♍
8	9.06	15	20	3	10	0♋	♅17♏
9	9.10	16	5♓	3	12	0	♆18♐R
10	9.13	17	20	3	13	1	♇17♎
11	9.17	18	5♈	3D	14	2	♃19♌
12	9.21	19	20	3	15	2	♄13♍
13	9.25	20	4♉	3	17	3	♅17♏
14	9.29	21	17	4	18	4	♆17♐R
15	9.33	22	0♊	4	19	4	♇17♎
16	9.37	23	13	5	20	5	♃20♌
17	9.41	24	26	5	21	6	♄14♍
18	9.45	25	8♋	6	23	6	♅17♏
19	9.49	26	20	7	24	7	♆17♐R
20	9.53	27	2♌	8	25	8	♇17♎
21	9.57	28	14	9	26	8	♃22♌
22	10.01	29	26	10	28	9	♄15♍
23	10.05	29	8♍	12	29	10	♅17♏
24	10.09	0♍	20	13	0♍	10	♆17♐
25	10.13	1	2♎	15	1	11	♇17♎
26	10.17	2	13	16	3	11	♃23♌
27	10.21	3	25	18	4	12	♄15♍
28	10.24	4	8♏	20	5	13	♅17♏
29	10.28	5	20	21	6	13	♆17♐
30	10.32	6	3♐	23	8	14	♇17♎
31	10.36	7	16	25	9	15	♃24♌

Sep	STime	☉	☽	☿	♀	♂	Plnts
1	10.40	8♍	0♑	27♌	10♍	15♋	♃24♌
2	10.44	9	14	29	11	16	♄16♍
3	10.48	10	28	1♍	13	17	♅17♏
4	10.52	11	13♒	3	14	17	♆17♐
5	10.56	12	28	5	15	18	♇17♎
6	11.00	13	14♓	7	16	18	♃25♌
7	11.04	14	29	9	18	19	♄17♍
8	11.08	15	14♈	11	19	20	♅17♏
9	11.12	16	28	12	20	20	♆17♐
10	11.16	17	13♉	14	21	21	♇18♎
11	11.20	18	26	16	22	22	♃26♌
12	11.24	19	10♊	18	24	22	♄17♍
13	11.28	20	23	20	25	23	♅18♏
14	11.31	21	5♋	22	26	23	♆17♐
15	11.35	22	17	24	27	24	♇18♎
16	11.39	23	0♌	26	29	25	♃27♌
17	11.43	24	11	27	0♎	25	♄18♍
18	11.47	25	23	29	1	26	♅18♏
19	11.51	26	5♍	1♎	2	26	♆18♐
20	11.55	27	17	3	4	27	♇18♎
21	11.59	28	29	4	5	28	♃28♌
22	12.03	29	11♎	6	6	28	♄18♍
23	12.07	0♎	23	8	7	29	♅18♏
24	12.11	1	5♏	10	9	29	♆18♐
25	12.15	2	17	11	10	0♌	♇18♎
26	12.19	3	0♐	13	11	1	♃29♌
27	12.23	3	13	15	12	1	♄19♍
28	12.27	4	26	16	14	2	♅18♏
29	12.31	5	9♑	18	15	2	♆18♐
30	12.35	6	23	19	16	3	♇18♎

Oct	STime	☉	☽	☿	♀	♂	Plnts
1	12.39	7♎	8♒	21♎	17♎	4♌	♃ 0♍
2	12.42	8	22	23	19	4	♄20♍
3	12.46	9	7♓	24	20	5	♅19♏
4	12.50	10	22	26	21	5	♆18♐
5	12.54	11	7♈	27	22	6	♇19♎
6	12.58	12	22	29	24	7	♃ 1♍
7	13.02	13	7♉	0♏	25	7	♄20♍
8	13.06	14	21	2	26	8	♅19♏
9	13.10	15	5♊	3	27	8	♆18♐
10	13.14	16	18	5	29	9	♇19♎
11	13.18	17	1♋	6	0♏	9	♃ 2♍
12	13.22	18	14	8	1	10	♄21♍
13	13.26	19	26	9	2	11	♅19♏
14	13.30	20	8♌	10	4	11	♆18♐
15	13.34	21	20	12	5	12	♇19♎
16	13.38	22	2♍	13	6	12	♃ 3♍
17	13.42	23	14	14	7	13	♄21♍
18	13.46	24	25	16	9	13	♅19♏
19	13.49	25	7♎	17	10	14	♆18♐
20	13.53	26	19	18	11	14	♇19♎
21	13.57	27	2♏	20	12	15	♃ 4♍
22	14.01	28	14	21	14	15	♄22♍
23	14.05	29	27	22	15	16	♅20♏
24	14.09	0♏	10♐	23	16	17	♆18♐
25	14.13	1	23	25	17	17	♇19♎
26	14.17	2	6♑	26	19	18	♃ 5♍
27	14.21	3	20	27	20	18	♄23♍
28	14.25	4	4♒	28	21	19	♅20♏
29	14.29	5	18	29	22	19	♆18♐
30	14.33	6	2♓	0♐	23	20	♇20♎
31	14.37	7	16	1	25	20	♃ 5♍

Nov	STime	☉	☽	☿	♀	♂	Plnts
1	14.41	8♏	1♈	2♐	26♏	21♌	♃ 5♍
2	14.45	9	15	2	27	21	♄23♍
3	14.49	10	0♉	3	28	22	♅20♏
4	14.53	11	15	4	0♐	22	♆19♐
5	14.56	12	29	4	1	23	♇20♎
6	15.00	13	13♊	5	2	23	♃ 6♍
7	15.04	14	26	5	3	24	♄24♍
8	15.08	15	9♋	5	5	24	♅21♏
9	15.12	16	22	6R	6	25	♆19♐
10	15.16	17	4♌	5	7	25	♇20♎
11	15.20	18	16	5	8	26	♃ 7♍
12	15.24	19	28	5	10	26	♄24♍
13	15.28	20	10♍	4	11	27	♅21♏
14	15.32	21	22	4	12	27	♆19♐
15	15.36	22	4♎	3	13	28	♇20♎
16	15.40	23	16	2	15	28	♃ 7♍
17	15.44	24	28	0	16	29	♄25♍
18	15.48	25	10♏	29♏	17	29	♅21♏
19	15.52	26	23	28	18	0♍	♆19♐
20	15.56	27	6♐	27	20	0	♇20♎
21	16.00	28	20	25	21	0	♃ 8♍
22	16.04	29	3♑	24	22	1	♄25♍
23	16.07	0♐	17	23	23	1	♅22♏
24	16.11	1	1♒	22	25	2	♆19♐
25	16.15	2	14	21	26	2	♇20♎
26	16.19	3	28	20	27	3	♃ 9♍
27	16.23	4	12♓	20	28	3	♄25♍
28	16.27	5	27	19	0♑	3	♅22♏
29	16.31	6	11♈	19D	1	4	♆19♐
30	16.35	7	25	19	2	4	♇21♎

Dec	STime	☉	☽	☿	♀	♂	Plnts
1	16.39	8♐	9♉	20♏	3♑	5♍	♃ 9♍
2	16.43	9	23	20	5	5	♄26♍
3	16.47	10	7♊	21	6	5	♅22♏
4	16.51	11	21	21	7	6	♆20♐
5	16.55	12	4♋	22	8	6	♇21♎
6	16.59	13	17	23	10	7	♃ 9♍
7	17.03	14	0♌	24	11	7	♄26♍
8	17.07	16	12	25	12	7	♅22♏
9	17.11	17	24	26	13	8	♆20♐
10	17.14	18	6♍	27	14	8	♇21♎
11	17.18	19	18	28	16	8	♃10♍
12	17.22	20	29	0♐	17	9	♄26♍
13	17.26	21	11♎	1	18	9	♅23♏
14	17.30	22	23	2	19	9	♆20♐
15	17.34	23	6♏	4	21	10	♇21♎
16	17.38	24	19	5	22	10	♃10♍
17	17.42	25	2♐	6	23	10	♄26♍
18	17.46	26	15	8	24	11	♅23♏
19	17.50	27	29	9	26	11	♆20♐
20	17.54	28	12♑	11	27	11	♇21♎
21	17.58	29	27	12	28	11	♃10♍
22	18.02	0♑	11♒	13	29	12	♄27♍
23	18.06	1	25	15	1♒	12	♅23♏
24	18.10	2	9♓	16	2	12	♆20♐
25	18.14	3	23	18	3	12	♇21♎
26	18.18	4	8♈	19	4	13	♃10♍
27	18.22	5	21	21	6	13	♄27♍
28	18.25	6	5♉	22	7	13	♅24♏
29	18.29	7	19	24	8	13	♆21♐
30	18.33	8	3♊	25	9	13	♇21♎
31	18.37	9	16	27	10	14	♃10♍R

Jan	STime	⊙	☽	☿	♀	♂	Plnts
1	18.41	10♑	29♊	28♐	12♒	14♍	♃10♍R
2	18.45	11	12♋	0♑	13	14	♄27♍
3	18.49	12	25	1	14	14	♅24♏
4	18.53	13	8♌	3	15	14	♆21♐
5	18.57	14	20	5	17	14	♇21♎
6	19.01	15	2♍	6	18	14	♃10♍R
7	19.05	16	14	8	19	15	♄27♍R
8	19.09	17	25	9	20	15	♅24♏
9	19.13	18	7♎	11	22	15	♆21♐
10	19.17	19	19	12	23	15	♇21♎
11	19.21	20	1♏	14	24	15	♃10♍R
12	19.25	21	14	16	25	15	♄27♍R
13	19.29	22	26	17	26	15	♅24♏
14	19.32	23	9♐	19	28	15	♆21♐
15	19.36	24	23	20	29	15	♇21♎
16	19.40	25	7♑	22	0♓	15R	♃ 9♍R
17	19.44	26	21	24	1	15	♄27♍R
18	19.48	27	5♒	25	3	15	♅24♏
19	19.52	28	20	27	4	15	♆21♐
20	19.56	29	5♓	29	5	15	♇21♎
21	20.00	0♒	20	0♒	6	15	♃ 9♍R
22	20.04	1	4♈	2	7	15	♄27♍R
23	20.08	2	18	4	9	15	♅25♏
24	20.12	3	2♉	5	10	15	♆21♐
25	20.16	4	16	7	11	14	♇21♎
26	20.20	5	0♊	9	12	14	♃ 8♍R
27	20.24	6	13	11	14	14	♄26♍R
28	20.28	7	26	12	15	14	♅25♏
29	20.32	8	9♋	14	16	14	♆22♐
30	20.36	9	21	16	17	14	♇21♎
31	20.40	10	4♌	18	18	14	♃ 8♍R

Feb	STime	⊙	☽	☿	♀	♂	Plnts
1	20.43	11♒	16♌	19♒	20♓	13♍	♃ 8♍R
2	20.47	12	28	21	21	13	♄26♍R
3	20.51	14	10♍	23	22	13	♅25♏
4	20.55	15	22	25	23	13	♆22♐
5	20.59	16	4♎	26	24	12	♇21♎
6	21.03	17	15	28	26	12	♃ 7♍R
7	21.07	18	27	0♓	27	12	♄26♍R
8	21.11	19	9♏	2	28	12	♅25♏
9	21.15	20	22	3	29	11	♆22♐
10	21.19	21	4♐	5	0♈	11	♇21♎R
11	21.23	22	17	7	1	11	♃ 7♍R
12	21.27	23	1♑	8	3	10	♄26♍R
13	21.31	24	15	10	4	10	♅25♏
14	21.35	25	29	11	5	10	♆22♐
15	21.39	26	14♒	13	6	9	♇21♎R
16	21.43	27	28	14	7	9	♃ 6♍R
17	21.47	28	14♓	16	9	8	♄25♍R
18	21.50	29	29	17	10	8	♅25♏
19	21.54	0♓	14♈	18	11	8	♆22♐
20	21.58	1	28	19	12	7	♇21♎R
21	22.02	2	12♉	20	13	7	♃ 5♍R
22	22.06	3	26	20	14	7	♄25♍R
23	22.10	4	10♊	21	16	6	♅25♏
24	22.14	5	23	21	17	6	♆22♐
25	22.18	6	6♋	21	18	5	♇21♎R
26	22.22	7	18	21R	19	5	♃ 5♍R
27	22.26	8	1♌	21	20	5	♄25♍R
28	22.30	9	13	21	21	4	♅25♏
29	22.34	10	25	20	23	4	♆22♐

Mar	STime	⊙	☽	☿	♀	♂	Plnts
1	22.38	11♓	7♍	20♓	24♈	3♍	♃ 4♍R
2	22.42	12	19	19	25	3	♄24♍R
3	22.46	13	0♎	18	26	3	♅25♏
4	22.50	14	12	17	27	2	♆22♐
5	22.54	15	24	16	28	2	♇21♎R
6	22.57	16	6♏	15	29	2	♃ 4♍R
7	23.01	17	18	14	0♉	1	♄24♍R
8	23.05	18	0♐	13	2	1	♅25♏R
9	23.09	19	13	12	3	0	♆22♐
10	23.13	20	26	11	4	0	♇21♎R
11	23.17	21	9♑	10	5	0	♃ 3♍R
12	23.21	22	23	10	6	0	♄23♍R
13	23.25	23	7♒	9	7	29♌	♅25♏R
14	23.29	24	22	8	8	29	♆22♐
15	23.33	25	7♓	8	9	29	♇21♎R
16	23.37	26	22	8	10	28	♃ 2♍R
17	23.41	27	7♈	7	12	28	♄23♍R
18	23.45	28	22	7	13	28	♅25♏R
19	23.49	29	7♉	7D	14	28	♆22♐
20	23.53	0♈	22	7	15	27	♇21♎R
21	23.57	1	6♊	7	16	27	♃ 2♍R
22	0.01	2	19	8	17	27	♄23♍R
23	0.05	3	2♋	8	18	27	♅25♏R
24	0.08	4	15	8	19	27	♆22♐
25	0.12	5	28	9	20	26	♇21♎R
26	0.16	6	10♌	9	21	26	♃ 1♍R
27	0.20	7	22	10	22	26	♄22♍R
28	0.24	8	4♍	11	23	26	♅25♏R
29	0.28	9	16	11	24	26	♆22♐
30	0.32	10	27	12	25	26	♇20♎R
31	0.36	11	9♎	13	26	26	♃ 1♍R

Apr	STime	⊙	☽	☿	♀	♂	Plnts
1	0.40	12♈	21♎	14♓	27♉	26♌	♃ 1♍R
2	0.44	13	3♏	15	28	26	♄22♍R
3	0.48	14	15	16	29	26	♅25♏R
4	0.52	15	27	17	0♊	26	♆22♐R
5	0.56	16	10♐	18	1	26	♇20♎R
6	1.00	17	22	19	2	26D	♃ 1♍R
7	1.04	18	5♑	20	3	26	♄22♍R
8	1.08	18	18	21	4	26	♅25♏R
9	1.12	19	2♒	23	5	26	♆22♐R
10	1.15	20	16	24	6	26	♇20♎R
11	1.19	21	0♓	25	7	26	♃ 0♍R
12	1.23	22	15	27	8	26	♄21♍R
13	1.27	23	0♈	28	9	26	♅24♏R
14	1.31	24	15	29	10	26	♆22♐R
15	1.35	25	0♉	1♈	11	26	♇20♎R
16	1.39	26	15	2	12	26	♃ 0♍R
17	1.43	27	0♊	4	13	26	♄21♍R
18	1.47	28	14	5	13	26	♅24♏R
19	1.51	29	28	7	14	27	♆22♐R
20	1.55	0♉	11♋	9	15	27	♇20♎R
21	1.59	1	24	10	16	27	♃ 0♍R
22	2.03	2	6♌	12	17	27	♄21♍R
23	2.07	3	19	13	18	27	♅24♏R
24	2.11	4	1♍	15	18	27	♆22♐R
25	2.15	5	12	17	19	28	♇20♎R
26	2.19	6	24	19	20	28	♃ 0♍
27	2.23	7	6♎	20	21	28	♄20♍R
28	2.26	8	18	22	21	28	♅24♏R
29	2.30	9	0♏	24	22	29	♆22♐R
30	2.34	10	12	26	23	29	♇20♎R

May	STime	⊙	☽	☿	♀	♂	Plnts
1	2.38	11♉	24♏	28♈	23♊	29♌	♃ 0♍
2	2.42	12	7♐	0♉	24	29	♄20♍R
3	2.46	13	19	2	25	0♍	♅24♏R
4	2.50	14	2♑	4	25	0	♆22♐R
5	2.54	15	15	6	26	0	♇19♎R
6	2.58	16	29	8	27	0	♃ 0♍
7	3.02	17	12♒	10	27	1	♄20♍R
8	3.06	18	26	12	28	1	♅24♏R
9	3.10	19	10♓	14	28	1	♆22♐R
10	3.14	20	24	16	29	2	♇19♎R
11	3.18	21	9♈	18	29	2	♃ 0♍
12	3.22	22	24	21	0♋	2	♄20♍R
13	3.26	23	9♉	23	0	3	♅23♏R
14	3.30	24	24	25	0	3	♆22♐R
15	3.33	24	8♊	27	1	3	♇19♎R
16	3.37	25	22	29	1	4	♃ 1♍
17	3.41	26	6♋	1♊	1	4	♄20♍R
18	3.45	27	19	4	2	4	♅23♏R
19	3.49	28	2♌	6	2	5	♆22♐R
20	3.53	29	15	8	2	5	♇19♎R
21	3.57	0♊	27	10	2	5	♃ 1♍
22	4.01	1	9♍	12	2	6	♄20♍
23	4.05	2	21	14	2	6	♅23♏R
24	4.09	3	3♎	16	2R	7	♆21♐R
25	4.13	4	14	18	2	7	♇19♎R
26	4.17	5	26	20	2	7	♃ 1♍
27	4.21	6	8♏	22	2	8	♄20♍
28	4.25	7	21	24	2	8	♅23♏R
29	4.29	8	3♐	26	2	9	♆21♐R
30	4.33	9	16	27	2	9	♇19♎R
31	4.37	10	29	29	1	10	♃ 2♍

Jun	STime	⊙	☽	☿	♀	♂	Plnts
1	4.41	11♊	12♑	1♋	1♋	10♍	♃ 2♍
2	4.44	12	25	2	1	10	♄20♍
3	4.48	13	9♒	4	0	11	♅22♏R
4	4.52	14	23	5	0	11	♆21♐R
5	4.56	15	7♓	7	0	12	♇19♎R
6	5.00	16	21	8	29♊	12	♃ 2♍
7	5.04	17	5♈	10	29	13	♄20♍
8	5.08	18	19	11	28	13	♅22♏R
9	5.12	18	4♉	12	28	14	♆21♐R
10	5.16	19	18	13	27	14	♇19♎R
11	5.20	20	2♊	15	26	15	♃ 3♍
12	5.24	21	17	16	26	15	♄20♍
13	5.28	22	1♋	17	25	16	♅22♏R
14	5.32	23	14	18	25	16	♆21♐R
15	5.36	24	27	19	24	16	♇19♎R
16	5.40	25	10♌	20	23	17	♃ 4♍
17	5.44	26	23	20	23	17	♄20♍
18	5.48	27	5♍	21	22	18	♅22♏R
19	5.51	28	17	22	21	18	♆21♐R
20	5.55	29	29	22	21	19	♇19♎R
21	5.59	0♋	11♎	23	20	19	♃ 4♍
22	6.03	1	22	23	20	20	♄21♍
23	6.07	2	5♏	24	19	20	♅22♏R
24	6.11	3	17	24	19	21	♆21♐R
25	6.15	4	29	24	18	22	♇19♎
26	6.19	5	12♐	25	18	22	♃ 5♍
27	6.23	6	25	25	18	23	♄21♍
28	6.27	7	8♑	25R	17	23	♅22♏R
29	6.31	8	22	25	17	24	♆21♐R
30	6.35	9	5♒	25	17	24	♇19♎

Jul	STime	⊙	☽	☿	♀	♂	Plnts
1	6.39	9♋	19♒	24♋	16♊	25♍	♃ 6♍
2	6.43	10	3♓	24	16	25	♄21♍
3	6.47	11	17	24	16	26	♅22♏R
4	6.51	12	2♈	23	16	26	♆20♐R
5	6.55	13	16	23	16	27	♇19♎
6	6.58	14	0♉	23	16D	27	♃ 7♍
7	7.02	15	14	22	16	28	♄22♍
8	7.06	16	28	21	16	28	♅21♏R
9	7.10	17	12♊	21	16	29	♆20♐R
10	7.14	18	26	20	16	0♎	♇19♎
11	7.18	19	9♋	19	16	0	♃ 8♍
12	7.22	20	23	19	16	1	♄22♍
13	7.26	21	6♌	18	17	1	♅21♏R
14	7.30	22	18	18	17	2	♆20♐R
15	7.34	23	1♍	17	17	2	♇19♎
16	7.38	24	13	17	17	3	♃ 8♍
17	7.42	25	25	16	18	4	♄22♍
18	7.46	26	7♎	16	18	4	♅21♏R
19	7.50	27	19	15	19	5	♆20♐R
20	7.54	28	0♏	15	19	5	♇19♎
21	7.58	29	12	15	19	6	♃ 9♍
22	8.02	0♌	25	15D	20	6	♄23♍
23	8.06	0	7♐	15	20	7	♅21♏R
24	8.09	1	20	15	21	8	♆20♐R
25	8.13	2	3♑	15	22	8	♇19♎
26	8.17	3	17	16	22	9	♃10♍
27	8.21	4	0♒	16	23	9	♄23♍
28	8.25	5	15	17	23	10	♅21♏
29	8.29	6	29	17	24	11	♆20♐R
30	8.33	7	13♓	18	25	11	♇19♎
31	8.37	8	28	19	25	12	♃11♍

Aug	STime	⊙	☽	☿	♀	♂	Plnts
1	8.41	9♌	12♈	20♋	26♊	12♎	♃11♍
2	8.45	10	27	21	27	13	♄24♍
3	8.49	11	11♉	22	27	14	♅21♏
4	8.53	12	25	23	28	14	♆20♐R
5	8.57	13	9♊	24	29	15	♇19♎
6	9.01	14	22	26	0♋	15	♃12♍
7	9.05	15	6♋	27	0	16	♄24♍
8	9.09	16	19	29	1	17	♅21♏
9	9.13	17	2♌	0♌	2	17	♆20♐R
10	9.16	18	14	2	3	18	♇19♎
11	9.20	19	27	4	4	18	♃13♍
12	9.24	20	9♍	6	5	19	♄25♍
13	9.28	21	21	7	5	20	♅21♏
14	9.32	22	3♎	9	6	20	♆20♐R
15	9.36	23	15	11	7	21	♇19♎
16	9.40	23	27	13	8	22	♃14♍
17	9.44	24	9♏	15	9	22	♄26♍
18	9.48	25	21	17	10	23	♅21♏
19	9.52	26	3♐	19	11	23	♆20♐R
20	9.56	27	15	21	12	24	♇19♎
21	10.00	28	28	23	13	25	♃16♍
22	10.04	29	11♑	25	13	25	♄26♍
23	10.08	0♍	25	27	14	26	♅21♏
24	10.12	1	9♒	29	15	27	♆20♐
25	10.16	2	23	1♍	16	27	♇20♎
26	10.20	3	8♓	3	17	28	♃17♍
27	10.24	4	23	5	18	29	♄27♍
28	10.27	5	8♈	7	19	29	♅22♏
29	10.31	6	23	9	20	0♏	♆20♐
30	10.35	7	7♉	11	21	1	♇20♎
31	10.39	8	22	13	22	1	♃18♍

Sep	STime	⊙	☽	☿	♀	♂	Plnts
1	10.43	9♍	6♊	15♍	23♋	2♏	♃18♍
2	10.47	10	19	16	24	2	♄27♍
3	10.51	11	3♋	18	25	3	♅22♏
4	10.55	12	16	20	26	4	♆20♐
5	10.59	13	28	22	27	4	♇20♎
6	11.03	14	11♌	24	28	5	♃19♍
7	11.07	15	23	25	29	6	♄28♍
8	11.11	16	5♍	27	0♌	6	♅22♏
9	11.15	17	18	29	2	7	♆20♐
10	11.19	18	29	0♎	3	8	♇20♎
11	11.23	19	11♎	2	4	8	♃20♍
12	11.27	20	23	4	5	9	♄29♍
13	11.31	21	5♏	5	6	10	♅22♏
14	11.34	22	17	7	7	10	♆20♐
15	11.38	22	29	9	8	11	♇20♎
16	11.42	23	11♐	10	9	12	♃21♍
17	11.46	24	24	12	10	12	♄29♍
18	11.50	25	6♑	13	11	13	♅22♏
19	11.54	26	19	15	12	14	♆20♐
20	11.58	27	3♒	16	13	15	♇20♎
21	12.02	28	17	18	15	15	♃22♍
22	12.06	29	1♓	19	16	16	♄ 0♎
23	12.10	0♎	16	21	17	17	♅22♏
24	12.14	1	1♈	22	18	17	♆20♐
25	12.18	2	16	23	19	18	♇21♎
26	12.22	3	2♉	25	20	19	♃23♍
27	12.26	4	17	26	21	19	♄ 0♎
28	12.30	5	1♊	28	22	20	♅23♏
29	12.34	6	15	29	23	21	♆20♐
30	12.38	7	29	0♏	25	21	♇21♎

Oct	STime	⊙	☽	☿	♀	♂	Plnts
1	12.41	8♎	13♋	2♏	26♌	22♏	♃24♍
2	12.45	9	26	3	27	23	♄ 1♎
3	12.49	10	8♌	4	28	24	♅23♏
4	12.53	11	20	5	29	24	♆20♐
5	12.57	12	3♍	7	0♍	25	♇21♎
6	13.01	13	15	8	1	26	♃25♍
7	13.05	14	26	9	3	26	♄ 2♎
8	13.09	15	8♎	10	4	27	♅23♏
9	13.13	16	20	11	5	28	♆20♐
10	13.17	17	2♏	12	6	28	♇21♎
11	13.21	18	14	13	7	29	♃26♍
12	13.25	19	26	14	8	0♐	♄ 2♎
13	13.29	20	8♐	15	10	1	♅23♏
14	13.33	21	20	16	11	1	♆20♐
15	13.37	22	2♑	16	12	2	♇21♎
16	13.41	23	15	17	13	3	♃28♍
17	13.45	24	28	18	14	3	♄ 3♎
18	13.49	25	11♒	18	15	4	♅24♏
19	13.52	26	25	19	17	5	♆20♐
20	13.56	27	10♓	19	18	6	♇22♎
21	14.00	28	24	19	19	6	♃29♍
22	14.04	29	9♈	20	20	7	♄ 3♎
23	14.08	0♏	25	20R	21	8	♅24♏
24	14.12	1	10♉	19	23	9	♆20♐
25	14.16	2	25	19	24	9	♇22♎
26	14.20	3	10♊	19	25	10	♃ 0♎
27	14.24	4	24	18	26	11	♄ 4♎
28	14.28	5	8♋	18	27	11	♅24♏
29	14.32	6	22	17	29	12	♆20♐
30	14.36	7	5♌	16	0♎	13	♇22♎
31	14.40	8	17	15	1	14	♃ 0♎

Nov	STime	⊙	☽	☿	♀	♂	Plnts
1	14.44	9♏	0♍	13♏	2♎	14♐	♃ 1♎
2	14.48	10	12	12	3	15	♄ 5♎
3	14.52	11	23	11	5	16	♅25♏
4	14.56	12	5♎	9	6	17	♆21♐
5	14.59	13	17	8	7	17	♇22♎
6	15.03	14	29	7	8	18	♃ 2♎
7	15.07	15	11♏	6	9	19	♄ 5♎
8	15.11	16	23	5	11	20	♅25♏
9	15.15	17	5♐	5	12	20	♆21♐
10	15.19	18	17	4	13	21	♇22♎
11	15.23	19	0♑	4	14	22	♃ 3♎
12	15.27	20	12	4D	16	23	♄ 6♎
13	15.31	21	25	4	17	23	♅25♏
14	15.35	22	8♒	4	18	24	♆21♐
15	15.39	23	21	4	19	25	♇23♎
16	15.43	24	5♓	5	20	26	♃ 3♎
17	15.47	25	19	6	22	26	♄ 6♎
18	15.51	26	3♈	7	23	27	♅26♏
19	15.55	27	18	8	24	28	♆21♐
20	15.59	28	3♉	9	25	29	♇23♎
21	16.03	29	18	10	27	29	♃ 4♎
22	16.07	0♐	3♊	11	28	0♑	♄ 7♎
23	16.10	1	18	12	29	1	♅26♏
24	16.14	2	2♋	13	0♏	2	♆21♐
25	16.18	3	16	15	1	2	♇23♎
26	16.22	4	0♌	16	3	3	♃ 5♎
27	16.26	5	13	17	4	4	♄ 7♎
28	16.30	6	26	19	5	5	♅26♏
29	16.34	7	8♍	20	6	5	♆22♐
30	16.38	8	20	22	8	6	♇23♎

Dec	STime	⊙	☽	☿	♀	♂	Plnts
1	16.42	9♐	2♎	23♏	9♏	7♑	♃ 6♎
2	16.46	10	14	25	10	8	♄ 8♎
3	16.50	11	26	26	11	8	♅27♏
4	16.54	12	8♏	28	13	9	♆22♐
5	16.58	13	20	29	14	10	♇23♎
6	17.02	14	2♐	1♐	15	11	♃ 7♎
7	17.06	15	14	2	16	11	♄ 8♎
8	17.10	16	26	4	18	12	♅27♏
9	17.14	17	9♑	5	19	13	♆22♐
10	17.17	18	22	7	20	14	♇23♎
11	17.21	19	5♒	8	21	15	♃ 7♎
12	17.25	20	18	10	23	15	♄ 8♎
13	17.29	21	1♓	11	24	16	♅27♏
14	17.33	22	15	13	25	17	♆22♐
15	17.37	23	29	15	26	18	♇24♎
16	17.41	24	13♈	16	28	18	♃ 8♎
17	17.45	25	28	18	29	19	♄ 9♎
18	17.49	26	12♉	19	0♐	20	♅27♏
19	17.53	27	27	21	1	21	♆22♐
20	17.57	28	12♊	22	2	22	♇24♎
21	18.01	29	26	24	4	22	♃ 8♎
22	18.05	1♑	10♋	25	5	23	♄ 9♎
23	18.09	2	24	27	6	24	♅28♏
24	18.13	3	8♌	29	7	25	♆22♐
25	18.17	4	21	0♑	9	25	♇24♎
26	18.21	5	4♍	2	10	26	♃ 9♎
27	18.24	6	16	3	11	27	♄ 9♎
28	18.28	7	28	5	12	28	♅28♏
29	18.32	8	10♎	7	14	29	♆23♐
30	18.36	9	22	8	15	29	♇24♎
31	18.40	10	4♏	10	16	0♒	♃ 9♎

1 9 8 1

Jan	STime	☉	☽	☿	♀	♂	Plnts
1	18.44	11♑	16♏	11♑	17♐	1♒	♃ 9♎
2	18.48	12	28	13	19	2	♄ 9♎
3	18.52	13	10♐	15	20	3	♅28♏
4	18.56	14	23	16	21	3	♆23♐
5	19.00	15	5♑	18	22	4	♇24♎
6	19.04	16	18	19	24	5	♃10♎
7	19.08	17	1♒	21	25	6	♄ 9♎
8	19.12	18	15	23	26	6	♅28♏
9	19.16	19	28	24	27	7	♆23♐
10	19.20	20	12♓	26	29	8	♇24♎
11	19.24	21	26	28	0♑	9	♃10♎
12	19.28	22	10♈	29	1	10	♄ 9♎
13	19.32	23	24	1♒	2	10	♅29♏
14	19.35	24	8♉	3	4	11	♆23♐
15	19.39	25	22	4	5	12	♇24♎
16	19.43	26	7♊	6	6	13	♃10♎
17	19.47	27	21	8	7	14	♄ 9♎
18	19.51	28	5♋	10	9	14	♅29♏
19	19.55	29	19	11	10	15	♆23♐
20	19.59	0♒	2♌	13	11	16	♇24♎
21	20.03	1	16	15	12	17	♃10♎
22	20.07	2	29	16	14	17	♄ 9♎R
23	20.11	3	11♍	18	15	18	♅29♏
24	20.15	4	24	19	16	19	♆24♐
25	20.19	5	6♎	21	17	20	♇24♎
26	20.23	6	18	23	19	21	♃10♎R
27	20.27	7	0♏	24	20	21	♄ 9♎R
28	20.31	8	12	26	21	22	♅29♏
29	20.35	9	24	27	22	23	♆24♐
30	20.39	10	6♐	28	24	24	♇24♎
31	20.42	11	18	29	25	25	♃10♎R

Apr	STime	☉	☽	☿	♀	♂	Plnts
1	0.39	11♈	26♒	19♓	10♈	12♈	♃ 4♎R
2	0.43	12	10♓	20	11	12	♄ 6♎R
3	0.47	13	25	22	12	13	♅29♏R
4	0.51	14	9♈	23	14	14	♆25♐
5	0.55	15	25	25	15	15	♇23♎R
6	0.59	16	10♉	27	16	15	♃ 4♎R
7	1.03	17	25	28	17	16	♄ 5♎R
8	1.07	18	10♊	0♈	19	17	♅29♏R
9	1.11	19	24	2	20	18	♆25♐R
10	1.15	20	8♋	3	21	18	♇23♎R
11	1.18	21	22	5	22	19	♃ 3♎R
12	1.22	22	5♌	7	23	20	♄ 5♎R
13	1.26	23	18	9	25	21	♅29♏R
14	1.30	24	0♍	11	26	22	♆24♐R
15	1.34	25	13	12	27	22	♇23♎R
16	1.38	26	25	14	28	23	♃ 3♎R
17	1.42	27	7♎	16	0♉	24	♄ 5♎R
18	1.46	28	19	18	1	25	♅29♏R
19	1.50	29	1♏	20	2	25	♆24♐R
20	1.54	0♉	13	22	3	26	♇22♎R
21	1.58	1	25	24	5	27	♃ 2♎R
22	2.02	2	7♐	26	6	28	♄ 4♎R
23	2.06	3	18	28	7	28	♅29♏R
24	2.10	4	0♑	0♉	8	29	♆24♐R
25	2.14	5	13	2	10	0♉	♇22♎R
26	2.18	6	25	4	11	1	♃ 2♎R
27	2.22	7	8♒	7	12	1	♄ 4♎R
28	2.25	8	21	9	13	2	♅29♏R
29	2.29	9	4♓	11	15	3	♆24♐R
30	2.33	10	18	13	16	4	♇22♎R

Jul	STime	☉	☽	☿	♀	♂	Plnts
1	6.38	9♋	5♋	26♊	2♌	18♊	♃ 2♎
2	6.42	10	20	26	3	19	♄ 3♎
3	6.46	11	4♌	26D	4	20	♅26♏R
4	6.50	12	18	26	5	20	♆23♐R
5	6.54	13	1♍	26	7	21	♇21♎
6	6.58	14	14	26	8	22	♃ 2♎
7	7.01	15	27	27	9	22	♄ 4♎
8	7.05	16	9♎	27	10	23	♅26♏R
9	7.09	17	21	28	11	24	♆23♐R
10	7.13	18	3♏	28	13	24	♇21♎
11	7.17	19	15	29	14	25	♃ 3♎
12	7.21	20	27	29	15	26	♄ 4♎
13	7.25	21	9♐	0♋	16	26	♅26♏R
14	7.29	22	21	1	18	27	♆22♐R
15	7.33	23	3♑	2	19	28	♇21♎
16	7.37	24	16	3	20	28	♃ 4♎
17	7.41	25	28	4	21	29	♄ 4♎
18	7.45	25	11♒	5	22	0♋	♅26♏R
19	7.49	26	24	7	24	0	♆22♐R
20	7.53	27	7♓	8	25	1	♇21♎
21	7.57	28	21	9	26	2	♃ 4♎
22	8.01	29	4♈	11	27	2	♄ 5♎
23	8.05	0♌	18	13	28	3	♅26♏R
24	8.08	1	2♉	14	0♍	4	♆22♐R
25	8.12	2	17	16	1	4	♇21♎
26	8.16	3	1♊	18	2	5	♃ 5♎
27	8.20	4	15	19	3	6	♄ 5♎
28	8.24	5	0♋	21	4	7	♅26♏
29	8.28	6	14	23	6	7	♆22♐R
30	8.32	7	28	25	7	8	♇21♎
31	8.36	8	12♌	27	8	9	♃ 6♎

Oct	STime	☉	☽	☿	♀	♂	Plnts
1	12.41	8♎	15♏	2♏	21♏	18♌	♃18♎
2	12.44	9	27	3	22	19	♄12♎
3	12.48	10	9♐	3	23	19	♅27♏
4	12.52	11	21	3	25	20	♆22♐
5	12.56	12	3♑	4	26	20	♇23♎
6	13.00	13	15	4R	27	21	♃19♎
7	13.04	14	27	3	28	22	♄13♎
8	13.08	15	10♒	3	29	22	♅27♏
9	13.12	16	23	3	0♐	23	♆22♐
10	13.16	17	6♓	2	1	23	♇24♎
11	13.20	18	20	2	3	24	♃20♎
12	13.24	19	4♈	1	4	25	♄13♎
13	13.28	20	19	0	5	25	♅28♏
14	13.32	21	4♉	29♎	6	26	♆22♐
15	13.36	22	19	28	7	26	♇24♎
16	13.40	23	4♊	27	8	27	♃21♎
17	13.44	24	19	26	9	28	♄14♎
18	13.48	25	3♋	25	10	28	♅28♏
19	13.52	26	17	23	11	29	♆22♐
20	13.55	27	1♌	22	13	29	♇24♎
21	13.59	28	14	21	14	0♍	♃22♎
22	14.03	29	28	20	15	1	♄15♎
23	14.07	0♏	10♍	19	16	1	♅28♏
24	14.11	1	23	19	17	2	♆22♐
25	14.15	2	5♎	18	18	2	♇24♎
26	14.19	3	18	18	19	3	♃23♎
27	14.23	4	0♏	18D	20	3	♄15♎
28	14.27	5	12	18	21	4	♅29♏
29	14.31	6	24	18	22	5	♆23♐
30	14.35	7	6♐	19	23	5	♇24♎
31	14.39	8	18	19	24	6	♃24♎

Feb	STime	☉	☽	☿	♀	♂	Plnts
1	20.46	12♒	0♑	1♓	26♑	25♒	♃10♎R
2	20.50	13	13	2	27	26	♄ 9♎R
3	20.54	14	26	2	29	27	♅29♏
4	20.58	15	10♒	3	0♒	28	♆24♐
5	21.02	16	24	4	1	29	♇24♎R
6	21.06	17	8♓	4	3	29	♃10♎R
7	21.10	18	22	5	4	0♓	♄ 9♎R
8	21.14	19	6♈	5R	5	1	♅ 0♐
9	21.18	20	21	5	6	2	♆24♐
10	21.22	21	5♉	4	8	3	♇24♎R
11	21.26	22	19	4	9	3	♃10♎R
12	21.30	23	3♊	3	10	4	♄ 9♎R
13	21.34	24	17	2	11	5	♅ 0♐
14	21.38	25	1♋	2	13	6	♆24♐
15	21.42	26	15	1	14	6	♇24♎R
16	21.46	27	28	0	15	7	♃ 9♎R
17	21.50	28	11♌	28♒	16	8	♄ 9♎R
18	21.53	29	24	27	18	9	♅ 0♐
19	21.57	0♓	7♍	26	19	10	♆24♐
20	22.01	1	19	25	20	10	♇24♎R
21	22.05	2	2♎	24	21	11	♃ 9♎R
22	22.09	3	14	23	23	12	♄ 8♎R
23	22.13	4	26	22	24	13	♅ 0♐
24	22.17	5	8♏	21	25	14	♆24♐
25	22.21	6	20	21	26	14	♇24♎R
26	22.25	8	2♐	20	28	15	♃ 8♎R
27	22.29	9	13	20	29	16	♄ 8♎R
28	22.33	10	26	20	0♓	17	♅ 0♐

May	STime	☉	☽	☿	♀	♂	Plnts
1	2.37	11♉	3♈	15♉	17♉	4♉	♃ 1♎R
2	2.41	12	18	17	18	5	♄ 4♎R
3	2.45	13	3♉	20	19	6	♅28♏R
4	2.49	14	18	22	21	7	♆24♐R
5	2.53	15	3♊	24	22	7	♇22♎R
6	2.57	16	18	26	23	8	♃ 1♎R
7	3.01	17	3♋	28	24	9	♄ 3♎R
8	3.05	17	17	0♊	26	10	♅28♏R
9	3.09	18	1♌	2	27	10	♆24♐R
10	3.13	19	14	4	28	11	♇22♎R
11	3.17	20	27	6	29	12	♃ 1♎R
12	3.21	21	10♍	8	1♊	12	♄ 3♎R
13	3.25	22	22	9	2	13	♅28♏R
14	3.29	23	4♎	11	3	14	♆24♐R
15	3.33	24	16	13	4	15	♇22♎R
16	3.36	25	28	14	5	15	♃ 0♎R
17	3.40	26	10♏	16	7	16	♄ 3♎R
18	3.44	27	22	18	8	17	♅28♏R
19	3.48	28	4♐	19	9	18	♆24♐R
20	3.52	29	16	20	10	18	♇22♎R
21	3.56	0♊	28	22	12	19	♃ 0♎R
22	4.00	1	10♑	23	13	20	♄ 3♎R
23	4.04	2	22	24	14	21	♅28♏R
24	4.08	3	4♒	25	15	21	♆24♐R
25	4.12	3	17	27	17	22	♇22♎R
26	4.16	5	0♓	28	18	23	♃ 0♎
27	4.20	6	14	29	19	23	♄ 3♎R
28	4.24	7	28	0♋	20	24	♅27♏R
29	4.28	8	12♈	0	21	25	♆24♐R
30	4.32	9	27	1	23	26	♇22♎R
31	4.36	10	12♉	2	24	26	♃ 0♎

Aug	STime	☉	☽	☿	♀	♂	Plnts
1	8.40	9♌	26♌	29♋	9♍	9♋	♃ 6♎
2	8.44	10	9♍	1♌	10	10	♄ 5♎
3	8.48	11	22	3	12	10	♅26♏
4	8.52	12	5♎	5	13	11	♆22♐R
5	8.56	13	17	7	14	12	♇22♎
6	9.00	14	29	9	15	12	♃ 7♎
7	9.04	15	11♏	12	16	13	♄ 6♎
8	9.08	16	23	14	18	14	♅26♏
9	9.12	17	5♐	16	19	14	♆22♐R
10	9.16	17	17	18	20	15	♇22♎
11	9.19	18	29	20	21	16	♃ 8♎
12	9.23	19	11♑	22	22	16	♄ 6♎
13	9.27	20	24	24	24	17	♅26♏
14	9.31	21	7♒	26	25	18	♆22♐R
15	9.35	22	20	28	26	18	♇22♎
16	9.39	23	3♓	0♍	27	19	♃ 8♎
17	9.43	24	17	2	28	20	♄ 7♎
18	9.47	25	1♈	3	0♎	20	♅26♏
19	9.51	26	15	5	1	21	♆22♐R
20	9.55	27	29	7	2	22	♇22♎
21	9.59	28	14♉	9	3	22	♃ 9♎
22	10.03	29	28	11	4	23	♄ 7♎
23	10.07	0♍	12♊	13	6	24	♅26♏
24	10.11	1	26	14	7	24	♆22♐
25	10.15	2	10♋	16	8	25	♇22♎
26	10.19	3	24	18	9	25	♃10♎
27	10.23	4	8♌	19	10	26	♄ 8♎
28	10.26	5	21	21	12	27	♅26♏
29	10.30	6	4♍	23	13	27	♆22♐
30	10.34	7	17	24	14	28	♇22♎
31	10.38	8	0♎	26	15	29	♃11♎

Nov	STime	☉	☽	☿	♀	♂	Plnts
1	14.43	9♏	29♐	20♎	25♐	6♍	♃24♎
2	14.47	10	11♑	21	27	7	♄16♎
3	14.51	11	23	22	28	7	♅29♏
4	14.55	12	5♒	23	29	8	♆23♐
5	14.59	13	18	24	0♑	9	♇25♎
6	15.02	14	1♓	26	1	9	♃25♎
7	15.06	15	14	27	2	10	♄16♎
8	15.10	16	28	28	3	10	♅29♏
9	15.14	17	13♈	0♏	4	11	♆23♐
10	15.18	18	27	1	5	11	♇25♎
11	15.22	19	12♉	3	6	12	♃27♎
12	15.26	20	28	4	7	12	♄17♎
13	15.30	21	13♊	6	8	13	♅ 0♐
14	15.34	22	28	7	9	14	♆23♐
15	15.38	23	13♋	9	10	14	♇25♎
16	15.42	24	27	10	11	15	♃28♎
17	15.46	25	11♌	12	12	15	♄18♎
18	15.50	26	24	13	13	16	♅ 0♐
19	15.54	27	7♍	15	14	16	♆23♐
20	15.58	28	20	16	15	17	♇25♎
21	16.02	29	3♎	18	15	17	♃29♎
22	16.06	0♐	15	20	16	18	♄18♎
23	16.09	1	27	21	17	18	♅ 0♐
24	16.13	2	9♏	23	18	19	♆23♐
25	16.17	3	21	24	19	19	♇25♎
26	16.21	4	3♐	26	20	20	♃ 0♏
27	16.25	5	15	28	21	21	♄19♎
28	16.29	6	26	29	22	21	♅ 0♐
29	16.33	7	8♑	1♐	23	22	♆24♐
30	16.37	8	20	2	23	22	♇26♎

Mar	STime	☉	☽	☿	♀	♂	Plnts
1	22.37	11♓	8♑	20♒	1♓	17♓	♃ 8♎R
2	22.41	12	21	20D	3	18	♄ 8♎R
3	22.45	13	4♒	20	4	19	♅ 0♐
4	22.49	14	18	20	5	20	♆24♐
5	22.53	15	2♓	20	6	21	♇24♎R
6	22.57	16	16	20	7	21	♃ 8♎R
7	23.00	17	1♈	21	9	22	♄ 8♎R
8	23.04	18	16	21	10	23	♅ 0♐R
9	23.08	19	1♉	22	11	24	♆24♐
10	23.12	20	15	23	12	25	♇24♎R
11	23.16	21	0♊	23	14	25	♃ 7♎R
12	23.20	22	14	24	15	26	♄ 7♎R
13	23.24	23	28	25	16	27	♅ 0♐R
14	23.28	24	11♋	26	17	28	♆25♐
15	23.32	25	25	27	19	28	♇23♎R
16	23.36	26	8♌	28	20	29	♃ 6♎R
17	23.40	27	21	29	21	0♈	♄ 7♎R
18	23.44	27	3♍	0♓	22	1	♅ 0♐R
19	23.48	28	16	1	24	2	♆25♐
20	23.52	29	28	2	25	2	♇23♎R
21	23.56	0♈	10♎	4	26	3	♃ 6♎R
22	0.00	1	22	5	27	4	♄ 7♎R
23	0.04	2	4♏	6	29	5	♅ 0♐R
24	0.08	3	16	7	0♈	5	♆25♐
25	0.11	4	28	9	1	6	♇23♎R
26	0.15	5	10♐	10	2	7	♃ 5♎R
27	0.19	6	22	11	4	8	♄ 6♎R
28	0.23	7	4♑	13	5	9	♅ 0♐R
29	0.27	8	16	14	6	9	♆25♐
30	0.31	9	29	16	7	10	♇23♎R
31	0.35	10	12♒	17	9	11	♃ 5♎R

Jun	STime	☉	☽	☿	♀	♂	Plnts
1	4.40	11♊	27♉	3♋	25♊	27♉	♃ 0♎
2	4.43	12	12♊	3	26	28	♄ 3♎
3	4.47	13	27	4	28	28	♅27♏R
4	4.51	13	11♋	4	29	29	♆23♐R
5	4.55	14	26	4	0♋	0♊	♇21♎R
6	4.59	15	10♌	5	1	1	♃ 0♎
7	5.03	16	23	5	2	1	♄ 3♎
8	5.07	17	6♍	5	4	2	♅27♏R
9	5.11	18	18	5R	5	3	♆23♐R
10	5.15	19	1♎	5	6	3	♇21♎R
11	5.19	20	13	5	7	4	♃ 0♎
12	5.23	21	25	5	9	5	♄ 3♎
13	5.27	22	7♏	4	10	6	♅27♏R
14	5.31	23	19	4	11	6	♆23♐R
15	5.35	24	0♐	4	12	7	♇21♎
16	5.39	25	12	3	13	8	♃ 1♎
17	5.43	26	24	3	15	8	♄ 3♎
18	5.47	27	7♑	3	16	9	♅27♏R
19	5.51	28	19	2	17	10	♆23♐R
20	5.54	29	1♒	1	18	11	♇21♎R
21	5.58	0♋	14	1	20	11	♃ 1♎
22	6.02	1	27	0	21	12	♄ 3♎
23	6.06	2	10♓	29♊	22	13	♅26♏R
24	6.10	3	24	29	23	13	♆23♐R
25	6.14	4	8♈	28	24	14	♇21♎
26	6.18	4	22	28	26	15	♃ 1♎
27	6.22	5	6♉	27	27	15	♄ 3♎
28	6.26	6	21	27	28	16	♅26♏R
29	6.30	7	6♊	27	29	17	♆23♐R
30	6.34	8	20	26	1♌	17	♇21♎

Sep	STime	☉	☽	☿	♀	♂	Plnts
1	10.42	9♍	13♎	27♍	16♎	29♋	♃11♎
2	10.46	10	25	29	17	0♌	♄ 9♎
3	10.50	11	7♏	1♎	19	1	♅26♏
4	10.54	12	19	2	20	1	♆22♐
5	10.58	13	1♐	4	21	2	♇22♎
6	11.02	14	13	5	22	3	♃12♎
7	11.06	14	25	6	23	3	♄ 9♎
8	11.10	15	7♑	8	24	4	♅26♏
9	11.14	16	19	9	26	4	♆22♐
10	11.18	17	2♒	11	27	5	♇23♎
11	11.22	18	15	12	28	6	♃13♎
12	11.26	19	28	13	29	6	♄10♎
13	11.30	20	12♓	15	0♏	7	♅26♏
14	11.34	21	26	16	2	8	♆22♐
15	11.37	22	11♈	17	3	8	♇23♎
16	11.41	23	25	18	4	9	♃15♎
17	11.45	24	10♉	20	5	9	♄10♎
18	11.49	25	24	21	6	10	♅27♏
19	11.53	26	9♊	22	7	11	♆22♐
20	11.57	27	23	23	8	11	♇23♎
21	12.01	28	7♋	24	10	12	♃16♎
22	12.05	29	21	25	11	13	♄11♎
23	12.09	0♎	4♌	26	12	13	♅27♏
24	12.13	1	17	27	13	14	♆22♐
25	12.17	2	1♍	28	14	14	♇23♎
26	12.21	3	13	29	15	15	♃17♎
27	12.25	4	26	0♏	17	15	♄11♎
28	12.29	5	9♎	0	18	16	♅27♏
29	12.33	6	21	1	19	17	♆22♐
30	12.37	7	3♏	2	20	17	♇23♎

Dec	STime	☉	☽	☿	♀	♂	Plnts
1	16.41	9♐	2♒	4♐	24♑	23♍	♃ 1♏
2	16.45	10	14	5	25	23	♄19♎
3	16.49	11	27	7	26	24	♅ 1♐
4	16.53	12	10♓	9	27	24	♆24♐
5	16.57	13	23	10	27	25	♇26♎
6	17.01	14	7♈	12	28	25	♃ 2♏
7	17.05	15	21	13	29	26	♄19♎
8	17.09	16	6♉	15	29	26	♅ 1♐
9	17.13	17	20	16	0♒	27	♆24♐
10	17.17	18	6♊	18	1	27	♇26♎
11	17.20	19	21	20	1	28	♃ 2♏
12	17.24	20	6♋	21	2	28	♄20♎
13	17.28	21	21	23	3	29	♅ 1♐
14	17.32	22	6♌	24	3	29	♆24♐
15	17.36	23	20	26	4	29	♇26♎
16	17.40	24	3♍	27	4	0♎	♃ 3♏
17	17.44	25	16	29	5	0	♄20♎
18	17.48	26	29	1♑	5	1	♅ 2♐
19	17.52	27	12♎	2	6	1	♆24♐
20	17.56	28	24	4	6	2	♇26♎
21	18.00	29	6♏	5	7	2	♃ 4♏
22	18.04	0♑	18	7	7	3	♄21♎
23	18.08	1	0♐	8	7	3	♅ 2♐
24	18.12	2	11	10	8	4	♆25♐
25	18.16	3	23	12	8	4	♇26♎
26	18.20	4	5♑	13	8	4	♃ 5♏
27	18.24	5	17	15	8	5	♄21♎
28	18.27	6	29	17	8	5	♅ 2♐
29	18.31	7	11♒	18	8	6	♆25♐
30	18.35	8	24	20	9	6	♇26♎
31	18.39	9	7♓	21	9R	7	♃ 6♏

Jan	STime	☉	☽	☿	♀	♂	Plnts
1	18.43	10♑	19♓	23♑	9♒	7♎	♃ 6♏
2	18.47	11	3♈	25	9	7	♄21♎
3	18.51	12	16	26	8	8	♅ 3♐
4	18.55	14	0♉	28	8	8	♆25♐
5	18.59	15	15	29	8	9	♇26♎
6	19.03	16	29	1♒	8	9	♃ 7♏
7	19.07	17	14♊	2	8	9	♄21♎
8	19.11	18	29	4	7	10	♅ 3♐
9	19.15	19	14♋	5	7	10	♆25♐
10	19.19	20	29	7	7	10	♇27♎
11	19.23	21	13♌	8	6	11	♃ 7♏
12	19.27	22	28	10	6	11	♄22♎
13	19.31	23	11♍	11	5	11	♅ 3♐
14	19.35	24	25	12	5	12	♆25♐
15	19.38	25	8♎	13	4	12	♇27♎
16	19.42	26	20	15	4	12	♃ 8♏
17	19.46	27	2♏	16	3	13	♄22♎
18	19.50	28	14	16	3	13	♅ 3♐
19	19.54	29	26	17	2	13	♆25♐
20	19.58	0♒	8♐	18	1	14	♇27♎
21	20.02	1	20	18	1	14	♃ 8♏
22	20.06	2	2♑	18	0	14	♄22♎
23	20.10	3	14	18R	29♑	15	♅ 3♐
24	20.14	4	26	18	29	15	♆26♐
25	20.18	5	8♒	18	28	15	♇27♎
26	20.22	6	21	17	28	15	♃ 9♏
27	20.26	7	4♓	17	27	16	♄22♎
28	20.30	8	17	16	27	16	♅ 4♐
29	20.34	9	0♈	15	26	16	♆26♐
30	20.38	10	13	14	26	16	♇27♎
31	20.42	11	27	12	25	17	♃ 9♏

Feb	STime	☉	☽	☿	♀	♂	Plnts
1	20.45	12♒	11♉	11♒	25♑	17♎	♃ 9♏
2	20.49	13	25	10	24	17	♄22♎
3	20.53	14	9♊	9	24	17	♅ 4♐
4	20.57	15	23	8	24	17	♆26♐
5	21.01	16	8♋	7	24	18	♇27♎
6	21.05	17	23	6	23	18	♃10♏
7	21.09	18	7♌	5	23	18	♄22♎R
8	21.13	19	21	4	23	18	♅ 4♐
9	21.17	20	5♍	4	23	18	♆26♐
10	21.21	21	19	3	23D	18	♇27♎R
11	21.25	22	2♎	3	23	18	♃10♏
12	21.29	23	15	3	23	18	♄22♎R
13	21.33	24	28	3D	23	19	♅ 4♐
14	21.37	25	10♏	3	23	19	♆26♐
15	21.41	26	22	3	23	19	♇27♎R
16	21.45	27	4♐	3	24	19	♃10♏
17	21.49	28	16	4	24	19	♄22♎R
18	21.53	29	28	4	24	19	♅ 4♐
19	21.56	0♓	10♑	5	24	19	♆26♐
20	22.00	1	22	5	25	19R	♇27♎R
21	22.04	2	4♒	6	25	19	♃10♏
22	22.08	3	17	7	26	19	♄22♎R
23	22.12	4	0♓	8	26	19	♅ 4♐
24	22.16	5	13	8	26	19	♆26♐
25	22.20	6	26	9	27	19	♇26♎R
26	22.24	7	10♈	10	27	19	♃10♏R
27	22.28	8	24	11	28	19	♄21♎R
28	22.32	9	8♉	12	29	18	♅ 4♐

Mar	STime	☉	☽	☿	♀	♂	Plnts
1	22.36	10♓	22♉	14♒	29♑	18♎	♃10♏R
2	22.40	11	6♊	15	0♒	18	♄21♎R
3	22.44	12	20	16	0	18	♅ 4♐
4	22.48	13	4♋	17	1	18	♆27♐
5	22.52	14	18	18	2	18	♇26♎R
6	22.56	15	2♌	20	2	18	♃10♏R
7	23.00	16	16	21	3	17	♄21♎R
8	23.03	17	0♍	22	4	17	♅ 4♐
9	23.07	18	14	24	4	17	♆27♐
10	23.11	19	27	25	5	17	♇26♎R
11	23.15	20	10♎	26	6	17	♃10♏R
12	23.19	21	23	28	7	16	♄21♎R
13	23.23	22	6♏	29	8	16	♅ 4♐
14	23.27	23	18	1♓	8	16	♆27♐
15	23.31	24	0♐	2	9	16	♇26♎R
16	23.35	25	12	4	10	15	♃ 9♏R
17	23.39	26	24	5	11	15	♄20♎R
18	23.43	27	6♑	7	12	15	♅ 4♐R
19	23.47	28	18	8	13	14	♆27♐
20	23.51	29	0♒	10	13	14	♇26♎R
21	23.55	0♈	12	12	14	14	♃ 9♏R
22	23.59	1	25	13	15	13	♄20♎R
23	0.03	2	8♓	15	16	13	♅ 4♐R
24	0.07	3	21	17	17	13	♆27♐
25	0.10	4	5♈	18	18	12	♇26♎R
26	0.14	5	19	20	19	12	♃ 9♏R
27	0.18	6	4♉	22	20	12	♄20♎R
28	0.22	7	18	24	21	11	♅ 4♐R
29	0.26	8	2♊	25	22	11	♆27♐
30	0.30	9	17	27	23	10	♇26♎R
31	0.34	10	1♋	29	24	10	♃ 8♏R

Apr	STime	☉	☽	☿	♀	♂	Plnts
1	0.38	11♈	15♋	1♈	25♒	10♎	♃ 8♏R
2	0.42	12	29	3	26	9	♄19♎R
3	0.46	13	13♌	5	27	9	♅ 4♐R
4	0.50	14	26	7	28	8	♆27♐R
5	0.54	15	10♍	9	29	8	♇26♎R
6	0.58	16	23	11	0♓	8	♃ 8♏R
7	1.02	17	6♎	13	1	7	♄19♎R
8	1.06	18	19	15	2	7	♅ 4♐R
9	1.10	19	2♏	17	3	7	♆27♐
10	1.14	20	14	19	4	6	♇25♎R
11	1.18	21	26	21	5	6	♃ 7♏R
12	1.21	22	8♐	23	6	6	♄18♎R
13	1.25	23	20	25	7	5	♅ 4♐R
14	1.29	24	2♑	27	8	5	♆27♐R
15	1.33	25	14	29	9	5	♇25♎R
16	1.37	26	26	1♉	10	4	♃ 6♏R
17	1.41	27	8♒	3	11	4	♄18♎R
18	1.45	28	20	5	12	4	♅ 4♐R
19	1.49	29	3♓	7	13	3	♆27♐R
20	1.53	0♉	16	10	14	3	♇25♎R
21	1.57	1	29	12	15	3	♃ 6♏R
22	2.01	2	14♈	14	16	2	♄18♎R
23	2.05	3	28	16	18	2	♅ 4♐R
24	2.09	4	13♉	18	19	2	♆27♐R
25	2.13	5	27	19	20	2	♇25♎R
26	2.17	6	12♊	21	21	2	♃ 5♏R
27	2.21	7	27	23	22	1	♄17♎R
28	2.25	8	11♋	25	23	1	♅ 3♐R
29	2.28	9	26	26	24	1	♆26♐R
30	2.32	10	9♌	28	25	1	♇25♎R

May	STime	☉	☽	☿	♀	♂	Plnts
1	2.36	10♉	23♌	0♊	26♓	1♎	♃ 4♏R
2	2.40	11	7♍	1	27	1	♄17♎R
3	2.44	12	20	2	29	1	♅ 3♐R
4	2.48	13	3♎	4	0♈	0	♆26♐R
5	2.52	14	15	5	1	0	♇25♎R
6	2.56	15	28	6	2	0	♃ 4♏R
7	3.00	16	10♏	7	3	0	♄17♎R
8	3.04	17	23	8	4	0	♅ 3♐R
9	3.08	18	5♐	9	5	0	♆26♐R
10	3.12	19	16	10	6	0D	♇25♎R
11	3.16	20	28	11	8	0	♃ 3♏R
12	3.20	21	10♑	12	9	0	♄16♎R
13	3.24	22	22	13	10	0	♅ 3♐R
14	3.28	23	4♒	13	11	0	♆26♐R
15	3.32	24	16	14	12	0	♇24♎R
16	3.36	25	28	14	13	0	♃ 3♏R
17	3.39	26	11♓	14	14	0	♄16♎R
18	3.43	27	24	15	15	0	♅ 3♐R
19	3.47	28	8♈	15	17	0	♆26♐R
20	3.51	29	22	15	18	1	♇24♎R
21	3.55	0♊	6♉	15R	19	1	♃ 2♏R
22	3.59	1	21	15	20	1	♄16♎R
23	4.03	2	6♊	15	21	1	♅ 2♐R
24	4.07	3	21	14	22	1	♆26♐R
25	4.11	4	6♋	14	23	1	♇24♎R
26	4.15	5	21	14	25	1	♃ 2♏R
27	4.19	6	5♌	13	26	2	♄16♎R
28	4.23	7	20	13	27	2	♅ 2♐R
29	4.27	7	3♍	12	28	2	♆26♐R
30	4.31	8	17	12	29	2	♇24♎R
31	4.35	9	0♎	11	0♉	2	♃ 1♏R

Jun	STime	☉	☽	☿	♀	♂	Plnts
1	4.39	10♊	12♎	11♊	2♉	3♎	♃ 1♏R
2	4.43	11	25	10	3	3	♄15♎R
3	4.46	12	7♏	10	4	3	♅ 2♐R
4	4.50	13	19	9	5	3	♆26♐R
5	4.54	14	1♐	9	6	4	♇24♎R
6	4.58	15	13	8	7	4	♃ 1♏R
7	5.02	16	25	8	9	4	♄15♎R
8	5.06	17	7♑	7	10	4	♅ 2♐R
9	5.10	18	19	7	11	5	♆26♐R
10	5.14	19	1♒	7	12	5	♇24♎R
11	5.18	20	13	7	13	5	♃ 1♏R
12	5.22	21	25	6	14	6	♄15♎R
13	5.26	22	7♓	6D	16	6	♅ 2♐R
14	5.30	23	20	6	17	6	♆25♐R
15	5.34	24	3♈	6	18	7	♇24♎R
16	5.38	25	16	7	19	7	♃ 0♏R
17	5.42	26	0♉	7	20	7	♄15♎
18	5.46	27	15	7	21	8	♅ 1♐R
19	5.50	28	29	7	23	8	♆25♐R
20	5.54	29	14♊	8	24	8	♇24♎R
21	5.57	29	0♋	8	25	9	♃ 0♏R
22	6.01	0♋	15	9	26	9	♄15♎
23	6.05	1	0♌	10	27	10	♅ 1♐R
24	6.09	2	14	11	29	10	♆25♐R
25	6.13	3	29	11	0♊	10	♇24♎R
26	6.17	4	13♍	12	1	11	♃ 0♏
27	6.21	5	26	13	2	11	♄15♎
28	6.25	6	9♎	14	3	12	♅ 1♐R
29	6.29	7	22	15	4	12	♆25♐R
30	6.33	8	4♏	16	6	12	♇24♎

Jul	STime	☉	☽	☿	♀	♂	Plnts
1	6.37	9♋	17♏	18♊	7♊	13♎	♃ 0♏
2	6.41	10	28	19	8	13	♄15♎
3	6.45	11	10♐	20	9	14	♅ 1♐R
4	6.49	12	22	22	10	14	♆25♐R
5	6.53	13	4♑	23	12	15	♇24♎
6	6.57	14	16	25	13	15	♃ 0♏
7	7.01	15	28	26	14	16	♄16♎
8	7.04	16	10♒	28	15	16	♅ 1♐R
9	7.08	17	22	0♋	16	17	♆25♐R
10	7.12	18	4♓	2	18	17	♇24♎
11	7.16	19	17	3	19	18	♃ 0♏
12	7.20	20	29	5	20	18	♄16♎
13	7.24	20	12♈	7	21	18	♅ 1♐R
14	7.28	21	26	9	22	19	♆25♐R
15	7.32	22	9♉	11	23	19	♇24♎
16	7.36	23	24	13	25	20	♃ 1♏
17	7.40	24	8♊	15	26	21	♄16♎
18	7.44	25	23	17	27	21	♅ 0♐R
19	7.48	26	8♋	19	28	22	♆25♐R
20	7.52	27	23	21	29	22	♇24♎
21	7.56	28	8♌	24	1♋	23	♃ 1♏
22	8.00	29	23	26	2	23	♄16♎
23	8.04	0♌	7♍	28	3	24	♅ 0♐R
24	8.08	1	21	0♌	4	24	♆24♐R
25	8.11	2	5♎	2	5	25	♇24♎
26	8.15	3	18	4	7	25	♃ 1♏
27	8.19	4	1♏	6	8	26	♄16♎
28	8.23	5	13	8	9	26	♅ 0♐R
29	8.27	6	25	10	10	27	♆24♐R
30	8.31	7	7♐	12	12	27	♇24♎
31	8.35	8	19	14	13	28	♃ 2♏

Aug	STime	☉	☽	☿	♀	♂	Plnts
1	8.39	9♌	1♑	16♌	14♋	29♎	♃ 2♏
2	8.43	10	13	18	15	29	♄17♎
3	8.47	11	25	20	16	0♏	♅ 0♐
4	8.51	11	7♒	22	18	0	♆24♐R
5	8.55	12	19	24	19	1	♇24♎
6	8.59	13	1♓	26	20	1	♃ 2♏
7	9.03	14	14	28	21	2	♄17♎
8	9.07	15	26	0♍	22	3	♅ 0♐
9	9.11	16	9♈	1	24	3	♆24♐R
10	9.15	17	22	3	25	4	♇24♎
11	9.19	18	6♉	5	26	4	♃ 3♏
12	9.22	19	20	6	27	5	♄18♎
13	9.26	20	4♊	8	29	6	♅ 0♐
14	9.30	21	18	10	0♌	6	♆24♐R
15	9.34	22	2♋	11	1	7	♇24♎
16	9.38	23	17	13	2	7	♃ 4♏
17	9.42	24	2♌	15	3	8	♄18♎
18	9.46	25	17	16	5	9	♅ 0♐
19	9.50	26	1♍	18	6	9	♆24♐R
20	9.54	27	15	19	7	10	♇24♎
21	9.58	28	29	21	8	10	♃ 4♏
22	10.02	29	13♎	22	10	11	♄18♎
23	10.06	0♍	26	23	11	12	♅ 0♐
24	10.10	1	9♏	25	12	12	♆24♐R
25	10.14	2	21	26	13	13	♇25♎
26	10.18	3	4♐	28	14	14	♃ 5♏
27	10.22	4	16	29	16	14	♄19♎
28	10.26	5	27	0♎	17	15	♅ 0♐
29	10.29	6	9♑	1	18	15	♆24♐
30	10.33	6	21	3	19	16	♇25♎
31	10.37	7	3♒	4	21	17	♃ 6♏

Sep	STime	☉	☽	☿	♀	♂	Plnts
1	10.41	8♍	15♒	5♎	22♌	17♏	♃ 6♏
2	10.45	9	28	6	23	18	♄20♎
3	10.49	10	10♓	7	24	19	♅ 1♐
4	10.53	11	23	8	26	19	♆24♐R
5	10.57	12	6♈	9	27	20	♇25♎
6	11.01	13	19	10	28	21	♃ 7♏
7	11.05	14	3♉	11	29	21	♄20♎
8	11.09	15	16	12	0♍	22	♅ 1♐
9	11.13	16	0♊	13	2	23	♆24♐
10	11.17	17	14	14	3	23	♇25♎
11	11.21	18	28	14	4	24	♃ 8♏
12	11.25	19	13♋	15	5	25	♄21♎
13	11.29	20	27	16	7	25	♅ 1♐
14	11.33	21	11♌	16	8	26	♆24♐
15	11.37	22	26	16	9	27	♇25♎
16	11.40	23	10♍	17	10	27	♃ 8♏
17	11.44	24	24	17	12	28	♄21♎
18	11.48	25	8♎	17	13	29	♅ 1♐
19	11.52	26	21	17R	14	29	♆24♐
20	11.56	27	4♏	17	15	0♐	♇25♎
21	12.00	28	17	17	17	1	♃ 9♏
22	12.04	29	29	17	18	1	♄22♎
23	12.08	0♎	12♐	16	19	2	♅ 1♐
24	12.12	1	24	16	20	3	♆24♐
25	12.16	2	5♑	15	22	3	♇26♎
26	12.20	3	17	14	23	4	♃10♏
27	12.24	4	29	13	24	5	♄22♎
28	12.28	5	11♒	13	25	6	♅ 1♐
29	12.32	6	23	11	27	6	♆24♐
30	12.36	7	6♓	10	28	7	♇26♎

Oct	STime	☉	☽	☿	♀	♂	Plnts
1	12.40	8♎	19♓	9♎	29♍	8♐	♃11♏
2	12.44	9	2♈	8	0♎	8	♄23♎
3	12.47	10	15	7	1	9	♅ 2♐
4	12.51	11	29	6	3	10	♆24♐
5	12.55	12	13♉	5	4	10	♇26♎
6	12.59	13	27	4	5	11	♃12♏
7	13.03	14	11♊	3	6	12	♄23♎
8	13.07	15	25	3	8	13	♅ 2♐
9	13.11	16	9♋	2	9	13	♆24♐
10	13.15	17	23	2	10	14	♇26♎
11	13.19	18	7♌	2D	11	15	♃13♏
12	13.23	19	21	2	13	15	♄24♎
13	13.27	20	5♍	3	14	16	♅ 2♐
14	13.31	21	19	3	15	17	♆24♐
15	13.35	22	3♎	4	16	18	♇26♎
16	13.39	22	16	4	18	18	♃14♏
17	13.43	23	0♏	5	19	19	♄25♎
18	13.47	24	12	6	20	20	♅ 2♐
19	13.51	25	25	8	21	21	♆24♐
20	13.55	26	7♐	9	23	21	♇27♎
21	13.58	27	19	10	24	22	♃16♏
22	14.02	28	1♑	11	25	23	♄25♎
23	14.06	29	13	13	27	23	♅ 3♐
24	14.10	0♏	25	14	28	24	♆25♐
25	14.14	1	7♒	16	29	25	♇27♎
26	14.18	2	19	17	0♏	26	♃17♏
27	14.22	3	1♓	19	2	26	♄26♎
28	14.26	4	14	21	3	27	♅ 3♐
29	14.30	5	27	22	4	28	♆25♐
30	14.34	6	10♈	24	5	29	♇27♎
31	14.38	7	24	26	7	29	♃18♏

Nov	STime	☉	☽	☿	♀	♂	Plnts
1	14.42	8♏	8♉	27♎	8♏	0♑	♃18♏
2	14.46	9	22	29	9	1	♄27♎
3	14.50	10	7♊	0♏	10	2	♅ 3♐
4	14.54	11	21	2	12	2	♆25♐
5	14.58	12	6♋	4	13	3	♇27♎
6	15.02	13	20	5	14	4	♃19♏
7	15.05	14	4♌	7	15	5	♄27♎
8	15.09	15	18	9	17	5	♅ 3♐
9	15.13	16	2♍	10	18	6	♆25♐
10	15.17	17	16	12	19	7	♇27♎
11	15.21	18	29	14	20	8	♃20♏
12	15.25	19	13♎	15	22	8	♄28♎
13	15.29	20	26	17	23	9	♅ 4♐
14	15.33	21	8♏	18	24	10	♆25♐
15	15.37	22	21	20	25	11	♇28♎
16	15.41	24	3♐	22	27	11	♃21♏
17	15.45	25	16	23	28	12	♄28♎
18	15.49	26	28	25	29	13	♅ 4♐
19	15.53	27	9♑	26	0♐	14	♆25♐
20	15.57	28	21	28	2	14	♇28♎
21	16.01	29	3♒	0♐	3	15	♃22♏
22	16.05	0♐	15	1	4	16	♄29♎
23	16.09	1	27	3	5	17	♅ 4♐
24	16.12	2	9♓	4	7	18	♆26♐
25	16.16	3	22	6	8	18	♇28♎
26	16.20	4	5♈	7	9	19	♃23♏
27	16.24	5	18	9	10	20	♄ 0♏
28	16.28	6	2♉	11	12	21	♅ 5♐
29	16.32	7	16	12	13	21	♆26♐
30	16.36	8	1♊	14	14	22	♇28♎

Dec	STime	☉	☽	☿	♀	♂	Plnts
1	16.40	9♐	15♊	15♐	15♐	23♑	♃25♏
2	16.44	10	0♋	17	17	24	♄ 0♏
3	16.48	11	15	18	18	24	♅ 5♐
4	16.52	12	0♌	20	19	25	♆26♐
5	16.56	13	15	21	20	26	♇28♎
6	17.00	14	29	23	22	27	♃26♏
7	17.04	15	13♍	25	23	28	♄ 1♏
8	17.08	16	26	26	24	28	♅ 5♐
9	17.12	17	10♎	28	25	29	♆26♐
10	17.16	18	22	29	27	0♒	♇28♎
11	17.20	19	5♏	1♑	28	1	♃27♏
12	17.23	20	18	2	29	1	♄ 1♏
13	17.27	21	0♐	4	1♑	2	♅ 6♐
14	17.31	22	12	5	2	3	♆26♐
15	17.35	23	24	7	3	4	♇29♎
16	17.39	24	6♑	8	4	5	♃28♏
17	17.43	25	18	10	6	5	♄ 1♏
18	17.47	26	0♒	11	7	6	♅ 6♐
19	17.51	27	11	13	8	7	♆26♐
20	17.55	28	23	14	9	8	♇29♎
21	17.59	29	5♓	16	11	8	♃29♏
22	18.03	0♑	17	17	12	9	♄ 2♏
23	18.07	1	0♈	19	13	10	♅ 6♐
24	18.11	2	13	20	14	11	♆27♐
25	18.15	3	26	22	16	12	♇29♎
26	18.19	4	10♉	23	17	12	♃ 0♐
27	18.23	5	24	24	18	13	♄ 2♏
28	18.27	6	8♊	25	19	14	♅ 6♐
29	18.30	7	23	27	21	15	♆27♐
30	18.34	8	8♋	28	22	16	♇29♎
31	18.38	9	24	29	23	16	♃ 1♐

1 9 8 3

Jan	STime	☉	☽	☿	♀	♂	Plnts
1	18.42	10♑	9♌	0♒	24♑	17♒	♃ 1♐
2	18.46	11	24	0	26	18	♄ 3♏
3	18.50	12	8♍	1	27	19	♅ 7♐
4	18.54	13	22	2	28	19	♆27♐
5	18.58	14	6♎	2	29	20	♇29♎
6	19.02	15	19	2	1♒	21	♃ 2♐
7	19.06	16	2♏	2R	2	22	♄ 3♏
8	19.10	17	15	2	3	23	♅ 7♐
9	19.14	18	27	2	4	23	♆27♐
10	19.18	19	9♐	1	6	24	♇29♎
11	19.22	20	21	0	7	25	♃ 3♐
12	19.26	21	3♑	29♑	8	26	♄ 3♏
13	19.30	22	15	28	9	27	♅ 7♐
14	19.34	23	27	27	11	27	♆27♐
15	19.38	24	8♒	26	12	28	♇29♎
16	19.41	25	20	25	13	29	♃ 4♐
17	19.45	26	2♓	23	14	0♓	♄ 4♏
18	19.49	28	14	22	16	0	♅ 8♐
19	19.53	29	26	21	17	1	♆28♐
20	19.57	0♒	9♈	20	18	2	♇29♎
21	20.01	1	22	19	19	3	♃ 5♐
22	20.05	2	5♉	18	21	4	♄ 4♏
23	20.09	3	18	17	22	4	♅ 8♐
24	20.13	4	2♊	17	23	5	♆28♐
25	20.17	5	17	16	24	6	♇29♎
26	20.21	6	1♋	16	26	7	♃ 5♐
27	20.25	7	16	16D	27	8	♄ 4♏
28	20.29	8	2♌	16	28	8	♅ 8♐
29	20.33	9	17	16	29	9	♆28♐
30	20.37	10	2♍	17	1♓	10	♇29♎
31	20.41	11	17	17	2	11	♃ 6♐

Feb	STime	☉	☽	☿	♀	♂	Plnts
1	20.45	12♒	1♎	18♑	3♓	11♓	♃ 6♐
2	20.48	13	15	18	4	12	♄ 4♏
3	20.52	14	28	19	6	13	♅ 8♐
4	20.56	15	11♏	20	7	14	♆28♐
5	21.00	16	24	20	8	15	♇29♎
6	21.04	17	6♐	21	9	15	♃ 7♐
7	21.08	18	18	22	11	16	♄ 4♏
8	21.12	19	0♑	23	12	17	♅ 8♐
9	21.16	20	12	24	13	18	♆28♐
10	21.20	21	23	25	14	18	♇29♎
11	21.24	22	5♒	26	16	19	♃ 8♐
12	21.28	23	17	27	17	20	♄ 4♏
13	21.32	24	29	29	18	21	♅ 8♐
14	21.36	25	11♓	0♒	19	22	♆28♐
15	21.40	26	24	1	21	22	♇29♎R
16	21.44	27	6♈	2	22	23	♃ 8♐
17	21.48	28	19	4	23	24	♄ 4♏R
18	21.52	29	2♉	5	24	25	♅ 9♐
19	21.55	0♓	15	6	25	25	♆28♐
20	21.59	1	28	8	27	26	♇29♎R
21	22.03	2	12♊	9	28	27	♃ 9♐
22	22.07	3	26	10	29	28	♄ 4♏R
23	22.11	4	10♋	12	0♈	29	♅ 9♐
24	22.15	5	25	13	2	29	♆29♐
25	22.19	6	10♌	15	3	0♈	♇29♎R
26	22.23	7	25	16	4	1	♃ 9♐
27	22.27	8	10♍	18	5	2	♄ 4♏R
28	22.31	9	25	19	7	2	♅ 9♐

Mar	STime	☉	☽	☿	♀	♂	Plnts
1	22.35	10♓	9♎	21♒	8♈	3♈	♃10♐
2	22.39	11	23	22	9	4	♄ 4♏R
3	22.43	12	6♏	24	10	5	♅ 9♐
4	22.47	13	20	25	12	5	♆29♐
5	22.51	14	2♐	27	13	6	♇29♎R
6	22.55	15	14	29	14	7	♃10♐
7	22.59	16	27	0♓	15	8	♄ 4♏R
8	23.03	17	8♑	2	16	9	♅ 9♐
9	23.06	18	20	4	18	9	♆29♐
10	23.10	19	2♒	5	19	10	♇29♎R
11	23.14	20	14	7	20	11	♃10♐
12	23.18	21	26	9	21	12	♄ 3♏R
13	23.22	22	8♓	10	23	12	♅ 9♐
14	23.26	23	20	12	24	13	♆29♐
15	23.30	24	3♈	14	25	14	♇29♎R
16	23.34	25	16	16	26	15	♃10♐
17	23.38	26	29	18	27	15	♄ 3♏R
18	23.42	27	12♉	19	29	16	♅ 9♐
19	23.46	28	25	21	0♉	17	♆29♐
20	23.50	29	9♊	23	1	18	♇29♎R
21	23.54	0♈	22	25	2	18	♃11♐
22	23.58	1	6♋	27	3	19	♄ 3♏R
23	0.02	2	20	29	5	20	♅ 9♐
24	0.06	3	5♌	1♈	6	21	♆29♐
25	0.10	4	19	3	7	21	♇29♎R
26	0.13	5	4♍	5	8	22	♃11♐
27	0.17	6	18	7	9	23	♄ 3♏R
28	0.21	7	3♎	9	11	24	♅ 9♐R
29	0.25	8	17	11	12	24	♆29♐
30	0.29	9	1♏	13	13	25	♇28♎R
31	0.33	10	14	15	14	26	♃11♐R

Apr	STime	☉	☽	☿	♀	♂	Plnts
1	0.37	11♈	27♏	17♈	15♉	27♈	♃11♐R
2	0.41	12	10♐	19	17	27	♄ 2♏R
3	0.45	13	22	21	18	28	♅ 9♐R
4	0.49	14	4♑	23	19	29	♆29♐
5	0.53	15	16	25	20	0♉	♇28♎R
6	0.57	16	28	27	21	0	♃10♐R
7	1.01	17	10♒	29	23	1	♄ 2♏R
8	1.05	18	22	1♉	24	2	♅ 9♐R
9	1.09	19	4♓	3	25	3	♆29♐R
10	1.13	20	16	5	26	3	♇28♎R
11	1.17	21	29	7	27	4	♃10♐R
12	1.21	22	12♈	8	29	5	♄ 2♏R
13	1.24	23	25	10	0♊	6	♅ 8♐R
14	1.28	24	8♉	12	1	6	♆29♐R
15	1.32	25	22	13	2	7	♇28♎R
16	1.36	26	5♊	15	3	8	♃10♐R
17	1.40	27	19	16	4	8	♄ 1♏R
18	1.44	28	3♋	17	6	9	♅ 8♐R
19	1.48	29	17	18	7	10	♆29♐R
20	1.52	0♉	1♌	19	8	11	♇28♎R
21	1.56	1	15	20	9	11	♃10♐R
22	2.00	1	0♍	21	10	12	♄ 1♏R
23	2.04	2	14	22	11	13	♅ 8♐R
24	2.08	3	28	23	13	14	♆29♐R
25	2.12	4	12♎	23	14	14	♇28♎R
26	2.16	5	26	24	15	15	♃ 9♐R
27	2.20	6	9♏	24	16	16	♄ 0♏R
28	2.24	7	22	25	17	17	♅ 8♐R
29	2.28	8	5♐	25	18	17	♆29♐R
30	2.31	9	18	25	20	18	♇28♎R

May	STime	☉	☽	☿	♀	♂	Plnts
1	2.35	10♉	0♑	25♉	21♊	19♉	♃ 9♐R
2	2.39	11	12	25	22	19	♄ 0♏R
3	2.43	12	24	25	23	20	♅ 8♐R
4	2.47	13	6♒	25	24	21	♆29♐R
5	2.51	14	18	25	25	22	♇27♎R
6	2.55	15	0♓	24	26	22	♃ 8♐R
7	2.59	16	12	24	27	23	♄ 0♏R
8	3.03	17	24	23	29	24	♅ 8♐R
9	3.07	18	7♈	23	0♋	24	♆29♐R
10	3.11	19	20	22	1	25	♇27♎R
11	3.15	20	3♉	22	2	26	♃ 8♐R
12	3.19	21	17	21	3	27	♄29♎R
13	3.23	22	1♊	21	4	27	♅ 7♐R
14	3.27	23	15	20	5	28	♆28♐R
15	3.31	24	29	19	6	29	♇27♎R
16	3.35	25	14♋	19	8	29	♃ 7♐R
17	3.38	26	28	18	9	0♊	♄29♎R
18	3.42	27	12♌	18	10	1	♅ 7♐R
19	3.46	28	26	17	11	2	♆28♐R
20	3.50	29	10♍	17	12	2	♇27♎R
21	3.54	0♊	24	17	13	3	♃ 7♐R
22	3.58	1	8♎	16	14	4	♄29♎R
23	4.02	1	22	16	15	4	♅ 7♐R
24	4.06	2	5♏	16	16	5	♆28♐R
25	4.10	3	18	16D	17	6	♇27♎R
26	4.14	4	1♐	16	18	6	♃ 6♐R
27	4.18	5	14	16	20	7	♄28♎R
28	4.22	6	26	16	21	8	♅ 7♐R
29	4.26	7	8♑	17	22	9	♆28♐R
30	4.30	8	20	17	23	9	♇27♎R
31	4.34	9	2♒	17	24	10	♃ 5♐R

Jun	STime	☉	☽	☿	♀	♂	Plnts
1	4.38	10♊	14♒	18♉	25♋	11♊	♃ 5♐R
2	4.42	11	26	18	26	11	♄28♎R
3	4.46	12	8♓	19	27	12	♅ 7♐R
4	4.49	13	20	20	28	13	♆28♐R
5	4.53	14	2♈	21	29	13	♇27♎R
6	4.57	15	15	21	0♌	14	♃ 5♐R
7	5.01	16	28	22	1	15	♄28♎R
8	5.05	17	11♉	23	2	16	♅ 6♐R
9	5.09	18	25	24	3	16	♆28♐R
10	5.13	19	9♊	25	4	17	♇27♎R
11	5.17	20	24	26	5	18	♃ 4♐R
12	5.21	21	9♋	27	6	18	♄28♎R
13	5.25	22	23	29	7	19	♅ 6♐R
14	5.29	23	8♌	0♊	8	20	♆28♐R
15	5.33	24	23	1	9	20	♇27♎R
16	5.37	24	7♍	3	10	21	♃ 3♐R
17	5.41	25	21	4	11	22	♄28♎R
18	5.45	26	5♎	6	12	22	♅ 6♐R
19	5.49	27	19	7	13	23	♆28♐R
20	5.53	28	2♏	9	14	24	♇27♎R
21	5.56	29	15	10	15	24	♃ 3♐R
22	6.00	0♋	28	12	15	25	♄27♎R
23	6.04	1	10♐	14	16	26	♅ 6♐R
24	6.08	2	23	15	17	26	♆27♐R
25	6.12	3	5♑	17	18	27	♇26♎R
26	6.16	4	17	19	19	28	♃ 2♐R
27	6.20	5	29	21	20	28	♄27♎R
28	6.24	6	10♒	23	21	29	♅ 6♐R
29	6.28	7	22	25	22	0♋	♆27♐R
30	6.32	8	4♓	27	22	1	♇26♎

Jul	STime	☉	☽	☿	♀	♂	Plnts
1	6.36	9♋	16♓	29♊	23♌	1♋	♃ 2♐R
2	6.40	10	28	1♋	24	2	♄27♎
3	6.44	11	11♈	3	25	3	♅ 5♐R
4	6.48	12	23	5	26	3	♆27♐R
5	6.52	13	6♉	8	26	4	♇26♎
6	6.56	14	20	10	27	5	♃ 2♐R
7	7.00	15	3♊	12	28	5	♄27♎
8	7.04	15	18	14	29	6	♅ 5♐R
9	7.07	16	2♋	16	29	7	♆27♐R
10	7.11	17	17	18	0♍	7	♇26♎
11	7.15	18	2♌	21	1	8	♃ 1♐R
12	7.19	19	17	23	1	9	♄28♎
13	7.23	20	2♍	25	2	9	♅ 5♐R
14	7.27	21	17	27	2	10	♆27♐R
15	7.31	22	1♎	29	3	11	♇26♎
16	7.35	23	15	1♌	4	11	♃ 1♐R
17	7.39	24	29	3	4	12	♄28♎
18	7.43	25	12♏	5	5	13	♅ 5♐R
19	7.47	26	25	7	5	13	♆27♐R
20	7.51	27	7♐	9	6	14	♇26♎
21	7.55	28	20	11	6	15	♃ 1♐R
22	7.59	29	2♑	13	7	15	♄28♎
23	8.03	0♌	14	15	7	16	♅ 5♐R
24	8.07	1	25	16	7	17	♆27♐R
25	8.11	2	7♒	18	8	17	♇27♎
26	8.14	3	19	20	8	18	♃ 1♐R
27	8.18	4	1♓	22	8	18	♄28♎
28	8.22	5	13	23	8	19	♅ 5♐R
29	8.26	6	25	25	9	20	♆27♐R
30	8.30	6	7♈	27	9	20	♇27♎
31	8.34	7	19	28	9	21	♃ 1♐

Aug	STime	☉	☽	☿	♀	♂	Plnts
1	8.38	8♌	2♉	0♍	9♍	22♋	♃ 1♐
2	8.42	9	15	1	9	22	♄28♎
3	8.46	10	28	3	9	23	♅ 5♐R
4	8.50	11	12♊	4	9R	24	♆26♐R
5	8.54	12	26	6	9	24	♇27♎
6	8.58	13	11♋	7	9	25	♃ 1♐
7	9.02	14	26	9	9	26	♄29♎
8	9.06	15	11♌	10	9	26	♅ 5♐
9	9.10	16	26	11	9	27	♆26♐R
10	9.14	17	11♍	13	8	28	♇27♎
11	9.18	18	26	14	8	28	♃ 1♐
12	9.22	19	11♎	15	8	29	♄29♎
13	9.25	20	25	17	7	0♌	♅ 5♐
14	9.29	21	8♏	18	7	0	♆26♐R
15	9.33	22	21	19	7	1	♇27♎
16	9.37	23	4♐	20	6	2	♃ 1♐
17	9.41	24	17	21	6	2	♄29♎
18	9.45	25	29	22	5	3	♅ 5♐
19	9.49	26	11♑	23	5	3	♆26♐R
20	9.53	27	23	24	4	4	♇27♎
21	9.57	28	4♒	25	3	5	♃ 2♐
22	10.01	29	16	26	3	5	♄ 0♏
23	10.05	0♍	28	26	2	6	♅ 5♐
24	10.09	0	10♓	27	2	7	♆26♐
25	10.13	1	22	28	1	7	♇27♎
26	10.17	2	4♈	28	0	8	♃ 2♐
27	10.21	3	16	29	0	9	♄ 0♏
28	10.25	4	29	29	29♌	9	♅ 5♐
29	10.29	5	11♉	0♎	29	10	♆26♐
30	10.32	6	24	0	28	10	♇27♎
31	10.36	7	8♊	0	27	11	♃ 2♐

Sep	STime	☉	☽	☿	♀	♂	Plnts
1	10.40	8♍	21♊	0♎	27♌	12♌	♃ 2♐
2	10.44	9	5♋	0R	26	12	♄ 0♏
3	10.48	10	19	0	26	13	♅ 5♐
4	10.52	11	4♌	0	25	14	♆26♐
5	10.56	12	19	0	25	14	♇27♎
6	11.00	13	4♍	0	25	15	♃ 3♐
7	11.04	14	20	29♍	24	16	♄ 1♏
8	11.08	15	4♎	28	24	16	♅ 5♐
9	11.12	16	19	28	24	17	♆26♐
10	11.16	17	3♏	27	23	17	♇28♎
11	11.20	18	17	26	23	18	♃ 4♐
12	11.24	19	0♐	25	23	19	♄ 1♏
13	11.28	20	13	24	23	19	♅ 5♐
14	11.32	21	25	23	23	20	♆26♐
15	11.36	22	7♑	22	23D	21	♇28♎
16	11.39	23	19	21	23	21	♃ 4♐
17	11.43	24	1♒	20	23	22	♄ 2♏
18	11.47	25	13	19	23	23	♅ 5♐
19	11.51	26	25	18	23	23	♆26♐
20	11.55	27	7♓	18	23	24	♇28♎
21	11.59	28	19	17	24	24	♃ 5♐
22	12.03	29	1♈	17	24	25	♄ 2♏
23	12.07	0♎	13	16	24	26	♅ 5♐
24	12.11	1	26	16D	24	26	♆26♐
25	12.15	2	9♉	16	25	27	♇28♎
26	12.19	3	21	16	25	28	♃ 6♐
27	12.23	4	4♊	17	25	28	♄ 3♏
28	12.27	5	18	17	26	29	♅ 6♐
29	12.31	5	1♋	18	26	29	♆26♐
30	12.35	6	15	19	27	0♍	♇28♎

Oct	STime	☉	☽	☿	♀	♂	Plnts
1	12.39	7♎	29♋	20♍	27♌	1♍	♃ 6♐
2	12.43	8	14♌	21	28	1	♄ 4♏
3	12.47	9	28	22	28	2	♅ 6♐
4	12.50	10	13♍	23	29	2	♆26♐
5	12.54	11	28	24	0♍	3	♇28♎
6	12.58	12	13♎	26	0	4	♃ 7♐
7	13.02	13	27	27	1	4	♄ 4♏
8	13.06	14	11♏	29	1	5	♅ 6♐
9	13.10	15	25	1♎	2	6	♆26♐
10	13.14	16	8♐	2	3	6	♇29♎
11	13.18	17	21	4	4	7	♃ 8♐
12	13.22	18	4♑	5	4	7	♄ 5♏
13	13.26	19	16	7	5	8	♅ 6♐
14	13.30	20	28	9	6	9	♆27♐
15	13.34	21	10♒	11	7	9	♇29♎
16	13.38	22	21	12	7	10	♃ 9♐
17	13.42	23	3♓	14	8	10	♄ 5♏
18	13.46	24	15	16	9	11	♅ 7♐
19	13.50	25	27	18	10	12	♆27♐
20	13.54	26	10♈	19	11	12	♇29♎
21	13.57	27	22	21	12	13	♃10♐
22	14.01	28	5♉	23	12	14	♄ 6♏
23	14.05	29	18	24	13	14	♅ 7♐
24	14.09	0♏	1♊	26	14	15	♆27♐
25	14.13	1	15	28	15	15	♇29♎
26	14.17	2	28	29	16	16	♃11♐
27	14.21	3	12♋	1♏	17	17	♄ 6♏
28	14.25	4	26	3	18	17	♅ 7♐
29	14.29	5	10♌	4	19	18	♆27♐
30	14.33	6	24	6	20	18	♇29♎
31	14.37	7	8♍	8	21	19	♃12♐

Nov	STime	☉	☽	☿	♀	♂	Plnts
1	14.41	8♏	23♍	9♏	22♍	20♍	♃12♐
2	14.45	9	7♎	11	23	20	♄ 7♏
3	14.49	10	21	13	24	21	♅ 7♐
4	14.53	11	6♏	14	25	21	♆27♐
5	14.57	12	19	16	26	22	♇ 0♏
6	15.01	13	3♐	17	27	23	♃13♐
7	15.05	14	16	19	28	23	♄ 8♏
8	15.08	15	29	21	29	24	♅ 8♐
9	15.12	16	11♑	22	0♎	24	♆27♐
10	15.16	17	24	24	1	25	♇ 0♏
11	15.20	18	6♒	25	2	26	♃14♐
12	15.24	19	17	27	3	26	♄ 8♏
13	15.28	20	29	28	4	27	♅ 8♐
14	15.32	21	11♓	0♐	5	27	♆27♐
15	15.36	22	23	1	6	28	♇ 0♏
16	15.40	23	6♈	3	7	29	♃15♐
17	15.44	24	18	5	8	29	♄ 9♏
18	15.48	25	1♉	6	9	0♎	♅ 8♐
19	15.52	26	14	8	10	0	♆27♐
20	15.56	27	27	9	11	1	♇ 0♏
21	16.00	28	11♊	11	13	2	♃16♐
22	16.04	29	24	12	14	2	♄10♏
23	16.08	0♐	8♋	14	15	3	♅ 9♐
24	16.12	1	22	15	16	3	♆28♐
25	16.15	2	7♌	17	17	4	♇ 0♏
26	16.19	3	21	18	18	4	♃18♐
27	16.23	4	5♍	20	19	5	♄10♏
28	16.27	5	19	21	20	6	♅ 9♐
29	16.31	6	3♎	23	22	6	♆28♐
30	16.35	7	17	24	23	7	♇ 1♏

Dec	STime	☉	☽	☿	♀	♂	Plnts
1	16.39	8♐	1♏	25♐	24♎	7♎	♃19♐
2	16.43	9	15	27	25	8	♄11♏
3	16.47	10	28	28	26	8	♅ 9♐
4	16.51	11	11♐	0♑	27	9	♆28♐
5	16.55	12	24	1	28	10	♇ 1♏
6	16.59	13	7♑	2	0♏	10	♃20♐
7	17.03	15	19	4	1	11	♄11♏
8	17.07	16	1♒	5	2	11	♅ 9♐
9	17.11	17	13	6	3	12	♆28♐
10	17.15	18	25	8	4	12	♇ 1♏
11	17.19	19	7♓	9	5	13	♃21♐
12	17.23	20	19	10	6	14	♄12♏
13	17.26	21	1♈	11	8	14	♅10♐
14	17.30	22	13	12	9	15	♆28♐
15	17.34	23	26	13	10	15	♇ 1♏
16	17.38	24	8♉	14	11	16	♃22♐
17	17.42	25	22	15	12	16	♄12♏
18	17.46	26	5♊	15	14	17	♅10♐
19	17.50	27	19	16	15	18	♆29♐
20	17.54	28	3♋	16	16	18	♇ 1♏
21	17.58	29	18	16	17	19	♃23♐
22	18.02	0♑	2♌	16R	18	19	♄13♏
23	18.06	1	17	16	19	20	♅10♐
24	18.10	2	2♍	16	21	20	♆29♐
25	18.14	3	16	15	22	21	♇ 1♏
26	18.18	4	0♎	14	23	21	♃24♐
27	18.22	5	14	13	24	22	♄13♏
28	18.26	6	28	12	25	22	♅11♐
29	18.30	7	11♏	11	27	23	♆29♐
30	18.33	8	24	10	28	24	♇ 1♏
31	18.37	9	7♐	9	29	24	♃25♐

Jan	STime	☉	☽	☿	♀	♂	Plnts
1	18.41	10♑	20♐	7♑	0♐	25♎	♃26♐
2	18.45	11	3♑	6	1	25	♄14♏
3	18.49	12	15	5	3	26	♅11♐
4	18.53	13	27	3	4	26	♆29♐
5	18.57	14	9♒	3	5	27	♇ 2♏
6	19.01	15	21	2	6	27	♃27♐
7	19.05	16	3♓	1	7	28	♄14♏
8	19.09	17	15	1	9	28	♅11♐
9	19.13	18	27	0	10	29	♆29♐
10	19.17	19	9♈	0D	11	29	♇ 2♏
11	19.21	20	21	0	12	0♏	♃28♐
12	19.25	21	4♉	0	14	0	♄15♏
13	19.29	22	16	0	15	1	♅12♐
14	19.33	23	29	1	16	1	♆ 0♑
15	19.37	24	13♊	1	17	2	♇ 2♏
16	19.40	25	27	2	18	2	♃29♐
17	19.44	26	11♋	3	20	3	♄15♏
18	19.48	27	26	3	21	3	♅12♐
19	19.52	28	11♌	4	22	4	♆ 0♑
20	19.56	29	26	5	23	4	♇ 2♏
21	20.00	0♒	11♍	6	24	5	♃ 0♑
22	20.04	1	26	7	26	5	♄15♏
23	20.08	2	10♎	8	27	6	♅12♐
24	20.12	3	24	9	28	6	♆ 0♑
25	20.16	4	8♏	10	29	7	♇ 2♏
26	20.20	5	21	11	1♑	7	♃ 1♑
27	20.24	6	4♐	13	2	8	♄15♏
28	20.28	7	17	14	3	8	♅12♐
29	20.32	8	0♑	15	4	9	♆ 0♑
30	20.36	9	12	16	5	9	♇ 2♏
31	20.40	10	24	18	7	10	♃ 2♑

Feb	STime	☉	☽	☿	♀	♂	Plnts
1	20.44	12♒	6♒	19♑	8♑	10♏	♃ 2♑
2	20.48	13	18	20	9	11	♄16♏
3	20.51	14	0♓	22	10	11	♅12♐
4	20.55	15	12	23	12	12	♆ 0♑
5	20.59	16	24	25	13	12	♇ 2♏
6	21.03	17	6♈	26	14	12	♃ 3♑
7	21.07	18	18	27	15	13	♄16♏
8	21.11	19	0♉	29	17	13	♅13♐
9	21.15	20	12	0♒	18	14	♆ 0♑
10	21.19	21	24	2	19	14	♇ 2♏
11	21.23	22	7♊	3	20	15	♃ 4♑
12	21.27	23	21	5	21	15	♄16♏
13	21.31	24	5♋	6	23	15	♅13♐
14	21.35	25	19	8	24	16	♆ 0♑
15	21.39	26	4♌	9	25	16	♇ 2♏
16	21.43	27	19	11	26	17	♃ 5♑
17	21.47	28	5♍	13	28	17	♄16♏
18	21.51	29	20	14	29	17	♅13♐
19	21.55	0♓	5♎	16	0♒	18	♆ 1♑
20	21.58	1	20	17	1	18	♇ 2♏R
21	22.02	2	4♏	19	3	19	♃ 6♑
22	22.06	3	18	21	4	19	♄16♏
23	22.10	4	1♐	22	5	19	♅13♐
24	22.14	5	14	24	6	20	♆ 1♑
25	22.18	6	27	26	7	20	♇ 2♏R
26	22.22	7	9♑	28	9	20	♃ 7♑
27	22.26	8	21	29	10	21	♄16♏R
28	22.30	9	3♒	1♓	11	21	♅13♐
29	22.34	10	15	3	12	21	♆ 1♑

Mar	STime	☉	☽	☿	♀	♂	Plnts
1	22.38	11♓	27♒	5♓	14♒	22♏	♃ 8♑
2	22.42	12	9♓	6	15	22	♄16♏R
3	22.46	13	21	8	16	22	♅13♐
4	22.50	14	3♈	10	17	23	♆ 1♑
5	22.54	15	15	12	19	23	♇ 2♏R
6	22.58	16	27	14	20	23	♃ 8♑
7	23.02	17	9♉	16	21	24	♄16♏R
8	23.06	18	21	18	22	24	♅13♐
9	23.09	19	4♊	20	23	24	♆ 1♑
10	23.13	20	17	21	25	24	♇ 1♏R
11	23.17	21	0♋	23	26	25	♃ 9♑
12	23.21	22	13	25	27	25	♄16♏R
13	23.25	23	28	27	28	25	♅13♐
14	23.29	24	12♌	29	0♓	25	♆ 1♑
15	23.33	25	27	1♈	1	26	♇ 1♏R
16	23.37	26	13♍	3	2	26	♃10♑
17	23.41	27	28	5	3	26	♄16♏R
18	23.45	28	13♎	7	5	26	♅13♐
19	23.49	29	28	9	6	26	♆ 1♑
20	23.53	0♈	12♏	11	7	27	♇ 1♏R
21	23.57	1	26	13	8	27	♃10♑
22	0.01	2	10♐	15	10	27	♄15♏R
23	0.05	3	23	17	11	27	♅13♐
24	0.09	4	6♑	19	12	27	♆ 1♑
25	0.13	5	18	20	13	27	♇ 1♏R
26	0.16	6	0♒	22	14	27	♃11♑
27	0.20	7	12	24	16	28	♄15♏R
28	0.24	8	24	25	17	28	♅13♐R
29	0.28	9	6♓	27	18	28	♆ 1♑
30	0.32	10	18	28	19	28	♇ 1♏R
31	0.36	11	0♈	29	21	28	♃11♑

Apr	STime	☉	☽	☿	♀	♂	Plnts
1	0.40	12♈	12♈	0♉	22♓	28♏	♃11♑
2	0.44	13	24	2	23	28	♄15♏R
3	0.48	14	6♉	3	24	28	♅13♐R
4	0.52	15	18	3	26	28	♆ 1♑
5	0.56	16	1♊	4	27	28	♇ 1♏R
6	1.00	17	13	5	28	28R	♃12♑
7	1.04	18	26	5	29	28	♄15♏R
8	1.08	19	10♋	6	1♈	28	♅13♐R
9	1.12	20	23	6	2	28	♆ 1♑
10	1.16	20	7♌	6	3	28	♇ 1♏R
11	1.20	21	22	6R	4	28	♃12♑
12	1.23	22	6♍	6	5	28	♄14♏R
13	1.27	23	21	6	7	28	♅13♐R
14	1.31	24	6♎	6	8	28	♆ 1♑R
15	1.35	25	21	6	9	27	♇ 1♏R
16	1.39	26	6♏	5	10	27	♃12♑
17	1.43	27	20	5	12	27	♄14♏R
18	1.47	28	4♐	4	13	27	♅13♐R
19	1.51	29	18	4	14	27	♆ 1♑R
20	1.55	0♉	1♑	3	15	27	♇ 0♏R
21	1.59	1	14	2	17	26	♃13♑
22	2.03	2	26	2	18	26	♄14♏R
23	2.07	3	9♒	1	19	26	♅13♐R
24	2.11	4	21	0	20	26	♆ 1♑R
25	2.15	5	2♓	0	21	26	♇ 0♏R
26	2.19	6	14	29♈	23	25	♃13♑
27	2.23	7	26	28	24	25	♄13♏R
28	2.27	8	8♈	28	25	25	♅13♐R
29	2.31	9	20	27	26	24	♆ 1♑R
30	2.34	10	2♉	27	28	24	♇ 0♏R

May	STime	☉	☽	☿	♀	♂	Plnts
1	2.38	11♉	15♉	27♈	29♈	24♏	♃13♑R
2	2.42	12	28	26	0♉	24	♄13♏R
3	2.46	13	10♊	26	1	23	♅12♐R
4	2.50	14	23	26	3	23	♆ 1♑R
5	2.54	15	7♋	26D	4	23	♇ 0♏R
6	2.58	16	20	26	5	22	♃13♑R
7	3.02	17	4♌	26	6	22	♄12♏R
8	3.06	18	18	26	7	22	♅12♐R
9	3.10	19	2♍	27	9	21	♆ 1♑R
10	3.14	20	16	27	10	21	♇ 0♏R
11	3.18	21	1♎	27	11	20	♃12♑R
12	3.22	22	16	28	12	20	♄12♏R
13	3.26	23	0♏	28	14	20	♅12♐R
14	3.30	24	14	29	15	19	♆ 1♑R
15	3.34	25	29	0♉	16	19	♇ 0♏R
16	3.38	25	12♐	0	17	19	♃12♑R
17	3.41	26	26	1	18	18	♄12♏R
18	3.45	27	9♑	2	20	18	♅12♐R
19	3.49	28	22	3	21	18	♆ 1♑R
20	3.53	29	4♒	4	22	17	♇ 0♏R
21	3.57	0♊	17	5	23	17	♃12♑R
22	4.01	1	29	6	25	17	♄11♏R
23	4.05	2	11♓	7	26	16	♅12♐R
24	4.09	3	22	8	27	16	♆ 0♑R
25	4.13	4	4♈	10	28	16	♇ 0♏R
26	4.17	5	16	11	0♊	15	♃12♑R
27	4.21	6	29	12	1	15	♄11♏R
28	4.25	7	11♉	14	2	15	♅11♐R
29	4.29	8	24	15	3	14	♆ 0♑R
30	4.33	9	7♊	16	4	14	♇29♎R
31	4.37	10	20	18	6	14	♃11♑R

Jun	STime	☉	☽	☿	♀	♂	Plnts
1	4.41	11♊	3♋	19♉	7♊	14♏	♃11♑R
2	4.45	12	17	21	8	13	♄11♏R
3	4.49	13	1♌	23	9	13	♅11♐R
4	4.52	14	15	24	11	13	♆ 0♑R
5	4.56	15	29	26	12	13	♇29♎R
6	5.00	16	13♍	28	13	13	♃11♑R
7	5.04	17	27	29	14	12	♄10♏R
8	5.08	18	11♎	1♊	16	12	♅11♐R
9	5.12	19	26	3	17	12	♆ 0♑R
10	5.16	19	10♏	5	18	12	♇29♎R
11	5.20	20	24	7	19	12	♃10♑R
12	5.24	21	7♐	9	20	12	♄10♏R
13	5.28	22	21	11	22	12	♅11♐R
14	5.32	23	4♑	13	23	12	♆ 0♑R
15	5.36	24	17	15	24	12	♇29♎R
16	5.40	25	0♒	17	25	11	♃ 9♑R
17	5.44	26	12	19	27	11	♄10♏R
18	5.48	27	24	21	28	11	♅11♐R
19	5.52	28	7♓	24	29	11D	♆ 0♑R
20	5.56	29	18	26	0♋	11	♇29♎R
21	5.59	0♋	0♈	28	2	11	♃ 9♑R
22	6.03	1	12	0♋	3	11	♄10♏R
23	6.07	2	24	2	4	11	♅10♐R
24	6.11	3	7♉	5	5	12	♆ 0♑R
25	6.15	4	19	7	6	12	♇29♎
26	6.19	5	2♊	9	8	12	♃ 8♑R
27	6.23	6	15	11	9	12	♄10♏R
28	6.27	7	28	13	10	12	♅10♐R
29	6.31	8	12♋	15	11	12	♆ 0♑R
30	6.35	9	26	17	13	12	♇29♎

Jul	STime	☉	☽	☿	♀	♂	Plnts
1	6.39	10♋	11♌	19♋	14♋	12♏	♃ 8♑R
2	6.43	10	25	21	15	12	♄ 9♏R
3	6.47	11	10♍	23	16	13	♅10♐R
4	6.51	12	24	25	17	13	♆29♐R
5	6.55	13	8♎	27	19	13	♇29♎
6	6.59	14	22	29	20	13	♃ 7♑R
7	7.03	15	6♏	1♌	21	13	♄ 9♏R
8	7.06	16	20	3	22	14	♅10♐R
9	7.10	17	4♐	5	24	14	♆29♐R
10	7.14	18	17	6	25	14	♇29♎
11	7.18	19	0♑	8	26	14	♃ 6♑R
12	7.22	20	13	10	27	15	♄ 9♏
13	7.26	21	26	11	29	15	♅10♐R
14	7.30	22	8♒	13	0♌	15	♆29♐R
15	7.34	23	21	15	1	15	♇29♎
16	7.38	24	3♓	16	2	16	♃ 6♑R
17	7.42	25	15	18	3	16	♄ 9♏
18	7.46	26	27	19	5	16	♅10♐R
19	7.50	27	8♈	21	6	17	♆29♐R
20	7.54	28	20	22	7	17	♇29♎
21	7.58	29	2♉	24	8	17	♃ 5♑R
22	8.02	0♌	15	25	10	18	♄ 9♏
23	8.06	1	27	26	11	18	♅10♐R
24	8.10	1	10♊	28	12	19	♆29♐R
25	8.14	2	23	29	13	19	♇29♎
26	8.17	3	7♋	0♍	15	19	♃ 5♑R
27	8.21	4	21	1	16	20	♄10♏
28	8.25	5	5♌	2	17	20	♅ 9♐R
29	8.29	6	20	3	18	21	♆29♐R
30	8.33	7	5♍	4	19	21	♇29♎
31	8.37	8	20	5	21	21	♃ 4♑R

Aug	STime	☉	☽	☿	♀	♂	Plnts
1	8.41	9♌	5♎	6♍	22♌	22♏	♃ 4♑R
2	8.45	10	19	7	23	22	♄10♏
3	8.49	11	3♏	8	24	23	♅ 9♐R
4	8.53	12	17	9	26	23	♆29♐R
5	8.57	13	1♐	10	27	24	♇29♎
6	9.01	14	14	10	28	24	♃ 4♑R
7	9.05	15	27	11	29	25	♄10♏
8	9.09	16	10♑	11	1♍	25	♅ 9♐R
9	9.13	17	22	12	2	25	♆29♐R
10	9.17	18	5♒	12	3	26	♇29♎
11	9.21	19	17	13	4	26	♃ 3♑R
12	9.24	20	29	13	5	27	♄10♏
13	9.28	21	11♓	13	7	27	♅ 9♐
14	9.32	22	23	13R	8	28	♆29♐R
15	9.36	23	5♈	13	9	28	♇29♎
16	9.40	23	17	13	10	29	♃ 3♑R
17	9.44	24	29	13	12	0♐	♄10♏
18	9.48	25	11♉	12	13	0	♅ 9♐
19	9.52	26	23	12	14	1	♆28♐R
20	9.56	27	5♊	12	15	1	♇ 0♏
21	10.00	28	18	11	17	2	♃ 3♑R
22	10.04	29	1♋	10	18	2	♄11♏
23	10.08	0♍	15	10	19	3	♅ 9♐
24	10.12	1	29	9	20	3	♆28♐R
25	10.16	2	14♌	8	21	4	♇ 0♏
26	10.20	3	29	7	23	4	♃ 3♑R
27	10.24	4	14♍	6	24	5	♄11♏
28	10.28	5	29	5	25	6	♅ 9♐
29	10.32	6	14♎	4	26	6	♆28♐
30	10.35	7	29	3	28	7	♇ 0♏
31	10.39	8	13♏	3	29	7	♃ 3♑

Sep	STime	☉	☽	☿	♀	♂	Plnts
1	10.43	9♍	27♏	2♍	0♎	8♐	♃ 3♑
2	10.47	10	11♐	1	1	9	♄11♏
3	10.51	11	24	1	3	9	♅ 9♐
4	10.55	12	7♑	0	4	10	♆28♐
5	10.59	13	19	0	5	10	♇ 0♏
6	11.03	14	2♒	0	6	11	♃ 3♑
7	11.07	15	14	0D	7	12	♄12♏
8	11.11	16	26	0	9	12	♅ 9♐
9	11.15	17	8♓	0	10	13	♆28♐
10	11.19	18	20	1	11	13	♇ 0♏
11	11.23	19	2♈	1	12	14	♃ 3♑
12	11.27	20	14	2	14	15	♄12♏
13	11.31	21	25	3	15	15	♅10♐
14	11.35	22	7♉	4	16	16	♆28♐
15	11.39	23	19	5	17	17	♇ 0♏
16	11.42	24	2♊	6	18	17	♃ 3♑
17	11.46	24	14	7	20	18	♄13♏
18	11.50	25	27	9	21	18	♅10♐
19	11.54	26	10♋	10	22	19	♆28♐
20	11.58	27	23	12	23	20	♇ 0♏
21	12.02	28	8♌	13	25	20	♃ 4♑
22	12.06	29	22	15	26	21	♄13♏
23	12.10	0♎	7♍	17	27	22	♅10♐
24	12.14	1	22	18	28	22	♆28♐
25	12.18	2	8♎	20	29	23	♇ 1♏
26	12.22	3	23	22	1♏	24	♃ 4♑
27	12.26	4	8♏	24	2	24	♄14♏
28	12.30	5	22	26	3	25	♅10♐
29	12.34	6	6♐	27	4	26	♆28♐
30	12.38	7	20	29	6	26	♇ 1♏

Oct	STime	☉	☽	☿	♀	♂	Plnts
1	12.42	8♎	3♑	1♎	7♏	27♐	♃ 4♑
2	12.46	9	16	3	8	28	♄14♏
3	12.50	10	29	5	9	28	♅10♐
4	12.53	11	11♒	6	11	29	♆29♐
5	12.57	12	23	8	12	0♑	♇ 1♏
6	13.01	13	5♓	10	13	1	♃ 5♑
7	13.05	14	17	12	14	1	♄15♏
8	13.09	15	29	13	15	2	♅10♐
9	13.13	16	11♈	15	17	3	♆29♐
10	13.17	17	23	17	18	3	♇ 1♏
11	13.21	18	4♉	19	19	4	♃ 6♑
12	13.25	19	16	20	20	5	♄15♏
13	13.29	20	29	22	21	5	♅11♐
14	13.33	21	11♊	24	23	6	♆29♐
15	13.37	22	23	25	24	7	♇ 1♏
16	13.41	23	6♋	27	25	8	♃ 6♑
17	13.45	24	19	29	26	8	♄16♏
18	13.49	25	3♌	0♏	28	9	♅11♐
19	13.53	26	17	2	29	10	♆29♐
20	13.57	27	1♍	4	0♐	10	♇ 2♏
21	14.00	28	16	5	1	11	♃ 7♑
22	14.04	29	1♎	7	2	12	♄16♏
23	14.08	0♏	16	8	4	13	♅11♐
24	14.12	1	1♏	10	5	13	♆29♐
25	14.16	2	16	12	6	14	♇ 2♏
26	14.20	3	0♐	13	7	15	♃ 8♑
27	14.24	4	15	15	9	15	♄17♏
28	14.28	5	29	16	10	16	♅11♐
29	14.32	6	12♑	18	11	17	♆29♐
30	14.36	7	25	19	12	18	♇ 2♏
31	14.40	8	7♒	21	13	18	♃ 8♑

Nov	STime	☉	☽	☿	♀	♂	Plnts
1	14.44	9♏	20♒	22♏	15♐	19♑	♃ 9♑
2	14.48	10	2♓	24	16	20	♄18♏
3	14.52	11	14	25	17	21	♅12♐
4	14.56	12	26	27	18	21	♆29♐
5	15.00	13	7♈	28	19	22	♇ 2♏
6	15.04	14	19	0♐	21	23	♃ 9♑
7	15.07	15	1♉	1	22	24	♄18♏
8	15.11	16	13	3	23	24	♅12♐
9	15.15	17	25	4	24	25	♆29♐
10	15.19	18	8♊	5	25	26	♇ 2♏
11	15.23	19	20	7	27	27	♃10♑
12	15.27	20	3♋	8	28	27	♄19♏
13	15.31	21	16	10	29	28	♅12♐
14	15.35	22	29	11	0♑	29	♆29♐
15	15.39	23	13♌	12	2	29	♇ 3♏
16	15.43	24	27	14	3	0♒	♃11♑
17	15.47	25	11♍	15	4	1	♄20♏
18	15.51	26	25	16	5	2	♅12♐
19	15.55	27	10♎	18	6	2	♆ 0♑
20	15.59	28	24	19	8	3	♇ 3♏
21	16.03	29	9♏	20	9	4	♃12♑
22	16.07	0♐	24	21	10	5	♄20♏
23	16.11	1	8♐	23	11	6	♅13♐
24	16.15	2	23	24	12	6	♆ 0♑
25	16.18	3	6♑	25	14	7	♇ 3♏
26	16.22	4	20	26	15	8	♃13♑
27	16.26	5	3♒	27	16	9	♄21♏
28	16.30	6	16	28	17	9	♅13♐
29	16.34	7	28	28	18	10	♆ 0♑
30	16.38	8	10♓	29	19	11	♇ 3♏

Dec	STime	☉	☽	☿	♀	♂	Plnts
1	16.42	9♐	22♓	0♑	21♑	12♒	♃14♑
2	16.46	10	4♈	0	22	12	♄21♏
3	16.50	11	16	0	23	13	♅13♐
4	16.54	12	28	0R	24	14	♆ 0♑
5	16.58	13	10♉	0	25	15	♇ 3♏
6	17.02	14	22	0	27	15	♃15♑
7	17.06	15	4♊	0	28	16	♄22♏
8	17.10	16	17	29♐	29	17	♅14♐
9	17.14	17	0♋	29	0♒	18	♆ 0♑
10	17.18	18	13	28	1	18	♇ 4♏
11	17.22	19	26	27	2	19	♃16♑
12	17.25	20	10♌	25	4	20	♄22♏
13	17.29	21	24	24	5	21	♅14♐
14	17.33	22	8♍	23	6	21	♆ 1♑
15	17.37	23	21	21	7	22	♇ 4♏
16	17.41	24	6♎	20	8	23	♃18♑
17	17.45	25	20	19	9	24	♄23♏
18	17.49	26	4♏	18	11	25	♅14♐
19	17.53	27	18	17	12	25	♆ 1♑
20	17.57	28	3♐	16	13	26	♇ 4♏
21	18.01	0♑	17	15	14	27	♃19♑
22	18.05	1	1♑	15	15	28	♄23♏
23	18.09	2	14	14	16	28	♅15♐
24	18.13	3	28	14D	18	29	♆ 1♑
25	18.17	4	11♒	14	19	0♓	♇ 4♏
26	18.21	5	23	14	20	1	♃20♑
27	18.25	6	6♓	15	21	1	♄24♏
28	18.29	7	18	15	22	2	♅15♐
29	18.33	8	0♈	16	23	3	♆ 1♑
30	18.36	9	12	16	24	4	♇ 4♏
31	18.40	10	23	17	25	4	♃21♑

1 9 8 5

Jan	STime	☉	☽	☿	♀	♂	Plnts
1	18.44	11♑	5♉	18♐	27♒	5♓	♃21♑
2	18.48	12	17	19	28	6	♄25♏
3	18.52	13	0♊	20	29	7	♅15♐
4	18.56	14	12	21	0♓	7	♆ 1♑
5	19.00	15	25	22	1	8	♇ 4♏
6	19.04	16	8♋	23	2	9	♃22♑
7	19.08	17	22	24	3	10	♄25♏
8	19.12	18	6♌	26	4	11	♅15♐
9	19.16	19	20	27	5	11	♆ 1♑
10	19.20	20	4♍	28	7	12	♇ 4♏
11	19.24	21	18	29	8	13	♃24♑
12	19.28	22	3♎	1♑	9	14	♄25♏
13	19.32	23	17	2	10	14	♅16♐
14	19.36	24	1♏	3	11	15	♆ 2♑
15	19.40	25	15	5	12	16	♇ 4♏
16	19.43	26	29	6	13	17	♃25♑
17	19.47	27	12♐	7	14	17	♄26♏
18	19.51	28	26	9	15	18	♅16♐
19	19.55	29	10♑	10	16	19	♆ 2♑
20	19.59	0♒	23	12	17	20	♇ 4♏
21	20.03	1	6♒	13	18	20	♃26♑
22	20.07	2	19	15	19	21	♄26♏
23	20.11	3	1♓	16	20	22	♅16♐
24	20.15	4	14	18	21	23	♆ 2♑
25	20.19	5	26	19	22	23	♇ 4♏
26	20.23	6	8♈	21	23	24	♃27♑
27	20.27	7	19	22	24	25	♄27♏
28	20.31	8	1♉	24	25	26	♅16♐
29	20.35	9	13	25	26	27	♆ 2♑
30	20.39	10	25	27	27	27	♇ 4♏
31	20.43	11	7♊	28	28	28	♃28♑

Feb	STime	☉	☽	☿	♀	♂	Plnts
1	20.47	12♒	20♊	0♒	29♓	29♓	♃29♑
2	20.51	13	3♋	2	0♈	0♈	♄27♏
3	20.54	14	16	3	1	0	♅17♐
4	20.58	15	0♌	5	2	1	♆ 2♑
5	21.02	16	14	6	3	2	♇ 4♏
6	21.06	17	29	8	3	3	♃ 0♒
7	21.10	18	14♍	10	4	3	♄27♏
8	21.14	19	28	11	5	4	♅17♐
9	21.18	20	13♎	13	6	5	♆ 3♑
10	21.22	21	27	15	7	6	♇ 4♏
11	21.26	22	12♏	16	8	6	♃ 1♒
12	21.30	23	26	18	8	7	♄27♏
13	21.34	24	9♐	20	9	8	♅17♐
14	21.38	25	23	22	10	9	♆ 3♑
15	21.42	26	6♑	23	11	9	♇ 4♏R
16	21.46	27	19	25	11	10	♃ 2♒
17	21.50	28	2♒	27	12	11	♄28♏
18	21.54	29	15	29	13	12	♅17♐
19	21.58	0♓	27	1♓	14	12	♆ 3♑
20	22.01	1	10♓	2	14	13	♇ 4♏R
21	22.05	3	22	4	15	14	♃ 3♒
22	22.09	4	4♈	6	16	14	♄28♏
23	22.13	5	16	8	16	15	♅17♐
24	22.17	6	28	10	17	16	♆ 3♑
25	22.21	7	9♉	12	17	17	♇ 4♏R
26	22.25	8	21	14	18	17	♃ 4♒
27	22.29	9	3♊	16	18	18	♄28♏
28	22.33	10	15	18	19	19	♅17♐

Mar	STime	☉	☽	☿	♀	♂	Plnts
1	22.37	11♓	28♊	19♓	19♈	20♈	♃ 5♒
2	22.41	12	11♋	21	20	20	♄28♏
3	22.45	13	24	23	20	21	♅18♐
4	22.49	14	8♌	25	20	22	♆ 3♑
5	22.53	15	23	27	21	23	♇ 4♏R
6	22.57	16	7♍	29	21	23	♃ 6♒
7	23.01	17	22	1♈	21	24	♄28♏
8	23.05	18	7♎	2	21	25	♅18♐
9	23.08	19	22	4	22	26	♆ 3♑
10	23.12	20	7♏	6	22	26	♇ 4♏R
11	23.16	21	22	7	22	27	♃ 7♒
12	23.20	22	6♐	9	22	28	♄28♏R
13	23.24	23	20	10	22R	28	♅18♐
14	23.28	24	3♑	12	22	29	♆ 3♑
15	23.32	25	16	13	22	0♉	♇ 4♏R
16	23.36	26	29	14	22	1	♃ 8♒
17	23.40	27	12♒	15	22	1	♄28♏R
18	23.44	28	24	16	22	2	♅18♐
19	23.48	29	6♓	17	21	3	♆ 3♑
20	23.52	0♈	19	17	21	4	♇ 4♏R
21	23.56	1	1♈	18	21	4	♃ 9♒
22	0.00	2	12	18	20	5	♄28♏R
23	0.04	2	24	18	20	6	♅18♐R
24	0.08	3	6♉	18R	20	6	♆ 3♑
25	0.12	4	18	18	19	7	♇ 4♏R
26	0.16	5	0♊	18	19	8	♃10♒
27	0.19	6	12	18	18	9	♄27♏R
28	0.23	7	24	18	18	9	♅18♐
29	0.27	8	6♋	17	17	10	♆ 3♑
30	0.31	9	19	16	17	11	♇ 4♏R
31	0.35	10	3♌	16	16	11	♃11♒

Apr	STime	☉	☽	☿	♀	♂	Plnts
1	0.39	11♈	16♌	15♈	15♈	12♉	♃11♒
2	0.43	12	1♍	14	15	13	♄27♏R
3	0.47	13	15	14	14	14	♅18♐R
4	0.51	14	0♎	13	13	14	♆ 3♑
5	0.55	15	16	12	13	15	♇ 4♏R
6	0.59	16	1♏	11	12	16	♃12♒
7	1.03	17	16	10	12	16	♄27♏R
8	1.07	18	1♐	10	11	17	♅18♐R
9	1.11	19	15	9	10	18	♆ 3♑
10	1.15	20	29	8	10	19	♇ 3♏R
11	1.19	21	13♑	8	9	19	♃12♒
12	1.23	22	26	7	9	20	♄27♏R
13	1.26	23	9♒	7	8	21	♅17♐R
14	1.30	24	21	7	8	21	♆ 3♑
15	1.34	25	4♓	7	8	22	♇ 3♏R
16	1.38	26	16	6	7	23	♃13♒
17	1.42	27	28	6D	7	23	♄27♏R
18	1.46	28	9♈	7	7	24	♅17♐R
19	1.50	29	21	7	6	25	♆ 3♑R
20	1.54	0♉	3♉	7	6	26	♇ 3♏R
21	1.58	1	15	7	6	26	♃14♒
22	2.02	2	27	8	6	27	♄26♏R
23	2.06	3	9♊	8	6	28	♅17♐R
24	2.10	4	21	9	6D	28	♆ 3♑R
25	2.14	5	3♋	9	6	29	♇ 3♏R
26	2.18	6	16	10	6	0♊	♃14♒
27	2.22	7	28	11	6	0	♄26♏R
28	2.26	8	12♌	11	6	1	♅17♐R
29	2.30	9	25	12	6	2	♆ 3♑R
30	2.34	10	9♍	13	6	3	♇ 3♏R

May	STime	☉	☽	☿	♀	♂	Plnts
1	2.37	11♉	24♍	14♈	7♈	3♊	♃15♒
2	2.41	12	9♎	15	7	4	♄26♏R
3	2.45	13	24	16	7	5	♅17♐R
4	2.49	14	9♏	17	7	5	♆ 3♑R
5	2.53	15	24	18	8	6	♇ 3♏R
6	2.57	16	9♐	19	8	7	♃15♒
7	3.01	17	24	21	9	7	♄25♏R
8	3.05	18	8♑	22	9	8	♅17♐R
9	3.09	18	22	23	9	9	♆ 3♑R
10	3.13	19	5♒	25	10	9	♇ 3♏R
11	3.17	20	18	26	10	10	♃16♒
12	3.21	21	0♓	27	11	11	♄25♏R
13	3.25	22	12	29	11	12	♅17♐R
14	3.29	23	25	0♉	12	12	♆ 3♑R
15	3.33	24	6♈	2	13	13	♇ 2♏R
16	3.37	25	18	3	13	14	♃16♒
17	3.41	26	0♉	5	14	14	♄24♏R
18	3.44	27	12	7	15	15	♅16♐R
19	3.48	28	24	8	15	16	♆ 3♑R
20	3.52	29	6♊	10	16	16	♇ 2♏R
21	3.56	0♊	18	12	17	17	♃16♒
22	4.00	1	0♋	14	17	18	♄24♏R
23	4.04	2	13	15	18	18	♅16♐R
24	4.08	3	25	17	19	19	♆ 3♑R
25	4.12	4	8♌	19	20	20	♇ 2♏R
26	4.16	5	22	21	20	20	♃17♒
27	4.20	6	5♍	23	21	21	♄24♏R
28	4.24	7	19	25	22	22	♅16♐R
29	4.28	8	3♎	27	23	22	♆ 3♑R
30	4.32	9	18	29	24	23	♇ 2♏R
31	4.36	10	3♏	1♊	25	24	♃17♒

Jun	STime	☉	☽	☿	♀	♂	Plnts
1	4.40	11♊	18♏	3♊	25♈	24♊	♃17♒
2	4.44	12	2♐	5	26	25	♄23♏R
3	4.48	13	17	8	27	26	♅16♐R
4	4.51	14	2♑	10	28	26	♆ 2♑R
5	4.55	14	16	12	29	27	♇ 2♏R
6	4.59	15	0♒	14	0♉	28	♃17♒R
7	5.03	16	13	16	1	28	♄23♏R
8	5.07	17	26	18	2	29	♅16♐R
9	5.11	18	9♓	21	3	0♋	♆ 2♑R
10	5.15	19	21	23	4	0	♇ 2♏R
11	5.19	20	3♈	25	4	1	♃17♒R
12	5.23	21	15	27	5	2	♄23♏R
13	5.27	22	27	29	6	2	♅15♐R
14	5.31	23	8♉	1♋	7	3	♆ 2♑R
15	5.35	24	20	4	8	4	♇ 2♏R
16	5.39	25	2♊	6	9	4	♃16♒R
17	5.43	26	14	8	10	5	♄22♏R
18	5.47	27	27	10	11	6	♅15♐R
19	5.51	28	9♋	12	12	6	♆ 2♑R
20	5.55	29	22	14	13	7	♇ 2♏R
21	5.59	0♋	5♌	15	14	8	♃16♒R
22	6.02	1	19	17	15	8	♄22♏R
23	6.06	2	2♍	19	16	9	♅15♐R
24	6.10	3	16	21	17	10	♆ 2♑R
25	6.14	4	0♎	23	18	10	♇ 2♏R
26	6.18	5	14	24	19	11	♃16♒R
27	6.22	5	28	26	20	12	♄22♏R
28	6.26	6	13♏	28	21	12	♅15♐R
29	6.30	7	27	29	22	13	♆ 2♑R
30	6.34	8	11♐	1♌	24	14	♇ 2♏R

Jul	STime	☉	☽	☿	♀	♂	Plnts
1	6.38	9♋	26♐	2♌	25♉	14♋	♃16♒R
2	6.42	10	10♑	4	26	15	♄22♏R
3	6.46	11	24	5	27	16	♅15♐R
4	6.50	12	8♒	7	28	16	♆ 2♑R
5	6.54	13	21	8	29	17	♇ 2♏
6	6.58	14	4♓	9	0♊	18	♃15♒R
7	7.02	15	17	11	1	18	♄21♏R
8	7.06	16	29	12	2	19	♅14♐R
9	7.09	17	11♈	13	3	20	♆ 2♑R
10	7.13	18	23	14	4	20	♇ 2♏
11	7.17	19	5♉	15	5	21	♃15♒R
12	7.21	20	17	16	6	21	♄21♏R
13	7.25	21	29	17	7	22	♅14♐R
14	7.29	22	11♊	18	9	23	♆ 1♑R
15	7.33	23	23	19	10	23	♇ 2♏
16	7.37	24	6♋	20	11	24	♃14♒R
17	7.41	25	18	21	12	25	♄21♏R
18	7.45	26	2♌	21	13	25	♅14♐R
19	7.49	26	15	22	14	26	♆ 1♑R
20	7.53	27	29	23	15	27	♇ 2♏
21	7.57	28	13♍	23	16	27	♃13♒R
22	8.01	29	27	24	17	28	♄21♏
23	8.05	0♌	11♎	24	19	29	♅14♐R
24	8.09	1	25	25	20	29	♆ 1♑R
25	8.13	2	9♏	25	21	0♌	♇ 2♏
26	8.17	3	23	25	22	1	♃13♒R
27	8.20	4	7♐	25	23	1	♄21♏
28	8.24	5	21	25R	24	2	♅14♐R
29	8.28	6	5♑	25	25	3	♆ 1♑R
30	8.32	7	19	25	26	3	♇ 2♏
31	8.36	8	3♒	25	28	4	♃12♒R

Aug	STime	☉	☽	☿	♀	♂	Plnts
1	8.40	9♌	16♒	24♌	29♊	4♌	♃12♒R
2	8.44	10	29	24	0♋	5	♄21♏
3	8.48	11	12♓	23	1	6	♅14♐R
4	8.52	12	25	23	2	6	♆ 1♑R
5	8.56	13	7♈	22	3	7	♇ 2♏
6	9.00	14	19	21	4	8	♃11♒R
7	9.04	15	1♉	21	6	8	♄21♏
8	9.08	16	13	20	7	9	♅14♐R
9	9.12	17	24	19	8	10	♆ 1♑R
10	9.16	17	6♊	18	9	10	♇ 2♏
11	9.20	18	19	17	10	11	♃11♒R
12	9.24	19	1♋	17	11	12	♄21♏
13	9.27	20	14	16	13	12	♅14♐R
14	9.31	21	27	15	14	13	♆ 1♑R
15	9.35	22	10♌	15	15	13	♇ 2♏
16	9.39	23	24	14	16	14	♃10♒R
17	9.43	24	8♍	14	17	15	♄22♏
18	9.47	25	23	13	18	15	♅14♐
19	9.51	26	7♎	13	20	16	♆ 1♑R
20	9.55	27	21	13D	21	17	♇ 2♏
21	9.59	28	6♏	13	22	17	♃10♒R
22	10.03	29	20	13	23	18	♄22♏
23	10.07	0♍	4♐	13	24	19	♅14♐
24	10.11	1	18	14	25	19	♆ 1♑R
25	10.15	2	2♑	14	27	20	♇ 2♏
26	10.19	3	15	15	28	20	♃ 9♒R
27	10.23	4	29	16	29	21	♄22♏
28	10.27	5	12♒	17	0♌	22	♅14♐
29	10.31	6	25	18	1	22	♆ 1♑R
30	10.34	7	8♓	19	2	23	♇ 2♏
31	10.38	8	21	20	4	24	♃ 9♒R

Sep	STime	☉	☽	☿	♀	♂	Plnts
1	10.42	9♍	3♈	21♌	5♌	24♌	♃ 8♒R
2	10.46	10	15	23	6	25	♄22♏
3	10.50	11	27	24	7	26	♅14♐
4	10.54	12	9♉	26	8	26	♆ 1♑R
5	10.58	13	21	27	10	27	♇ 2♏
6	11.02	14	2♊	29	11	27	♃ 8♒R
7	11.06	15	14	1♍	12	28	♄23♏
8	11.10	15	27	3	13	29	♅14♐
9	11.14	16	9♋	5	14	29	♆ 1♑
10	11.18	17	22	6	16	0♍	♇ 3♏
11	11.22	18	5♌	8	17	1	♃ 8♒R
12	11.26	19	19	10	18	1	♄23♏
13	11.30	20	3♍	12	19	2	♅14♐
14	11.34	21	17	14	20	3	♆ 1♑
15	11.38	22	2♎	16	22	3	♇ 3♏
16	11.42	23	17	18	23	4	♃ 7♒R
17	11.45	24	1♏	20	24	4	♄23♏
18	11.49	25	16	21	25	5	♅14♐
19	11.53	26	1♐	23	27	6	♆ 1♑
20	11.57	27	15	25	28	6	♇ 3♏
21	12.01	28	29	27	29	7	♃ 7♒R
22	12.05	29	12♑	29	0♍	8	♄24♏
23	12.09	0♎	26	1♎	1	8	♅14♐
24	12.13	1	9♒	2	3	9	♆ 1♑
25	12.17	2	22	4	4	9	♇ 3♏
26	12.21	3	5♓	6	5	10	♃ 7♒R
27	12.25	4	17	8	6	11	♄24♏
28	12.29	5	29	10	7	11	♅14♐
29	12.33	6	11♈	11	9	12	♆ 1♑
30	12.37	7	23	13	10	13	♇ 3♏

Oct	STime	☉	☽	☿	♀	♂	Plnts
1	12.41	8♎	5♉	15♎	11♍	13♍	♃ 7♒
2	12.45	9	17	16	12	14	♄25♏
3	12.49	10	29	18	14	15	♅14♐
4	12.52	11	11♊	20	15	15	♆ 1♑
5	12.56	12	23	21	16	16	♇ 3♏
6	13.00	13	5♋	23	17	16	♃ 7♒
7	13.04	14	17	25	19	17	♄25♏
8	13.08	15	0♌	26	20	18	♅15♐
9	13.12	16	13	28	21	18	♆ 1♑
10	13.16	17	27	29	22	19	♇ 4♏
11	13.20	18	11♍	1♏	23	20	♃ 7♒
12	13.24	19	25	2	25	20	♄26♏
13	13.28	20	10♎	4	26	21	♅15♐
14	13.32	21	25	5	27	21	♆ 1♑
15	13.36	22	10♏	7	28	22	♇ 4♏
16	13.40	23	25	8	0♎	23	♃ 7♒
17	13.44	24	10♐	10	1	23	♄26♏
18	13.48	25	25	11	2	24	♅15♐
19	13.52	26	9♑	13	3	25	♆ 1♑
20	13.56	27	23	14	5	25	♇ 4♏
21	14.00	28	6♒	16	6	26	♃ 7♒
22	14.03	29	19	17	7	26	♄27♏
23	14.07	0♏	2♓	19	8	27	♅15♐
24	14.11	1	14	20	10	28	♆ 1♑
25	14.15	2	26	21	11	28	♇ 4♏
26	14.19	3	8♈	23	12	29	♃ 8♒
27	14.23	4	20	24	13	0♎	♄27♏
28	14.27	5	2♉	26	15	0	♅15♐
29	14.31	6	14	27	16	1	♆ 1♑
30	14.35	7	26	28	17	1	♇ 4♏
31	14.39	8	8♊	29	18	2	♃ 8♒

Nov	STime	☉	☽	☿	♀	♂	Plnts
1	14.43	9♏	19♊	1♐	20♎	3♎	♃ 8♒
2	14.47	10	1♋	2	21	3	♄28♏
3	14.51	11	14	3	22	4	♅16♐
4	14.55	12	26	4	23	5	♆ 1♑
5	14.59	13	9♌	6	25	5	♇ 5♏
6	15.03	14	22	7	26	6	♃ 9♒
7	15.07	15	5♍	8	27	7	♄29♏
8	15.10	16	19	9	28	7	♅16♐
9	15.14	17	3♎	10	0♏	8	♆ 1♑
10	15.18	18	18	11	1	8	♇ 5♏
11	15.22	19	3♏	11	2	9	♃ 9♒
12	15.26	20	18	12	3	10	♄29♏
13	15.30	21	4♐	13	5	10	♅16♐
14	15.34	22	19	14	6	11	♆ 2♑
15	15.38	23	3♑	14	7	12	♇ 5♏
16	15.42	24	18	14	8	12	♃10♒
17	15.46	25	2♒	15	10	13	♄ 0♐
18	15.50	26	15	15R	11	13	♅17♐
19	15.54	27	28	15	12	14	♆ 2♑
20	15.58	28	11♓	14	13	15	♇ 5♏
21	16.02	29	23	14	15	15	♃11♒
22	16.06	0♐	5♈	13	16	16	♄ 0♐
23	16.10	1	17	13	17	16	♅17♐
24	16.14	2	29	12	18	17	♆ 2♑
25	16.18	3	11♉	11	20	18	♇ 6♏
26	16.21	4	23	10	21	18	♃11♒
27	16.25	5	5♊	8	22	19	♄ 1♐
28	16.29	6	16	7	23	20	♅17♐
29	16.33	7	29	6	25	20	♆ 2♑
30	16.37	8	11♋	4	26	21	♇ 6♏

Dec	STime	☉	☽	☿	♀	♂	Plnts
1	16.41	9♐	23♋	3♐	27♏	21♎	♃12♒
2	16.45	10	5♌	2	28	22	♄ 2♐
3	16.49	11	18	1	0♐	23	♅17♐
4	16.53	12	1♍	0	1	23	♆ 2♑
5	16.57	13	14	29♏	2	24	♇ 6♏
6	17.01	14	28	29	3	25	♃13♒
7	17.05	15	12♎	29	5	25	♄ 2♐
8	17.09	16	27	28D	6	26	♅18♐
9	17.13	17	11♏	29	7	26	♆ 2♑
10	17.17	18	26	29	8	27	♇ 6♏
11	17.21	19	12♐	29	10	28	♃14♒
12	17.25	20	27	0♐	11	28	♄ 3♐
13	17.28	21	11♑	0	12	29	♅18♐
14	17.32	22	26	1	13	0♏	♆ 3♑
15	17.36	23	10♒	2	15	0	♇ 6♏
16	17.40	24	24	3	16	1	♃15♒
17	17.44	25	7♓	4	17	1	♄ 3♐
18	17.48	26	20	5	19	2	♅18♐
19	17.52	27	2♈	6	20	3	♆ 3♑
20	17.56	28	14	7	21	3	♇ 6♏
21	18.00	29	26	8	22	4	♃16♒
22	18.04	0♑	8♉	10	24	4	♄ 4♐
23	18.08	1	19	11	25	5	♅19♐
24	18.12	2	1♊	12	26	6	♆ 3♑
25	18.16	3	13	14	27	6	♇ 6♏
26	18.20	4	25	15	29	7	♃17♒
27	18.24	5	7♋	16	0♑	8	♄ 4♐
28	18.28	6	20	18	1	8	♅19♐
29	18.32	7	2♌	19	2	9	♆ 3♑
30	18.36	8	15	20	4	9	♇ 7♏
31	18.39	9	28	22	5	10	♃18♒

Jan	STime	☉	☽	☿	♀	♂	Plnts
1	18.43	10♑	11♍	23♐	6♑	11♏	♃18♒
2	18.47	11	25	25	7	11	♄ 5♐
3	18.51	13	8♎	26	9	12	♅19♐
4	18.55	14	22	28	10	12	♆ 3♑
5	18.59	15	6♏	29	11	13	♇ 7♏
6	19.03	16	21	1♑	12	14	♃19♒
7	19.07	17	5♐	2	14	14	♄ 6♐
8	19.11	18	20	4	15	15	♅20♐
9	19.15	19	5♑	5	16	15	♆ 4♑
10	19.19	20	19	7	17	16	♇ 7♏
11	19.23	21	4♒	8	19	17	♃20♒
12	19.27	22	18	10	20	17	♄ 6♐
13	19.31	23	2♓	11	21	18	♅20♐
14	19.35	24	15	13	22	18	♆ 4♑
15	19.39	25	28	14	24	19	♇ 7♏
16	19.43	26	10♈	16	25	20	♃21♒
17	19.46	27	22	18	26	20	♄ 6♐
18	19.50	28	4♉	19	28	21	♅20♐
19	19.54	29	16	21	29	21	♆ 4♑
20	19.58	0♒	28	22	0♒	22	♇ 7♏
21	20.02	1	9♊	24	1	23	♃23♒
22	20.06	2	21	26	3	23	♄ 7♐
23	20.10	3	4♋	27	4	24	♅20♐
24	20.14	4	16	29	5	24	♆ 4♑
25	20.18	5	29	0♒	6	25	♇ 7♏
26	20.22	6	12♌	2	8	26	♃24♒
27	20.26	7	25	4	9	26	♄ 7♐
28	20.30	8	8♍	5	10	27	♅21♐
29	20.34	9	22	7	11	27	♆ 4♑
30	20.38	10	5♎	9	13	28	♇ 7♏
31	20.42	11	19	11	14	29	♃25♒

Feb	STime	☉	☽	☿	♀	♂	Plnts
1	20.46	12♒	3♏	12♒	15♒	29♏	♃25♒
2	20.50	13	17	14	16	0♐	♄ 8♐
3	20.53	14	1♐	16	18	0	♅21♐
4	20.57	15	15	18	19	1	♆ 4♑
5	21.01	16	0♑	19	20	2	♇ 7♏
6	21.05	17	14	21	21	2	♃26♒
7	21.09	18	28	23	23	3	♄ 8♐
8	21.13	19	12♒	25	24	3	♅21♐
9	21.17	20	26	27	25	4	♆ 5♑
10	21.21	21	9♓	28	26	5	♇ 7♏
11	21.25	22	23	0♓	28	5	♃27♒
12	21.29	23	5♈	2	29	6	♄ 8♐
13	21.33	24	18	4	0♓	6	♅21♐
14	21.37	25	0♉	6	1	7	♆ 5♑
15	21.41	26	12	7	3	7	♇ 7♏R
16	21.45	27	24	9	4	8	♃29♒
17	21.49	28	5♊	11	5	9	♄ 9♐
18	21.53	29	17	13	6	9	♅21♐
19	21.57	0♓	29	15	8	10	♆ 5♑
20	22.01	1	12♋	16	9	10	♇ 7♏R
21	22.04	2	24	18	10	11	♃ 0♓
22	22.08	3	7♌	19	11	11	♄ 9♐
23	22.12	4	20	21	13	12	♅22♐
24	22.16	5	4♍	22	14	13	♆ 5♑
25	22.20	6	17	24	15	13	♇ 7♏R
26	22.24	7	1♎	25	16	14	♃ 1♓
27	22.28	8	16	26	18	14	♄ 9♐
28	22.32	9	0♏	27	19	15	♅22♐

Mar	STime	☉	☽	☿	♀	♂	Plnts
1	22.36	10♓	14♏	28♓	20♓	15♐	♃ 2♓
2	22.40	11	28	29	21	16	♄ 9♐
3	22.44	12	12♐	0♈	23	17	♅22♐
4	22.48	13	26	0	24	17	♆ 5♑
5	22.52	14	10♑	1	25	18	♇ 7♏R
6	22.56	15	24	1	26	18	♃ 3♓
7	23.00	16	8♒	1R	28	19	♄ 9♐
8	23.04	17	21	1	29	19	♅22♐
9	23.08	18	5♓	1	0♈	20	♆ 5♑
10	23.11	19	18	0	1	20	♇ 7♏R
11	23.15	20	1♈	0	3	21	♃ 4♓
12	23.19	21	13	29♓	4	21	♄ 9♐
13	23.23	22	26	28	5	22	♅22♐
14	23.27	23	8♉	28	6	23	♆ 5♑
15	23.31	24	20	27	8	23	♇ 7♏R
16	23.35	25	1♊	26	9	24	♃ 5♓
17	23.39	26	13	25	10	24	♄ 9♐
18	23.43	27	25	24	11	25	♅22♐
19	23.47	28	7♋	23	13	25	♆ 5♑
20	23.51	29	19	22	14	26	♇ 7♏R
21	23.55	0♈	2♌	21	15	26	♃ 7♓
22	23.59	1	15	21	16	27	♄ 9♐R
23	0.03	2	28	20	18	27	♅22♐
24	0.07	3	12♍	19	19	28	♆ 5♑
25	0.11	4	26	19	20	28	♇ 7♏R
26	0.15	5	10♎	18	21	29	♃ 8♓
27	0.19	6	25	18	22	29	♄ 9♐R
28	0.22	7	9♏	18	24	0♑	♅22♐
29	0.26	8	24	18	25	0	♆ 5♑
30	0.30	9	9♐	18D	26	1	♇ 6♏R
31	0.34	10	23	18	27	1	♃ 9♓

Apr	STime	☉	☽	☿	♀	♂	Plnts
1	0.38	11♈	7♑	18♓	29♈	2♑	♃ 9♓
2	0.42	12	21	18	0♉	2	♄ 9♐R
3	0.46	13	5♒	18	1	3	♅22♐
4	0.50	14	18	19	2	3	♆ 6♑
5	0.54	15	1♓	19	4	4	♇ 6♏R
6	0.58	16	14	20	5	4	♃10♓
7	1.02	17	27	20	6	5	♄ 9♐R
8	1.06	18	9♈	21	7	5	♅22♐R
9	1.10	19	22	22	9	6	♆ 6♑
10	1.14	20	4♉	23	10	6	♇ 6♏R
11	1.18	21	16	24	11	7	♃11♓
12	1.22	22	28	24	12	7	♄ 9♐R
13	1.26	23	10♊	25	13	8	♅22♐R
14	1.29	24	21	26	15	8	♆ 5♑R
15	1.33	25	3♋	27	16	8	♇ 6♏R
16	1.37	26	15	29	17	9	♃12♓
17	1.41	27	28	0♈	18	9	♄ 9♐R
18	1.45	28	10♌	1	20	10	♅22♐R
19	1.49	29	23	2	21	10	♆ 5♑
20	1.53	0♉	6♍	3	22	11	♇ 6♏R
21	1.57	1	20	5	23	11	♃13♓
22	2.01	2	4♎	6	24	11	♄ 8♐R
23	2.05	3	18	7	26	12	♅22♐R
24	2.09	4	3♏	9	27	12	♆ 5♑
25	2.13	5	18	10	28	13	♇ 6♏R
26	2.17	6	3♐	12	29	13	♃14♓
27	2.21	7	18	13	1♊	13	♄ 8♐R
28	2.25	8	3♑	15	2	14	♅22♐R
29	2.29	9	17	16	3	14	♆ 5♑R
30	2.33	10	1♒	18	4	15	♇ 6♏R

May	STime	☉	☽	☿	♀	♂	Plnts
1	2.36	11♉	15♒	19♈	5♊	15♑	♃15♓
2	2.40	11	28	21	7	15	♄ 8♐R
3	2.44	12	11♓	23	8	16	♅22♐R
4	2.48	13	24	24	9	16	♆ 5♑R
5	2.52	14	6♈	26	10	16	♇ 5♏R
6	2.56	15	19	28	12	17	♃16♓
7	3.00	16	1♉	0♉	13	17	♄ 8♐R
8	3.04	17	13	1	14	17	♅21♐R
9	3.08	18	25	3	15	18	♆ 5♑R
10	3.12	19	6♊	5	16	18	♇ 5♏R
11	3.16	20	18	7	18	18	♃17♓
12	3.20	21	0♋	9	19	19	♄ 7♐R
13	3.24	22	12	11	20	19	♅21♐R
14	3.28	23	24	13	21	19	♆ 5♑R
15	3.32	24	6♌	15	22	19	♇ 5♏R
16	3.36	25	19	17	24	20	♃18♓
17	3.40	26	1♍	19	25	20	♄ 7♐R
18	3.44	27	15	21	26	20	♅21♐R
19	3.47	28	28	24	27	20	♆ 5♑R
20	3.51	29	12♎	26	28	21	♇ 5♏R
21	3.55	0♊	27	28	0♋	21	♃18♓
22	3.59	1	11♏	0♊	1	21	♄ 7♐R
23	4.03	2	27	2	2	21	♅21♐R
24	4.07	3	12♐	5	3	21	♆ 5♑R
25	4.11	4	27	7	4	22	♇ 5♏R
26	4.15	5	12♑	9	6	22	♃19♓
27	4.19	6	27	11	7	22	♄ 6♐R
28	4.23	7	11♒	13	8	22	♅21♐R
29	4.27	8	25	15	9	22	♆ 5♑R
30	4.31	8	8♓	17	10	22	♇ 5♏R
31	4.35	9	21	20	12	22	♃20♓

Jun	STime	☉	☽	☿	♀	♂	Plnts
1	4.39	10♊	3♈	22♊	13♋	22♑	♃20♓
2	4.43	11	16	24	14	23	♄ 6♐R
3	4.47	12	28	26	15	23	♅20♐R
4	4.51	13	10♉	28	16	23	♆ 5♑R
5	4.54	14	22	0♋	18	23	♇ 5♏R
6	4.58	15	3♊	1	19	23	♃21♓
7	5.02	16	15	3	20	23	♄ 5♐R
8	5.06	17	27	5	21	23	♅20♐R
9	5.10	18	9♋	7	22	23R	♆ 5♑R
10	5.14	19	21	9	23	23	♇ 5♏R
11	5.18	20	3♌	10	25	23	♃21♓
12	5.22	21	15	12	26	23	♄ 5♐R
13	5.26	22	28	13	27	23	♅20♐R
14	5.30	23	11♍	15	28	23	♆ 4♑R
15	5.34	24	24	16	29	23	♇ 4♏R
16	5.38	25	7♎	18	1♌	22	♃21♓
17	5.42	26	21	19	2	22	♄ 5♐R
18	5.46	27	5♏	21	3	22	♅20♐R
19	5.50	28	20	22	4	22	♆ 4♑R
20	5.54	29	5♐	23	5	22	♇ 4♏R
21	5.58	0♋	20	24	6	22	♃22♓
22	6.02	0	5♑	26	8	22	♄ 4♐R
23	6.05	1	21	27	9	22	♅20♐R
24	6.09	2	5♒	28	10	21	♆ 4♑R
25	6.13	3	20	29	11	21	♇ 4♏R
26	6.17	4	4♓	0♌	12	21	♃22♓
27	6.21	5	17	1	13	21	♄ 4♐R
28	6.25	6	0♈	1	15	20	♅19♐R
29	6.29	7	12	2	16	20	♆ 4♑R
30	6.33	8	25	3	17	20	♇ 4♏R

Jul	STime	☉	☽	☿	♀	♂	Plnts
1	6.37	9♋	7♉	3♌	18♌	20♑	♃22♓
2	6.41	10	19	4	19	20	♄ 4♐R
3	6.45	11	0♊	5	20	19	♅19♐R
4	6.49	12	12	5	21	19	♆ 4♑R
5	6.53	13	24	5	23	19	♇ 4♏R
6	6.57	14	6♋	6	24	18	♃22♓
7	7.01	15	18	6	25	18	♄ 3♐R
8	7.05	16	0♌	6	26	18	♅19♐R
9	7.09	17	13	6R	27	18	♆ 4♑R
10	7.12	18	25	6	28	17	♇ 4♏
11	7.16	19	8♍	6	29	17	♃23♓
12	7.20	20	21	6	1♍	17	♄ 3♐R
13	7.24	21	4♎	6	2	16	♅19♐R
14	7.28	21	17	5	3	16	♆ 4♑R
15	7.32	22	1♏	5	4	16	♇ 4♏
16	7.36	23	15	4	5	16	♃23♓R
17	7.40	24	29	4	6	15	♄ 3♐R
18	7.44	25	14♐	3	7	15	♅19♐R
19	7.48	26	29	3	9	15	♆ 4♑R
20	7.52	27	14♑	2	10	14	♇ 4♏
21	7.56	28	29	1	11	14	♃22♓R
22	8.00	29	14♒	1	12	14	♄ 3♐R
23	8.04	0♌	28	0	13	14	♅19♐R
24	8.08	1	12♓	29♋	14	13	♆ 3♑R
25	8.12	2	25	29	15	13	♇ 4♏
26	8.16	3	8♈	28	16	13	♃22♓R
27	8.19	4	21	27	17	13	♄ 3♐R
28	8.23	5	3♉	27	19	13	♅18♐R
29	8.27	6	15	26	20	12	♆ 3♑R
30	8.31	7	27	26	21	12	♇ 4♏
31	8.35	8	9♊	26	22	12	♃22♓R

Aug	STime	☉	☽	☿	♀	♂	Plnts
1	8.39	9♌	21♊	26♋	23♍	12♑	♃22♓R
2	8.43	10	3♋	25	24	12	♄ 3♐R
3	8.47	11	15	25D	25	12	♅18♐R
4	8.51	12	27	26	26	12	♆ 3♑R
5	8.55	12	9♌	26	27	11	♇ 4♏
6	8.59	13	22	26	28	11	♃22♓R
7	9.03	14	5♍	27	29	11	♄ 3♐
8	9.07	15	18	27	0♎	11	♅18♐R
9	9.11	16	1♎	28	1	11	♆ 3♑R
10	9.15	17	14	28	2	11	♇ 4♏
11	9.19	18	28	29	4	11	♃21♓R
12	9.23	19	11♏	0♌	5	11D	♄ 3♐
13	9.27	20	25	1	6	11	♅18♐R
14	9.30	21	10♐	3	7	11	♆ 3♑R
15	9.34	22	24	4	8	11	♇ 5♏
16	9.38	23	9♑	5	9	11	♃21♓R
17	9.42	24	23	7	10	11	♄ 3♐
18	9.46	25	8♒	8	11	11	♅18♐
19	9.50	26	22	10	12	11	♆ 3♑R
20	9.54	27	6♓	11	13	12	♇ 5♏
21	9.58	28	20	13	14	12	♃20♓R
22	10.02	29	3♈	15	15	12	♄ 3♐
23	10.06	0♍	16	17	16	12	♅18♐
24	10.10	1	29	19	17	12	♆ 3♑R
25	10.14	2	11♉	21	18	12	♇ 5♏
26	10.18	3	23	23	19	12	♃20♓R
27	10.22	4	5♊	24	20	13	♄ 3♐
28	10.26	5	17	26	21	13	♅18♐
29	10.30	6	29	28	22	13	♆ 3♑R
30	10.34	7	11♋	0♍	23	13	♇ 5♏
31	10.37	7	23	2	23	14	♃19♓R

Sep	STime	☉	☽	☿	♀	♂	Plnts
1	10.41	8♍	5♌	4♍	24♎	14♑	♃19♓R
2	10.45	9	18	6	25	14	♄ 3♐
3	10.49	10	1♍	8	26	14	♅18♐
4	10.53	11	14	10	27	15	♆ 3♑R
5	10.57	12	27	12	28	15	♇ 5♏
6	11.01	13	11♎	14	29	15	♃18♓R
7	11.05	14	24	16	0♏	16	♄ 4♐
8	11.09	15	8♏	18	1	16	♅18♐
9	11.13	16	22	20	1	16	♆ 3♑
10	11.17	17	6♐	21	2	17	♇ 5♏
11	11.21	18	21	23	3	17	♃17♓R
12	11.25	19	5♑	25	4	17	♄ 4♐
13	11.29	20	19	27	5	18	♅18♐
14	11.33	21	3♒	29	6	18	♆ 3♑
15	11.37	22	17	0♎	6	18	♇ 5♏
16	11.41	23	1♓	2	7	19	♃17♓R
17	11.45	24	15	4	8	19	♄ 4♐
18	11.48	25	28	6	9	20	♅18♐
19	11.52	26	11♈	7	9	20	♆ 3♑
20	11.56	27	24	9	10	21	♇ 5♏
21	12.00	28	7♉	10	11	21	♃16♓R
22	12.04	29	19	12	11	21	♄ 4♐
23	12.08	0♎	1♊	14	12	22	♅18♐
24	12.12	1	13	15	13	22	♆ 3♑
25	12.16	2	25	17	13	23	♇ 6♏
26	12.20	3	7♋	18	14	23	♃16♓R
27	12.24	4	19	20	14	24	♄ 5♐
28	12.28	5	1♌	22	15	24	♅18♐
29	12.32	6	13	23	16	25	♆ 3♑
30	12.36	7	26	25	16	25	♇ 6♏

Oct	STime	☉	☽	☿	♀	♂	Plnts
1	12.40	8♎	9♍	26♎	17♏	26♑	♃15♓R
2	12.44	9	22	28	17	26	♄ 5♐
3	12.48	10	6♎	29	17	27	♅19♐
4	12.52	11	20	0♏	18	27	♆ 3♑
5	12.55	12	4♏	2	18	28	♇ 6♏
6	12.59	13	18	3	19	28	♃14♓R
7	13.03	14	3♐	5	19	29	♄ 6♐
8	13.07	15	17	6	19	29	♅19♐
9	13.11	16	2♑	7	19	0♒	♆ 3♑
10	13.15	17	16	9	20	0	♇ 6♏
11	13.19	18	0♒	10	20	1	♃14♓R
12	13.23	19	14	11	20	2	♄ 6♐
13	13.27	20	27	13	20	2	♅19♐
14	13.31	21	11♓	14	20	3	♆ 3♑
15	13.35	22	24	15	20R	3	♇ 6♏
16	13.39	23	7♈	16	20	4	♃14♓R
17	13.43	24	20	17	20	4	♄ 7♐
18	13.47	25	3♉	19	20	5	♅19♐
19	13.51	26	15	20	20	6	♆ 3♑
20	13.55	27	27	21	20	6	♇ 7♏
21	13.59	28	9♊	22	19	7	♃13♓R
22	14.03	28	21	23	19	7	♄ 7♐
23	14.06	29	3♋	24	19	8	♅19♐
24	14.10	0♏	15	25	19	9	♆ 3♑
25	14.14	1	27	25	18	9	♇ 7♏
26	14.18	2	9♌	26	18	10	♃13♓R
27	14.22	3	21	27	17	10	♄ 8♐
28	14.26	4	4♍	27	17	11	♅20♐
29	14.30	5	17	28	16	12	♆ 3♑
30	14.34	6	0♎	28	16	12	♇ 7♏
31	14.38	7	14	29	15	13	♃13♓R

Nov	STime	☉	☽	☿	♀	♂	Plnts
1	14.42	8♏	28♎	29♏	15♏	14♒	♃13♓R
2	14.46	9	13♏	29R	14	14	♄ 8♐
3	14.50	10	28	29	14	15	♅20♐
4	14.54	11	13♐	29	13	15	♆ 3♑
5	14.58	12	27	28	12	16	♇ 7♏
6	15.02	13	12♑	28	12	17	♃13♓R
7	15.06	14	26	27	11	17	♄ 9♐
8	15.10	15	11♒	26	11	18	♅20♐
9	15.13	16	24	25	10	19	♆ 4♑
10	15.17	17	8♓	24	9	19	♇ 7♏
11	15.21	19	21	22	9	20	♃13♓
12	15.25	20	4♈	21	8	21	♄ 9♐
13	15.29	21	16	20	8	21	♅20♐
14	15.33	22	29	18	7	22	♆ 4♑
15	15.37	23	11♉	17	7	23	♇ 8♏
16	15.41	24	23	16	7	23	♃13♓
17	15.45	25	5♊	15	6	24	♄10♐
18	15.49	26	17	14	6	25	♅21♐
19	15.53	27	29	14	6	25	♆ 4♑
20	15.57	28	11♋	13	5	26	♇ 8♏
21	16.01	29	23	13	5	27	♃13♓
22	16.05	0♐	5♌	13D	5	27	♄10♐
23	16.09	1	17	13	5	28	♅21♐
24	16.13	2	29	13	5	29	♆ 4♑
25	16.17	3	12♍	14	5D	29	♇ 8♏
26	16.20	4	25	14	5	0♓	♃13♓
27	16.24	5	8♎	15	5	1	♄11♐
28	16.28	6	22	16	5	1	♅21♐
29	16.32	7	6♏	17	5	2	♆ 4♑
30	16.36	8	21	18	5	3	♇ 8♏

Dec	STime	☉	☽	☿	♀	♂	Plnts
1	16.40	9♐	6♐	19♏	5♏	3♓	♃14♓
2	16.44	10	21	20	5	4	♄12♐
3	16.48	11	6♑	21	6	5	♅22♐
4	16.52	12	21	22	6	5	♆ 4♑
5	16.56	13	6♒	24	6	6	♇ 8♏
6	17.00	14	21	25	7	7	♃14♓
7	17.04	15	4♓	26	7	7	♄12♐
8	17.08	16	18	28	7	8	♅22♐
9	17.12	17	1♈	29	8	9	♆ 5♑
10	17.16	18	14	0♐	8	10	♇ 9♏
11	17.20	19	26	2	9	10	♃14♓
12	17.24	20	8♉	3	9	11	♄13♐
13	17.28	21	20	5	10	12	♅22♐
14	17.31	22	2♊	6	11	12	♆ 5♑
15	17.35	23	14	8	11	13	♇ 9♏
16	17.39	24	26	9	12	14	♃15♓
17	17.43	25	8♋	11	12	14	♄13♐
18	17.47	26	20	12	13	15	♅22♐
19	17.51	27	2♌	14	14	16	♆ 5♑
20	17.55	28	14	15	15	16	♇ 9♏
21	17.59	29	26	17	15	17	♃16♓
22	18.03	0♑	8♍	18	16	18	♄14♐
23	18.07	1	21	20	17	19	♅23♐
24	18.11	2	3♎	21	18	19	♆ 5♑
25	18.15	3	17	23	18	20	♇ 9♏
26	18.19	4	0♏	24	19	21	♃16♓
27	18.23	5	14	26	20	21	♄15♐
28	18.27	6	29	27	21	22	♅23♐
29	18.31	7	14♐	29	22	23	♆ 5♑
30	18.35	8	29	1♑	22	23	♇ 9♏
31	18.38	9	14♑	2	23	24	♃17♓

1987

Jan	STime	☉	☽	☿	♀	♂	Plnts
1	18.42	10♑	0♒	4♏	24♐	25♏	♃17♐
2	18.46	11	15	5	25	25	♄15♐
3	18.50	12	29	7	26	26	♅23♐
4	18.54	13	13♓	8	27	27	♆6♑
5	18.58	14	27	10	28	28	♇9♏
6	19.02	15	10♈	13	0♑	29	♄16♐
7	19.06	16	23	13	0♒	29	♅16♐
8	19.10	17	5♉	15	1	0♐	♅24♐
9	19.14	18	17	16	2	0	♆6♑
10	19.18	19	29	18	3	1	♇9♏
11	19.22	20	11♊	20	4	2	♄16♐
12	19.26	21	23	21	5	2	♅16♐
13	19.30	22	5♋	23	6	3	♅24♐
14	19.34	23	17	25	7	4	♆6♑
15	19.38	24	29	26	8	5	♇9♏
16	19.42	26	11♌	28	9	5	♃20♐
17	19.46	27	23	0♒	10	6	♄17♐
18	19.49	28	5♍	1	11	7	♅24♐
19	19.53	29	18	3	12	7	♆6♑
20	19.57	0♒	0♎	5	13	8	♇10♏
21	20.01	1	13	6	14	9	♃21♐
22	20.05	2	26	8	15	9	♄17♐
23	20.09	3	10♏	10	16	10	♅25♐
24	20.13	4	23	12	17	11	♆6♑
25	20.17	5	8♐	13	18	11	♇10♏
26	20.21	6	22	15	19	12	♃22♐
27	20.25	7	7♑	17	20	14	♄18♐
28	20.29	8	23	19	21	14	♅25♐
29	20.33	9	8♒	20	22	14	♆6♑
30	20.37	10	23	22	23	15	♇10♏
31	20.41	11	7♓	24	25	16	♃23♐

Feb	STime	☉	☽	☿	♀	♂	Plnts
1	20.45	12♒	22♓	25♒	26♑	16♐	♃23♐
2	20.49	13	5♈	27	27	17	♄18♐
3	20.53	14	19	29	28	18	♅23♐
4	20.56	15	1♉	0♓	29	19	♆7♑
5	21.00	16	14	2	0♒	19	♇10♏
6	21.04	17	26	3	1	20	♃24♐
7	21.08	18	8♊	5	2	21	♄19♐
8	21.12	19	20	6	3	21	♅23♐
9	21.16	20	2♋	8	5	22	♆7♑
10	21.20	21	14	9	6	23	♇10♏
11	21.24	22	26	11	7	23	♃19♐
12	21.28	23	8♌	11	8	24	♄19♐
13	21.32	24	20	12	9	25	♅25♐
14	21.36	25	2♍	13	10	25	♆7♑
15	21.40	26	14	13	11	26	♇10♏
16	21.44	27	27	14	13	26	♃26♐
17	21.48	28	10♎	14	14	28	♄19♐
18	21.52	29	23	14R	15	28	♅26♐
19	21.56	0♓	6♏	14	17	29	♆7♑
20	22.00	1	20	14	17	0♑	♇10♏
21	22.03	2	4♐	14	18	0	♃28♓
22	22.07	3	18	13	19	1	♄20♐
23	22.11	4	2♑	12	21	2	♅26♐
24	22.15	5	17	11	22	2	♆7♑
25	22.19	6	1♒	10	23	3	♇10♏
26	22.23	7	16	10	24	4	♃29♓
27	22.27	8	1♓	9	25	4	♄20♐
28	22.31	9	15	7	26	4	♅26♐

Mar	STime	☉	☽	☿	♀	♂	Plnts
1	22.35	10♓	29♓	6♓	28♒	6♑	♃29♓
2	22.39	11	13♈	6	29	6	♄20♐
3	22.43	12	26	7	0♓	7	♅26♐
4	22.47	13	9♉	3	1	8	♆7♑
5	22.51	14	22	3	2	9	♇10♏R
6	22.55	15	4♊	3	3	9	♃2♈
7	22.59	16	17	1	5	10	♄20♐
8	23.03	17	28	1	6	11	♅26♐
9	23.07	18	10♋	0	7	11	♆7♑
10	23.11	19	22	0	8	12	♇9♏R
11	23.14	20	4♌	0♓	9	13	♃4♈
12	23.18	21	16	0♈	10	13	♄21♐
13	23.22	22	28	0	12	14	♅26♐
14	23.26	23	11♍	0	13	15	♆7♑
15	23.30	24	23	0	14	15	♇9♏R
16	23.34	25	6♎	0	15	16	♃5♈
17	23.38	26	20	1	16	17	♄21♐
18	23.42	27	3♏	1	18	17	♅26♐
19	23.46	28	17	2	19	18	♆7♑
20	23.50	29	1♐	2	20	19	♇9♏R
21	23.54	0♈	15	3	21	19	♃4♈
22	23.58	1	29	4	22	20	♄21♐
23	0.02	2	13♑	5	24	21	♅26♐
24	0.06	3	27	6	25	21	♆7♑
25	0.10	4	11♒	6	26	22	♇9♏R
26	0.14	5	26	7	27	23	♃5♈
27	0.18	6	10♓	8	29	24	♄21♐
28	0.21	7	24	9	0♈	24	♅26♐
29	0.25	8	8♈	10	1♓	25	♆8♑
30	0.29	9	21	11	2	26	♇9♏R
31	0.33	10	4♉	13	3	26	♃7♈

Apr	STime	☉	☽	☿	♀	♂	Plnts
1	0.37	11♈	17♉	14♈	4♓	27♑	♃7♈
2	0.41	12	0♊	15	5	28	♄21♐
3	0.45	13	12	16	7	28	♅26♐
4	0.49	14	24	18	8	29	♆8♑
5	0.53	15	6♋	19	9	0♒	♇9♏R
6	0.57	16	18	20	10	0	♃8♈
7	1.01	17	0♌	22	11	1	♄21♐
8	1.05	18	12	23	13	2	♅26♐
9	1.09	19	24	25	14	2	♆8♑
10	1.13	20	6♍	26	15	3	♇9♏
11	1.17	21	19	28	16	4	♃21♐
12	1.21	22	2♎	29	17	4	♄21♐
13	1.25	23	15	1♈	19	5	♅26♐
14	1.29	24	29	2	20	6	♆8♑
15	1.32	25	13♏	4	21	6	♇9♏R
16	1.36	26	27	6	22	7	♃10♈
17	1.40	27	11♐	7	23	8	♄21♐
18	1.44	28	25	9	25	8	♅26♐
19	1.48	29	10♑	11	26	9	♆9♑
20	1.52	0♉	24	12	27	10	♇9♏R
21	1.56	1	8♒	14	28	10	♃12♈
22	2.00	2	22	16	29	11	♄20♐
23	2.04	3	6♓	18	1♈	12	♅26♐
24	2.08	4	20	20	2	12	♆8♑
25	2.12	5	3♈	22	3	13	♇8♏R
26	2.16	6	17	23	4	14	♃13♈
27	2.20	7	0♉	25	5	14	♄20♐
28	2.24	8	13	27	6	15	♅26♐
29	2.28	9	25	29	8	16	♆8♑R
30	2.32	9	8♊	1♉	9	16	♇8♏R

May	STime	☉	☽	☿	♀	♂	Plnts
1	2.36	10♉	20♊	3♉	10♈	17♒	♃14♈
2	2.39	11	2♋	6	12	18	♄20♐R
3	2.43	12	14	8	13	19	♅26♐
4	2.47	13	26	10	14	19	♆8♑R
5	2.51	14	8♌	12	15	19	♇8♏R
6	2.55	15	20	14	16	20	♃15♈
7	2.59	16	2♍	16	17	20	♄20♐R
8	3.03	17	14	19	18	20	♅26♐
9	3.07	18	27	21	20	20	♆7♑R
10	3.11	19	10♎	23	21	23	♇8♏R
11	3.15	20	23	25	22	23	♃17♈
12	3.19	21	7♏	27	24	24	♄19♐R
13	3.23	22	21	0♊	25	25	♅26♐R
14	3.27	23	6♐	1	26	26	♆8♑R
15	3.31	24	21	3	27	27	♇8♏R
16	3.35	25	6♑	5	28	27	♃19♈
17	3.39	26	20	8	0♉	0♉	♄19♐R
18	3.43	27	5♒	10	1	1	♅26♐R
19	3.47	28	19	11	3	2	♆8♑R
20	3.50	29	3♓	13	4	3	♇8♏R
21	3.54	0♊	17	15	5	5	♃21♈
22	3.58	1	0♈	17	6	1	♄19♐R
23	4.02	2	13	19	7	1	♅25♐R
24	4.06	3	26	21	8	2	♆8♑R
25	4.10	4	9♉	23	9	3	♇8♏R
26	4.14	4	21	24	11	3	♃19♈
27	4.18	5	4♊	26	12	4	♄18♐R
28	4.22	6	16	27	13	4	♅25♐R
29	4.26	7	28	29	14	5	♆7♑R
30	4.30	8	10♋	0♋	15	6	♇8♏R
31	4.34	9	22	2	17	6	♃20♈

Jun	STime	☉	☽	☿	♀	♂	Plnts
1	4.38	10♊	4♋	3♋	18♉	7♉	♃21♈
2	4.42	11	16	4	19	8	♄18♐R
3	4.46	12	28	5	20	9	♅25♐R
4	4.50	13	10♍	7	22	9	♆7♑R
5	4.54	14	22	8	23	10	♇7♏R
6	4.57	15	5♎	9	24	11	♃22♈
7	5.01	16	18	10	25	11	♄18♐R
8	5.05	17	1♏	11	26	12	♅25♐R
9	5.09	18	15	11	28	13	♆7♑R
10	5.13	19	0♐	12	29	13	♇7♏R
11	5.17	20	15	13	0♊	14	♃22♈
12	5.21	21	0♑	14	1	15	♄17♐R
13	5.25	22	15	14	2	15	♅25♐R
14	5.29	23	0♒	14	5	16	♆7♑R
15	5.33	24	15	15	5	16	♇7♏R
16	5.37	25	29	15R	6	17	♃23♈
17	5.41	26	13♓	16	7	17	♄17♐R
18	5.45	26	27	16	9	18	♅24♐R
19	5.49	27	10♈	16	10	19	♆7♑R
20	5.53	28	23	17	11	19	♇7♏R
21	5.57	29	6♉	17R	12	20	♃24♈
22	6.01	0♋	18	16	13	20	♄17♐R
23	6.04	1	1♊	16	15	21	♅24♐R
24	6.08	2	13	16	16	22	♆7♑R
25	6.12	3	25	15	18	23	♇7♏R
26	6.16	4	7♋	15	18	23	♃25♈
27	6.20	5	19	15	20	24	♄16♐R
28	6.24	6	1♌	15	21	24	♅24♐R
29	6.28	7	13	14	22	25	♆6♑R
30	6.32	8	24	14	23	26	♇7♏R

Jul	STime	☉	☽	☿	♀	♂	Plnts
1	6.36	9♋	6♍	13♋	24♊	26♉	♃26♈
2	6.40	10	18	12	26	27	♄16♐R
3	6.44	11	1♎	11	27	28	♅24♐R
4	6.48	12	13	11	28	29	♆6♑R
5	6.52	13	26	11	29	29	♇7♏R
6	6.56	14	10♏	10♋	1♋	0♊	♃26♈
7	7.00	15	24	9	2	0	♄16♐R
8	7.04	16	8♐	9	3	1	♅24♐R
9	7.08	16	23	8	4	1	♆6♑R
10	7.12	17	8♑	8	5	2	♇7♏
11	7.15	18	23	8	7	3	♄15♐R
12	7.19	19	9♒	7	8	3	♅23♐R
13	7.23	20	24	7	9	4	♃28♈
14	7.27	21	8♓	7	10	5	♄15♐R
15	7.31	22	23	7D	11	5	♅23♐R
16	7.35	23	7♈	7	13	6	♃28♈
17	7.39	24	20	7	14	7	♄15♐R
18	7.43	24	3♉	8	15	7	♅23♐R
19	7.47	26	16	8	16	8	♆6♑R
20	7.51	27	28	8	18	8	♇7♏
21	7.55	28	10♊	9	19	9	♃28♈
22	7.59	29	22	9	20	10	♄15♐R
23	8.03	0♌	4♋	10	21	11	♅23♐R
24	8.07	1	16	11	23	11	♆6♑R
25	8.11	2	28	12	24	12	♇7♏
26	8.15	3	10♌	13	26	13	♃28♈
27	8.19	4	22	14	26	13	♄15♐R
28	8.22	5	3♍	15	28	14	♅23♐R
29	8.26	6	16	16	0♌	14	♆6♑R
30	8.30	7	28	18	0	15	♇7♏
31	8.34	7	10♎	19	1	16	♃29♈

Aug	STime	☉	☽	☿	♀	♂	Plnts
1	8.38	8♌	23♎	21♋	2♌	16♊	♃29♈
2	8.42	9	6♏	22	4	17	♄14♐R
3	8.46	10	19	24	5	17	♅22♐R
4	8.50	11	3♐	25	6	18	♆5♑R
5	8.54	12	17	27	7	19	♇7♏
6	8.58	13	2♑	29	9	20	♃29♈
7	9.02	14	17	1♌	10	20	♄14♐R
8	9.06	15	2♒	3	11	21	♅22♐R
9	9.10	16	17	4	13	22	♆5♑R
10	9.14	17	2♓	7	14	22	♇7♏
11	9.18	18	17	9	15	23	♃29♈
12	9.22	19	1♈	11	16	23	♄14♐R
13	9.26	20	15	13	17	24	♅22♐R
14	9.30	21	29	15	19	24	♆5♑R
15	9.33	22	12♉	17	21	25	♇7♏
16	9.37	23	25	19	21	26	♃29♈
17	9.41	24	7♊	21	23	27	♄14♐R
18	9.45	25	19	23	23	27	♄22♐R
19	9.49	26	1♋	25	25	28	♆5♑R
20	9.53	27	13	27	26	28	♇7♏
21	9.57	28	25	29	28	29	♃29♈R
22	10.01	29	7♌	1♍	29	29	♄14♐R
23	10.05	0♍	19	3	0♍	0♍	♅22♐R
24	10.09	1	1♍	5	1	0	♆5♑R
25	10.13	1	13	7	2	1	♇7♏
26	10.17	2	25	9	3	2	♃29♈R
27	10.21	3	7♎	10	5	2	♄14♐
28	10.25	4	20	12	6	3	♅22♐
29	10.29	5	2♏	14	7	4	♆5♑R
30	10.33	6	16	16	8	5	♇7♏
31	10.37	7	29	18	10	5	♃29♈R

Sep	STime	☉	☽	☿	♀	♂	Plnts
1	10.40	8♍	13♏	19♍	11♍	6♍	♃29♈R
2	10.44	9	27	21	12	6	♄14♐
3	10.48	10	11♐	23	13	7	♅22♐
4	10.52	11	26	25	14	8	♆5♑R
5	10.56	12	11♑	26	16	8	♇7♏
6	11.00	13	26	28	17	9	♃29♈R
7	11.04	14	10♓	0♎	18	10	♄15♐
8	11.08	15	25	1	19	10	♅22♐
9	11.12	16	9♈	3	21	11	♆5♑R
10	11.16	17	23	4	22	12	♇7♏
11	11.20	18	7♉	6	23	12	♃29♈R
12	11.24	19	20	7	24	13	♄15♐
13	11.28	20	3♊	9	26	14	♅22♐
14	11.32	21	15	10	27	14	♆5♑
15	11.36	22	27	12	28	15	♇8♏
16	11.40	23	9♋	13	0♎	15	♃28♈R
17	11.44	24	21	15	1♎	16	♄15♐
18	11.48	25	3♌	16	3	17	♅23♐
19	11.51	26	15	18	4	18	♆5♑
20	11.55	27	27	19	4	18	♇8♏
21	11.59	28	9♍	20	5	19	♃28♈R
22	12.03	29	21	22	7	19	♄15♐
23	12.07	0♎	4♎	23	9	20	♅23♐
24	12.11	1	16	24	10	21	♆5♑
25	12.15	2	28	25	11	22	♇8♏
26	12.19	3	13♍	27	13	22	♃27♈R
27	12.23	4	24	29	14	23	♄16♐
28	12.27	5	9♏	29	15	24	♅23♐
29	12.31	6	23	0♎	16	24	♆5♑
30	12.35	7	7♐	2	17	25	♇8♏

Oct	STime	☉	☽	☿	♀	♂	Plnts
1	12.39	7♎	21♐	3♎	18♎	25♍	♃27♈R
2	12.43	8	6♑	4	19	26	♄16♐
3	12.47	9	20	5	21	27	♅23♐
4	12.51	10	5♒	6	22	27	♆5♑
5	12.55	11	19	7	23	28	♇8♏
6	12.58	12	4♓	8	24	29	♄16♐
7	13.02	13	18	9	26	29	♅24♐
8	13.06	14	1♈	9	27	0♎	♅23♐
9	13.10	15	15	10	29	1	♆9♑...
10	13.14	16	28	11	29	1	♇9♏
11	13.18	17	11♊	11	0♏	2	♃25♈R
12	13.22	18	23	12	2	3	♄16♐
13	13.26	19	5♋	12	3	3	♅23♐
14	13.30	20	18	13	4	4	♆9♑
15	13.34	21	29	13	5	4	♇9♏
16	13.38	22	11♌	13R	7	5	♃25♈R
17	13.42	23	23	13	8	5	♄17♐
18	13.46	24	5♍	13	9	6	♅23♐
19	13.50	26	17	12	12	7	♆9♑
20	13.54	26	0♎	12	12	7	♇9♏
21	13.58	27	12	11	13	8	♃24♈R
22	14.02	28	25	10	15	9	♄17♐
23	14.05	29	9♏	10	15	9	♅24♐
24	14.09	0♏	22	9	17	10	♆5♑
25	14.13	1	6♐	8	19	11	♇9♏
26	14.17	2	20	6	19	11	♃23♈R
27	14.21	3	4♑	6	21	12	♄18♐
28	14.25	4	18	5	22	12	♅24♐
29	14.29	5	2♒	3	23	13	♆5♑
30	14.33	6	17	1	24	14	♇9♏
31	14.37	7	1♓	1	25	14	♃23♈R

Nov	STime	☉	☽	☿	♀	♂	Plnts
1	14.41	8♏	15♓	29♎	27♏	15♎	♃23♈R
2	14.45	9	29	29	28	16	♄18♐
3	14.49	10	13♈	29	29	16	♅24♐
4	14.53	11	26	27	0♏	17	♆6♑
5	14.57	12	10♉	27	2	18	♇10♏
6	15.01	13	23	27D	3	18	♃22♈R
7	15.05	14	6♊	27	4	19	♄19♐
8	15.09	15	19	28	5	20	♄24♐
9	15.13	16	1♋	28	7	20	♆6♑
10	15.16	17	13	29	8	21	♇10♏
11	15.20	18	25	1♏	9	22	♃22♈R
12	15.24	19	7♌	2	10	22	♄19♐
13	15.28	20	19	3	12	23	♅25♐
14	15.32	21	1♍	5	13	24	♆6♑
15	15.36	22	13	6	14	24	♇10♏
16	15.40	23	25	8	15	25	♃21♈R
17	15.44	24	7♎	10	16	25	♄20♐
18	15.48	25	20	11	18	26	♅25♐
19	15.52	26	2♏	13	19	26	♆6♑
20	15.56	27	15	14	20	27	♇10♏
21	16.00	28	1♐	16	22	28	♃20♈R
22	16.04	29	16	18	23	29	♄21♐
23	16.08	0♐	1♑	19	24	29	♅25♐
24	16.12	1	14	21	25	0♏	♆6♑
25	16.16	2	28	22	27	1	♇10♏
26	16.20	3	13♒	19	28	1	♃20♈R
27	16.23	4	28	22	29	2	♄21♐
28	16.27	5	12♓	25	0♐	3	♅25♐
29	16.31	6	25	23	1	3	♆6♑
30	16.35	7	9♈	25	2	4	♇11♏

Dec	STime	☉	☽	☿	♀	♂	Plnts
1	16.39	8♐	22♈	27♏	4♐	4♏	♃20♈R
2	16.43	9	6♉	28	5	5	♄22♐
3	16.47	10	19	0♐	6	6	♅26♐
4	16.51	12	2♊	1	8	6	♆6♑
5	16.55	13	14	3	9	7	♇11♏
6	16.59	14	27	4	11	8	♃20♈R
7	17.03	15	9♋	6	11	8	♄22♐
8	17.07	16	21	7	12	9	♅26♐
9	17.11	17	3♌	9	14	10	♆7♑
10	17.15	18	15	11	15	10	♇11♏
11	17.19	19	27	12	16	11	♃19♈R
12	17.23	20	9♍	14	18	12	♄23♐
13	17.27	21	21	15	19	12	♅26♐
14	17.31	23	3♎	17	21	13	♆7♑
15	17.34	24	15	18	21	14	♇11♏
16	17.38	25	28	20	23	14	♃19♈R
17	17.42	26	11♏	21	24	15	♄23♐
18	17.46	27	25	23	25	15	♅27♐
19	17.50	28	9♐	24	26	16	♆7♑
20	17.54	29	24	26	28	17	♇11♏
21	17.58	0♑	9♑	28	29	18	♃20♈R
22	18.02	0	24	29	0♑	0♑	♄24♐
23	18.06	1	9♒	1♑	1♒	19	♅27♐
24	18.10	2	23	2	2	20	♆7♑
25	18.14	3	8♓	4	4	20	♇11♏
26	18.18	4	22	6	6	21	♃20♈R
27	18.22	5	6♈	7	6	22	♄25♐
28	18.26	6	19	9	8	22	♅27♐
29	18.30	7	3♉	10	9	23	♆7♑
30	18.34	8	16	12	10	24	♇11♏
31	18.38	9	28	13	11	24	♃20♈

Jan	STime	☉	☽	☿	♀	♂	Plnts
1	18.41	10♑	11♊	15♑	12♒	25♏	♃20♈
2	18.45	11	23	17	14	26	♄25♐
3	18.49	12	6♋	19	15	26	♅28♐
4	18.53	13	18	20	16	27	♆ 8♑
5	18.57	14	0♌	22	17	28	♇12♏
6	19.01	15	12	24	18	28	♃20♈
7	19.05	16	24	25	20	29	♄26♐
8	19.09	17	5♍	27	21	0♐	♅28♐
9	19.13	18	17	28	22	0	♆ 8♑
10	19.17	19	29	0♒	23	1	♇12♏
11	19.21	20	11♎	2	25	2	♃21♈
12	19.25	21	24	3	26	2	♄26♐
13	19.29	22	6♏	5	27	3	♅28♐
14	19.33	23	20	7	28	4	♆ 8♑
15	19.37	24	3♐	8	29	4	♇12♏
16	19.41	25	17	10	1♓	5	♃21♈
17	19.45	26	2♑	12	2	6	♄27♐
18	19.48	27	17	13	3	6	♅28♐
19	19.52	28	2♒	15	4	7	♆ 8♑
20	19.56	29	17	16	6	8	♇12♏
21	20.00	0♒	3♓	18	7	8	♃22♈
22	20.04	1	17	19	8	9	♄28♐
23	20.08	2	2♈	20	9	10	♅29♐
24	20.12	3	16	22	10	10	♆ 8♑
25	20.16	4	29	23	12	11	♇12♏
26	20.20	5	13♉	24	13	12	♃22♈
27	20.24	6	25	25	14	12	♄28♐
28	20.28	7	8♊	26	15	13	♅29♐
29	20.32	8	20	27	16	14	♆ 9♑
30	20.36	10	3♋	27	18	14	♇12♏
31	20.40	11	15	27	19	15	♃23♈

Feb	STime	☉	☽	☿	♀	♂	Plnts
1	20.44	12♒	27♋	28♒	20♓	16♐	♃23♈
2	20.48	13	9♌	28R	21	16	♄29♐
3	20.52	14	20	28	22	17	♅29♐
4	20.56	15	2♍	27	24	18	♆ 9♑
5	20.59	16	14	27	25	18	♇12♏
6	21.03	17	26	26	26	19	♃24♈
7	21.07	18	8♎	25	27	20	♄29♐
8	21.11	19	20	24	28	20	♅29♐
9	21.15	20	2♏	23	0♈	21	♆ 9♑
10	21.19	21	15	22	1	22	♇12♏
11	21.23	22	28	21	2	22	♃25♈
12	21.27	23	12♐	20	3	23	♄ 0♑
13	21.31	24	26	19	4	24	♅ 0♑
14	21.35	25	10♑	18	6	24	♆ 9♑
15	21.39	26	25	17	7	25	♇12♏
16	21.43	27	10♒	16	8	26	♃26♈
17	21.47	28	25	15	9	26	♄ 0♑
18	21.51	29	11♓	14	10	27	♅ 0♑
19	21.55	0♓	26	13	11	28	♆ 9♑
20	21.59	1	10♈	13	13	28	♇12♏
21	22.03	2	25	13	14	29	♃27♈
22	22.06	3	8♉	12	15	0♑	♄ 0♑
23	22.10	4	22	12D	16	0	♅ 0♑
24	22.14	5	5♊	12	17	1	♆ 9♑
25	22.18	6	17	13	18	2	♇12♏R
26	22.22	7	0♋	13	20	2	♃27♈
27	22.26	8	12	13	21	3	♄ 1♑
28	22.30	9	24	14	22	4	♅ 0♑
29	22.34	10	6♌	14	23	4	♆ 9♑

Mar	STime	☉	☽	☿	♀	♂	Plnts
1	22.38	11♓	17♌	15♒	24♈	5♑	♃28♈
2	22.42	12	29	15	25	6	♄ 1♑
3	22.46	13	11♍	16	26	6	♅ 0♑
4	22.50	14	23	17	28	7	♆ 9♑
5	22.54	15	5♎	18	29	8	♇12♏R
6	22.58	16	17	19	0♉	9	♃29♈
7	23.02	17	29	19	1	9	♄ 1♑
8	23.06	18	12♏	20	2	10	♅ 0♑
9	23.10	19	25	22	3	11	♆10♑
10	23.14	20	8♐	23	4	11	♇12♏R
11	23.17	21	21	24	5	12	♃ 0♉
12	23.21	22	5♑	25	6	13	♄ 2♑
13	23.25	23	19	26	8	13	♅ 1♑
14	23.29	24	4♒	27	9	14	♆10♑
15	23.33	25	19	29	10	15	♇12♏R
16	23.37	26	4♓	0♓	11	15	♃ 1♉
17	23.41	27	19	1	12	16	♄ 2♑
18	23.45	28	4♈	2	13	17	♅ 1♑
19	23.49	29	18	4	14	17	♆10♑
20	23.53	0♈	3♉	5	15	18	♇12♏R
21	23.57	1	17	7	16	19	♃ 2♉
22	0.01	2	0♊	8	17	19	♄ 2♑
23	0.05	3	13	10	18	20	♅ 1♑
24	0.09	4	26	11	19	21	♆10♑
25	0.13	5	8♋	13	20	21	♇12♏R
26	0.17	6	20	14	21	22	♃ 4♉
27	0.21	7	2♌	16	22	23	♄ 2♑
28	0.24	8	14	17	23	23	♅ 1♑
29	0.28	9	26	19	24	24	♆10♑
30	0.32	10	8♍	20	26	25	♇12♏R
31	0.36	11	20	22	27	25	♃ 5♉

Apr	STime	☉	☽	☿	♀	♂	Plnts
1	0.40	12♈	2♎	24♓	28♉	26♑	♃ 5♉
2	0.44	13	14	25	28	27	♄ 2♑
3	0.48	14	26	27	29	27	♅ 1♑
4	0.52	15	9♏	29	0♊	28	♆10♑
5	0.56	16	22	1♈	1	29	♇12♏R
6	1.00	17	5♐	3	2	29	♃ 6♉
7	1.04	18	18	4	3	0♒	♄ 2♑
8	1.08	19	2♑	6	4	1	♅ 1♑
9	1.12	20	16	8	5	1	♆10♑
10	1.16	21	0♒	10	6	2	♇11♏R
11	1.20	22	14	12	7	3	♃ 7♉
12	1.24	22	28	14	8	3	♄ 2♑R
13	1.28	23	13♓	16	9	4	♅ 1♑
14	1.31	24	27	18	10	5	♆10♑
15	1.35	25	12♈	20	11	5	♇11♏R
16	1.39	26	26	22	12	6	♃ 8♉
17	1.43	27	11♉	24	12	7	♄ 2♑R
18	1.47	28	24	26	13	7	♅ 1♑R
19	1.51	29	8♊	28	14	8	♆10♑R
20	1.55	0♉	21	0♉	15	9	♇11♏R
21	1.59	1	4♋	2	16	9	♃10♉
22	2.03	2	16	4	16	10	♄ 2♑R
23	2.07	3	28	7	17	11	♅ 1♑R
24	2.11	4	10♌	9	18	11	♆10♑R
25	2.15	5	22	11	19	12	♇11♏R
26	2.19	6	4♍	13	19	13	♃11♉
27	2.23	7	16	15	20	13	♄ 2♑R
28	2.27	8	28	17	21	14	♅ 1♑R
29	2.31	9	10♎	19	22	15	♆10♑R
30	2.35	10	22	21	22	15	♇11♏R

May	STime	☉	☽	☿	♀	♂	Plnts
1	2.39	11♉	5♏	23♉	23♊	16♒	♃12♉
2	2.42	12	18	25	23	17	♄ 2♑R
3	2.46	13	1♐	27	24	17	♅ 0♑R
4	2.50	14	15	29	25	18	♆10♑R
5	2.54	15	29	1♊	25	19	♇11♏R
6	2.58	16	12♑	3	26	19	♃13♉
7	3.02	17	26	4	26	20	♄ 2♑R
8	3.06	18	10♒	6	27	21	♅ 0♑R
9	3.10	19	25	8	27	21	♆10♑R
10	3.14	20	9♓	9	28	22	♇11♏R
11	3.18	21	23	11	28	23	♃14♉
12	3.22	22	7♈	12	28	23	♄ 1♑R
13	3.26	23	21	14	29	24	♅ 0♑R
14	3.30	24	5♉	15	29	25	♆10♑R
15	3.34	25	19	16	29	25	♇11♏R
16	3.38	26	3♊	17	29	26	♃16♉
17	3.42	26	16	19	0♋	27	♄ 1♑R
18	3.46	27	29	20	0	27	♅ 0♑R
19	3.49	28	12♋	21	0	28	♆10♑R
20	3.53	29	24	21	0	29	♇10♏R
21	3.57	0♊	6♌	22	0	29	♃17♉
22	4.01	1	18	23	0R	0♓	♄ 1♑R
23	4.05	2	0♍	24	0	0	♅ 0♑R
24	4.09	3	12	24	0	1	♆ 9♑R
25	4.13	4	24	25	0	2	♇10♏R
26	4.17	5	6♎	25	0	2	♃18♉
27	4.21	6	18	26	0	3	♄ 1♑R
28	4.25	7	1♏	26	29♊	4	♅ 0♑R
29	4.29	8	14	26	29	4	♆ 9♑R
30	4.33	9	27	26	29	5	♇10♏R
31	4.37	10	11♐	26	29	5	♃19♉

Jun	STime	☉	☽	☿	♀	♂	Plnts
1	4.41	11♊	24♐	26♊	28♊	6♓	♃19♉
2	4.45	12	9♑	26	28	7	♄ 0♑R
3	4.49	13	23	26	27	7	♅29♐R
4	4.53	14	7♒	26	27	8	♆ 9♑R
5	4.57	15	21	26	26	9	♇10♏R
6	5.00	16	6♓	25	26	9	♃20♉
7	5.04	17	20	25	25	10	♄ 0♑R
8	5.08	18	4♈	25	25	10	♅29♐R
9	5.12	19	18	24	24	11	♆ 9♑R
10	5.16	20	1♉	24	23	12	♇10♏R
11	5.20	20	15	23	23	12	♃22♉
12	5.24	21	28	22	22	13	♄ 0♑R
13	5.28	22	12♊	22	22	13	♅29♐R
14	5.32	23	25	21	21	14	♆ 9♑R
15	5.36	24	7♋	21	20	15	♇10♏R
16	5.40	25	20	20	20	15	♃23♉
17	5.44	26	2♌	20	19	16	♄29♐R
18	5.48	27	14	19	19	16	♅29♐R
19	5.52	28	26	19	18	17	♆ 9♑R
20	5.56	29	8♍	19	17	18	♇10♏R
21	6.00	0♋	20	18	17	18	♃24♉
22	6.04	1	2♎	18	16	19	♄29♐R
23	6.07	2	14	18	16	19	♅29♐R
24	6.11	3	26	18D	16	20	♆ 9♑R
25	6.15	4	9♏	18	15	20	♇10♏R
26	6.19	5	22	18	15	21	♃25♉
27	6.23	6	5♐	18	15	21	♄28♐R
28	6.27	7	19	18	14	22	♅28♐R
29	6.31	8	3♑	19	14	23	♆ 9♑R
30	6.35	9	18	19	14	23	♇10♏R

Jul	STime	☉	☽	☿	♀	♂	Plnts
1	6.39	10♋	2♒	20♊	14♊	24♓	♃26♉
2	6.43	11	17	20	14	24	♄28♐R
3	6.47	11	2♓	21	14	25	♅28♐R
4	6.51	12	16	22	14D	25	♆ 8♑R
5	6.55	13	0♈	22	14	26	♇10♏R
6	6.59	14	15	23	14	26	♃27♉
7	7.03	15	28	24	14	27	♄28♐R
8	7.07	16	12♉	25	14	27	♅28♐R
9	7.11	17	25	26	14	28	♆ 8♑R
10	7.15	18	8♊	27	14	28	♇ 9♏
11	7.18	19	21	29	15	29	♃28♉
12	7.22	20	4♋	0♋	15	29	♄27♐R
13	7.26	21	16	1	15	0♈	♅28♐R
14	7.30	22	29	3	15	0	♆ 8♑R
15	7.34	23	11♌	4	16	0	♇ 9♏
16	7.38	24	23	6	16	1	♃29♉
17	7.42	25	4♍	8	17	1	♄27♐R
18	7.46	26	16	9	17	2	♅28♐R
19	7.50	27	28	11	17	2	♆ 8♑R
20	7.54	28	10♎	13	18	3	♇ 9♏
21	7.58	29	22	15	18	3	♃ 0♊
22	8.02	0♌	4♏	17	19	3	♄27♐R
23	8.06	1	17	19	20	4	♅27♐R
24	8.10	1	0♐	21	20	4	♆ 8♑R
25	8.14	2	13	23	21	5	♇ 9♏
26	8.18	3	27	25	21	5	♃ 0♊
27	8.22	4	12♑	27	22	5	♄27♐R
28	8.25	5	26	29	23	6	♅27♐R
29	8.29	6	11♒	1♌	23	6	♆ 8♑R
30	8.33	7	26	3	24	6	♇10♏
31	8.37	8	11♓	5	25	7	♃ 1♊

Aug	STime	☉	☽	☿	♀	♂	Plnts
1	8.41	9♌	26♓	7♌	25♊	7♈	♃ 1♊
2	8.45	10	11♈	9	26	7	♄26♐R
3	8.49	11	25	11	27	8	♅27♐R
4	8.53	12	9♉	14	28	8	♆ 8♑R
5	8.57	13	22	16	29	8	♇10♏
6	9.01	14	5♊	18	29	8	♃ 2♊
7	9.05	15	18	20	0♋	9	♄26♐R
8	9.09	16	1♋	22	1	9	♅27♐R
9	9.13	17	13	24	2	9	♆ 8♑R
10	9.17	18	25	25	3	9	♇10♏
11	9.21	19	8♌	27	3	10	♃ 3♊
12	9.25	20	19	29	4	10	♄26♐R
13	9.29	21	1♍	1♍	5	10	♅27♐R
14	9.33	22	13	3	6	10	♆ 7♑R
15	9.36	23	25	5	7	10	♇10♏
16	9.40	24	7♎	7	8	10	♃ 3♊
17	9.44	24	19	8	9	11	♄26♐R
18	9.48	25	1♏	10	10	11	♅27♐R
19	9.52	26	13	12	11	11	♆ 7♑R
20	9.56	27	25	14	12	11	♇10♏
21	10.00	28	8♐	15	13	11	♃ 4♊
22	10.04	29	22	17	14	11	♄26♐R
23	10.08	0♍	6♑	18	15	11	♅27♐R
24	10.12	1	20	20	15	11	♆ 7♑R
25	10.16	2	5♒	22	16	11	♇10♏
26	10.20	3	20	23	17	11R	♃ 4♊
27	10.24	4	5♓	25	18	11	♄26♐
28	10.28	5	20	26	19	11	♅27♐R
29	10.32	6	5♈	28	20	11	♆ 7♑R
30	10.36	7	20	29	21	11	♇10♏
31	10.40	8	4♉	1♎	22	11	♃ 5♊

Sep	STime	☉	☽	☿	♀	♂	Plnts
1	10.43	9♍	18♉	2♎	23♋	11♈	♃ 5♊
2	10.47	10	2♊	3	25	11	♄26♐
3	10.51	11	15	5	26	11	♅27♐
4	10.55	12	28	6	27	11	♆ 7♑R
5	10.59	13	10♋	7	28	11	♇10♏
6	11.03	14	23	9	29	10	♃ 5♊
7	11.07	15	5♌	10	0♌	10	♄26♐
8	11.11	16	17	11	1	10	♅27♐
9	11.15	17	28	13	2	10	♆ 7♑R
10	11.19	18	10♍	14	3	10	♇10♏
11	11.23	19	22	15	4	9	♃ 6♊
12	11.27	20	4♎	16	5	9	♄26♐
13	11.31	21	16	17	6	9	♅27♐
14	11.35	22	28	18	7	9	♆ 7♑R
15	11.39	23	10♏	19	8	9	♇10♏
16	11.43	24	22	20	9	8	♃ 6♊
17	11.47	25	5♐	21	11	8	♄26♐
18	11.50	25	18	22	12	8	♅27♐
19	11.54	26	1♑	23	13	7	♆ 7♑
20	11.58	27	15	23	14	7	♇11♏
21	12.02	28	29	24	15	7	♃ 6♊
22	12.06	29	13♒	25	16	7	♄26♐
23	12.10	0♎	28	25	17	6	♅27♐
24	12.14	1	13♓	26	18	6	♆ 7♑
25	12.18	2	28	26	19	6	♇11♏
26	12.22	3	13♈	26	21	5	♃ 6♊R
27	12.26	4	28	27	22	5	♄26♐
28	12.30	5	13♉	27R	23	5	♅27♐
29	12.34	6	27	27	24	5	♆ 7♑
30	12.38	7	11♊	27	25	4	♇11♏

Oct	STime	☉	☽	☿	♀	♂	Plnts
1	12.42	8♎	24♊	26♎	26♌	4♈	♃ 6♊R
2	12.46	9	7♋	26	27	4	♄26♐
3	12.50	10	19	25	29	3	♅27♐
4	12.54	11	1♌	25	0♍	3	♆ 7♑
5	12.58	12	13	24	1	3	♇11♏
6	13.01	13	25	23	2	3	♃ 6♊R
7	13.05	14	7♍	22	3	2	♄27♐
8	13.09	15	19	21	4	2	♅27♐
9	13.13	16	1♎	20	5	2	♆ 7♑
10	13.17	17	13	19	7	2	♇11♏
11	13.21	18	25	18	8	1	♃ 5♊R
12	13.25	19	7♏	16	9	1	♄27♐
13	13.29	20	19	15	10	1	♅27♐
14	13.33	21	2♐	14	11	1	♆ 7♑
15	13.37	22	15	13	12	1	♇11♏
16	13.41	23	28	13	14	1	♃ 5♊R
17	13.45	24	11♑	12	15	0	♄27♐
18	13.49	25	24	12	16	0	♅28♐
19	13.53	26	8♒	11	17	0	♆ 7♑
20	13.57	27	22	11D	18	0	♇12♏
21	14.01	28	7♓	12	20	0	♃ 5♊R
22	14.05	29	22	12	21	0	♄28♐
23	14.08	0♏	7♈	12	22	0	♅28♐
24	14.12	1	21	13	23	0	♆ 7♑
25	14.16	2	6♉	14	24	0	♇12♏
26	14.20	3	21	15	26	0	♃ 4♊R
27	14.24	4	5♊	16	27	0D	♄28♐
28	14.28	5	19	17	28	0	♅28♐
29	14.32	6	2♋	18	29	0	♆ 8♑
30	14.36	7	15	19	0♎	0	♇12♏
31	14.40	8	28	21	2	0	♃ 4♊R

Nov	STime	☉	☽	☿	♀	♂	Plnts
1	14.44	9♏	10♌	22♎	3♎	0♈	♃ 4♊R
2	14.48	10	22	23	4	0	♄29♐
3	14.52	11	4♍	25	5	0	♅28♐
4	14.56	12	15	26	6	0	♆ 8♑
5	15.00	13	27	28	8	0	♇12♏
6	15.04	14	9♎	0♏	9	0	♃ 3♊R
7	15.08	15	21	1	10	0	♄29♐
8	15.12	16	3♏	3	11	0	♅28♐
9	15.16	17	16	4	12	1	♆ 8♑
10	15.19	18	29	6	14	1	♇12♏
11	15.23	19	12♐	7	15	1	♃ 2♊R
12	15.27	20	25	9	16	1	♄ 0♑
13	15.31	21	8♑	11	17	1	♅29♐
14	15.35	22	21	12	19	1	♆ 8♑
15	15.39	23	5♒	14	20	2	♇13♏
16	15.43	24	19	15	21	2	♃ 2♊R
17	15.47	25	3♓	17	22	2	♄ 0♑
18	15.51	26	17	19	23	2	♅29♐
19	15.55	27	1♈	20	25	3	♆ 8♑
20	15.59	28	16	22	26	3	♇13♏
21	16.03	29	0♉	23	27	3	♃ 1♊R
22	16.07	0♐	15	25	28	3	♄ 1♑
23	16.11	1	29	27	0♏	4	♅29♐
24	16.15	2	13♊	28	1	4	♆ 8♑
25	16.19	3	27	0♐	2	4	♇13♏
26	16.23	4	10♋	1	3	5	♃ 0♊R
27	16.26	5	23	3	5	5	♄ 1♑
28	16.30	6	5♌	5	6	5	♅29♐
29	16.34	7	18	6	7	6	♆ 8♑
30	16.38	8	0♍	8	8	6	♇13♏

Dec	STime	☉	☽	☿	♀	♂	Plnts
1	16.42	9♐	12♍	9♐	10♏	6♈	♃ 0♊R
2	16.46	10	23	11	11	7	♄ 2♑
3	16.50	11	5♎	12	12	7	♅ 0♑
4	16.54	12	17	14	13	8	♆ 9♑
5	16.58	13	29	16	14	8	♇13♏
6	17.02	14	12♏	17	16	8	♃29♉R
7	17.06	15	24	19	17	9	♄ 2♑
8	17.10	16	7♐	20	18	9	♅ 0♑
9	17.14	17	21	22	19	9	♆ 9♑
10	17.18	18	4♑	23	21	10	♇14♏
11	17.22	19	18	25	22	10	♃28♉R
12	17.26	20	2♒	27	23	11	♄ 3♑
13	17.30	21	16	28	24	11	♅ 0♑
14	17.33	22	0♓	0♑	26	12	♆ 9♑
15	17.37	23	14	1	27	12	♇14♏
16	17.41	24	28	3	28	12	♃28♉R
17	17.45	25	12♈	4	29	13	♄ 4♑
18	17.49	26	26	6	1♐	13	♅ 1♑
19	17.53	28	10♉	8	2	14	♆ 9♑
20	17.57	29	24	9	3	14	♇14♏
21	18.01	0♑	8♊	11	4	15	♃27♉R
22	18.05	1	22	12	6	15	♄ 4♑
23	18.09	2	5♋	14	7	16	♅ 1♑
24	18.13	3	18	15	8	16	♆ 9♑
25	18.17	4	1♌	17	9	17	♇14♏
26	18.21	5	13	19	11	17	♃27♉R
27	18.25	6	25	20	12	18	♄ 5♑
28	18.29	7	7♍	22	13	18	♅ 1♑
29	18.33	8	19	23	14	19	♆10♑
30	18.37	9	1♎	25	16	19	♇14♏
31	18.41	10	13	26	17	20	♃26♉R

1 9 8 9

Jan	STime	☉	☽	☿	♀	♂	Plnts
1	18.44	11♑	25♎	28♑	18♐	20♈	♃26♉R
2	18.48	12	7♏	29	19	21	♄ 5♑
3	18.52	13	20	1♒	21	21	♅ 2♑
4	18.56	14	2♐	2	22	22	♆10♑
5	19.00	15	15	3	23	22	♇14♏
6	19.04	16	29	5	24	23	♃26♉R
7	19.08	17	13♑	6	26	23	♄ 6♑
8	19.12	18	27	7	27	24	♅ 2♑
9	19.16	19	11♒	8	28	24	♆10♑
10	19.20	20	26	9	29	25	♇14♏
11	19.24	21	10♓	10	1♑	25	♃26♉R
12	19.28	22	25	10	2	26	♄ 7♑
13	19.32	23	9♈	11	3	26	♅ 2♑
14	19.36	24	23	11	4	27	♆10♑
15	19.40	25	7♉	12	6	28	♇15♏
16	19.44	26	21	12R	7	28	♃26♉R
17	19.48	27	4♊	11	8	29	♄ 7♑
18	19.51	28	18	11	9	29	♅ 2♑
19	19.55	29	1♋	10	11	0♉	♆10♑
20	19.59	0♒	14	10	12	0	♇15♏
21	20.03	1	27	9	13	1	♃26♉
22	20.07	2	9♌	8	14	1	♄ 8♑
23	20.11	3	21	7	16	2	♅ 3♑
24	20.15	4	3♍	5	17	3	♆10♑
25	20.19	5	15	4	18	3	♇15♏
26	20.23	6	27	3	19	4	♃26♉
27	20.27	7	9♎	2	21	4	♄ 8♑
28	20.31	8	21	0	22	5	♅ 3♑
29	20.35	9	3♏	29♑	23	5	♆11♑
30	20.39	10	15	28	24	6	♇15♏
31	20.43	11	27	28	26	7	♃26♉

Feb	STime	☉	☽	☿	♀	♂	Plnts
1	20.47	12♒	10♐	27♑	27♑	7♉	♃26♉
2	20.51	13	23	26	28	8	♄ 9♑
3	20.55	14	7♑	26	29	8	♅ 3♑
4	20.59	15	21	26	1♒	9	♆11♑
5	21.02	16	5♒	26D	2	9	♇15♏
6	21.06	17	20	26	3	10	♃26♉
7	21.10	18	5♓	26	4	11	♄ 9♑
8	21.14	19	20	26	6	11	♅ 4♑
9	21.18	20	4♈	26	7	12	♆11♑
10	21.22	21	19	27	8	12	♇15♏
11	21.26	22	3♉	27	9	13	♃27♉
12	21.30	23	17	28	11	14	♄10♑
13	21.34	24	1♊	29	12	14	♅ 4♑
14	21.38	25	15	29	13	15	♆11♑
15	21.42	26	28	0♒	14	15	♇15♏
16	21.46	27	11♋	1	16	16	♃27♉
17	21.50	29	23	2	17	17	♄10♑
18	21.54	0♓	6♌	3	18	17	♅ 4♑
19	21.58	1	18	4	19	18	♆11♑
20	22.02	2	0♍	5	21	18	♇15♏
21	22.06	3	12	6	22	19	♃27♉
22	22.09	4	24	7	23	20	♄11♑
23	22.13	5	6♎	9	24	20	♅ 4♑
24	22.17	6	17	10	26	21	♆11♑
25	22.21	7	29	11	27	21	♇15♏
26	22.25	8	11♏	12	28	22	♃28♉
27	22.29	9	23	14	29	23	♄11♑
28	22.33	10	6♐	15	1♓	23	♅ 4♑

Mar	STime	☉	☽	☿	♀	♂	Plnts
1	22.37	11♓	18♐	16♒	2♓	24♉	♃28♉
2	22.41	12	1♑	18	3	24	♄12♑
3	22.45	13	15	19	4	25	♅ 4♑
4	22.49	14	29	20	6	26	♆12♑
5	22.53	15	13♒	22	7	26	♇15♏R
6	22.57	16	28	23	8	27	♃29♉
7	23.01	17	13♓	25	9	27	♄12♑
8	23.05	18	28	26	11	28	♅ 5♑
9	23.09	19	13♈	28	12	29	♆12♑
10	23.13	20	28	29	13	29	♇15♏R
11	23.16	21	13♉	1♓	14	0♊	♃ 0♊
12	23.20	22	27	2	16	0	♄12♑
13	23.24	23	11♊	4	17	1	♅ 5♑
14	23.28	24	25	6	18	2	♆12♑
15	23.32	25	8♋	7	19	2	♇15♏R
16	23.36	26	20	9	21	3	♃ 1♊
17	23.40	27	3♌	11	22	3	♄13♑
18	23.44	28	15	12	23	4	♅ 5♑
19	23.48	29	27	14	24	5	♆12♑
20	23.52	0♈	9♍	16	26	5	♇15♏R
21	23.56	1	21	17	27	6	♃ 1♊
22	0.00	2	2♎	19	28	7	♄13♑
23	0.04	3	14	21	29	7	♅ 5♑
24	0.08	4	26	23	1♈	8	♆12♑
25	0.12	5	8♏	25	2	8	♇15♏R
26	0.16	6	20	27	3	9	♃ 2♊
27	0.20	7	2♐	28	4	10	♄13♑
28	0.24	7	15	0♈	6	10	♅ 5♑
29	0.27	8	27	2	7	11	♆12♑
30	0.31	9	10♑	4	8	11	♇14♏R
31	0.35	10	24	6	9	12	♃ 3♊

Apr	STime	☉	☽	☿	♀	♂	Plnts
1	0.39	11♈	7♒	8♈	11♈	13♊	♃ 3♊
2	0.43	12	21	10	12	13	♄13♑
3	0.47	13	6♓	12	13	14	♅ 5♑
4	0.51	14	21	14	14	14	♆12♑
5	0.55	15	6♈	16	16	15	♇14♏R
6	0.59	16	21	18	17	16	♃ 4♊
7	1.03	17	7♉	21	18	16	♄13♑
8	1.07	18	21	23	19	17	♅ 5♑
9	1.11	19	6♊	25	20	18	♆12♑
10	1.15	20	20	27	22	18	♇14♏R
11	1.19	21	4♋	29	23	19	♃ 5♊
12	1.23	22	17	1♉	24	19	♄14♑
13	1.27	23	29	3	25	20	♅ 5♑R
14	1.31	24	12♌	5	27	21	♆12♑
15	1.34	25	24	7	28	21	♇14♏R
16	1.38	26	6♍	9	29	22	♃ 6♊
17	1.42	27	18	11	0♉	22	♄14♑
18	1.46	28	29	13	2	23	♅ 5♑R
19	1.50	29	11♎	15	3	24	♆12♑
20	1.54	0♉	23	16	4	24	♇14♏R
21	1.58	1	5♏	18	5	25	♃ 7♊
22	2.02	2	17	20	7	26	♄14♑
23	2.06	3	29	21	8	26	♅ 5♑R
24	2.10	4	12♐	23	9	27	♆12♑R
25	2.14	5	24	24	10	27	♇14♏R
26	2.18	6	7♑	26	11	28	♃ 8♊
27	2.22	7	20	27	13	29	♄14♑R
28	2.26	8	3♒	28	14	29	♅ 5♑R
29	2.30	9	17	29	15	0♋	♆12♑R
30	2.34	10	1♓	0♊	16	1	♇14♏R

May	STime	☉	☽	☿	♀	♂	Plnts
1	2.38	11♉	15♓	1♊	18♉	1♋	♃ 9♊
2	2.42	12	0♈	2	19	2	♄14♑R
3	2.45	13	15	3	20	2	♅ 5♑R
4	2.49	14	0♉	4	21	3	♆12♑R
5	2.53	15	15	4	23	4	♇13♏R
6	2.57	16	0♊	5	24	4	♃10♊
7	3.01	17	14	6	25	5	♄13♑R
8	3.05	18	28	6	26	5	♅ 5♑R
9	3.09	19	12♋	6	28	6	♆12♑R
10	3.13	19	25	6	29	7	♇13♏R
11	3.17	20	8♌	7	0♊	7	♃12♊
12	3.21	21	20	7R	1	8	♄13♑R
13	3.25	22	2♍	7	2	9	♅ 5♑R
14	3.29	23	14	6	4	9	♆12♑R
15	3.33	24	26	6	5	10	♇13♏R
16	3.37	25	8♎	6	6	10	♃13♊
17	3.41	26	20	6	7	11	♄13♑R
18	3.45	27	2♏	5	9	12	♅ 4♑R
19	3.49	28	14	5	10	12	♆12♑R
20	3.52	29	26	4	11	13	♇13♏R
21	3.56	0♊	9♐	4	12	14	♃14♊
22	4.00	1	21	3	14	14	♄13♑R
23	4.04	2	4♑	3	15	15	♅ 4♑R
24	4.08	3	17	2	16	15	♆12♑R
25	4.12	4	0♒	2	17	16	♇13♏R
26	4.16	5	14	1	18	17	♃15♊
27	4.20	6	27	0	20	17	♄13♑R
28	4.24	7	11♓	0	21	18	♅ 4♑R
29	4.28	8	25	29♉	22	18	♆12♑R
30	4.32	9	10♈	29	23	19	♇13♏R
31	4.36	10	24	29	25	20	♃16♊

Jun	STime	☉	☽	☿	♀	♂	Plnts
1	4.40	11♊	9♉	28♉	26♊	20♋	♃16♊
2	4.44	12	24	28	27	21	♄12♑R
3	4.48	13	8♊	28	28	22	♅ 4♑R
4	4.52	14	22	28	29	22	♆11♑R
5	4.56	15	6♋	28D	1♋	23	♇13♏R
6	5.00	15	20	28	2	23	♃18♊
7	5.03	16	3♌	28	3	24	♄12♑R
8	5.07	17	16	28	4	25	♅ 4♑R
9	5.11	18	28	29	6	25	♆11♑R
10	5.15	19	11♍	29	7	26	♇13♏R
11	5.19	20	22	29	8	27	♃19♊
12	5.23	21	4♎	0♊	9	27	♄12♑R
13	5.27	22	16	0	10	28	♅ 3♑R
14	5.31	23	28	1	12	28	♆11♑R
15	5.35	24	10♏	2	13	29	♇12♏R
16	5.39	25	22	2	14	0♌	♃20♊
17	5.43	26	5♐	3	15	0	♄11♑R
18	5.47	27	17	4	17	1	♅ 3♑R
19	5.51	28	0♑	5	18	2	♆11♑R
20	5.55	29	14	6	19	2	♇12♏R
21	5.59	0♋	27	7	20	3	♃21♊
22	6.03	1	10♒	8	21	3	♄11♑R
23	6.07	2	24	10	23	4	♅ 3♑R
24	6.10	3	8♓	11	24	5	♆11♑R
25	6.14	4	22	12	25	5	♇12♏R
26	6.18	5	6♈	14	26	6	♃22♊
27	6.22	6	20	15	28	6	♄11♑R
28	6.26	6	5♉	17	29	7	♅ 3♑R
29	6.30	7	19	18	0♌	8	♆11♑R
30	6.34	8	3♊	20	1	8	♇12♏R

Jul	STime	☉	☽	☿	♀	♂	Plnts
1	6.38	9♋	17♊	21♊	2♌	9♌	♃23♊
2	6.42	10	1♋	23	4	10	♄10♑R
3	6.46	11	15	25	5	10	♅ 3♑R
4	6.50	12	28	27	6	11	♆11♑R
5	6.54	13	11♌	29	7	11	♇12♏R
6	6.58	14	24	1♋	8	12	♃24♊
7	7.02	15	6♍	3	10	13	♄10♑R
8	7.06	16	18	5	11	13	♅ 2♑R
9	7.10	17	0♎	7	12	14	♆11♑R
10	7.14	18	12	9	13	15	♇12♏R
11	7.17	19	24	11	15	15	♃26♊
12	7.21	20	6♏	13	16	16	♄10♑R
13	7.25	21	18	15	17	16	♅ 2♑R
14	7.29	22	0♐	17	18	17	♆10♑R
15	7.33	23	13	19	19	18	♇12♏
16	7.37	24	26	21	21	18	♃27♊
17	7.41	25	9♑	24	22	19	♄ 9♑R
18	7.45	26	22	26	23	20	♅ 2♑R
19	7.49	26	6♒	28	24	20	♆10♑R
20	7.53	27	20	0♌	25	21	♇12♏R
21	7.57	28	4♓	2	27	21	♃28♊
22	8.01	29	19	4	28	22	♄ 9♑R
23	8.05	0♌	3♈	6	29	23	♅ 2♑R
24	8.09	1	17	8	0♍	23	♆10♑R
25	8.13	2	1♉	10	1	24	♇12♏
26	8.17	3	15	12	3	25	♃29♊
27	8.21	4	0♊	14	4	25	♄ 9♑R
28	8.25	5	13	16	5	26	♅ 2♑R
29	8.28	6	27	18	6	27	♆10♑R
30	8.32	7	11♋	20	7	27	♇12♏
31	8.36	8	24	22	9	28	♃ 0♋

Aug	STime	☉	☽	☿	♀	♂	Plnts
1	8.40	9♌	7♌	24♌	10♍	28♌	♃ 0♋
2	8.44	10	20	25	11	29	♄ 8♑R
3	8.48	11	2♍	27	12	0♍	♅ 2♑R
4	8.52	12	14	29	13	0	♆10♑R
5	8.56	13	26	0♍	15	1	♇12♏
6	9.00	14	8♎	2	16	2	♃ 1♋
7	9.04	15	20	4	17	2	♄ 8♑R
8	9.08	16	2♏	5	18	3	♅ 1♑R
9	9.12	17	14	7	19	3	♆10♑R
10	9.16	18	26	9	21	4	♇12♏
11	9.20	18	8♐	10	22	5	♃ 2♋
12	9.24	19	21	12	23	5	♄ 8♑R
13	9.28	20	4♑	13	24	6	♅ 1♑R
14	9.32	21	17	15	25	7	♆10♑R
15	9.35	22	1♒	16	27	7	♇12♏
16	9.39	23	15	17	28	8	♃ 3♋
17	9.43	24	29	19	29	9	♄ 7♑R
18	9.47	25	14♓	20	0♎	9	♅ 1♑R
19	9.51	26	28	22	1	10	♆10♑R
20	9.55	27	13♈	23	3	10	♇12♏
21	9.59	28	28	24	4	11	♃ 4♋
22	10.03	29	12♉	25	5	12	♄ 7♑R
23	10.07	0♍	26	27	6	12	♅ 1♑R
24	10.11	1	10♊	28	7	13	♆10♑R
25	10.15	2	24	29	9	14	♇12♏
26	10.19	3	7♋	0♎	10	14	♃ 5♋
27	10.23	4	20	1	11	15	♄ 7♑R
28	10.27	5	3♌	2	12	16	♅ 1♑R
29	10.31	6	16	3	13	16	♆ 9♑R
30	10.35	7	28	4	14	17	♇12♏
31	10.39	8	11♍	5	16	17	♃ 5♋

Sep	STime	☉	☽	☿	♀	♂	Plnts
1	10.43	9♍	23♍	6♎	17♎	18♍	♃ 6♋
2	10.46	10	5♎	6	18	19	♄ 7♑R
3	10.50	11	17	7	19	19	♅ 1♑R
4	10.54	12	29	8	20	20	♆ 9♑R
5	10.58	13	10♏	8	21	21	♇13♏
6	11.02	14	22	9	23	21	♃ 6♋
7	11.06	15	4♐	9	24	22	♄ 7♑R
8	11.10	16	17	10	25	23	♅ 1♑
9	11.14	16	29	10	26	23	♆ 9♑R
10	11.18	17	12♑	10	27	24	♇13♏
11	11.22	18	25	10R	29	24	♃ 7♋
12	11.26	19	9♒	10	0♏	25	♄ 7♑
13	11.30	20	23	10	1	26	♅ 1♑
14	11.34	21	8♓	10	2	26	♆ 9♑
15	11.38	22	22	10	3	27	♇13♏
16	11.42	23	7♈	9	4	28	♃ 8♋
17	11.46	24	23	9	6	28	♄ 7♑
18	11.50	25	8♉	8	7	29	♅ 1♑
19	11.53	26	22	7	8	0♎	♆ 9♑
20	11.57	27	7♊	6	9	0	♇13♏
21	12.01	28	21	5	10	1	♃ 8♋
22	12.05	29	4♋	4	11	2	♄ 7♑
23	12.09	0♎	18	3	12	2	♅ 1♑
24	12.13	1	0♌	2	14	3	♆ 9♑
25	12.17	2	13	1	15	4	♇13♏
26	12.21	3	25	0	16	4	♃ 9♋
27	12.25	4	8♍	29♍	17	5	♄ 7♑
28	12.29	5	20	28	18	5	♅ 1♑
29	12.33	6	2♎	27	19	6	♆ 9♑
30	12.37	7	13	26	20	7	♇13♏

Oct	STime	☉	☽	☿	♀	♂	Plnts
1	12.41	8♎	25♎	26♍	22♏	7♎	♃ 9♋
2	12.45	9	7♏	26	23	8	♄ 7♑
3	12.49	10	19	25D	24	9	♅ 1♑
4	12.53	11	1♐	25	25	9	♆ 9♑
5	12.57	12	13	26	26	10	♇14♏
6	13.00	13	25	26	27	11	♃10♋
7	13.04	14	8♑	27	28	11	♄ 8♑
8	13.08	15	20	27	0♐	12	♅ 1♑
9	13.12	16	3♒	28	1	13	♆ 9♑
10	13.16	17	17	29	2	13	♇14♏
11	13.20	18	1♓	0♎	3	14	♃10♋
12	13.24	19	16	1	4	15	♄ 8♑
13	13.28	20	1♈	2	5	15	♅ 2♑
14	13.32	21	16	4	6	16	♆ 9♑
15	13.36	22	1♉	5	7	17	♇14♏
16	13.40	23	16	7	8	17	♃10♋
17	13.44	24	1♊	8	10	18	♄ 8♑
18	13.48	25	16	10	11	19	♅ 2♑
19	13.52	26	0♋	11	12	19	♆10♑
20	13.56	27	14	13	13	20	♇14♏
21	14.00	28	27	15	14	21	♃10♋
22	14.04	29	10♌	16	15	21	♄ 8♑
23	14.08	0♏	22	18	16	22	♅ 2♑
24	14.11	1	5♍	20	17	23	♆10♑
25	14.15	2	17	21	18	23	♇14♏
26	14.19	3	29	23	19	24	♃11♋
27	14.23	4	10♎	25	20	25	♄ 9♑
28	14.27	5	22	26	21	25	♅ 2♑
29	14.31	6	4♏	28	22	26	♆10♑
30	14.35	7	16	0♏	24	27	♇14♏
31	14.39	8	28	1	25	27	♃11♋R

Nov	STime	☉	☽	☿	♀	♂	Plnts
1	14.43	9♏	10♐	3♏	26♐	28♎	♃11♋R
2	14.47	10	22	5	27	29	♄ 9♑
3	14.51	11	4♑	6	28	29	♅ 2♑
4	14.55	12	17	8	29	0♏	♆10♑
5	14.59	13	0♒	10	0♑	1	♇15♏
6	15.03	14	13	11	1	1	♃10♋R
7	15.07	15	26	13	2	2	♄10♑
8	15.11	16	10♓	14	3	3	♅ 2♑
9	15.15	17	24	16	4	3	♆10♑
10	15.18	18	9♈	18	5	4	♇15♏
11	15.22	19	24	19	6	5	♃10♋R
12	15.26	20	9♉	21	7	5	♄10♑
13	15.30	21	24	22	8	6	♅ 3♑
14	15.34	22	9♊	24	9	7	♆10♑
15	15.38	23	24	26	10	7	♇15♏
16	15.42	24	9♋	27	11	8	♃10♋R
17	15.46	25	23	29	12	9	♄10♑
18	15.50	26	6♌	0♐	12	9	♅ 3♑
19	15.54	27	19	2	13	10	♆10♑
20	15.58	28	1♍	3	14	11	♇15♏
21	16.02	29	13	5	15	11	♃10♋R
22	16.06	0♐	25	7	16	12	♄11♑
23	16.10	1	7♎	8	17	13	♅ 3♑
24	16.14	2	19	10	18	13	♆10♑
25	16.18	3	1♏	11	19	14	♇16♏
26	16.22	4	13	13	20	15	♃ 9♋R
27	16.26	5	25	14	20	15	♄11♑
28	16.29	6	7♐	16	21	16	♅ 3♑
29	16.33	7	19	17	22	17	♆11♑
30	16.37	8	2♑	19	23	17	♇16♏

Dec	STime	☉	☽	☿	♀	♂	Plnts
1	16.41	9♐	14♑	20♐	24♑	18♏	♃ 9♋R
2	16.45	10	27	22	24	19	♄12♑
3	16.49	11	10♒	23	25	20	♅ 4♑
4	16.53	12	23	25	26	20	♆11♑
5	16.57	13	6♓	27	27	21	♇16♏
6	17.01	14	20	28	27	22	♃ 8♋R
7	17.05	15	4♈	0♑	28	22	♄12♑
8	17.09	16	18	1	29	23	♅ 4♑
9	17.13	17	3♉	3	29	24	♆11♑
10	17.17	18	18	4	0♒	24	♇16♏
11	17.21	19	3♊	6	0	25	♃ 8♋R
12	17.25	20	18	7	1	26	♄13♑
13	17.29	21	2♋	8	2	26	♅ 4♑
14	17.33	22	17	10	2	27	♆11♑
15	17.36	23	0♌	11	3	28	♇16♏
16	17.40	24	14	13	3	29	♃ 7♋R
17	17.44	25	27	14	3	29	♄14♑
18	17.48	26	9♍	15	4	0♐	♅ 5♑
19	17.52	27	22	17	4	1	♆11♑
20	17.56	28	4♎	18	5	1	♇16♏
21	18.00	29	16	19	5	2	♃ 6♋R
22	18.04	0♑	28	20	5	3	♄14♑
23	18.08	1	9♏	21	5	3	♅ 5♑
24	18.12	2	21	22	6	4	♆11♑
25	18.16	3	3♐	23	6	5	♇17♏
26	18.20	4	16	24	6	5	♃ 6♋R
27	18.24	5	28	25	6	6	♄15♑
28	18.28	6	11♑	25	6	7	♅ 5♑
29	18.32	7	23	25	6R	8	♆12♑
30	18.36	8	6♒	26	6	8	♇17♏
31	18.40	9	20	26R	6	9	♃ 5♋R

1990

Jan	STime	☉	☽	☿	♀	♂	Plnts
1	18.44	11♑	3♓	25♑	6♒	10♐	♃ 5♋R
2	18.47	12	17	25	6	10	♄15♑
3	18.51	13	0♈	24	6	11	♅ 6♑
4	18.55	14	14	24	5	12	♆12♑
5	18.59	15	28	23	5	13	♇17♏
6	19.03	16	13♉	22	5	13	♃ 4♋R
7	19.07	17	27	20	4	14	♄16♑
8	19.11	18	12♊	19	4	15	♅ 6♑
9	19.15	19	26	18	4	15	♆12♑
10	19.19	20	10♋	16	3	16	♇17♏
11	19.23	21	24	15	3	17	♃ 4♋R
12	19.27	22	8♌	14	2	17	♄17♑
13	19.31	23	22	13	2	18	♅ 6♑
14	19.35	24	5♍	12	1	19	♆12♑
15	19.39	25	17	11	0	20	♇17♏
16	19.43	26	0♎	10	0	20	♃ 3♋R
17	19.47	27	12	10	29♑	21	♄17♑
18	19.51	28	24	10	29	22	♅ 6♑
19	19.54	29	5♏	9	28	22	♆12♑
20	19.58	0♒	17	9D	27	23	♇17♏
21	20.02	1	29	10	27	24	♃ 2♋R
22	20.06	2	11♐	10	26	25	♄18♑
23	20.10	3	24	10	26	25	♅ 7♑
24	20.14	4	6♑	11	25	26	♆13♑
25	20.18	5	19	11	24	27	♇17♏
26	20.22	6	2♒	12	24	27	♃ 2♋R
27	20.26	7	16	12	23	28	♄18♑
28	20.30	8	29	13	23	29	♅ 7♑
29	20.34	9	13♓	14	23	0♑	♆13♑
30	20.38	10	27	15	22	0	♇17♏
31	20.42	11	11♈	16	22	1	♃ 1♋R

Feb	STime	☉	☽	☿	♀	♂	Plnts
1	20.46	12♒	25♈	17♑	22♑	2♑	♃ 1♋R
2	20.50	13	9♉	18	21	3	♄19♑
3	20.54	14	24	19	21	3	♅ 7♑
4	20.58	15	8♊	20	21	4	♆13♑
5	21.01	16	22	21	21	5	♇17♏
6	21.05	17	6♋	23	21	5	♃ 1♋R
7	21.09	18	20	24	21	6	♄20♑
8	21.13	19	3♌	25	21D	7	♅ 8♑
9	21.17	20	16	26	21	8	♆13♑
10	21.21	21	0♍	28	21	8	♇17♏
11	21.25	22	12	29	21	9	♃ 1♋R
12	21.29	23	25	0♒	21	10	♄20♑
13	21.33	24	7♎	2	21	10	♅ 8♑
14	21.37	25	19	3	21	11	♆13♑
15	21.41	26	1♏	4	22	12	♇17♏
16	21.45	27	13	6	22	13	♃ 1♋R
17	21.49	28	25	7	22	13	♄21♑
18	21.53	29	7♐	9	23	14	♅ 8♑
19	21.57	0♓	19	10	23	15	♆13♑
20	22.01	1	2♑	12	23	16	♇18♏R
21	22.05	2	14	13	24	16	♃ 1♋R
22	22.09	3	27	15	24	17	♄21♑
23	22.12	4	10♒	16	25	18	♅ 8♑
24	22.16	5	24	18	25	19	♆14♑
25	22.20	6	8♓	20	26	19	♇17♏
26	22.24	7	22	21	26	20	♃ 1♋
27	22.28	8	7♈	23	27	21	♄22♑
28	22.32	9	21	24	28	21	♅ 8♑

Mar	STime	☉	☽	☿	♀	♂	Plnts
1	22.36	10♓	6♉	26♒	28♑	22♑	♃ 1♋
2	22.40	11	20	28	29	23	♄22♑
3	22.44	12	5♊	29	0♒	24	♅ 9♑
4	22.48	13	19	1♓	0	24	♆14♑
5	22.52	14	2♋	3	1	25	♇17♏R
6	22.56	15	16	4	2	26	♃ 1♋
7	23.00	16	29	6	2	27	♄22♑
8	23.04	17	13♌	8	3	27	♅ 9♑
9	23.08	18	26	10	4	28	♆14♑
10	23.12	19	8♍	12	5	29	♇17♏R
11	23.16	20	21	13	6	0♒	♃ 1♋
12	23.19	21	3♎	15	6	0	♄23♑
13	23.23	22	15	17	7	1	♅ 9♑
14	23.27	23	27	19	8	2	♆14♑
15	23.31	24	9♏	21	9	3	♇17♏R
16	23.35	25	21	23	10	3	♃ 1♋
17	23.39	26	3♐	25	11	4	♄23♑
18	23.43	27	15	27	11	5	♅ 9♑
19	23.47	28	27	29	12	6	♆14♑
20	23.51	29	9♑	1♈	13	6	♇17♏R
21	23.55	0♈	22	3	14	7	♃ 1♋
22	23.59	1	5♒	5	15	8	♄24♑
23	0.03	2	18	7	16	8	♅ 9♑
24	0.07	3	2♓	9	17	9	♆14♑
25	0.11	4	16	11	18	10	♇17♏R
26	0.15	5	1♈	13	19	11	♃ 2♋
27	0.19	6	16	15	20	11	♄24♑
28	0.23	7	1♉	17	21	12	♅ 9♑
29	0.27	8	16	19	22	13	♆14♑
30	0.30	9	0♊	21	23	14	♇17♏R
31	0.34	10	15	23	24	14	♃ 2♋

Apr	STime	☉	☽	☿	♀	♂	Plnts
1	0.38	11♈	29♊	25♈	25♒	15♒	♃ 3♋
2	0.42	12	13♋	26	26	16	♄24♑
3	0.46	13	26	28	27	17	♅ 9♑
4	0.50	14	10♌	0♉	28	17	♆14♑
5	0.54	15	22	2	29	18	♇17♏R
6	0.58	16	5♍	3	0♓	19	♃ 3♋
7	1.02	17	18	5	1	20	♄24♑
8	1.06	18	0♎	6	2	20	♅ 9♑
9	1.10	19	12	8	3	21	♆14♑
10	1.14	20	24	9	4	22	♇17♏R
11	1.18	21	6♏	10	5	23	♃ 4♋
12	1.22	22	18	11	6	23	♄25♑
13	1.26	23	0♐	12	7	24	♅ 9♑
14	1.30	24	12	13	8	25	♆14♑
15	1.34	25	24	14	9	26	♇17♏R
16	1.37	26	6♑	15	10	26	♃ 4♋
17	1.41	27	18	16	11	27	♄25♑
18	1.45	28	0♒	16	12	28	♅ 9♑
19	1.49	29	13	17	14	29	♆14♑
20	1.53	0♉	26	17	15	29	♇17♏R
21	1.57	1	10♓	17	16	0♓	♃ 5♋
22	2.01	2	24	17	17	1	♄25♑
23	2.05	3	9♈	17R	18	2	♅ 9♑R
24	2.09	4	24	17	19	2	♆14♑
25	2.13	5	9♉	17	20	3	♇16♏R
26	2.17	6	24	17	21	4	♃ 6♋
27	2.21	7	10♊	16	22	5	♄25♑
28	2.25	8	24	16	23	5	♅ 9♑R
29	2.29	9	9♋	16	25	6	♆14♑R
30	2.33	10	23	15	26	7	♇16♏R

May	STime	☉	☽	☿	♀	♂	Plnts
1	2.37	11♉	6♌	15♉	27♓	8♓	♃ 7♋
2	2.41	12	19	14	28	8	♄25♑
3	2.44	12	2♍	13	29	9	♅ 9♑R
4	2.48	13	15	13	0♈	10	♆14♑R
5	2.52	14	27	12	1	11	♇16♏R
6	2.56	15	9♎	11	2	11	♃ 8♋
7	3.00	16	21	11	3	12	♄25♑
8	3.04	17	3♏	10	5	13	♅ 9♑R
9	3.08	18	15	10	6	14	♆14♑R
10	3.12	19	27	9	7	14	♇16♏R
11	3.16	20	9♐	9	8	15	♃ 9♋
12	3.20	21	21	8	9	16	♄25♑R
13	3.24	22	3♑	8	10	17	♅ 9♑R
14	3.28	23	15	8	11	17	♆14♑R
15	3.32	24	27	8	13	18	♇16♏R
16	3.36	25	9♒	8	14	19	♃ 9♋
17	3.40	26	22	8D	15	20	♄25♑R
18	3.44	27	5♓	8	16	20	♅ 9♑R
19	3.48	28	19	8	17	21	♆14♑R
20	3.52	29	3♈	8	18	22	♇16♏R
21	3.55	0♊	18	8	19	22	♃10♋
22	3.59	1	2♉	9	21	23	♄25♑R
23	4.03	2	18	9	22	24	♅ 9♑R
24	4.07	3	3♊	10	23	25	♆14♑R
25	4.11	4	18	10	24	25	♇16♏R
26	4.15	5	3♋	11	25	26	♃11♋
27	4.19	6	18	12	26	27	♄25♑R
28	4.23	7	2♌	12	27	28	♅ 9♑R
29	4.27	8	15	13	29	28	♆14♑R
30	4.31	9	29	14	0♉	29	♇15♏R
31	4.35	9	11♍	15	1	0♈	♃12♋

Jun	STime	☉	☽	☿	♀	♂	Plnts
1	4.39	10♊	24♍	16♉	2♉	1♈	♃13♋
2	4.43	11	6♎	17	3	1	♄24♑R
3	4.47	12	18	18	4	2	♅ 8♑R
4	4.51	13	0♏	19	6	3	♆14♑R
5	4.55	14	12	21	7	3	♇15♏R
6	4.59	15	24	22	8	4	♃14♋
7	5.02	16	6♐	23	9	5	♄24♑R
8	5.06	17	18	25	10	6	♅ 8♑R
9	5.10	18	0♑	26	11	6	♆14♑R
10	5.14	19	12	27	13	7	♇15♏R
11	5.18	20	24	29	14	8	♃15♋
12	5.22	21	6♒	0♊	15	9	♄24♑R
13	5.26	22	19	2	16	9	♅ 8♑R
14	5.30	23	2♓	4	17	10	♆13♑R
15	5.34	24	15	5	18	11	♇15♏R
16	5.38	25	29	7	20	11	♃16♋
17	5.42	26	13♈	9	21	12	♄24♑R
18	5.46	27	27	11	22	13	♅ 8♑R
19	5.50	28	12♉	13	23	14	♆13♑R
20	5.54	29	26	15	24	14	♇15♏R
21	5.58	0♋	11♊	16	26	15	♃17♋
22	6.02	1	26	18	27	16	♄23♑R
23	6.06	1	11♋	21	28	16	♅ 8♑R
24	6.10	2	26	23	29	17	♆13♑R
25	6.13	3	10♌	25	0♊	18	♇15♏R
26	6.17	4	24	27	1	19	♃18♋
27	6.21	5	7♍	29	3	19	♄23♑R
28	6.25	6	20	1♋	4	20	♅ 7♑R
29	6.29	7	2♎	3	5	21	♆13♑R
30	6.33	8	15	5	6	21	♇15♏R

Jul	STime	☉	☽	☿	♀	♂	Plnts
1	6.37	9♋	27♎	8♋	7♊	22♈	♃19♋
2	6.41	10	9♏	10	9	23	♄23♑R
3	6.45	11	21	12	10	23	♅ 7♑R
4	6.49	12	2♐	14	11	24	♆13♑R
5	6.53	13	14	16	12	25	♇15♏R
6	6.57	14	26	18	13	26	♃20♋
7	7.01	15	9♑	21	15	26	♄22♑R
8	7.05	16	21	23	16	27	♅ 7♑R
9	7.09	17	3♒	25	17	28	♆13♑R
10	7.13	18	16	27	18	28	♇15♏
11	7.17	19	29	29	19	29	♃21♋
12	7.20	20	12♓	1♌	21	0♉	♄22♑R
13	7.24	21	25	3	22	0	♅ 7♑R
14	7.28	21	9♈	5	23	1	♆13♑R
15	7.32	22	23	6	24	2	♇15♏R
16	7.36	23	7♉	8	25	2	♃22♋
17	7.40	24	21	10	27	3	♄22♑R
18	7.44	25	6♊	12	28	4	♅ 7♑R
19	7.48	26	21	14	29	4	♆13♑R
20	7.52	27	5♋	15	0♋	5	♇15♏R
21	7.56	28	20	17	1	6	♃24♋
22	8.00	29	4♌	19	3	6	♄21♑R
23	8.04	0♌	18	21	4	7	♅ 6♑R
24	8.08	1	2♍	22	5	8	♆12♑R
25	8.12	2	15	24	6	8	♇15♏
26	8.16	3	28	25	7	9	♃25♋
27	8.20	4	10♎	27	9	9	♄21♑R
28	8.24	5	23	28	10	10	♅ 6♑R
29	8.28	6	5♏	0♍	11	11	♆12♑R
30	8.31	7	17	1	12	11	♇15♏
31	8.35	8	29	3	13	12	♃26♋

Aug	STime	☉	☽	☿	♀	♂	Plnts
1	8.39	9♌	11♐	4♍	15♋	13♉	♃26♋
2	8.43	10	23	5	16	13	♄20♑R
3	8.47	11	5♑	7	17	14	♅ 6♑R
4	8.51	12	17	8	18	15	♆12♑R
5	8.55	13	0♒	9	19	15	♇15♏
6	8.59	13	12	10	21	16	♃27♋
7	9.03	14	25	11	22	16	♄20♑R
8	9.07	15	9♓	13	23	17	♅ 6♑R
9	9.11	16	22	14	24	18	♆12♑R
10	9.15	17	6♈	15	26	18	♇15♏
11	9.19	18	20	16	27	19	♃28♋
12	9.23	19	4♉	17	28	19	♄20♑R
13	9.27	20	18	17	29	20	♅ 6♑R
14	9.31	21	2♊	18	0♌	20	♆12♑R
15	9.35	22	16	19	2	21	♇15♏
16	9.38	23	1♋	20	3	22	♃29♋
17	9.42	24	15	21	4	22	♄19♑R
18	9.46	25	29	21	5	23	♅ 6♑R
19	9.50	26	13♌	22	7	23	♆12♑R
20	9.54	27	27	22	8	24	♇15♏
21	9.58	28	10♍	23	9	24	♃ 0♌
22	10.02	29	23	23	10	25	♄19♑R
23	10.06	0♍	6♎	23	11	26	♅ 5♑R
24	10.10	1	18	23	13	26	♆12♑R
25	10.14	2	1♏	23R	14	27	♇15♏
26	10.18	3	13	23	15	27	♃ 1♌
27	10.22	4	25	23	16	28	♄19♑R
28	10.26	5	7♐	23	18	28	♅ 5♑R
29	10.30	6	19	23	19	29	♆12♑R
30	10.34	7	1♑	22	20	29	♇15♏
31	10.38	8	13	22	21	0♊	♃ 2♌

Sep	STime	☉	☽	☿	♀	♂	Plnts
1	10.42	8♍	25♑	21♍	22♌	0♊	♃ 3♌
2	10.45	9	8♒	20	24	1	♄19♑R
3	10.49	10	21	19	25	1	♅ 5♑R
4	10.53	11	4♓	18	26	2	♆12♑R
5	10.57	12	18	18	27	2	♇15♏
6	11.01	13	2♈	17	29	3	♃ 4♌
7	11.05	14	16	16	0♍	3	♄19♑R
8	11.09	15	0♉	15	1	3	♅ 5♑R
9	11.13	16	15	14	2	4	♆12♑R
10	11.17	17	29	13	4	4	♇15♏
11	11.21	18	13♊	12	5	5	♃ 5♌
12	11.25	19	27	11	6	5	♄18♑R
13	11.29	20	11♋	11	7	6	♅ 5♑
14	11.33	21	25	10	9	6	♆12♑
15	11.37	22	9♌	10	10	6	♇15♏
16	11.41	23	22	9	11	7	♃ 6♌
17	11.45	24	6♍	9D	12	7	♄18♑R
18	11.49	25	19	9	14	8	♅ 5♑
19	11.53	26	2♎	10	15	8	♆12♑R
20	11.56	27	14	10	16	8	♇16♏
21	12.00	28	27	11	17	9	♃ 6♌
22	12.04	29	9♏	11	18	9	♄18♑
23	12.08	0♎	21	12	20	9	♅ 5♑
24	12.12	1	3♐	13	21	10	♆11♑
25	12.16	2	15	14	22	10	♇16♏
26	12.20	3	26	15	23	10	♃ 7♌
27	12.24	4	8♑	17	25	11	♄18♑
28	12.28	5	20	18	26	11	♅ 5♑
29	12.32	6	3♒	19	27	11	♆12♑
30	12.36	7	16	21	28	11	♇16♏

Oct	STime	☉	☽	☿	♀	♂	Plnts
1	12.40	8♎	29♒	23♍	0♎	12♊	♃ 8♌
2	12.44	9	12♓	24	1	12	♄18♑
3	12.48	10	26	26	2	12	♅ 5♑
4	12.52	11	11♈	28	3	12	♆12♑
5	12.56	12	25	29	5	13	♇16♏
6	13.00	13	10♉	1♎	6	13	♃ 9♌
7	13.03	14	25	3	7	13	♄19♑
8	13.07	15	10♊	5	8	13	♅ 6♑
9	13.11	16	24	6	10	13	♆12♑
10	13.15	17	8♋	8	11	14	♇16♏
11	13.19	18	22	10	12	14	♃10♌
12	13.23	19	6♌	12	13	14	♄19♑
13	13.27	20	19	13	15	14	♅ 6♑
14	13.31	21	2♍	15	16	14	♆12♑
15	13.35	22	15	17	17	14	♇16♏
16	13.39	23	28	19	18	14	♃10♌
17	13.43	24	10♎	20	20	14	♄19♑
18	13.47	25	23	22	21	14	♅ 6♑
19	13.51	26	5♏	24	22	14	♆12♑
20	13.55	27	17	25	23	14R	♇17♏
21	13.59	28	29	27	25	14	♃11♌
22	14.03	29	11♐	29	26	14	♄19♑
23	14.07	0♏	23	0♏	27	14	♅ 6♑
24	14.11	1	5♑	2	28	14	♆12♑
25	14.14	2	16	4	0♏	14	♇17♏
26	14.18	3	29	5	1	14	♃11♌
27	14.22	4	11♒	7	2	14	♄19♑
28	14.26	5	24	9	3	14	♅ 6♑
29	14.30	6	7♓	10	5	14	♆12♑
30	14.34	7	20	12	6	14	♇17♏
31	14.38	8	4♈	13	7	13	♃12♌

Nov	STime	☉	☽	☿	♀	♂	Plnts
1	14.42	9♏	19♈	15♏	8♏	13♊	♃12♌
2	14.46	10	4♉	17	10	13	♄20♑
3	14.50	11	19	18	11	13	♅ 6♑
4	14.54	12	4♊	20	12	13	♆12♑
5	14.58	13	19	21	13	12	♇17♏
6	15.02	14	4♋	23	15	12	♃12♌
7	15.06	15	18	24	16	12	♄20♑
8	15.10	16	2♌	26	17	12	♅ 7♑
9	15.14	17	16	27	19	11	♆12♑
10	15.18	18	29	29	20	11	♇17♏
11	15.21	19	12♍	0♐	21	11	♃13♌
12	15.25	20	25	2	22	11	♄20♑
13	15.29	21	7♎	3	24	10	♅ 7♑
14	15.33	22	20	5	25	10	♆12♑
15	15.37	23	2♏	6	26	10	♇18♏
16	15.41	24	14	8	27	9	♃13♌
17	15.45	25	26	9	29	9	♄21♑
18	15.49	26	8♐	11	0♐	9	♅ 7♑
19	15.53	27	20	12	1	8	♆12♑
20	15.57	28	1♑	14	2	8	♇18♏
21	16.01	29	13	15	4	7	♃13♌
22	16.05	0♐	25	17	5	7	♄21♑
23	16.09	1	7♒	18	6	7	♅ 7♑
24	16.13	2	19	20	7	6	♆12♑
25	16.17	3	2♓	21	9	6	♇18♏
26	16.21	4	15	22	10	6	♃13♌
27	16.25	5	28	24	11	5	♄22♑
28	16.29	6	12♈	25	12	5	♅ 7♑
29	16.32	7	27	26	14	4	♆13♑
30	16.36	8	12♉	28	15	4	♇18♏

Dec	STime	☉	☽	☿	♀	♂	Plnts
1	16.40	9♐	27♉	29♐	16♐	4♊	♃13♌
2	16.44	10	12♊	0♑	17	3	♄22♑
3	16.48	11	27	2	19	3	♅ 8♑
4	16.52	12	13♋	3	20	3	♆13♑
5	16.56	13	27	4	21	2	♇18♏
6	17.00	14	12♌	5	22	2	♃13♌R
7	17.04	15	25	6	24	2	♄23♑
8	17.08	16	9♍	7	25	1	♅ 8♑
9	17.12	17	22	7	26	1	♆13♑
10	17.16	18	4♎	8	27	1	♇19♏
11	17.20	19	17	9	29	0	♃13♌R
12	17.24	20	29	9	0♑	0	♄23♑
13	17.28	21	11♏	10	1	0	♅ 8♑
14	17.32	22	23	10R	2	0	♆13♑
15	17.36	23	5♐	10	4	29♉	♇19♏
16	17.39	24	17	9	5	29	♃13♌R
17	17.43	25	28	9	6	29	♄24♑
18	17.47	26	10♑	8	7	29	♅ 9♑
19	17.51	27	22	8	9	29	♆13♑
20	17.55	28	4♒	7	10	28	♇19♏
21	17.59	29	16	6	11	28	♃13♌R
22	18.03	0♑	29	4	13	28	♄24♑
23	18.07	1	11♓	3	14	28	♅ 9♑
24	18.11	2	24	2	15	28	♆14♑
25	18.15	3	8♈	0	16	28	♇19♏
26	18.19	4	21	29♐	18	28	♃12♌R
27	18.23	5	6♉	28	19	28	♄25♑
28	18.27	6	20	27	20	28	♅ 9♑
29	18.31	7	5♊	26	21	28	♆14♑
30	18.35	8	20	25	23	27	♇19♏
31	18.39	9	5♋	24	24	27	♃12♌R

1 9 9 1

Jan	STime	☉	☽	☿	♀	♂	Plnts
1	18.43	10♑	20♋	24♐	25♑	27♉	♃12♌R
2	18.46	11	5♌	24	26	27	♄26♑
3	18.50	12	20	23D	28	27	♅10♑
4	18.54	13	4♍	23	29	28	♆14♑
5	18.58	14	17	24	0♒	28	♇19♏
6	19.02	15	0♎	24	1	28	♃11♌R
7	19.06	16	13	24	3	28	♄26♑
8	19.10	17	26	25	4	28	♅10♑
9	19.14	18	8♏	26	5	28	♆14♑
10	19.18	19	20	26	6	28	♇20♏
11	19.22	20	2♐	27	8	28	♃11♌R
12	19.26	21	13	28	9	28	♄27♑
13	19.30	22	25	29	10	28	♅10♑
14	19.34	24	7♑	0♑	11	28	♆14♑
15	19.38	25	19	1	13	29	♇20♏
16	19.42	26	1♒	2	14	29	♃10♌R
17	19.46	27	13	3	15	29	♄27♑
18	19.50	28	26	4	16	29	♅10♑
19	19.54	29	8♓	5	18	29	♆15♑
20	19.57	0♒	21	7	19	0♊	♇20♏
21	20.01	1	4♈	8	20	0	♃ 9♌R
22	20.05	2	18	9	21	0	♄28♑
23	20.09	3	1♉	11	23	0	♅11♑
24	20.13	4	15	12	24	1	♆15♑
25	20.17	5	0♊	13	25	1	♇20♏
26	20.21	6	14	15	26	1	♃ 9♌R
27	20.25	7	29	16	28	1	♄28♑
28	20.29	8	14♋	17	29	2	♅11♑
29	20.33	9	28	19	0♓	2	♆15♑
30	20.37	10	13♌	20	1	2	♇20♏
31	20.41	11	28	22	3	2	♃ 8♌R

Feb	STime	☉	☽	☿	♀	♂	Plnts
1	20.45	12♒	12♍	23♑	4♓	3♊	♃ 8♌R
2	20.49	13	25	25	5	3	♄29♑
3	20.53	14	8♎	26	6	3	♅11♑
4	20.57	15	21	28	8	4	♆15♑
5	21.01	16	4♏	29	9	4	♇20♏
6	21.04	17	16	1♒	10	4	♃ 7♌R
7	21.08	18	28	2	11	5	♄ 0♒
8	21.12	19	10♐	4	13	5	♅12♑
9	21.16	20	22	5	14	5	♆15♑
10	21.20	21	4♑	7	15	6	♇20♏
11	21.24	22	15	8	16	6	♃ 7♌R
12	21.28	23	28	10	17	7	♄ 0♒
13	21.32	24	10♒	12	19	7	♅12♑
14	21.36	25	22	13	20	7	♆15♑
15	21.40	26	5♓	15	21	8	♇20♏
16	21.44	27	18	17	22	8	♃ 6♌R
17	21.48	28	1♈	18	24	8	♄ 1♒
18	21.52	29	15	20	25	9	♅12♑
19	21.56	0♓	28	22	26	9	♆16♑
20	22.00	1	12♉	23	27	10	♇20♏
21	22.04	2	26	25	29	10	♃ 5♌R
22	22.08	3	10♊	27	0♈	11	♄ 1♒
23	22.12	4	24	29	1	11	♅12♑
24	22.15	5	9♋	0♓	2	11	♆16♑
25	22.19	6	23	2	4	12	♇20♏
26	22.23	7	7♌	4	5	12	♃ 5♌R
27	22.27	8	22	6	6	13	♄ 2♒
28	22.31	9	6♍	8	7	13	♅13♑

Mar	STime	☉	☽	☿	♀	♂	Plnts
1	22.35	10♓	20♍	10♓	8♈	14♊	♃ 5♌R
2	22.39	11	3♎	11	10	14	♄ 2♒
3	22.43	12	16	13	11	15	♅13♑
4	22.47	13	29	15	12	15	♆16♑
5	22.51	14	12♏	17	13	15	♇20♏R
6	22.55	15	24	19	15	16	♃ 4♌R
7	22.59	16	6♐	21	16	16	♄ 3♒
8	23.03	17	18	23	17	17	♅13♑
9	23.07	18	0♑	25	18	17	♆16♑
10	23.11	19	11	27	19	18	♇20♏R
11	23.15	20	23	29	21	18	♃ 4♌R
12	23.19	21	6♒	1♈	22	19	♄ 3♒
13	23.22	22	18	3	23	19	♅13♑
14	23.26	23	1♓	5	24	20	♆16♑
15	23.30	24	14	7	26	20	♇20♏R
16	23.34	25	27	8	27	21	♃ 4♌R
17	23.38	26	11♈	10	28	21	♄ 4♒
18	23.42	27	25	12	29	22	♅13♑
19	23.46	28	9♉	14	0♉	22	♆16♑
20	23.50	29	23	15	2	23	♇20♏R
21	23.54	0♈	7♊	17	3	23	♃ 3♌R
22	23.58	1	21	18	4	24	♄ 4♒
23	0.02	2	5♋	20	5	24	♅13♑
24	0.06	3	19	21	6	25	♆16♑
25	0.10	4	3♌	22	8	25	♇20♏R
26	0.14	5	17	24	9	26	♃ 3♌R
27	0.18	6	1♍	25	10	26	♄ 5♒
28	0.22	7	15	26	11	27	♅13♑
29	0.26	8	28	26	12	27	♆16♑
30	0.30	9	11♎	27	14	28	♇20♏R
31	0.33	10	24	28	15	28	♃ 3♌

Apr	STime	☉	☽	☿	♀	♂	Plnts
1	0.37	11♈	7♏	28♈	16♉	29♊	♃ 3♌
2	0.41	12	20	28	17	29	♄ 5♒
3	0.45	13	2♐	29	18	0♋	♅13♑
4	0.49	14	14	29R	20	0	♆16♑
5	0.53	15	26	29	21	1	♇20♏R
6	0.57	16	7♑	29	22	2	♃ 3♌
7	1.01	17	19	28	23	2	♄ 5♒
8	1.05	18	1♒	28	24	3	♅13♑
9	1.09	19	13	28	26	3	♆16♑
10	1.13	20	26	27	27	4	♇19♏R
11	1.17	21	9♓	26	28	4	♃ 3♌
12	1.21	22	22	26	29	5	♄ 6♒
13	1.25	23	5♈	25	0♊	5	♅14♑
14	1.29	24	20	24	1	6	♆16♑
15	1.33	25	4♉	24	3	6	♇19♏R
16	1.37	26	18	23	4	7	♃ 4♌
17	1.40	27	3♊	22	5	8	♄ 6♒
18	1.44	28	17	21	6	8	♅14♑
19	1.48	29	2♋	21	7	9	♆16♑
20	1.52	0♉	16	20	8	9	♇19♏R
21	1.56	1	0♌	20	10	10	♃ 4♌
22	2.00	2	14	19	11	10	♄ 6♒
23	2.04	3	28	19	12	11	♅13♑
24	2.08	4	11♍	18	13	11	♆16♑
25	2.12	4	24	18	14	12	♇19♏R
26	2.16	5	8♎	18	15	13	♃ 4♌
27	2.20	6	20	18	17	13	♄ 6♒
28	2.24	7	3♏	18D	18	14	♅13♑R
29	2.28	8	16	18	19	14	♆16♑R
30	2.32	9	28	18	20	15	♇19♏R

May	STime	☉	☽	☿	♀	♂	Plnts
1	2.36	10♉	10♐	18♈	21♊	15♋	♃ 5♌
2	2.40	11	22	18	22	16	♄ 6♒
3	2.44	12	4♑	19	23	16	♅13♑R
4	2.47	13	16	19	25	17	♆16♑R
5	2.51	14	27	20	26	18	♇19♏R
6	2.55	15	9♒	20	27	18	♃ 5♌
7	2.59	16	21	21	28	19	♄ 6♒
8	3.03	17	4♓	22	29	19	♅13♑R
9	3.07	18	17	22	0♋	20	♆16♑R
10	3.11	19	0♈	23	1	20	♇19♏R
11	3.15	20	14	24	2	21	♃ 6♌
12	3.19	21	28	25	4	22	♄ 7♒
13	3.23	22	12♉	26	5	22	♅13♑R
14	3.27	23	27	27	6	23	♆16♑R
15	3.31	24	12♊	28	7	23	♇19♏R
16	3.35	25	27	29	8	24	♃ 6♌
17	3.39	26	12♋	0♉	9	24	♄ 7♒
18	3.43	27	26	2	10	25	♅13♑R
19	3.47	28	11♌	3	11	26	♆16♑R
20	3.51	29	25	4	12	26	♇18♏R
21	3.55	0♊	8♍	5	13	27	♃ 7♌
22	3.58	1	21	7	14	27	♄ 7♒R
23	4.02	2	5♎	8	16	28	♅13♑R
24	4.06	3	17	10	17	29	♆16♑R
25	4.10	3	0♏	11	18	29	♇18♏R
26	4.14	4	12	13	19	0♌	♃ 8♌
27	4.18	5	24	14	20	0	♄ 6♒R
28	4.22	6	7♐	16	21	1	♅13♑R
29	4.26	7	18	18	22	1	♆16♑R
30	4.30	8	0♑	19	23	2	♇18♏R
31	4.34	9	12	21	24	3	♃ 9♌

Jun	STime	☉	☽	☿	♀	♂	Plnts
1	4.38	10♊	24♑	23♉	25♋	3♌	♃ 9♌
2	4.42	11	6♒	25	26	4	♄ 6♒R
3	4.46	12	18	27	27	4	♅13♑R
4	4.50	13	0♓	29	28	5	♆16♑R
5	4.54	14	12	0♊	29	6	♇18♏R
6	4.58	15	25	2	0♌	6	♃10♌
7	5.02	16	8♈	4	1	7	♄ 6♒R
8	5.05	17	22	7	2	7	♅13♑R
9	5.09	18	6♉	9	3	8	♆16♑R
10	5.13	19	21	11	4	9	♇18♏R
11	5.17	20	6♊	13	5	9	♃10♌
12	5.21	21	21	15	6	10	♄ 6♒R
13	5.25	22	6♋	17	7	10	♅12♑R
14	5.29	23	21	19	8	11	♆16♑R
15	5.33	24	6♌	22	9	12	♇18♏R
16	5.37	25	20	24	10	12	♃11♌
17	5.41	26	4♍	26	11	13	♄ 6♒R
18	5.45	26	18	28	12	13	♅12♑R
19	5.49	27	1♎	0♋	13	14	♆16♑R
20	5.53	28	14	2	14	15	♇18♏R
21	5.57	29	27	5	14	15	♃12♌
22	6.01	0♋	9♏	7	15	16	♄ 6♒R
23	6.05	1	22	9	16	16	♅12♑R
24	6.09	2	4♐	11	17	17	♆15♑R
25	6.13	3	15	13	18	18	♇18♏R
26	6.16	4	27	15	19	18	♃13♌
27	6.20	5	9♑	17	20	19	♄ 5♒R
28	6.24	6	21	19	20	19	♅12♑R
29	6.28	7	3♒	21	21	20	♆15♑R
30	6.32	8	15	23	22	21	♇17♏R

Jul	STime	☉	☽	☿	♀	♂	Plnts
1	6.36	9♋	27♒	25♋	23♌	21♌	♃14♌
2	6.40	10	9♓	27	24	22	♄ 5♒R
3	6.44	11	21	28	24	22	♅12♑R
4	6.48	12	4♈	0♌	25	23	♆15♑R
5	6.52	13	17	2	26	24	♇17♏R
6	6.56	14	1♉	4	27	24	♃15♌
7	7.00	15	15	5	27	25	♄ 5♒R
8	7.04	16	29	7	28	25	♅11♑R
9	7.08	16	14♊	8	29	26	♆15♑R
10	7.12	17	29	10	29	27	♇17♏R
11	7.16	18	14♋	12	0♍	27	♃16♌
12	7.20	19	29	13	0	28	♄ 4♒R
13	7.23	20	14♌	14	1	28	♅11♑R
14	7.27	21	29	16	2	29	♆15♑R
15	7.31	22	13♍	17	2	0♍	♇17♏
16	7.35	23	27	19	3	0	♃17♌
17	7.39	24	11♎	20	3	1	♄ 4♒R
18	7.43	25	24	21	4	2	♅11♑R
19	7.47	26	6♏	22	4	2	♆15♑R
20	7.51	27	18	24	4	3	♇17♏
21	7.55	28	1♐	25	5	3	♃18♌
22	7.59	29	12	26	5	4	♄ 4♒R
23	8.03	0♌	24	27	6	5	♅11♑R
24	8.07	1	6♑	28	6	5	♆15♑R
25	8.11	2	18	29	6	6	♇17♏R
26	8.15	3	0♒	0♍	6	6	♃19♌
27	8.19	4	12	1	7	7	♄ 3♒R
28	8.23	5	24	1	7	8	♅11♑R
29	8.27	6	6♓	2	7	8	♆15♑R
30	8.30	7	18	3	7	9	♇17♏
31	8.34	7	1♈	3	7	10	♃20♌

Aug	STime	☉	☽	☿	♀	♂	Plnts
1	8.38	8♌	14♈	4♍	7♍	10♍	♃21♌
2	8.42	9	27	4	7	11	♄ 3♒R
3	8.46	10	11♉	5	7	11	♅10♑R
4	8.50	11	24	5	7	12	♆14♑R
5	8.54	12	9♊	5	7	13	♇17♏
6	8.58	13	23	6	7	13	♃22♌
7	9.02	14	8♋	6	6	14	♄ 2♒R
8	9.06	15	23	6R	6	15	♅10♑R
9	9.10	16	8♌	6	6	15	♆14♑R
10	9.14	17	23	5	5	16	♇17♏
11	9.18	18	7♍	5	5	16	♃23♌
12	9.22	19	22	5	5	17	♄ 2♒R
13	9.26	20	6♎	4	4	18	♅10♑R
14	9.30	21	19	4	4	18	♆14♑R
15	9.34	22	2♏	3	3	19	♇17♏
16	9.38	23	15	2	3	20	♃24♌
17	9.41	24	27	2	2	20	♄ 2♒R
18	9.45	25	9♐	1	2	21	♅10♑R
19	9.49	26	21	0	1	22	♆14♑R
20	9.53	27	3♑	29♌	0	22	♇17♏
21	9.57	28	15	28	0	23	♃25♌
22	10.01	29	26	27	29♌	23	♄ 1♒R
23	10.05	0♍	8♒	27	29	24	♅10♑R
24	10.09	1	21	26	28	25	♆14♑R
25	10.13	2	3♓	25	27	25	♇17♏
26	10.17	2	15	24	27	26	♃26♌
27	10.21	3	28	24	26	27	♄ 1♒R
28	10.25	4	11♈	23	26	27	♅10♑R
29	10.29	5	24	23	25	28	♆14♑R
30	10.33	6	8♉	23	24	29	♇18♏
31	10.37	7	21	23D	24	29	♃27♌

Sep	STime	☉	☽	☿	♀	♂	Plnts
1	10.41	8♍	5♊	23♌	23♌	0♎	♃27♌
2	10.45	9	19	23	23	0	♄ 1♒R
3	10.48	10	3♋	23	23	1	♅10♑R
4	10.52	11	17	24	22	2	♆14♑R
5	10.56	12	2♌	24	22	2	♇18♏
6	11.00	13	17	25	22	3	♃28♌
7	11.04	14	1♍	26	21	4	♄ 0♒R
8	11.08	15	16	27	21	4	♅10♑
9	11.12	16	0♎	28	21	5	♆14♑R
10	11.16	17	14	29	21	6	♇18♏
11	11.20	18	27	1♍	21	6	♃ 0♍
12	11.24	19	10♏	2	21	7	♄ 0♒R
13	11.28	20	23	4	21D	8	♅10♑
14	11.32	21	5♐	5	21	8	♆14♑R
15	11.36	22	17	7	21	9	♇18♏
16	11.40	23	29	9	21	10	♃ 1♍
17	11.44	24	11♑	10	21	10	♄ 0♒R
18	11.48	25	23	12	21	11	♅10♑
19	11.52	26	5♒	14	21	12	♆14♑
20	11.56	27	17	16	22	12	♇18♏
21	11.59	28	29	17	22	13	♃ 2♍
22	12.03	29	11♓	19	22	14	♄ 0♒R
23	12.07	0♎	24	21	23	14	♅10♑
24	12.11	1	7♈	23	23	15	♆14♑
25	12.15	2	21	25	23	15	♇18♏
26	12.19	3	4♉	27	24	16	♃ 3♍
27	12.23	4	18	29	24	17	♄ 0♒R
28	12.27	5	2♊	0♎	25	17	♅10♑
29	12.31	6	16	2	25	18	♆14♑
30	12.35	7	0♋	4	26	19	♇18♏

Oct	STime	☉	☽	☿	♀	♂	Plnts
1	12.39	8♎	14♋	6♎	26♌	19♎	♃ 4♍
2	12.43	9	28	8	27	20	♄ 0♒
3	12.47	9	12♌	9	28	21	♅10♑
4	12.51	10	26	11	28	21	♆14♑
5	12.55	11	10♍	13	29	22	♇19♏
6	12.59	12	24	15	29	23	♃ 5♍
7	13.03	13	8♎	16	0♍	23	♄ 0♒
8	13.06	14	22	18	1	24	♅10♑
9	13.10	15	5♏	20	2	25	♆14♑
10	13.14	16	18	21	2	25	♇19♏
11	13.18	17	1♐	23	3	26	♃ 6♍
12	13.22	18	13	25	4	27	♄ 0♒
13	13.26	19	25	26	5	27	♅10♑
14	13.30	20	7♑	28	5	28	♆14♑
15	13.34	21	19	0♏	6	29	♇19♏
16	13.38	22	1♒	1	7	0♏	♃ 7♍
17	13.42	23	13	3	8	0	♄ 0♒
18	13.46	24	25	4	9	1	♅10♑
19	13.50	25	7♓	6	10	2	♆14♑
20	13.54	26	20	7	10	2	♇19♏
21	13.58	27	3♈	9	11	3	♃ 7♍
22	14.02	28	16	11	12	4	♄ 0♒
23	14.06	29	0♉	12	13	4	♅10♑
24	14.10	0♏	14	14	14	5	♆14♑
25	14.14	1	28	15	15	6	♇19♏
26	14.17	2	12♊	17	16	6	♃ 8♍
27	14.21	3	26	18	17	7	♄ 0♒
28	14.25	4	11♋	20	18	8	♅10♑
29	14.29	5	25	21	19	8	♆14♑
30	14.33	6	9♌	23	20	9	♇19♏
31	14.37	7	23	24	21	10	♃ 9♍

Nov	STime	☉	☽	☿	♀	♂	Plnts
1	14.41	8♏	7♍	25♏	22♍	10♏	♃ 9♍
2	14.45	9	20	27	23	11	♄ 1♒
3	14.49	10	4♎	28	24	12	♅10♑
4	14.53	11	17	0♐	25	12	♆14♑
5	14.57	12	1♏	1	26	13	♇20♏
6	15.01	13	14	3	27	14	♃10♍
7	15.05	14	26	4	28	15	♄ 1♒
8	15.09	15	9♐	5	29	15	♅11♑
9	15.13	16	21	7	0♎	16	♆14♑
10	15.17	17	3♑	8	1	17	♇20♏
11	15.21	18	15	9	2	17	♃11♍
12	15.24	19	27	11	3	18	♄ 1♒
13	15.28	20	8♒	12	4	19	♅11♑
14	15.32	21	20	13	5	19	♆14♑
15	15.36	22	2♓	14	6	20	♇20♏
16	15.40	23	15	15	7	21	♃11♍
17	15.44	24	27	16	9	22	♄ 1♒
18	15.48	25	11♈	18	10	22	♅11♑
19	15.52	26	24	19	11	23	♆14♑
20	15.56	27	8♉	20	12	24	♇20♏
21	16.00	28	22	20	13	24	♃12♍
22	16.04	29	7♊	21	14	25	♄ 2♒
23	16.08	0♐	21	22	15	26	♅11♑
24	16.12	1	6♋	23	16	26	♆15♑
25	16.16	2	21	23	17	27	♇21♏
26	16.20	3	5♌	24	18	28	♃13♍
27	16.24	4	20	24	20	29	♄ 2♒
28	16.28	5	4♍	24R	21	29	♅11♑
29	16.31	6	17	24	22	0♐	♆15♑
30	16.35	7	1♎	24	23	1	♇21♏

Dec	STime	☉	☽	☿	♀	♂	Plnts
1	16.39	8♐	14♎	23♐	24♎	1♐	♃13♍
2	16.43	10	27	23	25	2	♄ 3♒
3	16.47	11	10♏	22	26	3	♅12♑
4	16.51	12	23	21	28	4	♆15♑
5	16.55	13	5♐	20	29	4	♇21♏
6	16.59	14	17	19	0♏	5	♃13♍
7	17.03	15	29	17	1	6	♄ 3♒
8	17.07	16	11♑	16	2	6	♅12♑
9	17.11	17	23	15	3	7	♆15♑
10	17.15	18	5♒	13	5	8	♇21♏
11	17.19	19	17	12	6	9	♃14♍
12	17.23	20	29	11	7	9	♄ 4♒
13	17.27	21	11♓	10	8	10	♅12♑
14	17.31	22	23	9	9	11	♆15♑
15	17.35	23	5♈	8	10	11	♇21♏
16	17.39	24	18	8	12	12	♃14♍
17	17.42	25	2♉	8	13	13	♄ 4♒
18	17.46	26	16	8D	14	14	♅13♑
19	17.50	27	0♊	8	15	14	♆15♑
20	17.54	28	15	8	16	15	♇21♏
21	17.58	29	0♋	8	18	16	♃14♍
22	18.02	0♑	15	9	19	17	♄ 5♒
23	18.06	1	0♌	9	20	17	♅13♑
24	18.10	2	15	10	21	18	♆16♑
25	18.14	3	29	11	22	19	♇22♏
26	18.18	4	14♍	12	24	19	♃14♍
27	18.22	5	28	13	25	20	♄ 5♒
28	18.26	6	11♎	14	26	21	♅13♑
29	18.30	7	24	15	27	22	♆16♑
30	18.34	8	7♏	16	28	22	♇22♏
31	18.38	9	20	17	0♐	23	♃14♍

Jan	STime	☉	☽	☿	♀	♂	Plnts
1	18.42	10♑	2♐	18♐	1♐	24♐	♃14♍R
2	18.46	11	14	20	2	25	♄ 6♒
3	18.49	12	26	21	3	25	♅14♑
4	18.53	13	8♑	22	4	26	♆16♑
5	18.57	14	20	23	6	27	♇22♏
6	19.01	15	2♒	25	7	28	♃14♍R
7	19.05	16	13	26	8	28	♄ 6♒
8	19.09	17	25	28	9	29	♅14♑
9	19.13	18	7♓	29	10	0♑	♆16♑
10	19.17	19	19	0♑	12	1	♇22♏
11	19.21	20	2♈	2	13	1	♃14♍R
12	19.25	21	14	3	14	2	♄ 7♒
13	19.29	22	27	5	15	3	♅14♑
14	19.33	23	10♉	6	16	3	♆16♑
15	19.37	24	24	7	18	4	♇22♏
16	19.41	25	8♊	9	19	5	♃14♍R
17	19.45	26	23	10	20	6	♄ 7♒
18	19.49	27	8♋	12	21	6	♅14♑
19	19.53	28	23	13	23	7	♆17♑
20	19.57	29	8♌	15	24	8	♇22♏
21	20.00	0♒	23	16	25	9	♃14♍R
22	20.04	1	8♍	18	26	9	♄ 8♒
23	20.08	2	23	20	27	10	♅15♑
24	20.12	3	7♎	21	29	11	♆17♑
25	20.16	4	21	23	0♑	12	♇22♏
26	20.20	5	4♏	24	1	12	♃13♍R
27	20.24	6	17	26	2	13	♄ 9♒
28	20.28	8	29	27	4	14	♅15♑
29	20.32	9	11♐	29	5	15	♆17♑
30	20.36	10	23	1♒	6	15	♇22♏
31	20.40	11	5♑	2	7	16	♃13♍R

Feb	STime	☉	☽	☿	♀	♂	Plnts
1	20.44	12♒	17♑	4♒	9♑	17♑	♃13♍R
2	20.48	13	29	6	10	18	♄ 9♒
3	20.52	14	10♒	7	11	19	♅15♑
4	20.56	15	22	9	12	19	♆17♑
5	21.00	16	4♓	11	13	20	♇23♏
6	21.04	17	16	12	15	21	♃12♍R
7	21.07	18	29	14	16	22	♄10♒
8	21.11	19	11♈	16	17	22	♅16♑
9	21.15	20	23	18	18	23	♆17♑
10	21.19	21	6♉	19	20	24	♇23♏
11	21.23	22	19	21	21	25	♃12♍R
12	21.27	23	3♊	23	22	25	♄11♒
13	21.31	24	17	25	23	26	♅16♑
14	21.35	25	1♋	26	25	27	♆18♑
15	21.39	26	16	28	26	28	♇23♏
16	21.43	27	1♌	0♓	27	28	♃11♍R
17	21.47	28	16	2	28	29	♄11♒
18	21.51	29	1♍	4	29	0♒	♅16♑
19	21.55	0♓	16	6	1♒	1	♆18♑
20	21.59	1	1♎	7	2	1	♇23♏
21	22.03	2	15	9	3	2	♃10♍R
22	22.07	3	29	11	4	3	♄12♒
23	22.11	4	12♏	13	6	4	♅16♑
24	22.15	5	25	15	7	5	♆18♑
25	22.18	6	8♐	17	8	5	♇23♏
26	22.22	7	20	19	9	6	♃10♍R
27	22.26	8	2♑	20	11	7	♄12♒
28	22.30	9	14	22	12	8	♅17♑
29	22.34	10	25	24	13	8	♆18♑

Mar	STime	☉	☽	☿	♀	♂	Plnts
1	22.38	11♓	7♒	26♓	14♒	9♒	♃ 9♍R
2	22.42	12	19	27	15	10	♄13♒
3	22.46	13	1♓	29	17	11	♅17♑
4	22.50	14	13	1♈	18	11	♆18♑
5	22.54	15	25	2	19	12	♇23♏R
6	22.58	16	8♈	3	20	13	♃ 9♍R
7	23.02	17	21	5	22	14	♄13♒
8	23.06	18	3♉	6	23	15	♅17♑
9	23.10	19	16	7	24	15	♆18♑
10	23.14	20	0♊	8	25	16	♇23♏
11	23.18	21	13	9	27	17	♃ 8♍R
12	23.22	22	27	10	28	18	♄14♒
13	23.25	23	11♋	10	29	18	♅17♑
14	23.29	24	25	11	0♓	19	♆18♑
15	23.33	25	10♌	11	2	20	♇23♏R
16	23.37	26	25	11	3	21	♃ 7♍R
17	23.41	27	10♍	11R	4	22	♄14♒
18	23.45	28	24	11	5	22	♅17♑
19	23.49	29	9♎	11	6	23	♆18♑
20	23.53	0♈	23	10	8	24	♇22♏R
21	23.57	1	7♏	10	9	25	♃ 7♍R
22	0.01	2	20	9	10	25	♄15♒
23	0.05	3	3♐	8	11	26	♅17♑
24	0.09	4	16	8	13	27	♆18♑
25	0.13	5	28	7	14	28	♇22♏R
26	0.17	6	10♑	6	15	28	♃ 6♍R
27	0.21	7	22	5	16	29	♄15♒
28	0.25	8	4♒	4	18	0♓	♅17♑
29	0.29	9	16	3	19	1	♆19♑
30	0.32	10	27	3	20	2	♇22♏R
31	0.36	11	10♓	2	21	2	♃ 6♍R

Apr	STime	☉	☽	☿	♀	♂	Plnts
1	0.40	12♈	22♓	1♈	23♓	3♓	♃ 6♍R
2	0.44	13	4♈	1	24	4	♄16♒
3	0.48	14	17	0	25	5	♅18♑
4	0.52	15	0♉	29♓	26	5	♆19♑
5	0.56	16	13	29	27	6	♇22♏R
6	1.00	17	27	29	29	7	♃ 5♍R
7	1.04	18	10♊	29	0♈	8	♄16♒
8	1.08	19	24	28	1	9	♅18♑
9	1.12	20	8♋	28D	2	9	♆19♑
10	1.16	21	22	28	4	10	♇22♏R
11	1.20	22	6♌	29	5	11	♃ 5♍R
12	1.24	23	20	29	6	12	♄16♒
13	1.28	24	4♍	29	7	12	♅18♑
14	1.32	24	19	0♈	9	13	♆19♑
15	1.36	25	3♎	0	10	14	♇22♏R
16	1.40	26	17	1	11	15	♃ 5♍R
17	1.43	27	1♏	1	12	16	♄17♒
18	1.47	28	15	2	14	16	♅18♑
19	1.51	29	28	3	15	17	♆19♑
20	1.55	0♉	11♐	3	16	18	♇22♏R
21	1.59	1	24	4	17	19	♃ 4♍R
22	2.03	2	6♑	5	18	19	♄17♒
23	2.07	3	18	6	20	20	♅18♑
24	2.11	4	0♒	7	21	21	♆19♑R
25	2.15	5	12	8	22	22	♇22♏R
26	2.19	6	24	9	23	22	♃ 4♍R
27	2.23	7	6♓	10	25	23	♄17♒
28	2.27	8	18	12	26	24	♅18♑R
29	2.31	9	0♈	13	27	25	♆19♑R
30	2.35	10	13	14	28	26	♇22♏R

May	STime	☉	☽	☿	♀	♂	Plnts
1	2.39	11♉	26♈	15♈	0♉	26♓	♃ 4♍
2	2.43	12	9♉	17	1	27	♄18♒
3	2.47	13	23	18	2	28	♅18♑R
4	2.50	14	6♊	19	3	29	♆19♑R
5	2.54	15	20	21	4	29	♇21♏R
6	2.58	16	4♋	22	6	0♈	♃ 4♍
7	3.02	17	18	24	7	1	♄18♒
8	3.06	18	3♌	25	8	2	♅18♑R
9	3.10	19	17	27	9	2	♆19♑R
10	3.14	20	1♍	29	11	3	♇21♏R
11	3.18	21	15	0♉	12	4	♃ 5♍
12	3.22	22	29	2	13	5	♄18♒
13	3.26	23	13♎	4	14	6	♅18♑R
14	3.30	24	27	5	15	6	♆19♑R
15	3.34	25	10♏	7	17	7	♇21♏R
16	3.38	26	24	9	18	8	♃ 5♍
17	3.42	27	7♐	11	19	9	♄18♒
18	3.46	27	19	13	20	9	♅17♑R
19	3.50	28	2♑	15	22	10	♆18♑R
20	3.54	29	14	17	23	11	♇21♏R
21	3.57	0♊	26	19	24	12	♃ 5♍
22	4.01	1	8♒	21	25	12	♄18♒
23	4.05	2	20	23	27	13	♅17♑R
24	4.09	3	1♓	25	28	14	♆18♑R
25	4.13	4	13	27	29	15	♇21♏R
26	4.17	5	26	29	0♊	15	♃ 5♍
27	4.21	6	8♈	1♊	1	16	♄18♒
28	4.25	7	21	3	3	17	♅17♑R
29	4.29	8	4♉	5	4	18	♆18♑R
30	4.33	9	17	8	5	18	♇21♏R
31	4.37	10	1♊	10	6	19	♃ 6♍

Jun	STime	☉	☽	☿	♀	♂	Plnts
1	4.41	11♊	15♊	12♊	8♊	20♈	♃ 6♍
2	4.45	12	0♋	14	9	21	♄18♒R
3	4.49	13	14	16	10	21	♅17♑R
4	4.53	14	29	19	11	22	♆18♑R
5	4.57	15	13♌	21	13	23	♇21♏R
6	5.01	16	28	23	14	24	♃ 6♍
7	5.05	17	12♍	25	15	24	♄18♒R
8	5.08	18	26	27	16	25	♅17♑R
9	5.12	19	10♎	29	17	26	♆18♑R
10	5.16	20	23	1♋	19	27	♇21♏R
11	5.20	21	7♏	3	20	27	♃ 7♍
12	5.24	21	20	5	21	28	♄18♒R
13	5.28	22	3♐	7	22	29	♅17♑R
14	5.32	23	15	9	24	0♉	♆18♑R
15	5.36	24	28	11	25	0	♇20♏R
16	5.40	25	10♑	13	26	1	♃ 7♍
17	5.44	26	22	14	27	2	♄18♒R
18	5.48	27	4♒	16	29	3	♅16♑R
19	5.52	28	16	18	0♋	3	♆18♑R
20	5.56	29	28	20	1	4	♇20♏R
21	6.00	0♋	10♓	21	2	5	♃ 8♍
22	6.04	1	22	23	3	5	♄18♒R
23	6.08	2	4♈	24	5	6	♅16♑R
24	6.12	3	16	26	6	7	♆18♑R
25	6.15	4	29	27	7	8	♇20♏R
26	6.19	5	12♉	29	8	8	♃ 9♍
27	6.23	6	26	0♌	10	9	♄17♒R
28	6.27	7	9♊	1	11	10	♅16♑R
29	6.31	8	24	3	12	11	♆18♑R
30	6.35	9	8♋	4	13	11	♇20♏R

Jul	STime	☉	☽	☿	♀	♂	Plnts
1	6.39	10♋	23♋	5♌	14♋	12♉	♃10♍
2	6.43	11	8♌	6	16	13	♄17♒R
3	6.47	12	23	7	17	13	♅16♑R
4	6.51	12	8♍	8	18	14	♆17♑R
5	6.55	13	22	9	19	15	♇20♏R
6	6.59	14	6♎	10	21	16	♃10♍
7	7.03	15	20	11	22	16	♄17♒R
8	7.07	16	4♏	12	23	17	♅16♑R
9	7.11	17	17	13	24	18	♆17♑R
10	7.15	18	0♐	14	26	18	♇20♏R
11	7.19	19	12	14	27	19	♃11♍
12	7.23	20	24	15	28	20	♄17♒R
13	7.26	21	7♑	16	29	20	♅16♑R
14	7.30	22	19	16	0♌	21	♆17♑R
15	7.34	23	1♒	16	2	22	♇20♏
16	7.38	24	13	17	3	23	♃12♍
17	7.42	25	24	17	4	23	♄16♒R
18	7.46	26	6♓	17	5	24	♅15♑R
19	7.50	27	18	17	7	25	♆17♑R
20	7.54	28	0♈	17R	8	25	♇20♏R
21	7.58	29	12	17	9	26	♃13♍
22	8.02	0♌	25	17	10	27	♄16♒R
23	8.06	1	7♉	17	12	27	♅15♑R
24	8.10	2	20	16	13	28	♆17♑R
25	8.14	2	4♊	16	14	29	♇20♏R
26	8.18	3	18	16	15	29	♃14♍
27	8.22	4	2♋	15	16	0♊	♄16♒R
28	8.26	5	17	14	18	1	♅15♑R
29	8.30	6	2♌	14	19	2	♆17♑R
30	8.33	7	17	13	20	2	♇20♏
31	8.37	8	2♍	12	21	3	♃15♍

Aug	STime	☉	☽	☿	♀	♂	Plnts
1	8.41	9♌	17♍	12♌	23♌	4♊	♃15♍
2	8.45	10	2♎	11	24	4	♄15♒R
3	8.49	11	16	10	25	5	♅15♑R
4	8.53	12	0♏	9	26	6	♆17♑R
5	8.57	13	14	9	28	6	♇20♏
6	9.01	14	27	8	29	7	♃16♍
7	9.05	15	9♐	7	0♍	8	♄15♒R
8	9.09	16	22	7	1	8	♅15♑R
9	9.13	17	4♑	6	2	9	♆16♑R
10	9.17	18	16	6	4	10	♇20♏
11	9.21	19	28	6	5	10	♃17♍
12	9.25	20	10♒	6	6	11	♄14♒R
13	9.29	21	21	6D	7	11	♅14♑R
14	9.33	22	3♓	6	9	12	♆16♑R
15	9.37	23	15	6	10	13	♇20♏
16	9.41	24	27	6	11	13	♃18♍
17	9.44	25	9♈	7	12	14	♄14♒R
18	9.48	25	21	7	14	15	♅14♑R
19	9.52	26	4♉	8	15	15	♆16♑R
20	9.56	27	16	9	16	16	♇20♏
21	10.00	28	29	10	17	17	♃19♍
22	10.04	29	13♊	11	18	17	♄14♒R
23	10.08	0♍	26	12	20	18	♅14♑R
24	10.12	1	11♋	13	21	18	♆16♑R
25	10.16	2	25	15	22	19	♇20♏
26	10.20	3	10♌	16	23	20	♃20♍
27	10.24	4	25	18	25	20	♄13♒R
28	10.28	5	11♍	19	26	21	♅14♑R
29	10.32	6	26	21	27	22	♆16♑R
30	10.36	7	11♎	23	28	22	♇20♏
31	10.40	8	25	24	29	23	♃21♍

Sep	STime	☉	☽	☿	♀	♂	Plnts
1	10.44	9♍	9♏	26♌	1♎	23♊	♃21♍
2	10.48	10	23	28	2	24	♄13♒R
3	10.51	11	6♐	0♍	3	25	♅14♑R
4	10.55	12	18	2	4	25	♆16♑R
5	10.59	13	1♑	4	6	26	♇20♏
6	11.03	14	13	6	7	26	♃22♍
7	11.07	15	25	8	8	27	♄13♒R
8	11.11	16	7♒	10	9	28	♅14♑R
9	11.15	17	18	12	11	28	♆16♑R
10	11.19	18	0♓	13	12	29	♇20♏
11	11.23	19	12	15	13	29	♃23♍
12	11.27	20	24	17	14	0♋	♄12♒R
13	11.31	21	6♈	19	15	0	♅14♑R
14	11.35	22	18	21	17	1	♆16♑R
15	11.39	23	1♉	23	18	2	♇20♏
16	11.43	24	13	25	19	2	♃25♍
17	11.47	25	26	27	20	3	♄12♒R
18	11.51	26	9♊	28	22	3	♅14♑
19	11.55	27	22	0♎	23	4	♆16♑
20	11.59	27	6♋	2	24	4	♇21♏
21	12.02	28	20	4	25	5	♃26♍
22	12.06	29	4♌	5	26	5	♄12♒R
23	12.10	0♎	19	7	28	6	♅14♑
24	12.14	1	4♍	9	29	6	♆16♑R
25	12.18	2	19	11	0♏	7	♇21♏
26	12.22	3	4♎	12	1	7	♃27♍
27	12.26	4	19	14	3	8	♄12♒R
28	12.30	5	3♏	16	4	9	♅14♑
29	12.34	6	17	17	5	9	♆16♑
30	12.38	7	1♐	19	6	10	♇21♏

Oct	STime	☉	☽	☿	♀	♂	Plnts
1	12.42	8♎	14♐	20♎	7♏	10♋	♃28♍
2	12.46	9	27	22	9	11	♄12♒R
3	12.50	10	9♑	24	10	11	♅14♑
4	12.54	11	21	25	11	11	♆16♑
5	12.58	12	3♒	27	12	12	♇21♏
6	13.02	13	15	28	14	12	♃29♍
7	13.06	14	27	0♏	15	13	♄12♒R
8	13.09	15	9♓	1	16	13	♅14♑
9	13.13	16	21	3	17	14	♆16♑
10	13.17	17	3♈	4	18	14	♇21♏
11	13.21	18	15	6	20	15	♃ 0♎
12	13.25	19	28	7	21	15	♄12♒
13	13.29	20	10♉	9	22	16	♅14♑
14	13.33	21	23	10	23	16	♆16♑
15	13.37	22	6♊	12	25	17	♇21♏
16	13.41	23	19	13	26	17	♃ 1♎
17	13.45	24	3♋	14	27	17	♄12♒
18	13.49	25	16	16	28	18	♅14♑
19	13.53	26	0♌	17	29	18	♆16♑
20	13.57	27	14	18	1♐	19	♇22♏
21	14.01	28	29	20	2	19	♃ 2♎
22	14.05	29	13♍	21	3	19	♄12♒
23	14.09	0♏	28	22	4	20	♅14♑
24	14.13	1	13♎	24	5	20	♆16♑
25	14.16	2	27	25	7	20	♇22♏
26	14.20	3	12♏	26	8	21	♃ 3♎
27	14.24	4	25	27	9	21	♄12♒
28	14.28	5	9♐	28	10	21	♅14♑
29	14.32	6	22	29	12	22	♆16♑
30	14.36	7	5♑	1♐	13	22	♇22♏
31	14.40	8	17	2	14	22	♃ 4♎

Nov	STime	☉	☽	☿	♀	♂	Plnts
1	14.44	9♏	29♑	3♐	15♐	23♋	♃ 4♎
2	14.48	10	11♒	3	16	23	♄12♒
3	14.52	11	23	4	18	23	♅14♑
4	14.56	12	5♓	5	19	24	♆16♑
5	15.00	13	17	6	20	24	♇22♏
6	15.04	14	29	7	21	24	♃ 5♎
7	15.08	15	11♈	7	22	24	♄12♒
8	15.12	16	24	8	24	25	♅15♑
9	15.16	17	6♉	8	25	25	♆16♑
10	15.20	18	19	8	26	25	♇22♏
11	15.24	19	3♊	8R	27	25	♃ 6♎
12	15.27	20	16	8	28	26	♄12♒
13	15.31	21	0♋	8	0♑	26	♅15♑
14	15.35	22	13	7	1	26	♆16♑
15	15.39	23	27	7	2	26	♇23♏
16	15.43	24	11♌	6	3	26	♃ 7♎
17	15.47	25	25	5	4	26	♄12♒
18	15.51	26	9♍	4	6	27	♅15♑
19	15.55	27	24	3	7	27	♆17♑
20	15.59	28	8♎	1	8	27	♇23♏
21	16.03	29	22	0	9	27	♃ 8♎
22	16.07	0♐	6♏	29♏	10	27	♄13♒
23	16.11	1	20	27	12	27	♅15♑
24	16.15	2	4♐	26	13	27	♆17♑
25	16.19	3	17	25	14	27	♇23♏
26	16.23	4	0♑	24	15	27	♃ 9♎
27	16.27	5	13	23	16	27	♄13♒
28	16.31	6	25	23	18	27	♅16♑
29	16.34	7	7♒	22	19	27R	♆17♑
30	16.38	8	19	22	20	27	♇23♏

Dec	STime	☉	☽	☿	♀	♂	Plnts
1	16.42	9♐	1♓	22♏	21♑	27♋	♃ 9♎
2	16.46	10	13	22	22	27	♄13♒
3	16.50	11	25	22	24	27	♅16♑
4	16.54	12	7♈	23	25	27	♆17♑
5	16.58	13	19	23	26	27	♇23♏
6	17.02	14	2♉	24	27	27	♃10♎
7	17.06	15	14	25	28	27	♄14♒
8	17.10	16	28	26	29	27	♅16♑
9	17.14	17	11♊	27	1♒	27	♆17♑
10	17.18	18	25	28	2	26	♇24♏
11	17.22	19	9♋	29	3	26	♃11♎
12	17.26	20	23	0♐	4	26	♄14♒
13	17.30	21	8♌	1	5	26	♅16♑
14	17.34	22	22	2	6	26	♆17♑
15	17.38	23	6♍	4	8	25	♇24♏
16	17.42	24	21	5	9	25	♃12♎
17	17.45	26	5♎	6	10	25	♄15♒
18	17.49	27	19	8	11	25	♅17♑
19	17.53	28	2♏	9	12	24	♆18♑
20	17.57	29	16	10	13	24	♇24♏
21	18.01	0♑	29	12	14	24	♃12♎
22	18.05	1	12♐	13	16	23	♄15♒
23	18.09	2	25	15	17	23	♅17♑
24	18.13	3	8♑	16	18	23	♆18♑
25	18.17	4	21	18	19	23	♇24♏
26	18.21	5	3♒	19	20	22	♃13♎
27	18.25	6	15	20	21	22	♄16♒
28	18.29	7	27	22	22	21	♅17♑
29	18.33	8	9♓	23	24	21	♆18♑
30	18.37	9	21	25	25	21	♇24♏
31	18.41	10	3♈	26	26	20	♃13♎

Jan	STime	☉	☽	☿	♀	♂	Plnts
1	18.45	11♑	15♈	28♐	27♒	20♋	♃13♎
2	18.49	12	27	0♑	28	20	♄16♒
3	18.52	13	9♉	1	29	19	♅18♑
4	18.56	14	22	3	0♓	19	♆18♑
5	19.00	15	5♊	4	1	18	♇24♏
6	19.04	16	19	6	2	18	♃14♎
7	19.08	17	3♋	7	4	18	♄17♒
8	19.12	18	18	9	5	17	♅18♑
9	19.16	19	2♌	10	6	17	♆18♑
10	19.20	20	17	12	7	16	♇25♏
11	19.24	21	2♍	13	8	16	♃14♎
12	19.28	22	17	15	9	16	♄17♒
13	19.32	23	1♎	17	10	15	♅18♑
14	19.36	24	15	18	11	15	♆19♑
15	19.40	25	29	20	12	14	♇25♏
16	19.44	26	13♏	21	13	14	♃14♎
17	19.48	27	26	23	14	14	♄18♒
18	19.52	28	9♐	25	15	13	♅18♑
19	19.56	29	22	26	16	13	♆19♑
20	20.00	0♒	4♑	28	17	13	♇25♏
21	20.03	1	17	0♒	18	12	♃14♎
22	20.07	2	29	1	19	12	♄18♒
23	20.11	3	11♒	3	20	12	♅19♑
24	20.15	4	23	5	21	11	♆19♑
25	20.19	5	5♓	6	22	11	♇25♏
26	20.23	6	17	8	23	11	♃14♎
27	20.27	7	29	10	24	11	♄19♒
28	20.31	8	11♈	12	25	10	♅19♑
29	20.35	9	23	13	26	10	♆19♑
30	20.39	10	5♉	15	27	10	♇25♏
31	20.43	11	17	17	28	10	♃14♎R

Feb	STime	☉	☽	☿	♀	♂	Plnts
1	20.47	12♒	0♊	19♒	29♓	10♋	♃14♎R
2	20.51	13	13	20	0♈	9	♄20♒
3	20.55	14	27	22	1	9	♅19♑
4	20.59	15	11♋	24	1	9	♆19♑
5	21.03	16	25	26	2	9	♇25♏
6	21.07	17	10♌	28	3	9	♃14♎R
7	21.10	18	26	29	4	9	♄20♒
8	21.14	19	11♍	1♓	5	9	♅20♑
9	21.18	20	26	3	6	9	♆20♑
10	21.22	21	11♎	5	6	9	♇25♏
11	21.26	22	25	6	7	8	♃14♎R
12	21.30	23	9♏	8	8	8	♄21♒
13	21.34	24	23	10	9	8	♅20♑
14	21.38	26	6♐	11	9	8D	♆20♑
15	21.42	27	19	13	10	8	♇25♏
16	21.46	28	2♑	14	11	8	♃14♎R
17	21.50	29	14	16	12	8	♄22♒
18	21.54	0♓	26	17	12	8	♅20♑
19	21.58	1	8♒	18	13	8	♆20♑
20	22.02	2	20	20	13	9	♇25♏
21	22.06	3	2♓	21	14	9	♃14♎R
22	22.10	4	14	22	15	9	♄22♒
23	22.14	5	26	22	15	9	♅20♑
24	22.17	6	8♈	23	16	9	♆20♑
25	22.21	7	20	23	16	9	♇25♏
26	22.25	8	2♉	24	17	9	♃13♎R
27	22.29	9	14	24	17	9	♄23♒
28	22.33	10	26	24R	17	9	♅21♑

Mar	STime	☉	☽	☿	♀	♂	Plnts
1	22.37	11♓	9♊	24♓	18♈	10♋	♃13♎R
2	22.41	12	22	23	18	10	♄23♒
3	22.45	13	5♋	23	19	10	♅21♑
4	22.49	14	19	22	19	10	♆20♑
5	22.53	15	4♌	22	19	10	♇25♏
6	22.57	16	18	21	19	10	♃12♎R
7	23.01	17	4♍	20	19	11	♄24♒
8	23.05	18	19	19	20	11	♅21♑
9	23.09	19	4♎	18	20	11	♆20♑
10	23.13	20	19	17	20	11	♇25♏
11	23.17	21	4♏	16	20R	12	♃12♎R
12	23.21	22	18	15	20	12	♄24♒
13	23.25	23	2♐	14	20	12	♅21♑
14	23.28	24	16	13	20	12	♆20♑
15	23.32	25	28	13	19	13	♇25♏R
16	23.36	26	11♑	12	19	13	♃11♎R
17	23.40	27	23	11	19	13	♄25♒
18	23.44	28	5♒	11	19	14	♅21♑
19	23.48	29	17	10	18	14	♆21♑
20	23.52	0♈	29	10	18	14	♇25♏R
21	23.56	1	11♓	10	18	14	♃11♎R
22	0.00	2	23	10D	17	15	♄25♒
23	0.04	3	5♈	10	17	15	♅21♑
24	0.08	4	17	10	16	15	♆21♑
25	0.12	5	29	10	16	16	♇25♏R
26	0.16	6	11♉	11	15	16	♃10♎R
27	0.20	7	23	11	15	16	♄26♒
28	0.24	8	5♊	12	14	17	♅22♑
29	0.28	9	18	12	13	17	♆21♑
30	0.32	10	1♋	13	13	18	♇25♏R
31	0.35	10	15	13	12	18	♃ 9♎R

Apr	STime	☉	☽	☿	♀	♂	Plnts
1	0.39	11♈	28♋	14♓	12♈	18♋	♃ 9♎R
2	0.43	12	13♌	15	11	19	♄26♒
3	0.47	13	27	16	10	19	♅22♑
4	0.51	14	12♍	17	10	19	♆21♑
5	0.55	15	27	18	9	20	♇25♏R
6	0.59	16	12♎	19	9	20	♃ 9♎R
7	1.03	17	27	20	8	21	♄27♒
8	1.07	18	12♏	21	7	21	♅22♑
9	1.11	19	27	22	7	21	♆21♑
10	1.15	20	11♐	23	6	22	♇25♏R
11	1.19	21	24	24	6	22	♃ 8♎R
12	1.23	22	7♑	26	6	23	♄27♒
13	1.27	23	20	27	5	23	♅22♑
14	1.31	24	2♒	28	5	24	♆21♑
15	1.35	25	14	0♈	4	24	♇25♏R
16	1.39	26	26	1	4	24	♃ 7♎R
17	1.43	27	8♓	2	4	25	♄28♒
18	1.46	28	20	4	4	25	♅22♑
19	1.50	29	2♈	5	4	26	♆21♑
20	1.54	0♉	14	7	4	26	♇25♏R
21	1.58	1	26	8	3	27	♃ 7♎R
22	2.02	2	8♉	10	3D	27	♄28♒
23	2.06	3	20	11	3	28	♅22♑
24	2.10	4	3♊	13	4	28	♆21♑
25	2.14	5	15	15	4	29	♇24♏R
26	2.18	6	28	16	4	29	♃ 6♎R
27	2.22	7	11♋	18	4	29	♄28♒
28	2.26	8	25	20	4	0♌	♅22♑
29	2.30	9	8♌	22	4	0	♆21♑
30	2.34	10	23	23	5	1	♇24♏R

May	STime	☉	☽	☿	♀	♂	Plnts
1	2.38	11♉	7♍	25♈	5♈	1♌	♃ 6♎R
2	2.42	12	22	27	5	2	♄29♒
3	2.46	13	6♎	29	6	2	♅22♑R
4	2.50	14	21	1♉	6	3	♆21♑R
5	2.53	15	6♏	3	6	3	♇24♏R
6	2.57	16	20	5	7	4	♃ 5♎R
7	3.01	17	5♐	7	7	4	♄29♒
8	3.05	18	19	9	8	5	♅22♑R
9	3.09	19	2♑	11	8	5	♆21♑R
10	3.13	20	15	13	9	6	♇24♏R
11	3.17	21	28	15	9	6	♃ 5♎R
12	3.21	21	10♒	17	10	7	♄29♒
13	3.25	22	22	19	11	7	♅22♑R
14	3.29	23	4♓	21	11	8	♆21♑R
15	3.33	24	16	24	12	8	♇24♏R
16	3.37	25	28	26	13	9	♃ 5♎R
17	3.41	26	10♈	28	13	9	♄ 0♓
18	3.45	27	22	0♊	14	10	♅22♑R
19	3.49	28	4♉	2	15	10	♆21♑R
20	3.53	29	17	5	15	11	♇24♏R
21	3.57	0♊	29	7	16	12	♃ 5♎R
22	4.00	1	12♊	9	17	12	♄ 0♓
23	4.04	2	25	11	18	13	♅22♑R
24	4.08	3	8♋	13	19	13	♆21♑R
25	4.12	4	22	15	19	14	♇24♏R
26	4.16	5	5♌	17	20	14	♃ 5♎R
27	4.20	6	19	19	21	15	♄ 0♓
28	4.24	7	3♍	21	22	15	♅21♑R
29	4.28	8	18	23	23	16	♆21♑R
30	4.32	9	2♎	25	24	16	♇23♏R
31	4.36	10	16	27	24	17	♃ 4♎

Jun	STime	☉	☽	☿	♀	♂	Plnts
1	4.40	11♊	1♏	29♊	25♈	17♌	♃ 4♎
2	4.44	12	15	0♋	26	18	♄ 0♓
3	4.48	13	29	2	27	19	♅21♑R
4	4.52	14	13♐	4	28	19	♆20♑R
5	4.56	15	27	5	29	20	♇23♏R
6	5.00	15	10♑	7	0♉	20	♃ 5♎
7	5.04	16	23	8	1	21	♄ 0♓
8	5.08	17	6♒	10	2	21	♅21♑R
9	5.11	18	18	11	3	22	♆20♑R
10	5.15	19	0♓	13	4	22	♇23♏R
11	5.19	20	12	14	5	23	♃ 5♎
12	5.23	21	24	15	5	24	♄ 0♓R
13	5.27	22	6♈	16	6	24	♅21♑R
14	5.31	23	18	18	7	25	♆20♑R
15	5.35	24	0♉	19	8	25	♇23♏R
16	5.39	25	12	20	9	26	♃ 5♎
17	5.43	26	25	21	10	26	♄ 0♓R
18	5.47	27	8♊	22	11	27	♅21♑R
19	5.51	28	21	23	12	28	♆20♑R
20	5.55	29	4♋	23	13	28	♇23♏R
21	5.59	0♋	18	24	14	29	♃ 5♎
22	6.03	1	2♌	25	15	29	♄ 0♓R
23	6.07	2	16	25	16	0♍	♅21♑R
24	6.11	3	0♍	26	18	0	♆20♑R
25	6.15	4	14	27	19	1	♇23♏R
26	6.18	5	29	27	20	2	♃ 5♎
27	6.22	6	13♎	27	21	2	♄ 0♓R
28	6.26	7	27	28	22	3	♅20♑R
29	6.30	7	11♏	28	23	3	♆20♑R
30	6.34	8	25	28	24	4	♇23♏R

Jul	STime	☉	☽	☿	♀	♂	Plnts
1	6.38	9♋	9♐	28♋	25♉	4♍	♃ 6♎
2	6.42	10	22	28	26	5	♄ 0♓R
3	6.46	11	5♑	28	27	6	♅20♑R
4	6.50	12	18	28	28	6	♆20♑R
5	6.54	13	1♒	27	29	7	♇23♏R
6	6.58	14	14	27	0♊	7	♃ 6♎
7	7.02	15	26	27	1	8	♄29♒R
8	7.06	16	8♓	26	2	9	♅20♑R
9	7.10	17	20	26	3	9	♆20♑R
10	7.14	18	2♈	25	5	10	♇23♏R
11	7.18	19	14	25	6	10	♃ 7♎
12	7.22	20	26	24	7	11	♄29♒R
13	7.26	21	8♉	23	8	12	♅20♑R
14	7.29	22	20	23	9	12	♆19♑R
15	7.33	23	3♊	22	10	13	♇23♏R
16	7.37	24	16	21	11	13	♃ 7♎
17	7.41	25	29	21	12	14	♄29♒R
18	7.45	26	13♋	20	13	15	♅20♑R
19	7.49	27	27	20	15	15	♆19♑R
20	7.53	27	11♌	19	16	16	♇22♏R
21	7.57	28	26	19	17	16	♃ 8♎
22	8.01	29	10♍	18	18	17	♄29♒R
23	8.05	0♌	25	18	19	18	♅19♑R
24	8.09	1	10♎	18	20	18	♆19♑R
25	8.13	2	24	18D	21	19	♇22♏
26	8.17	3	8♏	18	22	19	♃ 9♎
27	8.21	4	22	18	24	20	♄28♒R
28	8.25	5	5♐	18	25	21	♅19♑R
29	8.29	6	18	19	26	21	♆19♑R
30	8.33	7	2♑	19	27	22	♇22♏
31	8.36	8	15	19	28	23	♃ 9♎

Aug	STime	☉	☽	☿	♀	♂	Plnts
1	8.40	9♌	27♑	20♋	29♊	23♍	♃10♎
2	8.44	10	10♒	21	0♋	24	♄28♒R
3	8.48	11	22	22	1	24	♅19♑R
4	8.52	12	4♓	23	3	25	♆19♑R
5	8.56	13	16	24	4	26	♇22♏
6	9.00	14	28	25	5	26	♃10♎
7	9.04	15	10♈	26	6	27	♄28♒R
8	9.08	16	22	27	7	27	♅19♑R
9	9.12	17	4♉	29	8	28	♆19♑R
10	9.16	18	16	0♌	10	29	♇22♏
11	9.20	19	28	2	11	29	♃11♎
12	9.24	19	11♊	3	12	0♎	♄27♒R
13	9.28	20	24	5	13	1	♅19♑R
14	9.32	21	7♋	7	14	1	♆19♑R
15	9.36	22	21	9	15	2	♇22♏
16	9.40	23	5♌	10	17	3	♃12♎
17	9.44	24	20	12	18	3	♄27♒R
18	9.47	25	5♍	14	19	4	♅19♑R
19	9.51	26	20	16	20	4	♆19♑R
20	9.55	27	5♎	18	21	5	♇23♏
21	9.59	28	20	20	22	6	♃13♎
22	10.03	29	4♏	22	24	6	♄26♒R
23	10.07	0♍	18	24	25	7	♅18♑R
24	10.11	1	2♐	26	26	8	♆18♑R
25	10.15	2	16	28	27	8	♇23♏
26	10.19	3	29	0♍	28	9	♃14♎
27	10.23	4	11♑	2	0♌	10	♄26♒R
28	10.27	5	24	4	1	10	♅18♑R
29	10.31	6	7♒	6	2	11	♆18♑R
30	10.35	7	19	8	3	11	♇23♏
31	10.39	8	1♓	10	4	12	♃15♎

Sep	STime	☉	☽	☿	♀	♂	Plnts
1	10.43	9♍	13♓	12♍	5♌	13♎	♃15♎
2	10.47	10	25	14	7	13	♄26♒R
3	10.51	11	7♈	16	8	14	♅18♑R
4	10.54	12	19	17	9	15	♆18♑R
5	10.58	13	1♉	19	10	15	♇23♏
6	11.02	14	12	21	11	16	♃16♎
7	11.06	15	24	23	13	17	♄25♒R
8	11.10	16	7♊	25	14	17	♅18♑R
9	11.14	17	19	26	15	18	♆18♑R
10	11.18	17	2♋	28	16	19	♇23♏
11	11.22	18	15	0♎	17	19	♃17♎
12	11.26	19	29	1	19	20	♄25♒R
13	11.30	20	14♌	3	20	21	♅18♑R
14	11.34	21	28	5	21	21	♆18♑R
15	11.38	22	13♍	6	22	22	♇23♏
16	11.42	23	29	8	24	23	♃18♎
17	11.46	24	14♎	10	25	23	♄25♒R
18	11.50	25	29	11	26	24	♅18♑R
19	11.54	26	14♏	13	27	25	♆18♑R
20	11.58	27	28	14	28	25	♇23♏
21	12.01	28	12♐	16	0♍	26	♃19♎
22	12.05	29	25	17	1	27	♄24♒R
23	12.09	0♎	8♑	19	2	27	♅18♑
24	12.13	1	21	20	3	28	♆18♑R
25	12.17	2	4♒	22	4	29	♇23♏
26	12.21	3	16	23	6	29	♃20♎
27	12.25	4	28	25	7	0♏	♄24♒R
28	12.29	5	10♓	26	8	1	♅18♑
29	12.33	6	22	28	9	1	♆18♑
30	12.37	7	4♈	29	11	2	♇23♏

Oct	STime	☉	☽	☿	♀	♂	Plnts
1	12.41	8♎	16♈	0♏	12♍	3♏	♃21♎
2	12.45	9	28	2	13	3	♄24♒R
3	12.49	10	10♉	3	14	4	♅18♑
4	12.53	11	21	4	15	5	♆18♑
5	12.57	12	4♊	5	17	5	♇24♏
6	13.01	13	16	7	18	6	♃22♎
7	13.05	14	28	8	19	7	♄24♒R
8	13.09	15	11♋	9	20	7	♅18♑
9	13.12	16	24	10	22	8	♆18♑
10	13.16	17	8♌	11	23	9	♇24♏
11	13.20	18	22	13	24	10	♃23♎
12	13.24	19	7♍	14	25	10	♄24♒R
13	13.28	20	22	15	27	11	♅18♑
14	13.32	21	7♎	16	28	12	♆18♑
15	13.36	22	22	17	29	12	♇24♏
16	13.40	23	7♏	18	0♎	13	♃24♎
17	13.44	24	22	18	2	14	♄23♒R
18	13.48	25	7♐	19	3	14	♅18♑
19	13.52	26	21	20	4	15	♆18♑
20	13.56	27	4♑	20	5	16	♇24♏
21	14.00	28	18	21	7	16	♃25♎
22	14.04	29	0♒	21	8	17	♄23♒R
23	14.08	0♏	13	22	9	18	♅18♑
24	14.12	1	25	22	10	19	♆18♑
25	14.16	2	7♓	22	11	19	♇24♏
26	14.19	3	19	22R	13	20	♃27♎
27	14.23	4	1♈	22	14	21	♄23♒
28	14.27	5	13	22	15	21	♅18♑
29	14.31	6	25	21	16	22	♆18♑
30	14.35	7	7♉	21	18	23	♇24♏
31	14.39	8	18	20	19	23	♃28♎

Nov	STime	☉	☽	☿	♀	♂	Plnts
1	14.43	9♏	1♊	19♏	20♎	24♏	♃28♎
2	14.47	10	13	18	21	25	♄23♒
3	14.51	11	25	17	23	26	♅18♑
4	14.55	12	8♋	16	24	26	♆18♑
5	14.59	13	21	14	25	27	♇25♏
6	15.03	14	4♌	13	26	28	♃29♎
7	15.07	15	18	12	28	28	♄23♒
8	15.11	16	2♍	10	29	29	♅19♑
9	15.15	17	16	9	0♏	0♐	♆19♑
10	15.19	18	0♎	8	1	1	♇25♏
11	15.23	19	15	8	3	1	♃ 0♏
12	15.26	20	0♏	7	4	2	♄24♒
13	15.30	21	15	7	5	3	♅19♑
14	15.34	22	0♐	6	6	3	♆19♑
15	15.38	23	15	6D	8	4	♇25♏
16	15.42	24	29	6	9	5	♃ 1♏
17	15.46	25	13♑	7	10	6	♄24♒
18	15.50	26	26	7	11	6	♅19♑
19	15.54	27	9♒	8	13	7	♆19♑
20	15.58	28	21	8	14	8	♇25♏
21	16.02	29	3♓	9	15	9	♃ 2♏
22	16.06	0♐	16	10	17	9	♄24♒
23	16.10	1	27	11	18	10	♅19♑
24	16.14	2	9♈	12	19	11	♆19♑
25	16.18	3	21	14	20	11	♇25♏
26	16.22	4	3♉	15	22	12	♃ 3♏
27	16.26	5	15	16	23	13	♄24♒
28	16.30	6	27	17	24	14	♅19♑
29	16.34	7	10♊	19	25	14	♆19♑
30	16.37	8	22	20	27	15	♇26♏

Dec	STime	☉	☽	☿	♀	♂	Plnts
1	16.41	9♐	5♋	22♏	28♏	16♐	♃ 4♏
2	16.45	10	18	23	29	17	♄24♒
3	16.49	11	1♌	24	0♐	17	♅20♑
4	16.53	12	14	26	2	18	♆19♑
5	16.57	13	28	27	3	19	♇26♏
6	17.01	14	12♍	29	4	20	♃ 5♏
7	17.05	15	26	0♐	5	20	♄25♒
8	17.09	16	10♎	2	7	21	♅20♑
9	17.13	17	25	3	8	22	♆19♑
10	17.17	18	9♏	5	9	23	♇26♏
11	17.21	19	24	6	10	23	♃ 6♏
12	17.25	20	8♐	8	12	24	♄25♒
13	17.29	21	23	9	13	25	♅20♑
14	17.33	22	7♑	11	14	26	♆20♑
15	17.37	23	20	13	15	26	♇26♏
16	17.41	24	4♒	14	17	27	♃ 7♏
17	17.44	25	17	16	18	28	♄25♒
18	17.48	26	29	17	19	29	♅21♑
19	17.52	27	11♓	19	20	29	♆20♑
20	17.56	28	24	20	22	0♑	♇26♏
21	18.00	29	5♈	22	23	1	♃ 8♏
22	18.04	0♑	17	23	24	2	♄26♒
23	18.08	1	29	25	25	2	♅21♑
24	18.12	2	11♉	26	27	3	♆20♑
25	18.16	3	23	28	28	4	♇27♏
26	18.20	4	5♊	0♑	29	5	♃ 9♏
27	18.24	5	18	1	1♑	5	♄26♒
28	18.28	6	1♋	3	2	6	♅21♑
29	18.32	7	14	4	3	7	♆20♑
30	18.36	9	27	6	4	8	♇27♏
31	18.40	10	11♌	8	6	8	♃ 9♏

Jan	STime	☉	☽	☿	♀	♂	Plnts
1	18.44	11♑	25♌	9♑	7♑	9♑	♃10♏
2	18.48	12	9♍	11	8	10	♄27♒
3	18.52	13	23	12	9	11	♅21♑
4	18.55	14	7♎	14	11	11	♆20♑
5	18.59	15	21	16	12	12	♇27♏
6	19.03	16	5♏	17	13	13	♃10♏
7	19.07	17	19	19	14	14	♄27♒
8	19.11	18	3♐	21	16	15	♅22♑
9	19.15	19	17	22	17	15	♆20♑
10	19.19	20	1♑	24	18	16	♇27♏
11	19.23	21	15	25	19	17	♃11♏
12	19.27	22	28	27	21	18	♄28♒
13	19.31	23	12♒	29	22	18	♅22♑
14	19.35	24	24	1♒	23	19	♆21♑
15	19.39	25	7♓	2	24	20	♇27♏
16	19.43	26	19	4	26	21	♃12♏
17	19.47	27	1♈	6	27	21	♄28♒
18	19.51	28	13	7	28	22	♅22♑
19	19.55	29	25	9	29	23	♆21♑
20	19.59	0♒	7♉	11	1♒	24	♇27♏
21	20.02	1	19	12	2	25	♃12♏
22	20.06	2	1♊	14	3	25	♄29♒
23	20.10	3	13	16	4	26	♅23♑
24	20.14	4	26	17	6	27	♆21♑
25	20.18	5	9♋	19	7	28	♇27♏
26	20.22	6	22	21	8	28	♃13♏
27	20.26	7	6♌	22	10	29	♄ 0♓
28	20.30	8	20	24	11	0♒	♅23♑
29	20.34	9	5♍	25	12	1	♆21♑
30	20.38	10	19	27	13	2	♇28♏
31	20.42	11	4♎	28	15	2	♃13♏

Feb	STime	☉	☽	☿	♀	♂	Plnts
1	20.46	12♒	18♎	0♓	16♒	3♒	♃13♏
2	20.50	13	2♏	1	17	4	♄ 0♓
3	20.54	14	16	2	18	5	♅23♑
4	20.58	15	0♐	3	20	5	♆21♑
5	21.02	16	14	4	21	6	♇28♏
6	21.06	17	27	5	22	7	♃14♏
7	21.09	18	11♑	6	23	8	♄ 1♓
8	21.13	19	24	7	25	9	♅24♑
9	21.17	20	7♒	7	26	9	♆22♑
10	21.21	21	20	7	27	10	♇28♏
11	21.25	22	3♓	7R	28	11	♃14♏
12	21.29	23	15	7	0♓	12	♄ 1♓
13	21.33	24	27	7	1	12	♅24♑
14	21.37	25	9♈	6	2	13	♆22♑
15	21.41	26	21	6	3	14	♇28♏
16	21.45	27	3♉	5	5	15	♃14♏
17	21.49	28	15	4	6	16	♄ 2♓
18	21.53	29	27	3	7	16	♅24♑
19	21.57	0♓	9♊	2	8	17	♆22♑
20	22.01	1	21	1	10	18	♇28♏
21	22.05	2	4♋	0	11	19	♃14♏
22	22.09	3	17	29♒	12	20	♄ 3♓
23	22.13	4	0♌	28	13	20	♅24♑
24	22.17	5	14	27	15	21	♆22♑
25	22.20	6	29	26	16	22	♇28♏
26	22.24	7	14♍	25	17	23	♃14♏
27	22.28	8	28	24	18	23	♄ 3♓
28	22.32	9	13♎	24	20	24	♅25♑

Mar	STime	☉	☽	☿	♀	♂	Plnts
1	22.36	10♓	28♎	23♒	21♓	25♒	♃14♏R
2	22.40	11	13♏	23	22	26	♄ 4♓
3	22.44	12	27	22	23	27	♅25♑
4	22.48	13	11♐	22	25	27	♆22♑
5	22.52	14	24	22D	26	28	♇28♏
6	22.56	15	8♑	22	27	29	♃14♏R
7	23.00	16	21	23	28	0♓	♄ 4♓
8	23.04	17	4♒	23	0♈	1	♅25♑
9	23.08	18	17	23	1	1	♆22♑
10	23.12	19	29	24	2	2	♇28♏
11	23.16	20	11♓	24	3	3	♃14♏R
12	23.20	21	24	25	5	4	♄ 5♓
13	23.24	22	6♈	25	6	4	♅25♑
14	23.28	23	18	26	7	5	♆23♑
15	23.31	24	29	27	8	6	♇28♏R
16	23.35	25	11♉	28	10	7	♃14♏R
17	23.39	26	23	29	11	8	♄ 5♓
18	23.43	27	5♊	0♓	12	8	♅25♑
19	23.47	28	17	1	13	9	♆23♑
20	23.51	29	29	2	14	10	♇28♏R
21	23.55	0♈	12♋	3	16	11	♃14♏R
22	23.59	1	25	4	17	12	♄ 6♓
23	0.03	2	8♌	5	18	12	♅25♑
24	0.07	3	22	6	19	13	♆23♑
25	0.11	4	7♍	8	21	14	♇28♏R
26	0.15	5	22	9	22	15	♃13♏R
27	0.19	6	7♎	10	23	15	♄ 7♓
28	0.23	7	22	11	24	16	♅26♑
29	0.27	8	7♏	13	26	17	♆23♑
30	0.31	9	22	14	27	18	♇28♏R
31	0.35	10	7♐	16	28	19	♃13♏R

Apr	STime	☉	☽	☿	♀	♂	Plnts
1	0.38	11♈	21♐	17♓	29♈	19♓	♃13♏R
2	0.42	12	4♑	18	1♉	20	♄ 7♓
3	0.46	13	18	20	2	21	♅26♑
4	0.50	14	1♒	21	3	22	♆23♑
5	0.54	15	14	23	4	22	♇27♏R
6	0.58	16	26	25	5	23	♃12♏R
7	1.02	17	8♓	26	7	24	♄ 8♓
8	1.06	18	21	28	8	25	♅26♑
9	1.10	19	3♈	29	9	26	♆23♑
10	1.14	20	15	1♈	10	26	♇27♏R
11	1.18	21	26	3	12	27	♃12♏R
12	1.22	22	8♉	4	13	28	♄ 8♓
13	1.26	23	20	6	14	29	♅26♑
14	1.30	24	2♊	8	15	0♈	♆23♑
15	1.34	25	14	10	17	0	♇27♏R
16	1.38	26	26	12	18	1	♃11♏R
17	1.42	27	8♋	13	19	2	♄ 9♓
18	1.45	28	21	15	20	3	♅26♑
19	1.49	29	4♌	17	21	3	♆23♑
20	1.53	0♉	17	19	23	4	♇27♏R
21	1.57	1	1♍	21	24	5	♃11♏R
22	2.01	2	15	23	25	6	♄ 9♓
23	2.05	3	0♎	25	26	6	♅26♑
24	2.09	4	15	27	28	7	♆23♑
25	2.13	5	0♏	29	29	8	♇27♏R
26	2.17	6	15	1♉	0♊	9	♃10♏R
27	2.21	7	0♐	3	1	10	♄10♓
28	2.25	8	15	5	2	10	♅26♑
29	2.29	9	0♑	8	4	11	♆23♑
30	2.33	10	14	10	5	12	♇27♏R

May	STime	☉	☽	☿	♀	♂	Plnts
1	2.37	11♉	27♑	12♉	6♊	13♈	♃ 9♏R
2	2.41	12	10♒	14	7	13	♄10♓
3	2.45	13	23	16	9	14	♅26♑
4	2.49	13	5♓	18	10	15	♆23♑
5	2.53	14	18	20	11	16	♇27♏R
6	2.56	15	0♈	23	12	16	♃ 9♏R
7	3.00	16	12	25	13	17	♄10♓
8	3.04	17	23	27	15	18	♅26♑R
9	3.08	18	5♉	29	16	19	♆23♑R
10	3.12	19	17	1♊	17	20	♇27♏R
11	3.16	20	29	3	18	20	♃ 8♏R
12	3.20	21	11♊	5	19	21	♄11♓
13	3.24	22	23	7	21	22	♅26♑R
14	3.28	23	5♋	9	22	23	♆23♑R
15	3.32	24	18	11	23	23	♇26♏R
16	3.36	25	0♌	12	24	24	♃ 7♏R
17	3.40	26	13	14	25	25	♄11♓
18	3.44	27	27	16	27	26	♅26♑R
19	3.48	28	10♍	17	28	26	♆23♑R
20	3.52	29	24	19	29	27	♇26♏R
21	3.56	0♊	9♎	21	0♋	28	♃ 7♏R
22	4.00	1	24	22	1	29	♄11♓
23	4.03	2	9♏	23	3	29	♅26♑R
24	4.07	3	24	25	4	0♉	♆23♑R
25	4.11	4	9♐	26	5	1	♇26♏R
26	4.15	5	23	27	6	2	♃ 6♏R
27	4.19	6	8♑	28	7	2	♄12♓
28	4.23	7	22	0♋	9	3	♅26♑R
29	4.27	8	6♒	1	10	4	♆23♑R
30	4.31	9	19	2	11	5	♇26♏R
31	4.35	10	2♓	3	12	5	♃ 6♏R

Jun	STime	☉	☽	☿	♀	♂	Plnts
1	4.39	10♊	14♓	3♋	13♋	6♉	♃ 6♏R
2	4.43	11	26	4	15	7	♄12♓
3	4.47	12	8♈	5	16	8	♅26♑R
4	4.51	13	20	6	17	8	♆23♑R
5	4.55	14	2♉	6	18	9	♇26♏R
6	4.59	15	14	7	19	10	♃ 5♏R
7	5.03	16	26	7	20	11	♄12♓
8	5.07	17	8♊	7	22	11	♅25♑R
9	5.11	18	20	8	23	12	♆23♑R
10	5.14	19	2♋	8	24	13	♇26♏R
11	5.18	20	15	8	25	13	♃ 5♏R
12	5.22	21	27	8R	26	14	♄12♓
13	5.26	22	10♌	8	28	15	♅25♑R
14	5.30	23	23	8	29	16	♆22♑R
15	5.34	24	7♍	8	0♌	16	♇26♏R
16	5.38	25	20	8	1	17	♃ 5♏R
17	5.42	26	4♎	7	2	18	♄12♓
18	5.46	27	19	7	3	19	♅25♑R
19	5.50	28	3♏	7	5	19	♆22♑R
20	5.54	29	18	6	6	20	♇26♏R
21	5.58	0♋	2♐	6	7	21	♃ 5♏R
22	6.02	1	17	5	8	22	♄12♓
23	6.06	2	2♑	4	9	22	♅25♑R
24	6.10	2	16	4	10	23	♆22♑R
25	6.14	3	0♒	3	12	24	♇25♏R
26	6.18	4	14	3	13	24	♃ 5♏R
27	6.21	5	27	2	14	25	♄12♓
28	6.25	6	10♓	2	15	26	♅25♑R
29	6.29	7	22	1	16	27	♆22♑R
30	6.33	8	5♈	1	17	27	♇25♏R

Jul	STime	☉	☽	☿	♀	♂	Plnts
1	6.37	9♋	17♈	0♋	19♌	28♉	♃ 4♏
2	6.41	10	29	0	20	29	♄12♓R
3	6.45	11	10♉	0	21	29	♅25♑R
4	6.49	12	22	29♊	22	0♊	♆22♑R
5	6.53	13	4♊	29	23	1	♇25♏R
6	6.57	14	16	29D	24	2	♃ 5♏
7	7.01	15	28	29	25	2	♄12♓R
8	7.05	16	11♋	29	27	3	♅24♑R
9	7.09	17	24	29	28	4	♆22♑R
10	7.13	18	7♌	0♋	29	4	♇25♏R
11	7.17	19	20	0	0♍	5	♃ 5♏
12	7.21	20	4♍	1	1	6	♄12♓R
13	7.25	21	17	1	2	6	♅24♑R
14	7.28	22	1♎	2	3	7	♆22♑R
15	7.32	22	15	2	4	8	♇25♏R
16	7.36	23	29	3	6	9	♃ 5♏
17	7.40	24	14♏	4	7	9	♄12♓R
18	7.44	25	28	5	8	10	♅24♑R
19	7.48	26	12♐	6	9	11	♆22♑R
20	7.52	27	26	7	10	11	♇25♏R
21	7.56	28	11♑	8	11	12	♃ 5♏
22	8.00	29	25	10	12	13	♄11♓R
23	8.04	0♌	9♒	11	13	13	♅24♑R
24	8.08	1	22	12	14	14	♆21♑R
25	8.12	2	5♓	14	16	15	♇25♏
26	8.16	3	18	16	17	15	♃ 5♏
27	8.20	4	0♈	17	18	16	♄11♓R
28	8.24	5	13	19	19	17	♅24♑R
29	8.28	6	25	21	20	17	♆21♑R
30	8.32	7	6♉	22	21	18	♇25♏
31	8.36	8	18	24	22	19	♃ 6♏

Aug	STime	☉	☽	☿	♀	♂	Plnts
1	8.39	9♌	0♊	26♋	23♍	20♊	♃ 6♏
2	8.43	10	12	28	24	20	♄11♓R
3	8.47	11	24	0♌	25	21	♅23♑R
4	8.51	12	7♋	2	26	22	♆21♑R
5	8.55	13	20	4	27	22	♇25♏
6	8.59	14	3♌	6	29	23	♃ 6♏
7	9.03	14	16	8	0♎	24	♄11♓R
8	9.07	15	0♍	10	1	24	♅23♑R
9	9.11	16	14	13	2	25	♆21♑R
10	9.15	17	28	15	3	26	♇25♏
11	9.19	18	12♎	17	4	26	♃ 7♏
12	9.23	19	26	19	5	27	♄10♓R
13	9.27	20	10♏	21	6	28	♅23♑R
14	9.31	21	25	23	7	28	♆21♑R
15	9.35	22	9♐	25	8	29	♇25♏
16	9.39	23	23	27	9	0♋	♃ 7♏
17	9.43	24	6♑	29	10	0	♄10♓R
18	9.46	25	20	1♍	11	1	♅23♑R
19	9.50	26	4♒	3	12	1	♆21♑R
20	9.54	27	17	4	13	2	♇25♏
21	9.58	28	1♓	6	14	3	♃ 8♏
22	10.02	29	13	8	15	3	♄ 9♓R
23	10.06	0♍	26	10	16	4	♅23♑R
24	10.10	1	8♈	12	17	5	♆21♑R
25	10.14	2	21	14	18	5	♇25♏
26	10.18	3	3♉	15	19	6	♃ 9♏
27	10.22	4	14	17	20	7	♄ 9♓R
28	10.26	5	26	19	21	7	♅23♑R
29	10.30	6	8♊	20	22	8	♆21♑R
30	10.34	7	20	22	22	9	♇25♏
31	10.38	8	2♋	24	23	9	♃ 9♏

Sep	STime	☉	☽	☿	♀	♂	Plnts
1	10.42	9♍	15♋	25♍	24♎	10♋	♃10♏
2	10.46	9	28	27	25	10	♄ 9♓R
3	10.50	10	11♌	29	26	11	♅22♑R
4	10.53	11	25	0♎	27	12	♆20♑R
5	10.57	12	9♍	2	28	12	♇25♏
6	11.01	13	23	3	29	13	♃10♏
7	11.05	14	8♎	5	0♏	14	♄ 8♓R
8	11.09	15	22	6	0	14	♅22♑R
9	11.13	16	7♏	8	1	15	♆20♑R
10	11.17	17	21	9	2	15	♇25♏
11	11.21	18	5♐	11	3	16	♃11♏
12	11.25	19	19	12	4	17	♄ 8♓R
13	11.29	20	3♑	13	4	17	♅22♑R
14	11.33	21	17	15	5	18	♆20♑R
15	11.37	22	0♒	16	6	18	♇25♏
16	11.41	23	14	17	7	19	♃12♏
17	11.45	24	27	19	7	20	♄ 8♓R
18	11.49	25	10♓	20	8	20	♅22♑R
19	11.53	26	22	21	9	21	♆20♑
20	11.57	27	5♈	22	9	21	♇26♏
21	12.01	28	17	23	10	22	♃13♏
22	12.04	29	29	25	11	23	♄ 7♓R
23	12.08	0♎	11♉	26	11	23	♅22♑R
24	12.12	1	22	27	12	24	♆20♑R
25	12.16	2	4♊	28	12	24	♇26♏
26	12.20	3	16	29	13	25	♃14♏
27	12.24	4	28	0♏	13	26	♄ 7♓R
28	12.28	5	10♋	1	14	26	♅22♑
29	12.32	6	23	2	14	27	♆20♑
30	12.36	7	6♌	2	15	27	♇26♏

Oct	STime	☉	☽	☿	♀	♂	Plnts
1	12.40	8♎	19♌	3♏	15♏	28♋	♃15♏
2	12.44	9	3♍	4	16	28	♄ 7♓R
3	12.48	10	17	4	16	29	♅22♑
4	12.52	11	2♎	5	16	0♌	♆20♑
5	12.56	12	16	5	17	0	♇26♏
6	13.00	13	1♏	6	17	1	♃16♏
7	13.04	14	16	6	17	1	♄ 6♓R
8	13.08	15	1♐	6	17	2	♅22♑
9	13.11	16	16	6R	17	2	♆20♑
10	13.15	17	0♑	6	18	3	♇26♏
11	13.19	18	14	6	18	4	♃17♏
12	13.23	19	27	6	18	4	♄ 6♓R
13	13.27	20	11♒	5	18R	5	♅22♑
14	13.31	21	24	4	18	5	♆20♑
15	13.35	22	6♓	4	18	6	♇26♏
16	13.39	23	19	3	17	6	♃18♏
17	13.43	24	1♈	2	17	7	♄ 6♓R
18	13.47	25	13	1	17	7	♅22♑
19	13.51	26	25	29♎	17	8	♆20♑
20	13.55	27	7♉	28	17	8	♇26♏
21	13.59	28	19	27	16	9	♃19♏
22	14.03	29	1♊	26	16	9	♄ 6♓R
23	14.07	0♏	13	25	16	10	♅22♑
24	14.11	1	25	24	15	10	♆20♑
25	14.15	2	7♋	23	15	11	♇27♏
26	14.19	3	19	22	14	11	♃20♏
27	14.22	4	1♌	21	14	12	♄ 6♓R
28	14.26	5	14	21	13	12	♅22♑
29	14.30	6	27	21	13	13	♆20♑
30	14.34	7	11♍	21D	12	13	♇27♏
31	14.38	8	25	21	11	14	♃21♏

Nov	STime	☉	☽	☿	♀	♂	Plnts
1	14.42	9♏	10♎	21♎	11♏	14♌	♃21♏
2	14.46	10	24	22	10	15	♄ 5♓R
3	14.50	11	10♏	22	10	15	♅23♑
4	14.54	12	25	23	9	16	♆21♑
5	14.58	13	10♐	24	8	16	♇27♏
6	15.02	14	25	25	8	17	♃22♏
7	15.06	15	9♑	26	7	17	♄ 5♓
8	15.10	16	23	27	7	18	♅23♑
9	15.14	17	7♒	28	6	18	♆21♑
10	15.18	18	20	0♏	6	19	♇27♏
11	15.22	19	3♓	1	5	19	♃24♏
12	15.26	20	16	2	5	19	♄ 5♓
13	15.29	21	28	4	4	20	♅23♑
14	15.33	22	10♈	5	4	20	♆21♑
15	15.37	23	22	7	4	21	♇27♏
16	15.41	24	4♉	8	3	21	♃25♏
17	15.45	25	16	10	3	21	♄ 5♓
18	15.49	26	28	11	3	22	♅23♑
19	15.53	27	10♊	13	3	22	♆21♑
20	15.57	28	22	14	2	23	♇28♏
21	16.01	29	4♋	16	2	23	♃26♏
22	16.05	0♐	16	18	2	23	♄ 6♓
23	16.09	1	28	19	2D	24	♅23♑
24	16.13	2	10♌	21	2	24	♆21♑
25	16.17	3	23	22	2	25	♇28♏
26	16.21	4	6♍	24	2	25	♃27♏
27	16.25	5	20	25	2	25	♄ 6♓
28	16.29	6	4♎	27	3	26	♅23♑
29	16.33	7	18	29	3	26	♆21♑
30	16.37	8	3♏	0♐	3	26	♇28♏

Dec	STime	☉	☽	☿	♀	♂	Plnts
1	16.40	9♐	18♏	2♐	3♏	27♌	♃28♏
2	16.44	10	3♐	3	4	27	♄ 6♓
3	16.48	11	18	5	4	27	♅24♑
4	16.52	12	3♑	6	4	28	♆21♑
5	16.56	13	18	8	5	28	♇28♏
6	17.00	14	2♒	10	5	28	♃29♏
7	17.04	15	16	11	6	28	♄ 6♓
8	17.08	16	0♓	13	6	29	♅24♑
9	17.12	17	12	14	7	29	♆21♑
10	17.16	18	25	16	7	29	♇28♏
11	17.20	19	7♈	17	8	29	♃ 0♐
12	17.24	20	19	19	8	0♍	♄ 6♓
13	17.28	21	1♉	21	9	0	♅24♑
14	17.32	22	13	22	10	0	♆22♑
15	17.36	23	25	24	10	0	♇29♏
16	17.40	24	7♊	25	11	1	♃ 1♐
17	17.44	25	18	27	12	1	♄ 7♓
18	17.47	26	0♋	28	12	1	♅24♑
19	17.51	27	13	0♑	13	1	♆22♑
20	17.55	28	25	2	14	1	♇29♏
21	17.59	29	7♌	3	15	1	♃ 2♐
22	18.03	0♑	20	5	15	2	♄ 7♓
23	18.07	1	3♍	6	16	2	♅25♑
24	18.11	2	16	8	17	2	♆22♑
25	18.15	3	29	10	18	2	♇29♏
26	18.19	4	13♎	11	19	2	♃ 3♐
27	18.23	5	27	13	20	2	♄ 7♓
28	18.27	6	11♏	14	20	2	♅25♑
29	18.31	7	26	16	21	2	♆22♑
30	18.35	8	11♐	18	22	2	♇29♏
31	18.39	9	26	19	23	2	♃ 4♐

Jan	STime	☉	☽	☿	♀	♂	Plnts
1	18.43	10♑	11♑	21♑	24♏	2♍	♃ 5♐
2	18.47	11	26	23	25	2	♄ 8♓
3	18.51	12	10♒	24	26	2R	♅25♑
4	18.54	13	24	26	27	2	♆22♑
5	18.58	14	8♓	27	28	2	♇29♏
6	19.02	15	21	29	29	2	♃ 6♐
7	19.06	16	3♈	1♒	0♐	2	♄ 8♓
8	19.10	17	16	2	1	2	♅26♑
9	19.14	18	28	4	2	2	♆23♑
10	19.18	19	10♉	5	3	2	♇ 0♐
11	19.22	20	21	7	4	2	♃ 6♐
12	19.26	22	3♊	8	5	2	♄ 9♓
13	19.30	23	15	10	6	2	♅26♑
14	19.34	24	27	11	7	1	♆23♑
15	19.38	25	9♋	13	8	1	♇ 0♐
16	19.42	26	22	14	9	1	♃ 7♐
17	19.46	27	4♌	15	10	1	♄ 9♓
18	19.50	28	17	16	11	1	♅26♑
19	19.54	29	0♍	17	12	1	♆23♑
20	19.58	0♒	13	18	13	0	♇ 0♐
21	20.02	1	26	19	14	0	♃ 8♐
22	20.05	2	10♎	20	15	0	♄10♓
23	20.09	3	24	20	16	0	♅26♑
24	20.13	4	7♏	21	17	29♌	♆23♑
25	20.17	5	22	21	18	29	♇ 0♐
26	20.21	6	6♐	21R	19	29	♃ 9♐
27	20.25	7	20	21	20	28	♄10♓
28	20.29	8	5♑	20	22	28	♅27♑
29	20.33	9	19	20	23	28	♆23♑
30	20.37	10	4♒	19	24	27	♇ 0♐
31	20.41	11	18	18	25	27	♃10♐

Feb	STime	☉	☽	☿	♀	♂	Plnts
1	20.45	12♒	2♓	17♒	26♐	27♌	♃10♐
2	20.49	13	15	16	27	26	♄11♓
3	20.53	14	28	15	28	26	♅27♑
4	20.57	15	11♈	14	29	26	♆24♑
5	21.01	16	24	12	0♑	25	♇ 0♐
6	21.05	17	6♉	11	2	25	♃11♐
7	21.09	18	18	10	3	24	♄11♓
8	21.13	19	29	9	4	24	♅27♑
9	21.16	20	11♊	8	5	24	♆24♑
10	21.20	21	23	7	6	23	♇ 0♐
11	21.24	22	5♋	7	7	23	♃12♐
12	21.28	23	17	6	8	22	♄12♓
13	21.32	24	0♌	6	9	22	♅28♑
14	21.36	25	13	5	11	22	♆24♑
15	21.40	26	26	5	12	21	♇ 0♐
16	21.44	27	9♍	5D	13	21	♃12♐
17	21.48	28	23	5	14	20	♄13♓
18	21.52	29	7♎	6	15	20	♅28♑
19	21.56	0♓	20	6	16	20	♆24♑
20	22.00	1	4♏	6	18	19	♇ 0♐
21	22.04	2	18	7	19	19	♃13♐
22	22.08	3	2♐	7	20	19	♄13♓
23	22.12	4	17	8	21	18	♅28♑
24	22.16	5	1♑	9	22	18	♆24♑
25	22.20	6	15	9	23	18	♇ 0♐
26	22.23	7	29	10	25	17	♃13♐
27	22.27	8	13♒	11	26	17	♄14♓
28	22.31	9	27	12	27	17	♅28♑

Mar	STime	☉	☽	☿	♀	♂	Plnts
1	22.35	10♓	10♓	13♒	28♑	16♌	♃14♐
2	22.39	11	23	14	29	16	♄14♓
3	22.43	12	6♈	15	0♒	16	♅29♑
4	22.47	13	19	16	2	15	♆24♑
5	22.51	14	1♉	17	3	15	♇ 0♐
6	22.55	15	13	19	4	15	♃14♐
7	22.59	16	25	20	5	15	♄15♓
8	23.03	17	7♊	21	6	15	♅29♑
9	23.07	18	19	22	7	14	♆25♑
10	23.11	19	1♋	24	9	14	♇ 0♐R
11	23.15	20	13	25	10	14	♃14♐
12	23.19	21	25	26	11	14	♄15♓
13	23.23	22	8♌	28	12	14	♅29♑
14	23.27	23	21	29	13	14	♆25♑
15	23.30	24	4♍	1♓	15	13	♇ 0♐R
16	23.34	25	18	2	16	13	♃15♐
17	23.38	26	2♎	3	17	13	♄16♓
18	23.42	27	16	5	18	13	♅29♑
19	23.46	28	0♏	6	19	13	♆25♑
20	23.50	29	15	8	20	13	♇ 0♐R
21	23.54	0♈	29	10	22	13	♃15♐
22	23.58	1	13♐	11	23	13	♄17♓
23	0.02	2	28	13	24	13	♅29♑
24	0.06	3	12♑	14	25	13D	♆25♑
25	0.10	4	26	16	26	13	♇ 0♐R
26	0.14	5	9♒	18	28	13	♃15♐
27	0.18	6	23	19	29	13	♄17♓
28	0.22	7	6♓	21	0♓	13	♅ 0♒
29	0.26	8	19	23	1	13	♆25♑
30	0.30	9	2♈	25	2	13	♇ 0♐R
31	0.34	10	15	26	4	13	♃15♐

Apr	STime	☉	☽	☿	♀	♂	Plnts
1	0.38	11♈	27♈	28♓	5♓	13♌	♃15♐
2	0.41	12	9♉	0♈	6	13	♄18♓
3	0.45	13	21	2	7	13	♅ 0♒
4	0.49	14	3♊	4	8	14	♆25♑
5	0.53	15	15	6	10	14	♇ 0♐R
6	0.57	16	27	8	11	14	♃15♐R
7	1.01	17	9♋	10	12	14	♄19♓
8	1.05	18	21	12	13	14	♅ 0♒
9	1.09	19	3♌	13	14	14	♆25♑
10	1.13	20	16	16	16	14	♇ 0♐R
11	1.17	21	29	18	17	15	♃15♐R
12	1.21	22	12♍	20	18	15	♄19♓
13	1.25	23	26	22	19	15	♅ 0♒
14	1.29	24	10♎	24	20	15	♆25♑
15	1.33	25	25	26	22	15	♇ 0♐R
16	1.37	26	9♏	28	23	16	♃15♐R
17	1.41	27	24	0♉	24	16	♄20♓
18	1.45	28	9♐	2	25	16	♅ 0♒
19	1.48	29	24	4	26	16	♆25♑
20	1.52	0♉	8♑	6	28	17	♇ 0♐R
21	1.56	1	22	9	29	17	♃14♐R
22	2.00	2	6♒	11	0♈	17	♄20♓
23	2.04	3	20	13	1	18	♅ 0♒
24	2.08	4	3♓	15	3	18	♆25♑
25	2.12	5	16	17	4	18	♇ 0♐R
26	2.16	5	29	19	5	18	♃14♐R
27	2.20	6	11♈	21	6	19	♄21♓
28	2.24	7	24	22	7	19	♅ 0♒
29	2.28	8	6♉	24	9	19	♆25♑
30	2.32	9	18	26	10	20	♇29♏R

May	STime	☉	☽	☿	♀	♂	Plnts
1	2.36	10♉	0♊	28♉	11♈	20♌	♃14♐R
2	2.40	11	12	29	12	20	♄21♓
3	2.44	12	23	1♊	13	21	♅ 0♒
4	2.48	13	5♋	3	15	21	♆25♑
5	2.52	14	17	4	16	21	♇29♏R
6	2.55	15	29	5	17	22	♃13♐R
7	2.59	16	12♌	7	18	22	♄22♓
8	3.03	17	24	8	19	23	♅ 0♒
9	3.07	18	7♍	9	21	23	♆25♑R
10	3.11	19	20	10	22	23	♇29♏R
11	3.15	20	4♎	11	23	24	♃13♐R
12	3.19	21	18	12	24	24	♄22♓
13	3.23	22	3♏	13	25	24	♅ 0♒R
14	3.27	23	18	14	27	25	♆25♑R
15	3.31	24	3♐	15	28	25	♇29♏R
16	3.35	25	18	16	29	26	♃12♐R
17	3.39	26	3♑	16	0♉	26	♄22♓
18	3.43	27	18	17	2	27	♅ 0♒R
19	3.47	28	2♒	17	3	27	♆25♑R
20	3.51	29	16	17	4	27	♇29♏R
21	3.55	0♊	0♓	18	5	28	♃12♐R
22	3.59	1	13	18	6	28	♄23♓
23	4.03	2	26	18	8	29	♅ 0♒R
24	4.06	3	8♈	18R	9	29	♆25♑R
25	4.10	4	21	18	10	0♍	♇29♏R
26	4.14	4	3♉	18	11	0	♃11♐R
27	4.18	5	15	18	12	1	♄23♓
28	4.22	6	27	17	14	1	♅ 0♒R
29	4.26	7	8♊	17	15	1	♆25♑R
30	4.30	8	20	17	16	2	♇29♏R
31	4.34	9	2♋	16	17	2	♃10♐R

Jun	STime	☉	☽	☿	♀	♂	Plnts
1	4.38	10♊	14♋	16♊	19♉	3♍	♃10♐R
2	4.42	11	26	15	20	3	♄24♓
3	4.46	12	8♌	15	21	4	♅ 0♒R
4	4.50	13	20	14	22	4	♆25♑R
5	4.54	14	3♍	14	23	5	♇29♏R
6	4.58	15	16	13	25	5	♃10♐R
7	5.02	16	29	13	26	6	♄24♓
8	5.06	17	13♎	12	27	6	♅ 0♒R
9	5.10	18	27	12	28	7	♆25♑R
10	5.13	19	11♏	11	29	7	♇28♏R
11	5.17	20	26	11	1♊	8	♃ 9♐R
12	5.21	21	11♐	10	2	8	♄24♓
13	5.25	22	26	10	3	9	♅ 0♒R
14	5.29	23	12♑	10	4	9	♆25♑R
15	5.33	24	27	10	6	10	♇28♏R
16	5.37	25	11♒	10	7	10	♃ 8♐R
17	5.41	26	25	10D	8	11	♄24♓
18	5.45	27	9♓	10	9	11	♅29♑R
19	5.49	27	22	10	10	12	♆25♑R
20	5.53	28	5♈	10	12	12	♇28♏R
21	5.57	29	18	10	13	13	♃ 8♐R
22	6.01	0♋	0♉	11	14	13	♄24♓
23	6.05	1	12	11	15	14	♅29♑R
24	6.09	2	24	12	17	15	♆24♑R
25	6.13	3	6♊	12	18	15	♇28♏R
26	6.17	4	17	13	19	16	♃ 7♐R
27	6.21	5	29	14	20	16	♄24♓
28	6.24	6	11♋	14	21	17	♅29♑R
29	6.28	7	23	15	23	17	♆24♑R
30	6.32	8	5♌	16	24	18	♇28♏R

Jul	STime	☉	☽	☿	♀	♂	Plnts
1	6.36	9♋	18♌	17♊	25♊	18♍	♃ 7♐R
2	6.40	10	0♍	18	26	19	♄24♓
3	6.44	11	13	19	28	19	♅29♑R
4	6.48	12	25	21	29	20	♆24♑R
5	6.52	13	9♎	22	0♋	21	♇28♏R
6	6.56	14	22	23	1	21	♃ 6♐R
7	7.00	15	6♏	25	2	22	♄24♓R
8	7.04	16	20	26	4	22	♅29♑R
9	7.08	17	5♐	28	5	23	♆24♑R
10	7.12	17	20	29	6	23	♇28♏R
11	7.16	18	5♑	1♋	7	24	♃ 6♐R
12	7.20	19	20	3	9	25	♄24♓R
13	7.24	20	5♒	5	10	25	♅29♑R
14	7.28	21	20	6	11	26	♆24♑R
15	7.31	22	4♓	8	12	26	♇28♏R
16	7.35	23	18	10	13	27	♃ 6♐R
17	7.39	24	1♈	12	15	27	♄24♓R
18	7.43	25	14	14	16	28	♅28♑R
19	7.47	26	26	16	17	29	♆24♑R
20	7.51	27	9♉	18	18	29	♇28♏R
21	7.55	28	21	20	20	0♎	♃ 5♐R
22	7.59	29	2♊	22	21	0	♄24♓R
23	8.03	0♌	14	25	22	1	♅28♑R
24	8.07	1	26	27	23	2	♆24♑R
25	8.11	2	8♋	29	24	2	♇28♏
26	8.15	3	20	1♌	26	3	♃ 5♐R
27	8.19	4	2♌	3	27	3	♄24♓R
28	8.23	5	14	5	28	4	♅28♑R
29	8.27	6	27	7	29	5	♆24♑R
30	8.31	7	10♍	9	1♌	5	♇28♏
31	8.35	8	22	11	2	6	♃ 5♐R

Aug	STime	☉	☽	☿	♀	♂	Plnts
1	8.38	8♌	5♎	13♌	3♌	6♎	♃ 5♐
2	8.42	9	19	15	4	7	♄24♓R
3	8.46	10	2♏	17	6	8	♅28♑R
4	8.50	11	16	19	7	8	♆23♑R
5	8.54	12	0♐	21	8	9	♇28♏
6	8.58	13	15	23	9	9	♃ 5♐
7	9.02	14	29	25	11	10	♄24♓R
8	9.06	15	14♑	27	12	11	♅27♑R
9	9.10	16	29	29	13	11	♆23♑R
10	9.14	17	14♒	1♍	14	12	♇28♏
11	9.18	18	28	2	15	13	♃ 5♐
12	9.22	19	12♓	4	17	13	♄23♓R
13	9.26	20	26	6	18	14	♅27♑R
14	9.30	21	9♈	8	19	14	♆23♑R
15	9.34	22	22	9	20	15	♇28♏
16	9.38	23	5♉	11	22	16	♃ 6♐
17	9.42	24	17	13	23	16	♄23♓R
18	9.46	25	29	14	24	17	♅27♑R
19	9.49	26	11♊	16	25	18	♆23♑R
20	9.53	27	23	17	27	18	♇28♏
21	9.57	28	4♋	19	28	19	♃ 6♐
22	10.01	29	16	20	29	19	♄23♓R
23	10.05	0♍	29	22	0♍	20	♅27♑R
24	10.09	1	11♌	23	2	21	♆23♑R
25	10.13	2	23	25	3	21	♇28♏
26	10.17	2	6♍	26	4	22	♃ 6♐
27	10.21	3	19	28	5	23	♄22♓R
28	10.25	4	2♎	29	6	23	♅27♑R
29	10.29	5	16	0♎	8	24	♆23♑R
30	10.33	6	29	2	9	25	♇28♏
31	10.37	7	13♏	3	10	25	♃ 6♐

Sep	STime	☉	☽	☿	♀	♂	Plnts
1	10.41	8♍	27♏	4♎	11♍	26♎	♃ 7♐
2	10.45	9	11♐	5	13	27	♄22♓R
3	10.49	10	25	7	14	27	♅27♑R
4	10.53	11	9♑	8	15	28	♆23♑R
5	10.56	12	24	9	16	29	♇28♏
6	11.00	13	8♒	10	18	29	♃ 7♐
7	11.04	14	23	11	19	0♏	♄22♓R
8	11.08	15	7♓	12	20	1	♅27♑R
9	11.12	16	21	13	21	1	♆23♑R
10	11.16	17	4♈	14	23	2	♇28♏
11	11.20	18	17	15	24	2	♃ 8♐
12	11.24	19	0♉	16	25	3	♄21♓R
13	11.28	20	12	16	26	4	♅26♑R
14	11.32	21	25	17	28	4	♆23♑R
15	11.36	22	7♊	18	29	5	♇28♏
16	11.40	23	19	18	0♎	6	♃ 8♐
17	11.44	24	1♋	19	1	7	♄21♓R
18	11.48	25	12	19	3	7	♅26♑R
19	11.52	26	24	19	4	8	♆23♑
20	11.56	27	7♌	20	5	9	♇28♏
21	12.00	28	19	20	6	9	♃ 9♐
22	12.04	29	2♍	20R	8	10	♄20♓R
23	12.07	0♎	15	20	9	11	♅26♑R
24	12.11	1	28	20	10	11	♆23♑R
25	12.15	2	12♎	19	11	12	♇28♏
26	12.19	3	25	19	13	13	♃ 9♐
27	12.23	4	9♏	18	14	13	♄20♓R
28	12.27	5	24	18	15	14	♅26♑
29	12.31	6	8♐	17	16	15	♆22♑R
30	12.35	7	22	16	17	15	♇28♏

Oct	STime	☉	☽	☿	♀	♂	Plnts
1	12.39	8♎	6♑	15♎	19♎	16♏	♃10♐
2	12.43	9	20	14	20	17	♄20♓R
3	12.47	10	4♒	13	21	17	♅26♑
4	12.51	11	18	12	22	18	♆22♑
5	12.55	11	2♓	11	24	19	♇28♏
6	12.59	12	16	9	25	20	♃11♐
7	13.03	13	29	8	26	20	♄19♓R
8	13.07	14	13♈	7	27	21	♅26♑
9	13.11	15	25	7	29	22	♆22♑
10	13.14	16	8♉	6	0♏	22	♇29♏
11	13.18	17	20	5	1	23	♃12♐
12	13.22	18	3♊	5	2	24	♄19♓R
13	13.26	19	15	5	4	24	♅26♑
14	13.30	20	27	5D	5	25	♆22♑
15	13.34	21	8♋	5	6	26	♇29♏
16	13.38	22	20	5	7	27	♃13♐
17	13.42	23	2♌	6	9	27	♄19♓R
18	13.46	24	15	6	10	28	♅26♑
19	13.50	25	27	7	11	29	♆23♑
20	13.54	26	10♍	8	12	29	♇29♏
21	13.58	27	23	9	14	0♐	♃14♐
22	14.02	28	6♎	10	15	1	♄18♓R
23	14.06	29	20	12	16	2	♅26♑
24	14.10	0♏	4♏	13	17	2	♆23♑
25	14.14	1	19	14	19	3	♇29♏
26	14.18	2	3♐	16	20	4	♃15♐
27	14.22	3	18	17	21	4	♄18♓R
28	14.25	4	3♑	19	22	5	♅26♑
29	14.29	5	17	20	24	6	♆23♑
30	14.33	6	1♒	22	25	7	♇29♏
31	14.37	7	15	23	26	7	♃16♐

Nov	STime	☉	☽	☿	♀	♂	Plnts
1	14.41	8♏	29♒	25♎	27♏	8♐	♃16♐
2	14.45	9	12♓	27	29	9	♄18♓R
3	14.49	10	26	28	0♐	10	♅27♑
4	14.53	11	9♈	0♏	1	10	♆23♑
5	14.57	12	21	2	2	11	♇ 0♐
6	15.01	13	4♉	3	4	12	♃17♐
7	15.05	14	16	5	5	12	♄18♓R
8	15.09	15	29	6	6	13	♅27♑
9	15.13	16	11♊	8	7	14	♆23♑
10	15.17	17	23	10	9	15	♇ 0♐
11	15.21	18	5♋	11	10	15	♃18♐
12	15.25	19	17	13	11	16	♄18♓R
13	15.29	20	28	15	12	17	♅27♑
14	15.32	21	10♌	16	13	18	♆23♑
15	15.36	22	23	18	15	18	♇ 0♐
16	15.40	23	5♍	19	16	19	♃19♐
17	15.44	24	18	21	17	20	♄18♓R
18	15.48	25	1♎	23	18	21	♅27♑
19	15.52	26	14	24	20	21	♆23♑
20	15.56	27	28	26	21	22	♇ 0♐
21	16.00	28	13♏	27	22	23	♃20♐
22	16.04	29	27	29	23	24	♄18♓
23	16.08	0♐	12♐	1♐	25	24	♅27♑
24	16.12	1	27	2	26	25	♆23♑
25	16.16	2	12♑	4	27	26	♇ 0♐
26	16.20	3	27	5	28	27	♃21♐
27	16.24	4	12♒	7	0♑	27	♄18♓
28	16.28	5	26	8	1	28	♅27♑
29	16.32	6	9♓	10	2	29	♆23♑
30	16.36	8	23	12	3	0♑	♇ 0♐

Dec	STime	☉	☽	☿	♀	♂	Plnts
1	16.39	9♐	6♈	13♐	5♑	0♑	♃22♐
2	16.43	10	18	15	6	1	♄18♓
3	16.47	11	1♉	16	7	2	♅28♑
4	16.51	12	13	18	8	3	♆23♑
5	16.55	13	25	19	10	3	♇ 1♐
6	16.59	14	7♊	21	11	4	♃23♐
7	17.03	15	19	22	12	5	♄18♓
8	17.07	16	1♋	24	13	6	♅28♑
9	17.11	17	13	26	15	6	♆24♑
10	17.15	18	25	27	16	7	♇ 1♐
11	17.19	19	7♌	29	17	8	♃25♐
12	17.23	20	19	0♑	18	9	♄18♓
13	17.27	21	1♍	2	19	10	♅28♑
14	17.31	22	13	3	21	10	♆24♑
15	17.35	23	26	5	22	11	♇ 1♐
16	17.39	24	9♎	7	23	12	♃26♐
17	17.43	25	22	8	24	13	♄18♓
18	17.47	26	6♏	10	26	13	♅28♑
19	17.50	27	20	11	27	14	♆24♑
20	17.54	28	5♐	13	28	15	♇ 1♐
21	17.58	29	20	14	29	16	♃27♐
22	18.02	0♑	6♑	16	1♒	16	♄19♓
23	18.06	1	21	17	2	17	♅29♑
24	18.10	2	6♒	19	3	18	♆24♑
25	18.14	3	21	20	4	19	♇ 1♐
26	18.18	4	5♓	22	6	20	♃28♐
27	18.22	5	19	23	7	20	♄19♓
28	18.26	6	2♈	24	8	21	♅29♑
29	18.30	7	15	26	9	22	♆24♑
30	18.34	8	28	27	10	23	♇ 2♐
31	18.38	9	10♉	28	12	23	♃29♐

Jan	STime	☉	☽	☿	♀	♂	Plnts
1	18.42	10♑	22♉	29♑	13♒	24♑	♃29♐
2	18.46	11	4♊	0♒	14	25	♄19♓
3	18.50	12	16	1	15	26	♅29♑
4	18.54	13	28	2	17	27	♆25♑
5	18.57	14	10♋	3	18	27	♇ 2♐
6	19.01	15	22	4	19	28	♃ 0♑
7	19.05	16	4♌	4	20	29	♄20♓
8	19.09	17	16	5	22	0♒	♅29♑
9	19.13	18	28	5R	23	1	♆25♑
10	19.17	19	10♍	5	24	1	♇ 2♐
11	19.21	20	22	5	25	2	♃ 2♑
12	19.25	21	5♎	4	26	3	♄20♓
13	19.29	22	18	4	28	4	♅ 0♒
14	19.33	23	1♏	3	29	4	♆25♑
15	19.37	24	15	2	0♓	5	♇ 2♐
16	19.41	25	29	1	1	6	♃ 3♑
17	19.45	26	13♐	0	3	7	♄20♓
18	19.49	27	28	28♑	4	8	♅ 0♒
19	19.53	28	14♑	27	5	8	♆25♑
20	19.57	29	29	26	6	9	♇ 2♐
21	20.01	0♒	14♒	24	7	10	♃ 4♑
22	20.05	1	29	23	9	11	♄21♓
23	20.08	2	14♓	22	10	12	♅ 0♒
24	20.12	3	28	21	11	12	♆25♑
25	20.16	4	11♈	21	12	13	♇ 2♐
26	20.20	6	24	20	13	14	♃ 5♑
27	20.24	7	7♉	19	15	15	♄21♓
28	20.28	8	19	19	16	15	♅ 1♒
29	20.32	9	1♊	19	17	16	♆25♑
30	20.36	10	13	19D	18	17	♇ 2♐
31	20.40	11	25	19	19	18	♃ 6♑

Feb	STime	☉	☽	☿	♀	♂	Plnts
1	20.44	12♒	7♋	19♑	21♓	19♒	♃ 6♑
2	20.48	13	19	19	22	19	♄22♓
3	20.52	14	1♌	20	23	20	♅ 1♒
4	20.56	15	13	20	24	21	♆26♑
5	21.00	16	25	21	25	22	♇ 3♐
6	21.04	17	7♍	22	27	23	♃ 7♑
7	21.08	18	20	22	28	23	♄22♓
8	21.12	19	2♎	23	29	24	♅ 1♒
9	21.15	20	15	24	0♈	25	♆26♑
10	21.19	21	28	25	1	26	♇ 3♐
11	21.23	22	11♏	26	3	27	♃ 8♑
12	21.27	23	24	27	4	27	♄23♓
13	21.31	24	8♐	28	5	28	♅ 2♒
14	21.35	25	23	29	6	29	♆26♑
15	21.39	26	7♑	0♒	7	0♓	♇ 3♐
16	21.43	27	22	1	8	0	♃ 9♑
17	21.47	28	7♒	2	10	1	♄24♓
18	21.51	29	22	4	11	2	♅ 2♒
19	21.55	0♓	7♓	5	12	3	♆26♑
20	21.59	1	21	6	13	4	♇ 3♐
21	22.03	2	6♈	8	14	4	♃10♑
22	22.07	3	19	9	15	5	♄24♓
23	22.11	4	2♉	10	17	6	♅ 2♒
24	22.15	5	15	12	18	7	♆26♑
25	22.19	6	27	13	19	8	♇ 3♐
26	22.23	7	10♊	14	20	8	♃11♑
27	22.26	8	22	16	21	9	♄25♓
28	22.30	9	4♋	17	22	10	♅ 2♒
29	22.34	10	15	19	23	11	♆27♑

Mar	STime	☉	☽	☿	♀	♂	Plnts
1	22.38	11♓	27♋	20♒	25♈	12♓	♃12♑
2	22.42	12	9♌	22	26	12	♄25♓
3	22.46	13	21	23	27	13	♅ 3♒
4	22.50	14	4♍	25	28	14	♆27♑
5	22.54	15	16	27	29	15	♇ 3♐
6	22.58	16	29	28	0♉	15	♃12♑
7	23.02	17	12♎	0♓	1	16	♄26♓
8	23.06	18	25	1	2	17	♅ 3♒
9	23.10	19	8♏	3	3	18	♆27♑
10	23.14	20	21	5	5	19	♇ 3♐
11	23.18	21	5♐	6	6	19	♃13♑
12	23.22	22	19	8	7	20	♄27♓
13	23.26	23	3♑	10	8	21	♅ 3♒
14	23.30	24	17	11	9	22	♆27♑
15	23.33	25	2♒	13	10	23	♇ 3♐
16	23.37	26	16	15	11	23	♃14♑
17	23.41	27	1♓	17	12	24	♄27♓
18	23.45	28	15	19	13	25	♅ 3♒
19	23.49	29	0♈	20	14	26	♆27♑
20	23.53	0♈	13	22	15	26	♇ 3♐R
21	23.57	1	27	24	16	27	♃14♑
22	0.01	2	10♉	26	17	28	♄28♓
23	0.05	3	23	28	19	29	♅ 3♒
24	0.09	4	5♊	0♈	20	0♈	♆27♑
25	0.13	5	18	2	21	0	♇ 3♐R
26	0.17	6	0♋	4	22	1	♃15♑
27	0.21	7	12	6	23	2	♄28♓
28	0.25	8	23	8	24	3	♅ 4♒
29	0.29	9	5♌	10	25	3	♆27♑
30	0.33	10	17	12	26	4	♇ 3♐R
31	0.37	11	0♍	14	27	5	♃16♑

Apr	STime	☉	☽	☿	♀	♂	Plnts
1	0.41	12♈	12♍	16♈	28♉	6♈	♃16♑
2	0.44	13	25	18	29	7	♄29♓
3	0.48	14	8♎	20	0♊	7	♅ 4♒
4	0.52	15	21	22	1	8	♆27♑
5	0.56	16	4♏	24	1	9	♇ 3♐R
6	1.00	17	18	26	2	10	♃16♑
7	1.04	18	2♐	28	3	10	♄ 0♈
8	1.08	19	16	0♉	4	11	♅ 4♒
9	1.12	20	0♑	2	5	12	♆27♑
10	1.16	21	14	4	6	13	♇ 2♐R
11	1.20	22	28	6	7	14	♃17♑
12	1.24	23	13♒	8	8	14	♄ 0♈
13	1.28	24	27	10	9	15	♅ 4♒
14	1.32	25	11♓	11	10	16	♆27♑
15	1.36	25	25	13	10	17	♇ 2♐R
16	1.40	26	8♈	15	11	17	♃17♑
17	1.44	27	22	16	12	18	♄ 1♈
18	1.48	28	5♉	18	13	19	♅ 4♒
19	1.51	29	18	19	14	20	♆27♑
20	1.55	0♉	1♊	20	15	20	♇ 2♐R
21	1.59	1	13	21	15	21	♃17♑
22	2.03	2	25	22	16	22	♄ 1♈
23	2.07	3	7♋	23	17	23	♅ 4♒
24	2.11	4	19	24	18	23	♆27♑
25	2.15	5	1♌	25	18	24	♇ 2♐R
26	2.19	6	13	26	19	25	♃17♑
27	2.23	7	25	26	20	26	♄ 2♈
28	2.27	8	7♍	27	20	26	♅ 4♒
29	2.31	9	20	27	21	27	♆27♑
30	2.35	10	3♎	28	21	28	♇ 2♐R

May	STime	☉	☽	☿	♀	♂	Plnts
1	2.39	11♉	16♎	28♉	22♊	29♈	♃17♑
2	2.43	12	29	28	23	0♉	♄ 3♈
3	2.47	13	13♏	28R	23	0	♅ 4♒
4	2.51	14	27	28	24	1	♆27♑
5	2.55	15	12♐	28	24	2	♇ 2♐R
6	2.58	16	26	28	25	3	♃17♑R
7	3.02	17	11♑	28	25	3	♄ 3♈
8	3.06	18	25	28	26	4	♅ 4♒
9	3.10	19	9♒	27	26	5	♆27♑R
10	3.14	20	24	27	26	5	♇ 2♐R
11	3.18	21	7♓	26	27	6	♃17♑R
12	3.22	22	21	26	27	7	♄ 4♈
13	3.26	23	5♈	25	27	8	♅ 4♒
14	3.30	24	18	25	27	8	♆27♑R
15	3.34	25	1♉	24	28	9	♇ 2♐R
16	3.38	26	14	23	28	10	♃17♑R
17	3.42	27	27	23	28	11	♄ 4♈
18	3.46	28	9♊	22	28	11	♅ 4♒
19	3.50	28	21	22	28	12	♆27♑R
20	3.54	29	4♋	21	28R	13	♇ 2♐R
21	3.58	0♊	16	21	28	14	♃17♑R
22	4.02	1	27	20	28	14	♄ 4♈
23	4.06	2	9♌	20	28	15	♅ 4♒R
24	4.09	3	21	20	28	16	♆27♑R
25	4.13	4	3♍	20	27	17	♇ 1♐R
26	4.17	5	15	19	27	17	♃17♑R
27	4.21	6	28	19D	27	18	♄ 5♈
28	4.25	7	11♎	19	27	19	♅ 4♒R
29	4.29	8	24	19	26	20	♆27♑R
30	4.33	9	7♏	20	26	20	♇ 1♐R
31	4.37	10	21	20	25	21	♃16♑R

Jun	STime	☉	☽	☿	♀	♂	Plnts
1	4.41	11♊	6♐	20♉	25♊	22♉	♃16♑R
2	4.45	12	21	21	25	22	♄ 5♈
3	4.49	13	6♑	21	24	23	♅ 4♒R
4	4.53	14	21	22	23	24	♆27♑R
5	4.57	15	5♒	22	23	25	♇ 1♐R
6	5.01	16	20	23	22	25	♃16♑R
7	5.05	17	4♓	24	22	26	♄ 6♈
8	5.09	18	18	24	21	27	♅ 4♒R
9	5.13	19	2♈	25	21	27	♆27♑R
10	5.16	20	15	26	20	28	♇ 1♐R
11	5.20	21	28	27	19	29	♃15♑R
12	5.24	21	11♉	28	19	0♊	♄ 6♈
13	5.28	22	23	29	18	0	♅ 4♒R
14	5.32	23	6♊	0♊	17	1	♆27♑R
15	5.36	24	18	2	17	2	♇ 1♐R
16	5.40	25	0♋	3	16	2	♃15♑R
17	5.44	26	12	4	16	3	♄ 6♈
18	5.48	27	24	6	15	4	♅ 4♒R
19	5.52	28	6♌	7	15	5	♆27♑R
20	5.56	29	18	8	14	5	♇ 1♐R
21	6.00	0♋	0♍	10	14	6	♃14♑R
22	6.04	1	12	12	13	7	♄ 7♈
23	6.08	2	24	13	13	7	♅ 3♒R
24	6.12	3	6♎	15	13	8	♆27♑R
25	6.16	4	19	17	12	9	♇ 1♐R
26	6.20	5	2♏	18	12	10	♃13♑R
27	6.24	6	16	20	12	10	♄ 7♈
28	6.27	7	0♐	22	12	11	♅ 3♒R
29	6.31	8	14	24	12	12	♆27♑R
30	6.35	9	29	26	12	12	♇ 0♐R

Jul	STime	☉	☽	☿	♀	♂	Plnts
1	6.39	10♋	14♑	28♊	12♊	13♊	♃13♑R
2	6.43	11	0♒	0♋	11D	14	♄ 7♈
3	6.47	12	15	2	12	14	♅ 3♒R
4	6.51	12	0♓	4	12	15	♆26♑R
5	6.55	13	14	6	12	16	♇ 0♐R
6	6.59	14	28	9	12	17	♃12♑R
7	7.03	15	12♈	11	12	17	♄ 7♈
8	7.07	16	25	13	12	18	♅ 3♒R
9	7.11	17	8♉	15	12	19	♆26♑R
10	7.15	18	20	17	13	19	♇ 0♐R
11	7.19	19	3♊	19	13	20	♃12♑R
12	7.23	20	15	21	13	21	♄ 7♈
13	7.27	21	27	24	14	21	♅ 3♒R
14	7.31	22	9♋	26	14	22	♆26♑R
15	7.34	23	21	28	15	23	♇ 0♐R
16	7.38	24	3♌	0♌	15	23	♃11♑R
17	7.42	25	15	2	15	24	♄ 7♈
18	7.46	26	27	4	16	25	♅ 3♒R
19	7.50	27	9♍	6	16	25	♆26♑R
20	7.54	28	21	8	17	26	♇ 0♐R
21	7.58	29	3♎	10	18	27	♃10♑R
22	8.02	0♌	15	12	18	27	♄ 7♈R
23	8.06	1	28	14	19	28	♅ 2♒R
24	8.10	2	11♏	16	19	29	♆26♑R
25	8.14	3	24	17	20	0♋	♇ 0♐R
26	8.18	3	8♐	19	21	0	♃10♑R
27	8.22	4	23	21	21	1	♄ 7♈R
28	8.26	5	8♑	23	22	2	♅ 2♒R
29	8.30	6	23	24	23	2	♆26♑R
30	8.34	7	8♒	26	24	3	♇ 0♐R
31	8.38	8	23	28	24	4	♃ 9♑R

Aug	STime	☉	☽	☿	♀	♂	Plnts
1	8.41	9♌	8♓	29♌	25♊	4♋	♃ 9♑R
2	8.45	10	23	1♍	26	5	♄ 7♈R
3	8.49	11	7♈	3	27	6	♅ 2♒R
4	8.53	12	21	4	27	6	♆26♑R
5	8.57	13	4♉	6	28	7	♇ 0♐
6	9.01	14	17	7	29	8	♃ 9♑R
7	9.05	15	0♊	9	0♋	8	♄ 7♈R
8	9.09	16	12	10	1	9	♅ 2♒R
9	9.13	17	24	11	2	10	♆25♑R
10	9.17	18	6♋	13	2	10	♇ 0♐
11	9.21	19	18	14	3	11	♃ 8♑R
12	9.25	20	0♌	15	4	12	♄ 7♈R
13	9.29	21	12	17	5	12	♅ 2♒R
14	9.33	22	24	18	6	13	♆25♑R
15	9.37	23	6♍	19	7	13	♇ 0♐
16	9.41	24	18	20	8	14	♃ 8♑R
17	9.45	25	0♎	22	9	15	♄ 6♈R
18	9.49	26	12	23	10	15	♅ 1♒R
19	9.52	26	24	24	11	16	♆25♑R
20	9.56	27	7♏	25	12	17	♇ 0♐
21	10.00	28	20	26	13	17	♃ 8♑R
22	10.04	29	4♐	27	14	18	♄ 6♈R
23	10.08	0♍	18	28	15	19	♅ 1♒R
24	10.12	1	2♑	28	16	19	♆25♑R
25	10.16	2	17	29	17	20	♇ 0♐
26	10.20	3	1♒	0♎	18	21	♃ 8♑R
27	10.24	4	17	1	19	21	♄ 6♈R
28	10.28	5	2♓	1	20	22	♅ 1♒R
29	10.32	6	17	2	21	23	♆25♑R
30	10.36	7	1♈	2	22	23	♇ 0♐
31	10.40	8	16	3	23	24	♃ 8♑R

Sep	STime	☉	☽	☿	♀	♂	Plnts
1	10.44	9♍	0♉	3♎	24♋	24♋	♃ 8♑R
2	10.48	10	13	3	25	25	♄ 5♈R
3	10.52	11	26	3	26	26	♅ 1♒R
4	10.56	12	9♊	3R	27	26	♆25♑R
5	10.59	13	21	3	28	27	♇ 0♐
6	11.03	14	3♋	3	29	28	♃ 8♑
7	11.07	15	15	3	0♌	28	♄ 5♈R
8	11.11	16	27	2	1	29	♅ 1♒R
9	11.15	17	9♌	2	2	29	♆25♑R
10	11.19	18	21	1	3	0♌	♇ 0♐
11	11.23	19	2♍	0	4	1	♃ 8♑
12	11.27	20	15	0	5	1	♄ 5♈R
13	11.31	21	27	29♍	6	2	♅ 1♒R
14	11.35	22	9♎	28	8	3	♆25♑R
15	11.39	23	22	27	9	3	♇ 0♐
16	11.43	24	4♏	26	10	4	♃ 8♑
17	11.47	25	17	25	11	4	♄ 4♈R
18	11.51	26	1♐	24	12	5	♅ 1♒R
19	11.55	27	14	23	13	6	♆25♑R
20	11.59	28	28	22	14	6	♇ 1♐
21	12.03	28	12♑	21	15	7	♃ 8♑
22	12.07	29	26	20	16	8	♄ 4♈R
23	12.10	0♎	11♒	20	18	8	♅ 0♒R
24	12.14	1	26	19	19	9	♆25♑R
25	12.18	2	10♓	19	20	9	♇ 1♐
26	12.22	3	25	19D	21	10	♃ 8♑
27	12.26	4	9♈	19	22	11	♄ 4♈R
28	12.30	5	24	19	23	11	♅ 0♒R
29	12.34	6	7♉	19	24	12	♆25♑
30	12.38	7	21	20	26	12	♇ 1♐

Oct	STime	☉	☽	☿	♀	♂	Plnts
1	12.42	8♎	4♊	21♍	27♌	13♌	♃ 9♑
2	12.46	9	17	21	28	14	♄ 3♈R
3	12.50	10	29	22	29	14	♅ 0♒R
4	12.54	11	11♋	23	0♍	15	♆25♑
5	12.58	12	23	25	1	15	♇ 1♐
6	13.02	13	5♌	26	2	16	♃ 9♑
7	13.06	14	17	27	4	17	♄ 3♈R
8	13.10	15	29	29	5	17	♅ 0♒
9	13.14	16	11♍	0♎	6	18	♆25♑
10	13.17	17	23	2	7	18	♇ 1♐
11	13.21	18	5♎	3	8	19	♃10♑
12	13.25	19	18	5	9	20	♄ 2♈R
13	13.29	20	1♏	7	11	20	♅ 0♒
14	13.33	21	14	8	12	21	♆25♑
15	13.37	22	27	10	13	21	♇ 1♐
16	13.41	23	11♐	12	14	22	♃10♑
17	13.45	24	25	13	15	22	♄ 2♈R
18	13.49	25	9♑	15	17	23	♅ 0♒
19	13.53	26	23	17	18	24	♆25♑
20	13.57	27	7♒	19	19	24	♇ 1♐
21	14.01	28	21	20	20	25	♃11♑
22	14.05	29	5♓	22	21	25	♄ 2♈R
23	14.09	0♏	20	24	23	26	♅ 0♒
24	14.13	1	4♈	25	24	26	♆25♑
25	14.17	2	18	27	25	27	♇ 2♐
26	14.21	3	2♉	29	26	28	♃12♑
27	14.25	4	16	0♏	27	28	♄ 1♈R
28	14.28	5	29	2	29	29	♅ 0♒
29	14.32	6	12♊	4	0♎	29	♆25♑
30	14.36	7	24	5	1	0♍	♇ 2♐
31	14.40	8	7♋	7	2	0	♃12♑

Nov	STime	☉	☽	☿	♀	♂	Plnts
1	14.44	9♏	19♋	9♏	3♎	1♍	♃13♑
2	14.48	10	1♌	10	5	1	♄ 1♈R
3	14.52	11	13	12	6	2	♅ 1♒
4	14.56	12	25	14	7	3	♆25♑
5	15.00	13	7♍	15	8	3	♇ 2♐
6	15.04	14	19	17	9	4	♃13♑
7	15.08	15	1♎	18	11	4	♄ 1♈R
8	15.12	16	14	20	12	5	♅ 1♒
9	15.16	17	26	22	13	5	♆25♑
10	15.20	18	10♏	23	14	6	♇ 2♐
11	15.24	19	23	25	15	6	♃14♑
12	15.28	20	7♐	26	17	7	♄ 1♈R
13	15.32	21	21	28	18	7	♅ 1♒
14	15.35	22	5♑	29	19	8	♆25♑
15	15.39	23	20	1♐	20	8	♇ 2♐
16	15.43	24	4♒	2	22	9	♃15♑
17	15.47	25	18	4	23	9	♄ 1♈R
18	15.51	26	2♓	6	24	10	♅ 1♒
19	15.55	27	16	7	25	10	♆25♑
20	15.59	28	0♈	9	27	11	♇ 3♐
21	16.03	29	14	10	28	12	♃16♑
22	16.07	0♐	27	12	29	12	♄ 0♈R
23	16.11	1	11♉	13	0♏	13	♅ 1♒
24	16.15	2	24	15	1	13	♆25♑
25	16.19	3	7♊	16	3	13	♇ 3♐
26	16.23	4	20	18	4	14	♃17♑
27	16.27	5	2♋	19	5	14	♄ 0♈R
28	16.31	6	15	21	6	15	♅ 1♒
29	16.35	7	27	22	8	15	♆25♑
30	16.39	8	9♌	24	9	16	♇ 3♐

Dec	STime	☉	☽	☿	♀	♂	Plnts
1	16.42	9♐	21♌	25♐	10♏	16♍	♃18♑
2	16.46	10	3♍	27	11	17	♄ 0♈
3	16.50	11	14	28	13	17	♅ 2♒
4	16.54	12	26	0♑	14	18	♆26♑
5	16.58	13	9♎	1	15	18	♇ 3♐
6	17.02	14	21	2	16	19	♃19♑
7	17.06	15	4♏	4	18	19	♄ 0♈
8	17.10	16	18	5	19	20	♅ 2♒
9	17.14	17	1♐	7	20	20	♆26♑
10	17.18	18	16	8	21	21	♇ 3♐
11	17.22	19	0♑	9	23	21	♃20♑
12	17.26	20	15	10	24	21	♄ 0♈
13	17.30	21	0♒	12	25	22	♅ 2♒
14	17.34	22	14	13	26	22	♆26♑
15	17.38	23	29	14	28	23	♇ 4♐
16	17.42	25	13♓	15	29	23	♃21♑
17	17.46	26	27	16	0♐	24	♄ 0♈
18	17.50	27	11♈	17	1	24	♅ 2♒
19	17.53	28	24	17	3	24	♆26♑
20	17.57	29	7♉	18	4	25	♇ 4♐
21	18.01	0♑	20	18	5	25	♃22♑
22	18.05	1	3♊	19	6	26	♄ 1♈
23	18.09	2	16	19R	8	26	♅ 3♒
24	18.13	3	29	19	9	26	♆26♑
25	18.17	4	11♋	19	10	27	♇ 4♐
26	18.21	5	23	18	11	27	♃24♑
27	18.25	6	5♌	18	13	27	♄ 1♈
28	18.29	7	17	17	14	28	♅ 3♒
29	18.33	8	29	16	15	28	♆26♑
30	18.37	9	11♍	15	16	28	♇ 4♐
31	18.41	10	23	13	18	29	♃25♑

1 9 9 7

Jan	STime	☉	☽	☿	♀	♂	Plnts
1	18.45	11♑	4♎	12♑	19♐	29♍	♃25♑
2	18.49	12	17	11	20	29	♄ 1♈
3	18.53	13	29	9	21	0♎	♅ 3♒
4	18.57	14	12♏	8	23	0	♆27♑
5	19.00	15	25	7	24	0	♇ 4♐
6	19.04	16	9♐	6	25	1	♃26♑
7	19.08	17	24	5	26	1	♄ 1♈
8	19.12	18	8♑	4	28	1	♅ 3♒
9	19.16	19	23	4	29	2	♆27♑
10	19.20	20	8♒	3	0♑	2	♇ 4♐
11	19.24	21	24	3	1	2	♃27♑
12	19.28	22	8♓	3D	3	2	♄ 2♈
13	19.32	23	23	3	4	3	♅ 4♒
14	19.36	24	7♈	3	5	3	♆27♑
15	19.40	25	21	3	6	3	♇ 5♐
16	19.44	26	4♉	4	8	3	♃28♑
17	19.48	27	17	4	9	3	♄ 2♈
18	19.52	28	0♊	5	10	4	♅ 4♒
19	19.56	29	13	5	11	4	♆27♑
20	20.00	0♒	25	6	13	4	♇ 5♐
21	20.04	1	8♋	7	14	4	♃ 0♒
22	20.08	2	20	8	15	4	♄ 2♈
23	20.11	3	2♌	9	16	5	♅ 4♒
24	20.15	4	14	10	18	5	♆27♑
25	20.19	5	26	11	19	5	♇ 5♐
26	20.23	6	7♍	12	20	5	♃ 1♒
27	20.27	7	19	13	21	5	♄ 3♈
28	20.31	8	1♎	14	23	5	♅ 5♒
29	20.35	9	13	15	24	5	♆28♑
30	20.39	10	25	17	25	5	♇ 5♐
31	20.43	11	8♏	18	26	5	♃ 2♒

Feb	STime	☉	☽	☿	♀	♂	Plnts
1	20.47	12♒	20♏	19♑	28♑	5♎	♃ 2♒
2	20.51	13	4♐	20	29	6	♄ 3♈
3	20.55	14	17	22	0♒	6	♅ 5♒
4	20.59	15	2♑	23	1	6	♆28♑
5	21.03	16	16	24	3	6	♇ 5♐
6	21.07	17	1♒	26	4	6R	♃ 3♒
7	21.11	18	17	27	5	6	♄ 4♈
8	21.15	19	2♓	29	6	6	♅ 5♒
9	21.18	20	17	0♒	8	6	♆28♑
10	21.22	21	2♈	2	9	5	♇ 5♐
11	21.26	23	16	3	10	5	♃ 5♒
12	21.30	24	0♉	4	11	5	♄ 4♈
13	21.34	25	14	6	13	5	♅ 5♒
14	21.38	26	27	7	14	5	♆28♑
15	21.42	27	10♊	9	15	5	♇ 5♐
16	21.46	28	22	11	16	5	♃ 6♒
17	21.50	29	5♋	12	18	5	♄ 5♈
18	21.54	0♓	17	14	19	5	♅ 6♒
19	21.58	1	29	15	20	4	♆28♑
20	22.02	2	11♌	17	21	4	♇ 5♐
21	22.06	3	23	18	23	4	♃ 7♒
22	22.10	4	4♍	20	24	4	♄ 6♈
23	22.14	5	16	22	25	4	♅ 6♒
24	22.18	6	28	23	26	3	♆29♑
25	22.22	7	10♎	25	28	3	♇ 5♐
26	22.25	8	22	27	29	3	♃ 8♒
27	22.29	9	4♏	29	0♓	3	♄ 6♈
28	22.33	10	17	0♓	1	2	♅ 6♒

Mar	STime	☉	☽	☿	♀	♂	Plnts
1	22.37	11♓	0♐	2♓	3♓	2♎	♃ 9♒
2	22.41	12	13	4	4	2	♄ 6♈
3	22.45	13	26	6	5	1	♅ 6♒
4	22.49	14	10♑	7	6	1	♆29♑
5	22.53	15	25	9	8	1	♇ 5♐
6	22.57	16	10♒	11	9	1	♃10♒
7	23.01	17	25	13	10	0	♄ 7♈
8	23.05	18	10♓	15	11	0	♅ 7♒
9	23.09	19	25	17	13	29♍	♆29♑
10	23.13	20	10♈	19	14	29	♇ 5♐R
11	23.17	21	25	21	15	29	♃11♒
12	23.21	22	9♉	22	16	28	♄ 8♈
13	23.25	23	23	24	18	28	♅ 7♒
14	23.29	24	6♊	26	19	28	♆29♑
15	23.33	25	19	28	20	27	♇ 5♐
16	23.36	26	1♋	0♈	21	27	♃12♒
17	23.40	27	14	2	23	26	♄ 8♈
18	23.44	28	26	4	24	26	♅ 7♒
19	23.48	29	8♌	6	25	26	♆29♑
20	23.52	0♈	19	8	26	25	♇ 5♐R
21	23.56	1	1♍	10	28	25	♃13♒
22	0.00	2	13	12	29	24	♄ 9♈
23	0.04	3	25	14	0♈	24	♅ 7♒
24	0.08	4	7♎	16	1	24	♆29♑
25	0.12	5	19	18	3	23	♇ 5♐R
26	0.16	6	1♏	20	4	23	♃14♒
27	0.20	7	14	22	5	23	♄10♈
28	0.24	8	27	23	6	22	♅ 8♒
29	0.28	9	10♐	25	8	22	♆29♑
30	0.32	10	23	27	9	22	♇ 5♐R
31	0.36	11	6♑	28	10	21	♃15♒

Apr	STime	☉	☽	☿	♀	♂	Plnts
1	0.40	12♈	20♑	0♉	11♈	21♍	♃15♒
2	0.43	12	4♒	1	12	21	♄10♈
3	0.47	13	19	2	14	20	♅ 8♒
4	0.51	14	4♓	3	15	20	♆29♑
5	0.55	15	18	4	16	20	♇ 5♐R
6	0.59	16	3♈	5	17	19	♃16♒
7	1.03	17	18	6	19	19	♄11♈
8	1.07	18	3♉	7	20	19	♅ 8♒
9	1.11	19	17	8	21	19	♆ 0♒
10	1.15	20	1♊	8	22	18	♇ 5♐R
11	1.19	21	14	9	24	18	♃16♒
12	1.23	22	27	9	25	18	♄12♈
13	1.27	23	10♋	9	26	18	♅ 8♒
14	1.31	24	22	9	27	18	♆ 0♒
15	1.35	25	4♌	9R	29	17	♇ 5♐R
16	1.39	26	16	9	0♉	17	♃17♒
17	1.43	27	28	9	1	17	♄12♈
18	1.47	28	10♍	9	2	17	♅ 8♒
19	1.51	29	21	8	4	17	♆ 0♒
20	1.54	0♉	3♎	8	5	17	♇ 5♐R
21	1.58	1	16	7	6	17	♃18♒
22	2.02	2	28	7	7	17	♄13♈
23	2.06	3	11♏	6	8	17	♅ 8♒
24	2.10	4	23	6	10	16	♆ 0♒
25	2.14	5	7♐	5	11	16	♇ 5♐R
26	2.18	6	20	4	12	16	♃19♒
27	2.22	7	3♑	4	13	16D	♄13♈
28	2.26	8	17	3	15	16	♅ 8♒
29	2.30	9	1♒	2	16	16	♆ 0♒
30	2.34	10	15	2	17	16	♇ 5♐R

May	STime	☉	☽	☿	♀	♂	Plnts
1	2.38	11♉	29♒	1♉	18♉	17♍	♃19♒
2	2.42	12	13♓	1	20	17	♄14♈
3	2.46	13	28	0	21	17	♅ 8♒
4	2.50	14	12♈	0	22	17	♆ 0♒
5	2.54	15	27	0	23	17	♇ 4♐R
6	2.58	16	11♉	29♈	25	17	♃20♒
7	3.01	17	25	29	26	17	♄15♈
8	3.05	18	9♊	29D	27	17	♅ 8♒
9	3.09	19	22	29	28	17	♆ 0♒R
10	3.13	20	5♋	29	29	17	♇ 4♐R
11	3.17	21	18	29	1♊	18	♃20♒
12	3.21	21	0♌	0♉	2	18	♄15♈
13	3.25	22	12	0	3	18	♅ 8♒
14	3.29	23	24	0	4	18	♆ 0♒R
15	3.33	24	6♍	1	6	18	♇ 4♐R
16	3.37	25	18	1	7	18	♃21♒
17	3.41	26	29	2	8	19	♄16♈
18	3.45	27	12♎	3	9	19	♅ 8♒
19	3.49	28	24	3	10	19	♆ 0♒R
20	3.53	29	6♏	4	12	19	♇ 4♐R
21	3.57	0♊	19	5	13	20	♃21♒
22	4.01	1	3♐	6	14	20	♄16♈
23	4.05	2	16	7	15	20	♅ 8♒R
24	4.09	3	0♑	8	17	20	♆ 0♒R
25	4.12	4	14	9	18	21	♇ 4♐R
26	4.16	5	28	10	19	21	♃21♒
27	4.20	6	12♒	11	20	21	♄17♈
28	4.24	7	26	13	22	22	♅ 8♒R
29	4.28	8	10♓	14	23	22	♆29♑R
30	4.32	9	24	15	24	22	♇ 4♐R
31	4.36	10	8♈	16	25	22	♃21♒

Jun	STime	☉	☽	☿	♀	♂	Plnts
1	4.40	11♊	22♈	18♉	26♊	23♍	♃22♒
2	4.44	12	6♉	19	28	23	♄17♈
3	4.48	13	20	21	29	23	♅ 8♒R
4	4.52	14	4♊	22	0♋	24	♆29♑R
5	4.56	15	17	24	1	24	♇ 4♐R
6	5.00	16	0♋	26	3	25	♃22♒
7	5.04	16	13	27	4	25	♄18♈
8	5.08	17	26	29	5	25	♅ 8♒R
9	5.12	18	8♌	1♊	6	26	♆29♑R
10	5.16	19	20	2	7	26	♇ 4♐R
11	5.19	20	2♍	4	9	26	♃22♒R
12	5.23	21	14	6	10	27	♄18♈
13	5.27	22	25	8	11	27	♅ 8♒R
14	5.31	23	7♎	10	12	28	♆29♑R
15	5.35	24	19	12	14	28	♇ 3♐R
16	5.39	25	2♏	14	15	28	♃22♒R
17	5.43	26	15	16	16	29	♄18♈
18	5.47	27	28	18	17	29	♅ 8♒R
19	5.51	28	11♐	20	18	0♎	♆29♑R
20	5.55	29	25	22	20	0	♇ 3♐R
21	5.59	0♋	9♑	25	21	1	♃21♒R
22	6.03	1	23	27	22	1	♄19♈
23	6.07	2	8♒	29	23	2	♅ 8♒R
24	6.11	3	22	1♋	25	2	♆29♑R
25	6.15	4	7♓	3	26	2	♇ 3♐R
26	6.19	5	21	5	27	3	♃21♒R
27	6.23	6	5♈	8	28	3	♄19♈
28	6.26	7	19	10	29	4	♅ 8♒R
29	6.30	7	3♉	12	1♌	4	♆29♑R
30	6.34	8	17	14	2	5	♇ 3♐R

Jul	STime	☉	☽	☿	♀	♂	Plnts
1	6.38	9♋	0♊	16♋	3♌	5♎	♃21♒R
2	6.42	10	13	18	4	6	♄19♈
3	6.46	11	26	20	5	6	♅ 7♒R
4	6.50	12	9♋	22	7	7	♆29♑R
5	6.54	13	22	24	8	7	♇ 3♐R
6	6.58	14	4♌	26	9	8	♃21♒R
7	7.02	15	16	28	10	8	♄20♈
8	7.06	16	28	0♌	12	9	♅ 7♒R
9	7.10	17	10♍	2	13	9	♆29♑R
10	7.14	18	22	4	14	10	♇ 3♐R
11	7.18	19	3♎	6	15	10	♃20♒R
12	7.22	20	15	8	16	11	♄20♈
13	7.26	21	27	9	18	11	♅ 7♒R
14	7.30	22	10♏	11	19	12	♆28♑R
15	7.34	23	23	13	20	12	♇ 3♐R
16	7.37	24	6♐	14	21	13	♃20♒R
17	7.41	25	19	16	22	14	♄20♈
18	7.45	26	3♑	18	24	14	♅ 7♒R
19	7.49	27	18	19	25	15	♆28♑R
20	7.53	28	2♒	21	26	15	♇ 3♐R
21	7.57	28	17	22	27	16	♃19♒R
22	8.01	29	2♓	24	28	16	♄20♈
23	8.05	0♌	17	25	0♍	17	♅ 7♒R
24	8.09	1	1♈	26	1	17	♆28♑R
25	8.13	2	16	28	2	18	♇ 3♐R
26	8.17	3	0♉	29	3	19	♃18♒R
27	8.21	4	13	0♍	4	19	♄20♈
28	8.25	5	27	2	6	20	♅ 6♒R
29	8.29	6	10♊	3	7	20	♆28♑R
30	8.33	7	23	4	8	21	♇ 3♐
31	8.37	8	6♋	5	9	21	♃18♒R

Aug	STime	☉	☽	☿	♀	♂	Plnts
1	8.41	9♌	18♋	6♍	10♍	22♎	♃18♒R
2	8.44	10	1♌	7	12	23	♄20♈
3	8.48	11	13	8	13	23	♅ 6♒R
4	8.52	12	25	9	14	24	♆28♑R
5	8.56	13	6♍	10	15	24	♇ 3♐R
6	9.00	14	18	11	16	25	♃17♒R
7	9.04	15	0♎	12	18	26	♄20♈R
8	9.08	16	12	12	19	26	♅ 6♒R
9	9.12	17	24	13	20	27	♆28♑R
10	9.16	18	6♏	14	21	27	♇ 3♐
11	9.20	19	18	14	22	28	♃16♒R
12	9.24	20	1♐	15	24	29	♄20♈R
13	9.28	20	14	15	25	29	♅ 6♒R
14	9.32	21	28	15	26	0♏	♆28♑R
15	9.36	22	12♑	16	27	0	♇ 3♐
16	9.40	23	26	16	28	1	♃16♒R
17	9.44	24	11♒	16R	0♎	2	♄20♈R
18	9.48	25	26	16	1	2	♅ 6♒R
19	9.52	26	11♓	16	2	3	♆28♑R
20	9.55	27	26	16	3	4	♇ 3♐
21	9.59	28	11♈	15	4	4	♃15♒R
22	10.03	29	26	15	6	5	♄20♈R
23	10.07	0♍	10♉	14	7	5	♅ 5♒R
24	10.11	1	24	14	8	6	♆27♑R
25	10.15	2	7♊	13	9	7	♇ 3♐
26	10.19	3	20	12	10	7	♃15♒R
27	10.23	4	3♋	12	11	8	♄19♈R
28	10.27	5	15	11	13	9	♅ 5♒R
29	10.31	6	28	10	14	9	♆27♑R
30	10.35	7	10♌	9	15	10	♇ 3♐
31	10.39	8	22	8	16	11	♃14♒R

Sep	STime	☉	☽	☿	♀	♂	Plnts
1	10.43	9♍	3♍	7♍	17♎	11♏	♃14♒R
2	10.47	10	15	6	18	12	♄19♈R
3	10.51	11	27	5	20	12	♅ 5♒R
4	10.55	12	9♎	5	21	13	♆27♑R
5	10.59	13	21	4	22	14	♇ 3♐
6	11.02	14	3♏	3	23	14	♃13♒R
7	11.06	15	15	3	24	15	♄19♈R
8	11.10	16	27	3	26	16	♅ 5♒R
9	11.14	17	10♐	2	27	16	♆27♑R
10	11.18	18	23	2D	28	17	♇ 3♐
11	11.22	18	6♑	3	29	18	♃13♒R
12	11.26	19	20	3	0♏	18	♄19♈R
13	11.30	20	4♒	3	1	19	♅ 5♒R
14	11.34	21	19	4	2	20	♆27♑R
15	11.38	22	4♓	5	4	20	♇ 3♐
16	11.42	23	19	5	5	21	♃13♒R
17	11.46	24	4♈	6	6	22	♄18♈R
18	11.50	25	20	8	7	23	♅ 5♒R
19	11.54	26	4♉	9	8	23	♆27♑R
20	11.58	27	19	10	9	24	♇ 3♐
21	12.02	28	3♊	12	11	25	♃12♒R
22	12.06	29	16	13	12	25	♄18♈R
23	12.10	0♎	29	15	13	26	♅ 5♒R
24	12.13	1	12♋	16	14	27	♆27♑R
25	12.17	2	25	18	15	27	♇ 3♐
26	12.21	3	7♌	20	16	28	♃12♒R
27	12.25	4	19	21	17	29	♄18♈R
28	12.29	5	0♍	23	19	29	♅ 5♒R
29	12.33	6	12	25	20	0♐	♆27♑R
30	12.37	7	24	27	21	1	♇ 3♐

Oct	STime	☉	☽	☿	♀	♂	Plnts
1	12.41	8♎	6♎	28♍	22♏	2♐	♃12♒R
2	12.45	9	18	0♎	23	2	♄17♈R
3	12.49	10	0♏	2	24	3	♅ 4♒R
4	12.53	11	12	4	25	4	♆27♑
5	12.57	12	24	6	27	4	♇ 3♐
6	13.01	13	7♐	7	28	5	♃12♒
7	13.05	14	19	9	29	6	♄17♈R
8	13.09	15	2♑	11	0♐	6	♅ 4♒
9	13.13	16	16	13	1	7	♆27♑
10	13.17	17	29	14	2	8	♇ 3♐
11	13.20	18	13♒	16	3	9	♃12♒
12	13.24	19	28	18	4	9	♄16♈R
13	13.28	20	13♓	20	5	10	♅ 4♒
14	13.32	21	28	21	7	11	♆27♑
15	13.36	22	13♈	23	8	11	♇ 4♐
16	13.40	23	28	25	9	12	♃12♒
17	13.44	24	12♉	26	10	13	♄16♈R
18	13.48	25	27	28	11	14	♅ 4♒
19	13.52	26	11♊	0♏	12	14	♆27♑
20	13.56	27	25	1	13	15	♇ 4♐
21	14.00	28	8♋	3	14	16	♃12♒
22	14.04	29	21	5	15	17	♄16♈R
23	14.08	0♏	3♌	6	16	17	♅ 4♒
24	14.12	1	15	8	17	18	♆27♑
25	14.16	2	27	9	18	19	♇ 4♐
26	14.20	3	9♍	11	19	19	♃12♒
27	14.24	4	21	13	21	20	♄15♈R
28	14.27	5	3♎	14	22	21	♅ 5♒
29	14.31	6	14	16	23	22	♆27♑
30	14.35	7	27	17	24	22	♇ 4♐
31	14.39	8	9♏	19	25	23	♃13♒

Nov	STime	☉	☽	☿	♀	♂	Plnts
1	14.43	9♏	21♏	20♏	26♐	24♐	♃13♒
2	14.47	10	4♐	22	27	25	♄15♈R
3	14.51	11	16	23	28	25	♅ 5♒
4	14.55	12	29	25	29	26	♆27♑
5	14.59	13	13♑	26	0♑	27	♇ 4♐
6	15.03	14	26	28	1	28	♃13♒
7	15.07	15	10♒	29	2	28	♄15♈R
8	15.11	16	23	1♐	3	29	♅ 5♒
9	15.15	17	8♓	2	4	0♑	♆27♑
10	15.19	18	22	4	5	1	♇ 5♐
11	15.23	19	7♈	5	6	1	♃14♒
12	15.27	20	21	7	7	2	♄14♈R
13	15.31	21	6♉	8	8	3	♅ 5♒
14	15.35	22	21	10	9	4	♆27♑
15	15.38	23	5♊	11	10	4	♇ 5♐
16	15.42	24	19	12	10	5	♃14♒
17	15.46	25	3♋	14	11	6	♄14♈R
18	15.50	26	16	15	12	7	♅ 5♒
19	15.54	27	29	16	13	7	♆27♑
20	15.58	28	11♌	18	14	8	♇ 5♐
21	16.02	29	23	19	15	9	♃15♒
22	16.06	0♐	5♍	20	16	10	♄14♈R
23	16.10	1	17	22	17	11	♅ 5♒
24	16.14	2	29	23	18	11	♆27♑
25	16.18	3	11♎	24	18	12	♇ 5♐
26	16.22	4	23	25	19	13	♃16♒
27	16.26	5	5♏	26	20	14	♄14♈R
28	16.30	6	17	28	21	14	♅ 5♒
29	16.34	7	0♐	29	22	15	♆28♑
30	16.38	8	13	29	22	16	♇ 5♐

Dec	STime	☉	☽	☿	♀	♂	Plnts
1	16.42	9♐	26♐	0♑	23♑	17♑	♃16♒
2	16.45	10	9♑	1	24	17	♄13♈R
3	16.49	11	23	2	24	18	♅ 5♒
4	16.53	12	7♒	2	25	19	♆28♑
5	16.57	13	20	3	26	20	♇ 5♐
6	17.01	14	4♓	3	26	21	♃17♒
7	17.05	15	18	3R	27	21	♄13♈R
8	17.09	16	2♈	3	28	22	♅ 6♒
9	17.13	17	17	3	28	23	♆28♑
10	17.17	18	1♉	2	29	24	♇ 6♐
11	17.21	19	15	2	29	24	♃18♒
12	17.25	20	29	1	0♒	25	♄13♈
13	17.29	21	13♊	0	0	26	♅ 6♒
14	17.33	22	27	29♐	1	27	♆28♑
15	17.37	23	11♋	28	1	28	♇ 6♐
16	17.41	24	24	26	2	28	♃19♒
17	17.45	25	7♌	25	2	29	♄13♈
18	17.49	26	19	24	2	0♒	♅ 6♒
19	17.53	27	1♍	22	3	1	♆28♑
20	17.56	28	13	21	3	1	♇ 6♐
21	18.00	29	25	20	3	2	♃20♒
22	18.04	0♑	7♎	19	3	3	♄13♈
23	18.08	1	19	18	3	4	♅ 6♒
24	18.12	2	1♏	18	4	5	♆28♑
25	18.16	3	13	17	4	5	♇ 6♐
26	18.20	4	25	17	4R	6	♃21♒
27	18.24	5	8♐	17D	4	7	♄13♈
28	18.28	6	21	17	4	8	♅ 7♒
29	18.32	8	5♑	17	4	8	♆29♑
30	18.36	9	19	17	3	9	♇ 6♐
31	18.40	10	3♒	18	3	10	♃22♒

Jan	STime	☉	☽	☿	♀	♂	Plnts
1	18.44	11♑	17♒	18♐	3♒	11♒	♃22♒
2	18.48	12	1♓	19	3	12	♄13♈
3	18.52	13	15	20	2	12	♅ 7♒
4	18.56	14	29	21	2	13	♆29♑
5	19.00	15	13♈	22	2	14	♇ 7♐
6	19.03	16	27	23	1	15	♃23♒
7	19.07	17	11♉	24	1	16	♄14♈
8	19.11	18	25	25	0	16	♅ 7♒
9	19.15	19	9♊	26	0	17	♆29♑
10	19.19	20	23	27	29♑	18	♇ 7♐
11	19.23	21	6♋	28	29	19	♃24♒
12	19.27	22	19	29	28	20	♄14♈
13	19.31	23	2♌	1♑	28	20	♅ 8♒
14	19.35	24	15	2	27	21	♆29♑
15	19.39	25	27	3	26	22	♇ 7♐
16	19.43	26	9♍	5	26	23	♃25♒
17	19.47	27	21	6	25	23	♄14♈
18	19.51	28	3♎	7	25	24	♅ 8♒
19	19.55	29	15	9	24	25	♆29♑
20	19.59	0♒	26	10	23	26	♇ 7♐
21	20.03	1	8♏	12	23	27	♃26♒
22	20.07	2	21	13	22	27	♄14♈
23	20.10	3	3♐	14	22	28	♅ 8♒
24	20.14	4	16	16	21	29	♆ 0♒
25	20.18	5	29	17	21	0♓	♇ 7♐
26	20.22	6	13♑	19	20	1	♃28♒
27	20.26	7	27	20	20	1	♄15♈
28	20.30	8	11♒	22	20	2	♅ 8♒
29	20.34	9	26	23	19	3	♆ 0♒
30	20.38	10	11♓	25	19	4	♇ 7♐
31	20.42	11	25	26	19	5	♃29♒

Feb	STime	☉	☽	☿	♀	♂	Plnts
1	20.46	12♒	10♈	28♑	19♑	5♓	♃29♒
2	20.50	13	24	29	18	6	♄15♈
3	20.54	14	8♉	1♒	18	7	♅ 9♒
4	20.58	15	22	3	18	8	♆ 0♒
5	21.02	16	6♊	4	18D	8	♇ 7♐
6	21.06	17	19	6	18	9	♃ 0♓
7	21.10	18	2♋	7	18	10	♄16♈
8	21.14	19	15	9	18	11	♅ 9♒
9	21.18	20	28	11	18	12	♆ 0♒
10	21.21	21	11♌	12	19	12	♇ 8♐
11	21.25	22	23	14	19	13	♃ 1♓
12	21.29	23	5♍	16	19	14	♄16♈
13	21.33	24	17	17	19	15	♅ 9♒
14	21.37	25	29	19	20	16	♆ 0♒
15	21.41	26	11♎	21	20	16	♇ 8♐
16	21.45	27	23	23	20	17	♃ 3♓
17	21.49	28	5♏	24	21	18	♄17♈
18	21.53	29	17	26	21	19	♅10♒
19	21.57	0♓	29	28	22	19	♆ 0♒
20	22.01	1	11♐	0♓	22	20	♇ 8♐
21	22.05	2	24	2	23	21	♃ 4♓
22	22.09	3	7♑	3	23	22	♄17♈
23	22.13	4	21	5	24	23	♅10♒
24	22.17	5	5♒	7	24	23	♆ 1♒
25	22.21	6	19	9	25	24	♇ 8♐
26	22.25	7	4♓	11	25	25	♃ 5♓
27	22.28	8	19	13	26	26	♄18♈
28	22.32	9	4♈	15	27	26	♅10♒

Mar	STime	☉	☽	☿	♀	♂	Plnts
1	22.36	10♓	19♈	17♓	27♑	27♓	♃ 6♓
2	22.40	11	4♉	19	28	28	♄18♈
3	22.44	12	18	21	29	29	♅10♒
4	22.48	13	2♊	22	0♒	0♈	♆ 1♒
5	22.52	14	16	24	0	0	♇ 8♐
6	22.56	15	29	26	1	1	♃ 7♓
7	23.00	16	12♋	28	2	2	♄19♈
8	23.04	17	25	0♈	3	3	♅11♒
9	23.08	18	8♌	2	3	3	♆ 1♒
10	23.12	19	20	4	4	4	♇ 8♐
11	23.16	20	2♍	5	5	5	♃ 8♓
12	23.20	21	14	7	6	6	♄19♈
13	23.24	22	26	9	7	7	♅11♒
14	23.28	23	8♎	10	8	7	♆ 1♒
15	23.32	24	19	12	9	8	♇ 8♐
16	23.36	25	1♏	13	9	9	♃ 9♓
17	23.39	26	13	14	10	10	♄20♈
18	23.43	27	25	16	11	10	♅11♒
19	23.47	28	7♐	17	12	11	♆ 1♒
20	23.51	29	20	18	13	12	♇ 8♐
21	23.55	0♈	3♑	19	14	13	♃10♓
22	23.59	1	16	19	15	13	♄20♈
23	0.03	2	29	20	16	14	♅11♒
24	0.07	3	13♒	20	17	15	♆ 1♒
25	0.11	4	27	21	18	16	♇ 8♐R
26	0.15	5	12♓	21	19	16	♃12♓
27	0.19	6	27	21R	20	17	♄21♈
28	0.23	7	13♈	21	21	18	♅11♒
29	0.27	8	28	21	22	19	♆ 2♒
30	0.31	9	13♉	21	23	19	♇ 8♐R
31	0.35	10	27	20	24	20	♃13♓

Apr	STime	☉	☽	☿	♀	♂	Plnts
1	0.39	11♈	12♊	20♈	25♒	21♈	♃13♓
2	0.43	12	26	19	26	22	♄22♈
3	0.46	13	9♋	19	27	23	♅12♒
4	0.50	14	22	18	28	23	♆ 2♒
5	0.54	15	5♌	17	29	24	♇ 8♐R
6	0.58	16	17	17	0♓	25	♃14♓
7	1.02	17	29	16	1	26	♄22♈
8	1.06	18	11♍	15	2	26	♅12♒
9	1.10	19	23	14	3	27	♆ 2♒
10	1.14	20	5♎	13	4	28	♇ 8♐R
11	1.18	21	16	13	5	29	♃15♓
12	1.22	22	28	12	6	29	♄23♈
13	1.26	23	10♏	11	7	0♉	♅12♒
14	1.30	24	22	11	8	1	♆ 2♒
15	1.34	25	4♐	11	10	2	♇ 7♐R
16	1.38	26	17	10	11	2	♃16♓
17	1.42	27	29	10	12	3	♄24♈
18	1.46	28	12♑	10	13	4	♅12♒
19	1.50	29	25	10	14	4	♆ 2♒
20	1.53	0♉	8♒	10D	15	5	♇ 7♐R
21	1.57	1	22	10	16	6	♃17♓
22	2.01	2	6♓	10	17	7	♄24♈
23	2.05	3	21	10	18	7	♅12♒
24	2.09	4	6♈	10	19	8	♆ 2♒
25	2.13	5	21	11	20	9	♇ 7♐R
26	2.17	6	6♉	11	22	10	♃18♓
27	2.21	7	21	12	23	10	♄25♈
28	2.25	8	6♊	12	24	11	♅12♒
29	2.29	9	20	13	25	12	♆ 2♒
30	2.33	10	4♋	14	26	13	♇ 7♐R

May	STime	☉	☽	☿	♀	♂	Plnts
1	2.37	11♉	18♋	14♈	27♓	13♉	♃19♓
2	2.41	12	1♌	15	28	14	♄25♈
3	2.45	13	13	16	29	15	♅12♒
4	2.49	14	26	17	0♈	16	♆ 2♒
5	2.53	14	8♍	18	2	16	♇ 7♐R
6	2.57	15	20	19	3	17	♃20♓
7	3.01	16	1♎	20	4	18	♄26♈
8	3.04	17	13	21	5	18	♅12♒
9	3.08	18	25	22	6	19	♆ 2♒
10	3.12	19	7♏	24	7	20	♇ 7♐R
11	3.16	20	19	25	8	21	♃21♓
12	3.20	21	1♐	26	10	21	♄27♈
13	3.24	22	14	27	11	22	♅12♒
14	3.28	23	26	29	12	23	♆ 2♒R
15	3.32	24	9♑	0♉	13	23	♇ 7♐R
16	3.36	25	22	2	14	24	♃22♓
17	3.40	26	5♒	3	15	25	♄27♈
18	3.44	27	18	5	16	26	♅12♒
19	3.48	28	2♓	6	18	26	♆ 2♒R
20	3.52	29	16	8	19	27	♇ 7♐R
21	3.56	0♊	0♈	10	20	28	♃23♓
22	4.00	1	15	11	21	29	♄28♈
23	4.04	2	0♉	13	22	29	♅12♒R
24	4.08	3	15	15	23	0♊	♆ 2♒R
25	4.11	4	29	17	24	1	♇ 6♐R
26	4.15	5	14♊	18	26	1	♃24♓
27	4.19	6	29	20	27	2	♄28♈
28	4.23	7	12♋	22	28	3	♅12♒R
29	4.27	8	26	24	29	3	♆ 2♒R
30	4.31	9	9♌	26	0♉	4	♇ 6♐R
31	4.35	10	22	28	1	5	♃24♓

Jun	STime	☉	☽	☿	♀	♂	Plnts
1	4.39	11♊	4♍	0♊	3♉	6♊	♃24♓
2	4.43	11	16	2	4	6	♄29♈
3	4.47	12	28	4	5	7	♅12♒R
4	4.51	13	10♎	6	6	8	♆ 2♒R
5	4.55	14	22	8	7	8	♇ 6♐R
6	4.59	15	4♏	11	8	9	♃25♓
7	5.03	16	16	13	10	10	♄ 0♉
8	5.07	17	28	15	11	11	♅12♒R
9	5.11	18	10♐	17	12	11	♆ 2♒R
10	5.15	19	23	19	13	12	♇ 6♐R
11	5.19	20	6♑	22	14	13	♃26♓
12	5.22	21	19	24	16	13	♄ 0♉
13	5.26	22	2♒	26	17	14	♅12♒R
14	5.30	23	15	28	18	15	♆ 1♒R
15	5.34	24	29	0♋	19	15	♇ 6♐R
16	5.38	25	13♓	2	20	16	♃26♓
17	5.42	26	27	5	21	17	♄ 0♉
18	5.46	27	11♈	7	23	17	♅12♒R
19	5.50	28	25	9	24	18	♆ 1♒R
20	5.54	29	9♉	11	25	19	♇ 6♐R
21	5.58	0♋	24	13	26	20	♃27♓
22	6.02	1	8♊	15	27	20	♄ 1♉
23	6.06	2	23	17	28	21	♅12♒R
24	6.10	2	7♋	18	0♊	22	♆ 1♒R
25	6.14	3	21	20	1	22	♇ 6♐R
26	6.18	4	4♌	22	2	23	♃27♓
27	6.22	5	17	24	3	24	♄ 1♉
28	6.26	6	0♍	26	4	24	♅12♒R
29	6.29	7	12	27	6	25	♆ 1♒R
30	6.33	8	24	29	7	26	♇ 6♐R

Jul	STime	☉	☽	☿	♀	♂	Plnts
1	6.37	9♋	6♎	1♌	8♊	26♊	♃27♓
2	6.41	10	18	2	9	27	♄ 2♉
3	6.45	11	0♏	4	10	28	♅12♒R
4	6.49	12	12	5	12	28	♆ 1♒R
5	6.53	13	24	7	13	29	♇ 5♐R
6	6.57	14	6♐	8	14	0♋	♃28♓
7	7.01	15	19	9	15	0	♄ 2♉
8	7.05	16	2♑	11	16	1	♅11♒R
9	7.09	17	15	12	18	2	♆ 1♒R
10	7.13	18	28	13	19	2	♇ 5♐R
11	7.17	19	12♒	15	20	3	♃28♓
12	7.21	20	25	16	21	4	♄ 2♉
13	7.25	21	9♓	17	22	5	♅11♒R
14	7.29	22	23	18	24	5	♆ 1♒R
15	7.33	23	8♈	19	25	6	♇ 5♐R
16	7.36	23	22	20	26	7	♃28♓
17	7.40	24	6♉	21	27	7	♄ 3♉
18	7.44	25	20	22	28	8	♅11♒R
19	7.48	26	4♊	23	0♋	9	♆ 1♒R
20	7.52	27	18	24	1	9	♇ 5♐R
21	7.56	28	2♋	24	2	10	♃28♓R
22	8.00	29	16	25	3	11	♄ 3♉
23	8.04	0♌	29	26	4	11	♅11♒R
24	8.08	1	12♌	26	6	12	♆ 0♒R
25	8.12	2	25	27	7	13	♇ 5♐R
26	8.16	3	8♍	27	8	13	♃28♓R
27	8.20	4	20	27	9	14	♄ 3♉
28	8.24	5	2♎	28	10	14	♅11♒R
29	8.28	6	14	28	12	15	♆ 0♒R
30	8.32	7	26	28	13	16	♇ 5♐R
31	8.36	8	8♏	28R	14	16	♃27♓R

Aug	STime	☉	☽	☿	♀	♂	Plnts
1	8.40	9♌	20♏	28♌	15♋	17♋	♃27♓R
2	8.44	10	2♐	28	16	18	♄ 3♉
3	8.47	11	14	27	18	18	♅10♒R
4	8.51	12	27	27	19	19	♆ 0♒R
5	8.55	13	10♑	27	20	20	♇ 5♐
6	8.59	14	23	26	21	20	♃27♓R
7	9.03	14	7♒	26	23	21	♄ 3♉
8	9.07	15	21	25	24	22	♅10♒R
9	9.11	16	5♓	24	25	22	♆ 0♒R
10	9.15	17	19	24	26	23	♇ 5♐
11	9.19	18	4♈	23	27	24	♃27♓R
12	9.23	19	18	22	29	24	♄ 3♉
13	9.27	20	3♉	21	0♌	25	♅10♒R
14	9.31	21	17	20	1	26	♆ 0♒R
15	9.35	22	1♊	20	2	26	♇ 5♐
16	9.39	23	15	19	4	27	♃26♓R
17	9.43	24	29	18	5	28	♄ 3♉R
18	9.47	25	12♋	17	6	28	♅10♒R
19	9.51	26	25	17	7	29	♆ 0♒R
20	9.54	27	8♌	16	8	0♌	♇ 5♐
21	9.58	28	21	16	10	0	♃26♓R
22	10.02	29	4♍	16	11	1	♄ 3♉R
23	10.06	0♍	16	16D	12	1	♅10♒R
24	10.10	1	28	16	13	2	♆ 0♒R
25	10.14	2	10♎	16	15	3	♇ 5♐
26	10.18	3	22	16	16	3	♃25♓R
27	10.22	4	4♏	16	17	4	♄ 3♉R
28	10.26	5	16	17	18	5	♅ 9♒R
29	10.30	6	28	18	19	5	♆ 0♒R
30	10.34	7	10♐	18	21	6	♇ 5♐
31	10.38	8	22	19	22	7	♃25♓R

Sep	STime	☉	☽	☿	♀	♂	Plnts
1	10.42	9♍	5♑	20♌	23♌	7♌	♃25♓R
2	10.46	10	18	22	24	8	♄ 3♉R
3	10.50	10	1♒	23	26	8	♅ 9♒R
4	10.54	11	15	24	27	9	♆29♑R
5	10.58	12	29	26	28	10	♇ 5♐
6	11.02	13	14♓	27	29	10	♃24♓R
7	11.05	14	29	29	1♍	11	♄ 3♉R
8	11.09	15	13♈	0♍	2	12	♅ 9♒R
9	11.13	16	28	2	3	12	♆29♑R
10	11.17	17	13♉	4	4	13	♇ 5♐
11	11.21	18	28	6	6	14	♃23♓R
12	11.25	19	12♊	7	7	14	♄ 3♉R
13	11.29	20	26	9	8	15	♅ 9♒R
14	11.33	21	9♋	11	9	15	♆29♑R
15	11.37	22	22	13	10	16	♇ 5♐
16	11.41	23	5♌	15	12	17	♃23♓R
17	11.45	24	18	17	13	17	♄ 2♉R
18	11.49	25	0♍	19	14	18	♅ 9♒R
19	11.53	26	13	21	15	19	♆29♑R
20	11.57	27	25	22	17	19	♇ 5♐
21	12.01	28	7♎	24	18	20	♃22♓R
22	12.05	29	19	26	19	20	♄ 2♉R
23	12.09	0♎	0♏	28	20	21	♅ 9♒R
24	12.12	1	12	0♎	22	22	♆29♑R
25	12.16	2	24	2	23	22	♇ 5♐
26	12.20	3	6♐	3	24	23	♃21♓R
27	12.24	4	18	5	25	24	♄ 2♉R
28	12.28	5	0♑	7	27	24	♅ 9♒R
29	12.32	6	13	9	28	25	♆29♑R
30	12.36	7	26	11	29	25	♇ 6♐

Oct	STime	☉	☽	☿	♀	♂	Plnts
1	12.40	8♎	9♒	12♎	0♎	26♌	♃21♓R
2	12.44	9	23	14	2	27	♄ 1♉R
3	12.48	10	7♓	16	3	27	♅ 9♒R
4	12.52	11	22	17	4	28	♆29♑
5	12.56	12	7♈	19	5	28	♇ 6♐
6	13.00	13	22	21	7	29	♃20♓R
7	13.04	14	7♉	22	8	0♍	♄ 1♉R
8	13.08	15	22	24	9	0	♅ 9♒
9	13.12	16	7♊	26	10	1	♆29♑
10	13.16	17	22	27	12	2	♇ 6♐
11	13.19	18	6♋	29	13	2	♃20♓R
12	13.23	19	19	0♏	14	3	♄ 1♉R
13	13.27	20	2♌	2	15	3	♅ 9♒
14	13.31	21	15	3	17	4	♆29♑
15	13.35	22	27	5	18	5	♇ 6♐
16	13.39	23	10♍	7	19	5	♃19♓R
17	13.43	24	22	8	20	6	♄ 0♉R
18	13.47	25	4♎	10	22	6	♅ 9♒
19	13.51	26	16	11	23	7	♆29♑
20	13.55	27	27	13	24	8	♇ 6♐
21	13.59	28	9♏	14	25	8	♃19♓R
22	14.03	29	21	15	27	9	♄ 0♉R
23	14.07	0♏	3♐	17	28	9	♅ 9♒
24	14.11	1	15	18	29	10	♆29♑
25	14.15	2	27	20	0♏	11	♇ 6♐
26	14.19	3	9♑	21	2	11	♃18♓R
27	14.23	4	22	23	3	12	♄ 0♉R
28	14.27	5	5♒	24	4	12	♅ 9♒
29	14.30	6	18	25	5	13	♆29♑
30	14.34	7	1♓	27	7	14	♇ 6♐
31	14.38	8	16	28	8	14	♃18♓R

Nov	STime	☉	☽	☿	♀	♂	Plnts
1	14.42	9♏	0♈	29♏	9♏	15♍	♃18♓R
2	14.46	10	15	1♐	10	15	♄29♈R
3	14.50	11	0♉	2	12	16	♅ 9♒
4	14.54	12	16	3	13	17	♆29♑
5	14.58	13	1♊	5	14	17	♇ 7♐
6	15.02	14	16	6	15	18	♃18♓R
7	15.06	15	0♋	7	17	18	♄29♈R
8	15.10	16	15	8	18	19	♅ 9♒
9	15.14	17	28	9	19	19	♆29♑
10	15.18	18	11♌	10	20	20	♇ 7♐
11	15.22	19	24	11	22	21	♃18♓R
12	15.26	20	7♍	12	23	21	♄28♈R
13	15.30	21	19	13	24	22	♅ 9♒
14	15.34	22	1♎	14	25	22	♆29♑
15	15.38	23	13	15	27	23	♇ 7♐
16	15.41	24	24	16	28	23	♃18♓
17	15.45	25	6♏	16	29	24	♄28♈R
18	15.49	26	18	17	0♐	25	♅ 9♒
19	15.53	27	0♐	17	2	25	♆ 0♒
20	15.57	28	12	17	3	26	♇ 7♐
21	16.01	29	24	17R	4	26	♃18♓
22	16.05	0♐	7♑	17	6	27	♄28♈R
23	16.09	1	19	17	7	27	♅ 9♒
24	16.13	2	1♒	16	8	28	♆ 0♒
25	16.17	3	14	16	9	29	♇ 7♐
26	16.21	4	27	15	11	29	♃18♓
27	16.25	5	11♓	14	12	0♎	♄27♈R
28	16.29	6	25	13	13	0	♅ 9♒
29	16.33	7	9♈	12	14	1	♆ 0♒
30	16.37	8	24	11	16	1	♇ 8♐

Dec	STime	☉	☽	☿	♀	♂	Plnts
1	16.41	9♐	9♉	9♐	17♐	2♎	♃18♓
2	16.45	10	24	8	18	3	♄27♈R
3	16.48	11	9♊	6	19	3	♅ 9♒
4	16.52	12	24	5	21	4	♆ 0♒
5	16.56	13	8♋	4	22	4	♇ 8♐
6	17.00	14	23	3	23	5	♃19♓
7	17.04	15	7♌	2	24	5	♄27♈R
8	17.08	16	20	2	26	6	♅10♒
9	17.12	17	3♍	1	27	6	♆ 0♒
10	17.16	18	15	1	28	7	♇ 8♐
11	17.20	19	27	1D	29	7	♃19♓
12	17.24	20	9♎	1	1♑	8	♄27♈R
13	17.28	21	21	1	2	9	♅10♒
14	17.32	22	3♏	2	3	9	♆ 0♒
15	17.36	23	15	2	4	10	♇ 8♐
16	17.40	24	27	3	6	10	♃20♓
17	17.44	25	9♐	4	7	11	♄27♈R
18	17.48	26	21	5	8	11	♅10♒
19	17.52	27	3♑	6	9	12	♆ 0♒
20	17.55	28	16	7	11	12	♇ 8♐
21	17.59	29	29	8	12	13	♃20♓
22	18.03	0♑	11♒	9	13	13	♄27♈R
23	18.07	1	24	10	14	14	♅10♒
24	18.11	2	8♓	11	16	14	♆ 0♒
25	18.15	3	21	12	17	15	♇ 9♐
26	18.19	4	5♈	14	18	15	♃21♓
27	18.23	5	19	15	19	16	♄26♈
28	18.27	6	3♉	16	21	16	♅10♒
29	18.31	7	18	18	22	17	♆ 1♒
30	18.35	8	3♊	19	23	17	♇ 9♐
31	18.39	9	17	20	24	18	♃22♓

Jan	STime	☉	☽	☿	♀	♂	Plnts
1	18.43	10♑	2♋	22♐	26♑	18♎	♃22♓
2	18.47	11	16	23	27	19	♄26♈
3	18.51	12	1♌	24	28	19	♅11♒
4	18.55	13	14	26	29	20	♆ 1♒
5	18.59	14	28	27	1♒	20	♇ 9♐
6	19.03	15	11♍	29	2	21	♃22♓
7	19.06	16	23	0♑	3	21	♄27♈
8	19.10	17	5♎	2	4	22	♅11♒
9	19.14	18	17	3	6	22	♆ 1♒
10	19.18	19	29	5	7	23	♇ 9♐
11	19.22	21	11♏	6	8	23	♃23♓
12	19.26	22	23	8	9	24	♄27♈
13	19.30	23	5♐	9	11	24	♅11♒
14	19.34	24	17	11	12	25	♆ 1♒
15	19.38	25	29	12	13	25	♇ 9♐
16	19.42	26	12♑	14	14	25	♃24♓
17	19.46	27	25	15	16	26	♄27♈
18	19.50	28	8♒	17	17	26	♅12♒
19	19.54	29	21	19	18	27	♆ 1♒
20	19.58	0♒	4♓	20	19	27	♇ 9♐
21	20.02	1	18	22	21	28	♃25♓
22	20.06	2	2♈	23	22	28	♄27♈
23	20.10	3	16	25	23	28	♅12♒
24	20.13	4	0♉	27	24	29	♆ 2♒
25	20.17	5	14	28	26	29	♇10♐
26	20.21	6	28	0♒	27	0♏	♃26♓
27	20.25	7	12♊	2	28	0	♄27♈
28	20.29	8	27	3	29	1	♅12♒
29	20.33	9	11♋	5	1♓	1	♆ 2♒
30	20.37	10	25	7	2	1	♇10♐
31	20.41	11	9♌	8	3	2	♃27♓

Apr	STime	☉	☽	☿	♀	♂	Plnts
1	0.38	11♈	17♎	21♓	17♉	11♏	♃11♈
2	0.42	12	29	21D	18	10	♄ 3♉
3	0.46	13	11♏	21	19	10	♅16♒
4	0.49	14	23	21	20	10	♆ 4♒
5	0.53	15	5♐	21	21	10	♇10♐R
6	0.57	16	17	21	23	10	♃12♈
7	1.01	17	29	22	24	9	♄ 4♉
8	1.05	18	11♑	22	25	9	♅16♒
9	1.09	19	23	23	26	9	♆ 4♒
10	1.13	20	6♒	23	27	9	♇10♐R
11	1.17	21	19	24	28	8	♃13♈
12	1.21	22	2♓	25	0♊	8	♄ 5♉
13	1.25	23	16	26	1	8	♅16♒
14	1.29	24	0♈	26	2	7	♆ 4♒
15	1.33	25	15	27	3	7	♇10♐R
16	1.37	26	0♉	28	4	7	♃14♈
17	1.41	27	15	29	5	6	♄ 5♉
18	1.45	28	0♊	0♈	7	6	♅16♒
19	1.49	29	15	1	8	6	♆ 4♒
20	1.53	0♉	0♋	3	9	5	♇10♐R
21	1.56	1	14	4	10	5	♃16♈
22	2.00	2	28	5	11	5	♄ 6♉
23	2.04	3	11♌	6	12	4	♅16♒
24	2.08	4	24	7	14	4	♆ 4♒
25	2.12	5	7♍	9	15	3	♇10♐R
26	2.16	6	20	10	16	3	♃17♈
27	2.20	6	2♎	12	17	3	♄ 6♉
28	2.24	7	14	13	18	2	♅16♒
29	2.28	8	26	14	19	2	♆ 4♒
30	2.32	9	8♏	16	20	2	♇10♐R

Jul	STime	☉	☽	☿	♀	♂	Plnts
1	6.36	9♋	8♒	4♌	22♌	29♎	♃ 0♉
2	6.40	10	21	5	23	29	♄14♉
3	6.44	11	4♓	6	24	29	♅16♒R
4	6.48	12	17	6	25	29	♆ 3♒R
5	6.52	13	0♈	7	25	0♏	♇ 8♐R
6	6.56	14	14	8	26	0	♃ 1♉
7	7.00	15	28	8	27	0	♄14♉
8	7.04	16	12♉	8	27	1	♅16♒R
9	7.08	17	27	9	28	1	♆ 3♒R
10	7.12	18	11♊	9	29	2	♇ 8♐R
11	7.16	18	26	9	29	2	♃ 2♉
12	7.20	19	11♋	9	0♍	2	♄15♉
13	7.24	20	26	9R	0	3	♅15♒R
14	7.28	21	10♌	9	1	3	♆ 3♒R
15	7.32	22	24	9	1	4	♇ 8♐R
16	7.36	23	8♍	9	2	4	♃ 2♉
17	7.39	24	21	8	2	4	♄15♉
18	7.43	25	4♎	8	2	5	♅15♒R
19	7.47	26	16	8	3	5	♆ 3♒R
20	7.51	27	28	7	3	6	♇ 8♐R
21	7.55	28	10♏	6	3	6	♃ 3♉
22	7.59	29	22	6	4	7	♄16♉
23	8.03	0♌	4♐	5	4	7	♅15♒R
24	8.07	1	16	4	4	7	♆ 3♒R
25	8.11	2	28	4	4	8	♇ 8♐R
26	8.15	3	10♑	3	5	8	♃ 3♉
27	8.19	4	23	2	5	9	♄16♉
28	8.23	5	5♒	2	5	9	♅15♒R
29	8.27	6	18	1	5	10	♆ 3♒R
30	8.31	7	1♓	0	5R	10	♇ 8♐R
31	8.35	8	14	0	5	11	♃ 4♉

Oct	STime	☉	☽	☿	♀	♂	Plnts
1	12.39	8♎	29♊	24♎	25♌	19♐	♃ 2♉R
2	12.43	9	13♋	26	26	19	♄16♉R
3	12.47	10	27	27	27	20	♅13♒R
4	12.51	11	10♌	29	27	21	♆ 1♒R
5	12.55	12	24	0♏	28	21	♇ 8♐
6	12.59	12	7♍	2	29	22	♃ 2♉R
7	13.03	13	20	3	0♍	23	♄16♉R
8	13.07	14	3♎	4	0	24	♅13♒R
9	13.11	15	16	6	1	24	♆ 1♒R
10	13.15	16	28	7	2	25	♇ 8♐
11	13.19	17	10♏	9	3	26	♃ 1♉R
12	13.23	18	23	10	3	26	♄15♉R
13	13.26	19	4♐	11	4	27	♅13♒R
14	13.30	20	16	13	5	28	♆ 1♒
15	13.34	21	28	14	6	29	♇ 8♐
16	13.38	22	10♑	15	7	29	♃ 1♉R
17	13.42	23	22	16	8	0♑	♄15♉R
18	13.46	24	4♒	18	9	1	♅13♒
19	13.50	25	17	19	9	1	♆ 1♒
20	13.54	26	29	20	10	2	♇ 8♐
21	13.58	27	13♓	21	11	3	♃ 0♉R
22	14.02	28	26	22	12	4	♄15♉R
23	14.06	29	11♈	23	13	4	♅13♒
24	14.10	0♏	25	24	14	5	♆ 1♒
25	14.14	1	10♉	25	15	6	♇ 9♐
26	14.18	2	25	26	16	7	♃29♈R
27	14.22	3	10♊	27	17	7	♄14♉R
28	14.26	4	25	28	18	8	♅13♒
29	14.30	5	9♋	29	19	9	♆ 1♒
30	14.33	6	23	29	20	10	♇ 9♐
31	14.37	7	7♌	0♐	21	10	♃29♈R

Feb	STime	☉	☽	☿	♀	♂	Plnts
1	20.45	12♒	22♌	10♒	4♓	2♏	♃27♓
2	20.49	13	5♍	12	6	2	♄28♈
3	20.53	14	18	13	7	3	♅13♒
4	20.57	15	1♎	15	8	3	♆ 2♒
5	21.01	16	13	17	9	4	♇10♐
6	21.05	17	25	19	11	4	♃28♓
7	21.09	18	7♏	20	12	4	♄28♈
8	21.13	19	19	22	13	5	♅13♒
9	21.17	20	1♐	24	14	5	♆ 2♒
10	21.21	21	13	26	16	5	♇10♐
11	21.24	22	25	28	17	6	♃29♓
12	21.28	23	7♑	29	18	6	♄28♈
13	21.32	24	20	1♓	19	6	♅13♒
14	21.36	25	3♒	3	21	7	♆ 2♒
15	21.40	26	16	5	22	7	♇10♐
16	21.44	27	0♓	7	23	7	♃ 0♈
17	21.48	28	14	9	24	7	♄29♈
18	21.52	29	28	10	26	8	♅13♒
19	21.56	0♓	12♈	12	27	8	♆ 3♒
20	22.00	1	26	14	28	8	♇10♐
21	22.04	2	11♉	16	29	8	♃ 2♈
22	22.08	3	25	18	0♈	9	♄29♈
23	22.12	4	9♊	19	2	9	♅14♒
24	22.16	5	23	21	3	9	♆ 3♒
25	22.20	6	7♋	22	4	9	♇10♐
26	22.24	7	21	24	5	10	♃ 3♈
27	22.28	8	4♌	25	7	10	♄ 0♉
28	22.31	9	18	27	8	10	♅14♒

May	STime	☉	☽	☿	♀	♂	Plnts
1	2.36	10♉	20♏	17♈	22♊	1♏	♃18♈
2	2.40	11	2♐	19	23	1	♄ 7♉
3	2.44	12	14	21	24	1	♅16♒
4	2.48	13	26	22	25	0	♆ 4♒
5	2.52	14	8♑	24	26	0	♇10♐R
6	2.56	15	20	26	27	29♎	♃19♈
7	3.00	16	2♒	27	28	29	♄ 8♉
8	3.04	17	14	29	29	29	♅16♒
9	3.07	18	27	1♉	1♋	28	♆ 4♒
10	3.11	19	11♓	3	2	28	♇ 9♐R
11	3.15	20	24	4	3	28	♃20♈
12	3.19	21	9♈	6	4	28	♄ 8♉
13	3.23	22	24	8	5	27	♅16♒
14	3.27	23	9♉	10	6	27	♆ 4♒R
15	3.31	24	24	12	7	27	♇ 9♐R
16	3.35	25	9♊	14	8	26	♃21♈
17	3.39	26	24	16	9	26	♄ 9♉
18	3.43	27	9♋	18	11	26	♅16♒
19	3.47	28	23	20	12	26	♆ 4♒R
20	3.51	29	7♌	22	13	26	♇ 9♐R
21	3.55	0♊	21	25	14	25	♃22♈
22	3.59	1	4♍	27	15	25	♄10♉
23	4.03	2	17	29	16	25	♅16♒
24	4.07	3	29	1♊	17	25	♆ 4♒R
25	4.11	4	11♎	3	18	25	♇ 9♐R
26	4.14	5	23	5	19	25	♃24♈
27	4.18	5	5♏	8	20	25	♄10♉
28	4.22	6	17	10	21	24	♅16♒
29	4.26	7	29	12	22	24	♆ 4♒R
30	4.30	8	11♐	14	23	24	♇ 9♐R
31	4.34	9	23	16	24	24	♃25♈

Aug	STime	☉	☽	☿	♀	♂	Plnts
1	8.39	9♌	27♓	29♋	5♍	11♏	♃ 4♉
2	8.43	9	11♈	29	5	12	♄16♉
3	8.47	10	24	29	4	12	♅15♒R
4	8.50	11	8♉	28	4	13	♆ 2♒R
5	8.54	12	23	28	4	13	♇ 8♐
6	8.58	13	7♊	28D	4	14	♃ 4♉
7	9.02	14	21	28	3	14	♄16♉
8	9.06	15	6♋	29	3	14	♅14♒R
9	9.10	16	20	29	3	15	♆ 2♒R
10	9.14	17	5♌	29	2	16	♇ 7♐
11	9.18	18	19	0♌	2	17	♃ 4♉
12	9.22	19	2♍	1	1	17	♄17♉
13	9.26	20	16	1	1	18	♅14♒R
14	9.30	21	29	2	0	18	♆ 2♒R
15	9.34	22	12♎	3	0	19	♇ 7♐R
16	9.38	23	24	4	29♌	19	♃ 5♉
17	9.42	24	6♏	5	29	20	♄17♉
18	9.46	25	18	7	28	20	♅14♒R
19	9.50	26	0♐	8	27	21	♆ 2♒R
20	9.54	27	12	10	27	22	♇ 7♐
21	9.57	28	24	11	26	22	♃ 5♉
22	10.01	29	6♑	13	25	23	♄17♉
23	10.05	0♍	18	14	25	23	♅14♒R
24	10.09	1	1♒	16	24	24	♆ 2♒R
25	10.13	2	14	18	24	25	♇ 7♐
26	10.17	3	26	20	23	25	♃ 5♉
27	10.21	3	10♓	22	23	26	♄17♉
28	10.25	4	23	24	22	26	♅14♒R
29	10.29	5	7♈	26	22	27	♆ 2♒R
30	10.33	6	21	27	21	28	♇ 7♐
31	10.37	7	5♉	29	21	28	♃ 5♉R

Nov	STime	☉	☽	☿	♀	♂	Plnts
1	14.41	8♏	21♌	1♐	22♍	11♑	♃28♈R
2	14.45	9	4♍	1	23	12	♄14♉R
3	14.49	10	17	1	24	12	♅13♒
4	14.53	11	0♎	1	25	13	♆ 1♒
5	14.57	12	12	1R	26	14	♇ 9♐
6	15.01	13	25	1	27	15	♃28♈R
7	15.05	14	7♏	1	28	15	♄13♉R
8	15.09	15	19	1	29	16	♅13♒
9	15.13	16	1♐	0	0♎	17	♆ 1♒
10	15.17	17	13	29♏	1	18	♇ 9♐
11	15.21	18	25	28	2	18	♃27♈R
12	15.25	19	7♑	27	3	19	♄13♉R
13	15.29	20	18	26	4	20	♅13♒
14	15.33	21	0♒	25	6	21	♆ 2♒
15	15.37	22	12	23	7	21	♇ 9♐
16	15.40	23	25	22	8	22	♃27♈R
17	15.44	24	7♓	21	9	23	♄13♉R
18	15.48	25	21	19	10	24	♅13♒
19	15.52	26	4♈	18	11	25	♆ 2♒
20	15.56	27	19	17	12	25	♇10♐
21	16.00	28	3♉	17	13	26	♃26♈R
22	16.04	29	18	16	14	27	♄12♉R
23	16.08	0♐	3♊	16	15	28	♅13♒
24	16.12	1	19	15	17	28	♆ 2♒
25	16.16	2	4♋	15D	18	29	♇10♐
26	16.20	3	19	15	19	0♒	♃26♈R
27	16.24	4	3♌	16	20	1	♄12♉R
28	16.28	6	17	16	21	1	♅13♒
29	16.32	7	1♍	17	22	2	♆ 2♒
30	16.36	8	14	18	23	3	♇10♐

Mar	STime	☉	☽	☿	♀	♂	Plnts
1	22.35	10♓	1♍	28♓	9♈	10♏	♃ 3♈
2	22.39	11	14	29	10	10	♄ 0♉
3	22.43	12	26	0♈	12	10	♅14♒
4	22.47	13	9♎	1	13	11	♆ 3♒
5	22.51	14	21	2	14	11	♇10♐
6	22.55	15	3♏	3	15	11	♃ 5♈
7	22.59	16	15	3	16	11	♄ 0♉
8	23.03	17	27	3	18	11	♅14♒
9	23.07	18	9♐	4	19	11	♆ 3♒
10	23.11	19	21	4R	20	11	♇10♐
11	23.15	20	3♑	4	21	12	♃ 6♈
12	23.19	21	15	3	23	12	♄ 1♉
13	23.23	22	28	3	24	12	♅15♒
14	23.27	23	11♒	3	25	12	♆ 3♒
15	23.31	24	24	2	26	12	♇10♐
16	23.35	25	8♓	1	27	12	♃ 7♈
17	23.38	26	22	0	29	12	♄ 1♉
18	23.42	27	7♈	0	0♉	12R	♅15♒
19	23.46	28	22	29♓	1	12	♆ 3♒
20	23.50	29	6♉	28	2	12	♇10♐
21	23.54	0♈	21	27	3	12	♃ 8♈
22	23.58	1	6♊	26	5	12	♄ 2♉
23	0.02	2	20	25	6	12	♅15♒
24	0.06	3	4♋	24	7	12	♆ 4♒
25	0.10	4	18	24	8	12	♇10♐
26	0.14	5	1♌	23	9	11	♃ 9♈
27	0.18	6	14	22	11	11	♄ 3♉
28	0.22	7	27	22	12	11	♅15♒
29	0.26	8	10♍	21	13	11	♆ 4♒
30	0.30	9	23	21	14	11	♇10♐R
31	0.34	10	5♎	21	15	11	♃11♈

Jun	STime	☉	☽	☿	♀	♂	Plnts
1	4.38	10♊	5♑	18♊	25♋	24♎	♃25♈
2	4.42	11	17	21	26	24	♄11♉
3	4.46	12	29	23	27	24	♅16♒R
4	4.50	13	11♒	25	28	24D	♆ 4♒R
5	4.54	14	24	27	29	24	♇ 9♐R
6	4.58	15	7♓	29	0♌	24	♃26♈
7	5.02	16	20	1♋	1	24	♄11♉
8	5.06	17	4♈	3	2	24	♅16♒R
9	5.10	18	18	4	3	24	♆ 4♒R
10	5.14	19	2♉	6	4	24	♇ 9♐R
11	5.18	20	17	8	5	24	♃27♈
12	5.21	21	2♊	10	6	25	♄12♉
13	5.25	22	18	11	7	25	♅16♒R
14	5.29	23	3♋	13	8	25	♆ 4♒R
15	5.33	24	17	15	9	25	♇ 8♐R
16	5.37	25	2♌	16	10	25	♃28♈
17	5.41	26	16	18	11	25	♄13♉
18	5.45	27	0♍	19	12	25	♅16♒R
19	5.49	27	13	21	12	26	♆ 4♒R
20	5.53	28	25	22	13	26	♇ 8♐R
21	5.57	29	8♎	23	14	26	♃29♈
22	6.01	0♋	20	25	15	26	♄13♉
23	6.05	1	2♏	26	16	26	♅16♒R
24	6.09	2	14	27	17	27	♆ 3♒R
25	6.13	3	26	28	18	27	♇ 8♐R
26	6.17	4	8♐	0♌	19	27	♃29♈
27	6.21	5	20	1	19	27	♄14♉
28	6.25	6	2♑	2	20	28	♅15♒R
29	6.29	7	14	3	21	28	♆ 3♒R
30	6.32	8	26	3	22	28	♇ 8♐R

Sep	STime	☉	☽	☿	♀	♂	Plnts
1	10.41	8♍	19♉	1♍	20♌	29♏	♃ 5♉R
2	10.45	9	4♊	3	20	29	♄17♉R
3	10.49	10	18	5	20	0♐	♅13♒R
4	10.53	11	2♋	7	19	1	♆ 2♒R
5	10.57	12	16	9	19	1	♇ 8♐
6	11.01	13	0♌	11	19	2	♃ 4♉R
7	11.04	14	14	13	19	3	♄17♉R
8	11.08	15	27	15	19	3	♅13♒R
9	11.12	16	11♍	17	19	4	♆ 2♒R
10	11.16	17	24	19	18D	4	♇ 8♐
11	11.20	18	7♎	21	18	5	♃ 4♉R
12	11.24	19	20	22	18	6	♄17♉R
13	11.28	20	2♏	24	19	7	♅13♒R
14	11.32	21	14	26	19	7	♆ 2♒R
15	11.36	22	26	28	19	8	♇ 8♐
16	11.40	23	8♐	0♎	19	9	♃ 4♉R
17	11.44	24	20	1	19	9	♄17♉R
18	11.48	25	2♑	3	20	10	♅13♒R
19	11.52	26	14	5	20	10	♆ 1♒R
20	11.56	27	26	7	20	11	♇ 8♐
21	12.00	28	9♒	8	20	12	♃ 3♉R
22	12.04	29	22	10	21	13	♄16♉R
23	12.08	0♎	5♓	12	21	13	♅13♒R
24	12.12	1	18	13	22	14	♆ 1♒R
25	12.15	2	2♈	15	22	15	♇ 8♐
26	12.19	3	17	16	23	15	♃ 3♉R
27	12.23	4	1♉	18	23	16	♄16♉R
28	12.27	5	16	20	24	17	♅13♒R
29	12.31	6	0♊	21	24	17	♆ 1♒R
30	12.35	7	15	23	25	18	♇ 8♐

Dec	STime	☉	☽	☿	♀	♂	Plnts
1	16.40	9♐	27♍	18♏	25♎	4♒	♃25♈R
2	16.44	10	9♎	19	26	4	♄11♉R
3	16.48	11	22	20	27	5	♅13♒
4	16.51	12	4♏	21	28	5	♆ 2♒
5	16.55	13	16	23	29	6	♇10♐
6	16.59	14	28	24	0♏	7	♃25♈R
7	17.03	15	10♐	25	2	8	♄11♉R
8	17.07	16	22	26	3	8	♅13♒
9	17.11	17	4♑	28	4	9	♆ 2♒
10	17.15	18	15	29	5	10	♇10♐
11	17.19	19	27	0♐	6	11	♃25♈R
12	17.23	20	9♒	2	7	11	♄11♉R
13	17.27	21	21	3	9	12	♅14♒
14	17.31	22	4♓	4	10	13	♆ 2♒
15	17.35	23	16	6	11	14	♇11♐
16	17.39	24	29	7	12	15	♃25♈R
17	17.43	25	13♈	9	13	15	♄11♉R
18	17.47	26	27	10	14	16	♅14♒
19	17.51	27	11♉	12	16	17	♆ 2♒
20	17.55	28	26	13	17	18	♇11♐
21	17.58	29	11♊	15	18	18	♃25♈
22	18.02	0♑	27	16	19	19	♄10♉R
23	18.06	1	12♋	18	20	20	♅14♒
24	18.10	2	27	19	21	21	♆ 3♒
25	18.14	3	12♌	21	23	22	♇11♐
26	18.18	4	26	22	24	23	♃25♈
27	18.22	5	10♍	24	25	23	♄10♉R
28	18.26	6	23	25	26	24	♅14♒
29	18.30	7	6♎	27	28	25	♆ 3♒
30	18.34	8	19	28	29	26	♇11♐
31	18.38	9	1♏	0♑	0♐	27	♃25♈

TABLES OF HOUSES

These Tables of Houses have been calculated for the Placidean system, in which the twelve houses are of unequal size. If you prefer to use the Equal House system, in which each house spans 30°, you only need the sign and degree of the Ascendant or first house cusp, and the MC (Midheaven). These give you your angles. Those using Placidus will require the house cusps for the second, third, 11th and 12th houses in addition. If you draw straight lines across the zodiac wheel, the second house cusp will give you that of the eighth, the third house cusp the ninth, the 11th house cusp the fifth and the 12th house cusp the sixth. The MC will mark the tenth house cusp and give you the degree of the fourth house cusp.

Reading the Tables is simple. Find the nearest latitude to the birthplace – London is 51 32N, for example – then locate local sidereal time at birth and read across the columns for the signs and degrees of the houses.

TABLES OF HOUSES FOR NORTHERN LATITUDES FOR NEW ORLEANS Latitude 30° 0'n

STime h. m.	10 ♈	11 ♉	12 ♊	Asc ♋	2 ♌	3 ♍	STime h. m.	10 ♉	11 ♊	12 ♋	Asc ♌	2 ♍	3 ♎	STime h. m.	10 ♊	11 ♋	12 ♌	Asc ♍	2 ♎	3 ♏	STime h. m.	10 ♋	11 ♌	12 ♍	Asc ♎	2 ♎	3 ♏	STime h. m.	10 ♋	11 ♍	12 ♎	Asc ♎	2 ♏	3 ♐	STime h. m.	10 ♌	11 ♎	12 ♎	Asc ♏	2 ♐	3 ♑
0. 0	0	5	11	13	5	0	2. 0	2	6	9	8	2	0	4. 0	2	4	5	4	0	0	6. 0	0	2	2	0	28	28	8. 0	28	0	0	26	25	26	10. 0	28	0	28	22	21	24
0. 5	1	6	12	14	6	1	2. 5	3	7	10	10	3	1	4. 5	3	6	6	5	1	1	6. 5	1	3	3	1	29	29	8. 5	29	1	1	27	26	27	10. 5	29	1	29	23	22	25
0.10	3	8	13	15	7	3	2.10	5	9	11	11	4	3	4.10	4	7	7	6	2	2	6.10	2	4	4	2	♏	♐	8.10	♌	3	2	28	27	28	10.10	♍	3	♏	24	23	26
0.15	4	9	14	16	9	4	2.15	6	10	12	12	6	4	4.15	6	8	9	7	4	3	6.15	3	5	6	3	1	2	8.15	2	4	4	29	28	29	10.15	2	4	1	25	25	27
0.20	5	10	16	17	10	5	2.20	7	11	13	13	7	5	4.20	7	9	10	8	5	5	6.20	5	6	7	4	2	3	8.20	3	5	5	0♏	29	♑	10.20	3	5	2	26	26	29
0.25	7	12	17	18	11	6	2.25	9	12	14	14	8	6	4.25	8	10	11	9	6	6	6.25	6	8	8	5	4	4	8.25	4	6	6	1	♐	1	10.25	4	6	4	27	27	♒
0.30	8	13	18	19	12	8	2.30	10	13	15	15	9	8	4.30	9	11	12	10	7	7	6.30	7	9	9	7	5	5	8.30	5	8	7	2	1	2	10.30	6	8	5	28	28	1
0.35	10	14	19	20	13	9	2.35	11	15	17	16	10	9	4.35	10	12	13	12	8	8	6.35	8	10	10	8	6	6	8.35	6	9	8	4	2	4	10.35	7	9	6	29	29	3
0.40	11	16	20	22	14	10	2.40	12	16	18	17	11	10	4.40	12	14	14	13	9	10	6.40	9	11	11	9	7	7	8.40	8	10	9	5	4	5	10.40	8	10	7	0♐	♑	4
0.45	12	17	22	23	15	11	2.45	14	17	19	18	13	11	4.45	13	15	15	14	10	11	6.45	10	12	13	10	8	9	8.45	9	11	10	6	5	6	10.45	10	11	8	1	1	5
0.50	14	18	23	24	16	12	2.50	15	18	20	19	14	13	4.50	14	16	16	15	12	12	6.50	11	13	14	11	9	10	8.50	10	12	12	7	6	7	10.50	11	13	9	2	3	6
0.55	15	20	24	25	17	14	2.55	16	19	21	20	15	14	4.55	15	17	17	16	13	13	6.55	13	15	15	12	10	11	8.55	11	14	13	8	7	8	10.55	12	14	10	3	4	8
1. 0	16	21	25	26	19	15	3. 0	17	21	22	21	16	15	5. 0	16	18	19	17	14	14	7. 0	14	16	16	13	11	12	9. 0	13	15	14	9	8	9	11. 0	14	15	11	4	5	9
1. 5	18	22	26	27	20	16	3. 5	19	22	23	22	17	16	5. 5	17	19	20	18	15	15	7. 5	15	17	17	14	13	13	9. 5	14	16	15	10	9	11	11. 5	15	16	13	5	6	10
1.10	19	24	27	28	21	17	3.10	20	23	24	23	18	18	5.10	19	20	21	19	16	17	7.10	16	18	18	15	14	14	9.10	15	17	16	11	10	12	11.10	16	18	14	6	7	12
1.15	20	25	29	29	22	19	3.15	21	24	25	24	20	19	5.15	20	21	22	20	17	18	7.15	17	19	20	16	15	15	9.15	16	19	17	12	11	13	11.15	18	19	15	7	8	13
1.20	22	26	♋	0♌	23	20	3.20	22	25	26	25	21	20	5.20	21	23	23	21	19	19	7.20	18	20	21	17	16	16	9.20	18	20	19	13	12	14	11.20	19	20	16	8	10	14
1.25	23	27	1	1	24	21	3.25	24	26	28	26	22	21	5.25	22	24	24	22	20	20	7.25	20	22	22	18	17	18	9.25	19	21	20	14	13	15	11.25	20	21	17	10	11	16
1.30	24	29	2	2	25	22	3.30	25	28	29	28	23	22	5.30	23	25	25	23	21	21	7.30	21	23	23	20	18	19	9.30	20	22	21	15	15	17	11.30	22	22	18	11	12	17
1.35	26	♊	3	3	26	24	3.35	26	29	♌	29	24	24	5.35	24	26	26	25	22	22	7.35	22	24	24	21	19	20	9.35	21	24	22	16	16	18	11.35	23	24	19	12	13	18
1.40	27	1	4	4	28	25	3.40	27	♋	1	0♍	25	25	5.40	25	27	28	26	23	24	7.40	23	25	25	22	20	21	9.40	23	25	23	17	17	19	11.40	25	25	20	13	14	20
1.45	28	3	5	5	29	26	3.45	28	1	2	1	26	26	5.45	27	28	29	27	24	25	7.45	24	27	26	23	21	22	9.45	24	26	24	18	18	20	11.45	26	26	21	14	16	21
1.50	♉	4	7	6	♍	27	3.50	♊	2	3	2	28	27	5.50	28	29	♍	28	26	26	7.50	26	28	28	24	23	23	9.50	25	27	26	19	19	21	11.50	27	27	23	15	17	22
1.55	1	5	8	7	1	29	3.55	1	3	4	3	29	29	5.55	29	♌	1	29	27	27	7.55	27	29	29	25	24	24	9.55	27	29	27	20	20	23	11.55	29	29	24	16	18	24
2. 0	2	6	9	8	2	♎	4. 0	2	4	5	4	♎	♏	6. 0	♋	2	2	0♎	28	28	8. 0	28	♍	♎	26	25	26	10. 0	28	♎	28	22	21	24	12. 0	♎	♏	25	17	19	25

STime h. m.	10 ♎	11 ♏	12 ♏	Asc ♐	2 ♑	3 ♒	STime h. m.	10 ♏	11 ♏	12 ♐	Asc ♑	2 ♒	3 ♈	STime h. m.	10 ♐	11 ♐	12 ♑	Asc ♒	2 ♈	3 ♉	STime h. m.	10 ♑	11 ♑	12 ♒	Asc ♈	2 ♉	3 ♊	STime h. m.	10 ♑	11 ♒	12 ♈	Asc ♉	2 ♊	3 ♋	STime h. m.	10 ♒	11 ♈	12 ♉	Asc ♊	2 ♋	3 ♌
12. 0	0	0	25	17	19	25	14. 0	2	28	21	15	22	0	16. 0	2	26	19	18	0	5	18. 0	0	24	22	0	8	6	20. 0	28	25	0	12	11	4	22. 0	28	0	8	15	9	2
12. 5	1	1	26	18	21	27	14. 5	3	29	22	16	24	1	16. 5	3	27	21	20	2	6	18. 5	1	25	24	2	9	7	20. 5	29	27	2	13	12	6	22. 5	29	1	9	16	10	3
12.10	3	2	27	19	22	28	14.10	5	♐	23	17	25	3	16.10	4	28	22	22	3	8	18.10	2	26	25	4	11	9	20.10	♒	28	3	15	13	7	22.10	♓	3	11	18	11	4
12.15	4	3	28	20	23	29	14.15	6	2	25	19	27	4	16.15	6	29	23	23	5	9	18.15	3	27	27	5	12	10	20.15	2	29	5	16	14	8	22.15	2	4	12	19	12	5
12.20	5	5	29	21	24	♓	14.20	7	3	26	20	28	6	16.20	7	♑	24	25	7	10	18.20	5	29	28	7	14	11	20.20	3	♓	7	18	16	9	22.20	3	6	14	20	13	6
12.25	7	6	♐	23	26	2	14.25	9	4	27	21	♓	7	16.25	8	1	26	27	8	12	18.25	6	♒	♓	9	15	12	20.25	4	2	8	19	17	10	22.25	4	7	15	21	14	8
12.30	8	7	1	24	27	4	14.30	10	5	28	23	1	9	16.30	9	2	27	28	10	13	18.30	7	1	1	11	17	13	20.30	5	4	10	21	18	11	22.30	6	9	17	23	15	9
12.35	10	8	2	25	28	5	14.35	11	6	29	24	3	10	16.35	10	4	28	0♓	11	14	18.35	8	3	3	13	18	15	20.35	6	5	11	22	19	12	22.35	7	10	18	24	17	10
12.40	11	10	4	26	♒	6	14.40	12	7	♑	25	4	12	16.40	12	5	♒	2	13	16	18.40	9	4	4	14	19	16	20.40	8	6	13	24	20	14	22.40	8	12	19	25	18	11
12.45	12	11	5	27	1	8	14.45	14	9	1	27	6	13	16.45	13	6	1	3	15	17	18.45	10	5	6	16	21	17	20.45	9	8	15	25	22	15	22.45	10	13	21	26	19	12
12.50	14	12	6	28	2	9	14.50	15	10	3	28	7	15	16.50	14	7	2	5	16	18	18.50	11	6	7	18	22	18	20.50	10	9	16	27	23	16	22.50	11	15	22	27	20	13
12.55	15	13	7	29	4	11	14.55	16	11	4	29	9	16	16.55	15	8	4	7	18	20	18.55	13	8	9	20	24	19	20.55	11	11	18	28	24	17	22.55	12	16	24	28	21	15
13. 0	16	14	8	0♑	5	12	15. 0	17	12	5	1♒	11	18	17. 0	16	9	5	8	19	21	19. 0	14	9	11	22	25	21	21. 0	13	12	19	29	25	18	23. 0	14	18	25	0♋	22	16
13. 5	18	15	9	2	6	14	15. 5	19	13	6	2	12	19	17. 5	17	11	6	10	21	22	19. 5	15	10	12	23	26	22	21. 5	14	14	21	1♊	26	19	23. 5	15	19	26	1	23	17
13.10	19	17	10	3	8	15	15.10	20	14	7	3	14	21	17.10	19	12	8	12	23	24	19.10	16	12	14	25	28	23	21.10	15	15	23	2	27	20	23.10	16	21	28	2	24	18
13.15	20	18	11	4	9	17	15.15	21	15	8	5	15	22	17.15	20	13	9	14	24	25	19.15	17	13	15	27	29	24	21.15	16	17	24	3	29	21	23.15	18	22	29	3	25	19
13.20	22	19	12	5	11	18	15.20	22	16	10	6	17	24	17.20	21	14	11	16	26	26	19.20	18	14	17	28	♊	25	21.20	18	18	26	5	♋	23	23.20	19	24	♊	4	26	20
13.25	23	20	13	6	12	20	15.25	24	18	11	8	19	25	17.25	22	15	12	17	27	27	19.25	20	16	19	0♉	2	26	21.25	19	20	27	6	1	24	23.25	20	25	2	5	28	22
13.30	24	21	15	7	13	21	15.30	25	19	12	9	20	26	17.30	23	17	13	19	29	29	19.30	21	17	20	2	3	28	21.30	20	21	29	7	2	25	23.30	22	26	3	6	29	23
13.35	26	22	16	9	15	23	15.35	26	20	13	11	22	28	17.35	24	18	15	21	♉	♊	19.35	22	18	22	3	4	29	21.35	21	23	♉	9	3	26	23.35	23	28	4	7	♌	24
13.40	27	24	17	10	16	24	15.40	27	21	14	12	23	29	17.40	25	19	16	23	2	1	19.40	23	20	23	5	6	♋	21.40	23	24	2	10	4	27	23.40	25	29	6	9	1	25
13.45	28	25	18	11	18	26	15.45	28	22	16	14	25	♉	17.45	27	20	18	25	3	3	19.45	24	21	25	7	7	1	21.45	24	26	3	11	5	28	23.45	26	♉	7	10	2	27
13.50	♏	26	19	12	19	27	15.50	♐	23	17	15	27	2	17.50	28	21	19	26	5	4	19.50	26	22	27	8	8	2	21.50	25	27	5	13	7	29	23.50	27	2	8	11	3	28
13.55	1	27	20	14	21	29	15.55	1	24	18	17	28	3	17.55	29	23	21	28	6	5	19.55	27	24	28	10	9	3	21.55	27	29	6	14	8	♌	23.55	29	3	9	12	4	29
14. 0	2	28	21	15	22	♈	16. 0	2	26	19	18	♈	5	18. 0	♑	24	22	0♈	8	6	20. 0	28	25	♈	12	11	4	22. 0	28	♈	8	15	9	2	24. 0	♈	5	11	13	5	♍

TABLES OF HOUSES FOR NORTHERN LATITUDES FOR LOS ANGELES Latitude 34° 0'n

STime h. m.	10 ♈	11 ♉	12 ♊	Asc ♋	2 ♌	3 ♍	STime h. m.	10 ♉	11 ♊	12 ♋	Asc ♌	2 ♍	3 ♎	STime h. m.	10 ♊	11 ♋	12 ♌	Asc ♍	2 ♎	3 ♎	STime h. m.	10 ♋	11 ♌	12 ♍	Asc ♎	2 ♎	3 ♏	STime h. m.	10 ♋	11 ♍	12 ♎	Asc ♎	2 ♏	3 ♐	STime h. m.	10 ♌	11 ♎	12 ♎	Asc ♏	2 ♐	3 ♑
0. 0	0	5	12	15	6	1	2. 0	2	7	10	10	3	0	4. 0	2	5	6	5	0	29	6. 0	0	2	3	0	27	28	8. 0	28	1	0	25	24	25	10. 0	28	0	27	20	20	23
0. 5	1	7	13	16	7	2	2. 5	3	8	11	11	4	1	4. 5	3	6	7	6	1	♏	6. 5	1	4	4	1	28	29	8. 5	29	2	1	26	25	26	10. 5	29	1	28	21	21	24
0.10	3	8	15	17	9	3	2.10	5	9	12	12	5	2	4.10	4	7	9	7	2	2	6.10	2	5	5	2	29	♐	8.10	♌	3	2	27	26	27	10.10	♍	2	29	22	22	26
0.15	4	10	16	18	10	4	2.15	6	11	14	13	6	4	4.15	6	9	10	8	3	3	6.15	3	6	6	3	♏	1	8.15	2	4	3	28	27	28	10.15	2	4	♏	23	23	27
0.20	5	11	17	19	11	5	2.20	7	12	15	14	7	5	4.20	7	10	11	9	5	4	6.20	5	7	7	4	2	2	8.20	3	5	5	29	28	29	10.20	3	5	2	24	24	28
0.25	7	12	18	20	12	7	2.25	9	13	16	15	8	6	4.25	8	11	12	10	6	5	6.25	6	8	8	5	3	3	8.25	4	7	6	0♏	29	♑	10.25	4	6	3	25	25	29
0.30	8	14	20	21	13	8	2.30	10	14	17	16	10	7	4.30	9	12	13	11	7	7	6.30	7	9	10	6	4	4	8.30	5	8	7	1	♐	2	10.30	6	7	4	26	27	♒
0.35	10	15	21	22	14	9	2.35	11	15	18	17	11	9	4.35	10	13	14	12	8	8	6.35	8	10	11	7	5	6	8.35	6	9	8	2	1	3	10.35	7	9	5	27	28	2
0.40	11	16	22	23	15	10	2.40	12	17	19	18	12	10	4.40	12	14	15	13	9	9	6.40	9	12	12	8	6	7	8.40	8	10	9	3	2	4	10.40	8	10	6	28	29	3
0.45	12	18	23	25	16	11	2.45	14	18	20	19	13	11	4.45	13	15	16	14	10	10	6.45	10	13	13	9	7	8	8.45	9	11	10	5	3	5	10.45	10	11	7	29	♑	4
0.50	14	19	24	26	17	13	2.50	15	19	21	20	14	12	4.50	14	16	17	15	11	11	6.50	11	14	14	11	8	9	8.50	10	13	11	6	4	6	10.50	11	12	8	0♐	1	6
0.55	15	20	25	27	18	14	2.55	16	20	22	21	15	14	4.55	15	18	18	16	13	13	6.55	13	15	15	12	9	10	8.55	11	14	13	7	6	7	10.55	12	14	9	1	2	7
1. 0	16	22	27	28	20	15	3. 0	17	21	23	22	16	15	5. 0	16	19	20	17	14	14	7. 0	14	16	16	13	10	11	9. 0	13	15	14	8	7	9	11. 0	14	15	10	2	3	8
1. 5	18	23	28	29	21	16	3. 5	19	23	24	23	17	16	5. 5	17	20	21	18	15	15	7. 5	15	17	17	14	12	12	9. 5	14	16	15	9	8	10	11. 5	15	16	12	3	5	10
1.10	19	24	29	0♌	22	18	3.10	20	24	26	24	19	17	5.10	19	21	22	19	16	16	7.10	16	19	19	15	13	14	9.10	15	18	16	10	9	11	11.10	16	17	13	4	6	11
1.15	20	26	♋	1	23	19	3.15	21	25	27	25	20	19	5.15	20	22	23	21	17	17	7.15	17	20	20	16	14	15	9.15	16	19	17	11	10	12	11.15	18	19	14	5	7	12
1.20	22	27	1	2	24	20	3.20	22	26	28	27	21	20	5.20	21	23	24	22	18	18	7.20	18	21	21	17	15	16	9.20	18	20	18	12	11	13	11.20	19	20	15	7	8	14
1.25	23	28	2	3	25	21	3.25	24	27	29	28	22	21	5.25	22	24	25	23	19	20	7.25	20	22	22	18	16	17	9.25	19	21	19	13	12	15	11.25	20	21	16	8	9	15
1.30	24	29	3	4	26	23	3.30	25	28	♌	29	23	22	5.30	23	26	26	24	20	21	7.30	21	23	23	19	17	18	9.30	20	23	20	14	13	16	11.30	22	22	17	9	10	16
1.35	26	♊	5	5	27	24	3.35	26	29	1	0♍	24	23	5.35	24	27	27	25	22	22	7.35	22	25	24	20	18	19	9.35	21	24	22	15	14	17	11.35	23	23	18	10	12	18
1.40	27	2	6	6	28	25	3.40	27	♋	2	1	25	25	5.40	25	28	28	26	23	23	7.40	23	26	25	21	19	20	9.40	23	25	23	16	15	18	11.40	25	25	19	11	13	19
1.45	28	3	7	7	29	26	3.45	28	2	3	2	27	26	5.45	27	29	29	27	24	24	7.45	24	27	27	22	20	21	9.45	24	26	24	17	16	19	11.45	26	26	20	12	14	20
1.50	♉	4	8	8	♍	28	3.50	♊	3	4	3	28	27	5.50	28	♌	♍	28	25	25	7.50	26	28	28	23	21	23	9.50	25	28	25	18	18	21	11.50	27	27	21	13	15	22
1.55	1	6	9	9	2	29	3.55	1	4	5	4	29	28	5.55	29	1	2	29	26	26	7.55	27	29	29	24	23	24	9.55	27	29	26	19	19	22	11.55	29	28	23	14	17	23
2. 0	2	7	10	10	3	♎	4. 0	2	5	6	5	♎	29	6. 0	♋	2	3	0♎	27	28	8. 0	28	♍	♎	25	24	25	10. 0	28	♎	27	20	20	23	12. 0	♎	29	24	15	18	25

STime h. m.	10 ♎	11 ♎	12 ♏	Asc ♐	2 ♑	3 ♒	STime h. m.	10 ♏	11 ♏	12 ♐	Asc ♑	2 ♒	3 ♈	STime h. m.	10 ♐	11 ♐	12 ♑	Asc ♒	2 ♈	3 ♉	STime h. m.	10 ♑	11 ♑	12 ♒	Asc ♈	2 ♉	3 ♊	STime h. m.	10 ♑	11 ♒	12 ♈	Asc ♉	2 ♊	3 ♋	STime h. m.	10 ♒	11 ♈	12 ♉	Asc ♊	2 ♋	3 ♌
12. 0	0	29	24	15	18	25	14. 0	2	28	20	12	21	0	16. 0	2	25	18	16	0	5	18. 0	0	23	21	0	9	7	20. 0	28	25	0	14	12	5	22. 0	28	0	9	18	10	2
12. 5	1	♏	25	16	19	26	14. 5	3	29	21	14	22	2	16. 5	3	26	19	18	2	7	18. 5	1	24	22	2	11	8	20. 5	29	26	2	15	13	6	22. 5	29	2	11	19	11	4
12.10	3	2	26	17	20	27	14.10	5	♐	22	15	24	3	16.10	4	27	20	20	3	8	18.10	2	26	24	4	12	9	20.10	♒	27	3	17	15	7	22.10	♓	3	12	20	12	5
12.15	4	3	27	18	22	29	14.15	6	1	23	16	25	5	16.15	6	28	22	21	5	10	18.15	3	27	25	6	14	11	20.15	2	29	5	18	16	9	22.15	2	5	14	21	14	6
12.20	5	4	28	19	23	♓	14.20	7	2	24	17	27	6	16.20	7	29	23	23	7	11	18.20	5	28	27	8	15	12	20.20	3	♓	7	20	17	10	22.20	3	6	15	22	15	7
12.25	7	5	29	20	24	2	14.25	9	3	25	19	29	8	16.25	8	♑	24	25	8	12	18.25	6	29	29	10	17	13	20.25	4	2	8	21	18	11	22.25	4	8	17	24	16	8
12.30	8	7	♐	21	26	3	14.30	10	4	27	20	♓	9	16.30	9	2	26	27	10	14	18.30	7	♒	♓	12	18	14	20.30	5	3	10	23	20	12	22.30	6	9	18	25	17	9
12.35	10	8	1	23	27	5	14.35	11	6	28	21	2	11	16.35	10	3	27	28	12	15	18.35	8	2	2	13	19	15	20.35	6	5	12	24	21	13	22.35	7	11	19	26	18	10
12.40	11	9	2	24	28	6	14.40	12	7	29	23	3	12	16.40	12	4	28	0♓	13	16	18.40	9	3	3	15	21	17	20.40	8	6	13	26	22	14	22.40	8	12	21	27	19	12
12.45	12	10	3	25	29	8	14.45	14	8	♑	24	5	14	16.45	13	5	29	2	15	18	18.45	10	4	5	17	22	18	20.45	9	8	15	27	23	15	22.45	10	14	22	28	20	13
12.50	14	11	4	26	♒	9	14.50	15	9	1	25	7	15	16.50	14	6	♒	4	17	19	18.50	11	6	7	19	24	19	20.50	10	9	17	29	24	16	22.50	11	15	24	0♋	21	14
12.55	15	13	6	27	2	11	14.55	16	10	2	27	8	17	16.55	15	7	2	5	18	20	18.55	13	7	8	21	25	20	20.55	11	11	18	0♊	25	18	22.55	12	17	25	1	22	15
13. 0	16	14	7	28	4	12	15. 0	17	11	3	28	10	18	17. 0	16	9	4	7	20	22	19. 0	14	8	10	23	26	21	21. 0	13	12	20	2	27	19	23. 0	14	18	26	2	23	16
13. 5	18	15	8	29	5	13	15. 5	19	12	5	0♒	12	19	17. 5	17	10	5	9	22	23	19. 5	15	10	12	25	28	23	21. 5	14	13	22	3	28	20	23. 5	15	19	28	3	24	17
13.10	19	16	9	0♑	6	15	15.10	20	14	6	1	13	21	17.10	19	11	6	11	23	24	19.10	16	11	13	26	29	24	21.10	15	15	23	5	29	21	23.10	16	21	29	4	26	19
13.15	20	17	10	2	8	16	15.15	21	15	7	3	15	22	17.15	20	12	8	13	25	26	19.15	17	12	15	28	♊	25	21.15	16	16	25	6	♋	22	23.15	18	22	♊	5	27	20
13.20	22	18	11	3	9	18	15.20	22	16	8	4	17	24	17.20	21	13	9	15	27	27	19.20	18	14	17	0♉	2	26	21.20	18	18	27	7	1	23	23.20	19	24	2	6	28	21
13.25	23	20	12	4	11	19	15.25	24	17	9	6	18	25	17.25	22	15	11	17	28	28	19.25	20	15	18	2	3	27	21.25	19	19	28	9	2	24	23.25	20	25	3	7	29	22
13.30	24	21	13	5	12	21	15.30	25	18	10	7	20	27	17.30	23	16	12	18	♉	29	19.30	21	16	20	3	4	28	21.30	20	21	♉	10	3	26	23.30	22	27	4	9	♌	23
13.35	26	22	14	6	13	22	15.35	26	19	12	9	22	28	17.35	24	17	13	20	1	♊	19.35	22	18	22	5	6	29	21.35	21	22	1	11	5	27	23.35	23	28	6	10	1	25
13.40	27	23	15	8	15	24	15.40	27	20	13	10	23	♉	17.40	25	18	15	22	3	2	19.40	23	19	23	7	7	♋	21.40	23	24	3	13	6	28	23.40	25	♉	7	11	2	26
13.45	28	24	16	9	16	25	15.45	28	21	14	12	25	1	17.45	27	19	16	24	5	3	19.45	24	20	25	9	8	2	21.45	24	25	5	14	7	29	23.45	26	1	8	12	3	27
13.50	♏	25	18	10	18	27	15.50	♐	23	15	13	27	3	17.50	28	21	18	26	6	4	19.50	26	22	27	10	10	3	21.50	25	27	6	15	8	♌	23.50	27	3	10	13	4	28
13.55	1	26	19	11	19	28	15.55	1	24	17	15	28	4	17.55	29	22	19	28	8	6	19.55	27	23	28	12	11	4	21.55	27	28	8	16	9	1	23.55	29	4	11	14	5	29
14. 0	2	28	20	12	21	♈	16. 0	2	25	18	16	♈	5	18. 0	♑	23	21	0♈	9	7	20. 0	28	25	♈	14	12	5	22. 0	28	♈	9	18	10	2	24. 0	♈	5	12	15	6	♍

TABLES OF HOUSES FOR NORTHERN LATITUDES FOR Latitude 35° 0'n

STime h. m.	10 ♈	11 ♉	12 ♊	Asc ♋	2 ♌	3 ♍	STime h. m.	10 ♉	11 ♊	12 ♋	Asc ♌	2 ♍	3 ♎	STime h. m.	10 ♊	11 ♋	12 ♌	Asc ♍	2 ♎	3 ♎	STime h. m.	10 ♋	11 ♌	12 ♍	Asc ♎	2 ♎	3 ♏	STime h. m.	10 ♋	11 ♍	12 ♎	Asc ♎	2 ♏	3 ♐	STime h. m.	10 ♌	11 ♎	12 ♎	Asc ♏	2 ♐	3 ♑
0. 0	0	5	13	16	7	1	2. 0	2	7	11	10	3	0	4. 0	2	5	7	5	0	29	6. 0	0	3	3	0	27	27	8. 0	28	1	0	25	23	25	10. 0	28	0	27	20	19	23
0. 5	1	7	14	17	8	2	2. 5	3	8	12	11	4	1	4. 5	3	7	8	6	1	♏	6. 5	1	4	4	1	28	29	8. 5	29	2	1	26	24	26	10. 5	29	1	28	21	20	24
0.10	3	8	15	18	9	3	2.10	5	10	13	12	5	2	4.10	4	8	9	7	2	2	6.10	2	5	5	2	29	♐	8.10	♌	3	2	27	25	27	10.10	♍	2	29	22	22	25
0.15	4	10	16	19	10	4	2.15	6	11	14	13	6	4	4.15	6	9	10	8	3	3	6.15	3	6	6	3	♏	1	8.15	2	4	3	28	27	28	10.15	2	4	♏	23	23	27
0.20	5	11	18	20	11	5	2.20	7	12	15	14	7	5	4.20	7	10	11	9	5	4	6.20	5	7	7	4	1	2	8.20	3	5	5	29	28	29	10.20	3	5	1	24	24	28
0.25	7	12	19	21	12	7	2.25	9	13	16	16	9	6	4.25	8	11	12	10	6	5	6.25	6	8	9	5	3	3	8.25	4	7	6	0♏	29	♑	10.25	4	6	3	25	25	29
0.30	8	14	20	22	13	8	2.30	10	14	17	17	10	7	4.30	9	12	13	11	7	7	6.30	7	9	10	6	4	4	8.30	5	8	7	1	♐	1	10.30	6	7	4	26	26	♒
0.35	10	15	21	23	14	9	2.35	11	16	18	18	11	9	4.35	10	13	14	12	8	8	6.35	8	11	11	7	5	5	8.35	6	9	8	2	1	3	10.35	7	9	5	27	27	2
0.40	11	17	22	24	15	10	2.40	12	17	19	19	12	10	4.40	12	14	15	13	9	9	6.40	9	12	12	8	6	7	8.40	8	10	9	3	2	4	10.40	8	10	6	28	28	3
0.45	12	18	24	25	16	12	2.45	14	18	20	20	13	11	4.45	13	16	16	14	10	10	6.45	10	13	13	9	7	8	8.45	9	12	10	4	3	5	10.45	10	11	7	29	♑	4
0.50	14	19	25	26	18	13	2.50	15	19	22	21	14	12	4.50	14	17	18	15	11	11	6.50	11	14	14	10	8	9	8.50	10	13	11	5	4	6	10.50	11	12	8	0♐	1	6
0.55	15	21	26	27	19	14	2.55	16	20	23	22	15	14	4.55	15	18	19	16	12	12	6.55	13	15	15	11	9	10	8.55	11	14	12	6	5	7	10.55	12	14	9	1	2	7
1. 0	16	22	27	28	20	15	3. 0	17	22	24	23	16	15	5. 0	16	19	20	17	14	14	7. 0	14	16	16	13	10	11	9. 0	13	15	14	7	6	8	11. 0	14	15	10	2	3	8
1. 5	18	23	28	29	21	16	3. 5	19	23	25	24	18	16	5. 5	17	20	21	19	15	15	7. 5	15	18	18	14	11	12	9. 5	14	16	15	8	7	10	11. 5	15	16	11	3	4	9
1.10	19	24	29	0♌	22	18	3.10	20	24	26	25	19	17	5.10	19	21	22	20	16	16	7.10	16	19	19	15	12	13	9.10	15	18	16	9	8	11	11.10	16	17	12	4	5	11
1.15	20	26	♋	1	23	19	3.15	21	25	27	26	20	18	5.15	20	22	23	21	17	17	7.15	17	20	20	16	14	14	9.15	16	19	17	10	10	12	11.15	18	18	14	5	6	12
1.20	22	27	2	2	24	20	3.20	22	26	28	27	21	20	5.20	21	23	24	22	18	18	7.20	18	21	21	17	15	16	9.20	18	20	18	11	11	13	11.20	19	20	15	6	8	13
1.25	23	28	3	3	25	21	3.25	24	27	29	28	22	21	5.25	22	25	25	23	19	19	7.25	20	22	22	18	16	17	9.25	19	21	19	12	12	14	11.25	20	21	16	7	9	15
1.30	24	♊	4	4	26	23	3.30	25	29	♌	29	23	22	5.30	23	26	26	24	20	21	7.30	21	23	23	19	17	18	9.30	20	23	20	13	13	16	11.30	22	22	17	8	10	16
1.35	26	1	5	5	27	24	3.35	26	♋	1	0♍	24	23	5.35	24	27	27	25	21	22	7.35	22	25	24	20	18	19	9.35	21	24	21	14	14	17	11.35	23	23	18	9	11	18
1.40	27	2	6	6	29	25	3.40	27	1	2	1	25	25	5.40	25	28	29	26	23	23	7.40	23	26	25	21	19	20	9.40	23	25	23	16	15	18	11.40	25	25	19	10	12	19
1.45	28	3	7	7	♍	26	3.45	28	2	3	2	27	26	5.45	27	29	♍	27	24	24	7.45	24	27	27	22	20	21	9.45	24	26	24	17	16	19	11.45	26	26	20	11	14	20
1.50	♉	5	8	8	1	28	3.50	♊	3	5	3	28	27	5.50	28	♌	1	28	25	25	7.50	26	28	28	23	21	22	9.50	25	28	25	18	17	20	11.50	27	27	21	12	15	22
1.55	1	6	10	9	2	29	3.55	1	4	6	4	29	28	5.55	29	1	2	29	26	26	7.55	27	29	29	24	22	23	9.55	27	29	26	19	18	22	11.55	29	28	22	13	16	23
2. 0	2	7	11	10	3	♎	4. 0	2	5	7	5	♎	29	6. 0	♋	3	3	0♎	27	27	8. 0	28	♍	♎	25	23	25	10. 0	28	♎	27	20	19	23	12. 0	♎	29	23	14	17	25

TABLE (top block)

STime h.m.	10 ♎	11 ♎	12 ♏	Asc ♐	2 ♑	3 ♒
12. 0	0	29	23	14	17	25
12. 5	1	♏	24	15	19	26
12.10	3	2	25	17	20	27
12.15	4	3	27	18	21	29
12.20	5	4	28	19	22	♓
12.25	7	5	29	20	24	2
12.30	8	7	♐	21	25	3
12.35	10	8	1	22	26	5
12.40	11	9	2	23	28	6
12.45	12	10	3	24	29	7
12.50	14	11	4	25	♒	9
12.55	15	12	5	26	2	10
13. 0	16	14	6	28	3	12
13. 5	18	15	7	29	5	13
13.10	19	16	8	♑	6	15
13.15	20	17	10	1	7	16
13.20	22	18	11	2	9	18
13.25	23	19	12	3	10	19
13.30	24	21	13	4	12	21
13.35	26	22	14	6	13	22
13.40	27	23	15	7	15	24
13.45	28	24	16	8	16	25
13.50	♏	25	17	9	18	27
13.55	1	26	18	11	19	28
14. 0	2	27	19	12	21	♈

STime h.m.	10 ♏	11 ♏	12 ♐	Asc ♑	2 ♒	3 ♈
14. 0	2	27	19	12	21	0
14. 5	3	29	20	13	22	1
14.10	5	♐	22	14	24	3
14.15	6	1	23	16	25	4
14.20	7	2	24	17	1	6
14.25	9	3	25	18	28	8
14.30	10	4	26	19	♓	9
14.35	11	5	27	21	2	11
14.40	12	7	28	22	3	12
14.45	14	8	♑	23	5	14
14.50	15	9	1	25	6	15
14.55	16	10	2	26	8	17
15. 0	17	11	3	28	10	18
15. 5	19	12	4	29	11	20
15.10	20	13	5	♒	13	21
15.15	21	14	6	1	16	25
15.20	22	16	8	3	18	27
15.25	24	17	9	5	19	28
15.30	25	18	11	6	20	♈
15.35	26	19	11	8	21	2
15.40	27	20	12	10	23	3
15.45	28	21	14	11	25	5
15.50	♐	22	15	13	26	6
15.55	1	23	16	14	28	8
16. 0	2	25	17	16	♈	9

STime h.m.	10 ♐	11 ♐	12 ♑	Asc ♒	2 ♈	3 ♉
16. 0	2	25	17	16	0	5
16. 5	3	26	19	18	2	7
16.10	4	27	20	19	3	8
16.15	6	28	21	21	5	10
16.20	7	29	23	23	6	11
16.25	8	♑	24	24	9	12
16.30	9	1	25	26	10	14
16.35	10	3	26	28	12	15
16.40	12	4	28	0♓	14	17
16.45	13	5	29	1	15	18
16.50	14	6	♒	3	17	19
16.55	15	7	2	5	18	21
17. 0	16	8	3	7	20	22
17. 5	17	10	5	9	22	23
17.10	19	11	6	11	24	25
17.15	20	12	7	13	25	26
17.20	21	13	9	14	27	27
17.25	22	14	10	16	28	28
17.30	23	15	12	18	♉	♊
17.35	24	17	13	20	2	1
17.40	25	18	15	22	3	2
17.45	27	19	16	24	5	3
17.50	28	20	18	26	6	5
17.55	29	22	19	28	8	6
18. 0	♑	23	21	0♈	9	7

STime h.m.	10 ♑	11 ♑	12 ♒	Asc ♈	2 ♉	3 ♊
18. 0	0	23	21	0	9	7
18. 5	1	24	22	2	11	8
18.10	2	25	24	4	12	10
18.15	3	27	25	6	14	11
18.20	5	28	27	8	15	12
18.25	6	29	28	10	17	13
18.30	7	♒	♓	12	18	14
18.35	8	2	2	14	20	16
18.40	9	3	3	16	21	17
18.45	10	4	5	17	23	18
18.50	11	6	6	19	24	19
18.55	13	7	8	21	26	21
19. 0	14	8	10	23	27	22
19. 5	15	9	11	25	28	23
19.10	16	11	13	27	♊	24
19.15	17	12	15	29	2	26
19.20	18	13	16	0♉	2	26
19.25	20	15	18	2	4	27
19.30	21	16	19	4	6	♊
19.35	22	18	21	6	7	1
19.40	23	19	23	7	8	1
19.45	24	20	25	9	9	2
19.50	26	22	26	11	11	3
19.55	27	23	28	12	11	4
20. 0	28	25	♈	14	13	5

STime h.m.	10 ♒	11 ♒	12 ♈	Asc ♉	2 ♊	3 ♋
20. 0	28	25	0	14	13	5
20. 5	29	26	2	16	14	7
20.10	♒	27	3	17	15	8
20.15	3	♓	5	19	17	10
20.20	3	♓	7	20	18	10
20.25	4	2	9	22	19	11
20.30	5	3	10	24	20	12
20.35	6	5	12	25	22	13
20.40	8	6	14	27	22	14
20.45	9	7	15	28	24	16
20.50	10	9	17	0♊	25	17
20.55	11	10	19	1	26	19
21. 0	13	12	20	3	27	19
21. 5	14	13	22	4	28	20
21.10	15	16	24	5	29	22
21.15	16	16	26	7	♋	23
21.20	18	18	27	8	2	23
21.25	19	19	29	9	3	25
21.30	20	21	♉	11	4	26
21.35	21	22	2	12	5	27
21.40	23	24	3	13	6	28
21.45	24	25	5	14	7	29
21.50	25	27	6	16	8	♌
21.55	27	28	8	17	10	1
22. 0	28	♈	9	18	11	3

STime h.m.	10 ♓	11 ♈	12 ♉	Asc ♊	2 ♋	3 ♌
22. 0	28	0	9	18	11	3
22. 5	29	2	11	19	12	4
22.10	♓	3	12	21	13	5
22.15	2	5	14	22	14	7
22.20	3	6	15	23	15	7
22.25	4	8	17	24	16	8
22.30	6	9	18	26	17	9
22.35	7	11	20	27	18	11
22.40	8	12	21	28	19	12
22.45	10	14	23	29	20	13
22.50	11	15	24	0♋	22	14
22.55	12	17	25	1	23	16
23. 0	14	18	27	2	24	16
23. 5	15	20	28	4	25	18
23.10	16	21	♊	5	♌	19
23.15	18	23	1	6	27	20
23.20	19	24	2	7	28	21
23.25	20	25	4	8	29	22
23.30	22	27	5	♋	1	24
23.35	23	28	6	10	2	25
23.40	25	♉	8	11	2	26
23.45	26	1	9	12	3	27
23.50	27	3	10	13	♌	29
23.55	29	4	11	15	5	♍
24. 0	♈	5	13	16	7	1

TABLES OF HOUSES FOR NORTHERN LATITUDES FOR SAN FRANCISCO   Latitude 37° 45'n

STime h.m.	10 ♈	11 ♉	12 ♊	Asc ♋	2 ♌	3 ♍
0. 0	0	6	14	17	8	1
0. 5	1	7	15	18	9	2
0.10	3	9	16	19	10	3
0.15	4	10	18	20	11	4
0.20	5	12	19	21	12	6
0.25	7	13	20	22	13	7
0.30	8	14	21	23	14	8
0.35	10	16	22	25	16	9
0.40	11	17	24	26	16	11
0.45	12	18	25	27	17	12
0.50	14	20	26	28	18	13
0.55	15	21	27	29	19	14
1. 0	16	22	28	0♌	20	15
1. 5	18	24	29	1	22	17
1.10	19	25	♋	2	23	18
1.15	20	26	2	3	24	20
1.20	22	28	3	4	25	20
1.25	23	29	4	5	26	21
1.30	24	♊	5	6	27	22
1.35	26	2	6	7	28	24
1.40	27	3	7	8	29	25
1.45	28	4	9	9	♍	26
1.50	♉	5	10	10	1	28
1.55	1	7	11	11	2	29
2. 0	2	8	12	12	3	♎

STime h.m.	10 ♉	11 ♊	12 ♋	Asc ♌	2 ♍	3 ♎
2. 0	2	8	12	12	3	0
2. 5	3	9	13	13	4	0
2.10	5	10	14	14	6	2
2.15	6	11	15	16	6	3
2.20	7	13	16	16	8	5
2.25	9	14	17	17	9	5
2.30	10	15	18	18	10	7
2.35	11	16	19	19	11	8
2.40	12	17	21	20	12	9
2.45	14	19	22	21	13	10
2.50	15	20	23	22	14	12
2.55	16	21	24	23	15	12
3. 0	17	22	25	24	17	15
3. 5	19	23	26	25	18	16
3.10	20	25	27	27	19	17
3.15	21	26	28	28	20	18
3.20	22	27	29	28	21	19
3.25	24	28	♌	29	22	21
3.30	25	♋	1	0♍	24	22
3.35	26	2	2	1	24	23
3.40	27	1	3	2	26	24
3.45	28	3	4	3	27	26
3.50	♊	4	5	5	27	26
3.55	1	5	7	5	29	28
4. 0	2	6	8	6	♎	29

STime h.m.	10 ♊	11 ♋	12 ♌	Asc ♍	2 ♎	3 ♏
4. 0	2	6	8	6	0	29
4. 5	4	8	9	7	2	1
4.10	4	8	10	8	2	1
4.15	6	9	11	9	3	3
4.20	7	11	12	10	4	4
4.25	8	12	13	11	6	5
4.30	9	13	14	12	7	6
4.35	10	14	15	13	8	7
4.40	12	15	16	14	9	9
4.45	13	16	17	15	10	10
4.50	14	17	18	16	11	11
4.55	15	18	19	17	12	12
5. 0	16	20	20	18	13	13
5. 5	17	21	22	19	14	14
5.10	19	22	23	20	16	16
5.15	20	23	24	21	17	17
5.20	21	24	25	21	18	18
5.25	22	25	26	23	19	19
5.30	23	26	27	24	20	20
5.35	24	27	28	25	21	21
5.40	25	29	29	26	22	22
5.45	27	♌	1	27	23	23
5.50	28	1	1	28	25	25
5.55	29	2	3	29	26	26
6. 0	♋	3	3	0♎	27	27

STime h.m.	10 ♋	11 ♌	12 ♍	Asc ♎	2 ♏	3 ♐
6. 0	0	3	3	0	27	27
6. 5	1	4	4	1	28	28
6.10	2	5	6	2	29	29
6.15	3	6	7	3	♏	♐
6.20	5	8	8	4	1	1
6.25	6	9	9	5	2	2
6.30	7	10	10	6	3	4
6.35	8	11	11	7	4	5
6.40	9	12	12	8	5	6
6.45	10	13	13	9	6	7
6.50	11	14	14	10	7	8
6.55	13	16	16	11	8	9
7. 0	14	17	17	12	10	10
7. 5	15	18	18	13	11	11
7.10	16	19	19	14	12	13
7.15	17	20	20	15	14	14
7.20	18	21	21	16	14	15
7.25	20	23	22	17	15	16
7.30	21	24	24	18	17	17
7.35	22	25	25	19	18	18
7.40	23	26	26	19	19	20
7.45	24	27	27	20	20	21
7.50	26	29	28	21	22	22
7.55	27	♍	29	23	22	23
8. 0	28	1	♎	24	24	24

STime h.m.	10 ♌	11 ♍	12 ♎	Asc ♏	2 ♐	3 ♑
8. 0	0	1	0	24	24	24
8. 5	1	2	1	25	25	25
8.10	2	3	2	26	26	26
8.15	3	5	3	27	27	27
8.20	4	6	4	28	29	29
8.25	5	7	6	29	1	0♑
8.30	6	8	7	0♏	1	1
8.35	8	9	8	1	2	2
8.40	9	11	9	2	3	4
8.45	10	12	10	3	4	5
8.50	11	13	11	4	5	6
8.55	13	14	12	5	7	7
9. 0	14	15	13	6	8	8
9. 5	15	17	14	7	9	9
9.10	16	18	16	8	10	11
9.15	18	19	17	9	11	12
9.20	18	20	18	10	13	13
9.25	19	21	19	11	14	14
9.30	20	22	20	13	15	16
9.35	22	23	21	13	16	17
9.40	23	25	22	14	17	18
9.45	24	26	23	15	19	19
9.50	25	27	24	16	20	21
9.55	27	28	25	17	21	22
10. 0	28	♎	26	18	22	23

STime h.m.	10 ♍	11 ♎	12 ♏	Asc ♐	2 ♑	3 ♒
10. 0	28	0	27	18	22	23
10. 5	29	1	28	19	24	25
10.10	♍	2	29	20	25	26
10.15	2	3	♏	21	26	27
10.20	3	5	1	22	27	29
10.25	4	6	2	23	29	28
10.30	6	7	3	24	♑	♒
10.35	7	8	4	25	1	1
10.40	8	10	5	26	2	2
10.45	10	11	6	27	4	4
10.50	11	12	7	28	5	5
10.55	12	13	8	29	6	7
11. 0	14	15	9	0♐	8	8
11. 5	15	16	11	1	9	9
11.10	16	17	12	2	10	11
11.15	18	19	13	4	12	12
11.20	19	19	14	5	13	13
11.25	20	21	15	6	14	14
11.30	22	22	16	8	16	16
11.35	23	23	17	9	16	17
11.40	25	24	18	9	18	18
11.45	26	26	19	10	19	20
11.50	27	27	20	11	21	21
11.55	29	28	21	12	22	23
12. 0	♎	29	22	13	23	24

TABLE (bottom block)

STime h.m.	10 ♎	11 ♎	12 ♏	Asc ♐	2 ♑	3 ♒
12. 0	0	29	22	13	16	24
12. 5	1	♏	23	14	17	26
12.10	3	1	25	15	19	27
12.15	4	3	26	16	20	28
12.20	5	4	27	17	21	♓
12.25	7	5	28	18	22	1
12.30	8	6	29	19	24	3
12.35	10	7	♐	20	25	4
12.40	11	9	1	21	26	6
12.45	12	10	2	22	28	7
12.50	14	11	3	23	29	9
12.55	15	12	4	25	♒	10
13. 0	16	13	5	26	2	12
13. 5	18	14	6	27	3	13
13.10	19	16	7	28	5	15
13.15	20	17	8	29	6	16
13.20	22	18	9	0♑	8	18
13.25	23	19	11	1	9	19
13.30	24	20	12	2	11	21
13.35	26	21	13	4	12	22
13.40	27	23	14	5	15	24
13.45	28	24	15	6	16	26
13.50	♏	25	16	7	17	27
13.55	1	26	17	8	18	28
14. 0	2	27	18	10	20	♈

STime h.m.	10 ♏	11 ♏	12 ♐	Asc ♑	2 ♒	3 ♈
14. 0	2	27	18	10	20	0
14. 5	3	28	19	11	22	2
14.10	5	29	20	12	23	3
14.15	6	♐	21	13	24	5
14.20	7	1	23	15	1	7
14.25	9	3	24	16	27	8
14.30	10	4	25	17	29	9
14.35	11	5	26	19	♓	11
14.40	12	6	27	20	2	12
14.45	14	7	28	21	4	14
14.50	15	8	29	23	5	15
14.55	16	9	♑	24	7	17
15. 0	17	11	2	26	8	18
15. 5	18	12	3	27	10	20
15.10	20	13	4	28	13	21
15.15	21	14	5	0♒	14	23
15.20	22	15	7	1	15	24
15.25	24	16	8	3	16	26
15.30	25	17	9	4	18	♈
15.35	26	18	10	6	19	1
15.40	28	20	12	7	21	3
15.45	♐	21	13	9	22	4
15.50	♐	22	14	11	24	6
15.55	1	23	15	12	26	7
16. 0	2	24	16	14	♈	9

STime h.m.	10 ♐	11 ♐	12 ♑	Asc ♒	2 ♈	3 ♉
16. 0	2	24	16	14	0	6
16. 5	3	25	17	16	2	7
16.10	4	26	19	17	3	9
16.15	6	27	20	19	5	10
16.20	7	29	21	21	6	12
16.25	8	♑	23	22	8	13
16.30	9	1	24	24	9	14
16.35	10	2	25	26	11	16
16.40	12	3	26	28	13	17
16.45	13	4	28	0♓	14	18
16.50	14	5	29	2	17	20
16.55	15	7	1	4	17	21
17. 0	16	8	2	6	19	23
17. 5	17	9	4	8	21	24
17.10	19	10	5	9	22	25
17.15	20	11	6	12	24	26
17.20	21	13	8	13	26	28
17.25	22	14	9	15	27	29
17.30	23	15	10	18	♉	♊
17.35	24	17	12	20	2	1
17.40	25	18	13	21	3	3
17.45	27	19	15	24	5	4
17.50	28	20	16	26	6	5
17.55	29	21	18	28	7	7
18. 0	♑	22	20	0♈	9	8

STime h.m.	10 ♑	11 ♑	12 ♒	Asc ♈	2 ♉	3 ♊
18. 0	0	22	20	0	9	8
18. 5	1	23	21	2	11	9
18.10	2	25	23	4	12	11
18.15	3	26	24	6	14	12
18.20	5	27	26	8	15	13
18.25	6	28	27	10	17	14
18.30	7	29	29	12	18	15
18.35	8	1	♓	14	20	17
18.40	9	3	2	16	21	18
18.45	10	4	4	18	23	19
18.50	11	5	6	20	24	20
18.55	13	6	7	22	26	21
19. 0	14	8	9	24	27	23
19. 5	15	9	11	25	28	24
19.10	16	10	13	27	♊	25
19.15	17	12	14	0♉	2	26
19.20	18	13	16	2	3	27
19.25	20	14	18	4	5	28
19.30	21	16	19	6	6	♊
19.35	22	17	21	8	7	1
19.40	23	19	23	9	9	2
19.45	24	20	25	11	10	3
19.50	26	21	26	13	11	4
19.55	27	23	28	15	13	6
20. 0	28	24	♈	16	14	7

STime h.m.	10 ♒	11 ♒	12 ♈	Asc ♉	2 ♊	3 ♋
20. 0	28	24	0	16	14	7
20. 5	29	25	2	18	15	8
20.10	♒	27	4	19	16	9
20.15	2	28	5	21	18	10
20.20	3	♓	7	22	19	12
20.25	4	1	9	24	20	13
20.30	5	3	11	25	21	13
20.35	6	4	12	27	22	14
20.40	8	6	14	28	24	16
20.45	9	7	16	0♊	25	17
20.50	10	9	17	2	26	17
20.55	11	10	19	3	27	19
21. 0	13	11	21	4	29	20
21. 5	14	13	22	6	♋	21
21.10	15	14	24	7	1	22
21.15	16	16	26	9	2	23
21.20	18	17	27	10	3	24
21.25	19	19	29	11	5	25
21.30	20	20	♉	13	6	26
21.35	21	22	2	14	7	27
21.40	23	24	4	16	8	28
21.45	24	25	5	17	9	♌
21.50	25	27	7	18	10	1
21.55	27	28	9	20	12	2
22. 0	28	♈	10	20	12	3

STime h.m.	10 ♓	11 ♈	12 ♉	Asc ♊	2 ♋	3 ♌
22. 0	28	0	10	20	12	3
22. 5	29	2	12	21	13	4
22.10	♓	3	14	23	14	5
22.15	2	5	15	24	15	6
22.20	3	6	17	25	16	7
22.25	4	8	18	26	18	8
22.30	6	9	20	28	19	10
22.35	7	11	21	29	20	11
22.40	8	12	22	0♊	21	12
22.45	10	14	24	2	22	13
22.50	11	15	25	2	23	14
22.55	12	17	27	3	24	16
23. 0	14	18	28	5	25	16
23. 5	15	20	♊	6	27	18
23.10	16	21	1	7	♌	19
23.15	18	23	2	8	29	20
23.20	19	24	4	9	♌	21
23.25	20	26	5	10	1	22
23.30	22	27	6	♋	2	24
23.35	23	28	8	11	3	25
23.40	25	♉	9	12	4	26
23.45	26	1	10	14	5	27
23.50	27	3	11	15	♌	29
23.55	29	4	13	16	7	♍
24. 0	♈	6	14	17	8	1

TABLES OF HOUSES FOR NORTHERN LATITUDES FOR NEW YORK Latitude 40° 43'n

STime h. m.	10 ♈	11 ♉	12 ♊	Asc ♋	2 ♌	3 ♍	STime h. m.	10 ♉	11 ♊	12 ♋	Asc ♌	2 ♍	3 ♎	STime h. m.	10 ♊	11 ♋	12 ♌	Asc ♍	2 ♎	3 ♎	STime h. m.	10 ♋	11 ♌	12 ♍	Asc ♎	2 ♎	3 ♏	STime h. m.	10 ♋	11 ♍	12 ♎	Asc ♎	2 ♏	3 ♐	STime h. m.	10 ♌	11 ♎	12 ♎	Asc ♏	2 ♐	3 ♑
0. 0	0	6	15	19	9	1	2. 0	2	8	13	13	4	0	4. 0	2	7	9	6	0	29	6. 0	0	4	4	0	26	26	8. 0	28	1	0	24	21	23	10. 0	28	0	26	17	17	22
0. 5	1	8	17	20	10	2	2. 5	3	10	14	14	5	1	4. 5	3	8	10	7	1	♏	6. 5	1	5	5	1	27	28	8. 5	29	2	1	25	22	24	10. 5	29	1	27	18	18	23
0.10	3	9	18	21	11	4	2.10	5	11	15	15	6	2	4.10	4	9	11	8	2	1	6.10	2	6	6	2	28	29	8.10	♌	4	2	26	24	26	10.10	♍	2	28	19	19	24
0.15	4	11	19	22	12	5	2.15	6	12	16	16	7	4	4.15	6	10	12	9	3	2	6.15	3	7	7	3	29	♐	8.15	2	5	3	27	25	27	10.15	2	4	29	20	20	25
0.20	5	12	20	23	13	6	2.20	7	13	17	17	8	5	4.20	7	11	13	10	4	3	6.20	5	8	8	4	♏	1	8.20	3	6	4	28	26	28	10.20	3	5	♏	21	21	27
0.25	7	13	22	24	14	7	2.25	9	15	19	18	9	6	4.25	8	12	14	11	5	5	6.25	6	9	9	5	1	2	8.25	4	7	5	29	27	29	10.25	4	6	1	22	22	28
0.30	8	15	23	25	15	8	2.30	10	16	20	19	10	7	4.30	9	13	15	12	7	6	6.30	7	10	10	6	2	3	8.30	5	8	7	0♏	28	♑	10.30	6	7	2	23	23	29
0.35	10	16	24	26	16	10	2.35	11	17	21	20	12	8	4.35	10	15	16	13	8	7	6.35	8	12	12	7	3	4	8.35	6	10	8	1	29	1	10.35	7	8	3	24	25	♒
0.40	11	18	25	27	17	11	2.40	12	18	22	21	13	10	4.40	12	16	17	14	9	8	6.40	9	13	13	8	5	5	8.40	8	11	9	2	♐	2	10.40	8	10	5	25	26	2
0.45	12	19	26	28	18	12	2.45	14	19	23	22	14	11	4.45	13	17	18	15	10	9	6.45	10	14	14	9	6	6	8.45	9	12	10	2	1	4	10.45	10	11	6	26	27	3
0.50	14	20	27	29	19	13	2.50	15	21	24	23	15	12	4.50	14	18	19	16	11	10	6.50	11	15	15	10	7	8	8.50	10	13	11	3	2	5	10.50	11	12	7	27	28	4
0.55	15	22	29	0♌	20	14	2.55	16	22	25	24	16	13	4.55	15	19	20	17	12	12	6.55	13	16	16	11	8	9	8.55	11	14	12	4	3	6	10.55	12	13	8	28	29	6
1. 0	16	23	♋	1	21	16	3. 0	17	23	26	25	17	14	5. 0	16	20	21	18	13	13	7. 0	14	17	17	12	9	10	9. 0	13	16	13	5	4	7	11. 0	14	14	9	29	♑	7
1. 5	18	24	1	2	22	17	3. 5	19	24	27	26	18	16	5. 5	17	21	22	19	14	14	7. 5	15	18	18	13	10	11	9. 5	14	17	14	6	5	8	11. 5	15	16	10	0♐	1	8
1.10	19	26	2	3	23	18	3.10	20	25	28	27	19	17	5.10	19	22	23	20	15	15	7.10	16	20	19	14	11	12	9.10	15	18	15	7	6	9	11.10	16	17	11	1	3	10
1.15	20	27	3	4	24	19	3.15	21	26	29	28	20	18	5.15	20	24	24	21	16	16	7.15	17	21	20	15	12	13	9.15	16	19	16	8	7	11	11.15	18	18	12	2	4	11
1.20	22	28	4	5	25	20	3.20	22	28	♌	28	21	19	5.20	21	25	25	22	17	17	7.20	18	22	21	16	13	14	9.20	18	20	17	9	8	12	11.20	19	19	13	3	5	12
1.25	23	♊	5	6	27	22	3.25	24	29	1	29	22	20	5.25	22	26	27	23	18	18	7.25	20	23	22	17	14	15	9.25	19	22	18	10	9	13	11.25	20	20	14	4	6	14
1.30	24	1	7	7	28	23	3.30	25	♋	2	0♍	23	22	5.30	23	27	28	24	20	20	7.30	21	24	23	18	15	17	9.30	20	23	20	11	10	14	11.30	22	22	15	5	7	15
1.35	26	2	8	8	29	24	3.35	26	1	3	1	25	23	5.35	24	28	29	25	21	21	7.35	22	25	25	19	16	18	9.35	21	24	21	12	11	15	11.35	23	23	16	6	8	17
1.40	27	3	9	9	♍	25	3.40	27	2	4	2	26	24	5.40	25	29	♍	26	22	22	7.40	23	27	26	20	17	19	9.40	23	25	22	13	13	17	11.40	25	24	17	7	10	18
1.45	28	5	10	10	1	26	3.45	28	3	5	3	27	25	5.45	27	♌	1	27	23	23	7.45	24	28	27	21	18	20	9.45	24	26	23	14	14	18	11.45	26	25	18	8	11	19
1.50	♉	6	11	11	2	28	3.50	♊	4	6	4	28	26	5.50	28	1	2	28	24	24	7.50	26	29	28	22	19	21	9.50	25	28	24	15	15	19	11.50	27	26	19	9	12	21
1.55	1	7	12	12	3	29	3.55	1	6	8	5	29	28	5.55	29	2	3	29	25	25	7.55	27	♍	29	23	20	22	9.55	27	29	25	16	16	20	11.55	29	28	20	10	13	22
2. 0	2	8	13	13	4	♎	4. 0	2	7	9	6	♎	29	6. 0	♋	4	4	0♎	26	26	8. 0	28	1	♎	24	21	23	10. 0	28	♎	26	17	17	22	12. 0	♎	29	21	11	15	24

STime h. m.	10 ♎	11 ♎	12 ♏	Asc ♐	2 ♑	3 ♒	STime h. m.	10 ♏	11 ♏	12 ♐	Asc ♑	2 ♒	3 ♈	STime h. m.	10 ♐	11 ♐	12 ♑	Asc ♒	2 ♈	3 ♉	STime h. m.	10 ♑	11 ♑	12 ♒	Asc ♈	2 ♉	3 ♊	STime h. m.	10 ♑	11 ♒	12 ♈	Asc ♉	2 ♊	3 ♋	STime h. m.	10 ♒	11 ♈	12 ♉	Asc ♊	2 ♋	3 ♌
12. 0	0	29	21	11	15	24	14. 0	2	26	17	7	18	0	16. 0	2	23	15	12	0	6	18. 0	0	22	18	0	12	8	20. 0	28	24	0	18	15	7	22. 0	28	0	12	23	13	4
12. 5	1	♏	22	12	16	25	14. 5	3	28	18	9	20	2	16. 5	3	24	16	14	2	8	18. 5	1	23	20	2	13	10	20. 5	29	25	2	20	17	8	22. 5	29	2	13	24	14	5
12.10	3	1	24	13	17	27	14.10	5	29	19	10	22	3	16.10	4	26	17	15	4	9	18.10	2	24	22	4	15	11	20.10	♒	27	4	21	18	9	22.10	♓	3	15	25	15	6
12.15	4	2	25	14	18	28	14.15	6	♐	20	11	23	5	16.15	6	27	18	17	5	11	18.15	3	25	23	7	16	12	20.15	2	28	5	23	19	10	22.15	2	5	16	26	16	7
12.20	5	3	26	15	20	29	14.20	7	1	21	12	25	6	16.20	7	28	20	19	7	12	18.20	5	27	25	9	18	13	20.20	3	29	7	25	20	11	22.20	3	6	18	27	17	8
12.25	7	5	27	16	21	♓	14.25	9	2	22	14	26	8	16.25	8	29	21	21	9	13	18.25	6	28	26	11	19	15	20.25	4	♓	9	26	22	12	22.25	4	8	19	29	19	9
12.30	8	6	28	17	22	2	14.30	10	3	23	15	28	9	16.30	9	♑	22	23	11	15	18.30	7	29	28	13	21	16	20.30	5	2	11	28	23	13	22.30	6	9	21	0♋	20	10
12.35	10	7	29	18	24	4	14.35	11	4	25	16	♓	11	16.35	10	1	24	25	13	16	18.35	8	♒	♓	15	22	17	20.35	6	4	13	29	24	15	22.35	7	11	22	1	21	12
12.40	11	8	♐	19	25	5	14.40	12	5	26	18	2	12	16.40	12	2	25	26	14	18	18.40	9	2	2	17	24	18	20.40	8	5	14	1♊	25	16	22.40	8	12	24	2	22	13
12.45	12	9	1	20	26	7	14.45	14	6	27	19	3	14	16.45	13	4	26	28	16	19	18.45	10	3	3	19	25	19	20.45	9	7	16	2	26	17	22.45	10	14	25	3	23	14
12.50	14	10	2	21	28	8	14.50	15	8	28	20	5	16	16.50	14	5	28	0♓	18	20	18.50	11	4	5	21	27	21	20.50	10	8	18	4	27	18	22.50	11	16	27	4	24	15
12.55	15	12	3	23	29	10	14.55	16	9	29	22	7	17	16.55	15	6	29	2	20	22	18.55	13	6	7	24	28	22	20.55	11	10	20	5	29	19	22.55	12	17	28	5	25	16
13. 0	16	13	4	24	♒	11	15. 0	17	10	♑	23	8	19	17. 0	16	7	♒	4	22	23	19. 0	14	7	8	26	♊	23	21. 0	13	11	22	7	♋	20	23. 0	14	19	♊	6	26	17
13. 5	18	14	5	25	2	13	15. 5	19	11	1	25	10	20	17. 5	17	8	2	6	23	24	19. 5	15	8	10	28	1	24	21. 5	14	13	23	8	1	21	23. 5	15	20	1	7	27	18
13.10	19	15	6	26	3	14	15.10	20	12	3	26	12	22	17.10	19	9	3	9	25	26	19.10	16	10	12	0♉	2	25	21.10	15	14	25	10	2	22	23.10	16	22	2	9	28	20
13.15	20	16	7	27	5	16	15.15	21	13	4	28	14	23	17.15	20	11	5	11	27	27	19.15	17	11	14	2	4	26	21.15	16	16	27	11	3	24	23.15	18	23	4	10	29	21
13.20	22	17	8	28	6	18	15.20	22	14	5	29	16	25	17.20	21	12	6	13	28	28	19.20	18	12	16	4	5	28	21.20	18	18	28	12	4	25	23.20	19	25	5	11	♌	22
13.25	23	18	9	29	8	19	15.25	24	15	6	1♒	17	26	17.25	22	13	8	15	♉	♊	19.25	20	14	17	5	6	29	21.25	19	19	♉	14	5	26	23.25	20	26	6	12	1	23
13.30	24	20	10	0♑	9	21	15.30	25	17	7	2	19	28	17.30	23	14	9	17	2	1	19.30	21	15	19	7	8	♋	21.30	20	21	2	15	7	27	23.30	22	28	8	13	2	24
13.35	26	21	11	1	11	22	15.35	26	18	8	4	21	29	17.35	24	15	11	19	4	2	19.35	22	17	21	9	9	1	21.35	21	22	4	16	8	28	23.35	23	29	9	14	3	25
13.40	27	22	13	3	12	24	15.40	27	19	10	5	23	♉	17.40	25	17	12	21	5	3	19.40	23	18	23	11	10	2	21.40	23	24	5	18	9	29	23.40	25	♉	10	15	4	27
13.45	28	23	14	4	14	25	15.45	28	20	11	7	25	2	17.45	27	18	14	23	7	5	19.45	24	19	25	13	12	3	21.45	24	25	7	19	10	♌	23.45	26	2	12	16	5	28
13.50	♏	24	15	5	15	27	15.50	♐	21	12	9	26	3	17.50	28	19	15	26	8	6	19.50	26	21	26	15	13	4	21.50	25	27	8	20	11	1	23.50	27	3	13	17	6	29
13.55	1	25	16	6	17	28	15.55	1	22	13	10	28	5	17.55	29	20	17	28	10	7	19.55	27	22	28	16	14	6	21.55	27	28	10	21	12	2	23.55	29	5	14	18	8	♍
14. 0	2	26	17	7	18	♈	16. 0	2	23	15	12	♈	6	18. 0	♑	22	18	0♈	12	8	20. 0	28	24	♈	18	15	7	22. 0	28	♈	12	23	13	4	24. 0	♈	6	15	19	9	1

TABLES OF HOUSES FOR NORTHERN LATITUDES FOR WASHINGTON D.C. Latitude 38° 55'n

STime h. m.	10 ♈	11 ♉	12 ♊	Asc ♋	2 ♌	3 ♍	STime h. m.	10 ♉	11 ♊	12 ♋	Asc ♌	2 ♍	3 ♎	STime h. m.	10 ♊	11 ♋	12 ♌	Asc ♍	2 ♎	3 ♎	STime h. m.	10 ♋	11 ♌	12 ♍	Asc ♎	2 ♎	3 ♏	STime h. m.	10 ♋	11 ♍	12 ♎	Asc ♎	2 ♏	3 ♐	STime h. m.	10 ♌	11 ♎	12 ♎	Asc ♏	2 ♐	3 ♑
0. 0	0	6	14	18	8	1	2. 0	2	8	12	12	4	0	4. 0	2	6	8	6	0	29	6. 0	0	3	4	0	26	27	8. 0	28	1	0	24	22	24	10. 0	28	0	26	18	18	22
0. 5	1	7	16	19	9	2	2. 5	3	9	13	13	5	1	4. 5	3	7	9	7	1	♏	6. 5	1	4	5	1	27	28	8. 5	29	2	1	25	23	25	10. 5	29	1	27	19	19	23
0.10	3	9	17	20	10	3	2.10	5	10	14	14	6	2	4.10	4	9	10	8	2	1	6.10	2	6	6	2	29	29	8.10	♌	3	2	26	24	26	10.10	♍	2	29	20	20	24
0.15	4	10	18	21	11	5	2.15	6	12	16	15	7	4	4.15	6	10	11	9	3	3	6.15	3	7	7	3	♏	♐	8.15	2	5	3	27	25	27	10.15	2	4	♏	21	21	26
0.20	5	12	19	22	12	6	2.20	7	13	17	16	8	5	4.20	7	11	12	10	4	4	6.20	5	8	8	4	1	1	8.20	3	6	4	28	26	28	10.20	3	5	1	22	22	27
0.25	7	13	21	23	13	7	2.25	9	14	18	17	9	6	4.25	8	12	13	11	6	5	6.25	6	9	9	5	2	2	8.25	4	7	6	29	27	29	10.25	4	6	2	23	23	28
0.30	8	14	22	24	14	8	2.30	10	15	19	18	10	7	4.30	9	13	14	12	7	6	6.30	7	10	10	6	3	4	8.30	5	8	7	0♏	28	♑	10.30	6	7	3	24	24	♒
0.35	10	16	23	25	15	9	2.35	11	17	20	19	11	9	4.35	10	14	15	13	8	7	6.35	8	11	11	7	4	5	8.35	6	9	8	1	29	2	10.35	7	9	4	25	25	1
0.40	11	17	24	26	16	11	2.40	12	18	21	20	12	10	4.40	12	15	16	14	9	8	6.40	9	12	12	8	5	6	8.40	8	11	9	2	♐	3	10.40	8	10	5	26	27	2
0.45	12	19	25	27	18	12	2.45	14	19	22	21	13	11	4.45	13	16	18	15	10	10	6.45	10	13	13	9	6	7	8.45	9	12	10	3	2	4	10.45	10	11	6	27	28	3
0.50	14	20	26	28	19	13	2.50	15	20	23	22	15	12	4.50	14	17	19	16	11	11	6.50	11	15	15	10	7	8	8.50	10	13	11	4	3	5	10.50	11	12	7	28	29	5
0.55	15	21	28	29	20	14	2.55	16	21	24	23	16	13	4.55	15	19	20	17	12	12	6.55	13	16	16	11	8	9	8.55	11	14	12	5	4	6	10.55	12	13	8	29	♑	6
1. 0	16	23	29	0♌	21	15	3. 0	17	22	25	24	17	15	5. 0	16	20	21	18	13	13	7. 0	14	17	17	12	9	10	9. 0	13	15	13	6	5	8	11. 0	14	15	9	0♐	1	7
1. 5	18	24	♋	1	22	17	3. 5	19	24	26	25	18	16	5. 5	17	21	22	19	14	14	7. 5	15	18	18	13	10	11	9. 5	14	17	14	7	6	9	11. 5	15	16	10	1	2	9
1.10	19	25	1	2	23	18	3.10	20	25	27	26	19	17	5.10	19	22	23	20	15	15	7.10	16	19	19	14	11	13	9.10	15	18	15	8	7	10	11.10	16	17	11	2	4	10
1.15	20	27	2	3	24	19	3.15	21	26	28	27	20	18	5.15	20	23	24	21	17	17	7.15	17	20	20	15	12	14	9.15	16	19	17	9	8	11	11.15	18	18	12	3	5	11
1.20	22	28	3	4	25	20	3.20	22	27	29	28	21	19	5.20	21	24	25	22	18	18	7.20	18	22	21	16	14	15	9.20	18	20	18	10	9	12	11.20	19	19	14	4	6	13
1.25	23	29	5	5	26	21	3.25	24	28	♌	29	22	21	5.25	22	25	26	23	19	19	7.25	20	23	22	17	15	16	9.25	19	21	19	11	10	13	11.25	20	21	15	5	7	14
1.30	24	♊	6	6	27	23	3.30	25	29	2	0♍	23	22	5.30	23	26	27	24	20	20	7.30	21	24	23	18	16	17	9.30	20	23	20	12	11	15	11.30	22	22	16	6	8	16
1.35	26	2	7	7	28	24	3.35	26	♋	3	1	24	23	5.35	24	28	28	25	21	21	7.35	22	25	24	19	17	18	9.35	21	24	21	13	12	16	11.35	23	23	17	7	9	17
1.40	27	3	8	8	29	25	3.40	27	2	4	2	26	24	5.40	25	29	29	26	22	22	7.40	23	26	26	20	18	19	9.40	23	25	22	14	13	17	11.40	25	24	18	8	11	18
1.45	28	4	9	9	♍	26	3.45	28	3	5	3	27	25	5.45	27	♌	♍	27	23	23	7.45	24	27	27	21	19	20	9.45	24	26	23	15	14	18	11.45	26	25	19	9	12	20
1.50	♉	6	10	10	1	28	3.50	♊	4	6	4	28	27	5.50	28	1	1	28	24	24	7.50	26	29	28	22	20	21	9.50	25	28	24	16	16	20	11.50	27	27	20	10	13	21
1.55	1	7	11	11	3	29	3.55	1	5	7	5	29	28	5.55	29	2	3	29	25	26	7.55	27	♍	29	23	21	23	9.55	27	29	25	17	17	21	11.55	29	28	21	11	14	23
2. 0	2	8	12	12	4	♎	4. 0	2	6	8	6	♎	29	6. 0	♋	3	4	0♎	26	27	8. 0	28	1	♎	24	22	24	10. 0	28	♎	26	18	18	22	12. 0	♎	29	22	12	16	24

STime h. m.	10 ♎	11 ♎	12 ♏	Asc ♐	2 ♑	3 ♒
12. 0	0	29	22	12	16	24
12. 5	1	♏	23	13	17	25
12.10	3	1	24	14	18	27
12.15	4	3	25	15	19	28
12.20	5	4	26	16	21	♓
12.25	7	5	27	17	22	1
12.30	8	6	28	18	23	3
12.35	10	7	29	20	25	4
12.40	11	8	♐	21	26	6
12.45	12	10	2	22	27	7
12.50	14	11	3	23	29	9
12.55	15	12	4	24	♒	10
13. 0	16	13	5	25	1	12
13. 5	18	14	6	26	3	13
13.10	19	15	7	27	4	15
13.15	20	17	8	28	6	16
13.20	22	18	9	29	7	18
13.25	23	19	10	1♑	9	19
13.30	24	20	11	2	10	21
13.35	26	21	12	3	12	22
13.40	27	22	13	4	13	24
13.45	28	23	14	5	15	25
13.50	♏	24	16	7	16	27
13.55	1	26	17	8	18	28
14. 0	2	27	18	9	19	♈

STime h. m.	10 ♏	11 ♏	12 ♐	Asc ♑	2 ♒	3 ♈
14. 0	2	27	18	9	19	0
14. 5	3	28	19	10	21	2
14.10	5	29	20	11	22	3
14.15	6	♐	21	13	24	5
14.20	7	1	22	14	26	6
14.25	9	2	23	15	27	8
14.30	10	4	24	17	29	9
14.35	11	5	25	18	♓	11
14.40	12	6	27	19	2	12
14.45	14	7	28	21	4	14
14.50	15	8	29	22	5	15
14.55	16	9	♑	23	7	17
15. 0	17	10	1	25	9	18
15. 5	19	11	2	26	11	20
15.10	20	13	4	28	12	21
15.15	21	14	5	29	14	23
15.20	22	15	6	1♒	16	24
15.25	24	16	7	2	18	26
15.30	25	17	8	4	19	27
15.35	26	18	9	5	21	29
15.40	27	19	11	7	23	♉
15.45	28	20	12	8	25	2
15.50	♐	21	13	10	26	3
15.55	1	23	14	12	28	5
16. 0	2	24	16	13	♈	6

STime h. m.	10 ♐	11 ♐	12 ♑	Asc ♒	2 ♈	3 ♉
16. 0	2	24	16	13	0	6
16. 5	3	25	17	15	2	7
16.10	4	26	18	17	4	9
16.15	6	27	19	19	5	10
16.20	7	28	21	20	7	12
16.25	8	29	22	22	9	13
16.30	9	♑	23	24	11	14
16.35	10	2	25	26	12	16
16.40	12	3	26	28	14	17
16.45	13	4	27	0♓	16	19
16.50	14	5	29	1	18	20
16.55	15	6	♒	3	19	21
17. 0	16	8	1	5	21	23
17. 5	17	9	3	7	23	24
17.10	19	10	4	9	25	25
17.15	20	11	6	11	26	27
17.20	21	12	7	13	28	28
17.25	22	13	9	15	♉	29
17.30	23	15	10	17	1	♊
17.35	24	16	12	20	3	2
17.40	25	17	13	22	4	3
17.45	27	18	15	24	6	4
17.50	28	20	16	26	8	6
17.55	29	21	18	28	9	7
18. 0	♑	22	19	0♈	11	8

STime h. m.	10 ♑	11 ♑	12 ♒	Asc ♈	2 ♉	3 ♊
18. 0	0	22	19	0	11	8
18. 5	1	23	21	2	12	9
18.10	2	24	22	4	14	10
18.15	3	26	24	6	15	12
18.20	5	27	26	8	17	13
18.25	6	28	27	10	18	14
18.30	7	♒	29	13	20	15
18.35	8	1	♓	15	21	17
18.40	9	2	2	17	23	18
18.45	10	3	4	19	24	19
18.50	11	5	5	21	26	20
18.55	13	6	7	23	27	21
19. 0	14	7	9	25	29	22
19. 5	15	9	11	27	♊	24
19.10	16	10	12	29	1	25
19.15	17	11	14	0♉	3	26
19.20	18	13	16	2	4	27
19.25	20	14	18	4	5	28
19.30	21	16	19	6	7	29
19.35	22	17	21	8	8	♋
19.40	23	18	23	10	9	2
19.45	24	20	25	11	11	3
19.50	26	21	26	13	12	4
19.55	27	23	28	15	13	5
20. 0	28	24	♈	17	14	6

STime h. m.	10 ♑	11 ♒	12 ♈	Asc ♉	2 ♊	3 ♋
20. 0	28	24	0	17	14	6
20. 5	29	25	2	18	16	7
20.10	♒	27	4	20	17	9
20.15	2	28	5	22	18	10
20.20	3	♓	7	23	19	11
20.25	4	1	9	25	21	12
20.30	5	3	11	26	22	13
20.35	6	4	12	28	23	14
20.40	8	6	14	29	24	15
20.45	9	7	16	1♊	25	16
20.50	10	9	18	2	26	17
20.55	11	10	19	4	28	19
21. 0	13	12	21	5	29	20
21. 5	14	13	23	7	♋	21
21.10	15	15	25	8	1	22
21.15	16	16	26	9	2	23
21.20	18	18	28	11	3	24
21.25	19	19	♉	12	5	25
21.30	20	21	1	13	6	26
21.35	21	22	3	15	7	28
21.40	23	24	4	16	8	29
21.45	24	25	6	17	9	♌
21.50	25	27	8	19	10	1
21.55	27	28	9	20	11	2
22. 0	28	♈	11	21	12	3

STime h. m.	10 ♒	11 ♈	12 ♉	Asc ♊	2 ♋	3 ♌
22. 0	28	0	11	21	12	3
22. 5	29	2	12	22	13	4
22.10	♓	3	14	23	14	6
22.15	2	5	15	25	16	7
22.20	3	6	17	26	17	8
22.25	4	8	18	27	18	9
22.30	6	9	20	28	19	10
22.35	7	11	21	29	20	11
22.40	8	12	23	1♋	21	12
22.45	10	14	24	2	22	13
22.50	11	15	26	3	23	15
22.55	12	17	27	4	24	16
23. 0	14	18	29	5	25	17
23. 5	15	20	♊	6	26	18
23.10	16	21	1	7	27	19
23.15	18	23	3	8	28	20
23.20	19	24	4	9	29	22
23.25	20	26	5	10	♌	23
23.30	22	27	7	12	2	24
23.35	23	29	8	13	3	25
23.40	25	♉	9	14	4	26
23.45	26	2	11	15	5	27
23.50	27	3	12	16	6	29
23.55	29	5	13	17	7	♍
24. 0	♈	6	14	18	8	1

TABLES OF HOUSES FOR NORTHERN LATITUDES FOR Latitude 45° 0'n

STime h. m.	10 ♈	11 ♉	12 ♊	Asc ♋	2 ♌	3 ♍
0. 0	0	7	18	22	10	2
0. 5	1	9	19	23	11	3
0.10	3	10	20	24	12	4
0.15	4	11	21	25	13	5
0.20	5	13	23	26	14	6
0.25	7	14	24	27	15	8
0.30	8	16	25	28	16	9
0.35	10	17	26	29	17	10
0.40	11	19	27	0♌	18	11
0.45	12	20	29	0	19	12
0.50	14	21	♋	1	20	13
0.55	15	23	1	2	21	15
1. 0	16	24	2	3	22	16
1. 5	18	25	3	4	23	17
1.10	19	27	4	5	24	18
1.15	20	28	5	6	25	19
1.20	22	29	6	7	26	20
1.25	23	♊	8	8	27	22
1.30	24	2	9	9	29	23
1.35	26	3	10	10	♍	24
1.40	27	5	11	11	1	25
1.45	28	6	12	12	2	26
1.50	♉	7	13	13	3	28
1.55	1	8	14	14	4	29
2. 0	2	10	15	15	5	♎

STime h. m.	10 ♉	11 ♊	12 ♋	Asc ♌	2 ♍	3 ♎
2. 0	2	10	15	15	5	0
2. 5	3	11	16	16	6	1
2.10	5	12	17	17	7	2
2.15	6	13	18	18	8	4
2.20	7	14	19	18	9	5
2.25	9	16	20	19	10	6
2.30	10	17	21	20	11	7
2.35	11	18	22	21	12	8
2.40	12	19	24	22	13	10
2.45	14	21	25	23	14	11
2.50	15	22	26	24	15	12
2.55	16	23	27	25	16	13
3. 0	17	24	28	26	17	14
3. 5	19	25	29	27	18	15
3.10	20	26	♌	28	19	17
3.15	21	28	1	29	20	18
3.20	22	29	2	0♍	22	19
3.25	24	♋	3	1	23	20
3.30	25	1	4	2	24	21
3.35	26	2	5	3	25	22
3.40	27	3	6	3	26	24
3.45	28	4	7	4	27	25
3.50	♊	6	8	5	28	26
3.55	1	7	9	6	29	27
4. 0	2	8	10	7	♎	28

STime h. m.	10 ♊	11 ♋	12 ♌	Asc ♍	2 ♎	3 ♎
4. 0	2	8	10	7	0	28
4. 5	3	9	11	8	1	29
4.10	4	10	12	9	2	♏
4.15	6	11	13	10	3	2
4.20	7	12	14	11	4	3
4.25	8	13	15	12	5	4
4.30	9	14	16	13	6	5
4.35	10	16	17	14	7	6
4.40	12	17	18	15	8	8
4.45	13	18	19	16	10	9
4.50	14	19	20	17	11	10
4.55	15	20	21	18	12	11
5. 0	16	21	22	19	13	12
5. 5	17	22	23	20	14	13
5.10	19	23	24	20	15	14
5.15	20	24	25	21	16	15
5.20	21	26	26	22	17	17
5.25	22	27	27	23	18	18
5.30	23	28	29	24	19	19
5.35	24	29	♍	25	20	20
5.40	25	♌	1	26	21	21
5.45	27	1	2	27	22	22
5.50	28	2	3	28	23	23
5.55	29	3	4	29	24	24
6. 0	♋	4	5	0♎	25	26

STime h. m.	10 ♋	11 ♌	12 ♍	Asc ♎	2 ♎	3 ♏
6. 0	0	4	5	0	25	26
6. 5	1	6	6	1	26	27
6.10	2	7	7	2	27	28
6.15	3	8	8	3	28	29
6.20	5	9	9	4	29	♐
6.25	6	10	10	5	♏	1
6.30	7	11	11	6	1	2
6.35	8	12	12	7	3	3
6.40	9	13	13	8	4	4
6.45	10	15	14	9	5	6
6.50	11	16	15	9	6	7
6.55	13	17	16	10	7	8
7. 0	14	18	17	11	8	9
7. 5	15	19	18	12	9	10
7.10	16	20	19	13	10	11
7.15	17	21	20	14	11	12
7.20	18	22	22	15	12	13
7.25	20	24	23	16	13	14
7.30	21	25	24	17	14	16
7.35	22	26	25	18	15	17
7.40	23	27	26	19	16	18
7.45	24	28	27	20	17	19
7.50	26	29	28	21	18	20
7.55	27	♍	29	22	19	21
8. 0	28	2	♎	23	20	22

STime h. m.	10 ♋	11 ♍	12 ♎	Asc ♎	2 ♏	3 ♐
8. 0	28	2	0	23	20	22
8. 5	29	3	1	24	21	23
8.10	♌	4	2	25	22	24
8.15	2	5	3	26	23	26
8.20	3	6	4	27	24	27
8.25	4	8	5	27	25	28
8.30	5	9	6	28	26	29
8.35	6	10	7	29	27	♑
8.40	8	11	8	0♏	28	1
8.45	9	12	10	1	29	2
8.50	10	13	11	2	♐	4
8.55	11	15	12	3	1	5
9. 0	13	16	13	4	2	6
9. 5	14	17	14	5	3	7
9.10	15	18	15	6	4	8
9.15	16	19	16	7	5	9
9.20	18	20	17	8	6	11
9.25	19	22	18	9	8	12
9.30	20	23	19	10	9	13
9.35	21	24	20	11	10	14
9.40	23	25	21	12	11	16
9.45	24	26	22	12	12	17
9.50	25	28	23	13	13	18
9.55	27	29	24	14	14	19
10. 0	28	♎	25	15	15	20

STime h. m.	10 ♌	11 ♎	12 ♎	Asc ♏	2 ♐	3 ♑
10. 0	28	0	25	15	15	20
10. 5	29	1	26	16	16	22
10.10	♍	2	27	17	17	23
10.15	2	4	28	18	18	24
10.20	3	5	29	19	19	25
10.25	4	6	♏	20	20	27
10.30	6	7	1	21	21	28
10.35	7	8	3	22	22	29
10.40	8	10	4	23	24	♒
10.45	10	11	5	24	25	2
10.50	11	12	6	25	26	3
10.55	12	13	7	26	27	5
11. 0	14	14	8	27	28	6
11. 5	15	15	9	28	29	7
11.10	16	17	10	29	♑	9
11.15	18	18	11	0♐	1	10
11.20	19	19	12	0	3	11
11.25	20	20	13	1	4	13
11.30	22	21	14	2	5	14
11.35	23	22	15	3	6	16
11.40	25	24	16	4	7	17
11.45	26	25	17	5	9	19
11.50	27	26	18	6	10	20
11.55	29	27	19	7	11	21
12. 0	♎	28	20	8	12	23

STime h. m.	10 ♎	11 ♎	12 ♏	Asc ♐	2 ♑	3 ♒
12. 0	0	28	20	8	12	23
12. 5	1	29	21	9	14	24
12.10	3	♏	22	10	15	26
12.15	4	2	23	11	16	27
12.20	5	3	24	12	17	29
12.25	7	4	25	13	19	♓
12.30	8	5	26	14	20	2
12.35	10	6	27	15	21	3
12.40	11	8	28	16	23	5
12.45	12	9	29	17	24	6
12.50	14	10	♐	18	25	8
12.55	15	11	1	20	27	9
13. 0	16	12	2	21	28	11
13. 5	18	13	3	22	♒	13
13.10	19	14	4	23	1	14
13.15	20	15	5	24	3	16
13.20	22	17	6	25	4	17
13.25	23	18	8	26	6	19
13.30	24	19	9	27	7	20
13.35	26	20	10	28	9	22
13.40	27	21	11	29	10	24
13.45	28	22	12	1♑	12	25
13.50	♏	23	13	2	13	27
13.55	1	24	14	3	15	28
14. 0	2	26	15	4	17	♈

STime h. m.	10 ♏	11 ♏	12 ♐	Asc ♑	2 ♒	3 ♈
14. 0	2	26	15	4	17	0
14. 5	3	27	16	5	18	2
14.10	5	28	17	6	20	3
14.15	6	29	18	8	21	5
14.20	7	♐	19	9	23	6
14.25	9	1	20	10	25	8
14.30	10	2	21	11	27	10
14.35	11	3	22	13	28	11
14.40	12	4	24	14	♓	13
14.45	14	6	25	15	2	14
14.50	15	7	26	17	4	16
14.55	16	8	27	18	6	17
15. 0	17	9	28	20	7	19
15. 5	19	10	29	21	9	21
15.10	20	11	♑	22	11	22
15.15	21	12	1	24	13	24
15.20	22	13	3	25	15	25
15.25	24	14	4	27	17	27
15.30	25	16	5	28	19	28
15.35	26	17	6	0♒	20	♉
15.40	27	18	7	2	22	1
15.45	28	19	9	3	24	3
15.50	♐	20	10	5	26	4
15.55	1	21	11	7	28	6
16. 0	2	22	12	8	♈	7

STime h. m.	10 ♐	11 ♐	12 ♑	Asc ♒	2 ♈	3 ♉
16. 0	2	22	12	8	0	7
16. 5	3	23	14	10	2	9
16.10	4	24	15	12	4	10
16.15	6	26	16	14	6	11
16.20	7	27	17	16	8	13
16.25	8	28	19	18	10	14
16.30	9	29	20	20	11	16
16.35	10	♑	21	22	13	17
16.40	12	1	23	24	15	19
16.45	13	2	24	26	17	20
16.50	14	4	25	28	19	21
16.55	15	5	27	0♓	21	23
17. 0	16	6	28	2	23	24
17. 5	17	7	♒	4	24	25
17.10	19	8	1	6	26	27
17.15	20	9	3	9	28	28
17.20	21	11	4	11	♉	29
17.25	22	12	6	13	2	♊
17.30	23	13	7	16	3	2
17.35	24	14	9	18	5	3
17.40	25	16	10	20	7	5
17.45	27	17	12	23	9	6
17.50	28	18	13	25	10	7
17.55	29	19	15	28	12	8
18. 0	♑	20	17	0♈	13	10

STime h. m.	10 ♑	11 ♑	12 ♒	Asc ♈	2 ♉	3 ♊
18. 0	0	20	17	0	13	10
18. 5	1	22	18	2	15	11
18.10	2	23	20	5	17	12
18.15	3	24	21	7	18	13
18.20	5	25	23	10	20	14
18.25	6	27	25	12	21	16
18.30	7	28	27	14	23	17
18.35	8	29	28	17	24	18
18.40	9	♒	♓	19	26	19
18.45	10	2	2	21	27	21
18.50	11	3	4	23	29	22
18.55	13	5	6	26	♊	23
19. 0	14	6	7	28	2	24
19. 5	15	7	9	0♉	3	25
19.10	16	9	11	2	5	26
19.15	17	10	13	4	6	28
19.20	18	11	15	6	7	29
19.25	20	13	17	8	9	♋
19.30	21	14	19	10	10	1
19.35	22	16	20	12	11	2
19.40	23	17	22	14	13	3
19.45	24	19	24	16	14	4
19.50	26	20	26	18	15	6
19.55	27	21	28	20	16	7
20. 0	28	23	♈	22	18	8

STime h. m.	10 ♑	11 ♒	12 ♈	Asc ♉	2 ♊	3 ♋
20. 0	28	23	0	22	18	8
20. 5	29	24	2	23	19	9
20.10	♒	26	4	25	20	10
20.15	2	27	6	27	21	11
20.20	3	29	8	28	23	12
20.25	4	♓	10	0♊	24	13
20.30	5	2	11	2	25	14
20.35	6	3	13	3	26	16
20.40	8	5	15	5	27	17
20.45	9	6	17	6	29	18
20.50	10	8	19	8	♋	19
20.55	11	9	21	9	1	20
21. 0	13	11	23	10	2	21
21. 5	14	13	24	12	3	22
21.10	15	14	26	13	4	23
21.15	16	16	28	15	5	24
21.20	18	17	♉	16	6	26
21.25	19	19	2	17	8	27
21.30	20	20	3	19	9	28
21.35	21	22	5	20	10	29
21.40	23	24	7	21	11	♌
21.45	24	25	9	22	12	1
21.50	25	27	10	24	13	2
21.55	27	28	12	25	14	3
22. 0	28	♈	13	26	15	4

STime h. m.	10 ♒	11 ♈	12 ♉	Asc ♊	2 ♋	3 ♌
22. 0	28	0	13	26	15	4
22. 5	29	2	15	27	16	6
22.10	♓	3	17	28	17	7
22.15	2	5	18	29	18	8
22.20	3	6	20	1♋	19	9
22.25	4	8	21	2	20	10
22.30	6	10	23	3	21	11
22.35	7	11	24	4	22	12
22.40	8	13	26	5	24	13
22.45	10	14	27	6	25	15
22.50	11	16	29	7	26	16
22.55	12	17	♊	8	27	17
23. 0	14	19	2	9	28	18
23. 5	15	21	3	10	29	19
23.10	16	22	5	12	♌	20
23.15	18	24	6	13	1	21
23.20	19	25	7	14	2	22
23.25	20	27	9	15	3	24
23.30	22	28	10	16	4	25
23.35	23	♉	11	17	5	26
23.40	25	1	13	18	6	27
23.45	26	3	14	19	7	28
23.50	27	4	15	20	8	29
23.55	29	6	16	21	9	♍
24. 0	♈	7	18	22	10	2

TABLES OF HOUSES FOR NORTHERN LATITUDES FOR LONDON Latitude 51° 32'n

STime h. m.	10 ♈	11 ♉	12 ♊	Asc ♋	2 ♌	3 ♍
0. 0	0	9	23	27	13	3
0. 5	1	10	24	28	14	4
0.10	3	12	25	29	15	5
0.15	4	13	26	0♌	16	6
0.20	5	15	28	1	17	7
0.25	7	16	29	1	18	8
0.30	8	18	♋	2	19	9
0.35	10	19	1	3	20	11
0.40	11	21	2	4	21	12
0.45	12	22	3	5	22	13
0.50	14	23	4	6	23	14
0.55	15	25	6	7	24	15
1. 0	16	26	7	8	24	16
1. 5	18	28	8	9	25	17
1.10	19	29	9	9	26	19
1.15	20	♊	10	10	27	20
1.20	22	2	11	11	28	21
1.25	23	3	12	12	29	22
1.30	24	4	13	13	♍	23
1.35	26	6	14	14	1	24
1.40	27	7	15	15	2	25
1.45	28	8	16	16	3	27
1.50	♉	9	17	16	4	28
1.55	1	11	18	17	5	29
2. 0	2	12	19	18	6	♎

STime h. m.	10 ♉	11 ♊	12 ♋	Asc ♌	2 ♍	3 ♎
2. 0	2	12	19	18	6	0
2. 5	3	13	20	19	7	1
2.10	5	15	21	20	8	2
2.15	6	16	22	21	9	3
2.20	7	17	23	22	10	5
2.25	9	18	24	23	11	6
2.30	10	19	25	23	12	7
2.35	11	21	26	24	13	8
2.40	12	22	27	25	14	9
2.45	14	23	28	26	15	10
2.50	15	24	29	27	16	11
2.55	16	25	♌	28	17	13
3. 0	17	27	1	29	18	14
3. 5	19	28	2	29	19	15
3.10	20	29	3	0♍	20	16
3.15	21	♋	4	1	21	17
3.20	22	1	5	2	22	18
3.25	24	2	6	3	23	19
3.30	25	3	7	4	24	21
3.35	26	5	8	5	25	22
3.40	27	6	9	5	26	23
3.45	28	7	10	6	27	24
3.50	♊	8	11	7	28	25
3.55	1	9	12	8	29	26
4. 0	2	10	13	9	♎	27

STime h. m.	10 ♊	11 ♋	12 ♌	Asc ♍	2 ♎	3 ♎
4. 0	2	10	13	9	0	27
4. 5	3	11	14	10	1	28
4.10	4	12	15	11	2	♏
4.15	6	13	16	12	3	1
4.20	7	15	17	12	4	2
4.25	8	16	18	13	5	3
4.30	9	17	19	14	6	4
4.35	10	18	20	15	7	5
4.40	12	19	21	16	8	6
4.45	13	20	22	17	9	7
4.50	14	21	23	18	10	9
4.55	15	22	24	19	11	10
5. 0	16	23	24	19	12	11
5. 5	17	24	25	20	13	12
5.10	19	25	26	21	14	13
5.15	20	26	27	22	15	14
5.20	21	28	28	23	16	15
5.25	22	29	29	24	17	16
5.30	23	♌	♍	25	18	17
5.35	24	1	1	26	19	18
5.40	25	2	2	26	20	19
5.45	27	3	3	27	21	21
5.50	28	4	4	28	22	22
5.55	29	5	5	29	23	23
6. 0	♋	6	6	0♎	24	24

STime h. m.	10 ♋	11 ♌	12 ♍	Asc ♎	2 ♎	3 ♏
6. 0	0	6	6	0	24	24
6. 5	1	7	7	1	25	25
6.10	2	8	8	2	26	26
6.15	3	9	9	3	27	27
6.20	5	11	10	3	28	28
6.25	6	12	11	4	29	29
6.30	7	13	12	5	♏	♐
6.35	8	14	13	6	1	1
6.40	9	15	14	7	2	2
6.45	10	16	15	8	3	4
6.50	11	17	16	9	4	5
6.55	13	18	17	10	5	6
7. 0	14	19	18	10	6	7
7. 5	15	20	19	11	6	8
7.10	16	21	20	12	7	9
7.15	17	23	21	13	8	10
7.20	18	24	22	14	9	11
7.25	20	25	23	15	10	12
7.30	21	26	24	16	11	13
7.35	22	27	25	17	12	14
7.40	23	28	26	17	13	15
7.45	24	29	27	18	14	17
7.50	26	♍	28	19	15	18
7.55	27	2	29	20	16	19
8. 0	28	3	♎	21	17	20

STime h. m.	10 ♋	11 ♍	12 ♎	Asc ♎	2 ♏	3 ♐
8. 0	28	3	0	21	17	20
8. 5	29	4	1	22	18	21
8.10	♌	5	2	23	19	22
8.15	2	6	3	24	20	23
8.20	3	7	4	24	21	24
8.25	4	8	5	25	22	25
8.30	5	9	6	26	23	27
8.35	6	11	7	27	24	28
8.40	8	12	8	28	25	29
8.45	9	13	9	29	26	♑
8.50	10	14	10	0♏	27	1
8.55	11	15	11	1	28	2
9. 0	13	16	12	1	29	3
9. 5	14	17	13	2	♐	5
9.10	15	19	14	3	1	6
9.15	16	20	15	4	2	7
9.20	18	21	16	5	3	8
9.25	19	22	17	6	4	9
9.30	20	23	18	7	5	11
9.35	21	24	19	7	6	12
9.40	23	25	20	8	7	13
9.45	24	27	21	9	8	14
9.50	25	28	22	10	9	15
9.55	27	29	23	11	10	17
10. 0	28	♎	24	12	11	18

STime h. m.	10 ♌	11 ♎	12 ♎	Asc ♏	2 ♐	3 ♑
10. 0	28	0	24	12	11	18
10. 5	29	1	25	13	12	19
10.10	♍	2	26	14	13	21
10.15	2	3	27	14	14	22
10.20	3	5	28	15	15	23
10.25	4	6	29	16	16	24
10.30	6	7	♏	17	17	26
10.35	7	8	1	18	18	27
10.40	8	9	2	19	19	28
10.45	10	10	3	20	20	♒
10.50	11	11	4	21	21	1
10.55	12	13	5	21	22	2
11. 0	14	14	6	22	23	4
11. 5	15	15	6	23	24	5
11.10	16	16	7	24	26	7
11.15	18	17	8	25	27	8
11.20	19	18	9	26	28	9
11.25	20	19	10	27	29	11
11.30	22	21	11	28	♑	12
11.35	23	22	12	29	1	14
11.40	25	23	13	29	2	15
11.45	26	24	14	0♐	4	17
11.50	27	25	15	1	5	18
11.55	29	26	16	2	6	20
12. 0	♎	27	17	3	7	21

STime h. m.	10 ♎	11 ♎	12 ♏	Asc ♐	2 ♑	3 ♒
12. 0	0	27	17	3	7	21
12. 5	1	28	18	4	8	23
12.10	3	♏	19	5	10	24
12.15	4	1	20	6	11	26
12.20	5	2	21	7	12	27
12.25	7	3	22	8	13	29
12.30	8	4	23	9	15	♓
12.35	10	5	24	9	16	2
12.40	11	6	25	10	17	4
12.45	12	7	26	11	19	5
12.50	14	9	27	12	20	7
12.55	15	10	28	13	22	8
13. 0	16	11	29	14	23	10
13. 5	18	12	♐	15	24	12
13.10	19	13	1	16	26	13
13.15	20	14	2	17	27	15
13.20	22	15	3	18	29	17
13.25	23	16	4	19	♒	18
13.30	24	17	5	20	2	20
13.35	26	18	6	21	4	22
13.40	27	19	7	22	5	23
13.45	28	21	8	23	7	25
13.50	♏	22	9	24	9	27
13.55	1	23	10	26	10	28
14. 0	2	24	11	27	12	♈

STime h. m.	10 ♏	11 ♏	12 ♐	Asc ♐	2 ♒	3 ♈
14. 0	2	24	11	27	12	0
14. 5	3	25	12	28	14	2
14.10	5	26	13	29	15	3
14.15	6	27	14	0♑	17	5
14.20	7	28	15	1	19	7
14.25	9	29	16	2	21	8
14.30	10	♐	17	4	23	10
14.35	11	1	18	5	25	12
14.40	12	2	19	6	27	13
14.45	14	4	20	7	29	15
14.50	15	5	21	9	♓	17
14.55	16	6	22	10	3	18
15. 0	17	7	23	11	5	20
15. 5	19	8	24	13	7	22
15.10	20	9	26	14	9	23
15.15	21	10	27	15	11	25
15.20	22	11	28	17	13	26
15.25	24	12	29	18	15	28
15.30	25	13	♑	20	17	♉
15.35	26	14	1	21	19	1
15.40	27	15	2	23	21	3
15.45	28	17	4	25	24	4
15.50	♐	18	5	26	26	6
15.55	1	19	6	28	28	7
16. 0	2	20	7	0♒	♈	9

STime h. m.	10 ♐	11 ♐	12 ♑	Asc ♒	2 ♈	3 ♉
16. 0	2	20	7	0	0	9
16. 5	3	21	8	2	2	10
16.10	4	22	10	3	4	12
16.15	6	23	11	5	6	13
16.20	7	24	12	7	9	15
16.25	8	25	13	9	11	16
16.30	9	27	15	11	13	18
16.35	10	28	16	14	15	19
16.40	12	29	17	16	17	21
16.45	13	♑	19	18	19	22
16.50	14	1	20	21	21	23
16.55	15	2	22	23	23	25
17. 0	16	3	23	26	25	26
17. 5	17	5	24	28	27	28
17.10	19	6	26	1♓	29	29
17.15	20	7	27	3	♉	♊
17.20	21	8	29	6	3	2
17.25	22	9	♒	9	5	3
17.30	23	11	2	12	7	4
17.35	24	12	4	15	9	6
17.40	25	13	5	18	11	7
17.45	27	14	7	21	13	8
17.50	28	15	9	24	15	9
17.55	29	17	10	27	16	11
18. 0	♑	18	12	0♈	18	12

STime h. m.	10 ♑	11 ♑	12 ♒	Asc ♈	2 ♉	3 ♊
18. 0	0	18	12	0	18	12
18. 5	1	19	14	3	20	13
18.10	2	21	15	6	21	15
18.15	3	22	17	9	23	16
18.20	5	23	19	12	25	17
18.25	6	24	21	15	26	18
18.30	7	26	23	18	28	19
18.35	8	27	25	21	♊	21
18.40	9	28	27	24	1	22
18.45	10	♒	29	26	3	23
18.50	11	1	♓	29	4	24
18.55	13	2	3	2♉	6	25
19. 0	14	4	5	4	7	27
19. 5	15	5	7	7	8	28
19.10	16	7	9	9	10	29
19.15	17	8	11	12	11	♋
19.20	18	9	13	14	13	1
19.25	20	11	15	16	14	2
19.30	21	12	17	19	15	3
19.35	22	14	19	21	17	5
19.40	23	15	21	23	18	6
19.45	24	17	24	25	19	7
19.50	26	18	26	27	20	8
19.55	27	20	28	28	22	9
20. 0	28	21	♈	0♊	23	10

STime h. m.	10 ♑	11 ♒	12 ♈	Asc ♊	2 ♊	3 ♋
20. 0	28	21	0	0	23	10
20. 5	29	23	2	2	24	11
20.10	♒	24	4	4	25	12
20.15	2	26	6	5	26	13
20.20	3	27	9	7	28	15
20.25	4	29	11	9	29	16
20.30	5	♓	13	10	♋	17
20.35	6	2	15	12	1	18
20.40	8	4	17	13	2	19
20.45	9	5	19	15	3	20
20.50	10	7	21	16	4	21
20.55	11	8	23	17	6	22
21. 0	13	10	25	19	7	23
21. 5	14	12	27	20	8	24
21.10	15	13	29	21	9	25
21.15	16	15	♉	23	10	26
21.20	18	17	3	24	11	28
21.25	19	18	5	25	12	29
21.30	20	20	7	26	13	♌
21.35	21	22	9	28	14	1
21.40	23	23	11	29	15	2
21.45	24	25	13	0♋	16	3
21.50	25	27	15	1	17	4
21.55	27	28	16	2	18	5
22. 0	28	♈	18	3	19	6

STime h. m.	10 ♒	11 ♈	12 ♉	Asc ♋	2 ♋	3 ♌
22. 0	28	0	18	3	19	6
22. 5	29	2	20	4	20	7
22.10	♓	3	21	6	21	8
22.15	2	5	23	7	22	9
22.20	3	7	25	8	23	11
22.25	4	8	26	9	24	12
22.30	6	10	28	10	25	13
22.35	7	12	♊	11	26	14
22.40	8	13	1	12	27	15
22.45	10	15	3	13	28	16
22.50	11	17	4	14	29	17
22.55	12	18	6	15	♌	18
23. 0	14	20	7	16	1	19
23. 5	15	22	8	17	2	20
23.10	16	23	10	18	3	21
23.15	18	25	11	19	4	23
23.20	19	26	13	20	5	24
23.25	20	28	14	21	6	25
23.30	22	♉	15	21	7	26
23.35	23	1	17	22	8	27
23.40	25	3	18	23	9	28
23.45	26	4	19	24	10	29
23.50	27	6	20	25	11	♍
23.55	29	7	22	26	12	2
24. 0	♈	9	23	27	13	3

TABLES OF HOUSES FOR NORTHERN LATITUDES FOR LIVERPOOL Latitude 53° 25'n

STime h. m	10 ♈	11 ♉	12 ♊	Asc ♋	2 ♌	3 ♍
0. 0	0	9	24	28	13	3
0. 5	1	11	25	29	14	4
0.10	3	12	26	0♌	15	5
0.15	4	14	27	1	16	6
0.20	5	15	29	1	17	7
0.25	7	17	♋	2	18	8
0.30	8	18	1	3	19	10
0.35	10	20	2	4	20	11
0.40	11	21	3	5	21	12
0.45	12	22	4	6	22	13
0.50	14	24	5	7	23	14
0.55	15	25	6	8	24	15
1. 0	16	27	7	8	25	16
1. 5	18	28	9	9	26	17
1.10	19	29	10	10	27	19
1.15	20	♊	11	11	28	20
1.20	22	2	12	12	29	21
1.25	23	3	13	13	♍	22
1.30	24	5	14	14	1	23
1.35	26	6	15	14	2	24
1.40	27	7	16	15	3	25
1.45	28	9	17	16	4	27
1.50	♉	10	18	17	5	28
1.55	1	11	19	18	5	29
2. 0	2	12	20	19	6	♎

STime h. m.	10 ♉	11 ♊	12 ♋	Asc ♌	2 ♍	3 ♎
2. 0	2	12	20	19	6	0
2. 5	3	14	21	20	7	1
2.10	5	15	22	20	8	2
2.15	6	16	23	21	9	3
2.20	7	17	24	22	10	5
2.25	9	19	25	23	11	6
2.30	10	20	26	24	12	7
2.35	11	21	27	25	13	8
2.40	12	22	28	26	14	9
2.45	14	23	29	26	15	10
2.50	15	25	♌	27	16	11
2.55	16	26	1	28	17	13
3. 0	17	27	2	29	18	14
3. 5	19	28	3	0♍	19	15
3.10	20	29	4	1	20	16
3.15	21	♋	5	2	21	17
3.20	22	2	6	2	22	18
3.25	24	3	7	3	23	19
3.30	25	4	8	4	24	20
3.35	26	5	9	5	25	22
3.40	27	6	9	6	26	23
3.45	28	7	10	7	27	24
3.50	♊	8	11	8	28	25
3.55	1	9	12	8	29	26
4. 0	2	11	13	9	♎	27

STime h. m.	10 ♊	11 ♋	12 ♌	Asc ♍	2 ♎	3 ♎
4. 0	2	11	13	9	0	27
4. 5	3	12	14	10	1	28
4.10	4	13	15	11	2	29
4.15	6	14	16	12	3	♏
4.20	7	15	17	13	4	2
4.25	8	16	18	14	5	3
4.30	9	17	19	14	6	4
4.35	10	18	20	15	7	5
4.40	12	19	21	16	8	6
4.45	13	20	22	17	9	7
4.50	14	21	23	18	10	8
4.55	15	22	24	19	11	9
5. 0	16	24	25	20	12	10
5. 5	17	25	26	20	13	12
5.10	19	26	27	21	14	13
5.15	20	27	28	22	15	14
5.20	21	28	29	23	16	15
5.25	22	29	♍	24	17	16
5.30	23	♌	1	25	18	17
5.35	24	1	2	26	19	18
5.40	25	2	3	26	20	19
5.45	27	3	4	27	21	20
5.50	28	4	5	28	22	21
5.55	29	5	5	29	23	22
6. 0	♋	6	6	0♎	24	24

STime h. m.	10 ♋	11 ♌	12 ♍	Asc ♎	2 ♎	3 ♏
6. 0	0	6	6	0	24	24
6. 5	1	8	7	1	25	25
6.10	2	9	8	2	25	26
6.15	3	10	9	3	26	27
6.20	5	11	10	3	27	28
6.25	6	12	11	4	28	29
6.30	7	13	12	5	29	♐
6.35	8	14	13	6	♏	1
6.40	9	15	14	7	1	2
6.45	10	16	15	8	2	3
6.50	11	17	16	9	3	4
6.55	13	18	17	9	4	5
7. 0	14	20	18	10	5	6
7. 5	15	21	19	11	6	8
7.10	16	22	20	12	7	9
7.15	17	23	21	13	8	10
7.20	18	24	22	14	9	11
7.25	20	25	23	15	10	12
7.30	21	26	24	15	11	13
7.35	22	27	25	16	12	14
7.40	23	28	26	17	13	15
7.45	24	29	27	18	14	16
7.50	26	♍	28	19	15	17
7.55	27	2	29	20	16	18
8. 0	28	3	♎	21	17	19

STime h. m.	10 ♋	11 ♍	12 ♎	Asc ♎	2 ♏	3 ♐
8. 0	28	3	0	21	17	19
8. 5	29	4	1	22	18	21
8.10	♌	5	2	22	19	22
8.15	2	6	3	23	20	23
8.20	3	7	4	24	21	24
8.25	4	8	5	25	21	25
8.30	5	10	6	26	22	26
8.35	6	11	7	27	23	27
8.40	8	12	8	28	24	28
8.45	9	13	9	28	25	♑
8.50	10	14	10	29	26	1
8.55	11	15	11	0♏	27	2
9. 0	13	16	12	1	28	3
9. 5	14	17	13	2	29	4
9.10	15	19	14	3	♐	5
9.15	16	20	15	4	1	7
9.20	18	21	16	4	2	8
9.25	19	22	17	5	3	9
9.30	20	23	18	6	4	10
9.35	21	24	19	7	5	11
9.40	23	25	20	8	6	13
9.45	24	27	21	9	7	14
9.50	25	28	22	10	8	15
9.55	27	29	23	10	9	16
10. 0	28	♎	24	11	10	18

STime h. m.	10 ♌	11 ♎	12 ♎	Asc ♏	2 ♐	3 ♑
10. 0	28	0	24	11	10	18
10. 5	29	1	25	12	11	19
10.10	♍	2	25	13	12	20
10.15	2	3	26	14	13	21
10.20	3	5	27	15	14	23
10.25	4	6	28	16	15	24
10.30	6	7	29	16	16	25
10.35	7	8	♏	17	17	27
10.40	8	9	1	18	18	28
10.45	10	10	2	19	19	29
10.50	11	11	3	20	20	♒
10.55	12	13	4	21	21	2
11. 0	14	14	5	22	23	3
11. 5	15	15	6	22	24	5
11.10	16	16	7	23	25	6
11.15	18	17	8	24	26	8
11.20	19	18	9	25	27	9
11.25	20	19	10	26	28	10
11.30	22	20	11	27	29	12
11.35	23	22	12	28	♑	13
11.40	25	23	13	29	1	15
11.45	26	24	14	29	3	16
11.50	27	25	15	0♐	4	18
11.55	29	26	16	1	5	19
12. 0	♎	27	17	2	6	21

STime h. m.	10 ♎	11 ♎	12 ♏	Asc ♐	2 ♑	3 ♒
12. 0	0	27	17	2	6	21
12. 5	1	28	18	3	7	22
12.10	3	29	19	4	9	24
12.15	4	♏	20	5	10	26
12.20	5	2	21	6	11	27
12.25	7	3	21	7	12	29
12.30	8	4	22	8	14	♓
12.35	10	5	23	9	15	2
12.40	11	6	24	9	16	3
12.45	12	7	25	10	18	5
12.50	14	8	26	11	19	7
12.55	15	9	27	12	21	8
13. 0	16	10	28	13	22	10
13. 5	18	12	29	14	24	12
13.10	19	13	♐	15	25	13
13.15	20	14	1	16	26	15
13.20	22	15	2	17	28	17
13.25	23	16	3	18	♒	18
13.30	24	17	4	19	1	20
13.35	26	18	5	20	3	22
13.40	27	19	6	21	4	23
13.45	28	20	7	22	6	25
13.50	♏	21	8	23	8	27
13.55	1	22	9	24	9	28
14. 0	2	24	10	25	11	♈

STime h. m.	10 ♏	11 ♏	12 ♐	Asc ♐	2 ♒	3 ♈
14. 0	2	24	10	25	11	0
14. 5	3	25	11	27	13	2
14.10	5	26	12	28	15	3
14.15	6	27	13	29	16	5
14.20	7	28	14	0♑	18	7
14.25	9	29	15	1	20	8
14.30	10	♐	16	2	22	10
14.35	11	1	17	3	24	12
14.40	12	2	18	5	26	13
14.45	14	3	19	6	28	15
14.50	15	4	20	7	♓	17
14.55	16	5	21	8	2	18
15. 0	17	6	23	10	4	20
15. 5	19	8	24	11	6	22
15.10	20	9	25	12	8	23
15.15	21	10	26	14	10	25
15.20	22	11	27	15	12	27
15.25	24	12	28	17	15	28
15.30	25	13	29	18	17	♉
15.35	26	14	♑	20	19	1
15.40	27	15	1	21	21	3
15.45	28	16	3	23	23	4
15.50	♐	17	4	25	26	6
15.55	1	18	5	26	28	8
16. 0	2	19	6	28	♈	9

STime h. m.	10 ♐	11 ♐	12 ♑	Asc ♑	2 ♈	3 ♉
16. 0	2	19	6	28	0	9
16. 5	3	21	7	0♒	2	11
16.10	4	22	9	2	4	12
16.15	6	23	10	4	7	14
16.20	7	24	11	6	9	15
16.25	8	25	12	8	11	17
16.30	9	26	14	10	13	18
16.35	10	27	15	12	15	20
16.40	12	28	16	14	18	21
16.45	13	♑	18	17	20	22
16.50	14	1	19	19	22	24
16.55	15	2	21	22	24	25
17. 0	16	3	22	24	26	27
17. 5	17	4	24	27	28	28
17.10	19	5	25	29	♉	29
17.15	20	7	26	2♓	2	♊
17.20	21	8	28	5	4	2
17.25	22	9	♒	8	6	3
17.30	23	10	1	11	8	5
17.35	24	11	3	14	10	6
17.40	25	13	4	17	12	7
17.45	27	14	6	20	14	9
17.50	28	15	8	23	15	10
17.55	29	16	9	27	17	11
18. 0	♑	18	11	0♈	19	12

STime h. m.	10 ♑	11 ♑	12 ♒	Asc ♈	2 ♉	3 ♊
18. 0	0	18	11	0	19	12
18. 5	1	19	13	3	21	14
18.10	2	20	15	6	22	15
18.15	3	21	16	9	24	16
18.20	5	23	18	13	26	17
18.25	6	24	20	16	27	19
18.30	7	25	22	19	29	20
18.35	8	27	24	22	♊	21
18.40	9	28	26	25	2	22
18.45	10	29	28	28	4	23
18.50	11	♒	♓	0♉	5	25
18.55	13	2	2	3	6	26
19. 0	14	3	4	6	8	27
19. 5	15	5	6	8	9	28
19.10	16	6	8	11	11	29
19.15	17	8	10	13	12	♋
19.20	18	9	12	16	14	2
19.25	20	10	15	18	15	3
19.30	21	12	17	20	16	4
19.35	22	13	19	22	18	5
19.40	23	15	21	24	19	6
19.45	24	16	23	26	20	7
19.50	26	18	26	28	21	8
19.55	27	19	28	0♊	23	9
20. 0	28	21	♈	2	24	11

STime h. m.	10 ♑	11 ♒	12 ♈	Asc ♊	2 ♊	3 ♋
20. 0	28	21	0	2	24	11
20. 5	29	22	2	4	25	12
20.10	♒	24	4	5	26	13
20.15	2	26	7	7	27	14
20.20	3	27	9	9	29	15
20.25	4	29	11	10	♋	16
20.30	5	♓	13	12	1	17
20.35	6	2	15	13	2	18
20.40	8	3	18	15	3	19
20.45	9	5	20	16	4	20
20.50	10	7	22	18	5	21
20.55	11	8	24	19	6	22
21. 0	13	10	26	20	7	24
21. 5	14	12	28	22	9	25
21.10	15	13	♉	23	10	26
21.15	16	15	2	24	11	27
21.20	18	17	4	25	12	28
21.25	19	18	6	27	13	29
21.30	20	20	8	28	14	♌
21.35	21	22	10	29	15	1
21.40	23	23	12	0♋	16	2
21.45	24	25	14	1	17	3
21.50	25	27	15	2	18	4
21.55	27	28	17	3	19	5
22. 0	28	♈	19	5	20	6

STime h. m.	10 ♒	11 ♈	12 ♉	Asc ♋	2 ♋	3 ♌
22. 0	28	0	19	5	20	6
22. 5	29	2	21	6	21	8
22.10	♓	3	22	7	22	9
22.15	2	5	24	8	23	10
22.20	3	7	26	9	24	11
22.25	4	8	27	10	25	12
22.30	6	10	29	11	26	13
22.35	7	12	♊	12	27	14
22.40	8	13	2	13	28	15
22.45	10	15	4	14	29	16
22.50	11	17	5	15	♌	17
22.55	12	18	6	16	1	18
23. 0	14	20	8	17	2	20
23. 5	15	22	9	18	3	21
23.10	16	23	11	19	4	22
23.15	18	25	12	20	5	23
23.20	19	27	14	21	6	24
23.25	20	28	15	21	7	25
23.30	22	♉	16	22	8	26
23.35	23	1	18	23	9	27
23.40	25	3	19	24	9	28
23.45	26	4	20	25	10	29
23.50	27	6	21	26	11	♍
23.55	29	8	23	27	12	2
24. 0	♈	9	24	28	13	3

TABLES OF HOUSES FOR NORTHERN LATITUDES FOR GLASGOW Latitude 55° 53'n

STime h. m.	10 ♈	11 ♉	12 ♊	Asc ♌	2 ♌	3 ♍
0. 0	0	10	27	1	15	3
0. 5	1	12	28	1	16	4
0.10	3	13	29	2	17	5
0.15	4	15	♋	3	18	7
0.20	5	16	2	4	19	8
0.25	7	18	3	5	19	9
0.30	8	19	4	6	20	10
0.35	10	21	5	6	21	11
0.40	11	22	6	7	22	12
0.45	12	24	7	8	23	13
0.50	14	25	8	9	24	14
0.55	15	27	9	10	25	15
1. 0	16	28	10	11	26	17
1. 5	18	29	11	11	27	18
1.10	19	♊	12	12	28	19
1.15	20	2	13	13	29	20
1.20	22	3	14	14	♍	21
1.25	23	5	15	15	1	22
1.30	24	6	16	15	2	23
1.35	26	8	17	16	3	24
1.40	27	9	18	17	3	26
1.45	28	10	19	18	4	27
1.50	♉	11	20	19	5	28
1.55	1	13	21	20	6	29
2. 0	2	14	22	20	7	♎

STime h. m.	10 ♉	11 ♊	12 ♋	Asc ♌	2 ♍	3 ♎
2. 0	2	14	22	20	7	0
2. 5	3	15	23	21	8	1
2.10	5	16	24	22	9	2
2.15	6	18	25	23	10	3
2.20	7	19	26	24	11	4
2.25	9	20	27	24	12	6
2.30	10	21	28	25	13	7
2.35	11	23	29	26	14	8
2.40	12	24	♌	27	15	9
2.45	14	25	1	28	16	10
2.50	15	26	2	29	17	11
2.55	16	27	3	29	18	12
3. 0	17	28	4	0♍	19	13
3. 5	19	♋	5	1	20	15
3.10	20	1	5	2	20	16
3.15	21	2	6	3	21	17
3.20	22	3	7	3	22	18
3.25	24	4	8	4	23	19
3.30	25	5	9	5	24	20
3.35	26	6	10	6	25	21
3.40	27	8	11	7	26	22
3.45	28	9	12	7	27	23
3.50	♊	10	13	8	28	25
3.55	1	11	14	9	29	26
4. 0	2	12	15	10	♎	27

STime h. m.	10 ♊	11 ♋	12 ♌	Asc ♍	2 ♎	3 ♎
4. 0	2	12	15	10	0	27
4. 5	3	13	16	11	1	28
4.10	4	14	17	12	2	29
4.15	6	15	18	12	3	♏
4.20	7	16	19	13	4	1
4.25	8	17	19	14	5	2
4.30	9	18	20	15	6	3
4.35	10	19	21	16	7	4
4.40	12	21	22	16	8	5
4.45	13	22	23	17	9	7
4.50	14	23	24	18	10	8
4.55	15	24	25	19	10	9
5. 0	16	25	26	20	11	10
5. 5	17	26	27	21	12	11
5.10	19	27	28	21	13	12
5.15	20	28	29	22	14	13
5.20	21	29	♍	23	15	14
5.25	22	♌	1	24	16	15
5.30	23	1	2	25	17	16
5.35	24	2	3	26	18	17
5.40	25	3	3	26	19	18
5.45	27	4	4	27	20	19
5.50	28	5	5	28	21	20
5.55	29	6	6	29	22	21
6. 0	♋	7	7	0♎	23	23

STime h. m.	10 ♋	11 ♌	12 ♍	Asc ♎	2 ♎	3 ♏
6. 0	0	7	7	0	23	23
6. 5	1	9	8	1	24	24
6.10	2	10	9	1	25	25
6.15	3	11	10	2	26	26
6.20	5	12	11	3	27	27
6.25	6	13	12	4	27	28
6.30	7	14	13	5	28	29
6.35	8	15	14	6	29	♐
6.40	9	16	15	6	♏	1
6.45	10	17	16	7	1	2
6.50	11	18	17	8	2	3
6.55	13	19	18	9	3	4
7. 0	14	20	19	10	4	5
7. 5	15	21	20	11	5	6
7.10	16	22	20	11	6	7
7.15	17	23	21	12	7	8
7.20	18	25	22	13	8	9
7.25	20	26	23	14	9	11
7.30	21	27	24	15	10	12
7.35	22	28	25	16	11	13
7.40	23	29	26	16	11	14
7.45	24	♍	27	17	12	15
7.50	26	1	28	18	13	16
7.55	27	2	29	19	14	17
8. 0	28	3	♎	20	15	18

STime h. m.	10 ♋	11 ♍	12 ♎	Asc ♎	2 ♏	3 ♐
8. 0	28	3	0	20	15	18
8. 5	29	4	1	21	16	19
8.10	♌	5	2	21	17	20
8.15	2	7	3	22	18	21
8.20	3	8	4	23	19	22
8.25	4	9	5	24	20	24
8.30	5	10	6	25	21	25
8.35	6	11	7	25	22	26
8.40	8	12	8	26	23	27
8.45	9	13	9	27	24	28
8.50	10	14	10	28	25	29
8.55	11	15	10	29	25	♑
9. 0	13	17	11	0♏	26	2
9. 5	14	18	12	0	27	3
9.10	15	19	13	1	28	4
9.15	16	20	14	2	29	5
9.20	18	21	15	3	♐	6
9.25	19	22	16	4	1	7
9.30	20	23	17	5	2	9
9.35	21	24	18	5	3	10
9.40	23	26	19	6	4	11
9.45	24	27	20	7	5	12
9.50	25	28	21	8	6	14
9.55	27	29	22	9	7	15
10. 0	28	♎	23	10	8	16

STime h. m.	10 ♌	11 ♎	12 ♎	Asc ♏	2 ♐	3 ♑
10. 0	28	0	23	10	8	16
10. 5	29	1	24	10	9	17
10.10	♍	2	25	11	10	19
10.15	2	3	26	12	11	20
10.20	3	4	27	13	12	21
10.25	4	6	27	14	13	22
10.30	6	7	28	14	14	24
10.35	7	8	29	15	15	25
10.40	8	9	♏	16	16	27
10.45	10	10	1	17	17	28
10.50	11	11	2	18	18	29
10.55	12	12	3	19	19	♒
11. 0	14	13	4	19	20	2
11. 5	15	15	5	20	21	3
11.10	16	16	6	21	22	5
11.15	18	17	7	22	23	6
11.20	19	18	8	23	24	8
11.25	20	19	9	24	25	9
11.30	22	20	10	24	26	11
11.35	23	21	11	25	27	12
11.40	25	22	11	26	28	14
11.45	26	23	12	27	♑	15
11.50	27	25	13	28	1	17
11.55	29	26	14	29	2	18
12. 0	♎	27	15	29	3	20

STime h. m.	10 ♎	11 ♎	12 ♏	Asc ♏	2 ♑	3 ♒
12. 0	0	27	15	29	3	20
12. 5	1	28	16	0♐	4	21
12.10	3	29	17	1	6	23
12.15	4	♏	18	2	7	25
12.20	5	1	19	3	8	26
12.25	7	2	20	4	9	28
12.30	8	3	21	5	11	29
12.35	10	4	22	6	12	♓
12.40	11	5	23	6	13	3
12.45	12	7	24	7	15	4
12.50	14	8	25	8	16	6
12.55	15	9	25	9	17	8
13. 0	16	10	26	10	19	9
13. 5	18	11	27	11	20	11
13.10	19	12	28	12	22	13
13.15	20	13	29	13	23	14
13.20	22	14	♐	14	25	16
13.25	23	15	1	15	26	18
13.30	24	16	2	16	28	20
13.35	26	17	3	16	29	21
13.40	27	18	4	17	♒	23
13.45	28	19	5	18	3	25
13.50	♏	20	6	19	5	27
13.55	1	21	7	20	6	28
14. 0	2	23	8	21	8	♈

STime h. m.	10 ♏	11 ♏	12 ♐	Asc ♐	2 ♒	3 ♈
14. 0	2	23	8	21	8	0
14. 5	3	24	9	22	10	2
14.10	5	25	10	23	12	3
14.15	6	26	11	24	14	5
14.20	7	27	12	26	16	7
14.25	9	28	13	27	18	9
14.30	10	29	14	28	20	10
14.35	11	♐	15	29	22	12
14.40	12	1	16	0♑	24	14
14.45	14	2	17	1	26	16
14.50	15	3	18	2	28	17
14.55	16	4	19	4	♓	19
15. 0	17	5	20	5	2	21
15. 5	19	6	21	6	4	22
15.10	20	7	22	7	7	24
15.15	21	8	23	9	9	26
15.20	22	9	24	10	11	27
15.25	24	11	25	11	13	29
15.30	25	12	26	13	16	♉
15.35	26	13	27	14	18	2
15.40	27	14	28	16	20	4
15.45	28	15	♑	17	23	5
15.50	♐	16	1	19	25	7
15.55	1	17	2	21	28	9
16. 0	2	18	3	22	♈	10

STime h. m.	10 ♐	11 ♐	12 ♑	Asc ♑	2 ♈	3 ♉
16. 0	2	18	3	22	0	10
16. 5	3	19	4	24	2	12
16.10	4	20	6	26	5	13
16.15	6	21	7	28	7	15
16.20	7	22	8	0♒	10	16
16.25	8	24	9	2	12	18
16.30	9	25	11	4	14	19
16.35	10	26	12	6	17	21
16.40	12	27	13	9	19	22
16.45	13	28	15	11	21	24
16.50	14	29	16	13	23	25
16.55	15	♑	17	16	26	27
17. 0	16	2	19	19	28	28
17. 5	17	3	20	22	♉	29
17.10	19	4	22	25	2	♊
17.15	20	5	23	28	4	2
17.20	21	6	25	1♓	6	3
17.25	22	7	26	4	8	5
17.30	23	9	28	8	10	6
17.35	24	10	29	11	12	8
17.40	25	11	♒	15	14	9
17.45	27	12	3	18	16	10
17.50	28	14	5	22	18	11
17.55	29	15	6	26	20	13
18. 0	♑	16	8	29	22	14

STime h. m.	10 ♑	11 ♑	12 ♒	Asc ♓	2 ♉	3 ♊
18. 0	0	16	8	29	22	14
18. 5	1	17	10	3♈	24	15
18.10	2	19	12	7	25	16
18.15	3	20	14	11	27	18
18.20	5	21	16	14	29	19
18.25	6	22	18	18	♊	20
18.30	7	24	20	22	2	21
18.35	8	25	22	25	4	23
18.40	9	27	24	28	5	24
18.45	10	28	26	2♉	7	25
18.50	11	29	28	5	8	26
18.55	13	♒	♓	8	10	27
19. 0	14	2	2	11	11	28
19. 5	15	3	4	14	13	♋
19.10	16	5	7	16	14	1
19.15	17	6	9	19	15	2
19.20	18	8	11	21	17	3
19.25	20	9	13	24	18	4
19.30	21	11	16	26	19	5
19.35	22	12	18	28	21	6
19.40	23	14	20	0♊	22	8
19.45	24	15	23	2	23	9
19.50	26	17	25	4	24	10
19.55	27	18	28	6	26	11
20. 0	28	20	♈	8	27	12

STime h. m.	10 ♑	11 ♒	12 ♈	Asc ♊	2 ♊	3 ♋
20. 0	28	20	0	8	27	12
20. 5	29	21	2	9	28	13
20.10	♒	23	5	11	29	14
20.15	2	25	7	13	♋	15
20.20	3	26	10	14	2	16
20.25	4	28	12	16	3	17
20.30	5	29	14	17	4	18
20.35	6	♓	17	19	5	19
20.40	8	3	19	20	6	21
20.45	9	4	21	21	7	22
20.50	10	6	23	23	8	23
20.55	11	8	26	24	9	24
21. 0	13	9	28	25	10	25
21. 5	14	11	♉	26	11	26
21.10	15	13	2	28	12	27
21.15	16	14	4	29	13	28
21.20	18	16	6	0♋	14	29
21.25	19	18	8	1	15	♌
21.30	20	20	10	2	16	1
21.35	21	21	12	3	17	2
21.40	23	23	14	4	18	3
21.45	24	25	16	6	19	4
21.50	25	27	18	7	20	5
21.55	27	28	20	8	21	6
22. 0	28	♈	22	9	22	7

STime h. m.	10 ♒	11 ♈	12 ♉	Asc ♋	2 ♋	3 ♌
22. 0	28	0	22	9	22	7
22. 5	29	2	24	10	23	9
22.10	♓	3	25	11	24	10
22.15	2	5	27	12	25	11
22.20	3	7	29	13	26	12
22.25	4	9	♊	14	27	13
22.30	6	10	2	14	28	14
22.35	7	12	4	15	29	15
22.40	8	14	5	16	♌	16
22.45	10	16	7	17	1	17
22.50	11	17	8	18	2	18
22.55	12	19	10	19	3	19
23. 0	14	21	11	20	4	20
23. 5	15	22	13	21	5	21
23.10	16	24	14	22	5	22
23.15	18	26	15	23	6	23
23.20	19	27	17	24	7	25
23.25	20	29	18	24	8	26
23.30	22	♉	19	25	9	27
23.35	23	2	21	26	10	28
23.40	25	4	22	27	11	29
23.45	26	5	23	28	12	♍
23.50	27	7	24	29	13	1
23.55	29	9	26	0♌	14	2
24. 0	♈	10	27	1	15	3

INDEX

ACKNOWLEDGMENTS

Ephemeris and Tables of Houses provided by Rose Elliot Horoscopes.

Birthcharts, Personality Profiles and Forecasts can be obtained from:
Rose Elliot Horoscopes
The Old Rectory
Church Road
Bishopstoke
Eastleigh
Hampshire SO5 6BH

9: Nick D'Allessio
10: (top right) Steven Hunt/Image Bank; (bottom left)
Images Colour Library; (bottom right) Joseph Drivas/Image Bank;
11: (top left) Joseph Devenney/Image Bank;
(bottom right) Werner Forman Archive/Naprstek Museum Prague
13, 23: John Barrat/ insets Katie Mynott
19: Ranald MacKechnie
20: (top) Paul Kime; (bottom left) Images Colour Library;
(bottom right) NASA/Science Photo Library
29: Steve Lyne
30: Musee Condé, Chantilly/Bridgeman Art Library
33: Gillian Sampson/ insets Katie Mynott
39: Johnny van Haeften Gallery/Bridgeman Art Library
40: Kobal Collection
41: Mansell Collection
42: Mary Evans Picture Library
43: Mary Evans Picture Library
44: E. T. Archive
45: Johnny van Haeften Gallery/Bridgeman Art Library
46: E. T. Archive
47: E. T. Archive
48: E. T. Archive
49: Kobal Collection
50: Bridgeman Art Library
53: Lorenzo Costa, detail from astrological ceiling,
Ducal Palace Mantua/Ancient Art and Architecture Collection
54: (bottom left) Tony Meadows
59: Michael Holford
64: Topham
65: (top) Mike Hewitt/Action Plus;
(bottom) Warner Bros/Kobal Collection;
66: (top) Frank Spooner/Gamma; (bottom) Kobal Collection
67: Images Colour Library
71: Joseph Devenney/Image Bank
73: David Jeffrey/Image Bank
75: Daily Telegraph Colour Library
77: Daily Telegraph Colour Library/Space Frontiers
79: Daily Telegraph Colour Library/Space Frontiers
81: NASA/Science Photo Library
83: Daily Telegraph Colour Library/Space Frontiers
85, 87: NASA/Science Photo Library
89: David A. Hardy/Science Photo Library
91: Images Colour Library
95: E. T. Archive
96: Kobal Collection
99: Images Colour Library
100: Acikalin/Rex Features
101: Hulton-Deutsch
102: Rex Features
102: Facelly/Rex/SIPA
103: T. I. Baker/Image Bank
104: Rex Features
104: Stills/Rex Features
107: Scott Snow/Image Bank
109: Warner Bros/Kobal Collection
110: (top) Ritts/LNS/Frank Spooner; (bottom) Frederic Regbin/Frank Spooner
113-137: Image Bank
141: Andrew Cameron
143/147: Mitchell Funk/Image Bank
153-157: Ray Duns
159: Steven Hunt/Image Bank
161: Image Bank